~~Durham's~~

Place-Names
of

California's
Gold Country
Including
Yosemite National Park

Includes Madera, Mariposa, Tuolumne,
Calaveras, Amador, El Dorado, Placer,
Sierra & Nevada Counties

David L. Durham

Word
Dancer
Press

Word Dancer Press books may be purchased at special prices for educational, fund-raising, business or promotional use. Please contact Special Markets, Quill Driver Books/Word Dancer Press, Inc. at the above address or phone number.

To order another copy of this book or another book in the Durham's Place-Names of California series, please call 1-800-497-4909.

Quill Driver Books/Word Dancer Press, Inc. project cadre:
Doris Hall, Dave Marion, Stephen Blake Mettee
ISBN 1-884995-25-X

Library of Congress Cataloging-in-Publication Data

Durham, David L., 1925-
 Durham's place names of California's Gold Country, including Yosemite National Park : including Madera, Mariposa, Tuolumne, Calaveras, Amador, El Dorado, Placer, Sierra & Nevada counties / David L. Durham.
 p. cm.
 Includes bibliographical references.
 ISBN 1-884995-25-X (trade paper)
 1. Names, Geographical--California, Northern. 2. California, Northern--History, Local. 3. Names, Geographical--California--Yosemite National Park. I. Title: Place names of California's Gold Country. II. Title.

F867.5 .D86 2001
917.94'4001'4--dc21

00-054631

Cover illustrations:

Panning for gold on Coyote Creek on north side of Natural Bridge, off Parrots Ferry Road, south of Vallecito, in Calaversas County. Photo by Dick James, courtesy of Dick James Stock Photography, 3023 Flume Court, P.O. Box 180, Arnold, California 95223-0180; 209-795-0864; djames@mlode.com.

Yosemite Valley. Photo by Stephen Blake Mettee

Contents

CALIFORNIA
GOLD COUNTRY COUNTIES
SHADED

INTRODUCTION

Purpose, organization and scope

This gazetteer, which lists geographic features of Madera, Mariposa, Tuolumne, Calaveras, Amador, El Dorado, Placer, Sierra & Nevada counties, California—Yosemite National Park extends over parts of Madera, Mariposa and Tuolumne counties—is one of a series of fourteen books that cover the whole state. This series is derived from *California's Geographic Names: A Gazetteer of Historic and Modern Names of the State,* David L. Durham's definitive gazetteer of California. Each book contains all the entries for the counties covered that are included in the larger volume.

United States government quadrangle maps, which are detailed, somewhat authoritative, and generally available, are the primary source of information. Included are features that are named on quadrangle maps, or that can be related to features named on the maps. The books list relief features, water features, and most kinds of cultural features, but omit names of streets, parks, schools, churches, cemeteries, dams and the like. Some names simply identify a person or family living at a site because such places are landmarks in sparsely settled parts of the state.

The listing of names is alphabetical, and multiword names are alphabetized as one word. Terms abbreviated on maps are given in full in the alphabetical list, and numerals in names are listed in alphabetical order rather than in numerical order. In addition to the principal entries, the list includes cross references to variant names, obsolete names and key words in multiword English-language names. For each principal entry, the name is followed by the name of the county or counties in which the feature lies, a classifying term, general and specific locations, identification of one or more quadrangle maps that show the name and other information. All features named in an entry generally belong to the same county. The classifying terms are defined under the heading "Geographic Terms" beginning on page *xi*.

Locations and measurements are from quadrangle maps, distances and directions are approximate, and latitude and longitude generally are to the nearest five seconds. Distances between post offices are measured by road, as the mail would be carried. Other distances are measured in a straight line unless the measurement is given with a qualifying expression such as "downstream" or "by road." For streams, the location given generally is the place that the stream joins another stream, enters a lake, or debouches into a canyon or valley. For features of considerable areal extent, the location given ordinarily is near the center, except for cities and towns, for which the location given is near the center of the downtown part, or at the city hall or civic center. Measurements to or from areal features usually are to or from the center. Specific locations are omitted for some very large or poorly defined places. Books, articles, and miscellaneous maps are listed under "References Cited" begining on page 363. The references identify sources of data and provide leads to additional information. If a name applies to more than one feature in a county, the features are numbered and identified elsewhere in the list by that number in parentheses following the name.

General.—This book concerns geographic features in nine counties—Madera, Amador, Calaveras, El Dorado, Mariposa, Nevada, Placer, Sierra, Tuolumne— in California's gold country. They are mainly east of the Central Valley, or Great Valley, of California, in and near the Sierra Nevada. The Central Valley is called Buena Ventura Valley on Wilkes' (1841) map. Garces gave the name "Sierra de San Marcos" to the present Sierra Nevada in 1776 (Boyd, p. 3), Wilkes (p. 44) called the feature California Range in 1841, Lyman (1849a, p. 307) called it "Sierra Nevada, or Snowy Mountains" in 1849, and Kip (p. 46) called it Snowy Range in 1850. United States Board on Geographic Names (1933, p. 692) ruled against the form "Sierra Nevadas" for the name. Whitney (1865, p. 2) pointed out that the feature long was known to the Spaniards as Sierra Nevada, or Snowy Range, because "the most distant and loftiest elevations are never entirely bare of snow, and for a large portion of the year are extensively covered with it." The map on page *iv* shows the location of the nine counties. Townships (T) and Ranges (R) given in the text refer to Mount Diablo Base and Meridian.

Madera County.—Madera County extends from the crest of the Sierra Nevada southwestward into the Central Valley. It was organized in 1893 from the part of Fresno County that lay north and west of San Joaquin River; the county boundaries have not changed (Coy, p. 157). The county name is from the principal town, Madera, which always has been the county seat (Hoover, Rensch, and Rensch, p. 170).

Amador County.—Amador County extends westward from near the crest of the Sierra Nevada into the Central Valley, generally between Cosumnes River and Mokelumne River. The state legislature created the county in 1854 from that part of previously established Calaveras County that lay north of Mokelumne River; later additions to the territory of the county came from El Dorado County in 1855, 1857, and 1863, before the east part of Amador County was lost to newly formed Alpine County in 1864 (Coy, p. 66-67). Jackson has been the county seat from the beginning. The name "Amador" commemorates Jose Maria Amador, for whom Amador City and Amador Creek were named (Hoover, Rensch, and Rensch, p. 29).

Calaveras County.—Calaveras County extends from near the crest of the Sierra Nevada westward between Tuolumne River and Stanislaus River to the edge of the Central Valley. It is one of 27 counties that the first state legislature created in 1850; part of its original territory was lost to Amador County in 1854, to Mono County in 1861, and to Alpine County in 1864 (Coy, p. 80-81). Pleasant Valley, later called Double Springs, was the first county seat; the county government moved to Jackson (now in Amador County) in 1851, to Mokelumne Hill in 1852, and to San Andreas in 1866, where it remains (Hoover, Rensch, and Rensch, p. 41-42).

El Dorado County.—El Dorado County is between the State of Nevada and the foothills of the Sierra Nevada east of the Central Valley. The first state legislature created the county in 1850; some of the original territory of El Dorado County was lost to Amador County and Alpine County in the 1850's and 1860's, and El Dorado-Placer County line was adjusted in 1863 and 1913 (Coy, p. 97-100). The county seat first was at Coloma, but it moved to Placerville in 1857; the Spanish term *El Dorado* has the connotation of "the gilded one" from a legend of golden wealth in South America—the name is appropriate for the county that has the site of the gold discovery that resulted in the California gold rush of 1849 (Hoover, Rensch, and Rensch, p. 73).

Mariposa County.—Mariposa County extends from the crest of the Sierra Nevada westward to near the east edge of the Central Valley, and is largely in the drainage area of Merced River. It was one of 27 counties that the first state legislature formed in 1850; the county originally covered a huge area that included present Fresno, Kern, Kings, Madera, Mariposa, and Merced Counties, as well as parts of present Inyo, Los Angeles, Mono, San Benito, and San Bernardino Counties. By 1856 Mariposa County was reduced to the present size, and later changes in the county boundaries have been minor (Coy, p. 161-165). Agua Fria was the first seat of government, and Mariposa has been the county seat since 1851 (Hoover, Rensch, and Rensch, p. 189).

Nevada County.—Nevada County extends westward from the State of Nevada across the crest of the Sierra Nevada into the foothills of that range. The county was created in 1851 from part of Yuba County; additions to the north part of Nevada County came in 1852 and 1856 (Coy, p. 194). Nevada City is and always as been the county seat (Hoover, Rensch, and Rensch, p. 247). The county took its name from Nevada City (Gudde, 1949, p. 233-234).

Placer County.—Placer County extends from the State of Nevada at Lake Tahoe westward across the crest of the Sierra Nevada into the Central Valley. It was created in 1851 from territory of the older Sutter County and Yuba County; only minor changes have been made in the original borders of Placer County (Coy, p. 200-202). Auburn has been the county seat from the beginning; the county name is from the Spanish term for surface mining (Hoover, Rensch, and Rensch, p. 265).

Sierra County.—Sierra County is in the Sierra Nevada between the State of Nevada and the lower elevations of the range near the Central Valley. It was formed in 1852 from the east part of Yuba County, and Downieville was made the county seat; the present boundaries of Sierra County are little changed from the original ones (Coy, p. 253-255). The county name obviously is from the location of the place in the Sierra Nevada.

Tuolumne County.—Tuolumne County extends from the crest of the Sierra Nevada westward to near the east edge of the Central Valley. It is one of the 27 counties that the first state legislature formed in 1850. Part of the original territory of Tuolumne County was lost to Stanislaus County when that county was organized in 1854, and part went to Alpine County when that county was formed in 1864 (Coy, p. 288-289). Sonora is the first and only seat of government for Tuolumne County (Hoover, Rensch, and Rensch, p. 565).

Geographic Terms

Area —A tract of land, either precisely or indefinitely defined.

Bay —A body of water connected to a larger body of water and nearly surrounded by land.

Beach —An expanse of sandy or pebbly material that borders a body of water.

Bend —A pronounced curve in the course of a stream, and the land partly enclosed therein.

Canyon —A narrow elongate depression in the land surface, generally confined between steep sides and usually drained by a stream.

Cave —A naturally formed subterranean chamber.

City —An inhabited place that has a population greater than about 25,000 in an urban setting.

District —Part of an inhabited place, either precisely or indefinitely defined.

Embayment —An indentation in the shoreline of a body of water.

Escarpment —A cliff or a nearly continuous line of steep slopes.

Glacier —A slowly moving mass of ice.

Hill —A prominent elevation on the land surface that has a well-defined outline on a map, and that rises less than 1000 feet above its surroundings.

Intermittent lake —A lake that ordinarily contains water only part of the time.

Island —A tract of normally dry land, or of marsh, that is surrounded by water.

Lake —A body of standing water, either natural or artificial.

Land grant —A gift of land made by Spanish or Mexican authority and eventually confirmed by the United States government.

Locality —A place that has past or present cultural associations.

Marsh —A poorly drained wet area.

Military installation —Land or facility used for military purposes.

Narrows —The constricted part of a channel, river, canyon, valley, or pass.

Pass —A saddle or natural depression that affords passage across a range or between peaks.

Peak —A prominent high point on a larger elevated land surface.

Peninsula —An elongate tract of land nearly surrounded by water.

Promontory —A conspicuous, but not necessarily high, elevation of the land surface that protrudes into a body of water or into a lowland.

Range —An elevated land surface of ridges and peaks.

Relief feature —A general term for a

recognizable form of the land surface produced by natural causes.

Ridge —A prominent elongate elevation on the land surface; occurs either independently or as part of a larger elevation.

Settlement —An informal inhabited place.

Spring —A natural flow of water from the ground.

Stream —A body of water that moves under gravity in a depression on the land surface; includes watercourses that have intermittent flow and watercourses that are modified by man.

Town —An inhabited place that has a population of about 500 to 25,000 in an urban setting.

Valley —A broad depression in the land surface, or a wide place in an otherwise narrow depression.

Village —An inhabited place that has a compact cluster of buildings and a population less than about 500.

Waterfall —A perpendicular or very steep descent of the water in a stream.

Water feature —A general term for something or some place involving water.

Well —A hole sunk into the ground to obtain water.

Place-Names
of

California's
Gold Country
Including
Yosemite National Park

– A –

Abbeys Ferry: see **Abbott Ferry** [CALA-VERAS-TUOLUMNE].

Abbott Ferry [CALAVERAS-TUOLUMNE]: *locality,* nearly 3 miles southeast of Vallecito along Stanislaus River on Calaveras-Tuolumne county line (lat. 38°03'30" N, long. 120°26' W). Named on Big Trees (1891) 30' quadrangle. Whitney (1865, p. 242) referred to Abby's Ferry, and Gudde (1975, p. 13) listed Abbeys Ferry.

Abbotts Peak [CALAVERAS]: *peak,* 1 mile east-southeast of Copperopolis near the southeast end of Copperopolis Mountain (lat. 37°58'35" N, long. 120°37'15" W; sec. 35, T 2 N, R 12 E). Altitude 1545 feet. Named on Melones Dam (1962) 7.5' quadrangle.

Abby's Ferry: see **Abbott Ferry** [CALA-VERAS-TUOLUMNE].

Abrams Ravine [PLACER]: *canyon,* drained by a stream that flows 0.5 mile to Pine Nut Canyon 6 miles south-southwest of Duncan Peak (lat. 39°04'20" N, long. 120°32'20" W; near SW cor. sec. 9, T 14 N, R 13 E). Named on Greek Store (1952) 7.5' quadrangle.

Ache: see **Billy Ache Canyon**, under **Bellyache Canyon** [MARIPOSA].

Aches: see **William Aches Canyon**, under **Bellyache Canyon** [MARIPOSA].

Acid Flat [NEVADA]: *area,* 9.5 miles northeast of Truckee (lat. 39° 23'55" N, long. 120°01'50" W; at E line sec. 24, T 18 N, R 17 E). Named on Boca (1955) 7.5' quadrangle.

Ackerman: see **Westville** [PLACER].

Acker Peak [TUOLUMNE]: *peak,* 3.25 miles southeast of Tower Peak (lat. 38°06'30" N, long. 119°30'30" W). Altitude 11,015 feet. Named on Tower Peak (1956) 15' quadrangle. Members of United States Geological Survey named the peak for William Bertrand Acker, head of National Park affairs for Department of the Interior (Browning, 1986, p. 1).

Ackerson Creek [TUOLUMNE]: *stream,* flows 6.25 miles to South Fork Tuolumne River 4.5 miles south-southwest of Mather (lat. 37°49'15" N, long. 119°52'30" W; sec. 27, T 1 S, R 19 E); the creek goes through Ackerson Meadow. Named on Lake Eleanor (1956) 15' quadrangle. The stream also was called Big Meadow Creek (Browning, 1986, p. 1).

Ackerson Meadow [TUOLUMNE]: *area,* 3 miles south-southeast of Mather (lat. 37°50'25" N, long. 119°50' W; mainly in sec. 24, T 1 S, R 19 E); the place is along Ackerson

Creek. Named on Lake Eleanor (1956) 15' quadrangle. The area first was known as Buckley Meadows; the name "Ackerson" commemorates James T. Ackerson, who lived at the site (Paden and Schlichtmann, p. 207). Hoffmann and Gardner's (1863-1867) map has the notation "Wade's or big meadows" at the place. Hoffmann referred to the feature as Reservoir Meadows in 1867 (Browning, 1988, p. 1).

Ackerson Mountain [TUOLUMNE]: *peak,* 3 miles south-southwest of Mather (lat. 37°50'20" N, long. 119°52' W; sec. 22, T 1 S, R 19 E); the peak is 1.5 miles west of Ackerson Meadow. Altitude 5249 feet. Named on Lake Eleanor (1956) 15' quadrangle.

Acorn Creek [EL DORADO]: *stream,* flows 2 miles to Skunk Canyon nearly 3.5 miles south of the village of Pilot Hill (lat. 38°46'55" N, long. 121°01'30" W; near NE cor. sec. 25, T 11 N, R 8 E). Named on Pilot Hill (1954) 7.5' quadrangle.

Acorn Lodge [MARIPOSA]: *locality,* 1.5 miles south of Midpines (lat. 37°31'25" N, long. 119°55'15" W; near W line sec. 5, T 5 S, R 19 E). Named on Feliciana Mountain (1947) 7.5' quadrangle. Laizure's (1935) map shows a place called Yosemite Oaks located a short distance west-northwest of Acorn Lodge (near E line sec. 6, T 5 S, R 19 E).

Acorn Peak: see **Ahwiyah Point** [MARIPOSA].

Adair Lake: see **Obelisk Lake** [MARIPOSA].

Adeline: see **Mount Adeline**, under **Mount Savage** [MARIPOSA].

Adobe Gulch [CALAVERAS]: *canyon,* nearly 2 miles long, opens into the canyon of McKinney Creek 9.5 miles east of San Andreas (lat. 38°12'40" N, long. 120°30'30" W; sec. 11, T 4 N, R 13 E). Named on Calaveritas (1962) 7.5' quadrangle.

A.E. Wood: see **Camp A.E. Wood**, under **Camp Hoyle** [MARIPOSA].

African Bar [EL DORADO-PLACER]: *locality,* 4 miles north-northwest of Georgetown along Middle Fork American River on El Dorado-Placer county line (lat. 38°57'55" N, long. 121°51'10" W; at N line sec. 22, T 13 N, R 10 E). Site named on Georgetown (1949) 7.5' quadrangle.

Agassiz Camp: see **Fallen Leaf** [EL DORADO].

Agate Bay [PLACER]: *embayment,* at and west of Kings Beach along Lake Tahoe between Stateline Point and Flick Point (lat. 39°14' N, long. 120°02'15" W). Named on Kings Beach (1955) 7.5' quadrangle. The name, given in

1863, is for the large number of agates on the beach at the place (Lekisch, p. 1).

Agua Fria [MARIPOSA]: *locality,* 5.25 miles northeast of the settlement of Catheys Valley (lat. 37°29'10" N, long. 120°01'10" W); the place is along Agua Fria Creek. Site named on Catheys Valley (1962) 7.5' quadrangle. Called Lower Agua Fria on Hoffmann and Gardner's (1863-1867) map, which shows a place called Upper Agua Fria located about 1 mile upstream from Lower Agua Fria. Postal authorities established Agua Fria post office in 1851 and discontinued it in 1862 (Frickstad, p. 90). The name, which is from Agua Fria Creek, also had the forms "Agua Frio," "Agua Frie," and "Aqua Fria" (Wood, p. 11-12).

Agua Fria Creek [MARIPOSA]: *stream,* flows 9 miles to Mariposa Creek 5 miles south of Mariposa (lat. 37°24'45" N, long. 119°59' W; sec. 15, T 6 S, R 18 E). Named on Catheys Valley (1962) and Mariposa (1947) 7.5' quadrangles. The name is from two springs of cold water at a bend in the creek just below Agua Fria—*agua fria* means "cold water" in Spanish (Eccleston, p. 7).

Ahart Camp [SIERRA]: *locality,* 8 miles southwest of Sierraville (lat. 39°30'05" N, long. 120°28' W; sec. 24, T 19 N, R 13 E). Named on Sattley (1981) 7.5' quadrangle.

Ahart Campground [PLACER]: *locality,* 7.5 miles west-southwest of Granite Chief along Middle Fork American River in French Meadows (lat. 39°08'45" N, long. 120°24'25" W; near SE cor. sec. 16, T 15 N, R 14 E). Named on Royal Gorge (1953) 7.5' quadrangle.

Ahart Sheep Camp [SIERRA]: *locality,* 3.5 miles southeast of Sierra City (lat. 39°32' N, long. 120°35'10" W; near NE cor. sec. 11, T 19 N, R 12 E). Named on Sierra City (1955) 15' quadrangle.

Ahwiyah Point [MARIPOSA]: *relief feature,* 2.5 miles east of Yosemite Village (lat. 37°45' N, long. 119°32'10" W). Named on Hetch Hetchy Reservoir (1956) 15' quadrangle. The name is of Indian origin; the feature also had the names "Acorn Peak," "The Old Piute," and "Old Man of the Mountains" (Browning, 1988, p. 3).

Aigare: see **Mount Aigare** [EL DORADO].

Airola Camp [CALAVERAS]: *locality,* 6 miles east of Blue Mountain (lat. 38°21'55" N, long. 120°15'20" W; sec. 30, T 6 N, R 16 E); the place is along Airola Creek. Named on Dorrington (1979) 7.5' quadrangle.

Airola Creek [CALAVERAS]: *stream,* flows 3 miles to South Fork Mokelumne River 5.25 miles east-northeast of Blue Mountain (lat. 38°21'35" N, long. 120°16'05" W; sec. 24, T 6 N, R 15 E). Named on Boards Crossing (1979) and Dorrington (1979) 7.5' quadrangles.

Alabama Bar [PLACER]: *locality,* 2.5 miles south of Michigan Bluff along Middle Fork American River (lat. 39°00'10" N, long. 120°

44'30" W; sec. 3, T 13 N, R 11 E). Named on Duncan Peak (1952) 15' quadrangle.

Alabama Flat: see **Johntown Creek** [EL DORADO].

Alabama Gulch: see **Alabama Hill** [CALAVERAS].

Alabama Hill [CALAVERAS]: *peak,* 4.25 miles west of Rail Road Flat near Glencoe (lat. 38°21'20" N, long. 120°35'25" W; sec. 19, T 6 N, R 13 E). Altitude 3012 feet. Named on Rail Road Flat (1948) 7.5' quadrangle. Miners from Alabama named the feature in 1849 (Camp *in* Doble, p. 297). Camp's (1962) map shows a canyon called Alabama Gulch that heads near Alabama Hill and opens into the canyon of Mokelumne River 2.5 miles southsouthwest of the confluence of Middle Fork and North Fork Mokelumne River. Doble (p. 39) noted that Alabama Gulch sometimes was called Spring Gulch because of the numerous springs there.

Alabama House [AMADOR]: *locality,* less than 1 mile south-southeast of present Carbondale (lat. 38°23'50" N, long. 121°00'15" W). Named on Carbondale (1909) 7.5' quadrangle.

Alabama House: see **Kentucky House** [CALAVERAS].

Alaska Hill [SIERRA]: *peak,* less than 1 mile north-northwest of Pike (lat. 39°26'55" N, long. 121°00'15" W; on N line sec. 7, T 18 N, R 9 E). Altitude 4027 feet. Named on Camptonville (1948) 7.5' quadrangle. United States Board on Geographic Names (1991, p. 2) approved the name "Alaska Peak" for the feature.

Alaska Peak: see **Alaska Hill** [SIERRA].

Albany Flat [CALAVERAS]: *area,* 2 miles south-southeast of Angels Camp (lat. 38°03' N, long. 120°31'40" W; near SE cor. sec. 3, T 2 N, R 13 E). Named on Angels Camp (1962) 7.5' quadrangle.

Alder: see **Alder Creek** [MARIPOSA].

Alder Creek [MARIPOSA]: *stream,* flows 6.5 miles to South Fork Merced River 3.5 miles northwest of Wawona (lat. 37°34'40" N, long. 119°41'50" W; sec. 20, T 4 S, R 21 E). Named on Yosemite (1956) 15' quadrangle. Laizure's (1935) map shows a place called Alder located along Alder Creek about 1 mile east of the mouth of the stream (sec. 21, T 4 S, R 21 E).

Alder Creek [TUOLUMNE]: *stream,* flows 4 miles to Tuolumne River 9.5 miles southsoutheast of Duckwall Mountain (lat. 37°50'55" N, long. 120°01'40" W; near SW cor. sec. 17, T 1 S, R 18 E). Named on Duckwall Mountain (1948) and Jawbone Ridge (1947) 7.5' quadrangles.

Alder Spring [TUOLUMNE]: *spring,* 2.25 miles east of Tuolumne (lat. 37°57'30" N, long. 120°11'35" W; near W line sec. 11, T 1 N, R 16 E). Named on Tuolumne (1948) 7.5' quadrangle.

Alberts Lake: see **Little Alberts Lake**, under **Elbert Lake** [EL DORADO].

Al Brass Creek [EL DORADO]: *stream,* flows 2 miles to Rock Creek 12.5 miles northwest of Pollock Pines (lat. 38°53'25" N, long. 120° 44'30" W; sec. 15, T 12 N, R 11 E). Named on Tunnel Hill (1950) 7.5' quadrangle.

Alder Creek [EL DORADO]: *stream,* flows 12.5 miles to South Fork American River nearly 4 miles east of Riverton (lat. 38°46' N, long. 120°22'45" W; sec. 26, T 11 N, R 14 E). Named on Kyburz (1952), Leek Spring Hill (1951), Riverton (1950), and Tragedy Spring (1979) 7.5' quadrangles.

Alder Creek [NEVADA]:
(1) *stream,* flows 1.5 miles to Fall Creek 6.5 miles southeast of Graniteville (lat. 39°22'40" N, long. 120°38'40" W; sec. 32, T 18 N, R 12 E). Named on Graniteville (1982) 7.5' quadrangle.
(2) *stream,* flows 7 miles to Prosser Creek Reservoir 3.25 miles north of Truckee (lat. 39°22'30" N, long. 120°10'25" W; near S line sec. 26, T 18 N, R 16 E). Named on Norden (1955) and Truckee (1955) 7.5' quadrangles.

Alder Creek [SIERRA]: *stream,* flows nearly 3 miles to Smithneck Creek 7 miles southeast of Loyalton (lat. 39°35'50" N, long. 120° 10'05" W; sec. 11, T 20 N, R 16 E). Named on Sardine Peak (1981) 7.5' quadrangle.

Alder Creek Camp Ground [EL DORADO]: *locality,* nearly 4 miles east of Riverton along South Fork American River (lat. 38°46' N, long. 120°22'40" W; sec. 26, T 11 N, R 14 E); the place is opposite the mouth of Alder Creek. Named on Riverton (1950) 7.5' quadrangle.

Alder Grove: see **Illinoistown** [PLACER].

Alder Hill [EL DORADO]: *peak,* 10.5 miles west-southwest of Kirkwood at the east end of Plummer Ridge (lat. 38°37'45" N, long. 120°14'15" W; near W line sec. 17, T 9 N, R 16 E). Named on Tragedy Spring (1979) 7.5' quadrangle.

Alder Hill [NEVADA]: *peak,* nearly 2 miles north-northwest of Truckee (lat. 39°21'10" N, long. 120°11'40" W; near W line sec. 3, T 17 N, R 16 E); the peak is south of Alder Creek (2). Altitude 6733 feet. Named on Truckee (1955) 7.5' quadrangle.

Alderman Creek [PLACER]: *stream,* flows 2 miles to Bear River 11 miles northwest of Auburn (lat. 39°00'45" N, long. 121°13'05" W; near N line sec. 5, T 13 N, R 7 E). Named on Gold Hill (1954) and Wolf (1949) 7'5' quadrangles.

Alder Ridge [EL DORADO]: *ridge,* generally northwest-trending, 10 miles long, center 6 miles north of Leek Spring Hill (lat. 38°43'20" N, long. 120°16'15" W). Named on Kyburz (1952), Leek Spring Hill (1951), and Tragedy Spring (1979) 7.5' quadrangles.

Algerine [TUOLUMNE]: *locality,* 5 miles south of Sonora (lat. 37°54'40" N, long. 120°22'55" W; sec. 25, T 1 N, R 14 E); the site is near Algerine Creek. Named on Sonora (1948) 7.5'

quadrangle. The place first was called Providence Camp, then Algiers and Algerine Camp (Gudde, 1975, p. 15).

Algerine Camp: see **Algerine** [TUOLUMNE].

Algerine Creek [TUOLUMNE]: *stream,* flows nearly 3 miles to Curtis Creek 4.5 miles south of Sonora (lat. 37°55' N, long. 120° 22'40" W; near NE cor. sec. 25, T 1 N, R 14 E). Named on Sonora (1948) and Standard (1948) 7.5' quadrangles.

Algiers: see **Algerine** [TUOLUMNE].

Alkali Creek [TUOLUMNE]: *stream,* flows 5.5 miles to Conness Creek 8 miles west of Tioga Pass (lat. 37°55'05" N, long. 119°24'20" W). Named on Tuolumne Meadows (1956) 15' quadrangle. The stream is called Middle Fork on a Wheeler survey map of 1878-79 (Browning, 1988, p. 3).

Alleghany [SIERRA]: *village,* 6.5 miles south of Downieville (lat. 39°28'20" N, long. 120°50'35" W; sec. 34, T 19 N, R 10 E). Named on Alleghany (1949) 7.5' quadrangle. Postal authorities established Alleghany post office in 1857 (Frickstad, p. 184). The name is from Alleghany tunnel, said to have been built in 1855 by gold miners from Alleghany, Pennsylvania (Hanna, p. 7).

Allegheny Creek [EL DORADO]: *stream,* flows 2 miles to Green Spring Creek nearly 4 miles north-northwest of Clarksville (lat. 38° 42'30" N, long. 121°04'05" W; sec. 23, T 10 N, R 8 E). Named on Clarksville (1953) 7.5' quadrangle.

Allen: see **John Allen Flat** [MARIPOSA].

Allen [AMADOR]: *locality,* 5.5 miles north of Mokelumne Peak along Bear River (lat. 38°37' N, long. 120°06'35" W; sec. 21, T 9 N, R 17 E). Named on Mokelumne Peak (1979) 7.5' quadrangle.

Allen Camp [EL DORADO]: *locality,* 10 miles southwest of Kirkwood at Corral Flat (lat. 38°37'50" N, long. 120°13'15" W; near NW cor. sec. 21, T 9 N, R 16 E). Named on Bear River Reservoir (1979) 7.5' quadrangle.

Allenwood Hill [NEVADA]: *peak,* 5 miles west of Pilot Peak (lat. 39°09'50" N, long. 121°06'20" W; sec. 11, T 15 N, R 6 E). Altitude 1320 feet. Named on Smartville (1951) 7.5' quadrangle.

Alma: see **Mount Alma** [SIERRA].

Aloha: see **Lake Aloha** [EL DORADO].

Alpha [NEVADA]: *locality,* 2 miles south-southeast of Washington (lat. 39°19'45" N, long. 120°47' W). Named on Colfax (1898) 30' quadrangle. Postal authorities established Alpha post office in 1855 and discontinued it in 1862 (Frickstad, p. 112). Prospectors discovered gold at the site in 1850 and settlers arrived in 1852; the place had the nickname "Hell Out for High Noon City" in the early days (Slyter and Slyter, p. 8).

Alpha Diggings [NEVADA]: *locality,* 2 miles south-southeast of Washington (lat. 39°20'10" N, long. 120°47' W; sec. 18, T 17 N, R 11 E);

the place is at or near the site of Alpha. Named on Washington (1950) 7.5' quadrangle.

Alpine Campground [EL DORADO]: *locality,* 1.5 miles south-southeast of Echo Summit along Upper Truckee River (lat. 38°47'45" N, long. 120°01'10" W; near SW cor. sec. 17, T 11 N, R 18 E). Named on Echo Lake (1955) 7.5' quadrangle.

Alpine Meadows [PLACER]: *settlement,* 5 miles west of Tahoe City along Bear Creek (lat. 39°10'30" N, long. 120°13'50" W). Named on Tahoe City (1955, photorevised 1969) 7.5' quadrangle.

Alta [PLACER]: *village,* 1.5 miles east of Dutch Flat (lat. 39°12'25" N, long. 120°48'40" W; near W line sec. 36, T 16 N, R 10 E). Named on Dutch Flat (1950) 7.5' quadrangle. Postal authorities established Alta post office in 1871 (Frickstad, p. 118). Officials of Central Pacific Railroad are said to have named the place in 1866 for the San Francisco newspaper *Alta California,* which favored the railroad (Gudde, 1949, p. 9).

Alta: see **Lake Alta** [PLACER].

Alta Hill [NEVADA]: *town,* 1 mile northwest of downtown Grass Valley (lat. 39°13'55" N, long. 121°04'30" W; near SE cor. sec. 21, T 16 N, R 8 E). Named on Grass Valley (1949) 7.5' quadrangle.

Alta Hill Reservoir [NEVADA]: *lakes,* 1 mile north of downtown Grass Valley (lat. 39°13'55" N, long. 121°03'55" W; sec. 22, T 16 N, R 8 E); the lakes are at the east edge of Alta Hill. Named on Grass Valley (1949) 7.5' quadrangle.

Al Tahoe [EL DORADO]: *district,* 7.5 miles northwest of Freel Peak in the town of South Lake Tahoe (lat. 38°56'30" N, long. 119° 59' W). Named on South Lake Tahoe (1955, photorevised 1969 and 1974) 7.5' quadrangle. Sinclair's (1901) map has the name "Rowlands" at the place. Lake House, the first lake-front hotel along Lake Tahoe, was located just west of present Al Tahoe; after Lake House burned, Tom Rowland rebuilt it and constructed a long pier that was a shipping point for lumber from Lake Valley—eventually Al Sprague replaced Rowland's establishment with a family hotel that he named Al Tahoe (Zauner, p. 8-9, 15). Postal authorities established Rowland post office in 1874 and discontinued it in 1888; they established Al Tahoe post office in 1908 (Salley, p. 5, 190). Sinclair (p. 272) noted a place called Goddard's Station that was situated 1.5 miles east of Lake House in the 1860's.

Alta Morris Lake [EL DORADO]: *lake,* 700 feet long, 4.25 miles south of Phipps Peak (lat. 38°53'35" N, long. 120°08'20" W). Named on Rockbound Valley (1955) 7.5' quadrangle.

Altaville [CALAVERAS]: *town,* less than 1 mile northwest of Angels Camp (lat. 38°05' N, long. 120°33'30" W; sec. 28, 29, T 3 N, R 13 E). Named on Angels Camp (1962) 7.5' quad-

rangle. Postal authorities established Altaville post office in 1904, discontinued it in 1943, and reestablished it in 1944 (Salley, p. 6). The community first was known as Cherokee Flat, then as Forks of the Road, and as Winterton; residents of the town selected the name "Altaville" in 1857 (Hanna, p. 9). Angels Camp annexed the place in 1972 (Leonard, p. 3). Gudde (1949, p. 8) noted that the site also had the name "Low Divide."

Amador: see **Amador City** [AMADOR].

Amador City [AMADOR]: *village,* 4.5 miles south-southeast of Plymouth (lat. 38°25'10" N, long. 120°49'25" W; sec. 36, T 7 N, R 10 E); the place is along Amador Creek. Named on Amador City (1962) 7.5' quadrangle. Called Amador on Jackson (1902) 30' quadrangle. Postal authorities established Amador City post office in 1863 (Frickstad, p. 5), and the community incorporated in 1915. The place first was situated about 0.5 mile upstream from the present site, but was moved when placer mining for gold threatened to destroy the original buildings (McKinstry, p. 317). The village grew around the camp of Jose Maria Amador, who came to the neighborhood seeking gold in 1848 (Gudde, 1975, p. 17). A place called Amador Crossing was east of Amador City where the stage road from Jackson to Dry Creek crossed Amador Creek; Amador Crossing also was known as Upper Crossing (Gudde, 1975, p. 17).

Amador Creek [AMADOR]: *stream,* flows 10.5 miles to Dry Creek nearly 4 miles south-southwest of Plymouth (lat. 38°25'45" N, long. 120°52'30" W; near E line sec. 28, T 7 N, R 10 E); the stream goes through and is named for Amador City (Hanna, p. 10). Named on Amador City (1962) and Pine Grove (1948) 7.5' quadrangles.

Amador Crossing: see **Amador City** [AMADOR].

Amador Reservoir: see **Icehouse Pond** [AMADOR].

Amelia Earhart Peak [TUOLUMNE]: *peak,* 8.5 miles south of Tioga Pass (lat. 37°47'15" N, long. 119°17'15" W). Altitude 11,982 feet. Named on Tuolumne Meadows (1956) 15' quadrangle. The name commemorates Amelia Earhart Putnam, who disappeared on a flight over the Pacific Ocean in 1937 (United States Board on Geographic Names, 1967b, p. 2). Rocketdyne Mountaineering Club proposed the name (Browning, 1988, p. 4).

American [PLACER]: *locality,* 4 miles east of Dutch Flat along Southern Pacific Railroad (lat. 39°12'05" N, long. 120°46' W; near N line sec. 5, T 15 N, R 11 E). Named on Colfax (1938) 30' quadrangle.

American Bar [PLACER]: *locality,* 3.5 miles east-southeast of Foresthill along Middle Fork American River (lat. 39°00'20" N, long. 120°45'10" W; near N line sec. 4, T 13 N, R 11 E). Named on Foresthill (1949) 7.5' quadrangle.

American Bar: see **Buckeye Bar** [EL DO-RADO-PLACER].

American Camp: see **American Camp Station** [TUOLUMNE]; **Columbia** [TUOLUMNE]; **Jamestown** [TUOLUMNE].

American Camp Station [TUOLUMNE]: *locality,* 4.5 miles northeast of Columbia in Silver Gulch (lat. 38°05'15" N, long. 120°20'40" W; sec. 29, T 3 N, R 15 E). Named on Columbia SE (1948) 7.5' quadrangle. Big Trees (1891) 30' quadrangle shows a place called American Camp near the site.

American Canyon [EL DORADO]: *canyon,* drained by a stream that flows 3.25 miles to Middle Fork American River 3 miles north-northwest of Greenwood at Poverty Bar (lat. 38°56'05" N, long. 120°56'30" W; sec. 35, T 13 N, R 9 E). Named on Greenwood (1949) 7.5' quadrangle.

American Flat [EL DORADO]: *locality,* 4.5 miles north of Chili Bar (lat. 38°50'05" N, long. 120°48'50" W; sec. 1, T 11 N, R 10 E). Named on Garden Valley (1949) 7.5' quadrangle. The name is from the term "American Company," the designation that the first group of miners at the place gave to themselves (Gernes, p. 45).

American Flat [SIERRA]: *area,* 1.25 miles northwest of Alleghany (lat. 39°29'05" N, long. 120°51'35" W; sec. 28, T 19 N, R 10 E). Named on Alleghany (1949) 7.5' quadrangle.

American Fork: see **American River** [EL DO-RADO-PLACER].

American Hill [PLACER]: *ridge,* south-south-west-trending, 1.5 miles long, 4.25 miles west-southwest of Duncan Peak (lat. 39°08'10" N, long. 120°35'20" W). Named on Duncan Peak (1952) 7.5' quadrangle.

American Hill [SIERRA]:

(1) *ridge,* south-southeast-trending, less than 0.5 mile long, 4.5 miles east-northeast of Alleghany (lat. 39°29'05" N, long. 120°45'35" W; sec. 29, T 19 N, R 11 E). Named on Alleghany (1949) 7.5' quadrangle.

(2) *locality,* nearly 5 miles east-northeast of Alleghany (lat. 39° 28'50" N, long. 120°45'30" W); the place is on present American Hill (1). Named on Colfax (1898) 30' quadrangle.

American Hill: see **Nevada City** [NEVADA].

American Hill Cabin [SIERRA]: *locality,* 4.25 miles east-northeast of Alleghany (lat. 39°29'45" N, long. 120°46' W; sec. 20, T 19 N, R 11 E); the place is 1 mile north-north-west of American Hill (1). Named on Alleghany (1949) 7.5' quadrangle.

American Lake [EL DORADO]: *lake,* 2200 feet long, 1.5 miles east-northeast of Pyramid Peak (lat. 38°51'20" N, long. 120°08'05" W). Named on Pyramid Peak (1955) 7.5' quadrangle.

American Ranch Hill [NEVADA]: *ridge,* 2 miles long, 4.5 miles southwest of Grass Valley (lat. 39°10'05" N, long. 121°06'45" W).

Named on Grass Valley (1949) and Rough and Ready (1949) 7.5' quadrangles.

American River [EL DORADO-PLACER]: *stream,* formed by the confluence of North Fork and South Fork in Folsom Lake, flows 30 miles to Sacramento River 1.5 miles north-northwest of downtown Sacramento (lat. 38°35'50" N, long. 121°30'25" W). Named on Carmichael (1967), Citrus Heights (1967), Folsom (1967), Sacramento East (1967), and Sacramento West (1967) 7.5' quadrangles. Called Rio de los Americanos on Fremont's (1845) map, and called American Fork on Williamson's (1849) map. The name "American River" is from a place called El Paso de los Americanos, where Canadian trappers, who were called Americanos by Spanish-speaking Indians, crossed the stream in the early days (Gudde, 1949, p. 10). North Fork heads near Granite Chief and flows 85 miles to join South Fork in Folsom Lake; it forms El Dorado-Placer county line below its junction with Middle Fork. North Fork is named on Auburn (1953), Colfax (1949), Duncan Peak (1952), Dutch Flat (1950), Folsom (1967), Foresthill (1949), Granite Chief (1953), Greenwood (1949), Norden (1955), Pilot Hill (1954, photorevised 1973), Rocklin (1967), Royal Gorge (1953), Soda Springs (1955), and Westville (1952) 7.5' quadrangles. North Fork of North Fork American River joins North Fork 4.5 miles east-southeast of Dutch Flat; it is 18 miles long and is named on Blue Canyon (1955), Cisco Grove (1955), Dutch Flat (1950), and Westville (1952) 7.5' quadrangles. On Whitney's (1873) map, the upper part, at least, of present North Fork of North Fork is called Little North Fork. East Fork of North Fork of North Fork American River joins North Fork of North Fork 4.5 miles north-northwest of Westville; it is 7.5 miles long and is named on Blue Canyon (1955), Cisco Grove (1955), Duncan Peak (1952), and Westville (1952) 7.5' quadrangles. Middle Fork American River joins North Fork 2.25 miles east-northeast of Auburn; it is 62 miles long and is named on Auburn (1953), Bunker Hill (1953), Foresthill (1949), Georgetown (1949), Granite Chief (1953), Greek Store (1952), Greenwood (1949), Michigan Bluff (1952), and Royal Gorge (1953) 7.5' quadrangles. Middle Fork forms El Dorado-Placer county line downstream from the mouth of Rubicon River to the junction with North Fork. North Fork of Middle Fork joins Middle Fork 2.25 miles south of Michigan Bluff; it is 17 miles long and is named on Duncan Peak (1952), Greek Store (1952), and Michigan Bluff (1952) 7.5' quadrangles. South Fork, which forms part of El Dorado-Sacramento county line, heads at Echo Summit and flows for 82 miles to join North Fork in Folsom Lake. South Fork is named on Clarksville (1953), Coloma (1949), Echo Lake (1955),

Folsom (1967), Garden Valley (1949), Kyburz (1952), Leek Spring Hill (1951), Pilot Hill (1954, photorevised 1973), Pollock Pines (1950), Pyramid Peak (1955), and Slate Mountain (1950) 7.5' quadrangles. Silver Fork heads at Silver Lake and flows 14 miles to South Fork 1 mile west-southwest of Kyburz, it is named on Caples Lake (1979), Kyburz (1952), Leek Spring Hill (1951), and Tragedy Spring (1979) 7.5' quadrangles. Gudde (1975) listed the several mining places situated along North Fork American River in Placer County: Calf Bar, located near the junction with Middle Fork (p. 56); Grizzly Bar, located 1 mile above the junction with Middle Fork (p. 146); Kellys Bar, located above Calf Bar (p. 183); Niggerhead Bar, located 2 miles below the mouth of Middle Fork (p. 243); and Portuguese Bar, located near Calf Bar (p. 273).

Anderson Canyon [EL DORADO]: *canyon,* drained by a stream that flows 4 miles to Middle Fork Cosumnes River 8 miles east of Caldor (lat. 38°35'25" N, long. 120°16'50" W; sec. 35, T 9 N, R 15 E). Named on Bear River Reservoir (1979) and Peddler Hill (1951) 7.5' quadrangles.

Anderson Creek [EL DORADO]: *stream,* flows 1 mile to Folsom Lake 6.25 miles southwest of the village of Pilot Hill (lat. 38°46'35" N, long. 121°06'05" W; sec. 29, T 11 N, R 8 E). Named on Pilot Hill (1954, photorevised 1973) 7.5' quadrangle.

Anderson Creek: see **Deep Ravine** [EL DORADO].

Anderson Flat [MARIPOSA]: *area,* 8 miles west-northwest of El Portal (lat. 37°44'25" N, long. 119°54'25" W; near SE cor. sec. 19, T 2 S, R 19 E). Named on Kinsley (1947) 7.5' quadrangle.

Anderson Meadow [SIERRA]: *area,* 8.5 miles south-southeast of Sierraville (lat. 39°28'40" N, long. 120°17'30" W; near SE cor. sec. 22, T 19 N, R 15 E). Named on Independence Lake (1981) 7.5' quadrangle.

Anderson Peak [PLACER]: *peak,* 4.25 miles south-southeast of Donner Pass (lat. 39°15'30" N, long. 120°17'45" W; near S line sec. 3, T 16 N, R 15 E). Altitude 8683 feet. Named on Norden (1955) 7.5' quadrangle.

Anderson Ridge [EL DORADO]: *ridge,* west-southwest-trending, 2 miles long, 11.5 miles southwest of Kirkwood (lat. 38°36'30" N, long. 120°14'15" W); the ridge is southeast of Anderson Canyon. Named on Bear River Reservoir (1979) 7.5' quadrangle.

Andesite Peak [NEVADA]: *peak,* 3.25 miles northwest of Donner Pass (lat. 39°21'05" N, long. 120°21'55" W; sec. 11, T 17 N, R 14 E). Altitude 8219 feet. Named on Norden (1955) 7.5' quadrangle. The name is from the kind of rock exposed at the peak (United States Board on Geographic Names, 1949b, p. 3).

Andesite Ridge [NEVADA]: *ridge,* southeast-trending, 1 mile long, 2.5 miles northwest of

Donner Pass (lat. 39°20'45" N, long. 120° 21'25" W); Andesite Peak is at the northwest end of the ridge. Named on Norden (1955) 7.5' quadrangle. The name is from the kind of rock exposed on the ridge (United States Board on Geographic Names, 1949b, p. 3).

Andover [PLACER]: *locality,* 11.5 miles west of Martis Peak along Southern Pacific Railroad (lat. 39°18'35" N, long. 120°14'45" W; sec. 19, T 17 N, R 16 E). Named on Truckee (1955) 7.5' quadrangle. A division superintendent of Southern Pacific Railroad named the place for his hometown in Massachusetts (Gudde, 1949, p. 11).

Andreason Mill [EL DORADO]: *locality,* 3.5 miles south of Omo Ranch (lat. 38°31'45" N, long. 120°34'35" W; sec. 19, T 8 N, R 13 E). Site named on Omo Ranch (1952) 7.5' quadrangle.

Andrew Creek [TUOLUMNE]: *stream,* flows 3 miles to Mountain Pass Creek 2 miles north of Keystone (lat. 37°52'40" N, long. 120° 30'40" W; sec. 2, T 1 S, R 13 E). Named on Keystone (1962) and Melones Dam (1962) 7.5' quadrangles.

Andrew Gray Creek [PLACER]: *stream,* flows nearly 2 miles to North Fork American River 6 miles northwest of Duncan Peak (lat. 39°12'45" N, long. 120°35'45" W; sec. 35, T 16 N, R 12 E). Named on Duncan Peak (1952) 7.5' quadrangle. The name is for Andrew Wheaton Gray, who came to the region in 1850 (United States Board on Geographic Names, 1967a, p. 2).

Andrews Lake [TUOLUMNE]: *lake,* 800 feet long, 10.5 miles southwest of Tower Peak (lat. 38°02'20" N, long. 119°41'20" W); the lake is 0.5 mile west of Andrews Peak. Named on Tower Peak (1956) 15' quadrangle.

Andrews Peak [TUOLUMNE]: *peak,* 10 miles southwest of Tower Peak (lat. 38°02'20" N, long. 119°40'45" W). Altitude 8570 feet. Named on Tower Peak (1956) 15' quadrangle.

Angela: see **Lake Angela** [NEVADA].

Angel Creek [EL DORADO]: *stream,* flows 3 miles to Gerle Creek 3 miles north of Robbs Peak (lat. 38°58'05" N, long. 120°23'35" W; sec. 15, T 13 N, R 14 E). Named on Loon Lake (1952) and Robbs Peak (1950) 7.5' quadrangles.

Angels: see **Angels Camp** [CALAVERAS].

Angels Camp [CALAVERAS]: *town,* 11 miles southeast of San Andreas (lat. 38°04'30" N, long. 120°32'45" W); the place is along Angels Creek. Named on Angels Camp (1962) 7.5' quadrangle. Called Angel's on Derby's (1849) map, and called Angels and Angels Camp P.O. on San Andreas (1947) 15' quadrangle. Postal authorities established Carson's Creek post office at the place in 1851, and changed the name to Angels Camp in 1853 (Frickstad, p. 14). The town incorporated in 1912 under the name "Angels," but the post office kept the name "Angels Camp." The name "Angels" commemorates Henry P. Angel, who came to the neighborhood in July, 1848, and set up a trading post; the community first was called Angels Trading Post, and later was named Angels Camp (Leonard, p. 3).

Angels Creek [CALAVERAS]: *stream,* flows 17 miles to Melones Reservoir 4.5 miles south of Angels Camp (lat. 38°00'25" N, long. 120°33' W; sec. 21 T 2 N, R 13 E); the stream passes through Angels Camp. Named on Angels Camp (1962), Columbia (1948), Melones Dam (1962), and Murphys (1948) 7.5' quadrangles. The name commemorates Henry P. Angel of Angels Camp (Hanna, p. 13).

Angel's Trading Post: see **Angels Camp** [CALAVERAS].

Angora Creek [EL DORADO]: *stream,* flows 4 miles to Upper Truckee River 4.25 miles north of Echo Summit (lat. 38°52'25" N, long. 120°00'45" W; sec. 20, T 12 N, R 18 E); the stream heads at Angora Lakes. Named on Echo Lake (1955) and Emerald Bay (1955) 7.5' quadrangles.

Angora Lakes [EL DORADO]: *lakes,* largest 1000 feet long, 4 miles north-northwest of Echo Summit (lat. 38°51'50" N, long. 120°03'55" W); the lakes are 0.25 mile east-southeast of Angora Peak at the head of Angora Creek. Named on Echo Lake (1955) 7.5' quadrangle. The name "Angora" is from the herd of Angora goats that Nathan Gilmore pastured in the neighborhood (Lekisch, p. 4).

Angora Peak [EL DORADO]: *peak,* 4.5 miles north-northwest of Echo Summit (lat. 38°52' N, long. 120°04'20" W). Altitude 8588 feet. Named on Echo Lake (1955) 7.5' quadrangle.

Ann: see **Fort Ann**, under **Volcano** [AMADOR].

Antelope [SIERRA]: *locality,* 12 miles east of Loyalton in Upper Long Valley (lat. 39°41'25" N, long. 120°00'55" W; at W line sec. 18, T 21 N, R 18 E). Named on Loyalton (1955) 15' quadrangle.

Antelope Creek [AMADOR]: *stream,* flows 5.5 miles to Mill Creek 9 miles east-northeast of Pine Grove (lat. 38°27'15" N, long. 120° 30'30" W; near N line sec. 23, T 7 N, R 13 E). Named on Caldor (1951), Devils Nose (1979), and West Point (1948) 7.5' quadrangles. On Mokelumne Hill (1948) 15' quadrangle, the name "Antelope Creek" seems to apply to present Mill Creek below the confluence of Antelope Creek and Mill Creek.

Antelope Creek [PLACER]: *stream,* flows 9.5 miles to join the stream in Miners Ravine and form Dry Creek (2) 1 mile east-northeast of downtown Roseville (lat. 38°45'20" N, long. 121° 16' W; near E line sec. 35, T 11 N, R 6 E). Named on Rocklin (1967) and Roseville (1967) 7.5' quadrangles. The canyon of the stream is called Antelope Rav. on Hobson's (1890b) map.

Antelope Creek: see **Dry Creek** [PLACER].

Antelope House: see **Jenny Lind** [CALAVERAS].

Antelope Ravine: see **Antelope Creek** [PLACER].

Antelope Springs [AMADOR]: *locality,* 6 miles west-southwest of present Hams Station (lat. 38°30'50" N, long. 120°38'40" W); the place is near Antelope Creek. Named on Pyramid Peak (1896) 30' quadrangle.

Antelope Valley [SIERRA]: *canyon,* drained by a stream that flows 5.5 miles to Sierra Valley nearly 7 miles north-northeast of Sierraville (lat. 39°40'45" N, long. 120°18'50" W; near NW cor. sec. 16, T 21 N, R 15 E). Named on Antelope Valley (1981) and Sierraville (1981) 7.5' quadrangles.

Anthony House [NEVADA]: *locality,* 5 miles north-northwest of Pilot Peak along Deer Creek (lat. 39°14'20" N, long. 120°12'45" W; at S line sec. 17, T 16 N, R 7 E). Named on Grass Valley (1949) 15' quadrangle. Water of a reservoir now covers the site. Postal authorities established Anthony House post office in 1862, discontinued it in 1866, reestablished it in 1867, discontinued it for a time in 1877, and discontinued it finally in 1906 (Frickstad, p. 113). The place was a stage station on the old turnpike that ran up San Juan Ridge (Hoover, Rensch, and Rensch, p. 250). Whitney's (1873) map shows a place called Texas Fl. [Flat] located 2 miles east of Anthony House along Deer Creek, and a relief feature called Beckman Hill located 2.25 miles northeast of Anthony House. Gudde (1975, p. 261) listed a place called Pearls Hill that was situated about 1 mile northwest of Anthony House near Deer Creek.

Antoine Canyon [PLACER]: *canyon,* drained by a stream that flows 3.25 miles to Screwauger Canyon 4 miles west-southwest of Duncan Peak (lat. 39°08'20" N, long. 120°35' W; near N line sec. 24, T 15 N, R 12 E). Named on Duncan Peak (1952) 7.5' quadrangle. Called Antone Canyon on Colfax (1898) 30' quadrangle. The name is for a half-breed Crow Indian who in 1850 was the first miner in the canyon (Hoover, Rensch, and Rensch, p. 277).

Antone Canyon: see **Antoine Canyon** [PLACER].

Antone Meadows [PLACER]: *area,* 2.25 miles north-northwest of Tahoe City (lat. 39°12'05" N, long. 120°09'10" W; near S line sec. 25, T 16 N, R 16 E). Named on Tahoe City (1955) 7.5' quadrangle. The name is for Antone Russi, who pastured cows at the place (Lekisch, p. 4).

Antwine Gulch [EL DORADO]: *canyon,* drained by a stream that flows 0.5 mile to Canyon Creek (1) 2.5 miles north-northeast of Georgetown (lat. 38°56'20" N, long. 120°49'10" W; near NE cor. sec. 35, T 13 N, R 10 E). Named on Georgetown (1949) 7.5' quadrangle.

Apex [EL DORADO]: *locality,* 1.25 miles west of downtown Placerville along Southern Pacific Railroad (lat. 38°43'40" N, long. 120° 49'20" W; near N line sec. 13, T 10 N, R 10 E). Named on Placerville (1949) 7.5' quadrangle.

Applegate [PLACER]: *town,* 7.25 miles south-southwest of Colfax (lat. 39°00'05" N, long. 120°59'25" W; near SE cor. sec. 5, T 13 N, R 9 E). Named on Colfax (1949) and Greenwood (1949) 7.5' quadrangles. California Division of Highways' (1934) map shows places called East Applegate and West Applegate located near Applegate. The name "Applegate" commemorates Lisbon Applegate and his son George; Lisbon settled at what was known as Bear River House in 1849—the place then was called Lisbon before the name was changed to Applegate (Hanna, p. 14). Postal authorities established Lisbon post office in 1855 and discontinued it in 1866; they established Applegate post office in 1875 (Salley, p. 8, 123).

Apple Tree Spring [MARIPOSA]: *spring,* 3.5 miles east-northeast of the settlement of Catheys Valley (lat. 37°27'05" N, long. 120° 02' W). Named on Catheys Valley (1962) 7.5' quadrangle.

Aqua Fria: see **Agua Fria** [MARIPOSA].

Aqueduct [AMADOR]: *locality,* nearly 2 miles southwest of Pine Grove (lat. 38°23'50" N, long. 120°37'55" W). Named on Jackson (1902) 30' quadrangle. Postal authorities established Aqueduct City post office in 1855 and discontinued it the same year (Frickstad, p. 5). The name is from a flume near the place (Andrews, p. 85).

Aqueduct City: see **Aqueduct** [AMADOR].

Ararat: see **Mount Ararat** [EL DORADO].

Ararat: see **Mount Ararat** [CALAVERAS].

Arastraville [TUOLUMNE]: *locality,* 2.5 miles north-northeast of Tuolumne (lat. 37°59'50" N, long. 120°13'30" W; sec. 28, T 2 N, R 16 E). Named on Tuolumne (1948) 7.5' quadrangle. Reynolds' (1899) map has the form "Arrastraville" for the name.

Arctic: see **Donner** [PLACER].

Ardeth Lake [TUOLUMNE]: *lake,* 1650 feet long, 10 miles southwest of Tower Peak (lat. 38°03'05" N, long. 119°41'25" W). Named on Tower Peak (1956) 15' quadrangle. Otto M. Brown, a ranger at Yosemite National Park from 1927 until 1946, named the lake for his wife (Browning, 1986, p. 7).

Arkansas Bar: see **Upper Arkansas Bar**, under **Green Valley** [PLACER].

Arkansas Creek [AMADOR]: *stream,* heads in Amador County and flows 9 miles to Cosumnes River 22 miles east-southeast of downtown Sacramento in Sacramento County (lat. 38°28'50" N, long. 121°06'20" W; near N line sec. 9, T 7 N, R 8 E). Named on Carbondale (1968) and Irish Hill (1962) 7.5' quadrangles.

Arkansas Ferry: see **Lancha Plana** [AMADOR].

Arkansas Flat: see **Carson** [MARIPOSA].

Armstrong Hill [EL DORADO]: *peak,* 5 miles south-southeast of Caldor (lat. 38°32'30" N, long. 120°23' W; near SW cor. sec. 13, T 8 N, R 14 E). Altitude 5701 feet. Named on Caldor (1951) 7.5' quadrangle.

Armstrong Pass [EL DORADO]: *pass,* nearly 2 miles south-southwest of Freel Peak on El Dorado-Alpine county line (lat. 38°49'55" N, long. 119°54'40" W; near E line sec. 1, T 11 N, R 18 E). Named on Freel Peak (1955) 7.5' quadrangle.

Armstrong's Mill: see **Pine Grove** [AMADOR].

Arndt Lake [TUOLUMNE]: *lake,* 1300 feet long, 5.25 miles south-southeast of Tower Peak (lat. 38°04'30" N, long. 119°30'10" W). Named on Tower Peak (1956) 15' quadrangle. Lieutenant H.C. Benson named the feature in 1896 for Sergeant Alvin Arndt of Fourth Cavalry (Gudde, 1949, p. 15).

Arnold [CALAVERAS]: *settlement,* 6 miles south of Blue Mountain (lat. 38°15'15" N, long. 120°21'15" W; mainly in sec. 29, 30, T 5 N, R 15 E). Named on Dorrington (1979) 7.5' quadrangle. Postal authorities established Arnold post office in 1934; they named it for Robert Arnold and Bernice Arnold, who operated the local store (Salley, p. 10).

Arrastraville: see **Arastraville** [TUOLUMNE].

Arroyo de los Osos: see **Bear River** [NEVADA-PLACER].

Arroyo Seco [AMADOR]: *land grant,* west of Ione in Amador, Sacramento, and San Joaquin Counties. Named on Carbondale (1968), Goose Creek (1968), Ione (1962), and Irish Hill (1962) 7.5' quadrangles. Teodosio Yorba received 11 leagues in 1840; Andres Pico claimed 48,858 acres patented in 1863 (Cowan, p. 17).

Arthur: see **Lake Arthur** [PLACER].

Artist Creek [MARIPOSA]: *stream,* flows 1.5 miles to Merced River 5.25 miles west-southwest of Yosemite Village (lat. 37°43'05" N, long. 119°40'20" W); the stream goes past Artist Point. Named on Yosemite (1956) 15' quadrangle.

Artist Point [MARIPOSA]: *relief feature,* 5.5 miles west-southwest of Yosemite Village on the south side of Yosemite Valley (lat. 37° 42'45" N, long. 119°40'30" W). Named on Yosemite (1956) 15' quadrangle. Artist Thomas Ayres drew the first picture of Yosemite Falls from the place; the feature is mislocated by 0.25 mile on early quadrangle maps (Browning, 1986, p. 8).

Ascension Mountain [TUOLUMNE]: *peak,* 4.25 miles southwest of Mather (lat. 37°50'05" N, long. 119°54'15" W; sec. 20, T 1 S, R 19 E). Named on Lake Eleanor (1956) 15' quadrangle.

Ashland: see **Ashland Creek** [AMADOR].

Ashland Creek [AMADOR]: *stream,* flows about 7 miles to Sutter Creek (1) 4 miles northeast of Pine Grove (lat. 38°27'20" N, long. 120°36'25" W; sec. 13, T 7 N, R 12 E). Named on Omo Ranch (1952) and West Point (1948) 7.5' quadrangles. Camp's (1962) map shows an inhabited place called Ashland located along Ashland Creek 2.25 miles east-northeast of Volcano.

Aspen Campgrounds [SIERRA]: *locality,* 6.5 miles southeast of Sierra City along Jackson Meadows Reservoir (lat. 39°30'20" N, long. 120°32'10" W; near N line sec. 20, T 19 N, R 13 E). Named on Haypress Valley (1981) 7.5' quadrangle.

Aspen Creek [EL DORADO]: *stream,* flows 1.25 miles to South Fork American River 3 miles west of Echo Summit (lat. 38°48'45" N, long. 120°05'05" W; sec. 10, T 11 N, R 17 E). Named on Echo Lake (1955) 7.5' quadrangle.

Aspen Meadow [TUOLUMNE]: *area,* 2.25 miles east-southeast of Pinecrest (lat. 38°10'40" N, long. 119°56'55" W; sec. 25, T 4 N, R 18 E). Named on Pinecrest (1979) 7.5' quadrangle.

Aspen Valley [TUOLUMNE]:
(1) *valley,* 6 miles southeast of Mather (lat. 37°50' N, long. 119°46'30" W). Named on Lake Eleanor (1956) 15' quadrangle.
(2) *settlement,* 6 miles southeast of Mather (lat. 37°49'40" N, long. 119°46'15" W; near E line sec. 28, T 1 S, R 20 E); the place is in Aspen Valley (1). Named on Lake Eleanor (1956) 15' quadrangle.

Atherton Flat [EL DORADO]: *area,* 2.25 miles northeast of Kyburz (lat. 38°48'05" N, long. 120°16' W; on W line sec. 18, T 11 N, R 16 E). Named on Kyburz (1952) 7.5' quadrangle.

Atlanta: see **Fordyce Lake** [NEVADA].

Auburn [PLACER]: *town,* in the center of the west half of Placer County (lat. 38°53'55" N, long. 121°04'25" W); the town is near the head of Auburn Ravine. Named on Auburn (1953) 7.5' quadrangle. Postal authorities established Auburn post office in 1853 (Frickstad, p. 119). The town incorporated in 1860, disincorporated about 1866, and incorporated again in 1888 (Hoover, Rensch, and Rensch, p. 269). Claude Chana discovered gold in Auburn Ravine in 1848; the mining camp that grew at the site later that same year was known as Wood's Dry Diggings, for John S. Wood, before it was named Auburn in the fall of 1849 (Davis, p. 5-7). The place also was called Rich Dry Diggin's (Jackson, J.H., p. 387). Postal authorities established East Auburn post office 1 mile east of Auburn post office in 1902 and discontinued it in 1919 (Salley, p. 63). They established Lone Star post office 6 miles north of Auburn in 1861 and discontinued it in 1863; the name was from Lone Star mine (Salley, p. 125). California Mining Bureau's (1917b) map shows a place called Leta located along the railroad about 3 miles west-southwest of Auburn. Gudde (1975, p. 195) listed a mining place called Little Rattlesnake

Bar that was situated 1 mile southeast of Auburn along North Fork American River.

Auburn Ravine [PLACER]: *relief feature,* drained by a stream that heads near Auburn and flows 28 miles to end in American Basin 7.25 miles northeast of Verona in Sutter County (lat. 38°51'10" N, long. 121°30'40" W; at S line sec. 27, T 12 N, R 4 E). Named on Auburn (1953), Gold Hill (1954), Lincoln (1953), Pleasant Grove (1967), Roseville (1967), and Verona (1967) 7.5' quadrangles.

Auburn Station: see **Newcastle** [PLACER].

Audrian Lake: see **Lake Audrian** [EL DORADO].

Aukum [EL DORADO]: *locality,* 13 miles south-southwest of Camino (lat. 38°33'25" N, long. 120°43'30" W; near SE cor. sec. 11, T 8 N, R 11 E); the place is 1.25 miles south of Mount Aukum. Named on Aukum (1952) 7.5' quadrangle. United States Board on Geographic Names (1976a, p. 5) gave the names "Aukum Fork" and "Mount Aukum" as variants. Postal authorities established Aukum post office in 1895, discontinued it in 1914, reestablished it in 1920, and changed the name to Mt. Aukum in 1961 (Salley, p. 148). California Mining Bureau's (1909a) map shows a place called Uno located nearly 3 miles east of Aukum by stage line. Postal authorities established Uno post office in 1892 and discontinued it in 1920 (Frickstad, p. 30).

Aukum: see **Mount Aukum** [EL DORADO].

Aukum Fork: see **Aukum** [EL DORADO].

Aurum City: see **El Dorado** [EL DORADO].

Austin Flat [NEVADA]: *area,* 6 miles west of Wolf (lat. 39°02'50" N, long. 121°14'50" W; near SE cor. sec. 24, T 14 N, R 6 E). Named on Wolf (1949) 7.5' quadrangle.

Austin Meadow [NEVADA]: *area,* 4 miles north-northwest of English Mountain (lat. 39°29'40" N, long. 120°35'20" W; near SE cor. sec. 23, T 19 N, R 12 E). Named on English Mountain (1983) 7.5' quadrangle.

Austin Ravine [NEVADA]: *canyon,* drained by a stream that flows 1 mile to Rock Creek (2) 8.5 miles south-southwest of Pilot Peak (lat. 39°03'50" N, long. 121°15'40" W; sec. 13, T 14 N, R 6 E). Named on Camp Far West (1949) 7.5' quadrangle.

Australia Gulch: see **Spring Creek** [MARIPOSA].

Aux-um-ne: see **Merced River** [MADERA-MARIPOSA].

Ave Maria: see **Stockton Creek** [MARIPOSA].

Ave Maria River: see **Stockton Creek** [MARIPOSA].

Avalanche Lake [EL DORADO]: *lake,* 650 feet long, 5.25 miles west-northwest of Echo Summit (lat. 38°50' N, long. 120°07'20" W). Named on Echo Lake (1955) 7.5' quadrangle.

Avalanche Ravine: see **Big Avalanche Ravine** [SIERRA].

Avery [CALAVERAS]: *settlement,* 7 miles northeast of Murphys (lat. 38°12'20" N, long.

120°22'05" W; near N line sec. 18, T 4 N, R 15 E). Named on Stanislaus (1948) 7.5' quadrangle. Postal authorities established Avery post office in 1885, discontinued it in 1943, and reestablished it in 1949; the name is for George J. Avery, first postmaster (Salley, p. 12).

Avinsino Corner [EL DORADO]: *locality,* 3 miles south of Camino (lat. 38°41'35" N, long. 120°40'30" W; sec. 29, T 10 N, R 12 E). Named on Camino (1952) 7.5' quadrangle. The name should have the form "Avansino" (Beverly Cola, personal communication, 1985).

Avonelle Lake [TUOLUMNE]: *lake,* 2400 feet long, 8 miles southwest of Tower Peak (lat. 38°03'15" N, long. 119°38'30" W). Named on Tower Peak (1956) 15' quadrangle. Otto M. Brown, a ranger at Yosemite National Park from 1927 until 1946, named the lake for his daughter (Browning, 1986, p. 9).

Azalea Lake [NEVADA]: *lake,* 950 feet long, 1.25 miles north of Donner Pass (lat. 39°20'05" N, long. 120°19'40" W; on E line sec. 8, T 17 N, R 15 E). Named on Norden (1955) 7.5' quadrangle.

Azure Lake [EL DORADO]: *lake,* 2300 feet long, 1.5 miles northwest of Mount Tallac (lat. 38°55'15" N, long. 120°07'25" W; on S line sec. 32, T 13 N, R 17 E). Named on Emerald Bay (1955) and Rockbound Valley (1955) 7.5' quadrangles.

– B –

Babbitt Peak [SIERRA]: *peak,* 3.25 miles north-northwest of Crystal Peak (lat. 39°36'10" N, long. 120°06'15" W; near E line sec. 8, T 20 N, R 17 E). Named on Dog Valley (1981) 7.5' quadrangle.

Babcock Lake [MARIPOSA]: *lake,* 1500 feet long, 6.25 miles south of Cathedral Peak (lat. 37°45'25" N, long. 119°23'45" W). Named on Tuolumne Meadows (1956) 15' quadrangle. Lieutenant N.F. McClure named the lake in 1895 for J.P. Babcock, chief deputy of California State Board of Fish Commissioners (United States Board on Geographic Names, 1934, p. 2).

Bacchis [EL DORADO]: *locality,* 11 miles east of Georgetown (lat. 38°54'50" N, long. 120°37'30" W). Named on Placerville (1893) 30' quadrangle.

Backbone House [NEVADA]: *locality,* 2 miles north of North Bloomfield (lat. 39°23'30" N, long. 120°54'35" W). Named on Colfax (1898) 30' quadrangle. Lindgren's (1911b) map shows a lake called Waldron Reservoir located about 650 feet southeast of Backbone House.

Bacon Canyon [EL DORADO]: *canyon,* drained by a stream that flows 1.5 miles to Pilot Creek (1) 12 miles north-northwest of

Pollock Pines (lat. 38°55'40" N, long. 120°38'45" W). Named on Tunnel Hill (1950) 7.5' quadrangle.

Badenaugh Canyon [SIERRA]: *canyon,* drained by a stream that flows 5.5 miles to Smithneck Creek 4 miles southeast of Loyalton (lat. 39°37'50" N, long. 120°11'55" W; sec. 33, T 21 N, R 16 E). Named on Loyalton (1981) and Sardine Peak (1981) 7.5' quadrangles.

Badger Hill [EL DORADO]: *peak,* 2.5 miles west-northwest of Pollock Pines (lat. 38°46'15" N, long. 120°37'55" W; sec. 27, T 11 N, R 12 E). Named on Slate Mountain (1950) 7.5' quadrangle.

Badger Hill [NEVADA]: *locality,* 4 miles east of North San Juan at present Badger Hill Diggings (lat. 39°22'50" N, long. 121°01'50" W). Named on Smartsville (1895) 30' quadrangle.

Badger Hill Diggings [NEVADA]: *locality,* 4 miles east-northeast of North San Juan (lat. 39°22'50" N, long. 121°01'50" W; sec. 36, T 18 N, R 8 E). Named on Camptonville (1948) 7.5' quadrangle.

Badger Pass [MARIPOSA]: *pass,* nearly 7 miles south-southwest of Yosemite Village (lat. 37°40' N, long. 119°39'15" W; near S line sec. 15, T 3 S, R 21 E). Named on Yosemite (1956) 15' quadrangle.

Bagby [MARIPOSA]: *locality,* 9.5 miles northeast of Hornitos along the north side of Merced River (lat. 37°36'45" N, long. 120°08' W). Named on Coulterville (1947) 15' quadrangle. Water of Lake McClure now covers the site. Postal authorities established Bagby post office in 1897 and discontinued it in 1951 (Frickstad, p. 90). The place opposite Bagby on the south side of the river was known from 1850 until 1860 as Ridleys Ferry for the ferry that Thomas E. Ridley operated there from 1850 until 1852 (Gudde, 1975, p. 32). John C. Fremont had a water-powered stamp mill built at the site of Ridleys Ferry and renamed the place Benton Mills for his father-in-law, Senator Thomas Hart Benton, but when postal authorities established the post office, they named it Bagby for Benjamin A. Bagby, who had a hotel, store, saloon, and boarding house across the river on the north side (Sargent, Shirley, 1976, p. 18). Stephen Bond had a store at a place called Bondville that was located 1 mile east of Benton Mills on the south side of the river (Gudde, 1975, p. 43). Postal authorities established Bondville post office in 1855 and discontinued it in 1860 (Frickstad, p. 90). A place called Kocher was situated 8 miles above Bagby along Yosemite Valley Railroad (Johnston, p. 51).

Bailey Ridge [CALAVERAS]: *ridge,* generally west-trending, 18 miles long, between Middle Fork Mokelumne River and Forest Creek. Named on Calaveras Dome (1979), Devils Nose (1979), and Garnet Hill (1979) 7.5' quadrangles.

Bailey Ridge [TUOLUMNE]: *ridge,* southwest-trending, about 3 miles long, 7 miles southwest of Tower Peak (lat. 38°03'45" N, long. 119°38' W). Named on Tower Peak (1956) 15' quadrangle.

Baileys [EL DORADO]: *locality,* 10.5 miles south-southeast of Placerville along Spanish Creek near the mouth of Grizzly Gulch (lat. 38°34'40" N, long. 120°45'30" W). Named on Placerville (1893) 30' quadrangle.

Baileys: see **Bayley House** [EL DORADO].

Bake Oven [PLACER]: *locality,* nearly 3 miles east of Michigan Bluff along North Fork of Middle Fork American River (lat. 39°02'40" N, long. 120°41' W; near W line sec. 19, T 14 N, R 12 E). Named on Michigan Bluff (1952) 7.5' quadrangle.

Baker: see **Baker Station** [TUOLUMNE].

Baker Campground [TUOLUMNE]: *locality,* 4.5 miles east-southeast of Dardanelle along Middle Fork Stanislaus River (lat. 38° 19'25" N, long. 119°45'10" W; sec. 35, T 6 N, R 20 E); the place is 0.5 mile south-southeast of Baker Station. Named on Dardanelle (1979) 7.5' quadrangle. Called Upper Baker Campground on Dardanelles Cone (1956) 15' quadrangle.

Baker Divide [PLACER]: *ridge,* west-north-west-trending, 1.25 miles long, 3.5 miles north-northeast of Foresthill (lat. 39°03'40" N, long. 120°46'40" W); the ridge is north-northwest of Baker Ranch. Named on Foresthill (1949) 7.5' quadrangle. Colfax (1898) 30' quadrangle has the name "Baker Divide" for a locality on the ridge.

Baker Peak: see **Fletcher Peak** [MARIPOSA].

Baker Ranch [PLACER]: *locality,* 4 miles northeast of Foresthill (lat. 39°03'20" N, long. 120°45'40" W; sec. 17, T 14 N, R 11 E). Named on Foresthill (1949) 7.5' quadrangle. J. Hull Baker operated a travelers stop at the place in the 1850's (Gudde, 1975, p. 25).

Bakers Crossing [TUOLUMNE]: *locality,* 5 miles west of Parsons (present Strawberry) along Middle Fork Stanislaus River (lat. 38° 11' N, long. 120°06'35" W). Named on Big Trees (1891) 30' quadrangle.

Bakers Ford [EL DORADO]: *locality,* 9 miles southeast of Placerville along Middle Fork Cosumnes River (lat. 38°37'30" N, long. 120°41'50" W). Named on Placerville (1893) 30' quadrangle.

Baker Station [TUOLUMNE]: *locality,* 4.25 miles east of Dardanelle along Middle Fork Stanislaus River (lat. 38°19'50" N, long. 119° 45'20" W; near NW cor. sec. 35, T 6 N, R 20 E). Named on Dardanelle (1979) 7.5' quadrangle. Called Baker on California Mining Bureau's (1917d) map. Postal authorities established Baker post office in 1880 and discontinued it in 1881; the name was for Greenbury C. Baker, who built a stage station at the site (Salley, p. 13).

Balaklava: see **Quaker Hill** [NEVADA] (2).

Balaklava Hill: see **Vallecito** [CALAVERAS].

Bald Eagle: see **Remington Hill** [NEVADA] (2).

Balderson Station [EL DORADO]: *locality,* 5 miles east-northeast of Georgetown (lat. 38°56'05" N, long. 120°45'10" W; sec. 33, T 13 N, R 11 E). Named on Georgetown (1949) 7.5' quadrangle. Allen Balderston lived at the place (Yohalem, p. 198). California Division of Highways' (1934) map has the name "Virner" at or near present Balderson Station. Postal authorities established Virner post office in 1897 and discontinued it in 1913; the name was from Camp Virner, a vacation resort (Salley, p. 232).

Bald Hill [CALAVERAS]: *hill,* 0.5 mile north of Angels Camp (lat. 38°05'05" N, long. 120°32'45" W; sec. 28, T 3 N, R 13 E). Altitude 1765 feet. Named on Angels Camp (1962) 7.5' quadrangle.

Bald Hill [EL DORADO]: *peak,* 2.25 miles south-southwest of Georgetown (lat. 38°52'35" N, long. 120°51'05" W; sec. 22, T 12 N, R 10 E). Altitude 2463 feet. Named on Georgetown (1949) 7.5' quadrangle.

Bald Hill [MARIPOSA]: *peak,* 3.5 miles north of the settlement of Catheys Valley (lat. 37°29'15" N, long. 120°05'35" W; sec. 22, T 5 S, R 17 E). Named on Catheys Valley (1962) 7.5' quadrangle.

Bald Hill [PLACER]: *ridge,* northwest-trending, 1 mile long, 2.25 miles west-northwest of Auburn (lat. 38°54'25" N, long. 121°06'45" W; sec. 7, 8, T 12 N, R 8 E). Named on Auburn (1953) 7.5' quadrangle.

Bald Mountain [CALAVERAS]:
(1) *ridge,* northwest-trending, 1 mile long, 3 miles south-southwest of Devils Nose (lat. 38°25'25" N, long. 120°27' W). Named on Devils Nose (1979) 7.5' quadrangle.
(2) *hill,* 7.5 miles west-southwest of Valley Springs (lat. 38°08'20" N, long. 120°56'55" W; sec. 2, T 3 N, R 9 E). Altitude 506 feet. Named on Wallace (1962) 7.5' quadrangle.
(3) *peak,* 1 mile east-northeast of Vallecito (lat. 38°05'30" N, long. 120°27'20" W; on S line sec. 20, T 3 N, R 14 E). Named on Columbia (1948) 7.5' quadrangle.

Bald Mountain [EL DORADO]:
(1) *peak,* 12 miles northwest of Pollock Pines (lat. 38°54'15" N, long. 120°42'15" W; sec. 12, T 12 N, R 11 E). Altitude 4592 feet. Named on Tunnel Hill (1950) 7.5' quadrangle.
(2) *peak,* 6.5 miles south-southwest of Pyramid Peak (lat. 38°46' N, long. 120°13'15" W; near S line sec. 28, T 11 N, R 16 E). Altitude 6980 feet. Named on Pyramid Peak (1955) 7.5' quadrangle.

Bald Mountain [MARIPOSA]: *peak,* 2 miles east-northeast of Coulterville (lat. 37°43'35" N, long. 120°09'45" W; near N line sec. 36, T 2 S, R 16 E). Named on Coulterville (1947) 7.5' quadrangle.

Bald Mountain [NEVADA]:
(1) *peak,* 5 miles north of Nevada City (lat.

39°20'05" N, long. 121° 00'45" W; sec. 18, T 17 N, R 9 E). Altitude 3125 feet. Named on Nevada City (1948) 7.5' quadrangle.

(2) *peak,* 4.5 miles north-northwest of Wolf (lat. 39°07'05" N, long. 121°10'30" W; near SE cor. sec. 27, T 15 N, R 7 E). Named on Wolf (1949) 7.5' quadrangle.

Bald Mountain [PLACER]: *peak,* 8 miles west of Martis Peak (lat. 39°17'50" N, long. 120°10'55" W; near E line sec. 27, T 17 N, R 16 E). Altitude 6760 feet. Named on Truckee (1955) 7.5' quadrangle.

Bald Mountain [SIERRA]:

(1) *peak,* 2.5 miles north-northwest of Goodyears Bar (lat. 39° 34'30" N, long. 120°53'50" W; near N line sec. 30, T 20 N, R 10 E). Altitude 5534 feet. Named on Goodyears Bar (1951) 7.5' quadrangle.

(2) *ridge,* southwest-trending, 1 mile long, 4 miles south of Downieville (lat. 39°30'15" N, long. 120°50' W). Named on Alleghany (1949) and Downieville (1951) 7.5' quadrangles.

Bald Mountain: see **Little Bald Mountain** [EL DORADO]; **Little Bald Mountain** [PLACER]; **Verdi Peak** [SIERRA].

Bald Mountain Canyon [EL DORADO]: *canyon,* drained by a stream that heads near Bald Mountain (1) and flows nearly 4 miles to Rock Creek 11.5 miles northwest of Pollock Pines (lat. 38°52'20" N, long. 120°44'35" W; sec. 22, T 12 N, R 11 E). Named on Slate Mountain (1950) and Tunnel Hill (1950) 7.5' quadrangles.

Bald Mountain Range [SIERRA]: *ridge,* generally south-southeast-trending, 8 miles long, center 8.5 miles east-southeast of Loyalton (lat. 39°36'15" N, long. 120°06'20" W). Named on Dog Valley (1981), Evans Canyon (1978), Loyalton (1981), and Sardine Peak (1981) 7.5' quadrangles.

Bald Mountain [TUOLUMNE]:

(1) *peak,* nearly 3 miles southeast of Columbia (lat. 38°00'30" N, long. 120°21'45" W; sec. 19, T 2 N, R 15 E). Altitude 3342 feet. Named on Columbia SE (1948) 7.5' quadrangle. Perkins (p. 100) used the designation "Bear or Bare Mountain" for the feature.

(2) *peak,* 5.5 miles southwest of Strawberry (lat. 38°08'40" N, long. 120°05'10" W; sec. 3, T 3 N, R 17 E). Altitude 5802 feet. Named on Strawberry (1979) 7.5' quadrangle.

(3) *peak,* 4 miles east-southeast of Mather (lat. 37°51'20" N, long. 119°47'20" W; near E line sec. 17, T 1 S, R 20 E). Altitude 7261 feet. Named on Lake Eleanor (1956) 15' quadrangle. Called Wade's Mt. on Hoffmann and Gardner's (1863-1867) map.

Bald Peak [TUOLUMNE]: *peak,* nearly 4 miles northeast of Dardanelle (lat. 38°22'20" N, long. 119°46'35" W). Altitude 9715 feet. Named on Dardanelle (1979) 7.5' quadrangle.

Bald Ridge [SIERRA]: *ridge,* generally northwest-trending, 3.5 miles long, 5.5 miles east-southeast of Sierra City (lat. 39°31'45" N, long. 120°31'40" W). Named on Haypress Valley (1981) and Sattley (1981) 7.5' quadrangles.

Bald Rock [MARIPOSA]:

(1) *peak,* 8 miles south-southeast of Mariposa (lat. 37°22'25" N, long. 119°56'05" W; near N line sec. 31, T 6 S, R 19 E). Altitude 2067 feet. Named on Ben Hur (1947) 7.5' quadrangle.

(2) *relief feature,* 3.25 miles west of Fish Camp (lat. 37°29' N, long. 119°41'50" W; sec. 20, T 5 S, R 21 E). Named on Bass Lake (1953) 15' quadrangle.

Bald Rock Mountain [PLACER]: *peak,* 9 miles north-northwest of Auburn (lat. 39°01'20" N, long. 121°08'35" W; sec. 36, T 14 N, R 7 E). Altitude 1695 feet. Named on Wolf (1949) 7.5' quadrangle.

Bald Top [SIERRA]: *peak,* 4.25 miles northwest of Goodyears Bar (lat. 39°34'45" N, long. 120°56'50" W; near SE cor. sec. 22, T 20 N, R 9 E). Named on Goodyears Bar (1951) 7.5' quadrangle.

Baldwin Beach [EL DORADO]: *beach,* 3 miles north-northeast of Mount Tallac along Lake Tahoe (lat. 38°56'35" N, long. 120° 04' W; sec. 26, T 13 N, R 17 E). Named on Emerald Bay (1955) 7.5' quadrangle. E.J. "Lucky" Baldwin owned the beach (Lekisch, p. 6).

Baldwin Reservoir [PLACER]: *lake,* 1500 feet long, 2.5 miles north of Folsom on Placer-Sacramento county line (lat. 38°42'50" N, long. 121°10'45" W; on S line sec. 14, T 10 N, R 7 E). Named on Folsom (1967) 7.5' quadrangle.

Ballarat Canyon [EL DORADO]: *canyon,* drained by a stream that flows 1.5 miles to Whaler Creek 9 miles northwest of Pollock Pines (lat. 38°51' N, long. 120°42'35" W; near NW cor. sec. 36, T 12 N, R 11 E). Named on Slate Mountain (1950) 7.5' quadrangle.

Ballard Ravine [EL DORADO]: *canyon,* drained by a stream that flows nearly 2 miles to Pilot Creek (1) 10.5 miles north-northwest of Pollock Pines (lat. 38°54'30" N, long. 120°37'35" W; sec. 10, T 12 N, R 12 E). Named on Devil Peak (1950) 7.5' quadrangle.

Ballards Humbug: see **Volcano** [AMADOR].

Balloon Dome [MADERA]: *peak,* 13 miles northeast of Shuteye Peak (lat. 37°27'50" N, long. 119°13'30" W; sec. 27, T 5 S, R 25 E). Altitude 6881 feet. Named on Kaiser Peak (1953) 15' quadrangle. The feature reminded Brewer "of the top of a gigantic balloon struggling to get up through the rock" (Whitney, 1865, p. 401). The peak also was called Dome or Great Dome (Gudde, 1949, p. 22).

Balls [AMADOR]: *locality,* 9 miles west of present Fiddletown on the south side of Cosumnes River near the mouth of present Grapevine Ravine (lat. 38°30'45" N, long. 120°55'30" W). Named on Placerville (1893) 30' quadrangle.

Balls Canyon [SIERRA]: *canyon,* drained by a stream that flows 3.5 miles to Upper Long Valley 10 miles east of Loyalton (lat. 39°39'25" N, long. 120°03'05" W; near W line sec. 23, T 21 N, R 17 E). Named on Evans Canyon (1978) 7.5' quadrangle, which shows Balls ranch in the canyon.

Balls Creek [SIERRA]: *stream,* flows 5.5 miles to Long Valley Creek 12 miles east of Loyalton (lat. 39°41' N, long. 120°00'55" W; at W line sec. 18, T 21 N, R 18 E); the stream drains Balls Canyon. Named on Loyalton (1955) 15' quadrangle.

Baloon Ridge [PLACER]: *ridge,* west-south-west-trending, 0.5 mile long, 4.25 miles east-northeast of Michigan Bluff (lat. 39°03'55" N, long. 120°39'45" W; sec. 17, T 14 N, R 12 E). Named on Michigan Bluff (1952) 7.5' quadrangle.

Balsam Flat [SIERRA]: *area,* 1 mile east-south-east of Alleghany (lat. 39°27'50" N, long. 120°49'35" W; on N line sec. 2, T 18 N, R 10 E). Named on Alleghany (1949) 7.5' quadrangle.

Baltic Creek [EL DORADO]: *stream,* flows nearly 3 miles to Camp Creek 8.5 miles east of Camino (lat. 38°43'20" N, long. 120°31'10" W; near N line sec. 15, T 10 N, R 13 E); the stream is north of Baltic Peak. Named on Sly Park (1952) 7.5' quadrangle.

Baltic Creek [NEVADA]: *stream,* flows 1 mile to Little Canyon Creek 4 miles south of Graniteville (lat. 39°22'55" N, long. 120° 44' W; near W line sec. 34, T 18 N, R 11 E). Named on Graniteville (1982) 7.5' quadrangle, which shows Baltic mine near the stream.

Baltic Peak [EL DORADO]: *peak,* 9 miles east-southeast of Camino (lat. 38°41'40" N, long. 120°30'50" W; near N line sec. 26, T 10 N, R 13 E); the peak is at the northwest end of Baltic Ridge. Altitude 5078 feet. Named on Sly Park (1952) 7.5' quadrangle. Forest Service officials named the feature for Baltic mine, located north of the peak (Gudde, 1969, p. 21).

Baltic Ridge [EL DORADO]: *ridge,* generally west-trending, 16 miles long, center 6 miles west-northwest of Leek Spring Hill (lat. 38°40'10" N, long. 120°22'15" W); Baltic Peak is at the northwest end of the ridge. Named on Leek Spring Hill (1951), Sly Park (1952), and Stump Spring (1951) 7.5' quadrangles.

Baltimore [PLACER]: *locality,* less than 1 mile southwest of Foresthill (lat. 39°00'50" N, long. 120°49'40" W; sec. 35, T 14 N, R 10 E). Named on Colfax (1938) 30' quadrangle.

Baltimore Lake [NEVADA]: *lake,* 1100 feet long, 4 miles south-southeast of English Mountain (lat. 39°23'30" N, long. 120°31'50" W; near SE cor. sec. 29, T 18 N, R 13 E); the lake is 0.25 mile north of the site of Baltimore Town. Named on English Mountain (1983) 7.5' quadrangle.

Baltimore Ravine [PLACER]: *canyon,* drained by a stream that flows less than 1 mile to Auburn Ravine 1.25 miles west-southwest of downtown Auburn (lat. 38°53'25" N, long. 121°05'35" W; sec. 16, T 12 N, R 8 E). Named on Auburn (1953) 7.5' quadrangle.

Baltimore Ravine: see **Scotchman Creek** [NEVADA].

Baltimore Town [NEVADA]: *locality,* 4.25 miles south-southeast of English Mountain (lat. 39°23'10" N, long. 120°31'50" W; near E line sec. 32, T 18 N, R 13 E). Site named on English Mountain (1983) 7.5' quadrangle. The place first was called Wightman's Camp (Fatout, p. 37).

Bandarita Ridge [MARIPOSA]: *ridge,* northwest-trending, 2 miles long, 5 miles northeast of Buckhorn Peak (lat. 37°42'20" N, long. 120°03'10" W). Named on Buckhorn Peak (1947) 7.5' quadrangle.

Bandereta: see **Coulterville** [MARIPOSA].

Banjo: see **Missouri Canyon** [NEVADA] (1).

Banner Hill: see **Banner Mountain** [NEVADA].

Banner Mountain [NEVADA]: *peak,* 7 miles north of Chicago Park (lat. 39°14'45" N, long. 120°57'55" W; near SE cor. sec. 16, T 16 N, R 9 E). Altitude 3899 feet. Named on Chicago Park (1949) 7.5' quadrangle. Called Banner Hill on Colfax (1898) 30' quadrangle.

Banner Reservoir [NEVADA]: *lake,* 750 feet long, 2.5 miles east-northeast of Grass Valley (lat. 39°14'15" N, long. 121°01' W; near W line sec. 19, T 16 N, R 9 E). Named on Grass Valley (1949) 7.5' quadrangle, which shows Banner Mtn. mine near the feature.

Bare Mountain: see **Bald Mountain** [TUOLUMNE] (1).

Bar Hill [MARIPOSA]: *peak,* 3 miles southeast of Mariposa (lat. 37°26'45" N, long. 119°56'30" W; near NW cor. sec. 6, T 6 S, R 19 E). Named on Mariposa (1912) 30' quadrangle.

Barker Creek [PLACER]: *stream,* flows nearly 7 miles to Rubicon River 3.5 miles east-north-east of Bunker Hill (lat. 39°03'50" N, long. 120°18'55" W; sec. 17, T 14 N, R 15 E); the stream goes through Barker Meadow. Named on Homewood (1955) and Wentworth Springs (1953) 7.5' quadrangles.

Barker Meadow [PLACER]: *area,* 5 miles west-southwest of Homewood (lat. 39°04' N, long. 120°14'45" W); the place is on upper reaches of Barker Creek. Named on Homewood (1955) and Wentworth Springs (1953) 7.5' quadrangles.

Barker Pass [PLACER]: *pass,* 4 miles west-southwest of Homewood (lat. 39°04'35" N, long. 120°13'55" W; sec. 8, T 14 N, R 16 E); the pass is at the head of Barker Creek. Named on Homewood (1955) 7.5' quadrangle.

Barker Peak [PLACER]: *peak,* 4.25 miles west of Homewood (lat. 39°04'45" N, long. 120°14'15" W; sec. 8, T 14 N, R 16 E); the

15

peak is 0.25 mile west-northwest of Barker Pass. Altitude 8166 feet. Named on Homewood (1955) 7.5' quadrangle.

Bark Shanty Canyon [EL DORADO]: *canyon*, drained by a stream that flows 4.25 miles to Silver Fork American River 8 miles west of Kirkwood (lat. 38°42'40" N, long. 120°13'15" W; near SE cor. sec. 17, T 10 N, R 16 E). Named on Tragedy Spring (1979) 7.5' quadrangle.

Barley Flat [EL DORADO]: *area*, 5.5 miles north-northeast of Chili Bar (lat. 38°50'25" N, long. 120°47'20" W; near S line sec. 31, T 12 N, R 11 E). Named on Garden Valley (1949) 7.5' quadrangle.

Barnett [CALAVERAS]: *locality*, 7.5 miles north-northeast of Blue Mountain (lat. 38°26'15" N, long. 120°17'35" W; near S line sec. 23, T 7 N, R 15 E). Named on Blue Mountain (1956) 15' quadrangle.

Barney Cavanah Ridge [PLACER]: *ridge*, generally southwest-trending, 5.5 miles long, 2.5 miles southwest of Duncan Peak (lat. 39°07'30" N, long. 120°32'30" W). Named on Duncan Peak (1952) and Greek Store (1952) 7.5' quadrangles. Logan's (1925) map shows Barney Kavanaugh cabin at or near the ridge.

Barney Meadow [EL DORADO]: *area*, 4.25 miles south-southwest of Caldor along Sopiago Creek (lat. 38°33' N, long. 120°27'50" W; on E line sec. 18, T 8 N, R 14 E); the place is north of the east end of Barney Ridge. Named on Caldor (1951) 7.5' quadrangle.

Barney Ridge [EL DORADO]: *ridge*, generally west-trending, 6.5 miles long, center 5.5 miles southwest of Caldor (lat. 38°32'40" N, long. 120°29'30" W). Named on Caldor (1951) and Omo Ranch (1952) 7.5' quadrangles. Pyramid Peak (1896) 30' quadrangle has the name "Barneys" for a place on the ridge.

Barneys: see **Barney Ridge** [EL DORADO].

Barn Meadow [TUOLUMNE]: *area*, 4 miles south-southwest of Dardanelle (lat. 38°17'20" N, long. 119°51'25" W; sec. 14, T 5 N, R 19 E). Named on Dardanelle (1979) 7.5' quadrangle.

Barrel Spring [MARIPOSA]:

(1) *spring*, 2.25 miles south-southeast of El Portal (lat. 37°38'50" N, long. 119°46'05" W; sec. 28, T 3 S, R 20 E). Named on El Portal (1947) 7.5' quadrangle.

(2) *spring*, 3 miles north-northeast of the settlement of Catheys Valley (lat. 37°28'35" N, long. 120°04'20" W). Named on Catheys Valley (1962) 7.5' quadrangle.

Barrett [MARIPOSA]: *locality*, 6.5 miles south-southwest of Penon Blanco Peak on the west side of Lake McClure (lat. 37°38'25" N, long. 120°17'05" W; sec. 26, T 3 S, R 15 E). Named on Penon Blanco Peak (1962) 7.5' quadrangle. Merced Falls (1944) 15' quadrangle shows the place situated along Yosemite Valley Railroad.

In 1926 water of Lake McClure covered the site of a community called Barrett (Sargent, Shirley, 1976, p. 27).

Barrett Lake [EL DORADO]: *lake*, 800 feet long, 5.5 miles southwest of Phipps Peak (lat. 38°54'15" N, long. 120°13'45" W; at W line sec. 9, T 12 N, R 16 E). Named on Rockbound Valley (1955) 7.5' quadrangle.

Barry Creek [SIERRA]: *stream*, heads in Plumas County and flows 2.5 miles in Sierra County before reentering Plumas County 11 miles north-northeast of Sierra City (lat. 39°42'25" N, long. 120° 31'35" W; near S line sec. 4, T 21 N, R 13 E). Named on Calpine (1981) and Clio (1981) 7.5' quadrangles.

Barth Mountain [CALAVERAS]: *peak*, 4.25 miles east of Copperopolis (lat. 37°59'10" N, long. 120°33'40" W; near E line sec. 32, T 2 N, R 13 E). Altitude 1916 feet. Named on Melones Dam (1962) 7.5' quadrangle.

Bartlett Creek [TUOLUMNE]: *stream*, flows 6.5 miles to join Kendrick Creek and form Eleanor Creek 16 miles southeast of Pinecrest (lat. 38°01'30" N, long. 119°48' W; near S line sec. 17, T 2 N, R 20 E); the stream heads near Bartlett Peak. Named on Pinecrest (1956) 15' quadrangle. The name is from Bartlett Peak (United States Board on Geographic Names, 1934, p. 2). The stream is called West Fork Eleanor Cr. on Dardanelles (1898) 30' quadrangle.

Bartlett Peak [TUOLUMNE]: *peak*, 14 miles east-southeast of Pinecrest (lat. 38°05'30" N, long. 119°46'35" W). Altitude 8238 feet. Named on Pinecrest (1956) 15' quadrangle.

Barton [AMADOR]: *locality*, 8 miles east-northeast of Pine Grove (lat. 38°27'20" N, long. 120°31'45" W; near S line sec. 15, T 7 N, R 13 E). Named on West Point (1948) 7.5' quadrangle.

Barts Creek [EL DORADO-PLACER]: *stream*, heads in Placer County and flows 5 miles to Gerle Creek 2 miles west of Wentworth Springs at Gerle Meadow in El Dorado County (lat. 39°00'50" N, long. 120°22'35" W; sec. 35, T 14 N, R 14 E); the stream goes through Barts Valley. Named on Bunker Hill (1953) and Wentworth Springs (1953) 7.5' quadrangles.

Barts Valley [PLACER]: *canyon*, 1 mile long, 1 mile east-southeast of Bunker Hill (lat. 39°02'30" N, long. 120°21'40" W; mainly in sec. 24, T 14 N, R 14 E); the canyon is along upper reaches of Barts Creek. Named on Wentworth Springs (1953) 7.5' quadrangle.

Base Line Camp [TUOLUMNE]: *locality*, 3 miles east-northeast of Mather (lat. 37°53'35" N, long. 119°48' W; near S line sec. 32, T 1 N, R 20 E); the place is near Mount Diablo Base line. Named on Lake Eleanor (1956) 15' quadrangle.

Basin: see **The Basin** [TUOLUMNE].

Basin Creek [TUOLUMNE]:

(1) *stream*, flows 2.5 miles to Shoofly Creek

5.5 miles southeast of Liberty Hill (lat. 38°18'40" N, long. 120°01'50" W; sec. 6, T 5 N, R 18 E). Named on Liberty Hill (1979) 7.5' quadrangle.
(2) *stream,* flows 4.5 miles to North Fork Tuolumne River 3.5 miles northeast of Tuolumne (lat. 37°59'35" N, long. 120°10'55" W; sec. 26, T 2 N, R 16 E); the stream goes through the feature called The Basin. Named on Duckwall Mountain (1948), Tuolumne (1948), and Twain Harte (1979) 7.5' quadrangles. Called Basin Slope Creek on Sonora (1897) 30' quadrangle.

Basin Peak [NEVADA]: *peak,* 5 miles north-northwest of Donner Pass (lat. 39°22'55" N, long. 120°21'45" W; near E line sec. 35, T 18 N, R 14 E). Altitude 9017 feet. Named on Independence Lake (1981) 7.5' quadrangle.

Basin Slope Creek: see **Basin Creek** [TUOLUMNE] (2).

Basket Dome [MARIPOSA]: *peak,* 2 miles east-northeast of Yosemite Village (lat. 37°45'50" N, long. 119°33' W). Altitude 7612 feet. Named on Hetch Hetchy Reservoir (1956) 15' quadrangle. The name is from an Indian legend concerning a basket that turned to stone (Browning, 1986, p. 12).

Bassella Creek [CALAVERAS]: *stream,* flows 3 miles to O'Neil Creek 6 miles north of Murphys (lat. 38°13'35" N, long. 120° 28' W; sec. 6, T 4 N, R 14 E). Named on Fort Mountain (1979) and Murphys (1948) 7.5' quadrangles.

Bassett's Gulch: see **Sonora Creek** [TUOLUMNE].

Bassetts [SIERRA]: *locality,* 4.25 miles north-northeast of Sierra City along North Yuba River (lat. 39°37' N, long. 120°35'25" W; sec. 11, R 20 N, R 12 E); the place is at the mouth of Howard Creek. Named on Haypress Valley (1981) 7.5' quadrangle. An inn called Hancock House opened at the site in the early 1860's; about 1865 the name of the place was changed to Howard Ranch for Howard Chris Tegerman, the owner; the name was changed again in the 1870's to Bassett's Station for Jacob Bassett and Mary Bassett (Gudde, 1975, p. 28).

Bassett's Station: see **Bassetts** [SIERRA].

Bassi [EL DORADO]: *locality,* 5.25 miles east of Robbs Peak (lat. 38° 55' N, long. 120°18'30" W). Named on Pyramid Peak (1896) 30' quadrangle.

Bassi Falls [EL DORADO]: *waterfall,* 4.5 miles east-southeast of Robbs Peak (lat. 38°53'35" N, long. 120°19'45" W; near NW cor. sec. 17, T 12 N, R 15 E); the feature is along Bassi Fork. Named on Loon Lake (1952) 7.5' quadrangle.

Bassi Fork [EL DORADO]: *stream,* flows 8 miles to Big Silver Creek 4.25 miles southeast of Robbs Peak (lat. 38°52'50" N, long. 120° 20'45" W; near SW cor. sec. 18, T 12 N, R 15 E). Named on Loon Lake (1952) 7.5' quadrangle.

Bass Lake [EL DORADO]: *lake,* 3550 feet long, 2.25 miles northeast of Clarksville (lat. 38°40'45" N, long. 121°01'15" W; on E line sec. 31, T 10 N, R 9 E). Named on Clarksville (1953, photorevised 1980) 7.5' quadrangle. Logan's (1938) map has the name "Bass Lake Reservoir" for the feature.

Bass Lake Reservoir: see **Bass Lake** [EL DORADO].

Bath [PLACER]: *locality,* 1.5 miles northeast of Foresthill (lat. 39° 02' N, long. 120°47'55" W). Named on Colfax (1898) 30' quadrangle. Postal authorities established Bath post office in 1858, discontinued it in 1859, reestablished it in 1861, discontinued it in 1890, reestablished it in 1891, and discontinued it in 1899 (Frickstad, p. 119). After prospectors discovered gold at the site in 1850, the mining camp there was called Volcano for nearby Volcano Canyon; the name of the camp was changed to Sarahsville to honor the first woman at the place, and then changed to Bath when the post office was established (Hoover, Rensch, and Rensch, p. 274). Whitney's (1873) map shows a place called Forest Shades located about halfway between Bath and Foresthill.

Bathhouse Ravine [NEVADA]: *canyon,* drained by a stream that flows 1.25 miles to Middle Yuba River 5.5 miles north-northeast of North Bloomfield (lat. 39°26'10" N, long. 120°50'45" W; near SW cor. sec. 10, T 18 N, R 10 E). Named on Alleghany (1949) 7.5' quadrangle.

Bath Mountain [TUOLUMNE]: *peak,* 5.25 miles west-southwest of Matterhorn Peak (lat. 38°03'30" N, long. 119°27'50" W). Named on Matterhorn Peak (1956) 15' quadrangle.

Bathtub Spring [MARIPOSA]: *spring,* 3.5 miles east of Santa Cruz Mountain (lat. 37°28' N, long. 120°08'15" W; near W line sec. 29, T 5 S, R 17 E). Named on Indian Gulch (1962) 7.5' quadrangle.

Battalion Pass [MARIPOSA]: *pass,* 3.25 miles southwest of Wawona (lat. 37°30'20" N, long. 119°41'45" W; sec. 8, T 5 S, R 21 E). Named on Yosemite (1956) 15' quadrangle. Chester Versteeg suggested the name because the Mariposa Battalion is believed to have used the pass in 1851 (Browning, 1986, p. 12).

Baville: see **Cooks Station** [AMADOR].

Baxter [MARIPOSA]: *locality,* 5 miles southwest of Coulterville (lat. 37°40' N, long. 120°16'15" W). Named on Sonora (1891) 30' quadrangle. Postal authorities established Baxter post office in 1890 and discontinued it in 1907 (Frickstad, p. 90).

Baxter [PLACER]: *village,* 3 miles east of Dutch Flat (lat. 39°12'50" N, long. 120°46'50" W; sec. 31, T 16 N, R 11 E). Named on Dutch Flat (1950) 7.5' quadrangle. Postal authorities established Baxter post office in 1935 (Frickstad, p. 119). The name originated with a travelers stop at the place (Stewart, p. 90).

Bayley House [EL DORADO]: *locality,* 1.25

miles north of the village of Pilot Hill (lat. 38°51'15" N, long. 121°00'50" W; sec. 31, T 12 N, R 9 E). Named on Auburn (1954) 15' quadrangle. Called Baileys on Sacramento (1892) 30' quadrangle.

Beacon Point [SIERRA]: *peak*, 2.5 miles southeast of Crystal Peak (lat. 39°32' N, long. 120°02'55" W; near NE cor. sec. 2, T 19 N, R 17 E). Altitude 7501 feet. Named on Dog Valley (1981) 7.5' quadrangle.

Beal Air Force Base [NEVADA]: *military installation*, east of Marysville between Yuba River and Bear River on Nevada-Yuba county line, mainly in Yuba County. Named on Browns Valley (1947), Camp Far West (1949), Rough and Ready (1949), Smartville (1951), Wheatland (1947), and Wolf (1949) 7.5' quadrangles. Called Camp Beal Military Reservation on Grass Valley (1949) and Wheatland (1949) 15' quadrangles. War Department officials established Camp Beal in 1942 and named it for Edward Fitzgerald Beal (Hoover, Rensch, and Rensch, p. 589).

Beals Bar: see **Beals Point** [PLACER].

Beals Point [PLACER]: *promontory*, 6 miles southeast of Rocklin along Folsom Lake (lat. 38°43'15" N, long. 120°10'10" W; at W line sec. 13, T 10 N, R 7 E). Named on Folsom (1967) 7.5' quadrangle. Arrowsmith's (1860) map shows Beals Bar situated east of present Beals Point on the west side of North Fork American River just above the junction with South Fork; water of Folsom Lake now covers the site of this old mining camp. Gudde (1975, p. 347) listed a mining place called Texas Bar that was located along North Fork near Beals Bar.

Bean Creek [MARIPOSA]: *stream*, flows 11 miles to North Fork Merced River 7 miles northeast of Buckhorn Peak (lat. 37°44'30" N, long. 120°02'35" W; sec. 24, T 2 S, R 17 E). Named on Buckhorn Peak (1947) and Groveland (1947) 7.5' quadrangles. Called Bean's Creek on Hoffmann and Gardner's (1863-1867) map, which shows Bean's Mill situated on upper reaches of the stream.

Bean Gulch [CALAVERAS]: *canyon*, drained by a stream that flows 2.25 miles to Stanislaus River 6.25 miles east-southeast of Copperopolis (lat. 37°57'35" N, long. 120°32'10" W; sec. 15, T 1 N, R 13 E). Named on Melones Dam (1962) 7.5' quadrangle.

Bean's Mill: see **Bean Creek** [MARIPOSA].

Beanville Creek [EL DORADO]: *stream*, flows 3.25 miles to Silver Fork American River 1 mile south-southwest of Kyburz (lat. 38°45'50" N, long. 120°18'05" W). Named on Kyburz (1952) and Leek Spring Hill (1951) 7.5' quadrangles.

Bear Creek [CALAVERAS]:
(1) *stream*, flows 9.5 miles to Middle Fork Mokelumne River nearly 7 miles southwest of Devils Nose (lat. 38°23'05" N, long. 120°29'45" W; sec. 12, T 6 N, R 13 E). Named

on Devils Nose (1979) and West Point (1948) 7.5' quadrangles.
(2) *stream*, flows 5.5 miles to New Hogan Reservoir 5 miles east of Jenny Lind (lat. 38°06'35" N, long. 120°46'35" W; near W line sec. 16, T 3 N, R 11 E). Named on Jenny Lind (1962), Salt Spring Valley (1962), and Valley Springs (1962) 7.5' quadrangles.
(3) *stream*, flows 5 miles to Cherokee Creek 6.5 miles west-northwest of Angels Camp (lat. 38°06'50" N, long. 120°39'05" W; sec. 16, T 3 N, R 12 E). Named on Salt Spring Valley (1962) 7.5' quadrangle.

Bear Creek [CALAVERAS]: *stream*, heads in Calaveras County and flows 39 miles to Disappointment Slough 7.5 miles southeast of Terminous in San Joaquin County (lat. 38°02'35" N, long. 121°23'10" W). Named on Clements (1968), Lockeford (1968), Lodi South (1968), Terminous (1978), Valley Springs (1962), Wallace (1962), and Waterloo (1968) 7.5' quadrangles.

Bear Creek [EL DORADO]:
(1) *stream*, flows 2 miles to Silver Creek 7 miles north-northeast of Pollock Pines (lat. 38°50'50" N, long. 120°30'20" W; sec. 34, T 12 N, R 13 E). Named on Pollock Pines (1950) and Riverton (1950) 7.5' quadrangles.
(2) *stream*, flows 7.25 miles to Rock Creek 4 miles north-northeast of Chili Bar (lat. 38°49' N, long. 120°46'50" W; near W line sec. 8, T 11 N, R 11 E). Named on Garden Valley (1949) and Georgetown (1949) 7.5' quadrangles. Called West Fork Rock Creek on Placerville (1893) 30' quadrangle.

Bear Creek [MARIPOSA]: *stream*, flows 8.5 miles to Merced River 5 miles north-northwest of Midpines at Briceburg (lat. 37°36'15" N, long. 119°57'55" W; sec. 10, T 4 S, R 18 E). Named on Feliciana Mountain (1947) 7.5' quadrangle.

Bear Creek [MARIPOSA]: *stream*, heads in Mariposa County and flows 69 miles to San Joaquin River 3.5 miles south-southeast of Stevinson in Merced County (lat. 37°16'45" N, long. 120°49'35" W; sec. 36, T 7 S, R 10 E). Named on Atwater (1961), Merced (1962), and Turlock (1962) 15' quadrangles, and on Bear Valley (1947), Catheys Valley (1962), Hornitos (1947), Indian Gulch (1962), and Owens Reservoir (1962), 7.5' quadrangles.

Bear Creek [PLACER]: *stream*, flows 3 miles to Truckee River 3.25 miles west-northwest of Tahoe City (lat. 39°11'25" N, long. 120°11'50" W; at W line sec. 34, T 16 N, R 16 E). Named on Tahoe City (1955) 7.5' quadrangle.

Bear Creek [SIERRA]: *stream*, flows 3.5 miles to Middle Yuba River 8 miles southeast of Downieville (lat. 39°28' N, long. 120°44'35" W; sec. 33, T 19 N, R 11 E). Named on Alleghany (1949), Graniteville (1982), and Sierra City (1981) 7.5' quadrangles.

Bear Creek [TUOLUMNE]:
(1) *stream*, flows 3 miles to New Melones Lake

6.5 miles west-southwest of Sonora (lat. 37°56'35" N, long. 120°39'15" W; near E line sec. 13, T 1 N, R 13 E). Named on Sonora (1948, photorevised 1973) 7.5' quadrangle.

(2) *stream,* flows 3.5 miles to Reed Creek 5.5 miles east of Duckwall Mountain (lat. 37°58'40" N, long. 120°01'05" W; near N line sec. 5, T 1 N, R 18 E). Named on Lake Eleanor (1956), Pinecrest (1956), and Tuolumne (1948) 15' quadrangles.

Bear Creek: see **Briceburg** [MARIPOSA].

Bear Creek: see **Bear River** [NEVADA-PLACER]; **Little Bear Creek** [PLACER].

Bear Creek Campground [PLACER]: *locality,* 3.5 miles west-northwest of Tahoe City (lat. 39°10'55" N, long. 120°12'25" W; near NW cor. sec. 3, T 15 N, R 16 E); the place is along Bear Creek. Named on Tahoe City (1955, photorevised 1969) 7.5' quadrangle.

Bear Den Canyon: see **Bear Pen Creek** [PLACER].

Beardsley Lake [TUOLUMNE]: *lake,* behind a dam on Middle Fork Stanislaus River 3.5 miles west of Strawberry (lat. 38°12'10" N, long. 120°04'30" W; sec. 14, T 4 N, R 17 E). Named on Strawberry (1979) 7.5' quadrangle.

Beardsley Point [TUOLUMNE]: *promontory,* 2.5 miles west-northwest of Strawberry on the south side of Beardsley Lake (lat. 38°12'40" N, long. 120°03'20" W; near S line sec. 12, T 4 N, R 17 E). Named on Strawberry (1979) 7.5' quadrangle.

Bear Flat [EL DORADO]: *area,* 2.5 miles north of Georgetown (lat. 38°56'40" N, long. 120°49'50" W; sec. 26, T 13 N, R 10 E). Named on Georgetown (1949) 7.5' quadrangle.

Bear Flat [SIERRA]: *area,* 5.5 miles east-northeast of Sierraville (lat. 39°36'30" N, long. 120°15'45" W; near SW cor. sec. 1, T 20 N, R 15 E). Named on Sierraville (1981) 7.5' quadrangle.

Bear Lake [PLACER]: *lake,* 700 feet long, 4.5 miles southwest of Homewood (lat. 39°02'55" N, long. 120°13'40" W; sec. 20, T 14 N, R 16 E). Named on Homewood (1955) 7.5' quadrangle.

Bear Lake [TUOLUMNE]:
(1) *lake,* 1750 feet long, 7.25 miles east of Pinecrest along Lily Creek (3) (lat. 38°10'30" N, long. 119°51'45" W; near W line sec. 26, T 4 N, R 19 E). Named on Pinecrest (1956) 15' quadrangle.
(2) *lake,* 1000 feet long, 9 miles west-south-west of Tower Peak (lat. 38°05'25" N, long. 119°41'55" W). Named on Tower Peak (1956) 15' quadrangle. Rangers Gallison and Wallis of Yosemite National Park named the lake in 1952 for a bear that they saw there (Browning, 1986, p. 13). United States Board on Geographic Names (1991, p. 3) approved the name "Big Island Lake" for the feature.

Bear Lake: see **Little Bear Lake** [TUOLUMNE].

Bear Lake Reservoir: see **Waterhouse Lake** [TUOLUMNE].

Bear Meadow [EL DORADO]: *area,* 5 miles southwest of Old Iron Mountain (lat. 38°39'55" N, long. 120°28'05" W; sec. 6, T 9 N, R 14 E). Named on Stump Spring (1951) 7.5' quadrangle.

Bear Meadow [TUOLUMNE]: *area,* 8 miles southeast of Pinecrest (lat. 38°05'30" N, long. 119°54'25" W). Named on Cherry Lake North (1979) 7.5' quadrangle.

Bear Meadow Creek [EL DORADO]: *stream,* flows 1.25 miles to North Fork Cosumnes River 5 miles west-southwest of Old Iron Mountain (lat. 38°40'45" N, long. 120°28'35" W; near W line sec. 31, T 10 N, R 14 E); the stream heads near Bear Meadow. Named on Stump Spring (1951) 7.5' quadrangle.

Bear Mountain [CALAVERAS]: *ridge,* north-west-trending, 2 miles long, 4.25 miles south-southwest of Angels Camp (lat. 38°01'20" N, long. 120°35'15" W). Named on Angels Camp (1962) 7.5' quadrangle.

Bear Mountain [TUOLUMNE]: *peak,* 2.5 miles southwest of Mather (lat. 37°51'20" N, long. 119°53'20" W; sec. 16, T 1 S, R 19 E). Altitude 5321 feet. Named on Lake Eleanor (1956) 15' quadrangle.

Bear Mountain: see **Bald Mountain** [TUOLUMNE] (1).

Bear Mountains [CALAVERAS]: *range,* extends southeast from Calaveras River to near Pools Station. Named on Jenny Lind (1962), Salt Spring Valley (1962), San Andreas (1962), and Valley Springs (1962) 7.5' quadrangles. On Jackson (1902) 30' quadrangle, application of the name extends farther southeast.

Bear Pen Creek [PLACER]: *stream,* flows 2.5 miles to Five Lakes Creek nearly 7 miles northeast of Bunker Hill (lat. 39°06'45" N, long. 120°17'15" W; near S line sec. 27, T 15 N, R 15 E). Named on Homewood (1955) and Wentworth Springs (1953) 7.5' quadrangles. On Truckee (1940) 30' quadrangle, the canyon of the stream is called Bear Den Canyon.

Bear Reservoir [MARIPOSA]: *lake,* behind a dam on Bear Creek (2) 9 miles west-south-west of the settlement of Catheys Valley (lat. 37°22'10" N, long. 120°13'40" W; sec. 33, T 6 S, R 16 E). Named on Indian Gulch (1962) and Owens Reservoir (1962) 7.5' quadrangles.

Bear River [AMADOR]: *stream,* flows 19 miles to North Fork Mokelumne River 6.5 miles southeast of Hams Station (lat. 38°28'35" N, long. 120°17'45" W; sec. 11, T 7 N, R 15 E). Named on Bear River Reservoir (1979), Garnet Hill (1979), Mokelumne Peak (1979), and Peddler Hill (1951) 7.5' quadrangles. United States Board on Geographic Names (1981b, p. 3) rejected the names "South Branch Bear River" and "Tragedy Creek" for any part of the stream.

Bear River [NEVADA-PLACER]: *stream,* flows

63 miles along Nevada-Placer county line and along and near Sutter-Yuba county line to Feather River 2.5 miles north of Nicolaus in Yuba County (lat. 38°56'20" N, long. 121°34'45" W); the river heads at Bear Valley [NEVADA-PLACER]. Named on Blue Canyon (1955), Camp Far West (1949), Chicago Park (1949), Colfax (1949), Dutch Flat (1950), Lake Combie (1949), Nicolaus (1952), Sheridan (1953), Washington (1950), Wheatland (1947), and Wolf (1949) 7.5' quadrangles. Called Arroyo de los Osos on a diseño of 1844 (Becker). Called Bear Creek on Ord's (1848) map.

Bear River: see **Chicago Park** [NEVADA]; **Little Bear River** [AMADOR].

Bear River Campground: see **Lower Bear River Campground** [AMADOR].

Bear River Group Campground [AMADOR]: *locality,* 7.25 miles west of Mokelumne Peak (lat. 38°32'05" N, long. 120°13'45" W; sec. 20, T 8 N, R 16 E). Named on Bear River Reservoir (1979) 7.5' quadrangle.

Bear River House: see **Applegate** [PLACER].

Bear River Lake: see **Bear River Reservoir** [AMADOR].

Bear River Pines [NEVADA]: *settlement,* 1.5 miles north of Chicago Park (lat. 39°10'10" N, long. 120°58' W; near NE cor. sec. 9, T 15 N, R 9 E). Named on Chicago Park (1949) 7.5' quadrangle.

Bear River Reservoir [AMADOR]: *lake,* 1 mile long, behind a dam on Bear River nearly 7 miles west-northwest of Mokelumne Peak (lat. 38°33'25" N, long. 120°12'55" W; sec. 9, T 8 N, R 16 E). Named on Bear River Reservoir (1979) 7.5' quadrangle. Postal authorities established Bear River Lake post office in 1967 to serve a vacation resort by the lake (Salley, p. 17).

Bear River Reservoir: see **Lower Bear River Reservoir** [AMADOR].

Bear Spring [PLACER]: *spring,* nearly 7 miles south-southwest of Duncan Peak (lat. 39°04'05" N, long. 120°34'05" W; sec. 18, T 14 N, R 13 E). Named on Greek Store (1952) 7.5' quadrangle.

Bear Springs [PLACER]: *spring,* 6.25 miles west-southwest of Bunker Hill (lat. 39°00'55" N, long. 120°29'10" W; sec. 35, T 14 N, R 13 E). Named on Bunker Hill (1953) 7.5' quadrangle.

Bear Springs Creek [TUOLUMNE]: *stream,* flows 3.5 miles to Clavey River 4.25 miles southeast of Duckwall Mountain (lat. 37° 55'20" N, long. 120°03'55" W; near W line sec. 24, T 1 N, R 17 E). Named on Duckwall Mountain (1948) 7.5' quadrangle.

Beartrap: see **The Beartrap** [NEVADA].

Bear Trap Basin [CALAVERAS]: *canyon,* drained by a stream that flows 2.25 miles to Jelmini Creek 3.25 miles north-northwest of Tamarack (lat. 38°28'45" N, long. 120°06'20" W; near N line sec. 9, T 7 N, R 17 E). Named

on Tamarack (1979) 7.5' quadrangle.

Bear Trap Creek [PLACER]: *stream,* flows 2 miles to Deep Canyon nearly 5 miles southwest of Duncan Peak (lat. 39°06'40" N, long. 120°34'40" W; near NW cor. sec. 31, T 15 N, R 13 E). Named on Greek Store (1952) 7.5' quadrangle. Logan's (1925) map has the name "Bear Trap Ravine" for the canyon of the stream.

Bear Trap Gap [CALAVERAS]: *pass,* 7.5 miles west of Angels Camp (lat. 38°04'40" N, long. 120°41'15" W; near SE cor. sec. 30, T 3 N, R 12 E); the pass is in Bear Mountains. Named on Salt Spring Valley (1962) 7.5' quadrangle.

Beartrap Meadow [SIERRA]: *area,* 9 miles northeast of Sierra City (lat. 39°38'30" N, long. 120°30'15" W; sec. 34, T 21 N, R 13 E). Named on Calpine (1981) and Clio (1981) 7.5' quadrangles.

Beartrap Meadow [TUOLUMNE]: *area,* 3.25 miles east of Liberty Hill (lat. 38°22'10" N, long. 120°02'20" W; sec. 18, T 6 N, R 18 E). Named on Liberty Hill (1979) 7.5' quadrangle.

Beartrap Mountain [SIERRA]: *peak,* 2.5 miles east-southeast of Mount Fillmore on Sierra-Plumas county line (lat. 39°43'15" N, long. 120°48'30" W; sec. 36, T 22 N, R 10 E). Altitude 7232 feet. Named on Mount Fillmore (1951) 7.5' quadrangle.

Bear Trap Ravine: see **Bear Trap Creek** [PLACER].

Bear Trap Spring [NEVADA]: *spring,* 2.25 miles northwest of North Bloomfield (lat. 39°23'45" N, long. 120°55'25" W; near W line sec. 25, T 18 N, R 9 E). Named on Pike (1949) 7.5' quadrangle.

Bearup Lake [TUOLUMNE]: *lake,* 4400 feet long, 10 miles southwest of Tower Peak (lat. 38°03'45" N, long. 119°42' W). Named on Tower Peak (1956) 15' quadrangle. Lieutenant N.F. McClure named the lake in 1894 for a soldier in his detachment (United States Board on Geographic Names, 1934, p. 2).

Bear Valley [MARIPOSA]:

(1) *valley,* south-southeast of the village of Bear Valley along Bear Creek (2) (lat. 37°32' N, long. 120°06' W). Named on Sonora (1897) 30' quadrangle. John C. Fremont named the feature in 1848 (Richards *in* Davis, p. 115).

(2) *village,* 10.5 miles south-southeast of Coulterville (lat. 37°34'05" N, long. 120°07'05" W); the village is near the north end of Bear Valley (1). Named on Bear Valley (1947) 7.5' quadrangle. The place first was called Haydensville for David Hayden, Charles Hayden, and Willard Hayden, who mined gold nearby; later it had several names: Biddle's Camp and Biddleville for William C. Biddle; Simpsonville for Robert Simpson, who had a store there; Johnsonville for John F. "Quartz" Johnson; finally it was given the name "Bear Valley" in 1858 (Gudde, 1975, p. 29-30). Postal authorities established

Haydensville post office before January 21, 1851, and discontinued it in 1852; they established Bear Valley post office in 1858, discontinued it in 1912, reestablished it in 1914, discontinued it in 1919, reestablished it in 1933, and discontinued it in 1955 (Salley, p. 17, 95).

Bear Valley [NEVADA]: *valley,* 9.5 miles northwest of Donner Pass (lat. 39°25'45" N, long. 120°25'40" W; sec. 17, T 18 N, R 14 E). Named on Webber Peak (1981) 7.5' quadrangle.

Bear Valley [NEVADA-PLACER]: *valley,* 1 mile west-northwest of Emigrant Gap [PLACER] (1) on Nevada-Placer county line (lat. 39°18'25" N, long. 120°41' W); the valley is along Bear River. Named on Blue Canyon (1955) 7.5' quadrangle.

Bear Valley [SIERRA]:
(1) *valley,* 8 miles south of Loyalton (lat. 39°33'45" N, long. 120° 13'30" W; at N line sec. 29, T 20 N, R 16 E). Named on Sardine Peak (1981) 7.5' quadrangle.
(2) *valley,* 5.25 miles southeast of Sierra City (lat. 39°31'15" N, long. 120°33'15" W; on S line sec. 7, T 19 N, R 13 E). Named on Haypress Valley (1981) 7.5' quadrangle.

Bear Valley [TUOLUMNE]: *area,* 8 miles south of Tower Peak (lat. 38°02' N, long. 119°34'30" W). Named on Tower Peak (1956) 15' quadrangle.

Bear Valley Campground [SIERRA]: *locality,* 8 miles south of Loyalton (lat. 39°33'25" N, long. 120°14'10" W; near E line sec. 30, T 20 N, R 16 E); the place is less than 1 mile southwest of Bear Valley (1). Named on Sardine Peak (1981) 7.5' quadrangle.

Bear Valley Creek [SIERRA]: *stream,* flows 8 miles to Smithneck Creek 2 miles southsoutheast of Loyalton (lat. 39°38'55" N, long. 120°13'20" W; near NE cor. sec. 30, T 21 N, R 16 E); the stream goes through Bear Valley (1). Named on Loyalton (1981) and Sardine Peak (1981) 7.5' quadrangles.

Bear Valley House [NEVADA]: *locality,* 8.5 miles south-southeast of Graniteville (lat. 39°18'30" N, long. 120°41'15" W); the place is in Bear Valley [NEVADA-PLACER] (1). Named on Colfax (1898) 30' quadrangle.

Bear Wallow [PLACER]: *relief feature,* 5.5 miles northeast of Michigan Bluff (lat. 39°06'05" N, long. 120°39'45" W; sec. 32, T 15 N, R 12 E). Named on Michigan Bluff (1952) 7.5' quadrangle.

Bear Wallows [PLACER]: *canyon,* drained by a stream that flows 1 mile to Grouse Creek 6.5 miles east-northeast of Michigan Bluff (lat. 39°05'30" N, long. 120°37'50" W; sec. 3, T 14 N, R 12 E). Named on Greek Store (1952) and Michigan Bluff (1952) 7.5' quadrangles.

Bear Wallow Spur [MARIPOSA]: *ridge,* north-trending, 1.5 miles long, 6 miles west-north-west of Wawona (lat. 37°34'40" N, long.

119°45' W). Named on El Portal (1947) and Yosemite (1956) 15' quadrangles.

Beatitude: see **Mount Beatitude**, under **Old Inspiration Point** [MARIPOSA].

Beauty Lake [EL DORADO]: *lake,* 650 feet long, 4.25 miles west of Pyramid Peak (lat. 38°51'20" N, long. 120°14'05" W; sec. 29, T 12 N, R 16 E). Named on Pyramid Peak (1955) 7.5' quadrangle. Shown as one of the group called Wrights Lakes on Pyramid Peak (1896) 30' quadrangle.

Beaver Bar: see **Rattlesnake Bar** [PLACER].

Beaver Canyon: see **Little Beaver Canyon** [TUOLUMNE].

Beaver Creek [AMADOR]: *stream,* flows 3.5 miles to Bear River 6.25 miles southeast of Hams Station (lat. 38°29'05" N, long. 120°17'45" W; sec. 2, T 7 N, R 15 E); the stream is east of Beaver Ridge. Named on Garnet Hill (1979) and Peddler Hill (1951) 7.5' quadrangles.

Beaver Creek [TUOLUMNE]: *stream,* flows 19 miles to North Fork Stanislaus River 5.5 miles north-northeast of Stanislaus (lat. 38°12'25" N, long. 120°19' W; near SW cor. sec. 10, T 4 N, R 15 E). Named on Boards Crossing (1979), Dorrington (1979), Liberty Hill (1979), and Stanislaus (1948) 7.5' quadrangles.

Beaver Creek: see **Little Beaver Creek** [TUOLUMNE].

Beaver Creek Camp [TUOLUMNE]: *locality,* 8.5 miles southwest of Liberty Hill (lat. 38°17'10" N, long. 120°13'15" W; sec. 16, T 5 N, R 16 E); the place is along Beaver Creek. Named on Big Meadow (1956) 15' quadrangle.

Beaver Ridge [AMADOR]: *ridge,* south-south-west-trending, 5 miles long, 3.5 miles southeast of Hams Station (lat. 38°30'45" N, long. 120°19'20" W); the ridge is west of Beaver Creek. Named on Garnet Hill (1979) and Peddler Hill (1951) 7.5' quadrangles.

Becker Peak [EL DORADO]: *peak,* 2 miles northwest of Echo Summit (lat. 38°49'55" N, long. 120°03'30" W; sec. 1, T 11 N, R 17 E). Named on Echo Lake (1955) 7.5' quadrangle. The name commemorates John S. Becker, who built a cabin in the region in 1886 and homesteaded in section 1 in 1904 (Lekisch, p. 7-8).

Beckman Hill: see **Anthony House** [NEVADA].

Beckmans Flat: see **Newtown** [NEVADA].

Becknell Creek [MARIPOSA]: *stream,* flows 6 miles to Chapman Creek 13 miles south of Mariposa (lat. 37°17'55" N, long. 119°58'05" W; sec. 26, T 7 S, R 18 E). Named on Ben Hur (1947) 7.5' quadrangle. The name is for John Becknell, a pioneer rancher (Sargent, Shirley, 1976, p. 29).

Bedbug: see **Ione** [AMADOR].

Beehive [TUOLUMNE]: *locality,* 9 miles north-northeast of Mather Station (present Mather) (lat. 37°59'35" N, long. 119°46'45" W; sec.

28, T 2 N, R 20 E). Named on Yosemite (1909) 30' quadrangle. United States Board on Geographic Names (1991, p. 3) approved the name "Beehive" for a flat 4 miles east-north-east of Lake Eleanor (lat. 37°59'46" N, long. 119°46'36" W; sec. 28, T 2 N, R 20 E), and rejected the name "Beehive Meadow" for the feature.

Beehive Meadow: see **Beehive** [TUOLUMNE].

Beeks Bight [PLACER]: *embayment,* 6 miles east-southeast of Rocklin along Folsom Lake (lat. 38°46'15" N, long. 121°07'45" W; near S line sec 30, T 11 N, R 8 E). Named on Rocklin (1967) 7.5' quadrangle.

Bella Union Ravine [SIERRA]: *canyon,* drained by a stream that flows nearly 1 mile to Canyon Creek 9 miles southwest of Mount Fillmore (lat. 39°37'30" N, long. 120°56'45" W; sec. 3, T 20 N, R 9 E). Named on La Porte (1951) 7.5' quadrangle.

Bell Creek [TUOLUMNE]: *stream,* flows about 7.5 miles to join Lily Creek (3) and form Clavey River nearly 4 miles south-southeast of Pinecrest (lat. 38°08'30" N, long. 119°58' W; sec. 2, T 3 N, R 18 E). Named on Pinecrest (1956) 15' quadrangle. Bell Creek and Clavey River together are called Middle Fork Tuolumne River on Dardanelles (1898) 30' quadrangle. United States Board on Geographic Names (1963a, p. 5) rejected the names "Belle Creek," "Clavey Creek," and "Clavey River" for present Bell Creek.

Belle Creek: see **Bell Creek** [TUOLUMNE].

Belle Meadow: see **Bell Meadow** [TUOLUMNE].

Belleview [TUOLUMNE]: *locality,* 6.25 miles east-southeast of Columbia along Sullivan Creek (lat. 38°00'45" N, long. 120°17'25" W; sec. 23, T 2 N, R 15 E). Named on Columbia SE (1948) 7.5' quadrangle.

Bellevue [EL DORADO]: *locality,* 1.25 miles northeast of the present town of Meeks Bay along Lake Tahoe (lat. 39°03'05" N, long. 120° 06'45" W). Named on Truckee (1895) 30' quadrangle.

Bellfour Canyon [CALAVERAS]: *canyon,* drained by a stream that flows 2.5 miles to Mattley Creek 5.25 miles northwest of Tamarack (lat. 38°29'45" N, long. 120°08'10" W). Named on Calaveras Dome (1979) 7.5' quadrangle.

Bell Hill [TUOLUMNE]: *peak,* 0.5 mile east-southeast of Columbia (lat. 38°02' N, long. 120°23'30" W; sec. 13, T 2 N, R 14 E). Named on Columbia (1948) 7.5' quadrangle. The feature was called Santiago Hill before about 1918 (Gudde, 1975, p. 305).

Bell Meadow [TUOLUMNE]: *area,* 4 miles east-southeast of Pinecrest (lat. 38°10' N, long. 119°55'45" W); the place is along Bell Creek. Named on Pinecrest (1979) 7.5' quadrangle. Called Belle Meadow on Dardanelles (1898) 30' quadrangle, but United States Board on Geographic Names (1963, p. 5) rejected the names "Belle Meadow" and "Bell Meadows" for the area.

Bell Mountain [TUOLUMNE]: *peak,* 5 miles southeast of Pinecrest (lat. 38°08'55" N, long. 119°55'15" W). Altitude 7950 feet. Named on Pinecrest (1979) 7.5' quadrangle.

Bellows' Butte: see **Liberty Cap** [MARIPOSA].

Bell Point [SIERRA]: *relief feature,* 3.5 miles east of Alleghany (lat. 39°28'20" N, long. 120°46'25" W; at E line sec. 31, T 19 N, E 11 E). Named on Alleghany (1949) 7.5' quadrangle.

Bells Diggings: see **Missouri Canyon** [EL DORADO].

Bell's Gulch: see **Hoffs Gulch** [MARIPOSA].

Bellyache Canyon [MARIPOSA]: *canyon,* drained by a stream that flows 1 mile to Cavallada Creek 4.25 miles north-northeast of the settlement of Catheys Valley (lat. 37°29'15" N, long. 120°03'10" W). Named on Catheys Valley (1962) 7.5' quadrangle. On Indian Gulch (1920) 15' quadrangle, the name applies to a canyon situated 1 to 2 miles farther southeast. United States Board on Geographic Names (1964a, p. 8) rejected the names "Billy Ache Canyon" and "William Aches Canyon" for the feature, but noted that the name "Bellyache" reportedly is derived from Billy Aike, or Ache, who was an early resident of the neighborhood.

Ben Bolt [EL DORADO]: *peak,* 5 miles south-southeast of Clarksville (lat. 38°35'05" N, long. 121°01'10" W; near SW cor. sec. 32, T 9 N, R 9 E); the feature is the high point on present Ben Bolt Ridge. Altitude 1139 feet. Named on Folsom (1941) 15' quadrangle.

Ben Bolt Ridge [EL DORADO]: *ridge,* northwest-trending, 3.5 miles long, 6 miles south-southeast of Clarksville (lat. 38°34'45" N, long. 121°00'45" W). Named on Folsom SE (1954) and Latrobe (1949) 7.5' quadrangles.

Ben Brow Hill [TUOLUMNE]: *peak,* 2.5 miles south of Don Pedro Camp (lat. 37°40'45" N, long. 120°24'35" W; near NE cor. sec. 15, T 3 S, R 14 E). Altitude 1074 feet. Named on La Grange (1962) 7.5' quadrangle.

Bendorf Spring [EL DORADO]: *spring,* 6 miles southwest of Old Iron Mountain (lat. 38°39'10" N, long. 120°28'45" W; at W line sec. 7, T 9 N, R 14 E). Named on Stump Spring (1951) 7.5' quadrangle.

Ben Hur [MARIPOSA]: *locality,* 9 miles south of Mariposa (lat. 37° 21'05" N, long. 119°57'25" W; sec. 1, T 7 S, R 18 E). Named on Ben Hur (1947) 7.5' quadrangle. Mariposa (1912) 30' quadrangle shows the place situated 1 mile farther north-northwest (near S line sec. 35, T 6 S, R 18 E). Postal authorities established Ben Hur post office in 1890, discontinued it in 1902, reestablished it 3 miles farther south in 1904, and discontinued it in 1951; the name is from the hero of Lew Wallace's romantic novel *Ben Hur* (Salley, p. 18).

Bennett: see **Shingle Springs** [EL DORADO].

Bennett Flat [NEVADA]: *area,* 2 miles northwest of Truckee (lat. 39°20'45" N, long. 120°12'40" W; on S line sec. 4, T 17 N, R 16 E). Named on Truckee (1955) 7.5' quadrangle.

Benson Lake [TUOLUMNE]: *lake,* 9 miles south of Tower Peak along Piute Creek (2) (lat. 38°00'55" N, long. 119°01'40" W). Named on Tower Peak (1956) 15' quadrangle. The name, given in 1895, commemorates Harry C. Benson, an army officer in Yosemite National Park from 1895 until 1897, and acting superintendent of the park from 1905 until 1908 (Hanna, p. 30).

Benson Pass [TUOLUMNE]: *pass,* 7 miles southwest of Matterhorn Peak (lat. 38°00'50" N, long. 119°27'40" W). Named on Matterhorn Peak (1956) 15' quadrangle.

Benton Mills: see **Bagby** [MARIPOSA].

Benwood Meadow [EL DORADO]: *marsh,* less than 1 mile south of Echo Summit (lat. 38°48'05" N, long. 120°01'50" W; sec. 18, T 11 N, R 18 E). Named on Echo Lake (1955) 7.5' quadrangle.

Berger Campground [SIERRA]: *locality,* 4.25 miles north of Sierra City (lat. 39°37'40" N, long. 120°38'35" W; near NE cor. sec. 5, T 20 N, R 12 E). Named on Gold Lake (1981) 7.5' quadrangle.

Berkeley Soda Springs: see **Soda Springs** [PLACER].

Bernice Lake [MARIPOSA]: *lake,* 1600 feet long, nearly 7 miles southeast of Cathedral Peak (lat. 37°46' N, long. 119°19'55" W). Named on Tuolumne Meadows (1956) 15' quadrangle. The name commemorates the wife of Superintendent W.B. Lewis of Yosemite National Park (United States Board on Geographic Names, 1934, p. 2).

Berry Creek [SIERRA]: *stream,* flows 5.5 miles to Sardine Valley 3.25 miles west-northwest of Sierraville (lat. 39°36'15" N, long. 120°25'25" W; near N line sec. 9, T 20 N, R 14 E). Named on Sattley (1981) 7.5' quadrangle. Sierraville (1955) 15' quadrangle shows Berry Creek extending up present Wild Bill Canyon.

Berry's Fish Camp: see **Fish Camp** [MARIPOSA].

Berts Lake [EL DORADO]: *lake,* 500 feet long, 5.25 miles northeast of Robbs Peak (lat. 38°58'35" N, long. 120°19'45" W; near E line sec. 18, T 13 N, R 15 E). Named on Loon Lake (1952, photorevised 1973) 7.5' quadrangle.

Beyers Lakes [NEVADA]: *lakes,* largest 1800 feet long, 4.25 miles south of English Mountain (lat. 39°23'05" N, long. 120°33'15" W; sec. 31, T 18 N, R 13 E). Named on English Mountain (1983) 7.5' quadrangle.

Biddle's Camp: see **Bear Valley** [MARIPOSA] (2)

Biddleville: see **Bear Valley** [MARIPOSA] (2).

Big Avalanche Ravine [SIERRA]: *canyon,* drained by a stream that flows nearly 2 miles to North Yuba River 1.5 miles west-southwest of Sierra City (lat. 39°33'45" N, long. 120°39'30" W; near NW cor. sec. 32, T 20 N, R 12 E). Named on Sierra City (1981) 7.5' quadrangle. Called Avalanche Ravine on Downieville (1897) 30' quadrangle, but United States Board on Geographic Names (1960a, p. 12) rejected this name for the feature.

Big Bar [CALAVERAS]: *locality,* 1 mile northwest of Mokelumne Hill along Mokelumne River (lat. 38°18'45" N, long. 120°43'05" W; sec. 1, T 5 N, R 11 E). Named on Mokelumne Hill (1948) 7.5' quadrangle. Gudde (1975, p. 34) noted that the place also had the names "Upper Bar" and "Upper Ferry." Whale Boat Ferry started at Big Bar in 1850 and operated until 1852 or 1853 (Hoover, Rensch, and Rensch, p. 29). Camp's (1962) map shows a place called Sandy Bar located less than 2 miles east-northeast of Big Bar, a place called Spanish Bar located nearly 3 miles east-northeast of Big Bar, and a place called Stony Bar located nearly 4 miles east-northeast of Big Bar—the map shows all three places on the south side of Moklumne River.

Big Bar [PLACER]: *locality,* 5.5 miles south of Duncan Peak in Duncan Canyon at the mouth of Spanish Ravine (lat. 39°04'30" N, long. 120°32' W; sec. 9, T 14 N, R 13 E). Named on Greek Store (1952) 7.5' quadrangle.

Big Bar: see **Grapevine Ravine** [AMADOR].

Big Bend [EL DORADO]: *bend,* 7 miles northnortheast of Pollock Pines along Silver Creek (lat. 38°51' N, long. 120°32' W). Named on Pollock Pines (1950) 7.5' quadrangle.

Big Bend [PLACER]:
(1) *bend,* 6.25 miles south-southeast of Colfax along North Fork American River (lat. 39°00'45" N, long. 120°55'05" W; at N line sec. 1, T 13 N, R 9 E). Named on Colfax (1949) 7.5' quadrangle.
(2) *settlement,* 1 mile east-southeast of Cisco Grove along South Yuba River (lat. 39°18'20" N, long. 120°31'10" W; sec. 28, T 17 N, R 13 E). Named on Cisco Grove (1955) 7.5' quadrangle.

Big Boulder Creek [SIERRA]: *stream,* flows 2.25 miles to Plumas County 10.5 miles northnortheast of Sierra City (lat. 39°42'35" N, long. 120°33'20" W; near S line sec. 6, T 21 N, R 13 E). Named on Clio (1981) 7.5' quadrangle.

Big Bowman Lake: see **Bowman Lake** [NEVADA].

Big Butte [EL DORADO]: *peak,* 7.5 miles southeast of Camino (lat. 38°40'35" N, long. 120°33'30" W; sec. 32, T 10 N, R 13 E); the peak is nearly 1 mile north-northwest of Little Butte. Altitude 4359 feet. Named on Sly Park (1952) 7.5' quadrangle. Big Butte, Middle Butte, and Little Butte together have the label "Buttes" on Placerville (1893) 30' quadrangle.

Big Canon Creek: see **Clavey River** [TUOLUMNE].

Big Canyon [EL DORADO]:
(1) *canyon,* 2.25 miles long, opens into the canyon of South Fork American River at Chili Bar (lat. 38°45'55" N, long. 120°49'15" W; near NW cor. sec. 36, T 11 N, R 10 E). Named on Garden Valley (1949) and Placerville (1949) 7.5' quadrangles. Gudde (1975, p. 276) listed a mining place called Poverty Point that was located on the east side of Big Canyon 2 miles north of Placerville.
(2) *canyon,* drained by a stream that flows 5 miles to North Fork Cosumnes River 10 miles east-southeast of Camino (lat. 38°39'55" N, long. 120°31'05" W; sec. 3, T 9 N, R 13 E). Named on Sly Park (1952) and Stump Spring (1951) 7.5' quadrangles.

Big Canyon [SIERRA]: *canyon,* drained by a stream that flows 2 miles to Turner Canyon (1) 5.5 miles west-northwest of Sierraville (lat. 39°37'20" N, long. 120°27'40" W; near SW cor. sec. 31, T 21 N, R 14 E). Named on Calpine (1981) and Sattley (1981) 7.5' quadrangles.

Big Canyon Creek [EL DORADO]: *stream,* flows 12 miles to Cosumnes River 3 miles southeast of Latrobe (lat. 38°31'40" N, long. 120°56'35" W; at S line sec. 24, T 8 N, R 9 E). Named on Latrobe (1949) and Shingle Springs (1949) 7.5' quadrangles.

Big Canyon Creek: see **East Big Canyon Creek** [EL DORADO].

Big Chief [PLACER]: *peak,* 5.5 miles north-northwest of Tahoe City (lat. 39°14'30" N, long. 120°11'45" W; near NW cor. sec. 15, T 16 N, R 16 E); the peak is 0.5 mile southeast of Little Chief. Altitude 7332 feet. Named on Tahoe City (1955) 7.5' quadrangle. California Division of Highways' (1934) map shows a place called Big Chief located along Southern Pacific Railroad less than 1 mile west of present Big Chief (near S line sec. 9, T 16 N, R 16 E), a place called McPhetres located along the railroad 1 mile farther north (sec. 4, T 16 N, R 16 E), and a place called Denvale situated along the railroad just north of McPhetres.

Big Crater [PLACER]: *relief feature,* 11 miles south-southwest of Duncan Peak (lat. 39°00'45" N, long. 120°36'15" W; on N line sec. 2, T 13 N, R 12 E); the feature is 2.5 miles west-southwest of Little Crater. Named on Greek Store (1952) 7.5' quadrangle.

Big Creek [MADERA-MARIPOSA]: *stream,* heads in Madera County and flows 15 miles to South Fork Merced River 0.5 mile west of Wawona in Mariposa County (lat. 37°32'20" N, long. 119°40' W; near E line sec. 33, T 4 S, R 21 E). Named on Bass Lake (1953) and Yosemite (1956) 15' quadrangles.

Big Creek [TUOLUMNE]:
(1) *stream,* flows 12.5 miles to Tuolumne River nearly 5 miles south of Tuolumne (lat. 37°53'35" N, long. 120°13'20" W; sec. 33, T 1 N, R 16 E). Named on Groveland (1947), Jawbone Ridge (1947), and Tuolumne (1948)

7.5' quadrangles. A large meadow at the head of the stream was called Savage Flat in the early days for James D. Savage, who probably grazed horses at the place (Gudde, 1975, p. 309).
(2) *stream,* flows nearly 7 miles to Don Pedro Reservoir 7.5 miles south of Chinese Camp (lat. 37°45'35" N, long. 120°25'05" W; sec. 15, T 2 S, R 14 E). Named on Chinese Camp (1947, photorevised 1973) and La Grange (1962) 7.5' quadrangles. Called Fortynine Creek on Merced Falls (1944) 15' quadrangle. West Fork enters from the northwest at the mouth of the main stream; it is nearly 5 miles long and is named on Chinese Camp (1947, photorevised 1973) 7.5' quadrangle.
(3) *stream,* flows 4.5 miles to South Fork Tuolumne River nearly 7 miles southwest of Mather (lat. 37°48'40" N, long. 119°56'20" W; near E line sec. 36, T 1 S, R 18 E). Named on Lake Eleanor (1956) 15' quadrangle. Called Hazel Green Creek on Yosemite (1909) 30' quadrangle, but United States Board on Geographic Names (1966, p. 7) rejected this name for the feature.
(4) *stream,* flows 3 miles to Tuolumne River 2 miles south-southwest of Don Pedro Camp (lat. 37°41'25" N, long. 120°25'20" W; sec. 10, T 3 S, R 14 E). Named on La Grange (1962) 7.5' quadrangle.

Big Creek: see **Hazel Green Creek** [TUOLUMNE].

Big Creek Basin [TUOLUMNE]: *valley,* 8 miles south-southwest of Mather (lat. 37°46'15" N, long. 119°54'15" W); the valley is at the head of Big Creek (3). Named on Lake Eleanor (1956) 15' quadrangle.

Big Dam Reservoir: see **Pinecrest Lake** [TUOLUMNE].

Big Dome [CALAVERAS]: *peak,* nearly 2 miles north-northwest of Paloma (lat. 38°17' N, long. 120°46'30" W; sec. 16, T 5 N, R 11 E). Altitude 1436 feet. Named on Jackson (1962) 7.5' quadrangle.

Bigelow Lake [TUOLUMNE]: *lake,* 2300 feet long, 5 miles west of Tower Peak (lat. 38°09'20" N, long. 119°38'10" W); the lake is 0.5 mile northwest of Bigelow Peak. Named on Tower Peak (1956) 15' quadrangle.

Bigelow Peak [TUOLUMNE]: *peak,* 4.5 miles west of Tower Peak (lat. 38°09' N, long. 119°37'35" W). Altitude 10,539 feet. Named on Tower Peak (1956) 15' quadrangle. The name commemorates Major John Bigelow, Jr., acting superintendent of Yosemite National Park in 1904 (United States Board on Geographic Names, 1934, p. 2).

Big Falls: see **La Grange Reservoir** [TUOLUMNE].

Big Granite Creek [PLACER]: *stream,* flows 6.5 miles to North Fork American River 5 miles north of Duncan Peak (lat. 39°13'25" N, long. 120°31'45" W; near W line sec. 28, T 16 N, R 13 E). Named on Cisco Grove

(1955), Duncan Peak (1952), and Soda Springs (1955) 7.5' quadrangles. Called Granite Creek on Truckee (1895) 30' quadrangle. The canyon of the stream is called Granite Canyon on Colfax (1898) 30' quadrangle.

Big Grizzly: see **Miller Gulch** [MARIPOSA].

Big Grizzly Canyon [PLACER]: *canyon,* drained by a stream that flows 8 miles to Rubicon River 4.25 miles west-southwest of Devil Peak (lat. 38°56'40" N, long. 120°37'20" W; sec. 27, T 13 N, R 12 E). Named on Devil Peak (1950) 7.5' quadrangle. On Placerville (1893) 30' quadrangle, the stream in the canyon is called Grizzly Creek.

Big Grizzly Creek [MARIPOSA]: *stream,* flows 1.5 miles to Ned Gulch (2) 5 miles west-north-west of El Portal (lat. 37°42'10" N, long. 119°51'50" W; sec. 4, T 3 S, R 19 E); the stream heads near Big Grizzly Mountain. Named on El Portal (1947) and Kinsley (1947) 7.5' quadrangles.

Big Grizzly Creek [SIERRA]: *stream,* flows 2.25 miles to Canyon Creek 2.5 miles south of Mount Fillmore at Poker Flat (lat. 39°41'35" N, long. 120°50'35" W). Named on Mount Fillmore (1951) 7.5' quadrangle. Called Grizzly Ck. on Downieville (1897) 30' quadrangle.

Big Grizzly Flat [MARIPOSA]: *area,* 6.25 miles west-northwest of El Portal (lat. 37°43'25" N, long. 119°52'40" W; at N line sec. 33, T 2 S, R 19 E); the place is 1 mile east-northeast of Big Grizzly Mountain. Named on El Portal (1947) and Kinsley (1947) 7.5' quadrangles.

Big Grizzly Mountain [MARIPOSA]: *peak,* 7 miles west-northwest of El Portal (lat. 37°43'05" N, long. 119°53'40" W; sec. 32, T 2 S, R 19 E); the peak is 1.25 miles east-northeast of Little Grizzly Mountain. Altitude 5192 feet. Named on Kinsley (1947) 7.5' quadrangle.

Big Hill [EL DORADO]: *peak,* 5.5 miles northnortheast of Riverton (lat. 38°50'35" N, long. 120°24'25" W; near E line sec. 33, T 12 N, R 14 E). Altitude 6155 feet. Named on Riverton (1950) 7.5' quadrangle.

Big Hill [PLACER]: *peak,* 7.5 miles northwest of Auburn (lat. 38°59'15" N, long. 121°09'30" W; near S line sec. 11, T 13 N, R 7 E). Altitude 1613 feet. Named on Gold Hill (1954) 7.5' quadrangle.

Big Hill: see **Rushing Mountain** [TUOLUMNE].

Big Hill Canyon [EL DORADO]: *canyon,* drained by a stream that flows 1.5 miles to South Fork Silver Creek 4 miles north of Riverton (lat. 38°49'55" N, long. 120°26'20" W; near W line sec. 5, T 11 N, R 14 E); the canyon is southwest of Big Hill. Named on Riverton (1950) 7.5' quadrangle.

Big Hill Ridge [EL DORADO]: *ridge,* south-to west-trending, 3 miles long, 4.25 miles north-northeast of Riverton (lat. 38°49'25" N, long. 120°24'30" W); Big Hill is at the north

end of the ridge. Named on Riverton (1950) 7.5' quadrangle.

Big House: see **Mosquito Valley**, under **Mosquito Creek** [EL DORADO].

Big Humbug Creek [TUOLUMNE]: *stream,* flows 3.5 miles to Tuolumne River nearly 5 miles south-southeast of Tuolumne (lat. 37°53'35" N, long. 120°13'05" W; sec. 33, T 1 N, R 16 E). Named on Groveland (1947) and Tuolumne (1948) 7.5' quadrangles.

Big Indian Creek [AMADOR]: *stream,* flows 17 miles to Cosumnes River 6 miles west-northwest of Fiddletown (lat. 38°33'05" N, long. 120°50'55" W; sec. 14, T 8 N, R 10 E). Named on Amador City (1962), Aukum (1952), and Fiddletown (1949) 7.5' quadrangles. Camp's (1962) map shows a canyon called Music Dale that opens into the canyon of Cosumnes River from the south nearly 3 miles southwest of the mouth of Big Indian Creek.

Big Iowa Canyon: see **Iowa Canyon** [EL DORADO].

Big Island [TUOLUMNE]: *island,* 325 feet long, 1 mile east-southeast of Don Pedro Camp in Don Pedro Reservoir (lat. 37°42'40" N, long. 120°23'10" W; near SW cor. sec. 36, T 2 N, R 14 E). Named on La Grange (1962) 7.5' quadrangle.

Big Island Lake: see **Bear Lake** [TUOLUMNE] (2).

Big Jackass Creek [TUOLUMNE]: *stream,* flows 7.5 miles to Moccasin Creek nearly 3 miles southeast of Moccasin (lat. 37°46'45" N, long. 120°16'15" W; sec. 12, T 2 S, R 15 E). Named on Groveland (1947) and Moccasin (1948) 7.5' quadrangles.

Big John Hill [PLACER]: *peak,* 5 miles south-southeast of Colfax (lat. 39°02' N, long. 120°55'25" W; sec. 25, T 14 N, R 9 E); the peak is near the east end of Big John Ridge. Altitude 2252 feet. Named on Colfax (1949) 7.5' quadrangle.

Big John Ridge [PLACER]: *ridge,* generally west-trending, 2.5 miles long, 4.5 miles south of Colfax (lat. 39°02'05" N, long. 120°56'25" W); Big John Hill is near the east end of the ridge. Named on Colfax (1949) 7.5' quadrangle.

Big Lake [TUOLUMNE]: *lake,* 0.5 mile long, 12 miles east-southeast of Pinecrest (lat. 38°07'20" N, long. 119°47'50" W). Named on Pinecrest (1956) 15' quadrangle.

Bigler: see **Lake Bigler**, under **Lake Tahoe** [EL DORADO-PLACER].

Bigler Lake Valley: see **Lake Valley** [EL DORADO].

Big Lick Spring [NEVADA]: *spring,* 2.5 miles north-northeast of Washington (lat. 39°23'25" N, long. 120°49'30" W; near SW cor. sec. 26, T 18 N, R 10 E). Named on Alleghany (1949) 7.5' quadrangle.

Big Meadow [CALAVERAS]:
(1) *area,* 2.25 miles southwest of Tamarack (lat. 38°25' N, long. 120°06'30" W; mainly in sec.

33, T 7 N, R 17 E). Named on Tamarack (1979) 7.5' quadrangle.

(2) *settlement,* 2.5 miles southwest of Tamarack (lat. 38°24'55" N, long. 120°06'50" W; sec. 33, T 7 N, R 17 E); the place is in Big Meadow (1). Named on Tamarack (1979) 7.5' quadrangle.

Big Meadow [EL DORADO]: *area,* 7.5 miles southwest of Freel Peak (lat. 38°46'45" N, long. 120°00' W; on S line sec. 21, T 11 N, R 18 E). Named on Echo Lake (1955) and Freel Peak (1955) 7.5' quadrangles.

Big Meadow [MARIPOSA]: *area,* 2.5 miles northeast of El Portal (lat. 37°42'20" N, long. 119°45' W; near N line sec. 3, T 3 S, R 20 E). Named on El Portal (1947) and Yosemite (1956) 15' quadrangles.

Big Meadow [PLACER]: *area,* 3 miles west-northwest of Bunker Hill (lat. 39°04'20" N, long. 120°25'35" W; on N line sec. 17, T 14 N, R 14 E). Named on Bunker Hill (1953) 7.5' quadrangle.

Big Meadow Creek [CALAVERAS]: *stream,* flows 5 miles to North Fork Stanislaus River 3.5 miles southwest of Tamarack (lat. 38° 24' N, long. 120°07'15" W); the stream goes through Big Meadow (1). Named on Tamarack (1979) 7.5' quadrangle.

Big Meadow Creek [EL DORADO]: *stream,* flows 3.5 miles to Upper Truckee River 1 mile southeast of Echo Summit (lat. 38°48'05" N, long. 120°00'55" W; sec. 17, T 11 N, R 18 E); the stream goes through Big Meadow. Named on Echo Lake (1955) and Freel Peak (1955) 7.5' quadrangles.

Big Meadow Creek [TUOLUMNE]: *stream,* flows 2.5 miles to Piute Creek (2) 5 miles southwest of Matterhorn Peak (lat. 38°03'10" N, long. 119°27'25" W). Named on Matterhorn Peak (1956) 15' quadrangle.

Big Meadow Creek: see **Ackerson Creek** [TUOLUMNE].

Big Meadow Creek: see **Rubicon River** [EL DORADO-PLACER].

Big Mosquito Creek [PLACER]: *stream,* flows 4.25 miles to Middle Fork American River 5.5 miles east of Michigan Bluff (lat. 39°02'25" N, long. 120°37'45" W; at S line sec. 22, T 14 N, R 12 E); the stream is south of Mosquito Ridge. Named on Greek Store (1952) and Michigan Bluff (1952) 7.5' quadrangle.

Big Mountain [EL DORADO]: *peak,* 3.5 miles east of Omo Ranch (lat. 38°34'35" N, long. 120°30'15" W; sec. 2, T 8 N, R 13 E). Altitude 4597 feet. Named on Omo Ranch (1952) 7.5' quadrangle.

Big Mountain Ridge [EL DORADO]: *ridge,* generally west-trending, 10 miles long, center 2 miles south-southwest of Caldor (lat. 38°34'50" N, long. 120°26'45" W); Big Mountain is near the west end of the ridge. Named on Caldor (1951), Omo Ranch (1952), and Peddler Hill (1951) 7.5' quadrangles.

Big Oak Flat [PLACER]: *area,* 5 miles east-

northeast of Michigan Bluff (lat. 39°03'30" N, long. 120°39' W; sec. 16, 17, T 14 N, R 12 E). Named on Michigan Bluff (1952) 7.5' quadrangle.

Big Oak Flat [TUOLUMNE]: *village,* 2.25 miles east-northeast of Moccasin near the head of Rattlesnake Creek (lat. 37°49'25" N, long. 120°15'25" W; sec. 30, T 1 S, R 16 E). Named on Moccasin (1948) 7.5' quadrangle. Postal authorities established Big Oak Flat post office in 1852 (Frickstad, p. 215). The name is from a huge oak tree at the place (Hanna, p. 33). James D. Savage began mining at the site in 1848, and it then became known as Savage Diggings; the place also was called Oak Flat and Oak Flats (Gudde, 1975, p. 37, 309).

Big Pebble Canyon [EL DORADO]: *canyon,* drained by a stream that flows 2 miles to Snow Creek 3 miles west-southwest of Old Iron Mountain (lat. 38°41'50" N, long. 120°26'50" W; sec. 29, T 10 N, R 14 E). Named on Stump Spring (1951) 7.5' quadrangle.

Big Prather Meadow [TUOLUMNE]: *valley,* less than 1 mile north of Liberty Hill (lat. 38°22'45" N, long. 120°06' W); the valley is 1 mile west of Little Prather Meadow. Named on Liberty Hill (1979) and Tamarack (1979) 7.5' quadrangles.

Big Rattlesnake Creek [TUOLUMNE]: *stream,* flows 5.25 miles to North Fork Stanislaus River 4.5 miles west of Liberty Hill (lat. 38° 21'30" N, long. 120°11'05" W; sec. 23, T 6 N, R 16 E); the stream generally is parallel to and about 1 mile north of Little Rattlesnake Creek. Named on Boards Crossing (1979) and Liberty Hill (1979) 7.5' quadrangles.

Big Ravine [EL DORADO]: *canyon,* 1 mile long, opens into the canyon of South Fork American River 5 miles south-southwest of the village of Pilot Hill (lat. 38°46'15" N, long. 121°03'10" W; sec. 26, T 11 N, R 8 E). Named on Pilot Hill (1954) 7.5' quadrangle.

Big Reservoir [EL DORADO]: *intermittent lake,* 500 feet long, 2.5 miles south-southeast of Omo Ranch (lat. 38°32'50" N, long. 120° 33'20" W; near W line sec. 16, T 8 N, R 13 E); the feature is 1.5 miles east-southeast of Little Reservoir. Named on Omo Ranch (1952) 7.5' quadrangle.

Big Reservoir [PLACER]: *lake,* behind a dam on a tributary of Forbes Creek 6.25 miles southeast of Dutch Flat (lat. 39°08'35" N, long. 120°45'20" W; sec. 17, T 15 N, R 11 E). Named on Dutch Flat (1950, photorevised 1973) and Westville (1952, photorevised 1973) 7.5' quadrangles. United States Board on Geographic Names (1986, p. 1) rejected the names "Morning Star Lake" and "Morning Star Reservoir" for the feature.

Big Sailor Creek [EL DORADO]: *stream,* flows 2.5 miles to Slate Creek (1) 3.5 miles north-northwest of Chili Bar (lat. 38°48'30" N, long. 120°51'25" W; near SW cor. sec. 10, T 11 N,

R 10 E). Named on Garden Valley (1949) 7.5' quadrangle.

Big Sandy Campground [MADERA]: *locality,* 7.25 miles north-northeast of Yosemite Forks (lat. 37°28' N, long. 119°34'55" W; sec. 29, T 5 S, R 22 E); the place is along Big Creek 1 mile downstream from Little Sandy Campground. Named on Bass Lake (1953) 15' quadrangle.

Big Seven Ridge [CALAVERAS]: *ridge,* northwest-trending, 2 miles long, 1.25 miles northeast of Copperopolis (lat. 37°59'45" N, long. 120°37'45" W); Big Seven mine is on the ridge. Named on Copperopolis (1962), Melones Dam (1962), and Salt Spring Valley (1962) 7.5' quadrangles.

Big Shady Creek: see **Shady Creek** [NEVADA].

Big Silver Campground [EL DORADO]: *locality,* 3 miles south-southeast of Robbs Peak along Big Silver Creek (lat. 38°52'55" N, long. 120°23'20" W; sec. 15, T 12 N, R 14 E). Named on Robbs Peak (1952) 15' quadrangle. Water of Union Valley Reservoir now covers the site.

Big Silver Creek [EL DORADO]: *stream,* flows 7.5 miles to Union Valley Reservoir 3.5 miles south-southeast of Robbs Peak (lat. 38° 52'45" N, long. 120°22' W; near SE cor. sec. 14, T 12 N, R 14 E). Named on Kyburz (1952) and Loon Lake (1952, photorevised 1973) 7.5' quadrangles. The lower part of present Big Silver Creek and all of present Bassi Fork above the confluence of the two streams are called North Fork Silver Creek on Pyramid Peak (1896) 30' quadrangle.

Big Sluice Box [EL DORADO]: *relief feature,* 4 miles east of Wentworth Springs (lat. 39°00'30" N, long. 120°15'45" W; at N line sec. 2, T 13 N, R 15 E); the feature is 1 mile southeast of Little Sluice Box. Named on Wentworth Springs (1953) 7.5' quadrangle.

Big Snyder Gulch [PLACER]: *canyon,* drained by a stream that flows 1 mile to Middle Fork American River 10.5 miles east-northeast of Auburn (lat. 38°57'35" N, long. 120°53'25" W; sec. 19, T 13 N, R 10 E). Named on Greenwood (1949) 7.5' quadrangle.

Big Spanish Hill: see **Spanish Ravine** [EL DORADO].

Big Spring [MARIPOSA]: *spring,* 3 miles southeast of Mariposa (lat. 37°27'35" N, long. 119°55'10" W; near NW cor. sec. 32, T 5 S, R 19 E); the spring is along a branch of Spring Creek. Named on Mariposa (1947) 7.5' quadrangle.

Big Spring [PLACER]: *spring,* 3.5 miles south-southeast of Granite Chief (lat. 39°08'55" N, long. 120°16'05" W; sec. 14, T 15 N, R 15 E). Named on Granite Chief (1953) 7.5' quadrangle.

Big Springs [SIERRA]: *springs,* 2.5 miles north-northeast of Sierra City (lat. 39°35'55" N, long. 120°36'40" W; sec. 15, T 20 N, R 12 E).

Named on Haypress Valley (1981) 7.5' quadrangle.

Big Springs Creek [CALAVERAS]: *stream,* flows 2.5 miles to Martells Creek 7.25 miles south-southwest of Copperopolis (lat. 37°53'10" N, long. 120°42'10" W). Named on Copperopolis (1962) 7.5' quadrangle. Called Big Spring Cr. on Copperopolis (1916) 15' quadrangle.

Big Sugar Loaf: see **China Mountain** [EL DORADO].

Big Tree [MARIPOSA]: *area,* 3.5 miles east-southeast of Wawona (lat. 37°30'30" N, long. 119°36' W). Named on Yosemite (1956) 15' quadrangle. The federal government gave the land to the State of California in 1864 as a park to preserve a grove of redwood trees (Whitney, 1870, p. 10). The place now is part of Yosemite National Park.

Big Trees [CALAVERAS]: *locality,* 5 miles south-southeast of Blue Mountain (lat. 38°16'45" N, long. 120°18'55" W; near NW cor. sec. 22, T 5 N, R 15 E); the place is in Calaveras Big Trees State Park. Named on Dorrington (1979) 7.5' quadrangle. Postal authorities established Big Trees post office in 1865, discontinued it for a time in 1903, and discontinued it finally in 1943 (Salley, p. 21).

Big Trees Creek [CALAVERAS]: *stream,* flows 3.5 miles to White Pine Lake 5.25 miles southsoutheast of Blue Mountain (lat. 38° 16' N, long. 120°20'25" W; sec. 20, T 5 N, R 15 E). Named on Dorrington (1979) 7.5' quadrangle.

Big Trees Creek [TUOLUMNE]: *stream,* flows 3.5 miles to Beaver Creek 9 miles northeast of Stanislaus (lat. 38°14'30" N, long. 120° 16'15" W; sec. 36, T 5 N, R 15 E). Named on Boards Crossing (1979), Crandall Peak (1979), and Stanislaus (1948) 7.5' quadrangles.

Big Tree Station: see **Wawona** [MARIPOSA].

Big Tunnel Spring [NEVADA]: *spring,* 4 miles south-southeast of Washington (lat. 39°18'05" N, long. 120°46'25" W; at NE cor. sec. 31, T 17 N, R 11 E); the spring is near a tunnel on South Yuba canal. Named on Washington (1950) 7.5' quadrangle.

Big Valley [PLACER]: *valley,* 3.25 miles south of Cisco Grove (lat. 39°15'50" N, long. 120°33' W; in and near sec. 7, T 16 N, R 13 E). Named on Cisco Grove (1955) 7.5' quadrangle.

Big Valley Bluff [PLACER]: *ridge,* southeast-trending, 1 mile long, 6.5 miles northwest of Duncan Peak (lat 39°14' N, long. 120°34'55" W; mainly in sec. 24, T 16 N, R 12 W); the ridge is west of Big Valley Canyon. Named on Duncan Peak (1952) 7.5' quadrangle.

Big Valley Canyon [PLACER]: *canyon,* 3 miles long, opens into the canyon of North Fork American River 5 miles north-northwest of Duncan Peak (lat. 39°13'10" N, long. 120°33'20" W; sec. 30, T 16 N, R 13 E); the feature heads at Big Valley. Named on Duncan Peak (1952) 7.5' quadrangle.

Big X Mountain [EL DORADO]: *peak,* 6 miles north-northwest of Pollock Pines (lat. 38°50'10" N, long. 120°38'10" W; near NE cor. sec. 4, T 11 N, R 12 E). Named on Slate Mountain (1950) 7.5' quadrangle.

Bijou [EL DORADO]: *district,* 7 miles north-northwest of Freel Peak in the town of South Lake Tahoe (lat. 38°56'45" N, long. 119° 58' W; sec. 33, T 13 N, R 18 E). Named on South Lake Tahoe (1955, photorevised 1969 and 1974) 7.5' quadrangle. Postal authorities established Bijou post office in 1888 and discontinued it in 1967 (Salley, p. 21). The name is from the French word for "jewel" (Hanna, p. 33). Almon M. Taylor patented land in section 33 in 1864, and Taylor's Landing there was a shipping point for lumber; the place took the name "Bijou" when the post office was established (Lekisch, p. 8).

Bijou Park [EL DORADO]: *district,* 7 miles north-northwest of Freel Peak in the town of South Lake Tahoe (lat. 38°56'55" N, long. 119°57'15" W); the feature is east of Bijou. Named on South Lake Tahoe (1955, photorevised 1969 and 1974) 7.5' quadrangle.

Biledo Meadow [MADERA]: *area,* 6.5 miles south-southwest of Buena Vista Peak (lat. 37°30'10" N, long. 119°34' W; on S line sec. 9, T 5 S, R 22 E). Named on Yosemite (1956) 15' quadrangle. United States Board on Geographic Names (1990, p. 5) rejected the form "Billiedo Meadow" for the feature. The name commemorates Thomas Biledo, or Biledeaux, a French-Canadian miner who built a log cabin at the place in 1890 (Uhte, p. 51).

Billiedo Meadow: see **Biledo Meadow** [MADERA].

Billy Ache Canyon: see **Bellyache Canyon** [MARIPOSA].

Billy Hill [NEVADA]: *peak,* 2 miles north of Hobart Mills (lat. 39° 25'25" N, long. 120°10'50" W; near NE cor. sec. 10, T 18 N, R 16 E). Altitude 6694 feet. Named on Hobart Mills (1981) 7.5' quadrangle.

Billy Mack Canyon [NEVADA]: *canyon,* 1.5 miles long, opens into the valley of Donner Lake 1.5 miles east-northeast of Donner Pass (lat. 39°19'30" N, long. 120°18'10" W; sec. 15, T 17 N, R 15 E). Named on Norden (1955) 7.5' quadrangle.

Billy Mack Flat [NEVADA]: *area,* 1.5 miles north-northeast of Donner Pass (lat. 39°20'10" N, long. 120°18'40" W; at E line sec. 9, T 17 N, R 15 E); the place is in Billy Mack Canyon. Named on Norden (1955) 7.5' quadrangle.

Billys Peak: see **Granite Chief** [PLACER].

Bingaman Lake [TUOLUMNE]: *lake,* 1400 feet long, 4.5 miles south of Tioga Pass (lat. 37°50'45" N, long. 119°14'40" W). Named on Mono Craters (1953) 15' quadrangle. The

name commemorates John W. Bingaman, a ranger at Yosemite National Park who planted trout in the lake in 1930, and who named the feature for himself (Browning, 1986, p. 19).

Bingham Lake: see **Calaveras Reservoir** [CALAVERAS].

Birch: see **Hildreth** [MADERA].

Birch Lake [TUOLUMNE]: *lake,* 850 feet long, at Mather (lat. 37°52'45" N, long. 119°51'15" W; sec. 2, T 1 S, R 19 E). Named on Lake Eleanor (1956) 15' quadrangle.

Birchville [NEVADA]: *locality,* nearly 2 miles north-northeast of French Corral (lat. 39°19'40" N, long. 121°08'35" W; at S line sec. 13, T 17 N, R 7 E). Named on French Corral (1948) 7.5' quadrangle. Called Birchy on California Mining Bureau's (1917b) map. The name commemorates L. Birch Adsit; until 1853 the place was called Johnson's Diggings for David Johnson, the first prospector there (Gudde, 1975, p. 38).

Birchy: see **Birchville** [NEVADA].

Birth Rock: see **Burst Rock** [TUOLUMNE].

Bisbee Lake: see **Loon Lake** [EL DORADO].

Bisbee Peak [AMADOR]: *peak,* 2.5 miles westnorthwest of Plymouth (lat. 38°29'30" N, long. 120°53'20" W; near W line sec. 4, T 7 N, R 10 E). Altitude 1207 feet. Named on Irish Hill (1962) 7.5' quadrangle. Camp's (1962) map has the name "Finn's Sugarloaf" as an alternate.

Bishop Creek [MARIPOSA]: *stream,* flows 4.5 miles to South Fork Merced River 6 miles northwest of Wawona (lat. 37°36'25" N, long. 119°43'10" W; near NW cor. sec. 12, T 4 S, R 20 E). Named on Yosemite (1956) 15' quadrangle. The name commemorates Samuel Addison Bishop, who served in the Mariposa Battalion during the Mariposa Indian War; the stream also is called Eleven Mile Creek (Mendershausen, p. 20).

Bitney Corner [NEVADA]: *locality,* 2.5 miles west-northwest of Grass Valley (lat. 39°13'55" N, long. 121°06'30" W; near W line sec. 20, T 16 N, R 8 E). Named on Grass Valley (1949) 7.5' quadrangle.

Black Bear Lake [TUOLUMNE]: *lake,* 1500 feet long, 5.5 miles west of Tower Peak (lat. 38°09'05" N, long. 119°38'55" W; sec. 34, T 4 N, R 21 E). Named on Tower Peak (1956) 15' quadrangle. Elden H. Vestal of California Department of Fish and Game named the lake in 1952 (Browning, 1986, p. 20).

Blackbird Camp Ground [EL DORADO]: *locality,* 0.5 mile west-northwest of Riverton along South Fork American River (lat. 38° 46'30" N, long. 120°27'30" W; sec. 30, T 11 N, R 14 E). Named on Riverton (1950) 7.5' quadrangle.

Blackbird Lake [TUOLUMNE]: *lake,* 700 feet long, 7.25 miles west-northwest of Tower Peak (lat. 38°10'35" N, long. 119°40'20" W; sec. 21, T 4 N, R 21 E). Named on Tower Peak (1956) 15' quadrangle.

Black Buttes [NEVADA]: *relief feature,* 3.5 miles south of English Mountain (lat. 39°23'40" N, long. 120°33'25" W). Named on English Mountain (1983) 7.5' quadrangle. Called Black Mountains on Colfax (1898) 30' quadrangle.

Black Camp [NEVADA]: *locality,* 4.25 miles east-southeast of Graniteville (lat. 39°24'45" N, long. 120°39'45" W; near E line sec. 19, T 18 N, R 12 E). Named on Graniteville (1982) 7.5' quadrangle.

Black Canyon [PLACER]: *canyon,* drained by a stream that flows nearly 3 miles to Secret Canyon 5.5 miles west of Duncan Peak (lat. 39°09'10" N, long. 120°37' W; at N line sec. 15, T 15 N, R 12 E). Named on Duncan Peak (1952) 7.5' quadrangle.

Black Canyon [SIERRA]: *canyon,* drained by a stream that flows 1 mile to Ladies Canyon 3.25 miles west-northwest of Sierra City (lat. 39°34'55" N, long. 120°41'25" W; sec. 24, T 20 N, R 11 E). Named on Sierra City (1981) 7.5' quadrangle. United States Board on Geographic Names (1960a, p. 12) rejected the name "Ladies Canyon" for the feature.

Black Creek [CALAVERAS]:
(1) *stream,* flows 11 miles to Tulloch Lake 4 miles south-southeast of Copperopolis (lat. 37°55'30" N, long. 120°36'45" W; near W line sec. 24, T 1 N, R 12 E). Named on Copperopolis (1962), Melones Dam (1962), and Salt Spring Valley (1962) 7.5' quadrangles.
(2) *stream,* flows 1 mile to Texas Charley Gulch 4.5 miles east-northeast of Copperopolis (lat. 37°59'50" N, long. 120°33'35" W). Named on Melones Dam (1962) 7.5' quadrangle.

Black Cut Ravine [NEVADA]: *canyon,* drained by a stream that flows 0.5 mile to Middle Yuba River nearly 7 miles northeast of North Bloomfield (lat. 39°26'10" N, long. 120°48'35" W; near W line sec. 12, T 18 N, R 10 E). Named on Alleghany (1949) 7.5' quadrangle.

Black Gulch [AMADOR]: *canyon,* drained by a stream that flows 1.5 miles to Mokelumne River 4 miles south of Jackson (lat. 38°17'25" N, long. 120°45'40" W; near sec. 16, T 5 N, R 11 E). Named on Jackson (1962) 7.5' quadrangle.

Blackhawk Canyon [PLACER]: *canyon,* drained by a stream that flows 2 miles to the head of Third Brushy Canyon 2.5 miles north of Foresthill (lat. 39°03'20" N, long. 120°49'25" W; sec. 14, T 14 N, R 10 E). Named on Foresthill (1949) 7.5' quadrangle.

Black Hawk Lake: see **Black Hawk Mountain** [TUOLUMNE].

Blackhawk Mountain [MADERA]: *ridge,* northeast-trending, 1.5 miles long, 2 miles north-northwest of O'Neals (lat. 37°09'15" N, long. 119°42'35" W). Named on O'Neals (1965) 7.5' quadrangle.

Black Hawk Mountain [TUOLUMNE]: *peak,* 9.5 miles west-northwest of Tower Peak (lat. 38°12'25" N, long. 119°42'30" W). Altitude 10,348 feet. Named on Tower Peak (1956) 15' quadrangle. United States Board on Geographic Names (1965c, p. 7) approved the name "Black Hawk Lake" for a lake, 600 feet long, that lies 0.5 mile north-northwest of Black Hawk Mountain (lat. 38°12'45" N, long. 119°42'50" W).

Black Hill [CALAVERAS]: *hill,* 9 miles west of Copperopolis on Calaveras-Stanislaus county line (lat. 37°58'30" N, long. 120°48'35" W; near S line sec. 31, T 2 N, R 11 E). Named on Bachelor Valley (1953) 7.5' quadrangle.

Blackie Lake [MADERA]: *lake,* 400 feet long, 4 miles south-southeast of Merced Peak (lat. 37°34'45" N, long. 119°22'40" W). Named on Merced Peak (1953) 15' quadrangle. Warden Herb Black told employees of California Department of Fish and Game in 1946 that the lake sometimes was called Blackie Lake after himself (Browning, 1986, p. 21).

Black Jack [SIERRA]: *locality,* 5.25 miles southeast of Downieville (lat. 39°30'30" N, long. 120°45' W). Named on Downieville (1897) 30' quadrangle.

Black Jack Ravine [SIERRA]: *canyon,* drained by a stream that flows 2.5 miles to Jim Crow Creek 4.5 miles southeast of Downieville (lat. 39°31'05" N, long. 120°45'45" W; sec. 17, T 19 N, R 11 E). Named on Downieville (1951) and Sierra City (1981) 7.5' quadrangles. On Downieville (1897) 30' quadrangle, the name "Jim Crow Ravine" appears to apply to present Black Jack Ravine together with the canyon of present Jim Crow Creek. United States Board on Geographic Names (1960a, p. 12) rejected the names "Jim Crow Ravine" and "Blackjack Ravine" for present Black Jack Ravine.

Blackmans Bar [MADERA]: *locality,* 3 miles northeast of Shuteye Peak along West Fork Chiquito Creek (lat. 37°22'30" N, long. 119°23' W; sec. 30, T 6 S, R 24 E). Named on Shuteye Peak (1953) 15' quadrangle.

Black Mountain: see **Madera Peak** [MADERA].

Black Mountain [MARIPOSA]: *peak,* 6.5 miles east of Buckeye Peak (lat. 37°40' N, long. 120°00'20" W; near S line sec. 17, T 3 S, R 18 E). Altitude 3316 feet. Named on Buckhorn Peak (1947) 7.5' quadrangle. Called Texas Hill on Sonora (1897) 30' quadrangle.

Black Mountain [PLACER]: *peak,* 4 miles west-southwest of Cisco Grove on Monumental Ridge (lat. 39°17' N, long. 120°36'20" W; near E line sec. 3, T 16 N, R 12 E). Altitude 6986 feet. Named on Cisco Grove (1955) 7.5' quadrangle.

Black Mountains: see **Black Buttes** [NEVADA].

Black Oak Spring [NEVADA]: *spring,* 2.5 miles northwest of Yuba Gap (lat. 39°20'05" N, long. 120°39'15" W; sec. 17, T 17 N, R 12

E). Named on Blue Canyon (1955) 7.5' quadrangle.

Black Peak: see **Madera Peak** [MADERA].

Black Peak Fork: see **Madera Creek** [MADERA].

Black Peak [TUOLUMNE]: *peak,* 2.5 miles southeast of Don Pedro Camp (lat. 37°41'40" N, long. 120°22'05" W; near NW cor. sec. 7, T 3 S, R 15 E). Altitude 1053 feet. Named on Penon Blanco Peak (1962) 7.5' quadrangle.

Black Rock Creek [EL DORADO]: *stream,* flows nearly 6 miles to join Blue Tent Creek and form Hastings Creek 5 miles west-north-west of Coloma (lat. 38°49'50" N, long. 120°58'35" W; sec. 4, T 11 N, R 9 E). Named on Coloma (1949) and Greenwood (1949) 7.5' quadrangles. Shown as part of Hastings Creek on Placerville (1893) 30' quadrangle.

Black Rock Lake [AMADOR]: *lake,* 650 feet long, 4 miles north-northeast of Mokelumne Peak on Amador-Alpine county line (lat. 38°35'30" N, long. 120°04'20" W). Named on Mokelumne Peak (1979) 7.5' quadrangle.

Black's Bridge: see **Edwards Crossing** [NEVADA].

Blacks Creek [MARIPOSA]: *stream,* flows 5.25 miles to Maxwell Creek 1.5 miles west-south-west of Coulterville (lat. 37°42'15" N, long. 120°13'30" W; sec. 5, T 3 S, R 16 E). Named on Coulterville (1947) 7.5' quadrangle.

Blacksmith Flat [PLACER]: *area,* 3 miles northwest of Devil Peak (lat. 38°59'20" N, long. 120°35'15" W; sec. 12, T 13 N, R 12 E). Named on Devil Peak (1950) 7.5' quadrangle.

Black Spring [CALAVERAS]: *spring,* 7.5 miles southwest of Tamarack (lat. 38°22'35" N, long. 120°11'35" W; sec. 15, T 6 N, R 16 E). Named on Calaveras Dome (1979) 7.5' quadrangle, which indicates that the spring is dry.

Black Spring [MARIPOSA]: *spring,* 4.5 miles west-southwest of Yosemite Village in Yosemite Valley (lat. 37°43'10" N, long. 119° 39'35" W). Named on Yosemite (1956) 15' quadrangle. The name is from the color of the ground at the spring (Browning, 1986, p. 20).

Black Spring Creek [CALAVERAS]: *stream,* flows 1.5 miles to Murray Creek 5 miles east of San Andeas (lat. 38°12'40" N, long. 120°40'05" W; near E line sec. 12, T 4 N, R 12 E). Named on Calaveritas (1962) 7.5' quadrangle.

Blackstone Creek [MARIPOSA]: *stream,* flows 2.5 miles to Smith Creek 3.25 miles south of Smith Peak (lat. 37°45'15" N, long. 120° 05'30" W; near NW cor. sec. 22, T 2 S, R 17 E). Named on Jawbone Ridge (1947) 7.5' quadrangle.

Blackwood Creek [PLACER]: *stream,* flows 5.5 miles to Lake Tahoe 1.5 miles north of Homewood (lat. 39°06'25" N, long. 120° 09'30" W; sec. 36, T 15 N, R 16 E); the stream is west and north of Blackwood Ridge. Named on Homewood (1955) 7.5' quadrangle. The name commemorates Hampton Craig Blackwood,

who settled at the mouth of the stream after July 1866 (Lekisch, p. 9). Middle Fork enters 4 miles above the mouth of the main stream and is 1.5 miles long. North Fork enters 3.5 miles above the mouth of the main stream and is 2 miles long. Both forks are named on Homewood (1955) 7.5' quadrangle.

Blackwood Ridge [PLACER]: *ridge,* northeast-trending, 1.5 miles long, center 1.5 miles west of Homewood (lat. 39°05'30" N, long. 120°11'15" W). Named on Homewood (1955) 7.5' quadrangle.

Blade Creek [MARIPOSA]: *stream,* flows 6.25 miles to West Fork Chowchilla River 10 miles southeast of Mariposa (lat. 37°22'20" N, long. 119°51'30" W; sec. 35, T 6 S, R 19 E). Named on Horsecamp Mountain (1947), Mariposa (1947), and Stumpfield Mountain (1947) 7.5' quadrangles.

Blair Saw Mill [EL DORADO]: *locality,* 11.5 miles east-northeast of Placerville (lat. 38°46'30" N, long. 120°36'05" W). Named on Placerville (1893) 30' quadrangle.

Blakeley [AMADOR]: *locality,* 6.5 miles southwest of present Hams Station (lat. 38°28'05" N, long. 120°26'40" W). Named on Big Trees (1891) 30' quadrangle.

Blakeley [EL DORADO]: *locality,* 4 miles west of Pyramid Peak (lat. 38°50'30" N, long. 120°14' W). Named on Pyramid Peak (1896) 30' quadrangle.

Blakeley Reservoir [EL DORADO]: *lake,* 1000 feet long, 1.5 miles west of Camino (lat. 38°44'25" N, long. 120°42'20" W; near NE cor. sec. 12, T 10 N, R 11 E). Named on Camino (1952) 7.5' quadrangle.

Blanchard [TUOLUMNE]: *locality,* 4.5 miles east-northeast of Don Pedro Camp (lat. 37°43'50" N, long. 120°19'25" W; sec. 28, T 2 S, R 15 E). Named on Penon Blanco Peak (1962) 7.5' quadrangle. Blanchard post office, named for Rosie M. Blanchard, first postmaster, was established in 1894, moved 0.5 mile southwest in 1938, and discontinued in 1953 (Salley p. 22).

Blanket Creek [TUOLUMNE]: *stream,* flows 5 miles to Rough and Ready Creek 7 miles south-southeast of Sonora (lat. 37°53'35" N, long. 120°19'50" W; sec. 33, T 1 N, R 15 E). Named on Standard (1948) 7.5' quadrangle. The stream received the name after some Indians stole blankets from a miner there (Gudde, 1975, p. 40).

Blatchley Canyon [SIERRA]: *canyon,* drained by a stream that flows 4 miles to Cold Stream (1) 3.25 miles southeast of Sierraville (lat. 39°32'50" N, long. 120°20' W; near N line sec. 32, T 20 N, R 15 E). Named on Sierraville (1981) 7.5' quadrangle.

Blewetts Point [TUOLUMNE]: *peak,* 2.5 miles northeast of Columbia (lat. 38°03'30" N, long. 120°21'55" W; sec. 6, T 2 N, R 15 E). Named on Columbia SE (1948) 7.5' quadrangle.

Blind Canyon [PLACER]: *canyon,* drained by

a stream that flows nearly 1 mile to Middle Fork American River 1.5 miles southeast of Foresthill (lat. 39°00'05" N, long. 120°48' W; sec. 1, T 13 N, R 10 E). Named on Foresthill (1949) 7.5' quadrangle.

Blind Shady: see **Blind Shady Creek** [NEVADA].

Blind Shady Creek [NEVADA]: *stream,* flows 2.25 miles to Shady Creek 2.5 miles east-southeast of North San Juan (lat. 39°20'55" N, long. 121°03'40" W; sec. 10, T 17 N, R 8 E). Named on Nevada City (1948) 7.5' quadrangle. Called Little Shady Creek on Whitney's (1873) map. The name "Blind Shady" was used for the canyon of the stream in 1852 (Canfield, p. 230).

Blood Gulch [AMADOR]: *canyon,* less than 1 mile long, 3 miles northwest of present Fiddletown and 1 mile west-southwest of Prospect Hill (lat. 38°31'40" N, long. 120°48'15" W). Named on Placerville (1893) 30' quadrangle.

Bloods Creek [CALAVERAS]: *stream,* heads in Alpine County and flows 2.5 miles in Calaveras County to North Fork Stanislaus River 1.5 miles southeast of Tamarack (lat. 38°33" N, long. 120° 03'30" W). Named on Tamarack (1979) 7.5' quadrangle. Browning (1986, p. 21) associated the name with Harvey S. Blood, who owned and operated the main tollgate for Big Trees-Carson Valley turnpike.

Bloodsucker Lake [EL DORADO]: *lake,* 800 feet long, 3 miles west-southwest of Pyramid Peak (lat. 38°50'10" N, long. 120°12'35" W; near NW cor. sec. 3, T 11 N, R 16 E). Named on Pyramid Peak (1955) 7.5' quadrangle.

Bloody Gulch: see **Enterprise** [AMADOR].

Bloody Ravine [PLACER]: *canyon,* drained by a stream that flows 1 mile to Duncan Creek (lat. 39°06'10" N, long. 120°31' W; sec. 34, T 15 N, R 13 E). Named on Greek Store (1952) 7.5' quadrangle.

Bloody Run [NEVADA]: *stream,* flows 7.5 miles to Middle Yuba River 3.5 miles north of North Bloomfield (lat. 39°29'15" N, long. 120°54'45" W; sec. 13, T 18 N, R 9 E). Named on Alleghany (1949) and Pike (1949) 7.5' quadrangles.

Bloomer Lake [TUOLUMNE]: *lake,* 325 feet long, 5.25 miles south-southwest of Dardanelle (lat. 38°16' N, long. 119°51'40" W; on E line sec. 22, T 5 N, R 19 E). Named on Dardanelle (1979) 7.5' quadrangle.

Bloomfield: see **North Bloomfield** [NEVADA].

Blue Bluffs: see **Midas** [PLACER].

Blue Canyon [PLACER]:

(1) *canyon,* drained by a stream that flows 7.25 miles to North Fork of North Fork American River 5.5 miles west-northwest of Westville (lat. 39°12'05" N, long. 120°44'45" W; at S line sec. 33, T 16 N, R 11 E). Named on Blue Canyon (1955) and Westville (1952) 7.5' quadrangles. The name is from blue smoke that hung over the canyon during the days of extensive lumbering, although according to

one account the name is from Old Jim Blue, a miner of the 1850's (Gudde, 1969, p. 32).

(2) *village,* nearly 4 miles southwest of Emigrant Gap (1) (lat. 39° 15'20" N, long. 120°42'35" W; sec. 14, T 16 N, R 11 E); the village is on the east side of Blue Canyon (1). Named on Blue Canyon (1955) 7.5' quadrangle, which shows Blue Canon P.O. at the place. Postal authorities established Blue Canyon post office in 1867, discontinued it in 1927, reestablished it with the name "Blue Cañon" in 1936, discontinued it in 1942, reestablished it in 1948, and discontinued it in 1964 (Salley, p. 23). Whitney's (1873) map shows a place called Gilsons Station situated 1.25 miles north-northwest of the present village of Blue Canyon along Donner Road, and shows a place called Lost Camp located 1 mile south-southeast of the present village. California Division of Highways' (1934) map shows a place called Knapp located less than 1 mile west-southwest of the village of Blue Canyon along Southern Pacific Railroad (at E line sec. 15, T 16 N, R 11 E).

Blue Canyon [TUOLUMNE]:

(1) *canyon,* drained by a stream that flows 2.25 miles to Beaver Creek 2.5 miles south of Liberty Hill (lat. 38°19'45" N, long. 120° 05'55" W; sec. 34, T 6 N, R 17 E). Named on Liberty Hill (1979) 7.5' quadrangle.

(2) *canyon,* drained by a stream that flows nearly 1.5 miles to Deadman Creek 1.5 miles west-southwest of Sonora Pass (lat. 38°19'05" N, long. 119°39'45" W). Named on Sonora Pass (1979) 7.5' quadrangle.

Blue Canyon Lake [TUOLUMNE]: *lake,* 1000 feet long, 2.5 miles southwest of Sonora Pass (lat. 38°17'50" N, long. 119°39'55" W); the lake is at the head of Blue Canyon (2). Named on Sonora Pass (1979) 7.5' quadrangle.

Blue Creek [CALAVERAS]: *stream,* flows 15 miles to North Fork Mokelumne River 6.5 miles west of Garnet Hill (lat. 38°27'45" N, long. 120°22'25" W; sec. 13, T 7 N, R 14 E). Named on Calaveras Dome (1979) and Garnet Hill (1979) 7.5' quadrangles.

Blue Cut [PLACER]: *locality,* 3 miles south-southwest of Colfax along Southern Pacific Railroad (lat. 39°03'35" N, long. 120°58'20" W; near SE cor. sec. 16, T 14 N, R 9 E). Named on Colfax (1949) 7.5' quadrangle.

Blue Eyes Canyon [PLACER]: *canyon,* drained by a stream that flows less than 1 mile to Duncan Canyon 4.5 miles south-southwest of Duncan Peak (lat. 39°05'20" N, long. 120°32' W; sec. 4, T 14 N, R 13 E). Named on Greek Store (1952) 7.5' quadrangle. Logan's (1925) map shows Old Blue Eyes cabin near the head of the canyon.

Blue Gulch [TUOLUMNE]: *canyon,* drained by a stream that flows 2 miles to Don Pedro Reservoir 2.25 miles east-southeast of Chinese Camp (lat. 37°51'45" N, long. 120°23'40" W; near E line sec. 11, T 1 S, R

14 E). Named on Chinese Camp (1947, photorevised 1973) and Sonora (1948) 7.5' quadrangles

Blue Hole [CALAVERAS]: *lake,* 200 feet long, 5.25 miles northwest of Tamarack at the mouth of Mattley Creek (lat. 38°29'50" N, long. 120°08'10" W). Named on Calaveras Dome (1979) 7.5' quadrangle.

Bluejay Creek [MARIPOSA]: *stream,* flows 2.5 miles to Yosemite Creek nearly 3 miles north-northwest of Yosemite Village (lat. 37° 46'55" N, long. 119°36'40" W). Named on Hetch Hetchy Reservoir (1956) 15' quadrangle.

Blue Jay Lakes [FRESNO]: *lakes,* largest 600 feet long, 6.5 miles northwest of Mount Abbot (lat. 37°26'45" N, long. 118°52'30" W). Named on Mount Abbot (1953) 15' quadrangle.

Blue Jay Point [CALAVERAS]: *peak,* 3 miles east-southeast of Mokelumne Hill (lat. 38°16'40" N, long. 120°39'35" W; near N line sec. 21, T 5 N, R 12 E). Named on Mokelumne Hill (1948) 7.5' quadrangle.

Blue Lake [MADERA]: *lake,* 1200 feet long, 7 miles east-northeast of Merced Peak (lat. 37°40'50" N, long. 119°16'55" W). Named on Merced Peak (1953) 15' quadrangle.

Blue Lake [NEVADA]: *lake,* 2350 feet long, 3 miles north-northwest of Yuba Gap (lat. 39°21'35" N, long. 120°37'55" W; near N line sec. 9, T 17 N, R 12 E). Named on Blue Canyon (1955) 7.5' quadrangle.

Blue Mountain [CALAVERAS]: *peak,* 20 miles east-northeast of San Andreas (lat. 38°20'30" N, long. 120°21'50" W; sec. 30, T 6 N, R 15 E). Altitude 6071 feet. Named on Dorrington (1979) 7.5' quadrangle.

Blue Mountain: see **Mountain Ranch** [CALAVERAS].

Blue Mountain [EL DORADO]: *peak,* 2.25 miles west of Pyramid Peak (lat. 38°50'55" N, long. 120°11'50" W; sec. 34, T 12 N, R 18 E). Altitude 8772 feet. Named on Pyramid Peak (1955) 7.5' quadrangle.

Blue Mountain City: see **Mountain Ranch** [CALAVERAS].

Blue Ravine [NEVADA]: *canyon,* drained by a stream that flows 1.5 miles to Squirrel Creek 4.5 miles north-northeast of Pilot Peak (lat. 39°13'30" N, long. 121°08'15" W; near N line sec. 25, T 16 N, T 7 E). Named on Rough and Ready (1949) 7.5' quadrangle.

Blue Ravine [SIERRA]: *canyon,* drained by a stream that flows 1.5 miles to Kanaka Creek nearly 4 miles west-southwest of Alleghany (lat. 39°26'20" N, long. 120°54'05" W; sec. 7, T 18 N, R 10 E). Named on Pike (1949) 7.5' quadrangle.

Blue Tent [NEVADA]: *locality,* 6 miles southwest of North Bloomfield (lat. 39°18'25" N, long. 120°59'10" W). Named on Colfax (1898) 30' quadrangle. Postal authorities established Blue Tent post office in 1878 and discontinued it in 1889; the name was for the first habitation at the place (Salley, p. 23).

Whitney's (1873) map shows Sailor Flat Cañon opening into the canyon of South Yuba River from the south-southeast 1.5 miles north-northeast of Blue Tent, shows a place called Mt. Vernon Ho. [House] situated 1.25 miles northwest of Blue Tent, and shows a feature called Gopher Hill located 1.25 miles north-northeast of Blue Tent.

Blue Tent Creek [EL DORADO]: *stream,* flows nearly 5 miles to join Black Rock Creek and form Hastings Creek 5 miles west-northwest of Coloma (lat. 38°49'50" N, long. 120°58'35" W; sec. 4, T 11 N, R 9 E). Named on Auburn (1953), Coloma (1949), and Pilot Hill (1954) 7.5' quadrangles.

Bluff Meadow [TUOLUMNE]: *area,* 6.5 miles northeast of Pinecrest (lat. 38°14'45" N, long. 119°53'45" W; near W line sec. 33, T 5 N, R 19 E). Named on Pinecrest (1979) 7.5' quadrangle.

Boards Crossing [CALAVERAS-TUOLUMNE]: *locality,* 8.5 miles west-southwest of Liberty Hill [TUOLUMNE] along North Fork Stanislaus River on Calaveras-Tuolumne county line (lat. 38°18'15" N, long. 120°14' W; sec. 8, T 5 N, R 16 E). Named on Boards Crossing (1979) 7.5' quadrangle.

Boca [NEVADA]: *locality,* 6.5 miles northeast of Truckee along Southern Pacific Railroad (lat. 39°23'10" N, long. 120°05'35" W; sec. 28, T 18 N, R 17 E). Named on Boca (1955) 7.5' quadrangle. Postal authorities established Boca post office in 1872 and discontinued it in 1945 (Frickstad, p. 113). Officials of Central Pacific Railroad named the place in 1867 for its location near the mouth of Little Truckee River—*boca* means "mouth" in Spanish (Gudde, 1949, p. 35). Postal authorities established Burckhalter post office 2 miles southeast of Boca in 1891 and discontinued it in 1896; the name, which also had the form "Burkhalter," was for Walter Burckhalter, first postmaster (Salley, p. 29). Wheeler's (1876-1877b) map shows a place called Virginia Ho. [House] located about 5 miles northwest of Boca. California Division of Highways' (1934) map shows an inhabited place called Prosser Creek situated about 1 mile southwest of Boca along the railroad (sec. 29, T 18 N, R 17 E).

Boca Canyon: see **East Boca Canyon** [NEVADA].

Boca Hill [NEVADA]: *peak,* 5 miles northeast of Truckee (lat. 39°22'50" N, long. 120°07' W; sec. 29, T 18 N, R 17 E); the peak is 1.5 miles west-southwest of Boca. Altitude 6669 feet. Named on Boca (1955) 7.5' quadrangle.

Boca Reservoir [NEVADA]: *lake,* behind a dam on Little Truckee River 6.5 miles northeast of Truckee (lat. 39°23'25" N, long. 120° 05'35" W; near S line sec. 21, T 18 N, R 17 E); the lake is north of Boca. Named on Boca (1955) 7.5' quadrangle.

Boca Ridge [NEVADA]: *ridge,* generally south-trending, 3.5 miles long, 10 miles northeast of Truckee (lat. 39°25'30" N, long. 120°03'05" W); the center of the ridge is 3.5 miles northeast of Boca. Named on Boca (1955) 7.5' quadrangle.

Boca Spring [NEVADA]: *spring,* 9 miles northeast of Truckee (lat. 39°25'45" N, long. 120°04'30" W; sec. 10, T 18 N, R 17 E); the spring is 3 miles north-northeast of Boca. Named on Boca (1955) 7.5' quadrangle.

Boca Spring: see **East Boca Spring** [NEVADA].

Boggy Meadow [MADERA]:
(1) *area,* 7.5 miles north-northeast of Yosemite Forks along Big Creek (lat. 37°27'30" N, long. 119°33' W; sec. 34, T 5 S, R 22 E). Named on Bass Lake (1953) 15' quadrangle. Called Boggy Meadows on Mariposa (1912) 30' quadrangle.
(2) *area,* 5.25 miles northeast of Shuteye Peak (lat. 37°24'10" N, long. 119°21'30" W; on W line sec. 16, T 6 S, R 24 E). Named on Shuteye Peak (1953) 15' quadrangle.

Bogus Point [PLACER]: *peak,* nearly 3 miles south of Dutch Flat (lat. 39°09'55" N, long. 120°49'45" W; near E line sec. 10, T 15 N, R 10 E). Named on Dutch Flat (1950) 7.5' quadrangle.

Bogus Thunder [PLACER]: *locality,* 3.5 miles east-northeast of Michigan Bluff along North Fork of Middle Fork American River (lat. 39°04'05" N, long. 120°40'55" W; near NW cor. sec. 18, T 14 N, R 12 E). Named on Michigan Bluff (1952) 7.5' quadrangle. The name is from the thunderlike sound of a nearby waterfall (Hoover, Rensch, and Rensch, p. 277).

Boles Gap [EL DORADO]: *pass,* 5.5 miles south-southeast of Camino (lat. 38°40'05" N, long. 120°37'15" W; at N line sec. 2, T 9 N, R 12 E). Named on Sly Park (1952) 7.5' quadrangle. Called Boulder Pass on Placerville (1893) 30' quadrangle.

Bond Pass [TUOLUMNE]: *pass,* 4 miles west-northwest of Tower Peak (lat. 38°10'20" N, long. 119°36'30" W). Named on Tower Peak (1956) 15' quadrangle. The name commemorates Frank Bond of General Land Office, a member of Yosemite Park Boundary Commission of 1904, and later chairman of United States Geographic Board (United States Board on Geographic Names, 1934, p. 3).

Bonds Flat [TUOLUMNE]: *area,* nearly 4 miles southeast of Don Pedro Camp (lat. 37°40'40" N, long. 120°21'40" W; sec. 18, T 3 S, R 15 E). Named on Penon Blanco Peak (1962) 7.5' quadrangle.

Bond's Flat: see **Rocky Gulch** [MARIPOSA].
Bond's Gulch: see **Rocky Gulch** [MARIPOSA].
Bondville: see **Bagby** [MARIPOSA].
Bonnel Gulch: see **Bonell Gulch** [MARIPOSA].
Bonell Gulch [MARIPOSA]: *canyon,* 2 miles long, 10.5 miles west of El Portal (lat.

37°41'30" N, long. 119°58'15" W). Named on Kinsley (1947) 7.5' quadrangle. United States Board on Geographic Names (1933, p. 156) rejected the form "Bonnel Gulch" for the name.

Bonetti [EL DORADO]: *locality,* 4 miles southwest of Old Iron Mountain (lat. 38°40'30" N, long. 120°27'10" W; sec. 32, T 10 N, R 14 E). Named on Stump Spring (1951) 7.5' quadrangle.

Boneyard Creek [MARIPOSA]: *stream,* flows 3.5 miles to Cuneo Creek 1 mile north-northeast of Coulterville (lat. 37°43'35" N, long. 120°11'10" W; near SE cor. sec. 27, T 2 S, R 16 E). Named on Coulterville (1947) and Groveland (1947) 7.5' quadrangles.

Boney Flat [TUOLUMNE]: *area,* 5.25 miles southeast of Long Barn (lat. 38°02'05" N, long. 120°04'05" W; near NE cor. sec. 14, T 2 N, R 17 E). Named on Hull Creek (1979) 7.5' quadrangle.

Bonnefoy [AMADOR]: *settlement,* 1.5 miles northeast of Jackson (lat. 38°21'40" N, long. 120°45' W; sec. 22, T 6 N, R 11 E). Named on Jackson (1962) and Mokelumne Hill (1948) 7.5' quadrangles.

Bonita [MADERA]: *locality,* 8 miles west of Madera (lat. 36°57'10" N, long. 120°12'05" W; near NE cor. sec. 27, T 11 S, R 16 E). Named on Bonita Ranch (1963) 7.5' quadrangle.

Bonny Nook [PLACER]: *locality,* 2.25 miles east of Dutch Flat (lat. 39°12'35" N, long. 120°47'35" W; at E line sec. 36, T 16 N, R 10 E). Named on Dutch Flat (1950) 7.5' quadrangle.

Bonpland: see **Lake Bonpland**, under **Lake Tahoe** [EL DORADO-PLACER].

Bonta Creek [SIERRA]: *stream,* flows about 6 miles to join Cold Stream (1) and form Sierraville Creek 1.5 miles south of Sierraville (lat. 39°34' N, long. 120°21'45" W; near E line sec. 24, T 20 N, R 14 E). Named on Sattley (1981) and Sierraville (1981) 7.5' quadrangles.

Bonta Saddle [SIERRA]: *pass,* 6 miles southwest of Sierraville (lat. 39°31'15" N, long. 120°25'55" W; sec. 8, T 19 N, R 14 E); the pass is at the head of Bonta Creek. Named on Sattley (1981) 7.5' quadrangle.

Bon Ton Ravine [SIERRA]: *canyon,* drained by a stream that flows 1 mile to Canyon Creek 8 miles southwest of Mount Fillmore (lat. 39°37'55" N, long. 120°56'25" W; sec. 35, T 21 N, R 9 E). Named on La Porte (1951) 7.5' quadrangle.

Boomerang Lake [EL DORADO]: *lake,* 325 feet long, nearly 3 miles northwest of Pyramid Peak (lat. 38°52'20" N, long. 120°11'35" W). Named on Pyramid Peak (1955) 7.5' quadrangle, where the outline of the lake has the shape of a boomerang.

Boomville: see **Butte City** [AMADOR].
Boonville: see **Butte City** [AMADOR].

Boothe Lake [MARIPOSA]: *lake,* 1300 feet long, 4.5 miles southeast of Cathedral Peak (lat. 37°48' N, long. 119°20'50" W). Named on Tuolumne Meadows (1956) 15' quadrangle. The name commemorates Clyde Boothe, a ranger at Yosemite National Park from 1915 until 1927 (Browning, 1986, p. 23).

Booth Point [NEVADA]: *relief feature,* 1.5 miles north-northeast of Graniteville (lat. 39°27'45" N, long. 120°43'35" W; at S line sec. 34, T 19 N, R 11 E). Named on Graniteville (1982) 7.5' quadrangle.

Bootjack [MARIPOSA]: *locality,* 4.5 miles east-southeast of Mariposa (lat. 37°27'55" N, long. 119°53'05" W; on W line sec. 27, T 5 S, R 19 E). Named on Mariposa (1947) 7.5' quadrangle. Shirley Sargent (1976, p. 31) listed three possible explanations given for the name: first, a road fork at the place makes a "Y" or bootjack shape; second, a large tree at the site had a bootjack shape; and third, a bootjack had to be used to remove the boots from a horsethief after he was hung at the spot.

Bope Ravine [SIERRA]: *canyon,* drained by a stream that flows 1.25 miles to Indian Creek (2) 2.25 miles east-southeast of Pike (lat. 39° 25'35" N, long. 120°57'40" W; near W line sec. 15, T 18 N, R 9 E); the feature heads near Plum Valley, where John Bope built Plum Valley House in 1854 (Hoover, Rensch, and Rensch, p. 496). Named on Pike (1949) 7.5' quadrangle.

Boreal Ridge [NEVADA]: *ridge,* west-south-west-trending, 2 miles long, 1.25 miles north-west of Donner Pass (lat. 39°19'50" N, long. 120°20'40" W). Named on Norden (1955) 7.5' quadrangle. The name, from *borealis,* the Latin word for "northern," was given because the ridge is north of Donner Pass and the rail-road crossing of the Sierra Nevada (Gudde, 1969, p. 35).

Bostick Bar [CALAVERAS]: *locality,* 6 miles east of Copperopolis along Stanislaus River (lat. 37°58'30" N, long. 120°31'45" W; near N line sec. 3, T 1 N, R 13 E). Named on Copperopolis (1916) 15' quadrangle. Water of New Melones Lake now covers the site. Gudde (1975, p. 44) called the place Bostwick Bar.

Bostick Mountain [CALAVERAS]: *ridge,* northwest-trending, 2 miles long, 6 miles east-southeast of Copperopolis (lat. 37°57'45" N, long. 120°31'45" W); the ridge is south of the site of Bostick Bar. Named on Melones Dam (1962) 7.5' quadrangle.

Boston Flat [CALAVERAS]: *area,* 4.5 miles south-southwest of Devils Nose (lat. 38°23'55" N, long. 120°26'30" W; near SW cor. sec. 4, T 6 N, R 14 E). Named on Devils Nose (1979) 7.5' quadrangle.

Boston Flat Gulch [CALAVERAS]: *canyon,* drained by a stream that flows 2.5 miles to Forest Creek 5.25 miles south-southwest of Devils Nose (lat. 38°23'35" N, long.

120°27'30" W); the stream goes past Boston Flat. Named on Devils Nose (1979) 7.5' quadrangle.

Boston House [AMADOR]: *locality,* 6.5 miles south-southeast of Ione (lat. 38°16'15" N, long. 120°52'35" W). Named on Jackson (1902) 30' quadrangle. The place was a combination store and inn (Hoover, Rensch, and Rensch, p. 30). It also was called Boston Store (Gudde, 1975, p. 43).

Boston Ravine [NEVADA]: *locality,* less than 1 mile south-southwest of downtown Grass Valley along Wolf Creek (lat. 39°12'30" N, long. 121°04'10" W; sec. 34, T 16 N, R 8 E). Named on Grass Valley (1949) 7.5' quadrangle. Postal authorities established Boston Ravine post office in 1889 and discontinued it in 1890 (Frickstad, p. 113). On United States Geological Survey's (1901) map, the name "Boston Ravine" applies to a canyon that opens into Wolf Creek from the west at the site of the locality called Boston Ravine. Men from Boston mined at the place in 1849 (Gudde, 1975, p. 43).

Boston Store: see **Boston House** [AMADOR].

Bostwick Bar: see **Bostick Bar** [CALA-VERAS].

Bosworth Meadow [EL DORADO]: *area,* 6.25 miles northwest of Kyburz (lat. 38°51'05" N, long. 120°21'45" W; near S line sec. 25, T 12 N, R 14 E). Named on Kyburz (1952) 7.5' quadrangle.

Botellas: see **Jackson** [AMADOR].

Botilleas Spring: see **Jackson** [AMADOR].

Bottle Hill [EL DORADO]: *peak,* 2.5 miles north-northwest of Georgetown (lat. 38°56'40" N, long. 120°51' W; sec. 27, T 13 N, R 10 E). Named on Georgetown (1949) 7.5' quadrangle. Postal authorities established Bottle Hill post office in 1855 and discontinued it in 1859 (Frickstad, p. 25). Gudde (1975, p. 44) listed a mining camp called Bottle Hill Diggings that was located 3 miles north of Georgetown and named in 1851 for the profusion of bottles at the site.

Bottle Hill Diggings: see **Bottle Hill** [EL DORADO].

Boucher Mountain [CALAVERAS]: *peak,* 4.5 miles west-southwest of Copperopolis on Gopher Ridge (lat. 37°57'25" N, long. 120°42'55" W; near N line sec. 12, T 1 N, R 11 E). Altitude 1549 feet. Named on Copperopolis (1962) 7.5' quadrangle.

Boughmans Mill [EL DORADO]: *locality,* 2 miles west-southwest of Omo Ranch (lat. 38°34'15" N, long. 120°36'45" W). Named on Placerville (1893) 30' quadrangle.

Boulder Bar: see **Scotchman Creek** [NE-VADA].

Boulder Creek: see **Big Boulder Creek** [SI-ERRA]; **Little Boulder Creek** [SIERRA].

Boulder Flat [TUOLUMNE]: *area,* 2 miles northwest of Dardanelle along Middle Fork Stanislaus River (lat. 38°21'20" N, long. 119°

51'35" W). Named on Dardanelle (1979) 7.5' quadrangle.

Boulder Pass: see **Boles Gap** [EL DORADO].

Boulder Ridge [PLACER]: *ridge,* west-south-west-trending, 1.25 miles long, 6.25 miles north-northeast of Rocklin (lat. 38°52'20" N, long. 121°10'45" W). Named on Rocklin (1967) 7.5' quadrangle.

Boundary Creek [MADERA]: *stream,* flows 2 miles to Middle Fork San Joaquin River 1.25 miles south of Devils Postpile (lat. 37°36'15" N, long. 119°04'35" W); the mouth of the stream is near the east boundary of Devils Postpile National Monument. Named on Devils Postpile (1953) 15' quadrangle.

Boundary Hill [MARIPOSA]: *peak,* 2.5 miles west-northwest of Yosemite Village (lat. 37°45'50" N, long. 119°37'40" W); the feature is at the boundary of the Yosemite grant. Named on Hetch Hetchy Reservoir (1956) 15' quadrangle. Lieutenant Macomb of the Wheeler survey named the feature (Browning, 1986, p. 24).

Boundary Lake [TUOLUMNE]: *lake,* 3500 feet long, 13 miles east-southeast of Pinecrest (lat. 38°05'15" N, long. 119°47'20" W); the lake is near the boundary of Yosemite National Park. Named on Pinecrest (1956) 15' quadrangle.

Bourland Creek [TUOLUMNE]: *stream,* flows 11 miles to join Reynolds Creek and form Reed Creek 8.5 miles southeast of Long Barn (lat. 38°01'10" N, long. 120°00'45" W; near W line sec. 21, T 2 N, R 18 E); the stream goes through Bourland Meadow. Named on Cherry Lake North (1979), Hull Creek (1979), and Pinecrest (1979) 7.5' quadrangles. The name commemorates John L. Bourland, sheriff of Tuolumne County from 1865 until 1868 (Browning, 1986, p. 24). Called Reed Creek on Big Trees (1891) and Dardanelles (1898) 30' quadrangles, but United States Board on Geographic Names (1963b, p. 5) rejected this name for the stream.

Bourland Meadow [TUOLUMNE]: *area,* 7.25 miles southeast of Pinecrest (lat. 38°06'55" N, long. 119°54'20" W; sec. 17, T 3 N, R 19 E); the place is along Bourland Creek. Named on Cherry Lake North (1979) 7.5' quadrangle.

Bourland Mountain [TUOLUMNE]: *peak,* 6.5 miles south-southeast of Pinecrest (lat. 38°06'30" N, long. 119°56'10" W; on N line sec. 19, T 3 N, R 19 E); the peak is north of Bourland Creek. Altitude 7691 feet. Named on Cherry Lake North (1979) 7.5' quadrangle.

Bow Creek [SIERRA]: *stream,* flows 1.5 miles to Fiddle Creek 3 miles west of Goodyears Bar (lat. 39°32'25" N, long. 120°56'15" W; sec. 2, T 19 N, R 9 E). Named on Goodyears Bar (1951) 7.5' quadrangle.

Bowen: see **Moore and Bowen Camp,** under **Hodgdon Ranch** [TUOLUMNE].

Bower Cave [MARIPOSA]: *cave,* 7.5 miles northeast of Buckhorn Peak near North Fork

Merced River (lat. 37°44'50" N, long. 120°02'05" W; sec. 19, T 2 S, R 18 E). Named on Buckhorn Peak (1947) 7.5' quadrangle. The name is from the leafy boughs of maple trees that grow in the pitlike feature, which was discovered in the 1850's and developed into a tourist attraction (Sargent, Shirley, 1976, p. 22).

Bowie Flat [CALAVERAS]: *valley,* 4.5 miles southeast of Copperopolis on upper reaches of Loucks Creek (lat. 37°56'20" N, long. 120°34' W). Named on Melones Dam (1962) 7.5' quadrangle.

Bowman [PLACER]: *locality,* 3.25 miles north-northeast of Auburn along Southern Pacific Railroad (lat. 38°56'30" N, long. 121°02'45" W; near N line sec. 35, T 13 N, R 8 E). Named on Auburn (1953) 7.5' quadrangle. Postal authorities established Bowman post office in 1893 (Frickstad, p. 119). The name commemorates Harry Hoisington Bowman, a pioneer fruit grower of the neighborhood (Hanna, p. 39).

Bowman Campground [NEVADA]: *locality,* 3.5 miles west-northwest of English Mountain (lat. 39°27'35" N, long. 120°36'40" W; sec. 3, T 18 N, R 12 E); the place is on the north side of the east end of Bowman Lake. Named on English Mountain (1983) 7.5' quadrangle.

Bowman Gulch [CALAVERAS]: *canyon,* drained by a stream that flows 1 mile to Bean Gulch 5 miles east-southeast of Copperopolis (lat. 37°57'20" N, long. 120°33'05" W; sec. 9, T 1 N, R 13 E). Named on Melones Dam (1962) 7.5' quadrangle.

Bowman House [NEVADA]: *locality,* 4.5 miles east of Graniteville (lat. 39°26'50" N, long. 120°39'20" W; at NW cor. sec. 8, T 18 N, E 12 E). Named on Graniteville (1982) 7.5' quadrangle.

Bowman Lake [NEVADA]: *lake,* behind a dam on Canyon Creek 4.5 miles east of Graniteville (lat. 39°26'55" N, long. 120°39'05" W; at S line sec. 5, T 18 N, R 12 E). Named on English Mountain (1983) and Graniteville (1982) 7.5' quadrangles. Called Bowman Reservoir on Logan's (1940) map. The name commemorates James F. Bowman, who settled in the early 1860's by what became known as Little Bowman Lake; this lake and nearby Big Bowman Lake were consolidated in 1873 into a single lake to provide water for hydraulic mining (Gudde, 1949, p. 38).

Bowman Mountain [NEVADA]: *peak,* 6 miles east of Graniteville (lat. 39°26' N, long. 120°37'45" W; at N line sec. 16, T 18 N, R 12 E); the peak is about 1 mile south of Bowman Lake. Altitude 7386 feet. Named on Graniteville (1982) 7.5' quadrangle.

Bowman Reservoir: see **Bowman Lake** [NEVADA].

Box Canyon [AMADOR]: *narrows,* 6 miles south-southwest of Jackson along Mokelumne River on Amador-Calaveras county line (lat. 38°16'25" N, long. 120°49'35" W; sec. 24, T 5 N, R 10 E). Named on Jackson (1962) 7.5' quadrangle.

Box Canyon [CALAVERAS]: *narrows,* 3.5 miles west-northwest of Paloma along Mokelumne River on Calaveras-Amador county line (lat. 38°16'25" N, long. 120°49'35" W; sec. 24, T 5 N, R 10 E). Named on Jackson (1962) 7.5' quadrangle.

Box Canyon Number 1 [NEVADA-SIERRA]: *canyon,* 4 miles south-southeast of Sierra City along Middle Yuba River on Nevada-Sierra county line (lat. 39°31'10" N, long. 120°40'20" W; near N line sec. 18, T 19 N, E 12 E); the feature is 3 miles upstream from Box Canyon Number 2. Named on Sierra City (1981) 7.5' quadrangle.

Box Canyon Number 3 [NEVADA-SIERRA]: *canyon,* 2 miles north of Graniteville [NEVADA] along Middle Yuba River on Nevada-Sierra county line (lat. 39°28'05" N, long. 120°44'20" W; near E line sec. 33, T 19 N, R 11 E); the feature is 2.5 miles downstream from Box Canyon Number 2. Named on Graniteville (1982) 7.5' quadrangle.

Box Canyon Number 2 [NEVADA-SIERRA]: *canyon,* 4 miles north-northeast of Graniteville along Middle Yuba River on Nevada-Sierra county line (lat. 39°29'30" N, long. 120°42'30" W; on N line sec. 26, T 19 N, R 11 E); the feature is about halfway between Box Canyon Number 1 and Box Canyon Number 3. Named on Graniteville (1982) 7.5' quadrangle.

Box Spring [TUOLUMNE]:
(1) *spring,* nearly 6 miles southeast of Long Barn (lat. 38°01'35" N, long. 120°04'05" W; near E line sec. 14, T 2 N, R 17 E). Named on Hull Creek (1979) 7.5' quadrangle.
(2) *spring,* 6.5 miles southeast of Pinecrest (lat. 38°07'50" N, long. 119°54'15" W). Named on Pinecrest (1979) 7.5' quadrangle.

Boyce Ravine [SIERRA]: *canyon,* drained by a stream that flows nearly 2 miles to Cherokee Creek 7.5 miles west of Goodyears Bar (lat. 39°31'10" N, long. 121°01'55" W; sec. 13, T 19 N, R 8 E). Named on Strawberry Valley (1948) 7.5' quadrangle.

Bradford [TUOLUMNE]: *locality,* 3 miles northeast of Long Barn along North Fork Tuolumne River (lat. 38°06'55" N, long. 120°05'30" W). Named on Big Trees (1891) 30' quadrangle.

Brady Mountain [NEVADA]: *peak,* nearly 3 miles north-northeast of Yuba Gap (lat. 39°21'15" N, long. 120°36'10" W; near W line sec. 11, T 17 N, R 12 E). Altitude 5956 feet. Named on Cisco Grove (1955) 7.5' quadrangle.

Brandon Canyon [EL DORADO]: *canyon,* drained by a stream that flows 1 mile to Camp Creek 1.5 miles south-southeast of Old Iron Mountain (lat. 38°40'55" N, long. 120°23'05" W; near NE cor. sec. 35, T 10 N, R 14 E).

Named on Stump Spring (1951) 7.5' quadrangle.

Brandon Corner [EL DORADO]: *locality,* 3 miles northeast of Latrobe (lat. 38°35'10" N, long. 120°55'55" W; near SE cor. sec. 36, T 9 N, R 9 E). Named on Latrobe (1949) 7.5' quadrangle. Called Brandons on Placerville (1893) 30' quadrangle.

Brandons: see **Brandon Corner** [EL DORADO].

Brandy City [SIERRA]: *locality,* 7.5 miles west of Goodyears Bar (lat. 39°32'15" N, long. 121°01'30" W; near SE cor. sec. 1, T 19 N, R 8 E). Named on Strawberry Valley (1948) 7.5' quadrangle. The place first was called Strychnine City (Gudde, 1975, p. 45).

Brandy Flat [CALAVERAS]: *area,* 3.5 miles southeast of San Andreas (lat. 38°10' N, long. 120°37'30" W; mainly in sec. 26, T 4 N, R 12 E). Named on Calaveritas (1962) and San Andreas (1962) 7.5' quadrangles.

Brandy Flat: see **Poorman Creek** [NEVADA] (1).

Branigan Lake [TUOLUMNE]: *lake,* 2200 feet long, 11 miles southwest of Tower Peak (lat. 38°01'50" N, long. 119°41'10" W). Named on Tower Peak (1956) 15' quadrangle. Lieutenant N.F. McClure named the lake for a soldier under his command while the lieutenant was exploring Yosemite National Park in 1894 (United States Board on Geographic Names, 1934, p. 3).

Branigan Lake: see **Middle Branigan Lake** [TUOLUMNE]; **Upper Branigan Lake** [TUOLUMNE].

Brant Lake: see **Crystal Lake** [NEVADA] (1).

Brass Wire Bar: see **Washington** [NEVADA].

Brazoria Bar: see **Moccasin Creek** [TUOLUMNE].

Breeze Creek [TUOLUMNE]: *stream,* flows 5.5 miles to Deep Canyon 7.5 miles north of White Wolf (lat. 37°58'50" N, long. 119°37'40" W). Named on Hetch Hetchy Reservoir (1956) and Tower Peak (1956) 15' quadrangles. The name commemorates William F. Breeze, brother-in-law of Lieutenant H.C. Benson; Breeze helped the lieutenant compile a map of Yosemite National Park (Browning, 1986, p. 25).

Breeze Lake [MADERA]: *lake,* 1600 feet long, 4 miles south of Merced Peak (lat. 37°34'35" N, long. 119°23'30" W). Named on Merced Peak (1953) 15' quadrangle. Lieutenant H.C. Benson named the lake for William H. Breeze of Breeze Creek (United States Board on Geographic Names, 1934, p. 3).

Brela [EL DORADO]: *locality,* 1.5 miles northeast of Latrobe along Southern Pacific Railroad (lat. 38°34'30" N, long. 120°57'50" W; near W line sec. 2, T 8 N, R 9 E). Named on Latrobe (1949) 7.5' quadrangle.

Brentwood Park [TUOLUMNE]: *settlement,* 1 mile west-northwest of Twain Harte (lat. 38°02'45" N, long. 120°14'45" W; on W line sec. 8, T 2 N, R 16 E). Named on Twain Harte (1979) 7.5' quadrangle.

Briceburg [MARIPOSA]: *locality,* 5 miles north-northwest of Midpines along Merced River (lat. 37°36'15" N, long. 119°57'55" W; sec. 10, T 4 S, R 18 E); the place is at the mouth of Bear Creek (1). Named on Feliciana Mountain (1947) 7.5' quadrangle. Called Bear Creek on Yosemite (1909) 30' quadrangle. The name "Briceburg" is for William M. Brice, who in 1909 started a general store across the river from the place, and who moved his business to the site of present Briceburg after a work camp there was abandoned in 1926 (Sargent, Shirley, 1976, p. 11). California Division of Highways' (1934) map shows a place called Drum located along the railroad 2.25 miles northeast of Briceburg (sec. 10, T 4 S, R 18 E).

Bridalveil Campground [MARIPOSA]: *locality,* 6.25 miles south-southwest of Yosemite Village (lat. 37°39'50" N, long. 119°37'15" W; sec. 24, T 3 S, R 21 E); the place is near Bridalveil Creek. Named on Yosemite (1956) 15' quadrangle.

Bridalveil Creek [MARIPOSA]: *stream,* flows 10.5 miles to Merced River 4.25 miles west-southwest of Yosemite Village (lat. 37°43'10" N, long. 119°39'10" W); Bridalveil Fall is along the stream. Named on Yosemite (1956) 15' quadrangle. King and Gardner's (1865) map has the form "Bridal Veil Creek" for the name.

Bridalveil Fall [MARIPOSA]: *waterfall,* 4 miles southwest of Yosemite Village (lat. 37°43' N, long. 119°38'45" W). Named on Yosemite (1956) 15' quadrangle. King and Gardner's (1865) map has the form "Bridal Veil Fall" for the name. Apparently Warren Baer, editor of the Mariposa *Democrat* newspaper, named the feature in 1856, although the Indian name "Pohono" still was in common use in the 1860's (Gudde, 1969, p. 38). United States Board on Geographic Names (1991, p. 3) approved the name "Bridalveil Moraine" for a ridge situated 0.6 mile west of Bridalveil Fall (lat. 37°43' N, long. 119°39'23" W).

Bridalveil Moraine: see **Bridalveil Fall** [MARIPOSA].

Bridgeport [MARIPOSA]: *locality,* 5 miles east of the settlement of Catheys Valley along Agua Fria Creek (lat. 37°26' N, long. 120°00'15" W). Named on Catheys Valley (1962) 7.5' quadrangle. The place was known as Suckertown (Hanna, p. 41) before Andrew Church opened a store there in 1852 and gave the present name (Gudde, 1975, p. 46).

Bridgeport [AMADOR]: *locality,* 3.25 miles north-northeast of present Fiddletown on the south side of South Fork Cosumnes River (lat. 38°32'35" N, long. 120°43'30" W). Named on Placerville (1893) 30' quadrangle.

Bridgeport [NEVADA]: *locality,* 2 miles west-southwest of French Corral along South Yuba River (lat. 39°17'30" N, long. 121°11'40" W; sec. 33, T 17 N, R 7 E). Named on French Corral (1948) 7.5' quadrangle. The name is from a wooden bridge across the river; the place also was known as Nyes Landing, for Urias Nye and Manuel Nye, who built a trading post there in 1849 (Gudde, 1975, p. 46), and as Nye's Crossing (Hoover, Rensch, and Rensch, p. 250).

Bright: see **Irwin Bright Lake** [TUOLUMNE]; **Irwin Bright Lake**, under **Saddle Horse Lake** [TUOLUMNE].

Brightman Flat [TUOLUMNE]: *area,* 1.25 miles northwest of Dardanelle along Middle Fork Stanislaus River (lat. 38°21'10" N, long. 119°51' W). Named on Dardanelle (1979) 7.5' quadrangle. Dardanelles Cone (1956) 15' quadrangle shows Brightman Flat Campground at the place. J.W. Brightman started a station at Brightman's Flat about 1860 (Wedertz, p. 61).

Brightman Flat Campground: see **Brightman Flat** [TUOLUMNE].

Brighton House: see **Grass Valley** [NEVADA].

Brimstone Creek [PLACER]: *stream,* flows 2 miles to the head of Shirttail Canyon 5 miles northeast of Foresthill (lat. 39°04'35" N, long. 120°45'45" W; sec. 8, T 14 N, R 11 E). Named on Foresthill (1949) 7.5' quadrangle. Hobson's (1890b) map has the name "Brimstone Plains" for the area at the head of present Brimstone Creek.

Brimstone Plains: see **Brimstone Creek** [PLACER].

Brock [PLACER]: *locality,* 5 miles northwest of Lincoln along Southern Pacific Railroad (lat. 38°56'35" N, long. 121°21'15" W; near SW cor. sec. 30, T 13 N, R 6 E). Named on Lincoln (1953) 7.5' quadrangle.

Brockliss Canyon [EL DORADO]: *canyon,* drained by a stream that flows 1.5 miles to South Fork American River 2.5 miles west of Riverton (lat. 38°46'05" N, long. 120°29'45" W; sec. 23, T 11 N, R 13 E). Named on Riverton (1950) 7.5' quadrangle.

Brockway [PLACER]: *settlement,* 1 mile south-southeast of Kings Beach along Lake Tahoe just west of Stateline Point (lat. 39°13'35" N, long. 120°00'30" W; sec. 30, T 16 N, R 18 E). Named on Kings Beach (1955) 7.5' quadrangle. Postal authorities established Brockway post office in 1901 and discontinued it in 1966; the name commemorates Nathaniel Brockway (Salley, p. 27), who was the uncle of Frank Brockway Alverson, first postmaster (Lekisch, p. 10). Truckee (1895) 30' quadrangle has the designation "Hot Springs" at the place. G.A. Waring (p. 131) described Brockway Hot Springs that rise in Lake Tahoe a few feet offshore from Brockway resort. The springs also were called Campbell's Hot Springs (Zauner, p. 32).

Brockway Hot Springs: see **Brockway** [PLACER].

Brockway Spring [PLACER]: *spring,* 1 mile north-northeast of Kings Beach (lat. 39°14'55" N, long. 120°00'45" W; sec. 18, T 16 N, R 18 E); the spring is 1.5 miles north of Brockway. Named on Kings Beach (1955) 7.5' quadrangle.

Brockway Summit [PLACER]: *pass,* 3 miles southwest of Martis Peak (lat. 39°15'40" N, long. 120°04'15" W; sec. 3, T 16 N, R 17 E). Named on Martis Peak (1955) 7.5' quadrangle.

Broderick: see **Mount Broderick** [MARIPOSA]; **Mount Broderick**, under **Liberty Cap** [MARIPOSA].

Broncho: see **Bronco** [NEVADA].

Broncho Creek: see **Bronco Creek** [NEVADA].

Bronco [NEVADA]: *locality,* 9.5 miles east-northeast of Truckee along Southern Pacific Railroad (lat. 39°23'10" N, long. 120°01'20" W); the place is north of the mouth of Bronco Creek. Named on Truckee (1895) 30' quadrangle. Postal authorities established Bronco post office in 1872 and discontinued it in 1891 (Frickstad, p. 113). United States Board on Geographic Names (1933, p. 166) rejected the form "Broncho" for the name.

Bronco Creek [NEVADA]: *stream,* heads in the State of Nevada and flows 1 mile in Nevada County to Truckee River 9.5 miles east-north-east of Truckee (lat. 39°23' N, long. 120°01'10" W; sec. 31, T 18 N, R 18 E). Named on Boca (1955) 7.5' quadrangle. United States Board on Geographic Names (1933, p. 166) rejected the form "Broncho Creek" for the name.

Bronson Meadows: see **Hodgdon Ranch** [TUOLUMNE].

Bronson's Meadow: see **Crocker's Meadow**, under **Rush Creek** [TUOLUMNE] (3).

Brooklin: see **Red Dog** [NEVADA].

Brooklyn: see **Red Dog** [NEVADA].

Brower Creek [CALAVERAS]: *stream,* flows nearly 3 miles to Angels Creek 2.5 miles south-southwest of Angels Camp (lat. 38°02'20" N, long. 120°33'35" W; near W line sec. 9, T 2 N, R 13 E). Named on Angels Camp (1962) 7.5' quadrangle.

Brown: see **Jimmy Brown Bar**, under **Scotchman Creek** [NEVADA]; **John Brown Flat** [PLACER].

Brown Bear Creek: see **Little Brown Bear Creek** [NEVADA].

Brown Bear Pass [TUOLUMNE]: *pass,* 8 miles northwest of Tower Peak (lat. 38°12'45" N, long. 119°39'45" W). Named on Tower Peak (1956) 15' quadrangle.

Brownell [EL DORADO]: *locality,* 10.5 miles south-southeast of Robbs Peak (lat. 38°46'15" N, long. 120°21' W). Named on Pyramid Peak (1896) 30' quadrangle.

Brownes Meadow [TUOLUMNE]: *area,* 3.5 miles northeast of Long Barn (lat. 38°07'15" N, long. 120°05' W; near NE cor. sec. 15, T 3 N, R 17 E). Named on Hull Creek (1979) 7.5'

quadrangle. United States Board on Geographic Names (1965c, p. 8) rejected the names "Browns Meadow" and "Brownes Meadows" for the feature.

Brown Flat: see **Browns Flat** [TUOLUMNE].

Brown Mountain [EL DORADO]: *peak,* 7.5 miles northeast of Robbs Peak (lat. 38°59'20" N, long. 120°17'15" W; sec. 10, T 13 N, R 15 E). Altitude 7144 feet. Named on Loon Lake (1952) 7.5' quadrangle.

Brown Peak [MARIPOSA]: *peak,* 3 miles south-southwest of El Portal on Pinoche Ridge (lat. 37°38'10" N, long. 119°48'10" W; near N line sec. 31, T 3 S, R 20 E). Altitude 5648 feet. Named on El Portal (1947) 7.5' quadrangle.

Brown Rock [EL DORADO]: *relief feature,* 2.5 miles north-northeast of Leek Spring Hill (lat. 38°39'40" N, long. 120°15'20" W; near E line sec. 1, T 9 N, R 15 E). Named on Leek Spring Hill (1951) 7.5' quadrangle.

Brown's: see **North Fork** [MADERA].

Browns Bar [EL DORADO]: *locality,* 4.5 miles west-northwest of Greenwood along Middle Fork American River (lat. 38°55'30" N, long. 120°59'25" W; near NE cor. sec. 5, T 12 N, R 9 E). Named on Greenwood (1949) 7.5' quadrangle.

Browns Bar Canyon [EL DORADO]: *canyon,* drained by a stream that flows 2.25 miles to Middle Fork American River 4.5 miles west-northwest of Greenwood (lat. 38°55'40" N, long. 120°59'15" W; near SW cor. sec. 33, T 13 N, R 9 E); Browns Bar is near the mouth of the canyon. Named on Greenwood (1949) 7.5' quadrangle.

Browns Creek [MADERA]: *stream,* flows 5.5 miles to join Sand Creek and form Willow Creek (2) 5 miles southwest of Shuteye Peak (lat. 37°17'55" N, long. 119°29'40" W; near NE cor. sec. 30, T 7 S, R 23 E); the stream heads at Browns Meadow. Named on Shuteye Peak (1953) 15' quadrangle.

Browns Creek [MARIPOSA]: *stream,* flows 8 miles to Dry Creek just inside Merced County 9 miles northwest of Hornitos (lat. 37°34'55" N, long. 120°21'30" W; sec. 18, T 4 S, R 15 E). Named on Merced Falls (1962) and Penon Blanco Peak (1962) 7.5' quadrangles.

Browns Flat [TUOLUMNE]: *village,* 2.5 miles south-southeast of Columbia along Woods Creek (lat. 38°00'15" N, long. 120°23' W; sec. 25, T 2 N, R 14 E). Named on Columbia (1948) 7.5' quadrangle. Wheeler (1879, p. 179) referred to Brown's Flat, and Bancroft (1888, p. 376) mentioned Brown Flat. The place was a mining camp started in 1851 (Hoover, Rensch, and Rensch, p. 573).

Brown's Hill: see **Mokelumne Hill** [CALAVERAS].

Browns Hill: see **You Bet** [NEVADA].

Browns Meadow [MADERA]: *area,* 1 mile southwest of Shuteye Peak (lat. 37°20'20" N, long. 119°26'25" W; sec. 10, T 7 S, R 23 E); the place is at the head of Browns Creek.

Named on Shuteye Peak (1953) 15' quadrangle.

Browns Meadow: see **Brownes Meadow** [TUOLUMNE].

Browns Pass: see **Tioga Pass** [TUOLUMNE].

Browns Ravine [EL DORADO]: *canyon,* drained by a stream that flows nearly 3 miles to South Fork American River 5.5 miles northwest of Clarksville (lat. 38°43'05" N, long. 121°06'55" W; near E line sec. 17, T 10 N, R 8 E). Named on Clarksville (1953) 7.5' quadrangle. Water of Folsom Lake now covers the lower part of the canyon.

Brownsville: see **Murphys** [CALAVERAS].

Brownsville [EL DORADO]: *locality,* 1 mile south-southeast of Omo Ranch (lat. 38°34'05" N, long. 120°33'30" W; near NE cor. sec. 8, T 8 N, R 13 E). Site named on Omo Ranch (1952) 7.5' quadrangle. Called Mendon on Placerville (1893) 30' quadrangle. The name "Brownsville" is for Henry Brown, one of the discoverers of gold at the locality (Hoover, Rensch, and Rensch, p. 84). Postal authorities established Mendon post office at the place in 1867, discontinued it for a time in 1869, and discontinued it finally in 1888; the name "Mendon" was coined from letters in the name of the first postmaster, J. Edmondson (Salley, p. 138).

Brownsville: see **Forest** [SIERRA].

Brownsville Creek [EL DORADO]: *stream,* flows 5 miles to Cedar Creek 5.5 miles east-northeast of Aukum (lat. 38°34'35" N, long. 120°32'40" W; sec. 2, T 8 N, R 12 E); the stream heads near the site of Brownsville. Named on Aukum (1952) and Omo Ranch (1952) 7.5' quadrangles.

Bruce: see **Mount Bruce**, under **Merced Peak** [MADERA].

Bruce Crossing [AMADOR]: *locality,* 5.5 miles south of Hams Station along North Fork Mokelumne River on Amador-Calaveras county line (lat. 38°27'40" N, long. 120°22'35" W; sec. 13, T 7 N, R 14 E). Named on Devils Nose (1979) 7.5' quadrangle.

Bruce Crossing [CALAVERAS]: *locality,* 2.25 miles east of Devils Nose along North Fork Mokelumne River on Calaveras-Amador county line (lat. 38°27'40" N, long. 120°22'35" W; sec. 13, T 7 N, R 14 E). Named on Devils Nose (1979) 7.5' quadrangle.

Bruener Meadow: see **Sonny Meadow** [MARIPOSA].

Brummel Ravine [SIERRA]: *canyon,* drained by a stream that flows 1.25 miles to North Yuba River 9 miles west of Goodyears Bar (lat. 39°31'05" N, long. 121°02'55" W; sec. 14, T 19 N, R 8 E). Named on Strawberry Valley (1948) 7.5' quadrangle.

Brunner Hill [CALAVERAS]: *peak,* nearly 2.25 miles northwest of Angels Camp (lat. 38°05'55" N, long. 120°34'35" W; on W line sec. 20, T 3 N, R 13 E). Altitude 1851 feet. Named on Angels Camp (1962) 7.5' quadrangle.

Brunt Flat [PLACER]: *valley,* 1 mile east-northeast of Colfax (lat. 39°06'20" N, long. 120°55'50" W; at E line sec. 35, T 15 N, R 9 E). Named on Colfax (1949) 7.5' quadrangle.

Brush Canyon [EL DORADO]: *canyon,* drained by a stream that flows 1 mile to Soldier Creek 2.5 miles northeast of Pollock Pines (lat. 38°47'10" N, long. 120°33'10" W; sec. 17, T 11 N, R 13 E). Named on Pollock Pines (1950) 7.5' quadrangle.

Brush Creek [EL DORADO]:
(1) *stream,* flows 6.5 miles to South Fork American River 4.25 miles west-northwest of Pollock Pines (lat. 38°47'40" N, long. 120° 39' W; near SW cor. sec. 16, T 11 N, R 12 E). Named on Pollock Pines (1950) and Slate Mountain (1950) 7.5' quadrangles.
(2) *stream,* flows 1.5 miles to South Fork American River 2.25 miles west-northwest of Coloma (lat. 38°49' N, long. 120°55'40" W; sec. 12, T 11 N, R 9 E). Named on Coloma (1949) 7.5' quadrangle.

Brush Creek [NEVADA]: *stream,* flows 2 miles to Rock Creek (1) 2.5 miles north of Nevada City in Lake Vera (lat. 39°18'05" N, long. 121°01'25" W; near S line sec. 25, T 17 N, R 8 E). Named on Nevada City (1948) 7.5' quadrangle.

Brush Creek [PLACER]: *stream,* flows 1 mile to Truckee River 9.5 miles west of Martis Peak (lat. 39°16'20" N, long. 120°12'20" W; at N line sec. 4, T 16 N, R 16 E). Named on Truckee (1955) 7.5' quadrangle.

Brush Creek [SIERRA]: *stream,* flows 1.5 miles to Oregon Creek nearly 3 miles west of Alleghany (lat. 39°28'40" N, long. 120°53'30" W; near NE cor. sec. 31, T 19 N, R 10 E). Named on Pike (1949) 7.5' quadrangle.

Brush Creek: see **Meyers Ravine** [NEVADA].

Brush Creek Ridge [SIERRA]: *ridge,* southeast-to south-trending, 1.25 miles long, 3.5 miles west-northwest of Alleghany (lat. 39°29'15" N, long. 120°54'10" W); the ridge is west of Brush Creek. Named on Pike (1949) 7.5' quadrangle.

Brush Gulch [TUOLUMNE]: *canyon,* drained by a stream that flows nearly 0.5 mile to Tuolumne River 1 mile southwest of Don Pedro Camp (lat. 37°42'25" N, long. 120°24'50" W; sec. 3, T 3 S, R 14 E). Named on La Grange (1962) 7.5' quadrangle.

Brush Ridge [MARIPOSA]: *ridge,* south-southeast-trending, 2 miles long, 3 miles east-southeast of Smith Peak (lat. 37°46'55" N, long. 120°03' W). Named on Jawbone Ridge (1947) 7.5' quadrangle.

Brushy Canyon [EL DORADO]:
(1) *canyon,* drained by a stream that flows 2.5 miles to Iowa Canyon 4 miles west of Pollock Pines (lat. 38°45'50" N, long. 120° 39'30" W; near N line sec. 32, T 11 N, R 12 E). Named on Pollock Pines (1950) and Slate Mountain (1950) 7.5' quadrangles. This appears to be the feature called Little Iowa Canyon on Plac-

erville (1893) 30' quadrangle.

(2) *canyon,* drained by a stream that flows nearly 3 miles to Cedar Creek 3.5 miles east of Aukum (lat. 38°33'35" N, long. 120°39'25" W; sec. 9, T 8 N, R 12 E). Named on Aukum (1952) 7.5' quadrangle. Called Cold Canyon on Placerville (1893) 30' quadrangle.

Brushy Canyon [MARIPOSA]: *canyon,* drained by a stream that flows 4 miles to Mariposa Creek 5.25 miles south-southeast of the settlement of Catheys Valley (lat. 37°21'40" N, long. 120°04'15" W; near SE cor. sec. 35, T 6 S, R 17 E). Named on Illinois Hill (1962) 7.5' quadrangle.

Brushy Canyon [PLACER]:

(1) *canyon,* 2.25 miles long, opens into Shirttail Canyon 3.5 miles northwest of Foresthill (lat. 39°03'30" N, long. 120°51'45" W). Named on Foresthill (1949) 7.5' quadrangle. The canyon divides at the head into First Brushy Canyon and Second Brushy Canyon. The stream in Brushy Canyon (1) and in Third Brushy Canyon is called Brushy Creek on Colfax (1898) 30' quadrangle.

(2) *canyon,* 2 miles long, opens into the canyon of Middle Fork American River 4.25 miles east-southeast of Michigan Bluff (lat. 39°01'10" N, long. 120°39'40" W; sec. 32, T 14 N, R 12 E); the canyon divides at the head into Middle Branch and South Branch. Named on Michigan Bluff (1952) 7.5' quadrangle. The stream in the canyon is called Brushy Creek on Colfax (1898) 30' quadrangle. Middle Branch is 1.5 miles long and is named on Greek Store (1952) and Michigan Bluff (1952) 7.5' quadrangles. South Branch is 3.5 miles long and is named on Devil Peak (1950), Greek Store (1952), Michigan Bluff (1952), and Tunnel Hill (1950) 7.5' quadrangles. North Branch enters less than 1 mile from the mouth of the main canyon; it is 2.5 miles long and is named on Greek Store (1952) and Michigan Bluff (1952) 7.5' quadrangles.

Brushy Canyon: see **First Brushy Canyon** [PLACER]; **Second Brushy Canyon** [PLACER]; **Third Brushy Canyon** [PLACER].

Brushy Creek [PLACER]: *stream,* flows 3.5 miles to North Fork American River 5.5 miles south-southeast of Colfax (lat. 39°01'25" N, long. 120°55' W; sec. 36, T 14 N, R 9 E). Named on Colfax (1949) 7.5' quadrangle.

Brushy Creek: see **Brushy Canyon** [PLACER] (1) and (2).

Brushy Creek [TUOLUMNE]: *stream,* flows 2 miles to Twomile Creek 5.25 miles southeast of Long Barn (lat. 38°02'25" N, long. 120°03'45" W; sec. 12, T 2 N, R 17 E). Named on Hull Creek (1979) 7.5' quadrangle.

Brushy Hollow Creek [TUOLUMNE]: *stream,* flows 3 miles to Beardsley Lake 3.25 miles north-northwest of Strawberry (lat. 38°14'15" N, long. 120°02'35" W; near SW cor. sec. 31, T 5 N, R 18 E). Named on Liberty Hill (1979)

and Strawberry (1979) 7.5' quadrangles.

Brushy Mountain [NEVADA]: *peak,* 4.25 miles west of Wolf (lat. 39°04'05" N, long. 121°13'05" W; near N line sec. 17, T 14 N, R 7 E). Named on Wolf (1949) 7.5' quadrangle.

Brushy Mountain Canyon [PLACER]: *canyon,* drained by a stream that flows 1.25 miles to Middle Fork American River 6.5 miles east-northeast of Auburn (lat. 38°56'10" N, long. 120°57'35" W; sec. 34, T 13 N, R 9 E). Named on Greenwood (1949) 7.5' quadrangle.

Brushy Spring [PLACER]: *spring,* 11 miles south-southwest of Duncan Peak (lat. 39°00'20" N, long. 120°34'55" W; sec. 1, T 13 N, R 12 E); the spring is at the head of Brushy Creek (present South Branch Brushy Canyon). Named on Colfax (1938) 30' quadrangle.

Bryan: see **Bryan Meadow** [EL DORADO].

Bryan Creek [EL DORADO]: *stream,* flows 1 mile to South Fork American River nearly 4 miles west of Echo Summit (lat. 38°48'10" N, long. 120°05'55" W; at E line sec. 16, T 11 N, R 17 E). Named on Echo Lake (1955) 7.5' quadrangle.

Bryan Meadow [EL DORADO]: *area,* 2.5 miles south-southwest of Echo Summit (lat. 38°46'50" N, long. 120°03'20" W; near S line sec. 24, T 11 N, R 17 E). Named on Echo Lake (1955) 7.5' quadrangle. Pyramid Peak (1896) 30' quadrangle has the name "Bryan" at the place.

Bryant Creek: see **Stonebreaker Creek** [EL DORADO].

Bryants [EL DORADO]: *locality,* 4.5 miles west of Old Iron Mountain (lat. 38°43'05" N, long. 120°28'30" W; near W line sec. 18, T 10 N, R 14 E). Named on Stump Spring (1951) 7.5' quadrangle.

Bryants Spring [EL DORADO]: *spring,* 3.5 miles north of Riverton (lat. 38°49'30" N, long. 120°27'20" W; sec. 6, T 11 N, R 14 E). Named on Riverton (1950) 7.5' quadrangle.

Buchanan [TUOLUMNE]: *locality,* 4 miles southeast of Tuolumne (lat. 37°54'55" N, long. 120°11'15" W; sec. 26, T 1 N, R 16 E). Named on Tuolumne (1948) 7.5' quadrangle.

Buchanan: see **Eastman Lake** [MADERA-MARIPOSA].

Buchanan Hollow: see **Eastman Lake** [MADERA-MARIPOSA].

Buchanan Reservoir: see **Eastman Lake** [MADERA-MARIPOSA].

Buck Camp [MADERA]: *locality,* 7.25 miles southwest of Merced Peak (lat. 37°33'50" N, long. 119°29'20" W; near N line sec. 30, T 4 S, R 23 E); the place is along Buck Creek. Named on Mount Lyell (1901) 30' quadrangle. The name supposedly is from the so-called buck privates who were on army duty at the place (Browning, 1988, p. 17).

Buck Creek [MADERA]: *stream,* flows 2.25 miles to South Fork Merced River 8 miles southwest of Merced Peak (lat. 37°32'30" N, long. 119°29'10" W); Buck Camp is along the stream.. Named on Merced Peak (1953) 15' quadrangle.

Buckeye [EL DORADO]: *locality,* 2.5 miles east-northeast of Georgetown (lat. 38°55'25" N, long. 120°47'45" W; near N line sec. 6, T 12 N, R 11 E). Named on Georgetown (1949) 7.5' quadrangle.

Buckeye Bar [EL DORADO-PLACER]: *locality,* 4 miles northwest of Greenwood along Middle Fork American River on El Dorado-Placer county line (lat. 38°56' N, long. 120°58'05" W; near W line sec. 34, T 13 N, R 7 E); the place is at the mouth of Buckeye Canyon. Named on Greenwood (1949) 7.5' quadrangle. Bancroft (1888, p. 354) listed a place called American Bar that was on the north side of Middle Fork between Buckeye Bar and Sardine Bar.

Buckeye Canyon [EL DORADO]: *canyon,* drained by a stream that flows 1 mile to Middle Fork American River nearly 4 miles northwest of Greenwood at Buckeye Bar (lat. 38°55'55" N, long. 120°57'55" W; sec. 34, T 13 N, R 9 E). Named on Greenwood (1949) 7.5' quadrangle.

Buckeye Creek [MARIPOSA]: *stream,* flows nearly 5 miles to Agua Fria Creek 4.25 miles south-southwest of Mariposa (lat. 37°25'25" N, long. 119°59'15" W; sec. 10, T 6 S, R 18 E). Named on Mariposa (1947) 7.5' quadrangle.

Buckeye Diggings [NEVADA]: *locality,* 8 miles north-northeast of Chicago Park (lat. 39°14'35" N, long. 120°53'25" W); the place is near the southwest end of Buckeye Ridge. Named on Chicago Park (1949) 7.5' quadrangle.

Buckeye Flat [PLACER]: *area,* 8.5 miles west-northwest of Devil Peak (lat. 38°59'15" N, long. 120°41'40" W; near S line sec. 12, T 13 N, R 11 E). Named on Tunnel Hill (1950) 7.5' quadrangle.

Buckeye Gulch: see **Happy Valley** [CALAVERAS].

Buckeye Hill [MARIPOSA]: *peak,* 10.5 miles south of Mariposa (lat. 37°19'50" N, long. 119°56'55" W; near N line sec. 13, T 7 S, 18 E). Altitude 1904 feet. Named on Ben Hur (1947) 7.5' quadrangle.

Buckeye Hill: see **Mokelumne Hill** [CALAVERAS].

Buckeye Mountain [MADERA]: *ridge,* northwest- to west-trending, 3 miles long, 7 miles southwest of Yosemite Forks (lat. 37°18'10" N, long. 119°43'40" W). Named on Bass Lake (1953) and Mariposa (1947) 15' quadrangles.

Buckeye Pass [TUOLUMNE]: *pass,* 6 miles west-northwest of Matterhorn Peak on Tuolumne-Mono county line (lat. 38°07'50" N, long. 119°28'40" W). Named on Matterhorn Peak (1956) 15' quadrangle. The name is from Buckeye Mill Company, which was active during the 1860's (Browning, 1986, p. 27).

Buckeye Point [EL DORADO]: *relief feature,* 5.5 miles north of Georgetown (lat. 38°59'05" N, long. 120°48'55" W; sec. 12, T 13 N, R 10 E). Named on Georgetown (1949) 7.5' quadrangle.

Buckeye Ravine [SIERRA]: *canyon,* drained by a stream that flows 1.5 miles to Wolf Creek nearly 3 miles southeast of Alleghany (lat. 39°26'40" N, long. 120°48'15" W; near N line sec. 12, T 18 N, R 10 E). Named on Alleghany (1949) 7.5' quadrangle.

Buckeye Ridge [NEVADA]: *ridge,* southwest-trending, 3 miles long, 8 miles north-north-east of Chicago Park (lat. 39°14'45" N, long. 120°53' W). Named on Chicago Park (1949), Dutch Flat (1950), North Bloomfield (1949), and Washington (1950) 7.5' quadrangles.

Buckeye Spring [NEVADA]: *spring,* 8 miles south-southwest of Washington (lat. 39°15'10" N, long. 120°51'50" W; sec. 16, T 16 N, R 10 E); the spring is on Buckeye Ridge. Named on Washington (1950) 7.5' quadrangle.

Buck Field [CALAVERAS]: *area,* 4.5 miles northwest of Angels Camp (lat. 38°07'30" N, long. 120°36'20" W; sec. 12, T 3 N, R 12 E). Named on Angels Camp (1962) and Calaveritas (1962) 7.5' quadrangles.

Buckham Gulch [CALAVERAS]: *canyon,* drained by a stream that flows nearly 4 miles to Snow Creek 7.5 miles west-southwest of Copperopolis (lat. 37°56'55" N, long. 120°46'25" W; sec. 9, T 1 N, R 11 E). Named on Bachelor Valley (1968) and Copperopolis (1962) 7.5' quadrangles.

Buckhorn Creek [MARIPOSA]: *stream,* flows nearly 4 miles to Maxwell Creek 1.5 miles south of Coulterville (lat. 37°41'20" N, long. 120°11'50" W; sec. 10, T 3 S, R 16 E); the stream heads at Buckhorn Flat. Named on Coulterville (1947) 7.5' quadrangle.

Buckhorn Flat [MARIPOSA]: *area,* 4 miles southeast of Coulterville (lat. 37°40'40" N, long. 120°08'10" W; mainly in sec. 7, 18, T 3 S, R 17 E); the place is northwest of Buckhorn Peak. Named on Coulterville (1947) 7.5' quadrangle.

Buckhorn Lodge [AMADOR]: *locality,* 7.25 miles east-northeast of Pine Grove (lat. 38°26'40" N, long. 120°31'50" W; sec. 22, T 7 N, R 13 E). Named on West Point (1948) 7.5' quadrangle.

Buckhorn Mountain [TUOLUMNE]: *peak,* 6 miles east-southeast of Sonora (lat. 37°57'35" N, long. 120°16'30" W; sec. 12, T 1 N, R 15 E). Altitude 3311 feet. Named on Standard (1948) 7.5' quadrangle.

Buckhorn Mountain: see **Buckhorn Peak** [MARIPOSA].

Buckhorn Peak [MARIPOSA]: *peak,* 5 miles southeast of Coulterville (lat. 37°39'50" N, long. 120°07'20" W; on N line sec. 20, T 3 S, R 17 E). Altitude 3774 feet. Named on Buckhorn Peak (1947) 7.5' quadrangle. Called Buckhorn Mt. on Hoffmann and Gardner's (1863-1867) map.

Buckingham Mountain [MARIPOSA]: *ridge,* northwest-trending, 2 miles long, 11 miles south-southwest of El Portal (lat. 37°31'45" N, long. 119°51'55" W). Named on Buckingham Mountain (1947) 7.5' quadrangle. Gudde (1975, p. 228), who called the feature Mount Buckingham, noted that William Buckingham opened the first gold mine on the ridge in 1850.

Buckingham Ridge [SIERRA]: *ridge,* west- to northwest-trending, 1.25 miles long, 3.5 miles east-southeast of Downieville (lat. 39° 32'35" N, long. 120°45'50" W; sec. 5, T 19 N, R 11 E). Named on Downieville (1951) 7.5' quadrangle.

Buck Island Lake [EL DORADO]: *lake,* 4.5 miles west of Wentworth Springs (lat. 39°00'05" N, long. 120°15'05" W). Named on Homewood (1955), Loon Lake (1952, photorevised 1973), and Wentworth Springs (1953, photorevised 1973) 7.5' quadrangles.

Buck Lake [PLACER]: *lake,* 1150 feet long, 3 miles south-southwest of Homewood (lat. 39°03' N, long. 120°11'25" W; sec. 22, T 14 N, R 16 E). Named on Homewood (1955) 7.5' quadrangle.

Buck Lakes [TUOLUMNE]: *lakes,* largest 4250 feet long, 10.5 miles west of Tower Peak (lat. 38°09'40" N, long. 119°44'25" W); the lakes are along Buck Meadow Creek. Named on Tower Peak (1956) 15' quadrangle.

Buckley Meadows: see **Ackerson Meadow** [TUOLUMNE].

Buck Meadow Creek [TUOLUMNE]: *stream,* flows 8.5 miles to West Fork Cherry Creek 10 miles east-southeast of Pinecrest (lat. 38°09'15" N, long. 119°48'45" W). Named on Pinecrest (1956) and Tower Peak (1956) 15' quadrangles.

Buck Meadows [MARIPOSA]: *locality,* 2 miles east-northeast of Smith Peak (lat. 37°48'50" N, long. 120°03'50" W; sec. 36, T 1 S, R 17 E). Named on Jawbone Ridge (1947) 7.5' quadrangle. Postal authorities established Buck Meadows post office in 1915 and discontinued it in 1925 (Frickstad, p. 90). Alva Hamilton started a stage stop called Hamilton's Station at the place in the early 1870's (Paden and Schlichtmann, p. 194).

Buck Mountain [CALAVERAS]: *ridge,* southwest-trending, 1 mile long, 7.5 miles northwest of Dorrington (lat. 38°22'20" N, long. 120°22'40" W). Named on Dorrington (1979), Fort Mountain (1979), and Garnet Hill (1979) 7.5' quadrangles.

Buck Meadow [PLACER]: *area,* 2 miles northnortheast of Bunker Hill (lat. 39°04'30" N, long. 120°22'05" W; at E line sec. 11, T 14 N, R 14 E). Named on Wentworth Springs (1953) 7.5' quadrangle. Truckee (1940) 30' quadrangle has the name for an area located 1 mile farther northeast (sec. 1, T 14 N, R 14 E).

Buck Meadows [NEVADA]: *area,* 6 miles east of Truckee (lat. 39°20'25" N, long. 120°04'25"

W; sec. 10, T 17 N, R 17 E); the place is northwest of Buck Ridge. Named on Martis Peak (1955) 7.5' quadrangle.

Buck Mountain [NEVADA]:
(1) *peak,* 1 mile southwest of North Bloomfield (lat. 39°21'35" N, long. 120°54'45" W; at S line sec. 1, T 17 N, R 9 E). Named on North Bloomfield (1949) 7.5' quadrangle.
(2) *peak,* 5 miles northeast of Higgins Corner (lat. 39°05'40" N, long. 121°01'45" W; near E line sec. 1, T 14 N, R 8 E). Altitude 2278 feet. Named on Lake Combie (1949) 7.5' quadrangle.

Buck Pasture [EL DORADO]: *area,* nearly 3 miles northwest of Kirkwood (lat. 38°44' N, long. 120°06'15" W; sec. 8, T 10 N, R 17 E). Named on Caples Lake (1979) 7.5' quadrangle.

Buck Point [MARIPOSA]: *peak,* 3.5 miles north-northeast of the settlement of Catheys Valley (lat. 37°29'05" N, long. 120°04'35" W). Altitude 2513 feet. Named on Catheys Valley (1962) 7.5' quadrangle.

Buck Ridge [NEVADA]: *ridge,* south- to westtrending, 2.5 miles long, 6.25 miles east of Truckee (lat. 39°20'15" N, long. 120°03'50" W). Named on Martis Peak (1955) 7.5' quadrangle.

Bucks Bar [EL DORADO]: *locality,* 6 miles south-southwest of Camino along North Fork Cosumnes River (lat. 38°39'20" N, long. 120°42' W; near SW cor. sec. 6, T 9 N, R 12 E). Named on Camino (1952) 7.5' quadrangle. Gudde (1975, p. 374) listed a place called Wisconsin Bar that was located along North Fork Cosumnes River above Bucks Bar.

Buckskin Creek [PLACER]: *stream,* flows 2 miles to Five Lakes Creek 5 miles northeast of Bunker Hill (lat. 39°05'50" N, long. 120°18'55" W; near N line sec. 5, T 14 N, R 15 E). Named on Wentworth Springs (1953) 7.5' quadrangle.

Buckskin Joe Spring [EL DORADO]: *spring,* 1.25 miles west of Leek Spring Hill (lat. 38°37'35" N, long. 120°17'50" W; sec. 15, T 9 N, R 15 E). Named on Leek Spring Hill (1951) 7.5' quadrangle.

Buck Spring [NEVADA]: *spring,* 5.5 miles eastnortheast of Truckee (lat. 39°20'40" N, long. 120°04'50" W; at N line sec. 10, T 17 N, R 17 E); the spring is 1 mile northwest of Buck Ridge. Named on Martis Peak (1955) 7.5' quadrangle.

Budd Creek [TUOLUMNE]: *stream,* flows 2.5 miles to Tuolumne River 7.5 miles west-southwest of Tioga Pass in Tuolumne Meadows (lat. 37°52'35" N, long. 119°23' W; sec. 6, T 1 S, R 24 E); the creek heads at Budd Lake. Named on Tuolumne Meadows (1956) 15' quadrangle. The stream was called Cathedral Creek in 1883, no doubt because it heads just east of Cathedral Peak (Browning, 1988, p. 17).

Budd Lake [TUOLUMNE]: *lake,* 1400 feet long, 9 miles west-southwest of Tioga Pass (lat. 37°50'30" N, long. 119°23'40" W; sec. 13, T 1 S, R 23 E); the lake is at the head of Budd Creek. Named on Tuolumne Meadows (1956) 15' quadrangle. The name probably commemorates Governor Budd of California (United States Board on Geographic Names, 1934, p. 4).

Buena Ventura Valley: see "Regional setting."

Buena Vista [AMADOR]: *locality,* 4 miles south-southeast of Ione in Jackson Valley (lat. 38°17'40" N, long. 120°54'45" W); the place is 1.5 miles north of Buena Vista Peaks. Named on Ione (1962) 7.5' quadrangle. Postal authorities established Buena Vista post office in 1866 and discontinued it in 1878 (Frickstad, p. 5). The place also was called the Corners (Sargent, p. 90).

Buena Vista [MARIPOSA]: *locality,* 2.5 miles north-northwest of El Portal (lat. 37°4240" N, long. 119°47'30" W; sec. 32, T 2 S, R 20 E). Named on El Portal (1947) 7.5' quadrangle.

Buena Vista [NEVADA]: *locality,* 3 miles north of present Chicago Park along Nevada County Narrow Gauge Railroad (lat. 39°11'15" N, long. 120°58'15" W). Named on Colfax (1898) 30' quadrangle.

Buena Vista Creek [MADERA-MARIPOSA]: *stream,* heads in Madera County and flows 6 miles to Illilouette Creek 7.25 miles southeast of Yosemite Village in Mariposa County (lat. 37° 40' N, long. 119°30'05" W; near NE cor. sec. 24, T 3 S, R 22 E). Named on Merced Peak (1953) and Yosemite (1956) 15' quadrangles.

Buena Vista Crest [MADERA]: *ridge,* east- to northeast-trending, 4 miles long, 5 miles west-southwest of Merced Peak (lat. 37°36' N, long. 119°28'30" W); the ridge is east of Buena Vista Peak. Named on Merced Peak (1953) 15' quadrangle.

Buena Vista Lake [MADERA]: *lake,* 1500 feet long, less than 0.5 mile north of Buena Vista Peak (lat. 37°36' N, long. 119°31' W; sec. 12, T 4 S, R 22 E). Named on Yosemite (1956) 15' quadrangle.

Buena Vista Mountain [CALAVERAS]: *peak,* 4.5 miles west-southwest of San Andreas (lat. 38°09'55" N, long. 120°45' W; near S line sec. 27, T 4 N, R 11 E). Named on San Andreas (1962) and Valley Springs (1962) 7.5' quadrangles.

Buena Vista Peaks [AMADOR]: *peaks,* nearly 6 miles south of Ione (lat. 38°16'05" N, long. 120°54'50" W; sec. 19, T 5 N, R 10 E); the peaks are 1.5 miles south of Buena Vista. Named on Ione (1962) 7.5' quadrangle. Jackson (1902) 30' quadrangle has the singular form "Buena Vista Peak" for the name.

Buffalo Hill [EL DORADO]: *locality,* 0.5 mile west-northwest of Georgetown (lat. 38°54'30" N, long. 120°50'45" W; sec. 10, T 12 N, R 10 E). Named on Georgetown (1949) 7.5' quadrangle.

Buffin Meadow [MADERA]: *area,* 8.5 miles

north of Yosemite Forks (lat. 37°29'20" N, long. 119°35'50" W; near N line sec. 19, T 5 S, R 22 E). Named on Bass Lake (1953) 15' quadrangle. The misspelled name is for businessman Edward Wheaton Buffum (Browning, 1986, p. 28).

Buford Mountain [MADERA]: *peak,* 2.5 miles east of Knowles (lat. 37°13'15" N, long. 119°49'50" W; sec. 19, T 8 S, R 20 E). Altitude 2066 feet. Named on Knowles (1962, photorevised 1981) 7.5' quadrangle.

Bugle Lake [EL DORADO-PLACER]: *lake,* 1050 feet long, 1 mile northeast of Wentworth Springs on El Dorado-Placer county line (lat. 39°01'20" N, long. 120°19'25" W; on N line sec. 32, T 14 N, R 15 E). Named on Wentworth Springs (1953) 7.5' quadrangle.

Bug Table [MADERA]: *ridge,* west-northwest-trending, 0.5 mile long, 8 miles south-southwest of the town of North Fork (lat. 37° 07'45" N, long. 119°34'45" W; sec. 21, T 9 S, R 22 E). Named on North Fork (1965) 7.5' quadrangle.

Bullard [EL DORADO]: *locality,* 3.5 miles north-northeast of Latrobe along Southern Pacific Railroad (lat. 38°36'35" N, long. 120°57'35" W; sec. 26, T 9 N, R 9 E). Named on Latrobe (1949) 7.5' quadrangle.

Bull Creek [EL DORADO]: *stream,* flows 1.5 miles to South Fork American River 1 mile east of Riverton (lat. 38°46'10" N, long. 120°25'55" W; sec. 29, T 11 N, R 14 E). Named on Riverton (1950) 7.5' quadrangle.

Bull Creek [MARIPOSA]: *stream,* flows 12 miles to North Fork Merced River 6 miles east-northeast of Buckhorn Peak (lat. 37°42'10" N, long. 120°01'40" W; sec. 6, T 3 S, R 18 E). Named on Coulterville (1947), El Portal (1947), and Lake Eleanor (1956) 15' quadrangles.

Bull Creek [TUOLUMNE]: *stream,* flows 1.25 miles to Middle Fork Stanislaus River 8.5 miles south-southeast of Liberty Hill (lat. 38° 15'30" N, long. 120°01'10" W; sec. 29, T 5 N, R 18 E). Named on Liberty Hill (1979) and Strawberry (1979) 7.5' quadrangles.

Bull Diggings: see **Mameluke Hill** [EL DORADO].

Bullet Ravine [EL DORADO]: *canyon,* less than 1 mile long, opens into the canyon of Camp Creek 11 miles east-southeast of Placerville (lat. 38°41' N, long. 120°36'10" W). Named on Placerville (1893) 30' quadrangle.

Bull Flat [NEVADA]: *area,* 7.5 miles northwest of Donner Pass (lat. 39°23'50" N, long. 120°25' W; on E line sec. 29, T 18 N, R 14 E). Named on Webber Peak (1981) 7.5' quadrangle.

Bullion: see **Mount Bullion** [MARIPOSA].
Bullion: see **Michigan Bluff** [PLACER].
Bullion Creek: see **West Branch**, under **El Dorado Canyon** [PLACER].
Bullion Hill [MARIPOSA]: *ridge,* north- to north-northwest-trending, less than 1 mile

long, 5 miles north-northwest of Hornitos (lat. 37° 34'15" N, long. 120°15'15" W). Named on Merced Falls (1962) 7.5' quadrangle.**Bullion Bend** [EL DORADO]: *bend,* 17 miles west-southwest of Pyramid Peak along South Fork American River (lat. 38°46'30" N, long. 120°28' W). Named on Pyramid Peak (1896) 30' quadrangle. Robbers held up a stage at the place and their loot supposedly is buried there (Paden, p. 453).

Bullion Mountain [MARIPOSA]: *ridge,* northwest-trending, 5 miles long, center 2.25 miles east-southeast of the village of Bear Valley (lat. 37°33'30" N, long. 120°04'30" W). Named on Bear Valley (1947) 7.5' quadrangle. Called Mount Bullion Spur Ridge on Laizure's (1928) map, which has the name "Mount Bullion" for a peak on the ridge. Whitney (1865, p. 224) used the name "Mount Bullion Range" for the ridge. John C. Fremont named the feature for his father-in-law, Senator Thomas Hart Benton, who had the nickname "Old Bullion" from his monetary policy (Chamberlain, p. 4).

Bull Meadow [TUOLUMNE]: *area,* 6 miles southeast of Duckwall Mountain (lat. 37°53'45" N, long. 120°03'20" W; sec. 36, T 1 N, R 17 E). Named on Duckwall Mountain (1948) 7.5' quadrangle.

Bull Meadow Creek [TUOLUMNE]: *stream,* flows 3.5 miles to Clavey River 7.5 miles south-southeast of Duckwall Mountain (lat. 37°52'05" N, long. 120°03'40" W; sec. 12, T 1 S, R 17 E); the stream goes through Bull Meadow. Named on Duckwall Mountain (1948) and Jawbone Ridge (1947) 7.5' quadrangles.

Bullpen Lake [NEVADA]: *lake,* 750 feet long, 5.5 miles east of Graniteville (lat. 39°25'20" N, long. 120°38'05" W; sec. 16, T 18 N, R 12 E). Named on Graniteville (1982) 7.5' quadrangle. Logan's (1940) map has the form "Bull Pen Lake" for the name.

Bull Run [MARIPOSA]: *stream,* flows 2.25 miles to Mariposa Creek 4.25 miles southsoutheast of the settlement of Catheys Valley (lat. 37°22'50" N, long. 120°03'10" W; sec. 25, T 6 S, R 17 E). Named on Catheys Valley (1962) 7.5' quadrangle.

Bull Run [TUOLUMNE]: *area,* 9 miles southwest of Dardanelle along Cow Creek (1) (lat. 38°15' N, long. 119°57' W). Named on Donnell Lake (1979) and Pinecrest (1979) 7.5' quadrangles.

Bull Run Rock [TUOLUMNE]: *peak,* 8.5 miles southwest of Dardanelle (lat. 38°15'20" N, long. 119°56'30" W; sec. 25, T 5 N, R 18 E); the peak is 0.5 mile northeast of Bull Run. Named on Donnell Lake (1979) 7.5' quadrangle.

Bull Run Valley [MARIPOSA]: *valley,* 3 miles southeast of the settlement of Catheys Valley (lat. 37°24' N, long. 120°03'15" W; sec. 24, T 6 S, R 17 E); Bull Run drains the valley.

Named on Catheys Valley (1962) 7.5' quadrangle.

Bullshead [PLACER]: *relief feature,* 5.5 miles northwest of Tahoe City (lat. 39°14'05" N, long. 120°12'05" W; sec. 16, T 16 N, R 16 E). Named on Tahoe City (1955) 7.5' quadrangle. California Division of Highways' (1934) map shows a place called Bulls Head located along Southern Pacific Railroad 0.5 mile south of Bullshead (near S line sec. 16, T 16 N, R 16 E).

Bumblebee [TUOLUMNE]: *settlement,* 2.25 miles north of Pinecrest (lat. 38°13'35" N, long. 119°59'45" W; near SE cor. sec. 4, T 4 N, R 18 E); the place is by Bumblebee Creek. Named on Pinecrest (1979) 7.5' quadrangle.

Bumblebee Creek [TUOLUMNE]: *stream,* flows 2.25 miles to Cow Creek (1) 2.5 miles north of Strawberry (lat. 38°14'05" N, long. 120°01' W; near W line sec. 5, T 4 N, R 18 E). Named on Pinecrest (1979) and Strawberry (1979) 7.5' quadrangles.

Bummers Flat [TUOLUMNE]: *area,* 5.5 miles east-southeast of Liberty Hill (lat. 38°20'30" N, long. 120°00'15" W; sec. 28, T 6 N, R 18 E). Named on Liberty Hill (1979) 7.5' quadrangle.

Bummerville [CALAVERAS]: *village,* 1.25 miles east of West Point (lat. 38°24'05" N, long. 120°30'20" W; near E line sec. 2, T 6 N, R 13 E). Named on West Point (1948) 7.5' quadrangle. Camp's (1962) map shows a place called Camp Spirito situated 1.25 miles northwest of Bummerville, and a peak called Valentine Hill located less than 1 mile northnorthwest of Bummerville. The name "Valentine" commemorates Valentine Granados, a Mexican prospector in Calaveras County (Camp *in* Doble, p. 300).

Bumpus Cañon: see **Iowa Hill** [PLACER].

Bunch Canyon [PLACER]: *canyon,* drained by a stream that flows 5.5 miles to North Fork American River 5 miles south-southeast of Colfax (lat. 39°02'10" N, long. 120°54'30" W; sec. 30, T 14 N, R 10 E). Named on Colfax (1949) 7.5' quadrangle.

Bunker Hill [AMADOR]:

(1) *peak,* 4 miles south-southeast of Plymouth (lat. 38°25'25" N, long. 120°49'05" W; near SE cor. sec. 25, T 7 N, R 10 E). Altitude 1344 feet. Named on Amador City (1962) 7.5' quadrangle.

(2) *locality,* nearly 4 miles south-southeast of Plymouth (lat. 38°25'35" N, long. 120°49'40" W; sec. 25, T 7 N, R 10 E); the place is 0.5 mile west-northwest of Bunker Hill (1). Named on Amador City (1962) 7.5' quadrangle. Called New Philadelphia on Sutter Creek (1944) 15' quadrangle. New Philadelphia also was known as Dog Town (Gudde, 1975, p. 97).

Bunker Hill [NEVADA]: *ridge,* southwest- to south-trending, 1 mile long, 5 miles northwest of Nevada City (lat. 39°18'40" N, long.

121°05'30" W; sec. 28, T 17 N, R 8 E). Named on Nevada City (1948) 7.5' quadrangle.

Bunker Hill [PLACER]: *peak,* 11.5 miles south-southeast of Granite Chief (lat. 39°03' N, long. 120°22'45" W; sec. 23, T 14 N, R 14 E). Altitude 7524 feet. Named on Bunker Hill (1953) 7.5' quadrangle.

Bunker Hill [SIERRA]: *peak,* 4.5 miles south-southeast of Mount Fillmore (lat. 39°40' N, long. 120°50' W). Altitude 6967 feet. Named on Mount Fillmore (1951) 7.5' quadrangle.

Bunker Hill Ridge [SIERRA]: *ridge,* southeast-trending, 2.25 miles long, 2.5 miles north of Mount Fillmore on Sierra-Plumas county line (lat. 39°45'50" N, long. 120°51'20" W). Named on Blue Nose Mountain (1951) 7.5' quadrangle.

Bunker Lake [PLACER]: *lake,* 950 feet long, less than 0.5 mile northwest of Bunker Hill (lat. 39°03'15" N, long. 120°23'10" W; at NE cor. sec. 22, T 14 N, R 14 E). Named on Bunker Hill (1953) 7.5' quadrangle.

Bunker Meadow [PLACER]: *area,* 0.5 mile south-southeast of Bunker Hill (lat. 39°02'25" N, long. 120°22'35" W; on S line sec. 23, T 14 N, R 14 E). Named on Bunker Hill (1953) 7.5' quadrangle.

Bunkerville: see **Little Deer Creek** [NEVADA].

Bunnell Cascade [MARIPOSA]: *waterfall,* 8 miles south-southwest of Cathedral Peak along Merced River (lat. 37°44'45" N, long. 119°28'10" W); the feature is north-northwest of Bunnell Point. Named on Merced Peak (1953) 15' quadrangle, where the name has the misspelled form "Bunnel Cascade." The name commemorates Lafayette H. Bunnell (United States Board on Geographic Names, 1933, p. 4). The feature also had the names "Washburn Cascade," "Diamond Shower Fall," and "Little Grizzly Falls" (Browning, 1986, p. 28).

Bunnell Point [MARIPOSA]: *peak,* 8.5 miles south-southwest of Cathedral Peak (lat. 37°44'20" N, long. 119°28' W). Altitude 8193 feet. Named on Merced Peak (1953) 15' quadrangle. The name commemorates Lafayette H. Bunnell, one of the group of men who discovered Yosemite Valley in 1851 (Hanna, p. 45). The peak was called Sugarbowl Dome before about 1920 (Browning, 1986, p. 28).

Burch Meadow [TUOLUMNE]: *area,* 6.5 miles east-southeast of Groveland (lat. 37°48'40" N, long. 120°07'05" W; near W line sec. 33, T 1 S, R 17 E). Named on Jawbone Ridge (1947) 7.5' quadrangle.

Burford [MADERA]: *locality,* 1.5 miles north-west of Yosemite Forks (lat. 37°22'55" N, long. 119°39'10" W; sec. 27, T 6 S, R 21 E). Site named on Bass Lake (1953) 15' quadrangle.

Burgeson Lake: see **Burgson Lake** [TUOLUMNE].

Burgson Lake [TUOLUMNE]: *lake,* 600 feet long, 6.5 miles west-northwest of Dardanelle (lat. 38°21'35" N, long. 119°56'50" W; sec. 24, T 6 N, R 18 E). Named on Donnell Lake (1979) 7.5' quadrangle. United States Board on Geographic Names (1981c, p. 3) rejected the form "Burgeson Lake" for the name.

Burks Bar: see **Relief** [NEVADA].

Burlington Ridge [NEVADA]: *ridge,* west-trending, 6 miles long, between North Fork and South Fork Deer Creek; center 4 miles south-southwest of Washington (lat. 39°18'30" N, long. 120° 50' W). Named on North Bloomfield (1949) and Washington (1950) 7.5' quadrangles.

Burma Summit [SIERRA]: *peak,* 7 miles east-southeast of Loyalton (lat. 39°38'25" N, long. 120°07'05" W; sec. 30, T 21 N, R 17 E). Altitude 8062 feet. Named on Evans Canyon (1978) 7.5' quadrangle.

Burned Hill [NEVADA]: *peak,* 8.5 miles east of Truckee (lat. 39°19'15" N, long. 120°01'20" W; sec. 19, T 17 N, R 18 E). Altitude 7925 feet. Named on Martis Peak (1955) 7.5' quadrangle.

Burnett Canyon [PLACER]: *canyon,* drained by a stream that flows 5 miles to East Fork of North Fork of North Fork American River 4.25 miles north-northwest of Westville (lat. 39°13'55" N, long. 120°41' W; sec. 24, T 16 N, R 11 E). Named on Duncan Peak (1952) and Westville (1952) 7.5' quadrangles.

Burns' Camp: see **Quartzburg**, under **Hornitos** [MARIPOSA].

Burns Creek [MARIPOSA]: *stream,* heads in Mariposa County and flows 26 miles to Bear Creek (1) nearly 3 miles north of Planada in Merced County (lat. 37°20' N, long. 120°19'10" W; sec. 10, T 7 S, R 15 E). Named on Haystack Mountain (1962), Hornitos (1947), Indian Gulch (1962), and Planada (1961) 7.5' quadrangles. Blake (p. 15) referred to Burns' creek, and Wheeler (1879, p. 168) referred to Burns's Creek.

Burns' Creek: see **Quartzburg**, under **Hornitos** [MARIPOSA].

Burns' Diggings: see **Quartzburg**, under **Hornitos** [MARIPOSA].

Burns' Ranch: see **Quartzburg**, under **Hornitos** [MARIPOSA].

Burnt Corral [TUOLUMNE]: *locality,* 6 miles southwest of Liberty Hill (lat. 38°19'10" N, long. 120°11'25" W; sec. 3, T 5 N, R 16 E). Named on Big Meadow (1956) 15' quadrangle.

Burnt Corral Spring [TUOLUMNE]: *spring,* 5.5 miles southwest of Liberty Hill (lat. 38°19'05" N, long. 120°10'35" W; sec. 2, T 5 N, R 16 E); the spring is less than 1 mile east of the site of Burnt Corral. Named on Boards Crossing (1979) 7.5' quadrangle.

Burnt Flat [NEVADA]: *area,* 6.5 miles northwest of Donner Pass (lat. 39°23'25" N, long. 120°23'45" W; near SW cor. sec. 27, T 18 N, R 14 E). Named on Webber Peak (1981) 7.5' quadrangle.

Burnt Flat [PLACER]: *area,* 1.25 miles east-northeast of Colfax (lat. 39°06'15" N, long. 120°55'50" W; near SE cor. sec. 35, T 15 N, R 9 E). Named on Colfax (1949) 7.5' quadrangle.

Burnt Shanty Creek [EL DORADO]: *stream,* flows 3 miles to South Fork American River nearly 5 miles west of Coloma (lat. 38°47'45" N, long. 120°58'45" W; sec. 21, T 11 N, R 9 E). Named on Coloma (1949) 7.5' quadrangle. Called Widow Creek on Placerville (1893) 30' quadrangle.

Burro Lake [MADERA]: *lake,* 400 feet long, 7 miles south-southeast of Merced Peak (lat. 37°31'55" N, long. 119°21'50" W; sec. 5, T 5 S, R 24 E); the lake is west-northwest of Jackass Lakes. Named on Merced Peak (1953) 15' quadrangle.

Burro Pass [TUOLUMNE]: *pass,* 0.5 mile west-southwest of Matterhorn Peak (lat. 38°05'20" N, long. 119°23'35" W). Named on Matterhorn Peak (1956) 15' quadrangle.

Burson [CALAVERAS]: *locality,* 3.25 miles west of Valley Springs (lat. 38°11' N, long. 120°53'20" W; on W line sec. 21, T 4 N, R 10 E). Named on Wallace (1962) 7.5' quadrangle. Jackson (1902) 30' quadrangle shows Burson along San Joaquin and Sierra Nevada Railroad. Postal authorities established Burson post office in 1884 (Frickstad, p. 14). The name commemorates David S. Burson, a railroad man (Gudde, 1969, p. 43).

Burst Rock [TUOLUMNE]: *relief feature,* 6.5 miles east of Pinecrest (lat. 38°12'05" N, long. 119°52'25" W; sec. 15, T 4 N, R 19 E). Named on Pinecrest (1956) 15' quadrangle. The feature also is known as Birth Rock because an emigrant mother gave birth there (Hoover, Rensch, and Rensch, p. 566).

Burton Creek [PLACER]: *stream,* flows 4 miles to Lake Tahoe 6.5 miles southwest of Kings Beach (lat. 39°10'55" N, long. 120°07'20" W; sec. 5, T 15 N, R 17 E). Named on Kings Beach (1955) and Tahoe City (1955) 7.5' quadrangles. The name commemorates Captain Homer D. Burton, who homesteaded in the region in 1871 (Lekisch, p. 12).

Butcher Corral [EL DORADO]: *locality,* 9.5 miles north-northwest of Pollock Pines (lat. 38°53'35" N, long. 120°37'15" W; sec. 15, T 12 N, R 12 E). Named on Devil Peak (1950) 7.5' quadrangle.

Butcher Flat [PLACER]: *area,* 6.5 miles south-southwest of Duncan Peak (lat. 39°03'50" N, long. 120°32'30" W; near E line sec. 17, T 14 N, R 13 E). Named on Greek Store (1952) 7.5' quadrangle.

Butcher Knife Pocket [TUOLUMNE]: *canyon,* drained by a stream that flows less than 1 mile to Don Pedro Reservoir 1.25 miles north-northwest of Don Pedro Camp (lat. 37°44' N, long. 120°24'35" W; sec. 27, T 2 S, R 14 E). Named on La Grange (1962) 7.5' quadrangle.

Butcher Knife Ridge [TUOLUMNE]: *ridge,* south- to west-trending, 1.25 miles long, 6 miles south of Duckwall Mountain (lat. 37°

53' N, long. 120°06'35" W). Named on Duckwall Mountain (1948) 7.5' quadrangle.

Butcher Ranch [PLACER]: *locality,* 11.5 miles east-northeast of Auburn (lat. 38°57'10" N, long. 120°57'15" W). Named on Greenwood (1949) 7.5' quadrangle. Called Butchers on Placerville (1893) 30' quadrangle. Postal authorities established Butcher Ranch post office in 1871 and discontinued it in 1935 (Frickstad, p. 119). They established McKeon post office 5.5 miles northeast of Butcher Ranch post office (SW quarter sec. 6, T 13 N, R 10 E) in 1920 and discontinued it in 1953 (Salley, p. 136).

Butcher Ranch Creek [SIERRA]: *stream,* flows 3.5 miles to Pauley Creek 6.25 miles northwest of Sierra City (lat. 39°37'25" N, long. 120°43'25" W; near S line sec. 3, T 20 N, R 11 E). Named on Gold Lake (1981) and Sierra City (1981) 7.5' quadrangles.

Butcher Ranch Meadow [SIERRA]: *area,* 5 miles northwest of Sierra City (lat. 39°37'50" N, long. 120°41'25" W; near S line sec. 1, T 20 N, R 11 E); the place is along Butcher Ranch Creek. Named on Sierra City (1981) 7.5' quadrangle.

Butchers: see **Butcher Ranch** [PLACER].

Butler Mountain [MARIPOSA]: *ridge,* south-trending, 2.5 miles long, 9.5 miles southeast of Mariposa (lat. 37°23'15" N, long. 119° 50'45" W). Named on Horsecamp Mountain (1947) and Stumpfield Mountain (1947) 7.5' quadrangles.

Butte Canyon [AMADOR]: *canyon,* 1.25 miles long, opens into the canyon of Mokelumne River nearly 2 miles south of Jackson Butte (lat. 38°18'45" N, long. 120°43'10" W; sec. 1, T 5 N, R 11 E). Named on Mokelumne Hill (1948) 7.5' quadrangle.

Butte City [AMADOR]: *locality,* 1.25 miles southwest of Jackson Butte (lat. 38°19'35" N, long. 120°44'05" W; sec. 35, T 6 N, R 11 E); the site is near the head of Butte Canyon. Ruins of the place are named on Mokelumne Hill (1948) 7.5' quadrangle. Postal authorities established Butte City post office in 1857 and discontinued it in 1858 (Frickstad, p. 5). Gudde (1975, p. 54) listed the possible early names "Boomville," "Boonville," "Greasertown," and "Greaserville" for the place.

Butte Creek [EL DORADO]: *stream,* flows 4 miles to North Fork Cosumnes River 6.25 miles south-southeast of Camino (lat. 38°39'10" N, long. 120°37'40" W; near NW cor. sec. 11, T 9 N, R 12 E). Named on Camino (1952) and Sly Park (1952) 7.5' quadrangles.

Butte Mountain: see **Jackson Butte** [AMADOR].

Buttermilk Bend [NEVADA]: *bend,* 1.25 miles southwest of French Corral along South Yuba River (lat. 39°17'40" N, long. 121°10'50" W; sec. 34, T 17 N, R 7 E). Named on French Corral (1948) 7.5' quadrangle.

Buttes Area Camp [NEVADA]: *locality,* 9 miles west-northwest of Donner Pass on the south shore of Lake Sterling (lat. 39°21'05" N, long. 120°29'30" W; at W line sec. 11, T 17 N, R 13 E). Named on Soda Springs (1955) 7.5' quadrangle.

Buttes Flat: see **Sierra City** [SIERRA].

Buttonwillow Slough [MADERA]: *water feature,* 21 miles west-southwest of Madera, and east of San Joaquin River. Named on Firebaugh (1956) and Poso Farm (1962) 7.5' quadrangles.

Buttresses: see **The Buttresses** [MADERA].

Buzzard Canyon [MADERA]: *canyon,* drained by a stream that flows 2 miles to Fresno River 5 miles south-southeast of Knowles (lat. 37°09' N, long. 119°51'20" W; sec. 13, T 9 S, R 19 E). Named on Knowles (1962) 7.5' quadrangle.

Buzzard Point [TUOLUMNE]: *peak,* 0.25 mile southwest of Don Pedro Camp (lat. 37°42'50" N, long. 120°24'35" W; near E line sec. 34, T 2 S, R 14 E). Named on La Grange (1962) 7.5' quadrangle.

Buzzard Roost [NEVADA]: *ridge,* west-south-west-trending, 0.5 long, 6.5 miles northwest of Donner Pass (lat. 39°22'20" N, long. 120°25'35" W; at N line sec. 5, T 17 N, R 14 E). Named on Soda Springs (1955) 7.5' quadrangle.

Buzzard Roost Lake [NEVADA]: *lake,* 850 feet long, 6.25 miles northwest of Donner Pass (lat. 39°22'45" N, long. 120°24'25" W; sec. 33, T 18 N, R 14 E); the lake is 1.25 miles east-northeast of Buzzard Roost. Named on Webber Peak (1981) 7.5' quadrangle.

Byrds Valley [PLACER]: *area,* 0.5 mile west of Michigan Bluff (lat. 39°02'25" N, long. 120°44'50" W; sec. 21, T 14 N, R 11 E). Named on Michigan Bluff (1952) 7.5' quadrangle. Whitney's (1873) map has the name for an inhabited place.

Byrnes Ferry: see **O'Byrnes Ferry** [CALAVERAS].

— C —

Cabbage Patch [CALAVERAS]: *area,* 3.25 miles west-southwest of Tamarack (lat. 38°24'55" N, long. 120°07'55" W; sec. 32, T 7 N, R 17 E). Named on Calaveras Dome (1979) 7.5' quadrangle.

Cabin Creek [EL DORADO]: *stream,* flows 1.5 miles to Oat Creek 6.5 miles east of Caldor (lat. 38°35'45" N, long. 120°18'50" W; near SE cor. sec. 28, T 9 N, R 15 E). Named on Peddler Hill (1951) 7.5' quadrangle.

Cabin Creek [PLACER]: *stream,* flows nearly 2 miles to Truckee River 9.5 miles west of Martis Peak (lat. 39°16'40" N, long. 120° 12'20" W; sec. 33, T 17 N, R 16 E). Named on Truckee (1955) 7.5' quadrangle. California Division of Highways' (1934) map shows

a place called Headland located along Southern Pacific Railroad about 0.5 mile north of the mouth of present Cabin Creek (at N line sec. 33, T 17 N, R 16 E).

Cabin Lake [MADERA]: *lake,* 900 feet long, 5.5 miles northwest of Devils Postpile (lat. 37°41'05" N, long. 119°09'05" W). Named on Devils Postpile (1953) 15' quadrangle. David Nidever built a log cabin by the lake in the early 1900's (Smith, p. 61).

Cable Point [EL DORADO]: *peak,* 5.5 miles west-northwest of Pollock Pines (lat. 38°47'30" N, long. 120°40'35" W; near NE cor. sec. 19, T 11 N, R 12 E). Altitude 2879 feet. Named on Slate Mountain (1950) 7.5' quadrangle.

Cagwin Lake [EL DORADO]: *lake,* 600 feet long, 4 miles west-northwest of Echo Summit (lat. 38°50'35" N, long. 120°05'40" W; sec. 34, T 12 N, R 17 E). Named on Echo Lake (1955) 7.5' quadrangle. The name commemorates Hamden El Dorado Cagwin, who settled at Lower Echo Lake in 1896 (Lekisch, p. 12).

Cain: see **Tommy Cain Ravine** [PLACER].

Cairns: see **Lincoln** [PLACER].

Calaveras Dome [CALAVERAS]: *relief feature,* 8.5 miles west-northwest of Tamarack on the south side of North Fork Mokelumne River (lat. 38°29'10" N, long. 120°13'35" W; on E line sec. 5, T 7 N, R 16 E). Named on Calaveras Dome (1979) 7.5' quadrangle.

Calaveras Reservoir [CALAVERAS]: *lake,* behind a dam on North Fork Calaveras River 7.5 miles west of Blue Mountain (lat. 38°19'30" N, long. 120°29'35" W; near S line sec. 36, T 6 N, R 13 E). Named on Fort Mountain (1979) 7.5' quadrangle. United States Board on Geographic Names (1990, p. 10) approved the name "Redhawk Lake" for the feature, and rejected the names "Calaveras Reservoir," "Bingham Lake," and "McCarty Reservoir."

Calaveras River [CALAVERAS]: *stream,* formed by the confluence of North Fork and South Fork in New Hogan Reservoir, flows 50 miles to San Joaquin River 4.25 miles west of downtown Stockton (lat. 37°58' N, long. 121°22' W). Named on Jenny Lind (1962), Linden (1968), Lodi South (1968), San Andreas (1962), Stockton West (1952), Valley Springs (1962), Valley Springs SW (1962) and Waterloo (1968) 7.5' quadrangles. Alfrez Gabriel Moraga discovered the stream in 1806 and named it Rio de la Pasion; later Moraga renamed the river Rio de las Calaveras for the discovery near the stream of many skulls left from an Indian battle—*calaveras* means "skulls" in Spanish (Hanna, p. 49-50. North Fork is 25 miles long and is named on Fort Mountain (1979), Mokelumne Hill (1948), Rail Road Flat (1948), and San Andreas (1962) 7.5' quadrangles. United States Board on Geographic Names (1980a, p. 3) rejected the name

"Calaveras River" for North Fork. South Fork, formed by the confluence of San Domingo Creek and Cherokee Creek, is 8 miles long; it is named on Salt Spring Valley (1962) and San Andreas (1962) 7.5' quadrangles.

Calaveras Valley [CALAVERAS]: *valley,* 1.25 miles south-southwest of Railroad Flat (present Rail Road Flat) (lat. 38°19'30" N, long. 120°31'15" W); the valley is along North Fork Calaveras River. Named on Jackson (1902) 30' quadrangle.

Calaveritas [CALAVERAS]: *village,* 4.5 miles southeast of San Andreas (lat. 38°09'25" N, long. 120°36'35" W; near W line sec. 36, T 4 N, R 12 E); the place is along Calaveritas Creek. Named on Calaveritas (1962) 7.5' quadrangle. The community was called Upper Calaveritas in the early days to distinguish it from Lower Calaveritas, which was located about 3.5 miles farther west and now has vanished (Gudde, 1975, p. 55-56).

Calaveritas Creek [CALAVERAS]: *stream,* formed by the confluence of McKinney Creek and O'Neil Creek, flows 10 miles to South Fork Calaveras River 2.5 miles south of San Andreas (lat. 38°09'35" N, long. 120°40'25" W; sec. 32, T 4 N, R 12 E); the stream goes past Calaveritas. Named on Calaveritas (1962) and San Andreas (1962) 7.5' quadrangles.

Caldor [EL DORADO]: *locality,* 8.5 miles west-southwest of Leek Spring Hill (lat. 38°36'20" N, long. 120°25'50" W; sec. 28, T 9 N, R 14 E). Named on Caldor (1951) 7.5' quadrangle

Caldwell's Upper Store: see **Nevada City** [NEVADA].

Calf Bar: see **American River** [EL DORADO-PLACER].

Cal-Ida [SIERRA]: *locality,* 7 miles west of Goodyears Bar (lat. 39° 31'35" N, long. 121°00'55" W; sec. 7, T 19 N, R 9 E). Named on Strawberry Valley (1948) 7.5' quadrangle.

Califa [MADERA]: *locality,* 1 mile northwest of Fairmead along Southern Pacific Railroad (lat. 37°05'05" N, long. 120°12'25" W; near S line sec. 3, T 10 S, R 16 E). Named on Berenda (1918) 7.5' quadrangle. Postal authorities established Califa post office in 1912 and discontinued it in 1915 (Frickstad, p. 85).

California Creek [MADERA]: *stream,* flows 3 miles to Nelder Creek 3.5 miles north-northeast of Yosemite Forks (lat. 37°24'40" N, long. 119°35'45" W; at W line sec. 17, T 6 S, R 22 E). Named on Bass Lake (1953) 15' quadrangle.

California Falls [TUOLUMNE]: *waterfall,* 10 miles west of Tioga Pass on Tuolumne River (lat. 37°55' N, long. 119°26'20" W). Named on Tuolumne Meadows (1956) 15' quadrangle.

California Falls: see **LeConte Falls** [TUOLUMNE].

California Range: see "Regional setting."

Calpine [SIERRA]: *village,* 6.5 miles northwest of Sierraville (lat. 39°39'55" N, long.

120°26'20" W; on S line sec. 17, T 21 N, R 14 E). Named on Calpine (1981) 7.5' quadrangle. Postal authorities established Calpine post office in 1921 and discontinued it in 1942 (Frickstad, p. 184). The place, which began in 1919 in connection with a lumber mill, first was called McAlpine; postal authorities rejected this name, but accepted the abbreviated form "Calpine" (Gudde, 1949, p. 52). California Division of Highways' (1934) map shows a place called Davis Jct. located along Western Pacific Railroad nearly 2 miles north of Calpine (sec. 8, T 21 N, R 14 E).

Calpine Reservoir [SIERRA]: *lake,* behind a dam on Fletcher Creek 1.25 miles west of Calpine (lat. 39°39'50" N, long. 120°27'40" W; near SW cor. sec. 18, T 21 N, R 14 E). Named on Calpine (1981) 7.5' quadrangle.

Calvada [SIERRA]: *locality,* 7.5 miles southeast of Crystal Peak along Southern Pacific Railroad (lat. 39°27'45" N, long. 120°00'15" W; near S line sec. 31, T 19 N, R 18 E). Named on Truckee (1940) 30' quadrangle.

Camanche [CALAVERAS]: *village,* 6 miles west-northwest of Valley Springs (lat. 38°12'45" N, long. 120°56' W; sec. 12, T 4 N, R 9 E); the place is along Camanche Creek. Named on Wallace (1962) 7.5' quadrangle. Water of Camanche Reservoir now covers the site. Postal authorities established Clay's Bar post office in 1861, changed the name to Camanche in 1864, discontinued it in 1886, reestablished it in 1887, and discontinued it in 1962; the name "Clay's Bar" was for the discoverer of gold at the place (Salley, p. 33, 45). Camanche first was called Limerick (Gudde, 1975, p. 56), but a miner renamed the place in 1849 for his hometown in Iowa (Cook, F.S., p. 3).

Camanche Creek [CALAVERAS]: *stream,* flows 1.5 miles to Camanche Reservoir 5 miles west of Valley Springs (lat. 38°12' N, long. 120°54'50" W; sec. 18, T 4 N, R 10 E); the stream once flowed past Camanche to Mokelumne River. Named on Wallace (1962) 7.5' quadrangle.

Camanche Reservoir [AMADOR]: *lake,* extends up Mokelumne River on Amador-Calaveras county line from a dam in San Joaquin County. Named on Clements (1968), Ione (1962), Jackson (1962), Valley Springs (1962), and Wallace (1962) 7.5' quadrangles. The name is from the village of Camanche, which was in Calaveras County; water of the lake now covers the site of the village. A miner named the village in 1849 for his hometown in Iowa (Cook, F.S., p. 3).

Camanche Reservoir [CALAVERAS]: *lake,* extends up Mokelumne River along Calaveras-Amador county line from a dam located in San Joaquin County 4.25 miles northeast of Clements (lat. 38°13'30" N, long. 121°01'20" W; sec. 6, T 4 N, R 9 E). Named on Clements (1968), Jackson (1962), Valley

Springs (1962), and Wallace (1962) 7.5' quadrangles. The name is from the village of Camanche; water of the reservoir now covers the site of the village.

Camel Hump [NEVADA]: *peak,* 8 miles northeast of present Chicago Park (lat. 39°13' N, long. 120°51' W). Named on Colfax (1898) 30' quadrangle. Dutch Flat (1950) 7.5' quadrangle shows Camels Hump L.O. [Lookout] at the place.

Camels Hump [PLACER]: *peak,* 4 miles south-southeast of Colfax at the south end of Gillis Hill (lat. 39°03'05" N, long. 120°54'45" W; on E line sec. 24, T 14 N, R 9 E). Altitude 2131 feet. Named on Colfax (1949) 7.5' quadrangle.

Camiaca Peak [TUOLUMNE]: *peak,* 4 miles southeast of Matterhorn Peak on Tuolumne-Mono county line (lat. 38°03'35" N, long. 119° 19'25" W). Altitude 11,739 feet. Named on Matterhorn Peak (1956) 15' quadrangle.

Caminettis: see **Silver Lake** [AMADOR].

Camino [EL DORADO]: *town,* 7 miles east of Placerville (lat. 38°44'20" N, long. 120°40'25" W; sec. 8, T 10 N, R 12 E). Named on Camino (1952) 7.5' quadrangle. Postal authorities established Camino post office in 1904; a travelers stop called Seven Mile House was at the site in the early days (Salley, p. 33).

Camino Campground [MADERA]: *locality,* 5.5 miles north of Shuteye Peak (lat. 37°25'55" N, long. 119°25'55" W; near SE cor. sec. 3, T 6 S, R 23 E); the place is along Camino Creek. Named on Shuteye Peak (1953) 15' quadrangle.

Camino Creek [MADERA]: *stream,* flows about 3 miles to Beasore Creek 5.25 miles north of Shuteye Peak (lat. 37°25'30" N, long. 119°24'25" W; sec. 12, T 6 S, R 23 E). Named on Shuteye Peak (1953) 15' quadrangle.

Camino Reservoir [EL DORADO]: *lake,* behind a dam on Silver Creek 5.25 miles north-northeast of Pollock Pines (lat. 38°49'40" N, long. 120°32'10" W; sec. 4, T 11 N, R 13 E). Named on Pollock Pines (1950, photorevised 1973) 7.5' quadrangle.

Camp A.E. Wood: see **Camp Hoyle** [MARIPOSA].

Campana [EL DORADO]: *locality,* 9 miles north-northeast of Pollock Pines (lat. 38°53'05" N, long. 120°31'10" W; sec. 16, T 12 N, R 13 E). Named on Devil Peak (1950) 7.5' quadrangle.

Camp Beal Military Reservation: see **Beal Air Force Base** [NEVADA].

Campbell Creek [CALAVERAS]: *stream,* flows 1.5 miles to Black Creek (1) 2 miles east-southeast of Copperopolis (lat. 37°58'25" N, long. 120°36'20" W; near N line sec. 1, T 1 N, R 12 E). Named on Melones Dam (1962) 7.5' quadrangle.

Campbell Creek [PLACER]: *stream,* flows 2 miles to Bear River 2.25 miles west-south-west of Colfax (lat. 39°05'05" N, long. 120°

59'15" W; near NE cor. sec. 8, T 14 N, R 9 E). Named on Colfax (1949) 7.5' quadrangle.

Campbell Gulch [SIERRA]: *canyon,* drained by a stream that heads in Sierra County and flows 3 miles to Willow Creek 0.5 mile north-north-west of Camptonville in Yuba County (lat. 39°27'40" N, long. 121°03'10" W; sec. 2, T 18 N, R 8 E). Named on Camptonville (1948) 7.5' quadrangle.

Campbell Hot Springs [SIERRA]: *locality,* 1.5 miles southeast of Sierraville (lat. 39°34'30" N, long. 120°20'50" W; near NE cor. sec. 19, T 20 N, R 15 E). Named on Sierraville (1981) 7.5' quadrangle. Called Sulphur Spring on Sierraville (1894) 30' quadrangle. Eight thermal springs at the site are the basis of a resort started in the 1880's (Waring, G.A., p. 129).

Campbell Sheep Camp [SIERRA]: *locality,* 7.25 miles north of Sierra City (lat. 39°40'05" N, long. 120°37' W; sec. 22, T 21 N, R 12 E). Named on Sierra City (1955) 15' quadrangle.

Campbell's Hot Springs: see **Brockway** [PLACER].

Camp Clavey [TUOLUMNE]: *locality,* 6.25 miles east-southeast of Long Barn (lat. 38°04'15" N, long. 120°01'30" W; sec. 32, T 3 N, R 18 E); the place is along a tributary to Clavey River. Named on Hull Creek (1979) 7.5' quadrangle.

Camp Cody [EL DORADO]: *locality,* 6 miles south of Pyramid Peak (lat. 38°45'30" N, long. 120°08'30" W; sec. 1, T 10 N, R 16 E); the place is at Cody Lake. Named on Pyramid Peak (1955) 7.5' quadrangle.

Camp Connell [CALAVERAS]: *settlement,* 5 miles east-southeast of Blue Mountain (lat. 38°18'45" N, long. 120°16'40" W; near W line sec. 1, T 5 N, R 15 E). Named on Dorrington (1979) 7.5' quadrangle. Postal authorities established Camp Connell post office in 1934; the name is for John F. Connell, first postmaster and owner of a vacation resort at the place (Salley, p. 34).

Camp Contreras: see **Pioneer** [AMADOR].

Camp Creek [AMADOR]: *stream,* flows 3 miles to North Fork Mokelumne River 5.5 miles south-southeast of Hams Station (lat. 38°27'55" N, long. 120°21'20" W; near NE cor. sec. 18, T 7 N, R 15 E). Named on Garnet Hill (1979) 7.5' quadrangle.

Camp Creek [EL DORADO]: *stream,* formed by the confluence of Middle Fork and North Fork, flows 29 miles to North Fork Cosumnes River 5.5 miles south of Camino (lat. 38°39'20" N, long. 120°39'55" W; near SW cor. sec. 4, T 9 N, R 12 E). Named on Camino (1952), Leek Spring Hill (1951), Sly Park (1952), and Stump Spring (1951) 7.5' quadrangles. A group of Mormons on the way across the Sierra Nevada to Salt Lake City in 1848 camped by the stream and named it (Ricketts, 1983, p. 19). Middle Fork is 1 mile long and North Fork is 1.25 miles long; both forks are named on Leek Spring Hill (1951)

7.5' quadrangle. South Fork enters the main creek from the southeast less than 1 mile downstream from the junction of North Fork and Middle Fork; it is 1 mile long and is named on Leek Spring Hill (1951) 7.5' quadrangle.

Camp Creek [TUOLUMNE]: *stream,* flows about 2 miles to Piute Creek (2) 5.5 miles southwest of Matterhorn Peak (lat. 38°02'50" N, long. 119°27'45" W). Named on Matterhorn Peak (1956) 15' quadrangle.

Camp Curry [MARIPOSA]: *locality,* 1 mile southeast of Yosemite Village in Yosemite Valley (lat. 37°44'15" N, long. 119°34'15" W). Named on Yosemite (1956) 15' quadrangle. Postal authorities established Camp Curry post office in 1909 and changed the name to Curry Village in 1970; David A. Curry and his wife founded the place in 1899 (Salley, p. 34).

Camp Curry [TUOLUMNE]: *locality,* 4 miles south-southwest of Liberty Hill near Beaver Creek (lat. 38°18'50" N, long. 120° 08' W). Named on Boards Crossing (1979) 7.5' quadrangle.

Camp Earnest [TUOLUMNE]: *settlement,* nearly 2 miles south of Twain Harte (lat. 38°00'50" N, long. 120°13'30" W; sec. 21, T 2 N, R 16 E). Named on Long Barn (1956) 15' quadrangle.

Camp 8 [TUOLUMNE]: *locality,* 5.5 miles east-southeast of Twain Harte (lat. 38°00'10" N, long. 120°08' W; sec. 29, T 2 N, R 17 E). Site named on Twain Harte (1979) 7.5' quadrangle.

Camp Eldorado: see **Camp Silverado** [AMADOR].

Camper Flat [EL DORADO]: *locality,* 2 miles west-southwest of Phipps Peak along Rubicon River in Rockbound Valley (lat. 38°56'30" N, long. 120°11' W; near SW cor. sec. 26, T 13 N, R 16 E). Named on Rockbound Valley (1955) 7.5' quadrangle.

Camp Far West Reservoir [PLACER]: *lake,* behind a dam on Bear River [NEVADA-PLACER] 5.5 miles north-northeast of Sheridan on Placer-Yuba county line (lat. 39°03' N, long. 121°18'55" W; sec. 21, T 14 N, R 6 E); the lake is 1.5 miles east-northeast of the site of Camp Far West. Named on Wheatland (1949) 15' quadrangle. Camp Far West (1949, photorevised 1973) 7.5' quadrangle shows a larger lake formed by a high dam that backs up water into Nevada County.

Camp 45 [TUOLUMNE]: *locality,* 5.5 miles east of Duckwall Mountain (lat. 37°57'35" N, long. 120°01'15" W; sec. 8, T 1 N, R 18 E). Named on Duckwall Mountain (1948) 7.5' quadrangle.

Camp 44 [TUOLUMNE]: *locality,* 6.5 miles northwest of Mather (lat. 37°56'45" N, long. 119°56'45" W; sec. 13, T 1 N, R 18 E). Named on Lake Eleanor (1956) 15' quadrangle.

Camp 43 [TUOLUMNE]: *locality,* 8.5 miles northwest of Mather along Crane Creek (2)

(lat. 37°58'30" N, long. 119°57'30" W; near E line sec. 2, T 1 N, R 18 E). Named on Lake Eleanor (1956) 15' quadrangle.

Camp Forward [EL DORADO]: *locality,* 12 miles north-northwest of Pollock Pines (lat. 38°55'05" N, long. 120°41'25" W; at W line sec. 6, T 12 N, R 12 E). Named on Tunnel Hill (1950) 7.5' quadrangle.

Camp Gleason [SIERRA]: *locality,* 4 miles north-northwest of Alleghany (lat. 39°29'40" N, long. 120°54'15" W; near SW cor. sec. 19, T 19 N, R 10 E). Named on Pike (1949) 7.5' quadrangle.

Camp Harvey West [EL DORADO]: *locality,* 3.5 miles northwest of Echo Summit at the west end of Upper Echo Lake (lat. 38°50'45" N, long. 120°04'50" W; at W line sec. 35, T 12 N, R 17 E). Named on Echo Lake (1955) 7.5' quadrangle. The name commemorates Harvey West, a lumberman who gave money to Boy Scouts for a camp that was dedicated in 1950 (Lekisch, p. 13).

Camp High Sierra [TUOLUMNE]: *locality,* nearly 4 miles south-southwest of Strawberry along North Fork Tuolumne River (lat. 38°09'05" N, long. 120°02'45" W; near NW cor. sec. 6, T 3 N, R 18 E). Named on Strawberry (1979) 7.5' quadrangle.

Camp Hoyle [MARIPOSA]: *locality,* 1 mile west-northwest of Wawona (lat. 37°32'35" N, long. 119°40'20" W; sec. 32, T 4 S, R 21 E). Named on Yosemite (1909) 30' quadrangle. Camp A.E. Wood, an army encampment that was the hub of the army administration of Yosemite National Park, occupied the site from 1891 until 1905; the name "Wood" was for Captain Abram Epperson Wood, first acting superintendent of the park (Sargent, Shirley, 1961, p. 16). Bert Hoyle started Camp Hoyle at the site in 1922 to provide camping facilities for touring families; the place later became a public campground operated by the National Park Service (Sargent, Shirley, 1961, p. 36).

Camp Ida Spring [TUOLUMNE]: *spring,* 3.5 miles east of Long Barn on Dodge Ridge (lat. 38°06'15" N, long. 120°04' W; near E line sec. 23, T 3 N, R 17 E). Named on Hull Creek (1979) 7.5' quadrangle.

Camp Lake [TUOLUMNE]: *lake,* 1100 feet long, 6.5 miles east-southeast of Pinecrest (lat. 38°10' N, long. 119°52'45" W; on N line sec. 34, T 4 N, R 19 E). Named on Pinecrest (1979) 7.5' quadrangle.

Camp Lundeen [NEVADA]: *locality,* 5.25 miles east-southeast of Graniteville along Lindsey Creek (lat. 39°24'40" N, long. 120°38'50" W; sec. 20, T 18 N, R 12 E). Named on Graniteville (1982) 7.5' quadrangle.

Camp MacBride [TUOLUMNE]: *locality,* 1.5 miles east-northeast of Pinecrest on the east shore of Pinecrest Lake (lat. 38°12' N, long. 119°58'15" W; sec. 14, T 4 N, R 18 E). Named on Pinecrest (1956) 15' quadrangle.

Camp Meeting Creek [MARIPOSA]: *stream,* flows 4 miles to DeLong Creek 9 miles east of Mariposa (lat. 37°28'40" N, long. 119°48'15" W; sec. 20, T 5 S, R 20 E). Named on Buckingham Mountain (1947) and Stumpfield Mountain (1947) 7.5' quadrangles.

Camp Meeting Gulch [TUOLUMNE]: *canyon,* 1.5 miles long, 5.25 miles south of Sonora along Algerine Creek (lat. 37°54'30" N, long. 120°22' W; sec. 30, T 1 N, R 15 E). Named on Standard (1948) 7.5' quadrangle.

Camp Minkalo [AMADOR]: *locality,* 8 miles north of Mokelumne Peak on the east side of Silver Lake (lat. 38°39'25" N, long. 120° 06'35" W; sec. 4, T 9 N, R 17 E). Named on Caples Lake (1979) 7.5' quadrangle.

Camp Niagara [TUOLUMNE]: *locality,* 9 miles southeast of Long Barn (lat. 38°00'25" N, long. 120°00'15" W); the place is near Niagara Creek (1). Named on Hull Creek (1979) 7.5' quadrangle.

Camp 19 [NEVADA]: *locality,* 5 miles northwest of Yuba Gap (lat. 39°22'05" N, long. 120°40'50" W; at E line sec. 1, T 17 N, R 11 E). Named on Blue Canyon (1955) 7.5' quadrangle.

Campoodle Creek [TUOLUMNE]: *stream,* flows 4.5 miles to Smoothwire Creek 8 miles south-southeast of Liberty Hill (lat. 38° 15'30" N, long. 120°02' W; sec. 30, T 5 N, R 18 E). Named on Liberty Hill (1979) 7.5' quadrangle. Called Compoodle Creek on Big Meadow (1956) 15' quadrangle, but United States Board on Geographic Names (1980a, p. 3) rejected this name for the stream.

Campo Salvador: see **Chinese Camp** [TUOLUMNE].

Camp Santa Teresita [MADERA]: *locality,* 3.5 miles southeast of Yosemite Forks at the northwest end of Bass Lake (1) (lat. 37°19'50" N, long 119°34'55" W; near SW cor. sec. 9, T 7 S, R 22 E). Named on Bass Lake (1953) 15' quadrangle.

Campo Seco [CALAVERAS]: *village,* nearly 3 miles north-northwest of Valley Springs along a stream that reaches Mokelumne River at Oregon Bar (lat. 38°13'40" N, long. 120°51'10" W; on E line sec. 3, T 4 N, R 10 E). Named on Valley Springs (1962) 7.5' quadrangle. Postal authorities established Campo Seco post office in 1854 (Frickstad, p. 14). Mexican miners settled at the place in the summer of 1849 to work placer deposits in Oregon Gulch, which extended through the community; the village got its present name after high water prevented work on the bars in the gulch and mining activity had to move to higher ground—*campo seco* indicates "dry camp" in Spanish (Hanna, p. 53).

Campo Seco [TUOLUMNE]: *locality,* 3.5 miles south-southwest of Sonora (lat. 37°56'20" N, long. 120°24'55" W; sec. 15, T 1 N, R 14 E). Named on Sonora (1948) 7.5' quadrangle. Postal authorities established Camp Seco post

office at the place in 1852 and discontinued it in 1853 (Salley, p. 35).

Camp O' pera: see **Lancha Plana**[AMADOR].

Camp Pahatsi [NEVADA]: *locality,* 5 miles west of Donner Pass (lat. 39°19'10" N, long. 120°24'55" W; near SW cor. sec. 21, T 17 N, R 14 E). Named on Soda Springs (1955) 7.5' quadrangle.

Camp Pardee [CALAVERAS]: *locality,* 4 miles north of Valley Springs (lat. 38°14'55" N, long. 120°50'40" W; sec. 35, T 5 N, R 10 E); the place is near Pardee Reservoir. Named on Valley Springs (1962) 7.5' quadrangle.

Camp Pendola [TUOLUMNE]: *locality,* nearly 4 miles north of Crandall Peak (lat. 38°12'55" N, long. 120°08'50" W; sec. 7, T 4 N, R 17 E); the place is near Soap Creek Pass. Named on Crandall Peak (1979) 7.5' quadrangle. Called Soap Cr. Pass Camp on Long Barn (1956) 15' quadrangle.

Camp Richardson [EL DORADO]: *village,* 4 miles northeast of Mount Tallac near Lake Tahoe (lat. 38°56'05" N, long. 120°02'20" W; at W line sec. 6, T 12 N, R 18 E). Named on Emerald Bay (1955) 7.5' quadrangle. Postal authorities established Camp Richardson post office in 1927, discontinued it in 1964, reestablished it in 1965, and discontinued it in 1973; the name was for Alonzo L. Richardson, first postmaster (Salley, p. 35), who had a resort at the place (Lekisch, p. 14).

Camp Seco: see **Campo Seco** [TUOLUMNE].

Camp Spirito: see **Bummerville** [CALAVERAS].

Camp Sacramento [EL DORADO]: *locality,* 4.5 miles west of Echo Summit along South Fork American River (lat. 38°48'10" N, long. 120°06'55" W; near W line sec. 16, T 11 N, R 17 E). Named on Echo Lake (1955) 7.5' quadrangle. Postal authorities established Camp Sacramento post office in 1929 and discontinued it in 1940 (Frickstad, p. 25).

Camp Seven [EL DORADO]: *locality,* 5 miles north of Pollock Pines (lat. 38°49'55" N, long. 120°34'20" W; sec. 6, T 11 N, R 13 E). Named on Pollock Pines (1950) 7.5' quadrangle. The place was a logging camp of Michigan California Lumber Company (Beverly Cola, personal communication, 1985).

Camp Silverado [AMADOR]: *locality,* 9 miles north of Mokelumne Peak (lat. 38°40' N, long. 120°06'20" W; near S line sec. 33, T 10 N, R 17 E); the place is east of Silver Lake. Named on Caples Lake (1979) 7.5' quadrangle. Called Camp Eldorado on Silver Lake (1956) 15' quadrangle.

Camp Spaulding [NEVADA]: *locality,* 1 mile west of Yuba Gap (lat. 39°19'05" N, long. 120°38'15" W; near S line sec. 21, T 17 N, R 12 E); the place is 0.5 mile south of Lake Spaulding. Named on Blue Canyon (1955) 7.5' quadrangle. Postal authorities established Ohm post office in 1913 at a power-plant construction camp called Spaulding (SW quarter sec. 21, T 17 N, R 12 E) and discontinued it the same year—the name "Ohm" is from a technical term for a unit of electrical resistance (Salley, p. 160).

Camp Springs [EL DORADO]: *locality,* 6.5 miles northwest of Leek Spring Hill (lat. 38°41'40" N, long. 120°21'30" W); the place is north of Camp Creek. Named on Pyramid Peak (1896) 30' quadrangle.

Camp Tamarack: see **Tamarack** [CALAVERAS].

Camp Ten [EL DORADO]: *locality,* 9 miles north-northeast of Pollock Pines (lat. 38°53'20" N, long. 120°32'10" W; sec. 17, T 12 N, R 13 E). Named on Devil Peak (1950) 7.5' quadrangle. The place was a logging camp of Michigan California Lumber Company (Beverly Cola, personal communication, 1985).

Camp Twentyfive Creek [TUOLUMNE]: *stream,* flows nearly 3 miles to Twomile Creek 5.5 miles southeast of Long Barn (lat. 38°02'10" N, long. 120°03'50" W; near S line sec. 12, T 2 N, R 17 E). Named on Hull Creek (1979) 7.5' quadrangle.

Camp Twentyfour [TUOLUMNE]: *locality,* 4.5 miles southeast of Long Barn (lat. 38°02'15" N, long. 120°05'20" W; near SE cor. sec. 10, T 2 N, R 17 E). Site named on Hull Creek (1979) 7.5' quadrangle.

Camp Twentyone Spring [TUOLUMNE]: *spring,* 6.5 miles south-southeast of Long Barn (lat. 38°00'25" N, long. 120°04'25" W; near N line sec. 26, T 2 N, R 17 E). Named on Hull Creek (1979) 7.5' quadrangle.

Camp Two Sentinels [EL DORADO]: *locality,* 0.5 mile west of Kirkwood (lat. 38°42'15" N, long. 120°04'55" W; on W line sec. 22, T 10 N, R 17 E); the place is 0.5 mile north-northeast of the peaks called Two Sentinels [AMADOR]. Named on Caples Lake (1979) 7.5' quadrangle.

Camp Union: see **Lancha Plana** [AMADOR].

Camp Virner: see **Balderson Station** [EL DORADO].

Camp Washington: see **Chinese Camp** [TUOLUMNE].

Camp Wasiu [EL DORADO]: *locality,* 1.5 miles southwest of the town of Meeks Bay near Meeks Creek (lat. 39°01'20" N, long. 120°08'45" W; near N line sec. 31, T 14 N, R 17 E). Named on Homewood (1955, photorevised 1969) 7.5' quadrangle.

Camp Winton [AMADOR]: *locality,* 7.5 miles west of Mokelumne Peak on the southeast side of Lower Bear River Reservoir (lat. 38°32'35" N, long. 120°13'35" W; sec. 17, T 8 N, R 16 E). Named on Bear River Reservoir (1979) 7.5' quadrangle.

Camp Wolfeboro [CALAVERAS]: *locality,* nearly 2 miles south of Tamarack along North Fork Stanislaus River (lat. 38°24'45" N, long. 120°04'40" W). Named on Tamarack (1979) 7.5' quadrangle.

Camp Yuba [SIERRA]: *locality,* 6.25 miles west of Sierra City along North Yuba River (lat. 39°33'35" N, long. 120°44'55" W; near W line sec. 33, T 20 N, R 11 E). Named on Sierra City (1981) 7.5' quadrangle.

Canada Hill [PLACER]: *ridge,* generally west-trending, 1.5 miles long, 1.5 miles north-northwest of Duncan Peak (lat. 39°10'40" N, long. 120°31'15" W; on E line sec. 4, T 15 N, R 13 E). Named on Duncan Peak (1952) 7.5' quadrangle. Whitney's (1880) map shows an inhabited place called Canada Hill on or near the ridge.

Canady Gulch [TUOLUMNE]: *canyon,* drained by a stream that flows 0.5 mile to Sawmill Gulch 2 miles southeast of Columbia (lat. 38°01'05" N, long. 120°22'20" W; sec. 19, T 2 N, R 15 E). Named on Columbia SE (1948) 7.5' quadrangle.

Canal Bar: see **Canyon Creek** [NEVADA].

Canon Creek: see **Big Canon Creek**, under **Clavey River** [TUOLUMNE].

Canty Meadow [MARIPOSA]: *locality,* 3 miles south-southwest of El Portal (lat. 37°38'05" N, long. 119°47'55" W; near NE cor. sec. 31, T 3 S, R 20 E). Named on El Portal (1947) 7.5' quadrangle.

Canyon: see **Shingle Springs** [EL DORADO].

Canyon Creek [EL DORADO]:
(1) *stream,* flows 9 miles to Middle Fork American River 4 miles north of Greenwood (lat. 38°57'10" N, long. 120°54'05" W; near N line sec. 30, T 13 N, R 10 E). Named on Georgetown (1949) and Greenwood (1949) 7.5' quadrangles. Whitney's (1880) map has the name "Jones Cr." for the next tributary—which enters from the south—to Middle Fork American River upstream from Canyon Creek (1), and shows a settlement called Jones Hill near the head of Jones Creek.
(2) *stream,* flows 2.5 miles to Rock Creek 13 miles northwest of Pollock Pines (lat. 38°55'05" N, long. 120°44'10" W; sec. 3, T 12 N, R 11 E). Named on Tunnel Hill (1950) 7.5' quadrangle.

Canyon Creek [NEVADA]: *stream,* flows 17 miles to South Yuba River 8 miles west-northwest of Yuba Gap (lat. 39°21'40" N, long. 120°44'55" W; at S line sec. 4, T 17 N, R 11 E). Named on Blue Canyon (1955), English Mountain (1983), and Graniteville (1982) 7.5' quadrangles. South Fork joins Canyon Creek in Sawmill Lake; it is 3.5 miles long and is named on English Mountain (1983) 7.5' quadrangle. A mining place called Canal Bar was located along South Yuba River at the mouth of Canyon Creek (Hoover, Rensch, and Rensch, p. 255). Early in 1850 miners started a settlement called Canyonville that was situated at the mouth of Canyon Creek, but by the end of the year the place was deserted (Slyter and Slyter, p. 9).

Canyon Creek [PLACER]: *stream,* flows 10.5 miles to North Fork American River 3.5 miles south of Dutch Flat (lat. 39°09'05" N, long. 120°50'05" W; sec. 15, T 15 N, R 10 E). Named on Blue Canyon (1955), Dutch Flat (1950), and Westville (1952) 7.5' quadrangles.

Canyon Creek [SIERRA]: *stream,* formed by the confluence of East Fork and North Fork in Sierra County, flows 22 miles to North Yuba River 9 miles west of Goodyears Bar (lat. 39°31'20" N, long. 121°03'10" W; at S line sec. 11, T 19 N, R 8 E). Named on Goodyears Bar (1951), La Porte (1951), Mount Fillmore (1951), and Strawberry Valley (1948) 7.5' quadrangles. The stream forms part of Sierra-Yuba county line. Marlette (p. 202) noted that the creek was correctly named, "for we had to send our pack mules some fifteen miles off our course to find a crossing." East Fork is 2 miles long and North Fork is nearly 1.5 miles long. South Fork, which enters the main stream just below the confluence of North Fork and East Fork, is 1.5 miles long. West Branch, which enters the main stream 2.25 miles southwest of Mount Fillmore, is 3.5 miles long. All four tributaries are named on Mount Fillmore (1951) 7.5' quadrangle.

Canyon Creek: see **Big Canyon Creek** [EL DORADO]; **Little Canyon Creek** [NEVADA]; **Little Canyon Creek** [SIERRA].

Canyon Creek Campground [NEVADA]: *locality,* 1.5 miles west-southwest of English Mountain (lat. 39°26'15" N, long. 120°34'45" W; sec. 12, T 18 N, R 12 E); the place is along Canyon Creek. Named on English Mountain (1983) 7.5' quadrangle.

Canyon 4 [SIERRA]: *canyon,* drained by a stream that flows 3.25 miles to Little Truckee River 6 miles south of Crystal Peak (lat. 39°27'55" N, long. 120°06'10" W; at E line sec. 29, T 19 N, R 17 E); the canyon is north of Canyon 3. Named on Boca (1955) 7.5' quadrangle.

Canyon 3 [SIERRA]: *canyon,* drained by a stream that flows 2 miles to Little Truckee River 7 miles south of Crystal Peak (lat. 39° 27' N, long. 120°06'10" W; near SW cor. sec. 33, T 19 N, R 17 E); the feature is between Canyon 2 and Canyon 4. Named on Boca (1955) 7.5' quadrangle.

Canyon 24 [NEVADA]: *canyon,* drained by a stream that flows 1.5 miles to Truckee River 11 miles northeast of Truckee (lat. 39°25'55" N, long. 120°01'45" W; near NE cor. sec. 12, T 18 N, R 17 E). Named on Boca (1955) 7.5' quadrangle.

Canyon 23 [NEVADA-SIERRA]: *canyon,* drained by a stream that heads in Sierra County and flows 2.5 miles to Truckee River 11.5 miles northeast of Truckee in Nevada County (lat. 39°26'05" N, long. 120°01'30" W; near SW cor sec. 7, T 18 N, R 18 E). Named on Boca (1955) 7.5' quadrangle.

Canyon 22 [NEVADA-SIERRA]: *canyon,* drained by a stream that heads in Sierra County and flows 2 miles to Truckee River

12 miles northeast of Truckee in Nevada County (lat. 39°26'30" N, long. 120°00'55" W; sec. 7, T 18 N, R 18 E); the canyon is northeast of Canyon 23. Named on Boca (1955) 7.5' quadrangle.

Canyon 2 [NEVADA-SIERRA]: *canyon,* drained by a stream that heads in Sierra County and flows nearly 3 miles to Little Truckee River 9 miles north-northeast of Truckee in Nevada County (lat. 39°26'15" N, long. 120°05'20" W; sec. 4, T 18 N, R 17 E). Named on Boca (1955) 7.5' quadrangle.

Canyonville: see **Canyon Creek** [NEVADA].

Canzatti Spring [AMADOR]: *spring,* 7.5 miles east-northeast of Pine Grove (lat. 38°26'35" N, long. 120°31'40" W; sec. 22, T 7 N, R 13 E). Named on West Point (1948) 7.5' quadrangle.

Cape Cod Bar: see **Enterprise** [AMADOR].

Cape Horn [PLACER]:
(1) *ridge,* south-trending, 1 mile long, 1.5 miles northeast of Colfax (lat. 39°07'10" N, long. 120°56' W). Named on Colfax (1949) 7.5' quadrangle. Builders of Central Pacific Railroad named the feature, which was a great obstacle during construction of the rail line (Stewart, p. 45).
(2) *locality,* 2.5 miles northeast of Colfax along Southern Pacific Railroad (lat. 39°07'45" N, long. 120°55'25" W; near N line sec. 25, T 15 N, R 9 E); the place is 1 mile northeast of Cape Horn (1). Named on Chicago Park (1949) 7.5' quadrangle.

Caperton Reservoir [PLACER]: *lake,* 450 feet long, 5 miles north of Rocklin (lat. 38°51'45" N, long. 121°13'10" W; sec. 29, T 12 N, R 7 E). Named on Rocklin (1967) 7.5' quadrangle.

Capitol Dome: see **Wawona Dome** [MARIPOSA].

Caples Creek [EL DORADO]: *stream,* heads at Caples Lake in Alpine County and flows 7.5 miles to Silver Fork American River 6.25 miles west of Kirkwood in El Dorado County (lat. 38°41'30" N, long. 120°11'05" W). Named on Caples Lake (1979) and Tragedy Spring (1979) 7.5' quadrangles. The name commemorates Dr. James Caples, who built a station near Caples Lake in the 1850's; the place became a regular stop on a wagon road into California (United States Board on Geographic Names, 1968b, p. 4).

Caple Spring [EL DORADO]: *spring,* 9.5 miles west-northwest of Leek Spring Hill (lat. 38°42'20" N, long. 120°24'40" W). Named on Pyramid Peak (1896) 30' quadrangle.

Cap of Liberty: see **Liberty Cap** [MARIPOSA].

Capps Crossing [EL DORADO]: *locality,* 4 miles south of Old Iron Mountain along North Fork Cosumnes River (lat. 38°38'50" N, long. 120°23'40" W; sec. 11, T 9 N, R 14 E). Named on Stump Spring (1951) 7.5' quadrangle.

Caps Ravine [PLACER]: *canyon,* drained by a stream that flows 4 miles to Doty Ravine 8

miles west-northwest of Auburn (lat. 38° 55'55" N, long. 121°13' W; sec. 32, T 13 N, R 7 E). Named on Gold Hill (1954) 7.5' quadrangle.

Carbondale [AMADOR]: *locality,* nearly 6 miles northwest of Ione along Southern Pacific Railroad (lat. 38°24'30" N, long. 121°00'30" W). Named on Carbondale (1968) 7.5' quadrangle. Carbondale (1909) 7.5' quadrangle shows the place situated 0.25 mile north of the railroad, and north of present Willow Creek. Postal authorities established Carbondale post office in 1922 and discontinued it in 1955 (Frickstad, p. 5). Carbondale also had the name "Buckeye" (Sargent, Mrs. J. L., p. 49). The place was a shipping point for coal after 1877 (Mosier, p. 4). Carbondale (1909) 7.5' quadrangle shows a place called May located less than 1 mile north of present Carbondale. Postal authorities established May post office in 1881 and discontinued it in 1920 (Frickstad, p. 6). California Division of Highways' (1934) map shows a place called Lignite situated about 0.5 mile southeast of Carbondale along Southern Pacific Railroad.

Cargyle Creek [MADERA]: *stream,* flows 4.5 miles to Middle Fork San Joaquin River 8 miles southwest of Devils Postpile (lat. 37° 31'55" N, long. 119°10'50" W; sec. 1, T 5 S, R 25 E). Named on Devils Postpile (1953) 15' quadrangle. East Fork enters from the northeast 2 miles upstream from the mouth of the main creek; it is 3.5 miles long and is named on Devils Postpile (1953) 15' quadrangle.

Cargyle Meadow [MADERA]: *area,* 5.5 miles southwest of Devils Postpile (lat. 37°34'25" N, long. 119°09'30" W); the place is east of East Fork Cargyle Creek. Named on Devils Postpile (1953) 15' quadrangle.

Carl Inn [TUOLUMNE]: *locality,* 4.5 miles south of Mather Station (present Mather) (lat. 37°48'50" N, long. 119°51'40" W; near NW cor. sec. 35, T 1 S, R 19 E). Named on Yosemite (1909) 30' quadrangle. Dan Carlon and Donna Carlon started a resort a the place in 1916 (Paden and Schlichtmann, p. 213).

Carlysle: see **Old Man Mountain** [NEVADA].

Carman Creek [SIERRA]: *stream,* formed by the confluence of East Fork and West Fork, flows 3.5 miles to Sierra Valley 2.5 miles northeast of Calpine (lat. 39°41'40" N, long. 120°24'30" W; near SE cor. sec. 4, T 21 N, 14 E). Named on Calpine (1981) 7.5' quadrangle. United States Board on Geographic Names (1974a, p. 2) gave the form "Carmen Creek" as a variant. East Fork and West Fork both head in Plumas County. Each fork is 5 miles long and each is named on Calpine (1981) 7.5' quadrangle.

Carmen City [CALAVERAS]: *locality,* 8 miles west-southwest of Angels Camp on the east side of Salt Spring Valley (lat. 38°02'50" N, long. 120°41'30" W; near S line sec. 6, T 2 N, R 12 E); the place is nearly 2 miles west-south-

west of Carmen Peak. Named on Salt Spring Valley (1962) 7.5' quadrangle.

Carmen Peak [CALAVERAS]: *peak,* 6.5 miles west-southwest of Angels Camp (lat. 38°0315" N, long. 120°39'40" W; sec. 4, T 2 N, R 12 E). Altitude 2603 feet. Named on Salt Spring Valley (1962) 7.5' quadrangle. Called Harmon Peak on Jackson (1902) 30' quadrangle.

Carnelian Bay [PLACER]:

(1) *embayment,* 4 miles southwest of Kings Beach along Lake Tahoe between Flick Point and Dollar Point (lat. 39°12'30" N, long. 120°05' W). Named on Kings Beach (1955) 7.5' quadrangle. Members of the Whitney survey named the embayment for the occurrence there of a variety of chalcedony called carnelian (Gudde, 1949, p. 57).

(2) *village,* 3.25 miles west-southwest of Kings Beach (lat. 39°13'40" N, long. 120°04'45" W; sec. 22, T 16 N, R 17 E); the village is at the north end of Carnelian Bay (1). Named on Kings Beach (1955) 7.5' quadrangle. Postal authorities established Cornelian post office in 1883, discontinued it in 1887, reestablished it in 1891, discontinued it in 1893, and reestablished it with the name "Carnelian Bay" in 1908 (Salley, p. 38).

Carnelian Canyon [PLACER]: *canyon,* drained by a stream that flows 1.25 miles to Lake Tahoe 3.25 miles west-southwest of Kings Beach (lat. 39°13'35" N, long. 120°04'50" W; sec. 22, T 16 N, R 17 E); the mouth of the canyon is at the village of Carnelian Bay. Named on Kings Beach (1955) 7.5' quadrangle.

Carney Creek [SIERRA]: *stream,* flows 1.5 miles to Jim Crow Creek 4 miles east-southeast of Downieville (lat. 39°31'40" N, long. 120°46'05" W; sec. 8, T 19 N, R 11 E). Named on Downieville (1951) and Sierra City (1981) 7.5' quadrangles.

Caroline Diggings: see **Last Chance** [PLACER].

Carpenter [EL DORADO]: *locality,* 13 miles east of Placerville (lat. 38°44'30" N, long. 120°33'05" W). Named on Placerville (1893) 30' quadrangle.

Carpenter Creek [EL DORADO]: *stream,* flows 2.5 miles to South Fork American River 2 miles west-southwest of Kyburz (lat. 38° 45'50" N, long. 120°19'35" W; near S line sec. 29, T 11 N, R 15 E). Named on Kyburz (1952) and Leek Spring Hill (1951) 7.5' quadrangles.

Carpenter Flat [PLACER]: *valley,* about 1.25 miles east of Emigrant Gap (1) along upper reaches of Fulda Creek (lat. 39°18'15" N, long. 121°38'40" W). Named on Blue Canyon (1955) 7.5' quadrangle. Called Wilson Valley on Colfax (1898) 30' quadrangle.

Carpenter Ridge [NEVADA]: *ridge,* east-trending, 2 miles long, 6.5 miles north of Donner Pass (lat. 39°24'50" N, long. 120°19' W); the ridge is northwest of Carpenter Valley. Named on Independence Lake (1981) 7.5' quadrangle.

Carpenters Bar: see **Green Valley** [PLACER].

Carpenter Valley [NEVADA]: *valley,* 6.25 miles north-northeast of Donner Pass along North Fork Prosser Creek (lat. 39°24' N, long. 120°16'45" W); the valley is southeast of Carpenter Ridge. Named on Independence Lake (1981) 7.5' quadrangle. Called Twin Valley on Truckee (1895) 30' quadrangle.

Carr Lake [NEVADA]: *lake,* 950 feet long, 6 miles east-southeast of Graniteville (lat. 39°24' N, long. 120°38'25" W; at W line sec. 28, T 18 N, R 12 E). Named on Graniteville (1982) 7.5' quadrangle. Colfax (1938) 30' quadrangle has the name "Feeley Lakes" for present Carr Lake and nearby Feeley Lake together.

Cars Creek [SIERRA]: *stream,* flows 2 miles to Canyon Creek 5.5 miles northwest of Goodyears Bar (lat. 39°35'50" N, long. 120°57'30" W). Named on Downieville (1897) 30' quadrangle.

Carson [EL DORADO]: *locality,* 6.25 miles north of Omo Ranch (lat. 38°40'15" N, long. 120°34'25" W). Named on Placerville (1893) 30' quadrangle.

Carson [MARIPOSA]: *locality,* 5.5 miles northeast of the settlement of Catheys Valley (lat. 37°28'50" N, long. 120°00'35" W); the place is along Carson Creek at Carson Flat. Named on Catheys Valley (1962) 7.5' quadrangle. Laizure's (1928) map shows a place called Arkansas Flat located nearly 1 mile east-northeast of the site of Carson, and a canyon called Goday Gulch that opens into the canyon of Carson Creek at Arkansas Flat. The misspelled name "Goday" commemorates Alex Godey (Sargent, Shirley, 1976, p. 9), who discovered gold deposits on Fremont's Las Mariposas grant in 1849 (Gudde, 1975, p. 63).

Carson Creek [CALAVERAS]: *stream,* flows 4 miles to Melones Reservoir 5 miles south-southeast of Angels Camp (lat. 38°00'25" N, long. 120°31' W; sec. 23, T 2 N, R 13 E). Named on Angels Camp (1962) 7.5' quadrangle. The name commemorates Sergeant James H. Carson, who discovered gold in the stream in 1848 while he was on furlough (Gudde, 1975, p. 62).

Carson Creek: see **McBrides Gulch** [MARIPOSA].

Carson Creek [AMADOR]: *stream,* flows 1.5 miles to Jackson Creek 4 miles southeast of Ione (lat. 38°18'15" N, long. 120°52'55" W; sec. 9, T 5 N, R 10 E). Named on Ione (1962) and Jackson (1962) 7.5' quadrangles.

Carson Creek [EL DORADO]: *stream,* heads in El Dorado County and flows 13 miles to Deer Creek 10 miles south of Folsom in Sacramento County (lat. 38°32' N, long. 121°08'25" W; sec. 19, T 8 N, R 8 E). Named on Buffalo Creek (1967), Clarksville (1953),

and Folsom SE (1954) 7.5' quadrangles.

Carson Creek [MARIPOSA]: *stream,* flows 2 miles to Agua Fria Creek 5 miles northeast of the settlement of Catheys Valley (lat. 37°28'55" N, long. 120°01'15" W); the stream goes past the site of Carson. Named on Catheys Valley (1962) and Mariposa (1947) 7.5' quadrangles. Alex Godey probably named the stream for Kit Carson (Gudde, 1975, p. 63).

Carson Flat [CALAVERAS]: *area,* 3 miles south-southeast of Angles Camp (lat. 38°02'25" N, long. 120°31' W; sec. 11, T 2 N, R 13 E); the place is near Carson Creek. Named on Angels Camp (1962) 7.5' quadrangle. Bancroft (1888, p. 513) referred to Carson's Flat, "the great camp of 1851."

Carson Flat [MARIPOSA]: *area,* 5.5 miles northeast of the settlement of Catheys Valley (lat. 37°28'50" N, long. 120°00'35" W); the place is along Carson Creek at the site of Carson. Named on Catheys Valley (1962) 7.5' quadrangle.

Carson Flat: see **Carson Hill** [CALAVERAS] (2).

Carson Gulch: see **McBrides Gulch** [MARIPOSA].

Carson Hill [CALAVERAS]:

(1) *peak,* 4.5 miles south-southeast of Angels Camp (lat. 38°01'20" N, long. 120°30'10" W; near SW cor. sec. 13, T 2 N, R 13 E); the peak is east of Carson Creek. Altitude 1983 feet. Named on Angels Camp (1962) and Columbia (1948) 7.5' quadrangles.

(2) *village,* nearly 4 miles south-southeast of Angels Camp (lat. 38°01'40" N, long. 120°30'20" W; near W line sec. 13, T 2 N, R 13 E); the village is north of Carson Hill (1) near Carson Creek. Named on Angels Camp (1962) 7.5' quadrangle. Called Carson Flat on Jackson (1902) 30' quadrangle, which shows the place along Sierra Railroad. The village originally was called Slumgullion, but later it was named for James H. Carson of Carson Creek (Gudde, 1949, p. 58). According to Hanna (p. 189), Slumgullion was the site of an 1849 gold camp called Melones, a name later applied to a place about 2 miles farther east. Postal authorities established Irvine post office in 1896, changed the name to Carson Hill in 1909, and discontinued it in 1935; the name "Irvine" was from a mining claim on Carson Hill (1) (Salley, p. 38, 105).

Carson Range [EL DORADO]: *range,* extends for 17 miles, largely on El Dorado-Alpine county line, north-northeast from Carson Pass in Alpine County to the State of Nevada. Named on Freel Peak (1955) and South Lake Tahoe (1955) 7.5' quadrangles. United States Board on Geographic Names (1939, p. 9) rejected the name "Rose Mountain Range" for the feature. Brewer (p. 437) used the name "Carson Spur" for the range in 1863.

Carson's Creek: see **Angels Camp** [CALAVERAS].

Carson's Flat: see **Carson Flat** [CALA-VERAS].

Carson Spur [AMADOR]: *peak*, 11.5 miles north of Mokelumne Peak (lat. 38°42'10" N, long. 120°06' W; sec. 21, T 10 N, R 17 E). Altitude 8290 feet. Named on Caples Lake (1979) 7.5' quadrangle.

Carson Spur: see **Carson Range** [EL DORADO].

Carter Creek [MADERA]: *stream*, flows 3.25 miles to Fine Gold Creek 4.5 miles northeast of O'Neals (lat. 37°10'20" N, long. 119° 38' W; sec. 1, T 9 S, R 21 E). Named on North Fork (1965) and O'Neals (1965) 7.5' quadrangles.

Carter Creek [MADERA-MARIPOSA]: *stream*, heads in Mariposa County and flows 7.5 miles to Miami Creek 4.25 miles west of Yosemite Forks in Madera County (lat. 37°21'45" N, long. 119°42'20" W; near W line sec. 32, T 6 S, R 21 E). Named on Bass Lake (1953) 15' quadrangle.

Carters: see **Summersville**, under **Soulsbyville** [TUOLUMNE].

Cart Wheel Valley: see **White Oak Flat** [EL DORADO].

Carvin Campground [SIERRA]: *locality*, 5 miles north-northeast of Sierra City along North Yuba River (lat. 39°37'20" N, long. 120° 34'55" W; near SW cor. sec. 1, T 20 N, R 12 E); the place is 0.5 mile downstream from the mouth of Carvin Creek. Named on Sierra City (1981) 7.5' quadrangle.

Carvin Creek [SIERRA]: *stream*, flows 1 mile to North Yuba River 5.25 miles northeast of Sierra City (lat. 39°37'35" N, long. 120° 34'30" W; sec. 1, T 20 N, R 12 E). Named on Clio (1981) 7.5' quadrangle.

Carvin Creek Homesites [SIERRA]: *locality*, 5.25 miles north-northeast of Sierra City (lat. 39°37'40" N, long. 120°34'40" W; sec. 1, T 20 N, R 12 E); the place is near the mouth of Carvin Creek. Named on Clio (1981) 7.5' quadrangle.

Casa Diablo [MARIPOSA]: *relief feature*, 4.5 miles southwest of El Portal (lat. 37°37'20" N, long. 119°49'55" W; near N line sec. 2, T 4 S, R 19 E). Named on Buckingham Mountain (1947) 7.5' quadrangle.

Casa Loma [PLACER]: *locality*, 3.25 miles east of Dutch Flat (lat. 39°12' N, long. 120°46'30" W; at N line sec. 6, T 15 N, R 11 E). Named on Dutch Flat (1950) 7.5' quadrangle.

Cascade Creek [EL DORADO]: *stream*, flows 4 miles to Lake Tahoe 3.25 miles north-northeast of Mount Tallac (lat. 38°57'05" N, long. 120°04'35" W). Named on Emerald Bay (1955) 7.5' quadrangle.

Cascade Creek [MARIPOSA]: *stream*, flows 8 miles to Merced River 7.25 miles west-south-west of Yosemite Village (lat. 37°43'20" N, long. 119°42'45" W; sec. 36, T 2 S, R 20 E). Named on Hetch Hetchy Reservoir (1956) and Yosemite (1956) 15' quadrangles.

Cascade Creek [TUOLUMNE]:

(1) *stream*, flows 5.5 miles to Middle Fork Stanislaus River 8 miles southeast of Liberty Hill (lat. 38°16'30" N, long. 120°00'40" W; sec. 20, T 5 N, R 18 E). Named on Donnell Lake (1979) and Liberty Hill (1979) 7.5' quadrangles.

(2) *locality*, 8.5 miles west-southwest of Dardanelle (lat. 38°16'45" N, long. 119°58'05" W; on N line sec. 23, T 5 N, R 18 E); the place is along Cascade Creek (1). Named on Donnell Lake (1979) 7.5" quadrangle.

Cascade Diggings: see **Quaker Hill** [NEVADA] (2).

Cascade Falls: see **The Cascades** [MARIPOSA].

Cascade Lake [EL DORADO]: *lake*, 1 mile long, 2.5 miles north of Mount Tallac (lat. 38°56'25" N, long. 120°05'25" W; mainly in sec. 27, T 13 N, R 17 E); the lake is along Cascade Creek. Named on Emerald Bay (1955) 7.5' quadrangle.

Cascade Lakes [PLACER]: *lakes*, two connected, largest 3500 feet long, 6 miles west-southwest of Donner Pass (lat. 39°18' N, long. 120°25'50" W; around NW cor. sec. 32, T 17 N, R 14 E). Named on Soda Springs (1955) 7.5' quadrangle. Hobson's (1890b) map shows a place called Cascade Station located north of present Cascade Lakes along Central Pacific Railroad.

Cascadel: see **North Fork** [MADERA].

Cascadel Point [MADERA]: *ridge*, east-trending, 1.5 miles long, 9.5 miles south of Shuteye Peak (lat. 37°13' N, long. 119°26'45" W). Named on Shaver Lake (1953) 15' quadrangle.

Cascades: see **The Cascades** [MARIPOSA].

Cascade Station: see **Cascade Lakes** [PLACER].

Casey [EL DORADO]: *locality*, 12 miles east of Placerville (lat. 38° 43'15" N, long. 120°34'40" W). Named on Placerville (1893) 30' quadrangle.

Casey Canyon [NEVADA]: *canyon*, drained by a stream that flows 2 miles to Truckee River 8 miles east-northeast of Truckee (lat. 39°22'05" N, long. 120°02'20" W; sec. 36, T 18 N, R 17 E). Named on Martis Peak (1955) 7.5' quadrangle.

Casey Corner [NEVADA]: *locality*, 2 miles north of Pilot Peak in Penn Valley (lat. 39°11'50" N, long. 121°10'35" W; near S line sec. 34, T 16 N, R 7 E). Named on Rough and Ready (1949) 7.5' quadrangle.

Casnau Creek [TUOLUMNE]: *stream*, flows 1.5 miles to Mountain Pass Creek 32 miles north-northwest of Keystone (lat. 37°52'30" N, long. 120°31'10" W; near E line sec. 3, T 1 S, R 13 E). Named on Melones Dam (1962) 7.5' quadrangle.

Cassidy Meadows [MADERA]: *areas*, 16 miles northeast of Shuteye Peak (lat. 37°28'45" N, long. 119°11'15" W; sec. 24, T 5 S, R 25 E). Named on Kaiser Peak (1953) 15' quadrangle.

Kaiser (1904) 30' quadrangle has the singular form "Cassidy Meadow" for the name, which commemorates James Cassidy, an early sheepman (Browning, 1986, p. 34).

Castle Cliffs [MARIPOSA]: *relief feature*, 0.5 mile north-northwest of Yosemite Village on the north side of Yosemite Valley (lat. 37° 45'20" N, long. 119°35'45" W). Named on Hetch Hetchy Reservoir (1956) 15' quadrangle.

Castle Creek: see **Lower Castle Creek** [NEVADA]; **Upper Castle Creek** [NEVADA].

Castle Lake [MADERA]: *lake*, 600 feet long, nearly 4 miles northwest of Devils Postpile (lat. 37°40'10" N, long. 119°07'10" W). Named on Devils Postpile (1953) 15' quadrangle.

Castle Meadow [TUOLUMNE]: *area*, 6.25 miles south-southwest of Dardanelle along Willow Creek (1) (lat. 38°15'05" N, long. 119°51'30" W; near SW cor. sec. 26, T 5 N, R 19 E). Named on Dardanelle (1979) 7.5' quadrangle.

Castle Peak [MADERA]: *peak*, 11.5 miles south of Shuteye Peak (lat. 37°11'05" N, long. 119°26'30" W; near S line sec. 34, T 8 S, R 23 E). Altitude 4082 feet. Named on Shaver Lake (1953) 15' quadrangle. Called Oat Mt. on Kaiser (1904) 30' quadrangle.

Castle Rock [TUOLUMNE]: *peak*, 9.5 miles east-northeast of Pinecrest (lat. 38°14'55" N, long. 119°50'15" W; sec. 36, T 5 N, R 19 E). Named on Pinecrest (1956) 15' quadrangle. Members of the Wheeler survey named the feature before 1878 (Browning, 1986, p. 34).

Castle Pass [NEVADA]: *pass*, 3.5 miles northwest of Donner Pass (lat. 39°21'30" N, long. 120°21'55" W; near NE cor. sec. 11, T 17 N, R 14 E); the pass is 1 mile west-southwest of Castle Peak. Named on Norden (1955) 7.5' quadrangle. United States Board on Geographic Names (1949b, p. 3) rejected the name "Castle Peak Pass" for the feature.

Castle Peak [NEVADA]: *peak*, 3.5 miles northnorthwest of Donner Pass (lat. 39°21'55" N, long. 120°20'55" W; sec. 1, T 17 N, R 14 E). Altitude 9103 feet. Named on Norden (1955) 7.5' quadrangle.

Castle Peak: see **Tower Peak** [TUOLUMNE].

Castle Peak Pass: see **Castle Pass** [NEVADA].

Castle Point [EL DORADO]: *peak*, 2.5 miles west of Kirkwood (lat. 38°42'15" N, long. 120°07'10" W; sec. 20, T 10 N, R 17 E). Altitude 8041 feet. Named on Caples Lake (1979) 7.5' quadrangle.

Castle Rock [CALAVERAS]: *relief feature*, 0.5 mile northeast of Valley Springs (lat. 38°11'50" N, long. 120°49'05" W; sec. 13, T 4 N, R 10 E). Named on Valley Springs (1962) 7.5' quadrangle.

Castle Valley [NEVADA]: *valley*, 2.5 miles north-northwest of Donner Pass (lat. 39°20'55" N, long. 120°21'10" W; mainly in sec. 12, T 17 N, R 14 E); the valley is 1 mile south-southwest of Castle Peak at the head of Upper Castle Creek. Named on Norden (1955) 7.5' quadrangle. United States Board on Geographic Names (1949c, p. 4) rejected the name "Willow Valley" for the feature.

Cataract Gulch [CALAVERAS]: *canyon*, drained by a stream that flows 1 mile to Stanislaus River 4 miles east-northeast of Vallecitos (lat. 38°06'25" N, long. 120°24'10" W; near S line sec. 14, T 3 N, R 14 E). Named on Columbia (1948) 7.5' quadrangle.

Cat Camp [CALAVERAS]: *locality*, 6.5 miles west of Valley Springs (lat. 38°12'20" N, long. 120°56'40" W; near NW cor. sec. 13, T 4 N, R 9 E). Named on Wallace (1962) 7.5' quadrangle.

Cat Canyon [SIERRA]: *canyon*, drained by a stream that flows nearly 3 miles to Balls Canyon 8.5 miles east of Loyalton (lat. 39° 39'20" N, long. 120°05'10" W; sec. 21, T 21 N, R 17 E). Named on Dog Valley (1981) and Evans Canyon (1978) 7.5' quadrangles.

Cat Creek [EL DORADO]: *stream*, flows 5.5 miles to Middle Fork Cosumnes River nearly 5 miles east-southeast of Caldor (lat. 38°34'20" N, long. 120°21'25" W; sec. 6, T 8 N, R 15 E). Named on Peddler Hill (1951) 7.5' quadrangle.

Cat Creek Ridge [EL DORADO]: *ridge*, westsouthwest-trending, 4.5 miles long, 6 miles east of Caldor (lat. 38°35'30" N, long. 120° 19' W); the ridge is south of Cat Creek. Named on Peddler Hill (1951) 7.5' quadrangle.

Catfish Lake [NEVADA]:

(1) *lake*, 1000 feet long, 1.5 miles north of English Mountain (lat. 39°28'15" N, long. 120°33'15" W; sec. 31, T 19 N, R 13 E). Named on English Mountain (1983) 7.5' quadrangle.

(2) *lake*, 850 feet long, 7.5 miles west of Donner Pass (lat. 39° 20'05" N, long. 120°27'50" W; sec. 13, T 17 N, R 13 E). Named on Soda Springs (1955) 7.5' quadrangle.

Catfish Lake: see **Little Catfish Lake**, under **Tollhouse Lake** [NEVADA].

Catfish Lake [TUOLUMNE]: *lake*, 350 feet long, 1.5 miles northeast of Pinecrest (lat. 38°12'25" N, long. 119°58'40" W; near NE cor. sec. 15, T 4 N, R 18 E). Named on Pinecrest (1979) 7.5' quadrangle.

Cathay: see **Catheys Valley** [MARIPOSA] (2).

Cathay Mountain: see **Catheys Mountain** [MARIPOSA].

Cathay Valley: see **Catheys Valley** [MARIPOSA] (1).

Cathedral Creek [EL DORADO]: *stream*, flows 1 mile to Fallen Leaf Lake 1.5 miles eastsoutheast of Mount Tallac (lat. 38°53'55" N, long. 120°04'10" W; sec. 11, T 12 N, R 17 E); the stream heads 0.5 mile north of Cathedral Peak. Named on Emerald Bay (1955) 7.5' quadrangle.

Cathedral Creek [TUOLUMNE]: *stream*, flows 10 miles to Tuolumne River 13 miles west of Tioga Pass (lat. 37°55'55" N, long. 119°30'

W); the creek heads near Cathedral Peak. Named on Hetch Hetchy Reservoir (1956) and Tuolumne Meadows (1956) 15' quadrangles. The stream was called Rocky Canyon Creek in the early 1880's (Browning, 1988, p. 22). South Fork enters from the south 2 miles upstream from the mouth of the main stream; it is 4.25 miles long and is named on Tuolumne Meadows (1956) 15' quadrangle.

Cathedral Creek: see **Budd Creek** [TUOLUMNE].

Cathedral Fork [MARIPOSA]: *stream,* flows 5 miles to Echo Creek 5.5 miles south of Cathedral Peak (lat. 37°46' N, long. 119°25' W); the stream heads south of Cathedral Peak. Named on Tuolumne Meadows (1956) 15' quadrangle. United States Board on Geographic Names (1970b, p. 2) gave the names "Cathedral Fork Merced Creek," "Cathedral Fork Merced River," and "Cathedral Fork of Merced River" as variants.

Cathedral Fork: see **Echo Creek** [MARIPOSA].

Cathedral Lake [EL DORADO]: *lake,* 400 feet long, 1.25 miles southeast of Mount Tallac (lat. 38°53'35" N, long. 120°04'50" W); the lake is 0.5 mile north-northeast of Cathedral Peak. Named on Emerald Bay (1955) 7.5' quadrangle.

Cathedral Lakes [MARIPOSA]: *lakes,* two, largest 1900 feet long, 1 mile southwest of Cathedral Peak (lat. 37°50'30" N, long. 119°25'10" W; mainly in sec. 14, T 1 S, R 23 E). Named on Tuolumne Meadows (1956) 15' quadrangle.

Cathedral Pass [MARIPOSA]: *pass,* 1.25 miles south-southwest of Cathedral Peak (lat. 37°50'10" N, long. 119°24'50" W; near N line sec. 23, T 1 S, R 23 E). Named on Tuolumne Meadows (1956) 15' quadrangle.

Cathedral Peak [EL DORADO]: *relief feature,* 1.5 miles south-southeast of Mount Tallac (lat. 38°53'15" N, long. 120°05' W; sec. 15, T 12 N, R 17 E). Named on Emerald Bay (1955) 7.5' quadrangle.

Cathedral Peak [MARIPOSA-TUOLUMNE]: *peak,* 9 miles west-southwest of Tioga Pass on Mariposa-Tuolumne county line (lat. 37°50'50" N, long. 119°24'20" W; near W line sec. 13, T 1 S, R 23 E). Altitude 10,940 feet. Named on Tuolumne Meadows (1956) 15' quadrangle. Brewer (p. 412) noted in 1863 that the peak is "something the shape of a huge cathedral."

Cathedral Point: see **Cathedral Rocks** [MARIPOSA].

Cathedral Range [MADERA-MARIPOSA-TUOLUMNE]: *ridge,* southeast-trending, 12 miles long, northwest of Mount Lyell; mainly on Mariposa-Tuolumne county line, but extends southeast for 4 miles along Madera-Tuolumne county line. Named on Merced Peak (1953) and Tuolumne Meadows (1956) 15' quadrangles.

Cathedral Rocks [MARIPOSA]: *relief feature,* 3.5 miles southwest of Yosemite Village on the south side of Yosemite Valley (lat. 37° 43' N, long. 119°38'15" W). Named on Yosemite (1956) 15' quadrangle. United States Board on Geographic Names (1933, p. 202) rejected the name "Cathedral Point" for the feature, which had the early name "The Three Graces" (Browning, 1986, p. 35).

Cathedral Spires [MARIPOSA]: *relief features,* 3.5 miles southwest of Yosemite Village on the south side of Yosemite Valley (lat. 37° 42'50" N, long. 119°37'45" W). Named on Yosemite (1956) 15' quadrangle. Henry G. Hanks, James Hutchings, and Captain Corcoran named the features in 1862 (Chalfant, p. 170).

Catherine: see **Lake Catherine** [MADERA].

Cathewood Saddle [MARIPOSA]: *pass,* 2.25 miles south-southeast of El Portal (lat. 37°38'35" N, long. 119°46' W; sec. 28, T 3 S, R 20 E). Named on El Portal (1947) 7.5' quadrangle.

Cathey Pond [MARIPOSA]: *intermittent lake,* 125 feet long, nearly 2 miles northwest of Santa Cruz Mountain (lat. 37°28'25" N, long. 120°13'35" W; sec. 28, T 5 S, R 16 E). Named on Indian Gulch (1962) 7.5' quadrangle.

Catheys Mountain [MARIPOSA]: *peak,* nearly 3 miles north-northeast of the settlement of Catheys Valley (lat. 37°28'10" N, long. 120°03'50" W; sec. 25, T 5 S, R 17 E). Altitude 2867 feet. Named on Catheys Valley (1962) 7.5' quadrangle. Called Cathay Mtn. on Indian Gulch (1920) 15' quadrangle, but United States Board on Geographic Names (1964a, p. 8) rejected this form of the name.

Catheys Valley [MARIPOSA]:

(1) *valley,* 8 miles west-southwest of Mariposa (lat. 37°25'30" N, long. 120°05' W). Named on Catheys Valley (1962) 7.5' quadrangle. Called Cathay Valley on Indian Gulch (1920) 15' quadrangle, but United States Board on Geographic Names (1964a, p. 8) rejected this name, and noted that the name "Cathey" is for Andrew Cathey of North Carolina, who settled in the valley about 1850. The feature first was called Vallecita (Sargent, Shirley, 1976, p. 8).

(2) *settlement,* 8 miles southwest of Mariposa (lat. 37°26'05" N, long. 120°05'35" W; sec. 3, 10, T 6 S, R 17 E); the place is in Catheys Valley (1). Named on Catheys Valley (1962) 7.5' quadrangle. Postal authorities established Cathey's Valley post office in 1879, discontinued it in 1881, reestablished it with the name "Cathey" in 1882, discontinued it in 1918, reestablished it in 1919, and changed the name to Catheys Valley in 1964 (Salley, p. 40). United States Board on Geographic Names (1964a, p. 8) rejected the name "Cathay" for the settlement.

Cattle Mountain [MADERA]: *peak,* 11 miles southwest of Devils Postpile (lat. 37°31'05"

N, long. 119°13'55" W; on W line sec. 3, T 5 S, R 25 E). Altitude 7946 feet. Named on Devils Postpile (1953) 15' quadrangle.

Cat Town [MARIPOSA]: *locality,* 2.25 miles southeast of Buckhorn Peak (lat. 37°38'40" N, long. 120°05'15" W; near W line sec. 27, T 3 S, R 17 E). Named on Buckhorn Peak (1947) 7.5' quadrangle.

Cavallada Creek [MARIPOSA]: *stream,* formed by the confluence of two unnamed streams and flows 1 mile to Sand Creek 4.25 miles northeast of the settlement of Catheys Valley (lat. 37°28'55" N, long. 120°02'15" W). Named on Catheys Valley (1962) 7.5' quadrangle. United States Board on Geographic Names (1964b, p. 12) rejected the name "Texas Creek" for the stream.

Cavallada Gulch: see **La Mineta Gulch** [MARIPOSA]; **Texas Gulch** [MARIPOSA].

Cavallado Creek: see **Sand Creek** [MARIPOSA].

Cavanah: see **Barney Cavanah Ridge** [PLACER].

Cave City [CALAVERAS]: *locality,* 9.5 miles east of San Andreas along McKinney Creek (lat. 38°12'10" N, long. 120°30'25" W; sec. 14, T 4 N, R 13 E). Named on Calaveritas (1962) 7.5' quadrangle. The place was a mining camp of the 1850's; Cave City cave was an early-day tourist attraction (Gudde, 1975, p. 64).

Cave Country [TUOLUMNE]: *area,* 3 miles north of Columbia (lat. 38°04'35" N, long. 120°23'50" W). Named on Columbia (1948) 7.5' quadrangle.

Cave Gulch [AMADOR]: *canyon,* less than 1 mile long, opens into the canyon of Mokelumne River 5.25 miles south-southwest of Jackson (lat. 38°16'50" N, long. 120°49'10" W; near S line sec. 13, T 5 N, R 10 E). Named on Jackson (1962) 7.5' quadrangle. Water of Pardee Reservoir now covers the lower part of the canyon.

Cecile Lake [MADERA]: *lake,* 1900 feet long, 5.5 miles west-northwest of Devils Postpile at the head of Shadow Creek (lat. 37°39'50" N, long. 119°10' W). Named on Devils Postpile (1953) 15' quadrangle. The feature also is called Upper Iceberg Lake (Smith, p. 62).

Cedarbrook [MARIPOSA]: *locality,* 5 miles southwest of Fish Camp (lat. 37°25'10" N, long. 119°41'20" W; near SE cor. sec. 8, T 6 S, R 21 E). Named on Bass Lake (1953) 15' quadrangle.

Cedar Canyon [EL DORADO]: *canyon,* drained by a stream that flows 2.5 miles to String Canyon 9 miles southeast of Camino (lat. 38°38'15" N, long. 120°33'50" W; sec. 17, T 9 N, R 13 E). Named on Sly Park (1952) 7.5' quadrangle.

Cedar Creek [CALAVERAS]: *stream,* flows 3.5 miles to North Fork Calaveras River 3 miles north of San Andreas (lat. 38°14'25" N, long. 120°41'25" W; sec. 31, T 5 N, R 12 E). Named

on Mokelumne Hill (1948) and San Andreas (1962) 7.5' quadrangles.

Cedar Creek [EL DORADO]: *stream,* flows 6.5 miles to Scott Creek 1.5 miles east-southeast of Aukum (lat. 38°32'45" N, long. 120°42'10" W; near W line sec. 18, T 8 N, R 12 E). Named on Aukum (1952) and Omo Ranch (1952) 7.5' quadrangles.

Cedar Creek [PLACER]: *stream,* flows 4.25 miles to North Fork American River nearly 5 miles south-southwest of Donner Pass (lat. 39°15'15" N, long. 120°22'10" W; sec. 14, T 16 N, R 14 E). Named on Norden (1955) 7.5' quadrangle

Cedar Creek Camp: see **Coyoteville** [EL DORADO].

Cedar Flat [PLACER]: *area,* 4 miles west-northwest of Kings Beach (lat. 39°12'55" N, long. 120°05'35" W; sec. 21, T 16 N, R 17 E). Named on Kings Beach (1955) 7.5' quadrangle.

Cedar Flat [TUOLUMNE]: *area,* 8.5 miles southwest of Liberty Hill (lat. 38°16'05" N, long. 120°11'25" W; sec. 22, T 5 N, R 16 E). Named on Boards Crossing (1979) 7.5' quadrangle.

Cedar Grove Ravine [SIERRA]: *canyon,* drained by a stream that flows 3.25 miles to Slate Creek 5.5 miles west-southwest of Mount Fillmore (lat. 39°41'25" N, long. 120°56'15" W; near S line sec. 11, T 21 N, R 9 E). Named on La Porte (1951) 7.5' quadrangle.

Cedar Gulch [TUOLUMNE]: *canyon,* drained by a stream that flows nearly 2 miles to North Fork Tuolumne River 1.5 miles southeast of Tuolumne (lat. 37°56'30" N, long. 120°13'05" W; sec. 16, T 1 N, R 16 E). Named on Tuolumne (1948) 7.5' quadrangle.

Cedar Kress: see **Union Hill** [NEVADA].

Cedar Mountain: see **Streeter Mountain** [MARIPOSA].

Cedar Ravine [EL DORADO]: *canyon,* drained by a stream that flows nearly 2 miles to Hangtown Creek in downtown Placerville (lat. 38°43'45" N, long. 120°47'45" W; at W line sec. 8, T 10 N, R 11 E). Named on Placerville (1949) 7.5' quadrangle.

Cedar Ravine [NEVADA]: *canyon,* drained by a stream that flows 2.5 miles to South Wolf Creek 5 miles north-northeast of Higgins Corner (lat. 39°06'05" N, long. 121°02'40" W; near NW cor. sec. 1, T 14 N, R 8 E). Named on Lake Combie (1949) 7.5' quadrangle.

Cedar Ridge [NEVADA]: *village,* 2.5 miles east-southeast of Grass Valley (lat. 39°12' N, long. 121°01'10" W; near SE cor. sec. 36, T 16 N, R 8 E). Named on Grass Valley (1949) 7.5' quadrangle. Postal authorities established Cedar Ridge post office in 1948 (Frickstad, p. 113).

Cedar Ridge [TUOLUMNE]: *settlement,* 7 miles east-northeast of Columbia (lat. 38°03'55" N, long. 120°16'40" W; sec. 36, T

3 N, R 15 E). Named on Columbia SE (1948) 7.5' quadrangle.

Cedar Rock Lodge [TUOLUMNE]: *locality,* 8 miles east of Columbia (lat. 38°01'15" N, long. 120°15' W; near N line sec. 19, T 2 N, R 16 E). Named on Columbia SE (1948) 7.5' quadrangle.

Cedars: see **The Cedars** [PLACER].

Cedar Spring [EL DORADO]: *spring,* nearly 3 miles north-northwest of Riverton (lat. 38°48'35" N, long. 120°27'55" W; sec. 12, T 11 N, R 13 E). Named on Riverton (1950) 7.5' quadrangle.

Cedarville [EL DORADO]: *locality,* 4.25 miles east-northeast of Aukum (lat. 38°34'05" N, long. 120°38'50" W; near SW cor. sec. 3, T 8 N, R 12 E); the place is along Cedar Creek. Site named on Aukum (1952) 7.5' quadrangle. Postal authorities established Cedarville post office in 1853 and discontinued it in 1863 (Frickstad, p. 25).

Celina Ridge [NEVADA]: *ridge,* south-trending, 2.25 miles long, 2.5 miles southeast of Graniteville (lat. 39°24'45" N, long. 120°42'20" W). Named on Graniteville (1982) 7.5' quadrangle.

Cement Hill [EL DORADO]:
(1) *peak,* 2.5 miles north-northwest of Georgetown (lat. 38°56'30" N, long. 120°51'10" W; near SW cor. sec. 27, T 13 N, R 10 E). Named on Georgetown (1949) 7.5' quadrangle.
(2) *peak,* 2.5 miles west-southwest of Omo Ranch (lat. 38°33'40" N, long. 120°36'40" W; near W line sec. 12, T 8 N, R 12 E). Named on Omo Ranch (1952) 7.5' quadrangle.

Cement Hill [NEVADA]: *ridge,* east-southeast-trending, 2.5 miles long, center 1.5 miles northwest of downtown Nevada City (lat. 39°16'50" N, long. 121°02'30" W). Named on Nevada City (1948) 7.5' quadrangle. California Division of Highways' (1934) map shows a lake called Cement Hill Res. located 3.25 miles west-northwest of Nevada City near the west end of present Cement Hill (near S line sec. 34, T 17 N, R 8 E).

Cement Hill Reservoir: see **Cement Hill** [NEVADA].

Cement Ravine [EL DORADO]: *canyon,* drained by a stream that flows 1.5 miles to Slab Creek 8 miles north of Pollock Pines (lat. 38°52'25" N, long. 120°36'20" W; sec. 23, T 12 N, R 12 E). Named on Devil Peak (1950) 7.5' quadrangle.

Cemetery Hill [MARIPOSA]: *hill,* 3.5 miles west-northwest of Hornitos on the south side of Merced River (lat. 37°30'55" N, long. 120°18' W; near W line sec. 11, T 5 S, R 15 E). Named on Merced Falls (1962) 7.5' quadrangle.

Cemetery Ridge [MARIPOSA]: *ridge,* south-southeast-trending, 1 mile long, 8.5 miles north-northwest of Hornitos (lat. 37°37'10" N, long. 120°16'30" W). Named on Merced Falls (1962) 7.5' quadrangle.

Centennial Ravine [SIERRA]: *canyon,* drained by a stream that flows 1 mile to Buckeye Ravine 2 miles southeast of Alleghany (lat. 39°27'15" N, long. 120°48'40" W; sec. 1, T 18 N, R 10 E). Named on Alleghany (1949) 7.5' quadrangle.

Center Mountain [TUOLUMNE]: *peak,* 7 miles west-northwest of Matterhorn Peak on Tuolumne-Mono county line (lat. 38°08'40" N, long. 119°29'20" W). Altitude 11,273 feet. Named on Matterhorn Peak (1956) 15' quadrangle.

Centerville: see **Pilot Hill** [EL DORADO] (2).

Central Camp [MADERA]: *locality,* 3 miles west of Shuteye Peak (lat. 37°21' N, long. 119°28'55" W; sec. 5, T 7 S, R 23 E). Named on Shuteye Peak (1953) 15' quadrangle. United States Board on Geographic Names (1994, p. 5) approved the name "Peckinpah Mountain" for a peak bounded by Peckinpah Creek 5.2 miles south-southeast of Central Camp (lat. 37°16'30" N, long. 119°28' W; sec. 33, T 17 S, R 23 E), and rejected the name "Mount Peckinpah" for it.

Central Ferry [CALAVERAS-TUOLUMNE]: *locality,* 6.25 miles east-southeast of Copperopolis along Stanislaus River on Calaveras-Tuolumne county line (lat. 37°56'20" N, long. 120°32'15" W; sec. 15, T 1 N, R 13 E). Site named on Melones Dam (1962) 7.5' quadrangle.

Central Hill [CALAVERAS]: *ridge,* south-southwest- to south-trending, 1.5 miles long, 3.5 miles west-northwest of San Andreas (lat. 38°13'30" N, long. 120°44'20" W). Named on San Andreas (1962) 7.5' quadrangle.

Central House [AMADOR]: *locality,* 2 miles south-southwest of Plymouth (lat. 38°27'20" N, long. 120°52' W; near S line sec. 15, T 7 N, R 10 E). Named on Sutter Creek (1944) 15' quadrangle.

Central House [NEVADA]: *locality,* 3.25 miles south-southeast of North Bloomfield (lat. 39°19'25" N, long. 120°52'45" W; sec. 20, T 17 N, R 10 E). Named on North Bloomfield (1949) 7.5' quadrangle. Called Galbraith on Colfax (1898) 30' quadrangle. Postal authorities established Galbraith post office in 1896 and discontinued it in 1899; the name was for Christopher Galbraith, first postmaster (Salley, p. 82).

Centreville: see **Grass Valley** [NEVADA].

Chain Lakes [MADERA]: *lakes,* largest 1600 feet long, 4.5 miles south of Merced Peak (lat. 37°34'05" N, long. 119°24'15" W). Named on Merced Peak (1953) 15' quadrangle.

Chaix Mountain [EL DORADO]: *peak,* 5 miles north of Pollock Pines (lat. 38°50'10" N, long. 120°34'30" W; near NW cor. sec. 6, T 11 N, R 13 E). Altitude 4935 feet. Named on Pollock Pines (1950) 7.5' quadrangle.

Chalk Bluff [NEVADA]: *relief feature,* 6.5 miles northeast of Chicago Park (lat. 39°13' N, long. 120°52'50" W; near S line sec. 29, T 16 N, R

10 E). Named on Chicago Park (1949) 7.5' quadrangle.

Chalk Bluff [PLACER]: *relief feature,* 8 miles west-southwest of Granite Chief (lat. 39°08'25" N, long. 120°24'45" W; sec. 21, T 15 N, R 14 E). Named on Royal Gorge (1953) 7.5' quadrangle.

Chalk Bluff Ridge [NEVADA]: *ridge,* generally southwest-trending, 8.5 miles long, center 7 miles south-southwest of Washington (lat. 39°15'45" N, long. 120°50'15" W); Chalk Bluff is near the southwest end of the ridge. Named on Chicago Park (1949), Dutch Flat (1950), and Washington (1950) 7.5' quadrangles.

Chalk Bluffs: see **Red Dog** [NEVADA].

Chalk Flat [SIERRA]: *area,* 1.5 miles north-northeast of Pike (lat. 39°27'30" N, long. 120°59'20" W; sec. 5, T 18 N, R 9 E); the place is north of Chalk Ridge. Named on Pike (1949) 7.5' quadrangle.

Chalk Ridge [SIERRA]: *ridge,* east-trending, 1.25 miles long, 1 mile north-northeast of Pike (lat. 39°27'15" N, long. 120°59'20" W). Named on Pike (1949) 7.5' quadrangle.

Challenge: see **Saint Louis** [SIERRA].

Chalybeate Spring: see **Iron Spring** [MARIPOSA].

Chambers Bar: see **Indian Bar** [TUOLUMNE].

Chambers Lodge [PLACER]: *locality,* 1.25 miles southeast of Homewood along Lake Tahoe at the mouth of McKinney Creek (lat. 39°04'25" N, long. 120°08'30" W; sec. 7, T 14 N, R 17 E). Named on Homewood (1955) 7.5' quadrangle. Called McKinney on Truckee (1940) 30' quadrangle, which shows Chambers Lodge at present Tahoma. Postal authorities established McKinney post office in 1884, changed the name to Chambers Lodge in 1928, and discontinued it in 1959 (Salley, p. 41, 136). The name "McKinney" was for John McKinney, who settled at the place in 1864; the name was changed in 1928 when David H. Chambers opened his lodge at the site (Hanna, p. 61).

Chamisal [MARIPOSA]: *locality,* 7 miles west-northwest of the village of Bear Valley (lat. 37°36'55" N, long. 120°14' W). Named on Sonora (1891) 30' quadrangle. The place was a gold-mining camp; the name also had the forms "Chemisal" and "Chimesal" (Gudde, 1975, p. 66).

Champion [NEVADA]: *locality,* 1.25 miles west-southwest of Nevada City on the north side of Deer Creek [NEVADA] (lat. 39°15'30" N, long. 121°02'20" W). Named on Smartsville (1895) 30' quadrangle. Grass Valley (1949) 7.5' quadrangle shows Champion mine situated across Deer Creek from the site.

Channel Arm: see **Pardee Reservoir** [CALAVERAS].

Channel Arm: see **Pardee Reservoir** [AMADOR].

Channel Lake [EL DORADO]: *lake,* 750 feet long, 1.5 miles east-northeast of Pyramid Peak (lat. 38°51'10" N, long. 120°07'50" W). Named on Pyramid Peak (1955) 7.5' quadrangle.

Chaparral Hill: see **Lancha Plana** [AMADOR].

Chapman Creek [MADERA-MARIPOSA]: *stream,* heads in Mariposa County and flows 12.5 miles to Chowchilla River 3 miles northwest of Raymond in Madera County (lat. 37°15'15" N, long. 119°56'40" W; sec. 12, T 8 S, R 18 E). Named on Ben Hur (1947) 7.5' quadrangle. On Mariposa (1912) 30' quadrangle, the part of the stream above the mouth of Becknell Creek is called West Branch.

Chapman Creek [SIERRA]: *stream,* flows 3.5 miles to North Yuba River 6.5 miles northeast of Sierra City (lat. 39°37'55" N, long. 120°32'50" W; near SW cor. sec. 32, T 21 N, R 13 E). Named on Clio (1981) 7.5' quadrangle.

Chapman Saddle [NEVADA]: *pass,* 9 miles northeast of Sierra City (lat. 39°39'25" N, long. 120°31'15" W; sec. 28, T 21 N, R 13 E); the pass is near the head of Chapman Creek. Named on Clio (1981) 7.5' quadrangle.

Charcoal Flat: see **Charcoal Ravine** [SIERRA].

Charcoal Ravine [SIERRA]: *canyon,* drained by a stream that flows 1.5 miles to North Yuba River 3.5 miles west of Sierra City (lat. 39°33'50" N, long. 120°42'05" W; near NE cor. sec. 35, T 20 N, R 11 E). Named on Sierra City (1981) 7.5' quadrangle. Gudde (1975, p. 68) listed a place called Charcoal Flat that was located at the mouth of Charcoal Ravine.

Charles Creek [EL DORADO]: *stream,* flows 1.5 miles to Deer Creek (1) 5 miles west of Wentworth Springs (lat. 39°00'10" N, long. 120°25'50" W; sec. 5, T 13 N, R 14 E). Named on Bunker Hill (1953) 7.5' quadrangle.

Charley's Flat: see **Dutch Flat** [PLACER].

Cheese Camp Creek [EL DORADO]: *stream,* flows 4 miles to Tells Creek 2.25 miles east-southeast of Robbs Peak (lat. 38°54'35" N, long. 120°21'50" W; near SW cor. sec. 1, T 12 N, R 14 E). Named on Loon Lake (1952) 7.5' quadrangle.

Chelalian Bar: see **Chili Bar** [EL DORADO].

Chemisal: see **Chamisal** [MARIPOSA].

Chemisal: see **The Chemisal** [AMADOR].

Chepo Saddle [MADERA]: *pass,* 2.5 miles east-southeast of Yosemite Forks (lat. 37°20'55" N, long. 119°35'20" W; sec. 5, T 7 S, R 22 E). Named on Bass Lake (1953) 15' quadrangle.

Cherokee [NEVADA]: *settlement,* 3.5 miles east of North San Juan (lat. 39°22'10" N, long. 121°02'30" W; on E line sec. 2, T 17 N, R 8 E). Named on Nevada City (1948) 7.5' quadrangle. Called Paterson on Smartsville (1895) 30' quadrangle. Postal authorities established Patterson post office at present Cherokee in

1855, discontinued it in 1895, reestablished it in 1905, discontinued it in 1909, reestablished it with the name "Melrose" in 1910, changed the name to Tyler the same year, and discontinued it in 1924 (Salley, p. 137, 168, 226). The name "Patterson," the middle name of Eugene P. Turney, first postmaster, was given to the post office because the name "Cherokee" was already in use for a post office in California; the name "Melrose" was for the hometown in Massachusetts of postmaster James L. Morgan (Salley, p. 137, 168). The name "Cherokee" recalls Cherokee Indians who prospected at the site in 1850 (Gudde, 1975, p. 68). Whitney's (1873) map shows Cherokee Ravine extending from Cherokee to Grizzly Cañon 1 mile northeast of Cherokee.

Cherokee [TUOLUMNE]: *locality,* 1.5 miles north-northwest of Tuolumne (lat. 37°58'55" N, long. 120°14'30" W; sec. 32, T 2 N, R 16 E). Named on Tuolumne (1948) 7.5' quadrangle. Called Cherokee Camp on Sonora (1897) 30' quadrangle. The Scott brothers, who were of Cherokee Indian ancestry, discovered gold at the place in 1853 (Gudde, 1969, p. 61).

Cherokee Bar [EL DORADO-PLACER]: *locality,* 4.25 miles north-northwest of Greenwood along Middle Fork American River on El Dorado-Placer county line (lat. 38°57'15" N, long. 120°56'15" W; on S line sec. 23, T 13 N, R 9 E); the place is west of Cherokee Flat. Named on Greenwood (1949) 7.5' quadrangle.

Cherokee Camp: see **Cherokee** [TUOLUMNE].

Cherokee Creek [CALAVERAS]: *stream,* flows 9.5 miles to join San Domingo Creek and form South Fork Calaveras River 6.5 miles west-northwest of Angels Camp (lat. 38°07'10" N, long. 120° 39' W; near S line sec. 9, T 3 N, R 12 E). Named on Angels Camp (1962) and Salt Spring Valley (1962) 7.5' quadrangles.

Cherokee Creek [SIERRA]: *stream,* flows 7 miles to North Yuba River 8 miles west of Goodyears Bar (lat. 39°30'50" N, long. 121° 02'05" W; sec. 13, T 19 N, R 8 E). Named on Goodyears Bar (1951) and Strawberry Valley (1948) 7.5' quadrangles.

Cherokee Diggings [NEVADA]: *locality,* 4 miles east of North San Juan (lat. 39°22'10" N, long. 121°01'55" W; sec. 1, T 17 N, R 8 E); the place is just east of Cherokee. Named on Nevada City (1948) 7.5' quadrangle.

Cherokee Flat [CALAVERAS]: *area,* northwest of downtown Angels Camp at Altaville (lat. 38°05' N, long. 120°34' W; sec. 29, T 3 N, R 13 E); the place is along Cherokee Creek. Named on Angels Camp (1962) 7.5' quadrangle. Leonard (p. 14) noted that a stopping place called Cherokee House was located just north of Cherokee Creek along the trail lead-

ing to Angels Camp from the north—this location suggests that the place must have been at or near Cherokee Flat.

Cherokee Flat [EL DORADO]: *area,* 4 miles north-northwest of Greenwood (lat. 38°57'20" N, long. 120°55'50" W; at NW cor. sec. 25, T 13 N, T 9 E); the area is east of Cherokee Bar. Named on Greenwood (1949) 7.5' quadrangle.

Cherokee Flat: see **Altaville** [CALAVERAS].

Cherokee House: see **Cherokee Flat** [CALAVERAS].

Cherokee Ravine: see **Cherokee** [NEVADA].

Cherry Creek [TUOLUMNE]: *stream,* formed by the confluence of East Fork and North Fork 13 miles east-southeast of Pinecrest, flows 26 miles to Tuolumne River 6.25 miles west of Mather (lat. 37°53'20" N, long. 119°58'15" W; sec. 2, T 1 S, R 18 E). Named on Lake Eleanor (1956) and Pinecrest (1956) 15' quadrangles. East Fork is 13 miles long and North Fork is 14 miles long; both forks are named on Pinecrest (1956) and Tower Peak (1956) 15' quadrangles. West Fork enters the main stream 11 miles south-southeast of Pinecrest; it is 16 miles long and is named on Pinecrest (1956) 15' quadrangle.

Cherry Creek Acres [NEVADA]: *settlement,* 4.25 miles north of Higgins Corner (lat. 39°06'20" N, long. 121°05'05" W; on and near W line sec. 34, T 15 N, R 8 E). Named on Lake Combie (1949) 7.5' quadrangle.

Cherry Creek Canyon [TUOLUMNE]: *canyon,* 7 miles long, along Cherry Creek above a point 11 miles south-southeast of Pinecrest (lat. 38°03'10" N, long. 119°54'05" W). Named on Pinecrest (1956) 15' quadrangle.

Cherry Creek Reservoir: see **Cherry Lake** [TUOLUMNE].

Cherry Hill [NEVADA]: *peak,* 6.5 miles east-northeast of North Bloomfield (lat. 39°25' N, long. 120°47'45" W; near NE cor. sec. 24, T 18 N, R 10 E). Altitude 5224 feet. Named on Alleghany (1949) 7.5' quadrangle.

Cherry Lake [TUOLUMNE]: *lake,* behind a dam on Cherry Creek 7 miles north-north-west of Mather (lat. 37°58'30" N, long. 119°54'30" W; sec. 5, T 1 N, R 19 E). Named on Lake Eleanor (1956) and Pinecrest (1956) 15' quadrangles. Called Cherry Creek Res. on California Mining Bureau's (1917d) map. Yosemite (1909) 30' quadrangle shows Cherry Valley at the site before the lake formed.

Cherry Point [PLACER]: *peak,* nearly 4 miles south-southeast of Cisco Grove (lat. 39°15'35" N, long. 120°30'45" W; at SE cor. sec. 9, T 16 N, R 13 E). Altitude 6728 feet. Named on Cisco Grove (1955) 7.5' quadrangle.

Cherry Ridge [TUOLUMNE]: *ridge,* south-west-trending, 6 miles long, 9 miles southeast of Pinecrest (lat. 38°06' N, long. 119°52'30" W); the ridge is between Cherry Creek and West Fork Cherry Creek. Named on Pinecrest (1956) 15' quadrangle.

Cherry Valley: see **Cherry Lake** [TUOLUMNE].

Chetwood Creek [MADERA]: *stream,* flows 2 miles to North Fork San Joaquin River 8.5 miles west-southwest of Devils Postpile (lat. 37°35'50" N, long. 119°14'10" W). Named on Devils Postpile (1953) and Merced Peak (1953) 15' quadrangles. Merced Peak (1953) 15' quadrangle shows Chetwood cabin near the stream.

Chewing Gum Lake [TUOLUMNE]: *lake,* 700 feet long, 8 miles east of Pinecrest (lat. 38°11'45" N, long. 119°51' W; near N line sec. 23, T 4 N, R 19 E). Named on Pinecrest (1956) 15' quadrangle.

Chicago: see **New Chicago** [AMADOR].

Chicago Park [NEVADA]: *settlement,* 7 miles southeast of Grass Valley (lat. 39°08'45" N, long. 120°57'55" W; around SW cor. sec. 15, T 15 N, R 9 E). Named on Chicago Park (1949) 7.5' quadrangle. On Colfax (1898) 30' quadrangle, the name applies to a place 1.5 miles farther north along Nevada County Narrow Gauge Railroad. Postal authorities established Chicago Park post office in 1888 and moved it 1 mile southeast in 1898 (Salley, p. 42). The name is from a real-estate promotion involving investors from Chicago, Illinois, who planned to develop a townsite near Storms' Station on the narrow-gauge railroad (Browne, J.K., p. 117). California Division of Highways' (1934) map shows a locality called Bear River located 1.5 miles south-southeast of Chicago Park along Nevada County Narrow Gauge Railroad near the stream called Bear River (sec. 22, T 15 N, R 9 E).

Chicago Park: see **Colfax** [PLACER].

Chichi: see **Mountain Ranch** [CALAVERAS].

Chickemasee Flat: see **Grizzly Flat** [EL DORADO].

Chicken Flat: see **Spanish Flat** [EL DORADO].

Chicken Hawk Campground [PLACER]: *locality,* 4 miles north of Michigan Bluff (lat. 39°05'55" N, long. 120°43'20" W; sec. 34, T 15 N, R 11 E); the place is near the north end of Chicken Hawk Ridge. Named on Michigan Bluff (1952) 7.5' quadrangle.

Chicken Hawk Ridge [PLACER]: *ridge,* generally south-trending, 4 miles long, center 2 miles north-northeast of Michigan Bluff (lat. 39°04'15" N, long. 120°43'35" W). Named on Michigan Bluff (1952) 7.5' quadrangle.

Chicken Hawk Spring [EL DORADO]: *spring,* 2 miles north-northeast of Riverton (lat. 38°48' N, long. 120°25'50" W; sec. 17, T 11 N, R 14 E). Named on Riverton (1950) 7.5' quadrangle.

Chief: see **Big Chief** [PLACER]; **Little Chief** [PLACER].

Chief Creek [PLACER]: *stream,* flows 2.25 miles to North Fork American River 2 miles north of Granite Chief (lat. 39°13'35" N, long. 120°17' W; near N line sec. 23, T 16 N, R 15 E). Named on Granite Chief (1953) 7.5' quadrangle.

Chilanoialna Creek: see **Chilnualna Creek** [MARIPOSA].

Chilanoialna Fall: see **Chilnualna Fall** [MARIPOSA].

Chilean Gulch: see **Chili Gulch** [CALAVERAS].

Chile Gulch [TUOLUMNE]: *canyon,* drained by a stream that flows 0.5 mile to Deadman Gulch 2.5 miles west of Columbia (lat. 38°02'15" N, long. 120°26'55" W; sec. 9, T 2 N, R 14 E). Named on Columbia (1948) 7.5' quadrangle.

Chilean Bar: see **Chili Bar** [EL DORADO].

Chili: see **Chili Gulch** [CALAVERAS].

Chili Bar [EL DORADO]: *locality,* 4.5 miles east-southeast of Coloma along South Fork American River (lat. 38°46' N, long. 120°49'15" W; at SW cor. sec. 25, T 11 N, R 10 E). Named on Garden Valley (1949) 7.5' quadrangle. Chilean miners worked at the place for a time after they were run out of Johntown (Gernes, p. 54). Gudde (1975, p. 70) gave the names "Chilean Bar," "Chelalian Bar," and "Chillean Bar" as alternates, and listed (p. 347) a place called Texas Bar that was located 0.5 mile upstream from present Chili Bar.

Chili Camp: see **Chili Camp Gulch** [CALAVERAS].

Chili Camp Gulch [CALAVERAS]: *canyon,* 1.25 miles long, 2 miles west-northwest of Valley Springs (lat. 38°11'55" N, long. 120°51'40" W; mainly in sec. 15, T 4 N, R 10 E). Named on Valley Springs (1962) 7.5' quadrangle. Camp's (1962) map shows a place called Chili Camp located in Chili Gulch (present Chili Camp Gulch).

Chili Gulch [CALAVERAS]: *canyon,* 7 miles long, opens into the canyon of North Fork Calaveras River 2 miles northwest of San Andreas (lat. 38°12'55" N, long. 120°42'25" W; sec. 12, T 4 N, R 11 E). Named on Mokelumne Hill (1948) and San Andreas (1962) 7.5' quadrangles. Apparently the original name was Chilean Gulch (Gudde, 1975, p. 70) for miners from Chili who worked in the canyon in 1848 and 1849 (Hanna, p. 62). Postal authorities established Chili post office 4 miles south of Mokelumne Hill in 1857, discontinued it in 1860, reestablished it in 1861, discontinued it in 1872, reestablished it in 1873, and discontinued it in 1877 (Salley, p. 43).

Chili Gulch: see **Chili Camp Gulch** [CALAVERAS].

Chili Hill [CALAVERAS]: *peak,* nearly 4 miles northwest of San Andreas (lat. 38°14'05" N, long. 120°43'50" W; sec. 2, T 4 N, R 11 E); the peak is west of Chili Gulch. Named on San Andreas (1962) 7.5' quadrangle.

Chilkoot Campground [MADERA]: *locality,* 5 miles east of Yosemite Forks (lat. 37°21'45" N, long. 119°32'20" W; sec. 35, T 6 S, R 22 E); the place is near the mouth of Chilkoot Creek. Named on Bass Lake (1953) 15' quadrangle.

Chilkoot Creek [MADERA]: *stream,* flows 5.5 miles to North Fork Willow Creek (2) 5 miles east of Yosemite Forks (lat. 37°21'55" N, long. 119°32'20" W; sec. 35, T 6 S, R 22 E); the stream heads at Chilkoot Lake. Named on Bass Lake (1953) and Shuteye Peak (1953) 15' quadrangles. United States Board on Geographic Names (1933, p. 216) rejected the name "Willow Creek" for the feature.

Chilkoot Lake [MADERA]: *lake,* 1000 feet long, 5 miles northwest of Shuteye Peak (lat. 37°24'40" N, long. 119°28'50" W; sec. 17, T 6 S, R 23 E); the lake is at the head of Chilkoot Creek. Named on Shuteye Peak (1953) 15' quadrangle.

Chillean Bar: see **Chili Bar** [EL DORADO].

Chilnualna Creek [MADERA-MARIPOSA]: *stream,* heads along Madera-Mariposa county line and flows 7.5 miles to South Fork Merced River 1.25 miles east-northeast of Wawona (lat. 37°32'45" N, long. 119°38' W; sec. 35, T 4 S, R 21 E). Named on Yosemite (1956) 15' quadrangle. Called Chilnoialny Cr. on Hoffmann and Gardner's (1863-1867) map, but United States Board on Geographic Names (1933, p. 216) rejected the forms "Chilnoialny Creek," "Chilanoialna Creek," and "Chilnoalna Creek" for the name.

Chilnoalna Fall [MARIPOSA]: *waterfall,* 3 miles northeast of Wawona (lat. 37°33'50" N, long. 119°36'50" W; sec. 25, T 4 S, R 21 E); the feature is along Chilnualna Creek. Named on Yosemite (1956) 15' quadrangle. United States Board on Geographic Names (1933, p. 216) rejected the forms "chilnoialny Fall," "Chilanoialna Fall," and "Chilnoalna Fall" for the name.

Chilnualna Lakes [MADERA-MARIPOSA]: *lakes,* 1 mile west of Buena Vista Peak on Madera-Mariposa county line (lat. 37°35'45" N, long. 119°32'15" W); the lakes are on upper reaches of Chilnualna Creek. Named on Yosemite (1956) 15' quadrangle.

Chilnoalna Creek: see **Chilnualna Creek** [MARIPOSA].

Chilnoalna Fall: see **Chilnualna Fall** [MARIPOSA].

Chilnoialny Creek: see **Chilnualna Creek** [MARIPOSA].

Chilnoialny Fall: see **Chilnualna Fall** [MARIPOSA].

Chilnualna Creek [MADERA-MARIPOSA]: *stream,* heads along Madera-Mariposa county line and flows 7.5 miles to South Fork Merced River 1.25 miles east-northeast of Wawona (lat. 37°32'45" N, long. 119°38' W; sec. 35, T 4 S, R 21 E). Named on Yosemite (1956) 15' quadrangle. Called Chilnoialny Cr. on Hoffmann and Gardner's (1863-1867) map, but United States Board on Geographic Names (1933, p. 216) rejected the forms "Chilnoialny Creek," "Chilanoialna Creek," and "Chilnoalna Creek" for the name.

Chilnualna Fall [MARIPOSA]: *waterfall,* 3 miles northeast of Wawona (lat. 37°33'50" N, long. 119°36'50" W; sec. 25, T 4 S, R 21 E); the feature is along Chilnualna Creek. Named on Yosemite (1956) 15' quadrangle. United States Board on Geographic Names (1933, p. 216) rejected the forms "Chilnoialny Fall," "Chilanoialna Fall," and "Chilnoalna Fall" for the name.

Chilnualna Lakes [MADERA-MARIPOSA]: *lakes,* 1 mile west of Buena Vista Peak on Madera-Mariposa county line (lat. 37°35'45" N, long. 119°32'15" W); the lakes are on upper reaches of Chilnualna Creek. Named on Yosemite (1956) 15' quadrangle.

Chimesal: see **Chamisal** [MARIPOSA].

Chimney Flat [EL DORADO]: *area,* 5.25 miles southwest of Pyramid Peak (lat. 38°48'10" N, long. 120°14'20" W; sec. 17, T 11 N, R 16 E). Named on Pyramid Peak (1955) 7.5' quadrangle.

Chimney Hill: see **Sugarloaf Peak** [NEVADA].

Chimney Rock [SIERRA]: *relief feature,* 4 miles south-southeast of Mount Fillmore (lat. 39°40'50" N, long. 120°48'55" W). Altitude 6698 feet. Named on Mount Fillmore (1951) 7.5' quadrangle.

China Bar [PLACER]: *locality,* nearly 6 miles south of Duncan Peak in Duncan Canyon (lat. 39°04'20" N, long. 120°32' W; sec. 9, T 14 N, R 13 E). Named on Greek Store (1952) 7.5' quadrangle.

China Bar [SIERRA]: *locality,* 9 miles southwest of Mount Fillmore along Slate Creek on Sierra-Plumas county line (lat. 39°38'55" N, long. 120°59' W; sec. 28, T 21 N, R 9 E). Named on La Porte (1951) 7.5' quadrangle.

China City: see **Electra** [AMADOR].

China Cove [NEVADA]: *embayment,* 4 miles east of Donner Pass along the south shore of Donner Lake (lat. 39°19'10" N, long. 120°15'10" W; at W line sec. 18, T 17 N, R 16 E). Named on Norden (1955) 7.5' quadrangle.

China Creek [EL DORADO]: *stream,* flows 2.5 miles to Weber Creek 2.5 miles west-southwest of Camino (lat. 38°43'05" N, long. 120°43' W; sec. 13, T 10 N, R 11 E). Named on Camino (1952) 7.5' quadrangle. Called Chunk Creek on Placerville (1893) 30' quadrangle.

China Creek [MADERA]: *stream,* flows 5.25 miles to Fresno River 3 miles south-southwest of Yosemite Forks at Oakhurst (lat. 37°19'45" N, long. 119°39'20" W; at N line sec. 15, T 7 S, R 21 E). Named on Bass Lake (1953) 15' quadrangle.

China Flat [EL DORADO]:
(1) *area,* 3.25 miles south-southwest of Phipps Peak along upper reaches of Rubicon River in Rockbound Valley (lat. 38°54'15" N, long. 120°10'30" W). Named on Rockbound Valley (1955) 7.5' quadrangle.
(2) *area,* 2 miles southeast of Kyburz along Silver Fork American River (lat. 38°45'15" N, long. 120°16' W; at E line sec. 35, T 11 N, R

15 E). Named on Kyburz (1952) 7.5' quadrangle.

China Flat [NEVADA]: *area,* 3.25 miles east of Higgins Corner (lat. 39°02'30" N, long. 121°02' W; near N line sec. 25, T 14 N, R 8 E). Named on Lake Combie (1949) 7.5' quadrangle.

China Flat [MARIPOSA]: *area,* 1 mile east-southeast of Smith Peak (lat. 37°47'45" N, long. 120°04'55" W; near sec. 3, T 2 S, R 17 E). Named on Jawbone Ridge (1947) 7.5' quadrangle.

China Flat [SIERRA]: *area,* 6 miles west of Sierra City along North Yuba River (lat. 39°33'45" N, long. 120°44'50" W; sec. 33, T 20 N, R 11 E). Named on Sierra City (1981) 7.5' quadrangle. The place also was called Chinese Flat (Gudde, 1975, p. 71).

China Garden [MADERA]: *area,* 11 miles south of Raymond on the southeast side of Fresno River (lat. 37°03'30" N, long. 119°55' W; mainly in sec. 17, T 10 S, R 19 E). Named on Daulton (1962) 7.5' quadrangle.

China Gulch [AMADOR]:
(1) *canyon,* 2.5 miles long, opens into the canyon of Mokelumne River 8.5 miles south of Ione (lat. 38°13'50" N, long. 120°54'50" W). Named on Ione (1962) and Wallace (1962) 7.5' quadrangles. Water of Camanche Reservoir.now covers the lower part of the canyon. Camp's (1962) map shows a place called Putts Bar located 1 mile west-southwest of the mouth of China Gulch along Mokelumne River. Andrews (p. 96) noted that a man named Putnam discovered gold at Put's Bar.
(2) *canyon,* 1 mile long, less than 1 mile west of Jackson Butte (lat. 38°20'20" N, long. 120°44' W; sec. 26, 35, T 6 N, R 11 E). Named on Mokelumne Hill (1948) 7.5' quadrangle.

China Gulch [MARIPOSA]: *canyon,* 3 miles long, opens into the canyon of Mariposa Creek 5.5 miles east-southeast of the settlement of Catheys Valley (lat. 37°24'10" N, long. 120°00'10"W). Named on Catheys Valley (1962) 7.5' quadrangle.

China Gulch: see **Little China Gulch** [AMADOR].

Chinaman Creek [TUOLUMNE]: *stream,* flows 3.5 miles to Middle Fork Stanislaus River 8 miles north-northeast of Long Barn (lat. 38°12'05" N, long. 120°04'50" W; sec. 14, T 4 S, R 17 E). Named on Long Barn (1956) 15' quadrangle.

China Mountain [EL DORADO]: *peak,* 6 miles east-northeast of Latrobe (lat. 38°35'35" N, long. 120°52'45" W; sec. 33, T 9 N, R 10 E). Altitude 1734 feet. Named on Latrobe (1949) 7.5' quadrangle. Called Big Sugar Loaf on Placerville (1893) 30' quadrangle.

China Ravine [SIERRA]: *canyon,* drained by a stream that flows less than 1 mile to Big Grizzly Creek 2.5 miles south of Mount Fillmore (lat. 39°41'30" N, long. 120°50'30" W). Named on Mount Fillmore (1951) 7.5' quadrangle.

China Slough [MADERA]: *stream,* flows 3 miles to South Fork Fresno River 13 miles south-southwest of Raymond (lat. 37°01'25" N, long. 119°57'20" W; at N line sec. 36, T 10 S, R 18 E); the stream heads at China Garden. Named on Daulton (1962) 7.5' quadrangle.

Chinatown: see **Dutch Flat Station** [PLACER].

China Wells [MADERA]: *locality,* 2 miles north-northwest of Yosemite Forks (lat. 37°23'25" N, long. 119°38'45" W; sec. 23, T 6 S, R 21 E). Site named on Bass Lake (1953) 15' quadrangle.

Chincapin: see **Chinquapin**, under **Wawona** [MARIPOSA].

Chinee: see **Chinese Camp** [TUOLUMNE].

Chinese: see **Chinese Station** [TUOLUMNE].

Chinese Bar [NEVADA-SIERRA]: *locality,* 4 miles east-southeast of Alleghany along Middle Yuba River on Nevada-Sierra county line (lat. 39°27' N, long. 120°46'25" W; near SE cor. sec. 6, T 18 N, R 11 E). Named on Alleghany (1949) 7.5' quadrangle.

Chinese Camp [TUOLUMNE]: *village,* 8 miles south-southwest of Sonora (lat. 37°52'15" N, long. 120°25'55" W; near SE cor. sec. 4, T 1 S, R 14 E). Named on Chinese Camp (1947) 7.5' quadrangle. Postal authorities established Chinese Camp post office in 1854 (Frickstad, p. 215). The first settlement at the place was called Camp Washington, but after a large number of Orientals began mining at the site it became known as Chinese Camp, or Chinee (Paden and Schlichtmann, p. 68). Whitney (1865, p. 233) called the place Chinese Diggings. Whitney's (1880) map shows a place called Salvado located less than 1 mile east of present Chinese Camp. Paden and Schlichtmann (p. 68, 69) called the same place Campo Salvador, and noted that the name was from a group of miners from San Salvador in Central America who settled at the site; they mentioned also that the place sometimes was called East Chinee. California Mining Bureau's (1909c) map shows a place called Shawmut situated 2 miles by stage east of Chinese Camp. Postal authorities established Shawmut post office in 1907 and discontinued it in 1925; the name was from Eagle Shawmut mine (Salley, p. 202). California Mining Bureau's (1917d) map shows a place called McAlpine located 7 miles south-southeast of Chinese Camp on the west side of Tuolumne River. Postal authorities established McAlpine post office in 1902 and discontinued it in 1907 (Frickstad, p. 216).

Chinese Camp Ridge [EL DORADO]: *ridge,* generally west-trending 2.25 miles long, 7 miles north-northwest of Kyburz (lat. 38°52'25" N, long. 120°20'15" W). Named on Kyburz (1952) 7.5' quadrangle.

Chinese Diggings: see **Chinese Camp** [TUOLUMNE].

Chinese Gulch [MARIPOSA]: *canyon,* drained

by a stream that flows about 1.5 miles to Indian Gulch (1) 1.5 miles northeast of Buckhorn Peak (lat. 37°40'40" N, long. 120°06' W; sec. 16, T 3 S, R 17 E). Named on Buckhorn Peak (1947) 7.5' quadrangle.

Chinese Station [TUOLUMNE]: *locality,* 8 miles south-southwest of Sonora along Sierra Railway (lat. 37°52'45" N, long. 120°27'25" W; sec. 5, T 1 S, R 14 E); the place is 1.5 miles west-northwest of Chinese Camp. Named on Sonora (1948) 15' quadrangle. Called Chinese on Sonora (1897) 30' quadrangle. A place called Shoemake, both a ranch house and a roadhouse for travelers, was located about 2 miles northeast of Chinese Station (Gudde, 1975, p. 318).

Chinese Flat: see **China Flat** [SIERRA].

Chinkapin: see **Chinquapin**, under **Wawona** [MARIPOSA].

Chinkapin Point: see **Dollar Point** [PLACER].

Chinquapin: see **Wawona** [MARIPOSA].

Chinquapin Creek: see **Indian Creek** [MARIPOSA].

Chinquapin Falls [MARIPOSA]: *waterfall,* 1.5 miles east-southeast of El Portal along Indian Creek (lat. 37°40' N, long. 119°45'20" W; sec. 15, T 3 S, R 20 E). Named on El Portal (1947) 7.5' quadrangle.

Chipmunk Bluff [EL DORADO]: *relief feature,* 4.5 miles northeast of Robbs Peak (lat. 38°58'05" N, long. 120°20'10" W; near S line sec. 18, T 13 N, R 15 E). Named on Loon Lake (1952) 7.5' quadrangle.

Chipmunk Creek [PLACER]: *stream,* flows 3.5 miles to Middle Fork American River nearly 6.5 miles south of Duncan Peak (lat. 39°03'45" N, long. 120°30'55" W; sec. 15, T 14 N, R 13 E); the stream heads on Chipmunk Ridge. Named on Bunker Hill (1953) and Greek Store (1952) 7.5' quadrangles.

Chipmunk Flat [TUOLUMNE]: *area,* 3 miles west of Sonora Pass (lat. 38°19'30" N, long. 119°41'30" W). Named on Sonora Pass (1979) 7.5' quadrangle.

Chipmunk Meadow [MADERA]: *area,* 7 miles east-northeast of Yosemite Forks along Chilkoot Creek (lat. 37°23'45" N, long. 119°30'30" W; near E line sec. 24, T 6 S, R 22 E). Named on Bass Lake (1953) 15' quadrangle.

Chipmunk Ridge [PLACER]: *ridge,* extends for 13 miles southwest from Mount Mildred between Middle Fork American River and South Fork Long Canyon. Named on Bunker Hill (1953), Granite Chief (1953), Greek Store (1952), and Royal Gorge (1953) 7.5' quadrangles.

Chips Flat [SIERRA]: *locality,* 1 mile southeast of Alleghany (lat. 39°27'35" N, long. 120°50' W; sec. 3, T 18 N, R 10 E). Named on Alleghany (1949) 7.5' quadrangle. Postal authorities established Chip's Flat post office in 1857 and discontinued it the same year (Salley, p. 43). The name is for the English sailor who discovered gold at the place; the sailor had the nickname "Chips" because he had been a ship's carpenter (Hoover, Rensch, and Rensch, p. 495). Gudde (1975, p. 261, 352) mentioned mining places called Peavine Flat and Tolpekocking Flat that were located near Chips Flat.

Chiquita: see **Chiquita Lake** [EL DORADO].

Chiquita Joaquin River: see **Chiquito Creek** [MADERA].

Chiquita Lake [EL DORADO]: *lake,* 850 feet long, 14 miles north-northwest of Pollock Pines (lat. 38°56'20" N, long. 120°43'40" W; near NE cor. sec. 34, T 13 N, R 11 E). Named on Tunnel Hill (1950) 7.5' quadrangle. Logan's (1938) map has the name "Chiquita" at the place.

Chiquita Pass: see **Chiquito Pass** [MADERA].

Chiquito Campground: see **Lower Chiquito Campground** [MADERA]; **Upper Chiquito Campground** [MADERA].

Chiquito Creek [MADERA]: *stream,* flows 20 miles to Mammoth Pool Reservoir on San Joaquin River 5 miles east of Shuteye Peak (lat. 37°20'30" N, long. 119°20' W; sec. 3, T 7 S, R 24 E). Named on Merced Peak (1953) and Shuteye Peak (1953) 15' quadrangles. Called Chiquito Joaquin on Hoffmann and Gardner's (1863-1867) map, and called Chiquita Joaquin River on Lippincott's (1902) map. East Fork enters from the north-northeast 9 miles south of Merced Peak; it is 3.5 miles long and is named on Merced Peak (1953) 15' quadrangle. West Fork enters from the west 2 miles upstream from the mouth of the main creek; it is 11 miles long and is named on Shuteye Peak (1953) 15' quadrangle.

Chiquito Joaquin: see **Chiquito Creek** [MADERA].

Chiquito Lake [MADERA]: *lake,* 1400 feet long, 7 miles south-southwest of Merced Peak (lat. 37°32'10" N, long. 119°26'10" W; on N line sec. 3, T 5 S, R 23 E); the lake is along Chiquito Creek. Named on Merced Peak (1953) 15' quadrangle.

Chiquito Meadows: see **Beasore Meadows** [MADERA].

Chiquito Pass [MADERA]: *pass,* nearly 7 miles south-southwest of Merced Peak (lat. 37°32'30" N, long. 119°26'15" W); the pass is north of Chiquito Lake. Named on Merced Peak (1953) 15' quadrangle. United States Board on Geographic Names (1991, p. 3) rejected the form "Chiquita Pass" for the name.

Chiquito Ridge [MADERA]: *ridge,* generally south-southeast-trending, 6 miles long, Shuteye Peak is near the center of the feature (lat. 37°21' N, long. 119°25'40" W); the ridge is west of Chiquito Creek. Named on Shuteye Peak (1953) 15' quadrangle.

Chittenden Lake [MADERA]: *lake,* 1200 feet long, 5.5 miles south of Merced Peak (lat. 37°33'15" N, long. 119°22'30" W). Named on Merced Peak (1953) 15' quadrangle. Billy Brown, a packer, named the feature in the

1920's for members of the Chittenden family of Fresno (Browning, 1988, p. 24).

Chittenden Peak [TUOLUMNE]: *peak,* 5 miles southwest of Tower Peak (lat. 38°05'55" N, long. 119°37' W). Altitude 9685 feet. Named on Tower Peak (1956) 15' quadrangle. The name commemorates Hiram M. Chittenden of the army, who was one of a group that made a report in 1904 on revision of the boundaries of Yosemite National Park (United States Board on Geographic Names, 1934, p. 5). Lieutenant McClure gave the name "Jack Main Mountain" to the feature in the mid-1890's (Browning, 1986, p. 39).

Chowchilla [MADERA]: *town,* 15 miles northwest of Madera (lat. 37°07'10" N, long. 120°15'50" W; in and near sec. 30, T 9 S, R 16 E). Named on Chowchilla (1960) 15' quadrangle. Postal authorities established Chowchilla post office in 1912 (Frickstad, p. 85), and the town incorporated in 1923.

Chowchilla Mountain: see **Chowchilla Mountains** [MARIPOSA].

Chowchilla Mountains [MARIPOSA]: *ridge,* northwest-trending, 6 miles long, 4 miles west of Wawona (lat. 37°31'30" N, long. 119° 44' W). Named on El Portal (1947) and Yosemite (1956) 15' quadrangles. Called Chowchilla Mtn. on Buckingham Mountain (1947) 7.5' quadrangle.

Chowchilla River [MADERA-MARIPOSA]: *stream,* formed by the confluence of Middle Fork and West Fork in Madera County 9.5 miles northwest of Raymond, flows 80 miles near Madera-Mariposa county line, and then in Merced County, before ending 6 miles northeast of Dos Palos Y (lat. 37°06'30" N, long. 120°32'50" W; sec. 33, T 9 S, R 13 E). Named on Chowchilla (1960), Le Grand (1961), Mariposa (1947), Raymond (1962), and Santa Rita Park (1962) 15' quadrangles. The word "Chowchilla" is a corruption of the name of a warlike Indian tribe that lived along the river; the Indian name is said to have the meaning "murderers" (Hanna, p. 64). Eccleston (p. 31) in 1851 referred to the Indians as the Chou Chili. East Fork heads in Mariposa County and flows 16 miles to Chowchilla River 13 miles southeast of Mariposa in Madera County; it is named on Bass Lake (1953) and Mariposa (1947) 15' quadrangles. Middle Fork is formed in Mariposa County by the confluence of Magoon Creek and Fox Creek; it is 11.5 miles long and is named on Horsecamp Mountain (1947) and Stumpfield Mountain (1947) 7.5' quadrangles. West Fork is formed in Mariposa County by the confluence of Jones Creek and Snow Creek (2); it is 12.5 miles long and is named on Horsecamp Mountain (1947), Mariposa (1947), and Stumpfield Mountain (1947) 7.5' quadrangles. Mendenhall's (1908) map shows a place called Newton Crossing situated along Chowchilla River about 12 miles

east-northeast of Chowchilla near the entrance of the river into lowlands (near SW cor. sec. 31, T 8 S, R 18 E). Goddard's (1857) map shows Newtons Crossing.

Christian Gulch [CALAVERAS]: *canyon,* drained by a stream that flows 2.25 miles to Black Creek 1.25 miles east-northeast of Copperopolis (lat. 37°59'05" N, long. 120°37' W; sec. 35, T 2 N, R 12 E). Named on Copperopolis (1962), Melones Dam (1962), and Salt Spring Valley (1962) 7.5' quadrangles.

Christian Valley [PLACER]: *valley,* 5.5 miles north-northeast of Auburn (lat. 38°58'30" N, long. 121°02'30" W; sec. 13, 14, T 13 N, R 8 E). Named on Auburn (1953) 7.5' quadrangle.

Christmas Hill Diggings [NEVADA]: *locality,* 6.5 miles northeast of Chicago Park (lat. 39°12' N, long. 120°52' W). Named on Dutch Flat (1950) 7.5' quadrangle.

Christopher: see **Lake Christopher** [EL DORADO].

Chrome Creek: see **Granite Ravine** [EL DORADO].

Chrome Mountain [AMADOR]: *peak,* 5.25 miles southwest of Jackson (lat. 38°17'15" N, long. 120°50'05" W; near E line sec. 14, T 5 N, R 10 E). Altitude 1202 feet. Named on Jackson (1962) 7.5' quadrangle.

Chubb Lake [NEVADA]: *lake,* 1300 feet long, 0.5 mile north of Yuba Gap (lat. 39°19'25" N, long. 120°36'50" W; sec. 22, T 17 N, R 12 E). Named on Cisco Grove (1955) 7.5' quadrangle.

Chuck Ravine [EL DORADO]: *canyon,* drained by a stream that flows 1 mile to South Fork American River less than 1 mile southeast of Coloma (lat. 38°47'30" N, long. 120°52'40" W; near E line sec. 20, T 11 N, R 10 E). Named on Coloma (1949) 7.5' quadrangle.

Chunk Creek: see **China Creek** [EL DORADO].

Church Bell Hill [AMADOR]: *ridge,* generally west-trending, less than 1 mile long, 2 miles northeast of Ione (lat. 38°22'25" N, long. 120°54'30" W; sec;. 17, 18, T 6 N, R 10 E). Named on Ione (1962) 7.5' quadrangle. Sutter Creek (1944) 15' quadrangle shows the feature located about 1 mile farther north. United States Board on Geographic Names (1964a, p. 9) rejected the form "Churchbell Hill" for the name.

Church Camp [SIERRA]: *locality,* nearly 7 miles southwest of Sierraville along Haypress Creek (lat. 39°31'50" N, long. 120° 28' W; sec. 12, T 19 N, R 13 E). Named on Sierraville (1955) 15' quadrangle.

Church Creek [SIERRA]: *stream,* flows 4.5 miles to Salmon Creek nearly 6 miles north of Sierra City (lat. 39°38'55" N, long. 120°37'55" W; sec. 28, T 21 N, R 12 E). Named on Clio (1981) 7.5' quadrangle.

Churchman Bar: see **North Yuba River** [SIERRA].

Church Meadows [SIERRA]: *area,* 7.5 miles

north of Sierra City (lat. 39°40'40" N, long. 120°37'05" W; at S line sec. 15, T 21 N, R 12 E); the place is along Church Creek. Named on Clio (1981) 7.5' quadrangle.

Churchs Camp [NEVADA]: *locality,* 1.5 miles north-northeast of English Mountain (lat. 39°27'55" N, long. 120°32'25" W; sec. 32, T 19 N, R 13 E). Named on English Mountain (1983) 7.5' quadrangle.

Churchs Corners: see **Sattley** [SIERRA].

Churchs Spring [CALAVERAS]: *spring,* 7 miles south-southwest of Copperopolis along Martells Creek (lat. 37°53'50" N, long. 120°42'40" W; sec. 36, T 1 N, R 11 E). Named on Copperopolis (1962) 7.5' quadrangle.

Church Tower [MARIPOSA]: *promontory,* 3.25 miles southwest of Yosemite Village on the south side of Yosemite Valley (lat. 37°42'55" N, long. 119°37'45" W). Named on Yosemite (1956) 15' quadrangle.

Ciatana Creek [MADERA]: *stream,* flows about 3.5 miles to Fish Creek (2) 4.25 miles south-southwest of the town of North Fork (lat. 37°10'05" N, long. 119°31'35" W; sec. 12, T 9 S, R 22 E). Named on North Fork (1965) 7.5' quadrangle.

Cincinnati: see **Kelsey** [EL DORADO].

Cirby Creek [PLACER]: *stream,* flows 3.5 miles to Dry Creek [PLACER] 1 mile south-southwest of downtown Roseville (lat. 38°44' N, long. 121°17'20" W; sec. 11, T 10 N, R 6 E). Named on Citrus Heights (1967) and Folsom (1967) 7.5' quadrangles. The canyon of the stream is called Walkers Ravine on Sacramento (1892) 30' quadrangle.

Cirby Creek: see **Linda Creek** [PLACER].

Cirque Lake: see **Adair Lake** [MADERA].

Cisco [PLACER]: *locality,* 0.5 mile south-southwest of Cisco Grove along Southern Pacific Railroad (lat. 39°18'05" N, long. 120°32'45" W; at N line sec. 32, T 17 N, R 13 E). Named on Cisco Grove (1955) 7.5' quadrangle. Officials of Central Pacific Railroad named the place in 1865 to honor John J. Cisco, treasurer of the railroad; it first was called Heaton Station (Gudde, 1949, p. 69). Postal authorities established Cisco post office in 1866 and discontinued it in 1941 (Frickstad, p. 119).

Cisco Butte [PLACER]: *peak,* 1.25 miles west of Cisco Grove (lat. 39°18'30" N, long. 120°33'40" W; sec. 30, T 17 N, R 13 E). Altitude 6639 feet. Named on Cisco Grove (1955) 7.5' quadrangle.

Cisco Grove [PLACER]: *village,* 7 miles east of Emigrant Gap (1) (lat. 39°18'35" N, long. 120°32'20" W; sec. 29, T 17 N, R 13 E); the village is 0.5 mile north-northeast of Cisco. Named on Cisco Grove (1955) 7.5' quadrangle.

City of Six Diggings: see **Slug Canyon** [SIERRA].

City of Six Ridge [SIERRA]: *ridge,* north-trending, 1 mile long, 1.25 miles south-southwest of Downieville (lat. 39°32'40" N, long. 120°

50'20" W). Named on Downieville (1951) 7.5' quadrangle, which shows City of Six mine near the south end of the ridge, which was named for a mining town of the 1850's (Gudde, 1969, p. 66).

Clamper Flat [SIERRA]: *area,* 7.5 miles south-southwest of Mount Fillmore (lat. 39°37'50" N, long. 120°54'25" W; near SW cor. sec. 31, T 21 N, R 10 E). Named on La Porte (1951) 7.5' quadrangle.

Clapboard Gulch: see **Volcano** [AMADOR].

Claraville: see **Squaw Creek** [PLACER].

Clarice Lake [MADERA]: *lake,* 600 feet long, 6.5 miles north-northwest of Devils Postpile (lat. 37°42'20" N, long. 119°08'35" W). Named on Devils Postpile (1953) 15' quadrangle.

Clark: see **Mount Clark** [MARIPOSA].

Clark [EL DORADO]: *locality,* 2.25 miles southwest of Robbs Peak (lat. 38°54' N, long. 120°25'55" W). Named on Pyramid Peak (1896) 30' quadrangle.

Clark and Moore's: see **Wawona** [MARIPOSA].

Clark Canyon [MARIPOSA]: *canyon,* drained by a stream that flows 3.5 miles to Merced River 7.5 miles south of Cathedral Peak (lat. 37°44'35" N, long. 119°25'50" W); the canyon heads near Mount Clark. Named on Merced Peak (1953) 15' quadrangle.

Clark Creek [EL DORADO]:
(1) *stream,* flows 1 mile to South Fork American River 3.25 miles west-northwest of Coloma (lat. 38°49'05" N, long. 121°56'50" W; sec. 11, T 11 N, R 9 E); the stream is east of Clark Mountain. Named on Coloma (1949) 7.5' quadrangle.
(2) *stream,* flows 3.5 miles to Cosumnes River 3 miles south-southeast of Latrobe (lat. 38°31'20" N, long. 120°57'15" W; sec. 26, T 8 N, R 9 E). Named on Latrobe (1949) 7.5' quadrangle.

Clarke: see **Sirey and Clarke's Ferry**, under **Stanislaus River** [CALAVERAS-TUOLUMNE].

Clark Flat: see **Clarks Flat** [CALAVERAS].

Clark Fork [MARIPOSA]: *stream,* flows 5 miles to Illilouette Creek 6.5 miles southeast of Yosemite Village (lat. 37°40'35" N, long. 119°30'30" W); the stream heads near Mount Clark. Named on Merced Peak (1953) and Yosemite (1956) 15' quadrangles. United States Board on Geographic Names (1991, p. 4) rejected the name "Clark Fork Creek" for the feature.

Clark Fork [TUOLUMNE]: *stream,* heads in Alpine County and flows 18 miles, approximately along Tuolumne-Alpine county line, to Middle Fork Stanislaus River 3 miles west-northwest of Dardanelle (lat. 38°21'40" N, long. 119°52'30" W). Named on Dardanelle (1979), Dardanelles Cone (1979), Disaster Peak (1979), and Sonora Pass (1979) 7.5' quadrangles. Called Clark's Fork Stanislaus

River on Wheeler's (1876-1877)a map. The name "Clark" commemorates a member of the commission that the state legislature authorized in 1862 to locate a wagon road from Sonora eastward over the Sierra Nevada to Aurora in the present State of Nevada; the route decided upon follows the stream (Browning, 1986, p. 40).

Clark Fork Campground [TUOLUMNE]: *locality,* 4.5 miles north-northeast of Dardanelle on Tuolumne-Alpine county line (lat. 38° 23'45" N, long. 119°48' W); the place is along Clark Fork. Named on Dardanelles Cone (1979) 7.5' quadrangle.

Clark Fork Creek: see **Clark Fork** [MARIPOSA].

Clark Mountain [EL DORADO]: *peak,* 3.5 miles west-northwest of Coloma (lat. 38°48'45" N, long. 120°57'25" W; on N line sec. 15, T 11 N, R 9 E); the peak is west of Clark Creek (1). Altitude 1585 feet. Named on Coloma (1949) 7.5' quadrangle.

Clark Range [MADERA]: *ridge,* northwest- to north-trending, 5 miles long, northwest of Merced Peak (lat. 37°39' N, long. 119°24'30" W). Named on Merced Peak (1953) 15' quadrangle. The feature was known as Obelisk Group and Merced Group at the time of the Whitney survey (Browning, 1986, p. 144).

Clark Reservoir [CALAVERAS]: *lake,* 600 feet long, 0.5 mile south of Rail Road Flat (lat. 38°20'05" N, long. 120°30'50" W; sec. 35, T 6 N, R 13 E). Named on Rail Road Flat (1948) 7.5' quadrangle.

Clarks Canyon [SIERRA]: *canyon,* drained by a stream that flows 1.5 miles to Rattlesnake Creek 5.5 miles south-southeast of Mount Fillmore (lat. 39°39'10" N, long. 120°48'50" W). Named on Mount Fillmore (1951) 7.5' quadrangle.

Clarks Flat [CALAVERAS]: *area,* 4.5 miles east of Murphys on the west side of Stanislaus River (lat. 38°08'35" N, long. 120°22'40" W; on E line sec. 1, T 3 N, R 14 E). Named on Stanislaus (1948) 7.5' quadrangle. Called Clark Flat on Murphys (1948) 7.5' quadrangle.

Clark's Fork Stanislaus River: see **Clark Fork** [TUOLUMNE].

Clarks Gulch [TUOLUMNE]: *canyon,* drained by a stream that flows 1 mile to South Fork Stanislaus River 3 miles northeast of Columbia (lat. 38°03'55" N, long. 120°21'25" W; near SE cor. sec. 31, T 3 N, R 15 E). Named on Columbia SE (1948) 7.5' quadrangle.

Clarks Mill [MARIPOSA]: *locality,* 9 miles east of Mariposa (lat. 37° 29'25" N, long. 119°48' W; near SE cor. sec. 17, T 5 S, R 20 E). Named on Mariposa (1912) 30' quadrangle.

Clarkson: see **Clarksona** [AMADOR].

Clarksona [AMADOR]: *locality,* 3 miles west-northwest of Ione along Southern Pacific Railroad (lat. 38°22'25" N, long. 120° 59' W). Named on Ione (1962) 7.5' quadrangle. Cali-

fornia Mining Bureau's (1917c) map has the name "Clarkson" for the place.

Clark's Ranch: see **Wawona** [MARIPOSA].

Clark's Station: see **Wawona** [MARIPOSA].

Clark Station Homesites [SIERRA]: *locality,* 7.25 miles northeast of Sierra City (lat. 39°37'20" N, long. 120°31'20" W; near S line sec. 4, T 20 N, R 13 E). Named on Sierra City (1955) 15' quadrangle.

Clarks Valley [MARIPOSA]: *valley,* 10 miles south-southwest of El Portal (lat. 37°32'45" N, long. 119°51'45" W). Named on Buckingham Mountain (1947) 7.5' quadrangle.

Clarksville [EL DORADO]: *locality,* 6 miles west-southwest of Placerville (lat. 38°39'20" N, long. 121°03' W; at N line sec. 12, T 9 N, R 8 E). Named on Clarksville (1953) 7.5' quadrangle. Postal authorities established Clarksville post office in 1855, discontinued it in 1924, reestablished it in 1927, and discontinued it in 1934 (Frickstad, p. 25). A travelers stop called Mormon Tavern was located 0.5 mile west of Clarksville along the emigrant road; it opened in 1849 and was a Pony Express stop in 1860 and 1861 (Hoover, Rensch, and Rensch, p. 83).

Claussenius [EL DORADO]: *locality,* 6 miles north-northwest of Pollock Pines (lat. 38°50'50" N, long. 120°36'45" W; near W line sec. 35, T 12 N, R 12 E). Named on Pollock Pines (1950) 7.5' quadrangle. The name should have the form "Clausenius" (Beverly Cola, personal communication, 1985).

Clavey: see **Camp Clavey** [TUOLUMNE].

Clavey Creek: see **Bell Creek** [TUOLUMNE]; **Clavey River** [TUOLUMNE].

Clavey Meadow [TUOLUMNE]: *area,* 8.5 miles south of Pinecrest along Looney Creek (lat. 38°04'05" N, long. 120°00' W; sec. 33, T 3 N, R 18 E). Named on Cherry Lake North (1979) and Hull Creek (1979) 7.5' quadrangles. Browning (1986, p. 41) associated the name with Jane A. Clavey, who patented land in the neighborhood in 1897.

Clavey River [TUOLUMNE]: *stream,* formed by the confluence of Bell Creek and Lily Creek (3), flows 30 miles to Tuolumne River 7.25 miles south of Duckwall Mountain (lat. 37°51'50" N, long. 120°06'55" W; sec. 9, T 1 S, R 17 E). Named on Cherry Lake North (1979), Duckwall Mountain (1948), Hull Creek (1979), Jawbone Ridge (1947), and Pinecrest (1979) 7.5' quadrangles. Present Clavey River is called Clavey Creek on Sonora (1897) 30' quadrangle, and present Clavey River and present Bell Creek together are called Middle Fork Tuolumne River on Dardanelles (1898) 30' quadrangle, but United States Board on Geographic Names (1963a, p. 6) rejected the names "Clavey Creek," "Middle Fork Tuolumne River," and "Big Canon Creek" for Clavey River.

Clavey River: see **Bell Creek** [TUOLUMNE].

Clay's Bar: see **Camanche** [CALAVERAS].

Clayton [EL DORADO]: *locality,* 12 miles east of Placerville (lat. 38° 44'25" N, long. 120°35'05" W). Named on Placerville (1893) 30' quadrangle.

Clayton [PLACER]: *locality,* 1.5 miles northwest of Lincoln along Southern Pacific Railroad (lat. 38°54'30" N, long. 121°18'40" W; sec. 9, T 12 N, R 6 E). Named on Lincoln (1953) 7.5' quadrangle, which shows clay pits near the place.

Clear Creek [EL DORADO]:

(1) *stream,* flows 8 miles to North Fork Cosumnes River 5.25 miles south of Camino (lat. 38°39'45" N, long. 120°41'10" W; near E line sec. 6, T 9 N, R 12 E). Named on Camino (1952) and Sly Park (1952) 7.5' quadrangles. North Fork enters from the northeast 6.5 miles above the mouth of the main stream; it is 2.5 miles long and is named on Sly Park (1952) 7.5' quadrangle.

(2) *stream,* flows 5.25 miles to Steely Fork Cosumnes River 2.5 miles north-northeast of Omo Ranch (lat. 38°36'50" N, long. 120° 33'35" W; near N line sec. 29, T 9 N, R 13 E). Named on Omo Ranch (1952) 7.5' quadrangle.

Clear Creek [NEVADA]:

(1) *stream,* flows 2 miles to Middle Yuba River nearly 1 mile north-northeast of North San Juan (lat. 39°22'55" N, long. 120°06' W; sec. 32, T 18 N, R 8 E). Named on Camptonville (1948) and Nevada City (1948) 7.5' quadrangles.

(2) *stream,* flows 3 miles to Fall Creek 5.25 miles northwest of Yuba Gap (lat. 39°22'10" N, long. 120°41' W; sec. 1, T 17 N, R 11 E). Named on Blue Canyon (1955) and Graniteville (1982) 7.5' quadrangles.

(3) *stream,* flows 5.5 miles to Squirrel Creek 2.25 miles north of Pilot Peak in Penn Valley (lat. 39°02'05" N, long. 121°10'30" W; sec. 34, T 16 N, R 7 E). Named on Grass Valley (1949) and Rough and Ready (1949) 7.5' quadrangles.

Clearing House [MARIPOSA]: *locality,* nearly 5 miles west of El Portal on the north side of Merced River (lat. 37°39'55" N, long. 119°52' W; sec. 21, T 3 S, R 19 E). Named on El Portal (1947) 7.5' quadrangle. Postal authorities established Clearinghouse post office in 1913 and discontinued it in 1933; the name is from Clearinghouse mine, which received its name because it was the exchange place for clearinghouse certificates and gold bullion in the panic of 1907 (Salley, p. 45). Hoffmann and Gardner's (1863-1867) map shows a place called Yosemite Mill situated at or near present Clearing House. California Division of Highways' (1934) map shows a place called Sloss located along Yosemite Valley Railroad 1 mile southeast of Clearinghouse (present Clearing House), and a place called Emory located along the railroad 1 mile west of Clearinghouse. The name "Emory" is for A. Emory

Wishon of Fresno, who headed a group that formed Yosemite Portland Cement Company in 1925 to use limestone at the site (Johnston, p. 51, 117, 119). The name "Emory" later was changed to "Richardsons" (Sargent, Shirley, 1976, p. 12).

Clear Lake [TUOLUMNE]: *lake,* 650 feet long, 5.5 miles southeast of Pinecrest (lat. 38°07'40" N, long. 119°56'15" W). Named on Pinecrest (1979) 7.5' quadrangle.

Clear View: see **Whiskey Slide** [CALAVERAS].

Clearwater Creek [MADERA]: *stream,* flows 2 miles to Ross Creek 9 miles south-south-east of Shuteye Peak (lat. 37°14'05" N, long. 119°21'10" W; sec. 16, T 8 S, R 24 E). Named on Shaver Lake (1953) 15' quadrangle.

Cleghorn Ravine [SIERRA]: *canyon,* drained by a stream that flows less than 1 mile to Canyon Creek 2.5 miles south of Mount Fillmore (lat. 39°41'30" N, long. 120°50'55" W). Named on Mount Fillmore (1951) 7.5' quadrangle.

Clementine: see **Lake Clementine,** under **North Fork Lake** [PLACER].

Cliff Canyon [PLACER]: *canyon,* drained by a stream that flows 1.5 miles to Screwauger Canyon less than 1 mile west of Duncan Peak (lat. 39°09'10" N, long. 120°31'35" W; near N line sec. 16, T 15 N, R 13 E). Named on Duncan Peak (1952) 7.5' quadrangle. This appears to be the feature called Van Cliffe Cañ. on Whitney's (1880) map.

Cliff Lake [EL DORADO]: *lake,* 750 feet long, 2.5 miles north of Phipps Peak (lat. 38°58'35" N, long. 120°08'50" W; sec. 18, T 13 N, R 17 E). Named on Rockbound Valley (1955) 7.5' quadrangle.

Clifton: see **Last Chance** [PLACER].

Cline Creek [TUOLUMNE]: *stream,* flows 2 miles to Big Jackass Creek 4.5 miles southeast of Groveland (lat. 37°46'50" N, long. 120°11'45" W; sec. 10, T 2 S, R 16 E). Named on Groveland (1947) 7.5' quadrangle.

Clinton [AMADOR]: *locality,* 2.5 miles south of Pine Grove (lat. 38° 22'35" N, long. 120°40' W; near W line sec. 16, T 6 N, R 12 E). Named on Pine Grove (1948) 7.5' quadrangle. The place also was called Sarahville or Sarahsville (Gudde, 1975, p. 75). Postal authorities established Sarahville post office in 1856 and discontinued it in 1859 (Frickstad, p. 6). Camp's (1962) map shows the alternate name "Lincoln" for the place. Doble (p. 76) mentioned a mining camp called Secreta that was situated along present South Fork Jackson Creek downstream from Clinton.

Clinton: see **Moores Flat** [NEVADA].

Clinton Peak [AMADOR]: *peak,* 2.5 miles south-southwest of Pine Grove (lat. 38°22'50" N, long. 120°40'30" W; near N line sec. 17, T 6 N, R 12 E); the peak is 0.5 mile northwest of Clinton. Altitude 2447 feet. Named on Pine Grove (1948) 7.5' quadrangle.

Clipper Creek [NEVADA]: *stream,* flows 5

miles to Little Greenhorn Creek 4 miles north of Chicago Park (lat. 39°12'10" N, long. 120°58'05" W; sec. 33, T 16 N, R 9 E). Named on Chicago Park (1949) and North Bloomfield (1949) 7.5' quadrangles.

Clipper Creek [PLACER]: *stream,* flows 6 miles to North Fork American River 3.25 miles northeast of Auburn (lat. 38°56' N, long. 121°02' W; sec. 36, T 13 N, R 8 E). Named on Auburn (1953) and Greenwood (1949) 7.5' quadrangles. The canyon of the stream is called Clipper Ravine on Placerville (1893) 30' quadrangle.

Clipper Creek: see **Little Clipper Creek** [NEVADA].

Clipper Gap [PLACER]: *locality,* 6 miles north-northeast of Auburn (lat. 38°58'10" N, long. 121°01'05" W; near N line sec. 19, T 13 N, R 9 E). Named on Auburn (1953) 7.5' quadrangle. Postal authorities established Clipper Gap post office in 1866, changed the name to Clippergap in 1894, moved it 2.5 miles southwest in 1881, changed the name back to Clipper Gap in 1950, and discontinued it in 1960 (Salley, p. 46).

Clipper Ravine: see **Clipper Creek** [PLACER].

Cloudman: see **Keystone** [TUOLUMNE].

Cloud Splitter [SIERRA]: *peak,* 4 miles south-southeast of Mount Fillmore (lat. 39°40'30" N, long. 120°50'10" W). Altitude 6491 feet. Named on Mount Fillmore (1951) 7.5' quadrangle.

Clouds Rest [MARIPOSA]: *peak,* 7 miles southwest of Cathedral Peak (lat. 37°46'05" N, long. 119°29'20" W). Altitude 9926 feet. Named on Tuolumne Meadows (1956) 15' quadrangle. Called Clouds' Rest on Hoffmann and Gardner's (1863-1867) map. Members of an exploring party gave the name in 1851 when they saw clouds settling on the peak before a snow storm (Gudde, 1969, p. 67).

Clover Creek [CALAVERAS]: *stream,* flows 4.5 miles to Littlejohns Creek 2.5 miles west-southwest of Copperopolis (lat. 37°58'10" N, long. 120°41' W; sec. 5, T 1 N, R 12 E). Named on Copperopolis (1962) and Salt Spring Valley (1962) 7.5' quadrangles.

Clover Meadow [TUOLUMNE]: *area,* 7.5 miles west-northwest of Dardanelle along Wheats Meadow Creek (lat. 38°22'10" N, long. 119°57'45" W; sec. 14, T 6 N, R 18 E). Named on Donnell Lake (1979) 7'5' quadrangle.

Clover Valley [PLACER]: *valley,* 2.5 miles north of Rocklin (lat. 38° 49'45" N, long. 121°13'30" W). Named on Rocklin (1967) 7.5' quadrangle.

Clover Valley Creek [PLACER]: *stream,* flows 6.25 miles to Antelope Creek 0.5 mile north-northwest of downtown Rocklin (lat. 38°47'50" N, long. 121°14'20" W; sec. 18, T 11 N, R 7 E); the stream goes through Clover Valley. Named on Rocklin (1967) 7.5' quadrangle.

Clover Valley Reservoir [PLACER]: *lake,* 625 feet long, behind a dam on Clover Valley Creek 5.5 miles north-northeast of Rocklin

(lat. 38°52'05" N, long. 121°11'45" W; at N line sec. 28, T 12 N, R 7 E). Named on Rocklin (1967) 7.5' quadrangle.

Clyde Lake [EL DORADO]: *lake,* 1300 feet long, 5.5 miles south of Phipps Peak (lat. 38°52'35" N, long. 120°10'05" W). Named on Pyramid Peak (1955) and Rockbound Valley (1955) 7.5' quadrangles.

Clyde Mountain [NEVADA]: *peak,* 3 miles northwest of Yuba Gap (lat. 39°20'35" N, long. 120°39'35" W; at W line sec. 17, T 17 N, R 12 E). Altitude 6052 feet. Named on Blue Canyon (1955) 7.5' quadrangle. Called Clydes Mt. on Colfax (1898) 30' quadrangle.

Coalpit Hill [MARIPOSA]: *peak,* 2.25 miles north of Buckhorn Peak (lat. 37°42' N, long. 120°07' W; sec. 5, T 3 S, R 17 E). Altitude 3375 feet. Named on Buckhorn Peak (1947) 7.5' quadrangle.

Coarsegold [MADERA]: *village,* 8 miles south-southwest of Yosemite Forks (lat. 37°15'45" N, long. 119°42' W; sec. 5, T 8 S, R 21 E); the village is along Coarse Gold Creek. Named on Bass Lake (1953) 15' quadrangle. Mariposa (1912) 30' quadrangle has the form "Coarse Gold" for the name. Postal authorities established Coarse Gold Gulch post office in 1878, changed the name to Goldgulch in 1895, and changed it to Coarsegold in 1899 (Frickstad, p. 85). Miners from Texas found gold at the place in 1849 and the community that developed there was known first as Texas Flat (Hoover, Rensch, and Rensch, p. 172). A map of 1874 has the name "Michaels" at the site—Charles Michael had a business there (Clough, p. 78). A Mexican mining camp called Oro Grosso probably was at the place (Gudde, 1975, p. 256). Postal authorities established Rallsville post office 20 miles northeast of Madera in 1881 and discontinued it in 1883, when they moved the service to Coarse Gold Gulch post office; the name "Rallsville" was for George W. Ralls, first postmaster (Salley, p. 180).

Coarse Gold Creek [MADERA]: *stream,* flows 23 miles to Fresno River 4 miles south-south-east of Knowles (lat. 37°10'05" N, long. 119°50'30" W; sec. 12, T 9 S, R 19 E). Named on Bass Lake (1953), Millerton Lake (1965), and Raymond (1962) 15' quadrangles. The name is from the coarseness of gold found in the stream (Hoover, Rensch, and Rensch, p. 172).

Coarse Gold Gulch: see **Coarsegold** [MADERA].

Cobbs Creek [TUOLUMNE]: *stream,* flows 2 miles to Big Jackass Creek 3.25 miles southeast of Moccasin (lat. 37°47' N, long. 120° 15'10" W; near N line sec. 7, T 2 S, R 16 E). Named on Groveland (1947) and Moccasin (1948) 7.5' quadrangles. Paden and Schlichtmann (p. 128) used the form "Cobb's Creek" for the name.

Coburn Lake [SIERRA]: *lake,* 600 feet long, 5

miles west-southwest of Sierraville at the head of Berry Creek (lat. 39°33'35" N, long. 120°27'10" W; near W line sec. 29, T 20 N, R 14 E). Named on Sattley (1981) 7.5' quadrangle.

Coburn Station: see **Truckee** [NEVADA].

Cock Robin Point [EL DORADO]: *peak*, 4 miles north of Georgetown (lat. 38°57'55" N, long. 120°50'30" W; near NE cor. sec. 22, T 13 N, R 10 E). Altitude 2479 feet. Named on Georgetown (1949) 7.5' quadrangle.

Cockscomb [MARIPOSA-TUOLUMNE]: *peak*, 1 mile south-southeast of Cathedral Peak on Mariposa-Tuolumne county line (lat. 37°50'05" N, long. 119°23'40" W; sec. 24, T 1 S, R 23 E). Named on Tuolumne Meadows (1956) 15' quadrangle. François Matthes named the feature before 1923 (O'Neill, p. 96). United States Board on Geographic Named (1970b, p. 2) gave the names "Cockscomb Crest" and "Cockscomb Peak" as variants.

Cockscomb Crest: see **Cockscomb** [MARIPOSA-TUOLUMNE].

Cockscomb Peak: see **Cockscomb** [MARIPOSA-TUOLUMNE].

Codfish Creek [PLACER]: *stream*, flows 3.25 miles to North Fork American River 9 miles northeast of Auburn (lat. 38°59'30" N, long. 120°57'15" W; sec. 10, T 13 N, R 9 E). Named on Colfax (1949) and Greenwood (1949) 7.5' quadrangles.

Codfish Creek: see **Little Codfish Creek** [PLACER].

Codfish Falls [PLACER]: *waterfall*, 9 miles northeast of Auburn along Codfish Creek (lat. 38°59'50" N, long. 120°57'15" W; sec. 10, T 13 N, R 9 E). Named on Greeenwood (1949) 7.5' quadrangle.

Codfish Point [PLACER]: *ridge*, south-southwest- to south-trending, 3 miles long, center 3.25 miles north-northeast of Michigan Bluff (lat. 39°05' N, long. 120°42'15" W). Named on Michigan Bluff (1952) 7.5' quadrangle.

Cody: see **Camp Cody** [EL DORADO].

Cody Creek [EL DORADO]: *stream*, flows 4 miles to Strawberry Creek 4.25 miles south of Pyramid Peak (lat. 38°47'05" N, long. 120°08'55" W; sec. 19, T 11 N, R 17 E). Named on Pyramid Peak (1955) and Tragedy Spring (1979) 7.5' quadrangles.

Cody Creek [PLACER]: *stream*, flows 1 mile to Andrew Gray Creek 7 miles northwest of Duncan Peak (lat. 39°13'35" N, long. 120°35'50" W; sec. 26, T 16 N, R 12 E). Named on Duncan Peak (1952) 7.5' quadrangle. The name commemorates George Milo Cody, pioneer rancher and fruit grower in the vicinity (United States Board on Geographic Names, 1967a, p. 2).

Cody Lake [EL DORADO]: *lake*, 950 feet long, 6 miles south of Pyramid Peak (lat. 38°45'35" N, long. 120°08'30" W; sec. 1, T 10 N, R 16 E); the lake is at the head of a branch of Cody Creek. Named on Pyramid Peak (1955) 7.5' quadrangle.

Cody Meadows [EL DORADO]: *area*, 4.5 miles northwest of Kirkwood (lat. 38°44'35" N, long. 120°07'55" W; sec. 6, T 10 N, R 17 E); the place is along Cody Creek. Named on Tragedy Spring (1979) 7.5' quadrangle.

Coe Gulch [MARIPOSA]: *canyon*, drained by a stream that flows nearly 1.5 miles to Whites Gulch 3 miles south-southeast of Coulterville (lat. 37°40'15" N, long. 120°10'40" W; sec. 14, T 3 S, R 16 E). Named on Coulterville (1947) 7.5' quadrangle.

Coffin Hollow [TUOLUMNE]: *canyon*, 2.25 miles long, 6 miles southeast of Pinecrest along Lily Creek (3) (lat. 38°08' N, long. 119°55'15" W). Named on Pinecrest (1979) 7.5' quadrangle.

Colby Mountain [TUOLUMNE]: *peak*, nearly 7 miles east-northeast of White Wolf (lat. 37°54'40" N, long. 119°32'20" W). Altitude 9631 feet. Named on Hetch Hetchy Reservoir (1956) 15' quadrangle. The name commemorates W.E. Colby of the Sierra Club (United States Board on Geographic Names, 1934, p. 5).

Cold Canyon [EL DORADO]: *canyon*, 1.25 miles long, on upper reaches of Park Canyon (present Sly Park Canyon) above a point 1.5 miles northwest of Old Iron Mountain (lat. 38°43'05" N, long. 120°24'35" W; sec. 18, T 10 N, R 14 E). Named on Stump Spring (1951) 7.5' quadrangle.

Cold Canyon [MARIPOSA]: *canyon*, drained by a stream that flows 3 miles to Merced River 1.5 miles west-southwest of El Portal (lat. 37°39'55" N, long. 119°48'30" W; near N line sec. 19, T 3 S, R 20 E). Named on El Portal (1947) 7.5' quadrangle.

Cold Canyon [TUOLUMNE]: *canyon*, drained by a stream that flows 5.25 miles to Tuolumne River 9 miles west of Tioga Pass (lat. 37°54'35" N, long. 119°25'05" W). Named on Tuolumne Meadows (1956) 15' quadrangle.

Cold Canyon: see **Brushy Canyon** [EL DORADO] (2).

Cold Creek [EL DORADO]: *stream*, heads at Star Lake and flows 6.5 miles to Trout Creek 5.5 miles northwest of Freel Peak (lat. 38°54'40" N, long. 119°58'10" W; sec. 3, T 12 N, R 18 E). Named on South Lake Tahoe (1955) 7.5' quadrangle.

Cold Creek [MADERA]: *stream*, flows 1 mile to Middle Fork San Joaquin River 4.5 miles south of Devils Postpile (lat. 37°33'20" N, long. 119°05'30" W). Named on Devils Postpile (1953) 15' quadrangle.

Cold Creek [NEVADA-PLACER]: *stream*, heads in Placer County and flows 6.5 miles to Donner Creek 2.25 miles west of downtown Truckee in Nevada County (lat. 39°19'25" N, long. 120°13'20" W; sec. 17, T 17 N, R 16 E). Named on Norden (1955) and Truckee (1955) 7.5' quadrangles. Mor-

CALIFORNIA'S GOLD COUNTRY

gan (p. 425) identified present Cold Creek as the stream called Summit Creek on Jefferson's (1849) map. South Fork enters from the south 3.5 miles east-southeast of Donner Pass in Coldstream Valley; it is 3 miles long and is named on Norden (1955) 7.5' quadrangle.

Cold Creek Campground [SIERRA]: *locality,* 4.25 miles southeast of Sierraville (lat. 39°32'30" N, long. 120°18'55" W; sec. 33, T 20 N, R 15 E); the place is along Cold Stream (1). Named on Sierraville (1981) 7.5' quadrangle.

Cold Mountain [TUOLUMNE]: *peak,* 9.5 miles west-northwest of Tioga Pass (lat. 37°57' N, long. 119°25'35" W); the peak is west of Cold Canyon. Altitude 10,301 feet. Named on Tuolumne Meadows (1956) 15' quadrangle.

Cold Spring [CALAVERAS]: *spring,* 5.5 miles east-southeast of Blue Mountain in Dorrington (lat. 38°18'05" N, long. 120°16'40" W; near W line sec. 12, T 5 N, R 15 E). Named on Dorrington (1979) 7.5' quadrangle.

Cold Spring [MARIPOSA]: *spring,* 6 miles west of Fish Camp (lat. 37°28'15" N, long. 119°44'30" W; near W line sec. 25, T 5 S, R 20 E). Named on Bass Lake (1953) 15' quadrangle. Laizure's (1935) map shows a locality called Cold Springs at or near the spring. Postal authorities established Cold Springs post office in 1879 and discontinued it in 1883 (Frickstad, p. 90).

Cold Spring [SIERRA]: *locality,* 3.5 miles east-northeast of Pike (lat. 39°27'50" N, long. 120°56' W). Named on Colfax (1898) 30' quadrangle.

Cold Spring: see **Cold Springs** [TUOLUMNE].

Cold Spring Hill [PLACER]: *peak,* 3 miles south-southwest of Dutch Flat (lat. 39°10'05" N, long. 120°51'50" W; at E line sec. 8, T 15 N, R 10 E). Altitude 3685 feet. Named on Dutch Flat (1950) 7.5' quadrangle. United States Board on Geographic Names (1933, p. 228) rejected the name "Gold Spring Hill" for the feature.

Cold Spring Meadow [MADERA]: *area,* 5 miles south-southeast of Shuteye Peak (lat. 37°17' N, long. 119°23'50" W; near NW cor. sec. 31, T 7 S, R 24 E). Named on Shuteye Peak (1953) 15' quadrangle.

Cold Spring Meadow [MARIPOSA]: *area,* nearly 6 miles west of Fish Camp (lat. 37°28'30" N, long. 119°44'30" W); Cold Spring is in the meadow. Named on Bass Lake (1953) 15' quadrangle.

Cold Springs [EL DORADO]: *locality,* 4 miles west of Placerville (lat. 38°44'30" N, long. 120°52'15" W; near NW cor. sec. 10, T 10 N, R 10 E). Site named on Placerville (1949) 7.5' quadrangle. Postal authorities established Cold Spring post office in or before 1852 and discontinued it in 1874 (Salley, p. 47).

Cold Springs [TUOLUMNE]: *settlement,* 3.5 miles southwest of Strawberry (lat. 38°09'45" N, long. 120°03'15" W; sec. 36, T 4 N, R 17 E). Named on Strawberry (1979) 7.5' quadrangle. Big Trees (1891) 30' quadrangle shows a place called Cold Spring at the site.

Cold Springs: see **Cold Spring** [MARIPOSA].

Cold Springs Creek [EL DORADO]: *stream,* flows 2.5 miles to Weber Creek 4 miles west of Placerville (lat. 38°44'25" N, long. 120°52'15" W; near W line sec. 10, T 10 N, R 10 E); Cold Springs is near the mouth of the stream. Named on Placerville (1949) 7.5' quadrangle.

Cold Springs Meadow [MADERA]:
(1) *area,* 9 miles south-southwest of Merced Peak (lat. 37°31'15" N, long. 119°28'45" W; near SW cor. sec. 5, T 5 S, R 23 E). Named on Merced Peak (1953) 15' quadrangle.
(2) *area,* nearly 6 miles northwest of Shuteye Peak (lat. 37°25' N, long. 119°29'30" W; near S line sec. 7, T 6 S, R 23 E). Named on Shuteye Peak (1953) 15' quadrangle.

Cold Springs Ranch: see **Dorrington** [CALAVERAS].

Cold Stream [NEVADA-SIERRA]: *stream,* heads in Nevada County and flows 4.5 miles to Little Truckee River 7 miles south of Sierraville in Sierra County (lat. 39°29'35" N, long. 120°20'55" W; near SE cor. sec. 24, T 19 N, R 14 E). Named on Independence Lake (1981) 7.5' quadrangle.

Cold Stream [SIERRA]: *stream,* flows 7 miles to join Bonta Creek and form Sierraville Creek 1.5 miles south of Sierraville (lat. 39° 34' N, long. 120°21'45" W; near E line sec. 24, T 20 N, R 14 E). Named on Sierraville (1981) 7.5' quadrangle.

Cold Stream Meadow [SIERRA]: *area,* 9.5 miles south of Sierraville (lat. 39°27'10" N, long. 120°20'45" W; near E line sec. 1, T 18 N, R 14 E); the place is along Cold Stream [NEVADA-SIERRA]. Named on Independence Lake (1981) 7.5' quadrangle.

Coldstream Valley [PLACER]: *valley,* along Cold Creek [NEVADA-PLACER] above a point 11 miles west of Martis Peak (lat. 39° 19' N, long. 120°13'40" W). Named on Norden (1955) and Truckee (1955) 7.5' quadrangles.

Cole Creek [AMADOR]: *stream,* flows 14 miles to North Fork Mokelumne River 8.5 miles west-southwest of Mokelumne Peak (lat. 38°29'10" N, long. 120°14'20" W; sec. 5, T 7 N, R 16 E). Named on Bear River Reservoir (1979), Calaveras Dome (1979), and Mokelumne Peak (1979) 7.5' quadrangles.

Cole Creek Lakes [AMADOR]: *lakes,* largest 700 feet long, 3 miles north of Mokelumne Peak (lat. 38°35' N, long. 120°05'30" W); the lakes are along a branch of Cole Creek. Named on Mokelumne Peak (1979) 7.5' quadrangle.

Cole Hill [NEVADA]: *peak,* 1.5 miles north-northwest of Wolf (lat. 39°04'45" N, long. 121°09'20" W; near E line sec. 11, T 14 N, R

73

7 E). Altitude 1827 feet. Named on Wolf (1949) 7.5' quadrangle.

Coleman [NEVADA]: *locality,* 2 miles north of Chicago Park along Nevada County Narrow Gauge Railroad (lat. 39°10'30" N, long. 120°58'30" W; near S line sec. 4, T 15 N, R 9 E). Named on Colfax (1938) 30' quadrangle.

Coleman Flat [MARIPOSA]: *area,* 10.5 miles south-southeast of Mariposa (lat. 37°21'10" N, long. 119°52'50" W; sec. 3, T 7 S, R 19 E). Named on Ben Hur (1947) 7.5' quadrangle.

Coleman Spring [NEVADA]: *spring,* nearly 2 miles east-northeast of North Bloomfield (lat. 39°22'35" N, long. 120°52'05" W; on E line sec. 32, T 18 N, R 10 E). Named on Alleghany (1949) 7.5' quadrangle.

Coles: see **Coles Station** [EL DORADO].

Coles Station [EL DORADO]: *locality,* 3 miles north-northwest of Omo Ranch (lat. 38°37'15" N, long. 120°35'30" W; near W line sec. 19, T 9 N, R 13 E). Named on Omo Ranch (1952) 7.5' quadrangle. Called Coles on Placerville (1893) 30' quadrangle.

Colfax [PLACER]: *town,* 15 miles north-northeast of Auburn (lat. 39°06'05" N, long. 120°57'10" W; around NE cor. sec. 3, T 14 N, R 9 E). Named on Colfax (1949) 7.5' quadrangle. The name commemorates Schuyler Colfax, Speaker of the House of Representatives, who inspected the new railroad through the place in the summer of 1865 (Stewart, p. 45). Postal authorities established Colfax post office in 1866 (Frickstad, p. 119), and the town incorporated in 1910. Whitney's (1873) map shows a place called Mineral Bar located due east of Colfax along North Fork American River. California Division of Highways' (1934) map shows a place called Chicago Park located along a narrow-gauge railroad about 1 mile north-northeast of Colfax (near N line sec. 35, T 15 N, R 9 E), a place called Smiths situated about 0.5 mile farther north (sec. 26, T 15 N, R 9 E), and a place called Oilville located 0.5 mile beyond Smiths along the railroad (sec. 26, T 15 N, R 9 E); the railroad goes to and beyond Chicago Park [NEVADA].

Colfax Gate: see **Colfax Spring** [TUOLUMNE].

Colfax Hill [PLACER]: *ridge,* south-trending, 1 mile long, just north of downtown Colfax (lat. 39°06'30" N, long. 120°57'10" W; near E line sec. 34, T 15 N, R 9 E). Named on Colfax (1949) 7.5' quadrangle.

Colfax Spring [TUOLUMNE]: *locality,* 11 miles east of Groveland (lat. 37°49'15" N, long. 120°01'30" W; sec. 29, T 1 S, R 18 E). Named on Jawbone Ridge (1947) 7.5' quadrangle. Sonora (1897) 30' quadrangle shows a place called Colfax Gate at the site. Charles Ewell built a modest stopping place at the locality for teamsters, who were attracted by an unfailing cold spring; about 1874 Ewell enlarged his establishment and called it Eagle

Hotel for an eagle that his small son shot (Paden and Schlichtmann, p. 197-198).

Collierville [CALAVERAS]: *locality,* 6 miles northeast of Vallecito (lat. 38°08' N, long. 120°23'10" W). Named on Big Trees (1891) 30' quadrangle. W. Collier owned nearby Homestake mine (Crawford, 1894, p. 93).

Collins Ravine [SIERRA]: *canyon,* drained by a stream that flows 2 miles to Goodyears Creek 2 miles north of Goodyears Bar (lat. 39°34'15" N, long. 120°52'30" W; sec. 29, T 20 N, R 10 E). Named on Goodyears Bar (1951) 7.5' quadrangle.

Colluma: see **Coloma** [EL DORADO].

Coloma [EL DORADO]: *village,* 7 miles northwest of Placerville along South Fork American River (lat. 38°48' N, long. 120°53'25" W; sec. 17, T 11 N, R 10 E). Named on Coloma (1949) 7.5' quadrangle. Called Colluma on Derby's (1849) map. Postal authorities established Culloma post office at the place in 1849 and changed the name to Coloma in 1851 (Frickstad, p. 26). The community grew at the site of Sutter's sawmill, where James Marshall made the gold discovery in 1848 that started the great California gold rush of 1849. In 1848 Marshall discovered and named a mining place called Live Oak Bar that was located 3 miles upstream from the sawmill (Bancroft, 1888, p. 47). A mining place called Stony Bar was situated about 5 miles upstream from Coloma, a mining place called Pleasant Flat was on the north side of South Fork American River 1 mile above Coloma, and a mining place called Snyders Bar was along South Fork 3 miles below Coloma (Gudde, 1975, p. 271, 326, 337).

Coloma Canyon [EL DORADO]: *canyon,* drained by a stream that flows 3.5 miles to Greenwood Creek less than 1 mile south of Greenwood (lat. 38°53'15" N, long. 120°54'35" W; sec. 18, T 12 N, R 10 E). Named on Coloma (1949), Garden Valley (1949), and Greenwood (1949) 7.5' quadrangles.

Colorado [MARIPOSA]: *locality,* 13 miles southwest of El Portal (lat. 37°33'25" N, long. 119°58' W; sec. 27, T 4 S, R 18 E). Named on Yosemite (1909) 30' quadrangle. El Portal (1947) 15' quadrangle shows Colorado mine near the site. Postal authorities established Colorado post office in 1858 and discontinued it in 1860; the name was from the mine (Salley, p. 48).

Columbia [TUOLUMNE]: *village,* 3.5 miles north-northwest of Sonora (lat. 38°02'10" N, long. 120°24' W; sec. 11, 14, T 2 N, R 14 E). Named on Columbia (1948) 7.5' quadrangle. Postal authorities established Columbia post office in 1852 (Frickstad, p. 215), and the community incorporated in 1854. Dr. Thaddeus Hildreth and his brother George were with a group that found gold at the place in 1850, and for a time the mining camp there was called Hildreth's Diggings (Hoover,

Rensch, and Rensch, p. 570). The camp also was called American Camp, Dry Diggings (Gudde, 1975, p. 78-79), and New Camp (Stoddart, p. 125) before Major Sullivan, the first alcalde, and others gave it the name "Columbia" in April of 1850 (Bancroft, 1888, p. 515). A feature called Main Gulch, first called Columbia Gulch, is in Columbia, and a feature called Lawnsdale Gulch is located about 1 mile west of the village (Gudde, 1975, p. 192, 203). A mining camp called Santiago, Santa Iago, or San Diego, was situated about 1 mile northeast of the site of Columbia; Mexicans mined there in 1849 before discovery of gold at Columbia (Morgan *in* Gardiner, p. 346).

Columbia: see **North Columbia** [NEVADA].

Columbia Bar: see **Grapevine Gulch** [AMADOR] (2).

Columbia Camp [TUOLUMNE]: *locality,* 5.5 miles west-southwest of Mather (lat. 37°51'15" N, long. 119°56'50" W; sec. 13, T 1 S, R 18 E). Named on Lake Eleanor (1956) 15' quadrangle.

Columbia Finger [MARIPOSA]: *relief feature,* 2.25 miles south-southwest of Cathedral Peak (lat. 37°49'10" N, long. 119°25'20" W; sec. 26, T 1 S, R 23 E). Named on Tuolumne Meadows (1956) 15' quadrangle. United States Board on Geographic Names (1933, p. 231) rejected the form "Columbia's Finger" for the name.

Columbia Flat: see **Kelsey** [EL DORADO].

Columbia Gulch: see **Main Gulch**, under **Columbia** [TUOLUMNE].

Columbia Hill [NEVADA]: *relief feature,* 4 miles west-northwest of North Bloomfield (lat. 39°23'25" N, long. 121°58' W; near SE cor. sec. 28, T 18 N, R 9 E). Named on Pike (1949) 7.5' quadrangle. Colfax (1898) 30' quadrangle has the name for a feature located about 3 miles farther east. N.L. Tisdale and others gave the name to the feature in 1853 for Columbia Consolidated Mining Company (Gudde, 1949, p. 75).

Columbia Hill: see **North Columbia** [NEVADA].

Columbia House: see **Kelsey** [EL DORADO].

Columbia Rock [MARIPOSA]: *relief feature,* 1 mile west-southwest of Yosemite Village on the north side of Yosemite Valley (lat. 37° 44'45" N, long. 119°36'05" W). Named on Yosemite (1956) 15' quadrangle.

Columbia's Finger: see **Columbia Finger** [MARIPOSA].

Columbia Well [MADERA]: *well,* 16 miles west of Madera (lat. 36° 56'25" N, long. 120°21'20" W; sec. 29, T 11 S, R 15 E). Named on Kentucky Well (1922) 7.5' quadrangle.

Columns of the Giants [TUOLUMNE]: *relief feature,* 1.5 miles east of Dardanelle (lat. 38°20'15" N, long. 119°48'10" W; sec. 29, T 6 N, R 20 E). Named on Dardanelle (1979) 7.5' quadrangle.

Combie: see **Lake Combie** [NEVADA-PLACER].

Combie Crossing [NEVADA-PLACER]: *locality,* 7 miles southwest of Colfax along Bear River on Nevada-Placer county line (lat. 39° 00'50" N, long. 121°02'15" W). Named on Smartsville (1895) 30' quadrangle. Water of Lake Combie now covers the site.

Compoodle Creek: see **Campoodle Creek** [TUOLUMNE].

Concord: see **Orleans Flat** [NEVADA].

Condemned Bar: see **Folsom Lake** [EL DORADO-PLACER].

Condon Gulch [AMADOR]: *canyon,* less than 1 mile long, opens into the canyon of Mokelumne River 5.5 miles south-southwest of Jackson (lat. 38°16'35" N, long. 120°49'20" W; sec. 24, T 5 N, R 10 E). Named on Jackson (1962) 7.5' quadrangle. Water of Pardee Reservoir now covers the lower part of the canyon.

Condon Mill: see **Old Condon Mill** [NEVADA].

Cone Hill [TUOLUMNE]: *peak,* 4 miles northeast of Stanislaus (lat. 38°11'05" N, long. 120°19'45" W; sec. 21, T 4 N, R 15 E). Altitude 2649 feet. Named on Stanislaus (1948) 7.5' quadrangle.

Confidence [TUOLUMNE]: *settlement,* nearly 2 miles east-northeast of Twain Harte (lat. 38°02'50" N, long. 120°11'55" W; near N line sec. 10, T 2 N, R 16 E). Named on Twain Harte (1979) 7.5' quadrangle, which shows Confidence mine situated 0.5 mile west-southwest of the place. Postal authorities established Confidence post office in 1899, changed the name to Middle Camp in 1906, changed it back to Confidence the same year, and discontinued it in 1925 (Frickstad, p. 215). The name "Confidence" is from Confidence mine (Hanna, p. 71). California Mining Bureau's (1917d) map shows a place called Newell located along a rail line between Soulsbyville and Confidence, and a place called Lyons situated at the end of the rail line beyond Confidence. Postal authorities operated Godfrey post office for a few months in 1901—it was situated 8 miles north of Confidence and named for Godfrey Willer, first postmaster; they established Conlin post office in 1903 and discontinued it in 1904—it was located 18 miles northeast of Confidence and named for George F. Conlin, first postmaster (Salley, p. 49, 86).

Conlin: see **Confidence** [TUOLUMNE].

Connell: see **Camp Connell** [CALAVERAS].

Conness: see **Mount Conness** [TUOLUMNE].

Conness Creek [TUOLUMNE]: *stream,* flows 7 miles to Tuolumne River 9 miles west of Tioga Pass (lat. 37°54'35" N, long. 119°25'05" W); the stream heads near Mount Conness. Named on Tuolumne Meadows (1956) 15' quadrangle.

Connor Cabin [EL DORADO]: *locality,* 10

miles north-northwest of Pollock Pines (lat. 38°53'15" N, long. 120°40'45" W; sec. 18, T 12 N, R 12 E). Named on Tunnel Hill (1950) 7.5' quadrangle.

Connor Hill: see **Nevada City** [NEVADA].

Contention Ridge [TUOLUMNE]: *ridge,* west-southwest-trending, 3.5 miles long, 6.5 miles north-northeast of Columbia (lat. 38° 07' N, long. 120°20'15" W). Named on Columbia SE (1948) 7.5' quadrangle.

Contreras: see **Camp Contreras**, under **Pioneer** [AMADOR].

Convict Meadow [EL DORADO]: *area,* 3.5 miles west of Kirkwood (lat. 38°42'35" N, long. 120°07'55" W). Named on Tragedy Spring (1979) 7.5' quadrangle.

Convicts Bar: see **Ramshorn Creek** [SIERRA].

Cony Crags [MADERA]: *ridge,* southwest-trending, 0.5 mile long, 7 miles north-northeast of Merced Peak (lat. 37°44' N, long. 119° 21' W). Named on Merced Peak (1953) 15' quadrangle. The name is for the numerous "conies" that live in talus on the ridge (United States Board on Geographic Names, 1963b, p. 14).

Cooks [EL DORADO]: *locality,* 5.25 miles east-southeast of Placerville (lat. 38°41'20" N, long. 120°43' W). Named on Placerville (1893) 30' quadrangle.

Cooks Station [AMADOR]: *locality,* 3.25 miles west-southwest of Hams Station (lat. 38°31'35" N, long. 120°25'55" W; near S line sec. 21, T 8 N, R 14 E). Named on Caldor (1951) 7.5' quadrangle. Called Wiley on Pyramid Peak (1896) 30' quadrangle. Sargent (p. 13) referred to Cook's, formerly Wiley's Station. Postal authorities established Wiley post office in 1883 and discontinued it in 1887; the name was for Edward Wiley, first postmaster (Salley, p. 240). Pyramid Peak (1896) 30' quadrangle also shows a place called Hewett located 2 miles south-southwest of Wiley. Salley (p. 16) noted that postal authorities established Baville post office 6 miles west of Wiley in 1886, moved it 5 miles east in 1892, and discontinued it in 1894.

Cooks Station Ridge [AMADOR]: *ridge,* south-southwest-trending, 4 miles long, 5 miles southwest of Hams Station (lat. 38°30'15" N, long. 120°27' W); Cooks Station is at the north end of the ridge. Named on Caldor (1951) and Devils Nose (1979) 7.5' quadrangles.

Cool [EL DORADO]: *village,* 16 miles northwest of Placerville (lat. 38°53'15" N, long. 121°00'55" W; sec. 18, T 12 N, R 9 E). Named on Auburn (1953) 7.5' quadrangle. Postal authorities established Cool post office in 1885 (Frickstad, p. 26).

Coolbrith: see **Mount Ina Coolbrith** [SIERRA].

Coon Canyon [NEVADA]: *canyon,* 1.5 miles long, along North Fork Prosser Creek above a point 4.5 miles north of Donner Pass (lat. 39°23'15" N, long. 120°19'45" W; near NE

cor. sec. 29, T 18 N, R 15 E). Named on Independence Lake (1981) and Norden (1955) 7.5' quadrangles.

Coon Creek [MADERA]: *stream,* flows nearly 3 miles to Fine Gold Creek 3.5 miles east-northeast of O'Neals (lat. 37°08'45" N, long. 119°38'15" W; sec. 13, T 9 S, R 21 E). Named on North Fork (1965) 7.5' quadrangle.

Coon Creek [PLACER]: *stream,* formed in Placer County by the confluence of Dry Creek (1) and Orr Creek, flows 35 miles to end at American Basin 4.5 miles north-northeast of Verona in Sutter County (lat. 38°50'45" N, long. 121°34'25" W). Named on Gold Hill (1954), Lincoln (1953), Nicolaus (1952), Sheridan (1953), and Verona (1967) 7.5' quadrangles.

Coon Creek: see **Ophir** [PLACER].

Coon Hollow [EL DORADO]: *area,* 1 mile southwest of downtown Placerville (lat. 38°43'05" N, long. 120°48'30" W; sec. 18, T 10 N, R 11 E). Named on Placerville (1949) 7.5' quadrangle.

Cooper Canyon [EL DORADO]: *canyon,* drained by a stream that flows 2.5 miles to Pilot Creek (2) 2.25 miles west of the village of Pilot Hill (lat. 38°50'30" N, long. 121°03'15" W; near S line sec. 35, T 12 N, R 8 E). Named on Pilot Hill (1954) 7.5' quadrangle.

Cooper Meadow [TUOLUMNE]: *area,* 9.5 miles east-northeast of Pinecrest (lat. 38°14' N, long. 119°49'40" W; near NE cor. sec. 1, T 4 N, R 19 E). Named on Pinecrest (1956) 15' quadrangle. Browning (1986, p. 46) associated the name with W.F. Cooper, who ran cattle in the neighborhood from 1861 until 1900.

Cooper Peak [TUOLUMNE]: *peak,* 8 miles east-northeast of Pinecrest (lat. 38°14'30" N, long. 119°51'25" W; sec. 35, T 5 N, R 19 E); the peak is 1.5 miles west-northwest of Cooper Meadow. Altitude 9603 feet. Named on Pinecrest (1956) 15' quadrangle.

Cooper Pocket [TUOLUMNE]: *area,* 11 miles east-northeast of Pinecrest at the head of a tributary to South Fork Stanislaus River (lat. 38°14'30" N, long. 119°48'10" W; near W line sec. 32, T 5 N, R 20 E); the place is 1.5 miles east-northeast of Cooper Meadow. Named on Pinecrest (1956) 15' quadrangle.

Coopers Creek [CALAVERAS]: *stream,* flows 3.25 miles to San Domingo Creek 4.5 miles west-northwest of Angels Camp (lat. 38° 06'40" N, long. 120°37'15" W; sec. 14, T 3 N, R 12 E). Named on Angels Camp (1962) 7.5' quadrangle.

Copper Center: see **Copper Mine Gulch** [AMADOR].

Copper Creek [AMADOR]: *stream,* flows 2.5 miles to Sutter Creek 1.25 miles east of Ione (lat. 38°21'05" N, long. 120°54'30" W; at W line sec. 29, T 6 N, R 10 E). Named on Ione (1962) 7.5' quadrangle. Called Mountain Spring Creek on Jackson (1902) 30' quadrangle, but United States Board on Geographic Names (1964a, p. 9) rejected the names "Mountain Spring Creek" and "Copperwater" for the stream.

Copper Creek [CALAVERAS]: *stream,* flows about 3 miles to Black Creek (1) 2 miles southeast of Copperopolis (lat. 37°5730" N, long. 120°37' W; sec. 11, T 1 N, R 12 E). Named on Copperopolis (1962) and Melones Dam (1962) 7.5' quadrangles.

Copper Gulch: see **Copper Mine Gulch** [AMADOR].

Copper Gulch [CALAVERAS]: *canyon,* drained by a stream that flows 2.5 miles to Stanislaus County 7.5 miles west-southwest of Copperopolis (lat. 37°56'25" N, long. 120°46'15" W; sec. 16, T 1 N, R 11 E). Named on Bachelor Valley (1968) and Copperopolis (1962) 7.5' quadrangles.

Copper Hill [MARIPOSA]: *peak,* 10 miles south-southeast of the settlement of Catheys Valley (lat. 37°17'25" N, long. 120°02'30" W; sec. 30, T 7 S, R 18 E). Named on Illinois Hill (1962) 7.5' quadrangle. Called Copper Mtn. on Indian Gulch (1920) 15' quadrangle.

Copper Hill: see **Forest Home** [AMADOR].

Copper Lead [EL DORADO]: *locality,* 2 miles northwest of Omo Ranch along Middle Fork Cosumnes River (lat. 38°36'15" N, long. 120°36'20" W). Named on Placerville (1893) 30' quadrangle.

Copper Mine Gulch [AMADOR]: *canyon,* less than 1 mile long, opens into the canyon of Mokelumne River nearly 7 miles south-southwest of Jackson (lat. 38°15'55" N, long. 120°50'25" W; near S line sec. 23, T 5 N, R 10 E). Named on Jackson (1962) 7.5' quadrangle. Water of Pardee Reservoir now covers most of the feature. Copper Center, a copper mining camp in the lower part of the canyon, boomed during the Civil War, but vanished when the price of copper fell after the war; water of Pardee Reservoir now covers the site (Andrews, p. 125-126; Andrews called the canyon Copper Gulch). Water of Pardee Reservoir also covers the site of a place called Townerville, named for a man who came to invest in copper mines and founded the community in the 1860's (Cook, F.S., p. 5).

Copper Mountain: see **Copper Hill** [MARIPOSA].

Copperopolis [CALAVERAS]: *village,* 15 miles south of San Andreas (lat. 37°58'50" N, long. 120°38'25" W; sec. 34, T 2 N, R 12 E). Named on Copperopolis (1962) 7.5' quadrangle. Postal authorities established Copperopolis post office in 1861 (Frickstad, p. 14). Copper was discovered and the first house was built at the place in 1861 (Whitney, 1865, p. 255)

Copperopolis Mountain [CALAVERAS]: *ridge,* northwest-trending, nearly 3 miles long, northeast of Copperopolis (lat. 37°59'15" N, long. 120°37'55" W). Named on Copperopolis (1962), Melones Dam (1962), and Salt Spring Valley (1962) 7.5' quadrangles.

Copperopolis Reservoir [CALAVERAS]: *lake,* 2100 feet long, behind a dam on Penny Creek 0.5 mile west-northwest of Copperopolis (lat. 37°59' N, long. 120°38'55" W; sec. 34, T 2 N, R 12 E). Named on Copperopolis (1962) 7.5' quadrangle.

Copperwater: see **Copper Creek** [AMADOR].

Coppins Meadow [SIERRA]: *area,* 7.5 miles south-southwest of Sierraville (lat. 39°29'50" N, long. 120°25'20" W). Named on Sattley (1981) and Webber Peak (1981) 7.5' quadrangles.

Cora Creek [MADERA]: *stream,* flows 3.5 miles to North Fork San Joaquin River 8.5 miles west-southwest of Devils Postpile (lat. 37° 35'25" N, long. 119°13'50" W); the stream heads at Cora Lakes. Named on Devils Postpile (1953) and Merced Peak (1953) 15' quadrangles.

Cora Lakes [MADERA]: *lakes,* largest 1300 feet long, 7.25 miles east-southeast of Merced Peak (lat. 37°35'45" N, long. 119°16'15" W); the lakes are at the head of Cora Creek. Named on Merced Peak (1953) 15' quadrangle. R.B. Marshall of United States Geological Survey named the lakes for Mrs. Cora Cressey Crow (Gudde, 1949, p. 78).

Corbet Creek [MARIPOSA]: *stream,* flows 6.5 miles to Bear Creek (2) 3 miles east-northeast of Santa Cruz Mountain (lat. 37°28'15" N, long. 120°09'05" W; sec. 30, T 5 S, R 17 E). Named on Hornitos (1947) and Indian Gulch (1962) 7.5' quadrangles. Called Corbett's Creek on Laizure's (1935) map. The name is for Alexander Corbett, who had mining claims, a store, and a hotel near the stream in the early 1850's; the hotel was called Dog Pump Hotel because Corbett had a Newfoundland dog that worked a water pump (Sargent, Shirley, 1976, p. 24).

Corbett's Creek: see **Corbet Creek** [MARIPOSA].

Corcoran Flat [TUOLUMNE]: *area,* 6.5 miles south-southeast of Tuolumne (lat. 37°52'35" N, long. 120°10'25" W; near SW cor. sec. 1, T 1 S, R 16 E). Named on Tuolumne (1948) 7.5' quadrangle.

Cornelian: see **Carnelian Bay** [PLACER] (2).

Cornish Flat [SIERRA]: *area,* 4.25 miles southeast of Downieville (lat. 39°30'35" N, long. 120°46'50" W; sec. 18, T 19 N, R 11 E). Named on Downieville (1951) 7.5' quadrangle.

Cornish House [SIERRA]: *locality,* 4.5 miles southeast of Downieville (lat. 39°30'20" N, long. 120°47' W; near N line sec. 19, T 19 N, R 11 E); the place is south of Cornish Flat. Site named on Downieville (1951) 7.5' quadrangle. The place also was called Nebraska Diggings, Nebraska City, and Nebraska Flat (Gudde, 1975, p. 235).

Corral Canyon [TUOLUMNE]: *canyon,* 1.5 miles long, 12.5 miles east of Pinecrest along Spring Creek (lat. 38°11'20" N, long. 119°

45'50" W). Named on Pinecrest (1956) 15' quadrangle.

Corral Creek: see **Latrobe Creek** [EL DORADO].

Corral Creek [TUOLUMNE]: *stream,* flows nearly 6 miles to Tuolumne River 8.5 miles southeast of Duckwall Mountain (lat. 37°52'45" N, long. 120°00'45" W; sec. 5, T 1 S, R 18 E). Named on Duckwall Mountain (1948) 7.5' quadrangle.

Corral Flat [AMADOR-EL DORADO]: *area,* 9 miles northwest of Mokelumne Peak on Amador-El Dorado county line (lat. 38°37'15" N, long. 120°13'10" W; near NW. cor. sec. 21, T 9 N, R 16 E). Named on Bear River Reservoir (1979) 7.5' quadrangle.

Corral Flat [EL DORADO]: *area,* 10 miles southwest of Kirkwood (lat. 38°37'25" N, long. 120°13'15" W; at NW cor. sec. 21, T 9 N, R 16 E). Named on Bear River Reservoir (1979) and Tragedy Spring (1979) 7.5' quadrangles.

Corral Flat: see **Mokelumne Hill** [CALAVERAS].

Corral Gulch [CALAVERAS]: *canyon,* drained by a stream that flows nearly 2 miles to Eldorado Creek 7.5 miles east-northeast of San Andreas (lat. 38°13'35" N, long. 120°32'40" W; sec. 4, T 4 N, R 13 E). Named on Calaveritas (1962) 7.5' quadrangle.

Corral Hollow [CALAVERAS]: *valley,* 3.5 miles north of Tamarack (lat. 38°29'15" N, long. 120°05' W; on W line sec. 2, T 7 N, R 17 E). Named on Tamarack (1979) 7'5' quadrangle.

Corral Meadow [MADERA]: *area,* 6 miles southwest of Devils Postpile (lat. 37°34'25" N, long. 119°10'10" W). Named on Devils Postpile (1953) 15' quadrangle. Mount Lyell (1901) 30' quadrangle shows "77" Corral at about the site of present Corral Meadow—this corral was named for the dry summer of 1877 because it was at one of the few feeding places for stock available that year (Smith, p. 58).

Corral Meadow [TUOLUMNE]: *area,* 4 miles northeast of Liberty Hill (lat. 38°23'50" N, long. 120°02'25" W). Named on Tamarack (1979) 7.5' quadrangle.

Corrine Lake [MADERA]: *lake,* 1100 feet long, 13 miles south-southwest of Shuteye Peak (lat. 37°09'35" N, long. 119°29'45" W; on E line sec. 7, T 9 S, R 23 E). Named on Shaver Lake (1953) 15' quadrangle.

Cosgrove Creek [CALAVERAS]: *stream,* flows 10.5 miles to Calaveras River nearly 3 miles south of Valley Springs (lat. 38°09' N, long. 120°49'50" W; sec. 36, T 5 N, R 10 E). Named on Valley Springs (1962) 7.5' quadrangle.

Cosumnes River [AMADOR-EL DORADO]: *stream,* formed by the confluence of Middle Fork and North Fork, flows 50 miles to Mokelumne River 11.5 miles south-southwest of Elk Grove in Sacramento County (lat. 38°15'20" N, long. 121°26'20" W). Amador-El Dorado county line follows Cosumnes River, its Middle Fork, and its South Fork. Named on Bruceville (1968), Carbondale (1968), Elk Grove (1968), Fiddletown (1949), Folsom SE (1954), Galt (1968), Latrobe (1949), and Sloughhouse (1968) 7.5' quadrangles. Called R. de los Cosumnes on Fremont's (1845) map, and called Cosumes River on Jackson's (1850) map. Wilkes (p. 137) referred to Rio Cosmenes, and Tyson (p. 12) mentioned Cosumes River. United States Board on Geographic Names (1933, p. 238) rejected the forms "Cosumne," "Cosumni," "Mokesumne," and "Mokosumne" for the name, which evidently is from the designation of an Indian village or tribe (Kroeber, p. 40). Middle Fork is 44 miles long and is named on Aukum (1952), Bear River Reservoir (1979), Caldor (1951), Camino (1952), Fiddletown (1949), Omo Ranch (1952), and Peddler Hill (1951) 7.5' quadrangles. On Pyramid Peak (1896) 30' quadrangle, present Dogtown Creek [EL DORADO] is called North Fork of Middle Fork Cosumnes River. South Fork enters Middle Fork 2 miles upstream from the confluence of Middle Fork and North Fork; it is 25 miles long and is named on Aukum (1952), Caldor (1951), Fiddletown (1949), and Omo Ranch (1952) 7.5' quadrangles. On Placerville (1893) 30' quadrangle, South Fork above the junction of present South Fork with Scott Creek [EL DORADO] is called South Fork of South Fork Cosumnes River. North Fork heads at Leek Spring Valley and is 48 miles long; it is named on Camino (1952), Fiddletown (1949), Leek Spring Hill (1951), Placerville (1949), Sly Park (1952), Stump Spring (1951), and Tragedy Spring (1979) 7.5' quadrangles. Steely Fork, formed by the confluence of North Steely Creek and South Steely Creek, flows 9 miles to North Fork Cosumnes River 8.5 miles southeast of Camino; is is named on Caldor (1951), Omo Ranch (1952), Sly Park (1952), and Stump Spring (1951) 7.5' quadrangles. Pyramid Peak (1896) 30' quadrangle has the form "Steeley Fork" for the name, which commemorates Dr. J.W. Steely, who found gold near the stream in 1852 and built two mills there (Gudde, 1949, p. 343; Gudde used the form "Steelys Fork" for the name).

Cosumni River: see **Cosumnes River** [AMADOR-EL DORADO].

Cothrin [EL DORADO]: *locality,* 4.25 miles south-southeast of Clarksville along Southern Pacific Railroad (lat. 38°35'50" N, long. 121°01'10" W; near N line sec. 32, T 9 N, R 9 E). Named on Folsom (1941) 15' quadrangle. Called Cothrins on Sacramento (1892) 30' quadrangle.

Cothrin Cove [PLACER]: *relief feature,* 4.5 miles west-southwest of Homewood (lat. 39°03'20" N, long. 120°14'05" W; mainly in

sec. 17, T 14 N, R 16 E). Named on
Homewood (1955) 7.5' quadrangle.

Cottage Hill [NEVADA]: *peak,* nearly 2 miles
north-northeast of Higgins Corner (lat.
39°03'55" N, long. 121°04'35" W; sec. 15, T
14 N, R 8 E). Altitude 1728 feet. Named on
Lake Combie (1949) 7.5' quadrangle.
Whitney's (1873) map shows Cottage Hill Ho.
[House] located 10.5 miles south of Grass
Valley near present Cottage Hill.

Cottage Hill House: see **Cottage Hill** [NE-
VADA].

Cottage Home Creek [PLACER]: *stream,* flows
1 mile to Shirttail Canyon 4.5 miles north-
northeast of Foresthill (lat. 39°04'50" N, long.
120°46'50" W; near S line sec. 6, T 14 N, R 11
E); the stream heads east of Cottage Home Hill.
Named on Foresthill (1949) 7.5' quadrangle.

Cottage Home Hill [PLACER]: *peak,* 5.5 miles
north-northeast of Foresthill (lat. 39°05'45"
N, long. 120°47'20" W; near SW cor. sec. 31,
T 15 N, R 11 E). Altitude 4100 feet. Named
on Foresthill (1949) 7.5' quadrangle.

Cottage Spring [CALAVERAS]:
(1) *spring,* 10 miles southwest of Tamarack (lat.
38°20'45" N, long. 120°12'45" W; sec. 28, T
6 N, R 16 E). Named on Boards Crossing
(1979) 7.5' quadrangle.
(2) *locality,* 4 miles east-northeast of Valley
Springs (lat. 38°12'45" N, long. 120°45'45"
W). Named on Jackson (1902) 30' quadrangle.

Cottage Springs [CALAVERAS]: *locality,* 9
miles southwest of Tamarack (lat. 38°21'20"
N, long. 120°12'40" W; sec. 21, T 6 N, R 16
E); the place is less than 1 mile north of Cottage Spring (1). Named on Boards Crossing
(1979) 7.5' quadrangle.

Cotton Arm: see **Lake McClure** [MARIPOSA].

Cotton Creek [MARIPOSA]: *stream,* flows
about 4 miles to Lake McClure 5.5 miles north
of Hornitos (lat. 37°34'45" N, long. 120°
13'10" W; at S line sec. 16, T 4 S, R 16 E).
Named on Hornitos (1947, photorevised
1973) 7.5' quadrangle.

Cotton Hill: see **Relief** [NEVADA].

Cottonwood Campground [SIERRA]: *locality,*
nearly 4 miles southeast of Sierraville (lat.
39°33' N, long. 120°19' W; at S line sec. 28,
T 20 N, R 15 E); the place is along Cottonwood Creek. Named on Sierraville (1981) 7.5'
quadrangle.

Cottonwood Campground [TUOLUMNE]:
locality, 3 miles north of present Dardanelle
along Clark Fork (lat. 38°23' N, long.
119°49'30" W). Named on Dardanelles Cone
(1956) 15' quadrangle.

Cottonwood Cow Camp [MADERA]: *locality,*
9.5 miles southwest of Madera along Cottonwood Creek (2) (lat. 36°52' N, long. 120°
11'10" W; near S line sec. 23, T 12 S, R 16
E). Named on Madera (1946) 15' quadrangle.

Cottonwood Creek [MADERA]:
(1) *stream,* flows 11.5 miles to San Joaquin
River 9 miles south of O'Neals (lat. 36°59'50"

N, long. 119°42'25" W; near W line sec. 5, T
11 S, R 21 E). Named on Little Table Mountain (1962) and Millerton Lake West (1965)
7.5' quadrangles.
(2) *stream,* diverges from Fresno River 10 miles
south of Raymond (lat. 37°04'10" N, long.
119°54'35" W; near SW cor. sec. 9, T 10 S, R
19 E) and flows more than 30 miles before
ending in lowlands southwest of Madera.
Named on Firebaugh (1946), Herndon (1965),
Madera (1946), and Raymond (1962) 15'
quadrangles.

Cottonwood Creek [PLACER]: *stream,* flows
3 miles to Hell Hole Reservoir 2.5 miles north
of Bunker Hill (lat. 39°05'15" N, long.
120°22'50" W; sec. 2, T 14 N, R 14 E). Named
on Bunker Hill (1953) and Wentworth Springs
(1953) 7.5' quadrangles.

Cottonwood Creek [SIERRA]: *stream,* flows
5.5 miles to Cold Stream 4 miles southeast of
Sierraville (lat. 39°32'50" N, long. 120°19'05"
W; near N line sec. 33, T 20 N, R 15 E).
Named on Sardine Peak (1981) and Sierraville
(1981) 7.5' quadrangles.

Cottonwood Creek [TUOLUMNE]:
(1) *stream,* flows 5 miles to Clavey River 3.5
miles east-northeast of Duckwall Mountain
(lat. 37°58'50" N, long. 120°03'15" W; sec.
36, T 2 N, R 17 E). Named on Duckwall
Mountain (1948) and Hull Creek (1979) 7.5'
quadrangles.
(2) *stream,* flows 3 miles to Cherry Lake 7.5
miles north-northwest of Mather (lat.
37°58'40" N, long. 119°55' W; near N line
sec. 5, T 1 N, R 19 E). Named on Lake Eleanor (1956) 15' quadrangle, and on Cherry
Lake North (1979) 7.5' quadrangle.
(3) *stream,* flows 6 miles to Middle Tuolumne
River 3.25 miles east of Mather (lat. 37°52'55"
N, long. 119°47'45" W; sec. 5, T 1 S, R 20 E).
Named on Hetch Hetchy Reservoir (1956)
and Lake Eleanor (1956) 15' quadrangles.

Cottonwood Creek: see **Willow Creek** [MA-
DERA] (3).

Cottonwood Gulch [CALAVERAS]: *canyon,*
drained by a stream that flows nearly 2 miles
to Blue Creek 5 miles west of Tamarack (lat.
38°26'20" N, long. 120°10'15" W; near SW
cor. sec. 24, T 7 N, R 16 E). Named on Calaveras Dome (1979) 7.5' quadrangle.

Cottonwood Peak: see **Smith Peak** [TUOL-
UMNE].

Council Hill: see **Scales** [SIERRA].

Coulterville [MARIPOSA]: *village,* 20 miles
northwest of Mariposa along Maxwell Creek
(lat. 37°42'45" N, long. 120°11'40" W; on S
line sec. 34, T 2 S, R 16 E). Named on Coulterville (1947) 7.5' quadrangle. Postal authorities established Maxwell's Creek post office
at the place in 1852 and changed the name to
Coulterville in 1872 (Frickstad, p. 92). The
name "Coulterville" commemorates George
W. Coulter, who came to the site in 1850 and
lived in a tent beneath an American flag; the

flag caused Mexican miners to call the place *bandereta*, which means "small flag" in Spanish (Hanna, p. 75). When Coulter and George Maxwell cast lots to determine whose name should be applied to the community, Coulter won and the place became Coulterville, while the stream and the post office there were called Maxwell's Creek·(Hanna, p. 75). Postal authorities established Opie post office 6 miles northeast of Coulterville in 1896 and discontinued it in 1898; they established Wenger post office 15 miles east of Coulterville in 1882 and discontinued it in 1883—the name was for Frederick Wenger, first postmaster (Salley, p. 162, 236).

Court House Rock: see **Medlicott Dome** [MADERA].

Courthouse Rock [MARIPOSA]: *hill*, 9.5 miles west of the settlement of Catheys Valley (lat. 37°25'20" N, long. 120°16'50" W; sec. 12, T 6 S, R 15 E). Named on Haystack Mountain (1962) 7.5' quadrangle.

Cow and Calf Gulch [MARIPOSA]: *canyon*, drained by a stream that flows 2.5 miles to Bear Creek (2) 4.25 miles south-southeast of the village of Bear Valley (lat. 37°30'25" N, long. 120°05'50" W). Named on Bear Valley (1947) 7.5' quadrangle. Laizure's (1928) map has the designation "Humbug or Cow and Calf Gulch" for the feature.

Cow and Calf Mountain [MARIPOSA]: *peak*, 9.5 miles south of the settlement of Catheys Valley (lat. 37°17'40" N, long. 120°05'20" W; near E line sec. 27, T 7 S, R 17 E). Named on Illinois Hill (1962) 7.5' quadrangle.

Coward: see **Ham Coward Gulch** [MARIPOSA].

Cow Creek [MARIPOSA]: *stream*, flows nearly 3 miles to Chapman Creek 14 miles south of Mariposa (lat. 37°16'15" N, long. 119°57'30" W; near NW cor. sec. 1, T 8 S, R 18 E). Named on Ben Hur (1947) 7.5' quadrangle.

Cow Creek [TUOLUMNE]:
(1) *stream*, flows 6 miles to Beardsley Lake 3 miles northwest of Strawberry (lat. 38°13'55" N, long. 120°02'35" W; sec. 6, T 4 N, R 18 E). Named on Donnell Lake (1979), Pinecrest (1979), and Strawberry (1979) 7.5' quadrangles.
(2) *settlement*, 3.5 miles north of Pinecrest (lat. 38°14'30" N, long. 119°59'25" W; on E line sec. 33, T 5 N, R 18 E); the place is near Cow Creek (1). Named on Pinecrest (1979) 7.5' quadrangle.

Cow Meadow Lake [TUOLUMNE]: *lake*, 2000 feet long, 10 miles west of Tower Peak along North Fork Cherry Creek (lat. 38°08'35" N, long. 119°44' W). Named on Tower Peak (1956) 15' quadrangle.

Cox Bar: see **Downieville** [SIERRA].

Cox Canyon [EL DORADO]: *canyon*, drained by a stream that flows 1.5 miles to join South Fork American River 1.5 miles east of Riverton (lat. 38°46'30" N, long. 120°25' W).

Named on Riverton (1950) 7.5' quadrangle.

Cox-Delaney Flat [NEVADA]: *area*, 8 miles east-northeast of Truckee (lat. 39°22'30" N, long. 120°02'40" W; near SW cor. sec. 25, T 18 N, R 17 E). Named on Boca (1955) and Martis Peak (1955) 7.5' quadrangles.

Coyote Creek [CALAVERAS]: *stream*, flows 12 miles to Stanislaus River 5.25 miles south of Vallecito (lat. 38°00'40" N, long. 120°29'30" W; sec. 24, T 2 N, R 13 E). Named on Columbia (1948) and Murphys (1948) 7.5' quadrangles. The name probably is from the so-called "coyote mining" done in the neighborhood (Goodman *in* Wood, p. 24).

Coyote Creek [PLACER]: *stream*, flows nearly 3 miles to Wooley Creek 6.5 miles south-southwest of Colfax (lat. 39°00'55" N, long. 121°00'10" W; near S line sec. 32, T 14 N, R 9 E); the stream heads east of Coyote Hill. Named on Colfax (1949) and Lake Combie (1949) 7.5' quadrangles.

Coyote Creek: see **Wooley Creek** [PLACER].

Coyote Hill [PLACER]: *ridge*, south-southwest-trending, 1 mile long, nearly 5 miles south-southwest of Colfax (lat. 39°02'15" N, long. 120°59'25" W; on and near E line sec. 29, T 14 N, R 9 E). Named on Colfax (1949) 7.5' quadrangle.

Coyote Meadow: see **Gully Meadow** [TUOLUMNE].

Coyote Meadows [TUOLUMNE]: *area*, 8 miles east-northeast of Pinecrest (lat. 38°14'30" N, long. 119°52'15" W; sec. 34, T 5 N, R 19 E). Named on Pinecrest (1979) 7.5' quadrangle.

Coyote Ravine [SIERRA]: *canyon*, drained by a stream that flows nearly 2 miles to North Yuba River 0.5 mile west of Downieville (lat. 39°33'35" N, long. 120°50'20" W; sec. 34, T 20 N, R 10 E). Named on Downieville (1951) 7.5' quadrangle.

Coyote Ridge [EL DORADO]: *ridge*, southwest- to west-trending, 2.5 miles long, 3 miles east-northeast of Aukum (lat. 38°33'50" N, long. 120°40'30" W). Named on Aukum (1952) 7.5' quadrangle.

Coyote Rocks [MARIPOSA]: *relief feature*, 5.25 miles north-northeast of Yosemite Village (lat. 37°48'50" N, long. 119°32'10" W; sec. 34, T 1 S, R 22 E). Named on Hetch Hetchy Reservoir (1956) 15' quadrangle.

Coyote Spring [PLACER]: *spring*, 7.5 miles southwest of Granite Chief in French Meadows (lat. 39°08'30" N, long. 120°24'05" W; sec. 22, T 15 N, R 14 E). Named on Royal Gorge (1953) 7.5' quadrangle.

Coyoteville [EL DORADO]: *locality*, 2 miles east of Aukum (lat. 38° 33'05" N, long. 120°41'51" W; near NE cor. sec. 18, T 8 N, R 12 E); the place is south of Coyote Ridge. Named on Aukum (1952) 7.5' quadrangle. Logan's (1938) map shows a place called Cedar Creek Camp located about 0.5 mile east of Coyteville along Cedar Creek (at N line sec. 17, T 8 N, R 12 E).

Coyoteville: see **Downieville** [SIERRA]; **Nevada City** [NEVADA].

Crabtree Campsite [TUOLUMNE]: *locality,* 5 miles east-southeast of Pinecrest (lat. 38°10'35" N, long. 119°54'20" W; sec. 29, T 4 N, R 19 E). Named on Pinecrest (1979) 7.5' quadrangle. Called Crabtree Camp on Pinecrest (1956) 15' quadrangle. O.S. Crabtree tried to patent 160 acres at the site in 1898 (Browning, 1986, p. 48).

Crabtree Canyon [NEVADA]: *canyon,* drained by a stream that flows nearly 2 miles to South Fork Prosser Creek 5.5 miles northeast of Donner Pass (lat. 39°22'35" N, long. 120°15'35" W; sec. 25, T 18 N, R 15 E). Named on Independence Lake (1981) 7.5' quadrangle.

Cracked Crag [EL DORADO]: *peak,* 2.25 miles northeast of Pyramid Peak (lat. 38°52'10" N, long. 120°07'40" W). Named on Pyramid Peak (1955) 7.5' quadrangle.

Crag Lake [EL DORADO]: *lake,* 2200 feet long, 2.5 miles north of Phipps Peak (lat. 38°59'30" N, long. 120°09'20" W; sec. 12, T 13 N, R 16 E). Named on Rockbound Valley (1955) 7.5' quadrangle.

Craig Peak [TUOLUMNE]: *peak,* 1.25 miles south-southwest of Tower Peak (lat. 38°07'45" N, long. 119°33'30" W). Altitude 11,090 feet. Named on Tower Peak (1956) 15' quadrangle. R.B. Marshall of United States Geological Survey named the feature for Colonel John W. Craig (United States Board on Geographic Names, 1934, p. 6).

Craigs Flat [SIERRA]: *area,* 7.25 miles south-southwest of Mount Fillmore (lat. 39°38'15" N, long. 120°54'45" W; on W line sec. 31, T 21 N, R 10 E). Named on La Porte (1951) 7.5' quadrangle. Bancroft (1888, p. 362) used the form "Craig's flat" for the name. Gudde (1975, p. 248) listed a mining camp called Oahu that was located at Craigs Flat, and (p. 226) a mining place called Morrisons Flat that was situated 1 mile from Craigs Flat.

Cranberry Gulch [MARIPOSA]: *canyon,* drained by a stream that flows 1.25 miles to the canyon of Merced River 4 miles west-southwest of El Portal (lat. 37°39'45" N, long. 119°51' W; sec. 22, T 3 S, R 19 E). Named on El Portal (1947) 7.5' quadrangle.

Cranberry Peak: see **Trumbull Peak** [MARIPOSA].

Crandall Peak [TUOLUMNE]: *peak,* 4.5 miles north of Long Barn (lat. 38°09'30" N, long. 120°08'35" W; sec. 31, T 4 N, R 17 E). Altitude 5449 feet. Named on Crandall Peak (1979) 7.5' quadrangle.

Crane: see **Joe Crane Lake** [MADERA].

Crane Creek [MARIPOSA]: *stream,* flows 8.5 miles to Merced River at El Portal (lat. 37°40'35" N, long. 119°46'30" W). Named on El Portal (1947) and Lake Eleanor (1956) 15' quadrangles. Crane Flat ranger station is 6 miles north-northwest of El Portal near the head of Crane Creek; Hoffmann and Gardner's (1863-1867) map shows Crane Flat at the site of the ranger station. Members of a group that included George W. Coulter and Lafayette H. Bunnell named the flat in 1856 after they heard the cries of sandhill cranes there (Paden and Schlichtmann, p. 219).

Crane Creek [TUOLUMNE]:
(1) *stream,* flows 4 miles to Beaver Creek 6 miles southwest of Liberty Hill (lat. 38°18'05" N, long. 120°10'25" W; sec. 11, T 5 N, R 16 E). Named on Boards Crossing (1979) and Liberty Hill (1979) 7.5' quadrangles. Called Little Beaver Creek on Big Meadow (1956) 15' quadrangle.
(2) *stream,* flows 3.25 miles to Jawbone Creek 9 miles northwest of Mather (lat. 38°58'20" N, long. 119°58'50" W; sec. 3, T 1 N, T 18 E); the stream goes through Crane Meadow. Named on Lake Eleanor (1956) 15' quadrangle.

Crane Creek: see **Little Crane Creek** [MARIPOSA]; **North Crane Creek** [TUOLUMNE].

Crane Flat: see **Crane Creek** [MARIPOSA].

Crane Meadow [TUOLUMNE]: *area,* 9 miles northwest of Mather (lat. 37°59'15" N, long. 119°56'50" W; sec. 36, T 2 N, R 18 E); the place is near the head of Crane Creek (2). Named on Lake Eleanor (1956) 15' quadrangle.

Crane Mountain: see **El Capitan** [MARIPOSA].

Crane's Gulch: see **Georgetown** [EL DORADO].

Crane Valley [MADERA]: *valley,* 5 miles southeast of Yosemite Forks along North Fork Willow Creek (2) (lat. 37°19' N, long. 119°33'30" W). Named on Bass Lake (1953) 15' quadrangle. Water of Bass Lake (1) now covers most of the valley.

Crane Valley Creek: see **North Fork**, under **Willow Creek** [MADERA] (2).

Crane Valley Lake: see **Bass Lake** [MADERA] (1).

Crater Creek [MADERA]: *stream,* flows 6.5 miles to Middle Fork San Joaquin River 4.5 miles south of Devils Postpile (lat. 37°33'30" N, long. 119°05'30" W). Named on Devils Postpile (1953) 15' quadrangle.

Crater Lake [NEVADA]: *lake,* 150 feet long, 1.5 miles west-northwest of Donner Pass (lat. 39°19'30" N, long. 120°20'20" W; sec. 24, T 17 N, R 14 E). Named on Norden (1955) 7.5' quadrangle.

Craycroft Diggings [SIERRA]: *locality,* 3.5 miles north-northeast of Downieville (lat. 39°36'50" N, long. 120°48'35" W; sec. 12, T 20 N, R 10 E); the place is on Craycroft Ridge. Named on Downieville (1951) 7.5' quadrangle.

Craycroft Ridge [SIERRA]: *ridge,* south- to south-southwest-trending, 6.5 miles long, center 7 miles south-southeast of Mount Fillmore (lat. 39°38' N, long. 120°47'35" W). Named on Downieville (1951) and Mount Fillmore (1951) 7.5' quadrangles.

Crazy Mule Gulch [TUOLUMNE]: *canyon,*

drained by a stream that flows 2.5 miles to Piute Creek (2) 6.25 miles southwest of Matterhorn Peak (lat. 38°02'30" N, long. 119°28'35" W). Named on Matterhorn Peak (1956) 15' quadrangle.

Crees Flat: see **Ophir** [PLACER].

Creighton: see **Creightons Meadow** [CALAVERAS].

Creightons Meadow [CALAVERAS]: *locality,* 2.5 miles north-northwest of Blue Mountain (lat. 38°22'20" N, long. 120°23'10" W; sec. 13, T 6 N, R 14 E). Named on Fort Mountain (1979) 7.5' quadrangle. Big Trees (1891) 30' quadrangle has the name "Creighton" at the spot.

Crescent Creek [MADERA]: *stream,* flows 4.5 miles to South Fork Merced River 4.25 miles south-southwest of Buena Vista Peak (lat. 37°32'15" N, long. 119°33' W; at S line sec. 34, T 4 S, R 22 E). Named on Yosemite (1956) 15' quadrangle.

Crescent Lake [MADERA]: *lake,* 1700 feet long, 2.25 miles south-southwest of Buena Vista Peak (lat. 37°33'55" N, long. 119°32' W; on N line sec. 26, T 4 S, R 22 E); the lake is along Crescent Creek. Named on Yosemite (1956) 15' quadrangle.

Crimea House [TUOLUMNE]: *locality,* 3.5 miles southwest of Chinese Camp (lat. 37°49'55" N, long. 120°28'40" W; sec. 19, T 1 S, R 14 E). Named on Chinese Camp (1947) 7.5' quadrangle. Paden and Schlichtmann (p. 61-62) believed that the name came from interest in the Crimean War, and also from the Chinese Tong War of 1856, which inhabitants of the neighborhood called their local Crimean War.

Critter Creek: see **Grass Valley** [NEVADA].

Crocker Creek [EL DORADO]: *stream,* flows 2.5 miles to Sweetwater Creek 5.5 miles north of Clarksville (lat. 38°44'15" N, long. 121°02'20" W; near W line sec. 7, T 10 N, R 9 E). Named on Clarksville (1953) 7.5' quadrangle.

Crocker Meadow: see **Harden Flat** [TUOLUMNE].

Crocker Point [MARIPOSA]: *promontory,* 5 miles southwest of Yosemite Village on the south side of Yosemite Valley (lat. 37°42'25" N, long. 119°39'30" W). Named on Yosemite (1956) 15' quadrangle. The name commemorates Charles Crocker of Central Pacific Railroad (Browning, 1988, p. 30).

Crocker Ridge [TUOLUMNE]: *ridge,* west-northwest-trending, 2.5 miles long, 7 miles south-southwest of Mather (lat. 37°47' N, long. 119°53'15" W); the ridge is 2 miles south of Rush Creek (3), which had the early name "Crockers Creek." Named on Lake Eleanor (1956) 15' quadrangle. The name is for Henry Robinson Crocker of Crocker's Sierra Resort (Browning, 1988, p. 30).

Crockers: see **Rush Creek** [TUOLUMNE] (3).

Crocker's Meadow: see **Rush Creek** [TUOLUMNE] (3).

Crocker's Sierra Resort: see **Rush Creek** [TUOLUMNE] (3).

Croft [EL DORADO]: *locality,* 1.5 miles south of Caldor (lat. 38°34'55" N, long. 120°26' W; near S line sec. 33, T 9 N, R 14 E). Named on Caldor (1951) 7.5' quadrangle.

Crook Creek [MADERA]: *stream,* flows 4.5 miles to Fresno River 6.5 miles west of Yosemite Forks (lat. 37°21' N, long. 119°44'45" W); the stream is east of Crook Mountain (1). Named on Bass Lake (1953) 15' quadrangle. United States Board on Geographic Names (1984a, p. 3) approved the name "Crooks Creek" for the feature; the name commemorates William H. Crooks, a rancher along the stream from the 1850's until 1912.

Crook Mountain [MADERA]:

(1) *ridge,* north-trending, 3 miles long, 13 miles north-northeast of Raymond (lat. 37°22'30" N, long. 119°46'15" W). Named on Horsecamp Mountain (1947) and Stumpfield Mountain (1947) 7.5' quadrangles. United States Board on Geographic Names (1984a, p. 3) approved the name "Crooks Mountain" for the feature; the name commemorates William H. Crooks, of present Crooks Creek.

(2) *peak,* nearly 6 miles southeast of O'Neals (lat. 37°04'20" N, long. 119°37'05" W; sec. 7, T 10 S, R 22 E). Altitude 2006 feet. Named on Millerton Lake East (1965) 7.5' quadrangle.

Crooked Lake: see **Crooked Lakes** [NEVADA].

Crooked Lakes [NEVADA]: *lakes,* 4 miles southwest of English Mountain (lat. 39°24'30" N, long. 120°36'30" W). Named on English Mountain (1983) 7.5' quadrangle. Colfax (1938) 30' quadrangle has the name "Crooked Lake" for one of the lakes.

Crooked Spring Gulch [CALAVERAS]: *canyon,* drained by a stream that flows nearly 1 mile to Straight Spring Gulch 3.5 miles east-northeast of San Andreas (lat. 38°12'50" N, long. 120°36'55" W; sec. 11, T 4 N, R 12 E). Named on Calaveritas (1962) 7.5' quadrangle.

Crooks Creek: see **Crook Creek** [MADERA].

Crooks Mountain: see **Crook Mountain** [MADERA] (1).

Crossman: see **Mount Crossman** [AMADOR].

Crown Point [TUOLUMNE]: *peak,* 4.25 miles west-northwest of Matterhorn Peak on Tuolumne-Mono county line (lat. 38°06'40" N, long. 119°27'25" W). Altitude 11,346 feet. Named on Matterhorn Peak (1956) 15' quadrangle. J.P. Walker named the peak in 1905 when he was surveying a new boundary for Yosemite National Park (Browning, 1988, p. 30).

Crowsfoot Campground [MARIPOSA]: *locality,* 4.25 miles west-southwest of Wawona (lat. 37°31'15" N, long. 119°43'45" W; near E cor. sec. 12, T 5 S, R 20 E). Named on Yosemite (1956) 15' quadrangle.

Crows Nest [PLACER]: *peak,* 2 miles southwest

of Donner Pass (lat. 39°17'50" N, long. 120°21' W; sec. 36, T 17 N, R 14 E). Altitude 7896 feet. Named on Norden (1955) 7.5' quadrangle.

Crumbecker Ravine: see **Krumbacher's Ravine**, under **Scotchman Creek** [NEVADA].

Crystal Lake [NEVADA]:
(1) *lake,* 1500 feet long, 2.25 miles east of Yuba Gap (lat. 39°19'10" N, long. 120°34'25" W; near S line sec. 24, T 17 N, R 12 E). Named on Cisco Grove (1955) 7.5' quadrangle. Morgan (p. 377) identified present Crystal Lake (1) as the feature called Brant Lake on Jefferson's (1849) map.
(2) *locality,* 2.5 miles east of Yuba Gap along Southern Pacific Railroad (lat. 39°19'20" N, long. 120°34'10" W; near E line sec. 24, T 17 N, R 12 E); the place is 0.25 mile northeast of Crystal Lake (1). Named on Cisco Grove (1955) 7.5' quadrangle.

Crystal Peak [SIERRA]: *peak,* 11.5 miles southeast of Loyalton (lat. 39°33'30" N, long. 120°05'15" W; near E line sec. 28, T 20 N, R 17 E). Altitude 8103 feet. Named on Dog Valley (1981) 7.5' quadrangle.

Crystal Peak: see **Mount Tallac** [EL DORADO]; **Verdi Peak** [SIERRA].

Crystal Peak Campground [SIERRA]: *locality,* 2.25 miles north-northeast of Crystal Peak (lat. 39°35'20" N, long. 120°04'20" W; sec. 15, T 20 N, R 17 E). Named on Dog Valley (1981) 7.5' quadrangle.

Crystal Range [EL DORADO]: *ridge,* extends for 9 miles north-northwest and northwest from Pyramid Peak; center 4.5 miles southwest of Phipps Peak (lat. 38°54' N, long. 120°11'45" W). Named on Pyramid Peak (1955) and Rockbound Valley (1955) 7.5' quadrangles.

Crystal Springs [NEVADA]: *locality,* 8 miles south-southwest of North Bloomfield (lat. 39°15'25" N, long. 120°58'35" W). Named on Colfax (1898) 30' quadrangle.

Cuba: see **Iceland** [NEVADA].

Cub Canyon [PLACER]: *canyon,* drained by a stream that flows 0.5 mile to New York Canyon (2) 4.5 miles north-northwest of Foresthill (lat. 39°05'05" N, long. 120°50'35" W; at W line sec. 3, T 14 N, R 10 E). Named on Foresthill (1949) 7.5' quadrangle.

Cuckoo Ridge [PLACER]: *ridge,* west- to southwest-trending, 3 miles long, 6 miles east-northeast of Michigan Bluff (lat. 39°04'50" N, long. 120°38'15" W). Named on Greek Store (1952) and Michigan Bluff (1952) 7.5' quadrangles.

Culbertson Lake [NEVADA]: *lake,* behind a dam 4.5 miles west-southwest of English Mountain on a tributary of Texas Creek (lat. 39°25'15" N, long. 120°37'20" W; near SW cor. sec. 16, T 18 N, R 12 E). Named on English Mountain (1983) 7.5' quadrangle.

Culbertson's: see **Moccasin** [TUOLUMNE].

Culloma: see **Coloma** [EL DORADO].

Cummings: see **El Dorado** [EL DORADO].

Cuneo Camp [CALAVERAS]: *locality,* 6 miles west of Tamarack (lat. 38°26'15" N, long. 120°11'25" W; near NW cor. sec. 26, T 7 N, R 16 E). Named on Calaveras Dome (1979) 7.5' quadrangle.

Cuneo Creek [MARIPOSA]: *stream,* flows 3 miles to Maxwell Creek nearly 1 mile northeast of Coulterville (lat. 37°43'15" N, long. 120° 11'05" W; near E line sec. 34, T 2 S, R 16 E). Named on Coulterville (1947) and Groveland (1947) 7.5' quadrangles.

Cunningham Flat: see **Rush Creek** [MARIPOSA].

Cup Lake [EL DORADO]: *lake,* 450 feet long, 3.5 miles west-northwest of Echo Summit (lat. 38°49'40" N, long. 120°05'35" W; sec. 3, T 11 N, R 17 E); the lake is 1 mile west-southwest of Saucer Lake. Named on Echo Lake (1955) 7.5' quadrangle.

Cups: see **The Cups** [SIERRA].

Curry: see **Camp Curry** [MARIPOSA]; **Camp Curry** [TUOLUMNE].

Curry Creek [PLACER]: *stream,* heads in Placer County and flows 13 miles to end at American Basin 4.5 miles east of Verona in Sutter County (lat. 38°47'05" N, long. 121°31'55" W; sec. 21, T 11 N, R 4 E). Named on Pleasant Grove (1967), Roseville (1967), and Verona (1967) 7.5' quadrangles. Called Sciata Creek on Sacramento (1892) 30' quadrangle.

Curry Village: see **Camp Curry** [MARIPOSA].

Curtis' Camp: see **Curtis Creek** [TUOLUMNE].

Curtis Creek [TUOLUMNE]: *stream,* flows 11 miles to Sullivan Creek 5 miles south-southwest of Sonora (lat. 37°54'40" N, long. 120°24'15" W; sec. 26, T 1 N, R 14 E). Named on Sonora (1948) and Standard (1948) 7.5' quadrangles. The name is for Kezia Darwin Curtis, a fortyniner (Dillon *in* Harris, p. 124). Curtis' Camp, or Curtisville, was located along Curtis Creek south of Sonora (Morgan and Scobie *in* Perkins, p. 198). Postal authorities established Curtisville post office in 1853 and discontinued it in 1856 (Frickstad, 215).

Curtisville: see **Curtis Creek** [TUOLUMNE]

Cut Eye Fosters Bar [SIERRA]: *locality,* 8 miles west of Goodyears Bar along North Yuba River at the mouth of Cherokee Creek (lat. 39°30'55" N, long. 121°02'05" W; sec. 13, T 19 N, R 8 E). Named on Strawberry Valley (1948) 7.5' quadrangle. The name reportedly commemorates a professional horse thief (Gudde, 1975, p. 89). The name also had the form "Cut Eye Foster's Bar" (Marlette, p. 202).

Cypress Point [CALAVERAS]: *promontory,* 4 miles west of Paloma on the east side of Pardee Reservoir (lat. 38°15'55" N, long. 120° 50'05" W; near NE cor. sec. 26, T 5 N, R 10 E). Named on Jackson (1962) 7.5' quadrangle.

– D –

Dad Youngs Spring [PLACER]: *spring,* 6.5 miles west of Devil Peak (lat. 38°58'25" N, long. 120°39'55" W; sec. 17, T 13 N, R 12 E). Named on Tunnel Hill (1950) 7.5' quadrangle.

Dagon [AMADOR]: *locality,* 1.5 miles west-southwest of Ione along Southern Pacific Railroad (lat. 38°20'40" N, long. 120°57'30" W). Named on Ione (1962) 7.5' quadrangle.

Dairyland [MADERA]: *locality,* 7.5 miles south-southwest of Chowchilla (lat. 37°01'05" N, long. 120°18'35" W; on W line sec. 35, T 10 S, R 15 E). Named on Chowchilla (1960) 7.5' quadrangle. Chowchilla (1918) 7.5' quadrangle shows the place 3 miles farther west at the end of Chowchilla Pacific Railroad, and California Division of Highways' (1934) map shows it at the end of a branch of Southern Pacific Railroad (SE quarter sec. 31, T 10 S, R 15 E).

Damascus [PLACER]: *locality,* 4.25 miles west-southwest of Westville (lat. 39°08'50" N, long. 120°43' W; sec. 15, T 15 N, R 11 E). Site named on Westville (1952) 7.5' quadrangle. Postal authorities established Damascus post office in 1856, discontinued it in 1860, reestablished it in 1861, discontinued it in 1867, reestablished it in 1888, moved it 1 mile east in 1892, moved it 1 mile east again in 1904, and discontinued it in 1908 (Salley, p. 55). The place first was known as Damascus Diggings or Strong Diggings (Hanna, p. 81).

Damascus Diggings: see **Damascus** [PLACER].

Damfine Spring [NEVADA]: *spring,* 2.25 miles north-northwest of English Mountain (lat. 39°28'40" N, long. 120°33'45" W; near SW cor. sec. 30, T 19 N, R 13 E). Named on English Mountain (1983) 7.5' quadrangle.

Dana Fork [TUOLUMNE]: *stream,* flows 8 miles to join Lyell Fork and form Tuolumne River nearly 6 miles west-southwest of Tioga Pass (lat. 37°52'30" N, long. 119°21' W; near SE cor. sec. 5, T 1 S, R 24 E); the stream heads 1 mile south of Mount Dana. Named on Mono Craters (1953) and Tuolumne Meadows (1956) 15' quadrangles. The name is from Mount Dana (United States Board on Geographic Names, 1934, p. 6).

Danaher: see **Mount Danaher** [EL DORADO].

Dana Meadows [TUOLUMNE]: *valley,* south of Tioga Pass (lat. 37° 53'30" N, long. 119°15'30" W). Named on Mono Craters (1953) and Tuolumne Meadows (1956) 15' quadrangles. The place first was known as Tioga Meadows (Browning, 1988, p. 31).

Dana Mountain: see **Mount Dana** [TUOLUMNE].

Dan Sullivan Gulch [MARIPOSA]: *canyon,* 1.25 miles long, opens into lowlands 8.5 miles southwest of Penon Blanco Peak near Hayward (lat. 37°38'40" N, long. 120°22'10" W; near W line sec. 30, T 3 S, R 15 E). Named on Penon Blanco Peak (1962) 7.5' quadrangle.

Darby Knob [CALAVERAS]: *peak,* 5 miles east-northeast of Murphys (lat. 38°10'15" N, long. 120°23'05" W; sec. 25, T 4 N, R 14 E). Altitude 3692 feet. Named on Murphys (1948) 7.5' quadrangle.

Dardanelle [TUOLUMNE]: *settlement,* 10.5 miles west of Sonora Pass (lat. 38°20'30" N, long. 119°50' W; sec. 25, T 6 N, R 19 E). Named on Dardanelle (1979) 7.5' quadrangle. Dardanelles Cone (1956) 15' quadrangle shows Dardanelle P.O. at the place. Postal authorities established Dardanelle post office in 1924 (Frickstad, p. 215).

Dardanelles Campground [TUOLUMNE]: *locality,* at present Dardanelle (lat. 38°20'30" N, long. 119°50' W; sec. 25, T 6 N, R 19 E). Named on Dardanelles Cone (1956) 15' quadrangle.

Dardanelles Creek [PLACER]: *stream,* flows 1.5 miles to Middle Fork American River 15 miles east-northeast of Auburn (lat. 38° 59'35" N, long. 120°49'20" W; near NE cor. sec. 11, T 13 N, R 10 E). Named on Foresthill (1949) and Georgetown (1949) 7.5' quadrangles.

Dardanelles Creek [TUOLUMNE]: *stream,* heads in Alpine County and flows 4.25 miles to Donnell Lake 5.5 miles west of Dardanelle (lat. 38°21' N, long. 119°56'05" W); the stream heads west of The Dardanelles, which is in Alpine County. Named on Donnell Lake (1979) and Spicer Meadow Reservoir (1979) 7.5' quadrangles.

Dardanelles Lake [EL DORADO]: *lake,* 1400 feet long, 3.5 miles south of Echo Summit (lat. 38°45'35" N, long. 120°01'15" W; sec. 5, T 10 N, R 18 E). Named on Echo Lake (1955) 7.5' quadrangle.

Dark Canyon [EL DORADO]:

(1) *canyon,* drained by a stream that flows nearly 2 miles to Canyon Creek (1) 2 miles north of Georgetown (lat. 38°56' N, long. 120° 50'15" W; near W line sec. 35, T 13 N, R 10 E). Named on Georgetown (1949) 7.5' quadrangle.

(2) *canyon,* drained by a stream that flows 1 mile to Otter Creek 5 miles northeast of Georgetown (lat. 38°57'10" N, long. 120°45'55" W; near NE cor. sec. 29, T 13 N, R 11 E). Named on Georgetown (1949) 7.5' quadrangle.

(3) *canyon,* drained by a stream that flows 1.25 miles to Slab Creek 5.5 miles northwest of Pollock Pines (lat. 38°48'40" N, long. 120° 39'35" W; sec. 8, T 11 N, R 12 E). Named on Slate Mountain (1950) 7.5' quadrangle.

(4) *canyon,* drained by a stream that flows 1.5 miles to South Fork American River 1.25 miles east of Chili Bar (lat. 38°46'10" N, long. 120°47'55" W; near W line sec. 30, T 11 N, R 11 E); the feature is 0.5 mile west of Light Canyon (1). Named on Garden Valley (1949) 7.5' quadrangle.

(5) *canyon,* drained by a stream that flows 1.25

miles to Camp Creek 6 miles northwest of Leek Spring Hill (lat. 38°01' N, long. 120°21'35" W; near S line sec 30, T 10 N, R 15 E). Named on Leek Spring Hill (1951) 7.5' quadrangle.

(6) *canyon,* drained by a stream that flows 2.25 miles to Cat Creek nearly 5 miles east of Caldor (lat. 38°35'20" N, long. 120°20'45" W; near W line sec. 32, T 9 N, R 15 E). Named on Peddler Hill (1951) 7.5' quadrangle.

Dark Canyon [PLACER]: *canyon,* drained by a stream that flows 1.5 miles to Secret Canyon 6 miles west of Duncan Peak (lat. 39° 09' N, long. 120°37'15" W; sec. 15, T 15 N, R 12 E). Named on Duncan Peak (1952) and Westville (1952) 7.5' quadrangles. On Colfax (1898) 30' quadrangle, the name applies to a nearby canyon.

Dark Canyon [SIERRA]:

(1) *canyon,* drained by a stream that flows 3.5 miles to Sierra Valley 2.25 miles west-south-west of Sierraville (lat. 39°34'40" N, long. 120°24'15" W; near N line sec. 22, T 20 N, R 14 E). Named on Sattley (1981) 7.5' quadrangle.

(2) *canyon,* drained by a stream that flows 3 miles to Lemon Canyon 3.5 miles east of Sierraville (lat. 39°34'50" N, long. 120° 18'05" W; sec. 15, T 20 N, R 15 E). Named on Sierraville (1981) 7.5' quadrangle.

(3) *canyon,* drained by a stream that flows 2.5 miles to Evans Canyon 7.25 miles east of Loyalton (lat. 39°41' N, long. 120°06'25" W; near SW cor. sec. 8, T 21 N, R 17 E). Named on Evans Canyon (1978) and Loyalton (1981) 7.5' quadrangles.

Dark Canyon Creek [EL DORADO]: *stream,* flows 2 miles to Brownsville Creek 1 mile south-southwest of Omo Ranch (lat. 38° 34' N, long. 120°34'30" W; at NW cor. sec. 8, T 8 N, R 13 E). Named on Omo Ranch (1952) 7.5' quadrangle.

Dark Hole [MARIPOSA]: *locality,* 7 miles north of Yosemite Village (lat. 37°50'45" N, long. 119°36' W; near NW cor. sec. 19, T 1 S, R 22 E). Named on Hetch Hetchy Reservoir (1956) 15' quadrangle. It is believed that the place was a stage stop (Browning, 1988, p. 31).

Dark Lake [EL DORADO]: *lake,* 1500 feet long, 4.5 miles west of Pyramid Peak (lat. 38°51'05" N, long. 120°14'25" W; at N line sec. 32, T 12 N, R 16 E). Named on Pyramid Peak (1955) 7.5' quadrangle. Shown as one of the group with the name "Wrights Lakes" on Pyramid Peak (1896) 30' quadrangle.

Darling Ridge [EL DORADO]: *ridge,* south-trending, 5.5 miles long, center 4.5 miles east-southeast of Georgetown (lat. 38°52'30" N, long. 120°45'40" W). Named on Garden Valley (1949) and Georgetown (1949) 7.5' quadrangles.

Darlings [EL DORADO]: *locality,* 5.25 miles southeast of Georgetown (lat. 38°51' N, long. 120°45'45" W); the place is on present Dar-

ling Ridge. Named on Placerville (1893) 30' quadrangle.

Darlington [EL DORADO]: *locality,* about 1.5 miles north-northwest of Old Iron Mountain along Plum Creek (2) (lat. 38°43'45" N, long. 120°24' W; near SE cor. sec. 10, T 10 N, R 14 E). Named on Stump Spring (1951) 7.5' quadrangle.

Darlington Flat [EL DORADO]: *area,* less than 0.25 mile east-southeast of Old Iron Mountain (lat. 38°42'15" N, long. 120°23'10" W; sec. 23, T 10 N, R 14 E). Named on Stump Spring (1951) 7.5' quadrangle.

Darrah [MARIPOSA]: *locality,* 11.5 miles south-southwest of El Portal (lat. 37°31' N, long. 119°50'05" W; near NE cor. sec. 12, T 5 S, R 19 E). Named on Buckingham Mountain (1947) 7.5' quadrangle. United States Board on Geographic Names (1933, p. 255) rejected the names "Darrah's" and "Snow Creek" for the place. Postal authorities established Darrah post office in 1880, discontinued it in 1889, reestablished it in 1890, and discontinued it in 1907; the name was for Richard Darrah, first postmaster (Salley, p. 55).

Date Flat [MARIPOSA]: *area,* 3 miles north-northeast of Buckhorn Peak (lat. 37°42'05" N, long. 120°05'35" W; near E line sec. 4, T 3 S, T 17 E). Named on Buckhorn Peak (1947) 7.5' quadrangle.

Daulton [MADERA]: *locality,* 8 miles south-southwest of Raymond (lat. 37°07'10" N, long. 119°58'50" W; sec. 26, T 9 S, R 18 E); the place is along Daulton Creek. Named on Daulton (1962) 7.5' quadrangle. Postal authorities established Daulton post office in 1899 and discontinued it in 1908 (Frickstad, p. 85). Daulton (1921) 7.5' quadrangle shows the place along Southern Pacific Railroad. Officials of the railroad named the station there in the 1860's for Henry C. Daulton, who gave right of way through his property—Mr. Daulton was chairman of the commission that organized Madera County (Gudde, 1949, p. 89).

Daulton Creek [MADERA]: *stream,* flows 16 miles to Dry Creek 10.5 miles south-south-west of Raymond (lat. 37°04'30" N, long. 119°59'20" W; sec. 10, T 10 S, R 18 E). Named on Daulton (1962) and Raymond (1962) 7.5' quadrangles. The part of the stream above the mouth of Rawls Gulch is called Gnat Creek on Raymond (1944) 15' quadrangle, but United States Board on Geographic Names (1964a, p. 9) rejected this name for the stream.

Daulton Spring [MADERA]: *spring,* 5.5 miles southeast of Knowles (lat. 37°10'20" N, long. 119°47'30" W; sec. 4, T 9 S, R 20 E). Named on Knowles (1962) 7.5' quadrangle.

Daves Ravine [SIERRA]: *canyon,* drained by a stream that flows 2.5 miles to Downie River 4.25 miles north of Downieville (lat. 37°37'20" N, long. 120°49'20" W; near S line sec. 2, T 20 N, R 10 E). Named on Downieville (1951) and Mount Fillmore (1951) 7.5' quadrangles.

David Gulch [MARIPOSA]: *canyon,* drained by a stream that flows 4 miles to Lake McClure 2.5 miles north of the village of Bear Valley (lat. 37°36'20" N, long. 120°07'05" W). Named on Bear Valley (1947, photorevised 1973) and Buckhorn Peak (1947) 7.5' quadrangles.

Davies Creek [SIERRA]: *stream,* flows 11.5 miles to Little Truckee River 5.5 miles south of Crystal Peak (lat. 39°28'35" N, long. 120°06'10" W; near NW cor. sec. 28, T 19 N, R 17 E). Named on Boca (1955), Dog Valley (1981), and Sardine Peak (1981) 7.5' quadrangles. The stream now enters Stampede Reservoir.

Davies Creek Campground [SIERRA]: *locality,* 3.5 miles south of Crystal Peak (lat. 39°30'20" N, long. 120°05'55" W; at N line sec. 16, T 19 N, R 17 E); the place is along Davies Creek. Named on Dog Valley (1981) 7.5' quadrangle.

Davis Creek [EL DORADO]: *stream,* flows 1.5 miles to Silver Creek 7 miles north-northeast of Pollock Pines (lat. 38°51'10" N, long. 120°31'35" W; sec. 28, T 12 N, R 13 E). Named on Devil Peak (1950) and Pollock Pines (1950) 7.5' quadrangles.

Davis Junction: see **Calpine** [SIERRA].

Davis Mountain: see **Mount Davis** [MADERA].

Dawson Spring [PLACER]: *spring,* 7 miles northwest of Duncan Peak (lat. 39°13'30" N, long. 120°36'20" W; near E line sec. 27, T 16 N, R 12 E). Named on Duncan Peak (1952) 7.5' quadrangle.

Deacon Long Ravine [SIERRA]: *canyon,* 2 miles long, opens into the canyon of Slate Creek 6 miles southwest of Mount Fillmore (lat. 39°40'55" N, long. 120°56'35" W; sec. 14, T 21 N, R 9 E). Named on La Porte (1951) 7.5' quadrangle.

Dead Horse Canyon [SIERRA]: *canyon,* drained by a stream that flows 1.5 miles to Haypress Creek 5 miles east of Sierra City (lat. 39°33'35" N, long. 120°32'30" W; sec. 32, T 20 N, R 13 E). Named on Haypress (1981) 7.5' quadrangle. Downieville (1897) 30' quadrangle has the name "Long Valley Ck." for the stream in the canyon.

Dead Horse Flat [CALAVERAS]: *area,* 1.5 miles north of Vallecito (lat. 38°06'30" N, long. 120°28'05" W; near SE cor. sec. 18, T 3 N, R 14 E). Named on Columbia (1948) 7.5' quadrangle.

Deadhorse Lake [MADERA]: *lake,* 1000 feet long, 4.5 miles west-northwest of Devils Postpile (lat. 37°39'05" N, long. 119°09'35" W). Named on Devils Postpile (1953) 15' quadrangle.

Deadman Bar [TUOLUMNE]: *locality,* 3 miles west of Columbia along Stanislaus River (lat. 38°02'20" N, long. 120°27'10" W; sec. 8, T 2

N, R 14 E); the place is at the mouth of Deadman Gulch. Named on Columbia (1948) 7.5' quadrangle.

Deadman Campground [TUOLUMNE]: *locality,* 6.25 miles west of Sonora Pass along Middle Fork Stanislaus River (lat. 38°19' N, long. 119°44'55" W; near N line sec. 2, T 5 N, R 20 E); the place is 0.25 mile north-northwest of the mouth of Deadman Creek. Named on Sonora Pass (1979) 7.5' quadrangle.

Deadman Canyon [PLACER]: *canyon,* drained by a stream that flows 4.25 miles to Coon Creek 7.25 miles northwest of Auburn (lat. 38°58' N, long. 121°10'40" W; sec. 22, T 13 N, R 7 E). Named on Gold Hill (1954) 7.5' quadrangle.

Deadman Creek [EL DORADO]: *stream,* flows 2.5 miles to Martinez Creek 5.5 miles south-southwest of Placerville (lat. 38°39'05" N, long. 120°49'30" W; sec. 12, T 9 N, R 10 E). Named on Placerville (1949) 7.5' quadrangle.

Deadman Creek [MARIPOSA]: *stream,* flows nearly 2 miles to Odom Creek 2.5 miles east-northeast of Santa Cruz Mountain (lat. 37°28'40" N, long. 120°09'45" W; sec. 24, T 5 S, R 16 E). Named on Indian Gulch (1962) 7.5' quadrangle.

Deadman Creek [MARIPOSA]: *stream,* heads in Mariposa County and flows 52 miles, partly in an artificial watercourse, to Duck Slough 11 miles north-northwest of Dos Palos Y in Merced County (lat. 37°12'20" N, long. 120°40'40" W; sec. 29, T 8 S, R 12 E). Named on Chowchilla (1960) and Santa Rita Park (1962) 15' quadrangles, and on Illinois Hill (1962), Le Grand (1961), and Raynor Creek (1961) 7.5' quadrangles. Called Deadman's Creek on Laizure's (1935) map.

Deadman Creek [NEVADA]: *stream,* flows 2.25 miles to Poorman Creek (1) 1 mile north of Washington (lat. 39°22'20" N, long. 120°48' W; near N line sec. 1, T 17 N, R 10 E). Named on Alleghany (1949) and Washington (1950) 7.5' quadrangles. Called Rob Roy Cr. on Colfax (1938) 30' quadrangle.

Deadman Creek [TUOLUMNE]: *stream,* heads in Alpine County and flows 8 miles to Middle Fork Stanislaus River 6 miles west of Sonora Pass (lat. 38°18'50" N, long. 119°44'50" W; sec. 2, T 5 N, R 20 E). Named on Sonora Pass (1979) 7.5' quadrangle.

Deadman Flat [CALAVERAS]: *area,* 8.5 miles west-northwest of Tamarack along North Fork Mokelumne River (lat. 38°29'45" N, long. 120°13' W; near S line sec. 33, T 8 N, R 16 E). Named on Calaveras Dome (1979) 7.5' quadrangle.

Deadman Flat [PLACER]: *area,* 5 miles west-southwest of Granite Chief along Middle Fork American River (lat. 39°11' N, long. 120°22'30" W; sec. 2, T 15 N, R 14 E). Named on Truckee (1940) 30" quadrangle.

Deadman Fork [AMADOR]: *stream,* flows 6.5 miles to South Fork Dry Creek 4.5 miles east of Plymouth (lat. 38°28'15" N, long. 120° 45'50" W; sec. 9, T 7 N, R 11 E). Named on Amador City (1962) and Pine Grove (1948) 7.5' quadrangles. Jackson (1902) 30' quadrangle has the form "Dead Man Fork" for the name.

Deadman Gulch [TUOLUMNE]: *canyon,* drained by a stream that flows 1 mile to Stanislaus River 3 miles west of Columbia (lat. 38° 02'20" N, long. 120°27'10" W; sec. 8, T 2 N, R 14 E); the mouth of the canyon is at Deadman Bar. Named on Columbia (1948) 7.5' quadrangle.

Deadman Lake [SIERRA]: *lake,* 650 feet long, 6 miles northeast of Sierra City (lat. 39°37'15" N, long. 120°33'05" W; on N line sec. 7, T 20 N, R 13 E); the lake is 0.25 mile north-northeast of Deadman Peak. Named on Haypress Valley (1981) 7.5' quadrangle. Called Deadmans Lake on Downieville (1897) 30' quadrangle.

Deadman Lake [TUOLUMNE]: *lake,* 950 feet long, nearly 3 miles south-southwest of Sonora Pass (lat. 38°17'35" N, long. 119°39'30" W). Named on Sonora Pass (1979) 7.5' quadrangle.

Deadman Pass [MADERA]: *pass,* 4.5 miles north of Devils Postpile on Madera-Mono county line (lat. 37°41'20" N, long. 119°04'10" W); the pass is near the head of Deadman Creek, which is in Mono County. Named on Devils Postpile (1953) 15' quadrangle. Deadman Creek was named for the headless body of a man found along it about 1868 (Browning, 1986, p. 53-54).

Deadman Peak [SIERRA]: *peak,* 5.5 miles northeast of Sierra City (lat 39°37' N, long. 120°33'10" W; sec. 7, T 20 N, R 13 E); the peak is 0.25 mile south-southwest of Deadman Lake. Altitude 7498 feet. Named on Haypress Valley (1981) 7.5' quadrangle. Called Deadmans Pk. on Downieville (1897) 30' quadrangle, and called Deadman's Pk. on Logan's (1929) map.

Deadmans Flat [NEVADA]:

(1) *area,* 3 miles west-southwest of Grass Valley at the head of Clear Creek (3) (lat. 39°12'05" N, long. 121°06'50" W; near E line sec. 31, T 16 N, R 8 E). Named on Grass Valley (1949) 7.5' quadrangle. United States Board on Geographic Names (1991, p. 6) approved the name "Osceola Ridge" for a ridge, 0.5 mile long, located 1 mile north of Deadmans Flat (lat. 39°12'58" N, long. 121°06'55" W; sec. 30, T 16 N, R 8 E).

(2) *area,* 7 miles south of Washington (lat. 39°15'35" N, long. 120° 47'10" W; on S line sec. 7, T 16 N, R 11 E). Named on Washington (1950) 7.5' quadrangle.

Deadmans Lake: see **Deadman Lake** [SIERRA].

Deadmans Peak: see **Deadman Peak** [SIERRA].

Deadman Spring [EL DORADO]: *spring,* 0.5 mile north-northwest of Pollock Pines (lat.

38°46'15" N, long. 120°35'15" W; sec. 25, T 11 N, R 12 E). Named on Pollock Pines (1950) 7.5' quadrangle.

Deadwood [PLACER]: *locality,* 3.5 miles northeast of Michigan Bluff (lat. 39°04'50" N, long. 120°41'15" W; sec. 12, T 14 N, R 11 E). Site named on Michigan Bluff (1952) 7.5' quadrangle. Colfax (1938) 30' quadrangle shows Deadwood House at the place. The name "Deadwood" is from a slang expression that has the meaning "a sure thing" (Hoover, Rensch, and Rensch, p. 276-277).

Deadwood [SIERRA]: *locality,* 3.5 miles south of Mount Fillmore (lat. 39°40'30" N, long. 120°51'15" W); the place is along present Deadwood Creek. Named on Downieville (1897) 30' quadrangle.

Deadwood [TUOLUMNE]: *locality,* 6 miles south-southeast of Long Barn along a logging railroad (lat. 38°00'20" N, long. 120°06'30" W; sec. 28, T 2 N, R 17 E). Named on Long Barn (1956) 15' quadrangle.

Deadwood Creek [SIERRA]: *stream,* flows 1.25 miles to Canyon Creek 3 miles south-southwest of Mount Fillmore (lat. 39°41'15" N, long. 120°51'55" W; at N line sec. 16, T 21 N, R 10 E); the stream is northeast of Deadwood Peak. Named on Mount Fillmore (1951) 7.5' quadrangle.

Deadwood Diggings [SIERRA]: *locality,* 3.5 miles south of Mount Fillmore (lat. 39°40'50" N, long. 120°51'20" W); the place is along Deadwood Creek. Named on Mount Fillmore (1951) 7.5' quadrangle.

Deadwood Gulch [MADERA]: *canyon,* 1.5 miles long, 7.25 miles south-southwest of Yosemite Forks (lat. 37°16'45" N, long. 119° 42' W). Named on Bass Lake (1953) 15' quadrangle.

Deadwood Peak [MADERA]: *peak,* 4.5 miles southwest of Yosemite Forks on Potter Ridge (lat. 37°18'50" N, long. 119°41'05" W; sec. 21, T 7 S, R 21 E). Altitude 4540 feet. Named on Bass Lake (1953) 15' quadrangle.

Deadwood House: see **Deadwood** [PLACER].

Deadwood Peak [SIERRA]: *peak,* 4 miles south-southwest of Mount Fillmore (lat. 39°40'25" N, long. 120°52'25" W; near NW cor. sec. 21, T 21 N, R 10 E). Altitude 6477 feet. Named on La Porte (1951) and Mount Fillmore (1951) 7.5' quadrangles.

Deadwood Ravine [SIERRA]: *canyon,* drained by a stream that flows less than 1 mile to Canyon Creek 4.25 miles south-southwest of Mount Fillmore (lat. 39°40'40" N, long. 120°53'25" W; sec. 17, T 21 N, R 10 E); the canyon is north of Deadwood Peak. Named on La Porte (1951) 7.5' quadrangle.

Deadwood Ridge [PLACER]: *ridge,* south-southwest- to south-trending, 11 miles long, extends from Foresthill Divide 1 mile east of Westville to the junction of El Dorado Canyon and North Fork of Middle Fork American River; the site of Deadwood is on the ridge. Named on Michigan Bluff (1952) and Westville (1952) 7.5' quadrangles.

Deadwood Spring [TUOLUMNE]: *spring,* 5 miles south-southeast of Long Barn (lat. 38°01'30" N, long. 120°06'40" W; sec. 16, T 2 N, R 17 E). Named on Hull Creek (1979) 7.5' quadrangle.

Deans Ravine [SIERRA]: *canyon,* drained by a stream that flows 1.25 miles to East Fork Canyon Creek 3.5 miles southeast of Mount Fillmore (lat. 39°41'50" N, long. 120°48'10" W). Named on Mount Fillmore (1951) 7.5' quadrangle.

Deep Canyon [EL DORADO]: *canyon,* drained by a stream that flows 1.5 miles to Pilot Creek (1) 13 miles north-northwest of Pollock Pines (lat. 38°56'20" N, long. 120°40'20" W). Named on Tunnel Hill (1950) 7.5' quadrangle.

Deep Canyon [PLACER]: *canyon,* drained by a stream that flows 7.5 miles to North Fork of Middle Fork American River 5 miles west-southwest of Duncan Peak (lat. 39°07'20" N, long. 120°35'35" W; sec. 25, T 15 N, R 12 E). Named on Duncan Peak (1952) and Greek Store (1952) 7.5' quadrangles.

Deep Canyon [SIERRA]: *canyon,* drained by a stream that heads in the State of Nevada and flows less than 0.5 mile in Sierra County to Truckee River 8 miles southeast of Crystal Peak (lat. 39°27'25" N, long. 120°00'25" W; sec. 6, T 18 N, R 18 E). Named on Boca (1955) 7.5' quadrangle.

Deep Canyon [TUOLUMNE]: *canyon,* 1.5 miles long, 7.5 miles north of White Wolf along a tributary to Rancheria Creek (lat. 37°58'50" N, long. 119°38'10" W). Named on Hetch Hetchy Reservoir (1956) 15' quadrangle.

Deep Creek [PLACER]: *stream,* flows 4.5 miles to Truckee River 10 miles west-southwest of Martis Peak (lat. 39°15'30" N, long. 120° 12'30" W; near S line sec. 4, T 16 N, R 16 E). Named on Granite Chief (1953), Norden (1955), and Truckee (1955) 7.5' quadrangles.

Deep Gulch [CALAVERAS]: *canyon,* drained by a stream that flows 0.5 mile to Stanislaus River 3 miles east of Vallecito (lat. 38°04'50" N, long. 120°25'05" W; sec. 27, T 3 N, R 14 E). Named on Columbia (1948) 7.5' quadrangle.

Deep Hollow [MADERA]: *canyon,* drained by a stream that flows nearly 2 miles to Willow Creek (1) 3.5 miles north-northeast of Raymond (lat. 37°15'45" N, long. 119°53'30" W). Named on Ben Hur (1947) and Raymond (1962) 7.5' quadrangles.

Deep Ravine [EL DORADO]: *canyon,* drained by a stream that flows 2 miles to South Fork American River 6.5 miles north-northwest of Clarksville (lat. 38°44'40" N, long. 121°05'25" W; near S line sec. 3, T 10 N, R 8 E). Named on Clarksville (1953) and Pilot Hill (1954) 7.5' quadrangles. Water of Folsom Lake now covers the lower part of the canyon. Auburn (1944) 15' quadrangle shows

Anderson Creek in the canyon.

Deer Camp [MARIPOSA]: *locality,* 5 miles north-northeast of Wawona (lat. 37°36'50" N, long. 119°37'45" W; at W line sec. 1, T 4 S, R 21 E). Named on Yosemite (1956) 15' quadrangle.

Deer Creek [AMADOR]: *stream,* flows nearly 2 miles to North Fork Mokelumne River 6 miles south-southeast of Hams Station (lat. 38°28'15" N, long. 120°25'35" W; near W line sec. 10, T 7 N, R 14 E). Named on Devils Nose (1979) 7.5' quadrangle.

Deer Creek [EL DORADO]:
(1) *stream,* flows 3.5 miles to Rubicon River 5.25 miles north-northwest of Robbs Peak (lat. 38°59'30" N, long. 120°27'05" W; sec. 7, T 13 N, R 14 E). Named on Bunker Hill (1953) and Robbs Peak (1950) 7.5' quadrangles.
(2) *locality,* 3.5 miles west of Shingle Springs along Deer Creek [EL DORADO] (lat. 38°39'30" N, long. 120°59'30" W). Named on Placerville (1893) 30' quadrangle.

Deer Creek [EL DORADO]: *stream,* heads in El Dorado County and flows 42 miles to Cosumnes River 7.5 miles north-northwest of Galt in Sacramento County (lat. 38°21'40" N, long. 121°20'25" W). Named on Buffalo Creek (1967), Clarksville (1953), Elk Grove (1968), Folsom SE (1954), Galt (1968), Latrobe (1949), Shingle Springs (1949), and Sloughhouse (1968) 7.5' quadrangles.

Deer Creek [NEVADA]: *stream,* formed in Nevada County by the confluence of North Fork and South Fork, flows 26 miles to Yuba River 6.5 miles northwest of Pilot Peak just inside of Yuba County (lat. 39°13'50" N, long. 121°16'50" W; near E line sec. 22, T 16 N, R 6 E). Named on Grass Valley (1949), Nevada City (1948), North Bloomfield (1949), Rough and Ready (1949), and Smartville (1951) 7.5' quadrangles. Some hunters named the stream in 1849 when they had to abandon a freshly killed deer there (Gudde, 1975, p. 93). North Fork is 6.5 miles long and South Fork is 7.25 miles long; both forks are named on North Bloomfield (1949) and Washington (1950) 7.5' quadrangles. Eddy's (1851) map shows a place called Deer Creek Crossing situated along Deer Creek 4 or 5 miles above the mouth, and a place called Matheus located along a southern tributary to Deer Creek southwest of Deer Creek Crossing. Gudde (1975, p. 115) listed a place called Fienes Crossing that was located along Deer Creek about 1 mile above the mouth of the stream.

Deer Creek [PLACER]: *stream,* flows 2.5 miles to Truckee River nearly 5 miles northwest of Tahoe City (lat. 39°13'20" N, long. 120°11'55" W; near E line sec. 21, T 16 N, R 16 E). Named on Tahoe City (1955) 7.5' quadrangle. Called Silver Creek on Hobson's (1890b) map.

Deer Creek [SIERRA]: *stream.* flows 4.5 miles to North Yuba River 4 miles north-northeast

of Sierra City (lat. 39°36'50" N, long. 120°
35'30" W; sec. 11, T 20 N, R 12 E). Named on
Haypress Valley (1981) 7.5' quadrangle. The
lower part of the stream is called Williams
Creek on Sierra City (1955) 15' quadrangle.

Deer Creek [TUOLUMNE]:
(1) *stream,* flows 7.25 miles to South Fork
Stanislaus River 8 miles east-northeast of
Columbia (lat. 38°05'30" N, long. 120°16'10"
W; near N line sec. 25, T 3 N, R 15 E). Named
on Columbia SE (1948), Crandall Peak
(1979), and Twain Harte (1979) 7.5' quadrangles.
(2) *stream,* flows 5 miles to Tuolumne River
4.25 miles north of Moccasin (lat. 37°52'25"
N, long. 120°17'45" W; sec. 2, T 1 S, R 15 E).
Named on Moccasin (1948) 7.5' quadrangle.

Deer Creek: see **Little Deer Creek** [EL DO-
RADO]; **Little Deer Creek** [NEVADA].

Deer Creek Crossing: see **Deer Creek** [NE-
VADA].

Deer Creek Dry Diggings: see **Nevada City**
[NEVADA].

Deer Creek Reservoir [NEVADA]: *lake,* behind
a dam on Deer Creek 7.5 miles south-southwest of North Bloomfield (lat. 39°16'10" N,
long. 120°57'10" W; sec. 10, T 16 N, R 9 E).
Named on North Bloomfield (1949) 7.5'
quadrangle.

Deer Flat [MARIPOSA]: *area,* 9.5 miles west-
northwest of El Portal (lat. 37°44'25" N, long.
119°56'15" W; near S line sec. 24, T 2 S, R
18 E). Named on Kinsley (1947) 7.5' quadrangle.

Deer Flat [TUOLUMNE]: *area,* 8 miles south
of Tuolumne on upper reaches of Deer Creek
(2) (lat. 37°50'30" N, long. 120°15'30" W).
Named on Sonora (1897) 30' quadrangle.

Deer Knob [EL DORADO]: *peak,* 3 miles
south-southwest of Robbs Peak (lat. 38°53'25"
N, long. 120°25'55" W; sec. 17, T 12 N, R 14
E). Altitude 5621 feet. Named on Robbs Peak
(1950) 7.5' quadrangle.

Deer Lake [SIERRA]: *lake,* 1850 feet long, 5.5
miles north-northwest of Sierra City (lat.
39°38'40" N, long. 120°39'55" W; near NE
cor. sec. 31, T 21 N, R 12 E). Named on Gold
Lake (1981) 7.5' quadrangle.

Deer Lake [TUOLUMNE]: *lake,* 0.5 mile long,
12.5 miles east of Pinecrest (lat. 38°09'55"
N, long. 119°45'50" W). Named on Pinecrest
(1956) 15' quadrangle.

Deer Lake: see **Little Deer Lake** [SIERRA].

Deer Lick Creek [MARIPOSA]: *stream,* flows
3.5 miles to Moore Creek 4.25 miles southeast of Smith Peak (lat. 37°45'45" N, long.
120°02'15" W; near E line sec. 13, T 2 S, R
17 E). Named on Jawbone Ridge (1947) 7.5'
quadrangle.

Deer Park [PLACER]: *locality,* 4.5 miles west
of Tahoe City along Bear Creek at present
Alpine Meadows (lat. 39°10'45" N, long.
120°13'35" W; at W line sec. 4, T 15 N, R 16
E); the place is 1.5 miles north of Scott Peak.

Named on Truckee (1940) 30' quadrangle.
Called Scotts Springs on Truckee (1895) 30'
quadrangle. G.A. Waring (p. 232-233) noted
that four springs, called Deer Park Springs,
were the basis of a resort at the place as early
as the 1880's. California Division of Highways' (1934) map shows a place called Deer
Park located along Southern Pacific Railroad
near the mouth of Bear Creek (at SW cor. sec.
34, T 16 N, R 16 E).

Deer Park Springs: see **Deer Park** [PLACER].

Deer Peak [CALAVERAS]: *peak,* 3.25 miles
west-southwest of San Andreas (lat. 38°10'15"
N, long. 120°43'50" W; sec. 26, T 4 N, R 11
E). Altitude 1921 feet. Named on San Andreas
(1962) 7.5' quadrangle.

Deer Ridge [CALAVERAS]: *ridge,* south-trending, 1.25 miles long, 4 miles north-northeast
of San Andreas (lat. 38°14'55" N, long. 120°
39'15" W). Named on Mokelumne Hill (1948)
and San Andreas (1962) 7.5' quadrangles.

Deer Valley [AMADOR]: *area,* 6 miles west of
Mokelumne Peak (lat. 38°32'55" N, long.
120°12'15" W; near NW cor. sec. 15, T 8 N,
R 16 E). Named on Bear River Reservoir
(1979) 7.5' quadrangle.

Deer View [EL DORADO]: *locality,* 7.25 miles
northwest of Pollock Pines (lat. 38°50'35" N,
long. 120°40' W; sec. 32, T 12 N, R 12 E).
Named on Slate Mountain (1950) 7.5' quadrangle.

Defender: see **Pine Grove** [AMADOR].

Defiance: see **Point Defiance** [NEVADA].

De Krusse Canyon [PLACER]: *canyon,* drained
by a stream that flows 1.5 miles to Indian
Creek (2) 6 miles north-northwest of Foresthill
(lat. 39°05'55" N, long. 120°51'55" W; at N
line sec. 4, T 14 N, R 10 E). Named on Colfax
(1950) 15' quadrangle. On Foresthill (1949)
7.5' quadrangle, the name has the misspell-
ing "DeKrruse Canyon."

Delahunty Lake [SIERRA]: *lake,* 750 feet long,
2.5 miles northwest of Mount Fillmore (lat.
39°45'05" N, long. 120°53'10" W; sec. 20, T
22 N, R 10 E). Named on Onion Valley (1950)
7.5' quadrangle.

Delaney: see **Cox-Delaney Flat** [NEVADA].

Delaney Creek [TUOLUMNE]: *stream,* flows
5.5 miles to Tuolumne River 7 miles west-
southwest of Tioga Pass (lat. 37°53' N, long.
119°23' W; sec. 6, T 1 S, R 24 E). Named on
Tuolumne Meadows (1956) 15' quadrangle.
John Muir named the stream for Pat Delaney,
who accompanied Muir to the Sierra Nevada
in 1869 (United States Board on Geographic
Names, 1934, p. 6).

Delaney's Bridge: see **Chaparral Hill**, under
Lancha Plana [AMADOR].

Delirium Tremens: see **Omega** [NEVADA].

Deller Creek [EL DORADO-PLACER]:
stream, heads in Placer County and flows 5
miles to Gerle Creek 2.5 miles west of Wentworth Springs in El Dorado County (lat.
39°00'35" N, long. 120° 22'55" W; near NW

cor. sec. 2, T 13 N, R 14 E). Named on Bunker Hill (1953) and Wentworth Springs (1953) 7.5' quadrangles.

Deller Meadow [PLACER]: *area,* 0.5 mile east of Bunker Hill (lat. 39°03'05" N, long. 120°22'10" W; near NE cor. sec. 23, T 14 N, R 14 E); the place is at the head of Deller Creek. Named on Wentworth Springs (1953) 7.5' quadrangle.

Deller Spring [PLACER]: *spring,* 9 miles southwest of Duncan Peak (lat. 39°03'05" N, long. 120°36'20" W; sec. 23, T 14 N, R 12 E). Named on Greek Store (1952) 7.5' quadrangle.

DeLong Creek [MARIPOSA]: *stream,* flows 4.5 miles to Oliver Creek 10 miles east-southeast of Mariposa (lat. 37°26'50" N, long. 119°47'15" W; near S line sec. 33, T 5 S, R 20 E). Named on Stumpfield Mountain (1947) 7.5' quadrangle. Mariposa (1947) 15' quadrangle has the name "DeLong Creek" for present Oliver Creek below the confluence of DeLong Creek and Oliver Creek. The name "DeLong" is for Charles DeLong, a rancher (Sargent, Shirley, 1976, p. 32).

Del Orto Camp [CALAVERAS]: *locality,* 2.25 miles west-southwest of Tamarack in Thompson Meadow (lat. 38°26' N, long. 120°06'55" W; sec. 28, T 7 N, R 17 E). Named on Tamarack (1979) 7.5' quadrangle.

Democrat [NEVADA]: *locality,* 5.25 miles south of Washington (lat. 39°16'45" N, long. 120°46'45" W). Named on Colfax (1898) 30' quadrangle.

Democrat Peak [SIERRA]: *peak,* 4.25 miles south of Mount Fillmore (lat. 39°40'05" N, long. 120°50'40" W). Altitude 6779 feet. Named on Mount Fillmore (1951) 7.5' quadrangle.

Demory Spring [NEVADA]: *spring,* 3.25 miles west-northwest of Washington (lat. 39°22'20" N, long. 120°51'35" W; near N line sec. 4, T 17 N, R 10 E). Named on Washington (1950) 7.5' quadrangle.

Dempsey Spring [NEVADA]: *spring,* 2.5 miles northwest of Washington (lat. 39°23'05" N, long. 121°50' W; near NE cor. sec. 34, T 18 N, R 10 E). Named on Alleghany (1949) 7.5' quadrangle.

Dennis Canyon [EL DORADO]: *canyon,* drained by a stream that flows 1 mile to Camp Creek 6.25 miles northwest of Leek Spring Hill (lat. 38°41'05" N, long. 120°22'10" W; near S line sec. 25, T 10 N, R 14 E). Named on Leek Spring Hill (1951) 7.5' quadrangle.

Dennis Spring [EL DORADO]: *spring,* 6.5 miles northwest of Leek Spring Hill (lat. 38°41'40" N, long. 120°22'05" W; sec. 25, T 10 N, R 14 E); the spring is in Dennis Canyon. Named on Leek Spring Hill (1951) 7.5' quadrangle.

Denvale: see **Big Chief** [PLACER].

Denver Church Campground [MADERA]: *locality,* 4.25 miles southeast of Yosemite Forks on the west side of Bass Lake (1) (lat.

37°19'20" N, long. 119°34'40" W; sec. 16, T 7 S, R 22 E). Named on Bass Lake (1953) 15' quadrangle.

Derbec Spring [NEVADA]: *spring,* 2 miles north-northeast of North Bloomfield (lat. 39°23'30" N, long. 121°52'45" W; sec. 29, T 18 N, R 10 E). Named on Pike (1949) 7.5' quadrangle.

Derbec Spring: see **Upper Derbec Spring** [NEVADA].

Desert Cold Spring [PLACER]: *spring,* 4 miles northeast of Devil Peak (lat. 38°59'55" N, long. 120°29'55" W; at S line sec. 2, T 13 N, R 13 E). Named on Robbs Peak (1950) 7.5' quadrangle.

Desolation Lake [EL DORADO]: *lake,* 750 feet long, 1.5 miles east of Pyramid Peak (lat. 38°50'50" N, long. 120°07'30" W); the lake is in Desolation Valley. Named on Pyramid Peak (1955) 7.5' quadrangle.

Desolation Valley [EL DORADO]: *valley,* 1.5 miles east-northeast of Pyramid Peak (lat. 38°51' N, long. 120°08' W). Named on Echo Lake (1955) and Pyramid Peak (1955) 7.5' quadrangles. The feature was known as Devil's Valley and Devil's Basin before it received the present name (Lekisch, p. 28).

Detachment Meadow [MADERA]: *area,* 7.25 miles east-southeast of Merced Peak (lat. 37°36'10" N, long. 119°16'05" W). Named on Merced Peak (1953) 15' quadrangle.

Detwiler: see **Jasper** [MARIPOSA].

Devil Gulch [MARIPOSA]: *canyon,* drained by a stream that flows 8.5 miles to South Fork Merced River 5 miles south-southwest of El Portal (lat. 37°36'35" N, long. 119°49'15" W). Named on Buckingham Mountain (1947) 7.5' quadrangle.

Devil Peak [MARIPOSA]: *peak,* 4.5 miles west of Wawona in Chowchilla Mountains (lat. 37°31'45" N, long. 119°44'25" W; sec. 1, T 5 S, R 20 E). Altitude 6989 feet. Named on Yosemite (1956) 15' quadrangle. Called Devil's Mt. on Hoffmann and Gardner's (1863-1867) map. United States Board on Geographic Names (1933, p. 263) rejected the names "Devil's Peak" and "Signal Peak" for the feature. According to Hanna (p. 306), the name "Signal Peak" was given because Indians used the place to send messages by smoke and fire.

Devil Peak [PLACER]: *peak,* 29 miles east of Auburn (lat. 38°57'30" N, long. 120°32'45" W; near S line sec. 20, T 13 N, R 13 E). Altitude 5302 feet. Named on Devil Peak (1950) 7.5' quadrangle.

Devil Peak: see **Devils Peak** [PLACER] (1).

Devils Basin [PLACER]: *relief feature,* 5.25 miles northeast of Michigan Bluff (lat. 39°05'35" N, long. 120°39'35" W; near N line sec. 5, T 14 N, R 12 E). Named on Michigan Bluff (1952) 7.5' quadrangle.

Devil's Basin: see **Desolation Valley** [EL DORADO].

Devils Canyon [NEVADA]: *canyon,* drained by a stream that flows 3 miles to Poorman Creek (1) 1 mile north of Washington (lat. 39° 22'25" N, long. 120°47'50" W; near N line sec. 1, T 17 N, R 10 E). Named on Alleghany (1949) and Washington (1950) 7.5' quadrangles.

Devils Canyon [PLACER]: *canyon,* drained by a stream that flows 5.5 miles to Shirttail Canyon 5.25 miles southeast of Colfax (lat. 39°02'20" N, long. 120°53'40" W; at S line sec. 19, T 14 N, R 10 E). Named on Colfax (1949) and Foresthill (1949) 7.5' quadrangles. Bancroft (1888, p. 355) used the form "Devil's cañon" for the name.

Devils Canyon [SIERRA]: *canyon,* drained by a stream that flows 1.5 miles to North Yuba River 1.5 miles west of Goodyears Bar (lat. 39°32'10" N, long. 120°54'50" W; sec. 1, T 19 N, R 9 E). Named on Goodyears Bar (1951) 7.5' quadrangle.

Devils Canyon [TUOLUMNE]: *canyon,* drained by a stream that flows nearly 2 miles to Stanislaus River 3.5 miles west-southwest of Columbia (lat. 38°00'40" N, long. 120°27'40" W; sec. 20, T 2 N, R 14 E). Named on Columbia (1948) 7.5' quadrangle.

Devils Gate [AMADOR]: *narrows,* 6 miles west-southwest of Jackson along Jackson Creek (lat. 38°18'25" N, long. 120°52'20" W; near NE cor. sec. 9, T 5 N, R 10 E). Named on Jackson (1962) 7.5' quadrangle.

Devils Gate [PLACER]: *narrows,* 4 miles east-northeast of Michigan Bluff along North Fork of Middle Fork American River (lat. 39°04'15" N, long. 120°40'10" W; near SE cor. sec. 7, T 14 N, R 12 E). Named on Michigan Bluff (1952) 7.5' quadrangle.

Devils Gate [SIERRA]: *narrows,* 3.25 miles south-southwest of Mount Fillmore along Canyon Creek (lat. 39°41'10" N, long. 120° 52'40" W; near N line sec. 17, T 21 N, R 10 E). Named on La Porte (1951) 7.5' quadrangle.

Devils Hole Lake [AMADOR]: *lake,* 500 feet long, 6.5 miles north of Mokelumne Peak (lat. 38°37'55" N, long. 120°04'35" W; sec. 15, T 9 N, R 17 E). Named on Caples Lake (1979) 7.5' quadrangle.

Devil's Horn: see **Devils Thumb** [PLACER].

Devils Lake [AMADOR]: *lake,* 1400 feet long, 6 miles west-northwest of Mokelumne Peak (lat. 38°34'55" N, long. 120°11'10" W; sec. 35, T 9 N, R 16 E). Named on Silver Lake (1956) 15' quadrangle.

Devil's Mountain: see **Devil Peak** [MARIPOSA].

Devils Nose [CALAVERAS]: *peak,* 9 miles north-northwest of Blue Mountain (lat. 38°27'45" N, long. 120°25'10" W; sec. 15, T 7 N, R 14 E). Altitude 4802 feet. Named on Devils Nose (1979) 7.5' quadrangle.

Devils Oven: see **Devils Oven Lake** [NEVADA].

Devils Oven Lake [NEVADA]: *lake,* 700 feet long, 5.25 miles north-northwest of Donner Pass (lat. 39°23'35" N, long. 120°21'25" W; near SW cor. sec. 25, T 18 N, R 14 E). Named on Independence Lake (1981) 7.5' quadrangle. Donner Pass (1955) 15' quadrangle has the name "Devils Oven" at the place.

Devil's Peak: see **Devil Peak** [MARIPOSA].

Devils Peak [PLACER]:
(1) *peak,* 6.5 miles west-southwest of Donner Pass (lat. 39°16'55" N, long. 120°26'25" W; sec. 6, T 16 N, R 14 E). Altitude 7704 feet. Named on Soda Springs (1955) 7.5' quadrangle. Called Devil Peak on Truckee (1895) 30' quadrangle.
(2) *peak,* 5 miles east-southeast of Bunker Hill (lat. 39°01'45" N, long. 120°17'25" W; at E line sec. 28, T 14 N, R 15 E). Altitude 7541 feet. Named on Wentworth Springs (1953) 7.5' quadrangle.

Devils Postpile [MADERA]: *relief feature,* 17 miles east of Merced Peak along Middle Fork San Joaquin River (lat. 37°37'30" N, long. 119°05' W). Named on Devils Postpile (1953) 15' quadrangle. The feature consists of columns of volcanic rock; it was known locally in 1894 as Devils Woodpile (Hanna, p. 86). McLaughlin and Bradley (p. 534) used the form "Devil's Post Pile" for the name. United States Board on Geographic Names (1954, p. 3) rejected the names "Devil Postpile" and "Devils Post Pile" for the feature.

Devils Post Pile [SIERRA]: *relief feature,* 4.25 miles south-southwest of Mount Fillmore (lat. 39°40'20" N, long. 120°52'50" W; near N line sec. 20, T 21 N, R 10 E). Named on La Porte (1951) 7.5' quadrangle.

Devils Punch Bowl: see **The Punchbowl** [NEVADA].

Devils Slide [NEVADA]: *relief feature,* 4 miles northwest of Nevada City on the southeast side of South Yuba River (lat. 39°18'25" N, long. 121°04' W; sec. 27, T 17 N, R 8 E). Named on Nevada City (1948) 7.5' quadrangle.

Devils Thumb [PLACER]: *relief feature,* 5.5 miles northeast of Michigan Bluff (lat. 39°05'45" N, long. 120°39'35" W; near S line sec. 32, T 15 N, R 12 E). Named on Michigan Bluff (1952) 7.5' quadrangle. C.A. Waring (p. 356) used the name "Devil's Horn" for the feature.

Devil's Valley: see **Desolation Valley** [EL DORADO].

Devine Gulch: see **Georgia Slide** [EL DORADO].

Dew Drop [NEVADA]: *locality,* 3 miles north of Higgins Corner (lat. 39°05'10" N, long. 121°05'05" W; near NW cor. sec. 10, T 14 N, R 8 E). Named on Lake Combie (1949) 7.5' quadrangle.

Dewey Campground [PLACER]: *locality,* 6.25 miles northwest of Bunker Hill along Middle Fork American River (lat. 39°06'45" N, long. 120°27'45" W; near NE cor. sec. 36, T 15 N, R 13 E). Named on Granite Chief (1953) 15' quadrangle. Water of French Meadows Reservoir now covers the site.

Dewey Point [MARIPOSA]: *promontory,* 4.5 miles southwest of Yosemite Village on the south side of Yosemite Valley (lat. 37°42'15" N, long. 119°39'05" W). Named on Yosemite (1956) 15' quadrangle.

Diablo Campground [SIERRA]: *locality,* 4.5 miles north of Sierra City along Packer Creek (lat. 39°37'50" N, long. 120°38'20" W; at S line sec. 33, T 21 N, R 12 E). Named on Gold Lake (1981) 7.5' quadrangle.

Diamond: see **Diamond Springs** [EL DORADO].

Diamond Bar: see **French Bar** [AMADOR].

Diamond Creek [EL DORADO]: *stream,* flows 3.25 miles to Camp Creek 9.5 miles east of Camino (lat. 38°43'10" N, long. 120°30'05" W; sec. 14, T 10 N, R 13 E). Named on Sly Park (1952) and Stump Spring (1951) 7.5' quadrangles.

Diamond Creek [NEVADA]: *stream,* flows 4.25 miles to South Yuba River 7.25 miles west-northwest of Yuba Gap (lat. 39°21'15" N, long. 120°44'20" W; sec. 9, T 17 N, R 11 E). Named on Blue Canyon (1955) 7.5' quadrangle.

Diamond Creek: see **Omega** [NEVADA].

Diamond Crossing [PLACER]: *locality,* 6.5 miles northeast of Bunker Hill along Five Lakes Creek (lat. 39°06'35" N, long. 120°17'25" W; near NW cor. sec. 34, T 15 N, R 15 E). Named on Wentworth Springs (1953) 7.5' quadrangle.

Diamond Shower Fall: see **Bunnell Cascade** [MARIPOSA].

Diamond Springs [EL DORADO]: *town,* 2.5 miles south-southwest of Placerville (lat. 38°41'40" N, long. 120°48'50" W; on W line sec. 30, T 10 N, R 11 E). Named on Placerville (1949) 7.5' quadrangle. Called Diamond Spring on Placerville (1893) 30' quadrangle, and called Diamond on California Mining Bureau's (1909a) map. Postal authorities established Diamond Spring post office in 1853 and changed the name to Diamond Springs in 1950 (Salley, p. 59). According to Hanna (p. 86), the name is from some crystal-clear springs. According to Paden (p. 455-456), the name is from the location of springs at the corners of a diamond-shaped area.

Dicks Lake [EL DORADO]: *lake,* 0.5 mile long, 3 miles south of Phipps Peak (lat. 38°54'45" N, long. 120°08'30" W; sec. 6, R 12 N, R 17 E); the lake is less than 1 mile north-northeast of Dicks Peak. Named on Rockbound Valley (1955) 7.5' quadrangle.

Dicks Pass [EL DORADO]: *pass,* 3.5 miles south-southeast of Phipps Peak (lat. 38°54'20" N, long. 120°08'05" W; sec. 7, T 12 N, R 17 E); the pass is 1 mile east-northeast of Dicks Peak. Named on Rockbound Valley (1955) 7.5' quadrangle.

Dicks Peak [EL DORADO]: *peak,* 3.5 miles

south of Phipps Peak (lat. 38°54' N, long. 120°09' W). Altitude 9974 feet. Named on Rockbound Valley (1955) 7.5' quadrangle. The name commemorates Captain Richard Barter, an eccentric English sailor who lived a lonely life at Emerald Bay in the 1860's and 1870's (Lekisch, p. 29-30).

Diggers Bar: see **Relief** [NEVADA].

Dingley Creek [TUOLUMNE]: *stream,* flows nearly 4 miles to Tuolumne River 7.5 miles west of Tioga Pass (lat. 37°53'50" N, long. 119°23'40" W). Named on Tuolumne Meadows (1956) 15' quadrangle.

Dillon [NEVADA]: *locality,* 6.5 miles east of North Bloomfield at the confluence of Poorman Creek (1) and its South Fork (lat. 39°23'05" N, long. 120°46'40" W; sec. 31, T 18 N, R 11 E). Named on Colfax (1938) 30' quadrangle.

Dirty Gulch [CALAVERAS]: *canyon,* drained by a stream that flows 2.5 miles to McKinney Creek 9 miles east of San Andreas (lat. 38°11'50" N, long. 120°30'50" W; sec. 14, T 4 N, R 13 E). Named on Calaveritas (1962) 7.5' quadrangle.

Disney: see **Mount Disney** [PLACER].

Ditch Camp [EL DORADO]: *locality,* nearly 2 miles north-northeast of Robbs Peak (lat. 38°57' N, long. 120°23'55" W; sec. 27, T 13 N, R 14 E). Named on Robbs Peak (1950) 7.5' quadrangle.

Ditch Camp [PLACER]: *locality,* 4 miles east of Michigan Bluff (lat. 39°02'45" N, long. 120°39'35" W; sec. 20, T 14 N, R 12 E). Site named on Michigan Bluff (1952) 7.5' quadrangle.

Ditch Camp Five [EL DORADO]: *locality,* 2 miles east of Pollock Pines (lat. 38°45'55" N, long. 120°32'50" W; at S line sec. 29, T 11 N, R 13 E). Named on Pollock Pines (1950) 7.5' quadrangle.

Ditch Camp Four [EL DORADO]: *locality,* 2.5 miles west-southwest of Riverton (lat. 38°45'20" N, long. 120°29'35" W; sec. 35, T 11 N, R 13 E). Named on Riverton (1950) 7.5' quadrangle.

Ditch Camp One [EL DORADO]: *locality,* 4.5 miles west of Kyburz (lat. 38°45'50" N, long. 120°22'30" W; at S line sec. 26, T 11 N, R 14 E). Named on Kyburz (1952) 7.5' quadrangle.

Ditch Camp Point [EL DORADO]: *ridge,* north-northeast- to north-trending, 1.5 miles long, 13 miles north-northwest of Pollock Pines (lat. 38°55'45" N, long. 120°41'05" W). Named on Tunnel Hill (1950) 7.5' quadrangle.

Ditch Camp Seven [EL DORADO]: *locality,* 1.25 miles southeast of Moores (present Riverton) (lat. 38°45'30" N, long. 120°25'45" W). Named on Pyramid Peak (1896) 30' quadrangle.

Ditch Camp Ten [EL DORADO]: *locality,* 4.25 miles west-southwest of Slippery Ford (present Kyburz) (lat. 38°45'15" N, long. 120°22'30" W). Named on Pyramid Peak (1896) 30' quadrangle.

Ditch Camp Three [EL DORADO]: *locality,* 1.25 miles west-southwest of Riverton (lat. 38°45'50" N, long. 120°28'10" W; sec. 36, T 11 N, R 13 E). Named on Riverton (1950) 7.5' quadrangle.

Ditch Camp Two [EL DORADO]: *locality,* less than 1 mile east-southeast of Riverton (lat. 38°45'55" N, long. 120°26'05" W; at N line sec. 32, T 11 N, R 14 E). Named on Riverton (1950) 7.5' quadrangle.

Diving Board [MARIPOSA]: *relief feature,* 2.5 miles east of Yosemite Village (lat. 37°44'30" N, long. 119°32'10" W). Named on Yosemite (1956) 15' quadrangle.

Doaks Ridge [AMADOR]: *ridge,* southwest-trending, 6 miles long, 3 miles south-south-west of Hams Station (lat. 38°30'15" N, long. 120°24'20" W). Named on Caldor (1951) and Devils Nose (1979) 7.5' quadrangles. Called Doak Ridge on Pyramid Peak (1896) 30' quadrangle.

Dobbas Cow Camp [PLACER]: *locality,* 6 miles northwest of Bunker Hill along Middle Fork American River (lat. 39°06'35" N, long. 120°27'35" W; sec. 36, T 15 N, R 13 E). Named on Granite Chief (1953) 15' quadrangle. Water of French Meadows Reservoir now covers the site.

Dodge Canyon [SIERRA]: *canyon,* drained by a stream that flows 3 miles to Badenaugh Canyon 4.5 miles southeast of Loyalton (lat. 39°37'45" N, long. 120°11'05" W; at W line sec. 34, T 21 N, R 16 E). Named on Loyalton (1981) 7.5' quadrangle.

Dodge Meadow [TUOLUMNE]: *area,* nearly 4 miles south of Pinecrest along Trout Creek (lat. 38°08'15" N, long. 119°59'10" W; on S line sec. 3, T 3 N, R 18 E). Named on Pinecrest (1979) 7.5' quadrangle.

Dodge Ridge [TUOLUMNE]: *ridge,* southwest-trending, 12 miles long, 5 miles east-north-east of Long Barn (lat. 38°07' N, long. 120°03'30" W). Named on Hull Creek (1979), Pinecrest (1979), and Strawberry (1979) 7.5' quadrangles.

Dodges [PLACER]: *locality,* 10 miles northeast of Auburn (lat. 38° 59'40" N, long. 120°55'30" W). Named on Placerville (1893) 30' quadrangle.

Doe Lake [TUOLUMNE]: *lake,* 1500 feet long, 6 miles southwest of Matterhorn Peak (lat. 38°02'10" N, long. 119°28' W). Named on Matterhorn Peak (1956) 15' quadrangle.

Dog Creek [SIERRA]: *stream,* flows 7 miles to the State of Nevada 5 miles east-southeast of Crystal Peak (lat. 39°31'40" N, long. 120°00'05" W; at E line sec. 7, T 19 N, R 18 E); the stream goes through Dog Valley. Named on Dog Valley (1981) 7.5' quadrangle. North Branch enters from the north 3 miles east of Crystal Peak and is nearly 4 miles long. South Branch enters at California-Nevada State line and is 2.5 miles long. Both branches are named on Dog Valley (1981) 7.5' quadrangle.

Doghead Peak [TUOLUMNE]: *peak,* nearly 4 miles southwest of Matterhorn Peak (lat. 38°03'10" N, long. 119°25'45" W). Altitude 11,102 feet. Named on Matterhorn Peak (1956) 15' quadrangle.

Dog Lake [TUOLUMNE]: *lake,* 2300 feet long, 4.5 miles west-southwest of Tioga Pass (lat. 37°53'25" N, long. 119°20'20" W; sec. 4, T 1 S, R 24 E). Named on Tuolumne Meadows (1956) 15' quadrangle. R.B. Marshall of United States Geological Survey named the lake in 1898 after he found a sheep dog and a litter of puppies there (Gudde, 1969, p. 91).

Dog Pump Hotel: see **Corbet Creek** [MARIPOSA].

Dogtown [CALAVERAS]: *locality,* 7.5 miles southeast of San Andreas along San Domingo Creek (lat. 38°07'30" N, long. 120° 34'15" W; sec. 8, T 3 N, R 13 E). Named on Angels Camp (1962) and Calaveritas (1962) 7.5' quadrangles. The place was a mining camp of 1849 that was named for a stray dog (Gudde, 1975, p. 97).

Dogtown [EL DORADO]: *locality,* 8 miles west-southwest of Leek Spring Hill (lat. 38°36'10" N, long. 120°25'30" W). Named on Pyramid Peak (1896) 30' quadrangle.

Dogtown [MARIPOSA]: *locality,* nearly 4 miles east of Coulterville along Maxwell Creek (lat. 37°42'10" N, long. 120°07'40" W; near E line sec. 6, T 3 S, R 17 E). Named on Coulterville (1947) 7.5' quadrangle.

Dog Town: see **Bunker Hill** [AMADOR] (2).

Dogtown: see **Newtown** [EL DORADO].

Dogtown Creek [EL DORADO]: *stream,* flows 10.5 miles to Middle Fork Cosumnes River 1 mile northeast of Omo Ranch (lat. 38° 35'30" N, long. 120°33'15" W; near W line sec. 33, T 9 N, R 13 E). Named on Caldor (1951), Omo Ranch (1952), and Stump Spring (1951) 7.5' quadrangles. Called North Fork of Middle Fork Cosumnes River on Pyramid Peak (1896) 30' quadrangle, which shows Dogtown situated along the stream.

Dog Valley [SIERRA]: *valley,* 2.5 miles east of Crystal Peak (lat. 39° 33'30" N, long. 120°02'30" W); the valley is along Dog Creek. Named on Dog Valley (1981) 7.5' quadrangle.

Dog Valley Campground [SIERRA]: *locality,* 1.25 miles east-northeast of Crystal Peak (lat. 39°33'55" N, long. 120°03'55" W; near SW cor. sec. 23, T 20 N, R 17 E); the place is 1.25 miles west-northwest of Dog Valley. Named on Dog Valley (1981) 7.5' quadrangle.

Dollar Creek [PLACER]: *stream,* flows 2.5 miles to Lake Tahoe nearly 5 miles southwest of Kings Beach (lat. 39°11'50" N, long. 120°05'40" W; near N line sec. 33, T 16 N, R 17 E); the stream is north of Dollar Point. Named on Kings Beach (1955) 7.5' quadrangle.

Dollar Point [PLACER]: *promontory,* 5.25 miles southwest of Kings Beach along Lake Tahoe (lat. 39°11'10" N, long. 120°05'30" W; sec.

33, T 16 N, R 17 E). Named on Kings Beach (1955) 7.5' quadrangle. Called Observatory Point on Truckee (1895) 30' quadrangle, but United States Board on Geographic Names (1963a, p. 6) rejected this name for the feature. The name "Dollar Point" is for Stanley Dollar, the millionaire who owned the promontory; the name "Observatory Point" came from James Lick's offer to finance an astronomical observatory at the place, a project that never materialized—earlier the feature had the name "Lousy Point" because the sole inhabitant of the place had lice (Zauner, p. 34). The feature was called Chinkapin Point on a map of 1863 (Lekisch, p. 31).

Dollar Reservoir [PLACER]: *lake,* 300 feet long, behind a dam on Dollar Creek 5.25 miles west-southwest of Kings Beach (lat. 39°12'05" N, long. 120°06'30" W; sec. 29, T 16 N, R 17 E). Named on Kings Beach (1955) 7.5' quadrangle.

Dolly Creek [PLACER]: *stream,* flows 3.5 miles to Middle Fork American River 7.25 miles west-southwest of Granite Chief (lat. 39°08'45" N, long. 120°24'10" W; sec. 15, T 15 N, R 14 E). Named on Granite Chief (1953) and Royal Gorge (1953) 7.5' quadrangles.

Dome: see **Balloon Dome** [MADERA].

Dome Rock [TUOLUMNE]: *peak,* 8 miles west of Dardanelle (lat. 38°20'20" N, long. 119°58'30" W). Named on Donnell Lake (1979) 7.5' quadrangle.

Domingo Flat [MARIPOSA]: *area,* 7 miles northwest of El Portal (lat. 37°43'55" N, long. 119°52'55" W; sec. 28, T 2 S, R 19 E). Named on Kinsley (1947) 7.5' quadrangle.

Domingo Peak [TUOLUMNE]: *peak,* 2.5 miles southwest of Moccasin (lat. 37°47'10" N, long. 120°19'50" W; sec. 4, T 2 S, R 15 E). Altitude 2486 feet. Named on Moccasin (1948) 7.5' quadrangle.

Donkey Canyon [SIERRA]: *canyon,* drained by a stream that flows 2 miles to Balls Canyon 7.5 miles east of Loyalton (lat. 39°39'25" N, long. 120°05'50" W; sec. 20, T 21 N, R 17 E). Named on Evans Canyon (1978) 7.5' quadrangle.

Donnell Lake [TUOLUMNE]: *lake,* behind a dam on Middle Fork Stanislaus River 7 miles west of Dardanelle (lat. 38°19'50" N, long. 119°57'35" W). Named on Donnell Lake (1979) 7.5' quadrangle. Called Donnells Reservoir on Dardanelles Cone (1956) 15' quadrangle, but United States Board on Geographic Names (1960a, p. 14) approved the form "Donnell Lake" for the name, which commemorates one of the partners of Donnell and Parson, who in 1855 built a system to bring water to Columbia (Gudde, 1969, p. 92).

Donnells Reservoir: see **Donnell Lake** [TUOLUMNE].

Donner [PLACER]: *locality,* nearly 2 miles east-southeast of Donner Pass along Southern Pacific Railroad (lat. 39°18'30" N, long. 120° 17'40" W; sec. 22, T 17 N, R 15 E). Named on Truckee (1940) 30' quadrangle. Truckee (1895) 30' quadrangle has the name "Donner" for a place along the railroad at Donner Pass. Postal authorities established Donner post office in 1882 and discontinued it in 1926 (Frickstad, p. 120). California Mining Bureau's (1917b) map shows a place called Arctic located along the railroad about 0.5 mile east of the site of Donner.

Donner Creek [NEVADA]: *stream,* flows 2.5 miles to Truckee River 1.25 miles southwest of Truckee (lat. 39°19' N, long. 120°12' W; near SE cor. sec. 16, T 17 N, R 16 E); the stream heads at Donner Lake. Named on Truckee (1955, photorevised 1969) 7.5' quadrangle.

Donner Lake [NEVADA]: *lake,* 2.5 miles long, center 3.25 miles east of Donner Pass (lat. 39°19'20" N, long. 120°15'50" W). Named on Norden (1955) and Truckee 1955) 7.5' quadrangles. Called Truckee Lake on Goddard's (1857) map. *Californian* newspaper for August 22, 1846, mentioned Trucky's Lake. The name "Donner Lake" commemorates the tragic Donner party of emigrants, who suffered near the lake in the winter of 1846 and 1847 (Gudde, 1949, p. 97). United States Board on Geographic Names (1994, p. 5) approved the name "Mount Stephens" for a peak located 1.9 miles west of Donner Lake (lat. 39°19'12" N, long. 120°19'19" W; sec. 16, T 17 N, R 15 E); the name is for Elisha Stephens, captain of the first party to cross the Sierra Nevada with a wagon.

Donner Lake: see **Truckee** [NEVADA].

Donner Pass [NEVADA-PLACER]: *pass,* 7.5 miles west of Truckee on Nevada-Placer county line (lat. 39°19' N, long. 120°19'30" W; near SW cor. sec. 16, T 17 N, R 15 E); the pass is 2 miles west of Donner Lake. Named on Norden (1955) 7.5' quadrangle. Jefferson's (1849) map has the designation "Truckey Pass of California Mountains" for the feature. Hobson's (1890b) map shows a place called Summit Station situated along the railroad in Placer County about 0.5 mile east-southeast of Donner Pass. United States Board on Geographic Names (1984b, p. 2) approved the name "George R. Stewart Peak" for a feature situated 0.5 mile northeast of Donner Pass (lat. 39°19'26" N, long. 120°19'07" W; sec. 16, T 17 N, R 15 E; altitude 7389 feet); the name commemorates George R. Stewart, place-name scholar, historian, and novelist, whose works include a study of the Donner party. United States Board on Geographic Names (1986, p. 1) also approved the name "McGlashan Point" for a peak 6920 feet east of Donner Pass (lat. 39°19'07" N, long. 120°19'06" W; sec. 16, T 17 N, R 15 E); the name commemorates Charles Fayette McGlashan, another historian of the Donner tragedy.

Donner Peak [PLACER]: *peak,* 1 mile southeast of Donner Pass (lat. 39°18'30" N, long. 120°18'40" W; near E line sec. 21, T 17 N, R 15 E). Altitude 8019 feet. Named on Norden (1955) 7.5' quadrangle. United States Board on Geographic Names (1942, p. 27) rejected the name "Donner Peak" for nearby Mount Judah.

Donner Ridge [NEVADA]: *ridge,* northeast- to southeast-trending, 2.5 miles long, 3 miles northeast of Donner Pass (lat. 39°21'10" N, long. 120°17'20" W). Named on Norden (1955) 7.5' quadrangle.

Donohue Pass [TUOLUMNE]: *pass,* 10.5 miles south of Tioga Pass on Tuolumne-Mono county line (lat. 37°45'40" N, long. 119°14'50" W). Named on Mono Craters (1953) 15' quadrangle. Lieutenant N.F. McClure named the pass in 1895 for a sergeant in his command (United States Board on Geographic Names, 1934, p. 7).

Donohue Peak [TUOLUMNE]: *peak,* 9.5 miles south of Tioga Pass (lat. 37°46'30" N, long. 119°13'45" W); the peak is 1.5 miles northeast of Donohue Pass. Altitude 12,023 feet. Named on Mono Craters (1953) 15' quadrangle. Lieutenant N.F. McClure named the feature in 1895 for Sergeant Donohue of Troop K, Fourth Cavalry, after the sergeant made the first ascent of the peak (Browning, 1986, p. 58).

Donovan Ridge [CALAVERAS]: *ridge,* west-southwest-trending, less than 1 mile long, 6.5 miles southeast of San Andreas (lat. 38° 08' N, long. 120°35'30" W). Named on Calaveritas (1962) 7.5' quadrangle.

Don Pedro Bar [TUOLUMNE]: *locality,* 10 miles south-southeast of Chinese Camp along Tuolumne River (lat. 37°43'45" N, long. 120° 22'45" W). Named on Sonora (1897) 30' quadrangle. Water of Don Pedro Reservoir now covers the site. Postal authorities established Don Pedro's Bar post office in 1853 and discontinued it in 1866 (Salley, p. 60). The name commemorates Pierre "Don Pedro" Sainsevain, a carpenter who went to the mines in 1848 (Morgan *in* Gardiner, p. 325).

Don Pedro Camp [TUOLUMNE]: *locality,* 10.5 miles south of Chinese Camp (lat. 37°42'55" N, long. 120°24'15" W; sec. 35, T 2 S, R 14 E); the place is near Don Pedro Reservoir. Named on La Grange (1962) 7.5' quadrangle.

Don Pedro Reservoir [TUOLUMNE]: *lake,* behind a dam on Tuolumne River 10.5 miles south of Chinese Camp (lat. 37°42'45" N, long. 120°24'05" W; sec. 35, T 2 N, R 14 E); water of the lake covers the site of Don Pedro Bar. Named on Chinese Camp (1947, photorevised 1973), La Grange (1962), Moccasin (1948, photorevised 1973), and Penon Blanco Peak (1962, photorevised 1973) 7.5' quadrangles. United States Board on Geographic Names (1977a, p. 4) gave the names "Lake Don Pedro" and "New Don Pedro Res-

ervoir" as variants. A dam completed in 1924 first formed the lake, and a dam completed in 1971 enlarged it (Gray, p. 38).

Doris: see **Lake Doris** [EL DORADO].

Dormodys [EL DORADO]: *locality,* 3.25 miles north-northeast of Clarksville (lat. 38°42' N, long. 121°02' W). Named on Sacramento (1892) 30' quadrangle.

Dorothy Lake [TUOLUMNE]: *lake,* 3250 feet long, 3.25 miles northwest of Tower Peak (lat. 38°10'40" N, long. 119°35'15" W). Named on Tower Peak (1956) 15' quadrangle. R.B. Marshall of United States Geological Survey named the lake for the daughter of Major W.W. Forsyth; the major was acting superintendent of Yosemite National Park from 1909 until 1912 (United States Board on Geographic Names, 1934, p. 7).

Dorothy Lake Pass [TUOLUMNE]: *pass,* 3.25 miles northwest of Tower Peak on Tuolumne-Mono county line (lat. 38°10'50" N, long. 119°34'50" W); the pass is northeast of Dorothy Lake. Named on Tower Peak (1956) 15' quadrangle.

Dorrington [CALAVERAS]: *settlement,* 5.5 miles east-southeast of Blue Mountain (lat. 38°18' N, long. 120°16'30" W). Named on Dorrington (1979) 7.5' quadrangle. Postal authorities established Dorrington post office in 1902, discontinued it in 1919, reestablished it in 1921, and discontinued it in 1934; the post office name was from the maiden name of the postmaster's wife—the place also was known as Cold Springs Ranch (Salley, p. 60).

Dorsey Creek [SIERRA]: *stream,* flows 1.25 miles to North Yuba River 7.5 miles east-northeast of Sierra City (lat. 39°36'55" N, long. 120°30'20" W; sec. 10, T 20 N, R 13 E). Named on Haypress Valley (1981) and Sattley (1981) 7.5' quadrangles.

Doschville: see **Indian Hill** [AMADOR] (1).

Dotons Bar [PLACER]: *locality,* 6.5 miles east of Rocklin along North Fork American River (lat. 38°46'25" N, long. 121°06'50" W; near W line sec. 29, T 11 N, R 8 E). Site named on Auburn (1954) 15' quadrangle. Water of Folsom Lake now covers the site.

Dotons Point [PLACER]: *peninsula,* 6 miles east-southeast of Rocklin along Folsom Lake (lat. 38°45'35" N, long. 121°07'40" W; sec. 31, T 11 N, R 8 E). Named on Rocklin (1967) 7.5' quadrangle.

Doty Creek: see **Doty Ravine** [PLACER].

Doty Flat [PLACER]: *area,* 4.25 miles west of Auburn (lat. 38°54'30" N, long. 121°09' W; sec. 11, 12, T 12 N, R 7 E); the place is in Doty Ravine. Named on Gold Hill (1954) 7.5' quadrangle. Myrick (p. 115) referred to a mining camp called Doty's Flat in 1852.

Doty Ravine [PLACER]: *canyon,* drained by a stream that flows 13 miles to Coon Creek 4 miles northwest of Lincoln (lat. 38°56'20" N, long. 121°20'20" W; near W line sec. 32, T 13 N, R 6 E). Named on Gold Hill (1954) and Lincoln (1953) 7.5' quadrangles. The stream in the canyon is called Doty Creek on Markham Ravine (1942) 15' quadrangle.

Double Dome Rock [TUOLUMNE]: *peaks,* two, 2.25 miles west of Dardanelle (lat. 38°20'30" N, long. 119°52'30" W). Named on Dardanelle (1979) and Donnell Lake (1979) 7.5' quadrangles.

Double Rock [MARIPOSA]: *peak,* 10.5 miles north of Yosemite Village on Mariposa-Tuolumne county line (lat. 37°54' N, long. 119°34'20" W). Altitude 9782 feet. Named on Hetch Hetchy Reservoir (1956) 15' quadrangle.

Double Rock [TUOLUMNE]: *peak,* 5 miles east-northeast of White Wolf on Tuolumne-Mariposa county line (lat. 37°54' N, long. 119° 34'20" W). Altitude 9782 feet. Named on Hetch Hetchy Reservoir (1956) 15' quadrangle.

Double Springs: see **Wheats** [CALAVERAS].

Doud Hill [CALAVERAS]: *peak,* 8.5 miles northeast of Murphys (lat. 38°12'45" N, long. 120°20'10" W; near E line sec. 8, T 4 N, R 15 E). Altitude 4155 feet. Named on Stanislaus (1948) 7.5' quadrangle.

Douds Landing [CALAVERAS]: *locality,* 9 miles northeast of Murphys and high above North Fork Stanislaus River (lat. 38°12'45" N, long. 120°19'25" W; sec. 9, T 4 N, R 15 E); the place is less than 1 mile east of Doud Hill. Named on Stanislaus (1948) 7.5' quadrangle.

Douglas Creek [TUOLUMNE]: *stream,* flows 4.25 miles to Middle Fork Stanislaus River 3 miles east of Dardanelle (lat. 38°20'15" N, long. 119°46'45" W; sec. 28, T 6 N, R 20 E). Named on Dardanelle (1979) and Sonora Pass (1979) 7.5' quadrangles. Browning (1986, p. 59) associated the name with Francis Douglass, who patented land in section 28 in 1891.

Douglas Flat [CALAVERAS]: *settlement,* 2.25 miles north-northeast of Vallecito (lat. 38°06'55" N, long. 120°27'10" W; sec. 17, T 3 N, R 14 E). Named on Columbia (1948) 7.5' quadrangle. Postal authorities established Douglas Flat post office in 1879, discontinued it in 1891, and reestablished it with the name "Douglasflat" the same year—the name "Douglas" commemorates Tom Douglas, who built a store at the place in the 1850's (Salley, p. 61). Whitney (1865, p. 259) called the settlement Douglass Flat, and mentioned a feature called Silver Knoll located less than 1 mile northwest of the place.

Douglas Resort [TUOLUMNE]: *locality,* 3 miles east of present Dardanelle (lat. 38°20'25" N, long. 119°46'30" W); the place is near the mouth of Douglas Creek. Named on Dardanelles Cone (1956) 15' quadrangle.

Douglasville: see **Union Hill** [TUOLUMNE].

Dover [EL DORADO]: *locality,* 6 miles north of Omo Ranch (lat. 38° 40' N, long. 120°34'25" W). Named on Placerville (1893) 30' quadrangle.

Dover: see **San Joaquin River** [MADERA].

Downerville: see **Downieville** [SIERRA].

Downey Lake [NEVADA]: *lake,* 1450 feet long, 4.25 miles south-southwest of English Mountain (lat. 39°23'40" N, long. 120°35'45" W; sec. 26, T 18 N, R 12 E). Named on English Mountain (1983) 7.5' quadrangle.

Downeyville: see **Downieville** [SIERRA].

Downie River [SIERRA]: *stream,* flows 8 miles to North Yuba River at Downieville (lat. 39°33'35" N, long. 120°49'40" W; sec. 35, T 20 N, R 10 E). Named on Downieville (1951) and Mount Fillmore (1951) 7.5' quadrangles. Called N. Fork of N. Fork Yuba River on Downieville (1897) 30' quadrangle, but United States Board on Geographic Names (1950, p. 5) rejected the names "North Fork of North Fork," "North Fork of North Fork of Yuba River," and "North Fork of North Fork Yuba River" for the stream. The name "Downie River" commemorates William Downie of Dowieville (Hanna, p. 90). West Branch enters from the northwest 6.5 miles south of Mount Fillmore; it is nearly 3 miles long and is named on Mount Fillmore (1951) 7.5' quadrangle.

Downieville [SIERRA]: *village,* in the west-central part of Sierra County along North Yuba River (lat. 39°33'35" N, long. 120°49'35" W; sec. 35, T 20 N, R 10 E); the village is at the mouth of Downie River. Named on Downieville (1951) 7.5' quadrangle. Called Downeyville on Eddy's (1851) map. Postal authorities established Downerville post office before October 1851 and changed the name to Downieville in 1852 (Salley, p. 61). William Downie came to the place late in 1849 and wintered just above present Downieville at Jersey Flat; the site at the mouth of present Downie River was called The Forks before the community there was named Downieville (Hoover, Rensch, and Rensch, p. 491-492). Jersey Flat was called Murraysville before Jersey Company acquired it in 1850 (Gudde, 1975, p. 176). The part of present Downieville south of North Yuba River was called Durgans Flat; it was known as Washingtonville before James Durgan built a sawmill there in 1850 (Gudde, 1975, p. 103). The following mining places were in the vicinity of present Downieville: Zumwalt Flat, located at the northeast end of the village, where William Downie mined in 1849 before Joseph Zumwalt arrived in 1850 (Gudde, 1975, p. 381); Tin Cup Diggings, where three men filled a tin cup with gold each day (Clark, p. 44); New York Flat, located about 1.5 miles east of Downieville (Gudde, 1975, p. 242); O' Donnells Flat, situated 2 miles east of Downieville, also called McCarty Flat and McDonald Flat (Gudde, 1975, p. 248); Coyoteville, located 1 mile west of Downieville (Gudde, 1975, p. 87); and Cox Bar, located 2 miles west of Downieville on the north side of North Yuba River (Gudde, 1975, p. 85).

Dragoon Flat: see **Shaws Flat** [TUOLUMNE].
Dragoon Gulch [TUOLUMNE]: *canyon,* drained by a stream that flows 1.25 miles to Woods Creek in Sonora (lat. 37°58'55" N, long. 120°23'25" W; sec. 36, T 2 N, R 14 E). Named on Sonora (1948) 7.5' quadrangle. The name is for a discharged dragoon who discovered gold in the canyon (Stoddart, p. 64).
Draper: see **Ralph** [TUOLUMNE].
Drew Creek [TUOLUMNE]:
(1) *stream,* flows 3 miles to Tuolumne River 10 miles south-southeast of Duckwall Mountain (lat. 37°50'35" N, long. 120°02'20" W; sec. 19, T 1 S, R 18 E); the stream heads at Drew Meadow. Named on Jawbone Ridge (1947) 7.5' quadrangle
(2) *stream,* heads in Alpine County and flows 3.5 miles, mainly in Alpine County, to Middle Fork Stanislaus River 3.25 miles west-northwest of Dardanelle (lat. 38°21'30" N, long. 119°53'15" W). Named on Donnell Lake (1979) 7.5' quadrangle.
Drew Meadow [TUOLUMNE]: *area,* 8 miles west-southwest of Mather (lat. 37°51'10" N, long. 120°00' W; sec. 16, T 1 S, R 18 E); the place is at the head of Drew Creek (1). Named on Lake Eleanor (1956) and Tuolumne (1948) 15' quadrangles.
Drivers Flat [PLACER]: *area,* 8 miles northeast of Auburn (lat. 38° 58'20" N, long. 120°57'10" W; near SE cor. sec. 15, T 13 N, R 9 E). Named on Greenwood (1949) 7.5' quadrangle.
Drum [PLACER]: *locality,* 5 miles east-northeast of Dutch Flat (lat. 39°14'55" N, long. 120°45'15" W; sec. 16, T 16 N, R 11 E). Named on Colfax (1938) 30' quadrangle. Postal authorities established Drum post office in 1913 and discontinued it in 1915 (Frickstad, p. 120).
Drum: see **Briceburg** [MARIPOSA].
Drum: see **Lang Crossing** [NEVADA].
Drum Forebay [PLACER]: *lake,* 5.5 miles east-northeast of Dutch Flat (lat. 39°15' N, long. 120°45' W). Named on Blue Canyon (1955, photorevised 1973), Dutch Flat (1950, photorevised 1979), Washington (1950, photorevised 1979), and Westville (1952, photorevised 1973) 7.5' quadrangles. The name "Drum Forebay" recalls Frank G. Drum, president of Pacific Gas and Electric Company (Gudde, 1969, p. 94).
Drummond Gulch [EL DORADO]: *canyon,* drained by a stream that flows less than 0.25 mile to Indian Creek (5) 2.5 miles southsouthwest of Omo Ranch (lat. 38°32'35" N, long. 120°34'55" W). Named on Omo Ranch (1952) 7.5' quadrangle.
Drunken Gulch [MARIPOSA]: *canyon,* drained by a stream that flows 2.25 miles to Sherlock Creek 3.25 miles east-northeast of the village of Bear Valley (lat. 37°35'15" N, long. 120°03'40" W; sec. 14, T 4 S, R 17 E). Named on Bear Valley (1947) 7.5' quadrangle.

Dry Creek [AMADOR]: *stream,* formed by the confluence of North Fork and South Fork in Amador County, flows 46 miles, including along Sacramento-San Joaquin county line, to Mokelumne River 6 miles west-southwest of Galt (lat. 38° 13'55" N, long. 121°24'35" W). Named on Amador City (1962), Clay (1968), Galt (1968), Goose Creek (1968), Ione (1962), Irish Hill (1962), Lockeford (1968), Lodi North (1968), and Thornton (1978) 7.5' quadrangles. North Fork is 10 miles long and is named on Amador City (1962), Aukum (1952), Fiddletown (1949), and Pine Grove (1948) 7.5' quadrangles. South Fork is 12.5 miles long and is named on Amador City (1962), Pine Grove (1948), and West Point (1948) 7.5' quadrangles; present South Fork is called Dry Creek on Jackson (1902) and Placerville (1893) 30' quadrangles. Camp's (1962) map shows a stream called Slate Creek that joins North Fork Dry Creek from the east 2.5 miles east of Plymouth, and a place called Suckertown located on the north side of Slate Creek nearly 5 miles east of Plymouth.
Dry Creek [CALAVERAS]:
(1) *stream,* flows 10 miles to Whisky Creek nearly 5 miles east of Jenny Lind (lat. 38°05'55" N, long. 120°46'55" W; sec. 20, T 3 N, R 11 E); the stream goes through Heiser Canyon. Named on Jenny Lind (1962) and Salt Spring Valley (1962) 7.5' quadrangles. On San Andreas (1947) 15' quadrangle, the part of the stream north of Salt Spring Valley is called Heiser Creek.
(2) *stream,* flows 2.25 miles to Coyote Creek 0.25 mile north-northeast of Vallecito (lat. 38°05'30" N, long. 120°28'15" W; near N line sec. 30, T 3 N, R 14 E). Named on Columbia (1948) 7.5' quadrangle.
Dry Creek [EL DORADO]: *stream,* flows 8 miles to Weber Creek 5 miles north-northwest of Shingle Springs (lat. 38°44'10" N, long. 120°57' W; sec. 11, T 10 N, R 9 E). Named on Placerville (1949) and Shingle Springs (1949) 7.5' quadrangles.
Dry Creek [MADERA]: *stream,* flows 20 miles to an artificial watercourse 8.5 miles west of Madera (lat. 36°59' N, long. 120°12'30" W; sec. 10, T 11 S, R 16 E). Named on Le Grand (1961), Madera (1946), and Raymond (1962) 15' quadrangles.
Dry Creek [MARIPOSA]: *stream,* heads in Mariposa County and flows 32 miles to Merced River 7 miles north of Atwood in Merced County (lat. 37°27'10" N, long. 120°37'10" W; sec. 35, T 5 S, R 12 E). Named on Merced Falls (1962), Snelling (1962), Turlock Lake (1968), and Winton (1961) 7.5' quadrangles. South Fork heads in Mariposa County and flows 10.5 miles to join the main stream 3.5 miles north of Snelling in Merced County; South Fork is named on Merced Falls (1962) and Snelling (1962) 7.5' quadrangles.

Dry Creek [NEVADA]: *stream,* heads in Nevada County and flows 19 miles to Bear River 8 miles south of Olivehurst in Yuba County (lat. 38°58'25" N, long. 121°31'25" W; near E line sec. 16, T 13 N, R 4 E). Named on Camp Far West (1949), Nicolaus (1952), Rough and Ready (1949), Sheridan (1953), Wheatland (1947, photorevised 1973), and Wolf (1949) 7.5' quadrangles.

Dry Creek [PLACER]: *stream,* flows 8 miles to join Orr Creek and form Coon Creek 6.25 miles north-northwest of Auburn (lat. 38° 58'30" N, long. 121°08'15" W; sec. 13, T 13 N, R 4 E). Named on Auburn (1953) and Gold Hill (1954) 7.5' quadrangles. Called South Fork Dry Creek on Sacramento (1892) 30' quadrangle. On Sacramento (1892) 30' quadrangle, present Orr Creek is called North Fork Dry Creek.

Dry Creek [PLACER]: *stream,* formed in Placer County by the confluence of Antelope Creek and the stream in Miners Ravine, flows 15 miles to a drainage canal 2.25 miles southwest of Rio Linda in Sacramento County (lat. 38°39'50" N, long. 121°28'35" W; sec. 6, T 9 N, R 5 E). Named on Citrus Heights (1967), Rio Linda (1967), and Roseville (1967) 7.5' quadrangles. Called Linda Creek on Antelope (1911) and Arcade (1911) 7.5' quadrangles, and called Antelope Creek above the junction with present Cirby Creek on Antelope (1911) 7.5' quadrangle. United States Board on Geographic Names (1968a, p. 6) rejected the names "Linda Creek" and "Rio Linda Creek" for the stream.

Dry Creek [SIERRA-NEVADA]: *stream,* heads in Sierra County and flows 3.5 miles to Boca Reservoir 8 miles north-northeast of Truckee in Nevada County (lat. 39°25'35" N, long. 120°06' W; sec. 9, T 18 N, R 17 E). Named on Boca (1955) and Hobart Mills (1981) 7.5' quadrangles.

Dry Creek: see **Linda Creek** [PLACER]; **Little Dry Creek** [NEVADA].

Dry Creek [TUOLUMNE]: *stream,* flows 2.5 miles to Deer Creek (1) 9 miles east-northeast of Columbia (lat. 38°05'30" N, long. 120°15'20" W; near N line sec. 30, T 3 N, R 16 E). Named on Columbia SE (1948) and Twain Harte (1979) 7.5' quadrangles.

Dry Creek: see **Gallup Creek** [TUOLUMNE]; **Little Dry Creek** [CALAVERAS]; **Rydberg Creek** [TUOLUMNE].

Dry Diggings: see **Columbia** [TUOLUMNE].

Dry Diggings: see **Placerville** [EL DORADO].

Dry Flat [SIERRA]: *area,* 6 miles south-southeast of Loyalton (lat. 39°36' N, long. 120°11'45" W; near W line sec. 10, T 20 N, R 16 E). Named on Sardine Peak (1981) 7.5' quadrangle.

Dry Gulch [EL DORADO]: *canyon,* drained by a stream that flows 2 miles to Clear Creek (1) 9.5 miles east-southeast of Placerville (lat. 38°41'45" N, long. 120°37'45" W). Named

on Placerville (1893) 30' quadrangle.

Dry Gulch [MARIPOSA]: *canyon,* drained by a stream that flows 2.5 miles to Merced River 3 miles west of El Portal (lat. 37°40'25" N, long. 119°50' W; sec. 14, T 3 S, R 19 E). Named on El Portal (1947) 7.5' quadrangle.

Dry Hollow [CALAVERAS]: *area,* 4 miles northeast of San Andreas (lat. 38°14'10" N, long. 120°37'40" W; near SW cor. sec. 35, T 5 N, R 12 E). Named on San Andreas (1962) 7.5' quadrangle.

Dry Lake [EL DORADO]: *intermittent lake,* 1500 feet long, 4.5 miles west-southwest of Pyramid Peak (lat. 38°49'05" N, long. 120°14'15" W; sec. 8, T 11 N, R 16 E). Named on Pyramid Peak (1955) 7.5' quadrangle.

Dry Lake [NEVADA]: *intermittent lake,* 0.5 mile long, 5.25 miles east of Truckee (lat. 39°19'40" N, long. 120°05'10" W; on E line sec. 16, T 17 N, R 17 E). Named on Martis Peak (1955) 7.5' quadrangle.

Dry Lakes [EL DORADO]: *intermittent lakes,* 4.5 miles north of Robbs Peak (lat. 38°59'30" N, long. 120°24'30" W; sec. 9, T 13 N, R 14 E). Named on Robbs Peak (1950) 7.5' quadrangle.

Dry Meadow [SIERRA]: *area,* 8.5 miles south-southeast of Sierraville (lat. 39°28'30" N, long. 120°19'40" W; at SE cor. sec. 20, T 19 N, R 15 E). Named on Independence Lake (1981) 7.5' quadrangle.

Dry Meadow [TUOLUMNE]: *area,* 6.25 miles west-northwest of Strawberry (lat. 38°13'25" N, long. 120°07'25" W; on N line sec. 8, T 4 N, R 17 E). Named on Strawberry (1979) 7.5' quadrangle.

Dry Meadow Creek [TUOLUMNE]: *stream,* flows 5.25 miles to Middle Fork Stanislaus River 2 miles north of Crandall Peak (lat. 38°11'10" N, long. 120°08'35" W; sec. 19, T 4 N, R 17 E); the stream goes through Dry Meadow. Named on Crandall Peak (1979) and Strawberry (1979) 7.5' quadrangles.

Dry Meadow Station [TUOLUMNE]: *locality,* nearly 5 miles north of Crandall Peak (lat. 38°13'35" N, long. 120°07'30" W; sec. 5, T 4 N, R 17 E); the place is at Dry Meadow. Named on Crandall Peak (1979) 7.5' quadrangle.

Drytown [AMADOR]: *village,* 2.5 miles south of Plymouth (lat. 38°26'25" N, long. 120°51'15" W; near SW cor. sec. 23, T 7 N, R 10 E); the village is along Dry Creek. Named on Amador City (1962) 7.5' quadrangle. Eddy's (1854) map has the form "Dry Town" for the name. Postal authorities established Drytown post office before January 21, 1852 (Salley, p. 62). Camp's (1962) map shows a place called Snake Flat located 1.5 miles east of Drytown, a place called Old Rancheria situated about 1 mile south-southeast of Drytown, and a place called Lower Rancheria located 2 miles east-southeast of Drytown along Rancheria Creek. Placer mining began at Lower

Rancheria in 1848 (Hoover, Rensch, and Rensch, p. 31).

Dry Valley Creek: see **Long Valley Creek** [SIERRA] (1).

Duck Bar [CALAVERAS]: *locality,* 3.25 miles east of Vallecito along Stanislaus River (lat. 38°05' N, long. 120°24'50" W; near E line sec. 27, T 3 N, R 14 E). Named on Columbia (1948) 7.5' quadrangle.

Duck Lake [EL DORADO]: *lake,* 1000 feet long, 3.5 miles southwest of the town of Meeks Bay (lat. 39°00'35" N, long. 120°10'45" W; on S line sec. 35, T 14 N, R 16 E). Named on Homewood (1955) 7.5' quadrangle.

Duckwall Creek [TUOLUMNE]: *stream,* flows 4 miles to North Fork Tuolumne River 1 mile east-southeast of Tuolumne (lat. 37°57'20" N, long. 120°13'05" W; sec. 9, T 1 N, R 16 E). Named on Tuolumne (1948) 7.5' quadrangle.

Duckwall Mountain [TUOLUMNE]: *peak,* 6.5 miles east of Tuolumne (lat. 37°58'05" N, long. 120°07'10" W; sec. 4, T 1 N, R 17 E). Altitude 5835 feet. Named on Duckwall Mountain (1948) 7.5' quadrangle. The name recalls the Duckwall family, emigrants who crossed Sonora Pass by wagon in 1853 (Hoover, Rensch, and Rensch, p. 566).

Duckwall Ridge [TUOLUMNE]: *ridge,* extends 3.5 miles east from Duckwall Mountain (lat. 37°57'20" N, long. 120°05'30" W). Named on Duckwall Mountain (1948) 7.5' quadrangle.

Dudley [MARIPOSA]: *locality,* 5.5 miles eastnortheast of Coulterville along Smith Creek (lat. 37°45'15" N, long. 120°06'30" W). Named on Sonora (1891) 30' quadrangle. Dudley's Station was a stage stop that Hosea E. Dudley and Fanny Chase Dudley operated on the road to Yosemite Valley (Sargent, Shirley, 1976, p. 21).

Dudley Hill [MARIPOSA]: *peak,* 6 miles north of Buckhorn Peak (lat. 37°44'50" N, long. 120°07'10" W; sec. 20, T 2 S, R 17 E). Named on Buckhorn Peak (1947) 7.5' quadrangle.

Dudley's Station: see **Dudley** [MARIPOSA].

Dufftown: see **Kelsey** [EL DORADO].

Dufrene Camp [AMADOR]: *locality,* 8 miles west-northwest of Mokelumne Peak (lat. 38°34'40" N, long. 120°14'05" W; sec. 5, T 8 N, R 16 E). Named on Bear River Reservoir (1979) 7.5' quadrangle.

Dufresne Gulch [AMADOR]: *canyon,* less than 1 mile long, opens into the canyon of Mokelumne River 5 miles south-southwest of Jackson (lat. 38°17' N, long. 120°49'05" W; sec. 13, T 5 N, R 10 E). Named on Jackson (1962) 7.5' quadrangle. Water of Pardee Reservoir now floods the lower part of the canyon.

Dugan [EL DORADO]: *locality,* 3.25 miles north-northeast of Latrobe along Southern Pacific Railroad (lat. 38°36'20" N, long. 120°57'25" W; sec. 26, T 9 N, R 9 E). Named on Latrobe (1949) 7.5' quadrangle.

Dugan Pond [SIERRA]: *lake,* 400 feet long,

nearly 4 miles north of Sierra City (lat. 39°37'10" N, long. 120°38'45" W; near N line sec. 8, T 20 N, R 12 E). Named on Sierra City (1981) 7.5' quadrangle.

Dulzura Lake: see **Ice Lakes** [PLACER].

Dunbar [CALAVERAS]: *locality,* nearly 7 miles south of Blue Mountain (lat. 38°14'30" N, long. 120°21'45" W). Named on Big Trees (1891) 30' quadrangle.

Duncan Canyon [PLACER]: *canyon,* drained by a stream that flows 13 miles to Middle Fork American River 8 miles south of Duncan Peak (lat. 39°02'20" N, long. 120°32'40" W; sec. 29, T 14 N, R 13 E). Named on Bunker Hill (1953), Greek Store (1952), and Royal Gorge (1953) 7.5' quadrangles. The name commemorates Thomas Duncan, who came to California in 1848 and led an expedition to the canyon in 1850 in a futile search for gold (Hoover, Rensch, and Rensch, p. 277). Colfax (1938) 30' quadrangle shows Duncan Creek in the canyon.

Duncan Canyon: see **Little Duncan Canyon** [PLACER].

Duncan Corral [EL DORADO]: *locality,* 4.5 miles south-southwest of Old Iron Mountain (lat. 38°38'45" N, long. 120°25'15" W; at W line sec. 10, T 9 N, R 14 E). Named on Stump Spring (1951) 7.5' quadrangle.

Duncan Creek: see **Duncan Canyon** [PLACER].

Duncan Hill [PLACER]: *peak,* 1.5 miles west of downtown Auburn (lat. 38°53'55" N, long. 121°05'45" W; at NW cor. sec. 16, T 12 N, R 8 E). Named on Auburn (1953) 7.5' quadrangle.

Duncan Peak [PLACER]: *peak,* 7.5 miles east of Westville (lat. 39° 09'15" N, long. 120°30'45" W; at S line sec. 10, T 15 N, R 13 E). Altitude 7116 feet. Named on Duncan Peak (1952) 7.5' quadrangle.

Dunlap Gulch [CALAVERAS]: *canyon,* drained by a stream that flows 2 miles to San Antonio Creek 5.5 miles north-northeast of Murphys (lat. 38°12'50" N, long. 120°25'30" W; sec. 10, T 4 N, R 14 E). Named on Murphys (1948) 7.5' quadrangle.

Dunn Creek [TUOLUMNE]: *stream,* flows 2.5 miles to Stanislaus County 4.5 miles south of Don Pedro Camp (lat. 37°38'55" N, long. 120°24'25" W; near W line sec. 26, T 3 S, R 14 E); the stream is west of Dunn Ridge. Named on La Grange (1962) 7.5' quadrangle.

Dunn Ridge [MARIPOSA-TUOLUMNE]: *ridge,* north- to northwest-trending, 2 miles long, 3.5 miles south-southeast of Don Pedro Camp on Tuolumne-Mariposa county line (lat. 37°40' N, long. 120°23'25" W). Named on La Grange (1962) 7.5' quadrangle.

Dunow's Camp: see **Keystone** [TUOLUMNE].

Durgans Flat: see **Downieville** [SIERRA].

Du Rock [EL DORADO]: *locality,* 2.5 miles west-southwest of Shingle Springs (lat. 38°39'05" N, long. 120°58'10" W). Named on Placerville (1893) 30' quadrangle. Postal authorities established El Dorado Ranch post office 8 miles west of El Dorado in 1857, changed the name to Duroc in 1858, and discontinued it in 1864 (Salley, p. 63, 66).

Dutch Canyon [EL DORADO]: *canyon,* drained by a stream that flows 2.25 miles to Rock Creek 11 miles northwest of Pollock Pines (lat. 38°51'10" N, long. 120°44'50" W; near NE cor. sec. 33, T 12 N, R 11 E). Named on Garden Valley (1949), Georgetown (1949), and Slate Mountain (1950) 7.5' quadrangles.

Dutch Charlie's Flat: see **Dutch Flat** [PLACER].

Dutch Creek [CALAVERAS]: *stream,* flows 2.5 miles to Licking Fork 3 miles west-northwest of Blue Mountain (lat. 38°21'10" N, long. 120°25'05" W; near S line sec. 22, T 6 N, R 14 E). Named on Fort Mountain (1979) 7.5' quadrangle.

Dutch Creek [EL DORADO]: *stream,* flows 5 miles to South Fork American River 0.5 mile east of Coloma (lat. 38°47'55" N, long. 120°52'50" W; near S line sec. 17, T 11 N, R 10 E). Named on Coloma (1949) and Garden Valley (1949) 7.5' quadrangles. Two mining camps, each called Dutch Creek, were located at the headwaters of the stream (Gernes, p. 34).

Dutch Creek [MARIPOSA]: *stream,* flows 4.5 miles to Bean Creek 6 miles north-northeast of Buckhorn Peak (lat. 37°44'25" N, long. 120°04'30" W; near NE cor. sec. 27, T 2 S, R 17 E). Named on Buckhorn Peak (1947) and Coulterville (1947) 7.5' quadrangles. The name is for "Dutch Frank" Laumeister, quartermaster of the Mariposa Battalion (Gudde, 1975, p. 104).

Dutch Ed Gulch [CALAVERAS]: *canyon,* drained by a stream that flows less than 1 mile to San Antonio Creek 5 miles south-southeast of San Andreas (lat. 38°08' N, long. 120°37'50" W; near SE cor. sec. 3, T 3 N, R 12 E). Named on Calaveritas (1962) and San Andreas (1962) 7.5' quadrangles.

Dutch Flat [PLACER]: *village,* 9.5 miles northeast of Colfax (lat. 39°12'20" N, long. 120°50'15" W; sec. 34, T 16 N, R 10 E). Named on Dutch Flat (1950) 7.5' quadrangle. Postal authorities established Dutch Flat post office in 1856 (Frickstad, p. 120). Charles Dornbach and Joseph Dornbach settled at the site in 1851; the place was known as Dutch Charlie's Flat, or Charley's Flat, before the post office opened (Gudde, 1975, p. 104).

Dutch Flat Canyon [PLACER]: *canyon,* drained by a stream that flows 1 mile to Bear River 1 mile west of Dutch Flat (lat. 39°12'15" N, long. 120°51'20" W; sec. 33, T 16 N, R 10 E); the canyon heads near Dutch Flat. Named on Dutch Flat (1950) 7.5' quadrangle.

Dutch Flat Station [PLACER]: *locality,* 1 mile south-southeast of Dutch Flat along Southern Pacific Railroad (lat. 39°11'30" N, long.

120°49'55" W; sec. 3, T 15 N, R 10 E). Named on Dutch Flat (1950) 7.5' quadrangle. Whitney's (1873) map has the designation "Station" for the locality. Colfax (1898) 30' quadrangle shows a place called Chinatown at or near present Dutch Flat Station.

Dutchman Creek [MARIPOSA]: *stream,* heads in Mariposa County and flows 35 miles to Deadman Creek 12 miles west-southwest of Le Grand in Merced County (lat. 37°11'35" N, long. 120°27'50" W; sec. 32, T 8 S, R 14 E). Named on Chowchilla (1960) and Le Grand (1961) 15' quadrangles, and on Illinois Hill (1962) and Raynor Creek (1961) 7.5' quadrangles. Laizure's (1935) map has the form "Dutchman's Cr." for the name.

Dutch Ravine [EL DORADO]: *canyon,* drained by a stream that flows less than 1 mile to Green Spring Creek 4 miles north-northwest of Clarksville (lat. 38°42'35" N, long. 121°04'10" W; sec. 23, T 10 N, R 8 E). Named on Clarksville (1953) 7.5' quadrangle.

Dutch Ravine [PLACER]: *canyon,* drained by a stream that flows nearly 7 miles to Auburn Ravine 6 miles west of Auburn (lat. 38° 54' N, long. 121°11'05" W; sec. 10, T 12 N, R 7 E). Named on Auburn (1953) and Gold Hill (1954) 7.5' quadrangles.

Dutchtown: see **Spanish Dry Diggings** [EL DORADO].

Dutschke Hill [AMADOR]: *hill,* 3.5 miles west-northwest of Ione (lat. 38°22' N, long 120°59'35" W). Altitude 648 feet. Named on Ione (1962) 7.5' quadrangle. Called Jones Butte on Jackson (1902) 30' quadrangle, but United States Board on Geographic Names (1964a, p. 9) rejected the name "Jones Butte" and pointed out that the name "Dutschke Hill" commemorates the pioneer family of Charles Dutschke.

Dyer Creek [TUOLUMNE]: *stream,* flows nearly 1 mile to North Fork Tuolumne River 2 miles northeast of Tuolumne (lat. 37°58'45" N, long. 120°12'15" W; sec. 34, T 2 N, R 16 E). Named on Tuolumne (1948) 7.5' quadrangle.

Dyers Mill [EL DORADO]: *locality,* 5.5 miles north-northeast of Omo Ranch (lat. 38°39'30" N, long. 120°33'20" W). Named on Placerville (1893) 30' quadrangle.

− E −

Eagle Bay: see **Emerald Bay** [EL DORADO] (1).

Eagle Bird [NEVADA]: *locality,* 6.25 miles south-southeast of Graniteville along South Fork Yuba River (present South Yuba River) (lat. 39°20'40" N, long. 120°41'40" W). Named on Colfax (1898) 30' quadrangle. Colfax (1938) 30' quadrangle shows Eagle Bird mine at the place.

Eagle Cliff: see **Eagle Rock** [PLACER].

Eagle Creek [MARIPOSA]: *stream,* flows 2

miles to Merced River nearly 2 miles south-west of Yosemite Village (lat. 37°43'55" N, long. 119°36'35" W); the stream heads west of Eagle Peak (1). Named on Yosemite (1956) 15' quadrangle.

Eagle Creek [TUOLUMNE]:
(1) *stream,* flows 8 miles to Rose Creek 6.25 miles northeast of Columbia (lat. 38°06'20" N, long. 120°19'50" W; near N line sec. 21, T 3 N, R 15 E). Named on Columbia SE (1948), Crandall Peak (1979), and Twain Hart (1979) 7.5' quadrangles.
(2) *stream,* flows 7.5 miles to Middle Fork Stanislaus River at Dardanelle (lat. 38°20'35" N, long. 119°49'55" W; sec. 25, T 6 N, R 19 E); the stream goes through Eagle Meadow. Named on Dardanelle (1979) 7.5' quadrangle. On Dardanelles (1898) 30' quadrangle, the name applies to present Long Valley Creek.

Eagle Creek Camp [TUOLUMNE]: *locality,* 3.5 miles west of Crandall Peak (lat. 38°09'15" N, long. 120°12'30" W; sec. 34, T 4 N, R 16 E); the place is along Eagle Creek (1). Named on Crandall Peak (1979) 7.5' quadrangle.

Eagle Falls [EL DORADO]: *waterfall,* 3.25 miles north-northwest of Mount Tallac (lat. 38°57'05" N, long. 120°06'35" W; near S line sec. 21, T 13 N, R 17 E). Named on Emerald Bay (1955) 7.5' quadrangle. The feature also was called Emerald Bay Falls—present Emerald Bay (1) had the name "Eagle Bay" in the early days (Lekisch, p. 32).

Eagle Falls Campground [EL DORADO]: *locality,* 3.25 miles north-northwest of Mount Tallac (lat. 38°57'10" N, long. 120°06'45" W; near SW cor. sec. 21, T 13 N, R 17 E); the place is near Eagle Falls. Named on Emerald Bay (1955) 7.5' quadrangle.

Eagle Lake [EL DORADO]: *lake,* 1350 feet long, nearly 3 miles north-northwest of Mount Tallac (lat. 38°56'30" N, long. 120°07'15" W; sec. 29, T 13 N, R 17 E). Named on Emerald Bay (1955) 7.5' quadrangle.

Eagle Lakes [NEVADA]: *lakes,* largest 2350 feet long, 3.5 miles northeast of Yuba Gap (lat. 39°21'15" N, long. 120°34'35" W; sec. 12, T 17 N, R 12 E). Named on Cisco Grove (1955) 7.5' quadrangle. Colfax (1938) 30' quadrangle has the name "Eagle Lake" for one of the lakes, but United States Board on Geographic Names (1962b, p. 18) rejected this name.

Eagle Meadow [TUOLUMNE]: *area,* 4 miles south of Dardanelle (lat. 38°16'50" N, long. 119°50'05" W; near S line sec. 13, T 5 N, R 19 E); the place is less than 1 mile east-north-east of Eagle Peak along Eagle Creek (2). Named on Dardanelle (1979) 7.5' quadrangle.

Eagle Pass [TUOLUMNE]: *pass,* 10 miles east-northeast of Pinecrest (lat. 38°14'55" N, long. 119°49'35" W; near NE cor. sec. 36, T 5 N, R 19 E); the pass is near the head of Eagle Creek (2). Named on Pinecrest (1956) 15' quadrangle.

Eagle Peak [MARIPOSA]:
(1) *peak,* 1.5 miles west of Yosemite Village

(lat. 37°44'45" N, long. 119°36'55" W). Altitude 7779 feet. Named on Yosemite (1956) 15' quadrangle. The feature also was called Eagle Point (Browning, 1986, p. 61). The peak is one of the group called Three Brothers.
(2) *peak,* 1 mile north-northwest of El Portal (lat. 37°41'20" N, long. 119°47'20" W; sec. 8, T 3 S, R 20 E). Altitude 4578 feet. Named on El Portal (1947) 7.5' quadrangle.

Eagle Peak [TUOLUMNE]: *peak,* 4.5 miles south of Dardanelle (lat. 38°16'30" N, long. 119°50'50" W; sec. 23, T 5 N, R 19 E); the peak is less than 1 mile west-southwest of Eagle Meadow. Altitude 9370 feet. Named on Dardanelle (1979) 7.5' quadrangle.

Eagle Peak Creek [MARIPOSA]: *stream,* flows 1.5 miles to Yosemite Creek 2 miles north-west of Yosemite Village (lat. 37° 46' N, long. 119°36'10" W); the stream heads near Eagle Peak (1). Named on Hetch Hetchy Reservoir (1956) 15' quadrangle.

Eagle Peak Meadows [MARIPOSA]: *area,* 2 miles west-northwest of Yosemite Village along Eagle Peak Creek (lat. 37°45'30" N, long. 119°36'45" W); the place is 1 mile north of Eagle Peak (1). Named on Hetch Hetchy Reservoir (1956) 15' quadrangle.

Eagle Point [EL DORADO]: *promontory,* 4.25 miles north-northeast of Mount Tallac along Lake Tahoe (lat. 38°57'55" N, long. 120°04'40" W). Named on Emerald Bay (1955) 7.5' quadrangle.

Eagle Point: see **Eagle Peak** [MARIPOSA] (1).

Eagle Ravine [NEVADA]: *canyon,* drained by a stream that flows less than 1 mile to Deer Creek 1 mile east-northeast of downtown Nevada City (lat. 39°16'05" N, long. 121°00'10" W; near E line sec. 7, T 16 N, R 9 E). Named on Nevada City (1948) 7.5' quadrangle.

Eagle Rock [EL DORADO]: *peak,* 1.5 miles east-southeast of Kyburz (lat. 38°46'05" N, long. 120°16'05" W; near E line sec. 26, T 11 N, R 15 E). Altitude 6270 feet. Named on Kyburz (1952) 7.5' quadrangle.

Eagle Rock [PLACER]: *hill,* 1.5 miles north of Homewood (lat. 39° 06'35" N, long. 120°09'40" W; near N line sec. 36, T 15 N, R 16 E). Named on Homewood (1955) 7.5' quadrangle. The feature also was called Eagle Cliff (Lekisch, p. 32).

Earhart: see **Amelia Earhart Peak** [TUOL-UMNE].

Earnest: see **Camp Earnest** [TUOLUMNE].

East Applegate: see **Applegate** [PLACER].

East Auburn: see **Auburn** [PLACER].

East Big Canyon Creek [EL DORADO]: *stream,* flows nearly 5 miles to North Fork Cosumnes River 12 miles south of Placerville (lat. 38°33'40" N, long. 120°50'40" W; sec. 11, T 8 N, R 10 E). Named on Fiddletown (1949) 7.5' quadrangle. Called Big Canyon Creek on Placerville (1893) 30' quadrangle.

East Boca Canyon [NEVADA]: *canyon,* drained by a stream that flows 3 miles to Boca Reservoir 7.5 miles northeast of Truckee (lat. 39°24'20" N, long. 120°05'05" W; near SW cor. sec. 15, T 18 N, R 17 E). Named on Boca (1955) 7.5' quadrangle.

East Boca Spring [NEVADA]: *spring,* 9 miles northeast of Truckee (lat. 39°24'55" N, long. 120°03'50" W; near NW cor. sec. 14, T 18 N, R 17 E); the spring is in East Boca Canyon. Named on Boca (1955) 7.5' quadrangle.

Eastern Canyon [NEVADA]: *canyon,* drained by a stream that flows 3 miles to South Yuba River 2 miles southeast of North Bloomfield (lat. 39°20'50" N, long. 120°52'35" W; near S line sec. 8, T 17 N, R 10 E). Named on Alleghany (1949), North Bloomfield (1949), and Washington (1950) 7.5' quadrangles.

East Chinee: see **Campo Salvador**, under **Chinese Camp** [TUOLUMNE].

East Flange Rock [TUOLUMNE]: *relief feature,* 3 miles east-northeast of Pinecrest (lat. 38°14'50" N, long. 119°46'10" W; near SW cor. sec. 27, T 5 N, R 20 E). Named on Pinecrest (1956) 15' quadrangle.

East Fork Creek [NEVADA]: *stream,* flows 8 miles to Middle Yuba River 3 miles northnortheast of Graniteville (lat. 39°29' N, long. 120°42'45" W; sec. 26, T 19 N, R 11 E). Named on English Mountain (1983) and Graniteville (1982) 7.5' quadrangles. Called South Fork [of Middle Fork Yuba River] on Colfax (1898) 30' quadrangle.

East Indian Creek: see **Indian Creek** [EL DORADO] (5).

Eastman Lake [MADERA-MARIPOSA]: *lake,* on Madera-Mariposa county line behind a dam on Chowchilla River 4.25 miles west of Raymond (lat. 37°13' N, long. 119°59' W; sec. 22, T 8 S, R 18 E). Named on Raymond (1962, photorevised 1981) 7.5' quadrangle, which has the name "Buchanan Dam" for the dam that forms the lake. United States Board on Geographic Names (1975, p. 5) noted that the name "H.V. Eastman Lake" was mandated by Congressional action and gave the name "Buchanan Reservoir" as a variant. Logan's (1950) map shows a place called Buchanan located about 5 miles west of Raymond near the site of the dam that forms the present lake. Buchanan took its name from Buchanan Hollow, which extends along Chowchilla River for about 2 miles just northeast of the place that Madera County, Mariposa County, and Merced County meet (Clough, p. 78). Postal authorities established Buchanan post office in 1873 and discontinued it in 1904—Buchanan Hollow was named for an early settler (Salley, p. 28).

East Martis Creek [PLACER]: *stream,* flows 5.25 miles to join Martis Creek near Nevada-Placer county line almost 5 miles west-north-west of Martis Peak (lat. 39°19'05" N, long. 120°06'50" W; near S line sec. 17, T 17 N, R 17 E). Named on Martis Peak (1955) 7.5' quadrangle.

East Meadow Campground [SIERRA]: *locality,* 7 miles southeast of Sierra City (lat. 39°30'05" N, long. 120°31'55" W; near E line sec. 20, T 19 N, R 13 E). Named on Haypress Valley (1981) 7.5' quadrangle.

East Panther Creek [AMADOR]: *stream,* flows 7.5 miles to join West Panther Creek and form Panther Creek 4.5 miles south-southwest of Hams Station (lat. 38°29'10" N, long. 120°24'05" W; sec. 2, T 7 N, R 14 E); the stream is east of Panther Ridge. Named on Devils Nose (1979), Garnet Hill (1979), and Peddler Hill (1951) 7.5' quadrangles.

Eastwoods [EL DORADO]: *locality,* 14 miles east of Placerville along Sly Park Creek (lat. 38°43'50" N, long. 120°32'15" W). Named on Placerville (1893) 30' quadrangle.

Eaton: see **Mount Eaton** [TUOLUMNE].

Echo [EL DORADO]: *locality,* 3.25 miles south-southeast of Pyramid Peak in Strawberry Valley at present Strawberry (lat. 38°47'55" N, long. 120°08'35" W). Named on Pyramid Peak (1896) 30' quadrangle.

Echo: see **Echo Lake** [EL DORADO].

Echo Creek [MARIPOSA]: *stream,* flows 8 miles to Merced River 7.5 miles south-southwest of Cathedral Peak (lat. 37°44'30" N, long. 119°26'35" W). Named on Merced Peak (1953) and Tuolumne Meadows (1956) 15' quadrangles. United States Board on Geographic Names (1970b, p. 2-3) gave the name "Cathedral Fork" as a variant.

Echo Lake [EL DORADO]: *locality,* 1.5 miles north-northwest of Echo Summit (lat. 38°50' N, long. 120°02'25" W; sec. 6, T 11 N, R 18 E); the place is near the east end of Lower Echo Lake. Named on Echo Lake (1955) 7.5' quadrangle. Postal authorities established Echo post office in 1888, discontinued it in 1910, reestablished it in 1911, discontinued it in 1913, reestablished it with the name "Echo Lake" in 1926, and discontinued it in 1973 (Salley, p. 65).

Echo Lake [MARIPOSA]: *lake,* 750 feet long, 2 miles south of Cathedral Peak (lat. 37°49' N, long. 119°24'30" W; near E line sec. 26, T 1 S, R 23 E); the lake is 1 mile south-south-west of Echo Peaks. Named on Tuolumne Meadows (1956) 15' quadrangle.

Echo Lake [NEVADA]: *lake,* 700 feet long, 900 feet east-northeast of English Mountain (lat. 39°26'50" N, long. 120°32'50" W; at NW cor. sec. 8, T 18 N, R 13 E). Named on English Mountain (1983) 7.5' quadrangle.

Echo Lake: see **Lower Echo Lake** [EL DORADO]; **Upper Echo Lake** [EL DORADO].

Echo Peak [EL DORADO]: *peak,* 4 miles north-west of Echo Summit (lat. 38°51'25" N, long. 120°04'20" W; sec. 26, T 12 N, R 17 E). Altitude 8895 feet. Named on Echo Lake (1955) 7.5' quadrangle.

Echo Peaks [MARIPOSA]: *relief features,* about 1 mile south of Cathedral Peak on Mariposa-Tuolumne county line (lat. 37°50' N, long. 119°24' W; sec. 24, T 1 S, R 23 E). Named on Tuolumne Meadows (1956) 15' quadrangle.

Echo Summit [EL DORADO]: *pass,* 7.25 miles east-southeast of Pyramid Peak (lat. 38°48'45" N, long. 120°01'45" W; sec. 7, T 11 N, R 18 E). Named on Echo Lake (1955) 7.5' quadrangle. The feature was called Johnson Pass in the early days (Zauner, p. 7).

Echo Valley [MARIPOSA]: *valley,* 7.25 miles south-southwest of Cathedral Peak (lat. 37°44'45" N, long. 119°26' W); the feature is at the mouth of Echo Creek. Named on Merced Peak (1953) 15' quadrangle.

Eden Valley [PLACER]: *canyon,* 1.5 miles long, 3.25 miles south-southwest of Colfax (lat. 39°03'35" N, long. 120°59' W). Named on Colfax (1949) 7.5' quadrangle.

Eder [PLACER]: *locality,* 2 miles southeast of Donner Pass along Southern Pacific Railroad (lat. 38°18' N, long. 120°17'30" W; at NE cor. sec. 27, T 17 N, R 15 E). Named on Norden (1955) 7.5' quadrangle.

Edison Cabin [EL DORADO]: *locality,* 16 miles north-northwest of Pollock Pines (lat. 38°58'15" N, long. 120°42'10" W; near SW cor. sec. 13, T 13 N, R 11 E). Named on Tunnel Hill (1950) 7.5' quadrangle. Called Edson Cabin on Saddle Mountain (1950) 15' quadrangle.

Edith Lake: see **Edyth Lake** [TUOLUMNE].

Ediza Lake [MADERA]: *lake,* 1700 feet long, 6.25 miles northwest of Devils Postpile along Shadow Creek (lat. 37°41'05" N, long. 119°09'55" W); the lake is 1.5 miles west-southwest of Shadow Lake. Named on Devils Postpile (1953) 15' quadrangle. The feature also was called Little Shadow Lake (Browning, 1988, p. 37).

Edna Lake [MADERA]: *lake,* 0.5 mile long, nearly 1 mile northeast of Merced Peak (lat. 37°38'35" N, long. 119°22'50" W). Named on Merced Peak (1953) 15' quadrangle. R.B. Marshall of United States Geological Survey named the lake for Edna Bowman of San Jose, who later became Mrs. Charles J. Kuhn (United States Board on Geographic Names, 1934, p. 7).

Edna Lake: see **Pinecrest Lake** [TUOLUMNE].

Edna Lake Reservoir: see **Pinecrest Lake** [TUOLUMNE].

Edson: see **Lake Edson** and **Mark Edson Reservoir**, under **Stumpy Meadows Lake** [EL DORADO].

Edson Cabin: see **Edison Cabin** [EL DORADO].

Edson Lake [MARIPOSA]: *lake,* 800 feet long, 9 miles south-southeast of Yosemite Village (lat. 37°37'55" N, long. 119°31'25" W; sec. 35, T 3 S, R 22 E). Named on Yosemite (1956) 15' quadrangle. This name is a perversion of the name "Edison Lake" suggested by park rangers Bingaman and Ernst (Browning, 1988, p, 38).

Edward's Bridge: see **Edwards Crossing** [NEVADA].

Edwards' Creek: see **Wildcat Creek** [TUOLUMNE].

Edwards Crossing [NEVADA]: *locality,* 5.25 miles west-southwest of North Bloomfield along South Yuba River (lat. 39°19'50" N, long. 120°59' W; near SE cor. sec. 17, T 17 N, R 9 E). Named on North Bloomfield (1949) 7.5' quadrangle. Called Edwards Bridge on Colfax (1898) 30' quadrangle. The place also was known as Edward's Bridge, Robinson's Crossing, and Black's Bridge (Hoover, Rensch, and Rensch, p. 249).

Edwin [AMADOR]: *locality,* 1.5 miles west-northwest of Ione along Southern Pacific Railroad (lat. 38°22'40" N, long. 120°59'10" W). Named on Irish Hill (1962) 7.5' quadrangle.

Edyth Lake [TUOLUMNE]: *lake,* 3500 feet long, 16 miles southeast of Pinecrest along Kendrick Creek (lat. 38°03'35" N, long. 119° 45' W; sec. 2, T 2 N, R 20 E). Named on Pinecrest (1956) and Tower Peak (1956) 15' quadrangles. Called Edith Lake on Dardanelles (1898, reprinted 1947) 30' quadrangle. Major W.W. Forsyth named the lake for Edyth Nance, daughter of Colonel Nance (United States Board on Geographic Names, 1934, p. 7). United States Board on Geographic Names (1990, p. 7) approved the form "Edith Lake" for the name—the daughter's name has the form "Edith."

Egbert Hill [NEVADA]: *peak,* 1.5 miles northeast of Higgins Corner (lat. 39°03'20" N, long. 121°04'15" W; near N line sec. 22, T 14 N, R 8 E). Altitude 1741 feet. Named on Lake Combie (1949) 7.5' quadrangle.

Eggers [EL DORADO]: *locality,* 3.5 miles north of Shingle Springs (lat. 38°42'50" N, long. 120°56'25" W). Named on Placerville (1893) 30' quadrangle.

Ehrnbeck Peak [TUOLUMNE]: *peak,* less than 2 miles east-southeast of Tower Peak on Tuolumne-Mono county line (lat. 38°08'15" N, long. 119°30'50" W). Altitude 11,240 feet. Named on Tower Peak (1956) 15' quadrangle. Browning (1986, p. 62-63) associated the name with Lieutenant Arthur R. Ehrnbeck, who reported in 1909 on a road and trail project for Yosemite National Park.

Eighteen Mile House [MADERA]: *locality,* 6.25 miles south-southeast of Raymond (lat. 37°07'40" N, long. 119°52'10" W; sec. 23, T 9 S, R 19 E). Named on Daulton (1921) 7.5' quadrangle.

Eightmile: see **Wawona** [MARIPOSA].

Eight Mile House [EL DORADO]: *locality,* 1 mile east-northeast of Camino (lat. 38°44'30" N, long. 120°39'35" W; near S line sec. 4, T 10 N, R 12 E). Named on Camino (1952) 15' quadrangle. Wheeler (1878, p. 60) called the place Painter's Station.

Elbert Lake [EL DORADO]: *lake,* 1100 feet long, 2.5 miles south of Echo Summit (lat.

38°46'30" N, long. 120°02' W; sec. 30, T 11 N, R 18 E). Named on Echo Lake (1955) 7.5' quadrangle. The feature also was called Little Alberts Lake (Lekisch, p. 38).

Elbow Hill [TUOLUMNE]: *peak,* 9 miles west-northwest of Tioga Pass (lat. 37°58'20" N, long. 119°24'10" W). Named on Tuolumne Meadows (1956) 15' quadrangle.

El Capitan [MARIPOSA]: *relief feature,* 3 miles west-southwest of Yosemite Village on the north side of Yosemite Valley (lat. 37° 44' N, long. 119°38'10" W). Named on Yosemite (1956) 15' quadrangle. Lafayette H. Bunnell named the feature in 1880 (United States Board on Geographic Names, 1934, p 8). According to Browning (1986, p. 63), the feature also had the names "Crane Mountain," from sandhill cranes that flew over it, and "Giant's Tower."

El Capitan Gully [MARIPOSA]: *canyon,* drained by a stream that flows 1 mile to Ribbon Creek 3.5 miles west-southwest of Yosemite Village (lat. 37°44' N, long. 119°38'40" W); the feature is 0.5 mile west of El Capitan. Named on Yosemite (1956) 15' quadrangle.

El Capitan Meadow [MARIPOSA]: *area,* 3.25 miles southwest of Yosemite Village (lat. 37°43'20" N, long. 119°38' W); the place is at the base of El Capitan. Named on Yosemite (1956) 15' quadrangle.

Elders Corner [PLACER]: *locality,* 4.25 miles north-northwest of downtown Auburn (lat. 38°57'25" N, long. 121°06' W; on S line sec. 20, T 13 N, R 8 E). Named on Auburn (1953) 7.5' quadrangle.

El Dorado [EL DORADO]: *town,* 4 miles southwest of Placerville (lat. 38°40'55" N, long. 120°50'45" W; sec. 35, T 10 N, R 10 E). Named on Placerville (1949) 7.5' quadrangle. Called Mud Springs on Placerville (1893) 30' quadrangle. California Mining Bureau's (1909a) map has the form "Eldorado" for the name. Postal authorities established Mud Spring post office in 1851 and changed the name to El Dorado in 1855 (Frickstad, p. 28). The town incorporated in 1855 and disincorporated in 1857 (Bancroft, 1888, p. 482). The name "Mud Springs" was from the muddy ground around springs that emigrants used to water their stock (Hoover, Rensch, and Rensch, p. 82). California Division of Highways' (1934) map shows a place called Cummings located about 2 miles west of El Dorado along Southern Pacific Railroad (sec. 33, T 10 N, R 10 E). Postal authorities established Aurum City post office 2 miles southeast of El Dorado in 1852 and discontinued it in 1853 (Salley, p. 12). A place called Uniontown was situated about 2 miles southeast of El Dorado along Martinez Creek; the name was from Union mine (Gudde, 1975, p. 356), which Placerville (1949) 7.5' quadrangle shows 2.5 miles south-southeast of El Dorado near Martinez Creek (sec. 12, T 9 N, R 10 E).

Eldorado: see **Camp Eldorado**, under **Camp Silverado** [AMADOR].

El Dorado: see **Mountain Ranch** [CALAVERAS].

El Dorado Bar: see **Melones** [CALAVERAS].

El Dorado Beach [EL DORADO]: *beach,* 7.25 miles north-northwest of Freel Peak along Lake Tahoe (lat. 38°56'45" N, long. 119°58'25" W). Named on South Lake Tahoe (1955) 7.5' quadrangle.

El Dorado Canyon [PLACER]: *canyon,* 2.25 miles long, opens into the canyon of North Fork of Middle Fork American River 1.5 miles east-southeast of Michigan Bluff (lat. 39°02' N, long. 120°42'30" W; sec. 26, T 14 N, R 11 E). Named on Michigan Bluff (1952) 7.5' quadrangle. The feature divides at the head into East Branch and West Branch. East Branch is 11 miles long and is named on Michigan Bluff (1952) and Westville (1952) 7.5' quadrangles. The stream in East Branch is called Indian Creek on Colfax (1898) 30' quadrangle. West Branch is 6.5 miles long and is named on Michigan Bluff (1952) and Westville (1952) 7.5' quadrangles. The upper part of West Branch is called Forks House Ravine on Colfax (1898) 30' quadrangle. The stream in West Branch is called El Dorado Creek on Colfax (1898) 30' quadrangle, and is called Bullion Creek on Colfax (1938) 30' quadrangle. Middle Branch opens into West Branch 4.25 miles north-northeast of Michigan Bluff; it is 1.5 miles long and is named on Michigan Bluff (1952) 7.5' quadrangle.

El Dorado Creek [CALAVERAS]: *stream,* flows 4.25 miles to Murry Creek 6.25 miles east-northeast of San Andreas (lat. 38°13'20" N, long. 120°34'15" W; sec. 5, T 4 N, R 13 E). Named on Calaveritas (1962) 7.5' quadrangle.

Eldorado Creek [MARIPOSA]: *stream,* flows 8 miles to Burns Creek 3.5 miles northwest of Santa Cruz Mountain (lat. 37°29'50" N, long. 120°14'15" W; sec. 17, T 5 S, R 16 E). Named on Indian Gulch (1962) 7.5' quadrangle. On Hornitos (1947) 7.5' quadrangle, the name has the form "El Dorado Creek."

El Dorado Creek: see **El Dorado Canyon** [PLACER].

El Dorado Hills [EL DORADO]: *town,* 1.5 miles west-northwest of Clarksville (lat. 38°39'45" N, long. 121°04'30" W). Named on Clarksville (1953, photorevised 1980) 7.5' quadrangle.

El Dorado Ranch: see **Du Rock** [EL DORADO].

Eleanor: see **Lake Eleanor**, under **Lake Eleanor Reservoir** [TUOLUMNE].

Eleanor Creek [TUOLUMNE]: *stream,* formed by the confluence of Bartlett Creek and Kendrick Creek, flows 9.5 miles to Cherry Creek 4.25 miles north-northwest of Mather (lat. 37°56'10" N, long. 119°53'45" W; near S line sec. 16, T 1 N, R 19 E). Named on Lake Eleanor (1956) and Pinecrest (1956) 15' quadrangles. United States Board on Geographic Names (1933, p. 285) rejected the name "Lake River" for present Eleanor Creek. On Dardanelles (1898) 30' quadrangle, present Kendrick Creek is called East Fork Eleanor Cr.

Eleanor Lake [TUOLUMNE]: *lake,* 2200 feet long, 1.5 miles east-northeast of present Pinecrest along South Fork Stanislaus River (lat. 38°12'05" N, long. 119°58'10" W). Named on Dardanelles (1898, reprinted 1947) 30' quadrangle. Pinecrest (1979) 7.5' quadrangle does not show Eleanor Lake, which apparently is encompassed by present Pinecrest Lake.

Eleanor Lake Reservoir: see **Lake Eleanor Reservoir** [TUOLUMNE].

Electra [AMADOR]: *locality,* nearly 3 miles east-southeast of Jackson Butte on the north side of Mokelumne River (lat. 38°19'55" N, long. 120°40'10" W; near E line sec. 32, T 6 N, R 12 E). Named on Mokelumne Hill (1948) 7.5' quadrangle. Postal authorities established Electra post office in 1900 and discontinued it in 1923; the name is from a generating plant for electricity located along the river (Salley, p. 67). Camp's (1962) map has the name "Whites Bar" at present Electra. The same map shows a place called China City located 1.5 miles east of present Electra on the north side of Mokelumne River, and a place called Watkins Bar situated 2 miles east-northeast of present Electra on the north side of the river.

Electra Peak [MADERA]: *peak,* 8.5 miles northeast of Merced Peak (lat. 37°42'20" N, long. 119°15'35" W). Altitude 12,442 feet. Named on Merced Peak (1953) 15' quadrangle.

Elephant Rock [MARIPOSA]: *relief feature,* 7.5 miles west-southwest of Yosemite Village (lat. 37°42'50" N, long. 119°42'45" W; sec. 36, T 2 S, R 20 E). Named on Yosemite (1956) 15' quadrangle.

Elephants Head [SIERRA]: *peak,* 2.5 miles northeast of Loyalton (lat. 39°41'50" N, long. 120°11'55" W; near W line sec. 4, T 21 N, R 16 E). Altitude 6608 feet. Named on Loyalton (1981) 7.5' quadrangle.

Elevenmile: see **Wawona** [MARIPOSA].

Elevenmile Creek [MARIPOSA]: *stream,* flows 4 miles to Bishop Creek 11 miles south-southwest of Yosemite Village (lat. 37°36'45" N, long. 119°41'40" W; sec. 5, T 4 S, R 21 E). Named on Yosemite (1956) 15' quadrangle. The name is from Eleven Mile Station, a stage stop located 11 miles from Wawona (Browning, 1986, p. 64). United States Board on Geographic Names (1991, p. 6) approved the name "Rail Creek" for a stream, 2 miles long, that joins Elevenmile Creek 6.4 miles north-northwest of Wawona (lat. 37°37'44" N, long. 119°41'40" W; sec. 32, T 3 S, R 21 E), and rejected the name "Elevenmile Creek" for this stream.

Eleven Mile Creek: see **Bishop Creek** [MARIPOSA].

11-Mile House: see **Wawona** [MARIPOSA].

Eleven Mile Station: see **Wawona** [MARIPOSA].

Eleven Pines [EL DORADO]: *locality,* 10.5 miles north-northeast of Pollock Pines (lat. 38°54'20" N, long. 120°31'10" W; sec. 9, T 12 N, R 13 E). Named on Devil Peak (1950) 7.5' quadrangle.

Elida: see **Rough and Ready** [NEVADA].

Elizabeth Hill: see **Refuge Canyon** [PLACER].

Elizabeth Lake [TUOLUMNE]: *lake,* 1500 feet long, 7.5 miles southwest of Tioga Pass (lat. 37°50'45" N, long. 119°22'05" W). Named on Tuolumne Meadows (1956) 15' quadrangle. R.B. Marshall of United States Geological Survey named the lake in 1909 for a daughter of Dr. and Mrs. Samuel E. Simmons (United States Board on Geographic Names, 1934, p. 8).

Elizabeth Peak [TUOLUMNE]: *peak,* 2 miles north-northwest of Twain Harte (lat. 38°03'45" N, long. 120°14'50" W; near NW cor. sec. 5, T 2 N, R 16 E). Altitude 4939 feet. Named on Twain Harte (1979) 7.5' quadrangle. Called Mount Elizabeth on Big Trees (1891) 30' quadrangle.

Elizabeth Town: see **Middle Martis Creek** [PLACER].

Elizaville: see **Forest** [SIERRA].

Elkhorn: see **Indian Gulch** [MARIPOSA] (3).

Elkhorn Station [CALAVERAS]: *locality,* 4.5 miles west-southwest of Angels Camp (lat. 38°03'05" N, long. 120°37'25" W; sec. 2, T 2 N, R 12 E). Named on Angels Camp (1962) 7.5' quadrangle.

Elkins Flat [EL DORADO]: *area,* 1.5 miles south-southwest of Caldor along Middle Dry Creek (lat. 38°35'10" N, long. 120°26'30" W; on E line sec. 32, T 9 N, R 14 E). Named on Caldor (1951) 7.5' quadrangle.

Ellens Creek: see **Grass Valley** [NEVADA].

Ellicott [PLACER]: *locality,* 4 miles east of Devil Peak (lat. 38°57'45" N, long. 120°29' W). Named on Pyramid Peak (1896) 30' quadrangle. Robbs Peak (1950) 7.5' quadrangle shows Ellicott bridge on Rubicon River just east of the place.

Elliott Corner [MARIPOSA]: *locality,* 10.5 miles east of Mariposa (lat. 37°27'45" N, long. 119°46'25" W; near SW cor. sec. 27, T 5 S, R 20 E). Named on Stumpfield Mountain (1947) 7.5' quadrangle.

Ellis [MARIPOSA]: *locality,* 8 miles north-northwest of Hornitos along Yosemite Valley Railroad (lat. 37°37' N, long. 120°16'20" W; sec. 1, T 4 S, R 15 E). Named on Merced Falls (1944) 15' quadrangle.

Ellis Creek [EL DORADO-PLACER]: *stream,* heads in Placer County and flows 2.5 miles to Pleasant Lake 2.5 miles east of Wentworth Springs in El Dorado County (lat. 39°00'45" N, long. 120°17'50" W; sec. 33, T 14 N, R 15 E). Named on Granite Chief (1953) 15' quadrangle. Wentworth Springs (1953,

105

photorevised 1973) 7.5' quadrangle shows the stream entering a larger Pleasant Lake.

Ellis Lake [PLACER]: *lake,* 550 feet long, 2.5 miles southwest of Homewood (lat. 39°04'05" N, long. 120°12'05" W; near NW cor. sec. 15, T 14 N, R 16 E); the lake is less than 0.25 mile west-southwest of Ellis Peak. Named on Homewood (1955) 7.5' quadrangle.

Ellis Peak [PLACER]: *peak,* 2.5 miles southwest of Homewood (lat. 39°04'05" N, long. 120°11'50" W; near S line sec. 10, T 14 N, R 16 E). Altitude 8740 feet. Named on Homewood (1955) 7.5' quadrangle. The name is for Jock Ellis, a dairyman and sheep rancher (Lekisch, p. 38).

El Portal [MARIPOSA]: *village,* 11.5 miles west-southwest of Yosemite Village along Merced River (lat. 37°40'35" N, long. 119°46'45" W; on E line sec. 17, T 3 S, R 20 E). Named on El Portal (1947) 7.5' quadrangle. Postal authorities established El Portal post office in 1907 (Frickstad, p. 91). The place was Yosemite Valley Railroad's railhead near the entrance to Yosemite National Park—*el portal* means "the gateway" in Spanish (Johnston, p. 15).

El Rio de Nuestra Senora de la Merced: see **Merced River** [MADERA-MARIPOSA].

Emerald Bay [EL DORADO]:
(1) *bay,* 3.5 miles north of Mount Tallac off Lake Tahoe (lat. 38°57'25" N, long. 120°05'35" W). Named on Emerald Bay (1955) 7.5' quadrangle. The feature also was called Eagle Bay (Lekisch, p. 32).
(2) *village,* 3.5 miles north of Mount Tallac (lat. 38°57'35" N, long. 120°05'50" W; on W line sec. 22, T 13 N, R 17 E); the village is on the northwest side of Emerald Bay (1). Named on Emerald Bay (1955) 7.5' quadrangle. Pyramid Peak (1896) 30' quadrangle has the name at a site farther southwest near the end of Emerald Bay (1). California Mining Bureau's (1917b) map shows a place called Rubicon located north of the village of Emerald Bay along Lake Tahoe about halfway from the village to Placer County. Postal authorities established Rubicon post office 4.5 miles north of Emerald Bay post office in 1901, discontinued it in 1906, reestablished it in 1909, and discontinued it in 1913 (Salley, p. 190).

Emerald Bay Falls: see **Eagle Falls** [EL DORADO].

Emerald Point [EL DORADO]: *promontory,* 4.25 miles north of Mount Tallac along Lake Tahoe (lat. 38°58' N, long. 120°05' W); the feature is on the north side of the entrance to Emerald Bay (1). Named on Emerald Bay (1955) 7.5' quadrangle.

Emerald Pool [MARIPOSA]: *lake,* 400 feet long, 3 miles east-southeast of Yosemite Village (lat. 37°43'40" N, long. 119°32'30" W). Named on Yosemite (1956) 15' quadrangle. The name dates from 1856; that same year the lake also was given the name "Frances"

for Mrs. Jane Frances Neal, the first white woman to visit the place (Browning, 1988, p. 40-41).

Emeric Creek [MARIPOSA]: *stream,* flows 3.25 miles to Fletcher Creek 5.25 miles south of Cathedral Peak (lat. 37°46'20" N, long. 119°23'15" W); the stream goes through Emeric Lake. Named on Tuolumne Meadows (1956) 15' quadrangle. Lieutenant N.F. McClure named the creek for Henry F. Emeric, for whom he named Emeric Lake (Browning, 1986, p. 65).

Emeric Lake [MARIPOSA]: *lake,* 2400 feet long, 5 miles south-southeast of Cathedral Peak (lat. 37°46'35" N, long. 119°23'05" W). Named on Tuolumne Meadows (1956) 15' quadrangle. Lieutenant N.F. McClure named the lake in 1895 for Henry F. Emeric, president of California Board of Fish Commissioners (United States Board on Geographic Names, 1934, p. 8).

Emery Reservoir [CALAVERAS]: *lake,* behind a dam on McKinney Creek 10 miles east-northeast of San Andreas (lat. 38°14'50" N, long. 120°30'10" W; sec. 35, T 5 N, R 13 E). Named on Calaveritas (1962), Murphys (1948), and Rail Road Flat (1948) 7.5' quadrangles.

Emigrant Canyon [PLACER]: *canyon,* drained by a stream that flows 2.5 miles to Cold Creek 3.5 miles east-southeast of Donner Pass (lat. 39°17'35" N, long. 120°16'10" W; near W line sec. 25, T 17 N, R 15 E). Named on Norden (1955) 7.5' quadrangle.

Emigrant Gap [PLACER]:
(1) *pass,* 35 miles northeast of Auburn (lat. 39°18' N, long. 120° 40' W; sec. 31, T 17 N, R 12 E). Named on Blue Canyon (1955) 7.5' quadrangle. The name is from the early days, when emigrants lowered their wagons through a gap in the ridge at the place (Stewart, p. 89).
(2) *village,* 0.25 mile southwest of Emigrant Gap (1) (lat. 39°17'50" N, long. 120°40'15" W; sec. 31, T 17 N, R 12 E). Named on Blue Canyon (1955) 7.5' quadrangle. Postal authorities established Wilsons Ranch post office in 1865; they moved it and changed the name to Emigrant Gap in 1868—the name "Wilsons Ranch" was for the operator of a stage stop on the emigrant trail (Salley, p. 241). California Mining Bureau's (1909a) map shows a place called Fulda located 2 miles southwest of the village of Emigrant Gap along the railroad. Postal authorities established Fulda post office in 1906 and discontinued it in 1912 (Frickstad, p. 120).

Emigrant Lake [TUOLUMNE]: *lake,* 1.5 miles long, 8.5 miles west-northwest of Tower Peak along North Fork Cherry Creek (lat. 38°10'25" N, long. 119°41'50" W). Named on Tower Peak (1956) 15' quadrangle. United States Board on Geographic Names (1965c, p. 9, 11, 12) approved the name "Fraser Lakes" for a group of four small lakes located about 0.3 mile south of Emigrant Lake (lat.

38°10'10" N, long. 119°41'55" W), approved the name "Ridge Lake" for a small lake situated about 4 miles northwest of Emigrant Lake (lat. 38°13'15" N, long. 119°44'40" W), and approved the name "W Lake" for a small lake found about 0.6 mile southeast of the northeast end of Emigrant Lake (lat. 38°10'18" N, long. 119° 40'45" W).

Emigrant Lake: see **High Emigrant Lake** [TUOLUMNE]; **Middle Emigrant Lake** [TUOLUMNE].

Emigrant Meadow [TUOLUMNE]: *valley,* 7 miles northwest of Tower Peak at the head of North Fork Cherry Creek (lat. 38°12'15" N, long. 119°39' W); the valley is west of Emigrant Pass. Named on Tower Peak (1956) 15' quadrangle.

Emigrant Meadow Lake [TUOLUMNE]: *lake,* 0.5 mile long, nearly 7 miles northwest of Tower Peak (lat. 38°12'05" N, long. 119°38'50" W); the lake is in Emigrant Meadow. Named on Tower Peak (1956) 15' quadrangle.

Emigrant Pass [TUOLUMNE]: *pass,* 6 miles northwest of Tower Peak on Tuolumne-Mono county line (lat. 38°12' N, long. 119°37'50" W); the pass is east of Emigrant Meadow. Named on Tower Peak (1956) 7.5' quadrangle.

Emily Lake [MADERA]: *lake,* 800 feet long, 4 miles northwest of Devils Postpile (lat. 37°40'20" N, long. 119°07'15" W). Named on Devils Postpile (1953) 15' quadrangle.

Emory Ford: see **Emory Island** [NEVADA].

Emory Island [NEVADA]: *island,* 3.5 miles northeast of North San Juan in Middle Yuba River on Nevada-Yuba county line (lat. 39°23'45" N, long. 121°02'55" W; sec. 26, T 18 N, R 8 E). Named on Camptonville (1948) 7.5' quadrangle. Smartsville (1895) 30' quadrangle shows Emory Ford at or near the place, and Wescoatt's (1861) map has Emorys Crossing there.

Emorys Crossing: see **Emory Island** [NEVADA].

Empire Camp: see **Empire Meadow** [MARIPOSA].

Empire Creek [CALAVERAS]: *stream,* flows 3.5 miles to Black Creek (1) nearly 2 miles east of Copperopolis (lat. 37°58'30" N, long. 120°36'20" W; at S line sec. 36, T 2 N, R 12 E). Named on Angels Camp (1962) and Melones Dam (1962) 7.5' quadrangles.

Empire Creek [EL DORADO]: *stream,* flows 4 miles to join Manhattan Creek and form Johntown Creek 6.5 miles north-northwest of Chili Bar (lat. 38°51'30" N, long. 120°51' W; sec. 27, T 12 N, R 10 E). Named on Garden Valley (1949) and Georgetown (1949) 7.5' quadrangles. Miners from New York, the Empire State, named the stream in 1849 (Gernes, p. 51).

Empire Creek [SIERRA]: *stream,* flows 5.5 miles to Lavezzola Creek 4 miles northeast of Downieville (lat. 39°36'10" N, long.

120°46'50" W; sec. 18, T 20 N, R 11 E). Named on Downieville (1951) and Mount Fillmore (1951) 7.5' quadrangles. Downieville (1951) 7.5' quadrangle shows Empire ranch located near the mouth of the stream. United States Board on Geographic Names (1950, p. 5) rejected the names "Little North Fork" and "Little North Fork of Middle Fork of North Fork Yuba River" for the stream, and noted that the name "Empire Creek" is from Empire ranch.

Empire Creek: see **Sly Park Creek** [EL DORADO].

Empire Meadow [MARIPOSA]: *area,* 5.5 miles north of Wawona (lat. 37°37' N, long. 119°38'30" W; sec. 2, T 4 S, R 21 E). Named on Yosemite (1956) 15' quadrangle. Hoffmann and Gardner's (1863-1867) map shows a place called Empire Camp located along Alder Creek, probably at or near present Empire Meadow.

Empire Reservoir [NEVADA]: *lake,* 900 feet long, nearly 6 miles north-northwest of Chicago Park (lat. 39°13'25" N, long. 120°59'45" W; near NW cor. sec. 29, T 16 N, R 9 E). Named on Colfax (1950) 15' quadrangle.

End of the World [PLACER]: *ridge,* south-southeast-trending, 0.5 mile long, 9.5 miles south-southwest of Duncan Peak (lat. 39°01'55" N, long. 120°35'50" W; at E line sec. 26, T 14 N, R 12 E). Named on Greek Store (1952) 7.5' quadrangle.

Englebright Lake [NEVADA]: *lake,* behind a dam on Yuba River 2.5 miles north-northeast of Smartville on Nevada-Yuba county line (lat. 39°14'25" N, long. 121°16'05" W; sec. 14, T 16 N, R 6 E). Named on Smartville (1951, photorevised 1973) 7.5' quadrangle. Called Englebright Reservoir on Oregon House (1948) 7.5' quadrangle, called Harry L. Englebright Lake on French Corral (1948) 7.5' quadrangle, and called Upper Narrows Reservoir on Bangor (1941) 15' quadrangle. United States Board on Geographic Names (1972, p. 4) gave the names "Englebright Reservoir," "Harry L. Englebright Lake," "Harry L. Englebright Reservoir," and "Upper Narrows Reservoir" as variants. Officials of California Hydraulic Miners Association named the dam that forms the lake in 1945 in memory of Harry L. Englebright of Nevada City, a congressman from 1926 until 1943 (Gudde, 1949, p. 108).

Englebright Reservoir: see **Englebright Lake** [NEVADA].

English Meadow [NEVADA-SIERRA]: *area,* 1.5 miles northeast of English Mountain along Middle Yuba River on Nevada-Sierra county line (lat. 39°27'35" N, long. 120°31'30" W). Named on English Mountain (1983) 7.5' quadrangle.

English Meadow: see **Moscove Meadow** [NEVADA-SIERRA].

English Mountain [NEVADA]: *peak,* 21 miles

west-northwest of Truckee (lat. 39°26'50" N, long. 120°33' W; near NE cor. sec. 7, T 18 N, R 13 E); the peak is 1.25 miles south-southeast of Jackson Lake. Altitude 8373 feet. Named on English Mountain (1983) 7.5' quadrangle. Called Jackson Peak on Hobson's (1890a) map, and called English Pk. on California Mining Bureau's (1917b) map. On Emigrant Gap (1955) 15' quadrangle, the name "English Mountain" applies to the ridge on which present English Mountain is the high point.

English Peak: see **English Mountain** [NEVADA].

Enterprise [AMADOR]: *locality,* 5.5 miles west-northwest of Fiddletown along Big Indian Creek (lat. 38°32'25" N, long. 120°50'45" W; near S line sec. 14, T 8 N, R 10 E). Named on Fiddletown (1949) 7.5' quadrangle. The old mining town of Yeomet was situated less than 1 mile north of Enterprise at the confluence of Middle Fork Cosumnes River and North Fork Cosumnes River; the name "Yeonet" reportedly is from an Indian word that has the meaning "rocky falls" and refers to some rapids upstream from the site of Yeomet (Andrews, p. 120-121). Postal authorities established Yornet post office at Yeomet in 1854 and discontinued it in 1861 (Salley, p. 245). Bancroft (1888, p. 372) gave the alternate name "Saratoga" for Yeomet, and Gudde (1975, p. 379) noted that the place also was known as Forks of the Cosumnes. Camp's (1962) map shows a place called Cape Cod Bar located 3 miles west-southwest of Enterprise on the south side of Cosumnes River, and a canyon called Bloody Gulch that opens into the canyon of Big Indian Creek from the east nearly 2.5 miles south of Enterprise.

Erie Point [NEVADA]: *ridge,* south- to southwest-trending, 2.5 miles long, 3.25 miles northeast of Washington (lat. 39°23'45" N, long. 120°45'30" W). Named on Alleghany (1949) 7.5' quadrangle.

Esmeralda [CALAVERAS]: *locality,* 8 miles east-southeast of San Andreas (lat. 38°09'15" N, long. 120°32'10" W). Named on Jackson (1902) 30' quadrangle. Postal authorities established Esmeralda post office in 1887, changed the name to Esmerelda in 1902, and discontinued it in 1943—the name is from Esmeralda mine (Salley, p. 70).

Esmeralda Creek [EL DORADO]: *stream,* flows 2 miles to South Fork American River 2.25 miles west of Riverton (lat. 38°46'05" N, long. 120°29'20" W; sec. 26, T 11 N, R 13 E). Named on Riverton (1950) and Stump Spring (1951) 7.5' quadrangles.

Esperanza: see **Esperanza Creek** [CALAVERAS].

Esperanza Creek [CALAVERAS]: *stream,* flows 11.5 miles to North Fork Calaveras River 5 miles west-southwest of Rail Road Flat (lat. 38°19'05" N, long. 120°35'50" W;

near E line sec. 1, T 5 N, R 12 E). Named on Fort Mountain (1979) and Rail Road Flat (1948) 7.5' quadrangles. Doble (p. 86) recorded a visit in 1852 to a mining camp called Esperanza that was along what he called "North fork of the Caliveras [River]." Camp (*in* Doble, p. 299) noted that Esperanza may have been a short distance up Esperanza Creek from the mouth.

Esperanza Valley [CALAVERAS]: *valley,* 6.5 miles west-southwest of Blue Mountain (lat. 38°17'55" N, long. 120°28'15" W; near S line sec. 7, T 5 N, R 14 E); the valley is along Esperanza Creek. Named on Fort Mountain (1979) 7.5' quadrangle.

Estelle: see **Lake Estelle** [PLACER].

Etna: see **Mount Etna** [SIERRA].

Etta: see **Randolph** [SIERRA].

Eucher Bar [PLACER]: *locality,* 4.5 miles east-southeast of Dutch Flat along North Fork American River (lat. 39°11'15" N, long. 120°45'35" W; sec. 5, T 15 N, R 11 E). Named on Dutch Flat (1950) 7.5' quadrangle. Gudde (1975, p. 237) noted that a place called Neutral Bar was located along North Fork just below Euchre Bar.

Eucher Diggings: see **Shngle Springs** [EL DORADO].

Euer Saddle [NEVADA]: *pass,* nearly 2 miles north-northwest of Donner Pass (lat. 39°20'30" N, long. 120°20'15" W; sec. 8, T 17 N, R 15 E). Named on Norden (1955) 7.5' quadrangle. United States Board on Geographic Names (1949b, p. 3) rejected the form "Euer's Saddle" for the name.

Euer Valley [NEVADA]: *valley,* 4.5 miles north-northeast of Donner Pass along South Fork Prosser Creek (lat. 39°22'20" N, long. 120° 16'50" W). Named on Independence Lake (1981) and Norden (1955) 7.5' quadrangles. Called Euers Valley on Truckee (1940) 30' quadrangle, but United States Board on Geographic Names (1949a, p. 3) rejected the forms "Euers Valley," "Euer's Valley," and "Evers Valley" for the name.

Eureka [SIERRA]: *locality,* 5 miles north of Goodyears Bar (lat. 39° 36'45" N, long. 120°53'35" W); the place is at present Eureka Diggings. Named on Downieville (1897) 30' quadrangle. Postal authorities established Eureka North post office in 1857 and discontinued it in 1861; the word "North" was added to the name to avoid confusion with Eureka South, which is in Nevada County (Salley, p. 71).

Eureka: see **Snow Point** [NEVADA].

Eureka Creek [SIERRA]: *stream,* flows 4 miles to Goodyears Creek 3 miles north of Goodyears Bar (lat. 39°35' N, long. 120°52'35" W; sec. 20, T 20 N, R 10 E). Named on Goodyears Bar (1951) 7.5' quadrangle.

Eureka Diggings [SIERRA]: *locality,* 5 miles north of Goodyears Bar (lat. 39°36'45" N, long. 120°53'40" W; sec. 7, T 20 N, R 10 E); the place is near Eureka Creek. Named on

Goodyears Bar (1951) 7.5' quadrangle.

Eureka North: see **Eureka** [SIERRA].

Eureka South: see **Graniteville** [NEVADA].

Eureka Valley [TUOLUMNE]: *area,* 2.5 miles east of Dardanelle along Middle Fork Stanislaus River (lat. 38°20'25" N, long. 119° 47'10" W; sec. 28, T 6 N, R 20 E). Named on Dardanelle (1979) 7.5' quadrangle.

Evans Canyon [SIERRA]: *canyon,* drained by a stream that flows 5 miles to Lassen County 10 miles east-northeast of Loyalton (lat. 39°42'30" N, long. 120°03'25" W; at N line sec. 3, T 21 N, R 17 E). Named on Evans Canyon (1978) and Loyalton (1981) 7.5' quadrangles.

Evans Gulch: see **Rocky Gulch** [MARIPOSA].

Evelyn Lake [TUOLUMNE]: *lake,* 2100 feet long, 8 miles south-southwest of Tioga Pass (lat. 37°48'20" N, long. 119°19'30" W). Named on Tuolumne Meadows (1956) 15' quadrangle. The name commemorates Evelyn Clough (United States Board on Geographic Names, 1934, p. 8).

Evergreen Lodge [TUOLUMNE]: *locality,* 0.5 mile south-southwest of Mather (lat. 37°52'30" N, long. 119°51'25" W; near N line sec. 11, T 1 S, R 19 E). Named on Lake Eleanor (1956) 15' quadrangle.

Evers Valley: see **Euer Valley** [NEVADA].

Ewing [PLACER]: *locality,* 4 miles northwest of Lincoln along Southern Pacific Railroad (lat. 38°55'55" N, long. 121°20'35" W; sec. 31, T 13 N, R 6 E). Named on Lincoln (1953) 7.5' quadrangle.

Excelsior: see **Monte Cristo** [SIERRA]; **Remington Hill** [NEVADA] (2); **Summit City** [NEVADA].

Excelsior Mountain [TUOLUMNE]: *peak,* 6.25 miles southeast of Matterhorn Peak on Tuolumne-Mono county line (lat. 38°01'25" N, long. 119°18'15" W; near W line sec. 14, T 2 N, R 24 E). Altitude 12,446 feet. Named on Matterhorn Peak (1956) 15' quadrangle.

Excelsior Point [NEVADA]: *relief feature,* 5.5 miles south-southeast of Washington (lat. 39°17' N, long. 120°46'15" W; near W line sec. 5, T 16 N, R 11 E). Named on Washington (1950) 7.5' quadrangle.

Excelsior Ravine [SIERRA]: *canyon,* drained by a stream that flows 1 mile to Downie River 3 miles north of Downieville (lat. 39°36'10" N, long. 120°49'55" W; near W line sec. 14, T 20 N, R 10 E). Named on Downieville (1951) 7.5' quadrangle, which shows Excelsior mine at the head of the canyon.

Exchequer [MARIPOSA]:

(1) *locality,* 6.25 miles north-northwest of Hornitos along Yosemite Valley Railroad (lat. 37°35'15" N, long. 120°16' W). Named on Sonora (1897) 30' quadrangle. Postal authorities established Exchequer post office in 1907, discontinued it in 1919, reestablished it in 1922, and discontinued it in 1926 (Frickstad, p. 91). Water of Lake McClure now covers

the site. California Mining Bureau's (1909c) map shows a place called Varain located along the railroad 5 miles north of Exchequer. Postal authorities established Varain post office in 1907 and discontinued it in 1919; the name was for John B. Varain, first postmaster (Salley, p. 230).

(2) *locality,* 6.25 miles north-northwest of Hornitos along Yosemite Valley Railroad (lat. 37°35' N, long. 120°17'15" W; sec. 14, T 4 S, R 15 E). Named on Merced Falls (1944) 15' quadrangle.

Exchequer Reservoir: see **Lake McClure** [MARIPOSA].

Experimental Gulch [TUOLUMNE]: *canyon,* drained by a stream that flows 1.25 miles to South Fork Stanislaus River 2.5 miles northnortheast of Columbia (lat. 38°04'05" N, long. 120°23'05" W; sec. 36, T 3 N, R 14 E). Named on Columbia (1948) 7.5' quadrangle, which shows Experimental mine in the canyon.

— F —

Fagan: see **Kirkwood** [AMADOR-EL DORADO].

Fahey Meadow [TUOLUMNE]: *area,* 4 miles south-southeast of Long Barn (lat. 38°02'10" N, long. 120°06'45" W; near S line sec. 9, T 2 N, R 17 E). Named on Hull Creek (1979) 7.5' quadrangle.

Fairbanks [EL DORADO]: *locality,* 8.5 miles north-northwest of Pollock Pines (lat. 38°51'55" N, long. 120°40'05" W; at NE cor. sec. 30, T 12 N, R 12 E). Named on Slate Mountain (1950) 7.5' quadrangle.

Fairmead [MADERA]: *village,* 11 miles northwest of Madera (lat. 37°04'35" N, long. 120°11'35" W; sec. 11, T 10 S, R 16 E). Named on Berenda (1961) 7.5' quadrangle. Postal authorities established Fairmead post office in 1913 and discontinued it in 1940 (Frickstad, p. 85).

Fair Play [EL DORADO]: *locality,* 4.5 miles northeast of Aukum (lat. 38°35'40" N, long. 120°39'30" W; sec. 33, T 9 N, R 12 E). Named on Aukum (1952) 7.5' quadrangle. Called Fairplay on California Mining Bureau's (1909a) map. Postal authorities established Fair Play post office in 1860 and discontinued it in 1944 (Frickstad, p. 26).

Fairview Dome [TUOLUMNE]: *peak,* 8.5 miles west-southwest of Tioga Pass (lat. 37°52'15" N, long. 119°24'10" W; near NW cor. sec. 12, T 1 S, R 23 E). Altitude 9731 feet. Named on Tuolumne Meadows (1956) 15' quadrangle. United States Board on Geographic Names (1933, p. 296) rejected the names "Soda Spring Dome" and "Soda Springs Butte" for the feature. John Muir used the names "Glacier Monument" and "Tuolumne Glacier Monument" for the peak (Browning, 1986, p. 67).

Fall Creek [NEVADA]: *stream,* flows 5 miles to South Yuba River 5.25 miles west-north-west of Yuba Gap (lat. 39°21'15" N, long. 120°41'55" W; at W line sec. 12, T 17 N, R 11 E). Named on Blue Canyon (1955), English Mountain (1983), and Graniteville (1982) 7.5' quadrangles

Fall Creek Mountain [NEVADA]: *peak,* 6.5 miles east-southeast of Graniteville (lat. 39°24'20" N, long. 120°37'40" W; at S line sec. 21, T 18 N, R 12 E). Altitude 7490 feet. Named on Graniteville (1982) 7.5' quadrangle.

Fallen Leaf [EL DORADO]: *town,* 2 miles southeast of Mount Tallac (lat. 38°52'55" N, long. 120°04'20" W; near SW cor. sec. 14, T 12 N, R 17 E); the town is at the south end of Fallen Leaf Lake. Named on Emerald Bay (1955) 7.5' quadrangle. Postal authorities established Fallen Leaf post office in 1908 (Frickstad, p. 26). William W. Price opened a resort called Fallen Leaf Lodge at the site in 1908; Price previously had operated Agassiz Camp there in connection with his Agassiz School for Boys at Auburn in Placer County (Hanna, p. 103).

Fallen Leaf Lake [EL DORADO]: *lake,* 3 miles long, 2 miles east of Mount Tallac (lat. 38°54' N, long. 120°03'45" W). Named on Emerald Bay (1955) 7.5' quadrangle. The name is from an Indian legend (Hanna, p. 103).

Fallen Leaf Lodge: see **Fallen Leaf** [EL DORADO].

Fall River: see **Falls Creek** [TUOLUMNE].

Falls: see **The Falls** [MADERA].

Falls Creek [TUOLUMNE]: *stream,* flows 21 miles to Hetch Hetchy Reservoir 7.5 miles northeast of Mather (lat. 37°57'50" N, long. 119°45'50" W; sec. 10, T 1 N, R 20 E). Named on Hetch Hetchy Reservoir (1956), Lake Eleanor (1956), and Tower Peak (1956) 15' quadrangles. United States Board on Geographic Names (1933, p. 297) rejected the name "Fall River" for the stream.

Falls Ridge [TUOLUMNE]: *ridge,* west-north-west-trending, 3.5 miles long, 11 miles west of Tioga Pass (lat. 37°55' N, long. 119°28' W); the ridge is southwest of Waterwheel Falls, LeConte Falls, and California Falls. Named on Tuolumne Meadows (1956) 15' quadrangle.

Fannette Island [EL DORADO]: *island,* 550 feet long, 3.25 miles north of Mount Tallac in Emerald Bay (1) (lat. 38°57'15" N, long. 120°06' W). Named on Emerald Bay (1955) 7.5' quadrangle.

Fanny Creek [EL DORADO]: *stream,* flows about 2 miles to Slate Creek (2) 5 miles east-northeast of Latrobe (lat. 38°35'05" N, long. 120°53'45" W; near S line sec. 32, T 9 N, R 10 E). Named on Fiddletown (1949) and Latrobe (1949) 7.5' quadrangles.

Farad: see **Mystic** [NEVADA].

Farnam Mill [EL DORADO]: *locality,* 4.5 miles south-southwest of Omo Ranch (lat.

38°31'20" N, long. 120°37' W); the place is along present Farnham Creek. Named on Placerville (1893) 30' quadrangle. The name should have the form "Farnham" (Beverly Cola, personal communication, 1985).

Farnham Creek [EL DORADO]: *stream,* flows nearly 5 miles to Scott Creek 4.5 miles east-southeast of Aukum (lat. 38°32'10" N, long. 120°38'40" W; sec. 22, T 8 N, R 12 E); the stream is south of Farnham Ridge. Named on Aukum (1952) and Omo Ranch (1952) 7.5' quadrangles.

Farnham Mill: see **Farnam Mill** [EL DORADO].

Farnham Ridge [EL DORADO]: *ridge,* generally west-trending, 10.5 miles long, center 4 miles south-southeast of Omo Ranch (lat. 38° 31'20" N, long. 120°32'45" W). Named on Aukum (1952), Caldor (1951), and Omo Ranch (1952) 7.5' quadrangles.

Fattebort Hill [NEVADA]: *peak,* 1.5 miles southeast of Higgins Corner (lat. 39°01'30" N, long. 121°04'30" W; near NW cor. sec. 34, T 14 N, R 8 E). Altitude 1931 feet. Named on Lake Combie (1949) 7.5' quadrangle. Called Flatbort Hill on Smartsville (1895) 30' quadrangle.

Faucherie Campground [NEVADA]: *locality,* 1.5 miles southwest of English Mountain (lat. 39°25'40" N, long. 120°34'10" W; near E line sec. 13, T 18 N, R 12 E); the place is on the north shore of Faucherie Lake. Named on English Mountain (1983) 7.5' quadrangle.

Faucherie Lake [NEVADA]: *lake,* behind a dam on Canyon Creek 1.5 miles southwest of English Mountain (lat. 39°25'45" N, long. 120°34'05" W; near E line sec. 13, T 18 N, R 12 E). Named on English Mountain (1983) 7.5' quadrangle. The name is for Mr. B. Faucherie, a pioneer hydraulic engineer (Gudde, 1949, p. 114).

Fawn Lake [EL DORADO]: *lake,* 1000 feet long, nearly 5 miles east of Wentworth Springs (lat. 39°00'35" N, long. 120°15' W; sec. 6, T 13 N, R 16 E). Named on Homewood (1955) and Wentworth Springs (1953, photorevised 1973) 7.5' quadrangles.

Fawn Lake [TUOLUMNE]: *lake,* 1000 feet long, 9 miles west-southwest of Tower Peak (lat. 38°06'50" N, long. 119°42'20" W). Named on Tower Peak (1956) 15' quadrangle.

Feeley Lake [NEVADA]: *lake,* 3000 feet long, 6.25 miles east-southeast of Graniteville (lat. 39°24' N, long. 120°37'55" W; sec. 28, T 18 N, R 12 E). Named on Graniteville (1982) 7.5' quadrangle. Present Feeley Lake and nearby Carr Lake together are called Feeley Lakes on Colfax (1938) 30' quadrangle.

Feeley Lakes: see **Feeley Lake** [NEVADA].

Feldspar Valley: see **Long Meadow** [MARIPOSA].

Feliciana Creek [MARIPOSA]: *stream,* flows 4.5 miles to Merced River 9 miles west-south-west of El Portal (lat. 37°38'05" N, long. 119°56' W; sec. 36, T 3 S, R 18 E). Named on

Feliciana Mountain (1947) and Kinsley (1947) 7.5' quadrangles. According to Gudde (1975, p. 114), this stream should be called Slate Gulch, and the name "Feliciana Creek" should be applied to a stream that heads near Feliciana mine and flows westerly into Bear Creek (1) about 1 mile south of the confluence of Bear Creek (1) and Merced River.

Feliciana Mountain [MARIPOSA]: *peak,* 3.5 miles north of Midpines (lat. 37°35'40" N, long. 119°55'05" W; near S line sec. 7, T 4 S, R 19 E). Altitude 4174 feet. Named on Feliciana Mountain (1947) 7.5' quadrangle.

Felix [CALAVERAS]: *locality,* 9.5 miles west-southwest of Angels Camp in Salt Spring Valley (lat. 38°01'45" N, long. 120°42'50" W; sec. 13, T 2 N, R 11 E). Named on Salt Spring Valley (1962) 7.5' quadrangle. Postal authorities established Felix post office in 1896 and discontinued it in 1923; the name is for Madame Felix of Salt Spring Valley (Salley, p. 73).

Femmon: see **Nipinnawasee** [MADERA].

Femmons [TUOLUMNE]: *locality,* nearly 6 miles east-southeast of Duckwall Mountain (lat. 37°56'20" N, long. 120°01'15" W; sec. 17, T 1 N, R 18 E). Named on Duckwall Mountain (1948) 7.5' quadrangle.

Fennessy [TUOLUMNE]: *locality,* 9.5 miles northwest of Parsons (present Strawberry) along Griswold Creek (present North Fork Griswold Creek) (lat. 38°16'40" N, long. 120°09'25" W). Named on Big Trees (1891) 30' quadrangle.

Fenton Ravine [PLACER]: *canyon,* drained by a stream that flows 2.5 miles to Bear River 7 miles northeast of Sheridan (lat. 39°01'55" N, long. 121°16'10" W; sec. 26, T 14 N, R 6 E). Named on Camp Far West (1949) 7.5' quadrangle.

Ferguson Point [AMADOR]: *promontory,* 9 miles north of Mokelumne Peak on the north shore of Silver Lake (lat. 38°40'05" N, long. 120°07'05" W). Named on Caples Lake (1979) 7.5' quadrangle.

Ferguson Ridge [MARIPOSA]: *ridge,* north-northwest-trending, 4 miles long, 7 miles west-southwest of El Portal (lat. 37°38'30" N, long. 119°54' W). Named on El Portal (1947) 15' quadrangle.

Fernandez Creek [MADERA]: *stream,* flows 1.25 miles to West Fork Granite Creek nearly 4 miles southeast of Merced Peak (lat. 37°35'25" N, long. 119°21'10" W); the stream heads near Fernandez Pass. Named on Merced Peak (1953) 15' quadrangle.

Fernandez Lakes [MADERA]: *lakes,* largest 800 feet long, nearly 4 miles south-southeast of Merced Peak (lat. 37°35' N, long. 119°22'20" W); the lakes are east of Fernandez Pass. Named on Merced Peak (1953) 15' quadrangle.

Fernandez Pass [MADERA]: *pass,* 3.25 miles south of Merced Peak (lat. 37°35'15" N, long. 119°23' W); the pass is near the head of

Fernandez Creek. Named on Merced Peak (1953) 15' quadrangle. Captain H.C. Benson, acting superintendent of Yosemite National Park, named the pass for First Sergeant Joseph Fernandez, who was commended for his assistance in planting fish (United States Board on Geographic Names, 1934, p. 9).

Fern Lake [MADERA]: *lake,* 750 feet long, 3 miles west-southwest of Devils Postpile (lat. 37°36'25" N, long. 119°08' W). Named on Devils Postpile (1953) 15' quadrangle.

Fern Lake [PLACER]: *lake,* 650 feet long, 6.5 miles east of Bunker Hill (lat. 39°02' N, long. 120°15'30" W; at W line sec. 30, T 14 N, R 16 E). Named on Wentworth Springs (1953, photorevised 1973) 7.5' quadrangle.

Fernley: see **Rough and Ready** [NEVADA].

Fern Spring [MARIPOSA]: *spring,* 5 miles west-southwest of Yosemite Village in Yosemite Valley (lat. 37°42'55" N, long. 119° 39'50" W). Named on Yosemite (1956) 15' quadrangle.

Fiddle Creek [SIERRA]: *stream,* flows 9 miles to North Yuba River 6.25 miles west-southwest of Goodyears Bar (lat. 39°31'05" N, long. 120°59'45" W; sec. 17, T 19 N, R 9 E). Named on Goodyears Bar (1951) 7.5' quadrangle.

Fiddle Creek: see **Little Fiddle Creek** [SIERRA].

Fiddle Creek Camp Ground [SIERRA]: *locality,* 6.25 miles west-southwest of Goodyears Bar along North Yuba River (lat. 39°31'05" N, long. 120°59'50" W; sec. 17, T 19 N, R 9 E); the place is at the mouth of Fiddle Creek. Named on Goodyears Bar (1951) 7.5' quadrangle. Called Fiddle Cr. Camp on Downieville (1951) 15' quadrangle.

Fiddle Creek Ridge [SIERRA]: *ridge,* south-to west-trending, 5 miles long, center 3.5 miles west of Goodyears Bar (lat. 39°31'55" N, long. 120°56'55" W); the ridge is between Fiddle Creek and North Yuba River. Named on Goodyears Bar (1951) 7.5' quadrangle.

Fiddlers Green [TUOLUMNE]: *area,* 2.5 miles north-northeast of Pinecrest (lat. 38°13'20" N, long. 119°58'20" W; sec. 11, T 4 N, R 18 E). Named on Pinecrest (1979) 7.5' quadrangle.

Fiddlers Spring [EL DORADO]: *spring,* 1 mile southwest of Old Iron Mountain (lat. 38°41'35" N, long. 120°24'10" W; sec. 27, T 10 N, R 14 E). Named on Stump Spring (1951) 7.5' quadrangle.

Fiddletown [AMADOR]: *village,* 10.5 miles north of Jackson along North Fork Dry Creek (lat. 38°30'15" N, long. 120°45'20" W; near W line sec. 34, T 8 N, R 11 E). Named on Fiddletown (1949) 7.5' quadrangle. Called Oleta on Placerville (1893) 30' quadrangle. Eddy's (1854) map has the form "Fiddle Town" for the name. Postal authorities established Fiddletown post office in 1853, changed the name to Oleta in 1878, and changed it back to Fiddletown in 1932 (Frickstad, p. 5). A group of Missourians who settled at the place in 1849 were "always fiddling," hence the designation; the name was changed to Oleta in 1878 to make it more respectable, but the Committee on Historic Landmarks of California Historical Society led a successful effort in 1932 to restore the old name (Hoover, Rensch, and Rensch, p. 32). Camp's (1962) map shows a canyon called Loafer Gulch that opens into the canyon of North Fork Dry Creek from the east nearly 2 miles west-southwest of Fiddletown.

Fienes Crossing: see **Deer Creek** [NEVADA].

Figtree: see **Plymouth** [AMADOR].

Fig Tree Gulch [SIERRA]: *canyon,* 0.25 mile long, 7.25 miles west-northwest of Sutter (lat. 39°12'25" N, long. 121°52'05" W; sec. 28, T 16 N, R 1 E). Named on Sutter Buttes (1954) 7.5' quadrangle.

Filipinis [EL DORADO]: *locality,* 4.5 miles east of Robbs Peak (lat. 38°56' N, long. 120°19'30" W). Named on Pyramid Peak (1896) 30' quadrangle.

Fillmore: see **Mount Fillmore** [SIERRA].

Fillmore Hill [SIERRA]: *ridge,* southwest-trending, less than 1 mile long, 4.5 miles east of Alleghany (lat. 39°28'20" N, long. 120°45'35" W; sec. 32, T 19 N, R 11 E). Named on Alleghany (1949) 7.5' quadrangle.

Findley Mountain: see **Findley Peak** [NEVADA].

Findley Peak [NEVADA]: *peak,* 3 miles north-northwest of English Mountain (lat. 39°29'05" N, long. 120°34'25" W; sec. 25, T 19 N, R 12 E). Altitude 7424 feet. Named on English Mountain (1983) 7.5' quadrangle. Called Findley Mtn. on Logan's (1940) map.

Fine Gold [MADERA]: *locality,* 6.5 miles west-southwest of North Fork (lat. 37°11'30" N, long. 119°37' W; near E line sec. 36, T 8 S, R 21 E); the place is along Fine Gold Creek. Named on Millerton Lake (1945) 15' quadrangle. Postal authorities established Fine Gold post office in 1881 and discontinued it in 1882 (Frickstad, p. 85). When they established a new post office called Gold a little way to the east in 1894, the inhabitants of the community called Fine Gold moved there; postal authorities discontinued Gold post office in 1907 (Clough, p. 79; Frickstad, p. 85). The name "Fine Gold" is the Anglicized form of the Spanish term *Oro Fino* (Gudde, 1975, p. 115).

Fine Gold Creek [MADERA]: *stream,* flows 18 miles to Millerton Lake 5.25 miles south-southeast of O'Neals (lat. 37°03'30" N, long. 119°38'55" W; sec. 14, T 10 S, R 21 E). Named on Bass Lake (1953) and Millerton Lake (1965) 15' quadrangles. North Fork enters from the northwest 6.5 miles northeast of O'Neals; it is 6.5 miles long and is named on Bass Lake (1953) and Millerton Lake (1965) 15' quadrangles. Clough (p. 79) used the name "Finegold Gulch" for the canyon of Fine Gold Creek.

Fine Gold Creek: see **Little Fine Gold Creek** [MADERA].

Finegold Gulch: see **Fine Gold Creek** [MADERA].

Finger Peaks [TUOLUMNE]: *relief features,* 1.5 miles west-southwest of Matterhorn Peak (lat. 38°05'15" N, long. 119°24'20" W). Named on Matterhorn Peak (1956) 15' quadrangle.

Finnon Reservoir [EL DORADO]: *lake,* 1700 feet long, behind a dam on Jaybird Creek 4.25 miles east-northeast of Chili Bar (lat. 38°47'50" N, long. 120°45'05" W; sec. 16, T 11 N, R 11 E). Named on Garden Valley (1949) and Slate Mountain (1950) 7.5' quadrangles.

Finn's Sugarloaf: see **Bisbee Peak** [AMADOR].

Fir Cap [SIERRA]: *peak,* 4.25 miles north-northwest of Downieville (lat. 39°37'10" N, long. 120°51'15" W; at NE cor. sec. 9, T 20 N, R 10 E). Named on Downieville (1951) 7.5' quadrangle. Called Fir Top Mt. on Downieville (1897) 30' quadrangle, and called Firtop Pk. on California Mining Bureau's (1917a) map.

Fir Cap: see **Monte Cristo** [SIERRA].

Fir Cap Diggings: see **Monte Cristo** [SIERRA].

Fir Crags [PLACER]: *relief feature,* nearly 3 miles west of Tahoe City near Truckee River (lat. 38°10'35" N, long. 120°11'30" W; near E line sec. 3, T 15 N, R 16 E). Named on Tahoe City (1955) 7.5' quadrangle.

Firebrick [AMADOR]: *locality,* 1.25 miles south-southeast of Ione along Amador Central Railroad (lat. 38°20'05" N, long. 120°55'25" W; sec. 31, T 6 N, R 10 E). Named on Ione (1962) 7.5' quadrangle.

Fireplace Bluffs [MARIPOSA]: *relief feature,* 5.5 miles west-southwest of Yosemite Village on the north side of Yosemite Valley (lat. 37°43'55" N, long. 119°41' W). Named on Yosemite (1956) 15' quadrangle.

Fireplace Creek [MARIPOSA]: *stream,* flows 2 miles to Merced River 5.5 miles west-southwest of Yosemite Village (lat. 37°43'10" N, long. 119°40'55" W); the stream goes past Fireplace Bluffs. Named on Yosemite (1956) 15' quadrangle.

Fir Hill [NEVADA]: *peak,* 3.25 miles northwest of English Mountain (lat. 39°28'40" N, long. 120°35'45" W; on S line sec. 26, T 19 N, R 12 E). Altitude 6926 feet. Named on English Mountain (1983) 7.5' quadrangle.

Firs Campground [EL DORADO]: *locality,* less than 1 mile north-northwest of Echo Summit (lat. 38°49'30" N, long. 120°02'10" W; near S line sec. 6, T 11 N, R 18 E). Named on Echo Lake (1955) 7.5' quadrangle.

First Brushy Canyon [PLACER]: *canyon,* 2.5 miles long, opens into the head of Brushy Canyon (1) 2.25 miles west-northwest of Foresthill (lat. 39°02'15" N, long. 120°51'15" W; near N line sec. 28, T 14 N, R 10 E).

Named on Foresthill (1949) 7.5' quadrangle.

First Creek [TUOLUMNE]: *stream,* flows nearly 3 miles to Hatch Creek 4.5 miles south-southwest of Moccasin (lat. 37°45'05" N, long. 120°19'45" W; sec. 21, T 2 S, R 15 E); the stream is south of Second Creek. Named on Moccasin (1948) 7.5' quadrangle.

First Divide [SIERRA]: *pass,* 2 miles north-northeast of Dowieville on the ridge between Larezzola Creek and Pauley Creek (lat. 39° 35'10" N, long. 120°48'35" W; sec. 24, T 20 N, R 10 E); the pass is 1 mile southwest of Second Divide. Named on Downieville (1951) 7.5' quadrangle.

First Garrote: see **Groveland** [TUOLUMNE].

First Sugarloaf [PLACER]: *peak,* 6.25 miles north-northwest of Foresthill (lat. 39°06'10" N, long. 120°52'05" W; sec. 32, T 15 N, R 10 E); the peak is less than 0.5 mile northeast of Second Sugarloaf. Altitude 3082 feet. Named on Foresthill (1949) 7.5' quadrangle. First Sugarloaf and Second Sugarloaf together are called Sugar Loaves on Colfax (1898) 30' quadrangle.

Fir Top Mountain: see **Fir Cap** [SIERRA].

Firtop Peak: see **Fir Cap** [SIERRA].

Fish Camp [MARIPOSA]: *settlement,* 18 miles east of Mariposa along Big Creek (lat. 37°28'40" N, long. 119°38'15" W; sec. 23, T 5 S, R 21 E). Named on Bass Lake (1953) 15' quadrangle. Called Happy Camp on Mariposa (1912) 30' quadrangle. Postal authorities established Fish Camp post office in 1924, discontinued it in 1933, and reestablished it in 1939; the name is from a fish hatchery at the site—the official name of the place is Berry's Fish Camp (Salley, p. 75).

Fish Creek [MADERA]:
(1) *stream,* flows 5 miles to San Joaquin River 8 miles southeast of Shuteye Peak (lat. 37°15'45" N, long. 119°19'30" W; sec. 2, T 8 S, R 24 E). Named on Shuteye Peak (1953) 15' quadrangle.
(2) *stream,* flows 4.5 miles to Kerckhoff Lake 5.25 miles south of the town of North Fork (lat. 37°09'05" N, long. 119°31'10" W; sec. 13, T 9 S, R 22 E). Named on North Fork (1965) 7.5' quadrangle.
(3) *stream,* heads in Fresno County and flows 2.5 miles in Madera County to Middle Fork San Joaquin River 6 miles south-southwest of Devils Postpile (lat. 37°32'40" N, long. 119°07'55" W). Named on Devils Postpile (1953) 15' quadrangle.

Fish Creek [NEVADA]: *stream,* flows 1.5 miles to South Yuba River 2.5 miles west-southwest of Washington (lat. 39°20'40" N, long. 120°50'45" W; near N line sec. 15, T 17 N, R 10 E). Named on Washington (1950) 7.5' quadrangle.

Fish Creek Campground [MADERA]: *locality,* 7.5 miles southeast of Shuteye Peak (lat. 37°15'35" N, long. 119°21'10" W; sec. 4, T 8 S, R 24 E); the place is along Fish Creek (1).

Named on Shuteye Peak (1953) 15' quadrangle.

Fish Creek Mountain [MADERA]: *ridge,* east-trending, 1.5 miles long, 5.5 miles southwest of the town of North Fork (lat. 37°09'50" N, long. 119°34'25" W); the ridge is south of the headwaters of Fish Creek (2). Named on North Fork (1965) 7.5' quadrangle.

Fisher Creek [TUOLUMNE]: *stream,* flows 6.25 miles to Skull Creek 6 miles north-north-west of Crandall Peak (lat. 38°14'15" N, long. 120°11'35" W; sec. 34, T 5 N, R 16 E). Named on Crandall Peak (1979), Liberty Hill (1979), and Strawberry (1979) 7.5' quadrangles.

Fisher Lake [PLACER]: *lake,* 600 feet long, 8.5 miles west-southwest of Donner Pass (lat. 39°17'05" N, long. 120°28'40" W; sec. 2, T 16 N, R 13 E). Named on Soda Springs (1955) 7.5' quadrangle.

Fisher Lakes: see **Lertora Lake** [TUOLUMNE].

Fish Ponds [EL DORADO]: *lakes,* largest 200 feet long, 3.5 miles south of Pyramid Peak at Strawberry (lat. 38°47'50" N, long. 120° 08'30" W; sec. 18, T 11 N, R 17 E). Named on Fallen Leaf Lake (1955) 15' quadrangle.

Fissures: see **The Fissures** [MARIPOSA].

Five Corners [EL DORADO]: *locality,* 3.5 miles south-southwest of Caldor (lat. 38°33'25" N, long. 120°27'20" W; sec. 8, T 8 N, R 14 E). Named on Caldor (1951) 7.5' quadrangle.

Five Lakes [PLACER]: *lakes,* largest 850 feet long, 6 miles west of Tahoe City (lat. 39°10'30" N, long. 120°15' W; sec. 6, T 15 N, R 16 E). Named on Granite Chief (1953) and Tahoe City (1955) 7.5' quadrangles.

Five Lakes Basin [NEVADA]: *relief feature,* 2.5 miles south of English Mountain (lat. 39°24'30" N, long. 120°33'25" W; mainly in sec. 19, T 18 N, R 13 E). Named on English Mountain (1983) 7.5' quadrangle.

Five Lakes Creek [PLACER]: *stream,* flows 10 miles to Rubicon River nearly 3 miles north-east of Bunker Hill (lat. 39°04'50" N, long. 120°20'50" W; near NE cor. sec. 12, T 14 N, R 14 E); the stream heads at Five Lakes. Named on Granite Chief (1953) and Wentworth Springs (1953) 7.5' quadrangles.

Fivemile Creek [TUOLUMNE]: *stream,* flows 6 miles to South Fork Stanislaus River 3.25 miles northeast of Columbia (lat. 38°04' N, long. 120°21'10" W; sec. 32, T 3 N, R 15 E). Named on Columbia SE (1948) 7.5' quadrangle.

Fivemile House [NEVADA]: *locality,* 6 miles south-southwest of North Bloomfield (lat. 39°17'10" N, long. 120°56'40" W; at NW cor. sec. 2, T 16 N, R 9 E). Named on North Bloomfield (1949) 7.5' quadrangle.

Five Mile Terrace [EL DORADO]: *locality,* 2 miles west of Camino (lat. 38°44'15" N, long. 120°42'45" W; sec. 12, T 10 N, R 11 E). Named on Camino (1952) 7.5' quadrangle.

Flagpole Peak [EL DORADO]: *peak,* 2.5 miles north-northwest of Echo Summit (lat.

38°50'45" N, long. 120°03'20" W; sec. 36, T 12 N, R 17 E). Altitude 8363 feet. Named on Echo Lake (1955) 7.5' quadrangle.

Flagpole Point [CALAVERAS]: *peak,* 2.25 miles northwest of Tamarack (lat. 38°27'35" N, long. 120°06'35" W; sec. 16, T 7 N, R 17 E). Altitude 7933 feet. Named on Tamarack (1979) 7.5' quadrangle.

Flagstaff Hill [EL DORADO]: *peak,* 6 miles southwest of the village of Pilot Hill (lat. 38°46'05" N, long. 121°05' W; near NW cor. sec. 33, T 11 N, R 8 E). Altitude 1421 feet. Named on Pilot Hill (1954) 7.5' quadrangle.

Flange Rock: see **East Flange Rock** [TUOL-UMNE].

Flatbort Hill: see **Fattebort Hill** [NEVADA].

Flat Creek [EL DORADO]: *stream,* flows 4.25 miles to Spanish Creek 11 miles south-south-east of Placerville (lat. 38°34'40" N, long. 120°45'20" W; sec. 3, T 8 N, R 11 E). Named on Aukum (1952) and Fiddletown (1949) 7.5' quadrangles.

Flat Lake [MADERA]: *lake,* 650 feet long, 4.5 miles south-southeast of Merced Peak (lat. 37°34'30" N, long. 119°21'40" W). Named on Merced Peak (1953) 15' quadrangle.

Flat Ravine [PLACER]: *canyon,* drained by a stream that flows 1 mile to Deep Canyon 1.5 miles south-southwest of Duncan Peak (lat. 39°07'55" N, long. 120°31'20" W; near E line sec. 21, T 15 N, R 13 E). Named on Duncan Peak (1952) 7.5' quadrangle. Colfax (1898) 30' quadrangle has the name for an inhabited place in the canyon.

Flat Top Mountain [MARIPOSA]: *peak,* 11.5 miles south of the settlement of Catheys Valley (lat. 37°16'15" N, long. 120°06'35" W; near NE cor. sec. 4, T 8 S, R 17 E). Altitude 838 feet. Named on Illinois Hill (1962) 7.5' quadrangle.

Fleetfoot Peak: see **Maggies Peaks** [EL DO-RADO].

Fleming Creek [TUOLUMNE]: *stream,* flows nearly 2 miles to Don Pedro Reservoir 3 miles east of Don Pedro Camp (lat. 37°42'45" N, long. 120°21'20" W; sec. 31, T 2 S, R 15 E). Named on Penon Blanco Peak (1962, photorevised 1973) 7.5' quadrangle.

Fleming Meadow [EL DORADO]: *locality,* 7 miles east-southeast of Camino (lat. 38°42'10" N, long. 120°33'10" W; on W line sec. 21, T 10 N, R 13 E). Named on Sly Park (1952) 7.5' quadrangle.

Fletcher Creek [MARIPOSA]: *stream,* flows 7 miles to Lewis Creek 7.25 miles south of Cathedral Peak (lat. 37°44'40" N, long. 119° 23'30" W). Named on Merced Peak (1953) and Tuolumne Meadows (1956) 15' quadrangles. Lieutenant N.F. McClure named the stream in 1895 for A.G. Fletcher, a state fish commissioner instrumental in having streams in Yosemite National Park stocked with fish (Gudde, 1949, p. 116).

Fletcher Creek [SIERRA]: *stream,* flows 3

miles to Sierra Valley 0.5 mile south-south-west of Calpine (lat. 39°3930" N, long. 120°26'45" W; at W line sec. 20, T 21 N, R 14 E). Named on Calpine (1981) 7.5' quadrangle.

Fletcher Gulch [CALAVERAS]: *canyon,* drained by a stream that flows 1.25 miles to Mokelumne River 2.25 miles north-northwest of Paloma (lat. 38°17'15" N, long. 120°46'50" W; sec. 17, T 5 N, R 11 E). Named on Jackson (1962) 7.5' quadrangle.

Fletcher Lake: see **Upper Fletcher Lake** [MARIPOSA]; **Upper Fletcher Lake**, under **Townsley Lake** [MARIPOSA].

Fletcher Peak [MARIPOSA]: *peak,* 5.5 miles southeast of Cathedral Peak (lat. 37°47'30" N, long. 119°20'10" W). Named on Tuolumne Meadows (1956) 15' quadrangle. The peak first was named for a Mr. Baker, who was a camp cook at Boothe Lake (United States Board on Geographic Names, 1934, p. 9).

Flick Point [PLACER]: *promontory,* 2.5 miles west-southwest of Kings Beach along Lake Tahoe between Carnelian Bay (1) and Agate Bay (lat. 39°13'45" N, long. 120°04' W; at S line sec. 15, T 16 N, R 17 E). Named on Kings Beach (1955) 7.5' quadrangle. The name is for the Flick brothers, William, Joseph, and Nicholas, who settled along Carnelian Bay (Lekisch, p. 44).

Flint: see **Lake Flint** [AMADOR].

Floating Island Lake [EL DORADO]: *lake,* 450 feet long, 1 mile east-southeast of Mount Tallac (lat. 38°54'10" N, long. 120°04'40" W). Named on Emerald Bay (1955) 7.5' quadrangle.

Flonellis [EL DORADO]: *locality,* 1 mile north-east of Latrobe along Southern Pacific Railroad (lat. 38°34'10" N, long. 120°57'45" W; near NW cor. sec. 11, T 8 N, R 9 E). Named on Latrobe (1949) 7.5' quadrangle. California Division of Highways' (1934) map shows a place called Swift located along the railroad just north of Flonellis.

Flood: see **Grass Valley** [NEVADA].

Flora Lake [NEVADA]: *lake,* 950 feet long, 1 mile north of Donner Pass (lat. 39°19'55" N, long. 120°19'30" W; near SW cor. sec. 9, T 17 N, R 15 E). Named on Norden (1955) 7.5' quadrangle. Called Lytton Lake on Truckee (1940) 30' quadrangle.

Flora Lake [TUOLUMNE]: *lake,* 1400 feet long, 14 miles southeast of Pinecrest (lat. 38°03' N, long. 119°48'25" W; near N line sec. 8, T 2 N, R 20 E). Named on Pinecrest (1956) 15' quadrangle. The name is for Flora Coleman of Mannsboro, Virginia, a cousin of R.B. Marshall of United States Geological Survey (Browning, 1986, p. 71).

Flora's: see **Volcanoville** [EL DORADO].

Florence: see **Mount Florence** [MADERA].

Florence Creek [MADERA-MARIPOSA]: *stream,* heads in Madera County and flows 6 miles to Lewis Creek 7 miles south-southeast of Cathedral Peak in Mariposa County (lat. 37°45'20" N, long. 119°21'15" W). Named on Merced Peak (1953) and Tuolumne Meadows (1956) 15' quadrangles. Browning (1986, p. 72) associated the name with Florence Hutchings, for whom Mount Florence was named.

Florence Lake [MADERA]: *lake,* 850 feet long, 8 miles north-northeast of Merced Peak (lat. 37°45' N, long. 119°20'35" W); the lake is along Florence Creek. Named on Merced Peak (1953) and Tuolumne Meadows (1956) 15' quadrangles. Browning (1986, p. 72) associated the name with Florence Hutchings, for whom Mount Florence was named.

Florence Spring: see **Soda Springs** [PLACER].

Floriston [NEVADA]: *village,* 10 miles east-northeast of Truckee on the east side of Truckee River (lat. 39°23'40" N, long. 120°01'15" W; sec. 30, T 18 N, R 18 E). Named on Boca (1955) 7.5' quadrangle. Postal authorities established Floriston post office in 1891 (Salley, p. 76). The name is from the abundant spring flowers at the place (Hanna, p. 107). California Division of Highways' (1934) map shows a place called Wickes located nearly 1 mile south of Floriston along Southern Pacific Railroad (sec. 31, T 18 N, R 18 E).

Flowers Mountain [CALAVERAS]: *ridge,* northwest-trending, 1 mile long, nearly 5 miles south-southwest of Copperopolis (lat. 37° 55' N, long. 120°40'30" W). Named on Copperopolis (1962) 7.5' quadrangle.

Flume Camp [SIERRA]: *locality,* 6 miles southwest of Mount Fillmore (lat. 39°39'45" N, long. 120°55'10" W; sec. 24, T 21 N, R 9 E). Named on La Porte (1951) 7.5' quadrangle.

Flume Creek [SIERRA]: *stream,* flows 2 miles to North Yuba River 2 miles northeast of Sierra City (lat. 39°35'25" N, long. 120°36'35" W; sec. 22, T 20 N, R 12 E). Named on Haypress Valley (1981) and Sierra City (1981) 7.5' quadrangles. The name is from a flume for irrigation water that crosses the stream (United States Board on Geographic Names, 1982, p. 2).

Flyaway Creek: see **Flyaway Gulch** [MARIPOSA].

Flyaway Gulch [MARIPOSA]: *canyon,* drained by a stream that flows 3.5 miles to Lake McClure 9.5 miles northeast of Hornitos near Bagby (lat. 37°36'45" N, long. 120°08'10" W). Named on Coulterville (1947) and Hornitos (1947, photorevised 1973) 7.5' quadrangles. Hoffmann and Gardner's (1863-1867) map has the form "Fly away Gulch" for the name. Laizure's (1928) map shows Flyaway Cr. in the canyon.

Foerster Creek [MADERA]: *stream,* flows 2.5 miles to Triple Peak Fork 4.5 miles northeast of Merced Peak (lat. 37°41' N, long. 119° 20'10" W); the stream heads near Foerster Peak. Named on Merced Peak (1953) 15' quadrangle.

Foerster Peak [MADERA]: *peak,* 7 miles north-east of Merced Peak (lat. 37°41'25" N, long. 119°17'20" W). Altitude 12,058 feet. Named on Merced Peak (1953) 15' quadrangle. Lieutenant N.F. McClure named the peak in 1895 for Sergeant Lewis Foerster (United States Board on Geographic Names, 1934, p. 9). United States Board on Geographic Names (1985a, p. 1) approved the name "Mount Ansel Adams" for a peak, altitude 11,760 feet, located 0.8 mile northeast of Foerster Peak (lat. 37°41'52" N, long. 119°16'49" W); the name honors Ansel Easton Adams, photographer and conservationist.

Folsom [CALAVERAS]: *locality,* nearly 7 miles north of Blue Mountain (lat. 38°26'25" N, long. 120°22'10" W). Named on Big Trees (1891) 30' quadrangle.

Folsom Campground [CALAVERAS]: *locality,* 5.5 miles north-northeast of Blue Mountain (lat. 38°25'10" N, long. 120°14'40" W; sec. 33, T 7 N, R 15 E). Named on Blue Mountain (1956) 15' quadrangle.

Folsom Lake [EL DORADO-PLACER]: *lake,* behind a dam on American River 7 miles westnorthwest of Clarksville in Sacramento County (lat. 38°42'25" N, long. 121°09'25" W; sec. 24, T 10 N, R 7 E), and less than 1 mile downstream from the confluence of North Fork and South Fork; the lake extends from Sacramento County into El Dorado and Placer Counties. Named on Clarksville (1953, photorevised 1980), Folsom (1967), and Pilot Hill (1954, photorevised 1973) 7.5' quadrangles. United States Board on Geographic Names (1960b, p. 8) rejected the name "Folsom Reservoir" for the feature. Arrowsmith's (1860) map shows a place called Negro Hill located less than 1 mile east of the confluence of North Fork and South Fork American River on the ridge north of South Fork; water of Folsom Lake now covers the site. The name "Negro Hill" was from the negro miners at the place in 1849 (Bancroft, 1888, p. 352). Arrowsmith's (1860) map also shows a place called McDowell Hill located on the south side of South Fork American River 2.5 miles northeast of the confluence of North Fork and South Fork—the place also was called McDowellsville (Gudde, 1975, p. 202). The same map shows a mining camp called Condemned Bar situated along North Fork American River 2.5 miles northeast of the confluence of North Fork and South Fork—water of Folsom Lake now covers the site.

Folsom Reservoir: see **Folsom Lake** [EL DORADO-PLACER].

Fontanillis Lake [EL DORADO]: *lake,* 0.5 mile long, 2.25 miles south of Phipps Peak (lat. 38°55'15" N, long. 120°09'05" W). Named on Rockbound Valley (1955) 7.5' quadrangle. The name should have the form "Fontanellis" (Beverly Cola, personal communication, 1985).

Foote Crossing [NEVADA-SIERRA]: *locality,* 4.25 miles northwest of North Bloomfield along Middle Yuba River on Nevada-Sierra county line (lat. 39°25' N, long. 120°57'05" W; near S line sec. 15, T 18 N, R 9 E). Named on Pike (1949) 7.5' quadrangle.

Footman Mountain: see **Footman Ridge** [MADERA].

Footman Ridge [MARIPOSA]: *ridge,* north-northwest-trending, 2.25 miles long, 9 miles south-southwest of El Portal (lat. 37°32'45" N, long. 119°49'20" W). Named on Buckingham Mountain (1947) 7.5' quadrangle. Called Footman Mtn. on Yosemite (1909) 30' quadrangle.

Forbes Campground [PLACER]: *locality,* 5.5 miles south-southeast of Dutch Flat (lat. 39°07'55" N, long. 120°47'10" W; near W line sec. 19, T 15 N, R 11 E); the place is along Forbes Creek. Named on Dutch Flat (1950) 7.5' quadrangle.

Forbes Creek [PLACER]: *stream,* flows 5 miles to North Shirttail Canyon 5.5 miles south-southeast of Dutch Flat (lat. 39°07'50" N, long. 120°47'40" W; sec. 24, T 15 N, R 10 E). Named on Dutch Flat (1950) and Westville (1952) 7.5' quadrangles.

Fordice Reservoir: see **Fordyce Lake** [NEVADA].

Ford Point [PLACER]: *ridge,* west-southwest-trending, 1.25 miles long, 3.5 miles northwest of Duncan Peak (lat. 39°11'05" N, long. 120°34'05" W; sec. 6, T 15 N, R 13 E). Named on Duncan Peak (1952) 7.5' quadrangle.

Ford Ravine [PLACER]: *canyon,* drained by a stream that flows 2 miles to North Fork American River 4.25 miles east-southeast of Dutch Flat near Euchre Bar (lat. 39°11'10" N, long. 120°45'45" W). Named on Colfax (1898) 30' quadrangle.

Fords Bar [EL DORADO]: *locality,* 3.5 miles north-northwest of Georgetown along Middle Fork American River at the mouth of Otter Creek (lat. 38°57'25" N, long. 120°51'20" W; near W line sec. 22, T 13 N, R 10 E). Named on Georgetown (1949) 7.5' quadrangle. Wierzbicki (p. 51-52) called the place Ford's, or Middle Bar.

Fordyce Creek [NEVADA]: *stream,* flows 9.5 miles to Lake Spaulding 2.5 miles north of Yuba Gap (lat. 39°21'05" N, long. 120°37' W; sec. 10, T 17 N, R 12 E); the stream heads at Fordyce Lake. Named on Cisco Grove (1955), English Mountain (1983), and Webber Peak (1981) 7.5' quadrangles.

Fordyce Lake [NEVADA]: *lake,* behind a dam on Fordyce Creek 10 miles west-northwest of Donner Pass (lat. 39°22'50" N, long. 120°29'45" W; sec. 34, T 18 N, R 13 E). Named on Soda Springs (1955) and Webber Peak (1981) 7.5' quadrangles. Officials of South Yuba Canal Company had the dam built that formed the lake in the 1870's, and named the lake for the engineer who began building

flumes and canals in the vicinity in 1853 (Gudde, 1949, p. 118). Called Fordice Res. on Hobson's (1890a) map. Water of the lake covers Fordyce Valley and the site of a mining camp called Atlanta, where Jerome Fordyce lived (Fatout, p. 48-49).

Fordyce Summit [NEVADA]: *pass,* 6.25 miles east-northeast of Yuba Gap (lat. 39°20'35" N, long. 120°30'15" W; near N line sec. 15, T 17 N, R 13 E). Named on Cisco Grove (1955) 7.5' quadrangle.

Fordyce Valley: see **Fordyce Lake** [NEVADA].

Forebay [PLACER]: *locality,* 6.5 miles northwest of Westville along Southern Pacific Railroad (lat. 39°14'10" N, long. 120°44'10" W; on W line sec. 22, T 16 N, R 11 E); the place is 1 mile southeast of Drum Forebay. Named on Westville (1952) 7.5' quadrangle.

Foremans: see **Fourth Crossing** [CALAVERAS].

Forest [SIERRA]: *village,* 1.5 miles north-northwest of Alleghany at the confluence of North Fork and South Fork Oregon Creek (lat. 39°29'25" N, long. 120°51'05" W; on W line sec. 27, T 19 N, R 10 E). Named on Alleghany (1949) 7.5' quadrangle. Postal authorities established Forest City post office in 1854, changed the name to Forest in 1895, and discontinued it in 1947 (Salley, p. 77). The place had a number of names, including: Brownsville, for I.E. Brown, who reportedly built a sawmill there in 1851; Forks of Oregon Creek, after gold was discovered there in 1853; Yomana, an Indian designation of a nearby bluff; Marietta and Elizaville, for Mary Davis, also called Eliza, the first woman at the place; and finally Forest City and Forest, after Mrs. Forest Mooney began contributing articles with the dateline "Forest City" to Marysville newspapers (Hanna, p. 108-109).

Forest: see **Lake Forest** [PLACER].

Foresta [MARIPOSA]: *settlement,* 2.25 miles northeast of El Portal (lat. 37°41'50" N, long. 119°45' W; sec. 3, T 3 S, R 20 E). Named on El Portal (1947) and Yosemite (1956) 15' quadrangles. Yosemite (1909) 30' quadrangle has the name "McCauley" at the place. The name "Foresta" recalls Foresta Land Company that A.B. Davis started in 1913; Davis built a resort at the site, but abandoned it in 1915 (Browning, 1986, p. 72-73). Postal authorities established Opim post office at the place in 1882 and discontinued it in 1884 (Salley, p. 162).

Foresta Falls [MARIPOSA]: *waterfall,* 1.5 miles northeast of El Portal along Crane Creek (lat. 37°41'35" N, long. 119°45'30" W; near W line sec. 10, T 3 S, R 20 E); the feature is 0.5 mile southwest of Foresta. Named on El Portal (1947) 7.5' quadrangle.

Forest City: see **Forest** [SIERRA].

Forest Creek [CALAVERAS]: *stream,* flows 17 miles to Middle Fork Mokelumne River 6 miles south-southwest of Devils Nose (lat.

38°23'05" N, long. 120°28'05" W; sec. 7, T 6 N, R 14 E). Named on Calaveras Dome (1979), Devils Nose (1979), and Garnet Hill (1979) 7.5' quadrangles. Called North Fork of Middle Fork Mokelumne River on Big Trees (1891) 30' quadrangle, but United States Board on Geographic Names (1960a, p. 14) rejected this name for the stream.

Foresthill [PLACER]: *town,* 9 miles southeast of Colfax (lat. 39° 01'10" N, long. 120°49' W; mainly in sec. 35, T 14 N, R 10 E). Named on Foresthill (1949) 7.5' quadrangle. Postal authorities established Forest Hill post office in 1859 and changed the post office name to Foresthill in 1895 (Salley, p. 77). The place had a trading post in 1850 and a hotel called Forest House in 1858 (Hoover, Rensch, and Rensch, p. 274).

Forest Hill Divide [PLACER]: *ridge,* extends generally southwest for 48 miles between North Fork American River and Middle Fork American River from near Granite Chief to the confluence of the two forks; Foresthill is on the ridge. Named on Auburn (1953), Colfax (1949), Duncan Peak (1952), Foresthill (1949), Granite Chief (1953), Greenwood (1949), Michigan Bluff (1952), Royal Gorge (1953), and Westville (1952) 7.5' quadrangles.

Forest Home [AMADOR]: *locality,* 6.25 miles west of Plymouth (lat. 38°27'55" N, long. 120°57'45" W; near W line sec. 14, T 7 N, R 9 E). Named on Sutter Creek (1944) 15' quadrangle. Postal authorities established Forest Home post office in 1862, moved it 4 miles south in 1886, and discontinued it in 1905; the name was from a hostelry (Salley, p. 77). Camp's (1962) map shows a place called Copper Hill located 3.5 miles north-northwest of Forest Home between Cosumnes River and Little Indian Creek.

Forest House: see **Foresthill** [PLACER].

Forest Shades: see **Bath** [PLACER].

Forest Spring [NEVADA]: *locality,* 3.5 miles south of Grass Valley along Wolf Creek (lat. 39°09'55" N, long. 121°03'55" W). Named on Smartsville (1895) 30' quadrangle.

Forgotten Flat [EL DORADO]: *area,* 5.5 miles west-southwest of Kirkwood along Silver Fork American River (lat. 38°41'10" N, long. 120°10'25" W). Named on Tragedy Spring (1979) 7.5' quadrangle.

Forked Meadow [MADERA]: *area,* 5.25 miles northeast of Shuteye Peak (lat. 37°23'35" N, long. 119°20'45" W; sec. 21, T 6 S, R 24 E). Named on Shuteye Peak (1953) 15' quadrangle.

Forks: see **The Forks** [MADERA]; **The Forks**, under **Downieville** [SIERRA].

Forks Campground [MADERA]: *locality,* 5 miles southeast of Yosemite Forks on the west side of Bass Lake (1) (lat. 37°18'45" N, long. 119°34'10" W; near N line sec. 21, T 7 S, R 22 E); the place is near The Forks. Named on Bass Lake (1953) 15' quadrangle.

Forks House [PLACER]: *locality,* nearly 4 miles southwest of Westville on Forest Hill Divide (lat. 39°08'10" N, long. 120°41'55" W; near NE cor. sec. 23, T 15 N, R 11 E). Site named on Westville (1952) 7.5' quadrangle. Postal authorities established Forks House post office in 1860 and discontinued it in 1861; the place was a hotel and stage stop (Salley, p. 77).

Forks House Ravine: see **West Branch**, under **El Dorado Canyon** [PLACER].

Forks of Oregon Creek: see **Forest** [SIERRA].

Forks of the Cosumnes: see **Yeomet**, under **Enterprise** [AMADOR].

Forni [EL DORADO]: *locality,* 3.5 miles northeast of Robbs Peak (lat. 38°57'30" N, long. 120°21' W). Named on Pyramid Peak (1896) 30' quadrangle.

Forks of the Road: see **Altaville** [CALAVERAS].

Forni: see **Lower Forni** [EL DORADO]; **Upper Forni** [EL DORADO].

Forni Creek [EL DORADO]: *stream,* flows 2.5 miles to South Fork American River 4 miles south of Pyramid Peak (lat. 38°47'15" N, long. 120°10'05" W; sec. 24, T 11 N, R 16 E). Named on Pyramid Peak (1955) 7.5' quadrangle.

Forni Lake [EL DORADO]:
(1) *lake,* 800 feet long, 8 miles east-northeast of Robbs Peak (lat. 38°57'20" N, long. 120°15'40" W; sec. 23, T 13 N, R 15 E). Named on Loon Lake (1952, photorevised 1973) 7.5' quadrangle.
(2) *lake,* 1000 feet long, 2.25 miles south of Pyramid Peak (lat. 38° 48'50" N, long. 120°09'50" W; sec. 12, T 11 N, R 16 E); the lake is near Forni Creek. Named on Pyramid Peak (1955) 7.5' quadrangle.

Fornis [EL DORADO]:
(1) *locality,* 1.5 miles southwest of Georgetown (lat. 38°53'30" N, long. 120°51'35" W; near E line sec. 16, T 12 N, R 10 E). Named on Georgetown (1949) 7.5' quadrangle.
(2) *locality,* 13 miles east of Georgetown (lat. 38°53'30" N, long. 120°35' W). Named on Placerville (1893) 30' quadrangle.

Forsyth Peak [TUOLUMNE]: *peak,* 2 miles west-northwest of Tower Peak (lat. 38°09'30" N, long. 119°34'50" W). Altitude 11,180 feet. Named on Tower Peak (1956) 15' quadrangle. The name commemorates Colonel William W. Forsyth, acting superintendent of Yosemite National Park from 1909 until 1912 (United States Board on Geographic Names, 1934, p. 9).

Fort Ann: see **Volcano** [AMADOR].

Fort Grizzly [EL DORADO]: *locality,* 6 miles south-southwest of Caldor near South Fork Cosumnes River (lat. 38°31'25" N, long. 120°28'40" W; near NW cor. sec. 30, T 8 N, R 14 E). Site named on Caldor (1951) 7.5' quadrangle.

Fort Hill: see **Fort Mountain** [CALAVERAS].

Fort Jim: see **Old Fort Jim** [EL DORADO].

Fort John: see **Volcano** [AMADOR].

Fort Monroe [MARIPOSA]: *locality,* 6.5 miles west-southwest of Yosemite (present Yosemite Village) (lat. 37°42'30" N, long. 119° 41'30" W). Named on Yosemite (1909) 30' quadrangle. The place was a stage station of the 1880's named for driver George F. Monroe (Whiting and Whiting, p. 49).

Fort Mountain [CALAVERAS]: *peak,* 6 miles west of Blue Mountain (lat. 38°20'35" N, long. 120°28'20" W; sec. 30, T 6 N, R 14 E). Altitude 3322 feet. Named on Fort Mountain (1979) 7.5' quadrangle. Blue Mountain (1956) 15' quadrangle shows the peak situated 0.5 mile farther south-southeast. Whitney (1865, p. 267), who illustrated the feature, called it Fort Hill.

Fort Trojan: see **Virginiatown** [PLACER].

45 Mile Campground [EL DORADO]: *locality,* 4.25 miles west of Echo Summit along South Fork American River (lat. 38°48'15" N, long. 120°06'30" W; sec. 16, T 11 N, R 17 E). Named on Echo Lake (1955) 7.5' quadrangle.

Fortynine Creek [TUOLUMNE]: *stream,* flows 3 miles to Don Pedro Reservoir 1.5 miles north of Don Pedro Camp (lat. 37°44'25" N, long. 120°24'35" W; sec. 22, T 2 S, R 14 E). Named on La Grange (1962) 7.5' quadrangle.

Fortynine Creek: see **Big Creek** [TUOLUMNE] (2).

Fortynine Gap [MARIPOSA]: *pass,* 7.5 miles south-southwest of Penon Blanco Peak (lat. 37°37'35" N, long. 120°18'25" W; sec. 34, T 3 S, R 15 E). Named on Penon Blanco Peak (1962) 7.5' quadrangle.

Fort Yosemite: see **Yosemite Village** [MARIPOSA].

Fosteria: see **Paloma** [CALAVERAS].

Fortytwo Mile Campground [EL DORADO]: *locality,* nearly 4 miles south of Pyramid Peak along South Fork American River (lat. 38° 47'25" N, long. 120°09'05" W; sec. 19, T 11 N, R 17 E). Named on Pyramid Peak (1955) 7.5' quadrangle.

Forward: see **Camp Forward** [EL DORADO].

Foster: see **Cut Eye Fosters Bar** [SIERRA].

Foster Meadow [EL DORADO]: *area,* 10 miles east of Caldor along Middle Fork Cosumnes River (lat. 38°35'25" N, long. 120°14'55" W; sec. 31, T 9 N, R 16 E). Named on Bear River Reservoir (1979) and Peddler Hill (1951) 7.5' quadrangles.

Foster Mountain [EL DORADO]: *peak,* 4.25 miles north of Chili Bar (lat. 38°49'40" N, long. 120°49'35" W; sec. 2, T 11 N, R 10 E). Altitude 2292 feet. Named on Garden Valley (1949) 7.5' quadrangle. The name commemorates William H. Foster, who bought land in the vicinity in 1854 (Gernes, p. 91).

Fosters: see **Lockwood** [AMADOR].

Foster's Station: see **Lockwood** [AMADOR].

Four Acres [PLACER]: *locality,* nearly 2 miles east-southeast of Foresthill (lat. 39°00'20" N, long. 120°47'15" W; near S line sec. 31, T 14 N, R 11 E). Named on Colfax (1938) 30' quadrangle.

Four Cornered Peak [EL DORADO]: *peak,* nearly 6 miles north of Kyburz (lat. 38°51'30" N, long. 120°17'15" W; sec. 27, T 12 N, R 15 E). Altitude 6858 feet. Named on Kyburz (1952) 7.5' quadrangle.

Four Corners [AMADOR]: *locality,* 4.5 miles west of Plymouth (lat. 38°28'50" N, long. 120°55'50" W; sec. 12, T 7 N, R 9 E). Named on Irish Hill (1962) 7.5' quadrangle.

Four Corners [EL DORADO]: *locality,* nearly 3 miles southwest of Coloma (lat. 38°46'05" N, long. 120°55'25" W; at N line sec. 36, T 11 N, R 9 E). Named on Coloma (1949) 7.5' quadrangle.

Four Corners [MADERA]: *locality,* 15 miles south-southeast of Raymond (lat. 37°00'35" N, long. 119°47'35" W; at S line sec. 33, T 10 S, R 20 E). Named on Little Table Mountain (1962) 7.5' quadrangle.

Four Horse Flat [PLACER]: *area,* 3.25 miles south-southeast of Cisco Grove along Little Granite Creek (lat. 39°15'50" N, long. 120°31'30" W; sec. 7, T 16 N, R 13 E). Named on Cisco Grove (1955) 7.5' quadrangle.

Four Lakes [EL DORADO]: *lakes,* largest 850 feet long, 4 miles northeast of Kirkwood (lat. 38°44'35" N, long. 120°01' W; sec. 4, 5, T 10 N, R 18 E). Named on Caples Lake (1979) 7.5' quadrangle.

Fourmile [MARIPOSA]: *locality,* 2.5 miles south-southeast of Wawona (lat. 37°30'20" N, long. 119°38' W; near W line sec. 12, T 5 S, R 21 E). Named on Yosemite (1909) 30' quadrangle.

4-Q Lakes [EL DORADO]: *lakes,* 3 miles west-northwest of Phipps Peak (lat. 38°56'35" N, long. 120°12'05" W; sec. 27, 28, T 13 N, R 16 E). Named on Rockbound Valley (1955) 7.5' quadrangle.

Fourteen Mile House [EL DORADO]: *locality,* 12 miles east-northeast of Placerville near present Pollock Pines (lat. 38°45'45" N, long. 120°34'40" W). Named on Placerville (1893) 30' quadrangle.

Fourth Crossing [CALAVERAS]: *locality,* 5 miles south-southeast of San Andreas along San Antonio Creek (lat. 38°07'20" N, long. 120°38' W; sec. 10, T 3 N, R 12 E). Named on San Andreas (1962) 7.5' quadrangle. Postal authorities established Fourth Crossing post office in 1855, discontinued it in 1888, reestablished it in 1892, and discontinued it in 1925 (Frickstad, p. 15). Alexander Beritzhoff and David Foreman operated a hotel and ferry at the place; the site was called Foremans—it also was called Fourth Crossing because it was at the fourth river crossing along the road from Stockton to the mines (Gudde, 1975, p. 118, 121).

Fourth of July Canyon [AMADOR]: *canyon,* 2 miles long, 1.5 miles east-northeast of Mokelumne Peak on Amador-Alpine county line (lat. 38°32'40" N, long. 120°04'20" W). Named on

Mokelumne Peak (1979) 7.5' quadrangle.

Fourth of July Flat [EL DORADO]: *area,* 4.25 miles west-northwest of Pyramid Peak (lat. 38°52'15" N, long. 120°13'40" W; near W line sec. 21, T 12 N, R 16 E). Named on Pyramid Peak (1955) 7.5' quadrangle.

Fowler Mountain [MADERA]: *ridge,* southsoutheast-trending, 1 mile long, 6 miles south of the town of North Fork (lat. 37°08'30" N, long. 119°31'40" W; on S line sec. 13, T 9 S, R 22 E). Named on North Fork (1965) 7.5' quadrangle.

Fowler Spring [NEVADA]: *spring,* 6 miles south of North Bloomfield (lat. 39°17' N, long. 120°53'10" W; sec. 5, T 16 N, R 10 E). Named on North Bloomfield (1949) 7.5' quadrangle.

Fox Creek [MARIPOSA]: *stream,* flows 2.25 miles to join Magoon Creek and form Middle Fork Chowchilla River 8 miles east of Mariposa (lat. 37°29'10" N, long. 119°49'10" W; sec. 19, T 5 S, R 20 E). Named on Buckingham Mountain (1947) and Stumpfield Mountain (1947) 7.5' quadrangles.

Fox Gulch [TUOLUMNE]: *canyon,* drained by a stream that flows less than 1 mile to South Fork Stanislaus River 2.5 miles north of Columbia (lat. 38°04'15" N, long. 120°23'50" W; near E line sec. 35, T 3 N, R 14 E). Named on Columbia (1948) 7.5' quadrangle.

Fox Lake [EL DORADO]: *lake,* 800 feet long, 5 miles west-northwest of Phipps Peak (lat. 38°59'35" N, long. 120°13'35" W; sec. 8, T 13 N, R 16 E). Named on Rockbound Valley (1955) 7.5' quadrangle.

Frances: see **Mount Frances**, under **Liberty Cap** [MARIPOSA].

Francis Cow Camp [EL DORADO]: *locality,* 5 miles north-northeast of Robbs Peak (lat. 38°59'25" N, long. 120°22'15" W; sec. 11, T 13 N, R 14 E). Named on Loon Lake (1952) 7.5' quadrangle.

Francis Lake [EL DORADO]: *lake,* 700 feet long, 6 miles north-northeast of Robbs Peak (lat. 38°59'35" N, long. 120°20'20" W; sec. 7, T 13 N, R 15 E). Named on Loon Lake (1952, photorevised 1973) 7.5' quadrangle.

Frank Harris Point [MARIPOSA]: *peak,* 4.5 miles east-southeast of Smith Peak (lat. 37°47'05" N, long. 120°01'20" W; near S line sec. 6, T 2 S, R 18 E). Named on Jawbone Ridge (1947) 7.5' quadrangle.

Frank Young Gulch [TUOLUMNE]: *canyon,* drained by a stream that flows less than 1 mile to Tuolumne River 0.5 mile south-southwest of Don Pedro Camp (lat. 37°42'35" N, long. 120°24'30" W; at NW cor. sec. 2, T 3 S, R 14 E). Named on La Grange (1962) 7.5' quadrangle.

Fraser Flat [TUOLUMNE]: *area,* nearly 4 miles west-southwest of Strawberry along South Fork Stanislaus River (lat. 38°10'10" N, long. 120°04'15" W; sec. 26, T 4 N, R 17 E). Named on Strawberry (1979) 7.5' quadrangle.

Fraser Lakes: see **Emigrant Lake** [TUOLUMNE].

Frata Lake [EL DORADO]: *lake,* 500 feet long, 5.5 miles west-northwest of Echo Summit (lat. 38°50'45" N, long. 120°07'15" W; sec. 32, T 12 N, R 17 E). Named on Echo Lake (1955) 7.5' quadrangle.

Frazier Creek [PLACER-SIERRA]: *stream,* heads at Gold Lake in Sierra County and flows 4.5 miles to Grouse Creek nearly 6 miles southwest of Duncan Peak in Placer County (lat. 39°05'45" N, long. 120°35'05" W; near N line sec. 1, T 14 N, R 12 E). Named on Gold Lake (1981) and Greek Store (1952) 7.5' quadrangles. Logan's (1925) map has the name "Frazier Ravine" for the canyon of the stream.

Frazier Ravine: see **Frazier Creek** [PLACER-SIERRA].

Freds Place [EL DORADO]: *locality,* 6 miles southwest of Pyramid Peak (lat. 38°47'10" N, long. 120°14'10" W; sec. 20. T 11 N, R 16 E). Named on Fallen Leaf Lake (1955) 15' quadrangle.

Freel Meadows [EL DORADO]: *area,* 4 miles southwest of Freel Peak (lat. 38°48'40" N, long. 119°56'50" W; on E line sec. 11, T 11 N, R 18 E). Named on Freel Peak (1955) 7.5' quadrangle.

Freel Peak [EL DORADO]: *peak,* 13 miles east of Pyramid Peak on El Dorado-Alpine county line (lat. 38°51'25" N, long. 119°53'55" W; on W line sec. 31, T 12 N, R 19 E). Altitude 10, 881 feet. Named on Freel Peak (1955) 7.5' quadrangle. The name commemorates James Freel, who lived at the foot of the peak; William Eimbeck of United States Coast Survey gave the name in 1874 to the highest of the peaks then known as Jobs Peaks (Gudde, 1969, p. 114). The feature also was called Sand Mountain because of its sandy summit (Lekisch, p. 48). United States Board on Geographic Names (1991, p. 7) approved the name "Trimmer Peak" for a peak, altitude 9915 feet, located 1.5 miles northwest of Freel Peak (lat. 38°52'18" N, long. 121°55'19" W; sec. 24, T 12 N, R 18 E); the name commemorates Arnold Robert Trimmer, rancher and former owner of the last working farm near Lake Tahoe.

Freeman Meadow [SIERRA]: *area,* 8 miles north of Sierra City along Church Creek (lat. 39°40'30" N, long. 120°36'15" W; near NW cor. sec. 23, T 21 N, R 12 E). Named on Clio (1981) 7.5' quadrangle.

Freemans Bridge: see **Freemans Crossing** [NEVADA].

Freemans Crossing [NEVADA]: *locality,* nearly 2 miles northeast of North San Juan along Middle Yuba River on Nevada-Yuba county line (lat. 39°23'20" N, long. 121°05'05" W; near N line sec. 33, T 18 N, R 8 E). Named on Camptonville (1948) 7.5' quadrangle. Called Freemans Bridge on Smartsville (1895) 30' quadrangle. A ferry at the site in 1850 was called Nyes Crossing; after Thomas Hesse built a bridge there in 1851 the place was called Hesse's Crossing until Thomas Freeman bought the bridge in 1854 (Gudde, 1975, p. 121).

Freezeout: see **Ione** [AMADOR].

Freeze-out Spring [TUOLUMNE]: *spring*, 2.25 miles north-northwest of Don Pedro Camp (lat. 37°44'45" N, long. 120°25'30" W; near W line sec. 22, T 2 S, R 14 E). Named on La Grange (1962) 7.5' quadrangle.

Fremont Peak [MARIPOSA]: *peak*, 2.25 miles east-southeast of the village of Bear Valley on Bullion Mountain (lat. 37°33'35" N, long. 120°04'30" W; sec. 27, T 4 S, R 17 E). Altitude 4199 feet. Named on Bear Valley (1947) 7.5' quadrangle.

Fremont Spring [MARIPOSA]: *spring*, 2.5 miles east of the village of Bear Valley (lat. 37°33'40" N, long. 120°04'20" W; sec. 27, T 4 S, R 17 E); the spring is 1000 feet northeast of Fremont Peak. Named on Bear Valley (1947) 7.5' quadrangle. Sonora (1891) 30' quadrangle has the plural form "Fremont Springs" for the name.

Fremont Valley: see **Jenny Lind** [CALAVERAS].

French Bar [AMADOR]: *locality*, 4.5 miles south-southwest of Jackson along Mokelumne River (lat. 38°17'10" N, long. 120°47'45" W; near W line sec. 17, T 5 N, R 11 E). Named on Jackson (1962) 7.5' quadrangle. Water of Pardee Reservoir now covers the site. The place also was called Frenchmans Bar (Gudde, 1975, p. 122). Camp's (1962) map shows a place called Diamond Bar located 3.25 miles west-southwest of French Bar on the north side of Mokelumne River.

French Bar [NEVADA]: *locality*, 2.5 miles west-northwest of French Corral along Yuba River on Nevada-Yuba county line (lat. 39°19'10" N, long. 121°12'10" W; near W line sec. 21, T 17 N, R 7 E). Named on French Corral (1948) 7.5' quadrangle. Called Frenchmans Bar on Wescoatt's (1861) map, and called French Corral Bar on Logan's (1940) map.

French Camp: see **Jackson Butte** [AMADOR]; **Lancha Plana** [AMADOR].

French Camp [TUOLUMNE]: *locality*, 3.5 miles north-northeast of Columbia (lat. 38°04'40" N, long. 120°22' W; near N line sec. 31, T 3 N, R 15 E). Site named on Columbia SE (1948) 7.5' quadrangle.

French Camp: see **Mariposa** [MARIPOSA].

French Corral [NEVADA]: *village*, 8 miles west-northwest of Nevada City (lat. 39°18'25" N, long. 121°09'40" W; sec. 26, T 17 N, R 7 E). Named on French Corral (1948) 7.5' quadrangle. Postal authorities established French Corral post office in 1859 and discontinued it in 1945 (Frickstad, p. 113). A Frenchman built a corral for his mules at the place in 1849 and a town developed there after the discovery of gold at the site (Hoover, Rensch, and Rensch, p. 256).

French Corral Bar: see **French Bar** [NEVADA].

French Corral Creek [NEVADA]: *stream*, flows 3 miles to South Yuba River 1.5 miles southwest of French Corral (lat. 39°17'40" N, long. 121°10'55" W; sec. 34, T 17 N, R 7 E); the stream goes past French Corral. Named on French Corral (1948) 7.5' quadrangle.

French Creek [CALAVERAS]: *stream*, flows 2.5 miles to Bean Gulch 6 miles east-south-east of Copperopolis (lat. 37°56'45" N, long. 120°32'20" W; near N line sec. 15, T 1 N, R 13 E). Named on Melones Dam (1962) 7.5' quadrangle.

French Creek [EL DORADO]: *stream*, flows 7 miles to Big Canyon Creek 4.25 miles east-northeast of Latrobe (lat. 38°35'10" N, long. 120°54'40" W; near SE cor. sec. 31, T 9 N, R 10 E); the stream goes past Frenchtown. Named on Latrobe (1949) and Shingle Springs (1949) 7.5' quadrangles.

French Creek [NEVADA]: *stream*, flows 1.5 miles to Middle Yuba River 1.5 miles northeast of English Mountain (lat. 39°27'50" N, long. 120°31'55" W; near SE cor. sec. 32, T 19 N, R 13 E). Named on English Mountain (1983) 7.5' quadrangle.

French Creek [SIERRA]: *stream*, heads in Sierra County and flows 2 miles to Willow Creek 1.25 miles north of Camptonville in Yuba County (lat. 39°28'15" N, long. 121°02'45" W; sec. 35, T 19 N, R 8 E). Named on Camptonville (1948) 7.5' quadrangle.

French Creek [TUOLUMNE]: *stream*, flows 1 mile to Silver Gulch 4.5 miles northeast of Columbia (lat. 38°04'45" N, long. 120°20'25" W; near SE cor. sec. 29, T 3 N, R 15 E). Named on Columbia SE (1948) 7.5' quadrangle.

French Creek: see **Frenchtown** [EL DORADO].

French Flat [TUOLUMNE]: *area*, 5 miles west of Sonora (lat. 37°58'25" N, long. 120°28'15" W; near NE cor. sec. 6, T 1 N, R 14 E). Named on Sonora (1948) 7.5' quadrangle.

French Gulch [CALAVERAS]:

(1) *canyon*, drained by a stream that flows 6.25 miles to San Domingo Creek 4 miles northwest of Angels Camp at Dogtown (lat. 38°07'35" N, long. 120°34'20" W; sec. 8, T 3 N, R 13 E). Named on Angels Camp (1962) 7.5' quadrangle.

(2) *canyon*, drained by a stream that flows 2 miles to Coyote Creek nearly 5 miles south of Vallecito (lat. 38°01'05" N, long. 120°29'20" W; near NE cor. sec. 24, T 2 N, R 13 E). Named on Columbia (1948) 7.5' quadrangle.

French Gulch [MADERA]: *canyon*, drained by a stream that flows 1.5 miles to Fresno River 7.25 miles west-southwest of Yosemite Forks (lat. 37°19' N, long. 119°44'45" W; near S line sec. 14, T 7 S, R 20 E). Named on Bass Lake (1953) 15' quadrangle.

French Hill [CALAVERAS]: *peak,* less than 1 mile northeast of Mokelumne Hill (lat. 38°18'25" N, long. 120°41'35" W; sec. 7, T 5 N, R 12 E). Named on Mokelumne Hill (1948) 7.5' quadrangle.

French Hill [EL DORADO]: *peak,* 3 miles north-northwest of Greenwood (lat. 38°56'20" N, long. 120°55'30" W; near N line sec. 36, T 13 N, R 9 E). Altitude 2146 feet. Named on Greenwood (1949) 7.5' quadrangle.

French House [PLACER]: *locality,* 7 miles south of Duncan Peak (lat. 39°03'05" N, long. 120°30'45" W; sec. 22, T 14 N, R 13 E). Site named on Greek Store (1952) 7.5' quadrangle.

French Lake [NEVADA]: *lake,* behind a dam on Canyon Creek nearly 2 miles south-southeast of English Mountain (lat. 39°25' N, long. 120°32' W). Named on English Mountain (1983) 7.5' quadrangle.

Frenchmans Bar: see **French Bar** [AMADOR]; **French Bar** [NEVADA]; **Washngton** [NEVADA].

Frenchman's Ranch: see **Paloma** [CALAVERAS].

French Meadow [CALAVERAS]: *area,* 6 miles east-southeast of Blue Mountain at Dorrington (lat. 38°17'45" N, long. 120°16'25" W; near S line sec. 12, T 5 N, R 15 E). Named on Dorrington (1979) 7.5' quadrangle.

French Meadow [SIERRA]: *area,* 8.5 miles southwest of Sierraville (lat. 39°29'55" N, long. 120°27'45" W; sec. 24, T 19 N, R 13 E). Named on Webber Peak (1981) 7.5' quadrangle.

French Meadows [PLACER]: *valley,* along Middle Fork American River above a point 12 miles west-southwest of Granite Chief (lat. 39°06'45" N, long. 120°28'25" W). Named on Granite Chief (1953) 15' quadrangle. Called French Meadow on Truckee (1940) 30' quadrangle. Water of French Meadows Reservoir now partly covers the place.

French Meadows Reservoir [PLACER]: *lake,* behind a dam on Middle Fork American River 12 miles west-southwest of Granite Chief (lat. 39°06'45" N, long. 120°28'15" W; sec. 36, T 15 N, R 13 E). Named on Bunker Hill (1953, photorevised 1973) and Royal Gorge (1953, photorevised 1973) 7.5' quadrangles.

French Ravine [NEVADA]:
(1) *canyon,* drained by a stream that flows 0.5 mile to Wolf Creek 0.5 mile south-southwest of downtown Grass Valley (lat. 39°12'35" N, long. 121°04'05" W; sec. 34, T 16 N, R 8 E). Named on Grass Valley (1949) 7.5' quadrangle.
(2) *canyon,* drained by a stream that flows 4.5 miles to Wolf Creek 4.5 miles south of Grass Valley (lat. 39°09'15" N, long. 121°04'40" W; sec. 15, T 15 N, R 8 E). Named on Grass Valley (1949) 7.5' quadrangle.

French Ravine [SIERRA]: *canyon,* drained by a stream that flows 1 mile to Kanaka Creek 1.25 miles southwest of Alleghany (lat. 39° 27'30" N, long. 120°51'30" W; sec. 4, T 18 N, R 10 E). Named on Alleghany (1949) 7.5' quadrangle.

Frenchtown [EL DORADO]: *locality,* nearly 2 miles south-southeast of Shingle Springs (lat. 38°38'30" N, long. 120°54'40" W; near NE cor. sec. 18, T 9 N, R 10 E); the site is along French Creek. Named on Shingle Springs (1949) 7.5' quadrangle. The place, which was an early mining camp settled largely by Frenchmen and French Canadians, also had the name "French Creek" (Hoover, Rensch, and Rensch, p. 83).

Fresh Pond [EL DORADO]: *locality,* 3 miles east of Pollock Pines (lat. 38°45'40" N, long. 120°31'45" W; sec. 33, T 11 N, R 13 E). Named on Pollock Pines (1950) 7.5' quadrangle.

Fresh Pond Ravine [EL DORADO]: *canyon,* drained by a stream that flows 1 mile to South Fork American River 3 miles east of Pollock Pines (lat. 38°45'55" N, long. 120°31'45" W; near S line sec. 28, T 11 N, R 13 E); the mouth of the canyon is near French Pond. Named on Pollock Pines (1950) 7.5' quadrangle.

Fresno Crossing [MADERA]: *locality,* 5.5 miles east-northeast of Knowles along Fresno River near the mouth of Spangle Gold Creek (lat. 37°14'15" N, long. 119°46'25" W; sec. 15, T 8 S, R 20 E). Named on Knowles (1962) 7.5' quadrangle. The place was the main crossing of Fresno River in the mining region (Crampton *in* Eccleston, p. 74).

Fresno Dome [MADERA]: *peak,* 8 miles northeast of Yosemite Forks (lat. 37°27'15" N, long. 119°32'10" W; sec. 35, T 5 S, R 22 E). Altitude 7540 feet. Named on Bass Lake (1953) 15' quadrangle. United States Board on Geographic Names (1991, p. 4) rejected the names "Hogans Dome," "Walemo Rock," "Wameloo Rock," and "Wamelo Rock" for the feature.

Fresno Dome Campground [MADERA]: *locality,* 7.5 miles northeast of Yosemite Forks along Big Creek (lat. 37°27'20" N, long. 119°32'50" W; sec. 34, T 5 S, R 22 E); the place is less than 1 mile west of Fresno Dome. Named on Bass Lake (1953) 15' quadrangle.

Fresno Flats [MADERA]: *valley,* 4.5 miles west-southwest of Yosemite Forks along Fresno River (lat. 37°20'15" N, long. 119° 42' W). Named on Bass Lake (1953) 15' quadrangle.

Fresno Flats: see **Oakhurst** [MADERA].

Fresno River [MADERA]: *stream,* formed by the confluence of Lewis Fork and Nelder Creek in Madera County, flows 80 miles to San Joaquin River 4.25 miles east-northeast of Dos Palos Y in Merced County (lat. 37°04'35" N, long. 120°33'30" W). Named on Bass Lake (1953), Chowchilla (1960), Firebaugh (1946), Le Grand (1961), Madera (1946), Mariposa (1947), Raymond (1962), and Santa Rita Park (1962) 15' quadrangles.

South Fork branches southwest from Fresno River 13 miles south of Raymond and flows 5.5 miles before rejoining the main stream 2.5 miles northeast of Madera; it is named on Herndon (1965) and Raymond (1962) 15' quadrangles. United States Board on Geographic Names (1964c, p. 15) rejected the name "North Fork of Fresno River" for present Lewis Fork [MADERA-MARIPOSA].

Frog Creek [TUOLUMNE]: *stream,* flows 16 miles to Lake Eleanor 7 miles north of Mather (lat. 37°59' N, long. 119°50'30" W; sec. 36, T 2 N, R 19 E). Named on Lake Eleanor (1956), Pinecrest (1956), and Tower Peak (1956) 15' quadrangles.

Frog Lake [NEVADA]: *lake,* 1850 feet long, 3.5 miles north of Donner Pass (lat. 39°22'05" N, long. 120°19'20" W; sec. 33, T 18 N, R 15 E). Named on Norden (1955) 7.5' quadrangle.

Frog Lake: see **Lertora Lake** [TUOLUMNE].

Frog Lake Cliff [NEVADA]: *relief feature,* 3.5 miles north of Donner Pass (lat. 39°22'05" N, long. 120°19'35" W; on W line sec. 33, T 18 N, R 15 E); the feature is west of Frog Lake. Named on Norden (1955) 7.5' quadrangle.

Frogtown [CALAVERAS]: *locality,* 2.25 miles south-southeast of Angles Camp (lat. 38°02'50" N, long. 120°31'35" W; near NE cor. sec. 10, T 2 N, R 13 E). Named on San Andreas (1947) 15' quadrangle.

Frost Hill [PLACER]: *peak,* 1 mile southeast of Dutch Flat (lat. 39° 11'45" N, long. 120°49'15" W; near NW cor. sec. 2, T 15 N, R 10 E). Named on Dutch Flat (1950) 7.5' quadrangle.

Frosts [EL DORADO]: *locality,* nearly 3 miles south-southeast of the present town of Meeks Bay (lat. 39°00'05" N, long. 120°06'05" W). Named on Truckee (1895) 30' quadrangle.

Fruit Ridge [EL DORADO]: *ridge,* generally west-trending, 1 mile long, 3 miles west of Camino (lat. 38°44'35" N, long. 120°43'45" W). Named on Camino (1952) 7.5' quadrangle.

Fry Creek [EL DORADO]: *stream,* flows 1.5 miles to South Fork American River 4.25 miles west of Kyburz (lat. 38°46'05" N, long. 120°22'20" W; sec. 26, T 11 N, R 14 E). Named on Kyburz (1952) 7.5' quadrangle.

Frytown: see **Ophir** [PLACER].

Fuchs [CALAVERAS]: *locality,* 5 miles west of Blue Mountain (lat. 38°21' N, long. 120°27'25" W; sec. 29, T 6 N, R 14 E). Named on Blue Mountain (1956) 15' quadrangle.

Fulda: see **Emigrant Gap** [PLACER] (2).

Fulda Creek [PLACER]: *stream,* flows 8 miles to North Fork of North Fork American River 4.5 miles north-northwest of Westville (lat. 39°14' N, long. 120°41'20" W; sec. 24, T 16 N, R 11 E). Named on Blue Canyon (1955) and Westville (1952) 7.5' quadrangles.

Fuller Lake [NEVADA]: *lake,* 0.5 mile long, 3 miles northwest of Yuba Gap (lat. 39°20'55"

N, long. 120°39' W; on S line sec. 8, T 17 N, R 12 E). Named on Blue Canyon (1955) 7.5' quadrangle.

Funk Hill [CALAVERAS]: *peak,* 4 miles east of Copperopolis (lat. 37°58'45" N, long. 120°33'55" W; sec. 32, T 2 N, R 13 E). Named on Melones Dam (1962) 7.5' quadrangle.

Funks Meadow [TUOLUMNE]: *area,* 3.5 miles southeast of Long Barn along Hull Creek (lat. 38°02'50" N, long. 120°05'45" W; sec. 10, T 2 N, R 17 E). Named on Hull Creek (1979) 7.5' quadrangle.

Fuqua Ridge [MARIPOSA]: *ridge,* south-trending, 1.5 miles long, 2.25 miles west-northwest of Coulterville (lat. 37°43'20" N, long. 120°14' W). Named on Coulterville (1947) 7.5' quadrangle.

Furnace Flat [NEVADA]: *area,* 6.5 miles east-northeast of Yuba Gap (lat. 39°21'15" N, long. 120°30'10" W; sec. 10, T 17 N, R 13 E). Named on Cisco Grove (1955) 7.5' quadrangle.

Fyffe [EL DORADO]: *locality,* 10.5 miles east of Placerville (lat. 38° 45' N, long. 120°36'20" W). Named on Placerville (1893) 30' quadrangle. Postal authorities established Fyffe post office in 1882 and discontinued it in 1913; the name is from the operator of a summer resort (Salley, p. 82).

– G –

Gaddis Creek [EL DORADO]: *stream,* flows 2.5 miles to Slab Creek 7.5 miles north-north-west of Pollock Pines (lat. 38°51'40" N, long. 120°38'10" W; sec. 28, T 12 N, R 12 E). Named on Slate Mountain (1950) and Tunnel Hill (1950) 7.5' quadrangles.

Gaddis Spring [EL DORADO]: *spring,* 9 miles north-northwest of Pollock Pines (lat. 38°52'55" N, long. 120°39'20" W; at S line sec. 17, T 12 N, R 12 E); the spring is west of the upper part of Gaddis Creek. Named on Tunnel Hill (1950) 7.5' quadrangle.

Gaggs Camp [MADERA]: *locality,* 2.5 miles west-northwest of Shuteye Peak (lat. 37°21'40" N, long. 119°28' W; sec. 33, T 6 S, R 23 E). Named on Shuteye Peak (1953) 15' quadrangle.

Galbraith: see **Central House** [NEVADA].

Gale Creek [SIERRA]: *stream,* flows 1.5 miles to Oregon Creek 3 miles northeast of Pike (lat. 39°28' N, long. 120°57'15" W; sec. 34, T 19 N, R 9 E). Named on Pike (1949) 7.5' quadrangle.

Gale Lake [MADERA]: *lake,* 300 feet long, 5.25 miles south of Merced Peak (lat. 37°33'40" N, long. 119°22'50" W); the lake is 0.5 mile south-southeast of Gale Peak. Named on Merced Peak (1953) 15' quadrangle. William A. Dill and a group from California Department of Fish and Game named the lake in 1946 for nearby Gale Peak (Browning, 1986, p. 77).

Gale Peak [MADERA]: *peak,* 4.5 miles south of Merced Peak (lat. 37°34'05" N, long. 119°23'10" W). Altitude 10,693 feet. Named on Merced Peak (1953) 15' quadrangle. Lieutenant N.F. McClure named the peak for Captain G.H.G. Gale, acting superintendent of Yosemite National Park in 1894 (United States Board on Geographic Names, 1934, p. 10).

Gales Orchard [SIERRA]: *locality,* 4 miles northeast of Pike (lat. 39°29' N, long. 120°57' W; sec. 27, T 19 N, R 9 E); the place is near the head of Gale Creek. Named on Pike (1949) 7.5' quadrangle.

Gales Ridge [CALAVERAS]: *ridge,* north-northwest-trending, 1.5 miles long, 1.5 miles northwest of Paloma (lat. 38°16'30" N, long. 120°46'50" W). Named on Jackson (1962) 7.5' quadrangle.

Gallison Lake [MARIPOSA]: *lake,* 1100 feet long, 6.5 miles southeast of Cathedral Peak (lat. 37°46'30" N, long. 119°19'40" W). Named on Tuolumne Meadows (1956) 15' quadrangle. Rangers Bingaman and Eastman of Yosemite National Park proposed the name to honor Arthur L. Gallison, a fellow ranger who planted fish in the lake in 1916 (Browning, 1986, p. 77).

Gallup Creek [TUOLUMNE]: *stream,* heads in Tuolumne County and flows 10 miles to Dry Creek nearly 3 miles south-southeast of Cooperstown in Stanislaus County (lat. 37°42'35" N, long. 120°31'05" W; near NE cor. sec. 3, T 3 S, R 13 E). Named on Cooperstown (1968) and La Grange (1962) 7.5' quadrangles. Called Salt Spring Creek on Merced Falls (1944) 15' quadrangle, and on Chinese Camp (1947) 7.5' quadrangle; called Dry Creek on La Grange (1919) 7.5' quadrangle.

Galloway Ridge: see **Old Galloway Ridge** [SIERRA].

Galt Basin [MADERA]: *area,* 7.5 miles southwest of the town of North Fork (lat. 37°08'50" N, long. 119°36'05" W; near W line sec. 17, T 9 S, R 22 E). Named on North Fork (1965) 7.5' quadrangle.

Gambler Creek [EL DORADO]: *stream,* flows nearly 1.5 miles to South Fork American River less than 1 mile north-northwest of Coloma (lat. 38°48'35" N, long. 120°53'45" W; near NE cor. sec. 18, T 11 N, R 10 E). Named on Coloma (1949) 7.5' quadrangle.

Gambler Creek: see **Little Gambler Creek** [EL DORADO].

Ganns [CALAVERAS]: *locality,* 5 miles west-southwest of Tamarack (lat. 38°24'15" N, long. 120°09'30" W; sec. 1, T 6 N, R 16 E). Named on Calaveras Dome (1979) 7.5' quadrangle.

Ganns Creek [MARIPOSA]: *stream,* flows 5.5 miles to Mariposa Reservoir 9.5 miles south-southwest of the settlement of Catheys Valley (lat. 37°18'05" N, long. 120°07'35" W; near N line sec. 29, T 7 S, R 17 E). Named on

Illinois Hill (1962) 7.5' quadrangle.

Garden Bar [PLACER]: *locality,* 11 miles northwest of Auburn along Bear River near the mouth of Alderman Creek (lat. 39°00'40" N, long. 121°13' W); sec. 5, T 13 N, R 7 E). Named on Wolf (1949) 7.5' quadrangle.

Gardeners Point [SIERRA]: *relief feature,* 5.5 miles southwest of Mount Fillmore (lat. 39°40'55" N, long. 120°55'45" W; sec. 13, T 21 N, R 9 E). Named on La Porte (1951) 7.5' quadrangle.

Gardener's Station: see **Gardner** [CALAVERAS].

Garden Valley [EL DORADO]: *settlement,* 6.25 miles north-northwest of Chili Bar (lat. 38°51'15" N, long. 120°51'30" W; around NE cor. sec. 33, T 12 N, R 10 E); the place is along Johntown Creek. Named on Garden Valley (1949) 7.5' quadrangle. Postal authorities established Garden Valley post office in 1852, discontinued it in 1853, reestablished it in 1854, discontinued it in 1862, reestablished it in 1872, discontinued it in 1895, reestablished it in 1896, and moved it 0.5 mile northwest in 1940 (Salley, p. 82). The place first was called Johntown for the sailor who discovered gold there; the name was changed to Garden Valley when raising vegetables became more profitable than mining gold (Hoover, Rensch, and Rensch, p. 88). A mining camp called Sailors Flat because it was founded by a group of sailors was located about 2 miles south and east of Garden Valley; a mining camp called Peru because it was founded by miners from Peru, Indiana, was situated close to Sailors Flat on the south side of Irish Creek near the head of that stream (Gernes, p. 58, 59).

Gardner [CALAVERAS]: *locality,* 5.5 miles east-southeast of Blue Mountain at present Dorrington (lat. 38°18' N, long. 120°16'30" W). Named on Big Trees (1891) 30' quadrangle. Wheeler (1879, p. 178) listed Gardener's Station.

Gardner Meadow [TUOLUMNE]: *area,* 4.25 miles northeast of Liberty Hill (lat. 38°24'40" N, long. 120°02'50" W). Named on Tamarack (1979) 7.5' quadrangle.

Gardner Mountain [EL DORADO]: *relief feature,* 4.5 miles east of Mount Tallac (lat. 38°54'40" N, long. 120°00'50" W; near S line sec. 5, T 12 N, R 18 E). Named on Emerald Bay (1955, photorevised 1969) 7.5' quadrangle.

Gardners [PLACER]: *locality,* less than 1 mile east-southeast of Devil Peak (lat. 38°57'10" N, long. 120°32'10" W). Named on Placerville (1893) 30' quadrangle.

Garnet Hill [CALAVERAS]: *peak,* 11 miles north-northeast of Blue Mountain (lat. 38°28'50" N, long. 120°15'10" W; near N line sec. 7, T 7 N, R 16 E). Altitude 4512 feet. Named on Garnet Hill (1979) 7.5' quadrangle.

Garnet Lake [MADERA]: *lake,* 1.5 miles long,

7.25 miles northwest of Devils Postpile (lat. 37°42'35" N, long. 119°09'30" W); the feature is south of Emerald Lake and Ruby Lake. Named on Devils Postpile (1953) 15' quadrangle. Called Badger Lake on maps of the 1890's, where the name "Garnet Lake" applies to present Shadow Lake (Browning, 1988, p. 48). United States Board on Geographic Names (1976c, p. 4) approved the name "Red Top Mountain" for a peak, altitude 10,532 feet, situated 5 miles southeast of Garnet Lake (lat. 37°38'12" N, long. 119°08'04" W).

Garnet Point [MARIPOSA]: *peak,* 3.5 miles north of the settlement of Catheys Valley (lat. 37°29'15" N, long. 120°06'05" W; on W line sec. 22, T 5 S, R 17 E). Altitude 2013 feet. Named on Catheys Valley (1962) 7.5' quadrangle.

Garrotte: see **Groveland** [TUOLUMNE]; **Second Garrotte** [TUOLUMNE].

Garrotte Creek [TUOLUMNE]: *stream,* flows nearly 3 miles to Pine Mountain Lake 1.5 miles east-northeast of Groveland (lat. 37°50'55" N, long. 120°12' W; near S line sec. 15, T 1 S, R 16 E); the stream goes through Second Garrotte. Named on Groveland (1947, photorevised 1973) 7.5' quadrangle.

Gasburg Creek [TUOLUMNE]: *stream,* heads in Tuolumne County and flows 6 miles to Tuolumne River opposite La Grange in Stanislaus County (lat. 37°40' N, long. 120°27'50" W; near S line sec. 18, T 3 S, R 14 E). Named on La Grange (1962) 7.5' quadrangle.

Gas Canyon [NEVADA]: *canyon,* 1.25 miles long, opens into the canyon of Greenhorn Creek 7.5 miles north-northeast of Chicago Park (lat. 39°14'35" N, long. 120°54'10" W; near NW cor. sec. 19, T 16 N, R 10 E). Named on Chicago Park (1949) and North Bloomfield (1949) 7.5' quadrangles.

Gas Canyon [PLACER]: *canyon,* drained by a stream that flows 3.5 miles to Middle Fork American River 8.5 miles east-northeast of Auburn (lat. 38°57'50" N, long. 120°56' W; at W line sec. 24, T 13 N, R 9 E). Named on Colfax (1949) and Greenwood (1949) 7.5' quadrangles.

Gasoline Alley [PLACER]: *locality,* 2 miles north-northwest of downtown Auburn (lat. 38°55'30" N, long. 121°05' W; sec. 4, T 12 N, R 8 E). Named on Auburn (1953) 7.5' quadrangle.

Gaston [NEVADA]: *locality,* 3.25 miles south of Graniteville (lat. 39°23'40" N, long. 120°44'30" W; sec. 28, T 18 N, R 11 E). Site named on Graniteville (1982) 7.5' quadrangle. Postal authorities established Gaston post office in 1899 and discontinued it in 1913 (Frickstad, p. 113).

Gaston Ridge [NEVADA]: *ridge,* south-south-west-trending, 2 miles long, 3.25 miles south of Graniteville (lat. 39°23'35" N, long. 120°44'25" W); the site of Gaston is on the ridge.

Named on Graniteville (1982) 7.5' quadrangle.

Gate: see **The Gate**, under **Jackson Gate** [AMADOR].

Gates Camp [PLACER]: *locality,* 7.5 miles west-southwest of Granite Chief (lat. 39°08'20" N, long. 120°24'10" W; sec. 22, T 15 N, R 14 E). Named on Truckee (1940) 30' quadrangle. Royal Gorge (1953) 7.5' quadrangle shows Gates cabin at the place.

Gates of the Antipodes [NEVADA-SIERRA]: *narrows,* 3 miles south-southwest of Sierra City along Middle Yuba River on Nevada-Sierra county line (lat. 39°31'35" N, long. 120°39'25" W; sec. 8, T 19 N, R 12 E). Named on Sierra City (1981) 7.5' quadrangle.

Gateway [NEVADA]: *locality,* 1 mile west of downtown Truckee (lat. 39°19'30" N, long. 120°12'10" W; sec. 16, T 17 N, R 16 E). Named on Truckee (1955) 7.5' quadrangle.

Gaylor Lakes [TUOLUMNE]: *lakes,* largest 2000 feet long, just west of Tioga Pass (lat. 37°54'45" N, long. 119°16'10" W). Named on Tuolumne Meadows (1956) 15' quadrangle. The name is for Jack Gaylor, a ranger in Yosemite National Park who died in service in 1921 (United States Board on Geographic Names, 1934, p. 10).

Gaylor Peak [TUOLUMNE]: *peak,* less than 1 mile north-northwest of Tioga Pass on Tuolumne-Mono county line (lat. 37°55'10" N, long. 119°15'50" W; sec. 30, T 1 N, R 25 E); the peak is east of Gaylor Lakes. Altitude 11,004 feet. Named on Tuolumne Meadows (1956) 15' quadrangle. Hubbard used the name "Tioga Hill" either for the peak, or for the ridge where it lies.

Geers Gulch [CALAVERAS]: *canyon,* drained by a stream that flows 0.5 mile to Chili Gulch 4.25 miles northwest of San Andreas (lat. 38°14'35" N, long. 120°43'45" W; sec. 35, T 5 N, R 11 E). Named on San Andreas (1962) 7.5' quadrangle.

Gefo Lake [EL DORADO]: *lake,* 950 feet long, 1 mile east-southeast of Pyramid Peak (lat. 38°50'30" N, long. 120°08'25" W). Named on Pyramid Peak (1955) 7.5' quadrangle. The word "Gefo" was coined from letters in the name "George Foss" (Lekisch, p. 65).

Gelatt [NEVADA]: *settlement,* 2 miles east of Donner Pass at the west end of Donner Lake (lat. 39°19'10" N, long. 120°17'10" W; near SW cor. sec. 14, T 17 N, R 15 E). Named on Truckee (1940) 30' quadrangle. Postal authorities established Gelatt post office in 1923 and discontinued it in 1935; the name was for Ethel M. Gelatt, first postmaster (Salley, p. 83).

Gem Lake [TUOLUMNE]: *lake,* 750 feet long, 11 miles east of Pinecrest (lat. 38°09'45" N, long. 119°47'35" W). Named on Pinecrest (1956) 15' quadrangle. Theodore C. Agnew, an early miner, gave the name "Gem-o'-the-Mountains" to the lake (Browning, 1986, p. 78).

General Creek [EL DORADO]: *stream,* flows 9 mile to Lake Tahoe 1.25 miles north-north-east of the town of Meeks Bay (lat. 39°03'20" N, long. 120°06'45" W; sec. 16, T 14 N, R 17 E); the stream heads 2 miles north-northwest of Phipps Peak. Named on Homewood (1955), Meeks Bay (1955), and Rockbound Valley (1955) 7.5' quadrangle. The name commemorates General William Phipps, for whom Phipps Peak was named (Gudde, 1949, p. 125).

Genevieve: see **Lake Genevieve** [EL DORADO].

Genness [TUOLUMNE]: *locality,* 2 miles north-northeast of Long Barn along Sugarpine Creek (lat. 38°06'50" N, long. 120°07'20" W). Named on Big Trees (1891) 30' quadrangle.

Gent Creek [NEVADA]: *stream,* flows 1.25 miles to Squirrel Creek 5 miles west of Grass Valley (lat. 39°13'10" N, long. 121°09'30" W). Named on Smartsville (1895) 30' quadrangle.

Gentry Gulch [MARIPOSA]: *canyon,* drained by a stream that flows 5 miles to North Fork Merced River 5 miles east-northeast of Buckhorn Peak (lat. 37°41'20" N, long. 120°02'15" W; near W line sec. 7, T 3 S, R 18 E). Named on Buckhorn Peak (1947) 7.5' quadrangle. Called Gentry's Gulch on Hoffmann and Gardner's (1863-1867) map.

George R. Stewart Peak: see **Donner Pass** [NEVADA-PLACER].

Georges Ravine [PLACER]: *canyon,* drained by a stream that flows 1 mile to Auburn Ravine 5 miles west of Auburn (lat. 38°54'05" N, long. 121°10'55" W; sec. 11, T 12 N, R 7 E). Named on Gold Hill (1954) 7.5' quadrangle.

Georgetown [EL DORADO]: *town,* 12.5 miles north of Placerville (lat. 38°54'25" N, long. 120°50'15" W; on W line sec. 11, T 12 N, R 10 E). Named on Georgetown (1949) 7.5' quadrangle. Postal authorities established Georgetown post office in 1851 (Frickstad, p. 26). According to Hoover, Rensch, and Rensch (p. 87), the first mining camp at the place was known as Growlersburg; after this community was destroyed by fire in 1852, the residents rebuilt the town on higher ground and renamed it Georgetown for George Phipps, who had led a company of sailors to the place. Bancroft (1888, p. 482), on the other hand, related the name to George Ehrenhaft, founder of the town. Whitney (1880, p. 85) mentioned a place called Crane's Gulch that was situated between Georgetown and Johntown.

Georgetown Creek [EL DORADO]: *stream,* flows 3.5 miles to Greenwood Creek 0.5 mile south-southeast of Greenwood (lat. 38° 53'20" N, long. 120°54'30" W; sec. 18, T 12 N, R 10 E); the stream heads near Georgetown. Named on Georgetown (1949) and Greenwood (1949) 7.5' quadrangles.

Georgetown Divide [EL DORADO]: *ridge,* generally west-trending, 9 miles long (center near

lat. 38°55'30" N, long. 120°46'45" W); Georgetown is near the west end of the ridge. Named on Georgetown (1949) and Tunnel Hill (1950) 7.5' quadrangles.

Georgetown Junction [EL DORADO]: *locality,* 5 miles southwest of Pyramid Peak (lat. 38°47'10" N, long. 120°12'55" W). Named on Pyramid Peak (1896) 30' quadrangle.

George Washington Hill [NEVADA]: *ridge,* generally south-southwest-trending, 1 mile long, 5.5 miles north-northwest of Pilot Peak (lat. 39°14'30" N, long. 121°13'20" W; on W line sec. 17, T 16 N, R 7 E). Named on Rough and Ready (1949) 7.5' quadrangle.

Georgia Flat: see **Georgia Slide** [EL DORADO].

Georgia Slide [EL DORADO]: *locality,* 1.5 miles north-northwest of Georgetown (lat. 38°55'35" N, long. 120°50'50" W; near N line sec. 3, T 12 N, R 10 E). Named on Georgetown (1949) 7.5' quadrangle. Miners from the State of Georgia started a mining camp called Georgia Flat at the place in 1849; the name was changed to Georgia Slide after a landslide occurred (Hoover, Rensch, and Rensch, p. 88). Gudde (1975, p. 95) listed a place called Devine Gulch that was located between Georgia Slide and Georgetown; the name was for Caleb Devine, who discovered gold at the site in 1850.

Gerle [EL DORADO]: *locality,* 2.25 miles west-northwest of Wentworth Springs (lat. 39°01'30" N, long. 120°22'45" W); the place is at present Gerle Meadow. Named on Truckee (1940) 30' quadrangle. United States Board on Geographic Names (1933, p. 321) rejected the form "Gurley" for the name.

Gerle Creek [EL DORADO]: *stream,* flows 9.5 miles to South Fork Rubicon River 2 miles north of Robbs Peak (lat. 38°57'15" N, long. 120°23'55" W). Named on Bunker Hill (1953), Loon Lake (1952), Robbs Peak (1950), and Wentworth Springs (1953, photorevised 1973) 7.5' quadrangles. United States Board on Geographic Names (1933, p. 321) rejected the form "Gurley Creek" for the name.

Gerle Meadow [EL DORADO]: *area,* 2 miles west of Wentworth Springs (lat. 39°00'50" N, long. 120°22'30" W); the place is along Gerle Creek. Named on Bunker Hill (1953) and Wentworth Springs (1953) 7.5' quadrangles.

German Ridge [CALAVERAS]: *ridge,* south-trending, 0.5 mile long, 2.5 miles north of Angels Camp (lat. 38°06'45" N, long. 120°32'20" W; near W line sec. 15, T 3 N, R 13 E). Named on Angels Camp (1962) 7.5' quadrangle.

Gertrude: see **Ahwahnee** [MADERA].

Gertrude Creek [MADERA]: *stream,* flows 3 miles to Whiskey Creek (2) 8 miles south of Shuteye Peak (lat. 37°14'10" N, long. 119°27'15" W; at W line sec. 15, T 8 S, R 23 E). Named on Shaver Lake (1953) and

Shuteye Peak (1953) 15' quadrangles.

Gertrude Lake [EL DORADO]: *lake,* 700 feet long, 5.5 miles south-southwest of Phipps Peak (lat. 38°53'05" N, long. 120°12' W). Named on Rockbound Valley (1955) 7.5' quadrangle.

Gertrude Lake [MADERA]: *lake,* 800 feet long, 3.5 miles west of Devils Postpile (lat. 37°37'10" N, long. 119°08'45" W). Named on Devils Postpile (1953) 15' quadrangle.

Gertrude Lake [TUOLUMNE]: *lake,* 3200 feet long, 6 miles east-northeast of present Pinecrest along South Fork Stanislaus River (lat. 38°12'55" N, long. 119°54'30" W). Named on Dardanelles (1898, reprinted 1947) 30' quadrangle. Pinecrest (1979) 7.5' quadrangle does not show a lake at the place.

Giant Gap [PLACER]: *narrows,* 3 miles southeast of Dutch Flat on North Fork American River (lat. 39°10'10" N, long. 120°48'15" W; near SW cor. sec. 1, T 15 N, R 10 E). Named on Dutch Flat (1950) 7.5' quadrangle. Called Grants Gap on Whitney's (1873) map.

Giant Gap Gulch [PLACER]: *canyon,* drained by a stream that flows nearly 2 miles to North Fork American River 3.25 miles southeast of Dutch Flat (lat. 39°10'20" N, long. 120°47'40" W; sec. 1, T 15 N, R 10 E); the mouth of the canyon is just upstream from Giant Gap. Named on Dutch Flat (1950) 7.5' quadrangle.

Giant Gap Ridge [PLACER]: *ridge,* north-northwest-trending, 1.25 miles long, 4 miles south-southeast of Dutch Flat (lat. 39°09'10" N, long. 120°48' W); the ridge is south of Giant Gap. Named on Dutch Flat (1950) 7.5' quadrangle.

Giant's Tower: see **El Capitan** [MARIPOSA].

Gibbs: see **Mount Gibbs** [TUOLUMNE].

Gibralter [SIERRA]: *peak,* 4.25 miles east-southeast of Mount Fillmore on Sierra-Plumas county line (lat. 39°42'45" N, long. 120° 46'35" W; near E line sec. 5, T 21 N, R 11 E). Altitude 7343 feet. Named on Mount Fillmore (1951) 7.5' quadrangle. Called Gibralta Pk. on Logan's (1929) map.

Gibson: see **Mount Gibson** [TUOLUMNE].

Gibson Creek [SIERRA]: *stream,* flows 1.5 miles to Slate Creek 3 miles west of Mount Fillmore and less than 0.5 mile south of Gibsonville (lat. 39°44'05" N, long. 120°54'20" W; sec. 30, T 22 N, R 10 E). Named on La Porte (1951) 7.5' quadrangle.

Gibsons New Diggings: see **Gibsonville** [SIERRA].

Gibsonville [SIERRA]: *locality,* 3 miles west-northwest of Mount Fillmore (lat. 39°44'30" N, long. 120°54'25" W; sec. 30, T 22 N, R 10 E). Named on La Porte (1951) 7.5' quadrangle. Postal authorities established Gibsonville post office in 1855, discontinued it for a time in 1869, and discontinued it finally in 1910 (Frickstad, p. 184). The name commemorates a prospector named Gibson, who discovered gold at the site (Hoover,

Rensch, and Rensch, p. 496). The place also was called Gibsons New Diggings (Gudde, 1969 p. 120).

Gibsonville Ridge [SIERRA]: *ridge,* generally southwest-trending, 8.5 miles long, 4.25 miles west of Mount Fillmore on Sierra-Plumas county line (lat. 39°44'30" N, long. 120°55'45" W). Named on Blue Nose Mountain (1951), La Porte (1951), and Onion Valley (1950) 7.5' quadrangles.

Gilberts [EL DORADO]: *locality,* 7.25 miles southwest of Old Iron Mountain (lat. 38°38'10" N, long 120°29'35" W; sec. 13, T 9 N, R 13 E). Named on Stump Spring (1951) 7.5' quadrangle.

Giles Pond [MARIPOSA]: *lake,* 500 feet long, 2.25 miles west-northwest of Santa Cruz Mountain (lat. 37°28'20" N, long. 120°14'20" W; sec. 29, T 5 S. R 16 E). Named on Indian Gulch (1962) 7.5' quadrangle.

Gillett Mountain [TUOLUMNE]: *peak,* 12.5 miles east-southeast of Pinecrest (lat. 38°06'50" N, long. 119°47'35" W). Altitude 8361 feet. Named on Pinecrest (1956) 15' quadrangle. R.B. Marshall of United States Geological Survey named the peak in 1909 for James Norris Gillett, governor of California from 1907 until 1911 (Hanna, p. 120).

Gillis Hill [PLACER]: *ridge,* south-southeast-trending, 3.5 miles long, 3 miles southeast of Colfax (lat. 39°04' N, long. 120°55'25" W). Named on Colfax (1949) 7.5' quadrangle.

Gillman Gulch [TUOLUMNE]: *canyon,* drained by a stream that flows 1.25 miles to Tuolumne River 0.25 mile south of Don Pedro Camp (lat. 37°42'40" N, long. 120°24'20" W; near S line sec. 35, T 2 S, R 14 E). Named on La Grange (1962) 7.5' quadrangle. Called Gilman Gulch on Merced Falls (1962) 15' quadrangle.

Gilman Gulch: see **Gillman Gulch** [TUOLUMNE].

Gilmore Creek [EL DORADO]: *stream,* flows 1.5 miles to Big Canyon Creek 2.5 miles east-southeast of Shingle Springs (lat. 38° 39'25" N, long. 120°52'55" W; at S line sec. 4, T 9 N, R 10 E). Named on Placerville (1949) and Shingle Springs (1949) 7.5' quadrangles.

Gilmore Lake [EL DORADO]: *lake,* 2250 feet long, 1 mile south-southwest of Mount Tallac (lat. 38°53'45" N, long. 120°06'55" W; near SE cor. sec. 8, T 12 N, R 17 E). Named on Emerald Bay (1955) 7.5' quadrangle. The name commemorates Nathan Gilmore, who pastured cattle in the summer on the shore of Fallen Leaf Lake in the 1860's (Patricia Loomis in *San Jose* [California] *Mercury,* October 6, 1980).

Gilmores Glen Alpine Springs: see **Glen Alpine Spring** [EL DORADO].

Gilsons Station: see **Blue Canyon** [PLACER] (2).

Gimasol Ridge [MARIPOSA]: *ridge,* east-trending, 2 miles long, 6 miles southwest of

El Portal (lat. 37°37'35" N, long. 119°52' W). Named on El Portal (1947) 15' quadrangle.

Gin Flat [MARIPOSA]: *area,* 6.25 miles north of El Portal (lat. 37° 45'55" N, long. 119°46'25" W; near N line sec. 16, T 2 S, R 20 E). Named on Lake Eleanor (1956) 15' quadrangle. Paden and Schlichtmann (p. 229) connected the name to a story about a barrel of gin that fell off of a wagon at the place.

Girard Creek [EL DORADO]: *stream,* flows nearly 3 miles to Silver Fork American River 9 miles west of Kirkwood (lat. 38°43'30" N, long. 120°14'10" W; near SW cor. sec. 8, T 10 N, R 16 E). Named on Leek Spring Hill (1951) and Tragedy Spring (1979) 7.5' quadrangles.

Girard Mill [EL DORADO]: *locality,* 12 miles northwest of Leek Spring Hill (lat. 38°44'35" N, long. 120°26'10" W; near SE cor. sec. 5, T 10 N, R 14 E). Site named on Stump Spring (1951) 7.5' quadrangle.

Gitana [CALAVERAS]: *locality,* 2.5 miles northwest of present Tamarack in or near present Jelmini Basin (lat. 38°28'05" N, long. 120°06'30" W). Named on Big Trees (1891) 30' quadrangle.

Givens Creek [MADERA]: *stream,* flows 4.5 miles to South Fork Merced River 7.5 miles south-southwest of Merced Peak (lat. 37° 32'40" N, long. 119°28'20" W). Named on Merced Peak (1953) 15' quadrangle.

Givens Gulch [MARIPOSA]: *canyon,* drained by a stream that flows 1.5 miles to Eldorado Creek 2.5 miles north-northwest of Santa Cruz Mountain (lat. 37°29'25" N, long. 120°13' W; at S line sec. 16, T 5 S, R 16 E). Named on Indian Gulch (1962) 7.5' quadrangle.

Givens Lake [MADERA]: *lake,* 900 feet long, 5.25 miles southwest of Merced Peak (lat. 37°35' N, long. 119°27'55" W); the lake is at the head of a branch of Givens Creek. Named on Merced Peak (1953) 15' quadrangle.

Givens Meadow [MADERA]: *area,* 6 miles southwest of Merced Peak (lat. 37°34'45" N, long. 119°28'20" W); the place is 0.5 mile southwest of Givens Lake along Givens Creek. Named on Merced Peak (1953) 15' quadrangle.

Glacier Brook: see **Snow Creek** [MARIPOSA] (1).

Glacier Lake: see **Johnson Lake** [MADERA].

Glacier Lake [NEVADA]: *lake,* 700 feet long, 3.25 miles south of English Mountain (lat. 39°23'55" N, long. 120°33'25" W; sec. 30, T 18 N, R 13 E). Named on English Mountain (1983) 7.5' quadrangle.

Glacier Monument: see **Fairview Dome** [TUOLUMNE].

Glacier Point [MARIPOSA]: *relief feature,* 1.5 miles south-southeast of Yosemite Village on the south side of Yosemite Valley (lat. 37°43'50" N, long. 119°34'20" W). Named on Yosemite (1956) 15' quadrangle.

Gladys Lake [MADERA]: *lake,* 600 feet long, 4.5 miles north-northwest of Devils Postpile (lat. 37°40'55" N, long. 119°07'05" W). Named on Devils Postpile (1953) 15' quadrangle.

Glasier Lake: see **Johnson Lake** [MADERA].

Gleason: see **Camp Gleason** [SIERRA].

Glen Alpine: see **Glen Alpine Spring** [EL DORADO].

Glen Alpine Creek [EL DORADO]: *stream,* flows 4 miles to Fallen Leaf Lake 2.25 miles southeast of Mount Tallac (lat. 38°52'50" N, long. 120°04'05" W; near S line sec. 14, T 12 N, R 17 E). Named on Echo Lake (1955) and Emerald Bay (1955) 7.5' quadrangles.

Glen Alpine Spring [EL DORADO]: *spring,* 2 miles south of Mount Tallac (lat. 38°52'30" N, long. 120°05'45" W); the spring is near Glen Alpine Creek. Named on Emerald Bay (1955) 7.5' quadrangle. Pyramid Peak (1896) 30' quadrangle has the name "Glen Alpine Springs" for buildings at the site. Nathan Gilmore discovered the spring in the 1850's and established a resort at the place (Hanna, p. 121). The resort also was known as Gilmores Glen Alpine Springs (Waring, G.A., p. 236). Gilmore's wife chose the name "Glen Alpine" from Walter Scott's romantic poem *Lady of the Lake* (Lekisch, p. 51). Postal authorities established Glen Alpine post office in 1904, discontinued it in 1918, reestablished it in 1929, and discontinued it in 1947 (Frickstad, p. 26).

Glen Aulin [TUOLUMNE]: *valley,* 9 miles west of Tioga Pass along Tuolumne River (lat. 37°54'45" N, long. 119°25'35" W). Named on Tuolumne Meadows (1956) 15' quadrangle. R.B. Marshall of United States Geological Survey named the place in 1913 or 1914 at the suggestion of James McCormick, who later was secretary of United States Geographic Board; the name is from *gleann alainn,* which means "beautiful valley" or "beautiful glen" in Gaelic (United States Board on Geographic Names, 1934, p. 10).

Glen Aulin High Sierra Camp [TUOLUMNE]: *locality,* 9 miles west of Tioga Pass (lat. 37°54'35" N, long. 119°25'05" W); the camp is at Glen Aulin. Named on Tuolumne Meadows (1956) 15' quadrangle.

Glencoe [CALAVERAS]: *village,* 4 miles west of Rail Road Flat near the head of Mosquito Gulch (lat. 38°21'15" N, long. 120°35' W; near S line sec. 19, T 6 N, R 13 E). Named on Rail Road Flat (1948) 7.5 quadrangle. The place formerly was called Mosquito Gulch (California Department of Parks and Recreation, p. 15). Postal authorities established Mosquito post office in 1858, discontinued it in 1869, and reestablished it in 1873 with the name "Musquito Gulch"; they changed the name to Glencoe in 1878, discontinued it in 1916, and reestablished it in 1947 (Salley, p. 85, 149). L.P. Terwilliger, a pioneer of Calaveras

County, applied the name "Glencoe" to the place (Hanna, p. 121).

Glenbrook [NEVADA]: *settlement*, 2 miles northeast of Grass Valley (lat. 39°14'30" N, long. 121°02'15" W; around northeast cor. sec. 23, T 16 N, R 8 E). Named on Grass Valley (1949) 7.5' quadrangle.

Globe Rock [MADERA]: *peak*, 9.5 miles north of Shuteye Peak (lat. 37°29'10" N, long. 119°24'45" W; sec. 23, T 5 S, R 23 E). Altitude 7152 feet. Named on Shuteye Peak (1953) 15' quadrangle.

Gnat Creek: see **Daulton Creek** [MADERA].

Goat Hill [AMADOR]: *peak*, 3.5 miles south of Jackson (lat. 38°17'40" N, long. 120°46'45" W; at SE cor. sec. 8, T 5 N, R 11 E). Altitude 1516 feet. Named on Jackson (1962) 7.5' quadrangle.

Goat Mountain [MADERA]: *ridge*, south- to southeast-trending, 3 miles long, 7 miles southeast of Yosemite Forks (lat. 37°17' N, long. 119°33'35" W). Named on Bass Lake (1953) 15' quadrangle.

Goat Rock [NEVADA]: *peak*, 1.5 miles west of Chicago Park (lat. 39°08'35" N, long. 120°59'35" W; near N line sec. 20, T 15 N, R 9 E). Named on Chicago Park (1949) 7.5' quadrangle.

Goat Spring [PLACER]: *spring*, 4.5 miles southwest of Westville (lat. 39°07'40" N, long. 120°42'35" W; sec. 23, T 15 N, R 11 E). Named on Westville (1952) 7.5' quadrangle.

Goday Gulch: see **Carson** [MARIPOSA].

Goddard's Station: see **Al Tahoe** [EL DORADO].

Godfrey: see **Confidence** [TUOLUMNE].

Goff [MARIPOSA]: *locality*, 10.5 miles southsouthwest of Coulterville along Yosemite Valley Railroad (lat. 37°34'40" N, long. 120° 17'30" W). Named on Sonora (1897) 30' quadrangle.

Goffinet Reservoir [AMADOR]: *lake*, 1800 feet long, behind a dam on Jackass Creek 3.25 miles east-northeast of Ione (lat. 38°22'40" N, long. 120°52'55" W; sec. 16, T 6 N, R 10 E). Named on Irish Hill (1962) 7.5' quadrangle.

Goffs Ravine [SIERRA]: *canyon*, drained by a stream that flows 2 miles to Downie River 2.25 miles north of Downieville (lat. 39° 35'35" N, long. 120°49'35" W; near S line sec. 14, T 20 N, R 10 E). Named on Downieville (1951) 7.5' quadrangle.

Goggins [PLACER]: *locality*, 8 miles south of Duncan Peak (lat. 39° 02'30" N, long. 120°30'30" W; near S line sec. 22, T 14 N, R 13 E). Named on Colfax (1938) 30' quadrangle. Greek Store (1952) 7.5' quadrangle shows Goggins mine at the place.

Golconda Ravine [NEVADA]: *canyon*, drained by a stream that flows less than 1 mile to Middle Yuba River nearly 7 miles northeast of North Bloomfield (lat. 39°26'10" N, long. 120°48'30" W; sec. 12, T 18 N, R 10 E). Named on Alleghany (1949) 7.5' quadrangle.

Gold: see **Fine Gold** [MADERA].

Gold Canyon [NEVADA-SIERRA]: *canyon*, 2.5 miles southeast of Alleghany along Middle Yuba River on Nevada-Sierra county line (lat. 39°26'15" N, long. 120°48'40" W; sec. 11, 12, T 18 N, R 10 E). Named on Alleghany (1949) 7.5' quadrangle.

Gold Canyon [SIERRA]: *canyon*, drained by a stream that flows 1 mile to Canyon Creek 2.25 miles south-southeast of Mount Fillmore (lat. 39°41'50" N, long. 120°50'20" W). Named on Mount Fillmore (1951) 7.5' quadrangle

Gold Canyon: see **Potosi Creek** [SIERRA].

Golden: see **Soapweed** [EL DORADO].

Golden Gate Butte: see **Golden Gate Hill** [CALAVERAS].

Golden Gate Creek [AMADOR]: *stream*, flows 4.5 miles to Sutter Creek (1) 4.5 miles northeast of Pine Grove (lat. 38°27'50" N, long. 120°36'15" W; sec. 13, T 7 N, R 12 E). Named on West Point (1948) 7.5' quadrangle.

Golden Gate Hill [CALAVERAS]: *peak*, 5 miles northwest of San Andreas (lat. 38°14'55" N, long. 120°44'35" W; near E line sec. 34, T 5 N, T 11 E). Altitude 2064 feet. Named on San Andreas (1962) 7.5' quadrangle. The feature also was known as Golden Gate Butte (Gudde, 1975, p. 133).

Gold Flat [NEVADA]: *locality*, 2.5 miles northeast of Grass Valley (lat. 39°14'45" N, long. 121°01'30" W; sec. 13, T 16 N, R 8 E). Named on Grass Valley (1949) 7.5' quadrangle.

Goldgulch: see **Coarsegold** [MADERA].

Gold Hill [EL DORADO]: *settlement*, 2.5 miles south of Coloma (lat. 38°45'45" N, long. 120°53' W; sec. 32, T 11 N, R 10 E). Named on Coloma (1949) 7.5' quadrangle. Called Granite Hill on Placerville (1893) 30' quadrangle. Postal authorities established Granite Hill post office in 1874 and discontinued it in 1908 (Frickstad, p. 27).

Gold Hill [NEVADA]: *peak*, 0.5 mile southwest of downtown Grass Valley (lat. 39°12'45" N, long. 121°04'10" W; near NW cor. sec. 34, T 16 N, R 8 E). Named on Grass Valley (1949) 7.5' quadrangle.

Gold Hill [PLACER]: *locality*, 6 miles west of Auburn along Auburn Ravine (lat. 38°54'10" N, long. 121°10'50" W; sec. 10, T 12 N, R 7 E). Named on Gold Hill (1954) 7.5' quadrangle. Gudde (1975, p. 135) noted that the place was called Orr City in 1855. Gudde (1975, p. 230, 237) also mentioned a mining place called Mugginsville, located 0.5 mile below Gold Hill, and a mining place called Nesbits Bar, situated in Auburn Ravine near Gold Hill.

Gold Hill: see **Washington** [NEVADA].

Gold Lake [SIERRA]: *lake*, 8500 feet long, 8 miles north of Sierra City (lat. 39°40'45" N, long. 120°39'15" W). Named on Gold Lake (1981) 7.5' quadrangle. The name is from the false report that gold was found at the lake in 1850 (Hanna, p. 123).

Gold Lake: see **Little Gold Lake** [SIERRA].
Gold Note Ridge [EL DORADO]: *ridge,* generally west-trending, 9 miles long, center 3.5 miles south-southwest of Caldor (lat. 38°33'45" N, long. 120°28'05" W). Named on Caldor (1951) and Omo Ranch (1952) 7.5' quadrangles.
Gold Point Ravine [SIERRA]: *canyon,* drained by a stream that flows 1.25 miles to North Yuba River 5.5 miles west of Sierra City (lat. 39°34'10" N, long. 120°44'15" W; near SE cor. sec. 28, T 20 N, R 11 E). Named on Sierra City (1981) 7.5' quadrangle, which shows Gold Point mine in the canyon.
Gold Run [NEVADA]: *stream,* flows 2 miles to Deer Creek in downtown Nevada City (lat. 39°15'40" N, long. 121°01'05" W; near W line sec. 7, T 16 N, R 9 E). Named on Grass Valley (1949) and Nevada City (1948) 7.5' quadrangles.
Gold Run [PLACER]: *village,* 2 miles south-southwest of Dutch Flat (lat. 39°10'55" N, long. 120°51'15" W; sec. 4, T 15 N, R 10 E). Named on Dutch Flat (1950) 7.5' quadrangle. Postal authorities established Mountain Springs post office in 1854; they moved it 1 mile north and changed the name to Gold Run in 1863—the name "Mountain Springs" was from Mountain Springs Hotel (Salley, p. 147). Whitney's (1873) map shows a mining camp called Indiana Hill located about 1 mile south of Gold Run, and a relief feature of the same name located less than 1 mile farther east-southeast.
Gold Run [SIERRA]: *stream,* heads in Sierra County and flows 4 miles to Slate Creek 5.5 miles northeast of Strawberry Valley in Yuba County (lat. 39°36'55" N, long. 121°01'50" W; near S line sec. 1, T 20 N, R 8 E). Named on Goodyears Bar (1951) and Strawberry Valley (1948) 7.5' quadrangles. Called Gold Run Cr. on La Porte (1951) 7.5' quadrangle.
Gold Run Creek: see **Gold Run** [SIERRA].
Gold Spring [TUOLUMNE]: *spring,* 1 mile north-northwest of Columbia (lat. 38°02'50" N, long. 120°24'35" W; sec. 11, T 2 N, R 14 E). Named on Columbia (1948) 7.5' quadrangle. Big Trees (1891) 30' quadrangle shows a locality called Gold Spring at the site. Charles M. Radcliff, justice of the peace for the mining camp at the spring, gave the name "Gold Spring" to the camp after watching an old man and his two sons mining there (Stoddart, p. 129). A place called Texas Flat was situated just south of Gold Spring (Gudde, 1975, p. 347).
Gold Spring Hill: see **Cold Spring Hill** [PLACER].
Gold Valley [SIERRA]: *valley,* 7.5 miles north-northwest of Sierra City along Pauley Creek (lat. 39°39' N, long. 120°42'35" W). Named on Gold Lake (1981) 7.5' quadrangle.
Gonelson Canyon [NEVADA]: *canyon,* drained by a stream that flows 1 mile to Lake Spaulding 1.25 miles north of Yuba Gap (lat. 39°20'05" N, long. 120°37' W; sec. 15, T 17 N, R 12 E). Named on Cisco Grove (1955) 7.5' quadrangle.
Good Gulch [MARIPOSA]: *canyon,* drained by a stream that flows 3 miles to Merced River 7 miles east-northeast of the village of Bear Valley (lat. 37°36'30" N, long. 120°00'10" W; near S line sec. 5, T 4 S, R 18 E). Named on Bear Valley (1947) and Feliciana Mountain (1947) 7.5' quadrangles. Called Goods Gulch on Kinsley (1947) 7.5' quadrangle.
Goodmans Corner [CALAVERAS]: *locality,* 5.5 miles east of Clements on San Joaquin-Calaveras county line (lat. 38°12'15" N, long. 120°59'10" W; sec. 16, T 4 N, R 9 E). Named on Wallace (1962) 7.5' quadrangle.
Goods Gulch: see **Good Gulch** [MARIPOSA].
Goodwin's: see **Yosemite Junction** [TUOLUMNE].
Goodyears Bar [SIERRA]: *village,* 3.25 miles west-southwest of Downieville along North Yuba River (lat. 39°32'25" N, long. 120° 53' W; sec. 5, T 19 N, R 10 E). Named on Goodyears Bar (1951) 7.5' quadrangle. Postal authorities established Goodyears Bar post office in 1851 and discontinued it briefly in 1888 (Frickstad, p. 184). The place first was called Slaughter's Bar, but in 1851 it took the name of the river bar opposite the community, where Miles Goodyear and Andrew Goodyear found gold in 1849 (Gudde, 1949, p. 131). Borthwick (p. 252) used the form "Goodyear's Bar" for the name. A mining place called Texas Bar was located 0.25 mile below Goodyears Bar opposite Hoodoo Bar (Gudde, 1975, p. 347), and a place called Rantedodler Bar was situated 0.5 mile below Goodyears Bar (Gudde, 1975, p 284). The name "Rantedodler Bar" also had the forms "Ranty Doddler Bar" (Bancroft, 1888, p. 361) and "Ranse Doddler Bar" (Hoover, Rensch, and Rensch, p. 491).
Goodyears Creek [SIERRA]: *stream,* flows nearly 7 miles to North Yuba River 0.25 mile west of Goodyears Bar (lat. 39°32'25" N, long. 120°53'15" W; sec. 5, T 19 N, R 10 E). Named on Downieville (1951) and Goodyears Bar (1951) 7.5' quadrangles.
Gooseberry Creek [TUOLUMNE]: *stream,* flows less than 1 mile to North Fork Tuolumne River 1.5 miles east of Pinecrest (lat. 38°11'20" N, long. 119°58'05" W; sec. 23, T 4 N, R 18 E). Named on Pinecrest (1979) 7.5' quadrangle.
Gooseberry Flat [MADERA]: *area,* 3.25 miles northeast of Yosemite Forks along Nelder Creek (lat. 37°24'20" N, long. 119°35'35" W; near SW cor. sec. 17, T 6 S, R 22 E). Named on Bass Lake (1953) 15' quadrangle.
Gooseberry Spring [CALAVERAS]: *spring,* 7 miles west-southwest of Angels Camp (lat. 38°01'35" N, long. 120°39'15" W; sec. 16, T 2 N, R 12 E). Named on Salt Spring Valley (1962) 7.5' quadrangle.

Goose Flat [EL DORADO]: *locality,* 4.25 miles west-southwest of the village of Pilot Hill (lat. 38°48'40" N, long. 120°05'35" W; on N line sec. 16, T 11 N, R 8 E). Site named on Pilot Hill (1954) 7.5' quadrangle. Called Wild Goose Flat on Arrowsmith's (1860) map.

Goose Lake [SIERRA]: *lake,* 2300 feet long, 7.5 miles north of Sierra City (lat. 39°40'25" N, long. 120°38'10" W; at N line sec. 21, T 21 N, R 12 E). Named on Gold Lake (1981) 7.5' quadrangle.

Gooseneck Flat [PLACER]: *area,* 6.5 miles west of Martis Peak (lat. 39°17'40" N, long. 120°09'20" W; sec. 25, T 17 N, R 16 E). Named on Truckee (1955) 7.5' quadrangle.

Gopher Gulch [AMADOR]: *canyon,* 1.5 miles long, opens into the canyon of Sutter Creek (1) 6.5 miles south-southeast of Plymouth at the town of Sutter Creek (lat. 38°23'40" N, long. 120°48' W). Named on Amador City (1962) 7.5' quadrangle.

Gopher Hill [EL DORADO]: *peak,* 3 miles north of Chili Bar (lat. 38° 48'35" N, long. 120°49'35" W; near S line sec. 11, T 11 N, R 10 E). Named on Garden Valley (1949) 7.5' quadrangle.

Gopher Hill: see **Blue Tent** [NEVADA]; **Nevada City** [NEVADA].

Gopher Hills: see **Gopher Ridge** [CALAVERAS].

Gopher Ridge [CALAVERAS]: *range,* extends south-southeast from Calaveras River to Littlejohns Creek. Named on Copperopolis (1962), Jenny Lind (1962), Salt Spring Valley (1962), and Valley Springs (1962) 7.5' quadrangles. Whitney (1865, p. 255) used the name "Gopher Hills" for the feature.

Gordon Creek [MADERA]: *stream,* flows 1.5 miles to Rock Creek 2.5 miles south-southeast of Shuteye Peak (lat. 37°19'05" N, long. 119°24'20" W; sec. 13, T 7 S, R 23 E); the stream heads at Gordon Meadow. Named on Shuteye Peak (1953) 15' quadrangle.

Gordon Meadow [MADERA]: *area,* 2.5 miles south of Shuteye Peak (lat. 37°18'45" N, long. 119°25'45" W; on S line sec. 14, T 7 S, R 23 E); the place is at the head of Gordon Creek. Named on Shuteye Peak (1953) 15' quadrangle.

Gorge: see **Towle** [PLACER].

Gothic Peak: see **Mount Clark** [MARIPOSA].

Gouge Eye: see **Hunts Hill** [NEVADA].

Gourley Reservoir [CALAVERAS]: *lake,* 650 feet long, 4 miles northwest of San Andreas (lat. 38°14'15" N, long. 120°44'10" W; on S line sec. 35, T 5 N, R 11 E). Named on San Andreas (1962) 7.5' quadrangle.

Government Meadow [EL DORADO]: *area,* 4.25 miles west of Kirkwood (lat. 38°42'35" N, long. 120°09'05" W; near SE cor. sec. 13, T 10 N, R 16 E). Named on Tragedy Spring (1979) 7.5' quadrangle.

Government Ridge [EL DORADO]: *ridge,* south- to south-southwest-trending, 2.5 miles long, 6.5 miles north-northwest of Riverton (lat. 38°51'30" N, long. 120°29'25" W). Named on Pollock Pines (1950) and Riverton (1950) 7.5' quadrangles.

Government Spring [PLACER]: *spring,* 2.5 miles north of Westville (lat. 39°12'50" N, long. 120°38'10" W; near N line sec. 33, T 16 N, R 12 E). Named on Westville (1952) 7.5' quadrangle. Called Manimoth Spring on Colfax (1938) 30' quadrangle.

Grace Meadow [TUOLUMNE]: *area,* 3.5 miles west of Tower Peak along Falls Creek (lat. 38°08'20" N, long. 119°36'50" W). Named on Tower Peak (1956) 15' quadrangle. The name commemorates Grace Sovulewski, whose father Gabriel Sovulewski was in government service at Yosemite National Park (United States Board on Geographic Names, 1934, p. 10).

Graham Meadow [MADERA]: *area,* 7.5 miles east-southeast of Yosemite Forks (lat. 37°18'45" N, long. 119°30'45" W; on N line sec. 24, T 7 S, R 22 E). Named on Bass Lake (1953) 15' quadrangle.

Graham Mountain [MADERA]: *ridge,* northwest-trending, 1 mile long, 6.25 miles east of Yosemite Forks (lat. 37°21'30" N, long. 119°30'55" W; on S line sec. 36, T 6 S, R 22 E). Named on Bass Lake (1953) 15' quadrangle.

Grand Canyon of the Tuolumne River [TUOLUMNE]: *canyon,* 18 miles long, along Tuolumne River above a point 6 miles northeast of Mather (lat. 37°56'50" N, long. 119°47'15" W). Named on Hetch Hetchy Reservoir (1956) 15' quadrangle. Called Grand Canyon of the Tuolumne on Yosemite (1909) 30' quadrangle.

Grand Mountain [TUOLUMNE]: *peak,* nearly 8 miles east-northeast of White Wolf (lat. 37°54'45" N, long. 119°31'05" W). Altitude 9491 feet. Named on Hetch Hetchy Reservoir (1956) 15' quadrangle. John Muir reportedly gave the name "Grand Mountain" to the peak, which Theodore S. Solomons called Tuolumne Castle (Browning, 1986, p. 85).

Grand Point [EL DORADO]: *ridge,* west-southwest-trending, 1.5 miles long, 5.5 miles southsoutheast of Camino (lat. 38°39'35" N, long. 120°39' W). Named on Camino (1952) 7.5' quadrangle.

Granite Bay [PLACER]: *embayment,* 6 miles east-southeast of Rocklin along Folsom Lake (lat. 38°45'15" N, long. 121°08'15" W). Named on Folsom (1967) and Rocklin (1967) 7.5' quadrangles.

Granite Canyon [EL DORADO]: *canyon,* 2 miles long, opens into the canyon of South Fork American River 1.25 miles west of Coloma (lat. 38°48' N, long. 120°54'45" W; near W line sec. 18, T 11 N, R 10 E). Named on Coloma (1949) 7.5' quadrangle.

Granite Canyon: see **Big Granite Creek** [PLACER]; **Little Granite Canyon**, under **Little Granite Creek** [PLACER].

Granite Chief [PLACER]: *peak,* 8.5 miles

south-southeast of Donner Pass (lat. 39°11'55" N, long. 120°17'10" W; sec. 35, T 16 N, R 15 E). Altitude 9006 feet. Named on Granite Chief (1953) 7.5' quadrangle. United States Board on Geographic Names (1992, p. 4) approved the name "Billys Peak" for a feature, altitude 8617 feet, located 2.8 miles north of Granite Chief (lat. 39°14'15" N, long, 120°16'23" W; sec. 14, T 16 N, R 15 E); the name is for William Albert Dutton, a deceased member of Tahoe Nordic Search and Rescue Team.

Granite Creek [EL DORADO]: *stream,* flows 2.5 miles to Granite Canyon nearly 2 miles southwest of Coloma (lat. 38°47'05" N, long. 120°54'55" W; near SE cor. sec. 24, T 11 N, R 9 E). Named on Coloma (1949) 7.5' quadrangle.

Granite Creek [MADERA]: *stream,* formed by the confluence of East Fork and West Fork, flows 6.5 miles to San Joaquin River 13 miles northeast of Shuteye Peak (lat. 37°28'35" N, long. 119° 14' W; near E line sec. 21, T 5 S, R 25 E). Named on Devils Postpile (1953), Kaiser Peak (1953), and Merced Peak (1953) 15' quadrangles. East Fork is 10 miles long and West Fork is 9.5 miles long; both forks are named on Merced Peak (1953) 15' quadrangle.

Granite Creek [MARIPOSA]: *stream,* flows 3 miles to South Fork Merced River 5 miles south-southeast of El Portal (lat. 37°36'10" N, long. 119°45'25" W). Named on Buckingham Mountain (1947) 7.5' quadrangle.

Granite Creek [NEVADA]: *stream,* flows 4.5 miles to Fordyce Creek 3.5 miles north-northeast of Yuba Gap (lat. 39°21'45" N, long. 120°35'20" W; near SE cor. sec. 2, T 17 N, R 12 E). Named on Cisco Grove (1955) and English Mountain (1983) 7.5' quadrangles.

Granite Creek [TUOLUMNE]: *stream,* flows 3.5 miles to Cherry Creek 6.25 miles west of Mather (lat. 37°53'45" N, long. 119°58' W; sec. 35, T 1 N, R 18 E). Named on Lake Eleanor (1956) 15' quadrangle.

Granite Creek: see **Big Granite Creek** [PLACER]; **Little Granite Creek** [PLACER].

Granite Creek Campground [MADERA]: *locality,* 9.5 miles southeast of Merced Peak near the confluence of East Fork Granite Creek and West Fork Granite Creek (lat. 37°32'30" N, long. 119° 16' W). Named on Merced Peak (1953) 15' quadrangle.

Granite Creek Saddle [MARIPOSA]: *pass,* 8 miles south of El Portal (lat. 37°33'25" N, long. 119°45'45" W); the pass is at the head of Granite Creek. Named on Buckingham Mountain (1947) 7.5' quadrangle.

Granite Dome [TUOLUMNE]: *peak,* 12 miles west-northwest of Tower Peak (lat. 38°12'55" N, long. 119°44'45" W). Altitude 10,322 feet. Named on Tower Peak (1956) 15' quadrangle. United States Board on Geographic Names

(1965c, p. 11) approved the name "Sardella Lake" for a lake, 0.1 mile across, located 0.7 mile northeast of Granite Dome (lat. 38°13'20" N, long. 119°44'05" W); the name is for Giovanni Domenico Sardella, who lived by the lake.

Granite Dome: see **Wawona Dome** [MARIPOSA].

Granite Hill [NEVADA]: *peak,* 1 mile southsouthwest of downtown Grass Valley (lat. 39°12'20" N, long. 121°03'55" W; sec. 34, T 16 N, R 8 E). Named on Grass Valley (1949) 7.5' quadrangle.

Granite Hill: see **Gold Hill** [EL DORADO].

Granite Lake [AMADOR]: *lake,* 750 feet long, 8 miles north of Mokelumne Peak (lat. 38°39' N, long. 120°06'30" W; on S line sec. 4, T 9 N, R 17 E). Named on Caples Lake (1979) 7.5' quadrangle.

Granite Lake [EL DORADO]: *lake,* 950 feet long, 2.25 miles north-northwest of Mount Tallac (lat. 38°56'15" N, long. 120°06'30" W; near S line sec. 28, T 13 N, R 17 E). Named on Emerald Bay (1955) 7.5' quadrangle.

Granite Lake [TUOLUMNE]: *lake,* 800 feet long, 9 miles east of Pinecrest (lat. 38°11' N, long. 119°50' W; sec. 24, T 4 N, R 19 E). Named on Pinecrest (1956) 15' quadrangle.

Granite Lakes [TUOLUMNE]: *lakes,* two, largest 0.5 mile long, 1.25 miles northwest of Tioga Pass (lat. 37°55'20" N, long. 119°16'35" W). Named on Tuolumne Meadows (1956) 15' quadrangle. United States Board on Geographic Names (1962a, p. 17) decided that Granite Lakes are not part of the group called Gaylor Lakes.

Granite Mountain [SIERRA]: *peak,* 6.25 miles west-southwest of Sierra City (lat. 39°31'35" N, long. 120°44'15" W; near E line sec. 9, T 19 N, R 11 E). Altitude 6482 feet. Named on Sierra City (1981) 7.5' quadrangle.

Granite Peak [SIERRA]: *peak,* 5.25 miles south-southeast of Crystal Peak (lat. 39°29'25" N, long. 120°02'30" W; near N line sec. 24, T 19 N, R 17 E). Altitude 8291 feet. Named on Boca (1955) 7.5' quadrangle.

Granite Ravine [EL DORADO]: *canyon,* drained by a stream that flows less than 1 mile to Folsom Lake 5.5 miles southwest of the village of Pilot Hill (lat. 38°47'10" N, long. 121°05'35" W; sec. 21, T 11 N, R 8 E). Named on Pilot Hill (1954, photorevised 1973) 7.5' quadrangle. The stream in the canyon is called Chrome Creek on Auburn (1944) 15' quadrangle.

Granite Ridge [TUOLUMNE]: *ridge,* southwest-trending, 5 miles long, 5 miles northeast of Twain Harte (lat. 38°06'45" N, long. 120°12'15" W). Named on Crandall Peak (1979) and Twain Harte (1979) 7.5' quadrangles.

Granite Spring [EL DORADO]: *spring,* 2.5 miles west-northwest of Kyburz (lat. 38°47'20" N, long. 120°20'30" W; sec. 19, T

11 N, R 15 E). Named on Kyburz (1952) 7.5' quadrangle.

Granite Springs [MARIPOSA]: *settlement*, nearly 3 miles southwest of Penon Blanco Peak (lat. 37°42' N, long. 120°17'30" W; near W line sec. 2, T 3 S, R 15 E). Named on Penon Blanco Peak (1962, photorevised 1973) 7.5' quadrangle.

Granite Stairway [MADERA]: *relief feature*, 3 miles southwest of Devils Postpile (lat. 37°35'40" N, long. 119°07'30" W). Named on Devils Postpile (1953) 15' quadrangle.

Graniteville [NEVADA]: *village*, 23 miles northeast of Grass Valley along Poorman Creek (1) (lat. 39°26'30" N, long. 120°44'15" W; on E line sec. 9, T 18 N, R 11 E). Named on Graniteville (1982) 7.5' quadrangle. Postal authorities established Graniteville post office in 1867 and discontinued it in 1959 (Salley, p. 88). The place also was called Eureka South (Hanna, p. 125).

Grant Lakes [MARIPOSA]: *lakes*, two, largest 1000 feet long, 10 miles north-northeast of Yosemite Village (lat. 37°53'15" N, long. 119°32' W; mainly in sec. 3, T 1 S, R 22 E). Named on Hetch Hetchy Reservoir (1956) 15' quadrangle.

Grant Ravine [SIERRA]:

(1) *canyon*, drained by a stream that flows 1 mile to Downie River 3 miles north of Downieville (lat. 39°36'20" N, long. 120°49'45" W; near NW cor. sec. 14, T 20 N, R 10 E). Named on Downieville (1951) 7.5' quadrangle.

(2) *canyon*, drained by a stream that flows 1.25 miles to Indian Creek (1) 6.25 miles west-southwest of Goodyears Bar (lat. 39°30'05" N, long. 120°59'20" W; sec. 20, T 19 N, R 9 E). Named on Pike (1949) 7.5' quadrangle.

Grants Gap: see **Giant Gap** [PLACER].

Grapevine Canyon [MADERA]: *canyon*, drained by a stream that flows 1.5 miles to San Joaquin River 6.5 miles south-southwest of the town of North Fork (lat. 37°08'30" N, long. 119°33'40" W; at S line sec. 15, T 9 S, R 22 E). Named on North Fork (1965) 7.5' quadrangle.

Grapevine Creek [TUOLUMNE]: *stream*, flows 3.5 miles to Tuolumne River 7 miles southeast of Tuolumne (lat. 37°53'10" N, long. 120°08'45" W; sec. 6, T 1 S, R 17 E). Named on Duckwall Mountain (1948) and Tuolumne (1948) 7.5' quadrangles.

Grapevine Gulch [AMADOR]:

(1) *canyon*, drained by a stream that flows 3.5 miles to Camanche Reservoir 7 miles south-southwest of Ione (lat. 38°15'10" N, long. 120°57'50" W; near SW cor. sec. 26, T 5 N, R 9 E). Named on Ione (1962) and Wallace (1962) 7.5' quadrangles.

(2) *canyon*, 2 miles long, opens into the canyon of Mokelumne River 4.5 miles south-southwest of Jackson (lat. 38°17'20" N, long. 120°48'20" W; sec. 18, T 5 N, R 11 E). Named

on Jackson (1962) 7.5' quadrangle. Water of Pardee Reservoir now covers the lower part of the canyon. Camp's (1962) map shows a place called Columbia Bar located on the north side of Mokelumne River just west of the mouth of Grapevine Gulch, and a place called Italian Bar situated on the same side of the river less than 0.5 mile downstream from Columbia Bar; water of Pardee Reservoir now covers both sites.

Grapevine Gulch [CALAVERAS]: *canyon*, drained by a stream that flows 2.5 miles to Stanislaus River 3.5 miles east of Vallecito (lat. 38°05'35" N, long. 120°24'35" W; near SW cor. sec. 23, T 3 N, R 14 E). Named on Columbia (1948) 7.5' quadrangle.

Grapevine Point [TUOLUMNE]: *peak*, 5.25 miles south of Duckwall Mountain (lat. 37°53'30" N, long. 120°07'25" W; near SE cor. sec. 32, T 1 N, R 17 E). Altitude 3650 feet. Named on Duckwall Mountain (1948) 7.5' quadrangle.

Grapevine Ravine [AMADOR]: *canyon*, drained by a stream that flows 1.5 miles to Cosumnes River 9 miles west of Fiddletown (lat. 38°30'55" N, long. 120°55'25" W; near SW cor. sec. 30, T 8 N, R 10 E). Named on Latrobe (1949) 7.5' quadrangle. Camp's (1962) map shows a place called Rich Bar located on the south side of Cosumnes River less than 1 mile west-northwest of the mouth of Grapevine Ravine, a place called Possum Bar situated on the south side of the river 1.25 miles northwest of the mouth of the ravine, a place called Big Bar located on the south side of the river 1.5 miles west-northwest of the mouth of the ravine, and a place called Wisconsin Bar positioned on the south side of the river 2 miles west-northwest of the mouth of the ravine.

Grass Flat [SIERRA]: *locality*, 5.5 miles southwest of Mount Fillmore (lat. 39°40'35" N, long. 120°56' W; near SE cor. sec. 14, T 21 N, R 9 E). Named on La Porte (1951) 7.5' quadrangle.

Grass Lake [EL DORADO]:

(1) *lake*, 1900 feet long, 6 miles northwest of Echo Summit (lat. 38° 52'20" N, long. 120°06'40" W). Named on Echo Lake (1955) 7.5' quadrangle.

(2) *lake*, 1650 feet long, 5.5 miles southwest of Freel Peak (lat. 38° 47'40" N, long. 119°57'50" W; near S line sec. 14, T 11 N, R 18 E). Named on Freel Peak (1955) 7.5' quadrangle.

Grass Lake [SIERRA]: *lake*, 400 feet long, 5.25 miles north-northwest of Sierra City (lat. 39°38'25" N, long. 120°39'20" W; sec. 32, T 21 N, R 12 E). Named on Gold Lake (1981) 7.5' quadrangle. On Sierra City (1955) 15' quadrangle, the name "Grass Lake" applies to a lake situated 0.5 mile south-southwest of present Grass Lake.

Grass Lake Creek [EL DORADO]: *stream*, flows 4.25 miles to Upper Truckee River 1 mile southeast of Echo Summit (lat. 38°48'05" N, long. 120°00'55" W; sec. 17, T 11 N, R 18 E); Grass Lake (2) is along the stream. Named on Echo Lake (1955) and Freel Peak (1955) 7.5' quadrangles.

Grass Valley [NEVADA]: *town,* near the center of the west half of Nevada County along Wolf Creek (lat. 39°13'05" N, long. 121°03'40" W; in and near sec. 27, T 16 N, R 8 E). Named on Grass Valley (1949) 7.5' quadrangle. Postal authorities established Centreville post office in 1851; they moved it and changed the name to Grass Valley in 1852 (Salley, p. 41). The town incorporated in 1861. The name "Grass Valley" is from the designation given by early emigrants to the valley where the town lies; the name "Centreville" was for the location of the place about halfway between the village of Rough and Ready and the town of Nevada City (Browne, p. 12). Doble (p. 76) referred to Grass Valley in 1852 as a beautiful flat some 1.5 miles long and 200 or 300 yards wide where the owners had a house that was a store and tavern. Whitney's (1873) map shows a place called Rays Flat located 2.5 miles southwest of Grass Valley, and a lake called Pine Tree Reservoir situated less than 1 mile southwest of downtown Grass Valley. United States Geological Survey's (1901) map shows a place called Brighton House located 1 mile southwest of downtown Grass Valley (at E line sec. 33, T 16 N, R 8 E). California Division of Highways' (1934) map shows a place called Pittsburg situated along Nevada County Narrow Gauge Railroad 1.25 miles south of Grass Valley (near SE cor. sec. 13, T 16 N, R 8 E), and a place called Mt. View along the railroad 0.5 mile farther west (near S line sec. 13, T 16 N, R 8 E). Postal authorities established Flood post office 3 miles south of Grass Valley in 1900 and discontinued in 1903; the name was for developer James L. Flood (Salley, p. 76). Gudde (1975, p. 190) listed a mining place called Lafayette Hill located 2 miles south of Grass Valley, and (p. 219) a mining place called Missouri Flat situated 1 mile south of Grass Valley. United States Board on Geographic Names (1992, p. 4) approved the name "Critter Creek" for a stream that flows 1.2 miles to Wolf Creek 2 miles south of Grass Valley (lat. 39°11'06" N, long. 121°03'33" W; sec. 2, T 15 N, R 8 E). The Board (1995, p. 5) approved the name "Ellens Creek" for a stream that flows 1 mile to join Wolf Creek 2 miles south of Grass Valley (lat. 39°11'06" N, long. 121°03'32" W; sec. 2, T 15 N, R 8 E); the name commemorates Ellen Bergman, who helped settle the region.

Grass Valley: see **Grass Valley Creek** [AMADOR].

Grass Valley Creek [AMADOR]: *stream,* flows 5.5 miles to Sutter Creek (1) nearly 2 miles north-northwest of Pine Grove (lat. 38°26'10"

N, long. 120°40'20" W; sec. 29, T 7 N, R 12 E). Named on Pine Grove (1948) 7.5' quadrangle.

Grass Valley Reservoir [NEVADA]: *lakes,* 0.5 mile north-northwest of downtown Grass Valley (lat. 39°13'40" N, long. 121°04' W; near S line sec. 22, T 16 N, R 8 E). Named on Grass Valley (1949) 7.5' quadrangle.

Gravelly Fork [MADERA]: *locality,* nearly 7 miles south-southwest of Merced Peak along South Fork Merced River (lat. 37°32'50" N, long. 119°27'10" W). Named on Merced Peak (1953) 15' quadrangle.

Gravel Pit Lake [TUOLUMNE]: *lake,* 1050 feet long, 6 miles north-northeast of Mather along Miguel Creek (lat. 37°57'55" N, long. 119°49'40" W; near NW cor. sec. 7, T 1 N, R 20 E). Named on Lake Eleanor (1956) 15' quadrangle.

Gravel Range [TUOLUMNE]: *ridge,* south-southwest-trending, 3 miles long, 10 miles southeast of Duckwall Mountain (lat. 37°51'30" N, long. 120°00'15" W). Named on Lake Eleanor (1956) and Tuolumne (1948) 15' quadrangles.

Graveyard Creek [TUOLUMNE]: *stream,* flows less than 1 mile to Don Pedro Reservoir 2 miles east-northeast of Don Pedro Camp (lat. 37°43'20" N, long. 120°22'30" W; near NE cor. sec. 36, T 2 S, R 14 E). Named on Penon Blanco Peak (1962, photorevised 1973) 7.5' quadrangle.

Graveyard Meadow [MADERA]: *area,* 11 miles northeast of Shuteye Peak (lat. 37°27'50" N, long. 119°17'40" W; sec. 25, T 5 S, R 24 E). Named on Shuteye Peak (1953) 15' quadrangle.

Gray Butte: see **Grey Butte** [TUOLUMNE].

Gray Creek [MARIPOSA]: *stream,* flows 2 miles to Clark Fork 12 miles south-southwest of Cathedral Peak (lat. 37°40'55" N, long. 119°27'50" W); the stream heads near Gray Peak [MADERA]. Named on Merced Peak (1953) 15' quadrangle.

Gray: see **Andrew Gray Creek** [PLACER]; **Harvey Gray Creek** [PLACER].

Gray Creek [NEVADA]: *stream,* formed by the confluence of North Fork and South Fork, flows 2.25 miles to Truckee River 9 miles east-northeast of Truckee (lat. 39°22'20" W; long. 120°01'50" W; near NE cor. sec. 36, T 18 N, R 17 E). Named on Martis Peak (1955) 7.5' quadrangle. North Fork heads in the State of Nevada and flows less than 0.25 mile in Nevada County to join South Fork. South Fork also heads in the State of Nevada and flows nearly 1.5 miles to join North Fork. Both forks are named on Martis Peak (1955) 7.5' quadrangle.

Gray Eagle Bar [EL DORADO]: *locality,* 2.25 miles north-northeast of Volcanoville along Middle Fork American River (lat. 39°00'35" N, long. 120°45'55" W). Named on Foresthill (1949) 7.5' quadrangle. Gudde (1975, p. 204) listed a mining place called Malcomb Bar that was located along Middle Fork below Gray Eagle Bar.

Gray Eagle Canyon [PLACER]: *canyon,* drained by a stream that flows 1 mile to Duncan Canyon 3.5 miles south of Duncan Peak (lat. 39°06'10" N, long. 120°30'55" W; sec. 34, T 15 N, R 13 E). Named on Greek Store (1952) 7.5' quadrangle.

Gray Eagle Hill: see **Grey Eagle Hill** [EL DORADO].

Gray Horse Creek [EL DORADO]: *stream,* flows 1.25 miles to Silver Creek 5.5 miles north-northwest of Riverton (lat. 38°50'45" N, long. 120°28'45" W; at W line sec. 36, T 12 N, R 13 E). Named on Riverton (1950) 7.5' quadrangle.

Grayhorse Creek [PLACER]: *stream,* flows 5 miles to Hell Hole Reservoir nearly 3 miles north-northeast of Bunker Hill (lat. 39°05'15" N, long. 120°21'50" W; near W line sec. 1, T 14 N, R 14 E). Named on Wentworth Springs (1953, photorevised 1973) 7.5' quadrangle.

Grayhorse Valley [PLACER]: *valley,* along Grayhorse Creek above a point 4 miles north-northeast of Bunker Hill (lat. 39°06'30" N, long. 120°21'45" W). Named on Granite Chief (1953) and Wentworth Springs (1953) 7.5' quadrangles.

Grayling Lake [MADERA]: *lake,* 750 feet long, 3.5 miles west-northwest of Merced Peak (lat. 37°39'40" N, long. 119°26'50" W). Named on Merced Peak (1953) 15' quadrangle. The name was given in 1930 when grayling first were planted in the lake (Browning, 1986, p. 87).

Gray Peak [MADERA]: *peak,* 3 miles north-northwest of Merced Peak (lat. 37°40'25" N, long. 119°25'05" W). Altitude 11,574 feet. Named on Merced Peak (1953) 15' quadrangle. Members of the Whitney survey named the peak for the color of its upper part (Browning, 1988, p. 53). United States Board on Geographic Names (1933, p. 336) rejected the name "Hayes Peak" for the feature.

Gray Peak Fork [MADERA-MARIPOSA]: *stream,* heads in Madera County and flows 7.5 miles to Merced River 8.5 miles south of Cathedral Peak in Mariposa County (lat. 37°43'45" N, long. 119° 23'25" W); the stream heads near Gray Peak [MADERA]. Named on Mount Lyell (1901) 30' quadrangle.

Grays Canyon [EL DORADO]: *canyon,* drained by a stream that flows 1.5 miles to South Fork American River 2.25 miles east-northeast of Pollock Pines (lat. 38°46'25" N, long. 120°32'35" W; sec. 20, T 11 N, R 13 E). Named on Pollock Pines (1950) 7.5' quadrangle.

Greaser Gulch [MARIPOSA]: *canyon,* drained by a stream that flows 4.5 miles to Burns Creek 1.25 miles east of Courthouse Rock (lat. 37°25'15" N, long. 120°15'25" W; sec. 7, T 6 S, R 16 E). Named on Haystack Mountain (1962) and Indian Gulch (1962) 7.5' quadrangles.

Greasertown: see **Butte City** [AMADOR].

Greasertown: see **San Andreas** [CALAVERAS].

Greaserville: see **Butte City** [AMADOR].

Great Dome: see **Balloon Dome** [MADERA].

Great Eastern Ravine [SIERRA]: *canyon,* drained by a stream that flows 1.5 miles to Haypress Creek 3 miles east of Sierra City (lat. 39°34'05" N, long. 120°34'40" W; sec. 25, T 20 N, R 12 E). Named on Haypress Valley (1981) 7.5' quadrangle.

Greek Store: see **Spruce Creek** [PLACER].

Greeley Hill [MARIPOSA]:
(1) *peak,* 3 miles northeast of Coulterville (lat. 37°44'35" N, long. 120°09'15" W; near S line sec. 24, T 2 S, R 16 E). Altitude 3629 feet. Named on Coulterville (1947) 7.5' quadrangle.
(2) *settlement,* 4.25 miles northeast of Coulterville (lat. 37°44'45" N, long. 120°07'50" W; on E line sec. 19, T 2 S, R 17 E); the place is 1.25 miles east of Greeley Hill (1). Named on Coulterville (1947) 7.5' quadrangle. The name commemorates Josiah F. Greely (who spelled his name without the third "e"), owner of a sawmill at the place (Sargent, Shirley, 1976, p. 21).

Green Creek [AMADOR]: *stream,* flows 2 miles to North Fork Mokelumne River 5.5 miles south-southeast of Hams Station (lat. 38°28' N, long. 120°20'45" W; near S line sec. 8, T 7 N, R 15 E). Named on Garnet Hill (1979) 7.5' quadrangle.

Green Gulch [MARIPOSA]: *canyon,* drained by a stream that flows 3 miles to Bear Creek (2) 4.25 miles south-southeast of Bear Valley (2) (lat. 37°30'30" N, long. 120°05'35" W). Named on Bear Valley (1947) 7.5' quadrangle. Called Green's Gulch on Laizure's (1928) map.

Greenhorn Creek [CALAVERAS]: *stream,* flows 3 miles to Angels Creek 2.5 miles south-southwest of Angels Camp (lat. 38°02'30" N, long. 120°33'30" W; sec. 9, T 2 N, R 13 E); the stream goes through Greenhorn Gulch. Named on Angels Camp (1962) 7.5' quadrangle.

Greenhorn Gulch [CALAVERAS]: *canyon,* 1 mile long, 2 miles south-southwest of Angels Camp (lat. 38°02'50" N, long. 120°33'50" W); the canyon is along lower reaches of Greenhorn Creek. Named on Angels Camp (1962) 7.5' quadrangle.

Greenhorn Creek [NEVADA]: *stream,* flows 12.5 miles to Rollins Reservoir 2.5 miles north-northeast of Chicago Park (lat. 39°10'35" N, long. 120°56'30" W; near SW cor. sec. 2, T 15 N, R 9 E). Named on Chicago Park (1949, photorevised 1973), North Bloomfield (1949), and Washington (1950) 7.5' quadrangles. South Fork enters nearly 7 miles north-northeast of Chicago Park. It is 4 miles long and is named on Chicago Park (1949), Dutch Flat (1950), and Washington (1950) 7.5' quadrangles.

Greenhorn Creek: see **Little Greenhorn Creek** [NEVADA].

Greenleaf: see **Gregg** [MADERA].

Green Mountain [MADERA]: *ridge,* east- to southeast-trending, 1.5 miles long, 10 miles west-southwest of Devils Postpile (lat. 37°34'20" N, long. 119°15' W). Named on Devils Postpile (1953) and Merced Peak (1953) 15' quadrangles.

Green Mountain [MARIPOSA]: *peak,* 15 miles south of Mariposa (lat. 37°15'50" N, long. 119°59'25" W; sec. 3, T 8 S, R 18 E). Altitude 1374 feet. Named on Ben Hur (1947) 7.5' quadrangle.

Green Mountain Bar: see **Maine Bar** [EL DORADO].

Green's Gulch: see **Green Gulch** [MARIPOSA].

Green Spring Creek [EL DORADO]: *stream,* flows 4.5 miles to New York Creek 4.25 miles north-northwest of Clarksville (lat. 38°42'50" N, long. 121°04'30" W; near NW cor. sec. 23, T 10 N, R 8 E). Named on Clarksville (1953) 7.5' quadrangle.

Green Spring Run [TUOLUMNE]: *stream,* flows nearly 7 miles to Tulloch Lake 3.5 miles northwest of Keystone (lat. 37°52'30" N, long. 120°32'55" W; sec. 4, T 1 S, R 13 E). Named on Keystone (1962) and Melones Dam (1962) 7.5' quadrangles.

Green Springs: see **Keystone** [TUOLUMNE].

Green Springs: see **Rescue** [EL DORADO].

Green Valley [EL DORADO]: *locality,* 3.25 miles north-northwest of Shingle Springs (lat. 38°42'30" N, long. 120°56'40" W). Named on Placerville (1893) 30' quadrangle. Postal authorities established Green Valley post office in 1854 and discontinued it in 1855; they established Hitchcock Ranch post office 7 miles southeast of Salmon Falls in 1860, changed the name to Green Valley in 1865, moved it 1.5 miles east in 1908, and discontinued it in 1911 (Salley, p. 89, 98).

Green Valley [PLACER]: *valley,* 3.5 miles east-southeast of Dutch Flat along North Fork American River (lat. 39°10'50" N, long. 120°46'55" W; sec. 6, T 15 N, R 11 E). Named on Dutch Flat (1950) 7.5' quadrangle. Gudde (1975, p. 62, 251, 357) noted mining places called Carpenters Bar, One Horse Bar, and Upper Arkansas Bar that were situated along North Fork in Green Valley.

Green Valley: see **Greenwood** [EL DORADO].

Green Valley Cañon: see **McIntyre Gulch** [PLACER].

Greenwood [EL DORADO]: *village,* 4 miles west of Georgetown (lat. 38°53'50" N, long. 120°54'45" W; near SW cor. sec. 7, T 12 N, R 10 E). Named on Greenwood (1949) 7.5' quadrangle. The place first was called Long Valley, then Green Valley and Lewisville before it was renamed Greenwood (Bancroft, 1888, p. 354)—John Greenwood had a trading post at the site in 1848 (Hoover, Rensch,

and Rensch, p. 87). Postal authorities established Louisville post office before July 28, 1851, and moved it in 1852 when they changed the name to Greenwood (Salley, p. 128). The name "Lewisville" or "Louisville" was for Lewis B. Meyers' son, the first child born near the site (Gudde, 1975, p. 145). Logan's (1938) map shows a place called Greenwood Camp about 2 miles north of Greenwood (near W line sec. 6, T 12 N, R 10 E).

Greenwood: see **John Greenwood's Creek**, under **Prosser Creek** [NEVADA].

Greenwood Camp: see **Greenwood** [EL DORADO].

Greenwood Creek [EL DORADO]: *stream,* flows 9 miles to South Fork American River 3.5 miles west-northwest of Coloma (lat. 38°49'30" N, long. 120°56'55" W; sec. 11, T 11 N, R 9 E); the stream goes past Greenwood. Named on Coloma (1949) and Greenwood (1949) 7.5' quadrangles.

Greenwood's Camp: see **Jefferson**, under **Jefferson Creek** [NEVADA].

Gregg [MADERA]: *locality,* 2.5 miles southeast of Trigo along Atchison, Topeka and Santa Fe Railroad (lat. 36°52'55" N, long. 119°56'10" W; near S line sec. 18, T 12 S, R 19 E). Named on Gregg (1965) 7.5' quadrangle. Called Greenleaf on Mendenhall's (1908) map. Postal authorities established Greenleaf post office in 1904 and discontinued it in 1905; they established Gregg post office in 1917, discontinued it for a time in 1928, and discontinued it finally in 1931 (Frickstad, p. 85).

Gregory [EL DORADO]: *locality,* 9 miles northwest of Leek Spring Hill (lat. 38°43'10" N, long. 120°23'30" W). Named on Pyramid Peak (1896) 30' quadrangle.

Gregory: see **Mount Gregory** [EL DORADO].

Greilich Camp [EL DORADO]: *locality,* 5 miles east-southeast of Caldor (lat. 38°34'05" N, long. 120°21' W; near SE cor. sec. 6, T 8 N, R 15 E). Named on Peddler Hill (1951) 7.5' quadrangle.

Greve [CALAVERAS]: *locality,* 3 miles west-northwest of Blue Mountain near present Hamilton Camp (lat. 38°21' N, long. 120° 25' W). Named on Big Trees (1891) 30' quadrangle.

Grey Butte [TUOLUMNE]: *peak,* 3.5 miles south-southeast of Matterhorn Peak (lat. 38°03'05" N, long. 119°20'50" W). Altitude 11,365 feet. Named on Matterhorn Peak (1956) 15' quadrangle. United States Board on Geographic Names (1970b, p. 3) gave the name "Gray Butte" as a variant.

Grey Eagle Hill [EL DORADO]: *peak,* 3.25 miles east of Georgetown (lat. 38°54'40" N, long. 120°46'30" W; at S line sec. 5, T 12 N, R 11 E). Named on Georgetown (1949) 7.5' quadrangle. Logan's (1938) map has the form "Gray" for the name.

135

Griders: see **Roseville** [PLACER].

Griff Creek [PLACER]: *stream,* flows 4 miles to Lake Tahoe at Kings Beach (lat. 39°14'15" N, long. 120°01'45" W; near E line sec. 13, T 16 N, R 17 E). Named on Kings Beach (1955) and Martis Peak (1955) 7.5' quadrangles.

Griminger [EL DORADO]: *locality,* 1.5 miles northwest of Old Iron Mountain (lat. 38°43'10" N, long. 120°24'30" W; sec. 15, T 10 N, R 14 E). Named on Stump Spring (1951) 7.5' quadrangle.

Griswold Creek [TUOLUMNE]: *stream,* formed by the confluence of North Fork and South Fork, flows 12.5 miles to North Fork Stanislaus River 3.25 miles north-northeast of Stanislaus (lat. 38°10'40" N, long. 120°20'10" W; at SW cor. sec. 21, T 4 N, R 15 E). Named on Boards Crossing (1979), Crandall Peak (1979), and Stanislaus (1948) 7.5' quadrangles. North Fork is 6 miles long and South Fork is 4 miles long; both forks are named on Boards Crossing (1979) and Liberty Hill (1979) 7.5' quadrangles.

Grizzly: see **Big Grizzly,** under **Miller Gulch** [MARIPOSA].

Grizzly: see **Fort Grizzly** [EL DORADO].

Grizzly Bar: see **American River** [EL DORADO-PLACER].

Grizzly Bear House [PLACER]: *locality,* 6 miles northeast of Auburn (lat. 38°56'35" N, long. 120°58'45" W; near S line sec. 28, T 13 N, R 9 E). Named on Greenwood (1949) 7.5' quadrangle. Postal authorities established Grizzly Bear House post office in 1858 and discontinued it in 1871 (Salley, p. 90).

Grizzly Canyon [EL DORADO]: *canyon,* drained by a stream that flows 1.25 miles to Missouri Canyon 5.5 miles northeast of Georgetown (lat. 38°58' N, long. 120°46'10" W; sec. 20, T 13 N, R 11 E). Named on Georgetown (1949) 7.5' quadrangle.

Grizzly Canyon [PLACER]: *canyon,* drained by a stream that flows 3.5 miles to Shirttail Canyon 3.5 miles north-northwest of Foresthill (lat. 39°04' N, long. 120°51'10" W; near N line sec. 16, T 14 N, R 10 E). Named on Foresthill (1949) 7.5' quadrangle.

Grizzly Canyon: see **Big Grizzly Canyon** [PLACER]; **Little Grizzly Canyon** [PLACER]; **Grizzly Creek** [NEVADA].

Grizzly Creek [EL DORADO]: *stream,* flows 1.5 miles to Steely Fork Cosumnes River 11 miles southeast of Camino (lat. 38°37'50" N, long. 120°31'40" W; near S line sec. 15, T 9 N, R 13 E); the stream flows past Grizzly Flat. Named on Camino (1952) 15' quadrangle.

Grizzly Creek [MADERA]: *stream,* flows 5 miles to South Fork Merced River 8 miles southwest of Merced Peak (lat. 37°32'30" N, long. 119°29' W); the stream heads at Grizzly Lake. Named on Merced Peak (1953) and Shuteye Peak (1953) 15' quadrangles. Called Quartz Cr. on Mount Lyell (1901) 30' quadrangle, but United States Board on Geo-

graphic Names (1969a, p. 3) rejected this name for the stream, which is west of Quartz Mountain (1).

Grizzly Creek [NEVADA]: *stream,* flows 7.25 miles to Middle Yuba River 4.5 miles east-northeast of North San Juan (lat. 39°23'20" N, long. 121°01'25" W; near NE cor. sec. 36, T 18 N, R 8 E). Named on Camptonville (1948) and Pike (1949) 7.5' quadrangles. Whitney's (1873) map has the name "Grizzly Cañon" along the stream.

Grizzly Creek [TUOLUMNE]: *stream,* flows 3.5 miles to Beaver Creek 10 miles southwest of Liberty Hill (lat. 38°16'10" N, long. 120°14'05" W; sec. 20, T 5 N, R 16 E). Named on Boards Crossing (1979) 7.5' quadrangle.

Grizzly Creek: see **Big Grizzly Creek** [MARIPOSA]; **Little Grizzly Creek** [MARIPOSA].

Grizzly Creek: see **Big Grizzly Canyon** [PLACER]; **Big Grizzly Creek** [SIERRA]; **Grizzly Gulch** [SIERRA]; **Little Grizzly Creek** [PLACER]; **Little Grizzly Creek** [SIERRA].

Grizzly Falls: see **Little Grizzly Falls,** under **Bunnel Cascade** [MARIPOSA].

Grizzly Flat [EL DORADO]: *village,* 11 miles southeast of Camino (lat. 38°38'10" N, long. 120°31'35" W; sec. 15, T 9 N, R 13 E). Named on Sly Park (1952) 7.5' quadrangle. California Mining Bureau's (1909a) map has the form "Grizzly Flats" for the name. Postal authorities established Grizzly Flats post office in 1855 (Frickstad, p. 27). Miners who were surprised by a grizzly bear at the place named the community in 1850 (Hoover, Rensch, and Rensch, p. 84). Doble (p. 79) referred to Chickemasee or Grizzly Flat in 1852.

Grizzly Flat [PLACER]: *area,* 4.5 miles north of Foresthill (lat. 39° 05'20" N, long. 120°49'40" W; at E line sec. 3, T 14 N, R 10 E); the place is in the upper part of Grizzly Canyon. Named on Foresthill (1949) 7.5' quadrangle. On Whitney's (1873) map, the name applies to an inhabited place at the site.

Grizzly Flat: see **Big Grizzly Flat** [MARIPOSA]; **Little Grizzly Flat** [MARIPOSA].**Grizzly Flat**: see **Big Grizzly Flat** [MARIPOSA]; **Little Grizzly Flat** [MARIPOSA].

Grizzly Flats: see **Grizzly Flat** [EL DORADO].

Grizzly Gulch [EL DORADO]: *canyon,* drained by a stream that flows 1.25 miles to Spanish Creek 11 miles south-southeast of Placerville (lat. 38°34'40" N, long. 120°45'15" W; sec. 3, T 8 N, R 11 E). Named on Fiddletown (1949) 7.5' quadrangle.

Grizzly Gulch [SIERRA]: *locality,* 1.5 miles northeast of Pike (lat. 39°27' N, long. 120°58' W); the place is at the head of Grizzly Creek, which is in present Grizzly Gulch [SIERRA]. Named on Colfax (1898) 30' quadrangle.

Grizzly Gulch [SIERRA]: *canyon,* drained by a stream that heads in Sierra County and flows 6 miles to Oregon Creek 1 mile south-southwest of Camptonville in Yuba County (lat. 39°26'25" N, long. 121°03'20" W; sec. 11, T 18 N, R 8 E). Named on Camptonville (1948) and Pike (1949) 7.5' quadrangles. On Colfax (1898) and Smartsville (1895) 30' quadrangles, the stream in the canyon has the name "Grizzly Creek."

Grizzly Gulch [TUOLUMNE]:
(1) *canyon,* drained by a stream that flows 0.5 mile to Devils Canyon 3.5 miles west-southwest of Columbia (lat. 38°00'35" N, long. 120°27'30" W; sec. 20, T 2 N, R 14 E). Named on Columbia (1948) 7.5' quadrangle.
(2) *canyon,* drained by a stream that flows nearly 3 miles to Moccasin Lake at Moccasin (lat. 37°48'40" N, long. 120°18'10" W; near N line sec. 34, T 1 S, R 15 E). Named on Moccasin (1948) 7.5' quadrangle.

Grizzly Hill: see **Relief** [NEVADA].

Grizzly Lake [MADERA]: *lake,* 600 feet long, 10 miles north-northwest of Shuteye Peak (lat. 37°29'10" N, long. 119°29' W; near W line sec. 20, T 5 S, R 23 E); the lake is at the head of Grizzly Creek. Named on Shuteye Peak (1953) 15' quadrangle.

Grizzly Meadow [MADERA]: *area,* 4 miles north of Shuteye Peak (lat. 37°24'15" N, long. 119°24'45" W; sec. 13, T 6 S, R 23 E). Named on Shuteye Peak (1953) 15' quadrangle.

Grizzly Meadow [TUOLUMNE]:
(1) *area,* 7 miles south-southwest of Liberty Hill (lat. 38°16'40" N, long. 120°09'10" W; sec. 24, T 5 N, R 16 E). Named on Boards Crossing (1979) 7.5' quadrangle.
(2) *area,* 5.5 miles northwest of Tower Peak (lat. 38°11'30" N, long. 119°37'45" W); the place is 0.5 mile west of Grizzly Peak. Named on Tower Peak (1956) 15' quadrangle.

Grizzly Mountain: see **Big Grizzly Mountain** [MARIPOSA]; **Little Grizzly Mountain** [MARIPOSA].

Grizzly Peak [MARIPOSA]: *peak,* 2.5 miles east-southeast of Yosemite Village (lat. 37°43'50" N, long. 119°33' W). Named on Yosemite (1956) 15' quadrangle. The feature was called Grizzly Point in the early days (Browning, 1986, p. 88).

Grizzly Peak [SIERRA]: *peak,* 2.25 miles west of Downieville (lat. 39°33'20" N, long. 120°52'05" W; near W line sec. 33, T 20 N, R 10 E). Altitude 4638 feet. Named on Downieville (1951) 7.5' quadrangle.

Grizzly Peak [TUOLUMNE]: *peak,* 5.25 miles northwest of Tower Peak on Tuolumne-Mono county line (lat. 38°11'35" N, long. 119° 37'15" W). Named on Tower Peak (1956) 15' quadrangle.

Grizzly Point: see **Grizzly Peak** [MARIPOSA].

Grizzly Ridge [NEVADA]: *ridge,* west-trending, 4 miles long, 4 miles northwest of North Bloomfield (lat. 39°24'30" N, long. 120° 57'30" W); the ridge is north of Grizzly Creek. Named on Colfax (1938) 30' quadrangle.

Grohl: see **Grohl Meadow** [TUOLUMNE].

Grohl Meadow [TUOLUMNE]: *area,* 4.5 miles northwest of Crandall Peak (lat. 38°12'15" N, long. 120°12'10" W; sec. 15, T 4 N, R 16 E). Named on Crandall Peak (1979) 7.5' quadrangle. Big Trees (1891) 30' quadrangle has the name "Grohl" at the place.

Grohls Upper Camp [TUOLUMNE]: *locality,* 4 miles east-southeast of Liberty Hill (lat. 38°20'25" N, long. 120°02'10" W; sec. 30, T 6 N, R 18 E). Named on Big Meadow (1956) 15' quadrangle.

Groundhog Meadow [TUOLUMNE]:
(1) *area,* 6 miles south-southwest of Dardanelle (lat. 38°15'35" N, long. 119°52' W; sec. 27, T 5 N, R 19 E). Named on Dardanelle (1979) 7.5' quadrangle.
(2) *area,* 9 miles east-southeast of Pinecrest along Piute Creek (1) (lat. 38°09'20" N, long. 119°50' W; sec. 36, T 4 N, R 19 E). Named on Pinecrest (1956) 15' quadrangle.

Groundhog Rock [SIERRA]: *relief feature,* 12 miles south-southeast of Loyalton (lat. 39°30'40" N, long. 120°10'55" W; sec. 10, T 19 N, R 16 E). Named on Sardine Peak (1981) 7.5' quadrangle.

Grouse Canyon [PLACER]: *canyon,* drained by a stream that flows 2 miles to the canyon of Five Lakes Creek 4.5 miles south of Granite Chief (lat. 39°07'50" N, long. 120°16'15" W; sec. 23, T 15 N, R 15 E). Named on Granite Chief (1953) and Tahoe City (1955) 7.5' quadrangles.

Grouse Creek [MARIPOSA]: *stream,* flows 4.5 miles to Merced River 9 miles west-southwest of Yosemite Village (lat. 37°41'20" N, long. 119°43'40" W; sec. 11, T 3 S, R 20 E). Named on Yosemite (1956) 15' quadrangle.

Grouse Creek [PLACER]: *stream,* flows 5.5 miles to North Fork of Middle Fork American River 6 miles northeast of Michigan Bluff (lat. 39°05'20" N, long. 120°38'40" W; sec. 4, T 14 N, R 12 E). Named on Greek Store (1952) and Michigan Bluff (1952) 7.5' quadrangles. South Branch enters from the east 1 mile from the mouth of the main stream; it is 2 miles long and is named on Greek Store (1952) and Michigan Bluff (1952) 7.5' quadrangles.

Grouse Creek [SIERRA]: *stream,* flows 2 miles to Indian Creek (2) 3 miles east of Pike (lat. 39°25'55" N, long. 120°56'35" W; near NW cor. sec. 14, T 18 N, R 9 E). Named on Pike (1949) 7.5' quadrangle.

Grouse Creek [TUOLUMNE]: *stream,* flows 2.25 miles to Relief Reservoir 6.5 miles southwest of Sonora Pass (lat. 38°16'10" N, long. 119°44' W; at W line sec. 24, T 5 N, R 20 E). Named on Sonora Pass (1979) 7.5' quadrangle.

Grouse Lake [EL DORADO]: *lake,* 750 feet long, 2.5 miles west-northwest of Pyramid Peak (lat. 38°51'25" N, long. 120°11'55" W). Named on Pyramid Peak (1955) 7.5' quadrangle.

Grouse Lake [MADERA]: *lake,* 500 feet long,

2.25 miles southwest of Buena Vista Peak (lat. 37°34'20" N, long. 119°32'45" W; sec. 22, T 4 S, R 22 E). Named on Yosemite (1956) 15' quadrangle.

Grouse Lake [TUOLUMNE]: *lake,* 650 feet long, 7.5 miles east-southeast of Pinecrest (lat. 38°09'05" N, long. 119°52'10" W; near S line sec. 34, T 4 N, R 19 E). Named on Pinecrest (1956) 15' quadrangle.

Grouse Lakes [EL DORADO]: *lakes,* largest 550 feet long, less than 1 mile east-northeast of Phipps Peak (lat. 38°57'40" N, long. 120°08'05" W; sec. 19, T 13 N, E 17 E). Named on Rockbound Valley (1955) 7.5' quadrangle.

Grouse Meadow [MADERA]: *area,* 6.25 miles north-northeast of Yosemite Forks (lat. 37°26'55" N, long. 119°34'40" W; at SW cor. sec. 33, T 5 S, R 22 E). Named on Bass Lake (1953) 15' quadrangle.

Grouse Ridge [NEVADA]: *ridge,* south- to southwest-trending, 2 miles long, 4 miles north of Yuba Gap (lat. 39°22'30" N, long. 120°37'10" W). Named on Blue Canyon (1955), Cisco Grove (1955), and English Mountain (1983) 7.5' quadrangles.

Groveland [TUOLUMNE]: *village,* 13 miles southeast of Sonora (lat. 37°50'20" N, long. 120°13'45" W; sec. 20, 21, T 1 S, R 16 E). Named on Groveland (1947) 7.5' quadrangle. Postal authorities established Garrotte post office in 1851 and changed the name to Groveland in 1875 (Frickstad, p. 215). Following the hanging of two Mexican thieves there in 1849, the place became known as Garrote from the Spanish term for death by choking or hanging; later the community was called First Garrote—to distinguish it from Second Garrote—until the middle 1870's, when Benjamin Savory suggested the more genteel name "Groveland," taken from his hometown in Massachusetts (Paden and Schlichtmann, p. 167-168).

Groves Meadow: see **Sonny Meadow** [MARIPOSA].

Growlersburg: see **Georgetown** [EL DORADO].

Grubb: see **Peter Grubb Hut** [NEVADA].

Grubb Creek [NEVADA]: *stream,* flows 3 miles to Squirrel Creek 3 miles north-northeast of Pilot Peak (lat. 39°12'30" N, long. 121° 10' W; near NW cor. sec. 35, T 16 N, R 7 E). Named on Grass Valley (1949) and Rough and Ready (1949) 7.5' quadrangles.

Grubb Gulch [TUOLUMNE]: *canyon,* drained by a stream that flows 1.5 miles to Rose Creek 5.5 miles north of Twain Harte (lat. 38° 07'10" N, long. 120°14'15" W; sec. 17, T 3 N, R 16 E). Named on Twain Harte (1979) 7.5' quadrangle.

Grub Gulch [MADERA]:
(1) *canyon,* 10.5 miles northeast of Raymond (lat. 37°19'25" N, long. 119°46'10" W; sec. 15, T 7 S, R 20 E). Named on Horsecamp

Mountain (1947) 7.5' quadrangle. The name is from the local tradition that miners, unsuccessful elsewhere, could always "grub out" enough gold in the canyon to make a living (Hanna, p. 128).
(2) *locality,* 10.5 miles northeast of Raymond (lat. 37°19'30" N, long. 119°46'15" W; sec. 15, T 7 S, R 20 E); the place is in Grub Gulch (1). Named on Mariposa (1912) 30' quadrangle. Postal authorities established Grubgulch post office in 1883 and discontinued it in 1918 (Salley, p 90). They established Miami post office 8 miles southwest of Grub Gulch (2) in 1884 and discontinued it in 1887; the name was from the Miami River region of Ohio (Salley, p. 139).

Grub Gulch [PLACER]: *canyon,* drained by a stream that flows 1 mile to Grouse Creek 6.25 miles west-southwest of Duncan Peak (lat. 39°06'30" N, long. 120°36'35" W; sec. 35, T 15 N, R 12 E). Named on Greek Store (1952) 7.5' quadrangle.

Guadalupe: see **Guadalupe Mountains** [MARIPOSA].

Guadalupe Creek [MARIPOSA]: *stream,* flows 2.5 miles to Agua Fria Creek 4 miles east-northeast of the settlement Catheys Valley (lat. 37°27'15" N, long. 120°01'10" W). Named on Catheys Valley (1962) 7.5' quadrangle. United States Board on Geographic Names (1964a, p. 10) rejected the names "La Minita Creek" and "Minita Creek" for the stream. The canyon of the creek is called Minita Gulch on Indian Gulch (1920) 15' quadrangle, and is called Guadalupe Gulch on Laizure's (1928) map.

Guadalupe Gulch: see **Guadalupe Creek** [MARIPOSA].

Guadalupe Mountains [MARIPOSA]: *ridge,* northwest-trending, 6 miles long, center 3 miles east of the settlement of Catheys Valley (lat. 37°25'45" N, long. 120°02'30" W). Named on Catheys Valley (1962) 7.5' quadrangle. The name is from the old mining town of Guadalupe (Gudde, 1949, p. 137), which Hoffmann and Gardner's (1863-1867) map shows situated nearly 2 miles north-northwest of Bridgeport along Agua Fria Creek.

Guadalupe Valley [MARIPOSA]: *valley,* 4.5 miles east of the settlement of Catheys Valley along Agua Fria Creek (lat. 37°26'50" N, long. 120°00'35" W); the valley is northeast of Guadalupe Mountains. Named on Catheys Valley (1962) 7.5' quadrangle.

Guide Peak [PLACER]: *peak,* nearly 4 miles east-southeast of Bunker Hill (lat. 39°02'15" N, long. 120°18'45" W; on S line sec. 20, T 14 N, R 15 E). Altitude 7741 feet. Named on Wentworth Springs (1953) 7.5' quadrangle.

Guishetti [CALAVERAS]: *locality,* 3.25 miles west-southwest of present Tamarack (lat. 38°25' N, long. 120°08' W). Named on Big Trees (1891) 30' quadrangle.

Gully Meadow [TUOLUMNE]: *area,* 7 miles

east-northeast of Pinecrest (lat. 38°14'45" N, long. 119°53'05" W; sec. 33, T 5 N, R 19 E). Named on Pinecrest (1979) 7.5' quadrangle. Called Coyote Meadows on Pinecrest (1956) 15' quadrangle. United States Board on Geographic Names (1980a, p. 3) described Gully Meadow as the northernmost of the group called Three Meadows, and rejected the names "Coyote Meadow" and "Coyote Meadows" for the feature.

Gunsite [MARIPOSA]: *relief feature,* nearly 4 miles west-southwest of Yosemite Village on the south side of Yosemite Valley (lat. 37°43'10" N, long. 119°38'45" W). Named on Yosemite (1956) 15' quadrangle. Rangers of Yosemite National Park named the feature because the view along it has Leaning Tower centered as in a gunsite (Browning, 1986, p. 89).

Gurley: see **Gerle** [EL DORADO].

Gurley Creek: see **Gerle Creek** [EL DORADO].

Gwin: see **Rich Gulch** [CALAVERAS] (1).

Gwin Mine: see **Rich Gulch** [CALAVERAS] (1).

Gwin Mine Canyon: see **Rich Gulch** [CALAVERAS] (1).

Gwin's Peak: see **Liberty Cap** [MARIPOSA].

— H —

Hackett Creek [NEVADA]: *stream,* flows nearly 3 miles to Little Dry Creek 4 miles west-southwest of Pilot Peak (lat. 39°08'45" N, long. 121°15'15" W; near S line sec. 13, T 15 N, R 6 E). Named on Smartville (1951) 7.5' quadrangle.

Hackmans Falls [SIERRA]: *waterfall,* 0.5 mile southeast of Sierra City (lat. 39°33'30" N, long. 120°37'35" W; sec. 33, T 20 N, R 12 E); the feature is in Hackmans Ravine. Named on Sierra City (1981) 7.5' quadrangle.

Hackmans Ravine [SIERRA]: *canyon,* drained by a stream that flows 2 miles to North Yuba River at Sierra City (lat. 39°33'55" N, long. 120°37'40" W; at N line sec. 33, T 20 N, R 12 E). Named on Sierra City (1981) 7.5' quadrangle.

Hadselville Creek [AMADOR]: *stream,* heads in Amador County and flows 12 miles to Laguna Creek 8.5 miles northeast of Galt in Sacramento County (lat. 38°20'05" N, long. 121°11' W; near NW cor. sec. 35, T 6 N, R 7 E). Named on Clay (1968) and Goose Creek (1968) 7.5' quadrangles.

Hale [TUOLUMNE]: *locality,* 3 miles north of Long Barn along South Fork Stanislaus River (lat. 38°07'50" N, long. 120°08'30" W). Named on Big Trees (1891) 30' quadrangle.

Half Dome [MARIPOSA]: *relief feature,* 3 miles east of Yosemite Village (lat. 37°44'40" N, long. 119°32' W). Named on Yosemite (1956) 15' quadrangle. The men who discovered Yosemite Valley named the domelike feature in

1851 (Hanna, p. 131). United States Board on Geographic Names (1934, p. 11) rejected the names "Tesaiyak," "Tisayac," and "Tissa-ack" for it.

Half Moon Meadow [MARIPOSA]: *area,* 10.5 miles north of Yosemite Village (lat. 37°53'40" N, long. 119°32'45" W). Named on Hetch Hetchy Reservoir (1956) 15' quadrangle.

Half Way Gulch [MARIPOSA]: *canyon,* drained by a stream that flows nearly 2 miles to Bear Creek (2) 2.5 miles south-southeast of the village of Bear Valley (lat. 37°32'15" N, long. 120°05'50" W). Named on Bear Valley (1947) 7.5' quadrangle. Coulterville (1947) 15' quadrangle has the form "Halfway Gulch" for the name. Laizure's (1928) map shows a place called Half Way House located along Half Way Gulch.

Half Way House: see **Half Way Gulch** [MARIPOSA].

Halfway House: see **Woods Creek** [TUOLUMNE].

Half Moon Lake [EL DORADO]: *lake,* 2100 feet long, 4 miles south of Phipps Peak (lat. 38°53'50" N, long. 120°08'10" W; sec. 7, T 12 N, R 17 E). Named on Rockbound Valley (1955) 7.5' quadrangle. The name is from the shape of the lake (Gudde, 1949, p. 140).

Halleck Hill [CALAVERAS]: *peak,* 1.5 miles south-southwest of Vallecito (lat. 38°03'55" N, long. 120°29'20" W; sec. 36, T 3 N, R 13 E). Altitude 2235 feet. Named on Columbia (1948) 7.5' quadrangle.

Halls Gulch [MARIPOSA]: *canyon,* drained by a stream that flows 8.5 miles to Merced River 6.5 miles northeast of the village of Bear Valley (lat. 37°37'15" N, long. 120°01'15" W; sec. 6, T 4 S, R 18 E). Named on Buckhorn Peak (1947) and Kinsley (1947) 7.5' quadrangles. Called Hall Gulch on Bear Valley (1947) 7.5' quadrangle, but United States Board on Geographic Names (1978b, p. 4) rejected this form of the name. North Fork opens into the main canyon from the north 5 miles above the mouth of the main canyon; it is nearly 4 miles long and is named on Kinsley (1947) 7.5' quadrangle.

Halsey Afterbay [PLACER]: *lake,* 1100 feet long, 4.5 miles north-northeast of Auburn (lat. 38°57'25" N, long. 121°02'25" W; at NW cor. sec. 25, T 13 N, R 8 E). Named on Auburn (1953) 7.5' quadrangle.

Halsey Forebay [PLACER]: *lake,* 1100 feet long, 5.5 miles north-northeast of Auburn (lat. 38°58'20" N, long. 121°02'10" W; on S line sec. 13, T 13 N, R 8 E). Named on Auburn (1953) 7.5' quadrangle.

Ham Coward Gulch [MARIPOSA]: *canyon,* drained by a stream that flows nearly 2 miles to Gentry Gulch 4 miles northeast of Buckhorn Peak (lat. 37°41'40" N, long. 120°03'55" W; near S line sec. 2, T 3 S, R 17 E). Named on Buckhorn Peak (1947) 7.5' quadrangle.

Hamilton Camp [CALAVERAS]: *locality,* 3

miles east of Fort Mountain along Licking Fork (lat. 38°21'05" N, long. 120°25' W; sec. 27, T 6 N, R 14 E). Named on Fort Mountain (1979) 7.5' quadrangle.

Hamilton's Station: see **Buck Meadows** [MARIPOSA].

Hamlin Creek [SIERRA]: *stream,* flows 2.5 miles to Sierra Valley 2 miles west-southwest of Sierraville (lat. 39°34'40" N, long. 120°24'10" W; at S line sec. 15, T 20 N, R 14 E). Named on Sattley (1981) 7.5' quadrangle.

Hammel Point [PLACER]: *ridge,* west-south-west-trending, 0.5 mile long, 4 miles north-northwest of Foresthill (lat. 39°04'20" N, long. 120°51' W; sec. 9, T 14 N, R 10 E). Named on Foresthill (1949) 7.5' quadrangle.

Hammill Canyon [TUOLUMNE]: *canyon,* 2.5 miles long, along Herring Creek above a point 7.5 miles southwest of Dardanelle (lat. 38°15'20" N, long. 119°55'15" W; sec. 30, T 5 N, R 19 E). Named on Donnell Lake (1979) 7.5' quadrangle.

Hammils Mountain [TUOLUMNE]: *peak,* 4 miles northwest of Keystone (lat. 37°52'35" N, long. 120°33'25" W; near E line sec. 5, T 1 S, R 13 E). Altitude 1044 feet. Named on Melones Dam (1962) 7.5' quadrangle.

Hampshire Rocks Campground [PLACER]: *locality,* 9 miles west of Donner Pass (lat. 39°18'40" N, long. 120°29'50" W; sec. 27, T 17 N, R 13 E). Named on Soda Springs (1955) 7.5' quadrangle.

Hams [CALAVERAS]: *locality,* 5.5 miles west-northwest of Blue Mountain (lat. 38°22'25" N, long. 120°27'40" W; sec. 17, T 6 N, R 14 E). Named on Blue Mountain (1956) 15' quadrangle.

Hams: see **Hams Station** [AMADOR].

Ham Spring [AMADOR]: *spring,* nearly 6 miles west-northwest of Mokelumne Peak (lat. 38°33'25" N, long. 120°11'45" W; sec. 10, T 8 N, R 16 E). Named on Bear River Reservoir (1979) 7.5' quadrangle.

Hams Station [AMADOR]: *locality,* 25 miles east-northeast of Jackson (lat. 38°32'40" N, long. 120°22'30" W; sec. 13, T 8 N, R 14 E). Named on Caldor (1951) and Peddler Hill (1951) 7.5' quadrangles. Called Hams on Pyramid Peak (1896) 30' quadrangle. Wheeler (1879, p. 177) called Ham's Station a public house.

Hancock Creek [EL DORADO]: *stream,* flows nearly 4 miles to Folsom Lake 6 miles south-southwest of the village of Pilot Hill (lat. 38°45'45" N, long. 121°04'25" W; sec. 34, T 11 N, R 8 E). Named on Pilot Hill (1954, photorevised 1973) 7.5' quadrangle.

Hancock House: see **Bassetts** [SIERRA].

Handy Camp [PLACER]: *locality,* nearly 6 miles west-southwest of Granite Chief near Middle Fork American River (lat. 39°10'35" N, long. 120°23'10" W; near SW cor. sec. 2, T 15 N, R 14 E). Named on Royal Gorge (1953) 7.5' quadrangle.

Haney Mountain [NEVADA]: *peak,* 2.5 miles south of Pilot Peak (lat. 39°07'50" N, long. 121°11' W; near S line sec. 22, T 15 N, R 7 E). Altitude 1813 feet. Named on Rough and Ready (1949) 7.5' quadrangle. Called Haney Pk. on California Mining Bureau's (1917b) map.

Haney Peak: see **Haney Mountain** [NEVADA].

Hanging Basket Lake [MARIPOSA]: *lake,* 750 feet long, 5.5 miles southeast of Cathedral Peak (lat. 37°47'20" N, long. 119°19'50" W). Named on Tuolumne Meadows (1956) 15' quadrangle.

Hangtown: see **Placerville** [EL DORADO].

Hangtown Creek [EL DORADO]: *stream,* flows nearly 7 miles to Weber Creek 3.5 miles west of Placerville (lat. 38°44'15" N, long. 120°51'50" W; sec. 10, T 10 N, R 10 E); the stream flows through Placerville, which had the nickname "Hangtown." Named on Placerville (1949) 7.5' quadrangle.

Hangtown Hill: see **Placerville** [EL DORADO].

Hanks Exchange [EL DORADO]: *locality,* 4.5 miles southeast of Placerville (lat. 38°40'35" N, long. 120°45'05" W; sec. 34, T 10 N, R 11 E). Named on Placerville (1949) 7.5' quadrangle.

Happy Camp [MARIPOSA]: *locality,* less than 1 mile south-southwest of Fish Camp (lat. 37°28'10" N, long. 119°38'40" W; sec. 26, T 5 S, R 21 E). Named on Bass Lake (1953) 15' quadrangle.

Happy Camp: see **Fish Camp** [MARIPOSA].

Happy Hollow [MADERA]: *canyon,* drained by a stream that flows 3.5 miles to Coarse Gold Creek 6 miles southeast of Knowles (lat. 37°09'35" N, long. 119°47'45" W; sec. 9, T 9 S, R 20 E). Named on Knowles (1962) and Little Table Mountain (1962) 7.5' quadrangles.

Happy Hol Ravine [SIERRA]: *canyon,* drained by a stream that flows less than 0.5 mile to Canyon Creek nearly 6 miles southwest of Mount Fillmore (lat. 39°39'50" N, long. 120°54'55" W; sec. 24, T 21 N, R 9 E). Named on La Porte (1951) 7.5' quadrangle.

Happy Isles [MARIPOSA]: *islands,* 2 miles southeast of Yosemite Village in Merced River (lat. 37°43'50" N, long. 119°33'30" W). Named on Yosemite (1956) 15' quadrangle. W.E. Dennison named the islands for their effect on the emotions of visitors; James M Hutchings earlier called the place Island Rapids (Browning, 1986, p. 92).

Happy Valley [CALAVERAS]: *valley,* 1 mile east of Mokelumne Hill (lat. 38°18' N, long. 120°41'05" W; sec. 7, 8, T 5 N, R 12 E). Named on Mokelumne Hill (1948) 7.5' quadrangle. According to McKinstry (p. 358, 369), two canyons, Indian Gulch and Buckeye Gulch, join near the valley.

Happy Valley [EL DORADO]:
(1) *valley,* 13 miles east-southeast of Placerville (lat. 38°40'50" N, long. 120°33'45" W). Named on Placerville (1893) 30' quadrangle.
(2) *locality,* 7.25 miles east-southeast of

Camino (lat. 38°40'55" N, long. 120°33'40" W); the place is in Happy Valley (1). Named on Sly Park (1952) 7.5' quadrangle.

Hardenburg: see **Jackson** [AMADOR].

Harden Flat [TUOLUMNE]: *settlement,* 7 miles southwest of Mather along South Fork Tuolumne River (lat. 37°48'40" N, long. 119°56'45" W; sec. 36, T 1 S, R 18 E). Named on Lake Eleanor (1956) 15' quadrangle. According to Paden and Schlichtmann (p. 202), the name recalls James Hardin, an Englishman who owned land at the place. Yosemite (1909) 30' quadrangle shows Harden ranch at the site. United States Board on Geographic Names (1991, p. 4) approved the name "Crocker Meadow" for a flat located 3 miles east of Harden Flat (lat. 37°48'40" N, long. 119°53'30" W; sec. 33, T 1 S, R 19 E).

Harden Lake [TUOLUMNE]: *lake,* 1050 feet long, 2.25 miles northwest of White Wolf (lat. 37°53'45" N, long. 119°40'30" W). Named on Hetch Hetchy Reservoir (1956) 15' quadrangle. United States Board on Geographic Names (1933, p. 352) rejected the names "Hardin Lake," "Hardins Lake," "Hardin's Lake," and "Rardin Lake" for the feature.

Harding Point [SIERRA]: *ridge,* northwest-trending, less than 1 mile long, 2.25 miles northeast of Sierraville (lat. 39°36'45" N, long. 120°20'10" W; sec. 5, T 20 N, R 15 E). Named on Sierraville (1981) 7.5' quadrangle.

Hardin Lake: see **Harden Lake** [TUOLUMNE].

Hardscrabble: see **Ione** [AMADOR].

Hardscrabble Gulch [TUOLUMNE]: *canyon,* drained by a stream that flows 1 mile to Rattlesnake Gulch 1.5 miles east of Columbia (lat. 38°02' N, long. 120°22'15" W; near N line sec. 18, T 2 N, R 15 E). Named on Columbia SE (1948) 7.5' quadrangle.

Harmon Peak: see **Carmen Peak** [CALAVERAS].

Harmony Ridge [NEVADA]: *ridge,* southwest-to west-trending, 6 miles long, between Deer Creek and Rock Creek (1); center 6.5 miles south-southwest of North Bloomfield (lat. 39°17'10" N, long. 120°57'30" W). Named on Nevada City (1948) and North Bloomfield (1949) 7.5' quadrangles.

Harricks Ravine [EL DORADO]: *canyon,* drained by a stream that flows 1.25 miles to Rock Creek 5.25 miles northeast of Chili Bar (lat. 38°49'30" N, long. 120°45'25" W; sec. 4, T 11 N, R 11 E). Named on Garden Valley (1949) 7.5' quadrangle.

Harriet Lake [MADERA]: *lake,* 2000 feet long, 5.5 miles east-northeast of Merced Peak (lat. 37°40'25" N, long. 119°18'25" W). Named on Merced Peak (1953) 15' quadrangle.

Harris: see **Frank Harris Point** [MARIPOSA].

Harris Meadow [SIERRA]: *area,* 6 miles southwest of Sierra City (lat. 39°31'05" N, long. 120°43'45" W; sec. 15, T 19 N, R 11 E). Named on Sierra City (1981) 7.5' quadrangle.

Harry L. Englebright Lake: see **Englebright Lake** [NEVADA].

Harry L. Englebright Reservoir: see **Englebright Lake** [NEVADA].

Hart Lakes [MARIPOSA]: *lakes,* three, largest 800 feet long, 9 miles northeast of Wawona (lat. 37°37'15" N, long. 119°36'40" W; sec. 2, T 4 S, R 22 E). Named on Yosemite (1956) 15' quadrangle.

Hartless [EL DORADO]: *locality,* 2 miles west-northwest of Robbs Peak (lat. 38°56'15" N, long. 120°26'20" W). Named on Pyramid Peak (1896) 30' quadrangle.

Hartley Butte [NEVADA]: *peak,* 4 miles southeast of English Mountain (lat. 39°24'05" N, long. 120°30'10" W; sec. 27, T 18 N, R 13 E). Altitude 7450 feet. Named on English Mountain (1983) 7.5' quadrangle. The name commemorates Henry Hartley, who discovered gold in the vicinity of Meadow Lake in 1863 (Gudde, 1975, p. 211-212).

Harvey: see **Malby Crossing** [EL DORADO].

Harvey Gray Creek [PLACER]: *stream,* flows nearly 1 mile to Andrew Gray Creek 6.5 miles northwest of Duncan Peak (lat. 39° 13'25" N, long. 120°35'45" W; sec. 26, T 16 N, R 12 E). Named on Duncan Peak (1952) 7.5' quadrangle. The name is for Harvey Purdy Gray, a pioneer of the dried-fruit industry in California (United States Board on Geographic Names, 1967a, p. 2).

Harveys Bar: see **Horseshoe Bend** [MARIPOSA].

Harvey West: see **Camp Harvey West** [EL DORADO].

Haskell Creek [SIERRA]: *stream,* flows 2.25 miles to North Yuba River 6.25 miles northeast of Sierra City (lat. 39°37'55" N, long. 120°33'20" W; at N line sec. 6, T 20 N, R 13 E); the stream heads near Haskell Peak. Named on Clio (1981) 7.5' quadrangle.

Haskell Creek Homesites [SIERRA]: *locality,* 6.5 miles northeast of Sierra City (lat. 39°38'05" N, long. 120°33'10" W; near SE cor. sec. 31, T 21 N, R 13 E); the place is near the mouth of Haskell Creek. Named on Clio (1981) 7.5' quadrangle.

Haskell Meadow [MADERA]: *area,* nearly 2 miles south of Shuteye Peak (lat. 37°19'25" N, long. 119°25'55" W; on W line sec. 14, T 7 S, R 23 E). Named on Shuteye Peak (1953) 15' quadrangle. The name is for Bill Haskell and John Haskell, early sheepmen in the neighborhood (Browning, 1986, p. 93).

Haskell Peak [SIERRA]: *peak,* 8 miles north-northeast of Sierra City (lat. 39°39'45" N, long. 120°33'05" W; near SE cor. sec. 19, T 21 N, R 13 E). Altitude 8107 feet. Named on Clio (1981) 7.5' quadrangle. Called Mt. Haskells on California Division of Highways' (1934) map, and called Haskells Pk. on Logan's (1929) map. The name commemorates Edward W. Haskell, who had a ranch at the base of the peak (Gudde, 1969, p. 135).

Haskell Ravine [SIERRA]: *canyon,* drained by a stream that flows 3.25 miles to Plumas County 11 miles north-northeast of Sierra City (lat. 39°42'25" N, long. 120°32'25" W; near S line sec. 5, T 21 N, R 13 E); the canyon heads near Haskell Peak. Named on Clio (1981) 7.5' quadrangle.

Hastings Creek [EL DORADO]: *stream,* formed by the confluence of Blue Tent Creek and Black Rock Creek, flows 1.5 miles to South Fork American River 4.25 miles west-northwest of Coloma (lat. 38°49'05" N, long. 120°57'45" W; sec. 10, T 11 N, R 9 E). Named on Coloma (1949) 7.5' quadrangle. On Placerville (1893) 30' quadrangle, the name also applies to present Black Rock Creek.

Hatch Creek [TUOLUMNE]: *stream,* flows 5.5 miles to Don Pedro Reservoir 4.5 miles southsouthwest of Moccasin (lat. 37°45'05" N, long. 120°20'35" W; sec. 20, T 2 S, R 15 E). Named on Moccasin (1948) and Penon Blanco Peak (1962) 7.5' quadrangles.

Hathaway Pines [CALAVERAS]: *settlement,* 6.5 miles northeast of Murphys (lat. 38°11'30" N, long. 120°21'50" W; sec. 18, 19, T 4 N, R 15 E). Named on Stanislaus (1948) 7.5' quadrangle. Postal authorities established Hathaway Pines post office in 1943; the name is for Robert B. Hathaway, first postmaster and promoter of a vacation resort at the place (Salley, p. 94).

Haupt Creek [CALAVERAS]: *stream,* flows 4 miles to New Hogan Reservoir 4 miles east of Valley Springs (lat. 38°12' N, long. 120° 45'20" W; sec. 15, T 4 N, R 11 E). Named on San Andreas (1962) and Valley Springs (1962) 7.5' quadrangles.

Haven Lake [SIERRA]: *lake,* 2050 feet long, 7.25 miles north of Sierra City (lat. 39°40'15" N, long. 120°38' W; sec. 21, T 21 N, R 12 E). Named on Gold Lake (1981) 7.5' quadrangle.

Hawkeye [CALAVERAS]: *locality,* 4.25 miles northwest of Angels Camp along present Coopers Creek (lat. 38°06'30" N, long. 120° 36' W). Named on Jackson (1902) 30' quadrangle. Gudde (1975, p. 153) used the form "Hawk Eye" for the name.

Hawkins Bar: see **Red Mountain Bar** [TUOLUMNE].

Hawkins Canyon [NEVADA]: *canyon,* drained by a stream that flows 1 mile to an unnamed canyon nearly 5 miles northeast of Chicago Park (lat. 39°11'20" N, long. 120°53'50" W; sec. 6, T 15 N, R 10 E). Named on Chicago Park (1949) 7.5' quadrangle.

Hawksbeak Peak [TUOLUMNE]: *peak,* 2.5 miles east-northeast of Tower Peak on Tuolumne-Mono county line (lat. 38°09'30" N, long. 119°30'10" W). Named on Tower Peak (1956) 15' quadrangle.

Hawley Lake [SIERRA]: *lake,* 700 feet long, 9 miles north-northwest of Sierra City (lat. 39°41' N, long. 120°42'35" W; sec. 14, T 21 N, R 11 E); the lake is northeast of Hawley Meadow. Named on Gold Lake (1981) 7.5' quadrangle. Called Lake Hawley on Downieville (1897) 30' quadrangle.

Hawley Meadow [SIERRA]: *area,* 9 miles north-northwest of Sierra City (lat. 39°40'45" N, long. 120°42'50" W; sec. 14, T 21 N, R 11 E); the place is southwest of Hawley Lake. Named on Gold Lake (1981) 7.5' quadrangle.

Hayden Hill [PLACER]: *peak,* 4.25 miles southeast of Dutch Flat (lat. 39°10'08" N, long. 120°45'30" W; near S line sec. 6, T 15 N, R 11 E). Named on Dutch Flat (1950) 7.5' quadrangle.

Haydensville: see **Bear Valley** [MARIPOSA] (2).

Hayes Peak: see **Gray Peak** [MADERA].

Hay Flat [EL DORADO]: *area,* 4.25 miles west-northwest of Kirkwood (lat. 38°43'25" N, long. 120°08'25" W). Named on Tragedy Spring (1979) 7.5' quadrangle.

Hayford Hill [PLACER]: *peak,* 4 miles northeast of Colfax (lat. 39°08'35" N, long. 120°54'05" W; near N line sec. 19, T 15 N, R 10 E). Altitude 3219 feet. Named on Chicago Park (1949) 7.5' quadrangle.

Hay Gulch [CALAVERAS]: *canyon,* drained by a stream that flows 2 miles to Blue Creek nearly 5 miles west of Tamarack (lat. 38°26'15" N, long. 120°09'50" W; at S line sec. 24, T 7 N, R 16 E). Named on Calaveras Dome (1979) 7.5' quadrangle.

Haypress Creek [SIERRA]: *stream,* flows 12 miles to North Yuba River 1 mile east of Sierra City (lat. 39°34'05" N, long. 120°36'55" W; sec. 27, T 20 N, R 12 E); the stream goes through Haypress Valley. Named on Haypress Valley (1981) and Sattley (1981) 7.5' quadrangles. Called South Fork of North Fork Yuba River on Downieville (1897) 30' quadrangle, but United States Board on Geographic Names (1950, p. 5) rejected this name for the stream.

Haypress Creek: see **Long Valley Creek** [SIERRA] (2).

Haypress Lake [TUOLUMNE]: *lake,* 1300 feet long, 4.5 miles east-southeast of Dardanelle (lat. 38°18'25" N, long. 119°45'50" W; sec. 3, T 5 N, R 20 E); the lake is in Haypress Meadow. Named on Dardanelle (1979) 7.5' quadrangle.

Haypress Meadow [TUOLUMNE]: *area,* 4.5 miles southeast of Dardanelle (lat. 38°18'15" N, long. 119°45'50" W; on S line sec. 3, T 5 N, R 20 E). Named on Dardanelle (1979) 7.5' quadrangle.

Haypress Meadows [EL DORADO]: *area,* 5 miles northwest of Echo Summit (lat. 38°51'15" N, long. 120°06'30" W; at S line sec. 28, T 12 N, R 17 E). Named on Echo Lake (1955) 7.5' quadrangle.

Haypress Valley [SIERRA]: *valley,* 6.25 miles east-southeast of Sierra City (lat. 39°32'30" N, long. 120°30'45" W); the valley is along Haypress Creek. Named on Haypress Valley (1981) 7.5' quadrangle. Called Tehuantepec

Val. on Downieville (1897) 30' quadrangle, which has the name "Hay Press Valley" for the canyon of present Long Valley Creek (2).

Hays Meadow [TUOLUMNE]: *area,* 10 miles east-northeast of Pinecrest (lat. 30°13'30" N, long. 119°49'15" W). Named on Pinecrest (1956) 15' quadrangle.

Hays Ravine [SIERRA]: *canyon,* drained by a stream that flows 0.5 mile to Canyon Creek 2.5 miles south of Mount Fillmore (lat. 39° 41'30" N, long. 120°51' W). Named on Mount Fillmore (1951) 7.5' quadrangle.

Haystack Mountain [NEVADA]: *peak,* 2.5 miles southwest of English Mountain (lat. 39°25'10" N, long. 120°35' W; at SW cor. sec. 13, T 18 N, R 12 E). Altitude 7391 feet. Named on English Mountain (1983) 7.5' quadrangle.

Haystack Peak [TUOLUMNE]: *peak,* 8 miles west-southwest of Tower Peak (lat. 38°06'20" N, long. 119°40' W). Altitude 10,015 feet. Named on Tower Peak (1956) 15' quadrangle.

Hayward [MARIPOSA]: *locality,* 8.5 miles southwest of Penon Blanco Peak (lat. 37°38'30" N, long. 120°22'15" W; near E line sec. 25, T 3 S, R 14 E); the place is near Hayward Creek. Named on Penon Blanco Peak (1962) 7.5' quadrangle.

Hayward Creek [CALAVERAS]: *stream,* flows 3.5 miles to South Fork Mokelumne River 3 miles east of Blue Mountain (lat. 38°20'40" N, long. 120°18'20" W; sec. 27, T 6 N, R 15 E). Named on Dorrington (1979) 7.5' quadrangle.

Hayward Creek [MARIPOSA]: *stream,* heads in Mariposa County and flows 9 miles to Dry Creek 4.5 miles north-northeast of Snelling in Merced County (lat. 37°34'50" N, long. 120°24'35" W; near SE cor. sec. 15, T 4 S, R 14 E). Named on La Grange (1962), Penon Blanco Peak (1962), and Snelling (1962) 7.5' quadrangles.

Hazel Creek [EL DORADO]: *stream,* flows 4 miles to Jenkinson Lake 8 miles east of Camino (lat. 38°44'15" N, long. 120°31'50" W; near NW cor. sec. 10, T 10 N, R 13 E). Named on Riverton (1950), Sly Park (1952, photorevised 1973), and Stump Spring (1951) 7.5' quadrangles. On Placerville (1893) 30' quadrangle, present Hazel Creek is shown as the upper part of Sly Park Creek.

Hazel Creek: see **Sly Park Creek** [EL DORADO].

Hazel Dell Gulch [CALAVERAS]: *canyon,* 1 mile long, opens into the canyon of Jack Nelson Creek 4 miles southwest of Rail Road Flat (lat. 38°17'50" N, long. 120°33'20" W; near SE cor. sec. 8, T 5 N, R 13 E). Named on Rail Road Flat (1948) 7.5' quadrangle.

Hazel Green [MARIPOSA]: *locality,* 8 miles northwest of El Portal (lat. 37°46' N, long. 119°52' W; at S line sec. 10, T 2 S, R 19 E). Named on Yosemite (1909) 30' quadrangle. Lake Eleanor (1956) 15' quadrangle shows Hazel Green ranch at the place.

Hazel Green Creek [TUOLUMNE]: *stream,* flows 2.5 miles to North Crane Creek 6 miles south of Mather (lat. 37°48' N, long. 119°50'45" W; near SE cor. sec. 35, T 1 S, R 19 E). Named on Lake Eleanor (1956) 15' quadrangle. United States Board on Geographic Names (1933, p. 358) rejected the name "Big Creek" for the stream. Lafayette H. Bunnell gave the name "Hazel Green" in 1856 to a campsite on the trail to Yosemite Valley because of the hazel bushes growing near the site (Hanna, p. 135).

Hazel Green Creek: see **Big Creek** [TUOLUMNE] (3).

Hazel Valley [EL DORADO]: *valley,* 7.5 miles east of Camino where Hazel Creek joined Sly Park Creek before creation of Jenkinson Lake (lat. 38°44' N, long. 120°32' W). Named on Camino (1952) 15' quadrangle.

Head Dam [SIERRA]: *locality,* 6 miles north-northwest of Goodyears Bar along Little Canyon Creek (lat. 39°36'55" N, long. 120° 56'35" W; near W line sec. 11, T 20 N, R 9 E). Site named on Goodyears Bar (1951) 7.5' quadrangle.

Headland: see **Cabin Creek** [PLACER].

Heather Glen [PLACER]: *area,* 6 miles south-southwest of Colfax (lat. 39°01'05" N, long. 120°58'55" W; sec. 33, T 14 N, R 9 E). Named on Colfax (1949) 7.5' quadrangle.

Heather Lake [EL DORADO]: *lake,* 2200 feet long, 5.5 miles south of Phipps Peak (lat. 38°52'40" N, long. 120°08'15" W; sec. 19, T 12 N, R 17 E). Named on Pyramid Peak (1955) and Rockbound Valley (1955) 7.5' quadrangles.

Heath Springs [PLACER]: *springs,* 7.5 miles west-northwest of Granite Chief (lat. 39°15' N, long. 120°16'50" W; sec. 16, T 16 N, R 14 E). Named on Royal Gorge (1953) 7.5' quadrangle.

Heaton Station: see **Cisco** [PLACER].

Heavenly Valley [EL DORADO]: *valley,* nearly 5 miles north of Freel Peak (lat. 38°55'25" N, long. 119°54'50" W; sec. 1, T 12 N, R 18 E). Named on South Lake Tahoe (1955) 7.5' quadrangle.

Heavenly Valley Creek [EL DORADO]: *stream,* flows 4.25 miles to Trout Creek 6 miles north-west of Freel Peak (lat. 38°55'15" N, long. 119°58'15" W; sec. 3, T 12 N, R 18 E); the creek goes through Heavenly Valley. Named on South Lake Tahoe (1955) 7.5' quadrangle. The stream first was called Miller Creek for John G. Miller, who built Miller House beside the creek in 1862 and ran a dairy (Lekisch, p. 61).

Heavens Gate [PLACER]: *pass,* 4 miles southwest of Granite Chief (lat. 39°08'55" N, long. 120°19'50" W; at E line sec. 18, T 15 N, R 15 E). Named on Granite Chief (1953) 7.5' quadrangle.

Hebron Mill [TUOLUMNE]: *locality,* 6.5 miles east-southeast of Groveland (lat. 37°47'30" N, long. 120°07'30" W); the place is 0.5 mile west of present Hobron Hill. Named on Sonora (1897) 30' quadrangle.

Heiser Canyon [CALAVERAS]: *canyon,* 3.5 miles long, on upper reaches of Dry Creek (1) above a point 9 miles west of Angels Camp (lat. 38°04'15" N, long. 120°42'50" W; sec. 36, T 3 N, R 11 E). Named on Salt Spring Valley (1962) 7.5' quadrangle. San Andreas (1947) 15' quadrangle has the name "Heiser Creek" for the stream in the canyon.

Heiser Creek: see **Dry Creek** [CALAVERAS] (1); **Heiser Canyon** [CALAVERAS].

Helen Lake [TUOLUMNE]: *lake,* 2100 feet long, 6 miles south-southeast of Tioga Pass (lat. 37°49'50" N, long. 119°13'40" W). Named on Mono Craters (1953) 15' quadrangle. R.B. Marshall of United States Geological Survey named the lake in 1900 for Helen Coburn Smith, daughter of George Otis Smith (United States Board on Geographic Names, 1934, p. 11).

Helen Lake: see **Maxwell Lake** [TUOLUMNE]; **Starr King Lake** [MARIPOSA].

Helester Point [PLACER]: *peak,* 3.5 miles northwest of Westville (lat. 39°12'50" N, long. 120°41'35" W; near N line sec. 36, T 16 N, R 11 E). Altitude 4930 feet. Named on Westville (1952) 7.5' quadrangle.

Helgeson Flat: see **Holbrook Flat** [NEVADA].

Helisma Station [CALAVERAS]: *locality,* 3.25 miles west of Valley Springs along Southern Pacific Railroad at Burson (lat. 38°11' N, long. 120°53'20" W; on W line sec. 21, T 4 N, R 10 E). Named on Wallace (1962) 7.5' quadrangle.

Hell Hole [EL DORADO]: *valley,* 3.25 miles southwest of Freel Peak (lat. 38°49'40" N, long. 119°56'35" W; near W line sec. 1, T 11 N, R 19 E). Named on Freel Peak (1955) 7.5' quadrangle.

Hell Hole: see **Lower Hell Hole** [PLACER]; **Upper Hell Hole** [PLACER].

Hell Hole Reservoir [PLACER]: *lake,* behind a dam on Rubicon River 1.5 miles west-northwest of Bunker Hill (lat. 39°03'30" N, long. 120°24'30" W; near S line sec. 16, T 14 N, R 14 E); water of the lake covers Lower Hell Hole and Upper Hell Hole. Named on Bunker Hill (1953, photorevised 1973) and Wentworth Springs (1953, photorevised 1973) 7.5' quadrangles.

Hell Out for High Noon City: see **Alpha** [NEVADA].

Hell Hollow [MARIPOSA]: *canyon,* 1.5 miles long, opens into the canyon of Merced River 9 miles northeast of Hornitos opposite Bagby (lat. 37°36'35" N, long. 120°08'10" W). Named on Hornitos (1947) 7.5' quadrangle. Called Hell's Hollow Gulch on Laizure's (1928) map. Shirley Sargent (1976, p. 17) called the feature Hell's Hollow, and attributed the name to the danger, difficulty of access, and summer heat of the place.

Hells Delight Creek [EL DORADO]: *stream,* flows 2.5 miles to Silver Fork American River 8 miles west of Kirkwood (lat. 38°42'45" N, long. 120°13'20" W; sec. 17, T 10 N, R 16 E); the stream goes through Hells Delight Valley. Named on Tragedy Spring (1979) 7.5' quadrangle.

Hells Delight Valley [EL DORADO]: *valley,* 9 miles west of Kirkwood (lat. 38°42'05" N, long. 120°14' W; near W line sec. 20, T 10 N, R 16 E). Named on Tragedy Spring (1979) 7.5' quadrangle.

Hells Half Acre [MADERA]: *area,* 9 miles east-northeast of Shuteye Peak near San Joaquin River (lat. 37°24'15" N, long. 119°16'25" W). Named on Shuteye Peak (1953) 15' quadrangle.

Hells Half Acre [PLACER]: *relief feature,* 2 miles northeast of Bunker Hill (lat. 39°03'40" N, long. 120°21'10" W; sec. 13, T 14 N, R 14 E). Named on Wentworth Springs (1953) 7.5' quadrangle.

Hells Half Acre [TUOLUMNE]: *area,* 3.5 miles north-northwest of Strawberry along Middle Fork Stanislaus River (lat. 38°14'50" N, long. 120°02' W; sec. 31, T 5 N, R 18 E). Named on Strawberry (1979) 7.5' quadrangle.

Hells Hollow [TUOLUMNE]: *area,* 5 miles east-southeast of Groveland (lat. 37°47'55" N, long. 120°09' W; near NE cor. sec. 1, T 2 S, R 16 E). Named on Groveland (1947) 7.5' quadrangle. Paden and Schlichtmann (p. 186) used the form "Hell's Hollow" for the name.

Hell's Hollow: see **Hell Hollow** [MARIPOSA].

Hells Hollow Creek [TUOLUMNE]: *stream,* flows 2.5 miles to Big Creek 5.5 miles east-southeast of Groveland (lat. 37°48'40" N, long. 120°08'05" W; sec. 32, T 1 S, R 17 E); the stream goes through Hells Hollow. Named on Groveland (1947) 7.5' quadrangle.

Hell's Hollow Gulch: see **Hell Hollow** [MARIPOSA].

Hells Hollow Ridge [TUOLUMNE]: *ridge,* northeast-trending, nearly 1 mile long, 4 miles southeast of Groveland (lat. 37°48'25" N, long. 120°10'10" W); the ridge is northwest of Hells Hollow. Named on Groveland (1947) 7.5' quadrangle.

Hells Kitchen [CALAVERAS-TUOLUMNE]: *area,* 2 miles south of Tamarack along North Fork Stanislaus River on Calaveras-Tuolumne county line (lat. 38°24'35" N, long. 120°04'45" W). Named on Tamarack (1979) 7.5' quadrangle.

Hells Mountain [TUOLUMNE]: *peak,* 9 miles south-southeast of Pinecrest (lat. 38°04'25" N, long. 119°54'55" W). Altitude 6996 feet. Named on Cherry Lake North (1979) 7.5' quadrangle.

Helms Creek [MADERA]: *stream,* flows 2.25 miles to Fine Gold Creek 5 miles west-southwest of the town of North Fork (lat. 37° 12'15" N, long. 119°35'45" W; sec. 29, T 8 S, R 22 E). Named on North Fork (1965) 7.5' quadrangle.

Hemlock Crossing [MADERA]: *locality,* 8

miles west of Devils Postpile along North Fork San Joaquin River (lat. 37°38'20" N, long. 119°13'25" W). Named on Devils Postpile (1953) 15' quadrangle.

Hemlock Lake [EL DORADO]: *lake,* 325 feet long, 2.25 miles west-northwest of Pyramid Peak (lat. 38°51'40" N, long. 120°11'35" W). Named on Pyramid Peak (1955) 7.5' quadrangle.

Henderson Reservoir [AMADOR]: *lake,* 1600 feet long, behind a dam on Jackass Creek nearly 4 miles northeast of Ione (lat. 38°23'05" N, long. 120°52'30" W; sec. 9, T 6 N, R 10 E). Named on Amador City (1962) and Irish Hill (1962) 7.5' quadrangles. Called Preston Res. on Sutter Creek (1944) 15' quadrangle, but United States Board on Geographic Names (1964a, p. 10) rejected this name for the feature.

Henly Canyon [AMADOR]: *canyon,* drained by a stream that flows 2.5 miles to Bear River 6 miles east-southeast of Hams Station (lat. 38°30'25" N, long. 120°16'30" W; sec. 36, T 8 N, R 15 E). Named on Peddler Hill (1951) 7.5' quadrangle.

Henness [MARIPOSA]: *locality,* 1.25 miles west of El Portal along Yosemite Valley Railroad (lat. 37°40'15" N, long. 119°48' W). Named on Yosemite (1909) 30' quadrangle. The name recalls James A. Hennessy, who had an extensive truck garden at present El Portal in the 1870's (Mendershausen, p. 21).

Henness Branch [MARIPOSA]: *stream,* flows 2 miles to Merced River 0.5 mile west-southwest of El Portal (lat. 37°40'15" N, long. 119°47'20" W). Named on El Portal (1947) 15' quadrangle. United States Board on Geographic Names (1933, p. 361) rejected the names "Hennessy Branch," "Ward's Branch," and "Wilsons Branch" for the stream.

Henness Pass [SIERRA]: *pass,* 7.25 miles south-southwest of Sierraville (lat. 39°30'05" N, long. 120°26'15" W; at E line sec. 19, T 19 N, R 14 E). Named on Sattley (1981) 7.5' quadrangle.

Henness Ridge [MARIPOSA]: *ridge,* generally west-trending, 2.5 miles long, 11 miles south-west of Yosemite Village (lat. 37°38'30" N, long. 119°43'45" W). Named on Yosemite (1956) 15' quadrangle.

Hennessy Branch: see **Henness Branch** [MARIPOSA].

Henrys Diggings [EL DORADO]: *locality,* 1.5 miles north-northeast of Omo Ranch (lat. 38°36'10" N, long. 120°33'20" W). Named on Omo Ranch (1952) 7.5' quadrangle. Called Henry Diggings on Placerville (1893) 30' quadrangle.

Hensley Lake [MADERA]: *lake,* behind a dam on Fresno River 7.5 miles south of Raymond (lat. 37°06'40" N, long. 119°53' W; near N line sec. 34, T 9 S, R 19 E). Named on Daulton (1962, photorevised 1981), Knowles (1962, photorevised 1981), Little Table Moun-

tain (1962, photorevised 1981), and Raymond (1962, photorevised 1981) 7.5' quadrangles.

Herbeck Flat [MARIPOSA]: *area,* 1 mile west-southwest of Penon Blanco Peak (lat. 37°43'45" N, long. 120°16'30" W; on W line sec. 25, T 2 S, R 15 E). Named on Penon Blanco Peak (1962) 7.5' quadrangle.

Herbert: see **Raymond** [MADERA].

Herleys [EL DORADO]: *locality,* 9 miles south-southeast of Placerville (lat. 38°36'10" N, long. 120°44'25" W). Named on Placerville (1893) 30' quadrangle.

Hermit Spring [CALAVERAS]: *spring,* 9 miles west of Tamarack (lat. 38°25'25" N, long. 120°14'15" W; sec. 29, T 7 N, R 16 E). Named on Calaveras Dome (1979) 7.5' quadrangle.

Herring Creek [TUOLUMNE]: *stream,* flows 11 miles to South Fork Stanislaus River 0.5 mile north of Pinecrest (lat. 38°12'05" N, long. 119°59'55" W; sec. 16, T 4 N, R 18 E). Named on Dardanelle (1979), Donnell Lake (1979), and Pinecrest (1979) 7.5' quadrangles.

Herring Creek Reservoir [TUOLUMNE]: *lake,* behind a dam on Herring Creek 8 miles southwest of Dardanelle (lat. 38°15'05" N, long. 119°55'35" W; sec. 30, T 5 N, R 19 E). Named on Donnell Lake (1979) 7.5' quadrangle. Called Herring Reservoir on California Division of Highways' (1934) map.

Herring Reservoir [NEVADA]: *lake,* 350 feet long, 3 miles east-northeast of Grass Valley (lat. 39°14'15" N, long. 121°00'30" W; sec. 19, T 16 N, R 9 E). Named on Grass Valley (1949) 7.5' quadrangle.

Herring Reservoir: see **Herring Creek Reservoir** [TUOLUMNE].

Hesse's Crossing: see **Freemans Crossing** [NEVADA].

Hess Mill [TUOLUMNE]: *locality,* 4.5 miles north of Twain Harte along Dry Creek (lat. 38°06'10" N, long. 120°14'15" W; sec. 20, T 3 N, R 16 E). Site named on Twain Harte (1979) 7.5' quadrangle.

Hetch Hetchy: see **Mather** [TUOLUMNE].

Hetch Hetchy Dome [TUOLUMNE]: *peak,* 8 miles northeast of Mather (lat. 37°57'55" N, long. 119°45'10" W; near NW cor. sec. 11, T 1 N, R 20 E); the peak is on the north side of Hetch Hetchy Reservoir. Named on Lake Eleanor (1956) 15' quadrangle. Called Hetch Hetchy Mtn. on Yosemite (1909) 30' quadrangle. United States Board on Geographic Names (1934, p. 11) rejected the name "North Dome" for the feature.

Hetch Hetchy Fall: see **Wapama Falls** [TUOLUMNE].

Hetch Hetchy Junction [TUOLUMNE]: *locality,* 5.5 miles south-southwest of Chinese Camp along Sierra Railway (lat. 37°48'05" N, long. 120°29'15" W; sec. 36, T 1 S, R 13 E); the place is near the railroad crossing of Hetch Hetchy aqueduct. Named on Chinese Camp (1947) 7.5' quadrangle. Postal authorities established Hetch Hetchy Junction post office in 1926 and discontinued it in 1930 (Frickstad, p. 215).

Hetch Hetchy Mountain: see **Hetch Hetchy Dome** [TUOLUMNE].

Hetch Hetchy Reservoir [TUOLUMNE]: *lake,* behind a dam on Tuolumne River 6 miles northeast of Mather (lat. 37°56'50" N, long. 119°47'15" W; sec. 16, T 1 N, R 20 E). Named on Hetch Hetchy Reservoir (1956) and Lake Eleanor (1956) 15' quadrangles.

Hetch Hetchy Valley [TUOLUMNE]: *valley,* 4 miles long, along Tuolumne River above a point 6 miles northeast of Mather Station (present Mather) (lat. 37°56'50" N, long. 119°47'15" W). Named on Yosemite (1909) 30' quadrangle. Water of Hetch Hetchy Reservoir now floods most of the Yosemitelike valley. The term "Hetch Hetchy" is from the Indian name for a kind of grass with edible seeds that was abundant in the valley (Kroeber, p. 42). Hoffmann (p. 266) referred to "Tuolumne Valley, or Hetch-Hetchy, as it is called by the Indians."

Hetch Hetchy Valley: see **Little Hetch Hetchy Valley** [TUOLUMNE].

Hewett: see **Cooks Station** [AMADOR].

Hewitt Valley [MADERA]: *valley,* 7 miles east-southeast of O'Neals (lat. 37°05'05" N, long. 119°34'55" W). Named on Millerton Lake East (1965) 7.5' quadrangle.

Hicks Gulch [AMADOR]: *canyon,* drained by a stream that flows 1 mile to Sutter Creek (1) nearly 2 miles east-northeast of Ione (lat. 38°21'30" N, long. 120°54' W; sec. 20, T 6 N, R 10 E). Named on Ione (1962) 7.5' quadrangle. Camp's (1962) map shows a feature called Hicks Hill located near present Hicks Gulch.

Hicks Hill: see **Hicks Gulch** [AMADOR].

Hicks Spring [CALAVERAS]: *spring,* 1.25 miles west-northwest of Copperopolis (lat. 37°59'15" N, long. 120°39'45" W; near N line sec. 33, T 2 N, R 12 E). Named on Copperopolis (1962) 7.5' quadrangle.

Hidden Gold Camp [PLACER]: *locality,* 3.25 miles south-southwest of Dutch Flat (lat. 39°09'55" N, long. 120°51'30" W; sec. 9, T 15 N, R 19 E). Named on Dutch Flat (1950) 7.5' quadrangle.

Hidden Lake [AMADOR]: *lake,* 650 feet long, 6.25 miles north of Mokelumne Peak (lat. 38°37'40" N, long. 120°06'30" W; sec. 16, T 9 N, R 17 E). Named on Caples Lake (1979) 7.5' quadrangle.

Hidden Lake [EL DORADO]:
(1) *lake,* 450 feet long, 3.25 miles east of Wentworth Springs (lat. 39°00'15" N, long. 120°16'45" W; sec. 3, T 13 N, R 15 E). Named on Wentworth Springs (1953, photorevised 1973) 7.5' quadrangle.
(2) *lake,* 750 feet long, 2.25 miles north of Phipps Peak (lat. 38° 59'10" N, long. 120°09'05" W; near SE cor. sec. 12, T 13 N, R 16 E). Named on Rockbound Valley (1955) 7.5' quadrangle.

Hidden Lake: see **Ruth Lake** [MADERA].

Hidden Lake [MARIPOSA]: *lake,* 800 feet long, nearly 6 miles west-southwest of Cathedral Peak (lat. 37°48'20" N, long. 119°29'40" W; near E line sec. 36, T 1 S, R 22 E). Named on Tuolumne Meadows (1956) 15' quadrangle.

Hidden Lake [NEVADA]: *lake,* 450 feet long, 5 miles southwest of English Mountain (lat. 39°24'05" N, long. 120°37'20" W; on E line sec. 28, T 18 N, R 12 E). Named on English Mountain (1983) 7.5' quadrangle.

Hidden Valley [PLACER]:
(1) *canyon,* drained by a stream that flows 1 mile to Campbell Creek 2 miles southwest of Colfax (lat. 39°05'10" N, long. 120° 59' W; near N line sec. 9, T 14 N, R 9 E). Named on Colfax (1949) 7.5' quadrangle.
(2) *locality,* 4.25 miles east-southeast of Rocklin (lat. 38°45'50" N, long. 121°09'45" W; near N line sec. 35, T 11 N, R 7 E). Named on Rocklin (1967) 7.5' quadrangle. Arrowsmith's (1860) map shows a place called Union House located at or near present Hidden Valley (2), and a place called Wildwood located about 0.5 mile farther northeast.

Hideaway Lake: see **Ruth Lake** [MADERA].

Higgins Corner [NEVADA]: *locality,* 12.5 miles south of Grass Valley (lat. 39°02'35" N, long. 121°05'40" W; at S line sec. 21, T 14 N, R 8 E). Named on Lake Combie (1949) 7.5' quadrangle.

Higgins Point: see **Salmon Falls** [EL DORADO] (2).

High Commission [SIERRA]: *peak,* less than 1 mile east-northeast of Downieville (lat. 39°34' N, long. 120°48'50" W; near SW cor. sec. 25, T 20 N, R 10 E). Altitude 4225 feet. Named on Downieville (1951) 7.5' quadrangle.

High Emigrant Lake [TUOLUMNE]: *lake,* 700 feet long, 6.5 miles northwest of Tower Peak (lat. 38°12'30" N, long. 119°37'50" W); the lake is 0.5 mile north of Emigrant Pass. Named on Tower Peak (1956) 15' quadrangle.

Highland Creek [TUOLUMNE]: *stream,* heads in Alpine County and flows 8 miles in Tuolumne County to North Fork Stanislaus River 2.5 miles north-northeast of Liberty Hill (lat. 38°24'15" N, long. 120°05'20" W). Named on Spicer Meadow Reservoir (1979) and Tamarack (1979) 7.5' quadrangles. The name recalls Highland City, an early mining camp in Alpine County (Gudde, 1949, p. 148).

Highland Lake [EL DORADO]: *lake,* 1250 feet long, 5 miles west of Phipps Peak (lat. 38°57'25" N, long. 120°14'25" W; on W line sec. 20, T 13 N, R 16 E). Named on Rockbound Valley (1955) 7.5' quadrangle.

High Loch Lake [PLACER]: *lake,* 850 feet long, 9.5 miles west-southwest of Donner Pass (lat. 39°17'10" N, long. 120°29'45" W; near NE cor. sec. 3, T 16 N, R 13 E). Named on Soda Springs (1955) 7.5' quadrangle. Truckee (1940) 30' quadrangle shows the lake as one of the group called Lac Leven Lakes. United States Board on Geographic Names (1962b, p. 19) rejected the name "High Loch Leven" for the feature.

High Loch Leven: see **High Loch Lake** [PLACER].

High Meadows [EL DORADO]: *area*, 2.5 miles north of Freel Peak along Cold Creek (lat. 38°53'45" N, long. 119°54'15" W; near SE cor. sec. 12, T 12 N, R 18 E). Named on South Lake Tahoe (1955) 7.5' quadrangle. Called High Meadow on Markleeville (1889) 30' quadrangle.

High Mountain [CALAVERAS]: *peak*, 9.5 miles east-southeast of San Andreas (lat. 38°10'10" N, long. 120°30'35" W; sec. 26, T 4 N, R 13 E). Altitude 2450 feet. Named on Calaveritas (1962) 7.5' quadrangle.

High Sierra: see **Camp High Sierra** [TUOLUMNE]; "Regional setting."

High Sierra Campground [MARIPOSA]: *locality*, 7.5 miles south of Cathedral Peak along Merced River (lat. 37°44'20" N, long. 119° 24'15" W); the place is in the Sierra Nevada. Named on Merced Peak (1953) 15' quadrangle.

High Sierra Park [TUOLUMNE]: *settlement*, 5.25 miles northeast of Twain Harte (lat. 38°04'45" N, long. 120°08'55" W; sec. 30, 31, T 3 N, R 17 E). Named on Twain Harte (1979) 7.5' quadrangle.

Hildreth [MADERA]: *locality*, 3.5 miles east-southeast of O'Neals (lat. 37°06'35" N, long. 119°37'55" W; sec. 36, T 9 N, R 21 E). Named on Millerton Lake West (1965) 7.5' quadrangle. Postal authorities established Hildreth post office in 1886 and discontinued it in 1896 (Frickstad, p. 86). The place began in the late 1870's when Tom Hildreth opened a store there (Clough, p. 85). Logan's (1950) map shows a place called Birch located about 3 miles west-northwest of Hildreth.

Hildreth Creek [MADERA]: *stream*, flows 14 miles to Cottonwood Creek (2) 5.5 miles north-northeast of Trigo (lat. 36°59'20" N, long. 119°56' W; sec. 7, T 11 S, R 19 E). Named on Herndon (1965) and Raymond (1962) 15' quadrangles.

Hildreth Mountain [MADERA]: *peak*, 3 miles east of O'Neals (lat. 37°07'15" N, long. 119°38'15" W; near W line sec. 25, T 9 S, R 21 E); the peak is less than 1 mile north-northwest of Hildreth. Altitude 2058 feet. Named on Millerton Lake West (1965) 7.5' quadrangle.

Hildreth's Diggings: see **Columbia** [TUOLUMNE].

Hill Crest [NEVADA]: *locality*, nearly 6 miles west-northwest of Pilot Peak (lat. 39°12'20" N, long. 121°16'40" W; at E line sec. 34, T 16 N, R 6 E). Named on Smartville (1951) 7.5' quadrangle.

Hills [CALAVERAS]: *locality*, 7.5 miles west-northwest of Valley Springs (lat. 38°12'50" N,

long. 120°57'50" W). Named on Jackson (1902) 30' quadrangle. Water of Camanche Reservoir now covers the site.

Hills Flat [NEVADA]: *locality*, 0.5 mile northeast of downtown Grass Valley (lat. 39°13'25" N, long. 121°03'10" W; near NW cor. sec. 26, T 16 N, R 8 E). Named on Grass Valley (1949) 7.5' quadrangle.

Hillside: see **Knowles** [MADERA].

Hillyer and Burnham Ferry: see **Stanislaus River** [CALAVERAS-TUOLUMNE].

Hinkle Reservoir [PLACER]: *lake*, 1400 feet long, 2.5 miles north of Folsom on Placer-Sacramento county line (lat. 38°42'50" N, long. 121°10'20" W; on N line sec. 23, T 10 N, R 7 E). Named on Folsom (1967) 7.5' quadrangle.

Hinton [NEVADA]: *locality*, 7 miles east-northeast of Truckee along Southern Pacific Railroad (lat. 39°22'30" N, long. 120°04'20" W; near S line sec. 27, T 18 N, R 17 E). Named on Boca (1955) 7.5' quadrangle.

Hirschdale [NEVADA]: *locality*, 6.25 miles east-northeast of Truckee (lat. 39°22'05" N, long. 120°04'35" W; sec. 34, T 18 N, R 17 E). Named on Martis Peak (1955) 7.5' quadrangle.

Hitchcock Ranch: see **Green Valley** [EL DORADO].

Hite: see **Hite Cove** [MARIPOSA].

Hite Cove [MARIPOSA]: *locality*, 4.5 miles west-southwest of El Portal along South Fork Merced River (lat. 37°38'25" N, long. 119°50'50" W; sec. 27, T 3 S, R 19 E). Named on El Portal (1947) 7.5' quadrangle. Hoffmann and Gardner's (1863-1867) map shows a place called Hite's Cove located near the confluence of South Fork with Merced River. The name commemorates John Hite, who discovered gold at the place (Chamberlain, p. 4). Postal authorities established Hites Cove post office in 1868, discontinued it in 1869, reestablished it in 1878, and discontinued it in 1889; they established Hite post office at a new site in 1901 and discontinued it in 1902 (Salley, p. 98).

Hites Cove: see **Hite Cove** [MARIPOSA].

Hobart Creek [TUOLUMNE]: *stream*, heads in Alpine County and flows 3 miles to Spicer Meadow Reservoir 9.5 miles west-northwest of Dardanelle (lat. 38°23'40" N, long. 119°59'45" W). Named on Spicer Meadow Reservoir (1979) 7.5' quadrangle.

Hobart Mills [NEVADA]: *locality*, 5 miles north of Truckee (lat. 39° 24'05" N, long. 120°11' W; near NE cor. sec. 22, T 18 N, R 16 E). Named on Hobart Mills (1981) 7.5' quadrangle. Postal authorities established Hobart Mills post office in 1900 and discontinued it in 1938 (Frickstad, p. 113). The name "Hobart" commemorates Walter Scott Hobart (Hanna, p. 139).

Hobart Reservoir [NEVADA]: *lake*, 400 feet long, 1.25 miles northwest of Hobart Mills (lat. 39°25' N, long. 120°11'50" W; near NW cor. sec. 15, T 18 N, R 16 E). Named on Hobart Mills (1981) 7.5' quadrangle.

Hoboken Canyon [EL DORADO]: *canyon,* drained by a stream that flows 1.5 miles to American Canyon 2.5 miles north-northwest of Greenwood (lat. 38°55'55" N, long. 120°56' W; near E line sec. 35, T 13 N, R 9 E). Named on Greenwood (1949) 7.5' quadrangle. On Placerville (1893) 30' quadrangle, the stream in the canyon has the name "Hoboken Creek."

Hoboken Creek: see **Hoboken Canyon** [EL DORADO].

Hobron Hill [MARIPOSA-TUOLUMNE]: *peak,* less than 1 mile southwest of Smith Peak on Mariposa-Tuolumne county line (lat. 37°47'40" N, long. 120°06'40" W; near E line sec. 5, T 2 S, R 17 E). Altitude 3805 feet. Named on Jawbone Ridge (1947) 7.5' quadrangle.

Hodgdon Meadows: see **Hodgdon Ranch** [TUOLUMNE].

Hodgdon Ranch [TUOLUMNE]: *locality,* 6 miles south of Mather (lat. 37°47'50" N, long. 119°51'25" W; near N line sec. 3, T 2 S, R 19 E). Named on Lake Eleanor (1956) 15' quadrangle. The site first was called Moore and Bowen Camp, then Bronson Meadows, and finally Hodgdon Meadows after T.J. Hodgdon settled there in 1865 (Uhte, p. 63-64). Hodgdon eventually built an inn for travelers going to Yosemite Valley (Paden and Schlichtmann, p. 216).

Hodson [CALAVERAS]: *village,* 2.5 miles west-northwest of Copperopolis (lat. 37°59'50" N, long. 120°41' W; sec. 29, T 2 N, R 12 E). Named on Copperopolis (1916) 15' quadrangle. Postal authorities established Hodson post office in 1898, discontinued it in 1906, reestablished it in 1915, and discontinued it in 1917; the name is for J.J. Hodson, a financier who backed copper mining (Salley, p. 99).

Hoffman Creek: see **Snow Creek** [MARIPOSA] (1).

Hoffmann: see **Mount Hoffmann** [MARIPOSA].

Hoffmann Creek [MARIPOSA]: *stream,* flows 2.25 miles to Snow Creek (1) 5.5 miles northeast of Yosemite Village (lat. 37°48'30" N, long. 119°31' W; sec. 35, T 1 S, R 22 E); the stream heads southwest of Mount Hoffmann. Named on Hetch Hetchy Reservoir (1956) 15' quadrangle.

Hoffmann Creek: see **Snow Creek** [MARIPOSA] (1).

Hoffs Gulch [MARIPOSA]: *canyon,* drained by a stream that flows 1 mile to Agua Fria Creek 5.5 miles northeast of the settlement of Catheys Valley (lat. 37°29'25" N, long. 120°01'05" W). Named on Catheys Valley (1962) 7.5' quadrangle. Laizure's (1928) map has the designation "Bell's Gulch (Hof's G.)" for the canyon.

Hogan Meadow: see **Sonny Meadow** [MARIPOSA].

Hogan Mountain [MARIPOSA]: *ridge,* west-

southwest-trending, 2.5 miles long, 2.25 miles west-northwest of Fish Camp (lat. 37°29' N, long. 119°40'45" W). Named on Bass Lake (1953) 15' quadrangle.

Hogan Reservoir: see **New Hogan Reservoir** [CALAVERAS].

Hogans Dome: see **Fresno Dome** [MADERA].

Hogan's Meadow: see **Sonny Meadow** [MARIPOSA].

Hogback Mountain [CALAVERAS]: *ridge,* north-northwest-trending, 5.5 miles long, 2.5 miles south-southwest of San Andreas (lat. 38°09'45" N, long. 120°42'15" W). Named on San Andreas (1962) 7.5' quadrangle.

Hogback [PLACER]: *ridge,* west-southwest-trending, 1 mile long, 5.25 miles west-north-west of Duncan Peak (lat. 39°11'10" N, long. 120°36'05" W; sec. 2, T 15 N, R 12 E). Named on Duncan Peak (1952) 7.5' quadrangle.

Hog Canyon [EL DORADO]: *canyon,* drained by a stream that flows 1.5 miles to Bear Creek (2) 7 miles north-northeast of Chili Bar (lat. 38°52' N, long. 120°46'45" W; sec. 29, T 12 N, R 11 E). Named on Garden Valley (1949) and Georgetown (1949) 7.5' quadrangles.

Hog Canyon [SIERRA]: *canyon,* drained by a stream that flows 4 miles to Pauley Creek 5 miles northeast of Downieville (lat. 39°36'05" N, long. 120°45'10" W; near W line sec. 16, T 20 N, R 11 E). Named on Sierra City (1981) 7.5' quadrangle.

Hoggem Lake [MADERA]: *lake,* 600 feet long, 10 miles north-northeast of Yosemite Forks (lat. 37°29'35" N, long. 119°31'45" W; sec. 14, T 5 S, R 22 E). Named on Bass Lake (1953) 15' quadrangle.

Hog Gulch [SIERRA]: *canyon,* drained by a stream that flows 1.5 miles to West Branch Canyon Creek 1.5 miles east-southeast of Mount Fillmore (lat. 39°43' N, long. 120°49'30" W; at S line sec. 35, T 22 N, R 10 E). Named on Mount Fillmore (1951) 7.5' quadrangle.

Hog Hill [CALAVERAS]: *peak,* 6.25 miles southwest of Copperopolis (lat. 37°55'15" N, long. 120°43'45" W; sec. 23, T 1 N, R 11 E). Altitude 1300 feet. Named on Copperopolis (1962) 7.5' quadrangle.

Hog Hill [NEVADA]: *peak,* 2 miles north of Wolf (lat. 39°05'20" N, long. 121°08'40" W; near S line sec. 1, T 14 N, R 7 E). Altitude 1652 feet. Named on Wolf (1949) 7.5' quadrangle.

Hog Mountain [TUOLUMNE]: *peak,* 7 miles south-southeast of Sonora (lat. 37°53' N, long. 120°21'10" W; sec. 5, T 1 S, R 15 E). Altitude 2481 feet. Named on Standard (1948) 7.5' quadrangle.

Hog Ranch: see **Mather** [TUOLUMNE].

Hoke Valley [SIERRA]: *valley,* 4 miles south of Crystal Peak (lat. 39°30' N, long. 120°05'25" W). Named on Boca (1955) and Dog Valley (1981) 7.5' quadrangles.

Holbrook Flat [NEVADA]: *area,* 2.5 miles east of Washington along South Yuba River (lat.

39°21'40" N, long. 120°45'05" W; near SW cor. sec. 4, T 17 N, R 11 E). Named on Blue Canyon (1955) and Washington (1950) 7.5' quadrangles. The place first was called Helgeson Flat in the 1880's for Charlie Helgeson, who had a store there (Slyter and Slyter, p. 7).

Holcomb Lake [MADERA]: *lake,* 1400 feet long, 4 miles west of Devils Postpile (lat. 37°37'45" N, long. 119°09'15" W). Named on Devils Postpile (1953) 15' quadrangle.

Holden Spring [NEVADA]: *spring,* 2.5 miles northwest of North Bloomfield (lat. 39°23'25" N, long. 120°56'25" W; near SW cor. sec. 26, T 18 N, R 9 E). Named on Pike (1949) 7.5' quadrangle.

Holdridge [EL DORADO]: *locality,* 4 miles northeast of Leek Spring Hill (lat. 38°39'45" N, long. 120°13'15" W). Named on Pyramid Peak (1896) 30' quadrangle.

Hole-in-Ground [NEVADA]: *lake,* 225 feet long, nearly 6 miles west-northwest of Donner Pass (lat. 39°21'20" N, long. 120°25'05" W; near E line sec. 8, T 17 N, R 14 E). Named on Soda Springs (1955) 7.5' quadrangle. Called Hole in Ground Reservoir on California Division of Highways' (1934) map. United States Board on Geographic Names (1994, p. 5) approved the name "Mount Marliave" for a peak situated 1 mile southeast of Hole-in-Ground (lat. 39°20'54" N, long. 120°24'02" W); the name commemorates Elmer C. Marliave and Burton H. Marliave, engineering geologists.

Hole in Ground Reservoir: see **Hole-in-Ground** [NEVADA].

Holley Ravine [NEVADA]: *canyon,* drained by a stream that flows 1 mile to Bloody Run 3.5 miles north-northeast of North Bloomfield (lat. 39°25' N, long. 120°54'45" W; at S line sec. 13, T 18 N, R 9 E). Named on Pike (1949) 7.5' quadrangle.

Hollow Log: see **Negro Tent** [SIERRA].

Homestead Ridge [CALAVERAS]: *ridge,* north-northwest-trending, 2 miles long, 1.25 miles northwest of Copperopolis (lat. 37°59'30" N, long. 120°39'35" W). Named on Copperopolis (1962) and Salt Spring Valley (1962) 7.5' quadrangles.

Homewood [PLACER]: *village,* 5.5 miles south of Tahoe City along Lake Tahoe (lat. 39°05'15" N, long. 120°09'40" W; sec. 1, T 14 N, R 16 E). Named on Homewood (1955) 7.5' quadrangle.

Homewood Canyon [PLACER]: *canyon,* drained by a stream that flows 2 miles to Lake Tahoe near the south end of Homewood (lat. 39°04'50" N, long. 120°09'20" W; sec. 12, T 14 N, R 16 E). Named on Homewood (1955) 7.5' quadrangle.

Honey Creek [EL DORADO]: *stream,* flows 1.25 miles to Plum Creek (1) 5 miles west-southwest of Robbs Peak (lat. 38°54'45" N, long. 120°29'35" W; near W line sec. 2, T 12

N, R 13 E). Named on Robbs Peak (1950) 7.5' quadrangle.

Hoodoo Bar: see **Goodyears Bar** [SIERRA].

Hoods Creek [CALAVERAS]: *stream,* heads in Calaveras County and flows 16 miles to Rock Creek 11 miles north-northwest of Oakdale in Stanislaus County (lat. 37°55'20" N, long. 120°54'20" W; sec. 20, T 1 N, R 10 E). Named on Bachelor Valley (1953), Copperopolis (1962), and Farmington (1968) 7.5' quadrangles.

Hoodsville: see **Slabtown**, under **Jackson Butte** [AMADOR].

Hookers Cove [MADERA]: *valley,* 11 miles south-southeast of Shuteye Peak (lat. 37°11'50" N, long. 119°22' W; sec. 29, 32, T 8 S, R 24 E); the valley is along Hookers Creek. Named on Shaver Lake (1953) 15' quadrangle.

Hookers Creek [MADERA]: *stream,* flows 3 miles to San Joaquin River 12 miles south-southeast of Shuteye Peak (lat. 37°11'10" N, long. 119°21'05" W; sec. 33, T 8 S, R 24 E); the stream goes through Hookers Cove. Named on Shaver Lake (1953) 15' quadrangle.

Hooper Creek: see **South Fork**, under **San Joaquin River** [MADERA].

Hooper Peak [TUOLUMNE]: *peak,* 12 miles west-northwest of Tioga Pass (lat. 37°57'15" N, long. 119°28'10" W). Named on Tuolumne Meadows (1956) 15' quadrangle.

Hoosier Bar [EL DORADO-PLACER]: *locality,* 4.25 miles west-northwest of Greenwood along Middle Fork American River on El Dorado-Placer county line (lat. 38°55'45" N, long. 120°58'45" W; near S line sec. 33, T 13 N, R 9 E). Named on Greenwood (1949) 7.5' quadrangle. Gudde (1975, p. 371, 372) listed a mining place called Wild Cat Bar that was located on the south side of Middle Fork between Kennebec Bar and Hoosier Bar, and a mining place called Willow Bar that was situated along Middle Fork between Hoosier Bar and Wildcat Bar.

Hoover Creek [MADERA-MARIPOSA]: *stream,* heads in Madera County and flows 3.5 miles to Buena Vista Creek 8.5 miles southeast of Yosemite Village in Mariposa County (lat. 37°38'55" N, long. 119°30'05" W); the stream heads at Hoover Lakes. Named on Merced Peak (1953) 15' quadrangle. Forest S. Townsley, chief ranger of Yosemite National Park, named Hoover Creek and Hoover Lakes for his friend Herbert C. Hoover (Browning, 1986, p. 99).

Hoover Lakes [MADERA]: *lakes,* three, largest 950 feet long, 4.5 miles west-southwest of Merced Peak (lat. 37°36'35" N, long. 119°28'20" W); the lakes are at the head of Hoover Creek. Named on Merced Peak (1953) 15' quadrangle.

Hope: see **Mount Hope** [EL DORADO].

Hope Ravine [SIERRA]: *canyon,* drained by a

stream that flows less than 1 mile to Jackass Ravine 2 miles southeast of Alleghany (lat. 39°26'55" N, long. 120°49'25" W; sec. 11, T 18 N, R 10 E). Named on Alleghany (1949) 7.5' quadrangle.

Hopkins: see **Soda Springs** [NEVADA].

Hopkins Springs: see **Soda Springs** [NEVADA].

Horizon Ridge [MARIPOSA]: *ridge*, northwest-trending, 2 miles long, 7.25 miles south of Yosemite Village (lat. 37°38'45" N, long. 119°34' W). Named on Yosemite (1956) 15' quadrangle.

Hornblende Mountains [EL DORADO]: *ridge,* south- to west-southwest-trending, 5 miles long, center 3.5 miles north-northeast of Georgetown (lat. 38°57'10" N, long. 120°48'30" W). Named on Georgetown (1949) 7.5' quadrangle.

Hornitas: see **Hornitos** [MARIPOSA].

Hornitos [MARIPOSA]: *village,* 14 miles south of Coulterville along Burns Creek (lat. 37°30'10" N, long. 120°14'15" W; sec. 17, T 5 S, R 16 E). Named on Hornitos (1947) 7.5' quadrangle. Postal authorities established Hornitas post office in 1856 and changed the name to Hornitos in 1877 (Frickstad, p. 91). The name is from the resemblance of above-ground graves at the place to little outdoor ovens—*hornitos* means "little ovens" in Spanish (Salazar, p. 2). A mining camp located about 2 miles upstream from Hornitos was called Burns' Creek, Burns' Camp, Burns' Ranch, or Burns' Diggings before it became known as Quartzburg in 1851 (Crampton *in* Eccleston, p. 11). The name "Burns" was for John Burns and Robert Burns, who settled at the place in 1847 (Gudde, 1975, p. 53). Postal authorities established Quartzburg post office in 1851 and discontinued it in 1861 (Frickstad, p. 92). Thomas Thorn gave the name "Quartzburg" to the community because of numerous quartz ledges nearby (Sargent, Shirley, 1976, p. 26). Postal authorities established Phillip's Flat post office on the bank of Merced River 7 miles north of Hornitos in 1857 and discontinued it in 1858 (Salley, p. 170).

Hornitos Creek [MARIPOSA]: *stream,* flow 4.5 miles to Burns Creek 1.25 miles north-northwest of Hornitos (lat. 37°31'05" N, long. 120°14'40" W; sec. 8, T 5 S, R 16 E). Named on Hornitos (1947) 7.5' quadrangle.

Horse and Cow Meadow [TUOLUMNE]: *area,* 8 miles east-northeast of Pinecrest (lat. 38°14'05" N, long. 119°51' W; on S line sec. 35, T 5 N, R 19 E). Named on Pinecrest (1956) 15' quadrangle.

Horse Bar: see **Rice Crossing** [NEVADA].

Horsecamp Mountain [MADERA]: *ridge,* north-northwest- to northwest-trending, 1.25 miles long, 8 miles north-northeast of Raymond (lat. 37°19'50" N, long. 119°50'45" W).

Named on Horsecamp Mountain (1947) 7.5' quadrangle.

Horse Canyon [EL DORADO]: *canyon,* drained by a stream that flows 2.25 miles to Middle Fork Cosumnes River 7.25 miles east-southeast of Caldor (lat. 38°35' N, long. 120°18'10" W; sec. 34, T 9 N, R 15 E). Named on Peddler Hill (1951) 7.5' quadrangle

Horse Creek [AMADOR]: *stream,* flows 5.25 miles to Dry Creek 4.5 miles north-northeast of Ione (lat. 38°24'55" N, long. 120°54'45" W; sec. 31, T 7 N, R 10 E). Named on Amador City (1962) and Irish Hill (1962) 7.5' quadrangles.

Horse Creek [MARIPOSA]: *stream,* flows 4.25 miles to Striped Rock Creek 10.5 miles south-southeast of Mariposa (lat. 37°20'45" N, long. 119°53'30" W; on S line sec. 4, T 7 S, R 19 E). Named on Ben Hur (1947) and Mariposa (1947) 7.5' quadrangles.

Horse Gulch [CALAVERAS]: *canyon,* drained by a stream that flows 1.25 miles to Hay Gulch 4.25 miles west of Tamarack (lat. 38° 26'30" N, long. 120°09'20" W; near E line sec. 24, T 7 N, R 16 E). Named on Calaveras Dome (1979) 7.5' quadrangle.

Horse Gulch [MARIPOSA]: *canyon,* drained by a stream that flows 1 mile to Agua Fria Creek 5.5 miles northeast of the settlement of Catheys Valley (lat. 37°29'25" N, long. 120°01'05" W). Named on Catheys Valley (1962) 7.5' quadrangle.

Horse Lake [SIERRA]: *lake,* 550 feet long, 6.25 miles north of Sierra City (lat. 39°39'10" N, long. 120°39'25" W; sec. 29, T 21 N, R 12 E). Named on Gold Lake (1981) 7.5' quadrangle.

Horse Meadow [TUOLUMNE]:
(1) *area,* 8 miles west of Dardanelle (lat. 38°20'40" N, long. 119° 58' W). Named on Donnell Lake (1979) 7.5' quadrangle.
(2) *area,* 6.25 miles west-northwest of Tower Peak along East Fork Cherry Creek (lat. 38°09'45" N, long. 119°39'35" W; sec. 27, T 4 N, R 21 E). Named on Tower Peak (1956) 15' quadrangle.

Horse Range [NEVADA]: *valley,* 2.5 miles north-northeast of Donner Pass (lat. 39°21'05" N, long. 120°18'35" W; on E line sec. 4, T 17 N, R 15 E). Named on Norden (1955) 7.5' quadrangle.

Horse Ridge [MARIPOSA]: *ridge,* west-north-west-trending, 2 miles long, 9.5 miles south-southeast of Yosemite Village (lat. 37°37' N, long. 119°32'25" W). Named on Yosemite (1956) 15' quadrangle.

Horseshoe Bar [EL DORADO-PLACER]:
(1) *locality,* 2 miles northeast of Volcanoville along Middle Fork American River on El Dorado-Placer county line (lat. 39°00'10" N, long. 120°45'30" W; sec. 4, T 13 N, R 11 E). Named on Foresthill (1949) 7.5' quadrangle.
(2) *locality,* 5 miles west-southwest of the village of Pilot Hill along North Fork American River on El Dorado-Placer county line

(lat. 38°48'30" N, long. 121°05'55" W; near W line sec. 16, T 11 N, R 8 E). Named on Auburn (1944) 15' quadrangle. Water of Folsom Lake now covers the site. Mormons mined for gold at the place in 1848; a mining spot called Little Horseshoe Bar was along North Fork below Horseshoe Bar (2) (Gudde, 1975, p. 160, 195).

Horseshoe Bend [CALAVERAS]: *bend,* 5.25 miles south of Vallecito along Stanislaus River (lat. 38°00'40" N, long. 120°27'45" W; near W line sec. 20, T 2 N, R 14 E). Named on Columbia (1948) 7.5' quadrangle.

Horseshoe Bend [MADERA]: *bend,* 16 miles south of Shuteye Peak along San Joaquin River on Madera-Fresno county line (lat. 37°06'40" N, long. 119°28'15" W). Named on Shaver Lake (1953) 15' quadrangle.

Horseshoe Bend [MARIPOSA]: *bend,* 3.25 miles southwest of Coulterville along Merced River (lat. 37°40'30" N, long. 120°13'45" W; sec. 17, T 3 S, R 16 E); the feature now is in Lake McClure. Named on Coulterville (1947) 15' quadrangle. A mining place called Harveys Bar was at Horseshoe Bend in the 1850's (Gudde, 1975, p. 152-153).

Horseshoe Bend [PLACER]: *locality,* 3.25 miles east-southeast of Donner Pass along Southern Pacific Railroad in Coldstream Valley (lat. 39°17'35" N, long. 120°16'15" W; near W line sec. 25, T 17 N, R 15 E). Named on Norden (1955) 7.5' quadrangle.

Horseshoe Bend Mountain [MARIPOSA]: *ridge,* southeast-trending, 3 miles long, 2.25 miles south-southwest of Coulterville (lat. 37° 40'30" N, long. 120°12'30" W); the ridge is northeast of Horseshoe Bend. Named on Coulterville (1947) 7.5' quadrangle.

Horseshoe Flat [NEVADA]: *area,* nearly 5 miles south of Smartville on Nevada-Yuba county line (lat. 39°08'15" N, long. 121°16'50" W; at W line sec. 23, T 15 N, R 6 E). Named on Smartville (1951) 7.5' quadrangle.

Horseshoe Lake [EL DORADO]: *lake,* 1000 feet long, nearly 4 miles west of Phipps Peak (lat. 38°57'15" N, long. 120°13'15" W; on S line sec. 21, T 13 N, R 16 E). Named on Rockbound Valley (1955) 7.5' quadrangle.

Horse Spring [PLACER]: *spring,* 2.25 miles north-northeast of Devil Peak (lat. 38°59'25" N, long. 120°31'50" W; sec. 9, T 13 N, R 13 E). Named on Devil Peak (1950) 7.5' quadrangle.

Horsetail Falls [EL DORADO]: *waterfall,* 5 miles west-northwest of Echo Summit along Pyramid Creek (lat. 38°49'50" N, long. 120° 07'20" W). Named on Echo Lake (1955) 7.5' Quadrangle.

Horse Thief Spring [AMADOR]: *spring,* 5 miles north of Mokelumne Peak (lat. 38°36'45" N, long. 120°05'20" W; sec. 22, T 9 N, R 18 E). Named on Mokelumne Peak (1979) 7.5' quadrangle.

Horton Ridge [NEVADA]: *ridge,* south-trend-

ing, 1 mile long, 2.25 miles north-northwest of Pilot Peak (lat. 39°11'50" N, long. 121° 12'15" W). Named on Rough and Ready (1949) 7.5' quadrangle.

Hotaling [PLACER]: *locality,* 6.25 miles north of Auburn (lat. 38° 59'20" N, long. 121°04'30" W; near SW cor. sec. 10, T 13 N, R 8 E). Site named on Auburn (1953) 7.5' quadrangle. Postal authorities established Hotaling post office in 1881 and discontinued it in 1886; the name was for Richard M. Hotaling, owner of Iron Mountain Company smelting works (Salley, p. 100).

Hotchkiss Hill [EL DORADO]: *peak,* 1.5 miles east-northeast of Georgetown (lat. 38°54'50" N, long. 120°48'45" W; sec. 1, T 12 N, R 10 E). Altitude 3245 feet. Named on Georgetown (1949) 7.5' quadrangle.

Hotchkiss Hill [PLACER]: *peak,* 6.5 miles south of Colfax (lat. 39° 00'25" N, long. 120°58'35" W; sec. 4, T 13 N, R 9 E). Altitude 2337 feet. Named on Colfax (1949) 7.5' quadrangle.

Hour House: see **Our House** [SIERRA].

Howard Creek [SIERRA]: *stream,* flows 5.5 miles to North Yuba River 4.25 miles north-northeast of Sierra City (lat. 39°36'50" N, long. 120°35'30" W; sec. 11, T 20 N, R 12 E). Named on Clio (1981) and Haypress Valley (1981) 7.5' quadrangles.

Howard Creek Meadows [SIERRA]: *marsh,* 7.5 miles north-northeast of Sierra City (lat. 39°40'15" N, long. 120°35'30" W; sec. 23, T 21 N, R 12 E); the feature is along Howard Creek. Named on Clio (1981) 7.5' quadrangle. Sierra City (1955) 15' quadrangle has the name for a dry area.

Howard Ranch: see **Bassetts** [SIERRA].

Howell Hill [PLACER]: *peak,* 2.5 miles south-southwest of Colfax (lat. 39°04'05" N, long. 120°58'15" W; near E line sec. 16, T 14 N, R 9 E). Altitude 2607 feet. Named on Colfax (1949) 7.5' quadrangle.

Howland Flat [SIERRA]: *settlement,* 2.25 miles west-southwest of Mount Fillmore (lat. 39°42'55" N, long. 120°53'10" W; near N line sec. 5, T 21 N, R 10 E); the place is less than 1 mile north-northwest of Table Rock. Named on La Porte (1951) 7.5' quadrangle. The post office at the site was called Table Rock (Hoover, Rensch, and Rensch, p. 496). Postal authorities established Table Rock post office in 1857 and discontinued it in 1922 (Frickstad, p. 185).

Hoyle: see **Camp Hoyle** [MARIPOSA].

Hoyt Crossing [NEVADA]: *locality,* 4.25 miles northwest of Grass Valley along South Yuba River (lat. 39°18'15" N, long. 120°04'40" W; near SE cor. sec. 28, T 17 N, R 8 E). Named on Nevada City (1948) 7.5' quadrangle. Called Hoyt's Crossing on Logan's (1940) map. M.F. Hoyt built a bridge at the site about 1854 (Gudde, 1975, p. 162).

Hubers [EL DORADO]: *locality,* 4.25 miles east-northeast of Georgetown (lat. 38°55'45"

N, long. 120°45'45" W). Named on Placerville (1893) 30' quadrangle.

Huckleberry Flat [EL DORADO]: *area,* 1.5 miles west of Echo Summit (lat. 38°48'50" N, long. 120°03'25" W; sec. 12, T 11 N, R 17 E). Named on Echo Lake (1955) 7.5' quadrangle.

Huckleberry Lake [TUOLUMNE]: *lake,* 2 miles long, 9 miles west of Tower Peak along East Fork Cherry Creek (lat. 38°07'45" N, long. 119°42'45" W). Named on Tower Peak (1956) 15' quadrangle. United States Board on Geographic Names (1965c, p. 10) approved the name "Olive Lake" for a feature, 0.2 mile long, located 0.6 mile north-north-west of the southwest end of Huckleberry Lake (lat. 38°07'30" N, long. 119°43'52" W); the name commemorates Olive Hall, a local resident and conservationist.

Hudsons Gulch [EL DORADO]: *canyon,* drained by a stream that flows less than 0.5 mile to Oregon Canyon 1.25 miles north-northwest of Georgetown (lat. 38°55'25" N, long. 120°50'55" W; near N line sec. 3, T 12 N, R 10 E). Named on Georgetown (1949) 7.5' quadrangle.

Hudsonville: see **Summit City** [NEVADA].

Hughes Mill [PLACER]: *locality,* 5.25 miles north-northeast of Foresthill (lat. 39°05'30" N, long. 120°46'40" W; sec. 6, T 14 N, R 11 E). Named on Foresthill (1949) 7.5' quadrangle.

Hulbert Mountain [MADERA]: *peak,* 5 miles south-southeast of O'Neals (lat. 37°03'20" N, long. 119°40'15" W; near S line sec. 15, T 10 S, R 21 E). Altitude 1847 feet. Named on Millerton Lake West (1965) 7.5' quadrangle.

Hull Creek [TUOLUMNE]: *stream,* flows 14 miles to Clavey River 7.5 miles southeast of Long Barn (lat. 38°00'05" N, long. 120°03'35" W; sec. 25, T 2 N, R 17 E). Named on Hull Creek (1979) and Strawberry (1979) 7.5' quadrangles.

Hull Creek Spring [TUOLUMNE]: *spring,* 5.25 miles east of Long Barn (lat. 38°05'35" N, long. 120°02'35" W); the spring is along Hull Creek. Named on Hull Creek (1979) 7.5' quadrangle.

Hulls Meadows [TUOLUMNE]: *area,* 4 miles east-southeast of Long Barn (lat. 38°04' N, long. 120°04'15" W; on S line sec. 35, T 3 N, R 17 E); the place is along Hull Creek. Named on Hull Creek (1979) 7.5' quadrangle.

Humbug: see **North Bloomfield** [NEVADA].

Humbug Bar [PLACER]: *locality,* 4.25 miles west of Westville at the mouth of Humbug Canyon (lat. 39°10'45" N, long. 120°43'35" W; sec. 3, T 15 N, R 11 E). Named on Westville (1952) 7.5' quadrangle.

Humbug Canyon [PLACER]: *canyon,* drained by a stream that flows 5 miles to North Fork American River 4.25 miles west of Westville (lat. 39°10'45" N, long. 120°43'35" W; sec. 3, T 15 N, R 11 E). Named on Westville (1952)

7.5' quadrangle. The feature was called Mississippi Canyon before early in 1850; miners renamed it because of poor luck that they had finding gold there (Hoover, Rensch, and Rensch, p. 269). On Colfax (1898) 30' quadrangle, the stream in the canyon is called Humbug Creek.

Humbug Creek [MARIPOSA]: *stream,* flows nearly 3 miles to West Fork Chowchilla River 6.25 miles southeast of Mariposa (lat. 37° 25'35" N, long. 119°52'35" W; sec. 10, T 6 S, R 19 E). Named on Mariposa (1947) 7.5' quadrangle.

Humbug Creek [NEVADA]: *stream,* flows 7.5 miles to South Yuba River 2.5 miles southwest of North Bloomfield (lat. 39°20'20" N, long. 120°55'50" W; sec. 14, T 17 N, R 9 E). Named on Alleghany (1949), North Bloomfield (1949), and Pike (1949) 7.5' quadrangles. Miners named the stream in 1851 after they failed to find gold there (Browne, p. 17).

Humbug Creek [SIERRA]: *stream,* flows 4 miles to North Yuba River nearly 5 miles west-southwest of Goodyears Bar (lat. 39°30'40" N, long. 120°57'55" W; near E line sec. 16, T 19 N, R 9 E). Named on Goodyears Bar (1951) 7.5' quadrangle.

Humbug Creek: see **Big Humbug Creek** [TUOLUMNE].

Humbug Creek: see **Humbug Canyon** [PLACER]; **Little Humbug Creek** [SIERRA].

Humbug Gulch [CALAVERAS]: *canyon,* drained by a stream that flows 1 mile to South Fork Mokelumne River 3.25 miles northwest of Rail Road Flat (lat. 38°22'15" N, long. 120°33'45" W; sec. 17, T 6 N, R 13 E). Named on Rail Road Flat (1948) 7.5' quadrangle. Camp's (1962) map shows Kohlberg's Humbug at the place.

Humbug Gulch: see **Cow and Calf Gulch** [MARIPOSA].

Humbug Ridge [PLACER]: *ridge,* generally west-trending, 3 miles long, center 1.25 miles west-northwest of Westville (lat. 39°10'45" N, long. 120°40'20" W); the ridge is north of Humbug Canyon. Named on Westville (1952) 7.5' quadrangle.

Hundred Ounce Gulch [AMADOR]: *canyon,* drained by a stream that flows 1 mile to Mokelumne River nearly 2 miles southeast of Jackson Butte (lat. 38°19'05" N, long. 120°42' W; sec. 6, T 5 N, R 12 E). Named on Mokelumne Hill (1948) 7.5' quadrangle.

Hungry Flat [TUOLUMNE]: *locality,* 4.5 miles northeast of Stanislaus (lat. 38°10'55" N, long. 120°18'10" W; sec. 22, T 4 N, R 15 E). Named on Stanislaus (1948) 7.5' quadrangle.

Hungry Hill [TUOLUMNE]: *peak,* 2.25 miles south-southeast of Chinese Camp (lat. 37°50'25" N, long. 120°24'50" W; near NE cor. sec. 22, T 1 S, R 14 E). Named on Chinese Camp (1947) 7.5' quadrangle.

Hungry Hollow [EL DORADO]: *relief feature,*

2.25 miles east of Latrobe (lat. 38°33'55" N, long. 120°56'20" W; sec. 12, T 8 N, R 9 E). Named on Latrobe (1949) 7.5' quadrangle.

Hungry Mouth Canyon [SIERRA]: *canyon,* drained by a stream that flows 2 miles to North Yuba River 0.5 mile east of Downieville (lat. 39°33'30" N, long. 120°49' W; near E line sec. 35, T 20 N, R 10 E). Named on Downieville (1951) 7.5' quadrangle.

Hunter Bend [TUOLUMNE]: *bend,* 8.5 miles south-southeast of Duckwall Mountain along Clavey River (lat. 37°51'25" N, long. 120°03'20" W; sec. 13, T 1 S, R 17 E); the feature is 1.25 miles southeast of Hunter Point. Named on Jawbone Ridge (1947) 7.5' quadrangle.

Hunter Creek [CALAVERAS]: *stream,* flows 4.5 miles to Forest Creek 3.5 miles south of Devils Nose (lat. 38°24'50" N, long. 120°25'35" W; sec. 34, T 7 N, R 14 E); the stream goes through Hunter Flat. Named on Devils Nose (1979) 7.5' quadrangle.

Hunter Creek [TUOLUMNE]: *stream,* flows 9 miles to North Fork Tuolumne River 2.5 miles south-southeast of Tuolumne (lat. 37° 55'35" N, long. 120°13'30" W; sec. 21, T 1 N, R 16 E). Named on Duckwall Mountain (1948) and Tuolumne (1948) 7.5' quadrangles.

Hunter Creek Camp Ground [TUOLUMNE]: *locality,* 5.5 miles east-southeast of Tuolumne (lat. 37°55'45" N, long. 120°08'40" W; sec. 19, T 1 N, R 17 E); the place is along Hunter Creek. Named on Tuolumne (1948) 7.5' quadrangle.

Hunter Flat [CALAVERAS]: *area,* 2.5 miles southeast of Devils Nose (lat. 38°26'15" N, long. 120°23'15" W; near NW cor. sec. 25, T 7 N, R 14 E); the place is along Hunter Creek. Named on Devils Nose (1979) 7.5' quadrangle.

Hunter Point [TUOLUMNE]: *peak,* 7 miles south-southeast of Duckwall Mountain (lat. 37°52' N, long. 120°04'25" W; sec. 11, T 1 S, R 17 E). Named on Jawbone Ridge (1947) 7.5' quadrangle.

Hunter Reservoir [CALAVERAS]: *lake,* behind a dam on Mill Creek (2) 7 miles northeast of Murphys (lat. 38°11'55" N, long. 120°21'30" W; sec. 18, T 4 N, R 15 E). Named on Stanislaus (1948) 7.5' quadrangle.

Hunters Creek: see **Hunters Valley** [EL DORADO].

Hunters Spring [PLACER]: *spring,* 4 miles northeast of Bunker Hill (lat. 39°05'50" N, long. 120°20'15" W; near N line sec. 6, T 14 N, R 15 E). Named on Wentworth Springs (1953) 7.5' quadrangle.

Hunters Valley [EL DORADO]: *canyon,* drained by a stream that flows 2 miles to Little Silver Creek (2) 4.5 miles southwest of Robbs Peak (lat. 38°52'35" N, long. 120°27'15" W; sec. 19, T 12 N, R 14 E). Named on Robbs Peak (1950) 7.5' quadrangle. The stream in the canyon is called Hunters Creek on Pyramid Peak (1896) 30' quadrangle.

Hunters Valley: see **Hunter Valley** [MARIPOSA].

Hunter Valley [MARIPOSA]: *area,* 7 miles north-northeast of Hornitos (lat. 37°36' N, long. 120°11'45" W). Named on Coulterville (1947) and Hornitos (1947) 7.5' quadrangles. Postal authorities established Hunters Valley post office 10 miles northeast of Hornitos in 1907 and discontinued it in 1923 (Salley, p. 102). The name commemorates William W. Hunter, a well-known engineer (Gudde, 1975, p. 164).

Hunter Valley Mountain [MARIPOSA]: *ridge,* east-southeast to southeast-trending, 2 miles long, 5 miles south of Coulterville (lat. 37°38'25" N, long. 120°12'50" W); the ridge is northeast of the northwest end of Hunter Valley. Named on Coulterville (1947) 7.5' quadrangle.

H.V. Eastman Lake: see **Eastman Lake** [MADERA-MARIPOSA].

Hunt Gulch [AMADOR]: *canyon,* 1.25 miles long. 2.25 miles south-southeast of Jackson (lat. 38°19'10" N, long. 120°45'05" W; mainly in sec. 3, T 5 N, R 11 E). Named on Jackson (1962) 7.5' quadrangle.

Huntley Mill Lake [PLACER]: *lake,* 700 feet long, 7.5 miles west-southwest of Donner Pass (lat. 39°16'05" N, long. 120°27'05" W; near W line sec. 7, T 16 N, R 14 E). Named on Soda Springs (1955) 7.5' quadrangle.

Hunts Hill [NEVADA]: *locality,* 6.5 miles north-northeast of present Chicago Park (lat. 39°14'10" N, long. 120°55'10" W). Named on Colfax (1898) 30' quadrangle. The place also was called Gouge Eye because a French miner lost an eye in a fight there in 1855 (Browne, p. 21).

Huse Bridge [AMADOR]: *locality,* less than 1 mile north of Enterprise along Cosumnes River (lat. 38°33' N, long. 120°51' W). Named on Placerville (1893) 30' quadrangle.

Hutching Creek [MADERA]: *stream,* flows 3.5 miles to Lyell Fork nearly 7 miles northeast of Merced Peak (lat. 37°42'35" N, long. 119°18'40" W). Named on Merced Peak (1953) 15' quadrangle. United States Board on Geographic Names (1978c, p. 2-3) approved the form "Hutchings Creek" for the name, and rejected the names "Hutching Creek" and "North Fork Merced River" for it; the name is for James M. Hutchings, who wrote of Yosemite Valley.

Hutchings Creek: see **Hutching Creek** [MADERA].

Huysink Lake [PLACER]: *lake,* 550 feet long, 1.5 miles south of Cisco Grove (lat. 39°17'15" N, long. 120°32'05" W; on S line sec. 32, T 17 N, R 13 E). Named on Cisco Grove (1955) 7.5' quadrangle. Called Huysinck Lake on Colfax (1898) 30' quadrangle.

H.V. Eastman Lake: see **Eastman Lake** [MADERA-MARIPOSA].

Hyatt Lake [TUOLUMNE]: *lake,* 3000 feet

long, 10 miles east-southeast of Pinecrest (lat. 38°07'20" N, long. 119°50' W). Named on Pinecrest (1956) 15' quadrangle. R.B. Marshall of United States Geological Survey named the lake in 1909 for Edward Hyatt, Jr., who was with a Survey field party that year, and who later was California state engineer (Browning, 1986, p. 104).

— I —

Iceberg Lake [MADERA]: *lake,* about 2000 feet long, 5.5 miles west-northwest of Devils Postpile along Shadow Creek (lat. 37°40'15" N, long. 119°10'05" W). Named on Devils Postpile (1953) 15' quadrangle. The name is for the ice that sometimes floats in the lake until the late summer months (Smith, p. 62).

Iceberg Lake: see **Upper Iceberg Lake**, under **Cecile Lake** [MADERA].

Iceberg Meadow [TUOLUMNE]: *area,* 8.5 miles northwest of Sonora Pass on Tuolumne-Alpine county line (lat. 38°25'05" N, long. 119°44'50" W); the place is 0.5 mile south-southwest of a feature called The Iceberg, which is in Alpine County. Named on Disaster Peak (1979) 7.5' quadrangle.

Icehouse Pond [AMADOR]: *lake,* 400 feet long, 5.25 miles south-southeast of Plymouth (lat. 38°24'30" N, long. 120°48'20" W; near N line sec. 6, T 6 N, R 11 N). Named on Amador City (1962) 7.5' quadrangle. Called Amador Reservoir on California Division of Highways' (1934) map.

Ice House Reservoir [EL DORADO]: *lake,* behind a dam on South Fork Silver Creek 5 miles northwest of Kyburz (lat. 38°49'25" N, long. 120°21'35" W; sec. 1, T 11 N, R 14 E). Named on Kyburz (1952, photorevised 1973) 7.5' quadrangle, which has the name "Ice House" for a building located 1 mile southwest of the dam.

Ice Lakes [PLACER]: *lakes,* two connected, each about 2000 feet long, 3.5 miles west-southwest of Donner Pass (lat. 39°18' N, long. 120°23' W). Named on Soda Springs (1955) 7.5' quadrangle. On Truckee (1940) 30' quadrangle, the southernmost lake is called Dulzura Lake, and the other is called Serena Lake, but United States Board on Geographic Names (1962b, p. 19) rejected these names. The lakes are called Sereno Lake on Truckee (1895) 15' quadrangle.

Iceland [NEVADA]: *locality,* 9 miles east-northeast of Truckee along Southern Pacific Railroad (lat. 39°22'30" N, long. 120°01'30" W; near SW cor. sec. 31, T 18 N, R 18 E). Named on Boca (1955) 7.5' quadrangle. Postal authorities established Iceland post office in 1897 and discontinued it in 1923 (Frickstad, p. 114). The name is from the cutting and storage of ice near the site; the place first was called Cuba (Hanna, p. 147).

Iceland Lake [TUOLUMNE]: *lake,* 1300 feet long, 12 miles west-northwest of Tower Peak (lat. 38°13'45" N, long. 119°44'40" W). Named on Tower Peak (1956) 15' quadrangle. United States Board on Geographic Names (1965a, p. 14) decided that Iceland Lake is not one of the group called Lewis Lakes.

Ida: see **Camp Ida Spring** [TUOLUMNE].

Idaho-Maryland Reservoir [NEVADA]: *lake,* 250 feet long, nearly 3 miles east of Grass Valley (lat. 39°13'25" N, long. 121°00'30" W; sec. 30, T 16 N, R 9 E). Named on Grass Valley (1949) 7.5' quadrangle, which shows Idaho-Maryland mine 1.5 miles west of the lake.

Idlewild [PLACER]: *settlement,* 1.5 miles north of Homewood along Lake Tahoe (lat. 39°06'30" N, long. 120°09'30" W; sec. 36, T 15 N, R 16 E). Named on Homewood (1955) 7.5' quadrangle.

Illilouette Creek [MADERA-MARIPOSA]: *stream,* heads in Madera County and flows 14 miles to Merced River 2.25 miles southeast of Yosemite Village in Mariposa County (lat. 37°43'30" N, long. 119°33'25" W). Named on Merced Peak (1953) and Yosemite (1956) 15' quadrangles. Called Illilouette Fork on Hoffmann and Gardner's (1863-1867) map. King and Gardner's (1865) map has the designation "Illilouette or South Fork" for the stream. Whitney (1870, p. 65) called it "the South Fork, or the Illilouette." He added: "This is the South Fork of the Middle Fork [Merced River] and not the main South Fork," and, "To avoid confusion, it will be well to call it by the Indian name, Illilouette, one not yet much in use in the Valley." United States Board on Geographic Names (1933, p. 385) rejected the names "South Canyon Creek" and "Tu-lu-la-wi-ak" for the stream.

Illilouette Fall [MARIPOSA]: *waterfall,* 3 miles south-southeast of Yosemite Village along Illilouette Creek (lat. 37°42'50" N, long. 119°33'40" W). Named on Yosemite (1956) 15' quadrangle.

Illilouette Fork: see **Illilouette Creek** [MADERA-MARIPOSA].

Illilouette Gorge [MARIPOSA]: *canyon,* less than 1 mile long, 2.25 miles southeast of Yosemite Village (lat. 37°43'10" N, long. 119°33'30" W); the canyon is along Illilouette Creek below Illilouette Fall. Named on Yosemite (1956) 15' quadrangle.

Illilouette Ridge [MARIPOSA]: *ridge,* north-trending, 2 miles long, 3 miles south of Yosemite Village (lat. 37°42'10" N, long. 119°34'30" W); the ridge is west of Illilouette Creek. Named on Yosemite (1956) 15' quadrangle.

Illinois Canyon [EL DORADO]: *canyon,* drained by a stream that flows 2.25 miles to Canyon Creek (1) 2 miles northwest of Georgetown (lat. 38°55'50" N, long. 120°51'25" W; near E line sec. 33, T 13 N, R

10 E). Named on Georgetown (1949) 7.5' quadrangle. Gudde (1975, p. 165) gave the names "Illinois Ravine," "South Canyon," and "Thousand Dollar Canyon" as other designations for the feature, and noted that a gold nugget worth one thousand dollars was found in the canyon in 1849.

Illinois Creek [SIERRA]: *stream,* flows 2 miles to Canyon Creek 2.25 miles south-southeast of Mount Fillmore (lat. 39°41'55" N, long. 120°50'10" W). Named on Mount Fillmore (1951) 7.5' quadrangle.

Illinois Hill [MARIPOSA]: *peak,* 8.5 miles south-southeast of the settlement of Catheys Valley (lat. 37°19'55" N, long. 120°00'45" W; near SW cor. sec. 9, T 7 S, R 18 E). Altitude 1670 feet. Named on Illinois Hill (1962) 7.5' quadrangle.

Illinois Ravine: see **Illinois Canyon** [EL DORADO]; **Newtown** [NEVADA].

Illinoistown [PLACER]: *locality,* less than 1 mile south of downtown Colfax (lat. 39°05'20" N, long. 120°57'20" W; sec. 3, T 14 N, R 9 E). Site named on Colfax (1949) 7.5' quadrangle. Postal authorities established Illinoistown post office in 1853 and discontinued it in 1866 (Salley, p. 103). The place first was called Alder Grove or Upper Corral (Bancroft, 1888, p. 483).

Ina Coolbrith: see **Mount Ina Coolbrith** [SIERRA].

Ina Coolbrith Summit: see **Mount Ina Coolbrith** [SIERRA].

Incline [MARIPOSA]: *locality,* 4 miles west-southwest of El Portal on the south side of Merced River (lat. 37°39'40" N, long. 119° 51' W; sec. 22, T 3 S, R 19 E). Named on El Portal (1947) 7.5' quadrangle. Postal authorities established Incline post office in 1924 and discontinued it in 1953 (Frickstad, p. 91). Officials of Yosemite Valley Railroad named the place in 1923 for a precipitous incline railway that carried logs to the railroad from the timber belt about 12 miles away (Gudde, 1949, p. 159; Johnston, p. 51).

Independence [CALAVERAS]: *settlement,* 0.5 mile north of Rail Road Flat (lat. 38°21' N, long. 120°30'40" W; near N line sec. 26, T 6 N, R 13 E). Named on Railroad Flat (1948) 7.5' quadrangle.

Independence Creek [SIERRA]: *stream,* flows 5 miles to Little Truckee River 8 miles southeast of Sierraville (lat. 39°30' N, long. 120°15'40" W; sec. 13, T 19 N, R 15 E); the stream heads at Independence Lake. Named on Independence Lake (1981) and Sierraville (1981) 7.5' quadrangles.

Independence Creek: see **Upper Independence Creek** [NEVADA].

Independence Flat: see **Mokelumne Hill** [CALAVERAS]; **Rail Road Flat** [CALAVERAS].

Independence Gulch [CALAVERAS]: *canyon,* drained by a stream that flows nearly 2 miles

to South Fork Mokelumne River 2 miles northwest of Rail Road Flat (lat. 38°21'55" N, long. 120°31'50" W; near N line sec. 22, T 6 N, R 13 E); the canyon heads at Independence. Named on Rail Road Flat (1948) 7.5' quadrangle.

Independence Hill: see **Monona Flat** [PLACER].

Independence Lake [NEVADA-SIERRA]: *lake,* 2.5 miles long, 9 miles north of Donner Pass on Nevada-Sierra county line (lat. 39° 26'35" N, long. 120°18'30" W). Named on Independence Lake (1981) 7.5' quadrangle. Actress Lola Montez named the lake when she picnicked there on Independence Day in 1853 (Hanna, p. 148).

Independence Point [EL DORADO]: *ridge,* west-trending, 1.5 miles long, 3.5 miles northwest of Pollock Pines (lat. 38°47' N, long. 120°38'30" W). Named on Slate Mountain (1950) 7.5' quadrangle.

Independence Point [SIERRA]: *ridge,* south-southeast- to south-trending, 1 mile long, 2 miles east-southeast of Alleghany (lat. 39° 27'45" N, long. 120°48'15" W; on N line sec. 1, T 18 N, R 10 E). Named on Alleghany (1949) 7.5' quadrangle.

Indiana Camp: see **Washington** [NEVADA].

Indiana Hill: see **Gold Run** [PLACER].

Indiana Ravine [PLACER]: *canyon,* drained by a stream that flows less than 1 mile to North Fork American River 4 miles south of Dutch Flat (lat. 39°08'55" N, long. 120°50'25" W; sec. 15, T 15 N, R 10 E); the canyon heads near Indiana Hill, which is shown on Whitney's (1873) map. Named on Dutch Flat (1950) 7.5' quadrangle.

Indian Bar [PLACER]: *locality,* 2.5 miles south-southwest of Michigan Bluff along Middle Fork American River (lat. 39°00'20" N, long. 120°44'50" W; near NE cor. sec. 4, T 13 N, R 11 E). Named on Michigan Bluff (1952) 7.5' quadrangle.

Indian Bar [TUOLUMNE]: *locality,* 7.5 miles south-southeast of Chinese Camp along Tuolumne River (lat. 37°46'30" N, long. 120° 22' W). Named on Sonora (1897) 30' quadrangle. Water of Don Pedro Reservoir now covers the site. A mining camp called Swetts Bar was located along the river 2 miles above Indian Bar (Gardiner, p. 229), and a mining camp called Chambers Bar was situated along the river 0.5 mile above Swetts Bar (Gudde, 1975, p. 66).

Indian Burying Gulch [CALAVERAS]: *canyon,* drained by a stream that flows 1.5 miles to San Antonio Creek 5.5 miles north-north-east of Murphys (lat. 38°12'55" N, long. 120°25'20" W; sec. 10, T 4 N, R 14 E). Named on Murphys (1948) 7.5' quadrangle.

Indian Cañon: see **Indian Creek** [PLACER] (2).

Indian Canyon Creek [MARIPOSA]: *stream,* flows 3.5 miles to Merced River at Yosemite

Village (lat. 37°44'45" N, long. 119°34'50" W). Named on Hetch Hetchy Reservoir (1956) 15' quadrangle. Indian prisoners of the Mariposa Battalion escaped up the stream course in 1851, and Mono Indians came down the stream to attack Indians in Yosemite Valley in 1853 (Browning, 1986, p. 105). United States Board on Geographic Names (1934, p. 12) rejected the name "Indian Creek" for the stream to avoid confusion with another tributary of Merced River that is called Indian Creek.

Indian Creek [CALAVERAS]:
(1) *stream,* flows 10 miles to San Antonio Creek 6.5 miles east-southeast of San Andreas (lat. 38°08'55" N, long. 120°34'25" W; near N line sec. 5, T 3 N, R 13 E). Named on Calaveritas (1962) and Murphys (1948) 7.5' quadrangles.
(2) *stream,* flows nearly 4 miles to Sixmile Creek 1.25 miles south-southeast of Angels Camp (lat. 38°03'25" N, long. 120°32'10" W; sec. 3, T 2 N, R 13 E). Named on Angels Camp (1962) 7.5' quadrangle.

Indian Creek [CALAVERAS]: *stream,* heads in Calaveras County and flows 14 miles to Calaveras River 8 miles east-northeast of Linden in San Joaquin County (lat. 38°04'10" N, long. 120°57' W; sec. 35, T 3 N, R 9 E). Named on Valley Springs (1962) and Valley Springs SW (1962) 7.5' quadrangles.

Indian Creek [EL DORADO]:
(1) *stream,* flows 3 miles to South Fork American River 1.25 miles northwest of Coloma (lat. 38°48'50" N, long. 120°54'10" W; sec. 7, T 11 N, R 10 E). Named on Coloma (1949) 7.5' quadrangle. Called North Indian Creek on Georgetown (1949) 15' quadrangle.
(2) *stream,* flows 2 miles to South Fork American River 1 mile southeast of Coloma (lat. 38°47'30" N, long. 120°52'35" W; near W line sec. 21, T 11 N, R 10 E). Named on Coloma (1949) and Garden Valley (1949) 7.5' quadrangles.
(3) *stream,* flows 7.5 miles to Weber Creek nearly 5 miles north of Shingle Springs (lat. 38°44'05" N, long. 120°56'25" W; sec. 12, T 10 N, R 9 E). Named on Placerville (1949) and Shingle Springs (1949) 7.5' quadrangles.
(4) *stream,* flows 2.5 miles to Cosumnes River 10 miles south-southeast of Clarksville (lat. 38°30'45" N, long. 121°00'40" W; near N line sec. 32, T 8 N, R 9 E). Named on Folsom SE (1954) 7.5' quadrangle.
(5) *stream,* flows 2 miles to Scott Creek nearly 4 miles south-southwest of Omo Ranch (lat. 38°31'50" N, long. 120°36' W; sec. 24, T 8 N, R 12 E); the stream heads at the site of Indian Diggins. Named on Omo Ranch (1952) 7.5' quadrangle. Logan's (1938) map has the name "East Indian Creek" for the feature, and has the name "Oregon Cr." for the next large tributary of Scott Creek to the east (mouth near E line sec. 20, T 8 N, R 13 E).

Indian Creek [MARIPOSA]: *stream,* flows 6

miles to Merced River 0.5 mile east of El Portal (lat. 37°40'35" N, long. 119°46'10" W; sec. 16, T 3 S, R 20 E). Named on El Portal (1947) and Yosemite (1956) 15' quadrangles. Chinquapin Falls is along the creek, but United States Board on Geographic Names (1933, p. 387) rejected the name "Chinquapin Creek" for the stream. Present Lehamite Creek once was called East Fork of Indian Creek (Browning, 1986, p. 125).

Indian Creek [PLACER]:
(1) *stream,* flows 1.25 miles to East Branch El Dorado Canyon 1.25 miles south of Westville (lat. 39°09'20" N, long. 120°38'40" W; sec. 9, T 15 N, R 12 E). Named on Westville (1952) 7.5' quadrangle. On Colfax (1898) 30' quadrangle, the canyon of the stream is called Indian Springs Ravine.
(2) *stream,* flows 10 miles to North Fork American River 4 miles southeast of Colfax (lat. 39°03'25" N, long. 120°54'25" W; near SW cor. sec. 18, T 14 N, R 10 E). Named on Colfax (1949), Dutch Flat (1950), and Foresthill (1949) 7.5' quadrangles. The canyon of the stream is called Indian Cañon on Whitney's (1873) map.

Indian Creek [SIERRA]:
(1) *stream,* flows 4.25 miles to North Yuba River 8 miles west-southwest of Goodyears Bar (lat. 39°30'20" N, long. 121°01'25" W; near NE cor. sec. 24, T 19 N, R 8 E); the stream is 1 mile west-southwest of Indian Hill (1). Named on Goodyears Bar (1951), Pike (1949), and Strawberry Valley (1948) 7.5' quadrangles.
(2) *stream,* flows 3.5 miles to Middle Yuba River 2 miles southeast of Pike (lat. 39°25'10" N, long. 120°58'20" W; near S line sec. 16, T 18 N, R 9 E). Named on Pike (1949) 7.5' quadrangle.

Indian Creek [TUOLUMNE]: *stream,* flows 4 miles to Tuolumne River 7 miles southeast of Tuolumne (lat. 37°53' N, long. 120°09'10" W; sec. 6, T 1 S, R 17 E). Named on Groveland (1947) and Tuolumne (1948) 7.5' quadrangles.

Indian Creek: see **Big Indian Creek** [AMADOR]; **East Branch**, under **El Dorado Canyon** [PLACER]; **Little Indian Creek** [AMADOR]; **Little Indian Creek** [EL DORADO]; **Little Indian Creek** [PLACER].

Indian Creek: see **Indian Canyon Creek** [MARIPOSA].

Indian Diggings: see **Indian Diggins** [EL DORADO].

Indian Diggins [EL DORADO]: *locality,* 2.25 miles south-southeast of Omo Ranch (lat. 38°32'50" N, long. 120°34'30" W); the place is near the head of Indian Creek (5). Named on Placerville (1893) 30' quadrangle. Postal authorities established Indian Diggings post office in 1853, discontinued it in 1869, reestablished it with the name "Indian Diggins" in 1888, and discontinued it in 1935 (Salley, p. 103). The name was given after a group of white prospectors discovered some Indians panning for gold at the site in 1850; the place had the nickname "Whore House Gulch" in the early days (Yohalem, p. 27, 29).

Indian Flat [NEVADA]: *valley,* 2 miles west of Nevada City along upper reaches of Rush Creek (lat. 39°16'05" N, long. 121°03'20" W; around NE cor. sec. 10, T 16 N, R 8 E). Named on Nevada City (1948) 7.5' quadrangle.

Indian Flat [PLACER]: *area,* 3.5 mile south-southwest of Colfax (lat. 39°03' N, long. 120°58'10" W; on W line sec. 22, T 14 N, R 9 E). Named on Colfax (1949) 7.5' quadrangle.

Indian Gulch [AMADOR]: *canyon,* 1.25 miles long, 4.5 miles south-southeast of Plymouth (lat. 38°25'10" N, long. 120°48' W; sec. 31, 32, T 7 N, R 11 E). Named on Amador City (1962) 7.5' quadrangle.

Indian Gulch [CALAVERAS]: *canyon,* drained by a stream that flows 1 mile to New Melones Lake 5.25 miles south-southeast of Angels Camp (lat. 38°00'30" N, long. 120°30' W; sec. 24, T 2 N, R 13 E). Named on Angels Camp (1962) 7.5' quadrangle.

Indian Gulch [MARIPOSA]:

(1) *canyon,* drained by a stream that flows 4.5 miles to North Fork Merced River 4 miles east of Buckhorn Peak (lat. 37°39'30" N, long. 120°03'05" W; near W line sec. 24, T 3 S, R 17 E). Named on Buckhorn Peak (1947) 7.5' quadrangle.

(2) *canyon,* drained by a stream that flows 3.5 miles to Slate Gulch 1.5 miles east-southeast of Santa Cruz Mountain (lat. 37°26'25" N, long. 120°10'25" W; sec. 1, T 6 S, R 16 E). Named on Indian Gulch (1962) 7.5' quadrangle.

(3) *locality,* 1.25 miles south-southeast of Santa Cruz Mountain (lat. 37°26'25" N, long. 120°11'45" W; near E line sec. 3, T 6 S, R 16 E); the place is in Indian Gulch (2). Named on Indian Gulch (1962) 7.5' quadrangle. California Mining Bureau's (1909c) map has the form "Indiangulch" for the name. Postal authorities established Indian Gulch post office in 1855, discontinued it for a time in 1901, and discontinued it finally in 1912 (Frickstad, p. 91). The place originally was called Santa Cruz (Chamberlain, p. 153). Laizure's (1935) map shows a place called Elkhorn located 3 miles north of Indiangulch.

Indian Gulch: see **Happy Valley** [CALAVERAS]; **Mokelumne River** [AMADOR-CALAVERAS]; **West Point** [CALAVERAS].

Indian Hatties [EL DORADO]: *locality,* 3 miles east-northeast of Pollock Pines (lat. 38°47' N, long. 120°32'15" W; near SW cor. sec. 16, T 11 N, R 13 E). Named on Pollock Pines (1950) 7.5' quadrangle.

Indian Hill [AMADOR]:

(1) *hill,* 3.25 miles northwest of Ione (lat. 38°22'45" N, long. 120° 58'50" W). Named on Irish Hill (1962) 7.5' quadrangle. A man named Dosch opened the first commercial clay pit in the Ione area at Indian Hill in 1854; a town called Doschville was near the pit (Andrews, p. 58).

(2) *locality,* 3.25 miles northwest of Ione along Southern Pacific Railroad (lat. 38°22'55" N, long. 120°59'20" W); the place is 0.25 mile northwest of Indian Hill (1). Named on Irish Hill (1962) 7.5' quadrangle.

Indian Hill [MADERA]: *peak,* 11 miles northeast of Raymond (lat. 37°19'40" N, long. 119°45'45" W; sec. 15, T 7 S, R 20 E). Named on Horsecamp Mountain (1947) 7.5' quadrangle.

Indian Hill [SIERRA]:

(1) *ridge,* west-trending, 0.5 mile long, 7 miles west-southwest of Goodyears Bar (lat. 39°30'35" N, long. 121°00'15" W; at S line sec. 18, T 19 N, R 9 E); the ridge is 1 mile east-northeast of the mouth of Indian Creek (1). Named on Goodyears Bar (1951) and Strawberry Valley (1948) 7.5' quadrangles.

(2) *locality,* 6 miles west-southwest of Goodyears Bar (lat. 39°30'30" N, long. 120°59'20" W); the place is east of present Indian Hill (1). Named on Downieville (1897) 30' quadrangle.

Indian Knoll [PLACER]: *relief feature,* 3.25 miles east of Colfax (lat. 39°05'55" N, long. 120°53'35" W; near N line sec. 6, T 14 N, R 10 E). Named on Colfax (1949) 7.5' quadrangle.

Indian Meadow [MADERA]: *area,* 10 miles southwest of Devils Postpile (lat. 37°32'35" N, long. 119°14'05" W). Named on Devils Postpile (1953) 15' quadrangle.

Indian Mountain [MARIPOSA]: *peak,* 2 miles east of Mariposa (lat. 37°29'25" N, long. 119°55'50" W; on N line sec. 19, T 5 S, R 19 E). Named on Mariposa (1947) 7.5' quadrangle.

Indian Peak [MARIPOSA]:

(1) *peak,* 1.5 miles south-southeast of Santa Cruz Mountain (lat. 37° 26'05" N, long. 120°11'15" W; sec. 2, T 6 S, R 16 E); the peak is 0.5 mile east-southeast of Indian Gulch (3). Named on Indian Gulch (1962) 7.5' quadrangle.

(2) *peak,* 10.5 miles southeast of Mariposa (lat. 37°23'35" N, long. 119°48'40" W; sec. 20, T 6 S, R 20 E). Altitude 3083 feet. Named on Stumpfield Mountain (1947) 7.5' quadrangle.

Indian Ridge [MARIPOSA]: *ridge,* south-southwest-trending, 2 miles long, 2 miles northeast of Yosemite Village (lat. 37°46'15" N, long. 119°33'25" W); Indian Rock is at the north-northeast end of the ridge. Named on Hetch Hetchy Reservoir (1956) 15' quadrangle.

Indian Rock [EL DORADO]: *peak,* 4.25 miles northwest of Echo Summit (lat. 38°51'50" N, long. 120°04'30" W). Named on Echo Lake (1955) 7.5' quadrangle.

Indian Rock [MARIPOSA]: *peak,* 3 miles northeast of Yosemite Village (lat. 37°47' N, long. 119°33' W); the peak is at the north-northeast end of Indian Ridge. Altitude 8522 feet. Named on Hetch Hetchy Reservoir (1956) 15' quadrangle.

Indian Spring [NEVADA]: *spring,* 4 miles south-southwest of Washington (lat. 39°18'25" N, long. 120°50' W; near E line sec. 27, T 17 N, R 10 E). Named on Washington (1950) 7.5' quadrangle.

Indian Spring [TUOLUMNE]:
(1) *spring,* 1.5 miles west-northwest of Crandall Peak (lat. 38°09'50" N, long. 120°10'20" W; at SE cor. sec. 26, T 4 N, R 16 E). Named on Crandall Peak (1979) 7.5' quadrangle.
(2) *spring,* 4.25 miles south-southeast of Duckwall Mountain (lat. 37°54'50" N, long. 120°05' W; near W line sec. 26, T 1 N, R 17 E). Named on Duckwall Mountain (1948) 7.5' quadrangle.

Indian Springs [MADERA]: *locality,* 5.5 miles south-southwest of O'Neals along Cottonwood Creek (1) (lat. 37°03'05" N, long. 119° 43'55" W; sec. 24, T 10 S, R 20 E). Named on Millerton Lake West (1965) 7.5' quadrangle.

Indian Springs [NEVADA]: *locality,* 1 mile northwest of Pilot Peak (lat. 39°10'45" N, long. 121°11'30" W; at E line sec. 4, T 15 N, R 7 E). Named on Rough and Ready (1949) 7.5' quadrangle. Postal authorities established Indian Springs post office in 1858, discontinued it in 1871, reestablished it in 1892, and discontinued it in 1893 (Frickstad, p. 114). They established Painsville post office 6 miles west of Indian Springs in 1864 and discontinued it in 1869; the name was for Philander Paine, rancher and hotel owner (Salley, p. 165).

Indian Springs Creek [EL DORADO]: *stream,* flows 2 miles to Folsom Lake 4.25 miles south-southwest of the village of Pilot Hill (lat. 38°46'35" N, long. 121°02'45" W). Named on Pilot Hill (1954, photorevised 1973) 7.5' quadrangle.

Indian Springs Creek [NEVADA]: *stream,* flows 5.5 miles to Dry Creek (2) 5 miles northwest of Wolf (lat. 39°06'50" N, long. 121° 12'10" W; near N line sec. 33, T 15 N, R 7 E); the stream heads near Indian Springs. Named on Rough and Ready (1949) and Wolf (1949) 7.5' quadrangles.

Indian Springs Hill: see **Pilot Peak** [NEVADA].

Indian Springs Ravine: see **Indian Creek** [PLACER] (1).

Indian Valley [SIERRA]: *valley,* 5.5 miles west-southwest of Goodyears Bar along North Yuba River (lat. 39°30'55" N, long. 120° 59' W; sec. 16, 17, T 19 N, R 9 E). Named on Goodyears Bar (1951) 7.5' quadrangle.

Indian Valley Camp Ground [SIERRA]: *locality,* 5.5 miles west-southwest of Goodyears Bar along North Yuba River (lat. 39°30'45" N, long. 120°58'50" W; at W line sec. 16, T 19 N, R 9 E); the place is in Indian Valley. Named on Goodyears Bar (1951) 7.5' quadrangle. Called Indian Valley Camp on Downieville (1951) 15' quadrangle.

Inferno Lakes [TUOLUMNE]: *lakes,* two, each about 1100 feet long, 15 miles east-southeast of Pinecrest (lat. 38°05'20" N, long. 119° 45'25" W). Named on Pinecrest (1956) 15' quadrangle.

Ingram Slough [PLACER]: *stream,* flows 2.5 miles to Orchard Creek 8 miles north-north-west of Roseville (lat. 38°51'15" N, long. 121°20'15" W; near SW cor. sec. 29, T 12 N, R 6 E). Named on Roseville (1967) 7.5' quadrangle.

Inspiration Lodge [AMADOR]: *locality,* 9 miles east-northeast of Pine Grove (lat. 38°29' N, long. 120°31'10" W; near SW cor. sec. 2, T 7 N, R 13 E); the place is less than 1 mile north-northeast of Inspiration Point. Named on West Point (1948) 7.5' quadrangle.

Inspiration Point [AMADOR]: *locality,* 8 miles east-northeast of Pine Grove (lat. 38°28'15" N, long. 120°31'35" W; sec. 10, T 7 N, R 13 E). Named on West Point (1948) 7.5' quadrangle.

Inspiration Point [EL DORADO]: *relief feature,* nearly 3 miles north of Mount Tallac (lat. 38°56'50" N, long. 120°06' W; sec. 28, T 13 N, R 17 E). Named on Emerald Bay (1955) 7.5' quadrangle.

Inspiration Point [MARIPOSA]: *relief feature,* 6 miles west-southwest of Yosemite Village on the south side of Yosemite Valley·(lat. 37°42'50" N, long. 119°41'15" W). Named on Yosemite (1956) 15' quadrangle.

Inspiration Point: see **Old Inspiration Point** [MARIPOSA].

Ione [AMADOR]: *town,* 9 miles west of Jackson (lat. 38°21'05" N, long. 120°55'50" W); the town is at the east end of Ione Valley. Named on Ione (1962) 7.5' quadrangle. The name is from Ione Valley (Sargent, Mrs. J.L., p. 49). Early names for the place include Bedbug, Freezeout (Hanna, p. 150), Rickeyville, Hardscrabble, and Woosterville (Gudde, 1949, p. 161). Postal authorities established Jone Valley post office in 1852, changed the name to Jone City in 1857, to Ione City almost immediately, to Ione Valley in 1861, and to Ione in 1880 (Salley, p. 105). The town incorporated in 1953. California Mining Bureau's (1909b) map shows a place called Ritchey located 5 miles south of Ione by stage line. Postal authorities established Ritchey post office in 1900 and discontinued it in 1914 (Frickstad, p. 6). A hostelry of the 1850's and 1860's called Q Ranch was located about 2 miles northwest of Ione; a group of men, one of whom had been in Company Q of the Ohio Volunteers during the Mexican War, started and named the hostelry in 1850 (Hoover, Rensch, and Rensch, p. 35).

Ione City: see **Ione** [AMADOR].

Ione Valley [AMADOR]: *valley,* mainly west of Ione along Sutter Creek (1) (lat. 38°21'15" N, long. 120°58' W). Named on Ione (1962) 7.5' quadrangle. Eddy's (1854) map has the name "Lone Valley" for the feature. The name "Ione" is from the heroine of Edward Bulwer-Lytton's novel *The Last Days of Pompeii*, published in London in 1834 (Hanna, p. 150).

Ione Valley: see **Ione** [AMADOR].

Iowa Cabin: see **North Branch** [CALA-VERAS].

Iowa Canyon [EL DORADO]: *canyon,* drained by a stream that flows 6 miles to South Fork American River 6.5 miles west of Pollock Pines (lat. 38°46'20" N, long. 120°42'05" W; sec. 25, T 11 N, R 11 E). Named on Pollock Pines (1950) and Slate Mountain (1950) 7.5' quadrangles. Called Big Iowa Canyon on Placerville (1893) 30' quadrangle, which has the name "Little Iowa Canyon" for a tributary of Iowa Canyon that probably is present Brushy Canyon (1).

Iowa City: see **Iowa Hill** [PLACER].

Iowa Hill [EL DORADO]: *peak,* 5.5 miles west of Pollock Pines (lat. 38°46'20" N, long. 120°41' W; sec. 30, T 11 N, R 12 E); the peak is north of the lower part of Iowa Canyon. Named on Slate Mountain (1950) 7.5' quadrangle.

Iowa Hill [PLACER]: *village,* 6.5 miles north-northwest of Foresthill (lat. 39°06'30" N, long. 120°51'30" W; sec. 33, T 15 N, R 10 E). Named on Foresthill (1949) 7.5' quadrangle. Miners from Iowa discovered gold at the place in 1853 (Hanna, p. 150). Postal authorities established Iowa City post office in 1854 and changed the name to Iowa Hill in 1901 (Frickstad, p. 120). United States Board on Geographic Names (1933, p. 390) rejected the name "Iowa City" for the village, and (1977b, p. 5) approved the name "Iowa Hill Divide" for the ridge on which the village stands; the ridge is 14 miles long and extends southwest from Forest Hill Divide to North Fork American River 5 miles east of Colfax. Whitney's (1873) map has the name "Bumpus Cañ." along present Indian Creek (2) just east of Iowa Hill.

Iowa Hill Divide: see **Iowa Hill** [PLACER].

Ireland Creek [TUOLUMNE]: *stream,* flows 3 miles to Lyell Fork 6 miles south of Tioga Pass (lat. 37°49'30" N, long. 119°16'40" W); the stream heads at Ireland Lake. Named on Tuolumne Meadows (1956) 15' quadrangle. Lieutenant H.C. Benson named the stream for Merritte Weber Ireland of the medical corps, who was on duty with the army in Yosemite National Park in 1897 (United States Board on Geographic Names, 1934, p. 12).

Ireland Lake [TUOLUMNE]: *lake,* 2900 feet long, 8.5 miles south-southwest of Tioga Pass (lat. 37°47'20" N, long. 119°18'15" W); the lake is at the head of Ireland Creek. Named on Tuolumne Meadows (1956) 15' quadrangle. Lieutenant H.C. Benson named the lake for Merritte Weber Ireland, for whom he named Ireland Creek (United States Board on Geographic Names, 1934, p. 12).

Irish Creek [EL DORADO]: *stream,* flows nearly 3 miles to Big Sailor Creek 4.25 miles north-northwest of Chili Bar (lat. 38°49'30" N, long. 120°50'45" W; sec. 3, T 11 N, R 10 E). Named on Garden Valley (1949) 7.5' quadrangle. Dredge tailings cover the lower part of the stream.

Irish Gulch [EL DORADO]: *canyon,* drained by a stream that flows 0.5 mile to String Canyon 9.5 miles southeast of Camino (lat. 38°38'40" N, long. 120°32'35" W; sec. 9, T 9 N, R 13 E). Named on Sly Park (1952) 7.5' quadrangle.

Irish Hill [AMADOR]: *ridge,* west-northwest-trending, less than 1 mile long, 3.5 miles north-northwest of Ione (lat. 38°24' N, long. 120°58' W). Named on Irish Hill (1962) 7.5' quadrangle. Hydraulic mining destroyed a mining camp called Irish Hill that was situated on or near the ridge (Andrews, p. 65).

Irish Town: see **Pine Grove** [AMADOR].

Iron Canyon [CALAVERAS-TUOLUMNE]: *narrows,* 7 miles east-southeast of Copperopolis along Stanislaus River on Calaveras-Tuolumne county line (lat. 37°57' N, long. 120°31'15" W; sec. 10, 11, T 1 N, R 13 E). Named on Melones Dam (1962) 7.5' quadrangle.

Iron Creek [MADERA]:

(1) *stream,* flows 3.5 miles to South Fork Merced River 4 miles south of Buena Vista Peak (lat. 37°32' N, long. 119°31'30" W; sec. 2, T 5 S, R 22 E); the stream heads at Iron Lakes. Named on Bass Lake (1953) and Yosemite (1956) 15' quadrangles.

(2) *stream,* flows 3 miles to Middle Fork San Joaquin River 7.5 miles west of Devils Postpile (lat. 37°37'10" N, long. 119°13'15" W); the stream heads at Iron Lake on the west side of Iron Mountain (2). Named on Devils Postpile (1953) 15' quadrangle.

Iron Creek [MARIPOSA]: *stream,* flows 3.5 miles to South Fork Merced River 3.25 miles northwest of Wawona (lat. 37°34'10" N, long. 119°41'55" W; sec. 20, T 4 S, R 21 E); the stream heads south of Iron Mountain. Named on Yosemite (1956) 15' quadrangle.

Iron Lake [MADERA]: *lake,* 950 feet long, nearly 5 miles west of Devils Postpile (lat. 37°36'45" N, long. 119°10'05" W); the lake is 0.25 mile west of Iron Mountain (2). Named on Devils Postpile (1953) 15' quadrangle.

Iron Lakes [MADERA]: *lakes,* largest 1400 feet long, 10.5 miles north-northwest of Shuteye Peak (lat. 37°29'30" N, long. 119°29'45" W; sec. 18, T 5 S, R 23 E). Named on Shuteye Peak (1953) 15' quadrangle.

Iron Mountain [CALAVERAS]: *peak,* 7.25 miles south-southwest of Copperopolis (lat. 37°52'50" N, long. 120°40'50" W). Altitude 990 feet. Named on Copperopolis (1962) 7.5' quadrangle.

Iron Mountain [EL DORADO]:

(1) *peak,* 6 miles north-northwest of Clarksville (lat. 38°44'25" N, long. 121°04'35" W; at W

line sec. 11, T 10 N, R 8 E). Altitude 911 feet. Named on Clarksville (1953) 7.5' quadrangle.

(2) *peak,* 6.5 miles northwest of Leek Spring Hill (lat. 38°42'15" N, long. 120°21'15" W; sec. 19, T 10 N, R 15 E); the peak is on Iron Mountain Ridge 2 miles east of Old Iron Mountain. Altitude 6242 feet. Named on Leek Spring Hill (1951) 7.5' quadrangle.

Iron Mountain [MADERA]:

(1) *peak,* 10 miles north-northwest of Shuteye Peak (lat. 37°28'55" N, long. 119°29'15" W; sec. 19, T 5 S, R 23 E). Altitude 9165 feet. Named on Shuteye Peak (1953) 15' quadrangle.

(2) *peak,* 4.5 miles west-southwest of Devils Postpile (lat. 37°36'45" N, long. 119°09'50" W). Altitude 11,149 feet. Named on Devils Postpile (1953) 15' quadrangle.

(3) *peak,* 3.5 miles southwest of Raymond (lat. 37°11'10" N, long. 119°57'35" W; at SW cor. sec. 36, T 8 S, R 18 E). Altitude 984 feet. Named on Raymond (1962) 7.5' quadrangle.

Iron Mountain [MARIPOSA]: *ridge,* north-trending, 2 miles long, 5.25 miles northwest of Wawona (lat. 37°35' N, long. 119°43'55" W). Named on Yosemite (1956) 15' quadrangle.

Iron Mountain [NEVADA]:

(1) *peak,* 1.5 miles northwest of Pilot Peak (lat. 39°10'55" N, long. 121°12'25" W; near W line sec. 4, T 15 N, R 7 E). Altitude 1921 feet. Named on Rough and Ready (1949) 7.5' quadrangle.

(2) *peak,* 4 miles northwest of Wolf (lat. 39°06'05" N, long. 121°11'15" W; on S line sec. 34, T 15 N, R 7 E). Altitude 1628 feet. Named on Wolf (1949) 7.5' quadrangle.

Iron Mountain: see **Old Iron Mountain** [EL DORADO].

Iron Mountain Ridge [EL DORADO]: *ridge,* generally northwest-trending, 4 miles long, center 6.5 miles northwest of Leek Spring Hill near Iron Mountain (2) (lat. 38°42'15" N, long. 120°21'15" W). Named on Leek Spring Hill (1951) and Stump Spring (1951) 7.5' quadrangles.

Iron Point [PLACER]: *ridge,* south-trending, 0.5 mile long, 4 miles east-southeast of Dutch Flat (lat. 39°11'30" N, long. 120°46'05" W; near W line sec. 5, T 15 N, R 11 E). Named on Dutch Flat (1950) 7.5' quadrangle.

Iron Spring [MARIPOSA]: *spring,* nearly 2 miles east-southeast of Yosemite Village along Tenaya Creek (lat. 37°44'35" N, long. 119° 33'10" W). Named on Yosemite (1956) 15' quadrangle. The feature also had the name "Chalybeate Spring" (Browning, 1986, p. 107).

Ironton Flats [MADERA]: *area,* 6.5 miles southwest of the town of North Fork (lat. 37°09'35" N, long. 119°35'45" W; sec. 8, T 9 S, R 22 E). Named on North Fork (1965) 7.5' quadrangle.

Irrigosa [MADERA]: *locality,* 2 miles south-west of Trigo along Southern Pacific Railroad (lat. 36°53'30" N, long. 119°59'10" W; sec.

15, T 12 S, R 18 E). Named on Gregg (1965) 7.5' quadrangle. California Division of Highways' (1934) map shows a place called Tharsa located along the railroad 3.25 miles southeast of Irrigosa (near SW cor. sec. 30, T 12 S, R 19 E).

Irvine: see **Carson Hill** [CALAVERAS] (2).

Irving Bright Lake: see **Irwin Bright Lake** [TUOLUMNE]; **Saddle Horse Lake** [TUOL-UMNE].

Irwin Bright Lake [TUOLUMNE]: *lake,* 1750 feet long, 9.5 miles north-northeast of White Wolf (lat. 37°59'25" N, long. 119°33'30" W). Named on Hetch Hetchy Reservoir (1956) 15' quadrangle. The name commemorates the man who planted rainbow trout in the lake (Browning, 1986, p. 107). United States Board on Geographic Names (1960c, p. 17) rejected the names "Lily Lake," "Irving Bright Lake," and "Saddle Horse Lake" for the feature.

Isberg Lakes [MADERA]: *lakes,* two, each about 700 feet long, 4.5 miles east of Merced Peak (lat. 37°38'50" N, long. 119°18'50" W); the lakes are less than 1 mile east of Isberg Pass. Named on Merced Peak (1953) 15' quadrangle.

Isberg Pass [MADERA]: *pass,* nearly 4 miles east of Merced Peak (lat. 37°38'40" N, long. 119°19'30" W). Named on Merced Peak (1953) 15' quadrangle. Lieutenant N.F. McClure named the pass for the soldier who found it in 1895 (United States Board on Geographic Names, 1934, p. 12).

Isberg Peak [MADERA]: *peak,* 4.25 miles east-northeast of Merced Peak (lat. 37°39'15" N, long. 119°19'15" W); the peak is less than 1 mile north-northeast of Isberg Pass. Altitude 10,996 feet. Named on Merced Peak (1953) 15' quadrangle.

Island Lake [EL DORADO]: *lake,* 2000 feet long, 5.5 miles south-southwest of Phipps Peak (lat. 38°52'35" N, long. 120°11'10" W). Named on Pyramid Peak (1955) and Rockbound Valley (1955) 7.5' quadrangles.

Island Lake [NEVADA]: *lake,* 2250 feet long, 5 miles southwest of English Mountain (lat. 39°23'55" N, long. 120°37'10" W; near W line sec. 27, T 18 N, R 12 E); the lake has three islands. Named on English Mountain (1983) 7.5' quadrangle.

Island Pass [MADERA]: *pass,* 10 miles north-west of Devils Postpile on Madera-Mono county line (lat. 37°44'10" N, long. 119°11'35" W); the pass is north of Thousand Island Lake. Named on Devils Postpile (1953) 15' quadrangle.

Island Rapids: see Happy Isles [MARIPOSA].

Italian Bar [MADERA]: *locality,* 13 miles south of Shuteye Peak along San Joaquin River on Madera-Fresno county line (lat. 37°09'25" N, long. 119°24'15" W; near SW cor. sec. 7, T 9 S, R 24 E). Named on Shaver Lake (1953) 15' quadrangle.

Italian Bar [PLACER]: *locality,* 2 miles north-northwest of Westville along North Fork American River (lat. 39°12'10" N, long. 120°39'55" W; near SE cor. sec. 31, T 16 N, R 12 E). Named on Westville (1952) 7.5' quadrangle.

Italian Bar [TUOLUMNE]: *locality,* 4.5 miles northeast of Columbia along South Fork Stanislaus River (lat. 38°04'30" N, long. 120°20'05" W; sec. 33, T 3 N, R 15 E). Named on Columbia SE (1948) 7.5' quadrangle.

Italian Bar: see **Grapevine Gulch** [AMADOR] (2).

Italian Creek [MARIPOSA]: *stream,* flows 5.5 miles to West Fork Chowchilla River 7.5 miles southeast of Mariposa (lat. 37°24'55" N, long. 119°51'45" W; sec. 14, T 6 S, R 19 E). Named on Stumpfield Mountain (1947) 7.5' quadrangle.

Italian Point [CALAVERAS]: *peak,* 5.5 miles southeast of San Andreas (lat. 38°08'25" N, long. 120°36'20" W; sec. 1, T 3 N, R 12 E). Named on Calaveritas (1962) 7.5' quadrangle.

Italian Ranch [TUOLUMNE]: *locality,* 4.25 miles east-southeast of Columbia (lat. 38°01'10" N, long. 120°19'35" W; near NE cor. sec. 21, T 2 N, R 15 E). Named on Columbia SE (1948) 7.5' quadrangle.

— J —

Jabu Lake [EL DORADO]: *lake,* 450 feet long, 6 miles northwest of Echo Summit (lat. 38°51'55" N, long. 120°07'15" W). Named on Echo Lake (1955) 7.5' quadrangle. The word "Jabu" was coined from letters in the name "Jack Butler" (Lekisch, p. 65).

Jackass Butte [MADERA]: *peak,* 11 miles north-northeast of Shuteye Peak (lat. 37°29' N, long. 119°18'30" W; sec. 23, T 5 S, R 24 E); the peak is near Jackass Creek. Altitude 7238 feet. Named on Shuteye Peak (1953) 15' quadrangle.

Jackass Campground: see **Little Jackass Campground** [MADERA].

Jackass Canyon [EL DORADO]: *canyon,* drained by a stream that flows 3 miles to North Fork Cosumnes River 6.25 miles south-southeast of Camino (lat. 38°39'10" N, long. 120°37'55" W; near NE cor. sec. 10, T 9 N, R 12 E). Named on Camino (1952), Omo Ranch (1952), and Sly Park (1952) 7.5' quadrangles.

Jackass Creek [AMADOR]: *stream,* flows 5 miles to Mule Creek 2.5 miles north-north-east of Ione (lat. 38°23'10" N, long. 120°54'50" W; sec. 7, T 6 N, R 10 E). Named on Amador City (1962), Ione (1962), and Irish Hill (1962) 7.5' quadrangles.

Jackass Creek [MADERA]: *stream,* flows 15 miles to Mammoth Pool Reservoir 7 miles east-northeast of Shuteye Peak (lat. 37°22'20" N, long. 119°18'15" W; sec. 25, T 6 S, R 24 E); the stream heads at Jackass Lakes and goes

past Jackass Butte and Jackass Rock. Named on Merced Peak (1953) and Shuteye Peak (1953) 15' quadrangles. West Fork enters from the northwest 0.5 mile upstream from the mouth of the main stream; it is 6.5 miles long and is named on Shuteye Peak (1953) 15' quadrangle.

Jackass Creek: see **Big Jackass Creek** [TUOLUMNE]; **Little Jackass Creek** [TUOLUMNE].

Jackass Gulch [AMADOR]: *canyon,* drained by a stream that flows 3.5 miles to Jackson Creek 3 miles southwest of Jackson (lat. 38° 19'20" N, long. 120°49' W; near NW cor. sec. 6, T 5 N, R 11 E). Named on Jackson (1962) 7.5' quadrangle.

Jackass Gulch [PLACER]: *canyon,* drained by a stream that flows less than 1 mile to Middle Fork American River 2.25 miles south-southwest of Michigan Bluff (lat. 39°00'35" N, long. 120°44'55" W; near S line sec. 33, T 33 N, R 11 E). Named on Foresthill (1949) and Michigan Bluff (1952) 7.5' quadrangles.

Jackass Gulch: see **Middle Bar** [CALAVERAS]; **Norwegian Gulch** [TUOLUMNE].

Jackass Gulch: see **Volcano** [AMADOR].

Jackass Hill [TUOLUMNE]: *locality,* 5.25 miles west-northwest of Sonora (lat. 37°59'50" N, long. 120°28'30" W; sec. 30, T 2 N, R 14 E). Named on Columbia (1948) and Sonora (1948) 7.5' quadrangles. The name is from noisy pack-train animals that paused overnight at the place on the way to and from the mines (Hoover, Rensch, and Rensch, p. 573).

Jackass Lakes [MADERA]: *lakes,* largest 1500 feet long, 7.5 miles south-southeast of Merced Peak (lat. 37°31'40" N, long. 119°21'10" W; sec. 4, 5, T 5 S, R 24 E); the lakes are at the head of Jackass Creek. Named on Merced Peak (1953) 15' quadrangle.

Jackass Meadow [MADERA]: *area,* 11.5 miles north-northeast of Shuteye Peak (lat. 37°30' N, long. 119°20' W); the place is along Jackass Creek. Named on Merced Peak (1953) and Shuteye Peak (1953) 15' quadrangles.

Jackass Meadow: see **Little Jackass Meadow,** under **Soldier Meadow** [MADERA].

Jackass Mountain [MARIPOSA]: *ridge,* west-trending, 1 mile long, 7.25 miles northeast of Buckhorn Peak (lat. 37°43'50" N, long. 120°01' W). Named on Buckhorn Peak (1947) 7.5' quadrangle.

Jackass Point [PLACER]: *peak,* 10.5 miles west of Martis Peak (lat. 39°18'40" N, long. 120°13'45" W; sec. 20, T 17 N, R 16 E). Named on Truckee (1955) 7.5' quadrangle.

Jackass Ravine [SIERRA]: *canyon,* drained by a stream that flows 1.5 miles to Middle Yuba River 2.5 miles south-southeast of Alleghany (lat. 39°26'15" N, long. 120°49' W; sec. 11, T 18 N, R 10 E). Named on Alleghany (1949) 7.5' quadrangle.

Jackass Ridge [TUOLUMNE]: *ridge,* north-northwest-trending, 2 miles long, 4 miles south-southeast of Groveland (lat. 37°46'50" N, long. 120°12'15" W). Named on Groveland (1947) 7.5' quadrangle.

Jackass Rock [MADERA]: *peak,* 9 miles northeast of Shuteye Peak (lat. 37°26' N, long. 119°18' W; sec. 1, T 6 S, R 24 E). Altitude 7112 feet. Named on Shuteye Peak (1953) 15' quadrangle.

Jackassville: see **City of Six Diggings,** under **Slug Canyon** [SIERRA].

Jackies Orchard Spring [NEVADA]: *spring,* 3.5 miles west-northwest of North Bloomfield (lat. 39°23'25" N, long. 120°57'35" W; near SW cor. sec. 27, T 18 N, R 9 E). Named on Pike (1949) 7.5' quadrangle.

Jack Main Canyon [TUOLUMNE]: *canyon,* 12 miles long, along upper reaches of Falls Creek above a point 11 miles southwest of Tower Peak (lat. 38°02'15" N, long. 119°42'15" W). Named on Tower Peak (1956) 15' quadrangle. The corrupted name commemorates Jack Means, an early-day sheepherder (United States Board on Geographic Names, 1934, p. 13).

Jack Main Mountain: see **Chittenden Peak** [TUOLUMNE].

Jack Nelson Creek [CALAVERAS]: *stream,* flows 3.25 miles to Esperanza Creek 4 miles southwest of Rail Road Flat (lat. 38°17'40" N, long. 120°33'20" W; near NE cor. sec. 17, T 5 N, R 13 E). Named on Rail Road Flat (1948) 7.5' quadrangle.

Jack Robinson Ravine [PLACER]: *canyon,* drained by a stream that flows less than 1 mile to Duncan Canyon 7 miles south of Duncan Peak (lat. 39°03'20" N, long. 120°32'15" W; near SW cor. sec. 16, T 14 N, R 13 E). Named on Greek Store (1952) 7.5' quadrangle.

Jackson [AMADOR]: *town,* along Jackson Creek where both North Fork and South Fork enter the main stream (lat. 38°21' N, long. 120°46'20" W; on N line sec. 28, T 6 N, R 11 E). Named on Jackson (1962) 7.5' quadrangle. Postal authorities established Jackson post office before July 10, 1851 (Salley, p. 106), and the town incorporated in 1905. The name commemorates Colonel Jackson, an early leader of the town; the site first was called Botilleas Spring (Bottle Spring) for the large number of bottles that campers had discarded at a spring there (Hoover, Rensch, and Rensch, p. 33). Mexican miners called the place Botellas in 1848 (Bancroft, 1888, p. 512). Jackson (1962) 7.5' quadrangle shows Hardenbergh mine situated 3.5 miles southsoutheast of Jackson near Mokelumne River. Postal authorities established Hardenburg post office in 1893 and discontinued it in 1896; the post office served the mine (Frickstad, p. 5; Gudde, 1975, p. 151). California Division of Highways' (1934) map shows a lake called New York Reservoir located 4.5 miles northeast of Jackson (sec. 1, T 6 N, R 11 E) near where Pine Grove (1948) 7.5' quadrangle indicates New York Ranch school.

Jackson [EL DORADO]: *locality,* 14 miles east of Georgetown (lat. 38°52'25" N, long. 120°34' W). Named on Placerville (1893) 30' quadrangle.

Jackson Butte [AMADOR]: *peak,* 3 miles eastsoutheast of Jackson (lat. 38°20'25" N, long. 120°43'15" W; near S line sec. 25, T 6 N, R 11 E). Altitude 2310 feet. Named on Mokelumne Hill (1948) 7.5' quadrangle. Camp (*in* Doble, p. 75) identified Jackson Butte as the feature that Doble called Butte Mountain in 1852. Camp's (1962) map shows a place called French Camp located 1 mile east-northeast of Jackson Butte, a canyon called Soldiers Gulch that opens into the canyon of South Fork Jackson Creek 1 mile northnortheast of Jackson Butte, a canyon called Sailors Gulch that opens into the canyon of South Fork Jackson Creek 1.5 miles northeast of Jackson Butte, and a place called Slabtown situated 1.5 miles east-northeast of Jackson Butte—the same map gives the alternate name "Hoodsville" for Slabtown. The first settlers of Slabtown were too poor to use anything better for building than rough slabs of wood with the bark left on (Hoover, Rensch, and Rensch, p. 34).

Jackson Creek [AMADOR]: *stream,* flows 26 miles to Dry Creek [AMADOR] 5 miles southwest of Ione (lat. 38°17'55" N, long. 121°00'45" W). Named on Ione (1962), Jackson (1962), Mokelumne Hill (1948) and Pine Grove (1948) 7.5' quadrangles. North Fork enters the main stream from the north in Jackson; it is 4 miles long and is named on Amador City (1962) and Jackson (1962) 7.5' quadrangles. South Fork enters the main stream from the southeast in Jackson; it is 10 miles long and is named on Jackson (1962), Mokelumne Hill (1948), and Pine Grove (1948) 7.5' quadrangles.

Jackson Creek [NEVADA]: *stream,* flows 3.5 miles to Bowman Lake 3 miles west-northwest of English Mountain (lat. 39°27'25" N, long. 120°36'25" W; near E line sec. 3, T 18 N, R 12 E); Jackson Lake is along the stream. Named on English Mountain (1983) 7.5' quadrangle.

Jackson Creek Campground [NEVADA]: *locality,* nearly 3 miles west-northwest of English Mountain (lat. 39°27'30" N, long. 120° 36' W; near W line sec. 2, T 18 N, R 12 E); the place is along Jackson Creek. Named on English Mountain (1983) 7.5' quadrangle.

Jackson Gate [AMADOR]: *locality,* 1 mile north of Jackson along North Fork Jackson Creek (lat. 38°21'55" N, long. 120°46'25" W; near N line sec. 21, T 6 N, R 11 E). Named on Jackson (1962) 7.5' quadrangle. The name is from a deep narrow chasm along the creek; the place also was called The Gate (Sargent, Mrs. J.L., p. 91).

Jackson Gulch [TUOLUMNE]: *canyon,* drained by a stream that flows nearly 2 miles to Big Jackass Creek 3.25 miles south-southeast of Groveland (lat. 37°47'40" N, long. 120°12'55" W; sec. 4, T 2 S, R 16 E). Named on Groveland (1947) 7.5' quadrangle.

Jackson Lake [NEVADA]: *lake,* 2350 feet long, 1.25 miles north-northwest of English Mountain (lat. 39°27'45" N, long. 120°33'40" W; on S line sec. 31, T 19 N, R 13 E). Named on English Mountain (1983) 7.5' quadrangle.

Jackson Meadow [NEVADA-SIERRA]: *area,* 3.5 miles north of English Mountain on Nevada-Sierra county line (lat. 39°29'45" N, long. 120°33' W). Named on Emigrant Gap (1955) and Sierra City (1955) 15' quadrangles. Water of Jackson Meadows Reservoir now covers the place.

Jackson Meadows Reservoir [NEVADA-SIERRA]: *lake,* behind a dam on Middle Yuba River 4 miles north of English Mountain on Nevada-Sierra county line (lat. 39°30'30" N, long. 120°33'20" W; near S line sec. 18, T 19 N, R 13 E); water of the lake covers Jackson Meadow. Named on English Mountain (1983) and Haypress Valley (1981) 7.5' quadrangles.

Jackson Meadows Station [NEVADA]: *locality,* 2.5 miles north of English Mountain (lat. 39°28'55" N, long. 120°33'25" W; sec. 30, T 19 N, R 13 E); the place is southwest of Jackson Meadows Reservoir. Named on English Mountain (1983) 7.5' quadrangle.

Jackson Peak: see **English Mountain** [NEVADA].

Jackson Point Campground [SIERRA]: *locality,* 7 miles southeast of Sierra City along Jackson Meadows Reservoir (lat. 39°29'55" N, long. 120°32'55" W; sec. 20, T 19 N, R 13 E). Named on English Mountain (1983) 7.5' quadrangle.

Jackson Spring [EL DORADO]: *spring,* 8 miles north of Pollock Pines (lat. 38°52'35" N, long. 120°34'05" W; sec. 19, T 12 N, R 13 E). Named on Devil Peak (1950) 7.5' quadrangle.

Jackson Valley [AMADOR]: *valley,* 4 miles south of Ione along Jackson Creek (lat. 38°17'30" N, long. 120°56' W). Named on Ione (1962) 7.5' quadrangle.

Jacksonville [TUOLUMNE]: *village,* 9.5 miles south of Sonora near the confluence of Woods Creek and Tuolumne River (lat. 37°50'45" N, long. 120°22'35" W; on E line sec. 13, T 1 S, R 14 E). Named on Sonora (1948) 15' quadrangle. Water of Don Pedro Reservoir now covers the site. Colonel Alden M. Jackson founded the place in June of 1849 (Paden and Schlichtmann, p. 97). Postal authorities established Jacksonville post office in 1851, discontinued it in 1868, reestablished it in 1895, discontinued it in 1896, reestablished it in 1900, and discontinued it in 1918 (Frickstad, p. 216).

Jacks Peak [EL DORADO]: *peak,* 4.5 miles south of Phipps Peak (lat. 38°53'25" N, long. 120°09'10" W). Altitude 9856 feet. Named on Rockbound Valley (1955) 7.5' quadrangle.

Jacobs Creek [EL DORADO]: *stream,* flows 2 miles to South Fork American River 2.5 miles west-northwest of Coloma (lat. 38°49'05" N, long. 120°56'05" W; sec. 11, T 11 N, R 9 E). Named on Coloma (1949) 7.5' quadrangle.

Jacobsen [EL DORADO]: *locality,* 2.5 miles west-southwest of Wentworth Springs at present Jacobsen Meadow (lat. 39°00'15" N, long. 120°23'05" W). Named on Truckee (1940) 30' quadrangle. Called Jacobsens on Truckee (1895) 30' quadrangle.

Jacobsen Meadow [EL DORADO]: *area,* 2.5 miles west-southwest of Wentworth Springs (lat. 39°00'15" N, long. 120°23'05" W; on E line sec. 3, T 13 N, R 14 E). Named on Bunker Hill (1953) 7.5' quadrangle.

Jake Schneider Meadow [EL DORADO]: *area,* 5.25 miles west of Kirkwood (lat. 38°42'10" N, long. 120°10'05" W). Named on Tragedy Spring (1979) 7.5' quadrangle.

Jakes Hill: see **Jakeys Hill** [EL DORADO].

Jakes Peak: see **South Lake Tahoe** [EL DORADO].

Jakeys Hill [EL DORADO]: *ridge,* north-trending, about 1 mile long, 5.25 miles north-northeast of Georgetown (lat. 38°58'35" N, long. 120°47'40" W; sec. 7, 18, T 13 N, R 11 E). Named on Georgetown (1949) 7.5' quadrangle. Called Jakes Hill on Logan's (1938) map.

James Bar: see **Rich Gulch** [CALAVERAS] (1).

Jamesons [EL DORADO]: *locality,* 11.5 miles south of Placerville (lat. 38°33'40" N, long. 120°47'40" W). Named on Placerville (1893) 30' quadrangle.

Jamestown [TUOLUMNE]: *town,* 3 miles southwest of Sonora (lat. 37°57'10" N, long. 120°25'20" W; sec. 10, T 1 N, R 14 E). Named on Sonora (1948) 7.5' quadrangle. The name commemorates Colonel James, a San Francisco lawyer and a mining speculator at the place in 1848; the town was called American Camp for a time after the colonel's departure (Stoddart, p. 61). Postal authorities established Jamestown post office in 1853 (Frickstad, p. 216). Gudde (1975, p. 186, 214, 369) listed a place called Whiskey Hill that was located 1 mile southwest of Jamestown, a place called Mexican Flat that was situated on the east side of Whiskey Hill, and a place called Kincades Flat that was located about 3 miles east of Jamestown. Rossland post office, located 5 miles northwest of Jamestown, operated for a few months in 1898 (Salley, p. 189).

Jamison Ravine [PLACER]: *canyon,* drained by a stream that flows 0.5 mile to Duncan Canyon 6.25 miles south of Duncan Peak (lat. 39°03'50" N, long. 120°32' W; sec. 16, T 14 N, R 13 E). Named on Greek Store (1952) 7.5' quadrangle.

Jammer Chair Flat [SIERRA]: *area,* 2.5 miles southwest of Crystal Peak (lat. 39°32' N, long. 120°07'30" W). Named on Dog Valley (1981) and Sardine Peak (1981) 7.5' quadrangles.

Janes Gulch [CALAVERAS]: *canyon,* drained by a stream that flows 1 mile to Walla Gulch 4 miles east of San Andreas (lat. 38°12'25" N, long. 120°36'35" W; near SW cor. sec. 12, T 4 N, R 12 E). Named on Calaveritas (1962) 7.5' quadrangle.

Jarbau Creek: see **Jawbone Creek** [TUOLUMNE].

Jasper [MARIPOSA]: *locality,* 5 miles southwest of Coulterville along Yosemite Valley Railroad (lat. 37°39'25" N, long. 120°15'20" W); the place is near present Jasper Point. Named on Sonora (1897) 30' quadrangle. Jasper Point post office, named for Jasper, was established 9 miles northwest of Bagby in 1909 and discontinued in 1916 (Salley, p. 106-107). California Division of Highways' (1934) map shows a place called Detwiler situated 1.5 miles east-northeast of Jasper along the railroad.

Jasper Point [MARIPOSA]: *promontory,* 5 miles south of Penon Blanco Peak on the south side of Lake McClure (lat. 37°39'35" N, long. 120°15'10" W; sec. 19, T 3 S, R 16 E). Named on Penon Blanco Peak (1962) 7.5' quadrangle.

Jasper Point: see **Jasper** [MARIPOSA].

Jawbone Creek [TUOLUMNE]: *stream,* flows 13 miles to Tuolumne River 7.5 miles west of Mather (lat. 37°53' N, long. 119°59'25" W; sec. 3, T 1 S, R 18 E). Named on Lake Eleanor (1956) and Pinecrest (1956) 15' quadrangles. A Frenchman named Jarbau had a cabin in the 1860's at the confluence of present Jawbone Creek and Skunk Creek; present Jawbone Creek was called Jarbau Creek before the name was corrupted to the form "Jawbone" (Browning, 1986, p. 109). United States Board on Geographic Names (1933, p. 397) rejected the name "Pile Creek" for present Jawbone Creek.

Jawbone Falls [TUOLUMNE]: *waterfall,* nearly 13 miles south of Pinecrest along Jawbone Creek (lat. 38°00'30" N, long. 119°58'15" W). Named on Cherry Lake North (1979) 7.5' quadrangle.

Jawbone Pass [TUOLUMNE]: *pass,* 11 miles south-southeast of Pinecrest (lat. 38°02'10" N, long. 119°56'25" W; near SE cor. sec. 12, T 2 N, R 18 E); the pass is near the head of Jawbone Creek. Named on Cherry Lake North (1979) 7.5' quadrangle.

Jawbone Pass Pond [TUOLUMNE]: *lake,* 150 feet long, 11 miles south of Pinecrest (lat. 38°02' N, long. 119°57'40" W; sec. 14, T 2 N, R 18 E); the lake is 1.25 miles west-southwest of Jawbone Pass. Named on Cherry Lake North (1979) 7.5' quadrangle.

Jawbone Ridge [TUOLUMNE]: *ridge,* south-to west-trending, 4.5 miles long, 8 miles south-southeast of Duckwall Mountain (lat. 37° 51' N, long. 120°03'30" W). Named on Jawbone Ridge (1947) 7.5' quadrangle.

Jay Bird Canyon [EL DORADO]: *canyon,* drained by a stream that flows 4 miles to Sil-

ver Creek 5.5 miles north-northeast of Pollock Pines (lat. 38°50' N, long. 120°31'50" W; near N line sec. 4, T 11 N, R 13 E). Named on Pollock Pines (1950) and Riverton (1950) 7.5' quadrangles.

Jaybird Creek [EL DORADO]: *stream,* flows 1.5 miles to South Fork American River 3 miles east-northeast of Chili Bar (lat. 38° 47' N, long. 120°46'15" W; sec. 20, T 11 N, R 11 E). Named on Garden Valley (1949) 7.5' quadrangle.

Jay Bird Spring [EL DORADO]: *spring,* 6 miles northeast of Pollock Pines (lat. 38°49'55" N, long. 120°30'50" W; near NW cor. sec. 3, T 11 N, R 13 E); the spring is north of Jay Bird Canyon. Named on Pollock Pines (1950) 7.5' quadrangle.

Jayhawk [EL DORADO]: *locality,* 6.5 miles southwest of Coloma (lat. 38°44'10" N, long. 120°58'40" W). Named on Placerville (1893) 30' quadrangle. Postal authorities established Jay Hawk post office in 1860 and discontinued it in 1863 (Frickstad, p. 27).

Jayhawk Creek [EL DORADO]: *stream,* flows 1.5 miles to Weber Creek 5.5 miles north-northwest of Shingle Springs (lat. 38°44'25" N, long. 120°57'30" W; sec. 11, T 10 N, R 9 E). Named on Shingle Springs (1949) 7.5' quadrangle.

Jefferson: see **Jefferson Creek** [NEVADA].

Jefferson Canyon [PLACER]: *canyon,* drained by a stream that flows 1.5 miles to North Fork American River 6.5 miles south of Colfax (lat. 39°00'10" N, long. 120°56'15" W; sec. 2, T 13 N, R 9 E). Named on Colfax (1949) 7.5' quadrangle.

Jefferson Creek [NEVADA]: *stream,* flows 2.5 miles to South Yuba River 1 mile west-southwest of Washington (lat. 39°21'05" N, long. 120°49'05" W; sec. 11, T 17 N, R 10 E). Named on Washington (1950) 7.5' quadrangle. Whitney's (1873) map shows a place called Jefferson located west of the mouth of Jefferson Creek, and a feature called Jefferson Hill situated less than 1 mile south of the mouth of the stream. Jefferson first was known as Greenwood's Camp for the leader of a group of miners that came to the place from the State of Oregon in 1849 (Slyter and Slyter, p. 2). Gudde (1975, p. 196) noted that a mining place called Lizard Flat was located opposite Jefferson at the mouth of Jefferson Creek.

Jefferson Hill: see **Jefferson Creek** [NEVADA].

Jeffersonville: see **Tuttletown** [TUOLUMNE].

Jelmini Basin [CALAVERAS]: *area,* nearly 3 miles northwest of Tamarack (lat. 38°28'15" N, long. 120°06'15" W; sec. 9, T 7 N, R 17 E); the place is near Jelmini Creek. Named on Tamarack (1979) 7.5' quadrangle.

Jelmini Creek [CALAVERAS]: *stream,* flows 3.25 miles to North Fork Mokelumne River 4.5 miles north-northwest of Tamarack (lat. 38°29'45" N, long 120°07'15" W); the stream goes past Jelmini Basin. Named on Tamarack (1979) 7.5' quadrangle.

Jenkins Hill [MARIPOSA]: *ridge,* south-south-east-trending, less than 1 mile long, 8.5 miles west of El Portal (lat. 37°39'50" N, long. 119°56'35" W). Named on Kinsley (1947) 7.5' quadrangle.

Jenkins Hill [TUOLUMNE]: *peak,* 1.5 miles east of Don Pedro Camp (lat. 37°43' N, long. 120°22'30" W; sec. 36, T 2 S, R 14 E). Named on La Grange (1962) and Penon Blanco Peak (1962) 7.5' quadrangles.

Jenkinson Lake [EL DORADO]: *lake,* behind a dam on Sly Park Creek 6.25 miles east-southeast of Camino (lat. 38°42'55" N, long. 120°33'35" W); water of the lake covers Sly Park. Named on Sly Park (1952, photorevised 1973) 7.5' quadrangle. United States Board on Geographic Names (1957, p. 2) rejected the name "Sly Park Reservoir" for the lake, and noted that the name "Jenkinson" commemorates Walter E. Jenkinson, who was chiefly responsible for creation of the feature.

Jenny Lind [CALAVERAS]: *village,* 7 miles south-southwest of Valley Springs near Calaveras River (lat. 38°05'45" N, long. 120° 52'10" W; near W line sec. 22, T 3 N, R 10 E). Named on Jenny Lind (1962) 7.5' quadrangle. Postal authorities established Jenny Lind post office in 1857, discontinued it in 1944, reestablished it in 1947, and discontinued it in 1951 (Frickstad, p. 15). The village, which began in the early 1850's as a mining camp, was named for the famous Swedish songstress who toured the eastern United States from 1850 until 1852 (Gudde, 1949, p. 166). Postal authorities operated Fremont Valley post office 6 miles northeast of Jenny Lind for a time in 1879; they established Pattees Ranch post office 8 miles northeast of Jenny Lind in 1865 and discontinued it in 1871 (Salley, p. 80, 168). A stopping place called Antelope House was situated across Calaveras River from Jenny Lind (Leonard, p. 14).

Jericho: see **Moores Flat** [NEVADA].

Jerrett Creek [EL DORADO-PLACER]: *stream,* heads in Placer County and flows 2.5 miles to Gerle Creek 0.5 mile west of Wentworth Springs in El Dorado County (lat. 39°00'45" N, long. 120° 20'50" W; near E line sec. 36, T 14 N, R 14 E). Named on Wentworth Springs (1953) 7.5' quadrangle.

Jerrett Peak [PLACER]: *peak,* 3 miles east-southeast of Bunker Hill (lat. 39°01'50" N, long. 120°19'50" W; sec. 30, T 14 N, R 15 E). Altitude 7504 feet. Named on Wentworth Springs (1953) 7.5' quadrangle.

Jerry Canyon [PLACER]: *canyon,* drained by a stream that flows 2 miles to Long Canyon 2.5 miles north-northwest of Devil Peak (lat. 38°59'50" N, long. 120°33'30" W; near NW cor. sec. 8, T 13 N, R 13 E). Named on Greek Store (1952) 7.5' quadrangle.

Jerry Lake [NEVADA]: *lake,* 800 feet long, 8 miles west-northwest of Donner Pass (lat. 39°21'55" N, long. 120°27'20" W; at E line sec. 1, T 17 N, R 13 E). Named on Soda Springs (1955, photorevised 1973) 7.5' quadrangle.

Jerseydale [MARIPOSA]: *locality,* nearly 9 miles south-southwest of El Portal (lat. 37°33'50" N, long. 119°51'20" W; near NW cor. sec. 27, T 4 S, R 19 E). Named on Buckingham Mountain (1947) 7.5' quadrangle. Postal authorities established Jerseydale post office in 1889 and discontinued it in 1930 (Frickstad, p. 91). They established Minear post office 6 miles north of Jerseydale in 1895 and discontinued it in 1896; the name was for John J. Minear, first postmaster (Salley, p. 141).

Jersey Flat: see **Downieville** [SIERRA].

Jersey Ravine [SIERRA]: *canyon,* drained by a stream that flows 1.25 miles to Oregon Creek 2.25 miles west-northwest of Alleghany (lat. 39°28'50" N, long. 120°52'45" W; near S line sec. 29, T 19 N, R 10 E). Named on Alleghany (1949) and Pike (1949) 7.5' quadrangles.

Jesbel [MADERA]: *locality,* 5.25 miles south-southwest of Raymond along Southern Pacific Railroad (lat. 37°09' N, long. 119°57'15" W; sec. 13, T 9 S, R 18 E). Named on Raymond (1944) 15' quadrangle.

Jesse Canyon [EL DORADO]: *canyon,* drained by a stream that flows 2 miles to Middle Fork American River 4.5 miles north of Georgetown (lat. 38°58'30" N, long. 120°49'55" W; sec. 14, T 13 N, R 10 E). Named on Georgetown (1949) 7.5' quadrangle. Called Republican Cañon on Whitney's (1880) map.

Jesus Maria [CALAVERAS]: *locality,* 3.25 miles east-southeast of Mokelumne Hill (lat. 38°17'10" N, long. 120°38'45" W; near W line sec. 15, T 5 N, R 12 E). Named on Mokelumne Hill (1948) 7.5' quadrangle. The site was settled in the early 1850's and named for a Mexican who grew vegetables and melons there (California Department of Parks and Recreation, p 16)

Jesus Maria Creek [CALAVERAS]: *stream,* flows 17 miles to North Fork Calaveras River 2.5 miles east-southeast of Mokelumne Hill (lat. 38°17'15" N, long. 120°39'35" W; sec. 16, T 5 N, R 12 E); the stream goes past Jesus Maria. Named on Fort Mountain (1979), Mokelumne Hill (1948), and Rail Road Flat (1948) 7.5' quadrangles.

Jewelry Lake [TUOLUMNE]: *lake,* 1200 feet long, 12 miles east of Pinecrest (lat. 38°09'45" N, long. 119°46'55" W). Named on Pinecrest (1956) 15' quadrangle. The name is from some jeweled spinners used by a fishermen at the lake about 1915 (Browning. 1986, p. 110).

Jim Crow Cañon: see **Jim Crow Creek** [SIERRA].

Jim Crow Creek [SIERRA]: *stream,* flows 4 miles to San Juan Canyon 2.5 miles east-southeast of Downieville (lat. 39°32'55" N, long. 120°46'55" W; sec. 6, T 19 N, R 11 E). Named on Downieville (1951) 7.5' quadrangle. On Downieville (1897) 30' quadrangle, the name "Jim Crow Ravine" appears to apply to the canyon of present Jim Crow Creek and to present Black Jack Ravine, but United States Board on Geographic Names (1960a, p. 15) rejected the name "Jim Crow Ravine." Logan's (1929) map shows Jim Crow Cañon. The name is for Jim Crow, a Kanaka who came to present Downieville with William Downie in 1849 (Hoover, Rensch, and Rensch, p. 491-492).

Jim Crow Ravine: see **Black Jack Ravine** [SIERRA]; **Jim Crow Creek** [SIERRA].

Jimmy Brown Bar: see **Scotchman Creek** [NEVADA].

Jim Quinn Spring [EL DORADO]: *spring,* 10 miles west-southwest of Kirkwood (lat. 38°39'25" N, long. 120°14'30" W; sec. 6, T 9 N, R 16 E). Named on Tragedy Spring (1979) 7.5' quadrangle.

Joaquin Gulch [CALAVERAS]: *canyon,* drained by a stream that flows 1.5 miles to Calaveritas Creek 8.5 miles east of San Andreas (lat. 38°10'55" N, long. 120°31'25" W; sec. 22, T 4 N, R 13 E). Named on Calaveritas (1962) 7.5' quadrangle.

Joaquin Peak [CALAVERAS]: *peak,* nearly 4 miles south of San Andreas near the south end of Hogback Mountain (lat. 38°08'30" N, long. 120°41'25" W; sec. 6, T 3 N, R 12 E). Altitude 2812 feet. Named on San Andreas (1962) 7.5' quadrangle. Called Mt. Joaquin on Jackson (1902) 30' quadrangle. The name "Joaquin" is for the Mexican outlaw Joaquin Murieta, who is said to have been involved in a skirmish near the peak in 1853 (Gudde, 1969, p. 215).

Job's Peaks: see **Jobs Sister** [EL DORADO].

Jobs Sister [EL DORADO]: *peak,* 1 mile east-northeast of Freel Peak on El Dorado-Alpine county line (lat. 38°51'45" N, long. 119° 53' W; sec. 31, T 12 N, R 19 E). Altitude 10,823 feet. Named on Freel Peak (1955) 7.5' quadrangle. Present Jobs Sister, Freel Peak, and Jobs Peak (Jobs Peak is in Alpine County) together were known as Job's Peaks; the name "Job" was for Moses Job, who had a store in the vicinity in the early 1850's (Gudde, 1949, p. 166-167).

Joe Crane Lake [MADERA]: *lake,* 1000 feet long, 4.5 miles east of Merced Peak (lat. 37°37'30" N, long. 119°18'50" W). Named on Merced Peak (1953) 15' quadrangle.

Joe Miller Ravine [NEVADA]: *canyon,* drained by a stream that flows 1 mile to Englebright Lake 7 miles north-northwest of Pilot Peak (lat. 39°14'25" N, long. 121°15'35" W; near SE cor. sec. 14, T 16 N, R 6 E). Named on Rough and Ready (1949) and Smartville (1951) 7.5' quadrangles.

Joes Point [TUOLUMNE]: *peak,* 5.5 miles west

of Mather (lat. 37°53'10" N, long. 119°57'15" W; near W line sec. 1, T 1 S, R 18 E). Altitude 4219 feet. Named on Lake Eleanor (1956) 15' quadrangle.

Joes Spring [PLACER]: *spring,* less than 0.5 mile east-southeast of Bunker Hill (lat. 39°02'45" N, long. 120°22'20" W; sec. 23, T 14 N, R 14 E). Named on Wentworth Springs (1953) 7.5' quadrangle.

John: see **Fort John**, under **Volcano** [AMADOR].

John Allen Flat [MARIPOSA]: *area,* 6.5 miles southeast of Mariposa along Blade Creek (lat. 37°24'40" N, long. 119°53'35" W; sec. 16, T 6 S, R 19 E). Named on Mariposa (1947) 7.5' quadrangle.

John Brown Flat [PLACER]: *area,* nearly 5 miles south of Colfax (lat. 39°01'55" N, long. 120°57'45" W; sec. 27, T 14 N, R 9 E). Named on Colfax (1949) 7.5' quadrangle.

John Bull Peak [CALAVERAS]: *peak,* 3.25 miles west of Paloma (lat. 38°15'25" N, long. 120°49'25" W; sec. 25, T 5 N, R 10 E). Altitude 1053 feet. Named on Jackson (1962) 7.5' quadrangle.

John Greenwood's Creek: see **Prosser Creek** [NEVADA].

Johnnie Gulch [TUOLUMNE]: *canyon,* drained by a stream that flows 1 mile to North Fork Tuolumne River 2.5 miles east of Twain Harte (lat. 38°02' N, long. 120°11' W; near N line sec. 14, T 2 N, R 16 E). Named on Twain Harte (1979) 7.5' quadrangle.

Johnnys Hill [EL DORADO]: *peak,* 2 miles west-southwest of Wentworth Springs (lat. 39°00'20" N, long. 120°22'35" W; sec. 2, T 13 N, R 14 E). Altitude 6559 feet. Named on Bunker Hill (1953) and Wentworth Springs (1953) 7.5' quadrangles.

Johns Creek: see **Prosser Creek** [NEVADA].

Johnson Canyon [EL DORADO]: *canyon,* 1.5 miles long, opens into North Canyon (2) 5.5 miles east-northeast of Placerville (lat. 38° 45'50" N, long. 120°43'50" W). Named on Placerville (1893) 30' quadrangle.

Johnson Creek [MADERA]:

(1) *stream,* flows 3.5 miles to South Fork Merced River 4 miles south of Buena Vista Peak (lat. 37°32'15" N, long. 119°31'20" W; near SE cor. sec. 35, T 4 S, R 22 E). Named on Yosemite (1956) 15' quadrangle.

(2) *stream,* flows 4.5 miles to Chiquito Creek 5.5 miles north-northeast of Shuteye Peak (lat. 37°25' N, long. 119°23'05" W; sec. 7, T 6 S, R 24 E). Named on Shuteye Peak (1953) 15' quadrangle.

Johnson Creek [TUOLUMNE]: *stream,* heads in Tuolumne County and flows 4 miles to Dry Creek 3.25 miles northwest of La Grange in Stanislaus County (lat. 37°42' N, long. 120°30' W; near W line sec. 1, T 3 S, R 13 E). Named on La Grange (1962) 7.5' quadrangle.

Johnson Lake [MADERA]: *lake,* 900 feet long, 1.5 miles south of Buena Vista Peak (lat.

37°34'05" N, long. 119°31' W; near SW cor. sec. 24, T 4 S, R 22 E); the lake is along Johnson Creek (1). Named on Yosemite (1956) 15' quadrangle. United States Board on Geographic Names (1933, p. 400) rejected the names "Glacier Lake" and "Glasier Lake" for the feature.

Johnson Lake: see **Johnston Lake** [MADERA].

Johnson Meadow: see **Johnston Meadow** [MADERA].

Johnson Meadows [MADERA]: *area,* 6 miles north-northeast of Shuteye Peak (lat. 37°25'50" N, long. 119°23'30" W; sec. 6, T 6 S, R 24 E). Named on Shuteye Peak (1953) 15' quadrangle.

Johnson Pass [EL DORADO]: *pass,* less than 1 mile north of Echo Summit (lat. 38°49'25" N, long. 120°01'50" W; near S line sec. 6, T 11 N, R 18 E). Named on Echo Lake (1955) 7.5' quadrangle. The name recalls John C. "Cock Eye" Johnson, who in 1848 blazed the first trail over present Echo Summit from Placerville to the south end of Lake Tahoe (Yohalem, p. 150). Echo Summit was called Johnson Pass in the early days (Zauner, p. 7).

Johnson Peak [TUOLUMNE]: *peak,* 7 miles southwest of Tioga Pass (lat. 37°50'10" N, long. 119°20'50" W). Altitude 11,070 feet. Named on Tuolumne Meadows (1956) 15' quadrangle. R.B. Marshall of United States Geological Survey named the peak in the 1890's for a teamster who worked for the Survey and was especially useful as a guide (United States Board on Geographic Names, 1934, p. 13).

Johnson Ravine [SIERRA]: *canyon,* drained by a stream that flows less than 1 mile to Canyon Creek 8 miles southwest of Mount Fillmore (lat. 39°38'15" N, long. 120°56'05" W; sec. 35, T 21 N, R 9 E). Named on La Porte (1951) 7.5' quadrangle.

Johnson's Diggings: see **Birchville** [NEVADA].

Johnsonville: see **Bear Valley** [MARIPOSA] (2).

Johnston Lake [MADERA]: *lake,* 600 feet long, nearly 2 miles northwest of Devils Postpile (lat. 37°38'45" N, long. 119°06' W); the lake is in Johnston Meadow. Named on Devils Postpile (1953) 15' quadrangle. It first was called Minaret Lake, but Stephen T. Mather suggested the name "Johnston Lake" to honor Taylor Johnston, as well as Mr. Johnston's father and brother—the three men began mining in the neighborhood in 1919 (Browning, 1988, p. 69). United States Board on Geographic Names (1962b, p. 20) rejected the names "Minaret Lake" and "Johnson Lake" for the feature.

Johnston Meadow [MADERA]: *area,* 2 miles northwest of Devils Postpile along Minaret Creek (lat. 37°38'45" N, long. 119°06' W). Named on Devils Postpile (1953) 15' quadrangle. Stephen T. Mather suggested the name

"Johnston Meadow" for what had been called Minaret Meadow; the new name honors the Johnstons for whom Johnston Lake was named (Browning, 1988, p. 69). United States Board on Geographic Names (1962b, p. 20) rejected the names "Johnson Meadow" and "Minaret Meadow" for the place.

Johntown: see **Garden Valley** [EL DORADO].

Johntown Creek [EL DORADO]: *stream,* formed by the confluence of Empire Creek and Manhattan Creek, flows 4.5 miles to Dutch Creek nearly 4 miles northwest of Chili Bar (lat. 38°48'20" N, long. 120°52'15" W; sec. 16, T 11 N, R 10 E). Named on Coloma (1949) and Garden Valley (1949) 7.5' quadrangles. The name recalls the old mining camp of Johntown (Gudde, 1975, p. 178). Whitney (1880, p. 85) mentioned a place called Alabama Flat that was located along Johntown Creek.

Jone City: see **Ione** [AMADOR].

Jones [EL DORADO]: *locality,* 5.25 miles south-southeast of Robbs Peak (lat. 38°51' N, long. 120°22' W). Named on Pyramid Peak (1896) 30' quadrangle. Kyburz (1952) 7.5' quadrangle shows Jones place at the site.

Jones Bar [NEVADA]: *locality,* 5.25 miles west-northwest of Nevada City along South Yuba River (lat. 39°17'40" N, long. 121° 06'35" W; sec. 32, T 17 N, R 8 E); the place is 0.5 mile upstream from the mouth of Jones Ravine. Named on Nevada City (1948) 7.5' quadrangle.

Jones Butte: see **Dutschke Hill** [AMADOR].

Jones Creek [MARIPOSA}: *stream,* flows 4.25 miles to join Snow Creek (2) and form West Fork Chowchilla River 5 miles east of Mariposa (lat. 37°28'55" N, long. 119°52'25" W; sec. 22, T 5 S, R 19 E). Named on Feliciana Mountain (1947) and Mariposa (1947) 7.5' quadrangles.

Jones Creek: see **Canyon Creek** [EL DORADO] (1).

Jones Flat [MARIPOSA]: *area,* 5 miles north-northwest of Hornitos (lat. 37°34'20" N, long. 120°16'15" W; sec. 24, T 4 S, R 15 E). Named on Merced Falls (1962) 7.5' quadrangle.

Jones Fork: see **Silver Creek** [EL DORADO].

Jones Hill [TUOLUMNE]: *ridge,* north-north-east-trending, 1 mile long, 1 mile north of Groveland (lat. 37°51'05" N, long. 120°13'50" W). Named on Groveland (1947) 7.5' quadrangle.

Jones Hill: see **Canyon Creek** [EL DORADO] (1).

Jones Ravine [NEVADA]: *canyon,* drained by a stream that flows 1.25 miles to South Yuba River 5.5 miles west-northwest of Nevada City (lat. 39°17'45" N, long. 121°06'55" W; sec. 31, T 17 N, R 8 E); the mouth of the canyon is nearly 0.5 mile downstream from Jones Bar. Named on Nevada City (1948) 7.5' quadrangle.

Jones Ridge [NEVADA]: *ridge,* south-southwest- to south-trending, 2 miles long, 6.25 miles north-northeast of Chicago Park (lat. 39° 14' N, long. 120°56'05" W). Named on Chicago Park (1949) 7.5' quadrangle.

Jones Valley [NEVADA]: *valley,* 7 miles west-northwest of Donner Pass along Rattlesnake Creek (2) (lat. 39°20'25" N, long. 120°27'15" W; on W line sec. 18, T 17 N, R 14 E). Named on Soda Springs (1955) 7.5' quadrangle.

Jones Valley [SIERRA]:
(1) *valley,* 1.25 miles west of Crystal Peak (lat. 39°33'35" N, long. 120°06'45" W). Named on Dog Valley (1981) 7.5' quadrangle, which shows marsh in much of the valley.
(2) *valley,* 9.5 miles south-southwest of Sierraville along Pass Creek (lat. 39°28'35" N, long. 120°27'30" W; on N line sec. 36, T 19 N, R 13 E). Named on Webber Peak (1981) 7.5' quadrangle.

Jones Valley: see **Upper Jones Valley** [NEVADA].

Jone Valley: see **Ione** [AMADOR].

Jordan Creek [MARIPOSA]: *stream,* flows 5.5 miles to North Fork Merced River 5 miles southeast of Smith Peak (lat. 37°45'05" N, long. 120°02'05" W; sec. 19, T 2 S, R 18 E). Named on Jawbone Ridge (1947) 7.5' quadrangle. West Fork enters from the northwest 3 miles upstream from the mouth of the main stream; it is 2.5 miles long and is named on Jawbone Ridge (1947) 7.5' quadrangle.

Jordan Creek [NEVADA]: *stream,* flows 1.5 miles to South Yuba River 2.25 miles west of Yuba Gap (lat. 39°19'15" N, long. 120°39'15" W; sec. 20, T 17 N, R 12 E). Named on Blue Canyon (1955) 7.5' quadrangle.

Jordan Flat [MARIPOSA]: *area,* 1 mile south of Smith Peak (lat. 37° 47'05" N, long. 120°06'10" W; near S line sec. 4, T 2 S, R 17 E); the place is along West Fork Jordan Creek. Named on Jawbone Ridge (1947) 7.5' quadrangle.

Josephine: see **Josephine Canyon** [EL DORADO].

Josephine Canyon [EL DORADO]: *canyon,* drained by a stream that flows nearly 1 mile to Middle Fork American River 7 miles north-northeast of Georgetown (lat. 39°00' N, long. 120°47'15" W; sec. 6, T 13 N, R 11 E). Named on Georgetown (1949) 7.5' quadrangle, which shows Josephine mine near the head of the canyon. Postal authorities established Josephine post office, named for the mine, in 1895, discontinued it in 1915, reestablished it in 1916, and discontinued it in 1917 (Salley, p. 108).

Joubert Diggins [SIERRA]: *locality,* 4 miles north-northwest of Pike along Willow Creek (lat. 39°29'40" N, long. 121°01'35" W; on S line sec. 24, T 19 N, R 8 E). Named on Camptonville (1948) 7.5' quadrangle. J. Joubert discovered gold at the place in 1852 (Gudde, 1975, p. 179).

Juba Creek: see **Yuba River** [NEVADA].

Judah: see **Mount Judah** [PLACER].

Judge Palmer's Bridge: see **Chaparral Hill**, under **Lancha Plana** [AMADOR].

Junction: see **Roseville** [PLACER].

Junction Bar [EL DORADO-PLACER]: *locality,* 3 miles northeast of Volcanoville along Middle Fork American River on El Dorado-Placer county line (lat. 39°00'35" N, long. 120°44'50" W; on N line sec. 4, T 13 N, R 11 E). Named on Michigan Bluff (1952) 7.5' quadrangle.

Junction Bluffs [MADERA]: *relief feature,* 7 miles south-southwest of Devils Postpile (lat. 37°31'30" N, long. 119°08' W); the feature is on the south side of Middle Fork San Joaquin River east of the junction with North Fork. Named on Devils Postpile (1953) 15' quadrangle.

Junction Butte [MADERA]: *ridge,* north-trending, 2 miles long, 9 miles southwest of Devils Postpile (lat. 37°31'40" N, long. 119°11'45" W; near E line sec. 2, T 5 S, R 25 E); the ridge is southwest of the junction of West Fork San Joaquin River and Middle Fork San Joaquin River. Named on Devils Postpile (1953) 15' quadrangle.

Junction Lake [MADERA]: *lake,* about 600 feet long, 10.5 miles north-northwest of Shuteye Peak (lat. 37°29'45" N, long. 119°29'45" W; sec. 18, T 5 S, R 23 E). Named on Shuteye Peak (1953) 15' quadrangle.

Junction House [NEVADA]: *locality,* 3 miles south-southwest of Washington (lat. 39°19' N, long. 120°48'40" W; near NW cor. sec. 25, T 17 N, R 10 E). Site named on Washington (1950) 7.5' quadrangle.

Juniper Creek [NEVADA-PLACER]: *stream,* heads in the State of Nevada and flows 7 miles through Placer County to Truckee River 6.5 miles east-northeast of Truckee in Nevada County (lat. 39° 21'55" N, long. 120°04'20" W; sec. 34, T 18 N, R 17 E). Named on Martis Peak (1955) 7.5' quadrangle.

Juniper Creek: see **West Juniper Creek** [NEVADA].

Juniper Flat [NEVADA]: *area,* 5.5 miles east-northeast of Truckee (lat. 39°22' N, long. 120°05'40" W; mainly in sec. 33, T 18 N, R 17 E). Named on Boca (1955) and Martis Peak (1955) 7.5' quadrangles.

Juniper Hill [NEVADA]: *peak,* 9 miles east of Truckee (lat. 39°20'45" N, long. 120°01'20" W; near SW cor. sec. 7, T 17 N, R 18 E). Altitude 7939 feet. Named on Martis Peak (1955) 7.5' quadrangle.

Juniper Ridge Spring [NEVADA]: *spring,* 8.5 miles east of Truckee (lat. 39°20'15" N, long. 120°01'20" W; sec. 18, T 17 N, R 18 E). Named on Martis Peak (1955) 7.5' quadrangle.

Jupiter [TUOLUMNE]: *locality,* 9 miles northeast of Columbia (lat. 38°07'20" N, long. 120°16'55" W; sec. 12, T 3 N, R 15 E). Named on Columbia SE (1948) 7.5' quadrangle. Postal authorities established Jupiter post office, named for Jupiter mine, in 1901 and discontinued it in 1922 (Salley, p. 109). The post office was at a place called Philadelphia Diggings (Gudde, 1975, p. 264).

Jurgens: see **Rescue** [EL DORADO].

– K –

Kalmeia Lake: see **Kalmia Lake** [EL DORADO].

Kalmia Lake [EL DORADO]: *lake,* 700 feet long, 1.5 miles west-northwest of Mount Tallac (lat. 38°54'40" N, long. 120°07'25" W; sec. 5, T 12 N, R 17 E). Named on Emerald Bay (1955) and Rockbound Valley (1955) 7.5' quadrangles. The name is from *Kalmia polifoia,* the botanical name for alpine laurel; the earlier form "Kalmeia Lake" was changed to conform with the botanical name (Lekisch, p. 68).

Kaiser Creek Ford [MADERA]: *locality,* 7 miles east of Shuteye Peak along San Joaquin River (lat. 37°22' N, long. 119°18' W; sec. 36, T 6 S, R 24 E); the place is above the mouth of Kaiser Creek, which is in Fresno County. Named on Kaiser (1904) 30' quadrangle.

Kanaka Bar: see **Kanaka Creek** [TUOLUMNE].

Kanaka Creek [SIERRA]: *stream,* formed by the confluence of Middle Fork and South Fork, flows 9 miles to Middle Yuba River 3.25 miles east-southeast of Pike (lat. 39°25'10" N, long. 120°56'35" W; at W line sec. 14, T 18 N, R 9 E). Named on Alleghany (1949) 7.5' quadrangle. A party of Kanaka (Hawaiian) prospectors discovered gold along the stream in 1850 (Hoover, Rensch, and Rensch, p. 494-495). Middle Fork is 3.25 miles long and is named on Alleghany (1949) and Downieville (1951) 7.5' quadrangles. South Fork is 3 miles long and is named on Alleghany (1949) 7.5' quadrangle. North Fork, which enters from the north 0.5 mile south-southwest of Alleghany, is 2.5 miles long and is named on Alleghany (1949) 7.5' quadrangle. Present North Fork is called Little Kanaka Creek on Colfax (1898) 30' quadrangle.

Kanaka Creek [TUOLUMNE]: *stream,* flows 3 miles to Don Pedro Reservoir 4 miles northwest of Moccasin (lat. 37°50'40" N, long. 120°21'25" W; sec. 18, T 1 S, R 15 E). Named on Moccasin (1948, photorevised 1973) 7.5' quadrangle. Kanaka Bar was located along Tuolumne River at the mouth of Kanaka Creek—water of Don Pedro Reservoir now covers the site of the bar (Gudde, 1975, p. 181).

Kanaka Gulch [AMADOR]: *canyon,* 1.5 miles long, 5.25 miles south-southeast of Plymouth (lat. 38°24'50" N, long. 120°47'50" W; sec. 31, 32, T 7 N, R 11 E). Named on Amador City (1962) 7.'5 quadrangle.

Kanaka Gulch [EL DORADO]: *canyon,* drained by a stream that flows 1.5 miles to Middle Fork American River 6.5 miles north-northeast of Georgetown (lat. 38°59'45" N, long. 120°47'50" W; near W line sec. 6, T 13 N, R 11 E). Named on Georgetown (1949) 7.5' quadrangle.

Kane Flat: see **Sierra City** [SIERRA].

Kanes [EL DORADO]: *locality,* 10 miles south-southeast of Placerville (lat. 38°35'50" N, long. 120°42'45" W). Named on Placerville (1893) 30' quadrangle.

Karls Lake [TUOLUMNE]: *lake,* 0.5 miles, long, 13 miles east-southeast of Pinecrest (lat. 38°08'50" N, long. 119°45'45" W). Named on Pinecrest (1956) 15' quadrangle. The name commemorates Karl Defiebre, a hotelman at Pinecrest before World War II (Browning, 1986, p. 114).

Kaseberg Creek [PLACER]: *stream,* flows 6 miles to Pleasant Grove Creek 5.25 miles northwest of Roseville (lat. 38°47'35" N, long. 121°21'45" W; sec. 24, T 11 N, R 5 E). Named on Roseville (1967) 7.5' quadrangle. The name commemorates James W. Kaseberg, a rancher in the neighborhood (Gudde, 1949, p. 170).

Kassabaum Flats [MARIPOSA]: *area,* 6.5 miles south-southwest of Penon Blanco Peak along Browns Creek (lat. 37°38'45" N, long. 120°19' W). Named on Penon Blanco Peak (1962) 7.5' quadrangle.

Kassabaum Meadow [TUOLUMNE]: *area,* 5.5 miles east of Groveland (lat. 37°49'25" N, long. 120°07'40" W; mainly in sec. 29, T 1 S, R 17 E). Named on Groveland (1947) 7.5' quadrangle.

Kates Cow Camp [MADERA]: *locality,* 8 miles north of Shuteye Peak (lat. 37°27'55" N, long. 119°24'15" W; sec. 25, T 5 S, R 23 E). Named on Shuteye Peak (1953) 15' quadrangle.

Katrine Lake: see **Snow Lake** [EL DORADO].

Keiths Dome [EL DORADO]: *peak,* 5.25 miles northwest of Echo Summit (lat. 38°51'35" N, long. 120°06'20" W; sec. 28, T 12 N, R 17 E). Altitude 8646 feet. Named on Echo Lake (1955) 7.5' quadrangle. The name commemorates W.F. Keith, a pioneer (Lekisch, p. 68).

Kelley Lake: see **Kelly Lake** [PLACER].

Kelly Creek [EL DORADO]: *stream,* flows 4 miles to Dry Creek 4.5 miles north-northwest of Shingle Springs (lat. 38°43'35" N, long. 120°56'50" W; near NE cor. sec. 14, T 10 N, R 9 E). Named on Shingle Springs (1949) 7.5' quadrangle.

Kelly Flat [TUOLUMNE]: *locality,* 6.25 miles west of Mather along Cherry Creek (lat. 37°53'30" N, long. 119°58'10" W; on S line sec. 35, T 1 N, R 18 E). Named on Lake Eleanor (1956) 15' quadrangle.

Kelly Lake [PLACER]: *lake,* 1800 feet long, 2 miles west of Cisco Grove (lat. 39°18'35" N, long. 120°34'40" W; sec. 25, T 17 N, R 12 E). Named on Cisco Grove (1955) 7.5' quadrangle. Called Kelley Lake on Emigrant Gap (1955) 15' quadrangle.

Kelly Ravine [EL DORADO]: *canyon,* drained by a stream that flows about 1 mile to Folsom Lake 4 miles west-southwest of the village of Pilot Hill (lat. 38°48'55" N, long. 121°04'50" W; at E line sec. 9, T 11 N, R 8 E). Named on Pilot Hill (1954, photorevised 1973) 7.5' quadrangle.

Kellys Bar: see **American River** [EL DORADO-PLACER].

Kelsey [EL DORADO]: *village,* 2 miles north of Chili Bar (lat. 38°47'45" N, long. 120°49'05" W; near SW cor. sec. 13, T 11 N, R 10 E). Named on Garden Valley (1949) 7.5' quadrangle, which shows Kelsey P.O. located nearly 1 mile north of Kelsey. Postal authorities established Kelsey post office in 1856, discontinued it in 1872, reestablished it in 1875, moved it 0.5 mile west in 1895, moved it 0.5 mile southeast in 1896, discontinued it in 1903, and reestablished it in 1920 (Salley, p. 110). Benjamin Kelsey, who came to California in 1841 with the Bidwell-Bartleson party, discovered gold in 1848 at the place, which became known as Kelsey's Diggings (Hoover, Rensch, and Rensch, p. 86). A mining camp called Dufftown was close to Kelsey; the place was named by sailors who lived there and had a concoction called plum duff each Sunday for dinner (Gernes, p. 33). Postal authorities established Saint Lawrenceburgh post office 4 miles north of Kelsey in 1872, discontinued it in 1875, reestablished it with the name "Saint Lawrence" in 1880, and discontinued it in 1882; the name was from Saint Lawrence mine (Salley, p. 191). They established Slatington post office in 1903, discontinued it in 1912, reestablished it in 1916, and discontinued it in 1920, when they moved it 1.5 miles northeast and changed the name to Kelsey; the name "Slatington" was from the hand-split slate shingles made at the place (Salley, p. 206). Gudde (1975, p. 80) listed a place called Lawrenceberg, also known as Columbia Flat, that was located near Kelsey. David Martin and his family moved to Columbia Flat in 1851 and built a travelers stop there called Columbia House; a mining camp called Cincinnati was situated near Kelsey between Columbia Flat and Irish Creek (Gernes, p. 34-35).

Kelsey Canyon [EL DORADO]: *canyon,* 2 miles long, opens into the canyon of South Fork American River less than 1 mile west-northwest of Chili Bar (lat. 38°46'15" N, long. 120°49'55" W; sec. 26, T 11 N, R 10 E). Named on Garden Valley (1949) 7.5' quadrangle.

Kelsey's Diggings: see **Kelsey** [EL DORADO].

Kelshaw Corners [MADERA]: *locality,* 2.5 miles northwest of O'Neals (lat. 37°09'05" N,

long. 119°44' W; sec. 13, T 9 S, R 20 E). Named on O'Neals (1965) 7.5' quadrangle.

Kelty Meadow [MADERA]: *area,* 7 miles northeast of Yosemite Forks (lat. 37°26'30" N, long. 119°32'35" W; near E line sec. 3, T 6 S, R 22 E). Named on Bass Lake (1953) 15' quadrangle. The misspelled name is for Frank Keltie, who homesteaded in sections 2 and 3 in 1886 (Browning, 1986, p. 116).

Kelty Meadow Campground [MADERA]: *locality,* 7 miles northeast of Yosemite Forks (lat. 37°26'25" N, long. 119°32'35" W; sec. 3, T 6 S, R 22 E); the place is at Kelty Meadow. Named on Bass Lake (1953) 15' quadrangle.

Kendrick Creek [TUOLUMNE]: *stream,* flows 13 miles to join Bartlett Creek and form Eleanor Creek 16 miles southeast of Pinecrest (lat. 38°01'30" N, long. 119°48' W; near S line sec. 17, T 2 N, R 20 E); the stream heads near Kendrick Peak. Named on Pinecrest (1956) and Tower Peak (1956) 15' quadrangles. The name is from Kendrick Peak (United States Board on Geographic Names, 1934, p. 13). Called East Fork Eleanor Cr. on Dardanelles (1898) 30' quadrangle.

Kendrick Peak [TUOLUMNE]: *peak,* 5 miles west-southwest of Tower Peak (lat. 38°07'30" N, long. 119°38'15" W). Altitude 10,390 feet. Named on Tower Peak (1956) 15' quadrangle. Colonel W.W. Forsyth named the peak in 1912 for Henry L. Kendrick, professor of chemistry at West Point (United States Board on Geographic Names, 1934, p. 13).

Kenebec Creek [NEVADA]: *stream,* flows 2 miles to South Yuba River 4.25 miles southwest of North Bloomfield (lat. 39°20'05" N, long. 120°58'05" W; sec. 16, T 17 N, R 9 E). Named on North Bloomfield (1949) 7.5' quadrangle. Whitney's (1873) map has the name "Kennebec Ravine" for the canyon of the stream.

Kennebec Hill: see **Kennebec House** [NEVADA].

Kennebec Hill [TUOLUMNE]: *hill,* 0.5 mile south-southeast of Columbia (lat. 38°01'40" N, long. 120°23'45" W; sec. 13, 14, T 2 N, R 14 E). Named on Columbia (1948) 7.5' quadrangle.

Kennebec House [NEVADA]: *locality,* 3.5 miles west-southwest of North Bloomfield (lat. 39°21' N, long. 120°58' W); the place is west of present Kenebec Creek. Named on Colfax (1898) 30' quadrangle. Whitney's (1873) map shows Kennebec Hill located 0.5 mile north of Kennebec Ho.

Kennebeck Bar [EL DORADO-PLACER]: *locality,* 4.5 miles west-northwest of Greenwood along Middle Fork American River on El Dorado-Placer county line (lat. 38°55'40" N, long. 120°59'10" W; near SW cor. sec. 33, T 13 N, R 9 E). Named on Greenwood (1949) 7.5' quadrangle.

Kennebec Ravine: see **Kenebec Creek** [NEVADA].

Kennedy Creek [TUOLUMNE]: *stream,* flows 8 miles to join Summit Creek and form Middle Fork Stanislaus River 5.5 miles west-southwest of Sonora Pass (lat. 38°17'40" N, long. 119°43'45" W; sec. 12, T 5 N, R 20 E). Named on Sonora Pass (1956) and Tower Peak (1956) 15' quadrangles. Called East Fork [Relief Creek] on Dardanelles (1898) 30' quadrangle, where present Summit Creek is called Relief Creek. United States Board on Geographic Names (1980a, p. 3) rejected the names "East Fork Summit Creek" and "Middle Fork Stanislaus River" for Kennedy Creek.

Kennedy Lake [TUOLUMNE]: *lake,* 0.5 mile long, 4.5 miles south-southwest of Sonora Pass along Kennedy Creek (lat. 38°15'35" N, long. 119°39'05" W; on S line sec. 22, T 5 N, R 21 E). Named on Sonora Pass (1979) 7.5' quadrangle. The name is for Andrew L. Kennedy, who patented land at the lake in 1886 (Gudde, 1949, p. 172).

Kennedy Meadow [TUOLUMNE]:
(1) *area,* 6 miles west-southwest of Sonora Pass along Middle Fork Stanislaus River (lat. 38°18'05" N, long. 119°44'20" W; near N line sec. 11, T 5 N, R 20 E). Named on Sonora Pass (1979) 7.5' quadrangle.
(2) *locality,* 6 miles west of Sonora Pass along Middle Fork Stanislaus River (lat. 38°18'40" N, long. 119°44'40" W; sec. 2, T 5 N, R 20 E). Named on Sonora Pass (1979) 7.5' quadrangle.

Kennedy Peak [TUOLUMNE]: *peak,* 9 miles northwest of Tower Peak (lat. 38°14'45" N, long. 119°39'15" W; near S line sec. 27, T 5 N, R 21 E); the peak is 1 mile south of Kennedy Lake. Altitude 10,718 feet. Named on Tower Peak (1956) 15' quadrangle. United States Board on Geographic Names (1976a, p. 5) approved the name "Molo Mountain" for a peak, altitude 10,885 feet, located less than 1 mile south of Kennedy Peak (lat. 38°14'04" N, long. 119°39'20" W; sec. 34, T 5 N, R 21 E).

Kennedy Reservoir [AMADOR]: *lake,* 350 feet long, 1.5 miles north-northwest of Jackson (lat. 38°22'05" N, long. 120°47'10" W; sec. 17, T 6 N, R 11 E). Named on Jackson (1962) 7.5' quadrangle.

Kennedy Table [MADERA]: *ridge,* south-southeast-trending, 4.5 miles long, 6 miles east-southeast of O'Neals (lat. 37°06'30" N, long. 119°35'45" W). Named on Millerton Lake East (1965) and North Fork (1965) 7.5' quadrangles.

Kentucky Well [MADERA]: *well,* 15 miles west of Madera (lat. 36°59'50" N, long. 120°20'20" W; near S line sec. 4, T 11 S, R 15 E). Named on Kentucky Well (1922) 7.5' quadrangle.

Kent Creek [PLACER]: *stream,* flows 1.5 miles to Shirttail Canyon 3.5 miles north-northeast of Foresthill (lat. 39°04'10" N, long. 120°47'40" W; sec. 12, T 14 N, R 10 E). Named

on Foresthill (1949) 7.5' quadrangle.

Kent Ravine: see **North San Juan** [NEVADA].

Kentucky Flat [EL DORADO]: *area,* 16 miles north-northwest of Pollock Pines (lat. 38°57'55" N, long. 120°44'20" W; sec. 22, T 13 N, R 11 E). Named on Tunnel Hill (1950) 7.5' quadrangle. Placerville (1893) 30' quadrangle has the name for a locality.

Kentucky House [CALAVERAS]: *locality,* 2.25 miles south of San Andreas near the confluence of Calaveritas Creek and South Fork Calaveras River (lat. 38°09'45" N, long. 120°40'20" W; near N line sec. 32, T 4 N, R 12 E). Named on San Andreas (1962) 7.5' quadrangle. Camp's (1962) map gives the name "Third Crossing" as an alternate, and shows a place called Alabama House situated 1 mile north-northwest of Kentucky House along South Fork Calaveras River. Postal authorities established Third Crossing post office in 1852 and discontinued it in 1854 (Salley, p. 221).

Kentucky Ravine [NEVADA]: *canyon,* drained by a stream that flows 5.5 miles to South Yuba River 2.25 miles west-southwest of French Corral (lat. 39°17'25" N, long. 121°11'50" W; sec. 33, T 17 N, R 7 E). Named on French Corral (1948) 7.5' quadrangle.

Kentucky Ridge [NEVADA]: *ridge,* west-trending, less than 1 mile long, 4.25 miles south-southeast of French Corral (lat. 39°15' N, long. 121°08' W); the ridge is south of upper Kentucky Ravine. Named on French Corral (1948) and Rough and Ready (1949) 7.5' quadrangles.

Kerckhoff Lake [MADERA]: *lake,* 2.25 miles long, behind a dam on San Joaquin River 7 miles south of the town of North Fork on Madera-Fresno county line (lat. 37°07'40" N, long. 119°31'30" W; near S line sec. 24, T 9 S, R 22 E). Named on North Fork (1965) 7.5' quadrangle. The name is from Kerckhoff power plant, which San Joaquin Power Company put into operation in 1920; the name of the plant commemorates William G. Kerckhoff, one of the organizers of the power company (Gudde, 1949, p. 173).

Kerrick Canon [TUOLUMNE]: *canyon,* 7 miles long, along Rancheria Creek above a point 8.5 miles south-southwest of Tower Peak (lat. 38°02' N, long. 119°36'45" W). Named on Tower Peak (1956) 15' quadrangle. Members of the Wheeler survey named the canyon for James D. Kerrick, who took sheep into the region about 1880 (Browning, 1986, p. 118).

Kerrick Meadow [TUOLUMNE]: *valley,* 5.5 miles west-northwest of Matterhorn Peak at the head of Rancheria Creek (lat. 38°06'30" N, long. 119°28'45" W). Named on Matterhorn Peak (1956) 15' quadrangle.

Keyes Peak [TUOLUMNE]: *peak,* 2.25 miles west of Tower Peak (lat. 38°08'25" N, long. 119°35'20" W). Altitude 10,670 feet. Named on Tower Peak (1956) 15' quadrangle. Colonel W.W. Forsyth named the peak in 1912 for his son-in-law, Edward Appleton Keyes (United States Board on Geographic Names, 1934, p. 13).

Keystone [TUOLUMNE]: *locality,* 12.5 miles south-southwest of Sonora along Sierra Railway (lat. 37°50'05" N, long. 120°30'25" W; sec. 23, T 1 S, R 13 E). Named on Keystone (1962) 7.5' quadrangle. Postal authorities established Cloudman post office in 1882, changed the name to Keystone in 1905, and discontinued it in 1913; the name "Cloudman" was for Daniel C. Cloudman, first postmaster (Salley, p. 46, 111). Paden and Schlichtmann (p. 60) noted both a place called Dunow's Camp, which was located less than 0.5 mile beyond Keystone at the site of Green Springs school, and (p. 55) "the forgotten community of Green Springs," a stopping place of the early 1850's situated 0.6 mile along the road to Sonora beyond the turnoff into present Keystone. Postal authorities established Green Springs post office in 1852 and discontinued it in 1869 (Frickstad, p. 215)—the name was from a double spring (Morgan *in* Gardiner, p. 315).

Keystone Gap [SIERRA]: *pass,* 2.5 miles southwest of Sierra City (lat. 39°32'15" N, long. 120°39'50" W; at S line sec. 6, T 19 N, R 12 E); the pass is at the head of Keystone Ravine. Named on Sierra City (1981) 7.5' quadrangle.

Keystone Mountain [SIERRA]: *peak,* nearly 3 miles southwest of Sierra City (lat. 39°32'20" N, long. 120°40'20" W; sec. 6, T 19 N, R 12 E); the peak is near the head of Keystone Ravine. Altitude 6912 feet. Named on Sierra City (1981) 7.5' quadrangle.

Keystone Ravine [NEVADA]: *canyon,* drained by a stream that flows 1.5 miles to Englebright Reservoir (present Englebright Lake) 6 miles southwest of French Corral (lat. 39°15'15" N, long. 121°15'05" W; near S line sec. 12, T 16 N, R 6 E). Named on French Corral (1948), Oregon House (1948), and Rough and Ready (1949) 7.5' quadrangles.

Keystone Ravine [SIERRA]: *canyon,* drained by a stream that flows 2 miles to North Yuba River 2.5 miles west of Sierra City (lat. 39°34'05" N, long. 120°40'35" W; near SW cor. sec. 30, T 20 N, R 12 E); the canyon heads near Keystone Mountain. Named on Sierra City (1981) 7.5' quadrangle, which shows Keystone mine in the canyon. The mine was developed before 1857 (Gudde, 1949, p. 174).

Kibbie Creek [TUOLUMNE]: *stream,* flows 8.5 miles to Lake Eleanor Reservoir 7.5 miles north of Mather (lat. 37°59'25" N, long. 119°51'55" W; near W line sec. 35, T 2 N, R 19 E). Named on Lake Eleanor (1956) and Pinecrest (1956) 15' quadrangles. Browning (1986, p. 119) associated the misspelled name with Horace G. Kibbe, who planted trout in Lake Eleanor and Lake Vernon in 1877.

Kibbie Lake [TUOLUMNE]: *lake,* 1 mile long, 12.5 miles southeast of Pinecrest (lat. 38°03'15" N, long. 119°50'45" W; sec. 1, 12, T 2 N, R 19 E); the lake is along Kibbie Creek. Named on Pinecrest (1956) 15' quadrangle.

Kibbie Ridge [TUOLUMNE]: *ridge,* generally south-southwest-trending, 12 miles long, 12 miles south-southeast of Pinecrest between Kibbie Creek and Cherry Creek. Named on Lake Eleanor (1956) and Pinecrest (1956) 15' quadrangles.

Kidd Lake [PLACER]: *lake,* 2950 feet long, 5.5 miles west of Donner Pass (lat. 39°18'35" N, long. 120°25'35" W; sec. 29, T 17 N, R 14 E). Named on Soda Springs (1955) 7.5' quadrangle. On Hobson's (1890b) map, the name "Kidds Lakes" applies to a group of lakes that includes present Kidd Lake.

Kidds Lakes: see **Kidd Lake** [PLACER].

Kiefer Reservoir [CALAVERAS]: *lake,* 950 feet long, 2.5 miles north-northeast of Angels Camp in French Gulch (1) (lat. 38°06'35" N, long. 120°32'10" W; sec. 15, T 3 N, R 13 E). Named on Angels Camp (1962) 7.5' quadrangle.

Kilaga Springs [PLACER]: *locality,* 10.5 miles west-northwest of Auburn (lat. 38°58'15" N, long. 121°14'50" W; at SE cor. sec. 13, T 13 N, R 6 E). Named on Gold Hill (1954) 7.5' quadrangle.

Kilborn Lake [NEVADA]: *lake,* 1000 feet long, nearly 5 miles west of Donner Pass (lat. 39°19'05" N, long. 120°24'55" W; near SW cor. sec. 21, T 17 N, R 14 E). Named on Soda Springs (1955) 7.5' quadrangle.

Kimberley Creek [SIERRA]: *stream,* flows 1.5 miles to Kanaka Creek 2.5 miles southwest of Alleghany (lat. 39°26'50" N, long. 120°52'50" W; near N line sec. 8, T 18 N, R 19 E). Named on Pike (1949) 7.5' quadrangle.

Kincades Flat: see **Jamestown** [TUOLUMNE].

Kinders Diggs: see **Lowell Hill** [NEVADA].

King: see **Mount Starr King** [MARIPOSA]; **Starr King Lake** [MARIPOSA]; **Starr King Meadow** [MARIPOSA].

King Creek [MADERA]: *stream,* flows 6 miles to Middle Fork San Joaquin River 2 miles south-southwest of Devils Postpile (lat. 37°35'50" N, long. 119°05'30" W). Named on Devils Postpile (1953) 15' quadrangle.

Kings Beach [PLACER]: *town,* 8 miles northeast of Tahoe City along Lake Tahoe (lat. 39°14'10" N, long. 120°01'15" W; mainly in sec. 19, T 16 N, R 18 E). Named on Kings Beach (1955) 7.5' quadrangle. Hobson's (1890b) map shows a place called Pine Grove located at the site of present Kings Beach. Postal authorities established Kings Beach post office in 1937, discontinued it in 1942, and reestablished it in 1945; the name is for Joe King, first postmaster (Salley, p. 112).

Kings Hill [PLACER]: *ridge,* west-southwest-trending, 1.5 miles long, 4.25 miles east-southeast of Colfax (lat. 39°04'40" N, long.

120°52'50" W). Named on Colfax (1949) and Foresthill (1949) 7.5' quadrangles. Gudde (1975, p. 187) gave the name "Parks Hill" as an apparent alternate.

King's Hill: see **Kings Hill Point** [PLACER].

Kings Hill Point [PLACER]: *ridge*, south-southwest-trending, 2 miles long, 4.5 miles southeast of Colfax (lat. 39°03'30" N, long. 120°53' W); the ridge extends south-southwest from Kings Hill. Named on Colfax (1949) 7.5' quadrangle. Whitney's (1873) map shows an inhabited place called King's Hill located on or near present Kings Hill Point.

King Slough [PLACER]: *stream*, heads in Placer County and flows 7 miles to American Basin 7 miles east-northeast of Verona in Sutter County (lat. 38°50'30" N, long. 121°30'35" W; sec. 34, T 12 N, R 4 E). Named on Pleasant Grove (1967) and Verona (1967) 7.5' quadrangles.

Kings Meadow [EL DORADO]: *area*, 7.25 miles north of Pollock Pines (lat. 38°52' N, long. 120°34'40" W; near SE cor. sec. 24, T 12 N, R 12 E). Named on Pollock Pines (1950) 7.5' quadrangle. Called Kings Meadows on Placerville (1893) 30' quadrangle.

Kings Store [EL DORADO]: *locality*, 8.5 miles east-northeast of Latrobe near North Fork Cosumnes River (lat. 38°36'40" N, long. 120°50'30" W). Named on Placerville (1893) 30' quadrangle.

Kingsville [EL DORADO]: *locality*, 5 miles southwest of Placerville (lat. 38°40'35" N, long. 120°52'30" W; sec. 33, T 10 N, R 10 E). Named on Placerville (1949) 7.5' quadrangle. Called Kingville on Placerville (1893) 30' quadrangle.

Kingvale [NEVADA]: *settlement*, 5.5 miles west of Donner Pass (lat. 39°19'15" N, long. 120°25'50" W; sec. 20, T 17 N, R 14 E). Named on Soda Springs (1955) 7.5' quadrangle.

Kingville: see **Kingsville** [EL DORADO].

King Woolford Mill [NEVADA]: *locality*, 7 miles south-southwest of Washington (lat. 39°15'45" N, long. 120°50'10" W; near SE cor. sec. 10, T 16 N, R 10 E). Site named on Washington (1950) 7.5' quadrangle.

Kinsley [MARIPOSA]: *locality*, 11.5 miles west of El Portal (lat. 37° 42'05" N, long. 119°59' W; near W line sec. 3, T 3 S, R 18 E). Named on Yosemite (1909) 30' quadrangle. Postal authorities established Kinsley post office in 1896, moved it 2 miles northwest in 1910, and discontinued it in 1928; the name was for James B. Kinsley, first postmaster (Salley, p. 112).

Kinsman Flat [MADERA]: *area*, 11 miles south-southeast of Shuteye Peak (lat. 37°12'15" N, long. 119°21'15" W; sec. 28, T 8 S, R 24 E). Named on Shaver Lake (1953) 15' quadrangle.

Kirby Peak [MARIPOSA]: *peak*, 10.5 miles south of El Portal (lat. 37°31'20" N, long. 119°47'45" W; near NW cor. sec. 9, T 5 S, R 20 E). Altitude 5448 feet. Named on Buckingham Mountain (1947) 7.5' quadrangle.

Kirk: see **Kirkwood** [AMADOR-EL DORADO].

Kirkwood [AMADOR-EL DORADO]: *locality*, 11.5 miles north of Mokelumne Peak at the junction of Amador County, El Dorado County, and Alpine County (lat. 38°42'10" N, long. 120°04'15" W; sec. 22, T 10 N, R 17 E). Named on Caples Lake (1979) 7.5' quadrangle. Called Kirk on Wheeler's (1876-1877a) map, but Wheeler (1878, p. 61) also referred to Kirkwood's. Zack Kirkwood built a stage station and inn at the place in 1864; Amador, El Dorado, and Alpine Counties met in the barroom of the inn, which housed Roundtop post office (Hoover, Rensch, and Rensch, p. 29). Postal authorities established Roundtop post office in 1887 and discontinued it in 1907; the name was from a nearby peak in Alpine County (Salley, p. 190). They established Fagan post office 5 miles west of Roundtop post office in 1891 and discontinued it in 1895; the name was for Maggie Fagan, first postmaster (Salley, p. 71).

Kirkwood Creek [AMADOR]: *stream*, heads in Alpine County and flows less than 1 mile in Amador County before reentering Alpine County 11.5 miles north of Mokelumne Peak at Kirkwood (lat. 38° 42'10" N, long. 120°04'15" W; sec. 22, T 10 N, R 17 E); the stream goes through Kirkwood Valley. Named on Caples Lake (1979) 7.5' quadrangle.

Kirkwood Lake [EL DORADO]: *lake*, 2100 feet long, 0.5 mile west-northwest of Kirkwood (lat. 38°42'20" N, long. 120°04'55" W; on W line sec. 22, T 10 N, R 17 E). Named on Caples Lake (1979) 7.5' quadrangle. Postal authorities established Lake Kirkwood post office at a resort in 1940 (Salley, p. 115).

Kirkwood Meadows [AMADOR]: *valley*, 10.5 miles north of Mokelumne Peak on Amador-Alpine county line (lat. 38°41'30" N, long. 120°04'15" W); the valley is south of Kirkwood along Kirkwood Creek. Named on Caples Lake (1979) 7.5' quadrangle.

Kirkwood Ridge [AMADOR]: *ridge*, southwest-trending, 1.25 miles long, 2.5 miles south of Jackson (lat. 38°18'45" N, long. 120° 46' W). Named on Jackson (1962) 7.5' quadrangle.

Kirkwood's: see **Kirkwood** [AMADOR-EL DORADO].

Kismet [MADERA]: *locality*, 6 miles east-southeast of Fairmead along Atchison, Topeka and Santa Fe Railroad (lat. 37°02'50" N, long. 120°05'35" W; near E line sec. 22, T 10 S, R 17 E). Named on Kismet (1961) 7.5' quadrangle. Called Miller on California Mining Bureau's (1917d) map.

Kit Carson [AMADOR]: *settlement*, 9 miles north of Mokelumne Peak at the north end of Silver Lake (lat. 38°40'10" N, long. 120° 06'50" W; near E line sec. 32, T 10 N, R 17 E). Named on Caples Lake (1979) 7.5' quadrangle. Postal authorities established Kit Carson post office in 1951 (Frickstad, p. 5).

Kittridge [MARIPOSA]: *locality,* 5 miles south-southeast of Coulterville along Yosemite Valley Railroad (lat. 37°38'25" N, long. 120° 10'30" W). Named on Sonora (1897) 30' quadrangle.

Kiva Beach [EL DORADO]: *beach,* 3.5 miles northeast of Mount Tallac along Lake Tahoe (lat. 38°56'25" N, long. 120°02'50" W; sec. 25, T 13 N, R 17 E). Named on Emerald Bay (1955, photorevised 1969) 7.5' quadrangle.

Klondike Meadow [PLACER]: *area,* 1.5 miles northwest of Martis Peak (lat. 39°18'20" N, long. 120°03' W; sec. 23, T 17 N, R 17 E). Named on Martis Peak (1955) 7.5' quadrangle.

Knapp: see **Blue Canyon** [PLACER] (2).

Knapp Creek: see **Spring Creek** [NEVADA].

Knee Ridge [PLACER]: *ridge,* east-trending, 1.25 miles long, about 2 miles southwest of Homewood (lat. 39°03'45" N, long. 120°11'05" W; sec. 14, 15, T 14 N, R 16 E). Named on Homewood (1955) 7.5' quadrangle.

Knickerbocker Canyon [EL DORADO]: *canyon,* 0.5 mile long, opens into the canyon of North Fork American River 3.25 miles northwest of the village of Pilot Hill (lat. 38°52'10" N, long. 121° 03'10" W; at S line sec. 23, T 12 N, R 8 E); the canyon is along lower reaches of Knickerbocker Creek. Named on Pilot Hill (1954) 7.5' quadrangle.

Knickerbocker Creek [EL DORADO]: *stream,* flows 5.5 miles to North Fork American River 3.25 miles northwest of the village of Pilot Hill (lat. 38°52'10" N, long. 121°03'10" W; at S line sec. 23, T 12 N, R 8 E). Named on Auburn (1953), Greenwood (1949), and Pilot Hill (1954) 7.5' quadrangles.

Knickerbocker Flat: see **Yankee Hill** [TUOLUMNE] (2).

Knight: see **Mount Knight** [TUOLUMNE].

Knight Creek [TUOLUMNE]: *stream,* flows 11 miles to Rose Creek nearly 5 miles north of Columbia (lat. 38°06'20" N, long. 120°23'40" W; near W line sec. 24, T 3 N, R 14 E). Named on Columbia (1948), Columbia SE (1948), Crandall Peak (1979), and Stanislaus (1948) 7.5' quadrangles.

Knob Hill [MARIPOSA]: *peak,* 9 miles south of Mariposa (lat. 37°21'15" N, long. 119°58'10" W; sec. 2, T 7 S, R 18 E). Altitude 2159 feet. Named on Ben Hur (1947) 7.5' quadrangle.

Knowles [MADERA]: *settlement,* less than 2 miles east of Raymond (lat. 37°13'10" N, long. 119°52'20" W; sec. 22, T 8 S, R 19 E). Named on Knowles (1962) and Raymond (1962) 7.5' quadrangles. Postal authorities established Knowles post office in 1902 and discontinued it in 1955; the name is for F.E. Knowles, who operated a granite quarry at the place (Salley, p. 113). California Division of Highways' (1934) map shows a place called Hillside located just southwest of Knowles along Southern Pacific Railroad (near N line sec. 27, T 8 S, R 19 E).

Knowles Junction [MADERA]: *locality,* 1 mile south of Raymond (lat. 37°12'10" N, long. 119°54'30" W; sec. 29, T 8 S, R 19 E); the place is 2.25 miles west-southwest of Knowles. Named on Raymond (1962) 7.5' quadrangle.

Knuthson Meadow [SIERRA]: *area,* 2.25 miles north of Calpine along Carman Creek (lat. 39°41'50" N, long. 120°26'35" W). Named on Calpine (1981) 7.5' quadrangle.

Knuts Spring [SIERRA]: *spring,* 3.25 miles west-southwest of Mount Fillmore (lat. 39°42'20" N, long. 120°54'15" W; sec. 6, T 21 N, R 10 E). Named on La Porte (1951) 7.5' quadrangle.

Kocher: see **Bagby** [MARIPOSA].

Kohlberg's Humbug: see **Humbug Gulch** [CALAVERAS].

Koip Crest [TUOLUMNE]: *ridge,* trends south along Tuolumne-Mono county line, then southeast into Mono County, 3.5 miles long, 9 miles south-southeast of Tioga Pass (lat. 37°47'30" N, long. 119°12'15" W). Named on Mono Craters (1953) 15' quadrangle. Kroeber (p. 45) considered the word "Koip" of Indian origin. United States Board on Geographic Names (1988, p. 4) rejected the names "Ko-it Ridge" and "Koip Ridge" for the feature.

Koip Ridge: see **Koip Crest** [TUOLUMNE].

Ko-it Ridge: see **Koip Crest** [TUOLUMNE].

Kolana Rock [TUOLUMNE]: *peak,* 7 miles northeast of Mather (lat. 37°57'10" N, long. 119°45'30" W; near S line sec. 10, T 1 N, R 20 E). Named on Lake Eleanor (1956) 15' quadrangle. The feature had the early name "Sugar Loaf" (Browning, 1988, p. 71).

Kramer Meadow [MADERA]: *area,* 7 miles north-northeast of Yosemite Forks (lat. 37°27'10" N, long. 119°33'35" W; at E line sec. 33, T 5 S, R 22 E). Named on Bass Lake (1953) 15' quadrangle.

Krappeau Gulch [CALAVERAS]: *canyon,* drained by a stream that flows 1.5 miles to Coyote Creek nearly 3 miles south-southwest of Vallecito (lat. 38°02'45" N, long. 120°29'05" W; sec. 7, T 2 N, R 14 E). Named on Columbia (1948) 7.5' quadrangle.

Kres [NEVADA]: *locality,* 3 miles east-southeast of Grass Valley along Nevada County Narrow Gauge Railroad (lat. 39°11'45" N, long. 121°00'30" W). Named on Smartsville (1895) 30' quadrangle.

Krumbacker's Ravine: see **Scotchman Creek** [NEVADA].

KT-22 [PLACER]: *peak,* 5.5 miles west of Tahoe City (lat. 39°11' N, long. 120°14'30" W; near NW cor. sec. 5, T 15 N, R 16 E). Altitude 8070 feet. Named on Tahoe City (1955) 7.5' quadrangle.

Kuna Creek [TUOLUMNE]: *stream,* flows 3 miles to Lyell Fork 8 miles south of Tioga Pass (lat. 37°47'30" N, long. 119°15'35" W); the stream heads near Kuna Peak. Named on Mono Craters (1953) and Tuolumne Meadows (1956) 15' quadrangles.

Kuna Crest [TUOLUMNE]: *ridge,* generally northwest-trending, 4.5 miles long, 6 miles south of Tioga Pass (lat. 37°49'45" N, long. 119°14'45" W); Kuna Peak is at the southeast end of the ridge. Named on Mono Craters (1953) and Tuolumne Meadows (1956) 15' quadrangles. W.D. Johnson of United States Geological Survey named the feature about 1883—the word "kuna" is of Indian origin (United States Board on Geographic Names, 1934, p. 13).

Kuna Lake [TUOLUMNE]: *lake,* 1800 feet long, 4 miles south of Tioga Pass (lat. 37°51'05" N, long. 119°15'05" W); the lake is northeast of Kuna Crest. Named on Mono Craters (1953) and Tuolumne Meadows (1956) 15' quadrangles.

Kuna Peak [TUOLUMNE]: *peak,* 7 miles south-southeast of Tioga Pass on Tuolumne-Mono county line (lat. 37°48'55" N, long. 119° 12'40" W); the peak is at the southeast end of Kuna Crest. Named on Mono Craters (1953) 15' quadrangle. W.D. Johnson of United States Geological Survey named the peak about 1883 (United States Board on Geographic Names, 1934, p. 13).

Kyburz [EL DORADO]: *village,* 9 miles west-southwest of Pyramid Peak (lat. 38°46'30" N, long. 120°17'40" W; at NW cor. sec. 27, T 11 N, R 15 E). Named on Kyburz (1952) 7.5' quadrangle. Pyramid Peak (1896) 30' quadrangle shows Slippery Ford at the place. Postal authorities established Slippery Ford post office in 1861, changed the name to Slipperyford in 1896, and changed it to Kyburz in 1911; Albert Kyburz, son of 1846 pioneer S.E. Kyburz, was the first postmaster of Kyburz post office (Salley, p. 113, 206). Another place called Slippery Ford was located northeast of Strawberry (Beverly Cola, personal communication, 1988).

Kyburz Flat [SIERRA]: *valley,* 12 miles south of Loyalton (lat. 39° 30'15" N, long. 120°14'05" W). Named on Hobart Mills (1981) and Sardine Peak (1981) 7.5' quadrangles.

— L —

La Barr Meadows [NEVADA]: *settlement,* 3 miles south-southeast of Grass Valley (lat. 39°10'30" N, long. 121°02'40" W; around SW cor. sec. 1, T 15 N, R 8 E). Named on Grass Valley (1949) 7.5' quadrangle.

La Commodedad: see **Pine Log** [TUOLUMNE].

Lacey Creek [NEVADA-SIERRA]: *stream,* heads in Nevada County and flows 4.5 miles to Webber Lake 8 miles south-southwest of Sierraville in Sierra County (lat. 39°28'55" N, long. 120°24'45" W; sec. 28, T 19 N, R 14 E). Named on Webber Peak (1981) 7.5' quadrangle.

Lacey Valley [SIERRA]: *valley,* 9 miles south-

southwest of Sierraville (lat. 39°28'30" N, long. 120°25' W); the valley is along Lacey Creek. Named on Webber Peak (1981) 7.5' quadrangle.

Lac Leven Lakes: see **High Loch Lake** [PLACER]; **Loch Leven Lakes** [PLACER].

Lacy Hill [MARIPOSA]: *peak,* 9.5 miles south of Mariposa (lat. 37° 20'50" N, long. 119°56'45" W; sec. 1, T 5 S, R 18 E). Altitude 2203 feet. Named on Ben Hur (1947) 7.5' quadrangle.

Ladd Creek [MADERA]: *stream,* flows 4.25 miles to Fine Gold Creek 4 miles northeast of O'Neals (lat. 37°09'50" N, long. 119°38'20" W; sec. 12, T 9 S, R 21 E). Named on O'Neals (1965) 7.5' quadrangle. Millerton Lake (1945) 15' quadrangle shows Ladd ranch near the mouth of the stream.

Laddies Cove [PLACER]: *relief feature,* 5.25 miles east-northeast of Bunker Hill (lat. 39°05'10" N, long. 120°17'40" W; near SE cor. sec. 4, T 14 N, R 15 E). Named on Wentworth Springs (1953) 7.5' quadrangle.

Ladeux: see **Ladeux Meadow** [AMADOR].

Ladeux Meadow [AMADOR]: *area,* 5 miles north of Mokelumne Peak (lat. 38°36'45" N, long. 120°04'45" W; sec. 22, T 9 N, R 17 E). Named on Mokelumne Peak (1979) 7.5' quadrangle. Pyramid Peak (1896) 30' quadrangle has the name "Ladeux" at the place.

Ladies Canyon [EL DORADO]: *canyon,* drained by a stream that flows 0.5 mile to South Fork American River 0.25 mile east-northeast of Chili Bar (lat. 38°46'45" N, long. 120°49' W; sec. 25, T 11 N, R 10 E). Named on Garden Valley (1949) 7.5' quadrangle.

Ladies Canyon [SIERRA]: *canyon,* drained by a stream that flows 4.5 miles to North Yuba River 4.5 miles west of Sierra City (lat. 39°34'10" N, long. 120°43'15" W; near SE cor. sec. 27, T 20 N, R 11 E). Named on Sierra City (1981) 7.5' quadrangle. Called Lady's Canyon on Logan's (1929) map.

Ladies Canyon: see **Black Canyon** [SIERRA]; **Ladys Canyon** [PLACER]; **Little Ladies Canyon** [SIERRA].

Ladies Paradise: see **Squaw Valley** [PLACER].

Ladybug Peak [SIERRA]: *peak,* 5.5 miles south-southeast of Crystal Peak (lat. 39°29'10" N, long. 120°02'40" W; near W line sec. 24, T 19 N, R 17 E). Altitude 8380 feet. Named on Boca (1955) 7.5' quadrangle. Called Lady Bug Peak on Truckee (1895) 30' quadrangle.

Lady Canyon: see **Ladys Canyon** [PLACER].

Lady Lake [MADERA]: *lake,* 1100 feet long, 6.5 miles south-southeast of Merced Peak (lat. 37°32'35" N, long. 119°21'40" W); the lake is one of the group called Madera Lakes. Named on Merced Peak (1953) 15' quadrangle.

Ladys Canyon [PLACER]: *canyon,* drained by a stream that flows nearly 2 miles to Middle Fork American River 2.5 miles east-southeast of Foresthill (lat. 39°00'25" N, long. 120°46'20" W; at S line sec. 32, T 14 N, R 11 E). Named on Foresthill (1949) 7.5' quadrangle. Called Lady Canyon on Colfax (1898) 30' quadrangle, and Ladies Cañon on Whitney's (1873) map.

Lady's Canyon: see **Ladies Canyon** [SIERRA].

Lafayette Hill: see **Grass Valley** [NEVADA].

Lafayette Ridge [SIERRA]: *ridge,* generally west-southwest-trending, 11 miles long, center 1.25 miles south of Alleghany (lat. 39°27'15" N, long. 120°50'30" W). Named on Alleghany (1949) and Pike (1949) 7.5' quadrangles.

Lagoon Lake [PLACER]: *lake,* 300 feet long, 3 miles north of Bunker Hill (lat. 39°05'25" N, long. 120°22'40" W; sec. 2, T 14 N, R 14 E). Named on Bunker Hill (1953) 7.5' quadrangle.

La Grange Reservoir [TUOLUMNE]: *lake,* on Stanislaus-Tuolumne county line behind a dam on Tuolumne River 3.5 miles southwest of Don Pedro Camp in Stanislaus County (lat. 37° 40'20" N, long. 120°26'35" W; on W line sec. 16, T 3 S, R 14 E). Named on La Grange (1962) 7.5' quadrangle. The dam that forms the lake was built at a place called Big Falls (Gray, p. 1).

Laguna [AMADOR]: *stream,* heads in Amador County and flows 32 miles to Cosumnes River 8.5 miles south of Elk Grove in Sacramento County (lat. 38°17'05" N, long. 121°22'40" W). Named on Bruceville (1968), Carbondale (1968), Clay (1968), Galt (1968), and Sloughhouse (1968) 7.5' quadrangles. United States Board on Geographic Names (1964a, p. 10) rejected the names "Laguna Creek," "The Laguna," and "Willow Creek" for the stream.

Laguna: see **Willow Creek** [AMADOR].

Laguna Creek: see **Laguna** [AMADOR].

La Honda Park [CALAVERAS]: *settlement,* 2.5 miles north-northwest of Vallecito (lat. 38°07'15" N, long. 120°29'40" W; near S line sec. 12, T 3 N, R 13 E). Named on Columbia (1948) 7.5' quadrangle.

Lake Aloha [EL DORADO]: *lake,* nearly 2 miles long, 1.5 miles north-northeast of Pyramid Peak (lat. 38°52' N, long. 120°08'25" W). Named on Pyramid Peak (1955) and Rockbound Valley (1955) 7.5' quadrangles.

Lake Alta [PLACER]: *lake,* 1250 feet long, 1 mile east of Dutch Flat (lat. 39°12'15" N, long. 120°48'55" W; sec. 35, T 16 N, R 10 E); the lake is 0.25 mile southwest of Alta. Named on Dutch Flat (1950) 7.5' quadrangle.

Lake Angela [NEVADA]: *lake,* 1350 feet long, 0.5 mile north of Donner Pass (lat. 39°19'25" N, long. 120°19'35" W; near W line sec. 16, T 17 N, R 15 E). Named on Norden (1955) 7.5' quadrangle. Surveyors working for Union Pacific Railroad named the lake in 1865 for Angela King, sister of Thomas Starr King (Gudde, 1949, p. 11).

Lake Arthur [PLACER]: *lake,* 950 feet long,

5.25 miles north-northeast of Auburn (lat. 38°57'55" N, long. 121°01'25" W; near W line sec. 19, T 13 N, R 9 E). Named on Auburn (1953) 7.5' quadrangle. The name commemorates W.R. Arthur, assistant manager of a water district (Gudde, 1949, p. 16).

Lake Audrian [EL DORADO]: *lake,* 1250 feet long, less than 1 mile west-northwest of Echo Summit (lat. 38°49'10" N, long. 120°02'35" W; on W line sec. 7, T 11 N, R 18 E). Named on Echo Lake (1955) 7.5' quadrangle. Called Audrian Lake on Pyramid Peak (1896) 30' quadrangle. The misspelled name commemorates Thomas Audrain, who had a station at Echo Summit in the 1860's (Gudde, 1969, p. 17).

Lake Bigler: see **Lake Tahoe** [EL DORADO-PLACER].

Lake Bonpland: see **Lake Tahoe** [EL DORADO-PLACER].

Lake Catherine [MADERA]: *lake,* 1800 feet long, 8 miles northwest of Devils Postpile (lat. 37°41'55" N, long. 119°11'25" W). Named on Devils Postpile (1953) 15' quadrangle.

Lake Christopher [EL DORADO]: *lake,* 1500 feet long, behind a dam on Cold Creek 5 miles northwest of Freel Peak (lat. 38°54'40" N, long. 120°58' W; near SE cor. sec. 3, T 12 N, R 18 E). Named on South Lake Tahoe (1955, photorevised 1969 and 1974) 7.5' quadrangle.

Lake City [NEVADA]: *locality,* 2.5 miles west-southwest of North Bloomfield (lat. 39°21'30" N, long. 120°56'30" W; near NW cor. sec. 11, T 17 N, R 9 E). Named on North Bloomfield (1949) 7.5' quadrangle. The Bell brothers built a hotel at the site in 1855; the name "Lake City," given in 1857, is from a lake at the place (Hanna, p. 166).

Lake Clementine: see **North Fork Lake** [PLACER].

Lake Combie [NEVADA-PLACER]: *lake,* behind a dam on Bear River 3 miles southeast of Higgins Corner on Nevada-Placer county line (lat. 39°00'35" N, long. 121°03'25" W; near W line sec. 2, T 13 N, R 8 E). Named on Lake Combie (1949) 7.5' quadrangle, which has the name "Van Geisen Dam" for the dam that forms the lake; the lake itself is called Vangeisen Combie Diversion Reservoir on Smartsville (1942) 30' quadrangle. The name "Combie" is for a Frenchman who had a ranch at a site now covered by water of the lake (Gudde, 1949, p. 76).

Lake Creek [NEVADA]: *stream,* flows 2.5 miles to Fall Creek 6 miles southeast of Graniteville (lat. 39°23' N, long. 120°30'30" W; near W line sec. 32, T 18 N, R 12 E); the stream heads at Carr Lake and Feely Lake. Named on Graniteville (1982) 7.5' quadrangle.

Lake Don Pedro: see **Don Pedro Reservoir** [TUOLUMNE].

Lake Doris [EL DORADO]: *lake,* 450 feet long, 4.25 miles southwest of Phipps Peak (lat. 38°54'20" N, long. 120°11'40" W). Named on Rockbound Valley (1955) 7.5' quadrangle.

Lake Edson: see **Stumpy Meadows Lake** [EL DORADO].

Lake Eleanor: see **Lake Eleanor Reservoir** [TUOLUMNE].

Lake Eleanor Reservoir [TUOLUMNE]: *lake,* behind a dam on Eleanor Creek 6.5 miles north of Mather (lat. 37°58'30" N, long. 119°52'45" W; sec. 3, T 1 N, R 19 E). Named on Lake Eleanor (1956) 15' quadrangle. The dam, constructed in 1917 and 1918, enlarged a natural lake (Hanna, p. 96) that is called Lake Eleanor on Yosemite (1909) 30' quadrangle. United States Board on Geographic Names (1965b, p. 11) approved the name "Lake Eleanor" for the present reservoir, and rejected the names "Lake Eleanor Reservoir" and "Eleanor Lake Reservoir." Members of the Whitney survey named the natural lake in the 1860's for Eleanor Goddard Whitney, daughter of Josiah Dwight Whitney (United States Board on Geographic Names, 1934, p. 8).

Lake Estelle [PLACER]: *lake,* 500 feet long, nearly 6 miles west of Tahoe City (lat. 39°09'50" N, long. 120°14'55" W; sec. 7, T 15 N, R 16 E). Named on Tahoe City (1955) 7.5' quadrangle.

Lake Flint [AMADOR]: *lake,* 1250 feet long, 1.5 miles south-southwest of Ione (lat. 38°19'55" N, long. 120°56'20" W). Named on Ione (1962) 7.5' quadrangle.

Lake Forest [PLACER]: *village,* 6.25 miles southwest of Kings Beach along Lake Tahoe (lat. 39°11'05" N, long. 120°06'45" W; on S line sec. 32, T 16 N, R 17 E). Named on Kings Beach (1955) 7.5' quadrangle. Postal authorities established Lake Forest post office in 1947 and discontinued it in 1953 (Frickstad, p. 120).

Lake Genevieve [EL DORADO]: *lake,* 850 feet long, 3 miles north of Phipps Peak (lat. 38°59'50" N, long. 120°09'35" W; at N line sec. 12, T 13 N, R 16 E). Named on Rockbound Valley (1955) 7.5' quadrangle.

Lake Hawley: see **Hawley Lake** [SIERRA].

Lake Helen: see **Maxwell Lake** [TUOLUMNE].

Lake House [NEVADA]: *locality,* 2.5 miles west of Truckee (lat. 39° 19'30" N, long. 120°13'50" W); the place is at the east end of Donner Lake. Named on Truckee (1895) 30' quadrangle.

Lake House: see **Al Tahoe** [EL DORADO].

Lake Kirkwood: see **Kirkwood Lake** [EL DORADO].

Lake LeConte [EL DORADO]: *lake,* 1050 feet long, 2 miles north-northeast of Pyramid Peak (lat. 38°52'15" N, long. 120°08'10" W). Named on Pyramid Peak (1955) 7.5' quadrangle. The name honors Professor Joseph LeConte of University of California (Lekisch, p. 72).

Lake Lois [EL DORADO]: *lake,* 1550 feet long, nearly 4 miles southwest of Phipps Peak (lat.

38°55' N, long. 120°12' W). Named on Rockbound Valley (1955) 7.5' quadrangle.

Lake Louise [PLACER]: *lake,* 800 feet long, 1.5 miles southwest of Homewood (lat. 39°04'30" N, long. 120°11'10" W; on E line sec. 10, T 14 N, R 16 E). Named on Homewood (1955, photorevised 1969) 7.5' quadrangle.

Lake Lucille [EL DORADO]: *lake,* 900 feet long, 5.5 miles northwest of Echo Summit (lat. 38°51'40" N, long. 120°06'40" W; sec. 28, T 12 N, R 17 E). Named on Echo Lake (1955) 7.5' quadrangle. The name is for Lucille Meredith, wife of a banker in Oakland, California (Lekisch, p. 76).

Lake Margaret [EL DORADO]: *lake,* 900 feet long, 1.5 miles north-northwest of Kirkwood (lat. 38°43'25" N, long. 120°05'10" W). Named on Caples Lake (1979) 7.5' quadrangle.

Lake Margery [EL DORADO]: *lake,* 800 feet long, 5.5 miles northwest of Echo Summit (lat. 38°51'30" N, long. 120°06'55" W; sec. 28, T 12 N, R 17 E). Named on Echo Lake (1955) 7.5' quadrangle.

Lake Mary [PLACER]: *lake,* 1500 feet long, 0.25 mile south-southwest of Donner Pass (lat. 39°18'45" N, long. 120°19'45" W; near NE cor. sec. 20, T 17 N, R 15 E). Named on Norden (1955) 7.5' quadrangle.

Lake McClure [MARIPOSA]: *lake,* behind a dam 6 miles north-northwest of Hornitos on Merced River (lat. 37°35'05" N, long. 120°16'10" W; sec. 13, T 4 S, R 15 E). Named on Bear Valley (1947, photorevised 1973), Coulterville (1947, photorevised 1973), Hornitos (1947, photorevised 1973), and Penon Blanco Peak (1962, photorevised 1973) 7.5' quadrangles. Called Lake McClure Reservoir on Sonora (1897) 30' quadrangle. Merced Falls (1962) 7.5' quadrangle has the designation "Lake McClure (Exchequer Reservoir)" for the lake, but United States Board on Geographic Names (1964c, p. 15) rejected the name "Exchequer Reservoir" for the feature. Exchequer dam formed the lake in 1926, and the lake was enlarged when the dam was raised; the name "Exchequer" is from the first bank in Mariposa County—water of the lake now covers the site of the bank (Sargent, Shirley, 1976, p. 26-27). The name "McClure" commemorates Wilbur Fiske McClure, who was state engineer of California from 1912 until 1926 (Hanna, p. 181). Cotton Arm of the lake occupies the lower part of the canyon of Cotton Creek, and Temperance Arm occupies the lower part of the canyon of Temperance Creek; both arms are named on Merced Falls (1962) 7.5' quadrangle.

Lake McClure Reservoir: see **Lake McClure** [MARIPOSA].

Lake Moic [MADERA]: *lake,* 600 feet long, 7.5 miles south-southeast of Yosemite Forks along Little Fine Gold Creek (lat. 37°16' N, long.

119°34'20" W; sec. 4, T 8 S, R 22 E). Named on Bass Lake (1953) 15' quadrangle.

Lake Moran [TUOLUMNE]: *lake,* 1400 feet long, nearly 2 miles northwest of Liberty Hill (lat. 38°23' N, long. 120°07'45" W). Named on Calaveras Dome (1979) 7.5' quadrangle.

Lake Nina: see **Tilden Lake** [TUOLUMNE].

Lake Number 5 [EL DORADO]: *lake,* 750 feet long, 5.25 miles southwest of Phipps Peak (lat. 38°54'55" N, long. 120°13'50" W; at E line sec. 5, T 12 N, R 16 E). Named on Rockbound Valley (1955) 7.5' quadrangle.

Lake Number 9 [EL DORADO]: *lake,* 400 feet long, nearly 5 miles southwest of Phipps Peak (lat. 38°54'30" N, long. 120°13' W; sec. 9, T 12 N, R 16 E). Named on Rockbound Valley (1955) 7.5' quadrangle.

Lake Number 3 [EL DORADO]: *lake,* 750 feet long, nearly 5 miles west-southwest of Phipps Peak (lat. 38°55'30" N, long. 120°13'45" W; at NE cor. sec. 5, T 12 N, R 16 E). Named on Rockbound Valley (1955) 7.5' quadrangle.

Lake of the Woods [EL DORADO]: *lake,* 0.5 mile long, 5.5 miles west-northwest of Echo Summit (lat. 38°51' N, long. 120°07'05" W; at NE cor. sec. 32, T 12 N, R 17 E). Named on Echo Lake (1955) 7.5' quadrangle.

Lake of the Woods [SIERRA]: *lake,* 1200 feet long, 6 miles south-southwest of Sierraville (lat. 39°30'15" N, long. 120°23'25" W; on N line sec. 22, T 19 N, R 14 E). Named on Sattley (1981) 7.5' quadrangle.

Lake Putt [PLACER]: *lake,* 1850 feet long, 1.25 miles southwest of Emigrant Gap (1) at the head of Blue Canyon (1) (lat. 38°17'25" N, long. 120°41'10" W; at S line sec. 36, T 17 N, R 11 E). Named on Blue Canyon (1955) 7.5' quadrangle.

Lake River: see **Eleanor Creek** [TUOLUMNE].

Lake Schmidell [EL DORADO]: *lake,* 1600 feet long, 3.5 miles west-southwest of Phipps Peak (lat. 38°55'45" N, long. 120°12'30" W; sec. 33, T 13 N, R 16 E). Named on Rockbound Valley (1955) 7.5' quadrangle.

Lakeside: see **Stateline** [EL DORADO].

Lakeside Campground [MADERA]: *locality,* nearly 6 miles southeast of Yosemite Forks on the southwest side of Bass Lake (1) (lat. 37°18'35" N, long. 119°32'45" W; near E line sec. 22, T 7 S, R 22 E). Named on Bass Lake (1953) 15' quadrangle.

Lakeside Campground [NEVADA]: *locality,* 1.25 miles south-southeast of Hobart Mills (lat. 39°23'05" N, long. 120°10'15" W; sec. 26, T 18 N, R 16 E); the place is along Prosser Creek Reservoir. Named on Hobart Mills (1981) 7.5' quadrangle.

Lake Spaulding [NEVADA]: *lake,* behind a dam on South Yuba River 1.5 miles west-northwest of Yuba Gap (lat. 39°19'35" N, long. 120°38'30" W; at E line sec. 20, T 17 N, R 12 E). Named on Blue Canyon (1955) and Cisco Grove (1955) 7.5' quadrangles. The name

commemorates John Spaulding, a water-company official (Stewart, p. 89).

Lake Sterling [NEVADA]: *lake,* 2850 feet long, 9 miles west-northwest of Donner Pass (lat. 39°21'20" N, long. 120°29'15" W; mainly in sec. 11, T 17 N, R 13 E). Named on Soda Springs (1955) 7.5' quadrangle.

Lake Sylvia [EL DORADO]: *lake,* 500 feet long, less than 1 mile west of Pyramid Peak (lat. 38°50'35" N, long. 120°10'20" W). Named on Pyramid Peak (1955) 7.5' quadrangle.

Lake Tabeaud [AMADOR]: *lake,* 0.5 mile long, 2 miles east of Jackson Butte (lat. 38°20'55" N, long. 120°39'45" W; sec. 28, T 6 N, R 12 E). Named on Mokelumne Hill (1948) 7.5' quadrangle. Called Tabeaud Reservoir on California Division of Highways' (1934) map, which also shows a smaller lake, called Petty Reservoir, in section 28.

Lake Tahoe [EL DORADO-PLACER]: *lake,* 21 miles long, 47 miles northeast of Placerville on California-Nevada State line in El Dorado County and Placer County of California (lat. 39°06' N, long. 120°30' W). Named on Emerald Bay (1955), Homewood (1955), Kings Beach (1955), Meeks Bay (1955), South Lake Tahoe (1955), and Tahoe City (1955) 7.5' quadrangles. Called L. Bonpland on Fremont's (1848) map, Mountain Lake on Gibbes' (1852) map, and Lake Bigler on Goddard's (1857) map. Fremont gave the feature the name "Bonpland" to honor Baron von Humbold's botanical associate, Aime Jacques Alexandre Bonpland (Farquhar, 1930, p. 87). Fremont (map following p. 246) also used the name "Mountain Lake" for the feature. The name "Bigler" was for John Bigler, governor of California in the 1850's (Gudde, 1949, p. 351). William H. Knight prepared a new map for H.H. Bancroft & Co. in 1863 and used the name "Lake Tahoe"—Knight reported that Henry DeGroot suggested the name "Tahoe" as one used by Indians to express the meaning "big water" or "high water" (Wheat, p. 71-72). DeGroot's (1853) map has the designation "Lake Tahoe or Bigler" for the feature.

Lake Tahoe: see **South Lake Tahoe** [EL DORADO[.

Lake Theodore [PLACER]: *lake,* 1550 feet long, 6.25 miles north-northeast of Auburn (lat. 38°58'30" N, long. 121°00'35" W; near SE cor. sec. 18, T 13 N, R 9 E). Named on Auburn (1953) 7.5' quadrangle.

Lake Valley [EL DORADO]: *valley,* extends for 8 miles south from Lake Tahoe along Upper Truckee River to Meyers; center 5.5 miles west-northwest of Freel Peak (lat. 38°53' N, long. 119°59'45" W). Named on Echo Lake (1955), Emerald Bay (1955), Freel Peak (1955), and South Lake Tahoe (1955) 7.5' quadrangles. The name was used as early as 1853 (Lekisch, p. 71). Day (p. 80) referred to Bigler Lake Valley in 1855.

Lake Valley [TUOLUMNE]: *valley,* 8 miles east

of Pinecrest (lat. 38° 12' N, long. 119°50'40" W; in and near sec. 13, T 4 N, R 19 E). Named on Pinecrest (1956) 15' quadrangle.

Lake Valley: see **Lake Valley Reservoir** [PLACER]; **Tallac** [EL DORADO].

Lake Valley Reservoir [PLACER]: *lake,* behind a dam on North Fork of North Fork American River 3.25 miles west-southwest of Cisco Grove (lat. 39°18' N, long. 120°35'50" W; sec. 35, T 17 N, R 12 E). Named on Cisco Grove (1955) 7.5' quadrangle. Colfax (1898) 30' quadrangle shows Lake Valley at the site of the lake.

Lake Van Norden [NEVADA-PLACER]: *lake,* behind a dam on South Yuba River 2.5 miles west of Donner Pass on Nevada-Placer county line (lat. 39°19'15" N, long. 120°22'35" W; sec. 23, T 17 N, R 14 E). Named on Norden (1955) and Soda Springs (1955) 7.5' quadrangles. Truckee (1895) 30' quadrangle has the name "Summit Valley" for the valley now partly covered by the lake. The name "Van Norden" commemorates Charles Van Norden, who was a water-company official (Stewart, p. 89).

Lake Vera [NEVADA]: *lake,* 1100 feet long, 2.5 miles north of Nevada City along Rock Creek (1) (lat. 39°18'05" N, long. 121°01'35" W; at S line sec. 25, T 17 N, R 8 E). Named on Nevada City (1948) 7.5' quadrangle.

Lake Vernon [TUOLUMNE]: *lake,* 0.5 mile long, 13 miles southwest of Tower Peak along Falls Creek (lat. 38°00'50" N, long. 119°43'25" W; sec. 24, T 2 N, R 20 E). Named on Tower Peak (1956) 15' quadrangle. Called Vernon Lake on Dardanelles (1898) 30' quadrangle.

Lakeview: see **Lakeview Canyon** [PLACER].

Lakeview Canyon [PLACER]: *canyon,* 1 mile long, 2 miles east-northeast of Donner Pass (lat. 39°18'30" N, long. 120°17'15" W); the canyon opens into the valley of Donner Lake. Named on Norden (1955) 7.5' quadrangle. California Division of Highways' (1934) map shows a place called Lakeview located along Southern Pacific Railroad on the northwest side of present Lakeview Canyon (sec. 22, T 17 N, R 15 E—the section is misnumbered "21" on the map).

Lake Winifred [EL DORADO]: *lake,* 1100 feet long, 4 miles east of Wentworth Springs (lat. 39°00'05" N, long. 120°16'10" W; sec. 2, T 13 N, R 15 E). Named on Wentworth Springs (1953, photorevised 1973) 7.5' quadrangle.

Lake Zitella [EL DORADO]: *lake,* 800 feet long, 4 miles west of Phipps Peak (lat. 38°57'35" N, long. 120°13'30" W; near E line sec. 20, T 13 N, R 16 E). Named on Rockbound Valley (1955) 7.5' quadrangle.

La Mar Flat [NEVADA]: *area,* 2 miles east-southeast of Higgins Corner (lat. 39°01'40" N, long. 121°03'45" W; at NW cor. sec. 35, T 14 N, R 8 E). Named on Lake Combie (1949) 7.5' quadrangle.

Lambert Dome: see **Lembert Dome** [TUOLUMNE].

Lambert Soda Springs: see **Soda Springs** [TUOLUMNE].

La Mineta: see **Mount Bullion** [MARIPOSA].

La Mineta Gulch [MARIPOSA]: *canyon,* drained by a stream that flows 2.5 miles to Agua Fria Creek 4.5 miles east-northeast of the settlement of Catheys Valley (lat. 37°28'05" N, long. 120°01'20" W). Named on Catheys Valley (1962) 7.5' quadrangle. Called Cavallada Gulch on Indian Gulch (1920) 15' quadrangle, but United States Board on Geographic Names (1964a, p. 11) rejected the names "Cavallada Gulch" and "Minita Gulch" for the feature.

La Minita Creek: see **Guadalupe Creek** [MARIPOSA].

Lancha Plana [AMADOR]: *locality,* 9 miles south-southeast of Ione on the north side of Mokelumne River (lat. 38°13'25" N, long. 120° 54'05" W; sec. 5, T 4 N, R 10 E). Named on Wallace (1962) 7.5' quadrangle. Water of Camanche Reservoir now covers the site. Messers. Kaiser and Winter came to the place in 1849 or 1850 and constructed a ferry made of empty whiskey barrels lashed to a timber frame; Mexicans referred to the ferry as *la lanche plana*—which means "the flat boat" in Spanish—and this term became the name of the community that grew at the ferry site (Andrews, p. 6). The place first was called Sonora Bar (Gudde, 1975, p. 190). Postal authorities established Lancha Plana post office in 1859, discontinued it in 1912, reestablished it in 1913, and discontinued it in 1919 (Frickstad, p. 5). Camp's (1962) map shows a place called Arkansas Ferry located about 1.5 miles northwest of Lancha Plana on Mokelumne River, a place called French Camp situated 2.25 miles northeast of Lancha Plana in a canyon north of Mokelumne River, and a place called Camp Union located nearly 2 miles northeast of Lancha Plana and just west of French Camp. The first settlers at French Camp were mainly of Gallic origin (Andrews, p. 24). A mining place called Camp O'pera was started near French Camp in the summer of 1849, when miners from Sonora dry washed gold there (Cook, F.S., p. 5; Andrews, p. 25). A mining camp of the 1850's called Chaparral Hill was located near Lancha Plana upstream along Mokelumne River; Chaparral Hill was the site of a river crossings called Judge Palmer's Bridge, Delaney's Bridge, Westmoreland's Ferry, and Westmoreland Bridge (Andrews, p. 115). Postal authorities established Pomegranate post office in 1888 and discontinued it in 1890; the name was from a pomegranate-growing project at the site (Salley, p. 175), which was about 4 miles west-northwest of Lancha Plana.

Lander: see **Lander Crossing** [PLACER].

Lander Crossing [PLACER]: *locality,* 2.5 miles

south-southwest of Colfax along Southern Pacific Railroad (lat. 39°04'10" N, long. 120°58'40" W; sec. 16, T 14 N, R 9 E). Named on Colfax (1949) 7.5' quadrangle. Called Lander on Colfax (1938) 30' quadrangle. The name commemorates Frederick West Lander, who was chief engineer and superintendent for the overland wagon road in 1858 (Hanna, p. 167).

Land Peak [SIERRA]: *peak,* 9 miles south-southeast of Loyalton (lat. 39°33'25" N, long. 120°11'20" W; sec. 27, T 20 N, R 16 E). Altitude 8030 feet. Named on Sardine Peak (1981) 7.5' quadrangle.

Lanes [AMADOR]: *locality,* 1.5 miles southeast of Ione along Amador Central Railroad (lat. 38°20'25" N, long. 120°54'50" W; near S line sec. 30, T 6 N, R 10 E). Named on Ione (1962) 7.5' quadrangle.

Lang Crossing [NEVADA]: *locality,* 2.25 miles west of Yuba Gap along South Yuba River (lat. 39°19'05" N, long. 120°39'25" W; near S line sec. 20, T 17 N, R 12 E). Named on Blue Canyon (1955) 7.5' quadrangle. Called Langs on Colfax (1898) 30' quadrangle. California Mining Bureau's (1917b) map shows a place called Drum located near present Lang Crossing.

Langs: see **Lang Crossing** [NEVADA].

Lankershim: see **Trigo** [MADERA].

Laphams: see **State Line** [EL DORADO].

Larsen Reservoir [EL DORADO]: *lake,* 925 feet long, 6 miles west of Pollock Pines in North Canyon (2) (lat. 38°45'25" N, long. 120° 41'40" W; sec. 36, T 11 N, R 11 E). Named on Slate Mountain (1950) 7.5' quadrangle.

Las Mariposas [MARIPOSA]: *land grant,* around Bear Valley (1). Named on Bear Valley (1947), Catheys Valley (1962), Feliciana Mountain (1947), Hornitos (1947), Indian Gulch (1962), and Mariposa (1947) 7.5' quadrangles. Called Mariposa Estate on Hoffmann and Gardner's (1863-1867) map. Juan Bautista Alvarado received 10 leagues in 1844; John C. Fremont purchased the grant in 1847 and claimed 44,387 acres patented in 1856 (Cowan, p. 46-47).

Last Chance [PLACER]: *locality,* 7.5 miles northeast of Michigan Bluff (lat. 39°06'35" N, long. 120°37'30" W; at S line sec. 27, T 15 N, R 12 E). Named on Greek Store (1952) and Michigan Bluff (1952) 7.5' quadrangles. Postal authorities established Last Chance post office in 1865, discontinued it in 1869, reestablished it in 1909, and discontinued it in 1919; the place also was known as Clifton (Salley, p. 119) and as Caroline Diggings (Gudde, 1975, p. 192).

Last Chance Meadow [MADERA]: *area,* 6.5 miles south-southwest of Buena Vista Peak (lat. 37°30'10" N, long. 119°33' W; near N line sec. 15, T 5 S, R 22 E). Named on Yosemite (1956) 15' quadrangle.

Latimer Gulch [CALAVERAS]: *canyon,* drained by a stream that flows 1.5 miles to New Hogan Reservoir 2 miles west of San Andreas (lat. 38°12'05" N, long. 120°43'20" W; near W line sec. 13, T 4 N, R 11 E). Named on San Andreas (1962) 7.5' quadrangle. David Latimer had a store in the canyon at the community of North Branch, where he was postmaster (Camp *in* Doble, p. 296-297).

Latrobe [EL DORADO]: *village,* 15 miles southwest of Placerville (lat. 38°33'35" N, long. 120°58'50" W; near SW cor. sec. 10, T 8 N, R 9 E). Named on Latrobe (1949) 7.5' quadrangle. California Mining Bureau's (1917b) map has the form "La Trobe" for the name. Postal authorities established Latrobe post office in 1864 and discontinued it in 1921 (Frickstad, p. 27). The village began as the terminus of Placerville and Sacramento Railroad; F.A. Bishop, chief engineer of the railroad, named the place to honor Benjamin H. Latrobe, chief engineer of Baltimore and Ohio Railroad, the first railroad in the United States (Gudde, 1949, p. 184).

Latrobe Creek [EL DORADO]: *stream,* flows 3.5 miles to Deer Creek (2) 4 miles south-southeast of Clarksville (lat. 38°36' N, long. 121°01'15" W; near SE cor. sec. 30, T 9 N, R 9 E); the stream heads near Latrobe. Named on Folsom SE (1954) and Latrobe (1949) 7.5' quadrangles. Called Corral Creek on Placerville (1893) 30' quadrangle.

Laughlin Ridge [TUOLUMNE]: *ridge,* west-northwest-trending, 0.5 mile long, 1.5 miles southeast of Don Pedro Camp (lat. 37°42'15" N, long. 120°23'05" W; sec. 1, T 3 S, R 14 E). Named on La Grange (1962) 7.5' quadrangle.

Laumann Ridge [EL DORADO]: *ridge,* northwest-trending, 2 miles long, 3 mile north-northeast of Chili Bar (lat. 38°48'20" N, long. 120°48' W). Named on Garden Valley (1949) 7.5' quadrangle.

Laura Lake [MADERA]: *lake,* 700 feet long, 6.25 miles north-northwest of Devils Postpile (lat. 37°42'20" N, long. 119°08'15" W). Named on Devils Postpile (1953) 15' quadrangle.

Laurel Creek [MARIPOSA]: *stream,* flows 3 miles to Big Creek 1.5 miles south-southwest of Wawona (lat. 37°30'55" N, long. 119°39'55" W; sec. 10, T 5 S, R 21 E). Named on Bass Lake (1953) and Yosemite (1956) 15' quadrangles.

Laurel Lake [TUOLUMNE]: *lake,* 2600 feet long, 8.5 miles north-northeast of Mather (lat. 37°59'55" N, long. 119°47'40" W; on E line sec. 29, T 2 N, R 20 E). Named on Lake Eleanor (1956) and Pinecrest (1956) 15' quadrangles.

Lava: see **Volcanoville** [EL DORADO].

Lava Cap Reservoir [NEVADA]: *lake,* 6.25 miles north of Chicago Park (lat. 39°14'15" N, long. 120°58'15" W; sec. 21, T 16 N, R 9 E). Named on Chicago Park (1949) 7.5' quadrangle, which shows Lava Cap mine 0.5 mile south of the lake.

Lavezzola Creek [SIERRA]: *stream,* flows 13 miles to Downie River 1.5 miles north-north-east of Downieville (lat. 39°35' N, long. 120° 49'10" W; sec. 23, T 20 N, R 10 E). Named on Downieville (1951), Gold Lake (1981), and Mount Fillmore (1951) 7.5' quadrangles. Downieville (1951) 7.5' quadrangle shows Lavezzola ranch near the stream. Called Middle Fork of North Fork Yuba River on Downieville (1897) 30' quadrangle, but United States Board on Geographic Names (1950, p. 5) rejected this name for the stream, and also rejected the name "North Fork of North Fork" for the upper part of the stream.

La Vina [MADERA]: *village,* 6.5 miles south-southwest of Madera (lat. 36°52'50" N long. 120°06'45" W; on S line sec. 16, T 12 S, R 17 E). Named on Madera (1963) 7.5' quadrangle. Postal authorities established La Vina post office in 1891 and discontinued it in 1895 (Frickstad, p. 86). The place began as part of an unsuccessful land-development scheme (Clough, p. 86).

Lawnsdale Gulch: see **Columbia** [TUOL-UMNE].

Lawrenceberg: see **Kelsey** [EL DORADO].

Lawrence Lake [EL DORADO]: *lake,* 750 feet long, 5 miles southwest of Phipps Peak (lat. 38°54'35" N, long. 120°13'30" W; near NW cor. sec. 9, T 12 N, R 16 E). Named on Rockbound Valley (1955) 7.5' quadrangle.

Lawrence Mill [EL DORADO]: *locality,* 5 miles east-southeast of Aukum (lat. 38°32'05" N, long. 120°38'20" W; sec. 22, T 8 N, R 12 E). Site named on Aukum (1952) 7.5' quadrangle.

Lawyer Cow Camp [EL DORADO]: *locality,* 2.5 miles west of Wentworth Springs in Gerle Meadow (lat. 39°10' N, long. 120° 23' W; near W line sec. 35, T 14 N, R 14 E). Named on Bunker Hill (1953) 7.5' quadrangle.

Leaning Tower [MARIPOSA]: *relief feature,* 4 miles southwest of Yosemite Village on the south side of Yosemite Valley (lat. 37°42'45" N, long. 119°38'50" W). Named on Yosemite (1956) 15' quadrangle.

Leavitt Peak [TUOLUMNE]: *peak,* 3 miles south-southeast of Sonora Pass on Tuolumne-Mono county line (lat. 38°17'10" N, long. 119° 39' W). Altitude 11,569 feet. Named on Sonora Pass (1979) 7.5' quadrangle. Called Leavitts Pk. on Wheeler's (1876-1877a) map. The name recalls Hiram L. Leavitt, who lived in Sonora about 1865 and later had a stage station in Mono County on the road that extended from Sonora into Mono County (Wedertz, p. 89).

LeConte: see **Lake LeConte** [EL DORADO].

LeConte Cascade: see **LeConte Falls** [TUOL-UMNE].

LeConte Falls [TUOLUMNE]: *waterfall,* 10.5 miles west of Tioga Pass along Tuolumne River (lat. 37°55'25" N, long. 119°27'05" W).

Named on Tuolumne Meadows (1956) 15' quadrangle. R.M. Price gave the name "LeConte Cascade" to present Waterwheel Falls in 1894 to honor Professor Joseph N. LeConte of University of California, but the name "LeConte" somehow was transferred to present LeConte Falls, which had been known as California Falls (Browning, 1988, p. 72-73).

LeConte Point [TUOLUMNE]: *peak,* 6 miles north-northwest of White Wolf (lat. 37°56'45" N, long. 119°42'20" W). Named on Hetch Hetchy Reservoir (1956) 15' quadrangle. R.B. Marshall of United States Geological Survey named the peak for Professor Joseph N. LeConte of University of California (United States Board on Geographic Names, 1934, p. 14).

Ledger Island [MADERA]: *area,* 18 miles east of Madera on the west side of San Joaquin River (lat. 36°56'55" N, long. 119°44'20" W; sec. 25, T 11 S, R 20 E). Named on Friant (1964) 7.5' quadrangle.

Leek Spring [EL DORADO]: *spring,* nearly 2 miles east-northeast of Leek Spring Hill (lat. 38°38' N, long. 120°14'45" W). Named on Pyramid Peak (1896) 30' quadrangle. Some Mormon men on their way over the Sierra Nevada to Salt Lake City in 1848 named the spring for the wild onions there (Dillon *in* Burrows and Hall, p. 67).

Leek Spring Hill [EL DORADO]: *peak,* 16 miles south-southwest of Pyramid Peak (lat. 38°37'45" N, long. 120°16'35" W; near E line sec. 14, T 9 N, R 15 E); the peak is nearly 2 miles west-southwest of Leek Spring. Altitude 7621 feet. Named on Leek Spring Hill (1951) 7.5' quadrangle.

Leek Spring Valley [EL DORADO]: *valley,* 1.5 miles east of Leek Spring Hill on upper reaches of North Fork Cosumnes River (lat. 38°38' N, long. 120°15' W). Named on Leek Spring Hill (1951) and Tragedy Spring (1979) 7.5' quadrangles.

Lee Price Camp [TUOLUMNE]: *locality,* 4 miles east-southeast of Long Barn in Hulls Meadows (lat. 38°03'50" N, long. 120°04'30" W; near N line sec. 2, T 2 N, R 17 E). Named on Hull Creek (1979) 7.5' quadrangle.

Lehamite Creek [MARIPOSA]: *stream,* flows 2.25 miles to Indian Canyon Creek 0.5 mile north-northwest of Yosemite Village (lat. 37°45'30" N, long. 119°34'50" W). Named on Hetch Hetchy Reservoir (1956) 15' quadrangle. The word "Lehamite" is of Indian origin (United States Board on Geographic Names, 1934, p. 14). Called Little Winkle Branch on a map of the Wheeler survey in 1883, and later called East Fork of Indian Creek (Browning, 1986, p. 125).

Leidig Meadow [MARIPOSA]: *area,* 1.25 miles southwest of Yosemite Village in Yosemite Valley (lat. 37°44'15" N, long. 119° 36'10" W). Named on Yosemite (1956) 15' quadrangle. The name commemorates Charlie Leidig, a ranger in Yosemite National Park (United States Board on Geographic Names, 1934, p. 14).

Leighton Lake [TUOLUMNE]: *lake,* 3300 feet long, 13 miles east-southeast of Pinegrove (lat. 38°08'30" N, long. 119°46'10" W). Named on Pinecrest (1956) 15' quadrangle. Browning (1986, p. 125) associated the name with Fred Leighton, a sportsman and conservationist.

Leland Creek [TUOLUMNE]: *stream,* flows 2.5 miles to Cow Creek (1) 3.25 miles north of Pinecrest (lat. 38°14'20" N, long. 119°59'55" W; sec. 33, T 5 N, R 18 E). Named on Pinecrest (1979) 7.5' quadrangle.

Leland Gulch [MADERA]: *canyon,* drained by a stream that flows 1.5 miles to Chowchilla River 8 miles northeast of Raymond (lat. 37°18'30" N, long. 119°49'05" W; sec. 19, T 7 S, R 20 E). Named on Horsecamp Mountain (1947) 7.5' quadrangle.

Leland Lakes [EL DORADO]: *lakes,* largest 1000 feet long, 4 miles west-southwest of Phipps Peak (lat. 38°56'05" N, long. 120°13'05" W; sec. 33, T 13 N, R 16 E). Named on Rockbound Valley (1955) 7.5' quadrangle.

Leland Meadow: see **Leland Reservoir** [TUOLUMNE].

Leland Reservoir [TUOLUMNE]: *lake,* 1000 feet long, 3 miles north-northeast of Pinecrest (lat. 38°14' N, long. 119°58'45" W; sec. 3, T 4 N, R 18 E); the lake is at the head of Leland Creek. Named on Pinecrest (1979) 7.5' quadrangle. Pinecrest (1956) 15' quadrangle shows Leland Mdw. at the site. G.A. Leland patented land there in 1898 (Browning, 1986, p. 125).

Lembert Dome [TUOLUMNE]: *peak,* 5.25 miles west-southwest of Tioga Pass on the north side of Tuolumne Meadows (lat. 37°52'55" N, long. 119°20'45" W; near W line sec. 4, T 1 S, R 24 E). Altitude 9450 feet. Named on Tuolumne Meadows (1956) 15' quadrangle. The name commemorates John Baptist Lembert, who homesteaded in Tuolumne Meadows in 1885 (Hanna, p. 170). United States Board on Geographic Names (1933, p. 454) rejected the form "Lambert Dome" for the name.

Lemon Canyon [SIERRA]: *canyon,* drained by a stream that flows nearly 6 miles to Sierra Valley 1.5 miles east-southeast of Sierraville (lat 39°35' N, long. 120°20' W). Named on Sardine Peak (1981) and Sierraville (1981) 7.5' quadrangles.

Leonardi [EL DORADO]: *locality,* 9 miles north-northeast of Pollock Pines (lat. 38°52'55" N, long. 120°32'05" W; near SE cor. sec. 17, T 12 N, R 13 E). Named on Devil Peak (1950) 7.5' quadrangle.

Leonardi Spring [EL DORADO]: *spring,* 10.5 miles north of Pollock Pines (lat. 38°54'35" N, long. 120°32'45" W; at S line sec. 5, T 12

N, R 13 E). Named on Devil Peak (1950) 7.5' quadrangle.

Leoni Meadow [EL DORADO]: *area,* 4 miles east-northeast of Omo Ranch (lat. 38°36'30" N, long. 120°30'15" W; sec. 26, T 9 N, R 13 E). Named on Omo Ranch (1952) 7.5' quadrangle. Logan's (1938) map shows a place called Leonis Station located about 1 mile southwest of present Leoni Meadow along Diamond Caldor Railroad (at SE cor. sec. 27, T 9 N, R 13 E).

Leonis Station: see **Leoni Meadow** [EL DORADO].

Leopold Lake [TUOLUMNE]: *lake,* 1350 feet long, 10.5 miles east of Pinecrest (lat. 38°10'40" N, long. 119°48'15" W). Named on Pinecrest (1956) 15' quadrangle.

Lertora Lake [TUOLUMNE]: *lake,* 2900 feet long, 9.5 miles west of Tower Peak (lat. 38°08'20" N, long. 119°43'10" W). Named on Tower Peak (1956) 15' quadrangle. United States Board on Geographic Names (1965c, p. 8) approved the name "Fisher Lakes" for a group of five small lakes situated just north of Lertora Lake (lat. 38°08'40" N, long. 119°43'10" W), and (p. 9) approved the name "Frog Lake" for a small lake located about 0.3 mile east-northeast of Lertora Lake (lat. 38°08'30" N, long. 119°42'40" W).

Leta: see **Auburn** [PLACER].

Levey Ditch Camp [NEVADA]: *locality,* 7 miles west-southwest of Yuba Gap (lat. 39°17'05" N, long. 120°44'25" W; sec. 4, T 16 N, R 11 E). Named on Blue Canyon (1955) 7.5' quadrangle.

Lewis [MARIPOSA]: *locality,* 8.5 miles south of the present settlement of Catheys Valley along Ganns Creek (lat. 37°18'15" N, long. 120°06'35" W; sec. 21, T 7 S, R 17 E). Named on Indian Gulch (1920) 15' quadrangle. Postal authorities established Lewis post office in 1879 and discontinued it in 1927 (Frickstad, p. 91).

Lewis [TUOLUMNE]: *locality,* 5 miles south-southwest of Long Barn (lat. 38°01'15" N, long. 120°10'15" W); the place is 1 mile southwest of Mount Lewis. Named on Big Trees (1891) 30' quadrangle.

Lewis: see **Mount Lewis** [TUOLUMNE].

Lewis Campground [PLACER]: *locality,* 8 miles southwest of Granite Chief along Middle Fork American River in French Meadows (lat. 39°08'20" N, long. 120°24'30" W; near E line sec. 21, T 15 N, R 14 E). Named on Royal Gorge (1953) 7.5' quadrangle.

Lewis Creek [MADERA-MARIPOSA]: *stream,* heads just inside Madera County and flows 7.5 miles to Merced River 7.5 miles south of Cathedral Peak (lat. 37°44'15" N, long. 119°24' W). Named on Merced Peak (1953) and Tuolumne Meadows (1956) 15' quadrangles. United States Board on Geographic Names (1934, p. 14) rejected the name "Maclure Fork" for the stream, and pointed out that the name "Lewis" is for W.B. Lewis, a superintendent of Yosemite National Park.

Lewis Creek: see **Lewis Fork** [MADERA-MARIPOSA].

Lewis Fork [MADERA-MARIPOSA]: *stream,* heads just inside Mariposa County and flows 8.5 miles to join Nelder Creek and form Fresno River less than 0.5 mile south-south-west of Yosemite Forks in Madera County (lat. 37°21'40" N, long. 119°37'55" W; near SW cor. sec. 36, T 6 S, R 21 E). Named on Bass Lake (1953) 15' quadrangle. Browning (1986, p. 127) associated the name with Jonathan Lewis, who homesteaded in the neighborhood in 1886. United States Board on Geographic Names (1964c, p. 15) rejected the names "Lewis Creek" and "North Fork of Fresno River" for the stream.

Lewis Gulch [MARIPOSA]: *canyon,* drained by a stream that flows 3 miles to Bull Creek 7.25 miles east-northeast of Buckhorn Peak (lat. 37°42'45" N, long. 120°00'20" W; sec. 32, T 2 S, R 18 E). Named on Buckhorn Peak (1947) and Kinsley (1947) 7.5' quadrangles.

Lewis Lakes [TUOLUMNE]: *lakes,* three, largest 2200 feet long, 11 miles west-northwest of Tower Peak (lat. 38°13'15" N, long. 119°43'40" W). Named on Tower Peak (1956) 15' quadrangle. The name honors Bert Lewis, a Forest Service employee who died in France during World War I (United States Board on Geographic Names, 1933, p. 456).

Lewisville: see **Greenwood** [EL DORADO].

Liars Flat: see **Rice Crossing** [NEVADA].

Liases Flat: see **Rice Crossing** [NEVADA].

Liberty Cap [MARIPOSA]: *peak,* 3 miles east-southeast of Yosemite Village (lat. 37°43'45" N, long. 119°31'55" W). Altitude 7076 feet. Named on Yosemite (1956) 15' quadrangle. King and Gardner's (1865) map has the designation "Cap of Liberty or Mt. Broderick" for the peak. The feature also was called Mount Frances, Gwin's Peak, and Bellows' Butte in the early days, but when Governor Leland Stanford viewed the peak he asked that a more appropriate name be found; he then approved the name "Liberty Cap" suggested by the resemblance of the feature to the Cap of Liberty depicted on the half-dollar coin of the time (Browning, 1986, p. 127).

Liberty Hill [TUOLUMNE]: *peak,* 28 miles northeast of Columbia (lat. 38°22'05" N, long. 120°06' W; near NE cor. sec. 21, T 6 N, R 17 E). Altitude 7537 feet. Named on Liberty Hill (1979) 7.5' quadrangle.

Liberty Hill: see **Liberty Hill Diggings** [NEVADA].

Liberty Hill Diggings [NEVADA]: *locality,* 10 miles northeast of Chicago Park (lat. 39°14'05" N, long. 120°49'10" W; sec. 23, T 16 N, R 10 E). Named on Dutch Flat (1950) 7.5' quadrangle. Whitney's (1873) map shows a community called Liberty Hill at or near the site of present Liberty Hill Diggings, and

a peak called Maguires Mt. located nearly 2 miles northeast of Liberty Hill.

Lichen Creek [EL DORADO]: *stream,* flows 3.5 miles to Greenwood Creek 3.5 miles northwest of Coloma (lat. 38°49'50" N, long. 120° 56'45" W; sec. 2, T 11 N, R 9 E). Named on Coloma (1949) 7.5' quadrangle.

Licking Fork [CALAVERAS]: *stream,* flows 14 miles to South Fork Mokelumne River 1.5 miles north of Rail Road Flat (lat. 38°21'45" N, long. 120°30'25" W; sec. 23, T 6 N, R 13 E). Named on Dorrington (1979), Fort Mountain (1979), Garnet Hill (1979), and Railroad Flat (1948) 7.5' quadrangles.

Light Canyon [EL DORADO]:
(1) *canyon,* drained by a stream that flows 1.25 miles to South Fork American River 1.5 miles east of Chili Bar (lat. 38°46'10" N, long. 120°47'30" W; sec. 30, T 11 N, R 11 E); the canyon is 0.5 mile east of Dark Canyon (4). Named on Garden Valley (1949) 7.5' quadrangle.
(2) *canyon,* drained by a stream that flows 1.5 miles to Alder Creek 7.25 miles north-northwest of Leek Spring Hill (lat. 38°43'30" N, long. 120°20'15" W; near N line sec. 17, T 10 N, R 15 E). Named on Leek Spring Hill (1951) 7.5' quadrangle.

Lignite: see **Carbondale** [AMADOR].

Lightner Peak [CALAVERAS]: *peak,* nearly 4 miles southeast of Copperopolis (lat. 37°56'40" N, long. 120°35'15" W; near N line sec. 18, T 1 N, R 13 E). Altitude 1543 feet. Named on Melones Dam (1962) 7.5' quadrangle.

Lightning Creek [CALAVERAS]: *stream,* flows 2 miles to South Fork Mokelumne River 2.5 miles east of Blue Mountain (lat. 38°20'20" N, long. 120°19'05" W; near SW cor. sec. 27, T 6 N, R 15 E). Named on Dorrington (1979) 7.5' quadrangle.

Lillian Lake [MADERA]: *lake,* 1550 feet long, 5.25 miles south-southeast of Merced Peak (lat. 37°33'45" N, long. 119°21'50" W). Named on Merced Peak (1953) 15' quadrangle.

Lilly Mountain [MADERA]: *peak,* 5 miles east-southeast of Knowles (lat. 37°10'55" N, long. 119°47'40" W; sec. 4, T 9 S, R 20 E). Named on Knowles (1962) 7.5' quadrangle.

Lily Lake [MADERA]: *lake,* 500 feet long, 8.5 miles west of Devils Postpile (lat. 37°36'15" N, long. 119°13'50" W). Named on Devils Postpile (1953) 15' quadrangle.

Lily Creek [TUOLUMNE]:
(1) *stream,* flows 2.25 miles to Middle Fork Stanislaus River 8.5 miles south-southeast of Liberty Hill (lat. 38°15'45" N, long. 120° 00'55" W; sec. 29, T 5 N, R 18 E). Named on Donnell Lake (1979) and Liberty Hill (1979) 7.5' quadrangles.
(2) *stream,* flows 4 miles to Hull Creek 3.5 miles southeast of Long Barn (lat. 38°03'25" N, long. 120°05' W; sec. 2, T 2 N, R 17 E).

Named on Hull Creek (1979) 7.5' quadrangle. (3) *stream,* flows 10 miles to join Bell Creek and form Clavey River nearly 4 miles south-southeast of Pinecrest (lat. 38°08'30" N, long. 119°58' W; sec. 2, T 3 N, R 18 E). Named on Pinecrest (1956) 15' quadrangle.

Lily Gap [CALAVERAS]: *locality,* nearly 3 miles southwest of Devils Nose along Bear Creek (1) (lat. 38°25'45" N, long. 120° 27' W; sec. 29, T 7 N, R 14 E). Named on Devils Nose (1979) 7.5' quadrangle.

Lily Lake [EL DORADO]: *lake,* 850 feet long, 2.25 miles south-southeast of Mount Tallac (lat. 38°52'30" N, long. 120°04'50" W). Named on Echo Lake (1955) and Emerald Bay (1955) 7.5' quadrangles.

Lily Lake [PLACER]: *lake,* 2000 feet long, nearly 4 miles south-southwest of Homewood (lat. 39°02'20" N, long. 120°11'20" W; on S line sec. 22, T 14 N, R 16 E). Named on Homewood (1955) 7.5' quadrangle.

Lily Lake [TUOLUMNE]: *intermittent lake,* 1000 feet long, 2.5 miles southeast of Pinecrest (lat. 38°09'35" N, long. 119°57'55" W; sec. 35, T 4 N, R 18 E). Named on Pinecrest (1979) 7.5' quadrangle.

Lily Lake: see **Irwin Bright Lake** [TUOLUMNE]; **Mud Lake** [TUOLUMNE].

Lily Pond [NEVADA]: *lake,* 300 feet long, 6.5 miles west-northwest of Donner Pass (lat. 39°21'55" N, long. 120°25'50" W; sec. 5, T 17 N, R 14 E). Named on Soda Springs (1955) 7.5' quadrangle.

Lily Valley [CALAVERAS]: *valley,* 1.5 miles south-southwest of Devils Nose (lat. 38°26'30" N, long. 120°25'45" W). Named on Devils Nose (1979) 7.5' quadrangle.

Limekiln [EL DORADO]: *locality,* 1.25 miles north of Cool (lat. 38° 54'15" N, long. 121°00'50" W). Named on Sacramento (1892) 30' quadrangle.

Limerick: see **Camanche** [CALAVERAS].

Lime Rock [PLACER]: *relief feature,* 5 miles northeast of Auburn (lat. 38°56'55" N, long. 121°00'30" W; sec. 30, T 13 N, R 9 E). Named on Auburn (1953) 7.5' quadrangle.

Lincoln [MADERA]: *locality,* 8 miles south-southwest of Chowchilla along Chowchilla Pacific Railroad (lat. 37°01'10" N, long. 120°20'40" W; near W line sec. 33, T 10 S, R 15 E). Named on Chowchilla (1918) 7.5' quadrangle.

Lincoln [PLACER]: *town,* 12 miles west of Auburn (lat. 38°53'30" N, long. 121°17'30" W; sec. 15, T 12 N, R 6 E). Named on Lincoln (1953) 7.5' quadrangle. Postal authorities established Lincoln post office in 1862 (Frickstad, p. 120), and the town incorporated in 1890. The name commemorates Charles Lincoln Wilson, head of the construction company that officials of California Central Railroad hired in 1858 to build a rail line from Sacramento to Marysville (Hanna, p. 171). California Mining Bureau's (1909a) map shows a place called Vantrent located 10 miles north of Lincoln by stage line. Postal authorities established Vantrent post office in 1904 and discontinued it in 1918 (Salley, p. 230). They established Cairns post office 11 miles northeast of Lincoln in 1906 and discontinued it in 1907 (Salley, p. 31).

Lincoln: see **Clinton** [AMADOR]; **Mount Lincoln** [PLACER].

Lincoln Creek [SIERRA]: *stream,* flows 5 miles to North Yuba River 7 miles northeast of Sierra City (lat. 39°37'10" N, long. 120° 31'20" W; near N line sec. 9, T 20 N, R 13 E); the stream goes through Lincoln Valley. Named on Haypress Valley (1981) and Sattley (1981) 7.5' quadrangles.

Lincoln Creek Campground [SIERRA]: *locality,* 7 miles northeast of Sierra City along North Yuba River (lat. 39°37'15" N, long. 120°31'25" W; at N line sec. 9, T 20 N, R 13 E); the place is near the mouth of Lincoln Creek. Named on Sierra City (1955) 15' quadrangle.

Lincoln Hill [EL DORADO]: *peak,* 10.5 miles east-southeast of Camino (lat. 38°39'45" N, long. 120°30'05" W; sec. 2, T 9 N, R 13 E). Named on Sly Park (1952) 7.5' quadrangle.

Lincoln Peak: see **Mount Lincoln** [PLACER].

Lincoln Valley [SIERRA]: *valley,* 7.5 miles east-northeast of Sierra City (lat. 39°35'30" N, long. 120°30' W); the valley is along Lincoln Creek. Named on Haypress Valley (1981) and Sattley (1981) 7.5' quadrangles.

Lind: see **Jenny Lind** [CALAVERAS].

Linda Creek [PLACER]: *stream,* heads in Placer County and flows 9.5 miles, partly in Sacramento County, to Cirby Creek 1 mile south-southeast of downtown Roseville in Placer County (lat. 38°44'05" N, long. 121°16'30" W; sec. 12, T 10 N, R 6 E). Named on Citrus Heights (1967) and Folsom (1967) 7.5' quadrangles. The upper part of the stream is called Rock Creek on Sacramento (1892) 30' quadrangle. United States Board on Geographic Names (1933, p. 461) rejected the name "Dry Creek" for the stream, and later (1968a, p. 8) rejected the name "Cirby Creek" for it.

Linda Creek: see **Dry Creek** [PLACER].

Lindsey Creek [NEVADA]: *stream,* flows 2.5 miles to Texas Creek 4.5 miles east-southeast of Graniteville (lat. 39°24'35" N, long. 120°40' W; sec. 19, T 18 N, R 12 E); the stream heads at Lindsey Lakes. Named on Graniteville (1982) 7.5' quadrangle.

Lindsey Lakes [NEVADA]: *lakes,* largest 1900 feet long, 6 miles east-southeast of Graniteville (lat. 39°24'45" N, long. 120°38' W; mainly in sec. 21, T 18 N, R 12 E). Named on Graniteville (1982) 7.5' quadrangle.

Lion Creek [CALAVERAS]: *stream,* flows 3.5 miles to Forest Creek 3.5 miles south of Devils Nose (lat. 38°24'35" N, long. 120°25'50" W; near SE cor. sec. 33, T 7 N, R 14 E). Named on Devils Nose (1979) 7.5' quadrangle.

Lion Creek [TUOLUMNE]: *stream,* flows 4.5 miles to Middle Fork Stanislaus River nearly 7 miles southeast of Liberty Hill (lat. 38° 18'25" N, long. 120°00'10" W; sec. 9, T 5 N, R 18 E). Named on Liberty Hill (1979) 7.5' quadrangle.

Lion Lake [CALAVERAS]: *lake,* 300 feet long, located 2 miles east of Tamarack (lat. 38°26'10" N, long. 120°02'25" W). Named on Tamarack (1979) 7.5' quadrangle.

Lion Point [MADERA]:

(1) *peak,* 11 miles south of Shuteye Peak (lat. 37°11'40" N, long. 119°23'35" W; sec. 31, T 8 S, R 24 E). Altitude 4970 feet. Named on Shaver Lake (1953) 15' quadrangle.

(2) *peak,* nearly 5 miles south-southwest of Devils Postpile (lat. 37° 33'50" N, long. 119°07'30" W). Altitude 8866 feet. Named on Devils Postpile (1953) 15' quadrangle.

Lisbon: see **Applegate** [PLACER].

Little Alberts Lake: see **Elbert Lake** [EL DORADO].

Little Ash Creek [MADERA]: *stream,* diverges west from Ash Creek (present Ash Slough) 8.5 miles west-southwest of Chowchilla (lat. 37°04'05" N, long. 120°23'50" W; near NW cor. sec. 13, T 10 S, R 14 E), and flows for 5 miles in a westerly direction. Named on Bliss Ranch (1918) 7.5' quadrangle.

Little Bald Mountain [EL DORADO]: *peak,* 3.5 miles north-northeast of Georgetown (lat. 38°57'10" N, long. 120°48'25" W; near N line sec. 25, T 13 N, R 10 E). Altitude 3083 feet. Named on Georgetown (1949) 7.5' quadrangle.

Little Bald Mountain [PLACER]: *ridge,* west-trending, 1.5 miles long, 1 mile southeast of Duncan Peak (lat. 39°08'45" N, long. 120°29'50" W). Named on Duncan Peak (1952) and Royal Gorge (1953) 7.5' quadrangles.

Little Bear Creek [PLACER]: *stream,* flows 4 miles to Bear River less than 1 mile north of Dutch Flat (lat. 39°12'55" N, long. 120° 50'25" W). Named on Colfax (1898) 30' quadrangle.

Little Bear Lake [TUOLUMNE]: *lake,* 2000 feet long, 14 miles southeast of Pinecrest (lat. 38°04'50" N, long. 119°47' W). Named on Pinecrest (1956) 15' quadrangle. Elden H. Vestal of California Department of Fish and Game named the lake in 1952 (Browning, 1986, p. 128).

Little Bear River [AMADOR]: *stream,* flows 2.25 miles to Lower Bear Reservoir 6.5 miles east of Hams Station (lat. 38°33'15" N, long. 120°15'05" W; sec. 7, T 8 N, R 16 E). Named on Bear River Reservoir (1979) and Peddler Hill (1951) 7.5' quadrangles.

Little Beaver Canyon [TUOLUMNE]: *canyon,* 1.25 miles long, on upper reaches of Beaver Creek above a point 2 miles south-southeast of Liberty Hill (lat. 38°20'30" N, long. 120°05'10" W). Named on Liberty Hill (1979) 7.5' quadrangle.

Little Beaver Creek [TUOLUMNE]: *stream,* flows 3 miles to Beaver Creek 8 miles southwest of Liberty Hill (lat. 38°17'15" N, long. 120°12'50" W; sec. 16, T 5 N, R 16 E). Named on Boards Crossing (1979) 7.5' quadrangle. On Big Meadow (1956) 15' quadrangle, the name applies to present Crane Creek (1).

Little Boulder Creek [SIERRA]: *stream,* flows 1 mile to Big Boulder Creek 10 miles north-northeast of Sierra City (lat. 39°41'50" N, long. 120°33'45" W; sec. 7, T 21 N, R 13 E). Named on Clio (1981) 7.5' quadrangle.

Little Bowman Lake: see **Bowman Lake** [NEVADA].

Little Brown Bear Creek [NEVADA]: *stream,* flows 1 mile to South Yuba River 3.5 miles west-southwest of Washington (lat. 39°20'35" N, long. 120°52' W; near NW cor. sec. 16, T 17 N, R 10 E). Named on Washington (1950) 7.5' quadrangle.

Little Butte [EL DORADO]: *peak,* 8.5 miles southeast of Camino (lat. 38°39'55" N, long. 120°33'05" W; near NW cor. sec. 4, T 9 N, R 13 E). Altitude 3835 feet. Named on Sly Park (1952) 7.5' quadrangle. Little Butte, Middle Butte, and Big Butte together have the label "Buttes" on Placerville (1893) 30' quadrangle.

Little Canyon Creek [NEVADA]: *stream,* flows 3.5 miles to Canyon Creek 7.5 miles west-northwest of Yuba Gap (lat. 39°22'15" N, long. 120°44'15" W; near E line sec. 4, T 17 N, R 11 E). Named on Blue Canyon (1955) and Graniteville (1982) 7.5' quadrangles.

Little Canyon Creek [SIERRA]: *stream,* flows 7.5 miles to Canyon Creek 6 miles northwest of Goodyears Bar (lat. 39°36'50" N, long. 120°56'55" W; sec. 10, T 20 N, R 9 E). Named on Goodyears Bar (1951) and La Port (1951) 7.5' quadrangles. East Branch enters from the east 7 miles south-southwest of Mount Fillmore; it is 2 miles long and is named on La Porte (1951) 7.5' quadrangle.

Little Catfish Lake: see **Tollhouse Lake** [NEVADA].

Little Chief [PLACER]: *peak,* 6 miles north-northwest of Tahoe City (lat. 39°14'40" N, long. 120°12'05" W; near SE cor. sec. 9, T 16 N, R 16 E); the peak is 0.5 mile northwest of Big Chief. Altitude 7255 feet. Named on Tahoe City (1955) 7.5' quadrangle.

Little China Gulch [AMADOR]: *canyon,* nearly 2 miles long, opens into China Gulch (1) 8 miles south of Ione (lat. 38°13'55" N, long. 120°54'50" W; sec. 6, T 4 N, R 10 E). Named on Wallace (1962) 7.5' quadrangle. Water of Camanche Reservoir covers the lower part of the canyon.

Little Clipper Creek [NEVADA]: *stream,* flows nearly 2 miles to Clipper Creek 4.5 miles north of Chicago Park (lat. 39°12'35" N, long. 120°58' W; sec. 33, T 16 N, R 9 E). Named on Chicago Park (1949) 7.5' quadrangle.

Little Codfish Creek [PLACER]: *stream,* flows nearly 2 miles to Codfish Creek 6.5 miles south of Colfax (lat. 39°00'10" N, long. 120°57'15" W; sec. 3, T 13 N, R 9 E). Named on Colfax (1949) 7.5' quadrangle.

Little Crane Creek [MARIPOSA]: *stream,* flows 4.5 miles to Crane Creek 1.25 miles north-northeast of El Portal (lat. 37°41'30" N, long. 119°46'15" W; sec. 9, T 3 S, R 20 E). Named on El Portal (1947) 7.5' quadrangle.

Little Crater [PLACER]: *relief feature,* 10 miles south-southwest of Duncan Peak (lat. 39°01'10" N, long. 120°33'30" W; near W line sec. 32, T 14 N, R 13 E); the feature is 2.5 miles east-northeast of Big Crater. Named on Greek Store (1952) 7.5' quadrangle.

Little Dry Creek [CALAVERAS]: *stream,* flows 1 mile to Dry Creek (2) 1 mile northeast of Vallecitos (lat. 38°05'50" N, long. 120°27'35" W; sec. 20, T 3 N, R 14 E). Named on Columbia (1948) 7.5' quadrangle.

Little Deer Creek [EL DORADO]: *stream,* flows 2.5 miles to Deer Creek (1) 5 miles west of Wentworth Springs (lat. 39°00'10" N, long. 120°25'50" W; sec. 5, T 13 N, R 14 E). Named on Bunker Hill (1953) 7.5' quadrangle.

Little Deer Creek [NEVADA]: *stream,* flows 4.25 miles to Deer Creek in downtown Nevada City (lat. 39°15'45" N, long. 121°00'55" W; near W line sec. 7, T 16 N, R 9 E). Named on Chicago Park (1949), Nevada City (1948), and North Bloomfield (1949) 7.5' quadrangles. Gudde (1975, p. 53) listed a place called Bunkerville that was located 0.5 mile south of Nevada City along Little Deer Creek.

Little Deer Lake [SIERRA]: *lake,* 900 feet long, 8 miles north-northwest of Sierra City (lat. 39°40'15" N, long. 120°41'20" W; sec. 24, T 21 N, R 11 E). Named on Gold Lake (1981) 7.5' quadrangle.

Little Dry Creek [MADERA]: *stream,* flows 16 miles to Cottonwood Creek (2) 3 miles northwest of Trigo (lat. 36°57' N, long. 119°59'15" W; sec. 27, T 11 S, R 18 E). Named on Herndon (1965) and Raymond (1962) 15' quadrangles.

Little Dry Creek [NEVADA]: *stream,* flows nearly 6 miles to Dry Creek (2) 6 miles southwest of Pilot Peak (lat. 39°06'50" N, long. 121°16'05" W; near NE cor. sec. 35, T 15 N, R 6 E). Named on Camp Far West (1949), Rough and Ready (1949), and Smartville (1951) 7.5' quadrangles.

Little Duncan Canyon [PLACER]: *canyon,* drained by a stream that flows 2.5 miles to Duncan Canyon 11 miles west-southwest of Granite Chief (lat. 39°08'30" N, long. 120°28'15" W; at S line sec. 13, T 15 N, R 13 E). Named on Royal Gorge (1953, photorevised 1973) 7.5' quadrangle. Called Little Duncan on Granite Chief (1953) 15' quadrangle. On Truckee (1940) 30' quadrangle, the stream in the canyon is called Little Duncan Creek.

Little Duncan Creek: see **Little Duncan Canyon** [PLACER].

Little Fiddle Creek [SIERRA]: *stream,* flows nearly 3 miles to Fiddle Creek 3.5 miles west of Goodyears Bar (lat. 39°32'05" N, long. 120°57'05" W; at N line sec. 10, T 19 N, R 9 E). Named on Goodyears Bar (1951) 7.5' quadrangle.

Little Fine Gold Creek [MADERA]: *stream,* flows 12 miles to Fine Gold Creek 6.25 miles west-southwest of North Fork (lat. 37°11'45" N, long. 119°37' W; near W line sec. 31, T 8 S, R 22 E). Named on Bass Lake (1953) and Millerton Lake (1965) 15' quadrangles.

Little Gambler Creek [EL DORADO]: *stream,* flows 0.5 mile to Gambler Creek less than 1 mile north of Coloma (lat. 38°48'40" N, long. 120°53'30" W; at N line sec. 17, T 11 N, R 10 E). Named on Coloma (1949) 7.5' quadrangle.

Little Gold Lake [SIERRA]: *lake,* 750 feet long, 7 miles north-northwest of Sierra City (lat. 39°40' N, long. 120°39'55" W; near E line sec. 19, T 21 N, R 12 E); the lake is 700 feet south of Gold Lake. Named on Gold Lake (1981) 7.5' quadrangle.

Little Granite Canyon: see **Little Granite Creek** [PLACER].

Little Granite Creek [PLACER]: *stream,* flows 5 miles to Big Granite Creek 5 miles north of Duncan Peak (lat. 39°13'40" N, long. 120°31'20" W; near N line sec. 28, T 16 N, R 13 E). Named on Cisco Grove (1955) and Duncan Peak (1952) 7.5' quadrangles. On Colfax (1898) 30' quadrangle, the canyon of the stream is called Little Granite Canyon.

Little Greenhorn Creek [NEVADA]: *stream,* flows 4.5 miles to Greenhorn Creek 3.25 miles north-northeast of Chicago Park (lat. 39°11'20" N, long. 120°56'25" W; sec. 2, T 15 N, R 9 E). Named on Chicago Park (1949) 7.5' quadrangle.

Little Grizzly Canyon [PLACER]: *canyon,* drained by a stream that flows 2 miles to Rubicon River 3 miles west-southwest of Devil Peak (lat. 38°56'10" N, long. 120°35'35" W; near W line sec. 36, T 13 N, R 12 E). Named on Devil Peak (1950) 7.5' quadrangle. On Placerville (1893) 30' quadrangle, the name applies to a branch of present Big Grizzly Canyon.

Little Grizzly Creek [MARIPOSA]: *stream,* flows 2.5 miles to Ned Gulch (2) 5.5 miles west-northwest of El Portal (lat. 37°41'25" N, long. 119°52'50" W); the stream heads at Big Grizzly Mountain. Named on Kinsley (1947) 7.5' quadrangle. Called Little Grizzly on Yosemite (1909) 30' quadrangle.

Little Grizzly Creek [PLACER]: *stream,* flows 1.5 miles to Deep Canyon 5.25 miles southwest of Duncan Peak (lat. 39°06'35" N, long. 120°35'15" W; sec. 36, T 15 N, R 12 E). Named on Greek Store (1952) 7.5' quadrangle.

Little Grizzly Creek [SIERRA]: *stream,* flows nearly 2 miles to Big Grizzly Creek 2.5 miles south of Mount Fillmore (lat. 39°41'35" N, long. 120°50'30" W). Named on Mount Fillmore (1951) 7.5' quadrangle.

Little Grizzly Falls: see **Bunnell Cascade** [MARIPOSA].

Little Grizzly Flat [MARIPOSA]: *area*, 7.5 miles west-northwest of El Portal (lat. 37°42'45" N, long. 119°54'35" W; near SE cor. sec. 31, T 2 S, R 19 E); the place is 0.25 mile east of Little Grizzly Mountain. Named on Kinsley (1947) 7.5' quadrangle.

Little Grizzly Mountain [MARIPOSA]: *peak*, 8 miles west-northwest of El Portal (lat. 37°42'40" N, long. 119°55' W; sec. 31, T 2 S, R 19 E); the peak is 1.25 miles west-southwest of Big Grizzly Mountain. Altitude 4341 feet. Named on Kinsley (1947) 7.5' quadrangle.

Littlehales [CALAVERAS]: *locality*, 3.25 miles north-northeast of Valley Springs (lat. 38°14' N, long. 120°48'30" W). Named on Jackson (1902) 7.5' quadrangle.

Little Hetch Hetchy Valley [TUOLUMNE]: *canyon*, 2 miles long, along Tuolumne River 5 miles north-northwest of White Wolf (lat. 37°56' N, long. 119°42' W); the valley is upstream from Hetch Hetchy Valley, and now holds part of the water of Hetch Hetchy Reservoir. Named on Yosemite (1909) 30' quadrangle.

Little Horseshoe Bar: see **Horseshoe Bar** [EL DORADO-PLACER] (2).

Little Humbug Creek [SIERRA]: *stream*, flows nearly 2 miles to Humbug Creek 4.25 miles southwest of Goodyears Bar (lat. 39°30'30" N, long. 120°57' W; sec. 15, T 19 N, R 9 E). Named on Goodyears Bar (1951) and Pike (1949) 7.5' quadrangles.

Little Indian Creek [AMADOR]: *stream*, flows 12.5 miles to Cosumnes River 12 miles northwest of Ione (lat. 38°30'40" N, long. 121°00'50" W; sec. 32, T 8 N, R 9 E). Named on Amador City (1962), Carbondale (1968), and Irish Hill (1962) 7.5' quadrangles. Called Indian Creek on Jackson (1902) 30' quadrangle, and called South Indian Creek on Folsom SE (1954) 7.5' quadrangle, but United States Board on Geographic Names (1964a, p. 11) rejected both names for the stream.

Little Indian Creek [EL DORADO]: *stream*, flows nearly 6 miles to Big Canyon Creek 3 miles east-southeast of Latrobe (lat. 38°33' N, long. 120°55'50" W; sec. 13, T 8 N, R 9 E). Named on Latrobe (1949) 7.5' quadrangle.

Little Indian Creek [PLACER]: *stream*, flows 1.25 miles to Indian Creek (2) 6.5 miles north of Foresthill (lat. 39°07'05" N, long. 120°49'55" W; sec. 27, T 15 N, R 10 E). Named on Foresthill (1949) 7.5' quadrangle.

Little Iowa Canyon: see **Brushy Canyon** [EL DORADO] (1).

Little Jackass Campground [MADERA]: *locality*, 6 miles northeast of Shuteye Peak (lat. 37°24' N, long. 119°20'10" W; near S line sec. 15, T 6 S, R 24 E); the place is along West Fork Jackass Creek. Named on Shuteye Peak (1953) 15' quadrangle.

Little Jackass Creek [TUOLUMNE]: *stream*, flows 2.25 miles to Big Jackass Creek 3.25 miles south of Groveland (lat. 37°47'35" N, long. 120°13'20" W; near E line sec. 5, T 2 S, R 16 E). Named on Groveland (1947) 7.5' quadrangle.

Little Jackass Meadow: see **Soldier Meadow** [MADERA].

Littlejohns Creek [CALAVERAS]: *stream*, heads in Calaveras County and flows 65 miles to join Lone Tree Creek (2) and form French Camp Slough 6 miles south-southeast of downtown Stockton in San Joaquin County (lat. 37°52'35" N, long. 121°14'05" W). Named on Bachelor Valley (1968), Copperopolis (1962), Farmington (1968), Knights Ferry (1962), Melones Dam (1962), Oakdale (1968), Peters (1952), Salt Spring Valley (1962), and Stockton East (1952) 7.5' quadrangles. Burnham (1914) and Peters (1915) 7.5' quadrangles have the form "Little Johns Creek" for the name. Watts (p. 685) called the feature Little John Creek. United States Board on Geographic Names (1954, p. 3) rejected the forms "Littlejohn Creek" and "Little Johns Creek" for the name.

Little Kanaka Creek: see **North Fork**, under **Kanaka Creek** [SIERRA].

Little Ladies Canyon [SIERRA]: *canyon*, drained by a stream that flows 1.5 miles to Ladies Canyon 4.5 miles west of Sierra City (lat. 39°34'10" N, long. 120°43'05" W; near E line sec. 27, T 20 N, R 11 E). Named on Sierra City (1981) 7.5' quadrangle.

Little Mad Canyon [PLACER]: *canyon*, drained by a stream that flows 1 mile to Mad Canyon 3 miles east of Foresthill (lat. 39°00'50" N, long. 120°45'55" W; sec. 32, T 14 N, R 11 E). Named on Foresthill (1949) 7.5' quadrangle.

Little McKinstry Meadow [PLACER]: *area*, 3.5 miles east of Bunker Hill (lat. 39°02'55" N, long. 120°18'45" W; near NE cor. sec. 20, T 14 N, R 15 E); the place is 1.5 miles east-northeast of McKinstry Meadow. Named on Wentworth Springs (1953) 7.5' quadrangle.

Little Mill Creek [AMADOR]: *stream*, flows 2.25 miles to Mill Creek 9 miles east-northeast of Pine Grove (lat. 38°27'45" N, long. 120°30'20" W; sec. 14, T 7 N, R 13 E). Named on Devils Nose (1979) 7.5' quadrangle.

Little Mokelumne River [CALAVERAS]: *stream*, flows 4 miles to South Fork Mokelumne River nearly 2 miles south of Blue Mountain (lat. 38°18'55" N, long. 120°22' W; sec. 6, T 5 N, R 15 E). Named on Dorrington (1979) 7.5' quadrangle.

Little Mosquito Creek [PLACER]: *stream*, flows 1.25 miles to Big Mosquito Creek 9 miles south-southwest of Duncan Peak (lat. 39°02'45" N, long. 120°36'05" W; sec. 23, T 14 N, R 12 E). Named on Greek Store (1952) 7.5' quadrangle.

Little Mountain [EL DORADO]: *peak,* 1.5 miles east-northeast of Omo Ranch (lat. 38°35'30" N, long. 120°32'30" W; sec. 33, T 9 N, R 13 E). Named on Omo Ranch (1952) 7.5' quadrangle.

Little Mountain Meadow [PLACER]: *area,* 1 mile north-northwest of Bunker Hill (lat. 39°03'45" N, long. 120°23'05" W; on W line sec. 14, T 14 N, R 14 E). Named on Bunker Hill (1953) 7.5' quadrangle.

Little Needle Lake [PLACER]: *lake,* 450 feet long, 1.25 miles south-southwest of Granite Chief (lat. 39°10'50" N, long. 120°17'55" W; sec. 4, T 15 N, R 15 E); the lake is 1.25 miles south of Needle Lake. Named on Granite Chief (1953) 7.5' quadrangle.

Little Nellie Falls [MARIPOSA]: *waterfall,* 3 miles north of El Portal along Little Crane Creek (lat. 37°43'15" N, long. 119°46'55" W; sec. 32, T 2 S, R 20 E). Named on El Portal (1947) 7.5' quadrangle.

Little New York: see **Little York** [NEVADA].

Little North Fork: see **North Fork of North Fork**, under **Sacramento River** [EL DORADO-PLACER].

Little Norway: see **Meyers** [EL DORADO].

Little Oak Flat [PLACER]: *area,* 3.5 miles east of Michigan Bluff on Mosquito Ridge (lat. 39°02' N, long. 120°40'15" W; on W line sec. 29, T 14 N, R 12 E); the place is 2 miles south-southwest of Big Oak Flat. Named on Michigan Bluff (1952) 7.5' quadrangle. Colfax (1938) 30' quadrangle shows the place situated 1 mile farther northeast (sec. 20, T 14 N, R 12 E) at the site of present Ditch Camp.

Little Otter Lake [TUOLUMNE]: *lake,* 1000 feet long, 7.25 miles southwest of Tower Peak (lat. 38°04'50" N, long. 119°39'20" W); the lake is 0.25 mile south of Otter Lake. Named on Tower Peak (1956) 15' quadrangle.

Little Pebble Canyon [EL DORADO]: *canyon,* drained by a stream that flows 1 mile to Big Pebble Canyon 2.25 miles west-southwest of Old Iron Mountain (lat. 38°41'40" N, long. 120°25'50" W; sec. 28, T 10 N, R 14 E). Named on Stump Spring (1951) 7.5' quadrangle.

Little Powderhorn Creek [PLACER]: *stream,* flows 1.5 miles to Five Lakes Creek 5.5 miles northeast of Bunker Hill (lat. 39°06' N, long. 120°18'10" W; sec. 33, T 15 N, R 15 E); the mouth of the stream is less than 1 mile southwest of the mouth of Powderhorn Creek. Named on Wentworth Springs (1953) 7.5' quadrangle.

Little Prather Meadow [TUOLUMNE]: *valley,* 1.5 miles east-northeast of Liberty Hill (lat. 38°22'20" N, long. 120°04'30" W; sec. 14, T 6 N, T 17 E); the valley is 1 mile east of Big Prather Meadow. Named on Liberty Hill (1979) and Tamarack (1979) 7.5' quadrangles.

Little Rattlesnake Bar: see **Auburn** [PLACER].

Little Rattlesnake Creek [TUOLUMNE]: *stream,* flows 5.25 miles to North Fork Stanis-

laus River 6 miles west-southwest of Liberty Hill (lat. 38°19'55" N, long. 120°12'10" W; sec. 34, T 6 N, R 16 E); the stream is generally parallel to and about 1 mile south of Big Rattlesnake Creek. Named on Boards Crossing (1979) and Liberty Hill (1979) 7.5' quadrangles.

Little Reservoir [EL DORADO]: *lake,* 350 feet long, 2 miles south-southwest of Omo Ranch (lat. 38°33'15" N, long. 120°34'55" W; near S line sec. 7, T 8 N, R 13 E); the lake is 1.5 miles west-northwest of Big Reservoir. Named on Omo Ranch (1952) 7.5' quadrangle.

Little Reynolds Creek [TUOLUMNE]: *stream,* flows 4 miles to Reynolds Creek 11 miles south of Pinecrest (lat. 38°01'45" N, long. 119°59'10" W; sec. 15, T 2 N, R 18 E). Named on Cherry Lake North (1979) 7.5' quadrangle.

Little Robertson Valley: see **Little Robinsons Valley** [PLACER].

Little Robinsons Valley [PLACER]: *valley,* 11.5 miles west-southwest of Granite Chief (lat. 39°09'10" N, long. 120°29'35" W; near N line sec. 14, T 15 N, R 13 E); the valley is 0.5 mile southeast of Robinsons Flat. Named on Royal Gorge (1953) 7.5' quadrangle. United States Board on Geographic Names (1961, p. 11) rejected the name "Little Robertson Valley" for the feature.

Little Rock Creek [SIERRA]: *stream,* flows 1.25 miles to Rock Creek (1) 7.25 miles west-northwest of Goodyears Bar (lat. 39°35'10" N, long. 121°00'30" W; sec. 19, T 20 N, R 9 E). Named on Strawberry Valley (1948) 7.5' quadrangle.

Little Round Top [EL DORADO]: *peak,* nearly 3 miles north-northeast of Kirkwood (lat. 38°44'25" N, long. 120°03' W; near W line sec. 6, T 10 N, R 18 E). Altitude 9590 feet. Named on Caples Lake (1979) 7.5' quadrangle.

Little Sage Hill [PLACER]: *ridge,* west-trending, less that 1 mile long, 4.5 miles southsouthwest of Colfax (lat. 39°02'45" N, long. 121°00'10" W; mainly in sec. 20, T 14 N, R 9 E). Named on Colfax (1949) and Lake Combie (1949) 7.5' quadrangles.

Little Sailor Creek [EL DORADO]: *stream,* flows 0.5 mile to Big Sailor Creek 4.5 miles northnorthwest of Chili Bar (lat. 38°49'35" N, long. 120°50'45" W; sec. 3, T 11 N, R 10 E). Named on Garden Valley (1949) 7.5' quadrangle.

Little Sandy Campground [MADERA]: *locality,* 7 miles north-northeast of Yosemite Forks (lat. 37°27'30" N, long. 119°34' W; sec. 33, T 5 S, R 22 E); the place is along Big Creek 1 mile upstream from Big Sandy Campground. Named on Bass Lake (1953) 15' quadrangle.

Little Secret Canyon [PLACER]: *canyon,* drained by a stream that flows 2.25 miles to Secret Canyon 4 miles west-northwest of Duncan Peak (lat. 39°10'35" N, long. 120°34'55" W; sec. 1, T 15 N, R 12 E). Named on Duncan Peak (1952) 7.5' quadrangle.

Little Shadow Lake: see **Ediza Lake** [MADERA].

Little Shady Creek [NEVADA]: *stream,* flows 2.5 miles to South Yuba River 1.5 miles east-southeast of French Corral (lat. 39°17'40" N, long. 121°08'15" W; sec. 36, T 17 N, R 7 E). Named on French Corral (1948) and Nevada City (1948) 7.5' quadrangles.

Little Shady Creek: see **Blind Shady Creek** [NEVADA].

Little Shuteye Pass [MADERA]: *pass,* 2 miles north-northwest of Shuteye Peak (lat. 37°22'45" N, long. 119°26'10" W; sec. 27, T 6 S, R 23 E); the pass is 2 miles east-southeast of Little Shuteye Peak. Named on Shuteye Peak (1953) 15' quadrangle.

Little Shuteye Peak [MADERA]: *peak,* 4 miles northwest of Shuteye Peak (lat. 37°23'40" N, long. 119°28'10" W; near E line sec. 20, T 6 S, R 23 E). Altitude 8362 feet. Named on Shuteye Peak (1953) 15' quadrangle.

Little Silver Creek [EL DORADO]:

(1) *stream,* flows 2.5 miles to Rock Creek 12.5 miles north of Pollock Pines (lat. 38°53'10" N, long. 120°44'40" W; near W line sec. 15, T 12 N, R 11 E). Named on Georgetown (1949) and Tunnel Hill (1950) 7.5' quadrangles.

(2) *stream,* flows 6 miles to Silver Creek 6.5 miles north of Riverton (lat. 38°51'55" N, long. 120°26'55" W; near N line sec. 30, T 12 N, R 14 E). Named on Riverton (1950, photorevised 1973) and Robbs Peak (1950) 7.5' quadrangles.

Little Slate Creek: see **Slate Creek** [SIERRA].

Little Sluice Box [EL DORADO]: *relief feature,* 3.5 miles east of Wentworth Springs (lat. 39°01'10" N, long. 120°16'25" W; near NE cor. sec. 34, T 14 N, R 15 E); the feature is 1 mile northwest of Big Sluice Box. Named on Wentworth Springs (1953) 7.5' quadrangle.

Little Soldier Creek [EL DORADO]: *stream,* flows 1.25 miles to Soldier Creek 3.5 miles northeast of Pollock Pines (lat. 38°47'40" N, long. 120°32' W; sec. 16, T 11 N, R 13 E). Named on Pollock Pines (1950) 7.5' quadrangle.

Little South Fork Rubicon River: see **South Fork**, under **Rubicon River** [EL DORADO].

Little Steamboat Mountain [PLACER]: *peak,* 4 miles north-northeast of Bunker Hill (lat. 39°05'55" N, long. 120°20'55" W; near SE cor. sec. 36, T 15 N, R 14 E); the peak is 1 mile south-southeast of Steamboat Mountain. Named on Wentworth Springs (1953) 7.5' quadrangle.

Little Sugar Pine Mountain [EL DORADO]: *peak,* 7 miles north of Pollock Pines (lat. 38°51'45" N, long. 120°35'55" W; sec. 26, T 12 N, R 12 E). Altitude 4914 feet. Named on Pollock Pines (1950) 7.5' quadrangle.

Little Table Mountain [MADERA]: *ridge,* south- to south-southeast-trending, 3 miles

long, 12 miles east-northeast of Trigo (lat. 36°59' N, long. 119°46' W). Named on Herndon (1965) and Raymond (1962) 15' quadrangles.

Little Table Rock [SIERRA]: *peak,* 3.5 miles southwest of Mount Fillmore (lat. 39°42' N, long. 120°54'30" W; near NW cor. sec. 7, T 21 N, R 10 E); the peak is 1.5 miles west of Table Rock. Named on La Porte (1951) 7.5' quadrangle.

Little Tiger Creek [AMADOR]: *stream,* flows nearly 3 miles to Tiger Creek 4.25 miles southwest of Hames Station (lat. 38°29'55" N, long. 120°25'50" W; sec. 33, T 8 N, R 14 E). Named on Caldor (1951) 7.5' quadrangle.

Little Truckee Lake: see **Webber Lake** [SIERRA].

Little Truckee River [NEVADA-SIERRA]: *stream,* heads in Sierra County and flows 28 miles to Truckee River 6.25 miles northeast of Truckee in Nevada County (lat. 39°23'05" N, long. 120°05'35" W; sec. 28, T 18 N, R 17 E); the stream heads at Webber Lake, which first was called Little Truckee Lake (Gudde, 1949, p. 385). Named on Boca (1955), Hobart Mills (1981), Independence Lake (1981), Sierraville (1981), and Webber Peak (1981) 7.5' quadrangles. According to Morgan (p. 377), James Clyman called the stream the Wind River in 1846.

Little Truckee Summit [SIERRA]: *pass,* 7.25 miles southeast of Sierraville at the head of Cold Stream (1) (lat. 39°30'20" N, long. 120°16'55" W; at S line sec. 11, T 19 N, R 15 E). Named on Sierraville (1981) 7.5' quadrangle.

Little Twin Gulch [TUOLUMNE]: *canyon,* drained by a stream that flows 0.25 mile to Twin Gulch (2) 3 miles south-southwest of Don Pedro Camp (lat. 37°40'45" N, long. 120°25'40" W; sec. 16, T 3 S, R 14 E). Named on La Grange (1962) 7.5' quadrangle.

Little Valley: see **McNair Meadow** [SIERRA].

Little Wallace Canyon [PLACER]: *canyon,* drained by a stream that flows 2.5 miles to Wallace Canyon 1.25 miles north of Devil Peak (lat. 38°58'40" N, long. 120°33' W; sec. 17, T 13 N, R 13 E). Named on Devil Peak (1950) 7.5' quadrangle.

Little Winkle Branch: see **Lehamite Creek** [MARIPOSA].

Little Wolf Creek [NEVADA]:

(1) *stream,* flows 2.5 miles to Wolf Creek 1 mile south-southwest of downtown Grass Valley (lat. 39°12'15" N, long. 121°04' W; sec. 34, T 16 N, R 8 E). Named on Grass Valley (1949) 7.5' quadrangle.

(2) *stream,* flows 9.5 miles to Bear River 5.5 miles west-southwest of Wolf (lat. 39°01'30" N, long. 121°13'55" W; sec. 31, T 14 N, R 7 E). Named on Wolf (1949) 7.5' quadrangle.

Little Wolf Creek [SIERRA]: *stream,* flows 2.25 miles to Wolf Creek 3.5 miles east of Alleghany (lat. 39°27'55" N, long. 120°46'35" W;

near SE cor. sec. 31, T 19 N, R 11 E). Named on Alleghany (1949) 7.5' quadrangle.

Little York [NEVADA]: *locality,* 6 miles northeast of present Chicago Park (lat. 39°11'35" N, long. 120°52'25" W). Named on Colfax (1898) 30' quadrangle. Postal authorities established Little York post office in 1855, discontinued it the same year, reestablished it in 1856, and discontinued it in 1886; the place first was called Little New York, but postal authorities shortened the name (Salley, p. 123).

Little York Diggings [NEVADA]: *locality,* 5.5 miles northeast of Chicago Park (lat. 39°12' N, long. 120°52'35" W; sec. 5, T 15 N, R 10 E). Named on Chicago Park (1949) and Dutch Flat (1950) 7.5' quadrangles.

Little Yosemite Valley [MARIPOSA]: *valley,* 4.5 miles east-southeast of Yosemite Village along Merced River above Nevada Fall (lat. 37°44' N, long. 119°30'30" W). Named on Merced Peak (1953) and Yosemite (1956) 15' quadrangles. Members of the Mariposa Battalion named the valley in 1851 (Browning, 1986, p. 129).

Live Oak Bar: see **Coloma** [EL DORADO].

Live Oak Ravine [PLACER]: *canyon,* drained by a stream that flows 2 miles to Bunch Canyon 3.5 miles south-southeast of Colfax (lat. 39°03' N, long. 120°56'05" W; sec. 23, T 14 N, R 9 E). Named on Colfax (1949) 7.5' quadrangle. Colfax (1898) 30' quadrangle has the form "Liveoak Ravine" for the name.

Lizard Flat: see **Jefferson Creek** [NEVADA].

Loafer Gulch: see **Fiddletown** [AMADOR].

Loch Lane [AMADOR]: *lake,* 3350 feet long, nearly 4 miles west of Ione (lat. 38°21'40" N, long. 121°00'10" W). Named on Goose Creek (1968) and Ione (1962) 7.5' quadrangles.

Loch Leven Lakes [PLACER]: *lakes,* largest 1750 feet long, 2.5 miles southeast of Cisco Grove (lat. 39°17'10" N, long. 120°30'10" W; sec. 34, T 17 N, R 13 E, and sec. 3, T 16 N, R 13 E). Named on Cisco Grove (1955) 7.5' quadrangle. Called Lac Leven Lakes on Colfax (1938) 30' quadrangle, but United States Board on Geographic Names (1962b, p. 20) rejected this name.

Lockwood [AMADOR]: *locality,* 7 miles northeast of Pine Grove (lat. 38°29'40" N, long. 120°34'45" W). Named on Jackson (1902) 30' quadrangle. Camp's (1962) map shows Lockwood Station, and gives the name "Fosters" as an alternate designation for the place. Wheeler (1879, p. 177) listed Foster's Station and called it a public house. Salley (p. 202) noted that postal authorities established Shake Ridge post office at the site in 1875 and discontinued it in 1878; the post office name was from the manufacture of shakes in the neighborhood.

Lockwood Station: see **Lockwood** [AMADOR].

Lodgepole Campground [SIERRA]: *locality,*

5.5 miles northeast of Sierra City along North Yuba River (lat. 39°37'45" N, long. 120°34'10" W; sec. 1, T 20 N, R 12 E). Named on Clio (1981) 7.5' quadrangle.

Logan Canyon [NEVADA]: *canyon,* drained by a stream that flows 3.25 miles to South Yuba River 3 miles west-southwest of Washington (lat. 39°20'50" N, long. 120°51'10" W; near SE cor. sec. 9, T 17 N, R 10 E). Named on Alleghany (1949) and Washington 1950) 7.5' quadrangles.

Logan Meadow [MADERA]: *area,* 5 miles east of Shuteye Peak (lat. 37°21' N, long. 118°20'10" W; in and near sec. 3, T 7 S, R 24 E). Named on Kaiser (1904) 30' quadrangle.

Logan Meadow Campground [MADERA]: *locality,* 5 miles east of Shuteye Peak along Chiquito Creek (lat. 37°21'05" N, long. 119°20'10" W; near N line sec. 3, T 7 S, R 24 E); the place is at Logan Meadow. Named on Shuteye Peak (1953) 15' quadrangle.

Loganville [SIERRA]: *locality,* nearly 2 miles west of Sierra City (lat. 39°34'05" N, long. 120°40' W; sec. 30, T 20 N, R 12 E). Named on Sierra City (1981) 7.5' quadrangle. Preston (p. 403) called it Logansville. A place called Missouri Flat was located about 1 mile west of Loganville (Gudde, 1975, p. 219).

Loggers Delight Canyon [EL DORADO]: *canyon,* drained by a stream that flows 1.5 miles to Cat Creek 5.25 miles east of Caldor (lat. 38°35'30" N, long. 120°20'05" W; sec. 32, T 9 N, R 15 E). Named on Peddler Hill (1951) 7.5' quadrangle.

Logtown [EL DORADO]: *locality,* 6.5 miles south-southwest of Placerville (lat. 38°38'40" N, long. 120°51' W; near SW cor. sec. 11, T 9 N, R 10 E). Site named on Placerville (1949) 7.5' quadrangle.

Logtown: see **Mariposa** [MARIPOSA].

Logtown Ravine [EL DORADO]: *canyon,* drained by a stream that flows 2.5 miles to Slate Creek (3) 4.5 miles southwest of Placerville (lat. 38°40'35" N, long. 120°51'20" W); the canyon heads near Logtown. Named on Placerville (1893) 30' quadrangle.

Logtown Ridge [EL DORADO]: *ridge,* south-trending, 10 miles long, center 9 miles south-southwest of Placerville (lat. 38°36'30" N, long. 120°51'30" W); Logtown was on the ridge. Named on Fiddletown (1949) and Placerville (1949) 7.5' quadrangles

Lohman Ridge [SIERRA]: *ridge,* generally west-trending, 2.5 miles long, 2 miles southsoutheast of Camptonville on Sierra-Yuba county line, mainly in Yuba County (lat. 39°25'30" N, long. 121°02'15" W). Named on Camptonville (1948) 7.5' quadrangle, which shows Lohman ranch on the ridge.

Lois: see **Lake Lois** [EL DORADO].

Lois Lake [MADERA]: *lake,* 650 feet long, 4.25 miles northwest of Devils Postpile (lat. 37°40'30" N, long. 119°07'40" W). Named on Devils Postpile (1953) 15' quadrangle.

Lola: see **Mount Lola** [NEVADA].

Lola Montez Lake: see **Lower Lola Montez Lake** [NEVADA]; **Upper Lola Montez Lake** [NEVADA].

Lombardi: see **Sherman Acres** [CALAVERAS].

Lombardi Gulch [CALAVERAS]: *canyon,* drained by a stream that flows less than 1 mile to North Fork Calaveras River 2 miles southeast of Mokelumne Hill (lat. 38°16'55" N, long. 120° 40'45" W; sec. 17, T 5 N, R 12 E). Named on Mokelumne Hill (1948) 7.5' quadrangle, which shows Lombardi ranch near the mouth of the canyon.

Lombardi Point [SIERRA]: *promontory,* 8 miles north-northeast of Sierraville at the edge of Sierra Valley (lat. 39°41' N, long. 120°16'50" W; sec. 10, T 21 N, R 15 E). Named on Antelope Valley (1981) 7.5' quadrangle.

Lone Gulch [CALAVERAS]: *canyon,* drained by a stream that flows 2.5 miles to Coopers Creek 4 miles northwest of Angels Camp (lat. 36°06'30" N, long. 120°36'40" W; near W line sec. 13, T 3 N, R 12 E). Named on Angels Camp (1962) 7.5' quadrangle.

Lone Gulch [TUOLUMNE]: *canyon,* drained by a stream that flows 0.25 mile to Don Pedro Reservoir 1 mile southeast of Don Pedro Camp (lat. 37°42'20" N, long. 120°23'25" W; sec. 2, T 3 S, R 14 E). Named on La Grange (1962) 7.5' quadrangle.

Lonely Gulch [EL DORADO]: *canyon,* drained by a stream that flows 2 miles to Lake Tahoe 1.25 miles south-southeast of the town of Meeks Bay (lat. 39°01'10" N, long. 120°07' W; sec. 32, T 14 N, R 17 E). Named on Homewood (1955) and Meeks Bay (1955) 7.5' quadrangles.

Lone Sequoia Campground [MARIPOSA]: *locality,* nearly 4 miles south-southwest of Fish Camp (lat. 37°25'40" N, long. 119°40' W; sec. 10, T 6 S, R 21 E). Named on Bass Lake (1953) 15' quadrangle.

Lone Star: see **Auburn** [PLACER].

Lone Valley: see **Ione Valley** [AMADOR].

Lone Willow Slough [MADERA]: *stream,* diverges northwest from San Joaquin River 18 miles southwest of Madera (lat. 36°46'25" N, long. 120°17'10" W; sec. 25, T 13 S, R 15 E) and flows 23 miles to an artificial watercourse. Named on Firebaugh (1956), Mendota Dam (1956), and Poso Farm (1962) 7.5' quadrangles.

Loney Lake [NEVADA]: *lake,* 800 feet long, 5 miles south-southwest of English Mountain (lat. 39°23'10" N, long. 120°35'40" W; sec. 35, T 18 N, R 12 E). Named on English Mountain (1983) 7.5' quadrangle.

Loney Meadow [NEVADA]: *area,* 4.5 miles east of Graniteville (lat. 39°25'30" N, long. 120°39'15" W; sec. 17, T 18 N, R 12 E). Named on Graniteville (1982) 7.5' quadrangle.

Long: see **Deacon Long Ravine** [SIERRA].

Long Bar: see **Scotchman Creek** [NEVADA].

Long Barn [TUOLUMNE]: *settlement,* 15 miles east-northeast of Sonora (lat. 38°05'30" N, long. 120°08' W; near N line sec. 29, T 3 N, R 17 E). Named on Twain Harte (1979) 7.5' quadrangle. Postal authorities established Long Barn post office in 1930 (Frickstad, p. 216). The name is from a large barn used in the early days to house logging and freighter teams (Quimby, p. 195).

Long Canyon [CALAVERAS]: *canyon,* drained by a stream that flows less than 1 mile to Stanislaus River 6.5 miles southeast of Copperopolis (lat. 37°55'20" N, long. 120°32'45" W; sec. 21, T 1 N, R 13 E). Named on Melones Dam (1962) 7.5' quadrangle.

Long Canyon [EL DORADO]:

(1) *canyon,* 3.25 miles long, opens into the canyon of South Fork American River nearly 5 miles west-northwest of Pollock Pines (lat. 38°47'05" N, long. 120°39'55" W; sec. 20, T 11 N, R 12 E). Named on Pollock Pines (1950) and Slate Mountain (1950) 7.5' quadrangles. The canyon splits at the head into North Fork and South Fork—each fork is 1.25 miles long and is named on Pollock Pines (1950) 7.5' quadrangle.

(2) *canyon,* drained by a stream that flows 6.25 miles to Silver Fork American River 8 miles north of Leek Spring Hill (lat. 38°44'35" N, long. 120°15'25" W). Named on Leek Spring Hill (1951), Pyramid Peak (1955), and Tragedy Spring (1979) 7.5' quadrangles.

(3) *canyon,* drained by a stream that flows about 2.5 miles to Big Canyon (2) 7 miles southwest of Old Iron Mountain (lat. 38°38'20" N, long. 120°29'05" W; sec. 13, T 9 N, R 13 E). Named on Stump Spring (1951) 7.5' quadrangle.

Long Canyon [MARIPOSA]: *canyon,* drained by a stream that flows 1.25 miles to Saxon Creek 3.25 miles west-northwest of Midpines (lat. 37°33'45" N, long. 119°58'25" W; sec. 27, T 4 S, R 18 E). Named on Feliciana Mountain (1947) 7.5' quadrangle.

Long Canyon [PLACER]: *canyon,* drained by a stream that flows 11 miles to Rubicon River 8 miles west-northwest of Devil Peak (lat. 38°59'25" N, long. 120°41'10" W; sec. 7, T 13 N, R 12 E). Named on Devil Peak (1950), Greek Store (1952), and Tunnel Hill (1950) 7.5' quadrangles. The canyon divides at the head into North Fork and South Fork. North Fork is nearly 7 miles long and is named on Bunker Hill (1953) and Greek Store (1952) 7.5' quadrangles—it is shown as part of Long Canyon on Truckee (1895) 30' quadrangle. South Fork is 10.5 miles long and is named on Bunker Hill (1953) and Greek Store (1952) 7.5' quadrangles.

Long Canyon [TUOLUMNE]: *canyon,* drained by a stream that flows 3 miles to Griswold Creek 7 miles northeast of Stanislaus (lat. 38° 12'20" N, long. 120°16'30" W; near N line sec. 13, T 4 N, R 15 E). Named on Crandall Peak (1979) and Stanislaus (1948) 7.5' quadrangles.

Long Creek [MADERA]: *stream,* flows 5 miles to North Fork San Joaquin River 8 miles west of Devils Postpile (lat. 37°38'35" N, long. 119°13'40" W); the stream heads near Long Mountain. Named on Devils Postpile (1953) and Merced Peak (1953) 15' quadrangles.

Long Gulch [CALAVERAS]:

(1) *canyon,* 2 miles long, opens into the canyon of Blue Creek 5.5 miles west of Tamarack (lat. 38°26'15" N, long. 120°10'45" W; near S line sec. 23, T 7 N, R 16 E). Named on Calaveras Dome (1979) 7.5' quadrangle.

(2) *canyon,* drained by a stream that flows 1.5 miles to Shad Gulch 2.5 miles west-northwest of Paloma (lat. 38°16'25" N, long. 120° 48'30" W; sec. 19, T 5 N, R 11 E). Named on Jackson (1962) 7.5' quadrangle.

(3) *canyon,* drained by a stream that flows nearly 2 miles to North Fork Calaveras River 2.5 miles south-southeast of Mokelumne Hill (lat. 38°15'55" N, long. 120°41'20" W; near S line sec. 19, T 5 N, R 12 E). Named on Mokelumne Hill (1948) 7.5' quadrangle.

(4) *canyon,* drained by a stream that flows 2.25 miles to Rock Creek nearly 7 miles southeast of Jenny Lind (lat. 38°01'15" N, long. 120°47'20" W; sec. 17, T 2 N, R 11 E). Named on Jenny Lind (1962) 7.5' quadrangle.

(5) *canyon,* drained by a stream that flows 1 mile to Coyote Creek 2.5 miles south of Vallecito (lat. 38°03' N, long. 120°28'50" W; near S line sec. 6, T 2 N, R 14 E). Named on Columbia (1948) 7.5' quadrangle.

(6) *canyon,* drained by a stream that flows 1.5 miles to Calaveritas Creek 7 miles east-south-east of San Andreas (lat. 38°10'15" N, long. 120°33'15" W; near W line sec. 28, T 4 N, R 13 E). Named on San Andreas (1947) 15' quadrangle.

Long Gulch [EL DORADO]: *canyon,* drained by a stream that flows 1.5 miles to One Eye Creek 5 miles northeast of Chili Bar (lat. 38° 49'05" N, long. 120°45'20" W; sec. 9, T 11 N, R 11 E). Named on Garden Valley (1949) 7.5' quadrangle.

Long Gulch [TUOLUMNE]:

(1) *canyon,* drained by a stream that flows 1.5 miles to South Fork Stanislaus River nearly 3 miles north-northeast of Columbia (lat. 38°04'10" N, long. 120°22'25" W; sec. 31, T 3 N, R 15 E). Named on Columbia (1948) 7.5' quadrangle.

(2) *canyon,* drained by a stream that flows 1.5 miles to New Melones Lake 6.5 miles west-southwest of Sonora (lat. 37°56'25" N, long. 120°29'15" W; sec. 13, T 1 N, R 13 E). Named on Sonora (1948, photorevised 1973) 7.5' quadrangle.

(3) *canyon,* drained by a stream that flows 2.5 miles to Big Creek (1) 3 miles east of Groveland (lat. 37°50'25" N, long. 120°

10'35" W; near W line sec. 24, T 1 S, R 16 E). Named on Groveland (1947) 7.5' quadrangle.

(4) *canyon,* drained by a stream that flows 4.5 miles to South Fork Tuolumne River 7.25 miles southeast of Mather (lat. 37°48'30" N, long. 119°45'40" W; sec. 34, T 1 S, R 20 E). Named on Hetch Hetchy Reservoir (1956) and Lake Eleanor (1956) 15' quadrangles.

Long Hollow [MADERA]: *canyon,* nearly 3 miles long, opens into the canyon of Coarse Gold Creek 7 miles east-southeast of Knowles (lat. 37°09'40" N, long. 119°46'25" W; sec. 10, T 9 S, R 20 E). Named on Knowles (1962) 7.5' quadrangle.

Long Hollow [NEVADA]: *canyon,* drained by a stream that flows 2.25 miles to Wolf Creek 1 mile northwest of Higgins Corner (lat. 39°03'10" N, long. 121°06'25" W; sec. 20, T 14 N, R 8 E). Named on Lake Combie (1949) 7.5' quadrangle.

Long John Creek [AMADOR]: *stream,* flows 1.25 miles to Mill Creek 6.25 miles southwest of Hams Station (lat. 38°29'45" N, long. 120°28'15" W; at S line sec. 31, T 8 N, R 14 E). Named on Caldor (1951) and Devils Nose (1979) 7.5' quadrangles.

Long John Creek [PLACER]: *stream,* flows 1.5 miles to Rubicon River 4 miles west-south-west of Bunker Hill (lat. 39°01'15" N, long. 120°26'30" W; near E line sec. 31, T 14 N, R 14 E). Named on Bunker Hill (1953) 7.5' quadrangle.

Long Lake [AMADOR]: *lake,* 1050 feet long, 2.5 miles north-northeast of Mokelumne Peak (lat. 38°34'30" N, long. 120°04'50" W). Named on Mokelumne Peak (1979) 7.5' quadrangle.

Long Lake [NEVADA]: *lake,* 1200 feet long, 4.5 miles southwest of English Mountain (lat. 39°23'55" N, long. 120°36'50" W; sec. 27, T 18 N, R 12 E). Named on English Mountain (1983) 7.5' quadrangle.

Long Lake [PLACER]:

(1) *lake,* 2350 feet long, 6 miles west-south-west of Donner Pass (lat. 39°17'35" N, long. 120°25'50" W; sec. 32, T 17 N, R 14 E). Named on Soda Springs (1955) 7.5' quadrangle.

(2) *lake,* 2150 feet long, 6.25 miles east of Bunker Hill (lat. 39° 02'20" N, long. 120°15'55" W; on S line sec. 23, T 14 N, R 15 E). Named on Wentworth Springs (1953) 7.5' quadrangle.

Long Lake [TUOLUMNE]: *lake,* 3500 feet long, 13 miles east of Pinecrest (lat. 38°10'30" N, long. 119°45'10" W). Named on Pinecrest (1956) and Tower Peak (1956) 15' quadrangles. Called Beulah Lake on Dardanelles (1898, reprinted 1947) 30' quadrangle, but United States Board on Geographic Names (1960c, p. 17) rejected this name for the feature.

Long Meadow [EL DORADO]: *area,* 3.5 miles north-northeast of Robbs Peak (lat. 38°58'15"

N, long. 120°22'15" W; sec. 14, T 13 N, R 14 E). Named on Loon Lake (1952) 7.5' quadrangle.

Long Meadow [MADERA]:
(1) *area*, 8.5 miles north-northeast of Yosemite Forks (lat. 37°29'10" N, long. 119°34'45" W; near E line sec. 20, T 5 S, R 22 E). Named on Bass Lake (1953) 15' quadrangle.
(2) *area*, 9 miles north of Shuteye Peak (lat. 37°29' N, long. 119° 25' W; sec. 23, T 5 S, R 23 E). Named on Shuteye Peak (1953) 15' quadrangle.
(3) *area*, 4.5 miles north-northeast of Shuteye Peak (lat. 37°24'30" N, long. 119°23'45" W; near W line sec. 18, T 6 S, R 24 E). Named on Shuteye Peak (1953) 15' quadrangle.

Long Meadow [MARIPOSA]: *area*, 3 miles south-southeast of Cathedral Peak (lat. 37°48'45" N, long. 119°25'45" W). Named on Tuolumne Meadows (1956) 15' quadrangle. Joseph LeConte gave the name "Feldspar Valley" to the feature in 1872 (Browning, 1988, p. 79).

Long Meadow Creek [MADERA]: *stream*, flows 2.5 miles to Rainier Creek 8 miles north-northeast of Yosemite Forks (lat. 37° 28'55" N, long. 119°35'55" W; sec. 19, T 5 S, R 22 E); the stream goes through Long Meadow (1). Named on Bass Lake (1953) 15' quadrangle.

Long Mountain [MADERA]: *peak*, 6 miles east-northeast of Merced Peak (lat. 37°40'05" N, long. 119°17'40" W). Altitude 11,502 feet. Named on Merced Peak (1953) 15' quadrangle.

Long Point [NEVADA]: *ridge*, south-trending, 1.5 miles long, 9 miles northeast of Chicago Park (lat. 39°14'05" N, long. 120°50'35" W; mainly in sec. 22, T 16 N, R 10 E). Named on Dutch Flat (1950) 7.5' quadrangle.

Long Point [PLACER]:
(1) *ridge*, southwest- to west-trending, 2 miles long, 3.5 miles north-northwest of Foresthill (lat. 39°04'15" N, long. 120°50' W). Named on Foresthill (1949) 7.5' quadrangle.
(2) *ridge*, east-trending, nearly 1 mile long, 7.5 miles northeast of Auburn (lat. 38°58'15" N, long. 120°58'15" W; at NE cor. sec. 21, T 13 N, R 9 E). Named on Greenwood (1949) 7.5' quadrangle.

Long Point: see **South Long Point** [PLACER].

Long Ravine [EL DORADO]: *canyon*, drained by a stream that flows 1.5 miles to North Fork Cosumnes River 6.5 miles south-southwest of Camino (lat. 38°39'05" N, long. 120°43'55" W; sec. 11, T 9 N, R 11 E). Named on Camino (1952) 7.5' quadrangle.

Long Ravine [NEVADA]: *canyon*, drained by a stream that flows 1.25 miles to South Wolf Creek 2 miles north-northeast of Higgins Corner (lat. 39°04'05" N, long. 121°04'20" W; sec. 15, T 14 N, R 8 E). Named on Lake Combie (1949) 7.5' quadrangle.

Long Ravine [PLACER]: *canyon*, drained by a

stream that flows 1 mile to Bear River 2.5 miles north of Colfax (lat. 39°08'15" N, long. 120°56'55" W; at E line sec. 22, T 15 N, R 9 E). Named on Colfax (1950) 15' quadrangle. The stream in the canyon now enters Rollins Reservoir.

Long Ridge [MADERA]: *ridge*, south-trending, 2.5 miles long, 15 miles south of Shuteye Peak (lat. 37°08'15" N, long. 119°28'30" W). Named on Shaver Lake (1953) 15' quadrangle.

Long Valley [AMADOR]: *valley*, 4.25 miles northwest of Mokelumne Peak (lat. 38°35'05" N, long. 120°08'30" W; sec. 31, T 9 N, R 17 E). Named on Bear River Reservoir (1979) 7.5' quadrangle.

Long Valley [PLACER]: *valley*, 7.25 miles southwest of Donner Pass (lat. 39°15'20" N, long. 120°26' W; sec 17, 18, T 16 N, R 14 E). Named on Soda Springs (1955) 7.5' quadrangle.

Long Valley [TUOLUMNE]: *valley*, 5 miles south-southeast of Dardanelle (lat. 38°16'30" N, long. 119°48' W). Named on Dardanelle (1979) 7.5' quadrangle.

Long Valley: see **Greenwood** [EL DORADO]; **Upper Long Valley** [SIERRA].

Long Valley Creek [SIERRA]:
(1) *stream*, flows 10.5 miles to Lassen County 11 miles east of Loyalton (lat. 39°42'30" N, long. 120°02'20" W; at N line sec. 2, T 21 N, R 17 E); the stream goes through Upper Long Valley. Named on Evans Canyon (1978) 7.5' quadrangle. United States Board on Geographic Names (1978a, p. 6) rejected the name "Dry Valley Creek" for the feature.
(2) *stream*, flows 3.25 miles to Haypress Creek 6 miles east of Sierra City (lat. 39°33'10" N, long. 120°31'35" W; near SW cor. sec. 33, T 20 N, R 13 E). Named on Haypress Valley (1981) and Sattley (1981) 7.5' quadrangles. Downieville (1897) 30' quadrangle used the name "Hay Press Valley" for the canyon of the stream, and has the name "Long Valley Creek" for a stream situated about 1 mile farther northwest. United States Board on Geographic Names (1960a, p. 15) rejected the name "Haypress Creek" for present Long Valley Creek (2).

Long Valley Creek [TUOLUMNE]: *stream*, flows 5 miles to Eagle Creek (2) nearly 3 miles south of Dardanelle (lat. 38°17'55" N, long. 119°49'55" W; sec. 12, T 5 N, R 19 E); the stream goes through Long Valley. Named on Dardanelles Cone (1956) 15' quadrangle. Called Eagle Creek on Dardanelles (1898) 30' quadrangle.

Long Valley Creek: see **Dead Horse Canyon** [SIERRA].

Lookout Mountain [EL DORADO]: *peak*, 8.5 miles north of Pollock Pines (lat. 38°53' N, long. 120°33'35" W; sec. 18, T 12 N, R 13 E). Altitude 5159 feet. Named on Devil Peak (1950) 7.5' quadrangle.

Lookout Mountain [MARIPOSA]: *peak,* 5.5 miles south-southeast of Mariposa (lat. 37°24'25" N, long. 119°56'25" W; on E line sec. 13, T 6 S, R 18 E). Altitude 2633 feet. Named on Mariposa (1947) 7.5' quadrangle.

Lookout Mountain [PLACER]: *peak,* 6.5 miles west-southwest of Martis Peak (lat. 39°15'45" N, long. 120°08'45" W; sec. 1, T 16 N, R 16 E). Altitude 8104 feet. Named on Truckee (1955) 7.5' quadrangle.

Lookout Point [TUOLUMNE]: *locality,* 11.5 miles southeast of Pinecrest (lat. 38°03'25" N, long. 119°52'40" W; sec. 3, T 2 N, R 19 E). Named on Cherry Lake North (1979) 7.5' quadrangle.

Loomis [PLACER]: *town,* 3 miles northeast of Rocklin (lat. 38°49'15" N, long. 121°11'35" W; near E line sec. 9, T 11 N, R 7 E). Named on Rocklin (1967) 7.5' quadrangle. Postal authorities established Placer post office in 1861, changed the name to Smithville in 1862, to Pino in 1869, and to Loomis in 1890 (Frickstad, p. 121, 122). The name "Smithville" recalls L.G. Smith, who kept a store at the place; the name "Pino" was from the old mining camp called Pine Grove, which was in Secret Ravine (2) about 1.5 miles from present Loomis (Hoover, Rensch, and Rensch, p. 272). Railroad officials named the town in 1884 for Jim Loomis, the local railroad agent, postmaster, and saloonkeeper (Gudde, 1949, p. 193).

Looney Creek [TUOLUMNE]: *stream,* flows 5.25 miles to Bourland Creek 8 miles east-southeast of Long Barn (lat. 38°01'50" N, long. 120°00'15" W; sec. 16, T 2 N, R 18 E). Named on Long Barn (1956) and Pinecrest (1956) 15' quadrangles. The misspelled name recalls Jerome Loney, Joseph Loney, and James Loney, all of whom patented land in the neighborhood about 1890 (Browning, 1986, p. 131).

Loon Lake [EL DORADO]: *lake,* behind a dam on Gerle Creek 1.5 miles east-southeast of Wentworth Springs (lat. 39°00'10" N, long. 120°18'35" W; on W line sec. 4, T 13 N, R 15 E). Named on Granite Chief (1953) and Robbs Peak (1952) 15' quadrangles. Loon Lake (1952, photorevised 1973) and Wentworth Springs (1953, photorevised 1973) 7.5' quadrangles show an enlarged lake. United States Board on Geographic Names (1978a, p. 6) rejected the names "Loon Lake Reservoir" and "Pleasant Lake" for the feature. California Division of Highways' (1934) map has the name "Bisbee Lake" for a southwest arm of Loon Lake (on W line sec. 8, T 13 N, R 15 E) that is shown as an unnamed part of Loon Lake on Robbs Peak (1952) 15' quadrangle.

Loon Lake Reservoir: see **Loon Lake** [EL DORADO].

Lord [TUOLUMNE]: *locality,* 3.5 miles southeast of Long Barn along Rush Creek (2) (lat. 38°03'30" N, long. 120°04'50" W). Named on Big Trees (1891) 30' quadrangle.

Lord Meadow [TUOLUMNE]: *area,* 13 miles east-southeast of Pinecrest along Cherry Creek (lat. 38°05'50" N, long. 119°47'30" W). Named on Pinecrest (1956) 15' quadrangle.

Lord Spring [TUOLUMNE]: *spring,* 2 miles north-northwest of Columbia (lat. 38°03'50" N, long. 120°24'50" W; near NE cor. sec. 3, T 2 N, R 14 E). Named on Columbia (1948) 7.5' quadrangle.

Lorenz Bar: see **Rattlesnake Bar** [EL DO-RADO-PLACER].

Lost Bear Meadow [MARIPOSA]: *area,* 7 miles south of Yosemite Village (lat. 37°38'45" N, long. 119°35'45" W; sec. 30, T 3 S, R 22 E). Named on Yosemite (1956) 15' quadrangle. Browning (1986, p. 132) attributed the name to an incident concerning a small girl who was lost in 1957, and after she was found unharmed she claimed that she was not lost, but that a bear that she saw went away and was lost.

Lost Camp: see **Blue Canyon** [PLACER] (2).

Lost Canyon [PLACER]: *canyon,* drained by a stream that flows 1.25 miles to North Fork of Middle Fork American River 5.5 miles west-southwest of Duncan Peak (lat. 39°07'35" N, long. 120°36'25" W; at S line sec. 23, T 15 N, R 12 E). Named on Duncan Peak (1952) 7.5' quadrangle.

Lost Canyon Creek [EL DORADO]: *stream,* flows 1.25 miles to Slab Creek 7 miles north-northwest of Pollock Pines (lat. 38°51'10" N, long. 120°38'35" W; near S line sec. 28, T 12 N, R 12 E). Named on Slate Mountain (1950) 7.5' quadrangle.

Lost City [CALAVERAS]: *locality,* 11 miles west of Angels Camp along Bear Creek (3) (lat. 38°05'10" N, long. 120°44'55" W; sec. 27, T 3 N, R 11 E). Named on Salt Spring Valley (1962) 7.5' quadrangle. The place also was called Stone City and Stone Creek Settlement (Gudde, 1975, p. 199).

Lost Claim Camp Ground [TUOLUMNE]: *locality,* 10 miles east of Groveland (lat. 37°49'15" N, long. 120°02'50" W; at E line sec. 25, T 1 S, R 17 E). Named on Jawbone Ridge (1947) 7.5' quadrangle.

Lost Corner Mountain [EL DORADO]: *peak,* 4.5 miles west-southwest of the town of Meeks Bay (lat. 39°00'50" N, long. 120°12'10" W; at W line sec. 34, T 14 N, R 16 E). Altitude 8261 feet. Named on Homewood (1955) 7.5' quadrangle.

Lost Creek [TUOLUMNE]: *stream,* flows 2.5 miles to Reynolds Creek 11 miles south of Pinecrest (lat. 38°01'50" N, long. 119°59'45" W; sec. 16, T 2 N, R 18 E). Named on Cherry Lake North (1979) 7.5' quadrangle.

Lost Dog Lake [MADERA]: *lake,* 300 feet long, 2.25 miles west-northwest of Devils Postpile (lat. 37°38'20" N, long. 119°07' W). Named on Devils Postpile (1953) 15' quadrangle.

Lost Lake [EL DORADO]:

(1) *lake,* 1000 feet long, 3.5 miles west-south-west of the town of Meeks Bay (lat. 39°00'50" N, long. 120°10'50" W; sec. 35, T 14 N, R 16 E). Named on Homewood (1955) 7.5' quadrangle.

(2) *lake,* 800 feet long, 5.5 miles southwest of Phipps Peak (lat. 38° 54'30" N, long. 120°14' W; near NE cor. sec. 8, T 12 N, R 16 E). Named on Rockbound Valley (1955) 7.5' quadrangle.

(3) *lake,* 450 feet long, 5 miles northwest of Echo Summit (lat. 38° 51'40" N, long. 120°05'45" W). Named on Echo Lake (1955) 7.5' quadrangle.

Lost Lake [MADERA]:
(1) *lake,* 750 feet long, 10 miles north of Shuteye Peak (lat. 37°29'45" N, long. 119°27'40" W; sec. 16, T 5 S, R 23 E). Named on Shuteye Peak (1953) 15' quadrangle.

(2) *lake,* 500 feet long, nearly 9 miles west of Devils Postpile (lat. 37°38'10" N, long. 119°14'30" W). Named on Devils Postpile (1953) 15' quadrangle.

Lost Lake [SIERRA]: *lake,* 200 feet long, 5.5 miles north of Sierra City (lat. 39°38'35" N, long. 120°39'05" W; sec. 32, T 21 N, R 12 E). Named on Gold Lake (1981) 7.5' quadrangle.

Lost Lake [TUOLUMNE]: *lake,* 1000 feet long, 8 miles northwest of Tower Peak (lat. 38°13'50" N, long. 119°38'50" W; on S line sec. 34, T 5 N, R 21 E). Named on Tower Peak (1956) 15' quadrangle.

Lost Lake Creek [MADERA]: *stream,* flows 1 mile to Mugler Creek nearly 10 miles north of Shuteye Peak (lat. 37°29'25" N, long. 119° 26'40" W; near SW cor. sec. 15, T 5 S, R 23 E); the stream heads at Lost Lake (1). Named on Shuteye Peak (1953) 15' quadrangle.

Lost Valley [MARIPOSA]: *area,* 8.5 miles south-southwest of Cathedral Peak along Merced River (lat. 37°44'35" N, long. 119° 28'25" W). Named on Merced Peak (1953) 15' quadrangle.

Lotus [EL DORADO]: *village,* 1 mile west of Coloma (lat. 38°48' N, long. 120°54'30" W; sec. 18, T 11 N, R 10 E). Named on Coloma (1949) 7.5' quadrangle, which shows Uniontown cemetery near the site. In 1849 the community was called Marshall, for James W. Marshall, but in 1850 the name was changed to Uniontown in honor of the admission of California to the Union that year; the name was changed to Lotus when postal authorities established Lotus post office at the place in 1881 (Frickstad, p. 27; Hoover, Rensch, and Rensch, p. 86). A mining camp called Michigan Flat was situated near present Lotus (Yohalem, p. 87).

Loucks Creek [CALAVERAS]: *stream,* flows 4 miles to Tulloch Lake 4.5 miles south-south-east of Copperopolis (lat. 37°55'30" N, long. 120°35'55" W; sec. 24, T 1 N, R 12 E). Named on Melones Dam (1962) 7.5' quadrangle.

Louisa: see **Relief** [NEVADA].

Louise: see **Lake Louise** [PLACER].

Louise Point [MARIPOSA]: *peak,* 0.5 mile south of Coulterville (lat. 37°42'20" N, long. 120°11'35" W; sec. 3, T 3 S, R 16 E). Named on Coulterville (1947) 7.5' quadrangle.

Louisiana Bar [EL DORADO] *locality,* 2 miles north-northwest of Cool along Middle Fork American River 0.25 mile above the mouth of Middle Fork (lat. 38°54'45" N, long. 121°01'55" W; near N line sec. 12, T 12 N, R 8 E). Named on Auburn (1953) 7.5' quadrangle.

Louisville [EL DORADO]: *locality,* 3.25 miles north of present Chili Bar (lat. 38°48'45" N, long. 120°49'15" W). Named on Placerville (1893) 30' quadrangle.

Louisville: see **Greenwood** [EL DORADO].

Louse Canyon [TUOLUMNE]: *canyon,* 2 miles long, 10 miles east-southeast of Pinecrest along West Fork Cherry Creek (lat. 38°08'40" N, long. 119°49'15" W). Named on Pinecrest (1956) 15' quadrangle.

Lousey Level: see **Rice Crossing** [NEVADA].

Lousy Point: see **Dollar Point** [PLACER].

Love Creek [CALAVERAS]: *stream,* flows 6 miles to join Moran Creek and form Mill Creek (2) 8 miles northeast of Murphys (lat. 38°13' N, long. 120°21'25" W; sec. 7, T 4 N, R 15 E). Named on Dorrington (1979) and Stanislaus (1948) 7.5' quadrangles.

Lovejoy Camp [EL DORADO]: *locality,* 6.5 miles north of Pollock Pines (lat. 38°51'30" N, long. 120°34'20" W; near W line sec. 30, T 12 N, R 13 E). Named on Pollock Pines (1950) 7.5' quadrangle.

Loveless Dredgings [EL DORADO]: *locality,* 2.25 miles west-southwest of Omo Ranch along Brownsville Creek (lat. 38°34' N, long. 120°36'25" W; at N line sec. 12, T 8 N, R 12 E). Named on Omo Ranch (1952) 7.5' quadrangle.

Lovers Leap [EL DORADO]: *relief feature,* 3.5 miles south-southeast of Pyramid Peak (lat. 38°48' N, long. 120°08' W; near W line sec. 17, T 11 N, R 17 E). Named on Pyramid Peak (1955) 7.5' quadrangle. Postal authorities established Lovers Leap post office, named for the relief feature, 1 mile southwest of Camp Sacramento post office in 1919 and discontinued it in 1929 (Salley, p. 128).

Lovers Leap [PLACER]: *relief feature,* 2.5 miles southeast of Dutch Flat above Giant Gap (lat. 39°10'25" N, long. 120°48'25" W; on E line sec. 2, T 15 N, R 10 E). Named on Dutch Flat (1950) 7.5' quadrangle.

Loves Falls [SIERRA]: *waterfall,* 2 miles northeast of Sierra City along North Yuba River (lat. 39°34'40" N, long. 120°36'25" W; near NE cor. sec. 27, T 20 N, R 12 E). Named on Haypress Valley (1981) 7.5' quadrangle.

Low Divide: see **Altaville** [CALAVERAS].

Lowell Hill [NEVADA]: *locality,* 6.5 miles south of Washington (lat. 39°15'55" N, long. 120°47'35" W; at E line sec. 12, T 16 N, R 10

E). Site named on Washington (1950) 7.5' quadrangle. Postal authorities established Lowell Hill post office in 1878 and discontinued it in 1918 (Frickstad, p. 114). Whitney's (1873) map shows a place called Mammoth Spring 1 mile east-southeast of Lowell Hill, and a place called Kinders Diggs 1.5 miles east of Lowell Hill.

Lowell Hill Ridge [NEVADA]: *ridge,* southwest-trending, 5.5 miles long, 7 miles west-south-west of Yuba Gap (lat. 39°17'10" N, long. 120°44'30" W); Lowell Hill is about 1 mile west of the southwest end of the ridge. Named on Blue Canyon (1955) and Washington (1950) 7.5' quadrangles.

Lower Agua Fria: see **Agua Fria** [MARIPOSA].

Lower Bear River Campground [AMADOR]: *locality,* 8.5 miles west of Mokelumne Peak on the north side of Lower Bear River Reservoir (lat. 38°33'10" N, long. 120°15' W; near S line sec. 7, T 8 N, R 16 E). Named on Bear River Reservoir (1979) 7.5' quadrangle.

Lower Bear River Reservoir [AMADOR]: *lake,* behind a dam on Bear River 6.5 miles east of Hams Station (lat. 38°32'15" N, long. 120°15'15" W; at S line sec. 18, T 8 N, R 16 E); the feature is below Bear River Reservoir. Named on Bear River Reservoir (1979) and Peddler Hill (1951, photorevised 1973) 7.5' quadrangles.

Lower Brother [MARIPOSA]: *relief feature,* nearly 2 miles west-southwest of Yosemite Village on the north side of Yosemite Valley (lat. 37°44'15" N, long. 119°36'50" W); the feature is one of the group called Three Brothers. Named on Yosemite (1956) 15' quadrangle.

Lower Calaveritas: see **Caliveritas** [CALAVERAS].

Lower Castle Creek [NEVADA]: *stream,* flows 4 miles to South Yuba River 4.25 miles west-northwest of Donner Pass (lat. 39°20'05" N, long. 120°24'05" W; near E line sec. 16, T 17 N, R 14 E); the stream heads west of Castle Peak. Named on Norden (1955) and Soda Springs (1955) 7.5' quadrangles.

Lower Chiquito Campground [MADERA]: *locality,* 5 miles north-northeast of Shuteye Peak (lat. 37°24'50" N, long. 119°23' W; near N line sec. 18, T 6 S, R 24 E); the place is along Chiquito Creek 7 miles downstream from Upper Chiquito Campground. Named on Shuteye Peak (1953) 15' quadrangle.

Lower Echo Lake [EL DORADO]: *lake,* nearly 1.5 miles long, 2.25 miles northwest of Echo Summit (lat. 38°50'20" N, long. 120°03'20" W); the feature is east of Upper Echo Lake. Named on Echo Lake (1955) 7.5' quadrangle. Called Echo Lake on Pyramid Peak (1896) 30' quadrangle.

Lower Falls [MADERA]: *waterfall,* 2 miles south of Devils Postpile on Middle Fork San Joaquin River (lat. 37°35'40" N, long.

119°05'15" W). Named on Devils Postpile (1953) 15' quadrangle.

Lower Forni [EL DORADO]: *locality,* nearly 5 miles southwest of Pyramid Peak (lat. 38°48'10" N, long. 120°13'40" W; near W line sec. 16, T 11 N, R 16 E); the place is 3.25 miles west-southwest of Upper Forni. Named on Pyramid Peak (1955) 7.5' quadrangle.

Lower Hell Hole [PLACER]: *valley,* 2.25 miles north-northwest of Bunker Hill along Rubicon River (lat. 39°05' N, long. 120°23'30" W). Named on Granite Chief (1953) 15' quadrangle. Truckee (1940) 30' quadrangle has the form "Lower Hellhole" for the name. Water of Hell Hole Reservoir now floods the valley.

Lower Lola Montez Lake [NEVADA]: *lake,* 1050 feet long, nearly 6 miles west-northwest of Donner Pass (lat. 39°20'55" N, long. 120°25'25" W; sec. 8, T 17 N, R 14 E); the feature is 0.25 mile east-southeast of Upper Lola Montez Lake. Named on Soda Springs (1955) 7.5' quadrangle.

Lower Meadow [PLACER]: *area,* 5.25 miles west of Bunker Hill in South Fork Long Canyon (lat. 39°02'30" N, long. 120°28'45" W; at SW cor. sec. 24, T 14 N, R 13 E). Named on Bunker Hill (1953) 7.5' quadrangle.

Lower Merced Pass Lake [MADERA]: *lake,* 1000 feet long, 3 miles west of Merced Peak (lat. 37°37'35" N, long. 119°26'50" W); the lake is less than 0.5 mile west-northwest of Upper Merced Pass Lake. Named on Merced Peak (1953) 15' quadrangle.

Lower Ottoway Lake [MADERA]: *lake,* 1900 feet long, 1.5 miles west-northwest of Merced Peak (lat. 37°38'35" N, long. 119°25'05" W); the lake is along Ottoway Creek 1.5 miles west of Ottoway Peak. Named on Merced Peak (1953) 15' quadrangle.

Lower Rancheria: see **Drytown** [AMADOR]; **Rancheria** [AMADOR].

Lower Relief Valley [TUOLUMNE]: *valley,* 13 miles east-northeast of Pinecrest (lat. 38°15' N, long. 119°45'30" W); the valley is along Relief Creek 1.5 miles north-northeast of Upper Relief Valley. Named on Dardanelles Cone (1956) and Pinecrest (1956) 15' quadrangles. Called Relief Valley on Dardanelles (1898) 30' quadrangle. Relief Valley took its name from an incident in the early 1850's, when a party of emigrants waited at the place until assistance arrived (Hoover, Rensch, and Rensch, p. 566).

Lower Rock Lake [NEVADA]: *lake,* 900 feet long, 4 miles west-southwest of English Mountain along Texas Creek (lat. 39°25'45" N, long. 120°37'15" W; near W line sec. 15, T 18 N, R 12 E); the feature is 600 feet downstream from Rock Lake. Named on English Mountain (1983) 7.5' quadrangle.

Lower Salmon Lake [SIERRA]: *lake,* 2500 feet long, 6 miles north of Sierra City (lat. 39°39' N, long. 120°38'30" W; at W line sec. 28, T 21 N, R 12 E); the feature is along Salmon

Creek 0.5 mile downstream from Upper Salmon Lake. Named on Gold Lake (1981) 7.5' quadrangle.

Lower Sardine Lake [SIERRA]: *lake,* 2200 feet long, 3.5 miles north of Sierra City (lat. 39°36'55" N, long. 120°37'35" W; mainly in sec. 9, T 20 N, R 12 E); the feature is along upper reaches of Sardine Creek less than 0.25 mile downstream from Upper Sardine Lake. Named on Haypress Valley (1981) and Sierra City (1981) 7.5' quadrangles.

Lower Town: see **Mosquito Creek** [EL DORADO].

Lower Velma Lake [EL DORADO]: *lake,* 2400 feet long, 1.25 miles south-southeast of Phipps Peak (lat. 38°56'20" N, long. 120°08'25" W; near S line sec. 30, T 13 N, R 17 E); the lake is less than 1 mile north-north-east of Upper Velma Lake. Named on Rockbound Valley (1955) 7.5' quadrangle. A Forest Service crew—at the father's request—named Lower Velma Lake, Middle Velma Lake, and Upper Velma Lake in 1900 for the baby daughter of Harry Oswald Comstock (Lekisch, p. 145).

Lower Virginia Falls: see **White Cascade** [TUOLUMNE].

Lower Yosemite Fall [MARIPOSA]: *waterfall,* 0.5 mile west-northwest of Yosemite Village along Yosemite Creek (lat. 37°45'05" N, long. 119°35'45" W); the feature is nearly 0.5 mile south of Upper Yosemite Fall. Named on Hetch Hetchy Reservoir (1956) 15' quadrangle. Upper Yosemite Fall and Lower Yosemite Fall together are called Yosemite Falls on Yosemite (1909) 30' quadrangle. Hoffmann and Gardner's (1863-1867) map has the name "Yosemite Fall" for the pair of waterfalls.

Loyalton [SIERRA]: *town,* 32 miles east-north-east of Downieville in Sierra Valley (lat. 39°40'35" N, long. 120°14'30" W; around NE cor. sec. 13, T 21 N, R 15 E); the town is along Smithneck Creek. Named on Loyalton (1981) 7.5' quadrangle. Postal authorities established Loyalton post office in 1864 (Frickstad, p. 184), and the town incorporated in 1901. The name is from Union sympathies among the townsfolk during the Civil War; the place first was called Smith's Neck (Gudde, 1949, p. 196). Postal Route (1884) map shows a place called Oneida located about 10 miles east of Loyalton. Postal authorities established Oneida post office in 1882 and discontinued it in 1885; the name was from a place in New York State (Salley, p. 161).

Lucas Gulch [TUOLUMNE]: *canyon,* drained by a stream that flows 1.5 miles to Don Pedro Reservoir 2 miles southeast of Don Pedro Camp (lat. 37°42'05" N, long. 120°22'35" W; sec. 1, T 3 S, R 14 E). Named on La Grange (1962) and Penon Blanco Peak (1962) 7.5' quadrangles.

Lucas Hill [NEVADA]: *peak,* 3 miles southwest of Wolf (lat. 39°01'35" N, long. 121°10'35"

W; sec. 34, T 14 N, R 7 E). Altitude 1490 feet. Named on Wolf (1949) 7.5' quadrangle.

Lucille: see **Lake Lucille** [EL DORADO].

Lucky Dog Creek [SIERRA]: *stream,* flows nearly 2.5 miles to Oregon Creek 2 miles west-northwest of Alleghany (lat. 39°29' N, long. 120°52'30" W; sec. 29, T 19 N, R 10 E). Named on Alleghany (1949), Downieville (1951), and Pike (1949) 7.5' quadrangles.

Lucky Hill Ravine [SIERRA]: *canyon,* drained by a stream that flows 1 mile to Slate Creek 9 miles southwest of Mount Fillmore (lat. 39°38'55" N, long. 120°58'40" W; sec. 28, T 21 N, R 9 E). Named on La Porte (1951) 7.5' quadrangle, which shows Lucky Hill mine near the head of the canyon.

Lucky Point [TUOLUMNE]: *peak,* 2 miles south-southeast of Don Pedro Camp (lat. 37°41'15" N, long. 120°23'45" W; sec. 11, T 3 S, R 14 E). Named on La Grange (1962) 7.5' quadrangle.

Luke Camp [TUOLUMNE]: *locality,* 3 miles south-southeast of Duckwall Mountain (lat. 37°55'30" N, long. 120°05'55" W). Named on Sonora (1897) 30' quadrangle.

Lukens Lake [TUOLUMNE]: *lake,* 1200 feet long, 2 miles east-southeast of White Wolf (lat. 37°51'35" N, long. 119°36'55" W; sec. 13, T 1 S, R 21 E). Named on Hetch Hetchy Reservoir (1956) 15' quadrangle. R.B. Marshall of United States Geological Survey named the lake in 1894 to honor Theodore Parker Lukens, mayor of Pasadena and a conservationist (Hanna, p. 178).

Lunch Creek [SIERRA]: *stream,* flows 1.5 miles to North Yuba River 7.5 miles east-northeast of Sierra City (lat. 39°37' N, long. 120°30'25" W; sec. 10, T 20 N, R 13 E). Named on Calpine (1981), Clio (1981), and Haypress Valley (1981) 7.5' quadrangles.

Lunch Meadow [TUOLUMNE]: *area,* 9 miles northwest of Tower Peak along Summit Creek (lat. 38°13'05" N, long. 119°41'20" W; near S line sec. 5, T 4 N, R 21 E). Named on Tower Peak (1956) 15' quadrangle.

Lundeen: see **Camp Lundeen** [NEVADA].

Lupine Campground [MADERA]: *locality,* 6.25 miles southeast of Yosemite Forks on the southwest side of Bass Lake (1) (lat. 37°18'30" N, long. 119°32'35" W; near W line sec. 23, T 7 S, R 22 E). Named on Bass Lake (1953) 15' quadrangle.

Lupine Point [NEVADA]: *relief feature,* 3.25 miles southwest of Washington (lat. 39°20' N, long. 120°51'10" W; at SW cor. sec. 15, T 17 N, R 10 E). Named on Washington (1950) 7.5' quadrangle.

Lusk Meadows [SIERRA]: *area,* 6.25 miles north of Sierra City (lat. 39°39'25" N, long. 120°37'55" W; sec. 28, T 21 N, R 12 E). Named on Gold Lake (1981) 7.5' quadrangle.

Luther Pass [EL DORADO]: *pass,* 5.5 miles south-southwest of Freel Peak on El Dorado-Alpine county line (lat. 38°47'15" N, long.

119°56'40" W; sec. 24, T 11 N, R 18 E). Named on Freel Peak (1955) 7.5' quadrangle. Called Luther's Pass on Wheeler's (1876-1877a) map. According to one account, the pass was named for Lieutenant Luther, who selected a route there for an army convoy in 1857; according to another account, the name is for Ira M. Luther, who crossed the pass in 1854 in a wagon (Gudde, 1969, p. 186; Long, p. 12).

Lyell: see **Mount Lyell** [MADERA-TUOLUMNE].

Lyell Canyon [TUOLUMNE]: *canyon,* 9 miles long, opens into Tuolumne Meadows 4.5 miles southwest of Tioga Pass (lat. 37°52'10" N, long. 119°20'15" W); the canyon is along Lyell Fork. Named on Tuolumne Meadows (1956) 15' quadrangle.

Lyell Fork [MADERA]: *stream,* flows 6 miles to join Merced Peak Fork and form Merced River 5.25 miles north-northeast of Merced Peak (lat. 37°42'05" N, long. 119°20'50" W). Named on Merced Peak (1953) 15' quadrangle. United States Board on Geographic Names (1978c, p. 3) rejected the names "Merced River" and "North Fork" for the stream.

Lyell Fork [TUOLUMNE]: *stream,* flows 12 miles to join Dana Fork and form Tuolumne River 5.5 miles west-southwest of Tioga Pass (lat. 37°52'30" N, long. 119°21' W; near SE cor. sec. 5, T 1 S, R 24 E); the stream heads near Mount Lyell and goes through Lyell Canyon. Named on Tuolumne Meadows (1956) 15' quadrangle.

Lyell Glacier [TUOLUMNE]: *glacier,* 11.5 miles south of Tioga Pass (lat. 37°44'35" N, long. 119°16'10" W); the glacier is north of Mount Lyell. Named on Merced Peak (1953) 15' quadrangle.

Lynchburg Hill [PLACER]: *peak,* 4.5 miles west-northwest of Devil Peak on Ralston Ridge (lat. 38°59'40" N, long. 120°37'15" W; sec. 10, T 13 N, R 12 E). Named on Devil Peak (1950) and Tunnel Hill (1950) 7.5' quadrangles.

Lyon Peak [PLACER]: *peak,* 1.5 miles west-northwest of Granite Chief (lat. 39°12'25" N, long. 120°18'50" W; sec. 28, T 16 N, R 15 E). Altitude 8891 feet. Named on Granite Chief (1953) 7.5' quadrangle.

Lyons [EL DORADO]: *locality,* 3.25 miles west-southwest of Pyramid Peak (lat. 38°49'15" N, long. 120°12'40" W; near NE cor. sec. 9, T 11 N, R 16 E). Site named on Pyramid Peak (1955) 7.5' quadrangle.

Lyons: see **Confidence** [TUOLUMNE].

Lyons Creek [EL DORADO]: *stream,* flows 7 miles to South Fork Silver Creek 3.25 miles north-northeast of Kyburz (lat. 38°48'55" N, long. 120°15'40" W; sec. 7, T 11 N, R 16 E); Lyons was along the stream. Named on Kyburz (1952) and Pyramid Peak (1955) 7.5' quadrangles.

Lyons Creek [TUOLUMNE]: *stream,* flows 4 miles to Lyons Reservoir 5.5 miles northeast of Twain Harte (lat. 38°05'50" N, long. 120°09'35" W; sec. 24, T 3 N, R 16 E). Named on Hull Creek (1979), Strawberry (1979), and Twain Harte (1979) 7.5' quadrangles.

Lyons Gulch [MARIPOSA]: *canyon,* drained by a stream that flows 4 miles to Sherlock Creek nearly 4 miles east-northeast of Bear Valley (2) (lat. 37°35' N, long. 120°03'05" W; sec. 13, T 4 S, R 17 E). Named on Bear Valley (1947) 7.5' quadrangle.

Lyons Lake [EL DORADO]: *lake,* 1150 feet long. 1.25 miles west-northwest of Pyramid Peak (lat. 38°51' N, long. 120°10'50" W). Named on Pyramid Peak (1955) 7.5' quadrangle.

Lyons Reservoir [TUOLUMNE]: *lake,* behind a dam on South Fork Stanislaus River 5 miles northeast of Twain Harte (lat. 38°05'40" N, long. 120°10' W); Lyons Creek joins South Fork Stanislaus River in the lake. Named on Twain Harte (1979) 7.5' quadrangle.

Lytton Lake [NEVADA]: *lake,* 400 feet long, 1 mile northwest of Donner Pass (lat. 39°19'30" N, long. 120°20'20" W; sec. 17, T 17 N, R 15 E). Named on Norden (1955) 7.5' quadrangle. On Truckee (1940) 30' quadrangle, present Flora Lake is called Lytton Lake.

– M –

MacBride: see **Camp MacBride** [TUOLUMNE].

Macedon Canyon [PLACER]: *canyon,* drained by a stream that flows 0.5 mile to Secret Canyon 4.5 miles west of Duncan Peak (lat. 39°09'55" N, long. 120°35'40" W; near W line sec. 12, T 15 N, R 12 E). Named on Duncan Peak (1952) 7.5' quadrangle.

Macedon Ridge [PLACER]: *ridge,* southwest-trending, 2.5 miles long, 5 miles west-north-west of Duncan Peak (lat. 39°10'15" N, long. 120°36'05" W). Named on Duncan Peak (1952) 7.5' quadrangle.

Mack: see **Billy Mack Canyon** [NEVADA]; **Billy Mack Flat** [NEVADA].

Mack House [SIERRA]: *locality,* 1.5 miles southwest of Alleghany (lat. 39°27'25" N, long. 120°52' W; on W line sec. 5, T 18 N, R 10 E). Named on Alleghany (1949) 7.5' quadrangle.

Macklin Creek [NEVADA]: *stream,* flows 2 miles to Middle Yuba River 7.5 miles northeast of Graniteville (lat. 39°31'10" N, long. 120°37'30" W; near NE cor. sec. 16, T 19 N, R 12 E). Named on Haypress Valley (1981) 7.5' quadrangle. The name commemorates Robert M. Macklin, fisheries management supervisor for California Department of Fish and Game from 1940 until 1970 (United States Board on Geographic Names, 1971, p. 3).

Macks Gulch [CALAVERAS]: *canyon,* drained by a stream that flows 3.5 miles to O'Neil

Creek 5.5 miles north of Murphys (lat. 38°13'15" N, long. 120°28'10" W; sec. 7, T 4 N, R 14 E). Named on Murphys (1948) 7.5' quadrangle.

Maclure: see **Mount Maclure** [MADERA-TUOLUMNE].

Maclure Creek [TUOLUMNE]: *stream,* flows 2 miles to Lyell Fork 9.5 miles south of Tioga Pass (lat. 37°46'30" N, long. 119°15'40" W); the stream heads north of Mount Maclure. Named on Tuolumne Meadows (1956) 15' quadrangle. The name is for William Maclure, a pioneer American geologist (United States Board on Geographic Names, 1934, p. 15).

Maclure Fork: see **Lewis Creek** [MADERA-MARIPOSA].

Macnider Switch [CALAVERAS]: *locality,* 1.5 miles west-southwest of San Andreas along Southern Pacific Railroad (lat. 38°11'25" N, long. 120°42'35" W; sec. 24, T 4 N, R 11 E). Named on San Andreas (1947) 15' quadrangle.

Macomb Falls: see **Wapama Falls** [TUOLUMNE].

Macomb Ridge [TUOLUMNE]: *ridge,* southwest-trending, 3.5 miles long, 6 miles south-southwest of Tower Peak (lat. 38°04'10" N, long. 119°36'30" W). Named on Tower Peak (1956) 15' quadrangle. The name commemorates Lieutenant M.M. Macomb, who was in charge of a party of the Wheeler survey in California in 1878 and 1879 (United States Board on Geographic Names, 1934, p. 15).\

Mad Canyon [PLACER]: *canyon,* drained by a stream that flows 2.5 miles to Middle Fork American River 2.5 miles east-southeast of Foresthill (lat. 39°00'25" N, long. 120°46'20" W; at S line sec. 32, T 14 N, R 11 E). Named on Foresthill (1949) 7.5' quadrangle.

Mad Canyon: see **Little Mad Canyon** [PLACER].

Madden Creek [PLACER]: *stream,* flows nearly 3 miles to Lake Tahoe at Homewood (lat. 39°05'25" N, long. 120°09'40" W; sec. 1, T 14 N, R 16 E). Named on Homewood (1955) 7.5' quadrangle. The name is for Dick Madden, who settled by the stream (Lekisch, p. 83).

Madera [MADERA]: *town,* in the southwest-central part of Madera County along Fresno River (lat. 36°57'45" N, long. 120°03'30" W). Named on Madera (1963) 7.5' quadrangle. Postal authorities established Madera post office in 1877 (Frickstad, p. 86), and the town incorporated in 1907. Officials of California Lumber Company had the town laid out in 1876 at the end of a flume that brought lumber 63 miles from the mountains to the railroad—madera means "wood" or "timber" in Spanish (Hoover, Rensch, and Rensch, p. 173).

Madera Creek [MADERA]: *stream,* flows 4 miles to West Fork Granite Creek 6.5 miles southeast of Merced Peak (lat. 37°33'45" N,

long. 119°18'50" W); the stream heads near Madera Peak. Named on Merced Peak (1953) 15' quadrangle. United States Board on Geographic Names (1933, p. 19) rejected the name "Black Peak Fork" for the stream.

Madera Equalization Reservoir [MADERA]: *lake,* 1 mile long, 10 miles south of Raymond (lat. 37°04' N, long. 119°56'15" W; on N line sec. 18, T 10 S, R 19 E). Named on Daulton (1962) 7.5' quadrangle.

Madera Lake [MADERA]: *lake,* 1.5 miles long, 14 miles south-southwest of Raymond near Fresno River (lat. 37°01'20" N, long. 119°59'15" W). Named on Daulton (1962) 7.5' quadrangle.

Madera Lakes [MADERA]: *lakes,* three, largest 1100 feet long, 6.5 miles south-southeast of Merced Peak along Madera Creek (lat. 37°32'40" N, long. 119°21'25" W); the group includes Lady Lake and Vandeburg Lake. Named on Merced Peak (1953) 15' quadrangle.

Madera Peak [MADERA]: *peak,* 6.5 miles south of Merced Peak (lat. 37°32'15" N, long. 119°22'30" W). Altitude 10,509 feet. Named on Merced Peak (1953) 15' quadrangle. Called Black Mt. on Hoffmann and Gardner's (1863-1867) map. Members of the Wheeler survey called the feature Black Peak (Browning, 1986, p. 134), but United States Board on Geographic Names (1933, p. 487) rejected this name.

Madera Station: see **Storey** [MADERA].

Maggie's Mountains: see **Maggies Peaks** [EL DORADO].

Maggies Peaks [EL DORADO]: *peaks,* two, 2 miles north-northwest of Mount Tallac (lat. 38°55'50" N, long. 120°06'45" W). Altitudes 8699 feet and 8499 feet. Named on Emerald Bay (1955) 7.5' quadrangle. Mary McConnell climbed the southernmost of the two features and called it Fleetfoot Peak; the two peaks also were known as Round Buttons and as Maggie's Mountains (Lekisch, p. 83-84).

Magnet: see **O'Neals** [MADERA].

Magnolia [EL DORADO]: *locality,* nearly 4 miles west-northwest of Coloma (lat. 38°49'35" N, long. 120°56'40" W). Named on Placerville (1893) 30' quadrangle.

Magnolia Creek [NEVADA]: *stream,* flows 6 miles to Bear River 2 miles southwest of Higgins Corner (lat. 39°01'25" N, long. 121°07'10" W; near NE cor. sec. 31, T 14 N, R 8 E). Named on Lake Combie (1949) 7.5' quadrangle.

Magonigal Camp [NEVADA]: *locality,* 8 miles west-northwest of Donner Pass (lat. 39°22'30" N, long. 120°27' W; at N line sec. 6, T 17 N, R 14 E); the place is nearly 1.5 miles northnortheast of Magonigal Summit. Named on Soda Springs (1955) 7.5' quadrangle.

Magonigal Summit [NEVADA]: *pass,* 8 miles west-northwest of Donner Pass (lat. 39°21'25" N, long. 120°27'50" W; sec. 12, T 17 N, R 13

E). Named on Soda Springs (1955) 7.5' quadrangle.

Magoon Creek [MARIPOSA]: *stream,* flows 3.5 miles to join Fox Creek and form Middle Fork Chowchilla River 8 miles east of Mariposa (lat. 37°29'10" N, long. 119°49'10" W; sec. 19, T 5 S, R 20 E); the stream is east of Magoon Hill. Named on Buckingham Mountain (1947) and Stumpfield Mountain (1947) 7.5' quadrangles.

Magoon Hill [MARIPOSA]: *peak,* 7 miles east of Mariposa (lat. 37° 29'35" N, long. 119°50'10" W; sec. 13, T 5 S, R 19 E). Named on Stumpfield Mountain (1947) 7.5' quadrangle.

Magra [PLACER]: *locality,* 4.5 miles northeast of Colfax along Southern Pacific Railroad (lat. 39°08'55" N, long. 120°53'45" W; sec. 18, T 15 N, R 10 E). Named on Chicago Park (1949) 7.5' quadrangle.

Maguires Mountain: see **Liberty Hill Diggings** [NEVADA].

Mahala Flat: see **Volcano** [AMADOR].

Mahan Lake [TUOLUMNE]: *lake,* 2400 feet long, 9 miles southwest of Tower Peak (lat. 38°03'15" N, long. 119°40' W); the lake is less than 1 mile east-northeast of Mahan Peak. Named on Tower Peak (1956) 15' quadrangle.

Mahan Peak [TUOLUMNE]: *peak,* 10 miles southwest of Tower Peak (lat. 38°03'10" N, long. 119°41'05" W). Altitude 9146 feet. Named on Tower Peak (1956) 15' quadrangle. Browning (1986, p. 135) associated the name with Dennis H. Mahan, professor of military engineering at West Point before the Civil War.

Mahon Camp [EL DORADO]: *locality,* 8 miles west-southwest of Kirkwood (lat. 38°40'05" N, long. 120°12'55" W; near SW cor. sec. 33, T 10 N, R 16 E). Named on Tragedy Spring (1979) 7.5' quadrangle.

Mahoney Gulch [MARIPOSA]: *canyon,* drained by a stream that flows 1 mile to Blacks Creek 1 mile west of Coulterville (lat. 37° 42'40" N, long. 120°13' W; sec. 4, T 3 S, R 16 E). Named on Coulterville (1947) 7.5' quadrangle.

Maiden Valley [SIERRA]: *valley,* 5 miles west-southwest of Sierraville at the head of Dark Canyon (1) (lat. 39°33'05" N, long. 120° 26'35" W; at S line sec. 29, T 20 N, R 14 E). Named on Sattley (1981) 7.5' quadrangle.

Main: see **Jack Main Canyon** [TUOLUMNE]; **Jack Main Mountain**, under **Chittenden Peak** [TUOLUMNE].

Maine Bar [EL DORADO]: *locality,* 3.5 miles northwest of Greenwood along Middle Fork American River (lat. 38°56'20" N, long. 120°57'25" W; sec. 34, T 13 N, R 9 E). Named on Greenwood (1949) 7.5' quadrangle. Bancroft (1888, p. 354) listed a place called Green Mountain Bar that was located on the south side of Middle Fork between Maine Bar and Hoosier Bar.

Maine Bar Canyon [EL DORADO]: *canyon,* drained by a stream that flows nearly 2 miles

to Middle Fork American River 3.5 miles northwest of Greenwood at Maine Bar (lat. 38°56'15" N, long. 120°57'30" W; sec. 34, T 13 N, R 9 E). Named on Greenwood (1949) 7.5' quadrangle.

Main Gulch: see **Columbia** [TUOLUMNE].

Maintop [PLACER]: *locality,* 4.5 miles north of Michigan Bluff (lat. 39°06'35" N, long. 120°43'05" W; near SE cor. sec. 27, T 15 N, R 11 E). Site named on Michigan Bluff (1952) 7.5' quadrangle.

Malakoff [NEVADA]: *locality,* 1.25 miles west of North Bloomfield (lat. 39°22'10" N, long. 120°55'30" W); the site is at present Malakoff Diggings. Named on Colfax (1898) 30' quadrangle.

Malakoff Diggings [NEVADA]: *locality,* less than 1 mile west of North Bloomfield (lat. 39°22'15" N, long. 120°54'45" W; on and near N line sec. 1, T 17 N, R 9 E). Named on North Bloomfield (1949) and Pike (1949) 7.5' quadrangles. The name was given at the time of the Crimean War for Malakoff Tower near Sebastopol in Russia (Gudde, 1975, p. 204).

Malby: see **Malby Crossing** [EL DORADO].

Malby Crossing [EL DORADO]: *locality,* 3 miles south-southwest of Clarksville along Southern Pacific Railroad at the rail crossing of Carson Creek (lat. 38°36'45" N, long. 121°04'05" W; on S line sec. 23, T 9 N, R 8 E). Named on Folsom SE (1954) 7.5' quadrangle. Called Malby on Folsom (1941) 15' quadrangle. California Division of Highways' (1934) map shows a place called Harvey 2 miles southeast of Malby along the railroad (at E line sec. 36, T 9 N, R 8 E).

Malcomb Bar: see **Gray Eagle Bar** [EL DORADO].

Males Station Campground [SIERRA]: *locality,* 3.25 miles east-southeast of Crystal Peak along South Branch Dog Creek (lat. 39° 32'30" N, long. 120°01'45" W; at W line sec. 6, T 19 N, R 18 E). Named on Dog Valley (1981) 7.5' quadrangle.

Malum Ridge [MADERA]: *ridge,* south-southeast-trending, 5 miles long, 10.5 miles southeast of Yosemite Forks (lat. 37°15' N, long. 119°30'30" W). Named on Bass Lake (1953), Millerton Lake (1965), and Shaver Lake (1953) 15' quadrangles.

Mameluke Hill [EL DORADO]: *peak,* 0.5 mile north-northwest of Georgetown (lat. 38°54'55" N, long. 120°50'25" W; near SE cor. sec. 3, T 12 N, R 10 E). Named on Georgetown (1949) 7.5' quadrangle. Gudde (1975, p. 52) listed a mining place called Bull Diggings that was located north of Mameluke Hill on the ridge between Illinois Canyon and Oregon Canyon; the name was from bulls used to haul gravel to be washed. Gudde (1975, p. 224) also listed a mining place called Mormon Gulch that was situated on Mameluke Hill.

Mammoth Bar [PLACER]: *locality,* 4 miles

east-northeast of Auburn along Middle Fork American River (lat. 38°55'05" N, long. 121°00' W; sec. 5, T 12 N, R 9 E). Named on Auburn (1953) and Greenwood (1949) 7.5' quadrangles.

Mammoth Cave: see **Mountain Ranch** [CALAVERAS].

Mammoth Crest [MADERA]: *ridge,* extends for 7 miles south-southeast and east from Mammoth Pass on Madera-Mono county line and on Fresno-Mono county line (center near lat. 37°34'15" N, long. 119°00' W). Named on Devils Postpile (1953) 15' quadrangle.

Mammoth Mountain [MADERA]: *peak,* nearly 3 miles east of Devils Postpile on Madera-Mono county line (lat. 37°37'50" N, long. 119°01'55" W); the peak is northwest of Mammoth Lakes, which are in Mono County. Altitude 11,053 feet. Named on Devils Postpile (1953) 15' quadrangle. Called Mammoth Pk. on California Mining Bureau's (1917d) map.

Mammoth Mountain: see **Banner Peak** [MADERA].

Mammoth Pass [MADERA]: *pass,* 3 miles east-southeast of Devils Postpile on Madera-Mono county line (lat. 37°36'35" N, long. 119°01'45" W); the pass is west of Mammoth Lakes, which are in Mono County. Named on Devils Postpile (1953) 15' quadrangle. The pass also is called Pumice Gap (Smith *in* Wright, p. 92).

Mammoth Peak: see **Mammoth Mountain** [MADERA].

Mammoth Peak [TUOLUMNE]: *peak,* nearly 4 miles east of Tioga Pass (lat. 37°51'20" N, long. 119°15'45" W). Altitude 12,117 feet. Named on Tuolumne Meadows (1956) 15' quadrangle.

Mammoth Pool Reservoir [MADERA]: *lake,* 7.5 miles long, behind a dam on San Joaquin River 6.5 miles east-southeast of Shuteye Peak on Madera-Fresno county line (lat. 37°19'25" N, long. 119° 18'55" W; near N line sec. 14, T 7 S, R 24 E. Named on Shuteye Peak (1953) 15' quadrangle.

Mammoth Spring [SIERRA]: *spring,* 2 miles northeast of Alleghany (lat. 39°29'25" N, long. 120°48'55" W; near NE. cor. sec. 26, T 19 N, R 10 E). Named on Alleghany (1949) 7.5' quadrangle. Called Mammoth Springs on Colfax (1938) 30' quadrangle.

Mammoth Spring: see **Lowell Hill** [NEVADA].

Manhattan Bar: see **Rattlesnake Bar** [PLACER].

Manhattan Creek [EL DORADO]: *stream,* flows nearly 3 miles to join Empire Creek and form Johntown Creek 6.5 miles north-northwest of Chili Bar (lat. 38°51'30" N, long. 120°51' W; sec. 27, T 12 N, R 10 E). Named on Garden Valley (1949) and Georgetown (1949) 7.5' quadrangles. Miners from New York named the stream in 1849 (Gernes, p. 51).

Manila Canyon [PLACER]: *canyon,* drained by

a stream that flows 2.5 miles to Screwauger Canyon 3.25 miles west-southwest of Duncan Peak (lat. 39°08'40" N, long. 120°34'20" W; sec. 18, T 15 N, R 13 E). Named on Duncan Peak (1952) 7.5' quadrangle.

Manimoth Spring: see **Government Spring** [PLACER].

Mann Creek [TUOLUMNE]: *stream,* flows 1.25 miles to South Fork Wildcat Creek 5.25 miles west of Keystone (lat. 37°49'20" N, long. 120°36'05" W; sec. 25, T 1 S, R 12 E). Named on Keystone (1962) 7.5' quadrangle.

Manuel Mill [CALAVERAS]: *locality,* 5.5 miles south of Blue Mountain along San Antonio Creek (lat. 38°15'40" N, long. 120° 21'30" W; sec. 30, T 5 N, R 15 E). Site named on Blue Mountain (1956) 15' quadrangle.

Many Island Lake [TUOLUMNE]: *lake,* 1850 feet long, 12.5 miles southeast of Pinecrest (lat. 38°05' N, long. 119°48'40" W). Named on Pinecrest (1956) 15' quadrangle.

Manzanita Lake [MADERA]: *lake,* behind a dam on North Fork Willow Creek (2) 1.25 miles north-northwest of North Fork (lat. 37°14'40" N, long. 119°30'55" W; sec. 12, T 8 S, R 22 E). Named on Bass Lake (1953) and Millerton Lake (1965) 15' quadrangles.

Maple Grove Camp Ground [EL DORADO]: *locality,* less than 0.5 mile west of Riverton along South Fork American River (lat. 38° 46'20" N, long. 120°27'20" W; sec. 30, T 11 N, R 14 E). Named on Riverton (1950, photorevised 1973) 7.5' quadrangle.

Marble Creek [EL DORADO]: *stream,* flows 3 miles to Deer Creek (2) 4.25 miles north-northwest of Latrobe (lat. 38°37'15" N, long. 120°59'50" W; sec. 21, T 9 N, R 9 E). Named on Clarksville (1953), Folsom SE (1954), and Latrobe (1949) 7.5' quadrangles.

Marble Gulch [MARIPOSA]: *canyon,* 1.5 miles long, 8 miles northeast of Buckhorn Peak (lat. 37°44'15" N, long. 120°00'40" W). Named on Buckhorn Peak (1947) 7.5' quadrangle.

Marble Mountain [TUOLUMNE]: *peak,* 5.5 miles east of Twain Harte (lat. 38°01'30" N, long. 120°07'40" W; sec. 17, T 2 N, R 17 E). Altitude 5477 feet. Named on Twain Harte (1979) 7.5' quadrangle.

Marble Point [MARIPOSA]: *promontory,* 5 miles southwest of El Portal on the west side of South Fork Merced River (lat. 37°37'15" N, long. 119°50'25" W; on W line sec. 2, T 4 S, R 19 E). Named on Buckingham Mountain (1947) 7.5' quadrangle.

Marble Point: see **Mokelumne River** [AMADOR-CALAVERAS].

Marble Spring [EL DORADO]: *locality,* 3 miles south of Omo Ranch near Indian Creek (5) (lat. 38°32'20" N, long. 120°35'30" W). Named on Placerville (1893) 30' quadrangle.

Marble Springs [EL DORADO]: *spring,* 2.25 miles south-southwest of Omo Ranch (lat. 38°32'50" N, long. 120°34'45" W; sec. 18, T 8 N, R 13 E). Named on Omo Ranch (1952)

7.5' quadrangle, which shows a marble quarry near the spring.

Marble Valley [EL DORADO]: *valley,* 2.25 miles east-southeast of Clarksville on the upper reaches of Marble Creek (lat. 38°38'40" N, long. 121°00'40" W; on S line sec. 8, T 9 N, R 9 E). Named on Clarksville (1953) 7.5' quadrangle.

Maredith Mill [SIERRA]: *locality,* 6.5 miles south-southwest of Mount Fillmore (lat. 39°38'25" N, long. 120°52'40" W; sec. 32, T 21 N, R 10 E). Named on La Porte (1951) 7.5' quadrangle.

Margaret: see **Lake Margaret** [EL DORADO].

Margery: see **Lake Margery** [EL DORADO].

Mariana Gulch [CALAVERAS]: *canyon,* drained by a stream that flows less than 1 mile to Stanislaus River 3.25 miles east of Vallecito (lat. 38°05'05" N, long. 120°24'50" W; near E line sec. 27, T 3 N, R 14 E). Named on Columbia (1948) 7.5' quadrangle.

Marietta: see **Forest** [SIERRA].

Marion Creek [SIERRA]: *stream,* flows 1.5 miles to Oregon Creek 1.5 miles north-northeast of Pike (lat. 39°27'50" N, long. 120°59'30" W; near N line sec. 5, T 18 N, R 9 E). Named on Pike (1949) 7.5' quadrangle.

Mariposa [MARIPOSA]: *town,* in the west-central part of Mariposa County along Mariposa Creek (lat. 37°29'05" N, long. 119°57'50" W); the town is on Las Mariposas grant. Named on Mariposa (1947) 7.5' quadrangle. Postal authorities established Mariposa post office in 1851 (Frickstad, p. 91). In 1849 the town was situated about 0.5 mile downstream from the present site (Chamberlain, p. 15). Miners who were flooded out of the town in the winter of 1849 and 1850 moved to slightly higher ground and formed a camp called Logtown (Sargent, Shirley, 1976, p. 15). Laizure's (1928) map shows a place called French Camp located 3.5 miles north-northwest of Mariposa (sec. 4, T 5 S, R 18 E).

Mariposa Creek [MARIPOSA]: *stream,* heads in Mariposa County and flows 35 miles to Merced County 12.5 miles south-southwest of the settlement of Catheys Valley (lat. 37°16'20" N, long. 120°11' W; near N line sec. 2, T 8 S, R 16 E). Named on Chowchilla (1960) and Le Grand (1961) 15' quadrangles, and on Bear Valley (1947), Catheys Valley (1962), Feliciana Mountain (1947), Illinois Hill (1962), Mariposa (1947), and Owens Reservoir (1962) 7.5' quadrangles. According to Bancroft (1886, p. 52), members of a Spanish expedition applied the name "Mariposas" in the region in 1806 because of the abundance of butterflies there—*mariposas* means "butterflies" in Spanish. Fremont in his memoirs attributed the name to the resemblance of wind-blown poppies to fluttering butterflies (Spence and Jackson, p. 37).

Mariposa Estate: see **Las Mariposas** [MARIPOSA].

Mariposa Reservoir [MARIPOSA]: *lake,* behind a dam on Mariposa Creek 10.5 miles south-southwest of the settlement of Catheys Valley (lat. 37°17'30" N, long. 120°08'50" W; sec. 30, T 7 S, R 17 E). Named on Illinois Hill (1962) and Owens Reservoir (1962) 7.5' quadrangles.

Mark Edson Reservoir: see **Stumpy Meadows Lake** [EL DORADO].

Markham Ravine [PLACER]: *canyon,* drained by a stream that heads in Placer County and flows 16 miles to a canal 8 miles northeast of Verona in Sutter County (lat. 38°52' N, long. 121°30'50" W; near N line sec. 27, T 12 N, R 4 E). Named on Lincoln (1953), Nicolaus (1952), Sheridan (1953, photorevised 1973), and Verona (1967) 7.5' quadrangles. Hobson's (1890b) map has the name "Markham Slough" for the feature.

Markham Slough: see **Markham Ravine** [PLACER].

Marliave: see **Mount Marliave**, under **Hole-in-Ground** [NEVADA].

Mars: see **Outingdale** [EL DORADO].

Marshall: see **Lotus** [EL DORADO].

Marsh Mill [NEVADA]: *locality,* 2 miles east of Graniteville (lat. 39°26'40" N, long. 120°42'10" W; sec. 11, T 18 N, R 11 E). Site named on Graniteville (1982) 7.5' quadrangle.

Marshs Flat [TUOLUMNE]: *valley,* 1.5 miles south-southwest of Moccasin (lat. 37°47'20" N, long. 120°18'20" W; sec. 3, T 2 S, R 15 E). Named on Moccasin (1948) 7.5' quadrangle. Sonora (1897) 30' quadrangle has the form "Marsh's Flat" for the name.

Martel Creek [CALAVERAS]: *stream,* flows 2 miles to South Fork Mokelumne River nearly 2 miles east-southeast of Blue Mountain (lat. 38°19'40" N, long. 120°20'05" W; sec. 33, T 6 N, R 15 E). Named on Dorrington (1979) 7.5' quadrangle.

Martells Creek [CALAVERAS]: *stream,* heads in Calaveras County and flows 12 miles to Littlejohns Creek 8 miles north-northeast of Oakdale in Stanislaus County (lat. 37°52'25" N, long. 120°47'45" W). Named on Copperopolis (1962), Knights Ferry (1962), and Oakdale (1968) 7.5' quadrangles.

Martel Creek [EL DORADO]: *stream,* flows 2.5 miles to Sweetwater Creek 5.25 miles north of Clarksville (lat. 38°43'55" N, long. 121° 02'10" W; sec. 7, T 10 N, R 9 E). Named on Clarksville (1953) 7.5' quadrangle.

Martell [AMADOR]: *village,* 1.5 miles northwest of Jackson (lat. 38° 22' N, long. 120°47'45" W; near NW cor. sec. 20, T 6 N, R 11 E). Named on Jackson (1962) 7.5' quadrangle. Postal authorities established Martell post office in 1905; the name commemorates Louis Martell, who settled in the region in the 1860's (Salley, p. 134). Camp's (1962) map gives the name "Oneida" as an alternate designation for the place.

Martin Creek [EL DORADO]: *stream,* flows

2.5 miles to Silver Fork American River 8 miles west of Krikwood (lat. 38°42'20" N, long. 120°12'55" W). Named on Tragedy Spring (1979) 7.5' quadrangle.

Martinez [TUOLUMNE]: *locality,* 1.5 miles southeast of Columbia (lat. 38°01'25" N, long. 120°22'45" W; near SE cor. sec. 13, T 2 N, R 14 E). Named on Columbia (1948) 7.5' quadrangle. The place was known as Spanish Camp in 1850, but later it was called Martinez to honor the first female resident there (Stoddart, p. 144).

Martinez Creek [EL DORADO]: *stream,* flows nearly 7 miles to North Fork Cosumnes River 7.5 miles south of Placerville (lat. 38°37'05" N, long. 120°48'40" W; sec. 19, T 9 N, R 11 E). Named on Fiddletown (1949) and Placerville (1949) 7.5' quadrangles.

Martin Gulch [CALAVERAS]: *canyon,* drained by a stream that flows 2 miles to McKinney Creek 9.5 miles east of San Andreas (lat. 38°12'15" N, long. 120°30'25" W; sec. 14, T 4 N, R 13 E). Named on Calaveritas (1962) and Murphys (1948) 7.5' quadrangles.

Martin Meadow [EL DORADO]: *area,* 2.5 miles west of Kirkwood near Amador-El Dorado county line (lat. 38°41'50" N, long. 120° 07'10" W; sec. 20, T 10 N, T 17 E). Named on Caples Lake (1979) 7.5' quadrangle.

Martin Point [AMADOR]: *peak,* 10.5 miles north of Mokelumne Peak (lat. 38°41'20" N, long. 120°05'30" W; sec. 28, T 10 N, R 17 E). Altitude 9250 feet. Named on Caples Lake (1979) 7.5' quadrangle.

Martins Cow Camp [TUOLUMNE]: *locality,* 3.5 miles south of Dardanelle (lat. 38°17'20" N, long. 119°50' W; sec. 13, T 5 N, R 19 E). Named on Dardanelle (1979) 7.5' quadrangle. Browning (1986, p. 138) related the name to Joe Martin, who had the cattle permit in Eagle Meadow in the 1850's.

Martis Creek [NEVADA-PLACER]: *stream,* heads in Placer County and flows 12 miles to Truckee River 3.5 miles east-northeast of Truckee in Nevada County (lat. 39°21' N, long. 120°07' W; sec. 5, T 17 N, R 17 E); the stream goes through Martis Valley. Named on Martis Peak (1955), Tahoe City (1955), and Truckee (1955) 7.5' quadrangles. United States Board on Geographic Names (1972, p. 4) approved the name "Martis Creek Lake" for a lake on Nevada-Placer county line that is formed by a dam on Martis Creek 3.5 miles east of Truckee (lat. 39°19'45" N, long. 120° 07' W; sec. 17, T 17 N, R 17 E), and gave the name "Martis Creek Reservoir" as a variant.

Martis Creek: see **East Martis Creek** [PLACER]; **Middle Martis Creek** [PLACER]; **West Martis Creek** [PLACER].

Martis Creek Lake: see **Martis Creek** [NEVADA-PLACER].

Martis Creek Reservoir: see **Martis Creek** [NEVADA-PLACER].

Martis Peak [PLACER]: *peak,* 15 miles east of

Donner Pass (lat. 39° 17'30" N, long. 120°01'55" W; sec. 25, T 17 N, R 17 E). Altitude 8742 feet. Named on Martis Peak (1955) 7.5' quadrangle.

Martis Valley [NEVADA-PLACER]: *valley,* 2.25 miles east-southeast of Truckee on Nevada-Placer county line (lat. 39°19' N, long. 120° 08'30" W); the valley is 6 miles west-northwest of Martis Peak along lower reaches of Martis Creek. Named on Martis Peak (1955) and Truckee (1955) 7.5' quadrangles.

Mary: see **Lake Mary** [PLACER].

Mary Lake [TUOLUMNE]: *lake,* 2900 feet long, 0.5 mile west of Tower Peak (lat. 38°08'40" N, long. 119°33'40" W). Named on Tower Peak (1956) 15' quadrangle. The name commemorates Mary Forsyth, daughter of Colonel W.W. Forsyth, acting superintendent of Yosemite National Park from 1909 until 1912 (Browning, 1988, p. 86).

Marys Lake [EL DORADO]: *lake,* 800 feet long, 6.5 miles northeast of Robbs Peak (lat. 38°59'40" N, long. 120°19'20" W; on S line sec. 5, T 13 N, R 15 E). Named on Robbs Peak (1952) 15' quadrangle. The feature now is part of an enlarged Loon Lake.

Mast [MARIPOSA]: *locality,* 3.5 miles south-southwest of Coulterville along Yosemite Valley Railroad (lat. 37°40' N, long. 120°13'25" W). Named on Sonora (1897) 30' quadrangle. Water of Lake McClure now covers the site.

Matelot Gulch [TUOLUMNE]: *canyon,* 1 mile long, opens into lowlands at Columbia (lat. 38°02'20" N, long. 120°24' W; sec. 11, T 2 N, R 14 E). Named on Columbia (1948) 7.5' quadrangle. Stoddart (p. 127) referred to Matelot or Sailor's gulch.

Matelot Reservoir [TUOLUMNE]: *lake,* 350 feet long, 1.25 miles north-northeast of Columbia (lat. 38°03'05" N, long. 120°23'35" W; sec. 1, T 2 N, R 14 E); the lake is at the head of Matelot Gulch. Named on Columbia (1948) 7.5' quadrangle.

Mather [TUOLUMNE]: *village,* 33 miles west of Tioga Pass (lat. 37° 53' N, long. 119°51'20" W; sec. 2, T 1 S, R 19 E). Named on Lake Eleanor (1956) 15' quadrangle. Called Mather Sta. on Yosemite (1909) 30' quadrangle, where it is shown at the end of Hetch Hetchy Railroad. Postal authorities established Mather post office in 1921 (Frickstad, p. 216). The name is for Stephen Tyng Mather, director of the National Park Service from 1917 until 1929 (Hanna, p. 187). Hoffmann and Gardner's (1863-1867) map shows a place called Hog Ranch located at or near present Mather—an early sheepman drew a picture of a sheep on a rock there, but because the drawing looked more like a hog than a sheep, the place became known as Hog Ranch (Browning, 1986, p. 138-139). Hetch Hetchy post office, located 9 miles northeast of Mather at the construction camp for the dam that forms Hetch Hetchy Reservoir, was established in 1921, discontinued in 1923, re-established in 1935, and discontinued in 1937 (Salley, p. 96).

Mather Station: see **Mather** [TUOLUMNE].

Matheus: see **Deer Creek** [NEVADA].

Matterhorn Canyon [TUOLUMNE]: *canyon,* drained by a stream that flows 9 miles to Regulation Creek 11 miles west-northwest of Tioga Pass (lat. 37°58'15" N, long. 119°26'50" W); the canyon heads near Matterhorn Peak. Named on Matterhorn Peak (1956) and Tuolumne Meadows (1956) 15' quadrangles.

Matterhorn Peak [TUOLUMNE]: *peak,* 21 miles southeast of Sonora Pass on Tuolumne-Mono county line (lat. 38°05'30" N, long. 119° 22'50" W). Altitude 12,264 feet. Named on Matterhorn Peak (1956) 15' quadrangle. Members of the Wheeler survey named the feature in 1878 (Browning, 1986, p. 139).

Matthes Crest [MARIPOSA]: *ridge,* south-southwest-trending, 2 miles long, 1.5 miles south-southeast of Cathedral Peak (lat. 37°49'20" N, long. 119°23'50" W). Named on Tuolumne Meadows (1956) 15' quadrangle. The name commemorates François Matthes of United States Geological Survey (O'Neill, p. 96).

Matthes Dome: see **Pywiak Dome** [MARIPOSA].

Matthes Lake [MARIPOSA]: *lake,* 900 feet long, 2.5 miles south of Cathedral Peak (lat. 37°48'35" N, long. 119°23'50" W; near S line sec. 25, T 1 S, R 23 E). Named on Tuolumne Meadows (1956) 15' quadrangle.

Mattie Lake [TUOLUMNE]: *lake,* 1250 feet long, 10 miles west of Tioga Pass (lat. 37°56' N, long. 119°26'20" W). Named on Tuolumne Meadows (1956) 15' quadrangle.

Mattley [CALAVERAS]: *locality,* 4.5 miles west-northwest of present Tamarack along Moore Creek (lat. 38°27'45" N, long. 120° 09'20" W). Named on Big Trees (1891) 30' quadrangle.

Mattley Creek [CALAVERAS]: *stream,* flows 3.25 miles to North Fork Mokelumne River 5.25 miles northwest of Tamarack (lat. 38° 29'50" N, long. 120°08'10" W); the stream is near Mattley Meadow. Named on Calaveras Dome (1979) and Tamarack (1979) 7.5' quadrangles.

Mattley Meadow [CALAVERAS]: *area,* 3 miles northwest of Tamarack (lat. 38°27'45" N, long. 120°07'30" W; sec. 17, T 7 N, R 17 E); the place is along a branch of Mattley Creek. Named on Calaveras Dome (1979) and Tamarack (1979) 7.5' quadrangles. Big Meadow (1956) 15' quadrangle shows Mattley cabin located 1.25 miles west of Mattley Meadow.

Matulich Meadow [EL DORADO]: *area,* 5 miles west of Old Iron Mountain (lat. 38°41'50" N, long. 120°29' W; near N line sec. 25, T 10 N, R 13 E). Named on Stump Spring (1951) 7.5' quadrangle.

Maud Lake [EL DORADO]: *lake,* 1000 feet long, 5.5 miles southwest of Phipps Peak (lat. 38°53'30" N, long. 120°12'30" W; on E line sec. 16, T 12 N, R 16 E). Named on Rockbound Valley (1955) 7.5' quadrangle.

Maxwell Creek [CALAVERAS]: *stream,* flows 3.5 miles to Bear Creek (4) 7 miles west of Angels Camp (lat. 38°05'30" N, long. 120°40'05" W; near NE cor. sec. 29, T 3 N, R 12 E). Named on Salt Spring Valley (1962) 7.5' quadrangle.

Maxwell Creek [MARIPOSA]: *stream,* flows 11.5 miles to Lake McClure 2 miles west-southwest of Coulterville (lat. 37°41'55" N, long. 120°13'40" W; near S line sec. 5, T 3 S, R 16 E). Named on Buckhorn Peak (1947) and Coulterville (1947, photorevised 1973) 7.5' quadrangles. The name commemorates George Maxwell, an early settler at Coulterville (Hanna, p. 75).

Maxwell Lake [TUOLUMNE]: *lake,* 2100 feet long, 7 miles west of Tower Peak (lat. 38°09'30" N, long. 119°40'20" W; on S line sec. 28, T 4 N, R 21 E). Named on Tower Peak (1956) 15' quadrangle. Called Helen Lake on Dardanelles (1898, reprinted 1947) 30' quadrangle, but United States Board on Geographic Names (1960c, p. 18) rejected the names "Helen Lake" and "Lake Helen" for the feature.

Maxwell's Creek: see **Coulterville** [MARIPOSA].

May: see **Carbondale** [AMADOR].

Maybert [NEVADA]: *locality,* 5.5 miles south-southeast of Graniteville along South Fork Yuba River (present South Yuba River) (lat. 39°21' N, long. 120°42'05" W). Named on Colfax (1898) 30' quadrangle. Postal authorities established Maybert post office in 1886, moved it 0.5 mile east in 1897, discontinued it in 1905, reestablished it in 1907, and discontinued it in 1910; the name is from a gold mine at the site (Salley, p. 135).

Mayers Ravine: see **Meyers Ravine** [NEVADA].

Mayflower [PLACER]: *locality,* 1.25 miles north of Foresthill (lat. 39°02'10" N, long. 120°49'30" W). Named on Colfax (1898) 30' quadrangle. Foresthill (1949) 7.5' quadrangle shows Mayflower mine at the place.

May Lake [MARIPOSA]: *lake,* 2100 feet long, nearly 5 miles west of Cathedral Peak (lat. 37°50'50" N, long. 119°29'30" W; on W line sec. 18, T 1 S, R 23 E). Named on Tuolumne Meadows (1956) 15' quadrangle. Charles F. Hoffmann of the Whitney survey named the peak for Lucy Mayotta Browne, daughter of J. Ross Browne (United States Board on Geographic Names, 1934, p. 16).

May Lake High Sierra Camp [MARIPOSA]: *locality,* 4.5 miles west of Cathedral Peak (lat. 37°50'40" N, long. 119°29'20" W; sec. 18, T 1 S, R 23 E); the place is on the east shore of May Lake. Named on Tuolumne Meadows (1956) 15' quadrangle.

May Rock [MARIPOSA]: *relief feature,* 2 miles southeast of the village of Bear Valley (lat. 37°32'40" N, long. 120°05'50" W). Named on Bear Valley (1947) 7.5' quadrangle. Jessie Fremont named the feature in remembrance of a picnic held there in the month of May (Sargent, Shirley, 1976, p. 16).

Mays: see **Tahoe Valley** [EL DORADO].

McAfee Gulch [CALAVERAS]: *canyon,* drained by a stream that flows less than 1 mile to Pardee Reservoir 3 miles west-northwest of Paloma (lat. 38°16'10" N, long. 120°49' W; near E line sec. 24, T 5 N, R 10 E). Named on Jackson (1962) 7.5' quadrangle.

McAlpine: see **Calpine** [SIERRA].

McAlpine: see **Chinese Camp** [TUOLUMNE].

McBride Creek [PLACER]: *stream,* flows 1.5 miles to the head of Shirttail Canyon 5 miles northeast of Foresthill (lat. 39°04'35" N, long. 120°45'45" W; sec. 8, T 14 N, R 11 E). Named on Foresthill (1949) and Michigan Bluff (1952) 7.5' quadrangles.

McBrides Gulch [MARIPOSA]: *canyon,* drained by a stream that flows 1 mile to Carson Creek 5.5 miles northeast of the settlement of Catheys Valley (lat. 37°28'50" N, long. 120°00'40" W). Named on Catheys Valley (1962) 7.5' quadrangle. Laizure's (1928) map has the form "McBride's Gulch" for the name. The stream in the canyon is called Carson Creek on Indian Gulch (1920) 15' quadrangle. United States Board on Geographic Names (1964a, p. 11) rejected the name "Carson Gulch" for the canyon.

McCabe Creek [TUOLUMNE]: *stream,* flows 3.5 miles to Return Creek 6 miles south of Matterhorn Peak (lat. 38°00'20" N, long. 119°22'35" W). Named on Matterhorn Peak (1956) 15' quadrangle. The stream also was called East Fork [Return Creek] (Browning, 1988, p. 89).

McCabe Flat [MARIPOSA]: *area,* 6.5 miles east-northeast of the village of Bear Valley along Merced River (lat. 37°35'50" N, long. 120°00'10" W; sec. 8, T 4 S, R 18 E). Named on Bear Valley (1947) 7.5' quadrangle. On Sonora (1891) 30' quadrangle, the name "McCabe Flat" applies to a place situated about 2 miles farther northwest along Merced River.

McCabe Lake: see **Upper McCabe Lake** [TUOLUMNE].

McCabe Lakes [TUOLUMNE]: *lakes,* largest 1900 feet long, 7 miles northwest of Tioga Pass (lat. 37°59'30" N, long. 119°20'30" W). Named on Tuolumne Meadows (1956) 15' quadrangle. The name is for Edward R.W. McCabe, son-in-law of Colonel W.W. Forsyth, acting superintendent of Yosemite National Park from 1909 until 1912 (Browning, 1986, p. 141).

McCarthy Creek: see **McCarty Creek** [CALAVERAS].

McCarty Creek [CALAVERAS]: *stream,* flows 7 miles to Littlejohns Creek 2.5 miles south-southwest of Copperopolis (lat. 37°56'50" N, long. 120°39'45" W; sec. 9, T 1 N, R 12 E). Named on Copperopolis (1962) and Salt Spring Valley (1962) 7.5' quadrangles. Called McCarthy Creek on Copperopolis (1916) 15' quadrangle, but United States Board on Geographic Names (1963b, p. 14) rejected this designation for the stream.

McCarty Flat [NEVADA]: *area,* 2.25 miles south-southeast of Higgins Corner (lat. 39°00'45" N, long. 121°04'20" W; at N line sec. 3, T 13 N, R 8 E). Named on Lake Combie (1949) 7.5' quadrangle.

McCarty Flat: see **O' Donnells Flat**, under **Downieville** [SIERRA].

McCarty Reservoir: see **Calaveras Reservoir** [CALAVERAS].

McCauley: see **Foresta** [MARIPOSA].

McCauley Hill [MARIPOSA]: *peak,* 12.5 miles west-northwest of El Portal (lat. 37°44'15" N, long. 119°59'30" W; sec. 28, T 2 S, R 18 E). Named on Kinsley (1947) 7.5' quadrangle, which has the designation "McCauley Ranch (Old Stage Station)" for a place located 0.5 mile north of the peak.

McCauley Ranch: see **McCauley Hill** [MARIPOSA].

McCleod Flat [MADERA]: *area,* 4 miles east of Yosemite Forks along North Fork Willow Creek (2) (lat. 37°21'20" N, long. 119° 33'25" W; near NW cor. sec. 3, T 7 S, R 22 E). Named on Bass Lake (1953) 15' quadrangle. United States Board on Geographic Names (1990, p. 9) approved the name "McLeod Flat" for the feature, and noted that the name is for Malcolm McLeod, district ranger for Fresno Flats in 1911.

McClure: see **Lake McClure** [MARIPOSA]; **Mount McClure**, under **Mount Maclure** [MADERA-TUOLUMNE].

McClure Lake [MADERA]: *lake,* 1100 feet long, 4.5 miles east of Merced Peak (lat. 37°38'30" N, long. 119°18'50" W). Named on Merced Peak (1953) 15' quadrangle. The name commemorates Lieutenant N.F. McClure, who was stationed in Yosemite National Park in 1894 and 1895 (Farquhar, 1924, p. 57).

McConnell Lake [EL DORADO]: *lake,* 750 feet long, 4.25 miles west-southwest of Phipps Peak (lat. 38°56'35" N, long. 120°13'30" W; sec. 29, T 13 N, R 16 E); the lake 1 mile east-southeast of McConnell Peak. Named on Rockbound Valley (1955) 7.5' quadrangle.

McConnell Peak [EL DORADO]: *peak,* 5 miles west of Phipps Peak (lat. 38°56'55" N, long. 120°14'30" W; at E line sec. 30, T 13 N, R 16 E). Altitude 9099 feet. Named on Rockbound Valley (1955) 7.5' quadrangle.

Mc. Cormick: see **McCormick Meadows** [TUOLUMNE].

McCormick Creek [TUOLUMNE]:
(1) *stream,* flows 2.5 miles to Griswold Creek 4 miles northeast of Stanislaus (lat. 38°10'55"

N, long. 120°19'30" W; sec. 21, T 4 N, R 15 E); the stream heads near McCormick Meadows. Named on Stanislaus (1948) 7.5' quadrangle.
(2) *stream,* heads in Alpine County and flows 5 miles to Middle Fork Stanislaus River 3.5 miles west-northwest of Dardanelle (lat. 38°21'30" N, long. 119°53'45" W). Named on Donnell Lake (1979) and Spicer Meadow Reservoir (1979) 7.5' quadrangles. The name commemorates an early settler (Browning, 1986, p. 141).

McCormick Meadows [TUOLUMNE]: *locality,* 5.5 miles northeast of Stanislaus (lat. 38°11'30" N, long. 120°17'20" W). Named on Stanislaus (1948) 7.5' quadrangle. Big Trees (1891) 30' quadrangle has the name "Mc. Cormick" at the place.

McCormick Pocket [TUOLUMNE]: *relief feature,* 5.5 miles south of Dardanelle (lat. 38°15'35" N, long. 119°50'45" W; near E line sec. 26, T 5 N, R 19 E). Named on Dardanelle (1979) 7.5' quadrangle.

McCormick Reservoir: see **Old McCormick Reservoir** [CALAVERAS].

McCourtney Crossing [PLACER]: *locality,* 6 miles northeast of Sheridan along Bear River on Placer-Yuba county line (lat. 39° 02'40" N, long. 121°17'35" W; at N line sec. 27, T 14 N, R 6 E); water of Camp Far West Reservoir now covers the site. Named on Wheatland (1949) 15' quadrangle.

McCreary Meadow [MADERA]: *area,* 13 miles northeast of Shuteye Peak (lat. 37°29'25" N, long. 119°16'20" W; sec. 18, T 5 S, R 25 E). Named on Shuteye Peak (1953) 15' quadrangle.

McCulloh [PLACER]: *locality,* 1.25 miles east-southeast of Devil Peak in Big Grizzly Canyon (lat. 38°57'15" N, long. 120°31'30" W; near N line sec. 28, T 13 N, R 13 E). Named on Devil Peak (1950) 7.5' quadrangle.

McCulloh Spring [PLACER]: *spring,* 0.5 mile north of Devil Peak (lat. 38°58'05" N, long. 120°32'50" W; sec. 20, T 13 N, R 13 E). Named on Devil Peak (1950) 7.5' quadrangle.

McDonald Flat: see **O' Donnells Flat**, under **Downieville** [SIERRA].

McDowell Hill: see **Folsom Lake** [EL DORADO-PLACER].

McDowellsville: see **McDowell Hill**, under **Folsom Lake** [EL DORADO-PLACER].

McGee Lake [MADERA]: *lake,* 550 feet long, 5.5 miles east-northeast of Merced Peak (lat. 37°39'15" N, long. 119°18' W). Named on Merced Peak (1953) 15' quadrangle.

McGee Lake [TUOLUMNE]: *lake,* 1400 feet long, 9.5 miles west of Tioga Pass (lat. 37°54'10" N, long. 119°25'45" W). Named on Tuolumne Meadows (1956) 15' quadrangle.

McGill Creek: see **Miguel Creek** [TUOLUMNE].

McGill Meadow: see **Miguel Meadow** [TUOLUMNE].

McGinnis Ravine [SIERRA]: *canyon,* drained by a stream that flows less than 1 mile to Middle Yuba River 3 miles south-southwest of Alleghany (lat. 39°25'55" N, long. 120°52'05" W; near NE cor. sec. 17, T 18 N, R 19 E). Named on Alleghany (1949) 7.5' quadrangle.

McGlashan Point: see **Donner Pass** [NEVADA-PLACER].

McGuire Campground [PLACER]: *locality,* 6 miles northwest of Bunker Hill along Middle Fork American River (lat. 39°06'45" N, long. 120°27'35" W; near NE cor. sec. 36, T 15 N, R 13 E). Named on Granite Chief (1953) 15' quadrangle. Water of French Meadows Reservoir now covers the site.

McGuire Mountain [NEVADA]: *peak,* 7.25 miles south of Washington (lat. 39°15'10" N, long. 120°47'40" W; near E line sec. 13, T 16 N, R 10 E). Named on Washington (1950) 7.5' quadrangle.

McGurk Meadow [MARIPOSA]: *area,* 5.25 miles south-southwest of Yosemite Village (lat. 37°40'50" N, long. 119°37'45" W; at SW cor. sec. 12, T 3 S, R 21 E). Named on Yosemite (1956) 15' quadrangle. The name commemorates John J. McGurk, who lived at the place in the 1890's (Uhte, p. 55).

McIntosh Hill [PLACER]: *peak,* 1.25 miles south of Cisco Grove at the east end of Monumental Ridge (lat. 39°17'20" N, long. 120°32'20" W; near S line sec. 32, T 17 N, R 13 E). Altitude 6762 feet. Named on Cisco Grove (1955) 7.5' quadrangle.

McIntyre Gulch [PLACER]: *canyon,* drained by a stream that flows 1.25 miles to North Fork American River 3.5 miles southeast of Dutch Flat (lat. 39°10'25" N, long. 120°47'15" W; near W line sec. 6, T 15 N, R 11 E); the mouth of the canyon is just below Green Valley. Named on Dutch Flat (1950) 7.5' quadrangle. Called Green Valley Cañon on Whitney's (1873) map.

McKay [CALAVERAS]: *locality,* 11.5 miles northeast of Murphys (lat. 38°14'50" N, long. 120°18'20" W; sec. 34, T 5 N, R 15 E). Named on Stanislaus (1948) 7.5' quadrangle.

McKays Point [CALAVERAS]: *relief feature,* 11.5 miles northeast of Murphys (lat. 38°14'40" N, long. 120°17'35" W; sec. 35, T 5 N, R 15 E); the feature is 0.5 mile east-southeast of McKay above North Fork Stanislaus River. Named on Stanislaus (1948) 7.5' quadrangle.

McKay Spring [NEVADA]: *spring,* 5.25 miles east-northeast of Truckee (lat. 39°20'50" N, long. 120°05'20" W; sec. 4, T 17 N, R 17 E). Named on Martis Peak (1955) 7.5' quadrangle.

McKee Hill [TUOLUMNE]: *peak,* 6.5 miles south of Liberty Hill (lat. 38°16'25" N, long. 120°07' W; sec. 20, T 5 N, R 17 E). Altitude 6363 feet. Named on Liberty Hill (1979) 7.5' quadrangle.

McKeon: see **Butchers** [PLACER].

McKilligan Creek [NEVADA]: *stream,* flows 2.25 miles to South Yuba River 1 mile west-southwest of Washington (lat. 39°21'10" N, long. 120°49'05" W; sec. 11, T 17 N, R 10 E). Named on Alleghany (1949) and Washington (1950) 7.5' quadrangles. Called McKillican Creek on Colfax (1938) 30' quadrangle.

McKinney: see **Chambers Lodge** [PLACER].

McKinney Bay [PLACER]: *embayment,* along Lake Tahoe at Homewood (lat. 39°05' N, long. 120°09' W). Named on Homewood (1955) 7.5' quadrangle. The name commemorates John McKinney, who came to the neighborhood in the early 1850's, and later opened a resort near the south end of the embayment (Gudde, 1949, p. 199).

McKinney Creek [CALAVERAS]: *stream,* flows 6.25 miles to join O'Neil Creek and form Calaveritas Creek 8.5 miles east of San Andreas (lat. 38°11' N, long. 120°31'15" W; near E line sec. 22, T 4 N, R 13 E). Named on Calaveritas (1962) and Murphys (1948) 7.5' quadrangles. Called McKinneys Creek on Jackson (1902) 30' quadrangle. Gudde (1975, p. 202) noted that a mining camp of the early 1850's located along McKinney Creek 9 miles east of San Andreas was called McKinneys Secret Diggings, McKinneys Humbug, or McKinneys.

McKinney Creek [EL DORADO]: *stream,* flows 4.5 miles to Dogtown Creek at Caldor (lat. 38°36'20" N, long. 120°26' W; sec. 28, T 9 N, R 14 E). Named on Caldor (1951) and Peddler Hill (1951) 7.5' quadrangles.

McKinney Creek [PLACER]: *stream,* flows 4 miles to Lake Tahoe 1.5 miles southeast of Homewood (lat. 39°04'25" N, long. 120°08'25" W; sec. 7, T 14 N, R 17 E); the stream enters the lake near the south end of McKinney Bay. Named on Homewood (1955) 7.5' quadrangle. The name commemorates John McKinney of McKinney Bay (Gudde, 1949, p. 199).

McKinney Lake [PLACER]: *lake,* 1650 feet long, 3.25 miles south-southwest of Homewood (lat. 39°02'25" N, long. 120°10'35" W; sec. 23, T 14 N, R 16 E); the lake is along McKinney Creek. Named on Homewood (1955) 7.5' quadrangle.

McKinneys: see **McKinney Creek** [CALAVERAS].

McKinneys Humbug: see **McKinney Creek** [CALAVERAS].

McKinneys Secret Diggings: see **McKinney Creek** [CALAVERAS].

McKinstry Lake [PLACER]: *lake,* 950 feet long, 2.5 miles east of Bunker Hill (lat. 39°02'30" N, long. 120°19'50" W; sec. 19, T 14 N, R 15 E); the lake is 1 mile southeast of McKinstry Peak in McKinstry Meadow. Named on Wentworth Springs (1953) 7.5' quadrangle.

McKinstry Meadow [PLACER]: *valley,* 2.5 miles east-southeast of Bunker Hill along Jerrett Creek (lat. 39°02'20" N, long. 120°20'10" W; sec. 19, 30, T 14 N, R 15 E); the valley is 1 mile south-southeast of McKinstry Peak. Named on Wentworth Springs (1953) 7.5' quadrangle.

McKinstry Meadow: see **Little McKinstry Meadow** [PLACER].

McKinstry Peak [PLACER]: *peak,* nearly 2 miles east of Bunker Hill (lat. 39°03'05" N, long. 120°20'45" W; at NW cor. sec. 19, T 14 N, R 15 E). Named on Wentworth Springs (1953) 7.5' quadrangle. The name commemorates George McKinstry, Jr., who came to California in 1846 (Hanna, p. 181).

McLeans Bar: see **Melones** [CALAVERAS].

McLeans Ferry: see **Melones** [CALAVERAS].

McLean's Pass: see **Tioga Pass** [TUOLUMNE].

McLeod Flat: see **McCleod Flat** [MADERA].

McMahons [SIERRA]: *locality,* 5.25 miles northwest of Goodyears Bar (lat. 39°36' N, long. 120°56'40" W). Named on Downieville (1897) 30' quadrangle.

McManus [EL DORADO]: *locality,* nearly 4 miles northeast of Pollock Pines (lat. 38°47'55" N, long. 120°32' W; sec. 9, T 11 N, R 13 E). Named on Pollock Pines (1950) 7.5' quadrangle.

McMurray Lake [NEVADA]: *lake,* 5 miles east-northeast of Graniteville (lat. 39°27'40" N, long. 120°38'50" W; near N line sec. 5, T 18 N, R 12 E). Named on Graniteville (1982) 7.5' quadrangle.

McNair Meadow [SIERRA]: *area,* 2.5 miles west-northwest of Calpine (lat. 39°40'50" N, long. 120°29'05" W; sec. 14, T 21 N, R 13 E). Named on Calpine (1981) 7.5' quadrangle. Called Little Valley on Sierraville (1894) 30' quadrangle.

McNulty Ridge [MARIPOSA-TUOLUMNE]: *ridge,* west-northwest-trending, 1 mile long, 2.5 miles south-southeast of Don Pedro Camp on Mariposa-Tuolumne county line (lat. 37°41'05" N, long. 120°23'05" W). Named on La Grange (1962) 7.5' quadrangle.

McNulty Spring [TUOLUMNE]: *spring,* 2 miles south of Don Pedro Camp (lat. 37°41'05" N, long. 120°24'20" W; near W line sec. 11, T 3 N, R 14 E). Named on La Grange (1962) 7.5' quadrangle.

McPherrin Camp [SIERRA]: *locality,* 2 miles north of Calpine (lat. 39°41'35" N, long. 120°26'35" W; near NW cor. sec. 8, T 21 N, R 14 E). Named on Calpine (1981) 7.5' quadrangle.

McPhetres: see **Big Chief** [PLACER].

McSwain Meadows [TUOLUMNE]: *area,* 1.25 miles southeast of White Wolf (lat. 37°51'20" N, long. 119°38' W; sec. 14, T 1 S, R 21 E). Named on Hetch Hetchy Reservoir (1956) 15' quadrangle.

Meadow Brook [EL DORADO]: *locality,* 6.5 miles north of Chili Bar (lat. 38°51'35" N, long. 120°19'55" W; sec. 26, T 12 N, R 10 E). Named on Garden Valley (1949) 7.5' quadrangle.

Meadow Brook [MARIPOSA]: *stream,* flows 2 miles to Yosemite Valley 5 miles west-southwest of Yosemite Village (lat. 37°42'50" N, long. 119°40' W). Named on Yosemite (1956) 15' quadrangle.

Meadow Creek: see **West Meadow Creek** [PLACER].

Meadow Lake [NEVADA]: *lake,* 1.25 miles long, 11 miles northwest of Donner Pass (lat. 39°24'45" N, long. 120°29'45" W). Named on English Mountain (1983) and Webber Peak (1981) 7.5' quadrangles.

Meadow Lake: see **Summit City** [NEVADA].

Meadow Lake Hill [NEVADA]: *peak,* 10 miles northwest of Donner Pass (lat. 39°24'55" N, long. 120°28'50" W; sec. 23, T 18 N, R 13 E); the peak is east of Meadow Lake. Altitude 7821 feet. Named on Webber Peak (1981) 7.5' quadrangle.

Meadow Spring [PLACER]: *spring,* 3.5 miles southwest of Cisco Grove (lat. 39°16'25" N, long. 120°35'05" W; at NW cor. sec. 12, T 16 N, R 12 E); the spring is in Mears Meadow. Named on Cisco Grove (1955) 7.5' quadrangle.

Meadow-Vale: see **Summit Valley** [NEVADA-PLACER].

Meadowview Campground [TUOLUMNE]: *locality,* less than 1 mile south-southeast of Strawberry (lat. 38°11'10" N, long. 120°00'15" W; sec. 21, T 4 N, R 18 E). Named on Strawberry (1979) 7.5' quadrangle.

Meadow Vista [PLACER]: *locality,* 7.5 miles south-southwest of Colfax (lat. 39°00'10" N, long. 121°01'15" W; near S line sec. 6, T 13 N, R 9 E). Named on Auburn (1953) and Lake Combie (1949) 7.5' quadrangles.

Mears Meadow [PLACER]: *area,* 3.5 miles southwest of Cisco (lat. 39°16'20" N, long. 120°35' W; at NW cor. sec. 12, T 16 N, R 12 E). Named on Cisco Grove (1955) 7.5' quadrangle.

Meathouse Meadow [SIERRA]: *area,* 8 miles south-southeast of Sierraville (lat. 39°28'35" N, long. 120°18'50" W; near S line sec. 21, T 19 N, R 15 E). Named on Independence Lake (1981) 7.5' quadrangle.

Medano [MADERA]: *locality,* 4.5 miles north-northeast of Fairmead (lat. 37°07'50" N, long. 120°09'10" W; sec. 19, T 9 S, R 17 E). Named on Le Grand (1918) 7.5' quadrangle.

Media: see **Bates Station** [MADERA].

Medlicott Dome [MARIPOSA]: *peak,* 1.25 miles west-northwest of Cathedral Peak (lat. 37°51'20" N, long. 119°25'30" W; near NE cor. sec. 15, T 1 S, R 23 E). Named on Tuolumne Meadows (1956) 15' quadrangle. The name commemorates Harry P. Medlicott, who helped survey the Tioga Road in 1882; the feature also had the names "Court House Rock" and "Mount Medlicott" (Browning, 1988, p. 91).

Meeks Bay [EL DORADO]:
(1) *embayment,* along Lake Tahoe at the town of Meeks Bay (lat. 38°02'25" N, long. 120°07' W). Named on Meeks Bay (1955) 7.5' quadrangle. United States Board on Geographic Names (1936, p. 30) rejected the name "Meigs Bay" for the feature. The name is for the Meeks brothers, who bailed 25 tons of wild hay at the place in 1862 (Zauner, p. 43).
(2) *town,* 13 miles north of Pyramid Peak (lat. 39°02'20" N, long. 120°07'20" W); the town is at the embayment of the same name. Named on Homewood (1955) and Meeks Bay (1955) 7.5' quadrangles. United States Board on Geographic Names (1936, p. 30) rejected the name "Meigs Bay" for the town. Postal authorities established Meeks Bay post office in 1929 and discontinued it in 1972 (Salley, p. 137). They established Rubicon Lodge post office at a summer resort situated 2.5 miles south of Meeks Bay post office in 1921, discontinued it in 1924, reestablished it in 1925, and discontinued it in 1931 (Salley, p. 190). Truckee (1895) 30' quadrangle has the name "Murphys" at the site of the present town of Meeks Bay.

Meeks Creek [EL DORADO]: *stream,* heads at Rubicon Lake and flows 7 miles to Lake Tahoe at Meeks Bay (1) (lat. 39°02'15" N, long. 120°07'15" W; sec. 29, T 14 N, R 17 E). Named on Homewood (1955) 7.5' quadrangle. United States Board on Geographic Names (1936, p. 30) rejected the name "Meigs Creek" for the stream.

Meentzen Gulch [TUOLUMNE]: *canyon,* drained by a stream that flows 0.5 mile to Sawmill Gulch 2.25 miles southeast of Columbia (lat. 38°01' N, long. 120°22'15" W; sec. 19, T 2 N, R 15 E). Named on Columbia SE (1948) 7.5' quadrangle.

Mehrten Creek [EL DORADO]: *stream,* flows 1.5 miles to Middle Fork Cosumnes River 7 miles east-southeast of Caldor (lat. 38° 35' N, long. 120°18'30" W; sec. 34, T 9 N, R 15 E). Named on Peddler Hill (1951) 7.5' quadrangle.

Mehrten Spring [EL DORADO]: *spring,* 7 miles east-southeast of Caldor (lat. 38°34'45" N, long. 120°18'35" W; near NW cor. sec. 3, T 8 N, R 15 E). Named on Peddler Hill (1951) 7.5' quadrangle.

Meigs Bay: see **Meeks Bay** [EL DORADO].

Meigs Creek: see **Meeks Creek** [EL DORADO].

Meinecke: see **Stanislaus River** [CALAVERAS-TUOLUMNE].

Meiss [EL DORADO]: *locality,* 3.25 miles west of Leek Spring Hill (lat. 38°38'20" N, long. 120°20'05" W; at S line sec. 8, T 9 N, R 15 E). Named on Leek Spring Hill (1951) 7.5' quadrangle.

Melburn Hill: see **Remington Hill** [NEVADA] (2).

Mello Canyon [SIERRA]: *canyon,* drained by a

stream that flows 2 miles to Sierra Valley 4.5 miles north of Sierraville (lat. 39°39'05" N, long. 120°21'15" W; near SE cor. sec. 24, T 21 N, R 14 E). Named on Antelope Valley (1981) 7.5' quadrangle.

Melones [CALAVERAS]: *settlement,* 5.25 miles south-southwest of Vallecito on the north side of Stanislaus River (lat. 38°00'40" N, long. 120°29'45" W; sec. 24, T 2 N, R 13 E). Named on Columbia (1948) 7.5' quadrangle. Called Robinson on Big Trees (1891) 30' quadrangle. The first community to have the name "Melones" was the present village of Carson Hill, which was situated about 2 miles west of present Melones on the west slope of Carson Hill (1); present Melones is at the site of Robinsons Ferry, where John W. Robinson and Stephen Mead settled in 1848, and later operated a ferry (Hanna, p. 189). Postal authorities established Robinson's Ferry post office in 1879, changed the name to Robinson's in 1895, changed it to Melones in 1902, discontinued it in 1932, reestablished it in 1933, and discontinued it in 1942 (Salley, p. 137, 187). Gudde (1975, p. 202) listed McLeans Bar and McLeans Ferry, both located about 1 mile upstream from Robinsons Ferry near the confluence of Coyote Creek and Stanislaus River. Wood (p. 24) noted a place called El Dorado Bar that was situated between McLeans Ferry and Coyote Creek.

Melones Lake: see **New Melones Lake** [CALAVERAS-TUOLUMNE].

Melones Reservoir: see **New Melones Lake** [CALAVERAS-TUOLUMNE].

Melrose: see **Cherokee** [NEVADA].

Melsons Corner [EL DORADO]: *locality,* 4 miles north-northeast of Aukum (lat. 38°36'35" N, long. 120°42'10" W; near NW cor. sec. 30, T 9 N, R 12 E). Named on Aukum (1952) 7.5' quadrangle.

Mendon: see **Brownsville** [EL DORADO].

Mendota Pool [MADERA]: *water feature,* behind a dam on San Joaquin River 21 miles south west of Madera on Madera-Fresno county line (lat. 36°47'15" N, long. 120°22'15" W; sec. 19, T 13 S, R 15 E). Named on Mendota Dam (1956) 7.5' quadrangle.

Mercedes River: see **Merced River** [MADERA-MARIPOSA].

Merced Gorge [MARIPOSA]: *canyon,* 4 miles long, along Merced River above a point about 10 miles west-southwest of Yosemite Village (lat. 37°40'30" N, long. 119°44'30" W). Named on Yosemite (1956) 15' quadrangle.

Merced Group: see **Clark Range** [MADERA].

Merced Lake [MARIPOSA]: *lake,* 2500 feet long, 7.5 miles south of Cathedral Peak (lat. 37°44'20" N, long. 119°24'45" W); the lake is along Merced River. Named on Merced Peak (1953) 15' quadrangle. John Muir called the feature Shadow Lake (Browning, 1986, p. 144).

Merced Pass [MADERA]: *pass,* 3 miles west-southwest of Merced Peak (lat. 37°37' N, long. 119°26'30" W). Named on Merced Peak (1953) 15' quadrangle.

Merced Pass Lake: see **Lower Merced Pass Lake** [MADERA]; **Upper Merced Pass Lake** [MADERA].

Merced Peak [MADERA]: *peak,* 22 miles north-northeast of Yosemite Forks (lat. 37°38'05" N, long. 119°23'35" W); the peak is near the headwaters of Merced River. Altitude 11,726 feet. Named on Merced Peak (1953) 15' quadrangle. United States Board on Geographic Names (1976b, p. 1-2) approved the name "Mount Bruce" for a peak (altitude 9728 feet) located 6 miles southwest of Merced Peak (lat. 37°35'48" N, long. 119°29'32" W); the name commemorates the Bruce family, pioneers in the region in the 1850's.

Merced Peak Fork [MADERA]: *stream,* flows 6 miles to join Lyell Fork and form Merced River 5.25 miles north-northeast of Merced Peak (lat. 37°42'05" N, long. 119°20'50" W); the stream heads north of Merced Peak. Named on Merced Peak (1953) 15' quadrangle.

Merced River [MADERA-MARIPOSA]: *stream,* formed in Madera County by the confluence of Lyell Fork and Merced Peak Fork, flows 140 miles, partly in Mariposa County, to San Joaquin River 27 miles west of Merced in Merced County (lat. 37°20'55" N, long. 120°58'30" W; near W line sec. 3, T 7 S, R 9 E). Named on Atwater (1961), Coulterville (1947), El Portal (1947), Merced (1962), Merced Falls (1962), Merced Peak (1953), Turlock (1962), and Yosemite (1956) 15' quadrangles. Called Rio de los Merced on Ord's (1848) map, R. de la Merced on Wyld's (1849) map, and Mercedes River on Ellis' (1850) map. United States, Board on Geographic Names (1978c, p. 3) rejected the names "Aux-um-ne," "Aux-um-nes," "Rio de la Merced," "Wa-kal-la," and "El Rio de Nuestra Senora de la Merced" for the stream, and pointed out that Spanish explorers under Sergeant Gabriel Moraga named the river on September 29, 1806, five days after the feast day of Our Lady of Mercy—*merced* means "mercy" in Spanish. North Fork enters the main stream from the north 4.5 miles northeast of the village of Bear Valley in Mariposa County; it is 18 miles long and is named on Coulterville (1947), Lake Eleanor (1956), and Tuolumne (1948) 15' quadrangles. South Fork heads in Madera County and enters the main stream from the southeast 6 miles west-southwest of El Portal in Mariposa County; it is 43 miles long and is named on El Portal (1947), Merced Peak (1953), and Yosemite (1956) 15' quadrangles. United States Board on Geographic Names (1978c, p. 3) rejected the name "North Fork Merced River" for Lyell Fork. Gardiner (p.

139) noted a place called New York Camp that was started in Mariposa County near the mouth of Merced River in 1850.

Merced River: see **Lyell Fork** [MADERA].

Mercer Cave [CALAVERAS]: *cave,* 1 mile northwest of Murphys (lat. 38°09'05" N, long. 120°28'35" W; sec. 31, T 4 N, R 14 E). Named on Murphys (1948) 7.5' quadrangle.

Mercer Mountain [MADERA]: *peak,* 1 mile east of O'Neals (lat. 37° 07'40" N, long. 119°40'40" W; near SE cor. sec. 21, T 9 S, R 21 E). Altitude 1921 feet. Named on O'Neals (1965) 7.5' quadrangle.

Mercur Peak [TUOLUMNE]: *peak,* 12 miles southeast of Pinecrest (lat. 38°05'45" N, long. 119°48'50" W). Named on Pinecrest (1956) 15' quadrangle. Colonel W.W. Forsyth named the peak in 1912 for James Mercur, professor of engineering at West Point (United States Board on Geographic Names, 1934, p. 16).

Merrill Spring [TUOLUMNE]: *spring,* 1.25 miles east-northeast of Long Barn (lat. 38°05'45" N, long. 120°06'55" W; sec. 21, T 3 N, R 17 E). Named on Hull Creek (1979) 7.5' quadrangle.

Merril Creek [SIERRA]: *stream,* flows nearly 7 miles to Davies Creek 3.5 miles south of Crystal Peak (lat. 39°30'20" N, long. 120° 05'50" W; at N line sec. 16, T 19 N, R 17 E); the stream goes through Merril Valley. Named on Dog Valley (1981) 7.5' quadrangle.

Merril Valley [SIERRA]: *valley,* 2 miles south-southwest of Crystal Peak (lat. 39°31'55" N, long. 120°05'50" W; mainly in sec. 4, T 19 N, R 17 E); the valley is along Merril Creek. Named on Dog Valley (1981) 7.5' quadrangle.

Metcalf Gap [MADERA]: *pass,* 15 miles north-northeast of Raymond (lat. 37°24'15" N, long. 119°45'55" W; sec, 15, T 6 S, R 20 E). Named on Stumpfield Mountain (1947) 7.5' quadrangle.

Mexican Flat: see **Jamestown** [TUOLUMNE].

Mexican Gulch [CALAVERAS]: *canyon,* drained by a stream that flows 2.5 miles to Jesus Maria Creek nearly 7 miles south-southwest of Rail Road Flat (lat. 38°15'30" N, long. 120°34'20" W; near W line sec. 29, T 5 N, R 13 E). Named on Calaveritas (1962) and Rail Road Flat (1948) 7.5' quadrangles.

Mexican Gulch [PLACER]: *canyon,* drained by a stream that flows 1.5 miles to Shirttail Canyon 5.25 miles southeast of Colfax (lat. 39°02'30" N, long. 120°53'15" W; near SE cor. sec. 19, T 14 N, R 10 E); the canyon heads near Yankee Jims. Named on Colfax (1949) and Foresthill (1949) 7.5' quadrangles. Called Yankee Jims Cañon on Whitney's (1873) map.

Mexican Gulch [TUOLUMNE]: *canyon,* drained by a stream that flows 1 mile to Tuolumne River 1.25 miles southwest of Don Pedro Camp (lat. 37°42'10" N, long. 120°25'15" W; sec. 3, T 3 S, R 14 E). Named on La Grange (1962) 7.5' quadrangle. On Merced Falls (1944) 15' quadrangle, the name

applies to a nearby canyon (sec. 34, T 2 S, R 14 E).

Meyer Ravine [NEVADA]: *canyon,* drained by a stream that flows 1.5 miles to Wolf Creek 1.5 miles west of Higgins Corner (lat. 39° 02'40" N, long. 121°07'20" W; near SE cor. sec. 19, T 14 N, R 8 E). Named on Lake Combie (1949) and Wolf (1949) 7.5' quadrangles.

Meyers [EL DORADO]: *village,* 3 miles north-northeast of Echo Summit in Lake Valley (lat. 38°51'20" N, long. 120°00'45" W; sec. 29, T 12 N, R 18 E). Named on Echo Lake (1955) 7.5' quadrangle. Called Yanks on Bancroft's (1864) map. Postal authorities established Meyers post office in 1904, discontinued it in 1957, reestablished it in 1958, and changed the name to Tahoe Paradise in 1962 (Salley, p. 139, 218). Martin Smith operated a trading post and travelers stop at the site in the early 1850's; Ephraim Clement, who had the nickname "Yank," took over the place from Smith, and it was known by the name "Yank's Station" before George Henry Dudly Meyers bought out Clement in 1873 (Farquhar, 1965, p. 96, 104). Postal authorities established Little Norway post office 9 miles west of Meyers in 1961 (Salley, p. 123).

Meyers Ravine [NEVADA]: *canyon,* drained by a stream that flows 2 miles to South Yuba River 3.5 miles north-northwest of Nevada City (lat. 39°18'40" N, long. 121°03' W; sec. 26, T 17 N, R 8 E). Named on Nevada City (1948) 7.5' quadrangle. Called Mayers Rav. on Whitney's (1873) map, and called Myers Ravine on Logan's (1940) map. On Smartsville (1895) 30' quadrangle, the stream in the canyon has the name "Brush Creek."

Miami: see **Grub Gulch** [MADERA] (2).

Miami [MARIPOSA]: *locality,* 5 miles west of Happy Camp (present Fish Camp) (lat. 37°28'35" N, long. 119°43'30" W; near SE cor. sec. 24, T 5 S, R 20 E). Named on Mariposa (1912) 30' quadrangle. Postal authorities established Miami post office in 1894, moved it 3 miles north in 1898, and discontinued it in 1926; the name is from Miami Mountain (Salley, p. 139). California Division of Highways' (1934) map shows a place called Oakvale Retreat located 3 miles south-southeast of Miami.

Miami Creek [MADERA-MARIPOSA]: *stream,* heads in Mariposa County and flows 17 miles to Fresno River 5.5 miles west-southwest of Yosemite Forks in Mariposa County (lat. 37°20'30" N, long. 119°43'40" W; near NE cor. sec. 12, T 7 S, R 20 E). Named on Bass Lake (1953) 15' quadrangle. Called North Fork on Mariposa (1912) 30' quadrangle, but United States Board on Geographic Names (1964b, p. 13) rejected the name "North Fork Fresno River" for the stream.

Miami Mill: see **Old Miami Mill**, under

Timberloft Camp [MARIPOSA].
Miami Mountain [MARIPOSA]: *peak,* 7 miles southwest of Fish Camp (lat. 37°25'10" N, long. 120°44'40" W; near SE cor. sec. 11, T 6 S, R 20 E). Altitude 4327 feet. Named on Bass Lake (1953) and Mariposa (1947) 15' quadrangles.
Michaels: see **Coarsegold** [MADERA].
Michie Peak [TUOLUMNE]: *peak,* 6 miles west-southwest of Tower Peak (lat. 38°07'25" N, long. 119°39'15" W). Altitude 10,365 feet. Named on Tower Peak (1956) 15' quadrangle. Colonel W.W. Forsyth named the peak for Peter Smith Michie, professor of engineering at West Point (Hanna, p. 191).
Michigan Bluff [PLACER]: *village,* 12.5 miles east-southeast of Colfax (lat. 39°02'30" N, long. 120°44'05" W; at W line sec. 22, T 14 N, R 11 E). Named on Michigan Bluff (1952) 7.5' quadrangle. Called Michigan Bluffs on Whitney's (1873) map. Postal authorities established Michigan Bluff post office in 1854 and discontinued it in 1943 (Frickstad, p. 121). The first community near the place was called Michigan City; when it threatened to slide away, the inhabitants moved higher up the slope and started a new community that they called Michigan Bluff (Hanna, p. 191-192). Lindgren's (1911a) map shows a place called Bullion located 4 miles north of Michigan Bluff. Postal authorities established Bullion post office in 1904 and discontinued it in 1915 (Frickstad, p. 119). They established Webster post office 6 miles northeast of Michigan Bluff in 1865 and discontinued it in 1867 (Salley, p. 236).
Michigan City: see **Michigan Bluff** [PLACER].
Michigan Flat: see **Lotus** [EL DORADO].
Midas [PLACER]: *locality,* 4.5 miles east of Dutch Flat along Southern Pacific Railroad (lat. 29°13' N, long. 120°45'25" W; near SE cor. sec. 29, T 16 N, R 11 E). Named on Dutch Flat (1950) 7.5' quadrangle. Hobson's (1890b) map shows a place called Shady Run located at or near present Midas. Postal authorities established Shady Run post office in 1872, discontinued it in 1879, reestablished it in 1903, and discontinued it in 1904 (Frickstad, p. 121). On Colfax (1898) 30' quadrangle, the name "Shady Run" applies to a stream near present Midas. Whitney's (1873) map shows a place called Blue Bluffs situated 0.5 mile north of Shady Run.
Middle Bar [CALAVERAS]: *locality,* 2.25 miles west of Mokelumne Hill along Mokelumne River (lat. 38°17'55" N, long. 120°44'50" W; sec. 10, T 5 N, R 11 E). Site named on Mokelumne Hill (1948) 7.5' quadrangle. Camp's (1962) map has the name "Jackass Gulch" for a canyon that opens into the canyon of Mokelumne River near Middle Bar.
Middle Bar: see **Fords Bar** [EL DORADO].
Middle Branigan Lake [TUOLUMNE]: *lake,*

3000 feet long, 10.5 miles southwest of Tower Peak (lat. 38°01'55" N, long. 119°40'40" W); the feature is between Branigan Lake and Upper Branigan Lake. Named on Tower Peak (1956) 15' quadrangle.
Middle Brother [MARIPOSA]: *relief feature,* 1.5 miles west-southwest of Yosemite Village on the north side of Yosemite Valley (lat. 37°44'35" N, long. 119°36'45" W); the feature is one of the group called Three Brothers. Named on Yosemite (1956) 15' quadrangle.
Middle Butte [EL DORADO]: *peak,* 8 miles southeast of Camino (lat. 38°40'15" N, long. 120°33'15" W; near W line sec. 33, T 10 N, R 13 E); the peak is between Big Butte and Little Butte. Altitude 4219 feet. Named on Sly Park (1952) 7.5' quadrangle. Middle Butte, Big Butte, and Little Butte together have the label "Buttes" on Placerville (1893) 30' quadrangle.
Middle Camp: see **Confidence** [TUOLUMNE].
Middle Creek [EL DORADO]: *stream,* flows 3 miles to Silver Fork American River 2.25 miles southeast of Kyburz (lat. 38°45'05" N, long. 120°15'50" W; near W line sec. 1, T 10 N, R 15 E). Named on Kyburz (1952) and Pyramid Peak (1955) 7.5' quadrangles.
Middle Dry Creek [EL DORADO]: *stream,* flows 5.5 miles to Dogtown Creek 3 miles west-southwest of Caldor (lat. 38°35'35" N, long. 120°29'10" W; sec. 36, T 9 N, R 13 E). Named on Caldor (1951) 7.5' quadrangle.
Middle Emigrant Lake [TUOLUMNE]: *lake,* 1400 feet long, 6.5 miles west-northwest of Tower Peak along North Fork Cherry Creek (lat. 38°11'25" N, long. 119°39'15" W); the feature is about halfway between Emigrant Lake and High Emigrant Lake. Named on Tower Peak (1956) 15' quadrangle.
Middle Fork Campground [TUOLUMNE]: *locality,* 2 miles south-southwest of Mather (lat. 37°51'20" N, long. 119°51'50" W; near E line sec. 15, T 1 S, R 19 E); the place is along Middle Tuolumne River; which formerly was called Middle Fork Tuolumne River. Named on Lake Eleanor (1956) 15' quadrangle.
Middle Gulch [CALAVERAS]: *canyon,* drained by a stream that flows 1.5 miles to Blue Creek 4.25 miles west of Tamarack (lat. 38°25'50" N, long 120°09'20" W; near E line sec. 25, T 7 N, R 16 E). Named on Calaveras Dome (1979) 7.5' quadrangle.
Middle Lake [NEVADA]: *lake,* 1450 feet long, 3.5 miles southwest of English Mountain along South Fork Canyon Creek (lat. 39°24'45" N, long. 120°36'10" W; on W line sec. 23, T 18 N, R 12 E). Named on English Mountain (1983) 7.5' quadrangle.
Middle Martis Creek [PLACER]: *stream,* flows 5.25 miles to Martis Creek nearly 5 miles west of Martis Peak (lat. 39°18'05" N, long. 120°07'15" W; near SW cor. sec. 20, T 17 N, R 17 E). Named on Martis Peak (1955) 7.5'

quadrangle. Hobson's (1890b) map shows a place called Elizabeth Town located along present Middle Martis Creek about 1.25 miles above the mouth of the stream (near W line sec. 28, T 17 N, R 17 E).

Middle Mountain [EL DORADO]: *peak,* 1.5 miles west of Phipps Peak (lat. 38°57'25" N, long. 120°10'50" W; sec. 23, T 13 N, R 16 E). Altitude 8333 feet. Named on Rockbound Valley (1955) 7.5' quadrangle.

Middle Three Meadow [TUOLUMNE]: *area,* 7.25 miles east-northeast of Pinecrest (lat. 38°14'40" N, long. 119°52'45" W; on E line sec. 33, T 5 N, R 19 E); the place is one of the group called Three Meadows. Named on Pinecrest (1979) 7.5' quadrangle.

Middle Tuolumne River [TUOLUMNE]: *stream,* flows 30 miles to South Fork Tuolumne River 11 miles south-southeast of Duckwall Mountain (lat. 37°49'40" N, long. 120°01'10" W; sec. 29, T 1 S, R 18 E). Named on Hetch Hetchy Reservoir (1956) and Lake Eleanor (1956) 15' quadrangles. Called Middle Fork Tuolumne River on Tuolumne (1948) 15' quadrangle, but United States Board on Geographic Names (1934, p. 17) rejected this name for the stream.

Middletown: see **Placerville** [EL DORADO].

Middle Velma Lake [EL DORADO]: *lake,* 2750 feet long, 1.25 miles south of Phipps Peak (lat. 38°56'10" N, long. 120°08'55" W; at SW cor. sec. 30, T 13 N, R 17 E); the lake is between Upper Velma Lake and Lower Velma Lake. Named on Rockbound Valley (1955) 7.5' quadrangle.

Middle Wallace Canyon: see **South Wallace Canyon** [PLACER].

Middle Waters Campground [SIERRA]: *locality,* 4 miles southwest of Sierra City (lat. 39°31'30" N, long. 120°41' W; near SE cor. sec. 12, T 19 N, R 11 E). Named on Sierra City (1981) 7.5' quadrangle.

Middle Yuba River [NEVADA-SIERRA]: *stream,* forms part of Nevada-Sierra county line and Nevada-Yuba county line, heads in Nevada County and flows 55 miles to join North Yuba River in Yuba County and form Yuba River nearly 4 miles east of Dobbins in Yuba County (lat. 39°22'05" N, long. 121°08'10" W; sec. 1, T 17 N, R 7 E). Named on Alleghany (1949), Camptonville (1948), Challenge (1948), English Mountain (1983), French Corral (1948), Graniteville (1982), Haypress Valley (1981), Pike (1949), Sierra City (1981), and Webber Peak (1981) 7.5' quadrangles. Called Middle Fork Yuba River on Downieville (1897), Smartsville (1895), and Truckee (1940) 30' quadrangles, but United States Board on Geographic Names (1950, p. 5-6) rejected this name and the name "Middle Fork" for the stream. On Smartsville (1895) 30' quadrangle, present Yuba River from the mouth of present Middle Yuba River downstream to the mouth of present South

Yuba River is called Middle Fork Yuba River.

Midpines [MARIPOSA]: *locality,* 12 miles southwest of El Portal (lat. 37°32'35" N, long. 119°55'10" W; sec. 31, T 4 S, R 19 E). Named on Feliciana Mountain (1947) 7.5' quadrangle. Postal authorities established Midpines post office in 1929 (Frickstad, p. 92). Newell D. Chamberlain began a resort at the place in 1926, and named the resort for its position in the pine forest midway between Merced and Yosemite Valley (Sargent, Shirley, 1976, p. 11).

Miguel Creek [TUOLUMNE]: *stream,* flows 4.5 miles to Eleanor Creek 5 miles north-northwest of Mather (lat. 37°57'15" N, long. 119°52'45" W; sec. 10, T 1 N, R 19 E); the stream goes through Miguel Meadow. Named on Lake Eleanor (1956) 15' quadrangle. United States Board on Geographic Names (1933, p. 519) rejected the name "McGill Creek" for the stream.

Miguel Meadow [TUOLUMNE]: *area,* 5.5 miles north of Mather (lat. 37°57'35" N, long. 119°50'15" W; sec. 12, T 1 N, R 19 E); the place is along Miguel Creek. Named on Lake Eleanor (1956) 15' quadrangle. Miguel Herrara and his partner owned the area and grazed cattle and horses there (Uhte, p. 66). The name "Miguel" was corrupted to "McGill" in the early days (Browning, 1986, p. 146), but United States Board on Geographic Names (1933, p. 519) rejected the name "McGill Meadow" for the place.

Mike Walker Canyon [MADERA]: *canyon,* drained by a stream that flows 1.5 miles to San Joaquin River 6.25 miles south-southwest of the town of North Fork (lat. 37°08'40" N, long. 119°33'15" W; sec. 15, T 9 S, R 22 E). Named on North Fork (1965) 7.5' quadrangle.

Mildred: see **Mount Mildred** [PLACER].

Mildred Lake [MARIPOSA]: *lake,* 1400 feet long, nearly 3 miles southwest of Cathedral Peak (lat. 37°49'15" N, long. 119°26'25" W; sec. 27, T 1 S, R 23 E). Named on Tuolumne Meadows (1956) 15' quadrangle. The name commemorates Mildred Sovulewski, who was the daughter of Gabriel Sovulewski, a ranger and supervisor in Yosemite National Park from 1906 until 1936 (Browning, 1986, p. 146).

Mildred Lakes [PLACER]: *lakes,* largest 500 feet long, 3.5 miles southwest of Granite Chief (lat. 39°09'40" N, long. 120°19'40" W; near W line sec. 8, T 15 N, R 15 E); the lakes are 1 mile north of Mount Mildred. Named on Granite Chief (1953) 7.5' quadrangle.

Mildred Ridge [PLACER]: *ridge,* north-trending, 1.5 miles long, nearly 4 miles southwest of Granite Chief (lat. 39°09'25" N, long. 120°19'50" W); Mount Mildred is at the south end of the ridge. Named on Granite Chief (1953) 7.5' quadrangle.

Mile High Curve [MADERA]: *locality,* 5.25 miles east-southeast of Shuteye Peak (lat.

37°18'40" N, long. 119°20'50" W); the feature is along a road 2500 feet above San Joaquin River. Named on Shuteye Peak (1953) 15' quadrangle.

Mile Hill Creek [PLACER]: *stream,* flows 1.5 miles to Middle Fork American River 8 miles east-northeast of Auburn (lat. 38°57'20" N, long. 120°56'15" W; near N line sec. 26, T 13 N, R 9 E). Named on Greenwood (1949) 7.5' quadrangle.

Mile Hill Toll House [PLACER]: *locality,* 9 miles northeast of Auburn (lat. 38°59' N, long. 120°56'20" W). Named on Placerville (1893) 30' quadrangle.

Miles Creek [MARIPOSA]: *stream,* heads in Mariposa County and flows 31 miles to Hartley Slough 14 miles north-northeast of Dos Palos Y in Merced County (lat. 37°14'40" N, long. 120°32'30" W; at SW cor. sec. 10, T 8 S, R 13 E). Named on El Nido (1960), Indian Gulch (1962), Merced (1961), Owens Reservoir (1962), Planada (1961), and Sandy Mush (1962) 7.5' quadrangles.

Milk Lake [NEVADA]: *lake,* 1100 feet long, 4.5 miles southwest of English Mountain (lat. 39°23'40" N, long. 120°36'25" W; near E line sec. 27, T 18 N, R 12 E). Named on English Mountain (1983) 7.5' quadrangle.

Milk Ranch Spring [TUOLUMNE]: *spring,* 4.5 miles southeast of Long Barn (lat. 38°02'40" N, long. 120°04'20" W; sec. 11, T 2 N, R 17 E). Named on Hull Creek (1979) 7.5' quadrangle.

Mill Creek [AMADOR]: *stream,* flows 7.25 miles to Tiger Creek Reservoir 9 miles east-northeast of Pine Grove (lat. 38°26'55" N, long. 120°30' W; sec. 24, T 7 N, R 13 E). Named on Caldor (1951), Devils Nose (1979), and West Point (1948) 7.5' quadrangles. On Mokelumne Hill (1948) 15' quadrangle, the name "Antelope Creek" seems to apply to present Mill Creek below the present junction of Antelope Creek and Mill Creek.

Mill Creek [CALAVERAS]:
(1) *stream,* flows 2.5 miles to North Fork Stanislaus River 12.5 miles southwest of Tamarack near Boards Crossing (lat. 38°18'25" N, long. 120°14' W; sec. 8, T 5 N, R 16 E). Named on Boards Crossing (1979) 7.5' quadrangle.
(2) *stream,* formed by the confluence of Love Creek and Moran Creek, flows 3.5 miles to North Fork Stanislaus River 7.5 miles east-northeast of Murphys (lat. 38°10'55" N, long. 120°20'15" W; near E line sec. 20, T 4 N, R 15 E). Named on Stanislaus (1948) 7.5' quadrangle.

Mill Creek [EL DORADO]:
(1) *stream,* flows nearly 1 mile to Slab Creek 8 miles north-northwest of Pollock Pines (lat. 38°52'10" N, long. 120°37'30" W; sec. 22, T 12 N, R 12 E). Named on Devil Peak (1950) and Slate Mountain (1950) 7.5' quadrangles.
(2) *stream,* flows 5.25 miles to South Fork American River 3 miles east of Riverton (lat.

38°46'25" N, long. 120°23'40" W; sec. 27, T 11 N, R 14 E). Named on Leek Spring Hill (1951), Riverton (1950), and Stump Spring (1951) 7.5' quadrangles. Called Wolf Creek on Pyramid Peak (1896) 30' quadrangle.

Mill Creek [PLACER]: *stream,* flows 2 miles to Shirttail Canyon nearly 4 miles north-northeast of Foresthill (lat. 39°04'15" N, long. 120°47'20" W; near W line sec. 7, T 14 N, R 11 E). Named on Foresthill (1949) 7.5' quadrangle.

Mill Creek [TUOLUMNE]: *stream,* flows 8 miles to Middle Fork Stanislaus River 7.5 miles southeast of Liberty Hill (lat. 38°17'20" N, long. 120°00'30" W; near E line sec. 17, T 5 N, R 18 E). Named on Donnell Lake (1979) and Liberty Hill (1979) 7.5' quadrangles.

Mill Creek: see **Little Mill Creek** [AMADOR]; **Old Mill Creek** [SIERRA].

Mill Creek Campground [TUOLUMNE]: *locality,* 6.25 miles west-southwest of Dardanelle (lat. 38°18'05" N, long. 118°56'10" W; near E line sec. 12, T 5 N, R 18 E); the place is along Mill Creek. Named on Dardanelles Cone (1956) 15' quadrangle.

Mill Creek Ridge [EL DORADO]: *ridge,* north-to northwest-trending, 4 miles long, center 8 miles north-northwest of Leek Spring Hill (lat. 38°43'45" N, long. 120°21'40" W); the feature is northeast of Mill Creek (2). Named on Leek Spring Hill (1951) and Stump Spring (1951) 7.5' quadrangles.

Miller: see **Joe Miller Ravine** [NEVADA]; **Kismet** [MADERA].

Miller Creek [MADERA]: *stream,* flows 4.5 miles to Granite Creek 14 miles northeast of Shuteye Peak (lat. 37°29'35" N, long. 119°14'40" W; sec. 16, T 5 S, R 25 E). Named on Kaiser Peak (1953), Merced Peak (1953), and Shuteye Peak (1953) 15' quadrangles.

Miller Creek [PLACER]: *stream,* flows nearly 4 miles to the canyon of Rubicon River 6.25 miles southwest of Homewood (lat. 39°01'40" N, long. 120°14'55" W; sec. 36, T 14 N, R 16 E). Named on Homewood (1955) 7.5' quadrangle.

Miller Creek [SIERRA]: *stream,* flows 1.5 miles to Oregon Creek 4.25 miles west of Alleghany (lat. 39°28'15" N, long. 120°55'15" W; sec. 36, T 19 N, R 9 E). Named on Pike (1949) 7.5' quadrangle, which shows Miller ranch near the stream.

Miller Creek: see **Heavenly Valley Creek** [EL DORADO]; **North Miller Creek** [PLACER].

Miller Crossing [MADERA]: *locality,* 10 miles southwest of Devils Postpile along San Joaquin River (lat. 37°30'35" N, long. 119° 12' W; sec. 11, T 5 S, R 25 E). Named on Devils Postpile (1953) 15' quadrangle. The name is for William C. Miller, an early-day sheepman (Browning, 1986, p. 147).

Miller Gulch [MARIPOSA]: *canyon,* drained by a stream that flows 3.25 miles to Merced River 8 miles west of El Portal (lat. 37°40'05" N, long. 119°55'15" W). Named on Kinsley (1947) 7.5' quadrangle. Yosemite (1909) 30' quadrangle has the name "Big Grizzly" for the stream in this canyon.

Miller House: see **Heavenly Valley Creek** [EL DORADO].

Miller Lake [PLACER]: *lake,* 2850 feet long, 4 miles south-southwest of Homewood (lat. 39°02'05" N, long. 120°12' W; at W line sec. 27, T 14 N, R 16 E); the lake is along Miller Creek. Named on Homewood (1955) 7.5' quadrangle.

Miller Lake [TUOLUMNE]: *lake,* 1600 feet long, 10.5 miles west-northwest of Tioga Pass (lat. 37°59'30" N, long. 119°25'05" W). Named on Tuolumne Meadows (1956) 15' quadrangle. Lieutenant N.F. McClure named the lake in 1894 for a soldier in his command (United States Board on Geographic Names, 1934, p. 17).

Miller Meadow [MADERA]: *area,* 12.5 miles northeast of Shuteye Peak (lat. 37°29'50" N, long. 119°17'30" W; sec. 13, T 5 S, R 24 E). Named on Shuteye Peak (1953) 15' quadrangle.

Miller Meadow Campground [MADERA]: *locality,* 10.5 miles south-southeast of Merced Peak (lat. 37°30'15" N, long. 119°17'20" W; near S line sec. 12, T 5 S, R 24 E). Named on Merced Peak (1953) 15' quadrangle.

Miller Meadows [PLACER]: *areas,* nearly 5 miles southwest of Homewood (lat. 39°02'05" N, long. 120°13' W; sec. 28, 29, T 14 N, R 16 E); the place is along Miller Creek. Named on Homewood (1955) 7.5' quadrangle.

Millers Corner: see **Twentytwo Mile House** [MADERA].

Millers Defeat Cañon: see **Starr Ravine** [PLACER].

Miller Spring [SIERRA]: *spring,* 4 miles west-northwest of Alleghany (lat. 39°29'10" N, long. 120°55' W; sec. 25, T 19 N, R 9 E). Named on Colfax (1938) 30' quadrangle. Pike (1949) 7.5' quadrangle shows the site of Miller ranch at the place.

Millerton Lake [MADERA]: *lake,* behind a dam on San Joaquin River 9 miles south of O'Neals on Madera-Fresno county line (lat. 37°00' N, long. 119°42'15" W; sec. 5, T 11 S, R 21 E). Named on Friant (1964), Millerton Lake East (1965), and Millerton Lake West (1965) 7.5' quadrangles. Water of the lake covers the site of Old Millerton in Fresno County.

Millerton Ridge [MADERA]: *ridge,* southwest-trending, 1.5 miles long, 5.5 miles south of O'Neals (lat. 37°02'45" N, long. 119° 41' W); the ridge is north of Millerton Lake. Named on Millerton Lake West (1965) 7.5' quadrangle.

Millertown [PLACER]: *locality,* 1.25 miles northwest of downtown Auburn (lat. 38°54'40" N, long. 121°05'30" W; near N line sec. 9, T 12 N, R 8 E). Site named on Auburn (1953) 7.5' quadrangle. Myrick (p. 115) used the form "Miller Town" for the name.

Millionaire Camp [EL DORADO]: *locality,* 4 miles southeast of Robbs Peak (lat. 38°53'05"

N, long. 120°21'15" W; sec. 13, T 12 N, R 14 E). Named on Loon Lake (1952) 7.5' quadrangle.

Million Dollar Creek [NEVADA]: *stream,* flows 1.5 miles to Steephollow Creek 7.5 miles northeast of Chicago Park (lat. 39°13'10" N, long. 120°51'35" W; sec. 28, T 16 N, R 10 E). Named on Dutch Flat (1950) 7.5' quadrangle.

Million Dollar Spring [TUOLUMNE]: *spring,* 10 miles northeast of Stanislaus (lat. 38°15'25" N, long. 120°15'15" W; sec. 30, T 5 N, R 16 E). Named on Dorrington (1979) 7.5' quadrangle.

Mill Pond [EL DORADO]: *lakes,* two connected, each 500 feet long, 7 miles west of Pollock Pines in South Canyon (lat. 38°45'15" N, long. 120°42'40" W; sec. 35, T 11 N, R 11 E). Named on Slate Mountain (1950, photorevised 1973) 7.5' quadrangle.

Mills Creek [EL DORADO]: *stream,* flows 2 miles to Squaw Hollow Creek 6 miles southwest of Camino (lat. 38°40'15" N, long. 120° 44'30" W; near SE cor. sec. 34, T 10 N, R 11 E). Named on Camino (1952) 7.5' quadrangle.

Mills Peak [SIERRA]: *peak,* 9.5 miles north of Sierra City (lat. 39° 42'20" N, long. 120°37'20" W; at N line sec. 10, T 21 N, R 12 E). Named on Clio (1981) 7.5' quadrangle.

Mills Spring [NEVADA]: *spring,* 7.5 miles northeast of Truckee (lat. 39°23'40" N, long. 120°04'30" W; sec. 22, T 18 N, R 17 E). Named on Boca (1955) 7.5' quadrangle.

Mill Valley: see **Mokelumne Hill** [CALAVERAS].

Milton [CALAVERAS]: *settlement,* 4.5 miles south-southeast of Jenny Lind (lat. 38°01'55" N, long. 120°51'05" W; near NW cor. sec. 14, T 2 N, R 10 E). Named on Jenny Lind (1962) 7.5' quadrangle. Jackson (1902) 30' quadrangle shows the place at the end of Stockton and Copperopolis Railroad. Postal authorities established Milton post office in 1871 and discontinued it in 1942 (Frickstad, p. 15). The name is for Milton Latham, a construction engineer for Southern Pacific Railroad when the rail line was built to the place in 1871 (Hanna, p. 193).

Milton [SIERRA]: *locality,* 3.5 miles southeast of Sierra City near Middle Fork Yuba River (present Middle Yuba River) (lat. 39°31'30" N, long. 120°35'30" W). Named on Downieville (1897) 30' quadrangle.

Milton Creek [SIERRA]: *stream,* flows nearly 5 miles to Haypress Creek 2.5 miles east of Sierra City (lat. 39°33'55" N, long. 120°35'05" W; near SW cor. sec. 25, T 20 N, R 12 E). Named on Haypress Valley (1981) 7.5' quadrangle.

Milton Reservoir [NEVADA]: *lake,* behind a dam on Middle Yuba River 5.5 miles north-northwest of English Mountain (lat. 39°31'20" N, long. 120°34'55" W; near SW cor. sec. 12, T 19 N, R 12 E). Named on Haypress Valley (1981) 7.5' quadrangle. Downieville (1897)

30' quadrangle shows Milton [SIERRA] near the lake.

Minaret Creek [MADERA]: *stream,* flows 5 miles to Middle Fork San Joaquin River less than 1 mile north-northwest of Devils Postpile (lat. 37°38'05" N, long. 119°05'05" W); the stream heads at Minaret Lake. Named on Devils Postpile (1953) 15' quadrangle.

Minaret Falls [MADERA]: *waterfall,* 1.25 miles north-northwest of Devils Postpile (lat. 37°38'25" N, long. 119°05'30" W); the feature is along Minaret Creek. Named on Devils Postpile (1953) 15' quadrangle.

Minaret Falls Campground [MADERA]: *locality,* 1 mile north of Devils Postpile along Middle Fork San Joaquin River (lat. 37°38'20" N, long. 119°05' W); the place is 0.5 mile east-southeast of Minaret Falls. Named on Devils Postpile (1953) 15' quadrangle.

Minaret Lake [MADERA]: *lake,* 2000 feet long, nearly 5 miles west-northwest of Devils Postpile (lat. 37°39'35" N, long. 119°09'25" W); the lake is 1 mile east of Minarets. Named on Devils Postpile (1953) 15' quadrangle.

Minaret Lake: see **Johnston Lake** [MADERA].

Minaret Meadow: see **Johnston Meadow** [MADERA].

Minarets [MADERA]: *relief features,* 6 miles west-northwest of Devils Postpile (lat. 37°39'50" N, long. 119°10'45" W). Named on Devils Postpile (1953) 15' quadrangle. Members of the Whitney survey named the features for their resemblance to mosque spires (Smith, p. 26).

Minarets: see **North Fork** [MADERA].

Minaret Summit [MADERA]: *pass,* 2.5 miles north-northeast of Devils Postpile on Madera-Mono county line (lat. 37°39'15" N, long. 119°03'25" W). Named on Devils Postpile (1953) 15' quadrangle.

Minear: see **Jerseydale** [MARIPOSA].

Mineral Bar: see **Colfax** [PLACER].

Mineral Point [PLACER]: *ridge,* south- to west-southwest-trending, 1 mile long, 7 miles northeast of Michigan Bluff (lat. 39°06' N, long. 120°37'30" W; sec. 24, T 15 N, R 12 E). Named on Greek Store (1952) and Michigan Bluff (1952) 7.5' quadrangles.

Miners Ravine [PLACER]: *canyon,* drained by a stream that flows 15 miles to join Antelope Creek and form Dry Creek (2) 1 mile east-northeast of downtown Roseville (lat. 38°45'20" N, long. 121° 16' W; near E line sec. 35, T 11 N, R 6 E). Named on Pilot Hill (1954), Rocklin (1967), and Roseville (1967) 7.5' quadrangles.

Minister Gulch [AMADOR]: *canyon,* drained by a stream that flows less than 1 mile to Hunt Gulch 2.25 miles south-southeast of Jackson (lat. 38°19'10" N, long. 120°45'05" W; sec. 3, T 5 N, R 11 E). Named on Mokelumne Hill (1948) 7.5' quadrangle. The name is for Peter Y. Cool and three other ministers who mined gold in the canyon (Watson, p. 206-207).

Minita Creek: see **Guadalupe Creek** [MARIPOSA].

Minita Gulch: see **Guadalupe Creek** [MARIPOSA]; **La Mineta Gulch** [MARIPOSA].

Minkalo: see **Camp Minkalo** [AMADOR].

Minnesota: see **Minnesota Flat** [SIERRA].

Minnesota Flat [SIERRA]: *locality,* 1.5 miles south-southeast of Alleghany (lat. 39°27' N, long. 120°49'50" W; near NW cor. sec. 11, T 18 N, R 10 E). Site named on Alleghany (1949) 7.5' quadrangle. Colfax (1898) 30' quadrangle has the name "Minnesota" at the place.

Minnow Gulch [TUOLUMNE]: *canyon,* drained by a stream that flows 1.5 miles to Six-bit Gulch 2.5 miles south of Chinese Camp (lat. 37°50'05" N, long. 120°25'55" W; sec. 21, T 1 S, R 14 E). Named on Chinese Camp (1947) 7.5' quadrangle.

Minnow Lake [MADERA]: *lake,* 600 feet long, 1 mile south of Buena Vista Peak (lat. 37°34'45" N, long. 119°30'50" W; sec. 24, T 4 S, R 22 E). Named on Yosemite (1956) 7.5' quadrangle.

Minturn [MADERA]: *locality,* 1.5 miles north-northwest of Chowchilla along Southern Pacific Railroad (lat. 37°08'25" N, long. 120° 16'25" W; on W line sec. 19, T 9 S, R 16 E). Named on Chowchilla (1960) 15' quadrangle. Postal authorities established Minturn post office in 1884 and discontinued it in 1922 (Frickstad, p. 86). The name commemorates Jonas Minturn and Thomas Minturn, who raised wheat and arranged for a freight siding when the railroad reached the place in 1872 (Clough, p. 80).

Mirror Lake [MARIPOSA]: *lake,* 900 feet long, 2 miles east of Yosemite Village along Tenaya Creek (lat. 37°44'55" N, long. 119°32'55" W). Named on Yosemite (1956) 15' quadrangle. C.H. Spencer of Utica, New York., a member of the Mariposa Battalion, named the lake (United States Board on Geographic Names, 1934, p. 17; Browning, 1988, p. 95).

Misery Creek [AMADOR]: *stream,* flows 4.25 miles to Pioneer Creek 4.25 miles northeast of Pine Grove (lat. 38°26'50" N, long. 120°55'50" W; near E line sec. 24, T 7 N, R 12 E). Named on West Point (1948) 7.5' quadrangle.

Mississippi Canyon: see **Humbug Canyon** [PLACER].

Missouri Bar [NEVADA]: *locality,* 1.5 miles south-southeast of North Bloomfield along South Yuba River (lat. 39°20'40" N, long. 120°53'05" W; at N line sec. 17, T 17 N, R 10 E); the place is at the mouth of Missouri Canyon (1). Named on North Bloomfield (1949) 7.5' quadrangle.

Missouri Bar: see **Moccasin Creek** [TUOLUMNE].

Missouri Canyon [EL DORADO]: *canyon,* drained by a stream that flows 3.5 miles to Otter Creek 5 miles northeast of Georgetown (lat. 38°57'35" N, long. 121°46'40" W; sec.

20, T 13 N, R 11 E). Named on Georgetown (1949) and Tunnel Hill (1950) 7.5' quadrangles. Gudde (1975, p. 31) listed a mining place called Bells Diggings that was located at the head of Missouri Canyon.

Missouri Canyon [NEVADA]:
(1) *canyon*, drained by a stream that flows 3.25 miles to South Yuba River 1.5 miles south-southeast of North Bloomfield at Missouri Bar (lat. 39°20'45" N, long. 120°53'05" W; at N line sec. 17, T 17 N, R 10 E). Named on Alleghany (1949), North Bloomfield (1949), and Washington (1950) 7.5' quadrangles. Whitney's (1873) map shows a place called Banjo located near the mouth of Missouri Cañon.
(2) *canyon*, drained by a stream that flows 2.25 miles to Greenhorn Creek 5.25 miles north-northeast of Chicago Park (lat. 39°12'50" N, long. 120°55'20" W; near NW cor. sec. 36, T 16 N, R 9 E). Named on Chicago Park (1949) 7.5' quadrangle.

Missouri Flat [EL DORADO]: *locality*, 2.5 miles west-southwest of downtown Placerville (lat. 38°43' N, long. 120°50'45" W; sec. 14, T 10 N, R 10 E). Named on Placerville (1949) 7.5' quadrangle.

Missouri Flat: see **Grass Valley** [NEVADA]; **Loganville** [SIERRA]

Missouri House: see **Placerville** [EL DORADO].

Mitchell Canyon [SIERRA]: *canyon*, drained by a stream that heads in the State of Nevada and flows 2 miles in Sierra County to North Branch Dog Creek 3 miles east-northeast of Crystal Peak (lat. 39° 34'05" N, long. 120°01'55" W; near E line sec. 24, T 20 N, R 17 E). Named on Dog Valley (1981) 7.5' quadrangle.

Mitchells Mill [CALAVERAS]: *locality*, 2.5 miles northeast of Fort Mountain (lat. 38°21'55" N, long. 120°25'55" W; near N line sec. 21, T 6 N, R 14 E). Named on Fort Mountain (1979) 7.5' quadrangle. Called Mitchell Mill on California Division of Highways' (1934) map. Postal authorities established Mitchells Mill post office in 1912 and discontinued it in 1955 (Salley, p. 143).

Miwok Lake [TUOLUMNE]: *lake*, 1700 feet long, 10 miles southwest of Tower Peak (lat. 38°03'20" N, long. 119°42' W). Named on Tower Peak (1956) 15' quadrangle.

Mi-Wuk Village [TUOLUMNE]: *town*, about 3 miles northeast of Twain Harte (lat. 38°03'45" N, long. 120°11' W; on S line sec. 35, T 3 N, R 16 E). Named on Twain Harte (1979) 7.5' quadrangle.

Moaning Caves [CALAVERAS]: *relief feature*, 1.25 miles south-southeast of Vallecito (lat. 38°04'10" N, long. 120°27'55" W; near W line sec. 32, T 3 N, R 14 E). Named on Columbia (1948) 7.5' quadrangle. The feature first was called Solomons Hole, and then renamed for the curious sound heard at the entrance to the place (Gudde, 1969, p. 205).

Mobile Flat: see **Mobile Ravine** [SIERRA].

Mobile Ravine [SIERRA]: *canyon*, drained by a stream that flows 1.25 miles to North Yuba River 3.5 miles east of Downieville, and 0.5 mile downstream from the mouth of Shaughnessy Ravine (lat. 39°33'35" N, long. 120°45'35" W; sec. 32, T 20 N, R 11 E). Named on Downieville (1951) 7.5' quadrangle. A place called Mobile Flat was located along North Yuba River 4 miles east of Downieville—it also was called Newhouse Place and Shaughnessy Place (Gudde, 1975, p. 219). A place called Shady Flat was situated 0.5 mile west of Mobile Flat (Gudde, 1975, p. 315).

Mobley Spring [NEVADA]: *spring*, 3.25 miles north-northeast of North Bloomfield (lat. 39°24'55" N, long. 120°53'05" W; near NW cor. sec. 27, T 18 N, R 10 E). Named on Pike (1949) 7.5' quadrangle.

Moccasin [TUOLUMNE]: *village*, 13 miles south-southeast of Sonora (lat. 37°48'40" N, long. 120°18' W; near NE cor. sec. 34, T 1 S, R 15 E); the village is near Moccasin Creek. Named on Moccasin (1948) 7.5' quadrangle. Postal authorities established Moccasin post office in 1923 (Frickstad, p. 216). George F. Culbertson settled at the place in 1856; the traveler's stop there was called Culbertson's in 1878 (Paden and Schlichtman, p. 114, 116).

Moccasin Creek [TUOLUMNE]: *stream*, flows 8.5 miles to Don Pedro Reservoir 2 miles northwest of Moccasin (lat. 37°49'50" N, long. 120°19'50" W; sec. 21, T 1 S, R 15 E). Named on Moccasin (1948, photorevised 1973) 7.5' quadrangle. Paden and Schlichtmann (p. 114) reported two theories concerning the name: one, it came from the abundance in the stream of water snakes that may have been mistaken for water moccasins; and the other, early prospectors found an Indian moccasin by the stream. A place called Brazoria Bar, and later called Missouri Bar, was on the south side of Tuolumne River a short distance above the mouth of Moccasin Creek (Gudde, 1975, p. 45)—water of Don Pedro Reservoir now covers the site.

Moccasin Peak [TUOLUMNE]: *peak*, 1.5 miles west-southwest of Moccasin (lat. 37°48'20" N, long. 120°19'40" W; sec. 33, T 1 S, R 15 E). Altitude 2948 feet. Named on Moccasin (1948) 7.5' quadrangle.

Moccasin Reservoir [TUOLUMNE]: *lake*, behind a dam on Moccasin Creek 0.25 mile west of Moccasin (lat. 37°48'40" N, long. 120°18'20" W; near N line sec. 34, T 1 S, R 15 E). Named on Moccasin (1948, photorevised 1973) 7.5' quadrangle.

Mockingbird Ridge [MARIPOSA]: *ridge*, east-southeast-trending, 1.5 miles long, 3.5 miles northeast of the settlement of Catheys Valley (lat. 37°27'45" N, long. 120°02'25" W). Named on Catheys Valley (1962) 7.5' quadrangle. On Indian Gulch (1920) 15' quadrangle, the name "Mocking Bird Ridge" applies to a feature located about 2 miles farther south. United States Board on Geographic Names (1964a, p. 11) rejected the form "Mocking Bird Ridge" for the name.

Moco Canyon [EL DORADO]: *canyon,* drained by a stream that flows 2.5 miles to Middle Fork Cosumnes River nearly 4 miles north-northwest of Aukum (lat. 38°36'30" N, long. 120°44'45" W; sec. 27, T 9 N, R 11 E). Named on Aukum (1952) 7.5' quadrangle.

Mohawk Creek [SIERRA]: *stream,* flows nearly 1 mile to Plumas County 10 miles north of Sierra City (lat. 39°42'25" N, long. 120° 36'10" W; near S line sec. 2, T 21 N, R 12 E). Named on Clio (1981) 7.5' quadrangle.

Mohawk Creek: see **Sulphur Creek** [SIERRA].

Mohawk Gap [SIERRA]: *pass,* 8.5 miles northeast of Sierra City (lat. 39°41'15" N, long. 120°35'45" W; sec. 14, T 21 N, R 12 E). Named on Clio (1981) 7.5' quadrangle.

Mohawk Ravine [NEVADA]: *canyon,* 7.25 miles northeast of North Bloomfield (lat. 39°26'15" N, long. 120°48'05" W; sec. 12, T 18 N, R 10 E). Named on Alleghany (1949) 7.5' quadrangle.

Mokelumne Hill [CALAVERAS]: *town,* 7.5 miles north-northwest of San Andreas on the ridge between Mokelumne River and North Fork Calaveras River (lat. 38°18' N, long. 120°42'15" W; on E line sec. 12, T 5 N, R 11 E). Named on Mokelumne Hill (1948) 7.5' quadrangle. Postal authorities established Mokelumne Hill post office in 1851 (Frickstad, p. 16). They established Mill Valley post office 9.5 miles northeast of Mokelumne Hill in 1856 and discontinued it in 1861 (Salley, p. 141). Camp's (1962) map shows a place called Independence Flat located less than 2 miles west of Mokelumne Hill. McKinstry (p. 355, 356, 358) noted a feature called Brown's Hill located at the north edge of the town, a shoulder of French Hill called Nigger Hill situated just east of Brown's Hill, a high meadow called Corral Flat found just south of the town, and a feature called Sport Hill located at the southeast edge of the town next to Corral Flat. Gudde (1975, p. 49-50) listed a place called Buckeye Hill that was 2 miles east of Mokelumne Hill; people from Ohio who had a store there named the place in 1849.

Mokelumne Peak [AMADOR]: *peak,* 38 miles east-northeast of Jackson (lat. 38°32'20" N, long. 120°05'35" W). Altitude 9334 feet. Named on Mokelumne Peak (1979) 7.5' quadrangle.

Mokelumne River [AMADOR-CALAVERAS]: *stream,* formed by the confluence of Middle Fork and North Fork 7.25 miles northeast of Mokelumne Hill, flows 75 miles to San Joaquin River 16 miles west of Lodi (lat. 38°05'50" N, long. 121°34'10" W). Named on Bouldin Island

(1978), Bruceville (1968), Clements (1968), Isleton (1978), Jackson (1962), Lockeford (1968), Lodi North (1968), Mokelumne Hill (1948), Rail Road Flat (1948), Thornton (1978), Valley Springs (1962), and Wallace (1962) 7.5' quadrangles. Calaveras-Amador county line follows the river and its North Fork. Ord's (1848) map has the names "Rio de las McGuelentes" and "Mokelamy" for the stream. Called R. de las Mukelemnes on Fremont's (1845) map, Mokelome River on Jackson's (1850) map, and Mokelomies R. on Scholfield's (1851) map. Early writers gave the name a variety of forms: "Mogueles" by Wilkes (p. 137) in 1841; "Mocalimo" by Ingersoll (p. 44) in 1847; "Mo-kel-um-ne" by Kelly (p. 6) in 1849; and "Mokelemy" by Tyson (p. 13) in 1850. The name "Mokelumne" is from an Indian expression meaning "people of Mokel"—Mokel was an Indian village near the stream (Kroeber, p. 48). The name "Mokelumne" is from an Indian expression meaning "people of Mokel"—Mokel was an Indian village near the stream (Kroeber, p. 48). Middle Fork is 28 miles long and is named on Calaveras Dome (1979), Devils Nose (1979), Garnet Hill (1979), Rail Road Flat (1948), and West Point (1948) 7.5' quadrangles. On Big Trees (1891) 30' quadrangle, present Forest Creek is called North Fork Middle Fork Mokelumne River. North Fork heads in Alpine County, is 32 miles long, and is named on Calaveras Dome (1979), Devils Nose (1979), Garnet Hill (1979), Mokelumne Peak (1979), Rail Road Flat (1948), Tamarack (1979), and West Point (1948) 7.5' quadrangles. South Fork joins Middle Fork 1.5 miles upstream from the confluence of Middle Fork and North Fork; it is 27 miles long and is named on Boards Crossing (1979), Calaveras Dome (1979), Dorrington (1979), Fort Mountain (1979), and Rail Road Flat (1948) 7.5' quadrangles. Camp's (1962) map shows a canyon called Indian Gulch that opens into the canyon of Mokelumne River 1 mile south-southwest of the confluence of Middle Fork and North Fork Mokelumne River, and shows a canyon called Nigger Gulch that opens into the canyon of Mokelumne River nearly 2 miles southwest of the confluence of North Fork and Middle Fork. Camp's (1962) map shows a feature called Marble Point located at the intersection of North Fork and Middle Fork Mokelumne River.

Mokelumne River: see **Little Mokelumne River** [CALAVERAS].

Mokelumne River Campground [AMADOR]: *locality,* 7.5 miles southeast of Hams Station (lat. 38°28'40" N, long. 120°16'10" W; sec. 12, T 7 N, R 15 E); the place is along North Fork Mokelumne River. Named on Garnet Hill (1979) 7.5' quadrangle.

Mokelumne Tetons [AMADOR]: *peaks,* 1.25

miles south of Mokelumne Peak on a south-east-trending ridge (lat. 38°31'15" N, long. 120°05'45" W). Named on Mokelumne Peak (1979) 7.5' quadrangle.

Mokesumne River: see **Cosumnes River** [AMADOR-EL DORADO].

Mokosumne River: see **Cosumnes River** [AMADOR-EL DORADO].

Molo Mountain: see **Kennedy Peak** [TUOLUMNE].

Monnona Town: see **Monona Flat** [PLACER].

Mono Camp [MARIPOSA]: *locality,* nearly 2 miles west-southwest of Midpines (lat. 37°32'10" N, long. 119°57'05" W; at S line sec. 35, T 4 S, R 18 E); the place is in Mono Gulch. Named on Feliciana Mountain (1947) 7.5' quadrangle.

Mono Gulch [MARIPOSA]: *canyon,* drained by a stream that flows nearly 2 miles to Stockton Creek 2.5 miles southwest of Midpines (lat. 37°31'10" N, long. 119°56'55" W). Named on Feliciana Mountain (1947) 7.5' quadrangle.

Mono Meadow [MARIPOSA]: *area,* 5 miles south of Yosemite Village (lat. 37°40'30" N, long. 119°34'55" W; sec. 17, T 3 S, R 22 E). Named on Yosemite (1956) 15' quadrangle.

Monona Flat [PLACER]: *area,* 7 miles north of Foresthill (lat. 38°07'15" N, long. 120°49'55" W; sec. 27, T 15 N, R 10 E). Named on Foresthill (1949) 7.5' quadrangles. Whitney's (1873) map shows an inhabited place called Monnona Town at or near present Monona Flat, an inhabited place called Independence Hill located about halfway from Monnona Town to Iowa Hill, and an inhabited place called Wolverine located about 0.25 mile northwest of Monnona Town.

Mono Pass [TUOLUMNE]: *pass,* 4.5 miles south-southeast of Tioga Pass on Tuolumne-Mono county line (lat. 37°51'20" N, long. 119° 12'45" W). Named on Mono Craters (1953) 15' quadrangle. The name "Mono" is from Mono Indians who lived in the region (Kroeber, p. 48).

Monotti Hill [MARIPOSA]: *peak,* nearly 5 miles north-northeast of Buckhorn Peak (lat. 37°43'55" N, long. 120°06' W; sec. 28, T 2 S, R 17 E). Named on Buckhorn Peak (1947) 7.5' quadrangle.

Mono Vista [TUOLUMNE]: *settlement,* 6.25 miles east of Sonora (lat. 37°59'50" N, long. 120°16'05" W; near E line sec. 25, T 2 N, R 15 E). Named on Standard (1948) 7.5' quadrangle.

Monroe: see **Fort Monroe** [MARIPOSA].

Monroe Meadows [MARIPOSA]: *area,* 7.5 miles southwest of Yosemite Village (lat. 37°39'45" N, long. 119°39'45" W; sec. 22, T 3 S, R 21 E). Named on Yosemite (1956) 15' quadrangle. The name commemorates George Monroe, a black man who came to California from Georgia as a child, and who became a Pony Express rider on the route between Merced and Mariposa, and a stage driver in Yosemite Valley (Hart, p. 280).

Monte Carlo Creek [PLACER]: *stream,* flows 2.25 miles to East Martis Creek 2.5 miles west-northwest of Martis Peak (lat. 39°18'20" N, long. 120°04'20" W; sec. 22, T 17 N, R 17 E); the stream goes through Monte Carlo Meadows. Named on Martis Peak (1955) 7.5' quadrangle.

Monte Carlo Meadows [PLACER]: *area,* 2.5 miles west of Martis Peak (lat. 39°17'50" N, long. 120°04'40" W; sec. 27, T 17 N, R 17 E); the place is along Monte Carlo Creek. Named on Martis Peak (1955) 7.5' quadrangle.

Monte Cristo [SIERRA]: *locality,* 3 miles northwest of Downieville (lat. 39°35'55" N, long. 120°51'30" W). Named on Downieville (1897) 30' quadrangle. Downieville (1951) 7.5' quadrangle shows Monte Cristo mine at or near the site. A place called Fir Cap Diggings was located about 4 miles northwest of Downieville, and a place called Excelsior was situated along Goodyears Creek near Monte Cristo (Gudde, 1975, p. 113, 115). Postal authorities established Fir Cap post office in 1869 and discontinued it in 1886 (Frickstad, p. 184).

Monte Vista [PLACER]: *locality,* 1.25 miles south-southeast of Dutch Flat (lat. 39°11'25" N, long. 120°49'50" W; sec. 3, T 15 N, R 10 E). Named on Dutch Flat (1950) 7.5' quadrangle.

Montez: see **Lower Lola Montez Lake** [NEVADA]; **Upper Lola Montez Lake** [NEVADA].

Montezuma [TUOLUMNE]: *locality,* 6.5 miles southwest of Sonora (lat. 37°54'15" N, long. 120°27'10" W; near SE cor. sec. 29, T 1 N, R 14 E). Named on Sonora (1948) 7.5' quadrangle. Postal authorities established Oak Spring post office 2 miles northwest of Chinese Camp in 1851 and moved it 1 mile northeast in 1854, when it took the name "Montezuma" from a trading post called Montezuma House; they discontinued Montezuma post office for a time in 1884 and discontinued it finally in 1887 (Salley, p. 145, 158).

Montezuma Hill [NEVADA]:

(1) *peak,* 5 miles north-northwest of Nevada City (lat. 39°19'30" N, long. 121°03'50" W; sec. 22, T 17 N, R 8 E); the peak is 2.5 miles southwest of Montezuma Ridge. Named on Nevada City (1948) 7.5' quadrangle. Whitney's (1873) map has the name "Robinson Rav." for a canyon that heads at Montezuma Hill (1) and extends west-northwest 1 mile to Shady Creek.

(2) *locality,* 5 miles north-northwest of Nevada City (lat. 39°19'40" N, long. 121°03'35" W); the place is at Montezuma Hill (1). Named on Smartsville (1895) 30' quadrangle.

Montezuma Ridge [NEVADA]: *ridge,* west-northwest- to west-southwest-trending, 1.5 miles long, 5.5 miles north of Nevada City (lat. 39°20'45" N, long. 121°01'30" W); the ridge is 2.5 miles northeast of Montezuma Hill (1). Named on Nevada City (1948) 7.5' quadrangle.

Montgomery Gulch [MARIPOSA]: *canyon,* drained by a stream that flows 5.25 miles to Bull Creek 10 miles west-northwest of El Portal (lat. 37°42'15" N, long. 119°57'10" W; sec. 2, T 3 S, R 18 E). Named on El Portal (1947) and Lake Eleanor (1956) 15' quadrangles.

Montgomery Meadow [TUOLUMNE]: *area,* 4.5 miles west-northwest of Dardanelle (lat. 38°21'45" N, long. 119°55'20" W). Named on Donnell Lake (1979) 7.5' quadrangle.

Montgomery Ridge [MARIPOSA]: *ridge,* southwest- to south-trending, 5.5 miles long, 11.5 miles west-northwest of El Portal (lat. 37° 44'30" N, long. 119°58'15" W). Named on El Portal (1947) and Lake Eleanor (1956) 15' quadrangles.

Monumental Creek [PLACER]: *stream,* flows 5 miles to East Fork of North Fork of North Fork American River 5 miles north of Westville (lat. 39°14'55" N, long. 120°38'30" W; at E line sec. 17, T 16 N, R 12 E); the stream heads on Monumental Ridge. Named on Blue Canyon (1955) and Cisco Grove (1955) 7.5' quadrangles.

Monumental Hill: see **Monumental Ridge** [PLACER].

Monumental Ridge [PLACER]: *ridge,* southwest- to west-trending, 5 miles long, center 3 miles southwest of Cisco Grove (lat. 39°16'45" N, long. 120°34'30" W). Named on Cisco Grove (1955) 7.5' quadrangle. Called Monumental Hill on Colfax (1898) 30' quadrangle.

Monument Lake [MADERA]: *lake,* 450 feet long, 4.25 miles south-southeast of Merced Peak (lat. 37°34'45" N, long. 119°21'40" W). Named on Merced Peak (1953) 15' quadrangle.

Monument Peak [EL DORADO]: *peak,* 4.5 miles north of Freel Peak on El Dorado-Alpine county line (lat. 38°55'25" N, long. 119°53'50" W; near NW cor. sec. 7, T 12 N, R 19 E); the peak is on the Von Schmidt California-Nevada State line of 1873. Altitude 10,067 feet. Named on South Lake Tahoe (1955) 7.5' quadrangle.

Moody Gap [TUOLUMNE]: *pass,* 7.5 miles northwest of Crandall Peak (lat. 38°14'40" N, long. 120°13'55" W; sec. 32, T 5 N, R 16 E). Named on Crandall Peak (1979) 7.5' quadrangle.

Moody Ridge [PLACER]: *ridge,* southwest-trending, 3 miles long, 2 miles southeast of Dutch Flat (lat. 39°11' N, long. 120°48'45" W). Named on Dutch Flat (1950) 7.5' quadrangle.

Mooney Creek [NEVADA]: *stream,* flows about 1.5 miles to Fall Creek 6 miles southeast of Graniteville (lat. 39°22'55" N, long. 120°39'10" W; sec. 32, T 18 N, R 12 E).

Named on Graniteville (1982) 7.5' quadrangle.

Mooney Flat [NEVADA]: *locality,* 6 miles northwest of Pilot Peak in Slacks Ravine (lat. 39°12'55" N, long. 121°16'20" W; sec. 26, T 16 N, R 6 E). Named on Smartville (1951) 7.5' quadrangle. Called Mooneys Fl. on Whitney's (1873) map, which shows a place called Zinc Ho. [House] located 6.5 miles south of Mooneys Flat near Dry Creek (2), and a peak called Pet Hill situated 2 miles east-southeast of Mooneys Flat. The name "Mooney" commemorates Thomas Mooney, who started a hotel and trading post near the site in 1851 (Gudde, 1949, p. 224).

Mooney Ridge [PLACER]: *ridge,* west-south-west-trending, 1 mile long, 6 miles southeast of Rocklin (lat. 38°44'25" N, long. 121°09'20" W). Named on Folsom (1967) 7.5' quadrangle.

Moore: see **Clark and Moore's**, under **Wawona** [MARIPOSA].

Moore and Bowen Camp: see **Hodgdon Ranch** [TUOLUMNE].

Moore Creek [CALAVERAS]: *stream,* flows nearly 7 miles to North Fork Mokelumne River less than 1 mile west of Garnet Hill (lat. 38°28'50" N, long. 120°15'55" W; near N line sec. 12, T 7 N, R 15 E); Moore mine is along the stream. Named on Calaveras Dome (1979) and Garnet Hill (1979) 7.5' quadrangles.

Moore Creek [MARIPOSA]: *stream,* flows 7 miles to Jordan Creek 4.5 miles southeast of Smith Peak (lat. 37°45'05" N, long. 120°02'25" W; sec. 24, T 2 S, R 17 E). Named on Jawbone Ridge (1947) 7.5' quadrangle.

Moore Hill [MARIPOSA]: *peak,* 6.5 miles south of Mariposa (lat. 37° 23'25" N, long. 119°59'10" W; near S line sec. 22, T 6 S, R 18 E). Named on Mariposa (1947) 7.5' quadrangle.

Moores: see **Riverton** [EL DORADO].

Moores Flat [NEVADA]: *locality,* 4.25 miles north-northeast of North Bloomfield (lat. 39°25'10" N, long. 120°51' W; near SE cor. sec. 16, T 18 N, R 10 E). Site named on Alleghany (1949) 7.5' quadrangle. Postal authorities established Clinton post office in 1854, changed the name to Moores Flat in 1857, discontinued it for a time in 1903, and discontinued it in 1914 (Frickstad, p. 113, 114). The name "Moores" is for H.M. Moore, who built the first house and store at the place in 1851 (Gudde, 1949, p. 224). Whitney's (1873) map shows a place called Jericho situated less than 0.5 mile south of Moores Flat.

Moores Flat Creek [NEVADA]: *stream,* flows 1.5 miles to Middle Yuba River 4.5 miles north-northeast of North Bloomfield (lat. 39° 25'50" N, long. 120°51'55" W; near NW cor. sec. 16, T 18 N, R 10 E); the stream heads near Moores Flat. Named on Alleghany (1949) 7.5' quadrangle.

Moore's Station: see **Riverton** [EL DORADO].

Moraine Dome [MARIPOSA]: *peak,* 8.5 miles southwest of Cathedral Peak (lat. 37°44'35" N, long. 119°29'20" W). Altitude 8055 feet. Named on Merced Peak (1953) 15' quadrangle.

Moraine Flat [TUOLUMNE]: *area,* 3 miles west-southwest of Tioga Pass (lat. 37°54' N, long. 119°18'35" W). Named on Tuolumne Meadows (1956) 15' quadrangle.

Moraine Meadow [MADERA]: *area,* 3 miles south-southwest of Merced Peak along South Fork Merced River (lat. 37°35'45" N, long. 119°25'30" W); the place is 1.5 miles east-northeast of Moraine Mountain. Named on Merced Peak (1953) 15' quadrangle. Mount Lyell (1901) 30' quadrangle has the form "Moraine Meadows" for the name.

Moraine Mountain [MADERA]: *peak,* 4.5 miles southwest of Merced Peak (lat. 37°35'30" N, long. 119°27'10" W). Altitude 9754 feet. Named on Merced Peak (1953) 15' quadrangle.

Moraine Ridge [TUOLUMNE]: *ridge,* southwest-trending, 4 miles long, 13 miles southwest of Tower Peak (lat. 38°01' N, long. 119°44'15" W). Named on Pinecrest (1956) and Tower Peak (1956) 15' quadrangles.

Moran [CALAVERAS]: *locality,* 6.25 miles south-southeast of Blue Mountain along Moran Creek (lat. 38°15' N, long. 120°20'10" W). Named on Big Trees (1891) 30' quadrangle.

Moran: see **Lake Moran** [TUOLUMNE].

Moran Creek [CALAVERAS]: *stream,* flows 5 miles to join Love Creek and form Mill Creek (2) 8 miles northeast of Murphys (lat. 38°13' N, long. 120°21'25" W; sec. 7, T 4 N, R 15 E). Named on Dorrington (1979) and Stanislaus (1948) 7.5' quadrangles.

Moran Point [MARIPOSA]: *promontory,* 1 mile south-southeast of Yosemite Village on the south side of Yosemite Valley (lat. 37° 44'05" N, long. 119°34'45" W). Named on Yosemite (1956) 15' quadrangle.

Morgan Meadow [MADERA]: *area,* 1.5 miles northwest of Shuteye Peak (lat. 37°21'40" N, long. 119°26'15" W; sec. 34, T 6 S, R 23 E). Named on Shuteye Peak (1953) 15' quadrangle.

Morgan's Bar: see **Red Mountain Bar** [TUOLUMNE].

Morattini [EL DORADO]: *locality,* nearly 7 miles east-southeast of Robbs Peak (lat. 38°53'50" N, long. 120°17' W). Named on Pyramid Peak (1896) 30' quadrangle.

Morattini Flat [EL DORADO]: *area,* 7.5 miles east-southeast of Robbs Peak (lat. 38°53'45" N, long. 120°16'20" W; at SE cor. sec. 10, T 12 N, R 15 E). Named on Loon Lake (1952) 7.5' quadrangle.

Morgan [EL DORADO]: *locality,* 9 miles west-southwest of Leek Spring Hill (lat. 38°34' N, long. 120°25'15" W). Named on Pyramid Peak (1896) 30' quadrangle.

Mormon Bar [MARIPOSA]: *locality,* 2 miles south-southeast of Mariposa near Mariposa Creek (lat. 37°27'45" N, long. 119°56'45" W). Named on Mariposa (1947) 7.5' quadrangle. Some Mormons camped at the place in the winter of 1849 and 1850 (Sargent, Shirley, 1976, p. 28).

Mormon Creek [TUOLUMNE]: *stream,* flows 8 miles to Melones Reservoir 9 miles north of Keystone (lat. 37°58' N, long. 120°30'20" W; at W line sec. 1, T 1 N, R 13 E). Named on Columbia (1948), Melones Dam (1962), and Sonora (1948) 7.5' quadrangles. The name is from Mormons who made the first discovery of gold along the creek—before the gold discovery, the stream was called Tuttle's Creek (Stoddart, p. 62).

Mormon Gulch: see **Tuttletown** [TUOLUMNE].

Mormon Gulch: see **Mameluke Hill** [EL DORADO].

Mormon Hill [EL DORADO]: *peak,* 6.5 miles north-northeast of Clarksville (lat. 38°44'45" N, long. 121°00'25" W; sec. 5, T 10 N, R 9 E). Altitude 1533 feet. Named on Clarksville (1953) 7.5' quadrangle.

Mormon Hill [MADERA]: *peak,* 8 miles south of Shuteye Peak (lat. 37°14' N, long. 119°25'35" W; sec. 14, T 8 S, R 23 E). Named on Shaver Lake (1953) 15' quadrangle.

Mormon Ravine [EL DORADO]: *canyon,* drained by a stream that flows 1.5 miles to Pinchem Creek 6 miles north-northwest of Shingle Springs (lat. 38°44'35" N, long. 120°58'35" W; near S line sec. 3, T 10 N, R 9 E); the canyon heads southeast of Mormon Hill. Named on Clarksville (1953) and Shingle Springs (1949) 7.5' quadrangles.

Mormon Ravine [PLACER]: *canyon,* drained by a stream that flows nearly 3 miles to Folsom Lake 8 miles east-northeast of Rocklin (lat. 38°50'10" N, long. 121°05'35" W; sec. 4, T 11 N, R 8 E). Named on Pilot Hill (1954, photorevised 1973) 7.5' quadrangle.

Mormon Tavern: see **Clarksville** [EL DORADO].

Morning Star Lake: see **Big Reservoir** [PLACER].

Morning Star Reservoir: see **Big Reservoir** [PLACER].

Morning Star Spring [MARIPOSA]: *spring,* 8 miles north-northeast of Hornitos (lat. 37°36'20" N, long. 120°09'55" W; sec. 12, T 4 S, R 16 E); the spring is 0.5 mile north-northwest of Morning Star mine. Named on Hornitos (1947) 7.5' quadrangle.

Morrison [EL DORADO]: *locality,* 6 miles north-northwest of Leek Spring Hill (lat. 38°42'35" N, long. 120°19'20" W; near NW cor. sec. 21, T 10 N, R 15 E). Named on Leek Spring Hill (1951) 7.5' quadrangle.

Morrison Creek [TUOLUMNE]: *stream,* flows 5.25 miles to Tuolumne River 3.5 miles northeast of White Wolf (lat. 37°55'05" N, long. 119°37'30" W). Named on Hetch Hetchy Reservoir (1956) 15' quadrangle.

Morrisons Flat: see **Craigs Flat** [SIERRA].

Morris Reservoir [NEVADA]: *lake,* 450 feet long, 1 mile southwest of North San Juan (lat. 39°21'30" N, long. 121°07' W; near SE cor. sec. 6, T 17 N, R 8 E). Named on Nevada City (1948) 7.5' quadrangle.

Morristown [SIERRA]: *locality,* 6 miles south-southwest of Mount Fillmore (lat. 39°39'10" N, long. 120°54'15" W; sec. 30, T 21 N, R 10 E). Named on La Porte (1951) 7.5' quadrangle.

Morristown Ravine [SIERRA]: *canyon,* drained by a stream that flows 0.5 mile to Canyon Creek 6.5 miles southwest of Mount Fillmore (lat. 39°39'15" N, long. 120°55'10" W; sec. 25, T 21 N, R 9 E); the canyon is west of Morristown. Named on La Porte (1951) 7.5' quadrangle.

Morristown Ridge [SIERRA]: *ridge,* southwest-trending, 5 miles long, center 7 miles south-southwest of Mount Fillmore (lat. 39°38'35" N, long. 120°54'35" W); Morristown is on the ridge. Named on Goodyears Bar (1951) and La Port (1951) 7.5' quadrangles.

Morrs Ravine [SIERRA]: *canyon,* drained by a stream that flows 1.5 miles to Canyon Creek 7.5 miles southwest of Mount Fillmore (lat. 39°38'20" N, long. 120°55'50" W; near W line sec. 36, T 21 N, R 9 E). Named on La Porte (1951) 7.5' quadrangle.

Morse [MARIPOSA]: *locality,* 3.25 miles west-northwest of Hornitos along Yosemite Valley Railroad (lat. 37°31'40" N, long. 120°17'10" W; sec. 2, T 5 S, R 15 E). Named on Merced Falls (1944) 15' quadrangle.

Mortimer Flat [EL DORADO]: *area,* 5 miles west-northwest of Pyramid Peak (lat. 38°52'25" N, long. 120°14'45" W; sec. 20, T 12 N, R 16 E). Named on Pyramid Peak (1955) 7.5' quadrangle.

Moscove Meadow [NEVADA-SIERRA]: *area,* 13 miles northwest of Donner Pass on Nevada-Sierra county line (lat. 39°26'45" N, long. 120°29'35" W; near NE cor. sec. 10, T 18 N, R 13 E). Named on Webber Peak (1981) 7.5' quadrangle. Called English Meadow on Truckee (1940) 30' quadrangle.

Mosquito [EL DORADO]: *locality,* 6.25 miles northeast of Placerville (lat. 38°47'40" N, long. 120°43'45" W). Named on Placerville (1893) 30' quadrangle. Postal authorities established Mosquito post office in 1880, discontinued it in 1881, reestablished it in 1892, and discontinued it in 1895; the name was from Mosquito Creek (Salley, p. 147).

Mosquito Camp [EL DORADO]: *locality,* 4 miles east-northeast of Chili Bar (lat. 38°47'45" N, long. 120°45'10" W; sec. 16, T 11 N, R 11 E). Named on Garden Valley (1949) 7.5' quadrangle.

Mosquito Creek [EL DORADO]: *stream,* flows 3.25 miles to South Fork American River 3.5

miles east-northeast of Chili Bar (lat. 38° 46'50" N, long. 120°45'25" W; at S line sec. 21, T 11 N, R 11 E). Named on Garden Valley (1949) and Slate Mountain (1950) 7.5' quadrangles. Gudde (1975, p. 227) listed a mining place called Mosquito Valley that apparently was located along or near present Mosquito Creek, and mentioned two mining camps in the valley—Lower Town or Big House, and Nelsonville.

Mosquito Creek [NEVADA]: *stream,* flows 2 miles to Deer Creek 8.5 miles southwest of North Bloomfield (lat. 39°16'05" N, long. 120°59'55" W; near W line sec. 8, T 16 N, R 9 E). Named on North Bloomfield (1949) 7.5' quadrangle.

Mosquito Creek: see **Big Mosquito Creek** [PLACER]; **Little Mosquito Creek** [PLACER].

Mosquito Gulch [CALAVERAS]: *canyon,* drained by a stream that flows 2 miles to South Fork Mokelumne River 4 miles northwest of Rail Road Flat (lat. 38°22'30" N, long. 120°34'20" W; sec. 17, T 6 N, R 13 E). Named on Rail Road Flat (1948) 7.5' quadrangle.

Mosquito Gulch: see **Glenco** [CALAVERAS].

Mosquito Lake [AMADOR]: *lake,* 1050 feet long, 3 miles north-northwest of Mokelumne Peak (lat. 38°34'35" N, long. 120°07' W). Named on Mokelumne Peak (1979) 7.5' quadrangle.

Mosquito Lake [TUOLUMNE]: *lake,* 1400 feet long, 8 miles west-northwest of Tower Peak (lat. 38°12'10" N, long. 119°40'20" W; at S line sec. 9, T 4 N, R 21 E). Named on Tower Peak (1956) 15' quadrangle.

Mosquito Narrows [PLACER]: *pass,* 5.25 miles east of Michigan Bluff (lat. 39°03'05" N, long. 120°38'15" W; near NE cor. sec. 21, T 14 N, R 12 E); the pass is on Mosquito Ridge. Named on Michigan Bluff (1952) 7.5' quadrangle.

Mosquito Pass [EL DORADO]: *pass,* 5.25 miles south of Phipps Peak (lat. 38°52'40" N, long. 120°09'35" W). Named on Rockbound Valley (1955) 7.5' quadrangle.

Mosquito Ridge [PLACER]: *ridge,* generally southwest-trending, 17 miles long, lies between Middle Fork American River and North Fork of Middle Fork American River from near Little Bald Mountain to the junction of the two streams. Named on Duncan Peak (1952), Greek Store (1952), and Michigan Bluff (1952) 7.5' quadrangles.

Mosquito Valley: see **Mosquito Creek** [EL DORADO].

Moss Canon: see **Moss Creek** [MARIPOSA].

Moss Canyon [MARIPOSA]:

(1) *canyon,* 3 miles long, 1.5 miles west-northwest of El Portal (lat. 37°41' N, long. 119°48'30" W); the canyon is along lower reaches of Moss Creek. Named on El Portal (1947) 7.5' quadrangle.

(2) *locality,* 2.25 miles west of El Portal along Yosemite Valley Railroad (lat. 37°40'15" N, long. 119°49'10" W); the place is near the

mouth of present Moss Canyon (1). Named on Yosemite (1909) 30' quadrangle.

Moss Creek [MARIPOSA]: *stream,* flows 7.25 miles to Merced River 2 miles west of El Portal (lat. 37°40'10" N, long. 119°49'05" W). Named on El Portal (1947) and Lake Eleanor (1956) 15' quadrangles. United States Board on Geographic Names (1933, p. 533) rejected the name "Moss Canon" for the feature.

Moss Hills: see **Rampart** [PLACER].

Moss Spring [MARIPOSA]: *spring,* 5 miles west-southwest of Yosemite Village in Yosemite Valley (lat. 37°42'50" N, long. 119° 39'50" W). Named on Yosemite (1956) 15' quadrangle.

Mossy Pond [NEVADA]: *intermittent lake,* 9 miles west-northwest of Donner Pass (lat. 39°22'40" N, long. 120°28'10" W; sec. 36, T 18 N, R 13 E). Named on Webber Peak (1981) 7.5' quadrangle. Donner Pass (1955) 15' quadrangle shows a permanent lake.

Mother Lode Acres [CALAVERAS]: *area,* 7.5 miles south-southwest of Valley Springs (lat. 38°05'45" N, long. 120°53'45" W; sec. 20, T 3 N, R 10 E). Named on Valley Springs SW (1962) 7.5' quadrangle.

Mount Adeline: see **Mount Savage** [MARIPOSA].

Motor City [EL DORADO]: *locality,* 3.5 miles west of Camino (lat. 38°44' N, long. 120°44'20" W; at W line sec. 11, T 10 N, R 11 E). Named on Camino (1952) 7.5' quadrangle.

Mounds: see **The Mounds** [SIERRA].

Mound Springs Creek [EL DORADO]: *stream,* flows nearly 3 miles to Indian Creek (3) 4.5 miles north-northeast of Shingle Springs (lat. 38°43'15" N, long. 120°53'05" W; sec. 16, T 10 N, R 10 E). Named on Placerville (1949) and Shingle Springs (1949) 7.5' quadrangles.

Mount Aigare [EL DORADO]: *peak,* 4.5 miles northeast of Latrobe (lat. 38°36'20" N, long. 120°55'05" W; sec. 30, T 9 N, R 10 E). Altitude 1564 feet. Named on Latrobe (1949) 7.5' quadrangle.

Mountain Chief Creek [PLACER]: *stream,* flows 2 miles to Sugar Pine Canyon 6.5 miles north-northeast of Foresthill (lat. 39°06' N, long. 120°45'10" W; near E line sec. 32, T 15 N, R 11 E). Named on Foresthill (1949) and Michigan Bluff (1952) 7.5' quadrangles.

Mountain Cottage [EL DORADO]: *locality,* nearly 3 miles south of the village of Pilot Hill (lat. 38°47'40" N, long. 121°01' W). Named on Sacramento (1892) 30' quadrangle.

Mountain House: see **Old Mountain House** [SIERRA].

Mountain King [MARIPOSA]: *locality,* 6 miles northeast of the village of Bear Valley along Yosemite Valley Railroad (lat. 37°37'15" N, long. 120°02' W). Named on Sonora (1897) 30' quadrangle. Postal authorities established Mountain King post office in 1907 and discontinued it in 1922; the name is from Mountain King mine (Salley, p. 147).

Mountain Lake: see **Lake Tahoe** [EL DORADO-PLACER].

Mountain Meadow [PLACER]: *area,* less than 1 mile northeast of Bunker Hill (lat. 39°03'25" N, long. 120°22'10" W; sec. 14, T 14 N, R 14 E). Named on Wentworth Springs (1953) 7.5' quadrangle.

Mountain Meadow: see **Little Mountain Meadow** [PLACER].

Mountain Meadow Lake [PLACER]: *lake,* 450 feet long, 1.5 miles north-northeast of Granite Chief at the head of North Fork American River (lat. 39°13' N, long. 120°16'25" W; sec. 23, T 16 N, R 15 E). Named on Granite Chief (1953) 7.5' quadrangle.

Mountain Pass [TUOLUMNE]: *pass,* 7.5 miles southwest of Sonora (lat. 37°54' N, long. 120°28'30" W). Named on Sonora (1897) 30' quadrangle.

Mountain Pass Creek [TUOLUMNE]: *stream,* flows 5 miles to Green Spring Run 3 miles north-northwest of Keystone (lat. 37°52'15" N, long. 120°32'20" W; near NE cor. sec. 9, T 1 S, R 13 E); the stream heads near Mountain Pass. Named on Keystone (1962), Melones Dam (1962), and Sonora (1948) 7.5' quadrangles.

Mountain Ranch [CALAVERAS]: *village,* 8 miles east-northeast of San Andreas along Eldorado Creek (lat. 38°13'45" N, long. 120°32'25" W; sec. 4, T 4 N, R 13 E). Named on Calaveritas (1962) 7.5' quadrangle. Postal authorities established Mountain Ranch post office in 1858 at a stopping place called Mountain Ranch House; they moved the post office 2 miles west in 1868 to the community of El Dorado, which then had its name changed to Mountain Ranch to match the post office designation (Hoover, Rensch, and Rensch, p. 46; Salley, p. 147). They established Blue Mountain post office 20 miles northeast of Mountain Ranch post office in 1863 and discontinued it in 1864 (Salley, p. 23); Blue Mountain City was along Licking Fork (Gudde, 1975, p. 41). They established Mammoth Cave post office 3 miles southeast of Mountain Ranch post office in 1883 and discontinued it in 1887; the name was from a nearby cave (Salley, p. 131). Gudde (1975, p. 69) noted a place called Chichi that was located 2 miles northwest of Mountain Ranch.

Mountain Ranch House: see **Mountain Ranch** [CALAVERAS].

Mountain Spring Creek [AMADOR]: *stream,* flows 4.25 miles to Jackson Creek 4 miles southeast of Ione (lat. 38°18'25" N, long. 120°52'45" W; sec. 9, T 5 N, R 10 E). Named on Ione (1962) and Jackson (1962) 7.5' quadrangles.

Mountain Spring Creek: see **Copper Creek** [AMADOR].

Mountain Spring House: see **Sunnybrook** [AMADOR].

Mountain Springs [AMADOR]: *locality,* 4

miles east of Ione (lat. 38°20'35" N, long. 120°51'45" W); the place is along Mountain Spring Creek. Named on Jackson (1902) 30' quadrangle.

Mountain Springs: see **Gold Run** [PLACER].

Mountain Top [CALAVERAS]: *peak,* 4 miles east-southeast of Copperopolis (lat. 37°57'45" N, long. 120°34'25" W; near S line sec. 5, T 1 N, R 13 E). Altitude 1716 feet. Named on Melones Dam (1962) 7.5' quadrangle.

Mountain View House: see **Westfall Meadows** [MARIPOSA].

Mountain View Peak [MADERA]: *ridge,* east-trending, 1 mile long, 6.5 miles southwest of North Fork (lat. 37°10'35" N, long. 119°36'30" W). Named on North Fork (1965) 7.5' quadrangle.

Mountain Well: see **North Bloomfield** [NEVADA].

Mount Alma [SIERRA]: *peak,* 5.25 miles south of Mount Fillmore (lat. 39°39'10" N, long. 120°51'20" W). Altitude 6477 feet. Named on Mount Fillmore (1951) 7.5' quadrangle.

Mount Ansel Adams: see **Foerster Peak** [MADERA].

Mount Ararat [CALAVERAS]: *peak,* 9 miles west-northwest of Angels Camp (lat. 38°06'55" N, long. 120°42'15" W; near E line sec. 13, T 3 N, R 11 E). Altitude 2279 feet. Named on Salt Spring Valley (1962) 7.5' quadrangle.

Mount Ararat [EL DORADO]: *peak,* 4.5 miles northwest of Coloma (lat. 38°51'10" N, long. 120°56'20" W; sec. 35, T 12 N, R 9 E). Altitude 2012 feet. Named on Coloma (1949) 7.5' quadrangle.

Mount Aukum [EL DORADO]: *peak,* 1.25 miles north of Aukum (lat. 38°34'25" N, long. 120°43'30" W; sec. 2, T 8 N, R 11 E). Altitude 2615 feet. Named on Aukum (1952) 7.5' quadrangle. Called Mt. Orcum on Placerville (1893) 30' quadrangle.

Mount Aukum: see **Aukum** [EL DORADO].

Mount Beatitude: see **Old Inspiration Point** [MARIPOSA].

Mount Broderick [MARIPOSA]: *peak,* 3 miles east-southeast of Yosemite Village (lat. 37°44' N, long. 119°32'05" W). Altitude 6706 feet. Named on Yosemite (1956) 15' quadrangle. The name commemorates David C. Broderick, senator from California from 1857 until 1859 (United States Board on Geographic Names, 1934, p. 3).

Mount Broderick: see **Liberty Cap** [MARIPOSA].

Mount Bruce: see **Merced Peak** [MADERA].

Mount Buckingham: see **Buckingham Mountain** [MARIPOSA].

Mount Bullion [MARIPOSA]: *village,* 6 miles southeast of the village of Bear Valley (lat. 37°30'30" N, long. 120°02'40" W). Named on Bear Valley (1947) 7.5' quadrangle. Called Princeton on Hoffmann and Gardner's (1863-1867) map. Postal authorities established

Mount Bullion post office in 1862, discontinued it for a time in 1887, and discontinued it finally in 1955 (Salley, p. 147). The place first was called La Mineta—*la mineta* means "the little mine" in Spanish; it then was called Princeton for Princeton mine, which in turn was named for one of its discoverers, Prince Steptoe; finally the place was renamed Mount Bullion in 1862 to honor Fremont's father-in-law, Senator Thomas Hart Benton, whose monetary policy earned him the nickname "Old Bullion" (Sargent, Shirley, 1976, p. 15).

Mount Bullion: see **Bullion Mountain** [MARIPOSA].

Mount Bullion Range: see **Bullion Mountain** [MARIPOSA].

Mount Bullion Spur Ridge: see **Bullion Mountain** [MARIPOSA].

Mount Clark [MARIPOSA]: *peak,* 10.5 miles south of Cathedral Peak (lat. 37°41'50" N, long. 119°25'40" W). Altitude 11,522 feet. Named on Merced Peak (1953) 15' quadrangle. Members of the Whitney survey called the peak the Obelisk for its peculiar shape (Whitney, 1870, p. 108). Browning (1986, p. 41) associated the name "Clark" with Galen Clark of Clark's Station (present Wawona), and pointed out that the feature also was called Gothic Peak.

Mount Conness [TUOLUMNE]: *peak,* 5.25 miles northwest of Tioga Pass on Tuolumne-Mono county line (lat. 37°58' N, long. 119°19'15" W). Altitude 12,590 feet. Named on Tuolumne Meadows (1956) 15' quadrangle. Members of the Whitney survey named the peak in 1864 for John Conness, senator from California (United States Board on Geographic Names, 1934, p. 6). Conness had promoted the Whitney survey while he was a member of the state legislature (Brewster, p. 184).

Mount Crossman [AMADOR]: *peak,* 8 miles east-northeast of Pine Grove (lat. 38°27'25" N, long. 120°31'55" W; sec. 15, T 7 N, R 13 E). Named on West Point (1948) 7.5' quadrangle.

Mount Dana [TUOLUMNE]: *peak,* 2.25 miles east-southeast of Tioga Pass on Tuolumne-Mono county line (lat. 37°54' N, long. 119°13'15" W); the feature is 1 mile north of the head of Dana Fork. Altitude 13,053 feet. Named on Mono Craters (1953) 15' quadrangle. Members of the Whitney survey named the peak in 1863 to honor geologist James Dwight Dana (United States Board on Geographic Names, 1934, p. 6). The feature also was called Dana Mountain (Browning, 1988, p. 31).

Mount Danaher [EL DORADO]: *peak,* 0.5 mile northeast of Camino (lat. 38°44'40" N, long. 120°40' W; near SE cor. sec. 5, T 10 N, R 12 E). Named on Camino (1952) 7.5' quadrangle.

Mount Davis [MADERA]: *peak,* 9.5 miles northwest of Devils Postpile on Madera-Mono county line (lat. 37°42'55" N, long.

119°13'05" W). Altitude 12,311 feet. Named on Devils Postpile (1953) 15' quadrangle. The name commemorates Milton F. Davis, who climbed the peak in 1891 when he was a Lieutenant under Captain A.E. Wood, first acting superintendent of Yosemite National Park (Farquhar, 1926, p. 305). The feature also was called Davis Mountain (Browning, 1988, p. 31).

Mount Disney [PLACER]: *peak*, 1.5 miles south-southeast of Donner Pass (lat. 39°17'40" N, long. 120°20'25" W; sec. 29, T 17 N, R 15 E). Altitude 7953 feet. Named on Norden (1955) 7.5' quadrangle. The name is for Walt Disney, who bought the first stock issued in Sugar Bowl Ski Corporation for operations near Donner Summit (Jackson, L.A., p. 145).

Mount Eaton [TUOLUMNE]: *peak*, 1.5 miles south-southeast of Tuolumne (lat. 37°56'25" N, long. 120°13'40" W; near W line sec. 16, T 1 N, T 16 E). Altitude 3134 feet. Named on Tuolumne (1948) 7.5' quadrangle. United States Board on Geographic Names (1978b, p. 4) rejected the name "Point Eaton" for the feature.

Mount Elizabeth: see **Elizabeth Peak** [TUOLUMNE].

Mount Etna [SIERRA]: *peak*, 1.25 miles northeast of Mount Fillmore on Sierra-Plumas county line (lat. 39°44'45" N, long. 120° 50'15" W; at NW cor. sec. 26, T 22 N, R 10 E). Altitude 7163 feet. Named on Mount Fillmore (1951) 7.5' quadrangle.

Mount Fillmore [SIERRA]: *peak*, 12 miles north of Downieville (lat. 39°43'50" N, long. 120°51'05" W; near NW cor. sec. 34, T 22 N, R 10 E). Altitude 7715 feet. Named on Mount Fillmore (1951) 7.5' quadrangle.

Mount Florence [MADERA]: *peak*, 8 miles north-northeast of Merced Peak (lat. 37°44'25" N, long. 119°19' W); the peak is south of Florence Creek. Altitude 12,561 feet. Named on Merced Peak (1953) 15' quadrangle. The name commemorates Florence Hutchings, daughter of James M. Hutchings and the first white child born in Yosemite Valley (United States Board on Geographic Names, 1934, p. 9).

Mount Frances: see **Liberty Cap** [MARIPOSA].

Mount Gibbs [TUOLUMNE]: *peak*, 3.5 miles southeast of Tioga Pass on Tuolumne-Mono county line (lat. 37°52'35" N, long. 119° 12'40" W). Altitude 12,764 feet. Named on Mono Craters (1953) 15' quadrangle. Frederick Law Olmsted named the peak in 1864 for Oliver Wolcott Gibbs, professor of science at Harvard (Farquhar *in* Brewer, p. 549).

Mount Gibson [TUOLUMNE]: *peak*, 9 miles north-northwest of White Wolf (lat. 37°59'55" N, long. 119°42'15" W). Named on Hetch Hetchy Reservoir (1956) 15' quadrangle.

Mount Gregory [EL DORADO]: *locality*, 7.25 miles northeast of Georgetown (lat. 38°59'05"

N, long. 120°44'55" W). Named on Placerville (1893) 30' quadrangle.

Mount Haskells: see **Haskell Peak** [SIERRA].

Mount Hoffmann [MARIPOSA]: *peak*, 8 miles north-northeast of Yosemite Village (lat. 37°50'50" N, long. 119°30'35" W; sec. 13, T 1 S, R 22 E). Altitude 10,850 feet. Named on Hetch Hetchy Reservoir (1956) 15' quadrangle. Members of the Whitney survey named the peak for Charles Frederick Hoffmann, topographer for the survey (Brewer, p. 407). United States Board on Geographic Names (1933, p. 368) rejected the form "Hoffman" for the name.

Mount Hope [EL DORADO]: *locality*, nearly 7 miles north-northeast of Georgetown (lat. 38°59'30" N, long. 120°46'20" W; sec. 8, T 13 N, R 11 E). Named on Georgetown (1949) 7.5' quadrangle.

Mount Ina Coolbrith [SIERRA]: *ridge*, northwest-trending, 1 mile long, 5.5 miles east-northeast of Loyalton (lat. 39°42'10" N, long. 120°08'30" W). Named on Loyalton (1981) 7.5' quadrangle. United States Board on Geographic Names (1933, p. 386) rejected the name "Ina Coolbrith Summit" for the feature, and noted that California State Geographic Board named the ridge for Ina Donna Coolbrith, former poet laureate of California.

Mount Joaquin: see **Joaquin Peak** [CALAVERAS].

Mount Judah [PLACER]: *peak*, 1.25 miles south-southeast of Donner Pass (lat. 39°17'55" N, long. 120°18'55" W; near N line sec. 28, T 17 N, R 15 E). Altitude 8243 feet. Named on Norden (1955) 7.5' quadrangle. United States Board on Geographic Names (1942, p. 27) rejected the name "Donner Peak" for the feature, and noted that the name "Judah" commemorates Theodore Judah.

Mount Knight [TUOLUMNE]: *peak*, 5.25 miles west of Crandall Peak (lat. 38°10' N, long. 120°14'20" W; sec. 29, T 4 N, R 16 E). Altitude 4783 feet. Named on Crandall Peak (1979) 7.5' quadrangle.

Mount Lewis [TUOLUMNE]: *peak*, 3.5 miles east of Twain Harte (lat. 38°02'10" N, long. 120°09'40" W; on S line sec. 12, T 2 N, R 16 E). Named on Twain Harte (1979) 7.5' quadrangle.

Mount Knight [TUOLUMNE]: *peak*, 5.25 miles west of Crandall Peak (lat. 38°10' N, long. 120°14'20" W; sec. 29, T 4 N, R 16 E). Altitude 4783 feet. Named on Crandall Peak (1979) 7.5' quadrangle.

Mount Lewis [TUOLUMNE]: *peak*, 3.5 miles east of Twain Harte (lat. 38°02'10" N, long. 120°09'40" W; on S line sec. 12, T 2 N, R 16 E). Named on Twain Harte (1979) 7.5' quadrangle.

Mount Lincoln [PLACER]: *peak*, 2 miles south of Donner Pass (lat. 39°17'15" N, long. 120°19'40" W; near SW cor. sec. 28, T 17 N, R 15 E). Named on Norden (1955) 7.5' quadrangle. Called Lincoln Pk. on Hobson's (1890b) map.

Mount Lola [NEVADA]: *peak,* 8.5 miles north-northwest of Donner Pass (lat. 39°26' N, long. 120°21'50" W; near SE cor. sec. 11, T 18 N, R 14 E). Altitude 9148 feet. Named on Independence Lake (1981) 7.5' quadrangle. The name is for actress Lola Montez (Gudde, 1949, p. 191).

Mount Lyell [MADERA-TUOLUMNE]: *peak,* 12 miles south of Tioga Pass on Madera-Tuolumne county line (lat. 37°44'25" N, long. 119°16'15" W); the peak is near the head of Lyell Fork [TUOLUMNE]. Altitude 13,114 feet. Named on Merced Peak (1953) 15' quadrangle. Members of the Whitney survey named the peak for Sir Charles Lyell, distinguished English geologist (United States Board on Geographic Names, 1934, p. 15).

Mount Maclure [MADERA-TUOLUMNE]: *peak,* 11.5 miles south of Tioga Pass on Madera-Tuolumne county line (lat. 37°44'40" N, long. 119°16'45" W). Named on Merced Peak (1953) 15' quadrangle. Members of the Whitney survey named the peak for William Maclure, pioneer American geologist (Whitney, 1870, p. 101). United States Board on Geographic Names (1933, p. 486) rejected the form "Mount McClure" for the name.

Mount Marliave: see **Hole-in-Ground** [NEVADA].

Mount McClure: see **Mount Maclure** [MADERA-TUOLUMNE].

Mount Medlicott: see **Medlicott Dome** [MARIPOSA].

Mount Mildred [PLACER]: *peak,* 4.25 miles south-southwest of Granite Chief (lat. 39°08'45" N, long. 120°19'45" W; near W line sec. 17, T 15 N, R 15 E). Altitude 8398 feet. Named on Granite Chief (1953) 7.5' quadrangle.

Mount Ophir [CALAVERAS]: *ridge,* south-southwest-trending, 0.5 mile long, 4.25 miles northwest of San Andreas (lat. 38°14'50" N, long. 120°43'35" W; near E line sec. 35, T 5 N, R 11 E). Named on San Andreas (1962) 7.5' quadrangle.

Mount Ophir [MARIPOSA]: *locality,* 4.5 miles southeast of the village of Bear Valley (lat. 37°30'55" N, long. 120°04' W); the place is in Norwegian Gulch. Named on Bear Valley (1947) 7.5' quadrangle. Postal authorities established Ophir post office before February 20, 1852, they changed the name to Mount Ophir in 1856, and discontinued it in 1868 (Salley, p. 148, 161). The place also was called Norwegian Gulch Center (Burchfield, p. 43).

Mount Olive [NEVADA]: *peak,* 1.5 miles west-southwest of Chicago Park (lat. 39°08'05" N, long. 120°59'35" W; sec. 20, T 15 N, R 9 E). Altitude 2569 feet. Named on Chicago Park (1949) 7.5' quadrangle.

Mount Orcum: see **Mount Aukum** [EL DORADO].

Mount Peckinpah: see **Peckinpah Mountain**, under **Central Camp** [MADERA].

Mount Pleasant [EL DORADO]: *locality,* 4.5 miles north-northeast of Omo Ranch (lat. 38°38'05" N, long. 120°32'40" W). Named on Placerville (1893) 30' quadrangle.

Mount Pleasant [SIERRA]: *locality,* 7 miles northwest of Goodyears Bar (lat. 39°36'35" N, long. 120°58'30" W). Named on Downieville (1897) 30' quadrangle. The place first was called Mount Pleasant Ranch (Gudde, 1975, p. 229).

Mount Pleasant: see **Taylor Hill** [TUOLUMNE].

Mount Pleasant Canyon [PLACER]: *canyon,* drained by a stream that flows 1 mile to Third Brushy Canyon 3 miles north-northwest of Foresthill (lat. 39°03'30" N, long. 120°50'40" W; sec. 15, T 14 N, R 10 E). Named on Foresthill (1949) 7.5' quadrangle.

Mount Pleasant Ranch: see **Mount Pleasant** [SIERRA].

Mount Pluto [PLACER]: *peak,* 5 miles north of Tahoe City (lat. 39° 14'30" N, long. 120°08'20" W; near NW cor. sec. 18, T 16 N, R 17 E). Named on Tahoe City (1955) 7.5' quadrangle. Called Pluto Pk. on Wheeler's (1876-1877b) map. The name "Pluto" is for plutonic rock at the peak (Lekisch, p. 97).

Mount Price [EL DORADO]: *peak,* 1.5 miles northwest of Pyramid Peak (lat. 38°51'50" N, long. 120°10'25" W). Altitude 9975 feet. Named on Pyramid Peak (1955) 7.5' quadrangle.

Mount Provo [TUOLUMNE]: *peak,* 2.25 miles southeast of Twain Harte (lat. 38°00'45" N, long. 120°12'20" W; sec. 22, T 2 N, R 16 E). Altitude 4845 feet. Named on Twain Harte (1979) 7.5' quadrangle.

Mount Raymond Camp [MADERA]: *locality,* 7 miles south-southwest of Buena Vista Peak (lat. 37°30' N, long. 119°29'20" W; sec. 16, T 5 S, R 22 E); the place is 1.5 miles west-southwest of Raymond Mountain. Named on Yosemite (1956) 15' quadrangle.

Mount Ritter [MADERA]: *peak,* 8 miles northwest of Devils Postpile (lat. 37°41'20" N, long. 119°11'55" W); the peak is on Ritter Ridge. Altitude 13,157 feet. Named on Devils Postpile (1953) 15' quadrangle. Members of the Whitney survey named the peak for German geographer Karl Ritter (Whitney, 1870, p. 101).

Mount Savage [MARIPOSA]: *peak,* 2 miles south of Wawona (lat. 37°30'35" N, long. 119°39' W; sec. 11, T 5 S, R 21 E). Altitude 5745 feet. Named on Yosemite (1956) 15' quadrangle. Chester Versteeg suggested the name in the early 1950's to commemorate Major James D. Savage of the Mariposa Battalion; the feature earlier was known locally as Twin Peaks and as Mount Adeline (Browning, 1986, p. 192).

Mount Starr King [MARIPOSA]: *peak,* 5 miles

southeast of Yosemite Village (lat. 37°42'10"
N, long. 119°31' W). Altitude 9092 feet.
Named on Yosemite (1956) 15' quadrangle.
The name honors Thomas Starr King, well-
known Unitarian preacher and orator for the
Union cause in California during the Civil War
(United States Board on Geographic Names,
1934, p. 24).

Mount Stephens: see **Donner Lake** [NEVADA]

Mount Tallac [EL DORADO]: *peak*, 5.25 miles
northwest of Pyramid Peak (lat. 38°54'20" N,
long. 120°05'50" W; near NE cor. sec. 9, T 12
N, R 17 E). Altitude 9735 feet. Named on
Emerald Bay (1955) 7.5' quadrangle. Called
Crystal Peak on early maps (Lekisch, p. 134).

Mount Trumbull: see **Trumbull Peak** [MARI-
POSA].

Mount Vernon House: see **Blue Tent** [NE-
VADA].

Mount View: see **Grass Valley** [NEVADA].

Mount Watkins [MARIPOSA]: *peak*, 4.5 miles
east-northeast of Yosemite Village (lat. 37°47'
N, long. 119°31' W). Altitude 8500 feet.
Named on Hetch Hetchy Reservoir (1956) 15'
quadrangle. The name commemorates photographer Carleton E. Watkins, whose early
photographs of Yosemite Valley did much to
publicize the place (Whitney, 1870, p. 69).

Mount Watson [PLACER]: *peak*, 3.5 miles
north of Tahoe City (lat. 39°13'15" N, long.
120°08'45" W; sec. 24, T 16 N, R 16 E). Altitude 8424 feet. Named on Tahoe City (1955)
7.5' quadrangle.

Mount Zion [AMADOR]: *peak*, 1.5 miles
south-southeast of Pine Grove (lat. 38°23'25"
N, long. 120°39'05" W; near E line sec. 9, T 6
N, R 12 E). Altitude 2968 feet. Named on Pine
Grove (1948) 7.5' quadrangle.

Mount Zion: see **Snow Tent** [NEVADA].

Mud Lake [AMADOR]: *lake*, 1250 feet long,
nearly 6 miles north-northeast of Mokelumne
Peak (lat. 38°36'35" N, long. 120°08'55" W;
near SW cor. sec. 19, T 9 N, R 17 E). Named
on Bear River Reservoir (1979) 7.5' quadrangle. Pyramid Peak (1896) 30' quadrangle
has the name "Mud Lakes" for three lakes in
a marsh at the site of present Mud Lake.

Mud Lake [CALAVERAS]: *lake*, 800 feet long,
3 miles east of Tamarack on Calaveras-Alpine
county line (lat. 38°26'10" N, long.
120°01'10" W). Named on Tamarack (1979)
7.5' quadrangle.

Mud Lake [EL DORADO]: *lake*, 200 feet long,
3.5 miles east of Wentworth Springs (lat.
39°01'10" N, long. 120°16'15" W; near W line
sec. 35, T 14 N, R 15 E). Named on Wentworth
Springs (1953) 7.5' quadrangle.

Mud Lake [NEVADA]: *lake*, 750 feet long, 3
miles northwest of English Mountain (lat.
39°28'40" N, long. 120°35'10" W; near SE
cor. sec. 26, T 19 N, R 12 E). Named on English Mountain (1983) 7.5' quadrangle.

Mud Lake [PLACER]: *lake*, 550 feet long, 6.5
miles east of Bunker Hill (lat. 39°03'05" N,

long. 120°15'25" W; near NW cor. sec. 19, T
14 N, R 16 E). Named on Wentworth Springs
(1953) 7.5' quadrangle.

Mud Lake [SIERRA]: *lake*, 350 feet long, 4
miles north of Sierra City (lat. 39°37'20" N,
long. 120°38'35" W; near SE cor. sec. 5, T 20
N, R 12 E). Named on Sierra City (1981) 7.5'
quadrangle.

Mud Lake [TUOLUMNE]: *lake*, 625 feet long,
nearly 6 miles east-southeast of Pinecrest (lat.
38°09'05" N, long. 119°54'10" W). Named
on Pinecrest (1979) 7.5' quadrangle, which
shows the lake in a marsh. On Dardanelles
(1898) 30' quadrangle, a feature called Lily
Lake covers present Mud Lake and its adjacent marsh. United States Board on Geographic Names (1963a, p. 7) rejected the name
"Lily Lake" for present Mud Lake.

Mud Lakes [EL DORADO]: *lakes*, largest 500
feet long, 3 miles east of Wentworth Springs
(lat. 39°01'10" N, long. 120°16'55" W; sec.
34, T 14 N, R 15 E). Named on Wentworth
Springs (1953, photorevised 1973) 7.5' quadrangle.

Mud Lakes: see **Mud Lake** [AMADOR].

Mud Spring [AMADOR]: *spring*, nearly 2 miles
east of Hams Station (lat. 38°32'45" N, long.
120°20'30" W; sec. 17, T 8 N, R 15 E). Named
on Peddler Hill (1951) 7.5' quadrangle.

Mud Spring [CALAVERAS]: *spring*, 7 miles
west-southwest of Tamarack (lat. 38°22'55"
N, long. 120°11'15" W; near SE cor. sec. 10,
T 6 N, R 16 E). Named on Calaveras Dome
(1979) 7.5' quadrangle, which indicates that
the spring is dry.

Mud Spring: see **El Dorado** [EL DORADO];
Upper Mud Spring [EL DORADO].

Mud Spring Creek [MADERA]: *stream*, flows
8 miles to Fresno River 9.5 miles south of Raymond (lat. 37°04'40" N, long. 119°53'55" W;
sec. 9, T 10 S, R 19 E). Named on Daulton
(1962), Knowles (1962), and Little Table
Mountain (1962) 7.5' quadrangles.

Mud Springs: see **El Dorado** [EL DORADO].

Mugginsville: see **Gold Hill** [PLACER].

Mugler Creek [MADERA]: *stream*, flows 6
miles to Chiquito Creek 6.5 miles north-northeast of Shuteye Peak (lat. 37°26'15" N, long.
119°23' W; sec. 6, T 6 S, R 24 E); the stream
goes through Muglers Meadow. Named on
Shuteye Peak (1953) 15' quadrangle.

Muglers Meadow [MADERA]: *area*, 9 miles
north of Shuteye Peak (lat. 37°28'45" N, long.
119°26' W; sec. 22, T 5 S, R 23 E); the place
is along Mugler Creek. Named on Shuteye
Peak (1953) 15' quadrangle. Christopher
Mugler, a sheepman who was in the neighborhood as early as 1852, had his base camp
at the place (Browning, 1986, p. 155).

Muir Gorge [TUOLUMNE]: *narrows*, 8 miles
northeast of White Wolf along Tuolumne
River (lat. 37°56'15" N, long. 119°31'45" W).
Named on Hetch Hetchy Reservoir (1956) 15'
quadrangle. R.M. Price named the feature in

1895 for naturalist John Muir (United States Board on Geographic Names, 1934, p. 17).

Mule Canyon [EL DORADO]: *canyon,* drained by a stream that flows 5 miles to Silver Fork American River 8 miles west of Kirkwood (lat. 38°42'20" N, long. 120°12'50" W; near W line sec. 21, T 10 N, R 16 E). Named on Tragedy Spring (1979) 7.5' quadrangle.

Mule Creek [AMADOR]: *stream,* flows 10 miles to Dry Creek nearly 3 miles west-northwest of Ione (lat. 38°21'40" N, long. 120° 58'55" W). Named on Amador City (1962), Ione (1962), and Irish Hill (1962) 7.5' quadrangles. Camp's (1962) map shows a place called Muletown located 2 miles north-northwest of Ione along Mule Creek. Muletown was a lively camp in the 1850's (Hoover, Rensch, and Rensch, p. 34).

Mule Spring [NEVADA]: *spring,* 11.5 miles northeast of Chicago Park (lat. 39°14'40" N, long. 120°48' W; near S line sec. 13, T 16 N, R 10 E). Named on Dutch Flat (1950) 7.5' quadrangle.

Muletown: see **Mule Creek** [AMADOR].

Mullen Ridge [MADERA-MARIPOSA]: *ridge,* south-trending, 2 miles long, 6.5 miles north of Raymond on Madera-Mariposa county line (lat. 37°18'40" N, long. 119°53'35" W). Named on Ben Hur (1947) 7.5' quadrangle.

Mumford Bar [PLACER]: *locality,* 6.5 miles west-northwest of Duncan Peak along North Fork American River (lat. 39°12'10" N, long. 120°37' W; near S line sec. 34, T 16 N, R 12 E). Named on Duncan Peak (1952) 7.5' quadrangle.

Mundys [EL DORADO]: *locality,* 16 miles east-southeast of Georgetown (lat. 38°50'30" N, long. 120°33'15" W). Named on Placerville (1893) 30' quadrangle.

Munson Meadow [AMADOR]: *area,* 1.5 miles north-northeast of Mokelumne Peak (lat. 38°33'35" N, long. 120°04'05" W). Named on Mokelumne Peak (1979) 7.5' quadrangle.

Murderers Bar [EL DORADO]: *locality,* 2 miles north of Cool along Middle Fork American River (lat. 38°55' N, long. 121°00'35" W; sec. 6, T 12 N, R 9 E). Named on Auburn (1953) 7.5' quadrangle. Indians massacred five miners at the place (Bancroft, 1888, p. 354).

Murderers Gulch [CALAVERAS]: *canyon,* drained by a stream that flows 1 mile to Coyote Creek 1 mile south of Vallecito (lat. 38°04'10" N, long. 120°28'20" W; sec. 31, T 3 N, R 14 E). Named on Columbia (1948) 7.5' quadrangle.

Murderers Gulch [PLACER]: *canyon,* drained by a stream that flows 1 mile to Middle Fork American River 4 miles east-northeast of Auburn (lat. 38°55'15" N, long. 121°00'15" W; at W line sec. 5, T 12 N, R 9 E). Named on Auburn (1953) 7.5' quadrangle.

Murderers' Gulch: see **Wards Ferry** [TUOLUMNE].

Murdock Lake [TUOLUMNE]: *lake,* 700 feet long, 10 miles south-southeast of Tower Peak (lat. 38°00'10" N, long. 119°30'15" W). Named on Tower Peak (1956) 15' quadrangle. Lieutenant N.F. McClure named the lake in 1895 for William C. Murdock of California State Board of Fish Commissioners (Gudde, 1949, p. 229).

Murphy: see **Murphys** [CALAVERAS].

Murphy Creek [AMADOR]: *stream,* flows 2.25 miles to San Joaquin County 7.5 miles southwest of Ione (lat. 38°15'40" N, long. 120° 00'35" W; sec. 29, T 5 N, R 9 E). Named on Goose Creek (1968) and Ione (1962) 7.5' quadrangles.

Murphy Creek [MARIPOSA]: *stream,* flows 3 miles to Tenaya Lake 3.25 miles west-southwest of Cathedral Peak (lat. 37°50' N, long. 119°27'45" W; near W line sec. 21, T 1 S, R 23 E). Named on Tuolumne Meadows (1956) 15' quadrangle. The name is for John L. Murphy, an early settler by Tenaya Lake (United States Board on Geographic Names, 1934, p. 17).

Murphy Flat [NEVADA]: *locality,* 2 miles east-southeast of Graniteville (lat. 39°25'35" N, long. 120°42'20" W; sec. 14, T 18 N, R 11 E). Named on Graniteville (1982) 7.5' quadrangle.

Murphy Gulch [AMADOR]: *canyon,* 1.25 miles long, 2.5 miles south-southeast of Jackson (lat. 38°19' N, long. 120°45'25" W; mainly in sec. 3, T 5 N, R 11 E). Named on Jackson (1962) 7.5' quadrangle. The name "Murphy's Gulch" was used for the feature as early as 1851 (McKinstry, p. 351).

Murphy Meadows [PLACER]: *area,* 2 miles north-northwest of Martis Peak (lat. 39°18'50" N, long. 120°00'40" W; near N line sec. 30, T 17 N, R 18 E). Named on Martis Peak (1955) 7.5' quadrangle.

Murphy Mountain [EL DORADO]: *peak,* 1 mile northeast of Coloma (lat. 38°48'30" N, long. 120°52'40" W; near NE cor. sec. 17, T 11 N, R 10 E). Named on Coloma (1949) and Garden Valley (1949) 7.5' quadrangles. The name commemorates Patrick O' Brien Murphy, a stone mason who soon after discovery of gold at Sutter's Mill built a stone fort on top of the peak for protection from Indian attack (Gernes, p. 8).

Murphy Peak [TUOLUMNE]: *peak,* 4 miles east-northeast of Tuolumne (lat. 37°58'55" N, long. 120°09'50" W; sec. 36, T 2 N, R 16 E). Named on Tuolumne (1948) 7.5' quadrangle.

Murphys [CALAVERAS]: *town,* 12 miles east-southeast of San Andreas (lat. 38°08'15" N, long. 120°27'45" W; in and near sec. 5, T 3 N, R 14 E). Named on Murphys (1948) 7.5' quadrangle. The place is called Murphy's on Ellis' (1850) map, and called Murphy on Big Trees (1891) 30' quadrangle. Postal authorities established Murphy's post office in 1851, changed the name to Murphy in 1894, and changed it to Murphys in 1935 (Frickstad, p. 16). The name is for Daniel Murphy and John

Murphy, brothers who set up a mining camp in 1848 that became known as Murphy's Diggings, Murphy's Camp, and Murphy's (Hoover, Rensch, and Rensch, p. 46). Gudde (1975, p. 258) noted that places called Owlsburg and Owlburrow Flat were rich diggings on a north-trending ridge located in present Murphys, and (p. 337) that a place called Stoutenburg, named for a German miner, was situated along Coyote Creek near Murphys. A mining camp of the 1850's and 1860's called Brownsville was located 1 mile east of Murphys; the name was for Alfred Brown (California Department of Parks and Recreation, p. 17).

Murphys: see **Meeks Bay** [EL DORADO] (2).

Murphy's Camp: see **Murphys** [CALAVERAS].

Murphy's Diggings: see **Murphys** [CALAVERAS].

Murphy's Dome: see **Pywiack Dome** [MARIPOSA].

Murray Creek [CALAVERAS]: *stream,* flows 14 miles to North Fork Calaveras River 1.5 miles northwest of San Andreas (lat. 38° 12'40" N, long. 120°42'15" W; near E line sec. 12, T 4 N, R 11 E). Named on Calaveritas (1962), Rail Road Flat (1948), and San Andreas (1962) 7.5' quadrangles. North Fork enters from the north 2.5 miles upstream from the mouth of Murray Creek; it is 5 miles long and is named on Mokelumne Hill (1948) and San Andreas (1962) 7.5' quadrangles.

Murraysville: see **Jersey Flat**, under **Downieville** [SIERRA].

Murry Camp [PLACER]: *locality,* about 1.5 miles south of Bunker Hill (lat. 39°01'40" N, long. 120°22'30" W; sec. 26, T 14 N, R 14 E). Named on Bunker Hill (1953) and Wentworth Springs (1953) 7.5' quadrangles.

Music Dale: see **Big Indian Creek** [AMADOR].

Musquito: see **Glencoe** [CALAVERAS].

Musquito Gulch: see **Glencoe** [CALAVERAS].

Mutton Canyon [EL DORADO]: *canyon,* drained by a stream that flows 1.25 miles to Pilot Creek (1) 12 miles north-northwest of Pollock Pines (lat. 38°55'20" N, long. 120°38'25" W). Named on Tunnel Hill (1950) 7.5' quadrangle.

Myers Creek [MARIPOSA]: *stream,* flows 2.5 miles to South Fork Dry Creek 6.5 miles northwest of Hornitos (lat. 37°34'10" N, long. 120°19'35" W; sec. 21, T 4 S, R 15 E). Named on Merced Falls (1962) 7.5' quadrangle.

Myers Ravine: see **Meyers Ravine** [NEVADA].

Mystic [NEVADA]: *locality,* 11.5 miles northeast of Truckee along Southern Pacific Railroad (lat. 39°26'15" N, long. 120°01'10" W; sec. 7, T 18 N, R 18 E). Named on Boca (1955) 7.5' quadrangle. California Division of Highways' (1934) map shows a place called Farad located along the railroad less than 1 mile south-southwest of Mystic (near E line sec. 12, T 18 N, R 17 E). Boca (1955) 7.5'

quadrangle shows Farad powerhouse near the site—the word "farad" is from a measure of electrical capacity.

Mystic Canyon [NEVADA]: *canyon,* drained by a stream that flows 1.5 miles to Truckee River 11 miles northeast of Truckee (lat. 39° 25'55" N, long. 120°01'30" W); near SW cor. sec. 7, T 18 N, R 18 E); the mouth of the canyon is 0.5 mile southwest of Mystic. Named on Boca (1955) 7.5' quadrangle.

– N –

Nance Peak [TUOLUMNE]: *peak,* 15 miles east-southeast of Pinecrest (lat. 38°04'05" N, long. 119°45'10" W). Named on Pinecrest (1956) 15' quadrangle. The name commemorates John Torrence Nance, professor of military science at University of California (United States Board on Geographic Names, 1934, p. 17).

Nancy Lake [PLACER]: *lake,* 750 feet long, 7.5 miles west-southwest of Donner Pass (lat. 39°17'25" N, long. 120°27'40" W; near S line sec. 36, T 17 N, R 13 E). Named on Soda Springs (1955, photorevised 1973) 7.5' quadrangle.

Narbo: see **Quartz Mountain** [MADERA] (2).

Nashton: see **Soulsbyville** [TUOLUMNE].

Nashville [EL DORADO]: *locality,* 10.5 miles south of Placerville along North Fork Cosumnes River (lat. 38°34'45" N, long. 120°50'35" W; sec. 2, T 8 N, R 10 E). Named on Fiddletown (1949) 7.5' quadrangle. Postal authorities established Nashville post office in 1852, discontinued it in 1854, reestablished it in 1870, and discontinued it in 1907 (Frickstad, p. 28). The place first was known as Nashville Bar (Hanna, p. 207). It also was called Quartzville and Quartzburg; the name "Nashville" is from the city in Tennessee (Gudde, 1975, p. 234).

Nashville Bar: see **Nashville** [EL DORADO].

Nassau: see **Nassau Valley** [CALAVERAS].

Nassau Creek [CALAVERAS]: *stream,* flows 7.5 miles to Cherokee Creek 5 miles west-northwest of Angels Camp (lat. 38°05'30" N, long. 120°37'55" W; near SE cor. sec. 22, T 3 N, R 12 E); the stream goes through Nassau Valley. Named on Angels Camp (1962) and Salt Spring Valley (1962) 7.5' quadrangles.

Nassau Valley [CALAVERAS]: *valley,* 5 miles southwest of Angels Camp (lat. 38°02' N, long. 120°37'10" W); the valley is on upper reaches of Nassau Creek. Named on Angels Camp (1962) 7.5' quadrangle. California Mining Bureau's (1909a) map shows a place called Nassau located 6.5 miles by stage line west-southwest of Altaville. Postal authorities established Nassau post office 6 miles west of Angels Camp in 1892, moved it 1.5 miles west in 1905, and discontinued it in 1910 (Salley, p. 150).

National Gulch [NEVADA]: *canyon,* drained by a stream that flows 1.25 miles to Middle Yuba River 9 miles northeast of North Bloomfield (lat. 39°26'55" N, long. 121°46'20" W; at SW cor. sec. 5, T 18 N, R 11 E). Named on Alleghany (1949) 7.5' quadrangle.

Neall Lake [TUOLUMNE]: *lake,* 950 feet long, 11.5 miles northwest of White Wolf (lat. 37°59'15" N, long. 119°30'15" W). Named on Hetch Hetchy Reservoir (1956) 15' quadrangle. The name is for John Mitchell Neall, who was stationed in Yosemite National Park with the Fourth Cavalry from 1892 until 1897 (United States Board on Geographic Names, 1934, p. 17). Lieutenant H.C. Benson named the feature, which first was called Rodgers Lake for Captain Alexander Rodgers—this name was dropped because it duplicated another name in the park (Browning, 1988, p. 102).

Nebenhorn [EL DORADO]: *locality,* less than 0.25 mile west-southwest of Echo Summit (lat. 38°48'40" N, long. 120°02' W; sec. 7, T 11 N, R 18 E). Named on Echo Lake (1955) 7.5' quadrangle.

Nebraska City: see **Cornish House** [SIERRA].

Nebraska Diggings: see **Cornish House** [SIERRA].

Nebraska Flat: see **Cornish House** [SIERRA].

Neck Meadow [EL DORADO]: *area,* 1 mile west of Wentworth Springs along Gerle Creek (lat. 39°00'50" N, long. 120°21'25" W; sec. 36, T 14 N, R 14 E). Named on Wentworth Springs (1953) 7.5' quadrangle.

Ned Gulch [MARIPOSA]:
(1) *canyon,* drained by a stream that flows 1.25 miles to Willow Creek 2.25 miles south of Penon Blanco Peak (lat. 37°42' N, long. 120°15'35" W; sec. 1, T 3 S, R 15 E). Named on Penon Blanco Peak (1962) 7.5' quadrangle.
(2) *canyon,* drained by a stream that flows 7.5 miles to Merced River 6.5 miles west of El Portal (lat. 37°40'10" N, long. 119° 54' W). Named on El Portal (1947) and Lake Eleanor (1956) 15' quadrangles. Called Ned's Gulch on Hoffmann and Gardner's (1863-1867) map.

Neds Gulch [CALAVERAS]: *canyon,* drained by a stream that flows nearly 3 miles to San Antonio Creek 5.5 miles north-northeast of Murphys (lat. 38°12'50" N, long. 120°25'50" W; sec. 9, T 4 N, R 14 E). Named on Murphys (1948) 7.5' quadrangle.

Needle: see **Needle Peak** [PLACER].

Needle Lake [PLACER]: *lake,* 450 feet long, 0.5 mile west-northwest of Granite Chief (lat. 39°12'05" N, long. 120°17'45" W; at N line sec. 34, T 16 N, R 15 E); the lake is 1000 feet east of Needle Peak. Named on Granite Chief (1953) 7.5' quadrangle.

Needle Lake: see **Little Needle Lake** [PLACER].

Needle Peak [PLACER]: *peak,* less than 1 mile west-northwest of Granite Chief (lat.

39°12'05" N, long. 120°18' W; at N line sec. 34, T 16 N, R 15 E). Altitude 8971 feet. Named on Granite Chief (1953) 7.5' quadrangle. Called Needle on Wheeler's (1876-1877b) map.

Needle Point [SIERRA]: *peak,* nearly 5 miles southeast of Mount Fillmore (lat. 39°40'35" N, long. 120°47'35" W; near SW cor. sec. 18, T 21 N, R 11 E). Altitude 7129 feet. Named on Mount Fillmore (1951) 7.5' quadrangle.

Negro Bar: see **Secret Canyon** [SIERRA].

Negro Canyon [EL DORADO]: *canyon,* drained by a stream that flows 2.25 miles to Mule Canyon 5.5 miles west-southwest of Kirkwood (lat. 38°43'10" N, long. 120°10'15" W; sec. 14, T 10 N, R 16 E). Named on Tregedy Spring (1979) 7.5' quadrangle.

Negro Canyon [NEVADA]: *canyon,* drained by a stream that flows 1 mile to Donner Lake 2.25 miles east-northeast of Donner Pass (lat. 39°19'30" N, long. 120°17'05" W; sec. 14, T 17 N, R 15 E). Named on Norden (1955) 7.5' quadrangle.

Negro Canyon [SIERRA]: *canyon,* drained by a stream that flows 6 miles to North Yuba River 4.5 miles west of Sierra City (lat. 39° 33'50" N, long. 120°43'05" W; near NE cor. sec. 34, T 20 N, R 11 E). Named on Sierra City (1981) 7.5' quadrangle.

Negro Creek [NEVADA]: *stream,* flows 4 miles to Deer Creek 5 miles north-northwest of Pilot Peak (lat. 39°14'10" N, long. 121° 12'50" W; sec. 20, T 16 N, R 7 E). Named on Grass Valley (1949) 15' quadrangle.

Negro Flat [EL DORADO]: *area,* nearly 5 miles west-northwest of Kirkwood (lat. 38°43'35" N, long. 120°09'10" W; sec. 12, T 10 N, R 16 E); the place is in Negro Canyon. Named on Tragedy Spring (1979) 7.5' quadrangle.

Negro Flat: see **Remington Hill** [NEVADA] (2).

Negro Hill [CALAVERAS]: *peak,* 2 miles west of Angels Camp (lat. 38°04'25" N, long. 120°34'55" W; sec. 31, T 3 N, R 13 E). Named on Angels Camp (1962) 7.5' quadrangle. Called Nigger Hill on San Andreas (1947) 15' quadrangle.

Negro Hill [MARIPOSA]: *ridge,* west-north-west-trending, 1.5 miles long, 5 miles northeast of the settlement of Catheys Valley (lat. 37° 28'30" N, long. 120°00'45" W). Named on Catheys Valley (1962) 7.5' quadrangle. Called Nigger Hill on Indian Gulch (1920) 15' quadrangle, but United States Board on Geographic Names (1964a, p. 12) rejected this name for the feature.

Negro Hill: see **Folsom Lake** [EL DORADO-PLACER].

Negro Jack Gulch [TUOLUMNE]: *canyon,* drained by a stream that flows nearly 1 mile to Tulloch Lake 5 miles northwest of Keystone (lat. 37°53'15" N, long. 120°34' W; at N line sec. 5, T 1 S, R 13 E); the canyon is east of Negro Jack Point. Named on Melones Dam (1962) 7.5' quadrangle. Called Nigger Jack

Gulch on Copperopolis (1916) 15' quadrangle.

Negro Jack Hill [NEVADA]: *peak,* 6.5 miles south-southeast of Washington (lat. 39°15'55" N, long. 120°46'30" W; at E line sec. 7, T 16 N, R 11 E). Altitude 4635 feet. Named on Washington (1950) 7.5' quadrangle. Called Nigger Jack Hill on Colfax (1938) 30' quadrangle.

Negro Jack Point [TUOLUMNE]: *promontory,* 5.5 miles northwest of Keystone on the south side of Tulloch Lake (lat. 37°53'20" N, long. 120°34'40" W; near SW cor. sec. 32, T 1 N, R 13 E). Named on Melones Dam (1962) 7.5' quadrangle. Called Nigger Jack Pt. on Copperopolis (1916) 15' quadrangle. The name is for Jack Wade, a slave who came to California, bought his freedom, and settled near the feature (Paden and Schlichtmann, p. 52-53).

Negro Tent [SIERRA]: *locality,* 4.25 miles northeast of Pike (lat. 39° 29'20" N, long. 120°57' W; sec. 27, T 19 N, R 9 E). Named on Alleghany (1950) 15' quadrangle. Called Nigger Tent on Colfax (1898) 30' quadrangle, and called Niger Tent on Trask's (1853) map. A black man erected a tent at the site for the accommodation of travelers, and although eventually a cabin replaced the tent, the place retained the original designation "Nigger Tent" (Borthwick, p. 215). The place also was known as Hollow Log in 1850 (Gudde, 1975, p. 244). Eddy's (1851) map shows Hollow Log situated 6 miles by trail south of Goodyears Bar.

Nehouse Creek [MADERA]: *stream,* flows 3 miles to West Fork Jackass Creek 6.5 miles east-northeast of Shuteye Peak (lat. 37°23'30" N, long. 119°19'20" W; sec. 23, T 6 S, R 24 E). Named on Shuteye Peak (1953) 15' quadrangle.

Neilsburg: see **Nielsburg** [PLACER].

Nelder Creek [MADERA]: *stream,* flows 7.5 miles to join Lewis Fork and form Fresno River less than 0.5 mile south-southwest of Yosemite Forks (lat. 37°21'40" N, long. 119°37'55" W; near SW cor. sec. 36, T 6 S, R 21 E). Named on Bass Lake (1953) 15' quadrangle.

Nelder Grove Campground [MADERA]: *locality,* 5 miles north-northeast of Yosemite Forks (lat. 37°15'20" N, long. 119°35' W; sec. 8, T 6 S, R 22 E). Named on Bass Lake (1953) 15' quadrangle. Nelder Grove is a group of redwood trees—John Muir found John A. Nelder living in a cabin at the place in 1875 (Browning, 1986, p. 157).

Nellie Falls: see **Little Nellie Falls** [MARIPOSA].

Nelson: see **Jack Nelson Creek** [CALAVERAS].

Nelson Canyon [EL DORADO]: *canyon,* drained by a stream that flows 1.5 miles to Rock Creek 2.5 miles northeast of Chili Bar (lat. 38°47'30" N, long. 120°46'50" W; near

W line sec. 20, T 11 N, R 11 E). Named on Garden Valley (1949) 7.5' quadrangle.

Nelson Cove [MARIPOSA]: *valley,* 11 miles east-southeast of Mariposa along East Fork Chowchilla Creek (lat. 37°24'35" N, long. 119°47' W; sec. 16, T 6 S, R 20 E). Named on Stumpfield Mountain (1947) 7.5' quadrangle.

Nelson Lake [MARIPOSA]: *lake,* 1400 feet long, 3 miles south-southeast of Cathedral Peak (lat. 37°48'35" N, long. 119°22'35" W). Named on Tuolumne Meadows (1956) 15' quadrangle. The name commemorates William Henry Nelson, a ranger in Yosemite National Park from 1917 until 1936, and from 1943 until 1945 (Browning, 1988, p. 103).

Nelson Mill [SIERRA]: *locality,* 0.5 mile south-southeast of Pike (lat. 39°26' N, long. 120°59'30" W). Named on Colfax (1898) 7.5' quadrangle.

Nelsonville: see **Mosquito Valley**, under **Mosquito Creek** [EL DORADO].

Nesbits Bar: see **Gold Hill** [PLACER].

Neutral Bar: see **Euchre Bar** [PLACER].

Nevada: see **Nevada City** [NEVADA].

Nevada City [NEVADA]: *town,* 4 miles northeast of Grass Valley along Deer Creek (lat. 39°15'50" N, long. 121°01'05" W; on W line sec. 7, T 16 N, R 9 E). Named on Nevada City (1948) 7.5' quadrangle. Called Nevada on Eddy's (1854) map. Postal authorities established Nevada City post office in 1850 (Frickstad, p. 114), and the town incorporated in 1856. Dr. A.B. Caldwell built a log cabin and store at the site in 1849, and for a time the place was known as Caldwell's Upper Store or Deer Creek Dry Diggings; the inhabitants changed the name of the community to Nevada in 1850, and to Nevada City ten years later to avoid confusion with the newly created State of Nevada (Hoover, Rensch, and Rensch, p. 253). After discovery of gold in the hills of the northwest part of present Nevada City, a community called Coyoteville grew there (Lindgren, 1897, p. 18). The name "Coyoteville" was from the fancied resemblance of holes dug for gold at the place to the burrows of coyotes (Gudde, 1975, p. 86). Whitney's (1873) map shows features called American Hill and Gopher Hill located just north of Nevada City and south of Sugar Loaf (present Sugarloaf Mountain). Whitney (1880, p. 190) described a feature called Connor Hill that was located about four miles west of Nevada City.

Nevada Fall [MARIPOSA]: *waterfall,* 3.5 miles east-southeast of Yosemite Village on Merced River (lat. 37°43'30" N, long. 119° 32' W). Named on Yosemite (1956) 15' quadrangle. Lafayette H. Bunnell, who was with the group that discovered the waterfall in 1851, suggested the name because the white foaming water resembled an avalanche of snow (United States Board on Geographic Names, 1934, p. 18)—*nevada* means "snowy" in Spanish.

Nevada Point [PLACER]: *ridge,* west-north-west-trending, 3.25 miles long, 6.25 miles west of Devil Peak (lat. 38°58'20" N, long. 120° 39'15" W); the ridge is at the west end of Nevada Point Ridge. Named on Tunnel Hill (1950) 7.5' quadrangle.

Nevada Point Ridge [PLACER]: *ridge,* extends generally southwest for 20 miles between Rubicon River and Long Canyon—as well as South Fork Long Canyon—from near Hell Hole Reservoir to the junction of Rubicon River and Long Canyon; Nevada Point is at the west end. Named on Bunker Hill (1953), Devil Peak (1950), Robbs Peak (1950), and Tunnel Hill (1950) 7.5' quadrangles.

Newark: see **Whiskey Diggings** [SIERRA].

New Camp: see **Columbia** [TUOLUMNE].

Newcastle [PLACER]: *town,* 8 miles northeast of Rocklin (lat. 38°52'25" N, long. 121°07'55" W; mainly in sec. 19, T 12 N, R 8 E). Named on Gold Hill (1954) and Rocklin (1967) 7.5' quadrangles. Postal authorities established Newcastle post office in 1864 (Frickstad, p. 121). They established Secret Ravine post office 3 miles southwest of Newcastle in 1854, changed the name to Auburn Station in 1863, changed it back to Secret Ravine the same year, and discontinued it in 1868 (Salley, p. 12, 200).

New Chicago [AMADOR]: *locality,* 3 miles south of Plymouth (lat. 38°26'15" N, long. 120°50'15" W; near NE cor. sec. 26, T 7 N, R 10 E). Named on Amador City (1962) 7.5' quadrangle. Called Chicago on Jackson (1902) 30' quadrangle.

New Don Pedro Reservoir: see **Don Pedro Reservoir** [TUOLUMNE].

Newell: see **Confidence** [TUOLUMNE].

New England Mills [PLACER]: *locality,* 4 miles south-southwest of Colfax (lat. 39°02'35" N, long. 120°58'20" W; near SE cor. sec. 21, T 14 N, R 9 E). Named on Colfax (1949) 7.5' quadrangle.

New Hogan Lake: see **New Hogan Reservoir** [CALAVERAS].

New Hogan Reservoir [CALAVERAS]: *lake,* behind a dam on Calaveras River 3 miles south-southeast of Valley Springs (lat. 38° 09' N, long. 120°48'45" W; near SW cor. sec. 31, T 4 N, R 11 E). Named on Jenny Lind (1962), San Andreas (1962), and Valley Springs (1962) 7.5' quadrangles. United States Board on Geographic Names (1972, p. 4) approved the name "New Hogan Lake" for the feature, and gave the names "Hogan Reservoir" and "Valley Springs Reservoir" as variants. Valley Springs (1944) 15' quadrangle shows a smaller, unnamed lake behind a dam just upstream from the dam that forms present New Hogan Lake.

New Hope: see **Stanislaus River** [CALAVERAS-TUOLUMNE].

Newhouse Place: see **Mobile Flat**, under **Mobile Ravine** [SIERRA].

Newman Hill [AMADOR]: *peak,* 3 miles west of Ione (lat. 38°21'10" N, long. 120°59'15" W). Altitude 474 feet. Named on Ione (1962) 7.5' quadrangle.

New Melones Lake [CALAVERAS-TUOLUMNE]: *lake,* behind a dam on Stanislaus River 7 miles east-southeast of Copperopolis on Calaveras-Tuolumne county line (lat. 37°57'10" N, long. 120°30'50" W; sec. 11, T 1 N, R 13 E). Named on Columbia (1948, photorevised 1973) and Sonora (1948, photorevised 1973) 7.5' quadrangles. Called Melones Reservoir on Columbia (1948) and Sonora (1948) 15' quadrangles, and on Angels Camp (1962) and Melones Dam (1962) 7.5' quadrangles. United States Board on Geographic Names (1972, p. 4) gave the names "Melones Reservoir" and "New Melones Reservoir" as variants.

New Melones Reservoir: see **New Melones Lake** [CALAVERAS-TUOLUMNE].

New Orleans Gulch [EL DORADO]: *canyon,* drained by a stream that flows 1.25 miles to Middle Fork American River 4.5 miles north-northeast of Greenwood (lat. 38°57'25" N, long. 120°52'35" W; sec. 20, T 13 N, R 10 E). Named on Georgetown (1949) and Greenwood (1949) 7.5' quadrangles.

New Philadelphia: see **Bunker Hill** [AMADOR] (2).

Newton: see **Newtown** [EL DORADO]; **Newtown** [NEVADA].

Newton Crossing: see **Chowchilla River** [MADERA-MARIPOSA].

Newtown [EL DORADO]: *locality,* 2.25 miles south of Camino (lat. 38°42'15" N, long. 120°40'40" W; sec. 20, T 10 N, R 12 E). Named on Camino (1952) 7.5' quadrangle. Called Newton on California Mining Bureau's (1917b) map. Logan's (1938) map has the form "New town" for the name. Postal authorities established Newtown post office in 1854, discontinued it for a time in 1875, and discontinued it finally in 1912 (Frickstad, p. 28). A mining camp called Dogtown was situated 0.5 mile northeast of Newtown (Hoover, Rensch, and Rensch, p. 84).

Newtown [NEVADA]: *locality,* 4.5 miles west of Nevada City (lat. 39°15'10" N, long. 121°06'10" W; near N line sec. 17, T 16 N, R 8 E). Named on Nevada City (1948) 7.5' quadrangle. A group of sailors made the first discovery of gold at the place, which for a time was called Sailors Flat; it also was called Newton (Gudde, 1975, p. 241). Whitney's (1873) map shows a place called Beckmans Fl. [Flat] located along Deer Creek about 1 mile southeast of Newtown, a place called Pleasant Fl. located along Deer Creek about 1 mile east-southeast of Newtown, and a place called Stockings Fl. located along Deer Creek 2.5 miles east of Newtown. Whitney (1880, p. 190) noted that a canyon called Illinois Ravine heads near Newtown and extends north to Rush Creek.

New York: see **Little New York**, under **Little York** [NEVADA].

New York Bar [EL DORADO-PLACER]: *locality,* 3 miles east-northeast of Auburn along Middle Fork American River on El Dorado-Placer county line nearly 1 mile above the mouth of Middle Fork (lat. 38°54'55" N, long. 121°01'25" W; near SW cor. sec. 6, T 12 N, R 9 E). Named on Auburn (1953) 7.5' quadrangle.

New York Camp: see **Merced River** [MADERA-MARIPOSA].

New York Canyon [NEVADA]: *canyon,* drained by a stream that flows 1 mile to South Yuba River 2.25 miles south of North Bloomfield (lat. 39°20'05" N, long. 120°54'10" W; sec. 18, T 17 N, R 10 E). Named on North Bloomfield (1949) 7.5' quadrangle.

New York Canyon [PLACER]:
(1) *canyon,* drained by a stream that flows 3 miles to North Fork American River 4.5 miles north of Duncan Peak (lat. 39°13'10" N, long. 120°30'30" W; sec. 27, T 16 N, R 13 E). Named on Duncan Peak (1952) 7.5' quadrangle.
(2) *canyon,* drained by a stream that flows 2 miles to Shirttail Canyon 4 miles northwest of Foresthill (lat. 39°04'10" N, long. 120°51'30" W; at S line sec. 9, T 14 N, R 10 E). Named on Foresthill (1949) 7.5' quadrangle.

New York Creek [EL DORADO]: *stream,* drained by a stream that flows 3.25 miles to Folsom Lake 5 miles north of Clarksville (lat. 38°43'35" N, long. 121°04'10" W; sec. 14, T 10 N, R 8 E). Named on Clarksville (1953, photorevised 1980) 7.5' quadrangle.

New York Flat: see **Downieville** [SIERRA]; **New York Gulch** [AMADOR].

New York Gulch [AMADOR]: *canyon,* drained by a stream that flows 1 mile to Dry Creek 4 miles south-southwest of Plymouth (lat. 38°25'35" N, long. 120°52'55" W; near S line sec. 28, T 7 N, R 10 E). Named on Irish Hill (1962) 7.5' quadrangle. Camp's (1962) map has the designation "New York Gulch & Flat" for the place.

New York Ranch Gulch [AMADOR]: *canyon,* 3 miles long, opens into the canyon of Jackson Creek nearly 2 miles north-northwest of Jackson Butte (lat. 38°21'45" N, long. 120°44'10" W; sec. 23, T 6 N, R 11 E). Named on Mokelumne Hill (1948) and Pine Grove (1948) 7.5' quadrangles.

New York Ravine [NEVADA]: *canyon,* drained by a stream that flows nearly 1.5 miles to Middle Yuba River 6 miles northeast of North Bloomfield (lat. 39°26'05" N, long. 120°49'30" W; sec. 11, T 18 N, R 10 E). Named on Alleghany (1949) 7.5' quadrangle.

New York Ravine [SIERRA]: *canyon,* drained by a stream that flows 2.25 miles to North Yuba River 2 miles east of Downieville (lat. 39°33'20" N, long. 120°47'20" W; sec. 31, T 20 N, R 11 E). Named on Downieville (1951) 7.5' quadrangle.

New York Reservoir: see **Jackson** [AMADOR].

New York Tent: see **Yosemite Junction** [TUOLUMNE].

Niagara: see **Camp Niagara** [TUOLUMNE].

Niagara Creek [TUOLUMNE]:
(1) *stream,* flows 4.5 miles to Reed Creek 5.5 miles east-northeast of Duckwall Mountain (lat. 37°59'40" N, long. 120°01'15" W; near S line sec. 29, T 2 N, R 18 E). Named on Cherry Lake North (1979), Duckwall Mountain (1948), and Hull Creek (1979) 7.5' quadrangles.
(2) *stream,* flows 6.5 miles to Donnell Reservoir 6 miles west of Dardanelle (lat. 38°19'55" N, long. 119°56'25" W). Named on Dardanelle (1979) and Donnell Lake (1979) 7.5' quadrangles.

Niagara Creek Campground [TUOLUMNE]: *locality,* 4.5 miles west-southwest of present Dardanelle (lat. 38°19'35" N, long. 119°54'45" W; sec. 32, T 6 N, R 19 E); the place is along Niagara Creek (2). Named on Dardanelles Cone (1956) 15' quadrangle.

Nichols: see **Robert Nichols Spring** [TUOLUMNE].

Nichols Mill [SIERRA]: *locality,* nearly 3 miles south-southwest of Sierraville along Bonta Creek (lat. 39°33'05" N, long. 120°23'15" W; sec. 26, T 20 N, R 14 E). Site named on Sattley (1981) 7.5' quadrangle.

Nick Welsh Spring [PLACER]: *spring,* 1.5 miles north-northeast of Foresthill (lat. 39°02'25" N, long. 120°48'10" W; sec. 24, T 14 N, R 10 E). Named on Foresthill (1949) 7.5' quadrangle.

Nielsburg [PLACER]: *locality,* 4.5 miles north-northeast of Auburn (lat. 38°57'25" N, long. 121°01'50" W; at S line sec. 24, T 13 N, R 8 E). Site named on Auburn (1953) 7.5' quadrangle. According to Salley (p. 152), postal authorities established Neilsburgh post office in 1855 and discontinued it in 1866; the name, which also had the form "Neillsburgh," was for Arthur C. Neill, first postmaster (Salley, p. 152).

Nigger Creek: see **White Fir Creek** [TUOLUMNE].

Nigger George Ravine [PLACER]: *canyon,* drained by a stream that flows 2.5 miles to North Fork American River 2.25 miles east-southeast of Colfax (lat. 39°05' N, long. 120°55' W; sec. 12, T 14 N, R 9 E). Named on Colfax (1949) 7.5' quadrangle.

Nigger Gulch: see **Mokelumne River** [CALAVERAS].

Niggerhead Bar: see **American River** [EL DORADO-PLACER].

Nigger Hill: see **Mokelumne Hill** [CALAVERAS]; **Negro Hill** [CALAVERAS]; **Negro Hill** [MARIPOSA].

Nigger Jack Gulch: see **Negro Jack Gulch** [TUOLUMNE].

Nigger Jack Hill: see Negro Jack Hill [NEVADA].

Nigger Jack Point: see Negro Jack Point [TUOLUMNE].

Nigger Slide: see Ramshorn Creek [SIERRA].

Niggers Ravine [PLACER]: *canyon,* drained by a stream that flows 1 mile to Bunch Canyon 4 miles south-southeast of Colfax (lat. 39° 02'55" N, long. 120°55'45" W; sec. 24, T 13 N, R 9 E). Named on Colfax (1949) 7.5' quadrangle.

Nigger Tent: see Negro Tent [SIERRA].

Night Cap: see Night Cap Peak [TUOLUMNE].

Night Cap Peak [TUOLUMNE]: *peak,* 3.25 miles west-southwest of Sonora Pass (lat. 38°18'25" N, long. 119°41'25" W). Named on Sonora Pass (1979) 7.5' quadrangle. Called simply Night Cap on Dardanelles (1898) 30' quadrangle.

Nina: see Lake Nina, under Tilden Lake [TUOLUMNE].

Nipinnawasee [MADERA]: *settlement,* 6.25 miles west-northwest of Yosemite Forks (lat. 37°24'15" N, long. 119°43'55" W; on S line sec. 13, T 6 S, R 20 E). Called Nipinnawassee on Bass Lake (1953) 15' quadrangle, but United States Board on Geographic Names (1981a, p. 2) rejected the forms "Nipinnawassee" and "Nippinnawasee" for the name. Postal authorities established Femmon post office 3 miles north of Ahwahnee in 1912, and then moved it and changed the name to Nipinnawasee the same year; the name "Femmon" honored Frank Femmon, who developed a prize-winning apple (Salley, p. 73-74). They discontinued Nipinnawasee post office in 1961; the name is of Indian origin and was transferred from Michigan (Salley, p. 154).

Noname Lake [MADERA]: *lake,* 500 feet long, 3.5 miles west of Devils Postpile (lat. 37°37'40" N, long. 119°08'50" W). Named on Devils Postpile (1953) 15' quadrangle.

Norden [NEVADA]: *village,* 1.5 miles west of Donner Pass (lat. 39° 19'05" N, long. 120°21'15" W; near S line sec. 24, T 17 N, R 14 E). Named on Norden (1955) 7.5' quadrangle. Postal authorities established Norden post office in 1926, discontinued it in 1943, and reestablished it in 1947 (Frickstad, p. 114). The name is for Charles Van Norden, a water-company official (Stewart, p. 89).

Norris Creek [MADERA]: *stream,* flows 4.5 miles to Jackass Creek 11.5 miles north-northeast of Shuteye Peak (lat. 37°29'45" N, long. 119°19'15" W); the stream heads near Norris Lake. Named on Merced Peak (1953) 15' quadrangle.

Norris Lake [MADERA]: *lake,* 400 feet long, 8 miles south-southeast of Merced Peak (lat. 37°31'35" N, long. 119°20'15" W; near W line sec. 3, T 5 S, R 24 E). Named on Merced Peak (1953) 15' quadrangle.

North American House: see Valley Springs [CALAVERAS].

North Arm: see Pardee Reservoir [AMADOR].

North Bloomfield [NEVADA]: *village,* 13 miles northeast of Grass Valley along Humbug Creek (lat. 39°22'05" N, long. 120°53'55" W; sec. 6, T 17 N, R 10 E). Named on North Bloomfield (1949) 7.5' quadrangle. Postal authorities established North Bloomfield post office in 1857, moved it to a new site in 1875, and discontinued it in 1942; the word "North" was added to the name "Bloomfield" to distinguish the place from Bloomfield in Sonoma County (Salley, p. 155). The place originally was called Humbug (Hanna, p. 34). Whitney's (1873) map shows a place called Mountain Wells situated 3.5 miles south of North Bloomfield. Postal authorities established Mountain Well post office in 1858 and discontinued it in 1866 (Frickstad, p. 114).

North Branch [CALAVERAS]: *locality,* 2.5 miles west-northwest of San Andreas (lat. 38°12'25" N, long. 120°43'30" W). Named on Jackson (1902) 30' quadrangle. Camp's (1962) map has the designation "North Branch (old site)" for a place located about 1 mile east-northeast of present North Branch at the confluence of North Fork Calaveras River and Murray Creek. The same map shows a place called Iowa Cabin, or Second Crossing, situated about 0.5 mile down North Fork Calaveras River from the confluence. Postal authorities established North Branch post office before March 19, 1852, discontinued it in 1870, and reestablished it in 1876; they changed the name to Northbranch in 1895, discontinued it in 1911, reestablished it in 1912, and discontinued it in 1925 (Salley, p. 155).

North Canyon [EL DORADO]:

(1) *canyon,* drained by a stream that flows 1.25 miles to Canyon Creek (1) 1.5 miles north-northwest of Georgetown (lat. 38°55'50" N, long. 120°50'40" W; sec. 34, T 13 N, R 10 E). Named on Georgetown (1949) 7.5' quadrangle.

(2) *canyon.* drained by a stream that flows 2.5 miles to South Fork American River 7 miles west of Pollock Pines (lat. 38°46'20" N, long. 120°42'30" W; sec. 26, T 11 N, R 11 E); the canyon is east of South Canyon. Named on Slate Mountain (1950) 7.5' quadrangle.

(3) *canyon,* drained by a stream that flows about 2 miles to Big Canyon (2) 11 miles east-southeast of Camino (lat. 38°39'15" N, long. 120°30'15" W; sec. 11, T 9 N, R 13 E). Named on Sly Park (1952) and Stump Spring (1951) 7.5' quadrangles.

North Canyon [NEVADA]: *canyon,* drained by a stream that flows nearly 1 mile to South Yuba River 3.25 miles southwest of North Bloomfield (lat. 39°20'35" N, long. 120°56'55" W; near N line sec. 15, T 17 N, R 9 E). Named on North Bloomfield (1949) 7.5' quadrangle.

North Columbia [NEVADA]: *settlement,* 4.5 miles west of North Bloomfield (lat. 39°22'20" N, long. 120°59'10" W; on S line sec. 32, T 18 N, R 9 E). Named on North Bloomfield (1949) and Pike (1949) 7.5' quadrangles. Postal authorities established North Columbia post office in 1860 and discontinued it in 1931; the word "North" was added to the name "Columbia" to distinguish the place from Columbia post office in Tuolumne County (Salley, p. 155). The community originally was called Columbia Hill (Hanna, p. 70).

North Crane Creek [TUOLUMNE]: *stream,* flows 4 miles to South Fork Tuolumne River 5.5 miles south of Mather (lat. 37°48'10" N, long. 19°50'50" W; sec. 35, T 1 S, R 19 E); the stream heads just north of the head of Crane Creek [MARIPOSA]. Named on Lake Eleanor (1956) 15' quadrangle.

North Creek [EL DORADO]: *stream,* flows 3.5 miles to Alder Creek 6.5 miles north-northwest of Leek Spring Hill (lat. 38°42'45" N, long. 120°19'50" W; sec. 17, T 10 N, R 15 E). Named on Leek Spring Hill (1951) 7.5' quadrangle.

North Creek [NEVADA]: *stream,* flows 5.5 miles to Fordyce Lake 9 miles northwest of Donner Pass (lat. 39°23'40" N, long. 120°27'20" W; near E line sec. 25, T 18 N, R 13 E). Named on Independence Lake (1981) and Webber Peak (1981) 7.5' quadrangles.

North Dome [MARIPOSA]: *peak,* 1.5 miles east-northeast of Yosemite Village (lat. 37°45'25" N, long. 119°33'35" W); the peak is on the north side of Yosemite Valley. Altitude 7542 feet. Named on Hetch Hetchy Reservoir (1956) 15' quadrangle. Members of the Mariposa Battalion named the peak in 1851 (Gudde, 1949, p. 238).

North Dome: see **Hetch Hetchy Dome** [TUOLUMNE].

North Fork [MADERA]: *town,* 22 miles east of Raymond (lat. 37°13'40" N, long. 119°30'30" W; around SE cor. sec. 13, T 8 S, R 22 E); the town is along North Fork Willow Creek (2). Named on North Fork (1965) 7.5' quadrangle. Called Northfork on California Mining Bureau's (1909b) map. Postal authorities established North Fork post office in 1888 (Frickstad, p. 86). Milton Brown was the first settler at the site, and the community that grew there was called Brown's; the place took the name "North Fork" after postal authorities started North Fork post office in the store building of North Fork Lumber Company (Clough, p. 80-81). Postal authorities established Cascadel post office 4 miles east of North Fork in 1892 and discontinued it in 1896; the name was from Cascadel ranch, which in turn was named for Cascadel Point (Salley, p. 39). Shaver Lake (1953) 15' quadrangle shows Cascadel ranch situated along Whiskey Creek (2) (sec. 16, T 8 S, R 23 E). Postal authorities established a post office called Minarets about 5 miles southeast of

North Fork in 1925 and discontinued it in 1933; the place was the terminus of Minarets and Western Railroad (Salley, p. 141). The name "Minarets" was used much earlier, however, when Madera County separated from Fresno County and residents of the mountainous part of Madera County planned to build a town called Minarets 15 miles east of Madera and have the county seat there (Clough, p. 15-16). Postal authorities established Bethel post office 4 miles west of North Fork in 1881 and discontinued it in 1885; James W. Bethel owned the store that housed the post office (Salley, p. 20).

North Fork [MARIPOSA]: *locality,* 4.5 miles northeast of the village of Bear Valley along Yosemite Valley Railroad (lat. 37°36'35" N, long. 120°23'40" W). Named on Sonora (1897) 30' quadrangle.

North Fork Lake [PLACER]: *lake,* behind a dam on North Fork American River 3.5 miles northeast of Auburn (lat. 38°56'10" N, long. 121°01'25" W; near W line sec. 31, T 13 N, R 9 E). Named on Auburn (1953) 7.5' quadrangle. Called Lake Clementine on Greenwood (1949) 7.5' quadrangle. United States Board on Geographic Names (1972, p. 4) gave the names "Lake Clementine" and "North Fork Reservoir" as variants.

North Fork Reservoir [PLACER]: *lake,* 1200 feet long, 2.5 miles north of Folsom on Placer-Sacramento county line (lat. 38°42'45" N, long. 121°10" W). Named on Folsom (1941) 15' quadrangle.

North Fork Reservoir: see **North Fork Lake** [PLACER].

North Grove Campground [CALAVERAS]: *locality,* 5.5 miles southeast of Blue Mountain along Big Trees Creek (lat. 38°16'30" N, long. 120°18'20" W; sec. 22, T 5 N, R 15 E). Named on Dorrington (1979) 7.5' quadrangle.

North Gulch [CALAVERAS]: *canyon,* drained by a stream that flows 2.5 miles to Calaveras River 1 mile east-northeast of Jenny Lind (lat. 38°06'15" N, long. 120°50'55" W; sec. 23, T 3 N, R 10 E). Named on Jenny Lind (1962) 7.2' quadrangle.

North Indian Creek: see **Indian Creek** [EL DORADO] (1).

North Miller Creek [PLACER]: *stream,* flows nearly 2 miles to Miller Creek 4.5 miles southwest of Homewood at Miller Meadows (lat. 39°02'05" N, long. 120°13' W; sec. 28, T 14 N, R 16 E). Named on Homewood (1955) 7.5' quadrangle.

North Mountain [TUOLUMNE]: *peak,* 2.5 miles northwest of Mather Station (present Mather) (lat. 37°54'05" N, long. 119°53'55" W; near N line sec. 33, T 1 N, R 19 E). Named on Yosemite (1909) 30' quadrangle.

North Park Creek: see **North Sly Park Creek** [EL DORADO].

North Peak [TUOLUMNE]: *peak,* 6 miles north-northwest of Tioga Pass on Tuolumne-

Mono county line (lat. 37°59' N, long. 119°18'50" W; sec. 34, T 2 N, R 24 E). Altitude 12,242 feet. Named on Tuolumne Meadows (1956) 15' quadrangle.

North Ravine [PLACER]: *canyon,* drained by a stream that flows 3.25 miles to Auburn Ravine 1.5 miles west-southwest of downtown Auburn (lat. 38°53'25" N, long. 121°06'10" W; sec. 17, T 12 N, R 8 E). Named on Auburn (1953) 7.5' quadrangle.

North San Juan [NEVADA]: *village,* 10.5 miles north of Grass Valley (lat. 39°22'10" N, long. 121°06'15" W; sec. 5, T 17 N, R 8 E); the village is on San Juan Ridge. Named on Nevada City (1948) 7.5' quadrangle. Postal authorities established North San Juan post office in 1857; the word "North" was added to the name to avoid confusion with San Juan in San Benito County (Salley, p. 156). Christian Kientz, a veteran of the Mexican War, settled at the site in 1853 and gave it the name "San Juan" because he thought he saw a resemblance between a bluff there and the Castle of San Juan de Ulloa at Vera Cruz, Mexico (Hanna, p. 279). Whitney's (1873) map has the name "Kent Rav." for a canyon just southwest of North San Juan.

North Shirttail Canyon [PLACER]: *canyon,* drained by a stream that flows 9 miles to Shirttail Canyon 3.5 miles north of Foresthill (lat. 39°04'15" N, long. 120°48'40" W; near E line sec. 11, T 14 N, R 10 E). Named on Dutch Flat (1950), Foresthill (1949), and Westville (1952) 7.5' quadrangles. Present North Shirttail Canyon is shown as the upper part of Shirttail Canyon on Colfax (1938) 30' quadrangle.

North Slate Creek: see **Slate Creek** [EL DORADO] (3).

North Sly Park Creek [EL DORADO]: *stream,* flows 2.5 miles to Sly Park Creek 4.5 miles west-northwest of Old Iron Mountain (lat. 38°43'50" N, long. 120°28'20" W; sec. 7, T 10 N, R 14 E). Named on Leek Spring Hill (1951) 15' quadrangle. Called North Park Creek on Stump Spring (1951) 7.5' quadrangle, which has the name "Park Creek" for present Sly Park Creek. United States Board on Geographic Names (1978a, p. 7) rejected the names "North Fork Park Creek" and "North Park Creek" for the stream.

North Steely Creek [EL DORADO]: *stream,* flows 4.5 miles to join South Steely Creek and form Steely Fork Cosumnes River 2 miles west-northwest of Caldor (lat. 38°37' N, long. 120°28' W; sec. 19, T 9 N, R 14 E). Named on Caldor (1951) and Stump Spring (1951) 7.5' quadrangles.

North Tragedy Creek [EL DORADO]: *stream,* flows 5.5 miles to Sherman Canyon 7 miles west of Kirkwood (lat. 38°41'20" N, long. 120°11'55" W); the stream heads near Tragedy Spring. Named on Tragedy Spring (1979) 7.5' quadrangle.

North Wallace Canyon [PLACER]: *canyon,*

drained by a stream that flows 3.25 miles to Wallace Canyon 2 miles north-northeast of Devil Peak (lat. 38°59' N, long. 120°31'35" W; near N line sec. 16, T 13 N, R 13 E). Named on Bunker Hill (1953), Devil Peak (1950), and Greek Store (1952) 7.5' quadrangles. Present North Wallace Canyon is shown as part of Wallace Canyon on Placerville (1893) 30' quadrangle.

North Wawona [MARIPOSA]: *settlement,* 1.25 miles northeast of Wawona (lat 37°32'50" N, long. 119°38'20" W; sec. 35, T 4 S, R 21 E); the place is 0.5 mile north of South Wawona. Named on Yosemite (1956) 15' quadrangle.

Norval [CALAVERAS]: *locality,* less than 1 mile southwest of Valley Springs along Southern Pacific Railroad (lat. 38°11'05" N, long. 120°50'20" W; sec. 23, T 4 N, R 10 E). Named on Valley Springs (1944) 15' quadrangle.

Norwegian Gulch [MARIPOSA]: *canyon,* 2.25 miles long, opens into the canyon of Bear Creek (2) 4 miles south-southeast of the village of Bear Valley (lat. 37°31'05" N, long. 120°05'15" W). Named on Bear Valley (1947) 7.5' quadrangle.

Norwegian Gulch [TUOLUMNE]: *canyon,* drained by a stream that flows nearly 1 mile to Stanislaus River 5 miles west-southwest of Columbia (lat. 38°00'30" N, long. 120°29'15" W; near E line sec. 24, T 2 N, R 13 E). Named on Columbia (1948) 7.5' quadrangle. The canyon also was called Jackass Gulch (Gudde, 1975, p. 247)—the owner of a strayed jackass discovered gold in the canyon while he was hunting for the animal (Stoddart, p. 62).

Norwegian Gulch Center: see **Mount Ophir** [MARIPOSA].

North Yuba River [SIERRA]: *stream,* flows 41 miles—the last mile along Sierra-Yuba county line—to join Middle Yuba River and form Yuba River nearly 4 miles east of Dobbins in Yuba County (lat. 39°22'05" N, long. 121°08'10" W; sec. 1, T 17 N, R 7 E); the stream heads at Yuba Pass. Named on Challenge (1948), Clipper Mills (1948), Clio (1981), Downieville (1951), French Corral (1948), Goodyears Bar (1951), Haypress Valley (1981), Sierra City (1981), and Strawberry Valley (1948) 7.5' quadrangles. Called North Fork Yuba River on Bidwell Bar (1897), Downieville (1897), and Smartsville (1895) 30' quadrangles, but United States Board on Geographic Names (1950, p. 6) rejected the names "North Fork," "North Fork of Yuba River," and "North Fork Yuba River" for the stream, and rejected the names "North Fork of North Yuba River" and "South Fork of North Fork Yuba River" for upper reaches of the stream. On Downieville (1897) 30' quadrangle, present Downie River [SIERRA] is called N. Fork of N. Fork Yuba River, and present Haypress Creek [SIERRA] is called South Fork of North Fork Yuba River; United States Board on Geographic Names (1950, p.

5) rejected both of these older names. On Downieville (1897) 30' quadrangle also, present Lavezzola Creek [SIERRA] is called Middle Fork of North Fork Yuba River, but United States Board on Geographic Names (1950, p. 5) rejected this name for the stream, and also rejected the name "North Fork of North Fork" for the upper part of the stream. On Downieville (1897) 30' quadrangle, present Pauley Creek [SIERRA] is called East Fork of North Fork Yuba River, but United States Board on Geographic Names (1950, p. 6) rejected this name. Gudde (1975, p. 73) listed a place called Churchman Bar that was situated on the east side of North Yuba River near the junction with Middle Yuba River.

Norton Ravine [EL DORADO]: *canyon,* drained by a stream that flows nearly 4 miles to South Fork American River 5 miles west of Coloma (lat. 38°47'35" N, long. 120°58'55" W; sec. 21, T 11 N, R 9 E). Named on Coloma (1949) and Pilot Hill (1954) 7.5' quadrangles.

Norway: see **Little Norway**, under **Meyers** [EL DORADO].

Notarb [MADERA]: *locality,* 6 miles southeast of Fairmead along Southern Pacific Railroad (lat. 37°00'40" N, long. 120°07'05" W; near N line sec. 4, T 11 S, R 17 E). Named on Kismet (1961) 7.5' quadrangle.

Number Nine [MARIPOSA]: *locality,* 6 miles southwest of Bear Valley (2) (lat. 37°30'45" N, long. 120°11'55" W). Named on Sonora (1891) 30' quadrangle. Coulterville (1947) 15' quadrangle shows Number Nine mine at the place.

Nutmeg Gulch [MARIPOSA]: *canyon,* drained by a stream that flows 3.25 miles to South Fork Merced River 5 miles southwest of El Portal (lat. 37°37'35" N, long. 119°50'40" W; sec. 34, T 3 S, R 19 E). Named on Buckingham Mountain (1947) 7.5' quadrangle.

Nutcracker Lake: see **Ruth Lake** [MADERA].

Nydiver Lakes [MADERA]: *lakes,* largest 1000 feet long, 7 miles northwest of Devils Postpile (lat. 37°41'35" N, long. 119°10'15" W). Named on Devils Postpile (1953) 15' quadrangle. Browning (1986, p. 160) associated the name with David Nidever, a prospector of the early 1900's.

Nye's Crossing: see **Bridgeport** [NEVADA]

Nyes Crossing: see **Freemans Crossing** [NEVADA].

Nyes Landing: see **Bridgeport** [NEVADA].

— O —

Oahu: see **Craigs Flat** [SIERRA].

Oak: see **Borden** [MADERA].

Oak Flat [PLACER]: *area,* 11.5 miles west of Granite Chief (lat. 39°11'50" N, long. 120°29'55" W; near N line sec. 2, T 15 N, R 13 E). Named on Royal Gorge (1953) 7.5' quadrangle.

Oak Flat [SIERRA]: *area,* 1.5 miles south-

southwest of Alleghany (lat. 39°27'10" N, long. 120°51'15" W; near S line sec. 4, T 18 N, R 10 E). Named on Alleghany (1949) 7.5' quadrangle.

Oak Flat: see **Big Oak Flat** [PLACER]; **Big Oak Flat** [TUOLUMNE]; **Little Oak Flat** [PLACER].

Oak Grove [CALAVERAS]: *locality,* 6 miles south-southwest of Valley Springs (lat. 38°07' N, long. 120°53'10" W; sec. 16, T 3 N, R 10 E). Named on Valley Springs SW (1962) 7.5' quadrangle.

Oak Grove [EL DORADO]: *locality,* 2.5 miles east-northeast of Placerville (lat. 38°44'40" N, long. 120°45'40" W). Named on Placerville (1893) 30' quadrangle.

Oakhurst [MADERA]: *settlement,* 3 miles south-southwest of Yosemite Forks along Fresno River (lat. 37°19'45" N, long. 119° 39' W; near NW cor. sec. 14, T 7 S, R 21 E); the place is at the east end of Fresno Flats. Named on Bass Lake (1953) 15' quadrangle. The settlement is called Fresno Flats on Mariposa (1912) 30' quadrangle. Postal authorities established Fresno Flats post office in 1873, and moved it and changed the name to Oakhurst in 1912 (Salley, p. 81, 158). They established Starville post office 23 miles northeast of Fresno Flats post office in 1889 and discontinued it in 1891; the name was from Star mine (Salley, p. 212).

Oakland Pond [SIERRA]: *lake,* 300 feet long, 8 miles north-northwest of Sierra City (lat. 39°40'40" N, long. 120°40'55" W; on W line sec. 18, T 21 N, R 12 E). Named on Gold Lake (1981) 7.5' quadrangle.

Oak Leaf Spring [TUOLUMNE]: *spring,* 10 miles north-northeast of Stanislaus (lat. 38°15'45" N, long. 120°15'55" W; sec. 25, T 5 N, R 15 E). Named on Dorrington (1979) 7.5' quadrangle.

Oaks: see **The Oaks** [NEVADA].

Oak Spring: see **Montezuma** [TUOLUMNE].

Oakvale Retreat: see **Miami** [MARIPOSA].

Oak Valley Creek [SIERRA]: *stream,* flows 1.25 miles to Willow Creek 4 miles north-northwest of Pike (lat. 39°29'35" N, long. 121° 01'35" W; near N line sec. 25, T 19 N, R 8 E). Named on Camptonville (1948) 7.5' quadrangle.

Oat Hills [TUOLUMNE]: *range,* 3.5 miles east-northeast of Don Pedro Camp (lat. 37°44'25" N, long. 120°21' W). Named on Penon Blanco Peak (1962) 7.5' quadrangle.

Oat Mountain: see **Castle Peak** [MADERA].

Obelisk: see **Mount Clark** [MARIPOSA].

Obelisk Group: see **Clark Range** [MADERA].

Obelisk Lake: see **Adair Lake** [MADERA].

Obelisk Lake [MARIPOSA]: *lake,* 1100 feet long, 10 miles south of Cathedral Peak (lat. 37°42'15" N, long. 119°24'55" W); the lake is less than 1 mile northeast of Mount Clark, which members of the Whitney survey called the Obelisk. Named on Merced Peak (1953) 15' quadrangle. United States Board on Geographic Names (1934, p. 18) rejected the name "Adair Lake" for the feature.

Observatory Point: see **Dollar Point** [PLACER].

O'Byrnes Ferry [CALAVERAS-TUOLUMNE]: *locality,* 7 miles south-southeast of Copperopolis along Stanislaus River on Calaveras-Tuolumne county line (lat. 37°53'40" N, long. 120°34'10" W; sec. 32, T 1 N, R 13 E). Named on Copperopolis (1916) 15' quadrangle. Water of Tulloch Lake now covers the site. Postal authorities established O'Byrnes Ferry post office in Calaveras County in 1855 and discontinued it in 1860 (Frickstad, p. 16). Patrick O. Byrne, or O'Byrne, operated a ferry there before the flood of 1852 (Paden and Schlichtmann, p. 58). A mining camp at the place in 1849 and 1850 was called Byrnes Ferry (Gudde, 1975, p. 55).

O'Connor Gulch [EL DORADO]: *canyon,* drained by a stream that flows 1 mile to Middle Fork Cosumnes River less than 1 mile north of Omo Ranch (lat. 38°35'30" N, long. 120°34'15" W; sec. 32, T 9 N, R 13 E). Named on Omo Ranch (1952) 7.5' quadrangle.

Odom Creek [MARIPOSA]: *stream,* flows nearly 4 miles to Bear Creek (2) 2.5 miles east-northeast of Santa Cruz Mountain (lat. 37° 28'05" N, long. 120°09'40" W; sec. 25, T 5 S, R 16 E). Named on Hornitos (1947) and Indian Gulch (1962) 7.5' quadrangles.

Ohio Diggings: see **Soulsbyville** [TUOLUMNE].

O'Donnells Flat: see **Downieville** [SIERRA].

Ogilby Canyon [EL DORADO]: *canyon,* drained by a stream that flows 2.5 miles to South Fork American River, 1.5 miles westsouthwest of Riverton (lat. 38°46' N, long. 120°28'45" W; sec. 25, T 11 N, R 11 E). Named on Riverton (1950) and Stump Spring (1951) 7.5' quadrangles.

Ohio Bar: see **South Yuba River** [NEVADA-PLACER].

Ohio Hill [AMADOR]: *peak,* 1.5 miles north of Jackson (lat. 38°22'15" N, long. 120°46'10" W; sec. 16, T 6 N, R 11 E). Named on Jackson (1962) 7.5' quadrangle.

Ohm: see **Camp Spaulding** [NEVADA].

Oilville: see **Colfax** [PLACER].

Oiyer Spring [EL DORADO]: *spring,* 6 miles northwest of Leek Spring Mill (lat. 38°41'45" N, long. 120°21' W; near N line sec. 30, T 10 N, R 15 E). Named on Leek Spring Hill (1951) 7.5' quadrangle.

Olaine Lake [MADERA]: *lake,* 1000 feet long, 5 miles north-northwest of Devils Postpile (lat. 37°41'40" N, long. 119°06'45" W). Named on Devils Postpile (1953) 15' quadrangle. Charles Olaine prospected at the lake about 1910 (Browning, 1986, p. 161).

Old Bar: see **Shirttail Canyon** [PLACER].

Old Condon Mill [NEVADA]: *locality,* 2.5 miles south of Graniteville (lat. 39°24'20" N, long. 120°44' W; near SW cor. sec. 22, T 18 N, R 11 E). Site named on Graniteville (1982) 7.5' quadrangle.

Old Dry Diggings: see **Placerville** [EL DORADO].

Old Fort Jim [EL DORADO]: *locality,* 3 miles southwest of Camino (lat. 38°42'40" N, long. 120°43' W; sec. 24, T 10 N, R 11 E). Named on Camino (1952) 7.5' quadrangle.

Old Galloway Ridge [SIERRA]: *ridge,* northnorthwest-trending, 1.5 miles long, center 1.5 miles south of Downieville (lat. 39°32'30" N, long. 120°49'30" W). Named on Downieville (1951) 7.5' quadrangle.

Old Gulch [CALAVERAS]:
(1) *canyon,* drained by a stream that flows 4.5 miles to Calaveritas Creek 5.5 miles eastsoutheast of San Andreas (lat. 38°09'25" N, long. 120°35'30" W; near W line sec. 31, T 4 N, R 13 E). Named on Calaveritas (1962) 7.5' quadrangle.
(2) *village,* 5 miles east-southeast of San Andreas (lat. 38°10'20" N, long. 120°35'40" W); the village was in present Old Gulch (1). Named on Jackson (1902) 30' quadrangle. The place also was known as Washington Flat (Gudde, 1975, p. 250).

Old Inspiration Point [MARIPOSA]: *relief feature,* 5.5 miles west-southwest of Yosemite Village on the south side of Yosemite Valley (lat. 37°42'20" N, long. 119°49'25" W); the feature is 1 mile southeast of Inspiration Point. Named on Yosemite (1956) 15' quadrangle. The place first was called Mount Beatitude (Browning, 1986, p. 14).

Old Iron Mountain [EL DORADO]: *peak,* 8 miles northwest of Leek Spring Hill (lat. 38°42'20" N, long. 120°23'25" W; sec. 23, T 10 N, R 14 E); the peak is on Iron Mountain Ridge 2 miles west of Iron Mountain (2). Altitude 5903 feet. Named on Stump Spring (1951) 7.5' quadrangle.

Old Man Mountain [NEVADA]: *peak,* 6.25 miles northeast of Yuba Gap (lat. 39°22'15" N, long. 120°31'15" W; sec. 4, T 17 N, R 13 E). Altitude 7789 feet. Named on Cisco Grove (1955) 7.5' quadrangle. Logan's (1940) map shows a place called Carlysle located less than 1 mile south of Old Man Mountain (on S line sec. 4, T 17 N, R 13 E), where Cisco Grove (1955) 7.5' quadrangle shows Carlisle mine—the name is for Thomas Carlyle, one of the locators of U.S. Grant claim in 1866 (Gudde, 1975, p. 61).

Old Man of the Mountains: see **Ahwiyah Point** [MARIPOSA].

Old McCormick Reservoir [CALAVERAS]: *intermittent lake,* 1000 feet long, 3.5 miles east-southeast of Jenny Lind (lat. 38°04'55" N, long. 120°48'20" W; sec. 30, T 3 N, R 11 E). Named on Jenny Lind (1962) 7.5' quadrangle.

Old Miami Mill: see **Timberloft Camp** [MARIPOSA].

Old Mill Creek [SIERRA]: *stream,* flows 3.5

miles to Little Canyon Creek 8 miles south-southwest of Mount Fillmore (lat. 39°37'35" N, long. 120°54'20" W; at W line sec. 6, T 20 N, R 10 E). Named on La Porte (1951) and Mount Fillmore (1951) 7.5' quadrangles.

Old Mountain House [SIERRA]: *locality,* nearly 3 miles south of Goodyears Bar (lat. 39°30'N, long. 120°53'25" W; near E line sec. 19, T 19 N, R 10 E). Site named on Goodyears Bar (1951) and Pike (1949) 7.5' quadrangles. Called Mountain House on Colfax (1898) 30' quadrangle. Postal authorities established Mountain House post office in 1874 and discontinued it in 1911 (Frickstad, p. 184).

Old Pino [EL DORADO]: *locality,* 5 miles northwest of Pollock Pines in Water Canyon (lat. 38°49'05" N, long. 120°38'45" W; sec. 9, T 11 N, R 12 E). Named on Slate Mountain (1950) 7.5' quadrangle.

Old Piute: see **The Old Piute**, under **Ahwiyah Point** [MARIPOSA].

Old Rancheria: see **Drytown** [AMADOR]; **Rancheria** [AMADOR].

Old Road: see **Squaw Creek** [PLACER].

Old Schaeffer Camp [PLACER]: *locality,* 7.25 miles west-southwest of Martis Peak (lat. 39°15'15" N, long. 120°09'35" W; on W line sec. 12, T 16 N, R 16 E). Site named on Truckee (1955) 7.5' quadrangle.

Old Schaeffer Mill [PLACER]: *locality,* 7 miles west of Martis Peak (lat. 39°16'50" N, long. 120°09'45" W; near E line sec. 35, T 17 N, R 16 E). Site named on Truckee (1955) 7.5' quadrangle.

Old Smith Mill [SIERRA]: *locality,* 15 miles south of Loyalton along Little Truckee River (lat. 39°27'55" N, long. 120°11'20" W; sec. 27, T 19 N, R 16 E). Site named on Hobart Mills (1981) 7.5' quadrangle.

Old Stanford Wood Camp [PLACER]: *locality,* 5 miles southeast of Donner Pass (lat. 39°16'15" N, long. 120°15'05" W; near NW cor. sec. 6, T 16 N, R 16 E). Site named on Norden (1955) 7.5' quadrangle.

Old Woman Gulch [CALAVERAS]: *canyon,* drained by a stream that flows 3 miles to Chili Gulch nearly 4 miles northwest of San Andreas (lat. 38°14'30" N, long. 120°43'15" W; near W line sec. 36, T 5 N, R 11 E). Named on Mokelumne Hill (1948) and San Andreas (1962) 7.5' quadrangles. On San Andreas (1947) 15' quadrangle, present Spring Gulch (3) is called Old Woman Gulch.

Oleta: see **Fiddletown** [AMADOR].

Olive: see **Mount Olive** [NEVADA].

Olive Lake: see **Huckleberry Lake** [TUOLUMNE].

Oliver Creek [MARIPOSA]: *stream,* flows 7.25 miles to East Fork Chowchilla River 11.5 miles east-southeast of Mariposa (lat. 37°25'20" N, long. 119°46'35" W; sec. 10, T 6 S, R 20 E). Named on Buckingham Mountain (1947) and Stumpfield Mountain (1947) 7.5' quadrangles. Mariposa (1947) 15' quadrangle

has the name "DeLong Creek" for present Oliver Creek below the confluence of DeLong and Oliver Creeks.

Olympic Valley: see **Squaw Valley** [PLACER].

Omega [NEVADA]: *locality,* 3.25 miles east-southeast of Washington (lat. 39°20' N, long. 120°45' W; near S line sec. 16, T 17 N, R 11 E). Named on Blue Canyon (1955) and Washington (1950) 7.5' quadrangles. Postal authorities established Omega post office in 1857 and discontinued it in 1891 (Frickstad, p. 114). Reportedly, the place first was called Delirum Tremens (Gudde, 1975, p. 251). Whitney's (1873) map shows a community called Diamond Creek located 1.5 miles east of Omega, a community called Shellback located 1 mile south-southwest of Omega, and a community called Spiritsville located 1.5 miles south-southwest of Omega.

Omega Diggings [NEVADA]: *locality,* 2.5 miles east-southeast of Washington (lat. 39°20'15" N, long. 120°45'25" W; sec. 16, 17, T 17 N, R 11 E); the place is near Omega. Named on Washington (1950) 7.5' quadrangle.

Omits Flat: see **Secret Canyon** [SIERRA].

Omo Ranch [EL DORADO]: *village,* 12.5 miles south-southeast of Camino (lat. 38°34'50" N, long. 120°34'05" W; at N line sec. 5, T 8 N, R 13 E). Named on Omo Ranch (1952) 7.5' quadrangle. Postal authorities established Omo Ranch post office in 1888 and discontinued it in 1974 (Salley, p. 161). The name "Omo" is from an Indian village (Kroeber, p. 52).

O'Neals [MADERA]: *locality,* 13 miles east-southeast of Raymond along Willow Creek (4) (lat. 37°07'40" N, long. 119°41'40" W; near SW cor. sec. 21, T 9 S, R 21 E). Named on O'Neals (1965) 7.5' quadrangle. Postal authorities established O'Neals post office in 1887 (Frickstad, p. 86). Charles O'Neal bought the store at the place in 1887, operated a small hotel, and was named postmaster of the new post office that took his name (Clough, p. 82). Postal authorities established Magnet post office 4 miles northeast of O'Neals in 1900 and discontinued it in 1907; the name was for Magnet mine (Salley, p. 131).

O'Neals Meadow [MARIPOSA]: *area,* 4.25 miles southwest of Fish Camp (lat. 37°26'05" N, long. 119°41'40" W; sec. 5, T 6 S, R 21 E). Named on Bass Lake (1953) 15' quadrangle. John Ruffin O'Neal patented land in section 5 in 1884, and homesteaded in sections 5 and 8 in 1892 (Browning, 1986, p. 162).

One Eye Creek [EL DORADO]: *stream,* formed by the confluence of North Fork and South Fork, flows 3.25 miles to Rock Creek nearly 5 miles northeast of Chili Bar (lat. 38°49'10" N, long. 120°45'50" W; at W line sec. 9, T 11 N, R 11 E). Named on Garden Valley (1949) and Slate Mountain (1950) 7.5' quadrangles. North Fork is 2.5 miles long and South Fork is 1.5 miles long; both forks are named on

Slate Mountain (1950) 7.5' quadrangle. The name "One Eye Creek" was given after one of the first prospectors along the stream lost an eye (Gudde, 1975, p. 251).

One Horse Bar: see **Green Valley** [PLACER].

Oneida: see **Loyalton** [SIERRA]; **Martell** [AMADOR].

Oneida Creek [AMADOR]: *stream,* flows 2 miles to North Fork Jackson Creek 1.25 miles north of Jackson (lat. 38°22'05" N, long. 120°46'30" W; sec. 16, T 6 N, R 11 E). Named on Amador City (1962) and Jackson (1962) 7.5' quadrangles.

O'Neil Creek [CALAVERAS]: *stream,* flows 13 miles to join McKinney Creek and form Calaveritas Creek 8.5 miles east of San Andreas (lat. 38°11' N, long. 120°31'15" W; near E line sec. 22, T 4 N, R 13 E). Named on Calaveritas (1962), Dorrington (1979), Fort Mountain (1979), and Murphys (1948) 7.5' quadrangles. Jackson (1902) 30' quadrangle has the form "O'Neils Creek" for the name.

O'Neil Reservoir [TUOLUMNE]: *lake,* 500 feet long, 3.25 miles west-southwest of Sonora (lat. 37°58'10" N, long. 120°26'10" W; sec. 4, T 1 N, R 14 E). Named on Sonora (1948, photorevised 1973) 7.5' quadrangle.

O'Neils Creek: see O'Neil Creek [CALAVERAS].

1001 Ridge [SIERRA]: *ridge,* generally west-trending, 5 miles long, center 5 miles east-northeast of Sierra City (lat. 39°35'15" N, long. 120°33' W). Named on Haypress Valley (1981) 7.5' quadrangle, which shows 1001 mine near the west end of the ridge.

Onion Creek [EL DORADO]: *stream,* flows 5.25 miles to Silver Creek 7 miles north-northeast of Pollock Pines (lat. 38°51'20" N, long. 120°32'05" W; near E line sec. 29, T 12 N, R 13 E). Named on Devil Peak (1950), Pollock Pines (1950), and Robbs Peak (1950) 7.5' quadrangles.

Onion Creek [PLACER]: *stream,* flows 3.25 miles to North Fork American River 5 miles south-southwest of Donner Pass (lat. 39° 15'15" N, long. 120°22'15" W; sec. 14, T 16 N, R 14 E). Named on Norden (1955) 7.5' quadrangle.

Onion Creek [SIERRA]: *stream,* flows 2.5 miles to Cold Stream (1) 6.5 miles southeast of Sierraville in Onion Valley (lat. 39°31'05" N, long. 120°17'05" W; near N line sec. 11, T 19 N, R 15 E). Named on Sierraville (1981) 7.5' quadrangle.

Onion Creek Campground [PLACER]: *locality,* 3.5 miles south-southwest of Donner Pass (lat. 39°16'30" N, long. 120°21'45" W; near SE cor. sec. 2, T 16 N, R 14 E); the place is along Onion Creek. Named on Norden (1955) 7.5' quadrangle.

Onion Flat [EL DORADO]: *area,* 4.5 miles west-northwest of Phipps Peak (lat. 38°59'10" N, long. 120°13'10" W; near SW cor. sec. 9, T 13 N, R 16 E). Named on Rockbound Valley (1955) 7.5' quadrangle. Water of Rubicon Reservoir now covers much of the area.

Onion Lake [TUOLUMNE]: *lake,* 600 feet long, nearly 5 miles southeast of Matterhorn Peak (lat. 38°02'30" N, long. 119°19'10" W; on N line sec. 10, T 2 N, R 24 E). Named on Matterhorn Peak (1956) 15' quadrangle.

Onion Valley [AMADOR]: *area,* 5.5 miles west-northwest of Mokelumne Peak (lat. 38°33'55" N, long. 120°06'15" W; near NW cor. sec. 11, T 8 N, R 16 E). Named on Bear River Reservoir (1979) 7.5' quadrangle.

Onion Valley [CALAVERAS]: *valley,* at Tamarack (lat. 38°26'25" N, long. 120°04'30" W; near S line sec. 23, T 7 N, R 17 E). Named on Big Meadow (1956) 15' quadrangle. The name is from the abundance of wild onions at the place (Browning, 1986, p. 212).

Onion Valley [PLACER]: *valley,* 2.25 miles south-southeast of Emigrant Gap (1) (lat. 39°16'10" N, long. 120°39'05" W; mainly in sec. 8, T 16 N, R 12 E). Named on Blue Canyon (1955) 7.5' quadrangle. On Colfax (1898) 30' quadrangle, the stream in the valley is called Onion Valley Cr.

Onion Valley [SIERRA]: *valley,* 6.5 miles southeast of Sierraville (lat. 39°30'50" N, long. 120°17'05" W; sec. 11, T 19 N, R 15 E); the valley is along Cold Stream (1) at the mouth of Onion Creek. Named on Sierraville (1981) 7.5' quadrangle.

Onion Valley: see **Upper Onion Valley** [AMADOR].

Onion Valley Creek: see **Onion Valley** [PLACER].

Onion Valley Spring 2 [PLACER]: *spring,* 3 miles south-southeast of Emigrant Gap (1) (lat. 39°15'25" N, long. 120°39'05" W; sec. 17, T 16 N, R 12 E); the spring is less than 1 mile south of Onion Valley. Named on Blue Canyon (1955) 7.5' quadrangle.

On It Creek [EL DORADO]: *stream,* flows 3.25 miles to Scott Creek 5.5 miles east-southeast of Aukum (lat. 38°32'05" N, long. 120°37'40" W; sec. 23, T 8 N, R 12 E). Named on Aukum (1952) and Omo Ranch (1952) 7.5' quadrangles. Justice of the Peace Jinkerson gave the name to the stream after he ordered destruction of the buildings along the creek that gave Indian Diggins the nickname "Whore House Gulch" (Yohalem, p. 27).

Opal Hill [CALAVERAS]: *hill,* 7.5 miles south-southwest of Valley Springs (lat. 38°05'35" N, long. 120°53'25" W; near SE cor. sec. 20, T 3 N, R 10 E). Altitude 385 feet. Named on Valley Springs SW (1962) 7.5' quadrangle.

O'Pera: see **Camp O'Pera**, under **Lancha Plana** [AMADOR].

Ophir [PLACER]: *village,* 2.5 miles west of Auburn in Auburn Ravine (lat. 38°53'30" N, long. 121°07'20" W; sec. 18, T 12 N, R 8 E). Named on Auburn (1953) 7.5' quadrangle. The place first was called Spanish Corral (Bancroft, 1888, p. 355). The name "Ophir" refers to the biblical source of King Solomon's treasure (Scamehorn, p. 191). Postal authorities established Ophirville post office before March 24, 1852, discontinued it in 1866, reestablished it with the name "Ophir" in 1872, and discontinued it in 1910 (Salley, p. 161). They established Coon Creek post office northwest of Ophir in 1856 and discontinued it in 1860 (Salley p. 50). A place called Frytown was located in Auburn Ravine 2 miles below Ophir—the name was from one of the owners of the merchandise firm of Fry and Bruce; a place called Crees Flat was situated on the road between Ophir and Auburn (Gudde, 1975, p. 88, 126).

Ophir: see **Mount Ophir** [CALAVERAS]; **Mount Ophir** [MARIPOSA].

Ophir Hill [NEVADA]: *peak,* 1.5 miles southeast of downtown Grass Valley (lat. 39°12'20" N, long. 121°02'30" W; sec. 35, T 16 N, R 8 E). Named on Grass Valley (1949) 7.5' quadrangle.

Ophirville: see **Ohir** [PLACER].

Opie: see **Coulterville** [MARIPOSA].

Opim: see **Forestsa** [MARIPOSA].

Ora Spring [EL DORADO]: *spring,* 7.5 miles north-northwest of Leek Spring Hill (lat. 38°43'50" N, long. 120°19'50" W; sec. 8, T 10 N, R 15 E). Named on Leek Spring Hill (1951) 7.5' quadrangle.

Orchard Creek [PLACER]: *stream,* flows 9 miles to Auburn Ravine 9 miles north-northwest of Roseville (lat. 38°51'45" N, long. 121° 22'10" W; sec. 25, T 12 N, R 5 E). Named on Rocklin (1967) and Roseville (1967) 7.5' quadrangles. Called Rock Creek on Markham Ravine (1942) 15' quadrangle.

Orcum: see **Mount Orcum**, under **Mount Aukum** [EL DORADO].

Oregon Bar [CALAVERAS]: *locality,* 4 miles northwest of Valley Springs along Mokelumne River (lat. 38°13'45" N, long. 120° 53' W; sec. 4, T 4 N, R 10 E). Named on Wallace (1962) 7.5' quadrangle. Water of Camanche Reservoir now covers the site.

Oregon Bar [EL DORADO]: *locality,* 3 miles northwest of the village of Pilot Hill along North Fork American River (lat. 38°51'50" N, long. 121°03'20" W; sec. 26, T 12 N, R 8 E). Named on Auburn (1954) 15' quadrangle.

Oregon Bar [PLACER]: *locality,* 9 miles east-northeast of Auburn along Middle Fork American River (lat. 38°57'45" N, long. 120° 55'45" W; sec. 24, T 13 N, R 9 E). Named on Greenwood (1949) 7.5' quadrangle.

Oregon Canyon [EL DORADO]: *canyon,* drained by a stream that flows 1.25 miles to Canyon Creek (1) 1.5 miles north-northwest of Georgetown (lat. 38°55'45" N, long. 120°51'05" W; sec. 34, T 13 N, R 10 E). Named on Georgetown (1949) 7.5' quadrangle. Three men from Oregon discovered gold in the canyon in 1848 or 1849 (Gudde, 1975, p. 254).

Oregon Creek [SIERRA]: *stream,* formed in Sierra County by the confluence of North Fork and South Fork, flows 18 miles to to Middle Yuba River 4.25 miles south-southwest of Camptonville in Yuba County (lat. 39°23'40" N, long. 121°05' W; sec. 28, T 18 N, R 8 E). Named on Alleghany (1949), Camptonville (1948), and Pike (1949) 7.5' quadrangles. North Fork is 2 miles long and South Fork is 2.25 miles long; both forks are named on Alleghany (1949) and Downieville (1951) 7.5' quadrangles.

Oregon Creek: see **Indian Creek** [EL DORADO] (5).

Oregon Gulch [EL DORADO]: *canyon,* drained by a stream that flows 1.5 miles to Scott Creek 4.5 miles southeast of Omo Ranch (lat. 38°32' N, long, 120°30'40" W; sec. 23, T 8 N, R 13 E). Named on Caldor (1951), and Omo Ranch (1952) 7.5' quadrangles.

Oregon Gulch: see **Campo Seco** [CALAVERAS].

Orelli [EL DORADO]: *locality,* 1 mile east of Robbs Peak (lat. 38°55'15" N, long. 120°23' W). Named on Pyramid Peak (1896) 30' quadrangle.

Orleans: see **Orleans Flat** [NEVADA].

Orleans Flat [NEVADA]: *locality,* 5.25 miles northeast of North Bloomfield (lat. 39°25'45" N, long. 120°50' W; near NE cor. sec. 15, T 18 N, R 10 E). Site named on Alleghany (1949) 7.5' quadrangle. Called Orleans on Colfax (1898) 30' quadrangle. The place first was called Concord (Bancroft, 1888, p. 486).

Oro Grosso: see **Coarsegold** [MADERA].

Orr City: see **Gold Hill** [PLACER].

Orr Creek [PLACER]: *stream,* flows 7.5 miles to join Dry Creek (1) and form Coon Creek 6.25 miles north-northwest of Auburn (lat. 38°58'30" N, long. 121°08'15" W; sec. 13, T 13 N, R 7 E). Named on Auburn (1953) and Gold Hill (1954) 7.5' quadrangles. Called North Fork Dry Creek on Sacramento (1892) 30' quadrangle.

Osborne Hill [NEVADA]: *peak,* 2.5 miles south-southeast of Nevada City (lat. 39°11'10" N, long. 121°02'10" W; sec. 1, T 15 N, R 8 E). Named on Grass Valley (1949) 7.5' quadrangle. On United States Geological Survey's (1901) map, the name "Osborne Hill" applies to the whole ridge on which present Osborne Hill is the high point.

Osceola Ravine [NEVADA]: *canyon,* drained by a stream that flows 1 mile to Squirrel Creek 4.5 miles north-northeast of Pilot Peak (lat. 39°13'30" N, long. 121°08'10" W; near N line sec. 25, T 16 N, R 7 E). Named on Rough and Ready (1949) 7.5' quadrangle.

Osceola Ridge: see **Deadmans Flat** [NEVADA] (1).

Osgood Swamp [EL DORADO]: *marsh,* 2.5 miles north-northwest of Echo Summit (lat. 38°50'50" N, long. 120°02'30" W; on E line sec. 36, T 12 N, R 17 E). Named on Echo

Lake (1955) 7.5' quadrangle.

Osma Lake [EL DORADO]: *lake,* 425 feet long, 1.5 miles east-southeast of Pyramid Peak (lat. 38°50'20" N, long. 120°08'05" W). Named on Pyramid Peak (1955) 7.5' quadrangle.

Oso Spring [EL DORADO]: *spring,* nearly 7 miles north of Leek Spring Hill (lat. 38°43'35" N, long. 120°17'10" W; near SW cor. sec. 11, T 10 N, R 15 E). Named on Leek Spring Hill (1951) 7.5' quadrangle.

Ostrander Lake [MARIPOSA]: *lake,* 1750 feet long, 9 miles south-southeast of Yosemite Village (lat. 37°37'30" N, long. 119°33' W; sec. 34, T 3 S, R 22 E). Named on Yosemite (1956) 15' quadrangle. Members of the Whitney survey named the lake for Harvey J. Ostrander, who homesteaded near it (Hanna, p. 222). The feature first was called Pohono Lake (Browning, 1986, p. 162).

Ostrander Rocks [MARIPOSA]: *relief feature,* 4 miles south of Yosemite Village (lat. 37°41'30" N, long. 119°35'30" W; near W line sec. 8, T 3 S, R 22 E). Named on Yosemite (1956) 15' quadrangle. Called Ostrander's Rocks on Hoffmann and Gardner's (1863-1867) map. Members of the Whitney survey named the feature for Harvey J. Ostrander of Ostrander Lake (Browning, 1986, p. 162).

Otter Creek [EL DORADO]: *stream,* flows 10.5 miles to Middle Fork American River 3.5 miles north-northwest of Georgetown at Fords Bar (lat. 38°57'25" N, long. 120°51'20" W; near SW cor. sec. 22, T 13 N, R 10 E). Named on Georgetown (1949) and Tunnel Hill (1950) 7.5' quadrangles. Gudde (1975, p. 337) listed a place called Stony Bar that was situated at the confluence of Otter Creek and Middle Fork American River.

Otter Lake [TUOLUMNE]: *lake,* 2200 feet long, 7 miles southwest of Tower Peak (lat. 38°05'20" N, long. 119°39'15" W). Named on Tower Peak (1956) 15' quadrangle.

Otter Lake: see **Little Otter Lake** [TUOLUMNE].

Ottoway Creek [MADERA]: *stream,* flows 3 miles to Illilouette Creek 3.25 miles west of Merced Peak (lat. 37°38' N, long. 119°27'10" W); the stream heads near Ottoway Peak. Named on Merced Peak (1953) 15' quadrangle.

Ottoway Lake: see **Lower Ottoway Lake** [MADERA]; **Upper Ottoway Lake** [MADERA].

Ottoway Peak [MADERA]: *peak,* 0.5 mile north of Merced Peak (lat. 37°38'30" N, long. 119°23'30" W). Named on Merced Peak (1953) 15' quadrangle. Lieutenant N.F. McClure named the peak in 1895 for a corporal in his detachment (United States Board on Geographic Names, 1934a, p. 18).

Our House [SIERRA]: *locality,* nearly 2 miles southwest of Pike (lat. 39°25'05" N, long. 121°01'10" W; near NW cor. sec. 19, T 18 N, R 9 E). Named on Camptonville (1948, photorevised 1969) 7.5' quadrangle. Called

Hour House on Nevada City (1948) 15' quadrangle. United States Board on Geographic Names (1970a, p. 2) approved the name "Our House" for a meadow at the place, and gave the name "Hour House" as a variant. The Board also noted that the name is from the custom of the Abe Harris family, who lived at the place from the 1860's until 1903, of inviting people to "our house," a station on the old stage route.

Outingdale [EL DORADO]: *settlement,* 4 miles north of Aukum along Middle Fork Cosumnes River (lat. 38°36'55" N, long. 120° 43'40" W; sec. 23, T 9 N, R 11 E). Named on Aukum (1952) 7.5' quadrangle. Called Mars on Placerville (1893) 30' quadrangle. Logan's (1938) map has the name "Outingdale Resort" at the place.

Ovejo: see **Tillman** [MADERA].

Owens Camp [EL DORADO]: *locality,* 9 miles west-northwest of Kirkwood (lat. 38°44'20" N, long. 120°14'10" W; near NE cor. sec. 7, T 10 N, R 16 E). Named on Silver Lake (1956) 15' quadrangle.

Owens Creek [MARIPOSA]: *stream,* heads in Mariposa County and flows 53 miles to join Duck Slough and form Deep Slough 12.5 miles north-northwest of Dos Palos Y in Merced County (lat. 37°13'15" N, long. 120°42'45" W; sec. 24, T 8 S, R 11 E). Named on Catheys Valley (1962), Indian Gulch (1962), Merced (1961), Owens Reservoir (1962), Planada (1961), Sandy Mush (1962), and Turner Ranch (1961) 7'5' quadrangles.

Owens Reservoir [MARIPOSA]: *lake,* behind a dam on Owens Creek 9.5 miles south-southwest of the settlement of Catheys Valley (lat. 37°18'55" N, long. 120°11'05" W; near N line sec. 23, T 7 S, R 16 E). Named on Owens Reservoir (1962) 7.5' quadrangle.

Owlburrow Flat: see **Murphys** [CALAVERAS].

Owl Creek [MADERA]: *stream,* flows 2 miles to Whiskey Creek (2) 5.5 miles south of Shuteye Peak (lat. 37°16' N, long. 119°26'15" W; sec. 3, T 8 S, R 23 E). Named on Shuteye Peak (1953) 15' quadrangle.

Owl Creek [MARIPOSA]:
(1) *stream,* flows 2.5 miles to Devil Gulch 9 miles south of El Portal (lat. 37°33'45" N, long. 119°48'20" W; near E line sec. 25, T 4 S, R 19 E). Named on Buckingham Mountain (1947) 7.5' quadrangle.
(2) *stream,* flows 3 miles to West Fork Chowchilla River 5.25 miles east-southeast of Mariposa (lat. 37°27'55" N, long. 119°52'25" W; sec. 27, T 5 S, R 19 E). Named on Stumpfield Mountain (1947) 7.5' quadrangle.

Owl Creek [NEVADA]: *stream,* flows 3 miles to South Yuba River nearly 2 miles south-southeast of French Corral (lat. 39°17'05" N, long. 121°08'40" W; near S line sec. 36, T 17 N, R 7 E). Named on French Corral (1948) and Nevada City (1948) 7.5' quadrangles.

Owl Creek [PLACER]: *stream,* formed by the

confluence of North Branch, Middle Branch, and South Branch, flows 1.5 miles to North Fork American River 6.25 miles south-southeast of Colfax (lat. 39°00'45" N, long. 120°55' W; near N line sec. 1, T 13 N, R 9 E). Named on Colfax (1949) 7.5' quadrangle. Middle Branch is 2.5 miles long, North Branch is 2 miles long, and South Branch is 1 mile long; all three branches are named on Colfax (1949) and Foresthill (1949) 7.5' quadrangles.

Owl Creek [TUOLUMNE]: *stream,* flows 5.5 miles to Stanislaus River 7.25 miles west of Keystone (lat. 37°51'05" N, long. 120°38'10" W; sec. 15, T 1 S, R 12 E). Named on Keystone (1962) and Knights Ferry (1962) 7.5' quadrangles.

Owlsburg: see **Murphys** [CALAVERAS].

Oxbow Bar [EL DORADO]: *locality,* 3 miles northeast of Volcanoville along Middle Fork American River (lat. 38°00'15" N, long. 120°44'40" W; near W line sec. 3, T 13 N, R 11 E). Named on Duncan Peak (1952) 15' quadrangle.

Oxendine [TUOLUMNE]: *locality,* 15 miles north-northeast of Columbia (lat. 38°12'55" N, long. 120°15'30" W). Named on Big Trees (1891) 30' quadrangle.

Oyster Creek [AMADOR-EL DORADO]: *stream,* heads in Amador County and flows 2 miles to Silver Fork American River 3.5 miles west-southwest of Kirkwood in El Dorado County (lat. 38°40'45" N, long. 120°07'45" W; near NW cor. sec. 32, T 10 N, R 17 E). Named on Caples Lake (1979) 7.5' quadrangle.

Oyster Lake [AMADOR]: *intermittent lake,* 750 feet long, 9 miles north of Mokelumne Peak (lat. 38°40'15" N, long. 120°07' W; sec. 32, T 10 N, R 17 E). Named on Caples Lake (1979) 7.5' quadrangle.

– P –

Pacific [EL DORADO]: *locality,* 4.25 miles east of Pollock Pines (lat. 38°45'35" N, long. 120°30'25" W; near E line sec. 34, T 11 N, R 13 E). Named on Pollock Pines (1950) 7.5' quadrangle. Postal authorities established Pacific post office in 1880, discontinued it in 1893, reestablished in it 1894, and changed the name to Pacific House in 1958 (Salley, p. 165). Pacific House was an early-day hostelry and Pony Express stop at the site (Hanna, p. 224).

Pacific House: see **Pacific** [EL DORADO].

Pacific Placer Reservoir [CALAVERAS]: *lake,* 450 feet long, nearly 2 miles east of Valley Springs (lat. 38°11'20" N, long. 120°47'45" W; on E line sec. 19, T 4 N, R 11 E). Named on Valley Springs (1962) 7.5' quadrangle.

Packer Creek [SIERRA]: *stream,* flows 3.25 miles to Salmon Creek 4.25 miles north of Sierra City (lat. 39°37'40" N, long. 120°37'05" W; sec. 3, T 20 N, R 12 E); the stream goes

through Packer Lake. Named on Gold Lake (1981) 7.5' quadrangles.

Packer Lake [SIERRA]: *lake,* 1150 feet long, 4 miles north-northwest of Sierra City (lat. 39°37'20" N, long. 120°39'20" W; near SW cor. sec. 5, T 20 N, R 12 E); the lake is along Packer Creek. Named on Sierra City (1981) 7.5' quadrangle.

Packer Lake Lodge [SIERRA]: *locality,* 4 miles north-northwest of Sierra City (lat. 39°37'20" N, long. 120°39'25" W; near SW cor. sec. 5, T 20 N, R 12 E); the place is along Packer Lake. Named on Sierra City (1981) 7.5' quadrangle.

Packer Lake Saddle [SIERRA]: *pass,* 4 miles north-northwest of Sierra City (lat. 39°37'10" N, long. 120°40' W; near N line sec. 7, T 20 N, R 12 E); the pass is 0.5 mile west-southwest of Packer Lake. Named on Sierra City (1981) 7.5' quadrangle.

Packsaddle Campground [SIERRA]: *locality,* about 4 miles north-northwest of Sierra City (lat. 39°37'25" N, long. 120°38'55" W; sec. 5, T 20 N, R 12 E). Named on Sierra City (1981) 7.5' quadrangle.

Paddle Creek [TUOLUMNE]: *stream,* flows 1.25 miles to Bourland Creek 9 miles south of Pinecrest (lat. 38°03'50" N, long. 119°59'25" W; near N line sec. 3, T 2 N, R 18 E). Named on Cherry Lake North (1979) 7.5' quadrangle.

Page Meadows [PLACER]: *area,* 3 miles west-southwest of Tahoe City (lat. 39°09' N, long. 120°11'15" W; sec. 14, 15, T 15 N, R 16 E). Named on Tahoe City (1955, photorevised 1969) 7.5' quadrangle. Called Paige Meadow on Tahoe (1955) 15' quadrangle, but United States Board on Geographic Names (1969b, p. 4) rejected this form of the name, which commemorates John Page and Frances Page, who grazed dairy cattle in the area from 1863 until 1880.

Page Mountain [TUOLUMNE]: *peak,* 6.5 miles south of Sonora (lat. 37°53'25" N, long. 120°22'45" W; on S line sec. 36, T 1 N, R 14 E). Altitude 2136 feet. Named on Sonora (1948) 7.5' quadrangle.

Pagge Creek [PLACER]: *stream,* flows 4.5 miles to North Shirttail Canyon 7 miles north of Foresthill (lat. 39°07'10" N, long. 120°47'45" W; sec. 25, T 15 N, R 10 E). Named on Foresthill (1949) and Michigan Bluff (1952) 7.5' quadrangles.

Pahatsi: see **Camp Pahatsi** [NEVADA].

Paige Meadow: see **Page Meadows** [PLACER].

Pain Flat: see **Payne Flat** [MARIPOSA].

Painsville: see **Indian Springs** [NEVADA].

Painted Rock [PLACER]:

(1) *peak,* 3.5 miles north-northwest of Granite Chief (lat. 39°14'30" N, long. 120°19'15" W; near N line sec. 16, T 16 N, R 15 E). Altitude 6682 feet. Named on Granite Chief (1953) 7.5' quadrangle.

(2) *ridge,* west-trending, 0.5 mile long, 3.5 miles north-northwest of Tahoe City (lat.

39°12'50" N, long. 120°10'35" W; at SW cor. sec. 23, T 16 N, R 16 E). Named on Tahoe City (1955) 7.5' quadrangle.

Painter's Station: see **Eight Mile House** [EL DORADO].

Palen Reservoir [SIERRA]: *lake,* 1150 feet long, 5.5 miles north-northwest of Sierraville in Antelope Valley (lat. 39°39'10" N, long. 120°18'25" W; near S line sec. 21, T 21 N, R 15 E). Named on Antelope Valley (1981) 7.5' quadrangle.

Palisade Creek [PLACER]: *stream,* flows nearly 5 miles to North Fork American River 8 miles west-northwest of Granite Chief (lat. 39°14'45" N, long. 120°25'05" W; at E line sec. 17, T 16 N, R 14 E); the stream heads at Palisade Lake. Named on Royal Gorge (1953) and Soda Springs (1955) 7.5' quadrangles.

Palisade Lake [PLACER]: *lake,* 2900 feet long, 5 miles west-southwest of Donner Pass (lat. 39°17'55" N, long. 120°24'50" W; sec. 33, T 17 N, R 14 E). Named on Soda Springs (1955) 7.5' quadrangle.

Palmer [EL DORADO]: *locality,* 3.25 miles south-southwest of Robbs Peak (lat. 38°52'40" N, long. 120°25'15" W). Named on Pyramid Peak (1896) 30' quadrangle.

Palmer Ridge [SIERRA]: *ridge,* southwest-trending, 5.25 miles long, center 4.5 miles east of Alleghany (lat. 39°28' N, long. 120°45'35" W). Named on Alleghany (1949) and Graniteville (1982) 7.5' quadrangles.

Paloma [CALAVERAS]: *village,* 6.5 miles northwest of San Andreas (lat. 38°15'35" N, long. 120°45'40" W; near E line sec. 28, T 5 N, R 11 E). Named on Jackson (1962) 7.5' quadrangle. Camp's (1962) map shows a place called Frenchman's Ranch at Paloma. California Mining Bureau's (1909a) map shows a place called Fosteria situated 7.5 miles northeast of Valley Springs by stage line, and Hanna (p. 110) noted that Fosteria had the early name "Paloma." Postal authorities established Fosteria post office in 1903 and discontinued it in 1918; the name was for the Foster family, pioneers of the neighborhood (Salley, p. 79).

Paloni Mountain [MARIPOSA]: *ridge,* north-northeast-trending, 1.25 miles long, 11 miles east-southeast of Mariposa (lat. 37°26'50" N, long. 119°46'25" W). Named on Stumpfield Mountain (1947) 7.5' quadrangle.

Pandola Ferry: see **Parrott Ferry** [CALAVERAS-TUOLUMNE].

Panorama Cliff [MARIPOSA]: *relief feature,* 2.5 miles southeast of Yosemite Village (lat. 37°43'10" N, long. 119°33' W); the feature is below Panorama Point. Named on Yosemite (1956) 15' quadrangle.

Panorama Point [MARIPOSA]: *peak,* 3 miles southeast of Yosemite Village (lat. 37°43' N, long. 119°33'05" W). Altitude 7007 feet. Named on Yosemite (1956) 15' quadrangle.

Pan Ravine [NEVADA]: *canyon,* drained by a stream that flows 1.5 miles to Humbug Creek 1.5 miles southwest of North Bloomfield (lat. 39°21'05" N, long. 120°55'20" W; near W line sec. 12, T 17 N, R 9 E). Named on North Bloomfield (1949) 7.5' quadrangle.

Panther Creek [AMADOR]: *stream,* formed by the confluence of East Panther Creek and West Panther Creek, flows 1.25 miles to North Fork Mokelumne River 5.25 miles south-southwest of Hams Station (lat. 38°28'25" N, long. 120°24'55" W; sec. 10, T 7 N, R 14 E). Named on Devils Nose (1979) 7.5' quadrangle.

Panther Creek: see **East Panther Creek** [AMADOR]; **West Panther Creek** [AMADOR].

Panther Ridge [AMADOR]: *ridge,* south-southeast of Hams Station (lat. 38°30'45" N, long. 120°21'10" W); the ridge is between East Panther Creek and West Panther Creek. Named on Devils Nose (1979) and Peddler Hill (1951) 7.5' quadrangles.

Paper Cabin Ridge [TUOLUMNE]: *ridge,* west- to south-trending, 3.5 miles long, 3 miles south-southeast of Tuolumne (lat. 37°55' N, long. 120°12'15" W). Named on Tuolumne (1948) 7.5' quadrangle.

Papoose Creek [SIERRA]: *stream,* flows less than 0.5 mile to Jim Crow Creek 3 miles east-southeast of Downieville (lat. 39°32'30" N, long. 120°46'25" W; near E line sec. 6, T 19 N, R 11 E). Named on Downieville (1951) 7.5' quadrangle.

Paps Gulch [MARIPOSA]: *canyon,* drained by a stream that flows 1.25 miles to Bull Creek 8.5 miles west-northwest of El Portal (lat. 37°43'30" N, long. 119°55'05" W; near S line sec. 30, T 2 S, R 19 E). Named on Kinsley (1947) 7.5' quadrangle.

Paradise [PLACER]: *locality,* 10 miles east-northeast of Auburn (lat. 38°58'20" N, long. 120°54'10" W); the place is along Todd Creek above present Paradise Canyon. Named on Placerville (1893) 30' quadrangle.

Paradise Canyon [PLACER]: *canyon,* 0.5 mile long, opens into the canyon of Middle Fork American River 9.5 miles east-northeast of Auburn (lat. 38°57'40" N, long. 120°55'20" W; sec. 24, T 13 N, R 9 E). Named on Greenwood (1949) 7.5' quadrangle.

Paradise Flat [EL DORADO]: *area,* 6.5 miles north of Mount Tallac (lat. 39°00' N, long. 120°06'30" W; sec. 4, T 13 N, R 17 E). Named on Emerald Bay (1955) and Meeks Bay (1955) 7.5' quadrangles.

Paradise Lake [NEVADA]: *lake,* 1950 feet long, 6 miles north-northwest of Donner Pass (lat. 39°24' N, long. 120°21'40" W; on W line sec. 25, T 18 N, R 14 E); the lake is east of Paradise Valley. Named on Independence Lake (1981) 7.5' quadrangle.

Paradise Valley [NEVADA]: *valley,* 6.25 miles north-northwest of Donner Pass (lat. 39°24' N, long. 120°22'20" W; near N line sec. 26, T 18 N, R 14 E). Named on Independence Lake

(1981) and Webber Peak (1981) 7.5' quadrangles.

Paramae Gulch [CALAVERAS]: *canyon,* 1 mile long, opens into the canyon of Jack Nelson Creek 4 miles southwest of Rail Road Flat (lat. 38°17'50" N, long. 120°33'20" W; near SE cor. sec. 8, T 5 N, R 13 E). Named on Rail Road Flat (1948) 7.5' quadrangle.

Parazo Canyon: see **Perazzo Canyon** [NEVADA-SIERRA].

Pardee: see **Camp Pardee** [CALAVERAS].

Pardee Reservoir [AMADOR]: *lake,* behind a dam on Mokelumne River 7.5 miles southwest of Jackson on Amador-Calaveras county line (lat. 38°15'25" N, long. 120°51' W; sec. 26, T 5 N, R 10 E). Named on Jackson (1962) and Mokelumne Hill (1948) 7.5' quadrangles. Channel Arm extends up Mokelumne River from the dam, and North Arm extends northwest from the river just behind the dam. Both arms are named on Jackson (1962) 7.5' quadrangle. The name "Pardee" honors George C. Pardee, mayor of Oakland from 1893 until 1895, governor of California from 1903 until 1907, and president of the board of directors of East Bay Municipal Utility District from 1924 until 1941 (Gudde, 1949, p. 253).

Pardee Reservoir [CALAVERAS]: *lake,* behind a dam on Mokelumne River nearly 5 miles west of Paloma on Calaveras-Amador county line (lat. 38°15'25" N, long. 120°51' W; sec. 26, T 5 N, R 10 E). Named on Jackson (1962), Mokelumne Hill (1948), and Valley Springs (1962) 7.5' quadrangles. Channel Arm extends up the river from the dam and is named on Jackson (1962) 7.5' quadrangle. South Arm extends south-southeast along a canyon that lies perpendicular to the river and is named on Jackson (1962) and Valley Springs (1962) 7.5' quadrangles. Officials of East Bay Utility District named the lake in 1929 for George C. Pardee, governor of California from 1903 to 1907, and president of the board of directors of the district from 1924 until 1941 (Gudde, 1949, p. 253).

Pardoe Lake [AMADOR]: *lake,* 850 feet long, 3.5 miles north-northwest of Mokelumne Peak (lat. 38°35'30" N, long. 120°06'20" W; near N line sec. 33, T 9 N, R 17 E). Named on Mokelumne Peak (1979) 7.5' quadrangle.

Pardoes Camp: see **Upper Pardoes Camp** [AMADOR].

Park: see **Sly Park** [EL DORADO].

Park Creek: see **Sly Park Creek** [EL DORADO].

Parker Pass [TUOLUMNE]: *pass,* 6 miles south-southeast of Tioga Pass on Tuolumne-Mono county line (lat. 37°50'20" N, long. 119° 12'25" W); the pass is at the head of Parker Creek, which is in Mono County. Named on Mono Craters (1953) 15' quadrangle.

Parker Pass Creek [TUOLUMNE]: *stream,* flows 5.5 miles to Dana Fork 2 miles southwest of Tioga Pass (lat. 37°52'50" N, long. 119°16' W); the stream heads at Parker Pass. Named on Mono Craters (1953) and Tuolumne Meadows (1956) 15' quadrangles.

Parker Pass Lake [TUOLUMNE]: *lake,* 1000 feet long, 6 miles south-southeast of Tioga Pass (lat. 37°50'05" N, long. 119°12'35" W); the lake is 0.25 mile southwest of Parker Pass. Named on Mono Craters (1953) 15' quadrangle.

Parks Hill: see **Kings Hill** [PLACER].

Parrott Ferry [CALAVERAS-TUOLUMNE]: *locality,* 2.5 miles west-northwest of Columbia along Stanislaus River on Calaveras-Tuolumne county line (lat. 38°02'35" N, long. 120°27' W). Named on Big Trees (1891) 30' quadrangle. Columbia (1948) 7.5' quadrangle shows Parrotts Ferry bridge at about the site of Parrott Ferry. Thomas H. Parrott started Parrott's Ferry in 1860 (Hoover, Rensch, and Rensch, p. 572). According to Wheeler (1879, p. 179), the place had the early name "Pandola Ferry."

Parsley Bar [PLACER]: *locality,* 3 miles west-southwest of Bunker Hill along Rubicon River (lat. 39°02'10" N, long. 120°25'55" W; sec. 29, T 14 N, R 14 E). Named on Bunker Hill (1953) 7.5' quadrangle.

Parsley Bar Crossing [EL DORADO-PLACER]: *locality,* 3.25 miles west-southwest of Bunker Hill along Rubicon River on El Dorado-Placer county line (lat. 39°01'40" N, long. 120°26'05" W; at N line sec. 32, T 14 N, R 14 E); the place is below Parsley Bar. Named on Bunker Hill (1953) 7.5' quadrangle.

Parson Rock [EL DORADO]: *promontory,* 3.5 miles north of Mount Tallac on the northwest side of Emerald Bay (1) (lat. 38°57'20" N, long. 120°06'05" W; sec. 21, T 13 N, R 17 E). Named on Emerald Bay (1955) 7.5' quadrangle. The name is from the resemblance of the feature to a pulpit (Lekisch, p. 95).

Parsons: see **Strawberry** [TUOLUMNE].

Parsons Peak [MADERA-TUOLUMNE]: *peak,* 9.5 miles south-southwest of Tioga Pass on Madera-Tuolumne county line (lat. 37°46'30" N, long. 119°18'25" W). Named on Tuolumne Meadows (1956) 15' quadrangle. R.B. Marshall of United States Geological Survey named the peak for Edward Taylor Parsons, who for many years was a director of the Sierra Club (United States Board on Geographic Names, 1934, p. 19).

Paso Del Pino: see **Pine Log** [TUOLUMNE].

Pass Creek [SIERRA]: *stream,* flows 7.25 miles to Jackson Meadows Reservoir 7 miles southeast of Sierra City (lat. 39°30'10" N, long. 120°31'55" W; near NE cor. sec. 20, T 19 N, R 13 E). Named on Haypress Valley (1981), Sattley (1981), and Webber Peak (1981) 7.5' quadrangles.

Pass Creek Campground [SIERRA]: *locality,* 7 miles southeast of Sierra City along Jackson Meadows Reservoir (lat. 39°30'15" N, long. 120°32' W; near NE cor. sec. 20, T 19

N, R 13 E); the place is near the mouth of Pass Creek. Named on Haypress Valley (1981) 7.5' quadrangle.

Paterson: see **Cherokee** [NEVADA].

Pate Valley [TUOLUMNE]: *area,* 5.5 miles northeast of White Wolf along Tuolumne River (lat. 37°56' N, long 119°35'50" W). Named on Hetch Hetchy Reservoir (1956) 15' quadrangle.

Pats Gulch [SIERRA]: *canyon,* drained by a stream that flows 2 miles to Slate Creek 8 miles southwest of Mount Fillmore (lat. 39° 39'35" N, long. 120°57'50" W; near SW cor. sec. 22, T 21 N, R 9 E). Named on La Porte (1951) 7.5' quadrangle.

Pats Meadow [SIERRA]: *area,* 9.5 miles southeast of Loyalton at the head of Smithneck Creek (lat. 39°33'35" N, long. 120°08'50" W; sec. 25, T 20 N, R 16 E). Named on Sardine Peak (1981) 7.5' quadrangle.

Pattees Ranch: see **Jenny Lind** [CALAVERAS].

Patterson: see **Cherokee** [NEVADA]; **Trigo** [MADERA].

Patterson Bend [MADERA]: *bend,* 6 miles south-southwest of the town of North Fork along San Joaquin River on Madera-Fresno county line (lat. 37°08'40" N, long. 119°33'15" W). Named on North Fork (1965) 7.5' quadrangle.

Pattison: see **Poorman Creek** [NEVADA] (1).

Pat Yore Flat [NEVADA]: *area,* 2.5 miles southeast of Graniteville (lat. 39°24'45" N, long. 120°42'20" W; sec. 23, T 18 N, R 11 E). Named on Graniteville (1982) 7.5' quadrangle. Logan's (1940) map shows a place called Salina Flat located about 1 mile south of Pat Yore Flat (sec. 26, T 18 N, R 11 E).

Pauley Creek [SIERRA]: *stream,* flows 14 miles to Downie River 0.5 mile north-northeast of Downieville (lat. 39°34'10" N, long. 120°49'15" W; sec. 26, T 20 N, R 10 E). Named on Downieville (1951), Gold Lake (1981), and Sierra City (1981) 7.5' quadrangles. Called East Fork of North Fork Yuba River on Downieville (1897) 30' quadrangle, but United States Board on Geographic Names (1950, p. 6) rejected this name for the feature.

Payne Flat [MARIPOSA]: *area,* 3.5 miles northnortheast of the settlement of Catheys Valley (lat. 37°28'50" N, long. 120°04' W). Named on Catheys Valley (1962) 7.5' quadrangle. Called Pain Flat on Indian Gulch (1920) 15' quadrangle, but United States Board on Geographic Names (1964a, p. 13) rejected this name for the feature. The place is called Payne's Flat on Laizure's (1928) map.

Payton Saddle [TUOLUMNE]: *pass,* nearly 3 miles southeast of Liberty Hill (lat. 38°20'40" N, long. 120°03'25" W; sec. 25, T 6 N, R 17 E). Named on Liberty Hill (1979) 7.5' quadrangle.

Peachstone Gulch [PLACER]: *canyon,* drained by a stream that flows nearly 2 miles to Middle Fork American River 13 miles east-northeast

of Auburn (lat. 38°58' N, long. 120°51'15" W; at S line sec. 16, T 13 N, R 10 E). Named on Georgetown (1949) 7.5' quadrangle.

Peachtree Bar [MARIPOSA]: *locality,* 4.5 miles south of El Portal along South Fork Merced River (lat. 37°36'40" N, long. 119°47'20" W). Named on Buckingham Mountain (1947) 7.5' quadrangle. A man named Blair, who mined at the place until 1919, planted peach trees there (Mendershausen, p. 18, 20).

Peachys Creek [CALAVERAS]: *stream,* heads in Calaveras County and flows 10 miles to Littlejohns Creek 2 miles north-northwest of Knights Ferry in Stanislaus County (lat. 37°50'45" N, long. 120°41'20" W). Named on Copperopolis (1962) and Knights Ferry (1962) 7.5' quadrangles.

Peacock Ravine [EL DORADO]: *canyon,* drained by a stream that flows 2.25 miles to Skunk Canyon 3.5 miles south of the village of Pilot Hill (lat. 38°46'55" N, long. 121°01'20" W; sec. 30, T 11 N, R 9 E). Named on Pilot Hill (1954) 7.5' quadrangle.

Peardale [NEVADA]: *settlement,* 3.5 miles north-northwest of Chicago Park (lat. 39°11'30" N, long. 120°59'45" W; mainly in sec. 5, T 15 N, R 9 E). Named on Chicago Park (1949) and Grass Valley (1949) 7.5' quadrangles. Postal authorities established Peardale post office in 1916 and discontinued it in 1927 (Frickstad, p. 114). Colfax (1938) 30' quadrangle shows the place located along Nevada County Narrow Gauge Railroad.

Peardon Hill [NEVADA]: *peak,* 5.25 miles northwest of Pilot Peak (lat. 39°12'45" N, long. 121°15'45" W; sec. 26, T 16 N, R 6 E). Altitude 1264 feet. Named on Smartville (1951) 7.5' quadrangle.

Pearl Lake [EL DORADO]: *lake,* 700 feet long, 8 miles east-southeast of Robbs Peak (lat. 38°53'30" N, long. 120°15'20" W; sec. 18, T 12 N, R 16 E). Named on Loon Lake (1952, photorevised 1973) 7.5' quadrangle.

Pearls Hill: see **Anthony House** [NEVADA].

Pearson Ravine [SIERRA]: *canyon,* drained by a stream that flows 2 miles to Potosi Creek 2.25 miles west of Mount Fillmore (lat. 39° 43'35" N, long. 120°53'35" W; near W line sec. 32, T 22 N, R 10 E). Named on La Porte (1951) and Mount Fillmore (1951) 7.5' quadrangles.

Peavine [SIERRA]: *locality,* 12.5 miles east of Loyalton along Western Pacific Railroad (lat. 39°40'40" N, long. 120°00'25" W; near N line sec. 19, T 21 N, R 18 E). Named on Evans Canyon (1978) 7.5' quadrangle.

Peavine Creek [EL DORADO]: *stream,* flows 3 miles to South Fork Silver Creek 4.5 miles northwest of Kyburz (lat. 38°49'05" N, long. 120°21'50" W; sec. 12, T 11 N, R 14 E); the stream heads on Peavine Ridge. Named on Kyburz (1952) 7.5' quadrangle.

Peavine Creek [PLACER]: *stream,* flows 7.5 miles to North Fork of Middle Fork American River 3 miles east-northeast of Michigan

Bluff (lat. 39°03'10" N, long. 120°40'40" W; sec. 19, T 14 N, R 12 E); upper reaches of the stream are south of Peavine Ridge. Named on Greek Store (1952) and Michigan Bluff (1952) 7.5' quadrangles.

Peavine Flat: see **Chips Flat** [SIERRA].

Peavine Point [EL DORADO]: *ridge,* west- to north-trending, 4.5 miles long, 13 miles north-northwest of Pollock Pines (lat. 38°56'30" N, long. 120°19'45" W). Named on Tunnel Hill (1950) 7.5' quadrangle.

Peavine Ridge [EL DORADO]: *ridge,* west-trending, 17 miles long, center 2 miles east-northeast of Riverton (lat. 38°47'45" N, long. 120°25'45" W). Named on Kyburz (1952), Pollock Pines (1950), and Riverton (1950) 7.5' quadrangles.

Peavine Ridge [PLACER]: *ridge,* generally southwest-trending, 5 miles long, 7.5 miles southwest of Duncan Peak (lat. 39°04'30" N, long. 120°36'15" W); the ridge is north of Peavine Creek. Named on Greek Store (1952) and Michigan Bluff (1952) 7.5' quadrangles.

Pebble Canyon: see **Big Pebble Canyon** [EL DORADO]; **Little Pebble Canyon** [EL DORADO].

Pecan Spring [MADERA]: *spring,* 5 miles southeast of Knowles (lat. 37°09'35" N, long. 119°49'05" W; sec. 8, T 9 S, R 20 E). Named on Knowles (1962) 7.5' quadrangle.

Peckinpah Creek [MADERA]: *stream,* flows 4 miles to South Fork Willow Creek (2) 9 miles south-southwest of Shuteye Peak (lat. 37°14'10" N, long. 119°29'45" W; sec. 18, T 8 S, R 23 E); the stream goes through Peckinpah Meadow. Named on Shaver Lake (1953) and Shuteye Peak (1953) 15' quadrangles.

Peckinpah Meadow [MADERA]: *area,* 6 miles south-southwest of Shuteye Peak (lat. 37°15'55" N, long. 119°27'45" W; sec. 4, T 8 S, R 23 E); the place is along Peckinpah Creek. Named on Shuteye Peak (1953) 15' quadrangle.

Peckinpah Mill [MADERA]: *locality,* 6.25 miles south-southwest of Shuteye Peak (lat. 37°15'50" N, long. 119°27'45" W; sec. 4, T 8 S, R 23 E); the place is along Peckinpah Creek. Named on Kaiser (1904) 30' quadrangle. Charlie Peckinpah and his brothers started a sawmill at the spot in 1884 (Browning, 1986, p. 167).

Peckinpah Mountain: see **Central Camp** [MADERA].

Peddler Creek [EL DORADO]: *stream,* flows 1.5 miles to Middle Fork Cosumnes River 8 miles east of Caldor (lat. 38°35'25" N, long. 120°17' W; sec. 35, T 9 N, R 15 E); the stream heads at Peddler Hill. Named on Peddler Hill (1951) 7.5' quadrangle.

Peddler Hill [AMADOR-EL DORADO]: *ridge,* south-southwest-trending, 1 mile long, 6.25 miles east-northeast of Hams Station on Amador-El Dorado county line (lat. 38°34'30"

N, long. 120°15'50" W). Named on Peddler Hill (1951) 7.5' quadrangle.

Pegleg Creek [EL DORADO]: *stream,* flows about 1.5 miles to Bear Creek (2) 3.5 miles southeast of Georgetown (lat. 38°52'35" N, long. 120°47'10" W; sec. 19, T 12 N, R 11 E). Named on Georgetown (1949) 7.5' quadrangle.

Pegleg Creek [MARIPOSA]: *stream,* flows 5 miles to West Fork Chowchilla River nearly 5 miles east-southeast of Mariposa (lat. 37°27'05" N, long. 119°53'20" W; sec. 33, T 5 S, R 19 E). Named on Mariposa (1947) 7.5' quadrangle.

Pelham Flat [PLACER]: *area,* 3 miles south of Cisco Grove (lat. 39° 16' N, long. 120°32'10" W; sec. 8, T 16 N, R 13 E). Named on Cisco Grove (1955) 7.5' quadrangle, which shows marsh and a lake at the place.

Pena Blanca Point: see **Penon Blanco Point** [MARIPOSA].

Pena Blanca Ridge: see **Penon Blanco Ridge** [MARIPOSA-TUOLUMNE].

Pendola: see **Camp Pendola** [TUOLUMNE].

Pendola Gardens [MARIPOSA]: *locality,* 3.5 miles south-southeast of the village of Bear Valley in Cow and Calf Gulch (lat. 37°31'05" N, long. 120°06'20" W). Named on Bear Valley (1947) 7.5' quadrangle.

Peninsula Lake [TUOLUMNE]: *lake,* 3300 feet long, 8 miles west-southwest of Tower Peak (lat. 38°06' N, long. 119°40'20" W); a peninsula divides the lake into two parts. Named on Tower Peak (1956) 15' quadrangle.

Peninsula Lake: see **Upper Peninsula Lake** [TUOLUMNE].

Penner Lake [NEVADA]: *lake,* 1650 feet long, 4 miles west-southwest of English Mountain (lat. 39°25'10" N, long. 120°36'55" W; on S line sec. 15, T 18 N, R 12 E). Named on English Mountain (1983) 7.5' quadrangle.

Pennsylvania Gulch [CALAVERAS]: *canyon,* 1 mile long, 1.5 miles east of Murphys (lat. 38°08'15" N, long. 120°26'05" W; sec. 4, 9, T 3 N, R 14 E). Named on Murphys (1948) 7.5' quadrangle. A group of men from Pennsylvania began mining in the canyon in December of 1849 (Gudde, 1975, p. 262).

Pennsylvania Point [PLACER]: *peak,* 9 miles west-northwest of Devil Peak (lat. 38°59'55" N, long. 120°42'05" W; on N line sec. 12, T 13 N, R 11 E). Altitude 3552 feet. Named on Tunnel Hill (1950) 7.5' quadrangle.

Penn Valley [NEVADA]: *valley,* 2.25 miles north of Pilot Peak along Squirrel Creek (lat. 39°12' N, long. 121°11' W). Named on Rough and Ready (1949) 7.5' quadrangle. Whitney's (1873) map shows Penn Valley Ho. [House] in or near present Penn Valley.

Penn Valley House: see **Penn Valley** [NEVADA].

Penny Creek [CALAVERAS]: *stream,* flows 2.5 miles to Sawmill Creek 1 mile south-south-west of Copperopolis (lat. 37°58'05" N, long. 120°38'55" W; sec. 3, T 1 N, R 12 E). Named on Copperopolis (1962) 7.5' quadrangle.

Penobscot Creek [EL DORADO]: *stream,* flows 3.5 miles to Greenwood Creek 1.25 miles south-southwest of Greenwood (lat. 38°52'55" N, long. 120°55'25" W; sec. 24, T 12 N, R 9 E). Named on Greenwood (1949) 7.5' quadrangle.

Penole Peak [TUOLUMNE]: *peak,* nearly 3 miles southeast of Don Pedro Camp (lat. 37°41'35" N, long. 120°21'50" W; sec. 7, T 3 S, R 15 E). Named on Penon Blanco Peak (1962) 7.5' quadrangle.

Penon Blanco [MARIPOSA]: *locality,* 2.5 miles northwest of Coulterville along Blacks Creek (lat. 37°44'15" N, long. 120°13'30" W); the site is 1 mile southeast of present Penon Blanco Point. Named on Sonora (1891) 30' quadrangle.

Penon Blanco Peak [MARIPOSA]: *peak,* 4 miles west-northwest of Coulterville (lat. 37°43'55" N, long. 120°15'35" W; sec. 25, T 2 S, R 15 E); the peak is near the southeast end of Penon Blanco Ridge. Altitude 2878 feet. Named on Penon Blanco Peak (1962) 7.5' quadrangle.

Penon Blanco Point [MARIPOSA]: *peak,* 3.25 miles northwest of Coulterville (lat. 37°44'45" N, long. 120°14'15" W; on E line sec. 19, T 2 S, R 16 E); the peak is near the southeast end of Penon Blanco Ridge. Altitude 2470 feet. Named on Coulterville (1947) 7.5' quadrangle. United States Board on Geographic Names (1933, p. 597) rejected the forms "Pena Blanca Point," "Peña Blanca Point," and "Peñon Blanco Point" for the name.

Penon Blanco Ridge [MARIPOSA-TUOLUMNE]: *ridge,* northwest-trending, 5 miles long, on Mariposa-Tuolumne county line, mainly in Tuolumne County; center 5 miles west-northwest of Coulterville (lat. 37°45' N, long. 120°16' W); the ridge extends northwest from Penon Blanco Peak. Named on Moccasin (1948) and Penon Blanco Peak (1962) 7.5' quadrangles. Whitney (1865, p. 231) noted that the feature is "a prominent elevation, of which the crest is a great white mass of quartz, visible from a great distance"—*peñon blanco* means "white rock" in Spanish. United States Board on Geographic Names (1933, p. 597) rejected the forms "Pena Blanca Ridge," "Peña Blanca Ridge," and "Peñon Blanco Ridge" for the name.

Penryn [PLACER]: *town,* 5.5 miles northeast of Rocklin (lat. 38°51'10" N, long. 121°10'10" W; near NW cor. sec. 35, T 12 N, R 7 E). Named on Rocklin (1967) 7.5' quadrangle. Postal authorities established Penryn post office in 1873 (Frickstad, p. 121). Griffith Griffith, a Welshman who had granite quarries nearby, named the place for Penrhyn, Wales; a mining town called Stewarts Flat was located 1.5 miles east of Penryn in Secret Ravine (Hoover, Rensch, and Rensch, p. 271-272).

Peon Gulch [CALAVERAS]: *canyon,* drained by a stream that flows 1.5 miles to Shad Gulch 2.5 miles west-northwest of Paloma (lat. 38°16'25" N, long. 120°48'30" W; sec. 19, T 5 N, R 11 E). Named on Jackson (1962) 7.5' quadrangle.

Peoria Basin [TUOLUMNE]: *valley,* 6.25 miles north of Keystone (lat. 37°55'20" N, long. 120°31'15" W; sec. 22, 23, T 1 N, R 13 E); Peoria Creek drains the place. Named on Melones Dam (1962) 7.5' quadrangle.

Peoria Creek [TUOLUMNE]: *stream,* flows 3.5 miles to Stanislaus River 6.5 miles north-northwest of Keystone (lat. 37°55'30" N, long. 120°32'10" W; sec. 22, T 1 N, R 13 E); the stream goes through Peoria Basin and Peoria Flat. Named on Melones Dam (1962) and Sonora (1948) 7.5' quadrangles.

Peoria Flat [TUOLUMNE]: *area,* 4.5 miles north of Keystone (lat. 37°54'15" N, long. 120°30' W; sec. 25, 36, T 1 N, R 13 E); the place is along Peoria Creek. Named on Melones Dam (1962) and Sonora (1948) 7.5' quadrangles.

Peoria Mountain [TUOLUMNE]: *ridge,* northwest-trending, 3 miles long, 7.25 miles west-southwest of Sonora (lat. 37°55'45" N, long. 120°29'45" W). Named on Melones Dam (1962) and Sonora (1948) 7.5' quadrangles.

Peoria Pass [TUOLUMNE]: *pass,* 4.25 miles north of Keystone (lat. 37°53'45" N, long. 120°30'10" W; sec. 36, T 1 N, R 13 E). Named on Melones Dam (1962) 7.5' quadrangle.

Peppermint Creek [CALAVERAS]: *stream,* flows 2.25 miles to Coyote Creek 2 miles east-southeast of Murphys (lat. 38°07'45" N, long. 120°25'50" W; at W line sec. 10, T 3 N, R 14 E). Named on Murphys (1948) 7.5' quadrangle.

Peppermint Creek [TUOLUMNE]: *stream,* flows 3.5 miles to Woods Creek 3 miles southwest of Sonora at Jamestown (lat. 37°57'20" N, long. 120°25'25" W; sec. 10, T 11 N, R 14 E). Named on Sonora (1948) 7.5' quadrangle.

Perazzo Canyon [NEVADA-SIERRA]: *canyon,* 9 miles south of Sierraville on Nevada-Sierra county line (lat. 39°26'45" N, long. 120°23'20" W). Named on Webber Peak (1981) 7.5' quadrangle. Called Parazo Canyon on Truckee (1940) 30' quadrangle, but United States Board on Geographic Names (1960a, p. 16) rejected the forms "Parazo" and "Perazza" for the name.

Perazzo Meadows [SIERRA]: *valley,* 7 miles south of Sierraville along Little Truckee River (lat. 39°29'15" N, long. 120°21'30" W). Named on Independence Lake (1981) and Webber Peak (1981) 7.5' quadrangles.

Peregoy Meadow [MARIPOSA]: *area,* 6 miles south-southwest of Yosemite Village (lat. 37°40'10" N, long. 119°37'20" W; sec. 13, T 3 S, R 21 E). Named on Yosemite (1956) 15' quadrangle. The name commemorates Charles E. Peregoy, a native of Maryland who built Mountain View House in 1869 (Hanna, p. 233).

Perkins Spring [NEVADA]: *spring,* 2.25 miles east of Higgins Corner along Magonlia Creek (lat. 39°02'45" N, long. 121°03'15" W; near S line sec. 23, T 14 N, R 8 E). Named on Lake Combie (1949) 7.5' quadrangle.

Perks Corner [EL DORADO]: *locality,* 2.5 miles west-southwest of Placerville (lat. 38°42'40" N, long. 120°50'15" W; sec. 23, T 10 N, R 10 E). Named on Placerville (1949) 7.5' quadrangle.

Perry Creek [EL DORADO]: *stream,* flows 7.5 miles to Middle Fork Cosumnes River 8 miles south of Camino (lat. 38°37'35" N, long. 120°42' W; at S line sec. 18, T 9 N, R 12 E). Named on Aukum (1952) and Omo Ranch (1952) 7.5' quadrangles.

Perry Creek [SIERRA]: *stream,* flows less than 0.25 mile to Sierra Valley 1.25 miles south of Sierraville (lat. 39°34'20" N, long. 120° 22' W; sec. 24, T 20 N, R 14 E). Named on Sattley (1981) and Sierraville (1981) 7.5' quadrangles.

Perry Mountain [EL DORADO]: *peak,* 1.5 miles north of Coloma (lat. 38°49'15" N, long. 120°53'20" W; sec. 8, T 11 N, R 10 E). Named on Coloma (1949) 7.5' quadrangle.

Perry Mountain Creek [EL DORADO]: *stream,* flows 1.5 miles to Indian Creek (1) 1.5 miles north-northwest of Coloma (lat. 38° 49'20" N, long. 120°54'15" W; sec. 7, T 11 N, R 10 E); the stream is west of Perry Mountain. Named on Coloma (1949) 7.5' quadrangle.

Peru: see **Garden Valley** [EL DORADO].

Peruvian Gulch [CALAVERAS]: *canyon,* drained by a stream that flows less than 1 mile to Coyote Creek nearly 3 miles south of Vallecito (lat. 38°02'50" N, long. 120°29' W; sec. 7, T 2 N, R 14 E). Named on Columbia (1948) 7.5' quadrangle.

Peter Grubb Hut [NEVADA]: *locality,* 4 miles north-northwest of Donner Pass in Round Valley (2) (lat. 39°22'05" N, long. 120° 22' W; sec. 2, T 17 N, R 14 E). Named on Norden (1955) 7.5' quadrangle.

Petersburg: see **San Andreas** [CALAVERAS].

Petersen [TUOLUMNE]: *locality,* 3.25 miles east of Columbia (lat. 38°02'30" N, long. 120°20'30" W). Named on Big Trees (1891) 30' quadrangle.

Peterson Creek [MADERA-MARIPOSA]: *stream,* heads in Mariposa County and flows 4.5 miles to Carter Creek 4.5 miles west of Yosemite Forks in Madera County (lat. 37°22'10" N, long. 119°42'40" W; sec. 31, T 6 S, R 21 E). Named on Bass Lake (1953) 15' quadrangle.

Petes Pond [MARIPOSA]: *lake,* 800 feet long, 3 miles south of Santa Cruz Mountain (lat. 37°24'45" N, long. 120°12'20" W; sec. 15, T 6 S, R 16 E). Named on Indian Gulch (1962) 7.5' quadrangle.

Pet Hill: see **Mooney Flat** [NEVADA].

Pettit Peak [TUOLUMNE]: *peak,* 13 miles west-northwest of Tioga Pass (lat. 37°59'10" N, long. 119°28'45" W). Altitude 10,788 feet. Named on Tuolumne Meadows (1956) 15' quadrangle. United States Board on Geographic Names (1934, p. 19) rejected the form "Petit Peak" for the name; Colonel W.W. Forsyth named the feature for James Seymour Pettit.

Petty Reservoir: see **Lake Tabeaud** [AMADOR]; **Stanislaus** [TUOLUMNE].

Phelps Hill: see **Washington** [NEVADA].

Phelps Point: see **Washington** [NEVADA].

Philadelphia: see **New Philadelphia**, under **Bunker Hill** [AMADOR] (2).

Philadelphia Bar [EL DORADO]: *locality,* 3.5 miles northwest of Greenwood along Middle Fork American River (lat. 38°56'20" N, long. 120°57' W; on W line sec. 35, T 13 N, R 9 E). Named on Greenwood (1949) 7.5' quadrangle.

Philadelphia Diggings: see **Jupiter** [TUOLUMNE].

Phillips [EL DORADO]: *village,* 2.5 miles west of Echo Summit along South Fork American River (lat. 38°49' N, long. 120°04'40" W; near W line sec. 11, T 11 N, R 17 E). Named on Echo Lake (1955) 7.5' quadrangle. Fallen Leaf Lake (1955) 15' quadrangle shows Vade P.O. at the place. Joseph Wells Davis Phillips brought cattle to the site in 1859 and built a hotel there in 1863 (Yohalem, p. 162). Postal authorities established Vade post office at the place in 1912 and discontinued it in 1961 (Salley, p. 228); the post office name was for Phillips' daughter, Sierra Nevada Phillips, who had the nickname "Vade" (Yohalem, p. 164-165).

Phillip's Flat: see **Hornitos** [MARIPOSA].

Phipps Creek [EL DORADO]: *stream,* flows 3.5 miles to Rubicon River 3 miles west-northwest of Phipps Peak in Rockbound Valley (lat. 38°57'55" N, long. 120°12'10" W; near W line sec. 22, T 13 N, R 16 E); the stream heads at Phipps Lake. Named on Rockbound Valley (1955) 7.5' quadrangle.

Phipps Lake [EL DORADO]: *lake,* 900 feet long, 0.5 mile north-northeast of Phipps Peak (lat. 38°57'40" N, long. 120°08'45" W; sec. 19, T 13 N, R 17 E). Named on Rockbound Valley (1955) 7.5' quadrangle.

Phipps Pass [EL DORADO]: *pass,* 0.5 mile east-northeast of Phipps Peak (lat. 38°57'30" N, long. 120°08'25" W; sec. 19, T 13 N, R 17 E). Named on Rockbound Valley (1955) 7.5' quadrangle.

Phipps Peak [EL DORADO]: *peak,* 7.5 miles north of Pyramid Peak (lat. 38°57'15" N, long. 120°08'55" W; at W line sec. 19, T 13 N, R 17 E). Named on Rockbound Valley (1955) 7.5' quadrangle. Altitude 9234 feet. The name commemorates General William Phipps, who came to Georgetown in 1854 (Gudde, 1949, p. 260).

Phoenix: see **Del Puerto Canyon** [MARIPOSA].

Phoenix Lake [NEVADA]: *lake,* 1500 feet long, 5 miles south-southeast of English Mountain (lat. 39°22'35" N, long. 120°31'15" W; on S line sec. 33, T 18 N, R 13 E). Named on Cisco Grove (1955) and English Mountain (1983) 7.5' quadrangles.

Phoenix Reservoir [TUOLUMNE]: *lake,* behind a dam on Sullivan Creek 3.25 miles east-northeast of Sonora (lat. 37°59'55" N, long. 120°19'35" W; sec. 28, T 2 N, R 15 E). Named on Columbia SE (1948) and Standard (1948) 7.5' quadrangles.

Picayune Creek [MADERA]: *stream,* flows 4.5 miles to Coarse Gold Creek 6.5 miles north of O'Neals (lat. 37°13'10" N, long. 119°42'35" W; sec. 19, T 8 S, R 21 E). Named on O'Neals (1965) 7.5' quadrangle.

Picayune Valley [PLACER]: *valley,* 2.5 miles south-southwest of Granite Chief (lat. 39°09'45" N, long. 120°18'40" W; at W line sec. 9, T 15 N, R 15 E). Named on Granite Chief (1953) 7.5' quadrangle.

Pickering Bar [PLACER]: *locality,* 4 miles south of Dutch Flat along North Fork American River (lat. 39°08'50" N, long. 120°50'30" W; sec. 15, T 15 N, R 10 E). Named on Dutch Flat (1950) 7.5' quadrangle.

Picture Gallery Gulch [MARIPOSA]: *canyon,* drained by a stream that flows 1.5 miles to Lake McClure 3.25 miles southwest of Coulterville (lat. 37°40'50" N, long. 120°14'20" W; near E line sec. 18, T 3 S, R 16 E). Named on Coulterville (1947, photorevised 1973) and Penon Blanco Peak (1962) 7.5' quadrangles.

Pierce Meadow [NEVADA]: *area,* 2.5 miles north-northeast of Yuba Gap (lat. 39°30'55" N, long. 120°35'35" W; at S line sec. 11, T 17 N, R 12 E). Named on Cisco Grove (1955) 7.5' quadrangle.

Pierces Bar: see **Ramshorn Creek** [SIERRA].

Pietra Blanca: see **Springfield** [TUOLUMNE].

Pig Canyon [SIERRA]: *canyon,* drained by a stream that flows 2.25 miles to Hog Canyon 6 miles west-northwest of Sierra City (lat. 39°35'45" N, long. 120°44'20" W; sec. 16, T 20 N, R 11 E). Named on Sierra City (1981) 7.5' quadrangle.

Pigeon Creek [AMADOR]: *stream,* flows 6 miles to Big Indian Creek 5.5 miles west-northwest of Fiddletown near Enterprise (lat. 38°32'35" N, long. 120°50'50" W; sec. 14, T 8 N, R 10 E). Named on Fiddletown (1949) 7.5' quadrangle.

Pigeon Creek Fall: see **Ribbon Fall** [MARIPOSA].

Pigeon Flat [MARIPOSA]: *area,* 4 miles east of Jawbone Ridge (lat. 37°48'10" N, long. 120°01'25" W; near SW cor. sec. 32, T 1 S, R 18 E). Named on Jawbone Ridge (1947) 7.5' quadrangle.

Pigeon Flat [TUOLUMNE]: *area,* 1.5 miles east of Dardanelle along Middle Fork Stanislaus River (lat. 38°20'20" N, long. 119°48'20" W).

Named on Dardanelle (1979) 7.5' quadrangle. Dardanelles Cone (1956) 15' quadrangle shows Pigeon Flat Campground at the place.

Pigeon Flat Campground: see **Pigeon Flat** [TUOLUMNE].

Pigeon Gulch [MARIPOSA]: *canyon,* drained by a stream that flows nearly 1 mile to the canyon of Merced River 1.5 miles west-southwest of El Portal (lat. 37°39'55" N, long. 119°48'20" W; sec. 19, T 3 S, R 20 E). Named on El Portal (1947) 7.5' quadrangle.

Pigeon Gulch [TUOLUMNE]: *canyon,* drained by a stream that flows nearly 1 mile to Woods Creek 1.25 miles east-southeast of Columbia (lat. 38°01'30" N, long. 120°22'50" W; sec. 13, T 2 N, R 14 E). Named on Columbia SE (1948) 7.5' quadrangle.

Pigeon Roost Canyon [PLACER]: *canyon,* drained by a stream that flows 1.5 miles to Rubicon River 3 miles southwest of Devil Peak (lat. 38°55'50" N, long. 120°35'10" W; sec. 36, T 13 N, R 12 E). Named on Devil Peak (1950) 7.5' quadrangle.

Pike [SIERRA]: *locality,* 8.5 miles west-southwest of Alleghany (lat. 39°26'20" N, long. 120°59'50" W; near W line sec. 8, T 18 N, R 9 E). Named on Pike (1949) 7.5' quadrangle. Postal authorities established Pike City post office in 1877, changed the name to Pike in 1895, discontinued it in 1901, reestablished it in 1902, and discontinued it in 1954; the named is for Pike County, Missouri (Salley, p. 171). Camptonville (1948) 7.5' quadrangle shows Pike P.O. located 0.5 mile northwest of Pike at Godfrey ranch.

Pike City: see **Pike** [SIERRA].

Pike Mountain: see **Vandervere Mountain** [NEVADA].

Pikes Peak [TUOLUMNE]: *peak,* 9 miles southwest of Dardanelle (lat. 38°15'40" N, long. 119°58'05" W; sec. 26, T 5 N, R 18 E). Altitude 7235 feet. Named on Donnell Lake (1979) 7.5' quadrangle.

Pile Creek: see **Jawbone Creek** [TUOLUMNE].

Pilliken [EL DORADO]: *locality,* 5.5 miles northwest of Leek Spring Hill (lat. 38°41'10" N, long. 120°21'10" W; sec. 30, T 10 N, R 15 E). Named on Leek Spring Hill (1951) 15' quadrangle.

Pilot Creek [EL DORADO]:
(1) *stream,* flows 18 miles to Rubicon River 15 miles north-northwest of Pollock Pines (lat. 38°58'15" N, long. 120°40'55" W; near S line sec. 18, T 13 N, R 12 E). Named on Devil Peak (1950), Robbs Peak (1950), and Tunnel Hill (1947) 7.5' quadrangles.
(2) *stream,* flows 3.5 miles to North Fork American River 2.5 miles west-northwest of the village of Pilot Hill (lat. 38°50'40" N, long. 121°03'35" W; sec. 35, T 12 N, R 8 E); the stream heads near Pilot Hill (1). Named on Pilot Hill (1954) 7.5' quadrangle.

Pilot Hill [EL DORADO]:

(1) *peak,* 1.5 miles southwest of the village of Pilot Hill (lat. 38°49'05" N, long. 121°01'45" W; sec. 12, T 11 N, R 8 E). Altitude 1869 feet. Named on Pilot Hill (1954) 7.5' quadrangle.
(2) *village,* 13 miles west-northwest of Placerville (lat. 38°50'05" N, long. 121°00'50" W; sec. 6, T 11 N, R 9 E); the village is 1.5 miles northeast of Pilot Hill (1). Named on Pilot Hill (1954) 7.5' quadrangle. Mining began near the place in 1849 and mining camps called Pilot Hill, Centerville, and Pittsfield developed near one another there; the three camps soon consolidated under the name "Centerville," a designation that persisted even after the post office at the place received the name "Pilot Hill" (Hoover, Rensch, and Rensch, p. 85). Postal authorities established Pilot Hill post office in 1854 (Frickstad, p. 28). Whitney (1880, p. 85) mentioned a place called Powningford that was located 3 or 4 miles east-northeast of Pilot Hill.

Pilot Hill: see **Pilot Peak** [NEVADA].

Pilot Peak [MARIPOSA]: *peak,* 4.5 miles southwest of Fish Camp (lat. 37°26'15" N, long. 119°42' W; sec. 5, T 6 S, R 21 E). Altitude 5246 feet. Named on Bass Lake (1953) 15' quadrangle.

Pilot Peak [MARIPOSA-TUOLUMNE]: *peak,* 10.5 miles northwest of El Portal on Mariposa-Tuolumne county line (lat. 37°45'45" N, long. 119°56'05" W; sec. 13, T 2 S, R 18 E); the peak is on Pilot Ridge. Altitude 6004 feet. Named on Lake Eleanor (1956) 15' quadrangle.

Pilot Peak [NEVADA]: *peak,* 7.25 miles west-southwest of Grass Valley (lat. 39°10'05" N, long. 121°10'55" W; sec. 10, T 15 N, R 7 E); the peak is 1 mile southeast of Indian Springs. Altitude 2239 feet. Named on Rough and Ready (1949) 7.5' quadrangle. Called Indian Springs Hill on Smartsville (1895) 30' quadrangle, and called Pilot Hill on Hobson's (1890a) map.

Pilot Ridge [MARIPOSA-TUOLUMNE]: *ridge,* northwest-trending, 9 miles long, 13 miles northwest of El Portal on Mariposa-Tuolumne county line (lat. 37°47' N, long. 119°58' W); Pilot Peak is on the ridge. Named on Lake Eleanor (1956) and Tuolumne (1948) 15' quadrangles.

Pinchem Creek [EL DORADO]: *stream,* flows nearly 2 miles to Weber Creek 5.25 miles southwest of Coloma (lat. 38°45'25" N, long. 120°58'15" W; near SE cor. sec. 33, T 11 N, R 9 E). Named on Coloma (1949) and Shingle Springs (1949) 7.5' quadrangles. The name recalls an early mining camp called Pinchemtight; the name of the camp supposedly originated from the exclamation "Pinch 'em tight!" made by miners to a storekeeper who measured gold dust by gathering some between his fingers (Hoover, Rensch, and Rensch, p. 85).

Pinchemtight: see **Pinchem Creek** [EL DORADO].

Pinecrest [NEVADA]: *locality,* 1 mile north of Chicago Park along Nevada County Narrow Gauge Railroad (lat. 39°09'40" N, long. 120°58' W; near S line sec. 9, T 15 N, R 9 E). Named on Colfax (1938) 30' quadrangle.

Pinecrest [TUOLUMNE]: *settlement,* 21 miles west-southwest of Sonora Pass (lat. 38°11'30" N, long. 119°59'45" W). Named on Pinecrest (1979) and Strawberry (1979) 7.5' quadrangles. Postal authorities established Pinecrest post office in 1917, discontinued it in 1921, and reestablished it in 1923 (Frickstad, p. 216).

Pinecrest Camp [EL DORADO]: *locality,* 4 miles west of Echo Summit along Tamarack Creek (lat. 38°48'35" N, long. 120°06'15" W; near S line sec. 9, T 11 N, R 17 E). Named on Echo Lake (1955) 7.5' quadrangle.

Pinecrest Lake [TUOLUMNE]: *lake,* behind a dam on South Fork Stanislaus River 0.5 mile northeast of Pinecrest (lat. 38°12' N, long. 119°59'15" W). Named on Pinecrest (1979) 7.5' quadrangle. Called Edna Lake on Dardanelles (1898, reprinted 1947) 30' quadrangle, and called Strawberry Lake on California Division of Highways' (1934) map, but United States Board on Geographic Names (1959b, p. 7) rejected the names "Edna Lake," "Edna Lake Reservoir," and "Strawberry Lake" for the feature. R.B. Marshall of United States Geological Survey gave the name "Edna Lake" to honor Edna Bowman, later Mrs. Charles J. Kuhn (Hanna, p. 95). California Division of Highways' (1934) map shows a lake called Big Dam Reservoir located 5.25 miles east-northeast of Strawberry Lake (present Pinecrest Lake) along South Fork Stanislaus River, where current maps show no lake.

Pinecrest Peak [TUOLUMNE]: *ridge,* southwest-trending, 1.5 miles long, 4.5 miles east-northeast of Pinecrest (lat. 38°13'45" N, long. 119°55'20" W). Named on Pinecrest (1979) 7.5' quadrangle.

Pinecroft [PLACER]: *locality,* 2 miles southwest of Colfax (lat. 39° 04'55" N, long. 120°58'35" W; sec. 9, T 14 N, R 9 E). Named on Colfax (1949) 7.5' quadrangle.

Pine Crossing: see **Pine Log** [TUOLUMNE].

Pine Flat [MADERA]: *area,* 9.5 miles southwest of Devils Postpile along San Joaquin River (lat. 37°30'50" N, long. 119°11'25" W; near NW cor. sec. 12, T 5 S, R 25 E). Named on Devils Postpile (1953) 15' quadrangle.

Pine Grove [AMADOR]: *village,* 7.5 miles northeast of Jackson (lat. 38°24'50" N, long. 120°39'30" W; sec. 33, T 7 N, R 12 E). Named on Pine Grove (1948) 7.5' quadrangle. Postal authorities established Pine Grove post office in 1856 (Frickstad, p. 6). Camp's (1962) map shows a place called Irish Town located 1.5 miles south-southwest of Pine Grove, and a place called Armstrong's Mill situated 1 mile southwest of Pine Grove. Postal authorities established Wieland post office 1.5 miles southwest of Pine Grove in 1892 and discontinued it in 1893; they established Defender post office 5 miles northeast of Pine Grove at Defender mine in 1900 and discontinued it in 1915 (Salley, p. 56, 240).

Pine Grove: see **Kings Beach** [PLACER]; **Loomis** [PLACER].

Pine Grove Creek [SIERRA]: *stream,* flows 1 mile to East Branch Slate Creek 3.25 miles west of Mount Fillmore (lat. 39°43'10" N, long. 120°54'35" W; near SW cor. sec. 31, T 22 N, R 10 E). Named on La Porte (1951) 7.5' quadrangle.

Pine Grove Reservoir [NEVADA]: *lake,* behind a dam on Little Shady Creek 2 miles east-northeast of French Corral (lat. 39°19'05" N, long. 121°07'40" W; sec. 19, T 17 N, R 8 E). Named on French Corral (1948, photorevised 1969) and Nevada City (1948) 7.5' quadrangles.

Pine Hill [EL DORADO]: *peak,* 5 miles northwest of Shingle Springs (lat. 38°43'10" N, long. 120°59'20" W; sec. 16, T 10 N, R 9 E). Altitude 2059 feet. Named on Shingle Springs (1949) 7.5' quadrangle. Logan's (1938) map has the form "Pinehill" for the name.

Pine Hill [NEVADA]:
(1) *peak,* 7 miles south-southwest of Grass Valley (lat. 39°07'50" N, long. 121°07'15" W; at SW cor. sec. 20, T 15 N, R 8 E). Altitude 2134 feet. Named on Grass Valley (1949) 7.5' quadrangle.
(2) *peak,* less than 1 mile north of Wolf (lat. 39°04'20" N, long. 120°08'25" W; on N line sec. 13, T 14 N, R 7 E). Named on Wolf (1949) 7.5' quadrangle.

Pine Log [TUOLUMNE]: *locality,* 2.5 miles north-northeast of Columbia along South Fork Stanislaus River (lat. 38°04'10" N, long. 120°23'15" W; sec. 36, T 3 N, R 14 E). Named on Columbia (1948) 7.5' quadrangle. The place also was called Paso Del Pino, Pine Crossing, and Pine Log Crossing (Todd *in* Wayman, p. 93). Gudde (1975, p. 189) listed a mining camp of the 1850's called La Commodedad that was located 5 miles northeast of Pine Log Crossing.

Pine Log Crossing: see **Pine Log** [TUOLUMNE].

Pine Mountain Lake [TUOLUMNE]: *lake,* 1.25 miles long, behind a dam on Big Creek 2 miles northeast of Groveland (lat. 37°51'25" N, long. 120°12' W; sec. 15, T 1 S, R 16 E). Named on Groveland (1947, photorevised 1973) 7.5' quadrangle.

Pine Nut Canyon [PLACER]: *canyon,* drained by a stream that flows less than 1 mile to Duncan Canyon 6 miles south of Duncan Peak (lat. 39°04'10" N, long. 120°32' W; at N line sec. 16, T 14 N, R 13 E). Named on Greek Store (1952) 7.5' quadrangle.

Pine Peak [CALAVERAS]: *peak,* 4 miles northnorthwest of San Andreas (lat. 38°14'55" N,

long. 120°42'40" W; sec. 36, T 5 N, R 11 E). Altitude 1402 feet. Named on San Andreas (1962) 7.5' quadrangle.

Pine Point Campground [MADERA]: *locality,* 6.5 miles southeast of Yosemite Forks on the southwest side of Bass Lake (1) (lat. 37° 18'20" N, long. 119°32'25" W; sec. 23, T 7 S, R 22 E). Named on Bass Lake (1953) 15' quadrangle.

Pine Ridge [CALAVERAS]: *ridge,* west-trending, 2 miles long, 5.5 miles west-southwest of Blue Mountain (lat. 38°18'35" N, long. 120°27'45" W). Named on Fort Mountain (1979) 7.5' quadrangle.

Pines: see **The Pines** [MADERA].

Pines Creek [MADERA]: *stream,* flows nearly 2 miles to Bass Lake (1) 5.5 miles southeast of Yosemite Forks (lat. 37°19'20" N, long. 119°32'45" W; near E line sec. 15, T 7 S, R 22 E). Named on Bass Lake (1953) 15' quadrangle.

Pine Slope Campground [MADERA]: *locality,* nearly 5 miles southeast of Yosemite Forks on the west side of Bass Lake (1) (lat. 37°18'55" N, long. 119°34'20" W; near S line sec. 16, T 7 S, R 22 E). Named on Bass Lake (1953) 15' quadrangle.

Pine Tree Reservoir: see **Grass Valley** [NEVADA].

Pine Tree Spring [PLACER]: *spring,* 3.5 miles northwest of Devil Peak (lat. 38°59'30" N, long. 120°36' W; sec. 11, T 13 N, R 12 E). Named on Devil Peak (1950) 7.5' quadrangle.

Pine Valley [TUOLUMNE]: *canyon,* nearly 1 mile long, 6.5 miles east-southeast of Pinecrest along Lily Creek (3) (lat. 38°09'25" N, long. 119°53'15" W; sec. 33, 34, T 4 N, R 19 E). Named on Pinecrest (1979) 7.5' quadrangle.

Piney Creek [MARIPOSA]: *stream,* flows 5 miles to Lake McClure 4.25 miles southwest of Penon Blanco Peak (lat. 37°41'25" N, long. 120°19' W; sec. 9, T 3 S, R 15 E); the stream is east of Piney Ridge. Named on Penon Blanco Peak (1962, photorevised 1973) 7.5' quadrangle. East Fork enters near the mouth of the main stream; it is 5.5 miles long and is named on Penon Blanco Peak (1962, photorevised 1973) 7.5' quadrangle.

Piney Ridge [MARIPOSA-TUOLUMNE]: *ridge,* south-southeast-trending, 4 miles long, 4.5 miles southwest of Penon Blanco Peak on Mariposa-Tuolumne county line (lat. 37°40'45" N, long. 120° 18'50" W); the ridge is west of Piney Creek. Named on Penon Blanco Peak (1962) 7.5' quadrangle.

Pingree Lake [TUOLUMNE]: *lake,* 1800 feet long, 11.5 miles east-southeast of Pinecrest (lat. 38°08'05" N, long. 119°47'55" W). Named on Pinecrest (1956) 15' quadrangle.

Pinnacles: see **The Pinnacles** [PLACER].

Pino: see **Loomis** [PLACER]; **Old Pino** [EL DORADO].

Pinoche Peak [MARIPOSA]: *peak,* 3 miles south of El Portal (lat. 37° 38'05" N, long.

119°46'30" W; near NW cor. sec. 33, T 3 S, R 20 E); the peak is on Pinoche Ridge. Altitude 5765 feet. Named on El Portal (1947) 7.5' quadrangle.

Pinoche Ridge [MARIPOSA]: *ridge,* mainly west-northwest-trending, 5 miles long, 3 miles south-southwest of El Portal (lat. 37°38'10" N, long. 119°48'W); Pinoche Peak is on the ridge. Named on El Portal (1947) 7.5' quadrangle.

Pino Grande [EL DORADO]: *locality,* 8 miles north-northwest of Pollock Pines (lat. 38°52'10" N, long. 120°37'35" W; sec. 22, T 12 N, R 12 E). Named on Saddle Mountain (1950) 15' quadrangle. Called Pinogrande on California Mining Bureau's (1909a) map. Postal authorities established Pino Grande post office in 1892, moved it 5.5 miles south in 1893, discontinued it in 1899, reestablished it in 1902, and discontinued it in 1909 (Salley, p. 172).

Pinoli Peak [NEVADA]: *peak,* 6 miles northeast of Graniteville (lat. 39°29'25" N, long. 120°38'55" W; near N line sec. 29, T 19 N, R 12 E); the peak is at the west end of Pinoli Ridge. Altitude 7297 feet. Named on Graniteville (1982) 7.5' quadrangle.

Pinoli Ridge [NEVADA]: *ridge,* extends for 2.5 miles east-northeast and east from Pinole Peak; center 7 miles east-northeast of Graniteville (lat. 39°29'40" N, long. 120°37'35" W). Named on English Mountain (1983) and Graniteville (1982) 7.5' quadrangles.

Pinto Lakes [TUOLUMNE]: *lakes,* two, largest 700 feet long, 13 miles east of Pinecrest (lat. 38°12'25" N, long. 119°45'10" W). Named on Pinecrest (1956) 15' quadrangle.

Pioneer [AMADOR]: *village,* 5 miles east-northeast of Pine Grove (lat. 38°25'55" N, long. 120°34'20" W; sec. 29, T 7 N, R 13 E). Named on West Point (1948) 7.5' quadrangle. The place is called Pioneer Station on Mokelumne Hill (1948) 15' quadrangle. Postal authorities established Pioneer post office in 1947 (Frickstad, p. 6). Camp's (1962) map shows a place called Camp Contreras located less than 1 mile south of Pioneer; the name honored Pablo Contreras, the most influential citizen of the place (Sargent, Mrs. J.L., p. 46).

Pioneer Campground [SIERRA]: *locality,* 6 miles northeast of Sierra City along North Yuba River (lat. 39°37'50" N, long. 120° 33'40" W; near N line sec. 6, T 20 N, R 13 E). Named on Clio (1981) 7.5' quadrangle. Sierra City (1955) 15' quadrangle has the name "Pioneer Lodge" near the site of the campground.

Pioneer Creek [AMADOR]: *stream,* flows about 5.5 miles to Sutter Creek (1) 3 miles northeast of Pine Grove (lat. 38°26'35" N; long. 120°37'20" W; sec. 23, T 7 N, R 12 E). Named on West Point (1948) 7.5' quadrangle.

Pioneer Lodge: see **Pioneer Campground** [SIERRA].

Pioneer Station: see **Pioneer** [AMADOR].

Pipe Creek [SIERRA]: *stream,* flows 2 miles to Canyon Creek 6 miles northwest of Goodyears Bar (lat. 39°36'35" N, long. 120° 57' W; sec. 10, T 20 N, R 9 E). Named on Goodyears Bar (1951) 7.5' quadrangle.

Piper Creek [NEVADA]: *stream,* flows 2 miles to Harry L. Englebright Lake (present Englebright Lake) 5 miles west-southwest of French Corral (lat. 39°16'45" N, long. 121°14'50" W; sec. 1, T 16 N, R 6 E); the stream heads at Piper Hill. Named on French Corral (1948) 7.5' quadrangle.

Piper Hill [NEVADA]: *peak,* 4.5 miles southwest of French Corral (lat. 39°15'40" N, long. 121°13'10" W; sec. 8, T 16 N, R 7 E). Named on French Corral (1948) 7.5' quadrangle.

Pi-Pi Creek [EL DORADO]: *stream,* flows 2.5 miles to Middle Fork Cosumnes River nearly 3 miles south of Caldor in Pi-Pi Valley (lat. 38°33'55" N, long. 120°25'50" W; near N line sec. 9, T 8 N, R 14 E). Named on Caldor (1951) 7.5' quadrangle.

Pi-Pi Valley [EL DORADO]: *valley,* 2.5 miles south of Caldor along Middle Fork Cosumnes River (lat. 38°34' N, long. 120°26' W; on S line sec. 4, T 8 N, R 14 E). Named on Caldor (1951) 7.5' quadrangle. Called Pi Pi Valley (without the hyphen) on Pyramid Peak (1896) 30' quadrangle.

Pitt Lake [EL DORADO]: *lake,* 400 feet long, 5.25 miles west-northwest of Echo Summit (lat. 38°50'10" N, long. 120°07'30" W). Named on Echo Lake (1955) and Pyramid Peak (1955) 7.5' quadrangles.

Pittsburg: see **Grass Valley** [NEVADA].

Pittsfield: see **Pilot Hill** [EL DORADO] (2).

Piute Creek [TUOLUMNE]:

(1) *stream,* flows 5 miles to West Fork Cherry Creek 9 miles east-southeast of Pinecrest (lat. 38°07'55" N, long. 119°51' W); the stream goes through Piute Meadow. Named on Pinecrest (1956) 15' quadrangle. Bill Woods, who named Piute Meadow, named the stream for Piute Indians who fished there (Browning, 1986, p. 171).

(2) *stream,* flows 20 miles to Tuolumne River 5 miles northeast of White Wolf in Pate Valley (lat. 37°55'50" N, long. 119°36' W). Named on Hetch Hetchy Reservoir (1956), Matterhorn Peak (1956), and Tower Peak (1956) 15' quadrangles.

Piute Lake [TUOLUMNE]: *lake,* 550 feet long, 10 miles east of Pinecrest (lat. 38°09'45" N, long. 119°48'35" W); the lake is 1.25 miles east of Piute Meadow. Named on Pinecrest (1956) 15' quadrangle. The name is from a Piute Indian that Bill Woods killed during a fight and then sank in the lake (Browning, 1986, p. 171-172).

Piute Meadow [TUOLUMNE]: *area,* 9 miles east-southeast of Pinecrest (lat. 38°09'45" N, long. 119°50' W; sec. 36, T 4 N, R 19 E); the area is along Piute Creek (1). Named on Pinecrest (1956) 15' quadrangle. Bill Woods named the place for Piute Indians that came there from Nevada to hunt and fish (Browning, 1986, p. 171).

Piute Mountain [TUOLUMNE]: *peak,* 7.5 miles south of Tower Peak (lat. 38°02' N, long. 119°32'50" W); the peak is northwest of Piute Creek (2). Altitude 10,541 feet. Named on Tower Peak (1956) 15' quadrangle.

Placer: see **Loomis** [PLACER].

Placerville [EL DORADO]: *town,* near the center of the west half of El Dorado County (lat. 38°43'45" N, long. 120°47'55" W; around SE cor. sec. 7, T 10 N, R 11 E). Named on Placerville (1949) 7.5' quadrangle. Postal authorities established Placerville post office in 1850 (Frickstad, p. 28), and the town incorporated in 1854. In 1848 prospectors found gold at the place, which became known as Old Dry Diggings; after the hanging of three robbers there, the community bore the nickname "Hangtown," but officially it became Placerville in 1850 (Bancroft, 1888, p. 468). The place also was called simply Dry Diggings; the name "Placerville" recalls placer mining carried on in the streets of the town (Gudde, 1975, p. 270). Whitney's (1880) map shows a feature called Hangtown Hill situated just south of Placerville between the town and Coon Hollow. Bancroft's (1864) map shows a place called Sportsmans Hall located east of Placerville along the road to the State of Nevada. Postal authorities established Sportsmans Hall post office 11 miles east of Placerville in 1865 and discontinued it in 1867; the post office name was from a building used for the entertainment of stage and freight drivers who stopped there (Salley, p. 210). Postal authorities established Zodoc post office 5 miles south of Placerville in 1887 and discontinued it in 1888 (Salley, p. 246). Borthwick (p. 125, 166) in 1857 mentioned a mining camp called Middletown that was located 2 or 3 miles from Hangtown (present Placerville) on the road to Cold Springs. An early-day stopping place called Missouri House was situated 12 miles below Placerville (Paden, p. 456).

Plains: see **Tillman** [MADERA].

Plasse [AMADOR]: *locality,* 7 miles north-northwest of Mokelumne Peak near Silver Lake (lat. 38°38'25" N, long. 120°07'40" W; sec. 8, T 9 N, R 17 E); Silver Lake post office is at the place. Both Silver Lake post office and Plasse are named on Tragedy Spring (1979) 7.5' quadrangle. Pyramid Peak (1896) 30' quadrangle has the form "Plassé" for the name. Postal authorities established Silver Lake post office in 1880, discontinued it in 1890, reestablished it in 1936, and discontinued it in 1973 (Salley, p. 205).

Plasse Trading Post [AMADOR]: *locality,* 5.25 miles north of Mokelumne Peak (lat. 38°36'50" N, long. 120°05'25" W; near W line

sec. 22, T 9 N, R 17 E). Site named on Mokelumne Peak (1979) 7.5' quadrangle. Raymond Plasse started the place (Sargent, Mrs. J.L., p. 13).

Pleasant: see **Mount Pleasant** [EL DORADO]; **Mount Pleasant** [SIERRA]; **Mount Pleasant**, under **Taylor Hill** [TUOLUMNE].

Pleasant Flat: see **Coloma** [EL DORADO]; **Newtown** [NEVADA].

Pleasant Grove Creek [PLACER]: *stream,* heads in Placer County and flows 10 miles to end in Sutter County nearly 6 miles east of Verona in American Basin (lat. 38°47'50" N, long. 121°30'30" W; sec. 15, T 11 N, R 4 E); the stream passes 1 mile south of Pleasant Grove in Sutter County (1). Named on Pleasant Grove (1967), Rocklin (1967), Roseville (1967), and Verona (1967) 7.5' quadrangles. South Branch enters from the southeast 5 miles northwest of Roseville; it is 6.5 miles long and is named on Roseville (1967) 7.5' quadrangle.

Pleasant Lake [EL DORADO]: *lake,* 2.5 miles east of Wentworth Springs (lat. 39°00'35" N, long. 120°17'40" W). Named on Granite Chief (1953) 15' quadrangle, where it is connected to Loon Lake. Wentworth Springs (1953, photorevised 1973) 7.5' quadrangle shows a larger lake with a wider connection to Loon Lake.

Pleasant Lake: see **Loon Lake** [EL DORADO].

Pleasant Point [NEVADA]: *peak,* 3.5 miles west of Washington (lat. 39°21'15" N, long. 120°52'10" W; at E line sec. 8, T 17 N, R 10 E). Named on Washington (1950) 7.5' quadrangle.

Pleasant Springs: see **Rich Gulch** [CALAVERAS] (5).

Pleasant Valley [EL DORADO]:

(1) *valley,* 8 miles east-southeast of Placerville (lat. 38°41' N, long. 120°40' W). Named on Placerville (1893) 30' quadrangle. Mormon men on their way across the Sierra Nevada to Salt Lake City in 1848 camped in the valley and named it (Hoover, Rensch, and Rensch, p. 83).

(2) *settlement,* 3.5 miles south of Camino (lat. 38°41' N, long. 120° 39'45" W; near SW cor. sec. 28, T 10 N, R 12 E); the place is near the south end of Pleasant Valley (1). Named on Camino (1952) 7.5' quadrangle. Postal authorities established Pleasant Valley post office in 1864 and discontinued it in 1917 (Frickstad, p. 28). They established Urban post office 5 miles southwest of Pleasant Valley post office in 1909 and discontinued it in 1912; the name was for Eva L. Urban, first postmaster (Salley, p. 228).

Pleasant Valley [MARIPOSA]:

(1) *canyon,* 5 miles long, along Merced River above a point 9.5 miles south-southwest of Coulterville (lat. 37°35'15" N, long. 120°16' W). Named on Sonora (1891) 30' quadrangle. Water of Lake McClure now floods the can-

yon. Postal authorities established Pleasant Valley post office on the bank of Merced River 12 miles northeast of La Grange in 1855 and discontinued it in 1856 (Salley, p. 174).

(2) *village,* 6.5 miles southwest of Coulterville along Yosemite Valley Railroad (lat. 37°39' N, long. 120°17'25" W); the village is near the north end of Pleasant Valley (1). Named on Sonora (1897) 30' quadrangle.

Pleasant Valley [NEVADA]: *valley,* 4 miles south-southwest of French Corral (lat. 39°15'30" N, long. 121°11'50" W; at and near sec. 9, T 16 N, R 7 E). Named on French Corral (1948) 7.5' quadrangle.

Pleasant Valley [TUOLUMNE]: *area,* about 9 miles north-northeast of White Wolf along Piute Creek (2) (lat. 37°59'10" N, long. 119°34'15" W). Named on Hetch Hetchy Reservoir (1956) 15' quadrangle. Members of the Bright family named the place and ran stock there before creation of Yosemite National Park (Browning, 1988, p. 109).

Pleasant Valley: see **Wheats** [CALAVERAS].

Pleasant View [SIERRA]: *locality,* 2 miles north-northeast of Pike (lat. 39°28' N, long. 120°58'50" W; near SW cor. sec. 33, T 19 N, R 9 E). Named on Pike (1949) 7.5' quadrangle.

Pliocene Ridge [SIERRA]: *ridge,* generally southwest-trending, 8 miles long, center 1 mile northwest of Alleghany (lat. 39°29' N, long. 120°51' W). Named on Alleghany (1949), Downieville (1951), and Pike (1949) 7.5' quadrangles.

Plug Point [SIERRA]: *peak,* 5.5 miles south-southwest of Mount Fillmore (lat. 39°39'10" N, long. 120°52'45" W; sec. 20, T 21 N, R 10 E). Altitude 5948 feet. Named on La Porte (1951) 7.5' quadrangle.

Plug Ugly Hill: see **Pug Ugly** [PLACER].

Plumbago [SIERRA]: *locality,* 2 miles southeast of Alleghany (lat. 39°27'10" N, long. 120°49' W; near SE cor. sec. 2, T 18 N, R 10 E). Named on Alleghany (1949) 7.5' quadrangle.

Plumbar Creek [MARIPOSA]: *stream,* flows 4.25 miles to Bear Creek (1) less than 0.5 mile southeast of Midpines (lat. 37°32'20" N, long. 119°54'55" W; sec. 31, T 4 S, R 19 E). Named on Feliciana Mountain (1947) 7.5' quadrangle.

Plum Creek [EL DORADO]:

(1) *stream,* flows 2.25 miles to Pilot Creek (1) 5 miles west of Robbs Peak (lat. 38°54'50" N, long. 120°30' W; sec. 3, T 12 N, R 13 E). Named on Robbs Peak (1950) 7.5' quadrangle.

(2) *stream,* flows 6.5 miles to South Fork American River 0.5 mile east-southeast of Riverton (lat. 38°46'05" N, long. 120°26'25" W; sec. 29, T 11 N, R 14 E). Named on Leek Spring Hill (1951), Riverton (1950), and Stump Spring (1951) 7.5' quadrangles. West Fork enters 1.25 miles north of Old Iron Mountain; it is 1.5 miles long and is named on Stump Spring (1951) 7.5' quadrangle.

Plum Creek Mill [EL DORADO]: *locality,* 3 miles north-northwest of Old Iron Mountain (lat. 38°44'40" N, long. 120°24'55" W; near W line sec. 3, T 10 N, R 14 E); the place is along Plum Creek (2). Site named on Stump Spring (1951) 7.5' quadrangle. A sawmill was at the site (Beverly Cola, personal communication, 1985).

Plum Creek Ridge [EL DORADO]: *ridge,* north-northwest-trending, 5 miles long, center 2 miles north of Old Iron Mountain (lat. 38° 44' N, long. 120°23'10" W); the ridge is northeast of Plum Creek (2). Named on Leek Spring Hill (1951) and Stump Spring (1951) 7.5' quadrangles.

Plum Flat [TUOLUMNE]: *area,* 4.5 miles west-northwest of Mather (lat. 37°54'20" N, long. 119°56'15" W; near SW cor. sec. 30, T 1 N, R 19 E). Named on Lake Eleanor (1956) 15' quadrangle.

Plummer Ridge [EL DORADO]: *ridge,* generally west-trending, 16 miles long, center 3.5 miles northeast of Caldor (lat. 38°38' N, long. 120°22'45" W). Named on Caldor (1951), Leek Spring Hill (1951), Omo Ranch (1952), Peddler Hill (1951), Stump Spring (1951), and Tragedy Spring (1979) 7.5' quadrangles.

Plum Tree Crossing [NEVADA-PLACER]: *locality,* 2.5 miles southwest of Colfax along Bear River on Nevada-Placer county line (lat. 39°04'50" N, long. 120°59'40" W; sec. 8, T 14 N, R 9 E). Named on Colfax (1949) 7.5' quadrangle. On Colfax (1950) 15' quadrangle, the name has the form "Plumtree Crossing."

Plum Valley [SIERRA]:

(1) *area,* 2 miles east-northeast of Pike (lat. 39°26'50" N, long. 120° 57'35" W; at NW cor. sec. 10, T 18 N, R 9 E). Named on Pike (1949) 7.5' quadrangle.

(2) *locality,* 2.25 miles east-northeast of Pike (lat. 39°26'55" N, long. 120°57'10" W); the place is at Plum Valley (1). Named on Colfax (1898) 30' quadrangle. Postal authorities established Plum Valley post office in 1855 and discontinued it in 1877 (Frickstad, p. 184).

Plunkett Creek [EL DORADO]: *stream,* flows nearly 3 miles to Deer Creek (2) 3.5 miles south-southeast of Clarksville (lat. 38°36'25" N, long. 121°01'10" W; near W line sec. 29, T 9 N, R 9 E). Named on Clarksville (1953) and Folsom SE (1954) 7.5' quadrangles.

Pluto Peak: see **Mount Pluto** [PLACER].

Plymouth [AMADOR]: *town,* 10 miles north-northwest of Jackson (lat. 38°28'45" N, long. 120°50'45" W; mainly in sec. 11, T 7 N, R 10 E). Named on Amador City (1962) 7.5' quadrangle. Postal authorities established Plymouth post office in 1871 and named it for the hotel that housed it (Salley, p. 174). The town incorporated in 1917. Camp's (1962) map has the name "Puckerville" as an alternate designation for Plymouth. Gudde (1975, p. 271) mentioned the terms "Pokerville" or "Poker Camp" as other possible names for the community. According to Andrews (p. 109-

110), the name "Pokerville" came when miners who were confined to the town in the winter of 1850 and 1851 played poker to relieve their boredom. Postal authorities established Figtree post office 4 miles northeast of Plymouth in 1917 and discontinued it in 1918; a fig tree was a landmark at the place (Salley, p. 74).

Podesta Camp [EL DORADO]: *locality,* 10.5 miles southwest of Kirkwood (lat. 38°37' N, long. 120°13'30" W; near E line sec. 20, T 9 N, R 16 E). Named on Bear River Reservoir (1979) 7.5' quadrangle.

Pohono: see **Bridalveil Fall** [MARIPOSA].

Pohono Lake: see **Ostrander Lake** [MARIPOSA].

Poho Ridge [EL DORADO]: *ridge,* generally west-trending, 3.25 miles long, center 3.5 miles northwest of Pollock Pines (lat. 38°48'10" N, long. 120°37'30" W). Named on Pollock Pines (1950) and Slate Mountain (1950) 7.5' quadrangles.

Point Defiance [NEVADA]: *relief feature,* 2.5 miles west-southwest of French Corral at the confluence of Yuba River and South Yuba River (lat. 39°17'45" N, long. 121°12'15" W; at SW cor. sec. 28, T 17 N, R 7 E). Named on French Corral (1948) 7.5' quadrangle.

Point Eaton: see **Mount Eaton** [TUOLUMNE].

Pointed Rocks [EL DORADO]: *peak,* 1.25 miles northwest of Cool (lat. 38°54' N, long. 121°02' W; near S line sec. 12, T 12 N, R 8 E). Altitude 1658 feet. Named on Auburn (1953) 7.5' quadrangle.

Poison Canyon [NEVADA]: *canyon,* 1 mile long, 4 miles west of English Mountain (lat. 39°26'40" N, long. 120°37'30" W). Named on English Mountain (1983) and Graniteville (1982) 7.5' quadrangles.

Poison Hole [EL DORADO]: *relief feature,* 5 miles east-northeast of Robbs Peak (lat. 38°56'55" N, long. 120°19'05" W; sec. 29, T 13 N, R 15 E). Named on Loon Lake (1952) 7.5' quadrangle.

Poison Meadow [MADERA]: *area,* 6.25 miles east-northeast of Yosemite Forks (lat. 37°23'50" N, long. 119°31'15" W; sec. 24, T 6 S, R 22 E). Named on Bass Lake (1953) 15' quadrangle.

Poison Spring [CALAVERAS]: *spring,* 6.5 miles west-southwest of Tamarack (lat. 38°23'40" N, long. 120°10'55" W; near N line sec. 11, T 6 N, R 16 E). Named on Calaveras Dome (1979) 7.5' quadrangle.

Poison Switch: see **Wassamma** [MADERA].

Poker Camp: see **Plymouth** [AMADOR].

Poker Flat [SIERRA]: *locality,* 2.5 miles south of Mount Fillmore along Canyon Creek (lat. 39°41'35" N, long. 120°50'40" W). Named on Mount Fillmore (1951) 7.5' quadrangle.

Pokerville: see **Plymouth** [AMADOR].

Polaris [NEVADA]: *locality,* 2.5 miles east-northeast of Truckee along Southern Pacific Railroad (lat. 39°20'20" N, long. 120°08'05" W; sec. 7, T 17 N, R 17 E). Named on Truckee (1955) 7.5' quadrangle. Postal authorities established Polaris post office in 1901 and discontinued it in 1923 (Frickstad, p. 114).

Pole Creek [PLACER]: *stream,* flows 3.5 miles to Truckee River nearly 6 miles northwest of Tahoe City (lat. 39°14'10" N, long. 120°12'25" W; sec. 16, T 16 N, R 16 E). Named on Granite Chief (1953) and Tahoe City (1955) 7.5' quadrangles.

Pollock Pines [EL DORADO]: *town,* 12 miles east-northeast of Placerville (lat. 38°45'45" N, long. 120°35' W; mainly in sec. 36, T 11 N, R 12 E). Named on Pollock Pines (1950) 7.5' quadrangle. Postal authorities established Pollock Pines post office in 1936 (Frickstad, p. 28). The name is from a grove of pine trees that belonged to the Pollock family, first settlers at the site (Gudde, 1949, p. 269).

Polly Dome [MARIPOSA]: *peak,* 2.5 miles west of Cathedral Peak (lat. 37°51'15" N, long. 119°26'55" W; near N line sec. 16, T 1 S, R 23 E). Altitude 8910 feet. Named on Tuolumne Meadows (1956) 15' quadrangle. R.B. Marshall of United States Geological Survey named the peak for Polly McCabe, daughter of Colonel W.W. Forsyth (United States Board on Geographic Names, 1934, p. 19).

Polly Dome Lakes [MARIPOSA]: *lakes,* largest 1300 feet long, 3 miles west-northwest of Cathedral Peak (lat. 37°51'45" N, long. 119°27'10" W; sec. 9, T 1 S, R 23 E); the lakes are 0.5 mile north-northwest of Polly Dome. Named on Tuolumne Meadows (1956) 15' quadrangle.

Pomegranate: see **Lancha Plana** [AMADOR].

Pomins [EL DORADO]: *locality,* 2 miles north of the present town of Meeks Bay along Lake Tahoe (lat. 39°04' N, long. 120°07'20" W; near N line sec. 17, T 14 N, R 17 E). Named on Truckee (1940) 30' quadrangle. Postal authorities established Pomins post office in 1915 and discontinued it in 1942; the name was for Frank J. Pomin, first postmaster (Salley, p. 176).

Pond Creek [PLACER]: *stream,* flows 1.25 miles to Middle Fork American River 15 miles east-northeast of Auburn (lat. 38°59'25" N, long. 120°49'40" W; sec. 11, T 13 N, R 10 E). Named on Foresthill (1949) and Georgetown (1949) 7.5' quadrangles.

Pond Lily Lake [MADERA]: *lake,* nearly 6 miles south of Devils Postpile (lat. 37°32'30" N, long. 119°06'05" W). Named on Devils Postpile (1953) 15' quadrangle.

Pond Lily Lake: see **Sotcher Lake** [MADERA].

Pooley's Ranch: see **Soulsbyville** [TUOLUMNE].

Pools Station [CALAVERAS]: *locality,* 6 miles west-southwest of Angels Camp (lat. 38°02'40" N, long. 120°38'50" W; sec. 10, T 2 N, R 12 E). Named on Salt Spring Valley (1962) 7.5' quadrangle.

Poopenaut Valley [TUOLUMNE]: *valley,* 4 miles northeast of Mather along Tuolumne River (lat.

37°55'30" N, long. 119°48'45" W). Named on Lake Eleanor (1956) 15' quadrangle. United States Board on Geographic Names (1933, p. 614) rejected the forms "Poo Poo Valley" and "Poopenant Valley" for the name.

Poo Poo Valley: see **Poopenaut Valley** [TUOLUMNE].

Poorman Gulch [CALAVERAS]: *canyon,* drained by a stream that flows 2.5 miles to Mokelumne River 2.5 miles west-southwest of Mokelumne Hill (lat. 38°17'25" N, long. 120°45'05" W; sec. 15, T 5 N, R 11 E). Named on Mokelumne Hill (1948) 7.5' quadrangle.

Poorman Creek [NEVADA]:
(1) *stream,* flows 13 miles to South Yuba River 0.5 mile southwest of Washington (lat. 39°21'10" N, long. 120°48'35" W; sec. 12, T 17 N, R 10 E). Named on Alleghany (1949), Graniteville (1982), and Washington (1950) 7.5' quadrangles. South Fork enters 2 miles north-northeast of Washington; it is 6 miles long and is named on Alleghany (1949) and Graniteville (1982) 7.5' quadrangles. A mining camp called South Fork was situated along South Fork Poorman Creek just above the mouth of the fork, and a mining place called Brandy Flat was located opposite the mouth of Poorman Creek (Slyter and Slyter, p. 7, 13). A place called Pattison was located along South Yuba River 0.5 mile above the mouth of Poorman Creek (Gudde, 1975, p. 261).
(2) *stream,* flows 2 miles to Rollins Reservoir 2 miles northeast of Chicago Park (lat. 39°09'55" N, long. 120°56'35" W; near W line sec. 11, T 15 N, R 9 E). Named on Chicago Park (1949, photorevised 1973) 7.5' quadrangle.

Poor Mans Canyon [PLACER]: *canyon,* drained by a stream that flows 1.5 miles to El Dorado Canyon 1.25 miles east-southeast of Michigan Bluff (lat. 39°02'15" N, long. 120°42'40" W; near N line sec. 26, T 14 N, R 11 E). Named on Michigan Bluff (1952) 7.5' quadrangle.

Poor Mans Gulch [TUOLUMNE]: *canyon,* drained by a stream that flows 3.5 miles to Don Pedro Reservoir 4.25 miles south-southeast of Chinese Camp (lat. 37°48'50" N, long. 120°24'25" W; near S line sec. 26, T 1 S, R 14 E). Named on Chinese Camp (1947) 7.5' quadrangle.

Poorman Valley [NEVADA]: *valley,* 4.5 miles northeast of Graniteville along East Fork Creek (lat. 39°29'05" N, long. 120°40'20" W; sec. 30, T 19 N, R 12 E). Named on Graniteville (1982) 7.5' quadrangle.

Pope Beach [EL DORADO]: *beach,* 4.25 miles east-northeast of Mount Tallac along Lake Tahoe (lat. 38°56'15" N, long. 120°01'40" W; sec. 6, T 12 N, R 18 E). Named on Emerald Bay (1955) 7.5' quadrangle. Lekisch (p. 97) associated the name with George A. Pope, who owned property at the place.

Poppy Campground [PLACER]: *locality,* 5.5 miles north-northwest of Bunker Hill along Middle Fork American River (lat. 39°07'10" N, long. 120°25'35" W; near E line sec. 29, T 15 N, R 14 E). Named on Granite Chief (1953) 15' quadrangle. Water of French Meadows Reservoir now covers the site.

Porath Gulch [MARIPOSA]: *canyon,* drained by a stream that flows 2.5 miles to Bull Creek 11 miles west-northwest of El Portal (lat. 37°42'25" N, long. 119°58'50" W; sec. 3, T 3 S, R 18 E). Named on Kinsley (1947) 7.5' quadrangle.

Porcupine Creek [MARIPOSA]: *stream,* flows 4.5 miles to Snow Creek (1) 4 miles northeast of Yosemite Village (lat. 37°47'30" N, long. 119°32'10" W). Named on Hetch Hetchy Reservoir (1956) 15' quadrangle.

Porcupine Flat [MARIPOSA]: *area,* 4.25 miles north-northeast of Yosemite Village (lat. 37°48'20" N, long. 119°33'50" W; near W line sec. 33, T 1 S, R 22 E); the place is along Porcupine Creek. Named on Hetch Hetchy Reservoir (1956) 15' quadrangle.

Porphyry Lake [MADERA]: *lake,* 500 feet long, 3.25 miles east of Merced Peak (lat. 37°37'45" N, long. 119°20' W). Named on Merced Peak (1953) 15' quadrangle.

Porter [CALAVERAS]: *locality,* nearly 5 miles northwest of Blue Mountain (lat. 38°23'40" N, long. 120°25'30" W; near N line sec. 10, T 6 N, R 14 E). Named on Blue Mountain (1956) 15' quadrangle.

Porthole Gap [AMADOR]: *pass,* 6.25 miles north-northwest of Mokelumne Peak (lat. 38°37'25" N, long. 120°07'55" W; near SE cor. sec. 18, T 9 N, R 17 E). Named on Bear River Reservoir (1979) 7.5' quadrangle.

Portuguese Bar: see **American River** [EL DORADO-PLACER].

Portuguese Creek [MADERA]: *stream,* flows 3.5 miles to Chiquito Creek 8.5 miles north-northeast of Shuteye Peak (lat. 37°28'10" N, long. 119°22'45" W; sec. 30, T 5 S, R 24 E). Named on Merced Peak (1953) and Shuteye Peak (1953) 15' quadrangles.

Portuguese Gulch [TUOLUMNE]: *canyon,* drained by a stream that flows nearly 1 mile to Woods Creek 2.5 miles south-southeast of Columbia (lat. 38°00'05" N, long. 120°22'55" W; sec. 25, T 2 N, R 14 E). Named on Columbia (1948) and Columbia SE (1948) 7.5' quadrangles.

Portuguese Point [PLACER]: *ridge,* generally west-trending, 1 mile long, 2.25 miles northwest of Foresthill (lat. 39°02'35" N, long. 120°50'50" W). Named on Foresthill (1949) 7.5' quadrangle.

Portuguese Ridge [MARIPOSA]: *ridge,* north-northwest-trending, 2.5 miles long, 9.5 miles south-southwest of El Portal (lat. 37°32'35" N, long. 119°51' W). Named on Buckingham Mountain (1947) 7.5' quadrangle.

Port Wine [SIERRA]: *locality,* 7 miles southwest of Mount Fillmore (lat. 39°39'40" N, long. 120°56'50" W; near SW cor. sec. 23, T 21 N, R 9 E). Named on La Porte (1951) 7.5' quadrangle. Called Portwine on California Mining Bureau's (1909a) map. Postal authorities established Port Wine post office in 1861, discontinued it in 1865, reestablished it in 1870, and discontinued it in 1918 (Frickstad, p. 184). Prospectors named the place after they found a cask of port wine hidden nearby (Hoover, Resnch, and Rensch, p. 497).

Port Wine Ravine [SIERRA]: *canyon,* drained by a stream that flows 1 mile to Pats Gulch 7.5 miles southwest of Mount Fillmore (lat. 39°39'35" N, long. 120°57'30" W; near S line sec. 22, T 21 N, R 9 E); the feature is south of Port Wine. Named on La Porte (1951) 7.5' quadrangle.

Port Wine Ridge [SIERRA]: *ridge,* southwest-trending, 6 miles long, between Slate Creek and Canyon Creek; center 6 miles southwest of Mount Fillmore (lat. 39°40' N, long. 120°55'40" W); the place called Port Wine is on the ridge. Named on La Porte (1951) 7.5' quadrangle. The feature first was called Sears Ridge (Gudde, 1975, p. 313)—Sears Ravine is on the side of the ridge.

Possum Bar: see **Grapevine Ravine** [AMADOR].

Post Corral [TUOLUMNE]: *locality,* 3 miles east of Liberty Hill (lat. 38°22'05" N, long. 120°02'45" W; near SW cor. sec. 18, T 6 N, R 18 E). Named on Liberty Hill (1979) 7.5' quadrangle.

Post Corral Canyon [TUOLUMNE]: *canyon,* 2 miles long, along Spring Creek above a point 11.5 miles east of Pinecrest (lat. 38°10'55" N, long. 119°47' W). Named on Pinecrest (1956) 15' quadrangle.

Post Corral Meadow [TUOLUMNE]: *area,* 2.5 miles east of Liberty Hill (lat. 38°21'45" N, long. 120°03'05" W; sec. 24, T 6 N, R 17 E); the place is 0.5 mile south-southwest of Post Corral. Named on Liberty Hill (1979) 7.5' quadrangle.

Post Creek [MADERA]: *stream,* flows 3.25 miles to West Fork Granite Creek 5.25 miles southeast of Merced Peak (lat. 37°34'50" N, long. 119°19'40" W); the stream heads near Post Peak. Named on Merced Peak (1953) 15' quadrangle.

Post Flat [EL DORADO]: *area,* 4.5 miles east-southeast of Camino (lat. 38°42'35" N, long. 120°35'40" W; at NE cor. sec. 24, T 10 N, R 12 E). Named on Sly Park (1952) 7.5' quadrangle.

Post Lakes [MADERA]: *lakes,* two, each about 700 feet long, nearly 3 miles east-southeast of Merced Peak (lat. 37°37'35" N, long. 119°20'40" W); the lakes are 1 mile west of Post Peak. Named on Merced Peak (1953) 15' quadrangle.

Post Peak [MADERA]: *peak,* 3.5 miles east of Merced Peak (lat. 37° 37'45" N, long. 119°19'40" W). Altitude 11,009 feet. Named on Merced Peak (1953) 15' quadrangle. R.B.

Marshall of United States Geological Survey named the peak for William S. Post, an employee of the Survey (United States Board on Geographic Names, 1934, p. 19).

Post Peak Pass [MADERA]: *pass,* 3.5 miles east of Merced Peak (lat. 37°37'50" N, long. 119°19'40" W); the pass is north of Post Peak. Named on Merced Peak (1953) 15' quadrangle.

Pothole Meadows [MARIPOSA]: *area,* 3.25 miles south of Yosemite Village (lat. 37°42'10" N, long. 119°35'10" W). Named on Yosemite (1956) 15' quadrangle. The name is from some bowl-shaped depressions about 5 feet in diameter (Browning, 1986, p. 173).

Potosi [SIERRA]: *locality,* 1.5 miles southwest of Mount Fillmore (lat. 39°43' N, long. 120°52'30" W; at NW cor. sec. 4, T 21 N, R 10 E). Named on La Porte (1951) and Mount Fillmore (1951) 7.5' quadrangles.

Potosi Creek [SIERRA]: *stream,* flows 2.5 mile to East Branch Slate Creek 2.25 miles west of Mount Fillmore (lat. 39°43'35" N, long. 120°53'35" W; near W line sec. 32, T 22 N, R 10 E); the stream goes past Potosi. Named on La Porte (1951) and Mount Fillmore (1951) 7.5' quadrangle. Downieville (1897) 30' quadrangle has the name "Gold Canyon" along the stream.

Potter Point [TUOLUMNE]: *peak,* 7 miles south of Tioga Pass (lat. 37°48'40" N, long. 119°16'45" W). Altitude 10,728 feet. Named on Tuolumne Meadows (1956) 15' quadrangle. R.B. Marshall of United States Geological Survey named the feature in 1909 for Dr. Charles Potter, an army doctor (Browning, 1988, p. 112).

Potter Ridge [MARIPOSA]: *ridge,* west- to northwest-trending, 6.5 miles long, 5.5 miles southwest of Yosemite Forks (lat. 37°18'30" N, long. 119°42' W). Named on Bass Lake (1953) 15' quadrangle.

Potts Cabin [EL DORADO]: *locality,* 5.5 miles north of Riverton (lat. 38°51' N, long. 120°26'40" W; near S line sec. 30, T 12 N, R 14 E). Named on Riverton (1950) 7.5' quadrangle.

Pourier Creek [SIERRA]: *stream,* flows 1.25 miles to Willow Creek 4 miles north-northwest of Pike (lat. 39°29'35" N, long. 121°01'45" W; near N line sec. 25, T 19 N, R 8 E). Named on Camptonville (1948) 7.5' quadrangle.

Poverty: see **Poverty Hill** [SIERRA] (2).

Poverty Bar [CALAVERAS]: *locality,* 5 miles west-northwest of Valley Springs along Mokelumne River (lat. 38°13'30" N, long. 120°54'30" W; on E line sec. 6, T 4 N, R 10 E). Named on Wallace (1962) 7.5' quadrangle. Postal authorities established Poverty Bar post office in 1858 and discontinued it in 1864 (Frickstad, p. 16). Water of Camanche Reservoir now covers the place.

Poverty Bar [EL DORADO-PLACER]: *locality,* 3 miles north-northwest of Greenwood along Middle Fork American River on El

Dorado-Placer county line (lat. 38°56'05" N, long. 120°56'25" W; sec. 35, T 13 N, R 9 E). Named on Greenwood (1949) 7.5' quadrangle.

Poverty Hill [SIERRA]:

(1) *peak,* 9.5 miles southwest of Mount Fillmore (lat. 39°37'50" N, long. 120°58'25" W; near SE cor. sec. 33, T 21 N, R 9 E). Altitude 5518 feet. Named on La Porte (1951) 7.5' quadrangle.

(2) *locality,* 8 miles northwest of Goodyears Bar (lat. 39°37'20" N, long. 121°00'20" W; near SE cor. sec. 6, T 20 N, R 9 E). Named on Strawberry Valley (1948) 7.5' quadrangle. Called Poverty on Logan's (1929) map.

Poverty Hill: see **Stent** [TUOLUMNE].

Powell Lake [TUOLUMNE]: *lake,* 600 feet long, 7.5 miles east of Pinecrest (lat. 38°12'15" N, long. 119°50'30" W; sec. 14, T 4 N, R 19 E). Named on Pinecrest (1956) 15' quadrangle.

Poverty Point: see **Big Canyon** [EL DORADO] (1).

Powderhorn Creek [PLACER]: *stream,* flows 3.25 miles to Five Lakes Creek 6.25 miles northeast of Bunker Hill (lat. 39°06'30" N, long. 120°17'25" W; near W line sec. 34, T 15 N, R 15 E). Named on Wentworth Springs (1953) 7.5' quadrangle.

Powderhorn Creek: see **Little Powderhorn Creek** [PLACER].

Powningville: see **Pilot Hill** [EL DORADO] (2).

Prairie Creek [NEVADA]: *stream,* flows 2 miles to Jackson Creek 3 miles west-northwest of English Mountain (lat. 39°27'25" N, long. 120°36'05" W; near W line sec. 2, T 18 N, R 12 E). Named on English Mountain (1983) 7.5' quadrangle.

Prather Meadow: see **Big Prather Meadow** [TUOLUMNE]; **Little Prather Meadow** [TUOLUMNE].

Prays [EL DORADO]: *locality,* 5 miles north of Omo Ranch (lat. 38° 39'15" N, long. 120°35' W). Named on Placerville (1893) 30' quadrangle.

Preston Reservoir [AMADOR]: *lake,* 1400 feet long, 1.25 miles north-northwest of Ione (lat. 38°22'10" N, long. 120°56'15" W). Named on Ione (1962) 7.5' quadrangle.

Preston Reservoir: see **Henderson Reservoir** [AMADOR].

Prewett Station: see **Bates Station** [MADERA].

Price: see **Mount Price** [EL DORADO]; **Lee Price Camp** [TUOLUMNE].

Price Peak [TUOLUMNE]: *peak,* 5.5 miles south of Tower Peak (lat. 38°03'50" N, long. 119°31'50" W). Altitude 10,716 feet. Named on Tower Peak (1956) 15' quadrangle. The name commemorates George Ehler Price of the Seventh Cavalry (United States Board on Geographic Names, 1934, p. 19).

Priest [TUOLUMNE]: *locality,* 1.5 miles east of Moccasin along Rattlesnake Creek (lat. 37°48'50" N, long. 120°16'20" W; near S line sec. 25, T 1 S, R 15 E). Named on Moccasin

(1948) 7.5' quadrangle. The name is for William Priest and his wife, who ran a hotel at the place; Alexander Kirkwood and his wife founded the hotel in 1855, and after Mr. Kirkwood's death Mrs. Kirkwood married William Priest (Paden and Schlichtmann, p. 118). The hotel was called Rattlesnake House before 1872, and later it usually was called Priest's Station (Gudde, 1975, p. 276).

Priest Reservoir [TUOLUMNE]: *lake,* behind a dam on Rattlesnake Creek 2 miles east-southeast of Moccasin (lat. 37°48'05" N, long. 120°15'55" W; near W line sec. 31, T 1 S, R 16 E); the lake is 1 mile south-southeast of Priest. Named on Moccasin (1948) 7.5' quadrangle.

Priest's Station: see **Priest** [TUOLUMNE].

Princeton: see **Mount Bullion** [MARIPOSA].

Profile Cliff [MARIPOSA]: *relief feature,* 2.5 miles south-southwest of Yosemite Village on the south side of Yosemite Valley (lat. 37° 42'55" N, long. 119°36' W). Named on Yosemite (1956) 15' quadrangle.

Prospect Creek [EL DORADO]: *stream,* flows 2 miles to Middle Fork Cosumnes River 4 miles southeast of Caldor (lat. 38°33'55" N, long. 120°22'35" W; sec. 12, T 8 N, R 14 E); Prospect Rock is near the head of the stream. Named on Peddler Hill (1951) 7.5' quadrangle.

Prospect Hill [AMADOR]: *hill,* 2.5 miles northwest of Fiddletown (lat. 38°31'55" N, long. 120°47'15" W; sec. 20, T 8 N, R 11 E). Named on Fiddletown (1949) 7.5' quadrangle.

Prospect Hill [PLACER]: *ridge,* generally south-trending, 1.5 miles long, 5 miles north of Foresthill (lat. 39°05'20" N, long. 120° 50' W). Named on Foresthill (1949) 7.5' quadrangle.

Prospect Rock [EL DORADO]: *relief feature,* 6 miles southeast of Caldor (lat. 38°33'05" N, long. 120°20'55" W; near NW cor. sec. 17, T 8 N, R 15 E). Named on Peddler Hill (1951) 7.5' quadrangle.

Prosser [NEVADA]: *locality,* 4.25 miles northeast of Truckee (lat. 39°22'10" N, long. 120°07'30" W); the place is along Prosser Creek. Named on Truckee (1895) 30' quadrangle.

Prosser Campground [NEVADA]: *locality,* 2 miles southeast of Hobart Mills (lat. 39°22'40" N, long. 120°09'40" W; near E line sec. 26, T 18 N, R 16 E); the place is along Prosser Creek Reservoir. Named on Hobart Mills (1981) 7.5' quadrangle.

Prosser Creek [NEVADA]: *stream,* formed by the confluence of North Fork and South Fork, flows 8.5 miles to Truckee River 4.5 miles northeast of Truckee (lat. 39°22'15" N, long. 120°07' W; sec. 32, T 18 N, R 17 E). Named on Hobart Mills (1981), Martis Peak (1955), and Truckee (1955) 7.5' quadrangles. The stream also was called John Greenwood's Creek (Morgan, p. 377) and Johns Creek (Clyman, p. 205). North Fork is 8 miles long and is named on Hobart Mills (1981) and Independence Lake (1981) 7.5' quadrangles. South Fork is 5.5 miles long and is named on Hobart Mills (1981), Independence Lake (1981), and Norden (1955) 7.5' quadrangles.

Prosser Creek: see **Boca** [NEVADA].

Prosser Creek Reservoir [NEVADA]: *lake,* behind a dam on Prosser Creek 3 miles east-southeast of Hobart Mills (lat. 39°22'45" N, long. 120°08'15" W; sec. 30, T 18 N, R 17 E). Named on Hobart Mills (1981) and Truckee (1955, photorevised 1969) 7.5' quadrangles. United States Board on Geographic Names (1977b, p. 5) gave the name "Prosser Reservoir" as a variant.

Prosser Hill [NEVADA]: *peak,* 2.5 miles southwest of Hobart Mills (lat. 39°22'30" N, long. 120°13' W; near SW cor. sec. 28, T 18 N, R 16 E). Altitude 7171 feet. Named on Hobart Mills (1981) and Truckee (1955) 7.5' quadrangles.

Prosser House [NEVADA]: *locality,* 4 miles north-northeast of Truckee (lat. 39°22'45" N, long. 120°09' W); the place is along Prosser Creek. Named on Truckee (1895) 30' quadrangle.

Prosser Reservoir: see **Prosser Creek Reservoir** [NEVADA].

Prothro Creek [EL DORADO]: *stream,* flows nearly 3 miles to Middle Fork Cosumnes River 5 miles east-southeast of Caldor (lat. 38°34'35" N, long. 120°20'45" W; sec. 5, T 8 N, R 15 E). Named on Peddler Hill (1951) 7.5' quadrangle.

Providence [NEVADA]: *locality,* 1.25 miles west-southwest of Nevada City on the south side of Deer Creek (lat. 39°15'25" N, long. 121°02'15" W). Named on Smartsville (1895) 30' quadrangle.

Providence Camp: see **Algerine** [TUOLUMNE].

Provo: see **Mount Provo** [TUOLUMNE].

Pruitt Lake [TUOLUMNE]: *lake,* 1150 feet long, 14 miles east-southeast of Pinecrest (lat. 38°06'45" N, long. 119°45'40" W). Named on Pinecrest (1956) 15' quadrangle.

Puckerville: see **Plymouth** [AMADOR].

Pug Ugly [PLACER]: *relief feature,* less than 1 mile southwest of Dutch Flat (lat. 39°12' N, long. 120°51' W; near NE cor. sec. 4, T 15 N, R 10 E). Named on Dutch Flat (1950) 7.5' quadrangle. Whitney's (1870) map shows Plug Ugly Hill.

Pulpit Rock [MARIPOSA]: *relief feature,* 5.5 miles west-southwest of Yosemite Village in Yosemite Valley (lat. 37°43' N, long. 119° 41' W). Named on Yosemite (1956) 15' quadrangle.

Pulpit Rock [TUOLUMNE]: *relief feature,* 3.25 miles west-southwest of Sonora (lat. 37°57'35" N, long. 120°26'05" W; sec. 9, T 1 N, R 14 E). Named on Sonora (1948) 7.5' quadrangle.

Pumice Flat [MADERA]: *area,* 1.5 miles north of Devils Postpile along Middle Fork San Joa-

quin River (lat. 37°39' N, long. 119°04'30" W). Named on Devils Postpile (1953) 15' quadrangle. G. A. Waring (p. 239) noted that a meadow located 2 miles south of Pumice Flat is known as Soda Spring Flat for a small spring of carbonated water there that is well known to campers.

Pumice Gap: see **Mammoth Pass** [MADERA].

Pumpkin Hollow [CALAVERAS]: *area,* 5 miles west-southwest of Tamarack (lat. 38°25'20" N, long. 120°10'10" W; at N line sec. 36, T 7 N, R 16 E). Named on Calaveras Dome (1979) 7.5' quadrangle.

Punch Bowl [TUOLUMNE]: *valley,* 4 miles north-northeast of Pinecrest (lat. 38°14'20" N, long. 119°57'30" W; sec. 35, T 5 N, R 18 E). Named on Pinecrest (1979) 7.5' quadrangle.

Punchbowl: see **The Punchbowl** [NEVADA].

Puny Dip Canyon [NEVADA]: *canyon,* drained by a stream that heads in the State of Nevada and flows less than 0.5 mile in Nevada County to Truckee River 12.5 miles northeast of Truckee (lat. 39°26'40" N, long. 120°00'30" W; sec. 7, T 18 N, R 18 E). Named on Boca (1955) 7.5' quadrangle.

Purdon Bridge: see **Purdon Crossing** [NEVADA].

Purdon Creek [NEVADA]: *stream,* flows 0.5 mile to South Yuba River 4.5 miles north-northwest of Nevada City (lat. 39°19'40" N, long. 121°02'50" W; sec. 23, T 17 N, R 8 E). Named on Nevada City (1948) 7.5' quadrangle.

Purdon Crossing [NEVADA]: *locality,* 4.5 miles north-northwest of Nevada City along South Yuba River (lat. 39°19'40" N, long. 121° 02'45" W; sec. 23, T 17 N, R 8 E); the place is near the mouth of Purdon Creek. Named on Nevada City (1948) 7.5' quadrangle. Called Purdon Bridge on Smartsville (1895) 30' quadrangle. The bridge at the place first was known as Wall's Bridge, then as Webber's Bridge, and finally as Purdon's Bridge (Hoover, Rensch, and Rensch, p. 249-250).

Purdy [SIERRA]: *locality,* 13 miles east of Loyalton along Western Pacific Railroad (lat. 39°40'20" N, long. 120°00'10" W; sec. 19, T 21 N, R 18 E). Named on Loyalton (1955) 15' quadrangle. Called Purdys on California Mining Bureau's (1909a) map. Postal authorities established Purdys post office in 1889, moved it 2 miles west in 1891, and discontinued it in 1911; the name was for the Purdy family, who operated a store and travelers stop (Salley, p. 179).

Purdy Creek [SIERRA]: *stream,* flows 4 miles to Upper Long Valley 12 miles east of Loyalton (lat. 39°38'55" N, long. 120°01'35" W; sec. 25, T 21 N, R 17 E). Named on Dog Valley (1981) and Evans Canyon (1978) 7.5' quadrangles.

Purdys: see **Purdy** [SIERRA].

Putnam Valley [PLACER]: *valley,* 1 mile south-southwest of Emigrant Gap (1) along present

Fulda Creek (lat. 38°17'15" N, long. 120°40'15" W). Named on Colfax (1898) 30' quadrangle.

Put's Bar: see **China Gulch** [AMADOR] (1).

Putt: see **Lake Putt** [PLACER].

Putts Bar: see **China Gulch** [AMADOR] (1).

Pyramid Campground [EL DORADO]: *locality,* 4 miles south-southwest of Pyramid Peak along South Fork American River (lat. 38°47'20" N, long. 120°11' W; sec. 23, T 11 N, R 16 E). Named on Pyramid Peak (1955) 7.5' quadrangle.

Pyramid Creek [EL DORADO]: *stream,* flows 5 miles to South Fork American River 3 miles south-southeast of Pyramid Peak (lat. 38° 48'25" N, long. 120°07'50" W; near N line sec. 17, T 11 N, R 17 E). Named on Echo Lake (1955) and Pyramid Peak (1955) 7.5' quadrangles.

Pyramid Lake [EL DORADO]: *lake,* 1500 feet long, 1 mile east-northeast of Pyramid Peak (lat. 38°50'55" N, long. 120°08'25" W). Named on Pyramid Peak (1955) 7.5' quadrangle.

Pyramid Peak [EL DORADO]: *peak,* 35 miles east of Placerville (lat. 38°50'45" N, long. 120°09'25" W). Altitude 9983 feet. Named on Pyramid Peak (1955) 7.5' quadrangle.

Pyramid Peak [NEVADA]: *peak,* 4.5 miles east-northeast of Graniteville (lat. 39°28'20" N, long. 120°39'50" W; sec. 31, T 19 N, R 12 E). Altitude 5925 feet. Named on Graniteville (1982) 7.5' quadrangle.

Pywiack Cascade [MARIPOSA]: *waterfall,* 6.25 miles southwest of Cathedral Peak along Tenaya Creek (lat. 37°47'15" N, long. 119° 29'20" W). Named on Tuolumne Meadows (1956) 15' quadrangle. United States Board on Geographic Names (1934, p. 20) rejected the name "Slide Fall" for the feature, and noted that the name "Pywiack" is of Indian origin.

Pywiack Dome [MARIPOSA]: *peak,* 2 miles west of Cathedral Peak (lat.. 37°50'45" N, long. 119°26'30" W; near W line sec. 15, T 1 S, R 23 E). Named on Tuolumne Meadows (1956) 15' quadrangle. David Brower recommended the name in the early 1950's; before that time the feature had the names "Murphy's Dome," "Teapot Dome," "Matthes Dome," "Ten-ieya Dome," and "Turtle Rock" (Browning, 1986, p. 176).

– Q –

Q Ranch: see **Ione** [AMADOR].

Quail Gulch [TUOLUMNE]: *canyon,* drained by a stream that flows 1.25 miles to Stanislaus River 3.5 miles west-southwest of Columbia (lat. 38°00'50" N, long. 120°27'45" W; sec. 20, T 2 N, R 14 E). Named on Columbia (1948) 7.5' quadrangle.

Quail Hill [CALAVERAS]: *peak,* 6 miles south-

west of Copperopolis (lat. 37°55'25" N, long. 120°43'15" W; sec. 24, T 1 N, R 11 E). Named on Copperopolis (1962) 7.5' quadrangle.

Quail Lake [PLACER]: *lake,* 1200 feet long, 1.25 miles south of Homewood (lat. 39°04'10" N, long. 120°09'55" W; on W line sec. 12, T 14 N, R 16 E). Named on Homewood (1955) 7.5' quadrangle.

Quail Trap Ravine [PLACER]: *canyon,* drained by a stream that flows less than 1 mile to Bunch Canyon 4.25 miles south-southeast of Colfax (lat. 39°02'35" N, long. 120°55'25" W; at N line sec. 25, T 14 N, R 9 E). Named on Colfax (1949) 7.5' quadrangle.

Quaker Hill [NEVADA]:
(1) *peak,* 7 miles south of North Bloomfield (lat. 39°16'05" N, long. 120°54'10" W; sec. 7, T 16 N, R 10 E). Named on North Bloomfield (1949) 7.5' quadrangle.
(2) *locality,* 7.25 miles south of North Bloomfield (lat. 39°15'45" N, long. 120°54'10" W; near W line sec. 7, T 16 N, R 10 E); the place is 0.25 mile south of present Quaker Hill (1). Named on Colfax (1938) 30' quadrangle. Gudde (1975, p. 25, 63, 286) listed a mining place called Red Diamond that was located about 3 miles northeast of Quaker Hill, a settlement called Balaklava that was located about 4 miles northeast of Quaker Hill, and a mining place called Cascade Diggings that was located about 3.5 miles northeast of Quaker Hill.

Quarry Peak [TUOLUMNE]: *peak,* 4 miles south-southwest of Matterhorn Peak (lat. 38°02'45" N, long. 119°25'05" W). Altitude 11,161 feet. Named on Matterhorn Peak (1956) 15' quadrangle.

Quarter Domes [MARIPOSA]: *relief feature,* 4.25 miles east-northeast of Yosemite Village (lat. 37°45'30" N, long. 119°30'30" W). Named on Hetch Hetchy Reservoir (1956) 15' quadrangle. François Matthes named the feature (Browning, 1986, p. 176).

Quartz [TUOLUMNE]: *settlement,* 4.25 miles south-southwest of Sonora (lat. 37°55'40" N, long. 120°25'15" W; sec. 22, T 1 N, R 14 E); the place is north of Quartz Mountain. Named on Sonora (1948) 7.5' quadrangle. Postal authorities established Quartz post office in 1897 and discontinued it in 1924 (Frickstad, p. 216). The settlement also was called Quartz Hill and Quartz Mountain (Gudde, 1975, p. 278).

Quartzburg: see **Nashville** [EL DORADO]; **Hornitos** [MARIPOSA].

Quartz Canyon [EL DORADO]: *canyon,* drained by a stream that flows 1.25 miles to Otter Creek 4.25 miles north-northeast of Georgetown (lat. 38°57'40" N, long. 120°47'55" W; near W line sec. 19, T 13 N, R 11 E). Named on Georgetown (1949) 7.5' quadrangle.

Quartz Creek [CALAVERAS]: *stream,* flows less than 1 mile to San Domingo Creek 1.5

miles northwest of Murphys (lat. 38°09'10" N, long. 120°29'05" W; sec. 36, T 4 N, R 13 E). Named on Murphys (1948) 7.5' quadrangle.

Quartz Creek: see **Grizzly Creek** [MADERA].

Quartz Hill [NEVADA]: *ridge,* southwest- to west-trending, 1 mile long, 4.25 miles west-northwest of English Mountain (lat. 39°28'10" N, long. 120°37'30" W; on E line sec. 33, T 19 N, R 12 E). Named on English Mountain (1983) and Graniteville (1982) 7.5' quadrangles.

Quartz Hill: see **Quartz** [TUOLUMNE].

Quartzite Peak [MARIPOSA]: *peak,* 9 miles south of Cathedral Peak (lat. 37°43' N, long. 119°25'30" W). Altitude 10,440 feet. Named on Merced Peak (1953) 15' quadrangle. Called Quartz Peak on Mount Lyell (1901) 30' quadrangle.

Quartz Mountain [AMADOR]: *peak,* 3 miles southeast of Plymouth (lat. 38°26'50" N, long. 120°48'35" W; sec. 19, T 7 N, R 11 E). Named on Amador City (1962) 7.5' quadrangle.

Quartz Mountain [MADERA]:
(1) *ridge,* northwest-trending, 1 mile long, 8.5 miles south-southwest of Merced Peak (lat. 37°31'10" N, long. 119°26'45" W). Named on Merced Peak (1953) 15' quadrangle.
(2) *peak,* 4.25 miles north of O'Neals (lat. 37°11'30" N, long. 119° 41'05" W; sec. 33, T 8 S, R 21 E). Altitude 2752 feet. Named on O'Neals (1965) 7.5' quadrangle. Quartz Mountain Mill Company, financed in France, started a mining community called Narbo on land that the company had near the peak (Clough, p. 89-90). Postal authorities established Narbo post office in 1884 (SW quarter sec. 33, T 8 S, R 21 E), moved it in 1887 (SW quarter sec. 20, T 8 S, R 21 E), and discontinued it the same year. The name "Narbo" was from the word "Narbonne," which was the name of one of the promoters of the French company (Salley, p. 150).

Quartz Mountain [MARIPOSA]:
(1) *peak,* 5 miles east-southeast of Buckhorn Peak (lat. 37°37'35" N, long. 120°02'35" W; sec. 36, T 3 S, R 17 E). Altitude 2475 feet. Named on Buckhorn Peak (1947) 7.5' quadrangle.
(2) *ridge,* west-trending, 1 mile long, nearly 2 miles northwest of Santa Cruz Mountain (lat. 37°28'35" N, long. 120°13'30" W). Named on Indian Gulch (1962) 7.5' quadrangle.

Quartz Mountain [TUOLUMNE]: *hill,* 4.5 miles south-southwest of Sonora (lat. 37°55'25" N, long. 120°25'10" W; sec. 22, T 1 N, R 14 E). Altitude 1673 feet. Named on Sonora (1948) 7.5' quadrangle.

Quartz Mountain: see **Quartz** [TUOLUMNE].

Quartz Peak: see **Quartzite Peak** [MARIPOSA].

Quartz Point [SIERRA]: *peak,* 4 miles east-southeast of Downieville (lat. 39°32'30" N, long. 120°45'10" W; near W line sec. 4, T 19 N, R 11 E). Altitude 5403 feet. Named on

Downieville (1951) 7.5' quadrangle.

Quartz Rock [MARIPOSA]: *relief feature,* 12 miles south of the settlement of Catheys Valley along Dutchman Creek (lat. 37°15'50" N, long. 120°03'15" W; sec. 1, T 8 S, R 17 E). Named on Illinois Hill (1962) 7.5' quadrangle.

Quartzville: see **Nashville** [EL DORADO].

Queen City [SIERRA]: *locality,* 6.5 miles southwest of Mount Fillmore (lat. 39°39'50" N, long. 120°56'25" W; sec. 23, T 21 N, R 9 E). Named on La Porte (1951) 7.5' quadrangle.

Quiggs Mountain [CALAVERAS]: *peak,* 4.25 miles east-northeast of San Andreas (lat. 38°13'50" N, long. 120°36'50" W; near E line sec. 2, T 4 N, R 12 E). Altitude 2785 feet. Named on Calaveritas (1962) 7.5' quadrangle. Called Sierra Vista Mountain on San Andreas (1947) 15' quadrangle.

Quigley Creek [TUOLUMNE]: *stream,* flows 4 miles to Rydberg Creek 8 miles south-southwest of Chinese Camp (lat. 37°46'05" N, long. 120°29'40" W; near N line sec. 13, T 2 S, R 13 E). Named on Chinese Camp (1947) 7.5' quadrangle.

Quilty Creek [TUOLUMNE]: *stream,* flows 2 miles to Clavey River 4.5 miles southeast of Duckwall Mountain (lat. 37°55'05" N, long. 120°04'10" W; sec. 26, T 1 N, R 17 E). Named on Duckwall Mountain (1948) 7.5' quadrangle.

Quinn: see **Jim Quinn Spring** [EL DORADO].

Quinn Canyon [NEVADA]: *canyon,* drained by a stream that flows 1.25 miles to Middle Yuba River 7.5 miles northeast of North Bloomfield (lat. 39°26'30" N, long. 120°47'35" W; sec. 7, T 18 N, R 11 E). Named on Alleghany (1949) 7.5' quadrangle, which shows Quinn ranch situated near the head of the canyon.

Quintette [EL DORADO]: *locality,* 12 miles north-northwest of Pollock Pines (lat. 38°54'55" N, long. 120°41'05" W; near SW cor. sec. 6, T 12 N, R 12 E). Named on Tunnel Hill (1950) 7.5' quadrangle. Postal authorities established Quintette post office in 1903, moved it 0.5 mile northwest in 1906, and discontinued it in 1912 (Salley, p. 180).

– R –

Rabbit Creek [AMADOR]: *stream,* flows 1.25 miles to Camanche Reservoir 6.5 miles south-southwest of Ione (lat. 38°15'50" N, long. 120°58'25" W). Named on Ione (1962) and Wallace (1962) 7.5' quadrangles.

Rabbit Flat [AMADOR]: *area,* 2.5 miles south-southwest of Jackson (lat. 38°18'40" N, long. 120°47'25" W; near S line sec. 5, T 5 N, R 11 E). Named on Jackson (1962) 7.5' quadrangle.

Rabbit Hill [MADERA]: *peak,* 5.5 miles south-southwest of Raymond (lat. 37°08'10" N, long. 119°55'50" W; near E line sec. 19, T 9

S, R 10 E). Altitude 886 feet. Named on Raymond (1962) 7.5' quadrangle.

Rab Ravine [NEVADA]: *canyon,* 1.25 miles long, 3 miles west of Wolf (lat. 39°03'20" N, long. 121°11'55" W; on S line sec. 16, T 14 N, R 7 E). Named on Wolf (1949) 7.5' quadrangle.

Race Track Hill [PLACER]: *ridge,* west- to south-southwest-trending, 1 mile long, 3 miles east-southeast of Colfax (lat. 39°05'25" N, long. 120°54' W; sec. 6, T 14 N, R 10 E). Named on Colfax (1949) 7.5' quadrangle.

Rackerby Jack Spring [TUOLUMNE]: *spring,* 5.25 miles east-southeast of Duckwall Mountain (lat. 37°56' N, long. 120°02' W; near N line sec. 19, T 1 N, R 18 E). Named on Duckwall Mountain (1948) 7.5' quadrangle.

Rafferty Creek [TUOLUMNE]: *stream,* flows 4.5 miles to Lyell Fork 4.5 miles southwest of Tioga Pass (lat. 37°52'10" N, long. 119°19'25" W); the stream heads near Rafferty Peak. Named on Tuolumne Meadows (1956) 15' quadrangle.

Rafferty Peak [MARIPOSA]: *peak,* 3.5 miles southeast of Cathedral Peak on Mariposa-Tuolumne county line (lat. 37°48'55" N, long. 119°21'15" W). Named on Tuolumne Meadows (1956) 15' quadrangle. Lieutenant N.F. McClure named the peak in 1895 for Captain Ogden Rafferty of the Medical Corps; the captain accompanied the lieutenant on a patrol of Yosemite National Park (United States Board on Geographic Names, 1934, p. 20).

Raffetto [EL DORADO]: *locality,* 6.25 miles north of Riverton (lat. 38°51'50" N, long. 120°26'20" W; near NW cor. sec. 29, T 12 N, R 14 E). Named on Riverton (1950) 7.5' quadrangle.

Ragged Peak [TUOLUMNE]: *peak,* 5.5 miles west-northwest of Tioga Pass (lat. 37°56' N, long. 119°21'10" W). Altitude 10,912 feet. Named on Tuolumne Meadows (1956) 15' quadrangle.

Ragsdale Creek [NEVADA]: *stream,* flows 2 miles to Wolf Creek less than 1 mile west-northwest of Higgins Corner (lat. 39°02'45" N, long. 121°06'30" W; sec. 20, T 14 N, R 8 E). Named on Lake Combie (1949) 7.5' quadrangle.

Ragtown: see **Salt Gulch** [CALAVERAS].

Rail Creek: see **Elevenmile Creek** [MARIPOSA].

Rail Road Flat [CALAVERAS]: *village,* 11 miles east-northeast of Mokelumne Hill (lat. 38°20'35" N, long. 120°30'40" W; sec. 26, T 6 N, R 13 E). Named on Rail Road Flat (1948) 7.5' quadrangle. Jackson (1902) 30' quadrangle has the form "Railroad Flat" for the name, and United States Board on Geographic Names (1972, p. 4) gave this form as a variant. Postal authorities established Rail Road Flat post office in 1857, discontinued it in 1858, and reestablished it in 1869 (Frickstad, p. 16). The name came into use because min-

ers at the place moved ore cars on rails; the place first was called Independence Flat (Cook, F. S., p. 17).

Rainbow [PLACER]: *settlement,* 1.5 miles east of Cisco Grove (lat. 38°18'35" N, long. 120°30'30" W; near W line sec. 27, T 17 N, R 13 E). Named on Cisco Grove (1955) 7.5' quadrangle.

Rainbow Falls [MADERA]: *waterfall,* 1.5 miles south of Devils Postpile on Middle Fork San Joaquin River (lat. 37°36'05" N, long. 119°05' W). Named on Devils Postpile (1953) 15' quadrangle.

Rainbow Lake [MADERA]: *lake,* 950 feet long, 4 miles south-southeast of Merced Peak (lat. 37°34'40" N, long. 119°22' W). Named on Merced Peak (1953) 15' quadrangle.

Rainbow View [MARIPOSA]: *locality,* 5.25 miles west-southwest of Yosemite Village on the north side of Yosemite Valley (lat. 37°43'25" N, long. 119°40'25" W). Named on Yosemite (1956) 15' quadrangle. A rainbow at Bridalveil Fall sometimes can be seen from the place (Browning, 1986, p. 178).

Rainier Creek [MADERA]: *stream,* flows 5 miles to Big Creek 7.5 miles north of Yosemite Forks (lat. 37°28'40" N, long. 119°36'50" W; near SW cor. sec. 19, T 5 S, R 22 E). Named on Bass Lake (1953) and Yosemite (1956) 15' quadrangles.

Rallsville: see **Coarsegold** [MADERA].

Ralph [TUOLUMNE]: *locality,* 6.25 miles east-southeast of Sonora along Sierra Railway (lat. 37°57'55" N, long. 120°16'10" W; sec. 1, T 1 N, R 15 E). Named on Standard (1948) 7.5' quadrangle. California Division of Highways' (1934) map shows a place called Draper located 1.25 miles northwest of Ralph along Sierra Railway.

Ralston [PLACER]: *locality,* 4 miles southeast of Michigan Bluff (lat. 39°00'20" N, long. 120°40'35" W; sec. 6, T 13 N, R 12 E). Named on Colfax (1938) 30' quadrangle. Michigan Bluff (1952) 7.5' quadrangle shows Ralston mine near the site—financier William C. Ralston owned a hydraulic-mining claim there (Salley, p. 180).

Ralston Divide: see **Ralston Ridge** [PLACER].

Ralston Lake [EL DORADO]: *lake,* 1150 feet long, 4.25 miles west-northwest of Echo Summit (lat. 38°50'30" N, long. 120°05'55" W; on W line sec. 34, T 12 N, R 17 E); the lake is 0.5 mile north of Ralston Peak. Named on Echo Lake (1955) 7.5' quadrangle.

Ralston Peak [EL DORADO]: *peak,* 4 miles west-northwest of Echo Summit (lat. 38°50' N, long. 120°06' W); the peak is 0.5 mile south of Ralston Lake. Altitude 9235 feet. Named on Echo Lake (1955) 7.5' quadrangle.

Ralston Ridge [PLACER]: *ridge,* extends southwest and west for 13 miles between Middle Fork American River and Long Canyon from near the site of French House to the junction of Middle Fork and Long Canyon. Named on

Devil Peak (1950), Greek Store (1952), Michigan Bluff (1952), and Tunnel Hill (1950) 7.5' quadrangles. Gudde (1975, p. 282) called the feature Ralston Divide, and noted that it was named for William C. Ralston.

Ramos Creek [TUOLUMNE]: *stream,* flows 1.25 miles to Don Pedro Reservoir 2.25 miles east of Don Pedro Camp (lat. 37°42'45" N, long. 120°21'50" W; sec. 31, T 2 S, R 15 E). Named on Merced Falls (1962) 15' quadrangle.

Rampart [PLACER]: *locality,* nearly 2 miles west-southwest of Tahoe City along Truckee River (lat. 39°09'55" N, long. 120°10'35" W; sec. 11, T 15 N, R 16 E). Named on Tahoe City (1955) 7.5' quadrangle. Truckee (1940) 30' quadrangle shows the place along Southern Pacific Railroad. California Division of Highways' (1934) map shows a place called Moss Hills situated along the railroad about halfway between Rampart and Tahoe (present Tahoe City) (sec. 12, T 15 N, R 16 E).

Ramsey [CALAVERAS]: *locality,* 7.25 miles southwest of Tamarack (lat. 38°22'20" N, long. 120°10'30" W; sec. 14, T 6 N, R 16 E). Site named on Boards Crossing (1979) 7.5' quadrangle.

Ramsey Crossing [PLACER]: *locality,* 2.5 miles north of Devil Peak in Long Canyon (lat. 38°59'55" N, long. 120°13'10" W; near N line sec. 8, T 13 N, R 13 E). Named on Devil Peak (1950) 7.5' quadrangle.

Ramsey Gulch [CALAVERAS]: *canyon,* less than 1 mile long, 4 miles south of Copperopolis (lat. 37°55'15" N, long. 120°38'05" W; in and near sec. 22, T 1 N, R 12 E). Named on Copperopolis (1962) 7.5' quadrangle.

Ramshorn Bar: see **Ramshorn Creek** [SIERRA].

Ramshorn Camp Ground [SIERRA]: *locality,* 1.5 miles west of Goodyears Bar (lat. 39°32'25" N, long. 120°54'45" W; sec. 1, T 19 N, R 9 E); the place is near the mouth of Ramshorn Creek. Named on Goodyears Bar (1951) 7.5' quadrangle. Called Ramshorn Camp on Downieville (1951) 15' quadrangle.

Ramshorn Creek [SIERRA]: *stream,* flows 2 miles to North Yuba River 1.5 miles west of Goodyears Bar (lat. 39°30'20" N, long. 120°54'40" W; sec. 1, T 19 N, R 9 E). Named on Goodyears Bar (1951) 7.5' quadrangle. A place called St. Joe Bar, or Ramshorn Bar, was located along Ramshorn Creek about 2 miles west of Goodyears Bar (Gudde, 1975, p. 301), and a place called Nigger Slide was situated on the steep slope above St. Joe's Bar (Hoover, Rensch, and Rensch, p. 491). A place called Pierces Bar was located near St. Joe Bar; later the name "Pierces Bar" was changed to Convicts Bar for the convicts who worked there on road crews between 1918 and 1920 (Gudde, 1975, p. 264).

Rancheria [AMADOR]: *locality,* 4 miles north-

west of Pine Grove (lat. 38°27'35" N, long. 120°42'10" W; near W line sec. 18, T 7 N, R 12 E); the site is 1 mile north of Rancheria Creek. Named on Pine Grove (1948) 7.5' quadrangle. The place also was known as Upper Rancheria (Gudde, 1975, p. 283). A community also called Rancheria—or Old Rancheria, or Lower Rancheria to distinguish it from Upper Rancheria—was located along Dry Creek southwest of Drytown (Watson, p. 413).

Rancheria Creek [AMADOR]: *stream,* flows 14 miles to Amador Creek 4 miles south-southwest of Plymouth (lat. 38°25'30" N, long. 120°52'20" W; near NW cor. sec. 34, T 7 N, R 10 E). Named on Amador City (1962) and Pine Grove (1948) 7.5' quadrangles. North Fork enters from the east 4 miles east-southeast of Plymouth; it is 6 miles long and is named on Amador City (1962) 7.5' quadrangle.

Rancheria Creek [MADERA]: *stream,* flows 1.5 miles to China Creek 4.25 miles south of Yosemite Forks (lat. 37°18'15" N, long. 119°37'20" W; sec. 24, T 7 S, R 21 E). Named on Bass Lake (1953) 15' quadrangle.

Rancheria Creek [MARIPOSA]: *stream,* flows about 1 mile to Bear Creek (1) nearly 4 miles northwest of Midpines (lat. 37°35'15" N, long. 119°57'35" W; near W line sec. 14, T 4 S, R 18 E). Named on Feliciana Mountain (1947) 7.5' quadrangle.

Rancheria Creek [TUOLUMNE]: *stream,* flows 23 miles to Hetch Hetchy Reservoir 7.25 miles northwest of White Wolf (lat. 37°57'10" N, long. 119°43'35" W; sec. 12, T 1 N, R 20 E). Named on Hetch Hetchy Reservoir (1956), Matterhorn Peak (1956), and Tower Peak (1956) 15' quadrangles.

Rancheria del Rio Estanislao [CALAVERAS]: *land grant,* near Stanislaus River on Calaveras-Stanislaus county line. Named on Bachelor Valley (1968), Copperopolis (1962), Keystone (1962), Knights Ferry (1962), Melones Dam (1962), and Oakdale (1968) 7.5' quadrangles. Francisco Rico and Jose Antonio Castro received the land in 1843 and claimed 48,887 acres patented in 1863 (Cowan, p. 35).

Rancheria Falls [TUOLUMNE]: *waterfall,* nearly 7 miles north-northwest of White Wolf on Rancheria Creek (lat. 37°57'20" N, long. 119°42'15" W). Named on Hetch Hetchy Reservoir (1956) 15' quadrangle.

Rancheria Flat [MARIPOSA]: *area,* 1.5 miles west of El Portal (lat. 37°40'20" N, long. 119°48'20" W; sec. 18, T 3 S, R 20 E). Named on El Portal (1947) 7.5' quadrangle.

Rancheria Mountain [TUOLUMNE]: *ridge,* west-southwest-trending, 3 miles long, 6.5 miles north-northeast of White Wolf (lat. 37°57'30" N, long. 119°36'30" W); the ridge is southeast of Rancheria Creek. Named on Hetch Hetchy Reservoir (1956) 15' quadrangle.

Ranchero Creek [TUOLUMNE]: *stream,* flows

about 2 miles to Big Creek (2) 2.25 miles north-northwest of Don Pedro Camp (lat. 37° 44'50" N, long. 120°25'05" W; sec. 22, T 2 S, R 14 E). Named on La Grange (1962) 7.5' quadrangle.

Rancho del Oro Gulch [MARIPOSA]: *canyon,* drained by a stream that flows 1.25 miles to Lake McClure 4 miles southwest of Coulterville (lat. 37°40'20" N, long. 120°14'50" W). Named on Penon Blanco Peak (1962) 7.5' quadrangle.

Randall: see **White Hall** [EL DORADO].

Randall Canon: see **Spiller Creek** [TUOL-UMNE].

Randalls Meadow [TUOLUMNE]: *valley,* 2 miles east of Liberty Hill (lat. 38°22' N, long. 120°03'45" W). Named on Liberty Hill (1979) 7.5' quadrangle.

Randolph [SIERRA]: *locality,* less than 1 mile south of Sierraville (lat. 39°34'45" N, long. 120°22'10" W; near S line sec. 13, T 20 N, R 14 E). Named on Sierraville (1981) 7.5' quad-rangle. Called Etta on Sierraville (1894) 30' quadrangle. Postal authorities established Etta post office in 1883 and discontinued it in 1895 (Frickstad, p. 184).

Randolph Canyon [EL DORADO]:
(1) *canyon,* drained by a stream that flows 1.25 miles to South Fork American River 1.5 miles northeast of Pollock Pines (lat. 38°46'35" N, long. 120°34' W; sec. 30, T 11 N, R 13 E). Named on Pollock Pines (1950) 7.5' quad-rangle.
(2) *canyon,* drained by a stream that flows nearly 3 miles to Hangtown Creek 0.25 mile east-northeast of downtown Placerville (lat. 38°43'50" N, long. 120°47'25" W; sec. 8, T 10 N, R 11 E). Named on Placerville (1949) 7.5' quadrangle.

Randolph Flat [NEVADA]: *area,* nearly 3 miles west-northwest of Grass Valley (lat. 39°14'05" N, long. 121°06'30" W; on W line sec. 20, T 16 N, R 8 E). Named on Grass Valley (1949) 7.5' quadrangle.

Randolph Hill [SIERRA]: *hill,* 1.25 miles south-southwest of Sierraville (lat. 39°34'25" N, long. 120°22'35" W; sec. 24, T 20 N, R 14 E); the hill is 0.5 mile southwest of Randolph. Altitude 5619 feet. Named on Sattley (1981) and Sierraville (1981) 7.5' quadrangles.

Randolph House: see **Rough and Ready** [NE-VADA].

Ranlett: see **Sunnybrook** [AMADOR].

Ranse Doddler Bar: see **Rantedodler Bar**, under **Goodyears Bar** [SIERRA].

Rantedodler Bar: see **Goodyears Bar** [SI-ERRA].

Ranty Doddler Bar: see **Rantedodler Bar**, under **Goodyears Bar** [SIERRA].

Rapp Ravine [NEVADA]: *canyon,* drained by a stream that flows 1.5 miles to Kentucky Ravine 2.25 miles southwest of French Cor-ral (lat. 39°16'50" N, long. 121°11'25" W; near NE cor. sec. 4, T 16 N, R 7 E). Named on

French Corral (1948) 7.5' quadrangle. Smartsville (1895) 30' quadrangle shows Rapps ranch at the head of the canyon.

Rapps Ravine [SIERRA]: *canyon,* drained by a stream that flows 1 mile to Kanaka Creek 2 miles southwest of Alleghany (lat. 39°27'15" N, long. 120°52'05" W; near SE cor. sec. 5, T 18 N, R 10 E). Named on Alleghany (1949) 7.5' quadrangle.

Rardin Lake: see **Harden Lake** [TUOL-UMNE].

Raspberry: see **Sugarpine** [TUOLUMNE].

Raster Gulch [MARIPOSA]: *canyon,* drained by a stream that flows 2.5 miles to Bear Creek (2) 2.5 miles north-northwest of the settlement of Catheys Valley (lat. 37°28' N, long. 120°06'45" W; sec. 28, T 5 S, R 17 E). Named on Catheys Valley (1962) 7.5' quadrangle.

Rattlesnake: see **Rattlesnake Bar** [PLACER].

Rattlesnake Bar [NEVADA-SIERRA]: *locality,* 3.5 miles east-southeast of Alleghany along Middle Yuba River on Nevada-Sierra county line (lat. 39°26'50" N, long. 120°47'50" W; at S line sec. 6, T 18 N, R 11 E). Named on Alleghany (1949) 7.5' quadrangle.

Rattlesnake Bar [PLACER]: *locality,* 6 miles south of Auburn along North Fork American River (lat. 38°49' N, long. 121°05'30" W; sec. 9, T 11 N, R 8 E). Site named on Auburn (1954) 15' quadrangle. Water of Folsom Lake now covers the site. Postal authorities estab-lished Rattlesnake Bar post office in 1854, discontinued it in 1869, reestablished it with the name "Rattlesnake" in 1882, and discon-tinued it in 1883 (Salley, p. 181). The com-munity, which was named for a mining place along North Fork, was above the river on a level place known as Rattlesnake Flat (Hoover, Rensch, and Rensch, p. 268-269). Arrowsmith's (1860) map shows a place called Manhattan Bar located along North Fork about 1.5 miles north-northeast of Rattle-snake Bar. Gudde (1975, p. 199) listed a min-ing place called Lorenz Bar that was located on both sides of North Fork American River above Rattlesnake Bar, and (p. 30) a place called Beaver Bar, or Rich Bar, that was lo-cated on both sides of North Fork below Rattlesnake Bar.

Rattlesnake Bar: see **Little Rattlesnake Bar**, under **Auburn** [PLACER].

Rattlesnake Bridge [EL DORADO]: *locality,* 4.5 miles west-southwest of the village of Pi-lot Hill along North Fork American River (lat. 38°48'50" N, long. 121°05'20" W; near S line sec. 9, T 11 N, R 8 E). Named on Auburn (1944) 15' quadrangle, which shows the site of Rattlesnake Bar [PLACER] across North Fork from Rattlesnake Bridge. Water of Folsom Lake now covers the site.

Rattlesnake Creek [AMADOR]:
(1) *stream,* flows 3 miles to Bear River 6 miles east-southeast of Hams Station (lat. 38°31'10" N, long. 120°15'55" W; sec. 25, T 8 N, R 15

E). Named on Peddler Hill (1951) 7.5' quadrangle.

(2) *stream,* flows 1.5 miles to Butte Canyon 1.5 miles south of Jackson Butte (lat. 38°19' N, long. 120°43'15" W; sec. 1, T 5 N, R 11 E). Named on Mokelumne Hill (1948) 7.5' quadrangle.

Rattlesnake Creek [NEVADA]:
(1) *stream,* flows 1.5 miles to Middle Yuba River 1.5 miles north of Graniteville (lat. 39°27'40" N, long. 120°44'30" W; near N line sec. 4, T 18 N, R 11 E). Named on Graniteville (1982) 7.5' quadrangle.

(2) *stream,* flows 5.25 miles to Wolf Creek 6.5 miles south of Grass Valley (lat. 39°07'35" N, long. 121°05'05" W; near E line sec. 28, T 15 N, R 8 E). Named on Grass Valley (1949) 7.5' quadrangle.

Rattlesnake Creek [NEVADA-PLACER]: *stream,* heads in Nevada County and flows 7 miles to South Yuba River 3.5 miles east of Yuba Gap just inside Placer County (lat. 39°18'50" N, long. 120° 33' W; near NE cor. sec. 30, T 17 N, R 13 E). Named on Cisco Grove (1955) and Soda Springs (1955) 7.5' quadrangles.

Rattlesnake Creek [SIERRA]: *stream,* flows nearly 3 miles to Downie River 6 miles south of Mount Fillmore (lat. 39°38'30" N, long. 120°49'40" W). Named on Mount Fillmore (1951) 7.5' quadrangle.

Rattlesnake Creek [TUOLUMNE]: *stream,* flows 4 miles to Big Jackass Creek 3 miles southeast of Moccasin (lat. 37°46'55" N, long. 120°15'30" W; near NE cor. sec. 12, T 2 S, R 15 E). Named on Moccasin (1948) 7.5' quadrangle.

Rattlesnake Creek: see **Big Rattlesnake Creek** [TUOLUMNE]; **Little Rattlesnake Creek** [TUOLUMNE].

Rattlesnake Flat: see **Rattlesnake Bar** [PLACER].

Rattlesnake Gulch [MARIPOSA]: *canyon,* 1.5 miles long, 2.5 miles south-southwest of Santa Cruz Mountain (lat. 37°25'20" N, long. 120°13'15" W). Named on Indian Gulch (1962) 7.5' quadrangle.

Rattlesnake Gulch [TUOLUMNE]: *canyon,* drained by a stream that flows nearly 2 miles to Woods Creek 1.25 miles east-southeast of Columbia (lat. 38°01'50" N, long. 120°22'40" W; near E line sec. 13, T 2 N, R 14 E). Named on Columbia SE (1948) 7.5' quadrangle.

Rattlesnake Hill [CALAVERAS]: *peak,* 6.5 miles east-northeast of Murphys (lat. 38°10'40" N, long. 120°21'30" W; at S line sec. 19, T 4 N, R 15 E). Altitude 3414 feet. Named on Stanislaus (1948) 7.5' quadrangle.

Rattlesnake House: see **Priest** [TUOLUMNE].

Rattlesnake Lake [MADERA]: *lake,* 850 feet long, 15 miles northeast of Shuteye Peak (lat. 37°28'40" N, long. 119°11'20" W; sec. 24, T 5 N, R 25 E). Named on Kaiser Peak (1953) 15' quadrangle.

Rattlesnake Mountain [NEVADA-PLACER]: *peak,* 0.5 mile northeast of Cisco Grove on Nevada-Placer county line (lat. 39°18'55" N, long. 120°31'45" W; at NE cor. sec. 29, T 17 N, R 13 E); the peak is 1 mile east of the mouth of Rattlesnake Creek [NEVADA-PLACER]. Altitude 6959 feet. Named on Cisco Grove (1955) 7.5' quadrangle.

Rattlesnake Peak [SIERRA]: *peak,* 4.5 miles southeast of Mount Fillmore (lat. 39°41' N, long. 120°47'15" W; sec. 18, T 21 N, R 11 E). Altitude 7219 feet. Named on Mount Fillmore (1951) 7.5' quadrangle.

Rattlesnake Well [MADERA]: *well,* 12.5 miles west of Madera (lat. 36°57'10" N, long. 120°16'45" W; near N line sec. 25, T 11 S, R 15 E). Named on Kentucky Well (1922) 7.5' quadrangle.

Rawhide [PLACER]: *locality,* nearly 5 miles east of Dutch Flat (lat. 39°12'05" N, long. 120°44'45" W; at N line sec. 4, T 15 N, R 11 E). Named on Colfax (1938) 30' quadrangle. Westville (1952) 7.5' quadrangle shows Rawhide mine near the site.

Rawhide [TUOLUMNE]: *locality,* 4 miles west-southwest of Sonora (lat. 37°57'30" N, long. 120°27'05" W); the place is at present Rawhide Flat. Named on Sonora (1897) 30' quadrangle. Postal authorities established Rawhide post office in 1904 and discontinued it in 1906 (Frickstad, p. 216).

Rawhide Flat [TUOLUMNE]: *area,* 3.5 miles west-southwest of Sonora (lat. 37°57'45" N, long. 120°26'35" W; on S line sec. 4, T 1 N, R 14 E). Named on Sonora (1948) 7.5' quadrangle.

Rawls Gulch [MADERA]: *canyon,* drained by a stream that flows 2.5 miles to Daulton Creek 4 miles south-southwest of Raymond (lat. 37°09'50" N, long. 119°56' W; sec. 7, T 9 S, R 19 E). Named on Raymond (1962) 7.5' quadrangle.

Raymond [MADERA]: *village,* 20 miles north-northeast of Madera (lat. 37°13'10" N, long. 119°54'20" W; mainly in sec. 20, 21, T 8 S, R 19 E). Named on Raymond (1962) 7.5' quadrangle. Postal authorities established Raymond post office in 1886 (Frickstad, p. 86). The place first was called Wildcat Station, but when Southern Pacific Railroad reached the site in 1886, the rail stop there was called Raymond for Mr. T. Raymond of Raymond-Whitcomb Travel Association (Clough, p. 90). California Division of Highways' (1934) map shows a place called Herbert located along the railroad 2.25 miles south of Raymond.

Raymond: see **Mount Raymond Camp** [MADERA].

Raymond Mountain [MADERA]: *peak,* 6 miles south-southwest of Buena Vista Peak (lat. 37°30'30" N, long. 119°32'50" W; sec. 10, T 5 S, R 22 E). Altitude 8712 feet. Named on Yosemite (1956) 15' quadrangle. Members of the Whitney survey named the peak for Israel Ward Raymond, who played an active part in persuading the federal government to give Yosemite Valley to the State of California for a park, and who served on the supervisory commission for the park from 1864 until 1866 (Hanna, p. 251).

Raynor Creek [MADERA-MARIPOSA]: *stream,* heads in Mariposa County and flows 10 miles to Chowchilla River 13 miles northeast of Fairmead in Madera County (lat. 37°12'05" N, long. 120°00'25" W; sec. 28, T 8 S, R 18 E). Named on Ben Hur (1947), Illinois Hill (1962), and Raynor Creek (1961) 7.5' quadrangles.

Rays Flat: see **Grass Valley** [NEVADA].

Real Pass: see **Vogelsang Pass**, under **Vogelsang Lake** [MARIPOSA].

Red Ant [SIERRA]: *locality,* 2.5 miles northwest of Downieville (lat. 39°35'05" N, long. 120°51'30" W; sec. 21, T 20 N, R 10 E). Named on Downieville (1951) 7.5' quadrangle.

Red Apple [CALAVERAS]: *locality,* 5.25 miles east-northeast of Murphys (lat. 38°10'45" N, long. 120°22'50" W; near S line sec. 24, T 4 N, R 14 E). Named on Murphys (1948) 7.5' quadrangle.

Redbird Canyon [EL DORADO]: *canyon,* 0.5 mile long, opens into the canyon of South Fork American River 7.25 miles west of Pollock Pines (lat. 38°46'40" N, long. 120°43' W; near N line sec. 26, T 11 N, R 11 E); the canyon is along lower reaches of Redbird Creek. Named on Slate Mountain (1950) 7.5' quadrangle.

Redbird Creek [EL DORADO]: *stream,* flows 2 miles to South Fork American River 7.25 miles west of Pollock Pines (lat. 38°46'40" N, long. 120°43' W; near N line sec. 26, T 11 N, R 11 E). Named on Slate Mountain (1950) 7.5' quadrangle. Placerville (1893) 30' quadrangle has the form "Red Bird Creek" for the name.

Red Can Lake [TUOLUMNE]: *lake,* 1000 feet long, 13 miles east-southeast of Pinecrest (lat. 38°08'40" N, long. 119°45'10" W). Named on Pinecrest (1956) 15' quadrangle.

Red Cliffs [PLACER]: *relief feature,* 2 miles east-northeast of Bunker Hill (lat. 39°03'20" N, long. 120°20'40" W; on W line sec. 18, T 14 N, R 15 E). Named on Wentworth Springs (1953) 7.5' quadrangle.

Red Cones [MADERA]: *peaks,* two, 2.5 miles south-southeast of Devils Postpile (lat. 37°35'30" N, long. 119°03'25" W). Altitudes 8985 and 9015 feet. Named on Devils Postpile (1953) 15' quadrangle.

Red Creek [MADERA-MARIPOSA]: *stream,* heads near Red Peak in Madera County and flows 4.5 miles to Clark Fork 12.5 miles south-southwest of Cathedral Peak in Mariposa County (lat. 37° 40'55" N, long. 119°29'15" W). Named on Merced Peak (1953) 15' quadrangle.

Red Devil Lake [MADERA]: *lake,* 1500 feet long, 2 miles north of Merced Peak (lat.

37°39'55" N, long. 119°23'10" W). Named on Merced Peak (1953) 15' quadrangle.

Red Diamond: see **Quaker Hill** [NEVADA] (2).

Red Diggins [EL DORADO]: *locality,* 5.5 miles northeast of Georgetown in Missouri Canyon (lat. 38°57'55" N, long. 120°46'15" W; sec. 20, T 13 N, R 11 E). Named on Georgetown (1949) 7.5' quadrangle.

Red Dog [NEVADA]: *locality,* 6 miles north-northeast of Chicago Park (lat. 39°13' N, long. 120°53'55" W; at S line sec. 30, T 16 N, R 10 E); the place is 1 mile west of Chalk Bluff. Named on Chicago Park (1949) 7.5' quadrangle. Postal authorities established Red Dog post office in 1855 and discontinued it in 1869 (Frickstad, p. 114). Goddard's (1857) map has the name "Brooklin" for a place located just south of Red Dog, and Whitney's (1873) map shows a community called Chalk Bluffs situated 1.5 miles east of Red Dog. Charlie Wilson of Illinois and his companions found gold in 1850 on an elevation that they named Red Dog Hill after a place in Illinois where Wilson had mined lead and zinc; two camps, called Red Dog and Chalk Bluffs, were started, but soon the residents of Chalk Bluffs moved to Red Dog, where the inhabitants voted to change the name of the place to Brooklyn, but postal authorities rejected the name "Brooklyn" and accepted the name "Red Dog" (Gudde, 1975, p. 286).

Red Dog Hill: see **Red Dog** [NEVADA].

Red Dog You Bet Diggings [NEVADA]: *locality,* 6.25 miles northeast of Chicago Park (lat. 39°12'45" N, long. 120°53'15" W); the place is east of Red Dog and You Bet. Named on Chicago Park (1949) 7.5' quadrangle.

Red Gulch [TUOLUMNE]: *canyon,* less than 0.5 mile long, opens into the canyon of Woods Creek 1.25 miles southeast of Columbia (lat. 38°01'25" N, long. 120°22'55" W; sec. 13, T 2 N, R 14 E). Named on Columbia (1948) 7.5' quadrangle.

Redhawk Lake: see **Calaveras Reservoir** [CALAVERAS].

Red Hill [CALAVERAS]: *peak,* less than 1 mile west-southwest of Vallecito (lat. 38°04'55" N, long. 120°29'10" W; near E line sec. 25, T 3 N, R 13 E). Named on Columbia (1948) 7.5' quadrangle.

Red Hill [NEVADA]: *peak,* 3.5 miles west of English Mountain (lat. 39°26'40" N, long. 120°37' W; sec. 10, T 18 N, R 12 E). Altitude 7060 feet. Named on English Mountain (1983) 7.5' quadrangle.

Red Hill [PLACER]: *peak,* nearly 4 miles east of Colfax (lat. 39°05'50" N, long. 120°52'55" W; near NE cor. sec. 6, T 14 N, R 10 E). Named on Colfax (1949) 7.5' quadrangle.

Red Hills [TUOLUMNE]: *range,* south and west of Chinese Camp. Named on Chinese Camp (1947) and Keystone (1962) 7.5' quadrangles.

Red Hill Spring [NEVADA]: *spring,* 10 miles northeast of Chicago Park (lat. 39°14'55" N, long. 120°50'50" W; sec. 15, T 16 N, R 10 E). Named on Dutch Flat (1950) 7.5' quadrangle.

Red Mountain [EL DORADO]: *peak,* 1 mile west-southwest of Wentworth Springs (lat. 39°00'25" N, long. 120°21'20" W; near N line sec. 1, T 13 N, R 14 E). Altitude 6872 feet. Named on Wentworth Springs (1953) 7.5' quadrangle. Called Red Peak on Truckee (1895) 30' quadrangle.

Red Mountain [MARIPOSA]: *peak,* 10 miles south-southeast of Mariposa (lat. 37°21'35" N, long. 119°53'05" W; on S line sec. 34, T 6 S, R 19 E). Altitude 1821 feet. Named on Ben Hur (1947) 7.5' quadrangle. Postal authorities established Red Mountain post office in 1918 and discontinued in 1919; it was located 2 miles north-northeast of the peak (near NE cor. sec. 27, T 6 S, R 19 E) and was named for the peak (Salley, p. 182).

Red Mountain [NEVADA]:
(1) *ridge,* east-northeast-trending, 1 mile long, 5 miles north-northeast of Donner Pass (lat. 39°23'05" N, long. 120°17'50" W; mainly in sec. 27, T 18 N, R 15 E). Named on Independence Lake (1981) 7.5' quadrangle. On Donner Pass (1955) 15' quadrangle, the name applies to a peak on the ridge.
(2) *ridge,* west-southwest-trending, 2.5 miles long, 4.5 miles east-northeast of Yuba Gap (lat. 39°20'15" N, long. 120°32'15" W). Named on Cisco Grove (1955) 7.5' quadrangle.

Red Mountain: see **Red Peak** [MADERA]; **Taylor Hill** [TUOLUMNE].

Red Mountain Bar [TUOLUMNE]: *locality,* 5 miles south-southeast of Chinese Camp along Tuolumne River (lat. 37°48' N, long. 120°24'35" W). Named on Sonora (1897) 30' quadrangle. Water of Don Pedro Reservoir now covers the site. Several mining camps were located along Tuolumne River near Red Mountain Bar: Hawkins Bar, named for "Old Hawkins," who kept a store at the place (Gudde, 1975, p. 153), was about 1 mile by path down the river from Red Mountain Bar (Gardiner, p. 80); Morgan's Bar was about 7 miles below Hawkins Bar along the river (Gardiner, p. 104); and Texas Bar was 9 miles below Hawkins Bar (Gudde, 1975, p. 347)

Red Oak Canyon [SIERRA]: *canyon,* drained by a stream that flows 3 miles to Empire Creek 7.25 miles southeast of Mount Fillmore (lat. 39°38'40" N, long. 120°46'30" W; near N line sec. 32, T 21 N, R 11 E). Named on Mount Fillmore (1951) 7.5' quadrangle.

Red Peak [EL DORADO]: *peak,* 4.25 miles west-southwest of Phipps Peak (lat. 38°55'30" N, long. 120°13'15" W; at N line sec. 4, T 12 N, R 16 E). Altitude 9307 feet. Named on Rockbound Valley (1955) 7.5' quadrangle.

Red Peak [MADERA]: *peak,* 1.5 miles north-northwest of Merced Peak (lat. 37°39'15" N, long. 119°24'30" W). Altitude 11,699 feet. Named on Merced Peak (1953) 15' quad-

rangle. Members of the Whitney survey gave the name "Red Mountain" to the feature for the dominant color of its upper part (Browning, 1988, p. 116).

Red Peak [TUOLUMNE]: *peak,* 7 miles west-northwest of Sonora Pass (lat. 38°22'55" N, long. 119°44'30" W). Altitude 10,009 feet. Named on Disaster Peak (1979) 7.5' quadrangle.

Red Peak: see **Red Mountain** [EL DORADO]; **Virginia Peak** [TUOLUMNE].

Red Peak Fork [MADERA]: *stream,* flows 4 miles to Merced River 5.25 miles north-north-east of Merced Peak (lat. 37°42'20" N, long. 119°21'40" W); the stream heads near Red Peak. Named on Merced Peak (1953) 15' quadrangle.

Red Point [PLACER]: *relief feature,* 3.5 miles southwest of Westville (lat. 39°08'55" N, long. 120°42' W; sec. 14, T 15 N, R 11 E). Named on Westville (1952) 7.5' quadrangle. Colfax (1898) 30' quadrangle has the name "Red Point" for an inhabited place near the feature.

Red Rock Meadow [TUOLUMNE]: *area,* 4 miles southeast of Dardanelle (lat. 38°18'05" N, long. 119°46'40" W; near N line sec. 9, T 5 N, R 20 E). Named on Dardanelle (1979) 7.5' quadrangle.

Reds Creek [MADERA]: *stream,* flows 1.5 miles to Middle Fork San Joaquin River 1.25 miles north of Devils Postpile (lat. 37°38'35" N, long. 119°04'40" W); the stream heads near Reds Lake. Named on Devils Postpile (1953) 15' quadrangle.

Reds Creek: see **Reds Meadow Hot Springs** [MADERA].

Reds Lake [MADERA]: *lake,* 500 feet long, 1.5 miles northeast of Devils Postpile (lat. 37°38'20" N, long. 119°03'20" W); the lake is near the head of Reds Creek. Named on Devils Postpile (1953) 15' quadrangle.

Reds Meadow Hot Springs [MADERA]: *springs,* 0.5 mile southeast of Devils Postpile (lat. 37°37'05" N, long. 119°04'25" W); the springs are at Reds Meadows. Named on Devils Postpile (1953) 15' quadrangle. G. A. Waring (p. 55) reported that water in a bathing pool at the largest of several small thermal springs at the east side of Reds Meadows has a temperature of 120° Fahrenheit. United States Board on Geographic Names (1984b, p. 2) approved the name "Reds Creek" for a stream that flows 3.5 miles to San Joaquin River 0.5 mile west-southwest of Reds Meadow Hot Springs (lat. 37°36'58" N, long. 119°04'57" W)—the hot springs are along this stream.

Reds Meadows [MADERA]: *area,* 0.5 mile southeast of Devils Postpile (lat. 37°37' N, long. 119°04'30" W). Named on Mount Lyell (1901) 30' quadrangle. The name commemorates Red Sotcher, or Satcher, who came to the place in 1879 to herd sheep (Smith, p. 14).

Red Star Point [PLACER]: *peak,* 7 miles south of Duncan Peak (lat. 39°03'10" N, long.

120°32' W; sec. 21, T 14 N, R 13 E); the peak is near the southwest end of Red Star Ridge. Altitude 4883 feet. Named on Greek Store (1952) 7.5' quadrangle.

Red Star Ravine [SIERRA]: *canyon,* drained by a stream that flows 0.5 mile to North Fork Kanaka Creek 0.25 mile east-northeast of Alleghany (lat. 39°28'25" N, long. 120°50'10" W; sec. 34, T 19 N, R 10 E). Named on Alleghany (1949) 7.5' quadrangle.

Red Star Ridge [PLACER]: *ridge,* south-south-west-trending, 13 miles long, between Duncan Canyon and Middle Fork American River; center 10 miles west-southwest of Granite Chief (lat. 39° 08' N, long. 120°27' W); Red Star Point is near the southwest end of the ridge. Named on Bunker Hill (1953), Greek Store (1952), and Royal Gorge (1953) 7.5' quadrangles.

Red Top [MADERA]:
(1) *locality,* 12 miles west-southwest of Chowchilla (lat. 37°05' N, long. 120°29'30" W; near SW cor. sec. 6, T 10 S, R 14 E). Named on Bliss Ranch (1960) 7.5' quadrangle. Postal authorities established Red Top post office in 1952 (Salley, p. 183).
(2) *peak,* 6 miles south of Merced Peak (lat. 37°32'45" N, long. 119°24'10" W). Altitude 9977 feet. Named on Merced Peak (1953) 15' quadrangle. The name also had the form "Redtop" (Browning, 1986, p. 180).

Red Top Mountain: see **Garnet Lake** [MADERA].

Redwood Creek [MADERA]: *stream,* flows 1.5 miles to Nelder Creek 1 mile east of Yosemite Forks (lat. 37°22' N, long. 119°36'35" W; sec. 13, T 6 S, R 22 E). Named on Bass Lake (1953) 15' quadrangle.

Reed Creek [TUOLUMNE]: *stream,* formed by the confluence of Bourland Creek and Reynolds Creek, flows 6 miles to Clavey River nearly 4 miles east of Duckwall Mountain (lat. 37°57'40" N, long. 120°02'55" W; near E line sec. 12, T 1 N, R 17 E). Named on Duckwall Mountain (1948) and Hull Creek (1979) 7.5' quadrangles.

Reed Creek: see **Bourland Creek** [TUOLUMNE].

Reese Ravine [SIERRA]: *canyon,* drained by a stream that flows 1.5 miles to Little Canyon Creek nearly 5 miles south-southwest of Mount Fillmore (lat. 39°39'45" N, long. 120°52'30" W; at W line sec. 21, T 21 N, R 10 E). Named on Mount Fillmore (1951) 7.5' quadrangle, which shows Reese mine near the head of the canyon.

Refuge Canyon [PLACER]: *canyon,* drained by a stream that flows 1.5 miles to New York Canyon 4 miles north-northwest of Foresthill (lat. 39°04'20" N, long. 120°51'30" W; sec. 9, T 14 N, R 10 E). Named on Foresthill (1949) 7.5' quadrangle. Whitney's (1880) map shows an inhabited place called Wisconsin Hill located on the ridge between Refuge Canyon and

New York Canyon, and shows an inhabited place called Elizabeth Hill situated between Refuge Canyon and Indian Canyon, which holds Indian Creek (2) of modern maps.

Register Creek [TUOLUMNE]: *stream,* flows 6.5 miles to Tuolumne River 8 miles northeast of White Wolf (lat. 37°56'25" N, long. 119°32' W). Named on Hetch Hetchy Reservoir (1956) and Tuolumne Meadows (1956) 15' quadrangles.

Regulation Creek [TUOLUMNE]: *stream,* flows 2.5 miles to Return Creek 11 miles west-northwest of Tioga Pass (lat. 38°57'55" N, long. 119°26'45" W); the creek is east of Regulation Peak. Named on Tuolumne Meadows (1956) 15' quadrangle. The stream first was called West Fork Return Creek (Browning, 1986, p. 181).

Regulation Peak [TUOLUMNE]: *peak,* 13 miles west-northwest of Tioga Pass (lat. 38°55'10" N, long. 119°28'15" W). Named on Tuolumne Meadows (1956) 15' quadrangle. A trumpeter named McBride suggested the name to Lieutenant H.C. Benson after he and the lieutenant had posted regulations for Yosemite National Park throughout the park—the name originally was meant for present Volunteer Peak (Browning, 1986, p. 181).

Regulation Peak: see **West Peak** [TUOLUMNE].

Relief [NEVADA]: *locality,* 3.25 miles west of Washington (lat. 39° 21'40" N, long. 120°51'35" W; sec. 4, T 17 N, R 10 E). Named on Washington (1950) 7.5' quadrangle. Called Relief Hill on Whitney's (1873) map, which shows a place called Louisa situated less than 1 mile south of Relief Hill along South Yuba River, and shows a feature called Cotton Hill located 1.5 miles southeast of Relief Hill. The name "Relief" is from a station established at the site by the first relief group sent to rescue Donner Party survivors in 1847 (Hanna, p. 253). The place also was called Grizzly Hill (Bancroft, 1888, p. 358). Gudde (1975, p. 96) listed a mining place called Diggers Bar that was located 1 mile below Relief on the south side of South Yuba River, and (p. 53) a mining place called Burks Bar that was situated 3 miles above Relief on the south side of the river.

Relief Creek [TUOLUMNE]: *stream,* flows 3.5 miles to Summit Creek 13 miles northwest of Tower Peak (lat. 38°14'55" N, long. 119°44'30" W; sec. 26, T 5 N, R 20 E); the stream heads in Upper Relief Valley and goes through Lower Relief Valley. Named on Pinecrest (1956) and Tower Peak (1956) 15' quadrangles.

Relief Creek: see **Summit Creek** [TUOLUMNE].

Relief Hill [NEVADA]: *ridge,* west-southwest-trending, 2 miles long, 3 miles east-northeast of North Bloomfield (lat. 39°23' N, long.

120°51'30" W); the ridge is 2 miles north of Relief. Named on Colfax (1898) 30' quadrangle.

Relief Hill: see **Relief** [NEVADA].

Relief Peak [TUOLUMNE]: *peak,* 10.5 miles northwest of Tower Peak (lat. 38°14'15" N, long. 119°41'45" W); the peak is 3 miles east of Lower Relief Valley. Altitude 10,808 feet. Named on Tower Peak (1956) 15' quadrangle.

Relief Reservoir [TUOLUMNE]: *lake,* 1.5 miles long, behind a dam on Summit Creek 6 miles west-southwest of Sonora Pass (lat. 38° 16'50" N, long. 119°43'55" W; near W line sec. 13, T 5 N, R 20 E). Named on Sonora Pass (1979) 7.5' quadrangle.

Relief Valley: see **Lower Relief Valley** [TUOLUMNE]; **Upper Relief Valley** [TUOLUMNE].

Remington Hill [NEVADA]:

(1) *ridge,* southwest-trending, 1.5 miles long, 4.5 miles south of Washington (lat. 39°17'25" N, long. 120°47'05" W). Named on Washington (1950) 7.5' quadrangle.

(2) *locality,* 5.5 miles south of Washington (lat. 39°16'30" N, long. 120°47'40" W). Named on Colfax (1898) 30' quadrangle. Whitney's (1873) map shows a community called Melburn Hill located 1 mile southwest of Remington Hill (2), a community called Excelsior located 1.25 miles east-northeast of Remington Hill (2), a community called Bald Eagle located 1.25 miles northeast of Remington Hill (2), and a community called Negro Flat situated 0.25 mile southwest of Remington Hill (2).

Repeater Hill [TUOLUMNE]: *peak,* 10 miles southwest of Liberty Hill (lat. 38°15'10" N, long. 120°13'10" W; near S line sec. 28, T 5 N, R 16 E). Altitude 5510 feet. Named on Boards Crossing (1979) 7.5' quadrangle.

Republican Cañon: see **Jesse Canyon** [EL DORADO].

Rescue [EL DORADO]: *locality,* 3.5 miles north-northwest of Shingle Springs (lat. 38°42'40" N, long. 120°57'05" W; sec. 23, T 10 N, R 9 E). Named on Shingle Springs (1949) 7.5' quadrangle. Postal authorities established Rescue post office in 1895; the name is for a nearby mine (Salley, p. 184). California Mining Bureau's (1909a) map shows a place called Jurgens located 6 miles by stage line northwest of Rescue. Postal authorities established Jurgens post office in 1903 and discontinued it in 1914; the name was for Annie C. Jurgens, first postmaster (Salley, p. 109). They established Green Springs post office in 1851 and discontinued it in 1852; it was located along Weber Creek 8 miles southwest of Coloma in the neighborhood of present Rescue (Salley, p. 89).

Reservoir Meadows: see **Ackerson Meadow** [TUOLUMNE].

Return Creek [TUOLUMNE]: *stream,* flows 14 miles to Tuolumne River 11.5 miles west of Tioga Pass (lat. 37°55'55" N, long. 119° 27'55" W). Named on Matterhorn Peak (1956) 15' quadrangle. United States Board on Geographic Names (1934, p. 21) rejected the name "North Fork of Tuolumne River" for the stream. Present Regulation Creek first was called West Fork Return Creek (Browning, 1986, p. 181).

Return Creek: see **North Fork**, under **Tuolumne River** [TUOLUMNE].

Revis Mountain [MADERA]: *peak,* 5.5 miles north-northwest of O'Neals (lat. 37°11'40" N, long. 119°44'45" W; near E line sec. 35, T 8 S, R 20 E). Named on Knowles (1962) and O'Neals (1965) 7.5' quadrangles.

Reymann Lake [MARIPOSA]: *lake,* 900 feet long, 3 miles southeast of Cathedral Peak (lat. 37°49'15" N, long. 119°21'30" W). Named on Tuolumne Meadows (1956) 15' quadrangle. The name commemorates William M. Reymann, who was a ranger in Yosemite National Park (Browning, 1986, p. 182).

Reynolds Creek [TUOLUMNE]: *stream,* flows 8.5 miles to join Bourland Creek and form Reed Creek 8.5 miles southeast of Long Barn (lat. 38°01'10" N, long. 120°00'45" W; near W line sec. 21, T 2 N, R 18 E). Named on Cherry Lake North (1979) and Hull Creek (1979) 7.5' quadrangles.

Reynolds Creek: see **Little Reynolds Creek** [TUOLUMNE].

Reynolds Ferry [CALAVERAS-TUOLUMNE]: *locality,* 5.5 miles east of Copperopolis along Stanislaus River on Calaveras-Tuolumne county line (lat. 37°58'50" N, long. 120°32'20" W; sec. 34, T 2 N, R 13 E). Named on Copperopolis (1916) 15' quadrangle. Water of New Melones Lake now covers the site. Postal authorities established Reynolds Ferry post office in Calaveras County in 1856, discontinued it for a time in 1860, and discontinued it finally in 1868 (Frickstad, p. 16).

Rex Reservoir [NEVADA]: *lake,* 700 feet long, 3.5 miles northeast of Pilot Peak (lat. 39°12'30" N, long. 121°08'10" W; sec. 36, T 16 N, R 7 E). Named on Rough and Ready (1949) 7.5' quadrangle.

Rhode Island Ravine [NEVADA]: *canyon,* drained by a stream that flows less than 1 mile to Wolf Creek 0.5 mile south-southwest of downtown Grass Valley (lat. 39°12'40" N, long. 121°04' W; near N line sec. 34, T 16 N, R 8 E). Named on Grass Valley (1949) 7.5' quadrangle. Rhode Island Company mined gold in the canyon (Morley and Foley, p. 22).

Rhodes Lake [TUOLUMNE]: *lake,* 600 feet long, 4.25 miles east of Liberty Hill (lat. 38°22'15" N, long. 120°01'15" W; sec. 17, T 6 N, R 18 E). Named on Liberty Hill (1979) 7.5' quadrangle.

Ribbon Creek [MARIPOSA]: *stream,* flows 3.5 miles to Merced River 3.5 miles west-southwest of Yosemite Village (lat. 37°43'25" N, long. 119°38'20" W); Ribbon Fall is along the stream.

Named on Hetch Hetchy Reservoir (1956) and Yosemite (1956) 15' quadrangles. Called Virgin Tears Creek on King and Gardner's (1865) map. Whitney (1870, p. 60) used the the form "Virgin's Tears Creek" for the name.

Ribbon Fall [MARIPOSA]: *waterfall*, 3.5 miles west-southwest of Yosemite Village on the north side of Yosemite Valley (lat. 37°44'10" N, long. 119°38'50" W). Named on Yosemite (1956) 15' quadrangle. Called Virgin Tear's Fall on King and Gardner's (1865) map. The Mariposa Battalion knew the feature as Pigeon Creek Fall (Browning, 1988, p. 118). James M. Hutchings gave it the name "Ribbon Fall" (Gudde, 1969, p. 268).

Ribbon Meadow [MARIPOSA]: *area*, 4 miles west of Yosemite Village (lat. 37°44'50" N, long. 119°39'30" W); the place is along a tributary to Ribbon Creek. Named on Yosemite (1956) 15' quadrangle.

Rice Canyon [SIERRA]: *canyon*, drained by a stream that flows 4 miles to Cold Stream (1) 5 miles southeast of Sierraville (lat. 39° 31'55" N, long. 120°18'15" W; near N line sec. 3, T 19 N, R 15 E). Named on Sierraville (1981) 7.5' quadrangle.

Rice Creek [PLACER]: *stream*, flows 3.5 miles to Middle Fork American River nearly 7 miles west-southwest of Granite Chief (lat. 39°09'15" N, long. 120°23'45" W; sec. 15, T 15 N, R 14 E). Named on Granite Chief (1953) and Royal Gorge (1953) 7.5' quadrangles.

Rice Crossing [NEVADA]: *locality*, 2.5 miles west of French Corral along Yuba River on Nevada-Yuba county line (lat. 39°18'45" N, long. 121°12'15" W; near SE cor. sec. 20, T 17 N, R 7 E). Site named on French Corral (1948) 7.5' quadrangle. Called Rices Ford on Smartsville (1895) 30' quadrangle, and called Rices Bridge on Wescoatt's (1861) map. It also was called Lousey Level (Bancroft, 1888, p. 360), Liars Flat, and Liases Flat (Gudde, 1975, p. 290). Wescoatt's (1861) map shows a place called Horse Bar located 1.25 miles south-southwest of Rices Bridge.

Rice Hill [SIERRA]: *peak*, 4 miles north of Sierraville (lat. 39°38'40" N, long. 120°21'35" W; sec. 25, T 21 N, R 14 E). Altitude 5406 feet. Named on Antelope Valley (1981) 7.5' quadrangle.

Rices [EL DORADO]: *locality*, 3.5 mile northwest of Omo Ranch (lat. 38°37'15" N, long. 120°37'20" W). Named on Placerville (1893) 30' quadrangle.

Rices Bridge: see **Rice Crossing** [NEVADA].

Rices Ford: see **Rice Crossing** [NEVADA].

Richards Creek [TUOLUMNE]: *stream*, flows nearly 2 miles to Cherry Lake 14 miles south-southeast of Pinecrest (lat. 38°00'05" N, long. 119°54'55" W; sec. 29, T 2 N, R 19 E). Named on Cherry Lake North (1979) 7.5' quadrangle.

Richardson: see **Camp Richardson** [EL DORADO].

Richardson Lake [EL DORADO]: *lake*, 1100 feet long, 5 miles west-southwest of the town of Meeks Bay (lat. 39°01'20" N, long. 120° 12'40" W; on N line sec. 33, T 14 N, R 16 E). Named on Homewood (1955) 7.5' quadrangle.

Richardson Peak [TUOLUMNE]: *peak*, 9 miles west-southwest of Tower Peak (lat. 38°05' N, long. 119°41'30" W). Altitude 9884 feet. Named on Tower Peak (1956) 15' quadrangle. Lieutenant M.M. Macomb named the peak in 1897 for Thomas Richardson, who ran sheep in the neighborhood (United States Board on Geographic Names, 1934, p. 21).

Richardsons: see **Emory**, under **Clearing House** [MARIPOSA].

Rich Bar: see **Grapevine Ravine** [AMADOR]; **Rattlesnake Bar** [PLACER].

Rich Dry Diggins: see **Auburn** [PLACER].

Rich Gulch [CALAVERAS]:

(1) *canyon*, drained by a stream that flows 2.25 miles to Mokelumne River 2 miles north of Paloma (lat. 38°17'15" N, long. 120° 45'25" W; sec. 15, T 5 N, R 11 E). Named on Jackson (1962) 7.5' quadrangle. Camp's (1962) map shows a place called James Bar located on the south side of Mokelumne River just downstream from the mouth of Rich Gulch (1). The name "James" was for Colonel George F. James, who mined at the place in 1849, and for whom Jamestown [TUOLUMNE] was named (Gudde, 1975, p. 174). Gwin mine is in Rich Gulch (1), which also had the name "Gwin Mine Canyon" (Sargent, Mrs. J.L., p. 65). Postal authorities established Gwin Mine post office at the mine in 1870, discontinued it in 1882, reestablished it with the name "Gwin" in 1895, changed the name to Gwinmine in 1895; and discontinued it in 1910—the name "Gwin" was for W.M. Gwin, who had the mine in the 1850's (Salley, p. 91).

(2) *canyon*, drained by a stream that flows 3 miles to North Fork Calaveras River 2.5 miles east of Mokelumne Hill (lat. 38°18'25" N, long. 120°39'20" W; near N line sec. 9, T 5 N, R 12 E). Named on Mokelumne Hill (1948) 7.5' quadrangle. Camp's (1962) map has the designation "Rich Gulch (upper)" for the canyon.

(3) *canyon*, drained by a stream that flows 1.5 miles to Calaveras River nearly 1 mile east-southeast of Jenny Lind (lat. 38°05'20" N, long. 120°51'20" W; near NE cor. sec. 27, T 3 N, R 10 E). Named on Jenny Lind (1962) 7.5' quadrangle.

(4) *canyon*, drained by a stream that flows 0.5 mile to Snake Gulch 3.5 miles south-southeast of Vallecito (lat. 38°02'20" N, long. 120° 27'20" W; sec. 8, T 2 N, R 14 E). Named on Columbia (1948) 7.5' quadrangle.

(5) *locality*, 5 miles east-northeast of Mokelumne Hill (lat. 38°19'50" N, long. 120°37'30" W; sec. 35, T 6 N, R 12 E); the place is near the head of Rich Gulch (2). Named on Mokelumne Hill (1948) and Rail Road Flat (1948) 7.5' quadrangles. Postal

authorities established Pleasant Springs post office in 1855, changed the name to Rich Gulch in 1857, discontinued it in 1867, reestablished it in 1887, and discontinued it in 1903 (Salley, p. 174, 185).

Rickeyville: see **Ione** [AMADOR].

Ridge Lake: see **Emigrant Lake** [TUOLUMNE].

Ridleys Ferry: see **Bagby** [MARIPOSA].

Riego [PLACER]: *locality*, 11 miles west of Roseville along the abandoned line of Sacramento Northern Railroad (lat. 38°45'05" N, long. 121°29' W; at NW cor. sec. 6, T 10 N, R 6 E). Named on Pleasant Grove (1967) and Rio Linda (1967) 7.5' quadrangles. Postal authorities established Riego post office in 1908 and discontinued it in 1919 (Frickstad, p. 121).

Riffle Box Ravine [NEVADA]: *canyon*, 2 miles long, opens into an unnamed canyon 5 miles west-northwest of Pilot Peak (lat. 39°11'45" N, long. 121°15'50" W; near S line sec. 35, T 16 N, R 6 E). Named on Rough and Ready (1949) and Smartville (1951) 7.5' quadrangles.

Riley Ridge [TUOLUMNE]: *ridge,* north-northwest-trending, 0.5 mile long, 1.25 miles south-southwest of Don Pedro Camp (lat. 37° 41'55" N, long. 120°24'55" W; sec. 3, T 3 N, R 14 E). Named on La Grange (1962) 7.5' quadrangle.

Ringgold: see **Weber Creek** [EL DORADO].

Ringgold Creek: see **Ringold Creek** [EL DORADO].

Ringold Creek [EL DORADO]: *stream,* flows 4.5 miles to Weber Creek 2 miles south of downtown Placerville (lat. 38°42'15" N, long. 120°47'30" W; sec. 20, T 10 N, R 11 E). Named on Camino (1952) and Placerville (1949) 7.5' quadrangles. United States Board on Geographic Names (1984a, p. 4) approved the name "Ringgold Creek" for the stream, and noted that the name is for Commander Cadwallader Ringgold, who was in charge of a party sent into the region in 1841 as part of Charles Wilkes' United States Exploring Expedition.

Rio de la Merced: see **Merced River** [MADERA-MARIPOSA].

Rio de la Pasion: see **Calaveras River** [CALAVERAS].

Rio de las Calaveras: see **Calaveras River** [CALAVERAS].

Rio de las Mukelemnes: see **Mokelumne River** [AMADOR-CALAVERAS].

Rio de la Towalumnes: see **Tuolumne River** [TUOLUMNE].

Rio del Laquisimes: see **Stanislaus River** [CALAVERAS-TUOLUMNE].

Rio de los Americanos: see **American River** [EL DORADO-PLACER].

Rio de los Cosumnes: see **Cosumnes River** [AMADOR-EL DORADO].

Rio de los Merced: see **Merced River** [MADERA-MARIPOSA].

Rio de Nuestra Señora de Guadalupe: see **Stanislaus River** [CALAVERAS-TUOLUMNE].

Rio de Yuba: see **Yuba River** [NEVADA].

Rio Estanislao: see **Stanislaus River** [CALAVERAS-TUOLUMNE].

Rio Linda Creek: see **Dry Creek** [PLACER].

Rio San Joaquin: see **San Joaquin River** [MADERA].

Rio Tulare: see **San Joaquin River** [MADERA].

Ripperdan [MADERA]: *village,* 7.5 miles south of Madera (lat. 36° 51'05" N, long. 120°03'20" W; at NE cor. sec. 36, T 12 S, R 17 E). Named on Biola (1963) 7.5' quadrangle.

Ritchey: see **Ione** [AMADOR].

Ritter: see **Mount Ritter** [MADERA].

Ritter Range [MADERA]: *ridge,* north-northwest-trending, 8 miles long, 8 miles northwest of Devils Postpile (lat. 37°41'30" N, long. 119°12' W); Mount Ritter is near the middle of the ridge. Named on Devils Postpile (1953) 15' quadrangle.

River Hill: see **Somerset** [EL DORADO].

River Pines [AMADOR]: *settlement,* 3 miles north-northeast of Fiddletown (lat. 38°32'45" N, long. 120°44'30" W; sec. 14, 15, T 8 N, R 11 E). Named on Aukum (1952) 7.5' quadrangle. Postal authorities established River Pines post office in 1948 (Frickstad, p. 6).

Riverside Station [TUOLUMNE]: *locality,* 2.25 miles northeast of Tuolumne along North Fork Tuolumne River (lat. 37°58'55" N, long. 120°12'20" W; sec. 34, T 2 N, R 16 E). Named on Tuolumne (1948) 7.5' quadrangle.

Riverton [EL DORADO]: *locality,* 8.5 miles west of Kyburz along South Fork American River (lat. 38°46'15" N, long. 120°26'50" W; sec. 30, T 11 N, R 14 E). Named on Riverton (1950) 7.5' quadrangle. Called Moores on Pyramid Peak (1896) 30' quadrangle. Postal authorities established Riverton post office in 1893 and discontinued it in 1898; the name was for the location of the site along a river (Salley, p. 186). The place first was known as Moore's Station—it was along a toll road built and operated by John M. Moore (Gudde, 1949, p. 287-288).

River View: see **Valley View** [MARIPOSA].

Roach Hill [PLACER]: *ridge,* south-southwest-to west-trending, 2 miles long, 5.5 miles south of Dutch Flat (lat. 39°07'45" N, long. 120°49'45" W). Named on Dutch Flat (1950) and Foresthill (1949) 7.5' quadrangles.

Robbers Ravine [PLACER]: *canyon,* 1.5 miles long, opens into an unnamed canyon 1.5 miles east-northeast of Colfax (lat. 39°06'50" N, long. 120°55'40" W; near NW cor. sec. 36, T 15 N, R 9 E). Named on Chicago Park (1949) and Colfax (1949) 7.5' quadrangles. Present Secret Ravine (1) is called Robbers Ravine on Colfax (1938) 30' quadrangle.

Robbs Peak [EL DORADO]: *peak,* 12 miles north-northwest of Kyburz (lat. 38°55'30" N, long. 120°24'10" W; near SW cor. sec. 34, T 13 N, R 14 E). Altitude 6686 feet. Named on Robbs Peak (1950) 7.5' quadrangle. The name commemorates either Hamilton D. Robb, a stockman in the early days, or Lieutenant Robb, who climbed the peak while he was exploring with a cavalry detachment (Gudde, 1969, p. 271).

Robbs Valley [EL DORADO]: *valley,* 1.5 miles east-northeast of Robbs Peak (lat. 38°55'40" N, long. 120°22'30" W). Named on Loon Lake (1952) and Robbs Peak (1950) 7.5' quadrangles.

Robert Nichols Spring [TUOLUMNE]: *spring,* 5 miles east-northeast of Twain Harte (lat. 38°04'30" N, long. 120°08'55" W; sec. 31, T 3 N, R 17 E). Named on Twain Harte (1979) 7.5' quadrangle.

Robert's Flat: see **Robinsons Flat** [PLACER].

Robertson Flat: see **Robinsons Flat** [PLACER].

Robertson Valley: see **Little Robertson Valley**, under **Little Robinsons Valley** [PLACER].

Robie Point [PLACER]: *peak,* 1.25 miles east-southeast of downtown Auburn (lat. 38°53'35" N, long. 121°03'05" W; sec. 14, T 12 N, R 8 E). Named on Auburn (1953) 7.5' quadrangle.

Robinson: see **Jack Robinson Ravine** [PLACER]; **Melones** [CALAVERAS].

Robinson Cow Camp [SIERRA]: *locality,* 4.5 miles northwest of Sierra City (lat. 39°37'15" N, long. 120°40'50" W; near SE cor. sec. 1, T 20 N, R 11 E). Named on Sierra City (1981) 7.5' quadrangle.

Robinson Flat: see **Robinsons Flat** [PLACER].

Robinson Ravine: see **Montezuma Hill** [NEVADA] (1).

Robinson's: see **Melones** [CALAVERAS].

Robinson's Ferry: see **Melones** [CALAVERAS].

Robinson's Crossing: see **Edwards Crossing** [NEVADA].

Robinsons Flat [PLACER]: *area,* 0.5 mile east of Duncan Peak (lat. 39°09'20" N, long. 120°30'05" W; around SW cor. sec. 11, T 15 N, R 13 E). Named on Duncan Peak (1952) and Royal Gorge (1953) 7.5' quadrangles. Called Robert's Flat on Whitney's (1880) map. United States Board on Geographic Names (1961, p. 14) rejected the forms "Robertson Flat," "Robinson Flat," and "Robinson's Flat" for the name.

Robinsons Valley: see **Little Robinsons Valley** [PLACER].

Rob Roy Creek: see **Deadman Creek** [NEVADA].

Rockbound Lake [EL DORADO]: *lake,* 4000 feet long, 5.5 miles west-northwest of Phipps Peak (lat. 38°59'50" N, long. 120°14'10" W). Named on Homewood (1955) and Rockbound Valley (1955) 7.5' quadrangles.

Rockbound Lake [MADERA]: *lake,* 6.5 miles east-northeast of Merced Peak (lat. 37°40'10" N, long. 119°16'50" W). Named on Merced Peak (1953) 15' quadrangle.

Rockbound Pass [EL DORADO]: *pass,* 4.5 miles southwest of Phipps Peak (lat. 38°54'10" N, long. 120°11'50" W); the pass is west of the upper end of Rockbound Valley. Named on Rockbound Valley (1955) 7.5' quadrangle.

Rockbound Valley [EL DORADO]: *valley,* on upper reaches of Rubicon River above a point 4.5 miles west-northwest of Phipps Peak (lat. 38°59'30" N, long. 120°13'15" W). Named on Rockbound Valley (1955) 7.5' quadrangle.

Rock Canyon [EL DORADO]: *canyon,* drained by a stream that flows 4.5 miles to Traverse Creek 2.5 miles south-southeast of Georgetown (lat. 38°52'25" N, long. 120°49' W; sec. 24, T 12 N, R 10 E). Named on Georgetown (1949) 7.5' quadrangle.

Rock Canyon [TUOLUMNE]: *canyon,* 1 mile long, 5.5 miles west-southwest of Matterhorn Peak (lat. 38°03'35" N, long. 119°28'35" W); the canyon is along lower reaches of Rock Creek (2). Named on Matterhorn Peak (1956) 15' quadrangle.

Rock Creek [AMADOR]: *stream,* flows 6.5 miles to Jackson Creek 6 miles west-southwest of Jackson (lat. 38°18'25" N, long. 120°52'15" W; at E line sec. 9, T 5 N, R 10 E). Named on Jackson (1962) 7.5' quadrangle.

Rock Creek [CALAVERAS]: *stream,* heads in Calaveras County and flows 19 miles, partly in Stanislaus County, to Littlejohns Creek 2.5 miles east-southeast of Farmington in San Joaquin County (lat. 37°54'50" N, long. 121°57'35" W; sec. 26, T 1 N, R 9 E). Named on Bachelor Valley (1968), Farmington (1968), and Jenny Lind (1962) 7.5' quadrangles.

Rock Creek [EL DORADO]: *stream,* flows 14 miles to South Fork American River 2.5 miles east-northeast of Chili Bar (lat. 38°47' N, long. 120°46'40" W; sec. 20, T 11 N, R 11 E). Named on Garden Valley (1949), Slate Mountain (1950), and Tunnel Hill (1950) 7.5' quadrangles.

Rock Creek [MADERA]: *stream,* flows 7 miles to San Joaquin River 7.5 miles southeast of Shuteye Peak (lat. 37°16'30" N, long. 119°19'55" W; sec. 34, T 7 S, R 24 E). Named on Shuteye Peak (1953) 15' quadrangle.

Rock Creek [NEVADA]: *stream,* flows 8.5 miles to South Yuba River 3.5 miles north-northwest of Nevada City (lat. 39°18'45" N, long. 121°02'55" W; sec. 26, T 17 N, R 8 E). Named on Nevada City (1948) and North Bloomfield (1949) 7.5' quadrangles.

Rock Creek [NEVADA]: *stream,* heads in Nevada County and flows 8 miles to Camp Far West Reservoir 7.5 miles east-northeast of Wheatland in Yuba County (lat. 39°03'25" N, long. 121°17'50" W; near N line sec. 22, T 14 N, R 6 E). Named on Grass Valley (1949) and Wheatland (1949) 15' quadrangles. Camp Far West (1949, photorevised 1973) 7.5' quadrangle shows the stream entering an enlarged Camp Far West Reservoir in Nevada County (lat. 39°03'40" N, long. 121°16'40" W; sec. 14, T 14 N, R 6 E).

Rock Creek [PLACER]: *stream,* flows 4 miles to Dry Creek (1) 5 miles north-northwest of Auburn (lat. 38°58' N, long. 121°06'35" W; sec. 20, T 13 N, R 8 E). Named on Auburn (1953) 7.5' quadrangle.

Rock Creek [SIERRA]:

(1) *stream,* flows 3.5 miles to Smithneck Creek 8.5 miles southeast of Loyalton (lat. 39°34'20" N, long. 120°09'20" W; sec. 24, T 20 N, R 16 E). Named on Dog Valley (1981) and Sardine Peak (1981) 7.5' quadrangles.

(2) *stream,* flows 4.5 miles to North Yuba River at Goodyears Bar (lat. 39°32'20" N, long. 120°53'10" W; near SW cor. sec. 5, T 19 N, R 10 E). Named on Downieville (1951) and Goodyears Bar (1951) 7.5' quadrangles.

Rock Creek [SIERRA]: *stream,* heads in Sierra County and flows 7.5 miles to Canyon Creek 4 miles east of Strawberry Valley in Yuba County (lat. 39°33'20" N, long. 121°01'55" W; near S line sec. 25, T 20 N, R 8 E). Named on Goodyears Bar (1951), La Porte (1951), and Strawberry Valley (1948) 7.5' quadrangles.

Rock Creek [TUOLUMNE]:

(1) *stream,* flows 5.5 miles to Clavey River 7 miles east of Long Barn (lat. 38°05'45" N, long. 120°00'20" W; sec. 21, T 3 N, R 18 E). Named on Cherry Lake North (1979) and Hull Creek (1979) 7.5' quadrangles.

(2) *stream,* flows 3.5 miles to Crazy Mule Gulch 6 miles west-southwest of Matterhorn Peak (lat. 38°03'05" N, long. 119°28'30" W); the stream goes through Rock Canyon. Named on Matterhorn Peak (1956) 15' quadrangle.

Rock Creek: see **Linda Creek** [PLACER]; **Little Rock Creek** [SIERRA]; **Orchard Creek** [PLACER].

Rock Creek Lake [PLACER]: *lake,* behind a dam on Rock Creek 3.5 miles north-north-west of downtown Auburn (lat. 38°56'50" N, long. 121°05'20" W; sec. 28, T 13 N, R 8 E). Named on Auburn (1953) 7.5' quadrangle.

Rock Island Lake [TUOLUMNE]: *lake,* 3800 feet long, 5.25 miles west-southwest of Matterhorn Peak (lat. 38°04'20" N, long. 119° 28'25" W); the lake is along Rock Creek (2). Named on Matterhorn Peak (1956) 15' quadrangle. Lieutenant N.F. McClure named the lake for a large island of granite near the north end (United States Board on Geographic Names, 1934, p. 21).

Rock Island Pass [TUOLUMNE]: *pass,* 4.5 miles west of Tower Peak on Tuolumne-Mono county line (lat. 38°05'55" N, long. 119°27'50" W); the pass is 1.5 miles north-northeast of Rock Island Lake. Named on Matterhorn Peak (1956) 15' quadrangle.

Rock Lake [NEVADA]: *lake,* 1650 feet long, 3.5 miles west-southwest of English Mountain at the head of Texas Creek (lat. 39°29'55" N, long. 120°36'55" W; near N line sec. 15, T 18 N, R 12 E). Named on English Mountain (1983) 7.5' quadrangle.

Rock Lake: see **Lower Rock Lake** [NEVADA].

Rocklin [PLACER]: *town,* 11 miles southwest of Auburn (lat. 38°47'25" N, long. 121°14'05" W). Named on Rocklin (1967) and Roseville (1967) 7.5' quadrangles. Postal authorities established Rocklin post office in 1868 (Frickstad, p. 121), and the town incorporated in 1893. The name is from rock quarries near the place (Hanna, p. 257).

Rock Mountain [NEVADA]: *peak,* 5 miles west of Wolf (lat. 39°03'35" N, long. 121°13'55" W; near SE cor. sec. 18, T 14 N, R 7 E); the peak is south of Rock Creek (2). Altitude 1409 feet. Named on Wolf (1949) 7.5' quadrangle.

Rockslides [MARIPOSA]: *relief feature,* 4 miles west-southwest of Yosemite Village on the north side of Yosemite Valley (lat. 37°43'40" N, long. 119°39'10" W). Named on Yosemite (1956) 15' quadrangle.

Rock Spring [MARIPOSA]: *locality,* 3.5 miles south-southwest of Coulterville along Yosemite Valley Railroad (lat. 37°39'30" N, long. 120°12'30" W). Named on Sonora (1897) 30' quadrangle.

Rocky Bar: see **Scotchman Creek** [NEVADA].

Rocky Basin Creek [EL DORADO]: *stream,* flows 2.5 miles to Gerle Creek nearly 5 miles north-northeast of Robbs Peak (lat. 38°59'25" N, long. 120°22'25" W; sec. 11, T 13 N, R 14 E). Named on Loon Lake (1952) 7.5' quadrangle.

Rocky Canyon [EL DORADO]: *canyon,* drained by a stream that flows 2 miles to South Fork American River 3 miles south-southeast of Pyramid Peak (lat. 38°48'25" N, long. 120°08'05" W; near NE cor. sec. 18, T 11 N, R 17 E). Named on Pyramid Peak (1955) 7.5' quadrangle.

Rocky Canyon [NEVADA]: *canyon,* drained by a stream that flows 2.25 miles to Boca Reservoir 7.5 miles northeast of Truckee (lat. 39°24'20" N, long. 120°05'05" W; near SW cor. sec. 15, T 18 N, R 17 E). Named on Boca (1955) 7.5' quadrangle.

Rocky Canyon Creek: see **Cathedral Creek** [TUOLUMNE].

Rocky Canyon Spring [NEVADA]: *spring,* 8 miles northeast of Truckee (lat. 39°24' N, long. 120°04'05" W; near NE cor. sec. 22, T 18 N, R 17 E); the spring is in Rocky Canyon. Named on Boca (1955) 7.5' quadrangle.

Rocky Creek [CALAVERAS]: *stream,* flows 1.25 miles to Littlejohns Creek 3.5 miles south-southwest of Copperopolis (lat. 37° 56' N, long. 120°39'45" W; sec. 16, T 1 N, R 12 E). Named on Copperopolis (1962) 7.5' quadrangle.

Rocky Glen [NEVADA]: *canyon,* drained by a stream that flows 1 mile to Poorman Creek (1) 9 miles east-northeast of North Bloomfield (lat. 39°25'40" N, long. 120°45'15" W; near W line sec. 16, T 18 N, R 11 E). Named on Alleghany (1949) and Graniteville (1982) 7.5' quadrangles.

Rocky Gulch [MARIPOSA]: *canyon,* drained

by a stream that flows 1.5 miles to Lake McClure 2.5 miles north-northeast of the village of Bear Valley (lat. 37°36'20" N, long. 120°06'30" W). Named on Bear Valley (1947, photorevised 1973) 7.5' quadrangle. Called Bond's Gulch on Laizure's (1928) map, which shows Bond's Flat at the mouth of the canyon. The same map shows a canyon called Evans Gulch located about 0.5 mile east of Bond's Gulch (present Rocky Gulch).

Rocky Gulch [TUOLUMNE]: *canyon,* drained by a stream that flows nearly 0.5 mile to Tulloch Lake 5 miles northwest of Keystone (lat. 37°53'25" N, long. 120°34'10" W; sec. 32, T 1 N, R 13 E). Named on Melones Dam (1962) 7.5' quadrangle.

Rocky Hill [CALAVERAS]: *peak,* 4 miles east-southeast of San Andreas (lat. 38°10'25" N, long. 120°36'40" W; on E line sec. 26, T 4 N, R 12 E). Altitude 1803 feet. Named on Calaveritas (1962) 7.5' quadrangle.

Rocky Peak [SIERRA]: *peak,* 4.25 miles west-northwest of Goodyears Bar (lat. 39°34'25" N, long. 120°57'10" W; sec. 27, T 20 N, R 9 E). Altitude 5344 feet. Named on Goodyears Bar (1951) 7.5' quadrangle.

Rocky Point [AMADOR]: *peak,* 4.5 miles south-southwest of Plymouth (lat. 38°25'10" N, long. 120°53'20" W; near W line sec. 33, T 7 N, R 10 E). Altitude 760 feet. Named on Irish Hill (1962) 7.5' quadrangle.

Rocky Point [MARIPOSA]: *relief feature,* 2 miles southwest of Yosemite Village on the north side of Yosemite Valley (lat. 37° 44' N, long. 119°36'50" W). Named on Yosemite (1956) 7.5' quadrangle. United States Board on Geographic Names (1991, p. 6) rejected the name "We-ack" for the feature.

Rocky Point: see **Sattley** [SIERRA].

Rocky Point Campground [MADERA]: *locality,* 6.5 miles southeast of Yosemite Forks on the southwest side of Bass Lake (1) (lat. 37° 18'10" N, long. 119°32'20" W; sec. 23, T 7 S, R 22 E). Named on Bass Lake (1953) 15' quadrangle.

Rocky Wash [PLACER]: *stream,* flows less than 0.5 mile to Truckee River 10 miles west-southwest of Martis Peak (lat. 39°15'55" N, long. 120°12'30" W; sec. 4, T 16 N, R 16 E). Named on Truckee (1955) 7.5' quadrangle.

Rodger Peak [MADERA]: *peak,* 9.5 miles northeast of Merced Peak on Madera-Mono county line (lat. 37°43'30" N, long. 119°15'25" W). Altitude 12,978 feet. Named on Merced Peak (1953) 15' quadrangle. Called Rodgers Peak on Mount Lyell (1901) 30' quadrangle. United States Board on Geographic Names (1934, p. 21) approved the form "Rodgers Peak" for the name, which Lieutenant N.F. McClure gave in 1895 to honor Captain Alexander Rodgers.

Rodgers Canyon [TUOLUMNE]: *canyon,* drained by a stream that flows 4.5 miles to Tuolumne River 8 miles northeast of White

Wolf (lat. 37°56'25" N, long. 119°32' W). Named on Hetch Hetchy Reservoir (1956) 15' quadrangle.

Rodgers Lake [TUOLUMNE]: *lake,* 3400 feet long, 14 miles west-northwest of Tioga Pass (lat. 37°59'45" N, long. 119°29'30" W). Named on Tuolumne Meadows (1956) 15' quadrangle. The name commemorates Captain Alexander Rodgers of the Fourth Cavalry, who was acting superintendent of Yosemite National Park from 1895 until 1897 (United States Board on Geographic Names, 1934, p. 21).

Rodgers Lake: see **Neall Lake** [TUOLUMNE].

Rodgers Peak: see **Rodger Peak** [MADERA].

Rodwell: see **Somerset** [EL DORADO].

Roger Creek [TUOLUMNE]: *stream,* flows 3.5 miles to Don Pedro Reservoir 4 miles southeast of Don Pedro Camp (lat. 37°41' N, long. 120°20'40" W; near S line sec. 8, T 3 S, R 15 E). Named on Penon Blanco Peak (1962, photorevised 1973) 7.5' quadrangle.

Rogers Creek [CALAVERAS]: *stream,* flows less than 1 mile to French Creek 6 miles east-southeast of Copperopolis (lat. 37°56'35" N, long. 120°32'35" W; near E line sec. 16, T 1 N, R 13 E). Named on Melones Dam (1962) 7.5' quadrangle.

Rogers Meadow [TUOLUMNE]: *area,* 11.5 miles northeast of White Wolf (lat. 37°59'35" N, long. 119°30'15" W). Named on Hetch Hetchy Reservoir (1956) 15' quadrangle.

Rogers Spring [MADERA]: *spring,* 2.5 miles east of Knowles (lat. 37°13'30" N, long. 119°49'40" W; sec. 19, T 8 S, R 20 E). Named on Knowles (1962) 7.5' quadrangle. Called Rogers Sprs. on Raymond (1944) 15' quadrangle, but United States Board on Geographic Names (1965c, p. 11) rejected this form of the name.

Rollins Reservoir [NEVADA-PLACER]: *lake,* behind a dam on Bear River 1 mile southeast of Chicago Park on Nevada-Placer county line (lat. 39°08'10" N, long. 120°57'05" W; sec. 22, T 15 N, R 9 E). Named on Chicago Park (1949, photorevised 1973) 7.5' quadrangle.

Roosevelt Lake [TUOLUMNE]: *lake,* 4600 feet long, 6 miles northwest of Tioga Pass (lat. 37°58'15" N, long. 119°20' W; on S line sec. 33, T 2 N, R 24 E). Named on Tuolumne Meadows (1956) 15' quadrangle. The name commemorates Eleanor Roosevelt, who visited Tuolumne Meadows in 1934 (O'Neill, p 116).

Root Creek [MADERA]: *stream,* flows 11.5 miles before ending in lowlands 2 miles east-southeast of Trigo (lat. 36°53'50" N, long. 119°55'45" W; sec. 8, T 12 S, R 19 E). Named on Herndon (1965) 15' quadrangle.

Ropi Lake [EL DORADO]: *lake,* 1900 feet long, 1.5 miles east-southeast of Pyramid Peak (lat. 38°50'20" N, long. 120°07'50" W). Named on Pyramid Peak (1955) 7.5' quadrangle. The word "Ropi" was coined from letters in the name "Ross Pierce" (Lekisch, p. 65).

Rosalie Lake [MADERA]: *lake,* 1100 feet long, nearly 5 miles north-northwest of Devils Postpile (lat. 37°41'15" N, long. 119°07'20" W). Named on Devils Postpile (1953) 15' quadrangle.

Rosasco: see **Rosasco Meadow** [TUOLUMNE].

Rosasco Lake [TUOLUMNE]: *lake,* 700 feet long, 10 miles east-southeast of Pinecrest (lat. 38°08'30" N, long. 119°49' W). Named on Pinecrest (1956) 15' quadrangle. The name commemorates Dave Rosasco, an early cattleman (Browning, 1986, p. 187).

Rosasco Meadow [TUOLUMNE]: *area,* 9 miles southeast of Long Barn (lat. 38°00'25" N, long. 120°00'45" W; at NW cor. sec. 28, T 2 N, R 18 E). Named on Hull Creek (1979) 7.5' quadrangle. Big Trees (1891) 30' quadrangle has the name "Rosasco" at or near the place.

Roscoe Creek [NEVADA]: *stream,* flows 2.25 miles to McKilligan Creek 1.5 miles west of Washington (lat. 39°21'50" N, long. 120° 49'50" W; at E line sec. 3, T 17 N, R 10 E). Named on Alleghany (1949) and Washington (1950) 7.5' quadrangles. The canyon of the stream is called Roscoe's Cañon on Whitney's (1873) map.

Roscoe's Cañon: see **Roscoe Creek** [NEVADA].

Rose Creek [TUOLUMNE]: *stream,* flows 16 miles to Stanislaus River 5 miles north of Columbia (lat. 38°06'35" N, long. 120°23'50" W; near SE cor. sec. 14, T 3 N, R 14 E). Named on Columbia (1948), Columbia SE (1948), Crandall Peak (1979), and Twain Harte (1979) 7.5' quadrangles.

Rosedale [MADERA]: *locality,* 4.5 miles north-northwest of O'Neals (lat. 37°11'25" N, long. 119°43'40" W; near W line sec. 31, T 8 S, R 21 E). Named on Mariposa (1912) 30' quadrangle.

Rose Mountain Range: see **Carson Range** [EL DORADO].

Roseville [PLACER]: *city,* 15 miles southwest of Auburn (lat. 38° 45' N, long. 121°17' W; around NE cor. sec. 2, T 10 N, R 6 E). Named on Citrus Heights (1967), Folsom (1967), Rocklin (1967), and Roseville (1967) 7.5' quadrangles. Postal authorities established Roseville post office in 1864 (Frickstad, p. 121), and the city incorporated in 1909. A stage station called Griders was at the place before the railroad came; trainmen called the place Junction before the name "Roseville" was applied (Hanna, p. 260).

Roseville Reservoir [PLACER]: *lake,* 950 feet long, 1.5 miles south of Rocklin (lat. 38°46'05" N, long. 121°14'05" W; near S line sec. 30, T 11 N, R 7 E). Named on Rocklin (1967) 7.5' quadrangle.

Rossassco Ravine [SIERRA]: *canyon,* drained by a stream that flows 1 mile to North Yuba River 1.25 miles west of Downieville (lat. 39°33'30" N, long. 120°51'05" W; near E line

sec. 33, T 20 N, R 10 E). Named on Downieville (1951) 7.5' quadrangle.

Ross Creek [MADERA]: *stream,* flows 5 miles to San Joaquin River 10 miles southeast of Shuteye Peak (lat. 37°13'35" N, long. 119° 20' W; near N line sec. 22, T 8 S, R 24 E). Named on Shaver Lake (1953) and Shuteye Peak (1953) 15' quadrangles.

Rossland: see **Jamestown** [TUOLUMNE].

Ross Reservoir [CALAVERAS]: *lake,* 1300 feet long, 3.25 miles northeast of Angels Camp (lat. 38°07' N, long. 120°30'45" W; sec. 14, T 3 N, R 13 E). Named on Angels Camp (1962) 7.5' quadrangle. Called Utica Reservoir on San Andreas (1947) 15' quadrangle.

Rough and Ready [NEVADA]: *village,* 5 miles north-northeast of Pilot Peak (lat. 39°13'50" N, long. 121°08'10" W; sec. 24, T 16 N, R 7 E). Named on Rough and Ready (1949) 7.5' quadrangle. Postal authorities established Rough and Ready post office before July 28, 1851, discontinued it for a time in 1855, discontinued it again for a time in 1913, discontinued it in 1942, and reestablished it in 1948 (Salley, p. 189). Miners of Rough and Ready Company came to the place in 1849 and the community that developed there took the company's name; Captain A.A. Townsend, leader of the company, had served under General Zachary Taylor, who had the nickname "Old Rough and Ready" (Hoover, Rensch, and Rensch, p. 251). Whitney's (1873) map shows a place called Randolph Ho. [House] located 1.25 miles east of Rough and Ready. California Mining Bureau's (1909a) map shows a place called Fernley located 5 miles southwest of Rough and Ready. Postal authorities established Fernley post office in 1898 and discontinued it in 1913 (Frickstad, p. 113). They established Elida post office 5 miles southwest of Rough and Ready in 1882 and discontinued it in 1883; the name war for the postmaster's wife (Salley, p. 67).

Rough and Ready Creek [TUOLUMNE]: *stream,* flows 6.25 miles to Tuolumne River 8 miles south-southeast of Sonora (lat. 37°52'30" N, long. 120°20' W; sec. 4, T 1 S, R 15 E). Named on Standard (1948) 7.5' quadrangle.

Rough and Ready Reservoir [NEVADA]: *intermittent lake,* 350 feet long, 5.25 miles north-northeast of Pilot Peak (lat. 39°14'10" N, long. 121°08' W; sec. 24, T 16 N, R 7 E); the feature is 0.5 mile north-northeast of Rough and Ready. Named on Rough and Ready (1949) 7.5' quadrangle.

Round Buttons: see **Maggies Peaks** [EL DORADO].

Round Hill [EL DORADO]: *peak,* 4.5 miles north-northeast of Chili Bar (lat. 38°49'40" N, long. 120°47'10" W; sec. 6, T 11 N, R 11 E). Altitude 2555 feet. Named on Garden Valley (1949) 7.5' quadrangle.

Round Hills [MARIPOSA]: *peaks,* two, nearly 4 miles south of the settlement of Catheys

Valley (lat. 37°22'50" N, long. 120°05'30" W; sec. 27, T 6 S, R 17 E). Altitudes 1455 feet and 1588 feet. Named on Catheys Valley (1962) 7.5' quadrangle.

Round Lake [EL DORADO]: *lake,* 2100 feet long, 4.5 miles south-southeast of Echo Summit (lat. 38°45' N, long. 120°00'20" W; sec. 4, T 10 N, R 18 E). Named on Caples Lake (1979) and Echo Lake (1955) 7.5' quadrangles.

Round Lake [NEVADA]: *lake,* 850 feet long, 5 miles southwest of English Mountain (lat. 39°23'45" N, long. 120°36'45" W; sec. 27, T 18 N, R 12 E). Named on English Mountain (1983) 7.5' quadrangle.

Round Meadow [TUOLUMNE]: *area,* 3 miles south of Duckwall Mountain (lat. 37°55'20" N, long. 120°07'25" W; near SE cor. sec. 20, T 1 N, R 17 E). Named on Duckwall Mountain (1948) 7.5' quadrangle.

Round Mountain [EL DORADO]: *peak,* 4 miles southwest of Omo Ranch (lat. 38°32'20" N, long. 120°36'55" W; near SE cor. sec. 14, T 8 N, R 12 E). Altitude 3501 feet. Named on Omo Ranch (1952) 7.5' quadrangle.

Round Mountain [NEVADA]: *peak,* 3.25 miles north-northeast of Nevada City (lat. 39°18'50" N, long. 121°00'05" W; near NE cor. sec. 30, T 17 N, R 9 E). Named on Nevada City (1948) and North Bloomfield (1949) 7.5' quadrangles.

Round Tent Canyon [EL DORADO]: *canyon,* drained by a stream that flows 4.5 miles to Silver Creek 5 miles north-northeast of Pollock Pines (lat. 38°49'30" N, long. 120°32'15" W; near W line sec. 4, T 11 N, R 13 E). Named on Pollock Pines (1950) and Riverton (1950) 7.5' quadrangles.

Round Top: see **Little Round Top** [EL DORADO].

Roundtop: see **Kirkwood** [AMADOR].

Roundtree Saddle [MARIPOSA]: *pass,* 11.5 miles south of El Portal (lat. 37°30'35" N, long. 119°45'45" W; near SE cor. sec. 10, T 5 S, R 20 E). Named on Buckingham Mountain (1947) 7.5' quadrangle.

Round Valley [NEVADA]:

(1) *valley,* 4 miles north-northwest of English Mountain (lat. 39°30'20" N, long. 120°33'50" W; near NW cor. sec. 19, T 19 N, R 13 E). Named on Haypress Valley (1981) 7.5' quadrangle.

(2) *valley,* 4.25 miles north-northwest of Donner Pass (lat. 39°22'10" N, long. 120°21'50" W; near E line sec. 2, T 17 N, R 14 E). Named on Norden (1955) 7.5' quadrangle.

Roush Creek [MADERA]: *stream,* flows nearly 2 miles to Whiskey Creek (2) 5.5 miles south of Shuteye Peak (lat. 37°15'50" N, long. 119°26'15" W; sec. 3, T 8 S, R 23 E). Named on Shuteye Peak (1953) 15' quadrangle. Charley Roush had a sawmill in section 3 in the 1920's (Browning, 1986, p. 188).

Rowland: see **Al Tahoe** [EL DORADO].

Royal Arch Cascade [MARIPOSA]: *waterfall,* less than 1 mile east of Yosemite Village on the north side of Yosemite Valley (lat. 37°44'55" N, long. 119°34'15" W); the waterfall is along Royal Arch Creek. Named on Yosemite (1956) 15' quadrangle.

Royal Arch Creek [MARIPOSA]: *stream,* flows 2.25 miles to Merced River less than 1 mile east-southeast of Yosemite Village (lat. 37°44'45" N, long. 119°34'15" W); the stream is west of Royal Arches. Named on Hetch Hetchy Reservoir (1956) 15' quadrangle.

Royal Arches [MARIPOSA]: *relief feature,* 1 mile east of Yosemite Village on the north side of Yosemite Valley (lat. 37°44'55" N, long. 119°33'50" W). Named on Yosemite (1956) 15' quadrangle. The name was used as early as 1851 (Browning, 1986, p. 188).

Royal Arch Lake [MADERA]: *lake,* 900 feet long, 1.25 miles southeast of Buena Vista Peak (lat. 37°34'40" N, long. 119°30'10" W; near E line sec. 24, T 4 S, R 22 E). Named on Yosemite (1956) 15' quadrangle.

Royal Gorge [PLACER]: *canyon,* 2.5 miles long, along North Fork American River above a point 9.5 miles west of Granite Chief (lat. 39°13'15" N, long. 120°27'30" W; at E line sec. 25, T 16 N, R 13 E). Named on Royal Gorge (1953) 7.5' quadrangle.

Rubicon: see **Emerald Bay** [EL DORADO] (2).

Rubicon Bay [EL DORADO]: *embayment,* 1.5 miles south-southeast of the town of Meeks Bay along Lake Tahoe (lat. 39°01'55" N, long. 120°06'30" W). Named on Meeks Bay (1955) 7.5' quadrangle.

Rubicon Creek [EL DORADO]: *stream,* flows nearly 2 miles to Lake Tahoe 2.5 miles south-southeast of the town of Meeks Bay (lat. 39°00'05" N, long. 120°06'05" W; sec. 4, T 13 N, R 17 E). Named on Emerald Bay (1955) 7.5' quadrangle.

Rubicon Creek: see **Rubicon River** [EL DORADO-PLACER].

Rubicon Lake [EL DORADO]: *lake,* 1100 feet long, 1 mile northeast of Phipps Peak (lat. 38°58' N, long. 120°08' W; near SE cor. sec. 18, T 13 N, R 17 E). Named on Rockbound Valley (1955) 7.5' quadrangle.

Rubicon Lodge: see **Meeks Bay** [EL DORADO] (2).

Rubicon Peak [EL DORADO]: *peak,* 2.5 miles north-northeast of Phipps Peak (lat. 38°59'20" N, long. 120°07'55" W; on W line sec. 8, T 13 N, R 17 E). Altitude 9183 feet. Named on Rockbound Valley (1955) 7.5' quadrangle.

Rubicon Point [EL DORADO]: *promontory,* 6.5 miles north of Mount Tallac along Lake Tahoe (lat. 38°59'55" N, long. 120°05'40" W; sec. 3, T 13 N, R 17 E). Named on Emerald Bay (1955) 7.5' quadrangle.

Rubicon Reservoir [EL DORADO]: *lake,* 3500 feet long, behind a dam on Rubicon River 4.5 miles west-northwest of Phipps Peak (lat. 38°59'20" N, long. 120°13'20" W; at W line sec. 9, T 13 N, R 16 E); the lake covers most of Onion Flat. Named on Rockbound Valley (1955, photorevised 1969) 7.5' quadrangle.

Rubicon River [EL DORADO-PLACER]: *stream,* flows for 55 miles, first in El Dorado County, then in Placer County, and finally along El Dorado-Placer county line, to Middle Fork American River 3.25 miles east-northeast of Volcanoville (lat. 39°00'10" N, long. 120°43'50" W; sec. 3, T 13 N, R 11 E). Named on Bunker Hill (1953), Devil Peak (1950), Homewood (1955), Michigan Bluff (1952), Robbs Peak (1950), Rockbound Valley (1955), Tunnel Hill (1950), and Wentworth Springs (1953) 7.5' quadrangles. Wheeler's (1876-1877b) map has the name "Rubicon Creek" for the upper part of the stream, and has the name "Big Meadow Creek" for the lower part. South Fork enters from the east 4.5 miles northwest of Robbs Peak; it is 15 miles long and is named on Loon Lake (1952, photorevised 1973) and Robbs Peak (1950) 7.5' quadrangles. South Fork is called Little South Fork Rubicon River on Pyramid Peak (1896) 30' quadrangle.

Rubicon Springs [EL DORADO]: *springs,* nearly 7 miles west-southwest of the town of Meeks Bay (lat. 39°01'05" N, long. 120° 14'40" W; sec. 31, T 14 N, R 16 E). Named on Homewood (1955) 7.5' quadrangle. Truckee (1895) 30' quadrangle has the name for a locality at the site. The springs were the basis of a resort as early as the 1860's; in 1909 a small hotel and three log cabins were open to guests in the summer (Waring, G.A., p. 234).

Ruby Bluff [SIERRA]: *relief feature,* 3.5 miles south-southwest of Downieville (lat. 39°30'45" N, long. 120°50'50" W; sec. 15, T 19 N, R 10 E). Named on Downieville (1951) 7.5' quadrangle.

Ruby Canyon [EL DORADO]: *canyon,* drained by a stream that flows 1 mile to Pilot Creek (1) 9.5 miles north of Pollock Pines (lat. 38°53'50" N, long. 120°33'55" W; near S line sec. 7, T 12 N, R 13 E). Named on Devil Peak (1950) 7.5' quadrangle.

Ruby Hill Spring [TUOLUMNE]: *spring,* 5 miles north of Twain Harte (lat. 38°06'50" N, long. 120°14'10" W; sec. 17, T 3 N, R 16 E). Named on Twain Harte (1979) 7.5' quadrangle.

Ruby Lake [MADERA]: *lake,* 1000 feet long, 8 miles north-northwest of Devils Postpile (lat. 37°43'20" N, long. 119°09'35" W); the feature is between Emerald Lake and Garnet Lake. Named on Devils Postpile (1953) 15' quadrangle.

Ruck-A-Chuncky Rapids [EL DORADO-PLACER]: *water feature,* 4 miles north of Greenwood along Middle Fork American River on El Dorado-Placer county line (lat. 38°57'20" N, long. 120°54'45" W; on E line sec. 24, T 13 N, R 9 E). Named on Greenwood (1949) 7.5' quadrangle.

Rucker Creek [NEVADA]: *stream,* flows 3 miles to South Yuba River 4 miles west-north-west of Yuba Gap (lat. 39°20'40" N, long. 120°40'40" W; near NW cor. sec. 18, T 17 N, R 12 E); the stream goes through Rucker Lake. Named on Blue Canyon (1955) 7.5' quadrangle.

Rucker Lake [NEVADA]: *lake,* 3350 feet long, 3.25 miles northwest of Yuba Gap (lat. 39°21'20" N, long. 120°39'05" W; sec. 8, T 17 N, R 12 E); the lake is along Rucker Creek. Named on Blue Canyon (1955) 7.5' quadrangle.

Rudberg Creek: see **Rydberg Creek** [TUOLUMNE].

Rupley Cabin [EL DORADO]: *locality,* 8 miles east-southeast of Robbs Peak (lat. 38°53'10" N, long. 120°15'35" W; sec. 18, T 12 N, R 16 E). Named on Loon Lake (1952) 7.5' quadrangle.

Rush Creek [MARIPOSA]: *stream,* flows 4.5 miles to South Fork Merced River 1.5 miles west-northwest of Wawona (lat. 37°32'50" N, long. 119°40'45" W; sec. 33, T 4 S, R 21 E). Named on Yosemite (1956) 15' quadrangle. Shirley Sargent (1961, p. 28) referred to a place called Cunningham Flat that was located at the mouth of Rush Creek and named for Stephen Mandeville Cunningham, who homesteaded there.

Rush Creek [TUOLUMNE]:
(1) *stream,* flows 2.25 miles to South Fork Tuolumne River 4.5 miles south-southwest of Mather (lat. 37°49'20" N, long. 119°53'35" W; in sec. 28, T 1 S, R 19 E). Named on Lake Eleanor (1956) 15' quadrangle.
(2) *stream,* flows 2.25 miles to Hull Creek 5.25 miles east of Long Barn (lat. 38°05'25" N, long. 120°02'30" W; sec. 30, T 3 N, R 18 E). Named on Hull Creek (1979) 7.5' quadrangle.
(3) *locality,* 5.25 miles south-southwest of Mather (lat. 37°48'40" N, long. 119°53'25" W; sec. 33, T 1 S, R 19 E); the place is near Rush Creek (1). Named on Lake Eleanor (1956) 15' quadrangle. Called Crockers on Yosemite (1909) 30' quadrangle. Henry Robinson Crocker arrived in California in 1853 and eventually built a cabin in what then was called Bronson's Meadow, and later became known as Crocker's Meadow; the cabin was the nucleus of a stage stop (Paden and Schlichtmann, p. 207, 211). Crocker built an inn at the place in 1880 that he called Crocker's Sierra Resort (Gudde, 1949, p. 84). California Mining Bureau's (1910) map shows a place called Sequoia located at or near present Rush Creek (3). Postal authorities established Sequoia post office in 1886 and discontinued it in 1915 (Salley, p. 201). Sequoia first was called Santa Maria because the group of Mexicans who started the community worked at Santa Maria mine (Paden and Schlichtmann, p. 205). United States Board on Geographic Names (1933, p. 682) rejected the names "Crocker" and "Crocker's" for Se-

quoia.

Rushing Hill: see **Rushing Mountain** [TUOLUMNE].

Rushing Meadow [TUOLUMNE]: *area,* nearly 7 miles northeast of Twain Harte along South Fork Stanislaus River (lat. 38°06'50" N, long. 120°09' W; sec. 18, T 3 N, R 17 E). Named on Twain Harte (1979) 7.5' quadrangle.

Rushing Mountain [TUOLUMNE]: *peak,* 3.25 miles west of Keystone (lat. 37°49'40" N, long. 120°34'05" W; near S line sec. 20, T 1 S, R 13 E). Altitude 1519 feet. Named on Keystone (1962) 7.5' quadrangle. Called Big Hill on Copperopolis (1916) 15' quadrangle, which shows Rushing ranch located 1 mile south-southeast of the peak. United States Board on Geographic Names (1965c, p. 11) rejected the names "Big Hill," "Rushing Hill," "Rushings Hill," and "Rushings Mountain" for the feature.

Rush Creek [NEVADA]: *stream,* flows nearly 4 miles to South Yuba River 5 miles west-northwest of Nevada City (lat. 39°17'35" N, long. 121°06'15" W; sec. 32, T 17 N, R 8 E). Named on Nevada City (1948) 7.5' quadrangle.

Russell Creek [TUOLUMNE]: *stream,* flows 1.5 miles to Clavey River 3.5 miles east of Duckwall Mountain (lat. 37°58'15" N, long. 120°03'10" W; sec. 1, T 1 N, R 17 E). Named on Duckwall Mountain (1948) 7.5' quadrangle.

Russell Hollow [EL DORADO]: *canyon,* 2 miles long, on upper reaches of Hancock Creek above a point 4.5 miles southwest of the village of Pilot Hill (lat. 38°47'20" N, long. 121°04'20" W; sec. 22, T 11 N, R 8 E). Named on Pilot Hill (1954) 7.5' quadrangle.

Russell Valley [NEVADA]: *valley,* 4 miles northeast of Hobart Mills along Dry Creek (1) (lat. 39°26'10" N, long. 120°07'30" W). Named on Boca (1955) and Hobart Mills (1981) 7.5' quadrangles.

Rutherford Lake [MADERA]: *lake,* 1900 feet long, nearly 3 miles south-southeast of Merced Peak (lat. 37°35'55" N, long. 119°22'15" W). Named on Merced Peak (1953) 15' quadrangle. The name commemorates Lieutenant Samuel M. Rutherford, who was stationed in Yosemite National Park in 1896 (Farquhar, 1925, p. 130).

Ruth Lake [MADERA]: *lake,* 700 feet long, 4.25 miles south-southeast of Merced Peak (lat. 37°34'35" N, long. 119°22'15" W). Named on Merced Peak (1953) 15' quadrangle. A group from California Department of Fish and Game and from the Forest Service named the lake in 1934 to honor Ruth Burghduff, wife of A.E. Burghduff of the Department of Fish and Game; the feature had been called Hidden Lake, Nutcracker Lake, and Hideaway Lake (Browning, 1986. p. 189).

Ryans Lower Cow Camp [MADERA]: *locality,* 4 miles north of Shuteye Peak (lat. 37°24'15" N, long. 119°25' W; near E line sec.

14, T 6 S, R 23 E); the place is 2 miles southeast of Ryans Upper Cow Camp. Named on Shuteye Peak (1953) 15' quadrangle.

Ryans Upper Cow Camp [MADERA]: *locality,* 5.5 miles north of Shuteye Peak (lat. 37°26' N, long. 119°25'55" W; near SW cor. sec. 2, T 6 S, R 23 E); the place is 2 miles northwest of Ryans Lower Cow Camp. Named on Shuteye Peak (1953) 15' quadrangle.

Rydberg Creek [TUOLUMNE]: *stream,* heads in Tuolumne County and flows 10.5 miles to Dry Creek 1.25 miles south-southwest of Cooperstown in Stanislaus County (lat. 37°43'30" N, long. 120°33'10" W; near SW cor. sec. 28, T 2 S, R 13 E). Named on Chinese Camp (1947), Cooperstown (1968), Keystone (1962), and La Grange (1962) 7.5' quadrangles. Called Dry Creek on Copperopolis (1916) 15' quadrangle. United States Board on Geographic Names (1978b, p. 5) rejected the name "Rudberg Creek" for the stream.

– S –

Sachse Monument [TUOLUMNE]: *peak,* nearly 7 miles west of Tower Peak (lat. 38°09'10" N, long. 119°40'15" W; sec. 33, T 4 N, R 21 E). Altitude 9405 feet. Named on Tower Peak (1956) 15' quadrangle. The name commemorates a cowboy who was credited with discovering routes that later became trails (Browning, 1986, p. 190).

Sacketts Gulch [SIERRA]: *canyon,* drained by a stream that flows 2 miles to Slate Creek 4.25 miles west-southwest of Mount Fillmore (lat. 39°42'35" N, long. 120°55'30" W; sec. 1, T 21 N, R 9 E). Named on La Porte (1951) 7.5' quadrangle.

Sacramento: see **Camp Sacramento** [EL DORADO].

Sacramento Hill [EL DORADO]: *ridge,* west-northwest- to west-trending, 1 mile long, less than 1 mile west-southwest of downtown Placerville (lat. 38°43'30" N, long. 120°48'35" W; near N line sec. 18, T 10 N, R 11 E). Named on Placerville (1949) 7.5' quadrangle.

Saddle Back: see **Saddleback Mountain** [SIERRA].

Saddleback Mountain [SIERRA]: *peak,* 6.5 miles south of Mount Fillmore (lat. 39°38'10" N, long. 120°51'45" W; sec. 33, T 21 N, R 10 E). Altitude 6690 feet. Named on Mount Fillmore (1951) 7.5' quadrangle Called Saddle Back on Logan's (1929) map.

Saddle Horse Lake [TUOLUMNE]: *lake,* 2400 feet long, 9.5 miles north-northeast of White Wolf (lat. 37°59'50" N, long. 119°34'10" W). Named on Hetch Hetchy Reservoir (1956) 15' quadrangle. Members of the Bright family pastured saddle horses at the lake and named it (Browning, 1988, p. 124). The United States Board on Geographic Names (1960c, p. 18) rejected the names "Irving Bright Lake" and "Irwin Bright Lake" for the feature.

Saddle Meadow [SIERRA]: *area,* 7.5 miles south-southeast of Sierraville (lat. 39°29'20" N, long. 120°18'30" W; at NE cor. sec. 21, T 19 N, R 15 E). Named on Independence Lake (1981) 7.5' quadrangle.

Saddle Mountain [EL DORADO]: *peak,* nearly 6 miles north of Pollock Pines (lat. 38°50'50" N, long. 120°34'55" W; sec. 36, T 12 N, R 12 E). Altitude 5165 feet. Named on Pollock Pines (1950) 7.5' quadrangle.

Sadler Lake [MADERA]: *lake,* 1100 feet long, 5 miles east of Merced Peak (lat. 37°38'35" N, long. 119°18'10" W); the lake is 1.5 miles west of Sadler Peak. Named on Merced Peak (1953) 15' quadrangle.

Sadler Peak [MADERA]: *peak,* 6.5 miles east of Merced Peak (lat. 37°38'20" N, long. 119°16'20" W). Altitude 10,567 feet. Named on Merced Peak (1953) 15' quadrangle. Lieutenant N.F. McClure named the peak in 1895 for a corporal in his detachment (Farquhar, 1925, p. 130).

Sagehen Campground [NEVADA]: *locality,* 9 miles north-northeast of Donner Pass (lat. 39°26'05" N, long. 120°15'25" W; near SE cor. sec. 1, T 18 N, R 15 E); the place is near Sagehen Creek. Named on Independence Lake (1981) 7.5' quadrangle.

Sagehen Creek [NEVADA-SIERRA]: *stream,* heads in Nevada County and flows 9.5 miles to Stampede Reservoir 15 miles south-southeast of Loyalton in Sierra County (lat. 39°27'15" N, long. 120°10'40" W; near W line sec. 35, T 19 N, R 16 E). Named on Hobart Mills (1981) and Independence Lake (1981) 7.5' quadrangles. The name has the form "Sage Hen Creek" on Truckee (1895) 30' quadrangle.

Sagehen Hills [NEVADA]: *ridge,* southwest- to west-northwest-trending, 4 miles long, center 3 miles west of Hobart Mills (lat. 39° 24'25" N, long. 120°14'40" W); the ridge is south of Sagehen Creek. Named on Hobart Mills (1981) and Independence Lake (1981) 7.5' quadrangles.

Sage Mill [MADERA]: *locality,* 5.5 miles south of Shuteye Peak (lat. 37°16'15" N, long. 119°25'30" W; near S line sec. 35, T 7 S, R 23 E). Named on Kaiser (1904) 30' quadrangle.

Sage Hill [PLACER]: *peak,* 3.5 miles east-northeast of Foresthill (lat. 39°02' N, long. 120°45'15" W; near W line sec. 28, T 14 N, R 11 E). Altitude 3655 feet. Named on Foresthill (1949) 7.5' quadrangle.

Sage Hill: see **Little Sage Hill** [PLACER].

Saginaw Creek [MADERA]: *stream,* flows 4.5 miles to San Joaquin River 13 miles south of Shuteye Peak (lat. 37°09'50" N, long. 119° 25' W; sec. 12, T 9 S, R 23 E). Named on Shaver Lake (1953) 15' quadrangle.

Sailor Canyon [PLACER]: *canyon,* drained by a stream that flows nearly 4 miles to North Fork American River 11.5 miles west of Granite Chief (lat. 39°13'05" N, long. 120°29'45" W; near SE cor. sec. 27, T 16 N, R 13 E). Named on Royal Gorge (1953) 7.5' quadrangle. Called Sailor Ravine on Truckee (1940) 30' quadrangle.

Sailor Creek: see **Big Sailor Creek** [EL DORADO]; **Little Sailor Creek** [EL DORADO].

Sailor Flat [NEVADA]:
(1) *area,* 5 miles southwest of North Bloomfield (lat. 39°18'50" N, long. 120°57'45" W; near NW cor. sec. 27, T 17 N, R 9 E). Named on North Bloomfield (1949) 7.5' quadrangle.
(2) *area,* 6 miles south of North Bloomfield (lat. 39°16'50" N, long. 120°53'05" W; sec. 5, T 16 N, R 10 E). Named on North Bloomfield (1949) 7.5' quadrangle.

Sailor Flat [PLACER]: *locality,* 1.25 miles north-northeast of Duncan Peak (lat. 39°10'25" N, long. 120°30'20" W; near SE cor. sec. 3, T 15 N, R 13 E). Named on Duncan Peak (1952) 7.5' quadrangle.

Sailor Flat Cañon: see **Blue Tent** [NEVADA].

Sailor Gulch [CALAVERAS]: *canyon,* drained by a stream that flows 0.5 mile to Shirley Gulch 5 miles southwest of Copperopolis (lat. 37°56'15" N, long. 120°42'45" W; sec. 13, T 1 N, R 11 E). Named on Copperopolis (1962) 7.5' quadrangle.

Sailor's Gulch: see **Matelot Gulch** [TUOLUMNE].

Sailor Meadow [PLACER]: *area,* 10 miles west of Granite Chief (lat. 39°11'10" N, long. 120°28'30" W; sec. 1, T 15 N, R 13 E); the place is at the head of a branch of Sailor Canyon. Named on Royal Gorge (1953) 7.5' quadrangle.

Sailor Point [PLACER]: *ridge,* south-southwest-trending, 1 mile long, 3 miles south of Emigrant Gap (1) (lat. 39°15'30" N, long. 120°40'35" W); the ridge is east of Sailor Ravine. Named on Blue Canyon (1955) 7.5' quadrangle.

Sailor Ravine [EL DORADO]: *canyon,* drained by a stream that flows 2.5 miles to Whaler Creek 9 miles northwest of Pollock Pines (lat. 38°51'10" N, long. 120°42'10" W; at S line sec. 25, T 12 N, R 11 E). Named on Slate Mountain (1950) 7.5' quadrangle.

Sailor Ravine [PLACER]: *canyon,* drained by a stream that flows 2.5 miles to Fulda Creek 5 miles north-northwest of Westville (lat. 39°14'20" N, long. 120°41'20" W; sec. 24, T 16 N, R 11 E); the canyon is west of Sailor Point. Named on Blue Canyon (1955) and Westville (1952) 7.5' quadrangles.

Sailor Ravine [SIERRA]: *canyon,* drained by a stream that flows 1.25 miles to Downie River nearly 2 miles north of Downieville (lat. 39°35'05" N, long. 120°49'30" W; sec. 23, T 20 N, R 10 E). Named on Downieville (1951) 7.5' quadrangle.

Sailor Ravine: see **Sailor Canyon** [PLACER].

Sailors Flat: see **Garden Valley** [EL DORADO]; **Newtown** [NEVADA].

Sailors Gulch: see **Jackson Butte** [AMADOR].

Sailors Ravine [PLACER]: *canyon,* drained by a stream that flows nearly 4 miles to Doty Ravine 6.5 miles west of Auburn (lat. 38° 55'05" N, long. 121°11'20" W; near W line sec. 3, T 12 N, R 7 E). Named on Gold Hill (1954) 7.5' quadrangle.

Saint Catherine Creek [SIERRA]: *stream,* flows 2 miles to North Yuba River 3 miles west-southwest of Goodyears Bar (lat. 39°31'30" N, long. 120°56'10" W; sec. 11, T 19 N, R 9 E). Named on Goodyears Bar (1951) 7.5' quadrangle.

Saint Charles Hill [SIERRA]: *peak,* 2.5 miles northwest of Goodyears Bar (lat. 39°34'05" N, long. 120°54'40" W; sec. 25, T 20 N, R 9 E). Altitude 5411 feet. Named on Goodyears Bar (1951) 7.5' quadrangle.

Saint Joe Bar: see **Ramshorn Creek** [SIERRA].

Saint Lawrence: see **Kelsey** [EL DORADO].

Saint Lawrenceburgh: see **Kelsey** [EL DORADO].

Saint Louis [SIERRA]: *locality,* 4.5 miles west-southwest of Mount Fillmore (lat. 39°41'55" N, long. 120°55'25" W; sec. 12, T 21 N, R 9 E). Named on La Porte (1951) 7.5' quadrangle. Postal authorities established Saint Louis post office in 1855, discontinued it in 1895, reestablished it in 1898, and discontinued it in 1915 (Frickstad, p. 185). Miners from Missouri laid out a community in 1852 at a mining place called Sears' Diggings, and named it St. Louis for the city in their home state (Hoover, Rensch, and Rensch, p. 496). The name "Sears" was for Captain Sears, who discovered gold at the place in 1850 (Gudde, 1975, p. 313). A mining place called Challenge was located 2 miles south of St. Louis along a tributary to Slate Creek (Gudde, 1975, p. 66).

Saint Michele Meadow [CALAVERAS]: *area,* 3.25 miles west-southwest of Tamarack (lat. 38°25'15" N, long. 120°08' W; near NW cor. sec. 32, T 7 N, R 17 E). Named on Calaveras Dome (1979) 7.5' quadrangle.

Salamander Creek [CALAVERAS]: *stream,* flows 3 miles to Jesus Maria Creek 8 miles southwest of Rail Road Flat (lat. 38°15'50" N, long. 120°36'45" W; near NE cor. sec. 26, T 5 N, R 12 E). Named on Calaveritas (1962) and Rail Road Flat (1948) 7.5' quadrangles.

Salina Flat: see **Pat Yore Flat** [NEVADA].

Salmon Creek [SIERRA]: *stream,* flows 4.25 miles to Sardine Creek 4.25 miles north of Sierra City (lat. 39°37'10" N, long. 120°36'35" W; near N line sec. 10, T 20 N, R 12 E); the stream goes through Upper Salmon Lake and Lower Salmon Lake. Named on Clio (1981), Gold Lake (1981), and Haypress Valley (1981) 7.5' quadrangles.

Salmon Creek Campground [SIERRA]: *locality,* 4 miles north-northeast of Sierra City (lat.

39°37'20" N, long. 120°36'35" W; at S line sec. sec. 3, T 20 N, R 12 E); the place is along Salmon Creek. Named on Sierra City (1955) 15' quadrangle.

Salmon Falls [EL DORADO]:

(1) *waterfall,* 6 miles south-southwest of the village of Pilot Hill along South Fork American River (lat. 38°45'30" N, long. 121°04'15" W; sec. 34, T 11 N, R 8 E). Named on Auburn (1954) 15' quadrangle. Water of Folsom Lake now covers the site. The place was a favorite fishing spot of aboriginal Indians (Hoover, Rensch, and Rensch, p. 85).

(2) *locality,* 5.5 miles south-southwest of the village of Pilot Hill along South Fork American River near Salmon Falls (1) (lat. 38° 45'40" N, long. 121°03'35" W; near E line sec. 34, T 11 N, R 8 E). Named on Auburn (1944) 15' quadrangle. Water of Folsom Lake now covers the site. Postal authorities established Salmon Falls post office in 1851, discontinued it for a time in 1875, discontinued it again for a time in 1893, and discontinued it finally in 1912 (Frickstad, p. 29). Mining began at the place in 1848, and a town was laid out in 1850 (Hoover, Rensch, and Rensch, p. 85). Arrowsmith's (1860) map shows a place called Higgins Point located along South Fork 0.5 mile west of Salmon Falls (2). The name was for an Australian who opened the first store at the place; gold was discovered there in 1849 (Gudde, 1975, p. 156).

Salmon Lake [PLACER]: *lake,* 650 feet long, 2.25 miles southeast of Cisco Grove (lat. 39°16'55" N, long. 120°30'55" W; sec. 4, T 16 N, R 13 E). Named on Cisco Grove (1955) 7.5' quadrangle.

Salmon Lake: see **Lower Salmon Lake** [SIERRA]; **Upper Salmon Lake** [SIERRA].

Salmon Lake Resort [SIERRA]: *locality,* 6.5 miles north of Sierra City (lat. 39°39'20" N, long. 120°39'15" W; sec. 29, T 21 N, R 12 E); the place is by Upper Salmon Lake. Named on Gold Lake (1981) 7.5' quadrangle.

Salmon Trout River: see **Truckee River** [NEVADA-PLACER-SIERRA].

Salt Creek [CALAVERAS]: *stream,* flows 4.5 miles to Salt Spring Valley Reservoir 10 miles west-southwest of Angels Camp (lat. 38°02' N, long. 120°43'20" W; at E line sec. 11, T 2 N, R 11 E). Named on Salt Spring Valley (1962) 7.5' quadrangle.

Salt Creek [EL DORADO]: *stream,* flows 2 miles to North Fork American River nearly 2 miles west of Cool (lat. 38°53'15" N, long. 121°02'55" W; sec. 14, T 12 N, R 8 E). Named on Auburn (1953) 7.5' quadrangle.

Salt Creek [NEVADA]: *stream,* flows 3.5 miles to South Wolf Creek 2.25 miles north-north-east of Higgins Corner (lat. 39°04'10" N, long. 121°04'05" W; near NE cor. sec. 15, T 14 N, R 8 E). Named on Lake Combie (1949) 7.5' quadrangle.

Salt Gulch [CALAVERAS]: *canyon,* drained by

a stream that flows 0.5 mile to Pardee Reservoir 3 miles north of Valley Springs (lat. 38°14'05" N, long. 120°49'20" W; near N line sec. 1, T 4 N, R 10 E). Named on Valley Springs (1962) 7.5' quadrangle. Water of South Arm Pardee Reservoir now floods most of the canyon of the stream. Camp's (1962) map shows a place called Ragtown situated 2 miles north-northeast of Campo Seco in the part of Salt Gulch now under water.

Salt Lick Meadow [TUOLUMNE]: *area,* 11.5 miles east of Pinecrest (lat. 38°11'55" N, long. 119°47'15" W). Named on Pinecrest (1956) 15' quadrangle.

Salt Rock Creek [EL DORADO]: *stream,* flows 2 miles to Steely Fork Cosumnes River 7.5 miles southwest of Old Iron Mountain (lat. 38°37'35" N, long. 120°29'05" W; near N line sec. 24, T 9 N, R 13 E). Named on Stump Spring (1951) 7.5' quadrangle.

Salt Spring [MARIPOSA]: *spring,* 11.5 miles east-southeast of Mariposa (lat. 37°25'15" N, long. 119°46'15" W; sec. 10, T 6 S, R 20 E). Named on Mariposa (1947) 15' quadrangle. Mariposa (1912) 30' quadrangle has the plural form "Salt Springs" for the name.

Salt Spring [TUOLUMNE]:
(1) *spring,* 3.5 miles west of Don Pedro Camp (lat. 37°43'30" N, long. 120°28'05" W; near S line sec. 30, T 2 S, R 14 E). Named on La Grange (1962) 7.5' quadrangle.
(2) *spring,* 3 miles south of Dardanelle (lat. 38°17'50" N, long. 119° 49'15" W; sec. 7, T 5 N, R 20 E). Named on Dardanelle (1979) 7.5' quadrangle.

Salt Spring Creek: see **Gallup Creek** [TUOLUMNE].

Salt Springs [CALAVERAS]: *lake,* 300 feet long, 5.25 miles northwest of Tamarack (lat. 38°29'45" N, long. 120°08'10" W). Named on Calaveras Dome (1979) 7.5' quadrangle.

Salt Springs: see **Salt Spring** [MARIPOSA].

Salt Springs Reservoir [CALAVERAS]: *lake,* 4 miles long, behind a dam on North Fork Mokelumne River 8.5 miles west-northwest of Tamarack on Calaveras-Amador county line (lat. 38°29'55" N, long. 120°12'50" W; sec. 33, T 8 N, R 16 E). Named on Calaveras Dome (1979) 7.5' quadrangle.

Salt Spring Valley [CALAVERAS]: *valley,* 10 miles west-southwest of Angels Camp (lat. 38°02'30" N, long. 120°43'30" W). Named on Jenny Lind (1962) and Salt Spring Valley (1962) 7.5' quadrangles. Postal authorities established Salt Spring Valley post office about 8 miles east of Milton in 1878 and discontinued it in 1880 (Salley, p. 192).

Salt Spring Valley Reservoir [CALAVERAS]: *lake,* behind a dam on Rock Creek 7.5 miles southeast of Jenny Lind (lat. 38°01'40" N, long. 120°45'40" W; near E line sec. 16, T 2 N, R 11 E); the lake is in Salt Spring Valley. Named on Jenny Lind (1962) and Salt Spring Valley (1962) 7.5' quadrangles.

Salvada Gulch [TUOLUMNE]: *canyon,* drained by a stream that flows 1 mile to Woods Creek 1.25 miles east of Chinese Camp (lat. 37°52'25" N, long. 120°24'40" W; sec. 2, T 1 S, R 14 E). Named on Sonora (1948) 15' quadrangle.

Salvado: see **Chinese Camp** [TUOLUMNE].

Salt Springs Reservoir [AMADOR]: *lake,* behind a dam on North Fork Mokelumne River 7 miles west-southwest of Mokelumne Peak on Amador-Calaveras county line (lat. 38°29'55" N, long. 120°12'55" W; sec. 33, T 8 N, R 16 E). Named on Bear River Reservoir (1979) and Calaveras Dome (1979) 7.5' quadrangles.

Salvation Ravine [PLACER]: *canyon,* drained by a stream that flows 2 miles to North Fork American River 4 miles southeast of Colfax (lat. 39°03'15" N, long. 120°54'15" W; at N line sec. 19, T 14 N, R 10 E). Named on Colfax (1949) 7.5' quadrangle.

Sam Williams Spring [TUOLUMNE]: *spring,* 1.5 miles east-southeast of Long Barn (lat. 38°05'15" N, long. 120°06'10" W; near E line sec. 28, T 3 N, R 17 E). Named on Hull Creek (1979) 7.5' quadrangle.

San Andreas [CALAVERAS]: *town,* 2 miles east of the confluence of North Fork Calaveras River and South Fork Calaveras River (lat. 38°11'45" N, long. 120°40'45" W; in and near sec. 17, T 4 N, R 12 E). Named on San Andreas (1962) 7.5' quadrangle. Postal authorities established San Andreas post office in 1854 (Salley, p. 192). Camp's (1962) map shows a place called Greasertown, or Petersburg, located 4 miles west of San Andreas on the west side of Calaveras River, a place called Taylors Bar situated 6 miles west-southwest of San Andreas on the south side of the river, and a place called Yaqui Camp located 2 miles southeast of San Andreas along Willow Creek.

San Andreas Creek [CALAVERAS]: *stream,* flows 3 miles to Murray Creek less than 1 mile northwest of San Andreas (lat. 38° 12'25" N, long. 120°41'20" W; near N line sec. 18, T 4 N, R 12 E). Named on San Andreas (1962) 7.5' quadrangle.

San Antone: see **San Antonio Camp** [CALAVERAS].

San Antonio Camp [CALAVERAS]: *locality,* 8 miles east-southeast of San Andreas (lat. 38°09'45" N, long. 120°32'15" W; near NW cor. sec. 34, T 4 N, R 13 E); the place is along San Antonio Creek. Named on Calaveritas (1962) 7.5' quadrangle. A Mexican mining camp probably was at the site by 1849 or 1850; the place also was called San Antone (Gudde, 1975, p. 304).

San Antonio Creek [CALAVERAS]: *stream,* flows 31 miles to South Fork Calaveras River nearly 4 miles south-southeast of San Andreas (lat. 38°08'35" N, long. 120°39'45" W; sec. 4, T 3 N, R 12 E). Named on Calaveritas (1962), Dorrington (1979), Fort Mountain (1979), Murphys (1948), and San Andreas

281

(1962) 7.5' quadrangles.

San Antonio Spring [CALAVERAS]: *spring,* 4.5 miles south-southeast of Blue Mountain (lat. 38°17' N, long. 120°19'10" W; sec. 16, T 5 N, R 15 E); the spring is above San Antonio Creek. Named on Dorrington (1979) 7.5' quadrangle.

Sand Bar [TUOLUMNE]: *locality,* 4 miles southeast of Duckwall Mountain along Clavey River (lat. 37°56' N, long. 120°03'30" W; near N line sec. 24, T 1 N, R 17 E). Named on Duckwall Mountain (1948) 7.5' quadrangle.

Sand Creek [MADERA]: *stream,* flows 7 miles to join Browns Creek and form South Fork Willow Creek (2) 5 miles southwest of Shuteye Peak (lat. 37°17'55" N, long. 119°29'40" W; near NE cor. sec. 30, T 7 S, R 23 E). Named on Shuteye Peak (1953) 15' quadrangle. North Fork enters from the northnorthwest 2.25 miles upstream from the mouth of the main creek; it is 4.5 miles long and is named on Shuteye Peak (1953) 15' quadrangle. Kaiser (1904) 30' quadrangle shows present North Fork as the main stream.

Sand Creek [MARIPOSA]: *stream,* flows 2 miles to Agua Fria Creek 4.5 miles northeast of the settlement of Catheys Valley (lat. 37°28'45" N, long. 120°01'45" W). Named on Catheys Valley (1962) 7.5' quadrangle. United States Board on Geographic Names (1964a, p. 14) rejected the name "Cavallado Creek" for the stream.

Sand Flat [CALAVERAS-TUOLUMNE]: *area,* 3.25 miles north-northeast of Liberty Hill along North Fork Stanislaus River on Calaveras-Tuolumne county line (lat. 38°24'35" N, long. 120° 04'35" W). Named on Tamarack (1979) 7.5' quadrangle.

Sand Flat [NEVADA]: *area,* 3 miles northeast of Higgins Corner (lat. 39°04'15" N, long. 121°03'25" W; near N line sec. 14, T 14 N, R 8 E). Named on Lake Combie (1949) 7.5' quadrangle.

Sand Flat Campground [CALAVERAS]: *locality,* 2 miles south of Tamarack along North Fork Stanislaus River (lat. 38°24'35" N, long. 120°04'50" W); the place is at Sand Flat. Named on Tamarack (1979) 7.5' quadrangle.

Sand Hill [CALAVERAS]: *hill,* 6.5 miles westnorthwest of Valley Springs (lat. 38°13'10" N, long. 120°56'50" W). Altitude 205 feet. Named on Wallace (1962) 7.5' quadrangle. The feature now is in Camanche Reservoir.

San Diego: see **Columbia** [TUOLUMNE].

San Diego Reservoir [TUOLUMNE]: *lake,* 600 feet long, 0.5 mile east-southeast of Columbia (lat. 38°01'50" N, long. 120°23'20" W; sec. 13, T 2 N, R 14 E). Named on Columbia (1948) 7.5' quadrangle.

Sand Mountain [EL DORADO]: *peak,* 8.5 miles north-northwest of Pollock Pines (lat. 38°52'20" N, long. 120°39'20" W; sec. 20, T 12 N, R 12 E). Altitude 4762 feet. Named on Slate Mountain (1950) 7.5' quadrangle.

Sand Mountain: see **Freel Peak** [EL DORADO].

San Domingo Creek [CALAVERAS]: *stream,* flows 19 miles to join Cherokee Creek and form South Fork Calaveras River 6.5 miles west-northwest of Angels Camp (lat. 38°07'10" N, long. 120° 39' W; near S line sec. 9, T 3 N, R 12 E). Named on Angels Camp (1962), Calaveritas (1962), Murphys (1948), and Salt Spring Valley (1962) 7.5' quadrangles.

Sand Pond [SIERRA]: *lake,* 350 feet long, 3.5 miles north of Sierra City (lat. 39°37' N, long. 120°37'15" W; near W line sec. 10, T 20 N, R 12 E). Named on Haypress Valley (1981) 7.5' quadrangle.

Sand Ridge [NEVADA]:

(1) *ridge,* east-trending, 1.25 miles long, 3 miles south-southwest of English Mountain (lat. 39°24'25" N, long. 120°34'45" W). Named on English Mountain (1983) 7.5' quadrangle.

(2) *ridge,* west-southwest-trending, 1 mile long, 5.5 miles northwest of Donner Pass (lat. 39°22'05" N, long. 120°23'55" W; on W line sec. 3, T 17 N, R 14 E). Named on Soda Springs (1955) 7.5' quadrangle.

Sand Ridge Lake [NEVADA]: *lake,* 600 feet long, 5.25 miles northwest of Donner Pass (lat. 39°22'35" N, long. 120°23'15" W; near S line sec. 34, T 18 N, R 14 E); the lake is northeast of Sand Ridge (2). Named on Webber Peak (1981) 7.5' quadrangle.

Sands Meadow [TUOLUMNE]: *area,* nearly 2 miles southeast of Liberty Hill (lat. 38°20'55" N, long. 120°04'35" W; sec. 26, T 6 N, R 17 E). Named on Liberty Hill (1979) 7.5' quadrangle.

Sandusky Creek [SIERRA]: *stream,* flows 1.5 miles to Lucky Dog Creek 2 miles west-northwest of Alleghany (lat. 39°29'15" N, long. 120°52'20" W; near E line sec. 29, T 19 N, R 10 E). Named on Alleghany (1949) and Downieville (1951) 7.5' quadrangles.

Sandy Bar: see **Big Bar** [CALAVERAS].

Sandy Campground: see **Big Sandy Campground** [MADERA]; **Little Sandy Campground** [MADERA].

Sandy Gulch [CALAVERAS]: *locality,* 1.25 miles south of West Point (lat. 38°22'50" N, long. 120°31'55" W; near N line sec. 15, T 6 N, R 13 E). Named on West Point (1948) 7.5' quadrangle. The place was named for a nearby canyon and was a trading center in 1849 (California Department of Parks and Recreation, p. 12).

Sandy Wash [TUOLUMNE]: *stream,* flows nearly 2 miles to Wolf Gulch 2.25 miles northwest of Columbia (lat. 38°03'30" N, long. 120°25'45" W; sec. 3, T 2 N, R 14 E). Named on Columbia (1948) 7.5' quadrangle.

Sanford Lake [NEVADA]: *lake,* 1150 feet long, 5 miles south-southwest of English Mountain (lat. 39°23'15" N, long. 120°36'10" W; near NW cor. sec. 35, T 18 N, R 12 E). Named on English Mountain (1983) 7.5' quadrangle.

San Joaquin Mountain [MADERA]: *peak,* 6.5 miles north of Devils Postpile on Madera-Mono county line (lat. 37°43'10" N, long. 119°06'20" W). Altitude 11,600 feet. Named on Devils Postpile (1953) 15' quadrangle. A pair of peaks, this one and the nearby peak now called Two Teats, together formerly had the name "Two Teats" (Gudde, 1949, p. 373-374).

San Joaquin River [MADERA]: *stream,* formed by the confluence of North Fork and Middle Fork in Madera County 8.5 miles southwest of Devils Postpile, flows 320 miles to Contra Costa and Sacramento Counties 17 miles west of Lodi (lat. 38°05'55" N, long. 121°34'40" W). Named on Fresno (1962, revised 1967), Mariposa (1957, revised 1970), Sacramento (1957, limited revision 1964), San Jose (1962), and Santa Cruz (1958) 1°x 2° quadrangles. Present San Joaquin River is called R. San Joachim on Wilkes' (1841) map, Rio San Joaquin on Fremont's (1848) map, River San Joarquin on Derby's (1850) map, and Rio Tulare or San Joaquin on Sage's (1846) map. Gabriel Moraga named the river about 1805 for Saint Joaquin, father of the Virgin Mary (Hart, p. 379). North Fork is 16 miles long and Middle Fork is 21 miles long; both forks are named on Devils Postpile (1953) 15' quadrangle. South Fork heads in Fresno County and flows 4 miles in Madera County to join San Joaquin River 12 miles east-northeast of Shuteye Peak; it is named on Kaiser Peak (1953) 15' quadrangle. United States Board on Geographic Names (1965b, p. 12) rejected the name "Hooper Creek" for South Fork. A landing place called Dover was situated along San Joaquin River 5 miles above the mouth of Merced River in present Merced County (Hoover, Rensch, and Rensch, p. 206). Postal authorities established Dover post office in 1870 and discontinued it in 1874; wheat was shipped from the place to Dover, England, which suggested the name (Salley, p. 61).

San Juan: see **North San Juan** [NEVADA].

San Juan Canyon [SIERRA]: *canyon,* drained by a stream that flows 2.5 miles to North Yuba River 2.5 miles east of Downieville (lat. 39°33'05" N, long. 120°46'45" W; near S line sec. 31, T 20 N, R 11 E). Named on Downieville (1951) 7.5' quadrangle.

San Juan Ridge [NEVADA]: *ridge,* extends for about 24 miles east-northeast between Middle Yuba River and South Yuba River. Named on Alleghany (1949), Camptonville (1948), French Corral (1948), Nevada City (1948), North Bloomfield (1949), and Pike (1949) 7.5' quadrangles.

Santa Cruz: see **Indian Gulch** [MARIPOSA] (3).

Santa Cruz Mountain [MARIPOSA]: *peak,* 6.25 miles west-northwest of the settlement of Catheys Valley (lat. 37°27'25" N, long.

120°12'05" W; sec. 34, T 5 S, T 16 E). Altitude 1525 feet. Named on Indian Gulch (1962) 7.5' quadrangle.

Santa Iago: see **Columbia** [TUOLUMNE].

Santa Maria: see **Sequoia**, under **Rush Creek** [TUOLUMNE] (3).

Santa Maria Gulch [AMADOR]: *canyon,* drained by a stream that flows 1.5 miles to Grapevine Gulch (2) 3.5 miles south-south-west of Jackson (lat. 38°18'10" N, long. 120°48'30" W; sec. 7, T 5 N, R 11 E). Named on Jackson (1962) 7.5' quadrangle.

Santa Teresita: see **Camp Santa Teresita** [MADERA].

Santiago: see **Columbia** [TUOLUMNE].

Santiago Hill: see **Bell Hill** [TUOLUMNE].

Sapps Camp: see **Sapps Meadow** [TUOLUMNE].

Sapps Hill [TUOLUMNE]: *peak,* 5 miles northeast of Liberty Hill (lat. 38°24'50" N, long. 120°01'35" W); the peak is 1.25 miles west-northwest of Sapps Meadow. Altitude 7307 feet. Named on Tamarack (1979) 7.5' quadrangle.

Sapps Meadow [TUOLUMNE]: *area,* 6 miles east-northeast of Liberty Hill (lat. 38°24'35" N, long. 120°00'20" W); the place is 1.25 miles east-southeast of Sapps Hill. Named on Tamarack (1979) 7.5' quadrangle. Big Meadow (1956) 15' quadrangle shows a place called Sapps Camp at the site.

Sarahsville: see **Bath** [PLACER]; **Clinton** [AMADOR].

Sarahville: see **Clinton** [AMADOR].

Saratoga: see **Yeomet**, under **Entrprise** [AMADOR].

Sardella Lake: see **Granite Dome** [TUOLUMNE].

Sardine Bar [EL DORADO-PLACER]: *locality,* 3.5 miles northwest of Greenwood along Middle Fork American River on El Dorado-Placer county line (lat. 38°56'05" N, long. 121°56'05" W; sec. 34, T 13 N, R 9 E). Named on Greenwood (1949) 7.5' quadrangle.

Sardine Campground [SIERRA]: *locality,* 3.5 miles north-northeast of Sierra City (lat. 39°37'10" N, long. 120°37'05" W; sec. 10, T 20 N, R 12 E); the place is along Sardine Creek. Named on Sierra City (1955) 15' quadrangle.

Sardine Creek [SIERRA]: *stream,* flows 2 miles from Lower Sardine Lake to North Yuba River 3 miles north-northeast of Sierra City (lat. 39°36'15" N, long. 120°36'25" W; near NE cor. sec. 15, T 20 N, R 12 E). Named on Haypress Valley (1981) 7.5' quadrangle.

Sardine Lake: see **Lower Sardine Lake** [SIERRA]; **Upper Sardine Lake** [SIERRA].

Sardine Lake Resort [SIERRA]: *locality,* 3.5 miles north of Sierra City (lat. 39°37' N, long. 120°37'20" W; on W line sec. 10, T 20 N, R 12 E); the place is at the east end of Lower Sardine Lake. Named on Haypress Valley (1981) 7.5' quadrangle.

Sardine Meadow [TUOLUMNE]: *area,* 3.25

miles southeast of Dardanelle (lat. 38°18'25"
N, long. 119°47'15" W; on W line sec. 4, T 5
N, R 20 E). Named on Dardanelle (1979) 7.5'
quadrangle.

Sardine Peak [SIERRA]: *peak,* 10 miles south-
southeast of Loyalton (lat. 39°32'25" N, long.
120°11'10" W; sec. 34, T 20 N, R 16 E). Altitude 8135 feet. Named on Sardine Peak
(1981) 7.5' quadrangle.

Sardine Point [SIERRA]: *peak,* 9 miles south-
southeast of Loyalton (lat. 39°33' N, long.
120°12'15" W; near S line sec. 28, T 20 N, R
16 E); the peak is 1 mile northwest of Sardine Peak. Altitude 7578 feet. Named on Sardine Peak (1981) 7.5' quadrangle.

Sardine Spring [NEVADA]: *spring,* nearly 4
miles south-southeast of Washington (lat.
39°18'35" N, long. 120°45'55" W; sec. 29, T
17 N, R 11 E). Named on Washington (1950)
7.5' quadrangle.

Sardine Spring [SIERRA]: *spring,* 9 miles
south-southeast of Loyalton (lat. 39°32'20" N,
long. 120°11'45" W; near NW cor. sec. 34, T
20 N, R 16 E); the spring is 3500 feet northwest of Sardine Peak. Named on Sardine Peak
(1981) 7.5' quadrangle.

Sardine Valley [SIERRA]: *valley,* 12.5 miles
south-southeast of Loyalton (lat. 39°31'10" N,
long. 120°08' W). Named on Dog Valley
(1981) and Sardine Peak (1981) 7.5' quadrangles, which show marsh in most of the
valley.

Satcher Lake: see **Sotcher Lake** [MADERA].

Sattley [SIERRA]: *village,* 3.5 miles west-northwest of Sierraville (lat. 39°36'55" N, long.
120°25'30" W; sec. 4, T 20 N, R 14 E). Named
on Sattley (1981) 7.5' quadrangle. Postal
authorities established Sattley post office in
1884, discontinued it in 1918, and reestablished it in 1919 (Frickstad, p. 185). The name
commemorates Harriet Sattley Church, wife
of Ezra Bliss Church; the place first was called
Churchs Corners (Hanna, p. 296). Postal authorities established Rocky Point post office
5 miles north of Sattley in 1876, changed the
name to Rockypoint in 1895, and discontinued it in 1897 (Salley, p. 187).

Saucer Lake [EL DORADO]: *lake,* 350 feet
long, 3 miles west-northwest of Echo Summit (lat. 38°50' N, long. 120°04'35" W; sec.
2, T 11 N, R 17 E); the lake is 1 mile east-
northeast of Cup Lake. Named on Echo Lake
(1955) 7.5' quadrangle.

Saucer Meadow [TUOLUMNE]: *area,* 12 miles
northwest of Tower Peak along Summit Creek
(lat. 38°14'35" N, long. 119°43'40" W; near
N line sec. 36, T 5 N, R 20 E). Named on
Tower Peak (1956) 15' quadrangle.

Saurian Crest [TUOLUMNE]: *ridge,* southwest-trending, 1.5 miles long, 1 mile west-
northwest of Tower Peak (lat. 38°08'45" N,
long. 119°34'15" W). Named on Tower Peak
(1956) 15' quadrangle. William E. Colby
named the ridge in 1911 for its supposed re-

semblance to the serrated back of some ancient saurian creature (Gudde, 1949, p. 321).

Savage: see **Mount Savage** [MARIPOSA].

Savage Diggings: see **Big Oak Flat** [TUOL-
UMNE].

Savage Flat: see **Big Creek** [TUOLUMNE] (1).

Savages Trading Post [MARIPOSA]: *locality,*
4.5 miles southeast of the settlement of
Catheys Valley along Mariposa Creek (lat. 37°
23' N, long. 120°02'35" W; sec. 30, T 6 S, R
18 E). Named on Catheys Valley (1962) 7.5'
quadrangle.

Sawmill Creek [CALAVERAS]: *stream,* flows
4.5 miles to Black Creek (1) 3.25 miles south-
southeast of Copperopolis (lat. 37°56'05" N,
long. 120°37'20" W; sec. 14, T 1 N, R 12 E).
Named on Copperopolis (1962) and Melones
Dam (1962) 7.5' quadrangles.

Sawmill Creek [EL DORADO]: *stream,* flows
2.25 miles to French Creek 1.5 miles south-
southeast of Shingle Springs (lat. 38°38'40"
N, long. 120°54'30" W; near SW cor. sec. 8,
T 9 N, R 10 E). Named on Shingle Springs
(1949) 7.5' quadrangle.

Sawmill Creek [SIERRA]: *stream,* flows 2 miles
to Salmon Creek 5 miles north of Sierra City
(lat. 39°38'20" N, long. 120°37'30" W; near
W line sec. 34, T 21 N, R 12 E). Named on
Gold Lake (1981) 7.5' quadrangle.

Sawmill Flat [PLACER]: *area,* 5 miles southwest of Martis Peak (lat. 39°15'15" N, long.
120°06'30" W; sec. 8, T 16 N, R 17 E). Named
on Martis Peak (1955) 7.5' quadrangle.

Sawmill Flat [TUOLUMNE]: *locality,* 1.5 miles
southeast of Columbia along Woods Creek
(lat. 38°01'10" N, long. 120°22'50" W; near
S line sec. 13, T 2 N, R 14 E). Named on
Columbia (1948) 7.5' quadrangle. The name
is from two sawmills built at the place to sup-
ply timbers for mines in the early 1850's; it
also has the form "Saw Mill Flat" (Hoover,
Rensch, and Rensch, p. 572).

Sawmill Gulch [TUOLUMNE]: *canyon,*
drained by a stream that flows 1 mile to Woods
Creek 1.5 miles southeast of Columbia at
Sawmill Flat (lat. 38°01'15" N, long.
120°22'50" W; near S line sec. 13, T 2 N, R
14 E). Named on Columbia (1948) and Columbia SE (1948) 7.5' quadrangles.

Sawmill Lake [NEVADA]: *lake,* behind a dam
on Canyon Creek 2.5 miles west of English
Mountain (lat. 39°26'45" N, long. 120°36'05"
W; near NW cor. sec. 11, T 18 N, R 12 E).
Named on English Mountain (1983) 7.5'
quadrangle.

Sawmill Mountain [TUOLUMNE]: *peak,* 6
miles southwest of Mather (lat. 37°49'35" N,
long. 119°56'05" W; near W line sec. 30, T 1
S, R 19 E). Altitude 5300 feet. Named on Lake
Eleanor (1956) 15' quadrangle.

Sawmill Ravine [SIERRA]:
(1) *canyon,* drained by a stream that flows 1.5
miles to Slate Creek nearly 6 miles southwest
of Mount Fillmore (lat. 39°41'05" N, long.

120°56'25" W; sec. 14, T 21 N, R 9 E). Named on La Porte (1951) 7.5' quadrangle.

(2) *canyon,* drained by a stream that flows 2 miles to Canyon Creek 6 miles northwest of Goodyears Bar (lat. 39°36'15" N, long. 120°57'35" W; sec. 15, T 20 N, R 9 E). Named on Goodyears Bar (1951) 7.5' quadrangle.

Sawmill Ridge [SIERRA]: *ridge,* generally southwest-trending, 4 miles long, 2 miles west-northwest of Mount Fillmore (lat. 39°44' N, long. 120°53'15" W). Named on Blue Nose Mountain (1951), La Porte (1951), and Mount Fillmore (1951) 7.5' quadrangles.

Sawpit Spring [PLACER]: *spring,* less than 1 mile west-northwest of Devil Peak (lat. 38°57'55" N, long. 120°33'30" W; near W line sec. 20, T 13 N, R 13 E). Named on Devil Peak (1950) 7.5' quadrangle.

Sawtooth Ridge [PLACER]:

(1) *ridge,* generally northwest-trending, 3 miles long, 5.5 miles north-northwest of Tahoe City (lat. 39°14'50" N, long. 120°10'15" W). Named on Tahoe City (1955) and Truckee (1955) 7.5' quadrangles.

(2) *ridge,* generally west-trending, 9 miles long, center 3.5 miles northwest of Westville (lat. 39°13' N, long. 120°41'15" W). Named on Duncan Peak (1952), Dutch Flat (1950), and Westville (1952) 7.5' quadrangles.

Sawtooth Ridge [TUOLUMNE]: *ridge,* extends for 2.5 miles west-northwest from Matterhorn Peak along Tuolumne-Mono county line (lat. 38°06'15" N, long. 119°23'45" W). Named on Matterhorn Peak (1956) 15' quadrangle.

Saxon Creek [EL DORADO]: *stream,* flows 6 miles to Trout Creek 4.5 miles west-northwest of Freel Peak (lat. 38°53' N, long. 119° 58'45" W; sec. 15, T 12 N, R 18 E). Named on Freel Peak (1955) and South Lake Tahoe (1955) 7.5' quadrangles.

Saxon Creek [MARIPOSA]: *stream,* flows 5 miles to Merced River 5 miles northwest of Midpines (lat. 37°35'35" N, long. 119°59'15" W; near S line sec. 9, T 4 S, R 18 E). Named on Feliciana Mountain (1947) 7.5' quadrangle. Yosemite (1909) 30' quadrangle has the name "Saxon Gulch" for the canyon of the stream.

Saxon Gulch: see **Saxon Creek** [MARIPOSA].

Saxonia Lake [SIERRA]: *lake,* 1050 feet long, 3.5 miles north of Sierra City (lat. 39°37'05" N, long. 120°38'15" W; near NW cor. sec. 9, T 20 N, R 12 E). Named on Sierra City (1981) 7.5' quadrangle.

Sayles Canyon [EL DORADO]: *canyon,* drained by a stream that flows nearly 5 miles to South Fork American River 4.5 miles west of Echo Summit (lat. 38°48'05" N, long. 120°06'40" W; sec. 16, T 11 N, R 17 E). Named on Echo Lake (1955) 7.5' quadrangle.

Sayles Flat [EL DORADO]: *locality,* nearly 5 miles west of Echo Summit along South Fork American River (lat. 38°48'10" N, long. 120°07' W; on W line sec. 16, T 11 N, R 17 E). Named on Echo Lake (1955) 7.5' quad-

rangle.

Scadden Flat [NEVADA]: *area,* 1 mile southwest of downtown Grass Valley (lat. 39°12'35" N, long. 121°04'40" W; near NE cor. sec. 33, T 16 N, R 8 E). Named on Grass Valley (1949) 7.5' quadrangle.

Scales [SIERRA]: *locality,* 7 miles northwest of Goodyears Bar (lat. 39°35'50" N, long. 120°59'30" W; sec. 17, T 20 N, R 9 E). Named on Goodyears Bar (1951) 7.5' quadrangle. Postal authorities established Scales Diggings post office in 1871, discontinued it in 1875, reestablished it with the name "Scales" in 1880, and discontinued it in 1923 (Salley, p. 199). A mining place called Council Hill was situated about 1.5 miles southwest of Scales Diggings on the same ridge (Marlette, p. 202).

Scales Diggings: see **Scales** [SIERRA].

Schaads Reservoir [CALAVERAS]: *lake,* behind a dam on Middle Fork Mokelumne River 5.5 miles south of Devils Nose (lat. 38° 23'05" N, long. 120°26'30" W; sec. 9, T 6 N, R 14 E). Named on Devils Nose (1979) 7.5' quadrangle.

Schaeffer Camp: see **Old Schaeffer Camp** [PLACER]

Schaeffer Mill: see **Old Schaeffer Mill** [PLACER].

Schallenberger Ridge [PLACER]: *ridge,* west-southwest- to southwest-trending, 2.5 miles long, 3 miles east-southeast of Donner Pass (lat. 39°18'20" N, long. 120°16'20" W). Named on Norden (1955) 7.5' quadrangle. The name is for Moses Schallenberger, a young emigrant who spent the winter of 1844 and 1845 in a log cabin below the ridge (Stewart, p. 11).

Schenck Camp [EL DORADO]: *locality,* 10 miles west-southwest of Kirkwood (lat. 38°39'20" N, long. 120°14'50" W; sec. 6, T 9 N, R 16 E). Named on Tragedy Spring (1979) 7.5' quadrangle.

Schleins Diggings: see **Tipton Hill** [EL DORADO].

Schmidell: see **Lake Schmidell** [EL DORADO].

Schmidt Creek [MADERA]: *stream,* flows 7.5 miles to end 6.5 miles southeast of Fairmead near Notarb (lat. 37°00'15" N, long. 120°07'05" W; sec. 4, T 11 S, R 17 E). Named on Kismet (1961) 7.5' quadrangle.

Schneider: see **Jake Schneider Meadow** [EL DORADO].

Schneider Camp [EL DORADO]: *locality,* 2 miles northeast of Kirkwood (lat. 38°43'30" N, long. 120°03' W; sec. 7, T 10 N, R 18 E). Named on Caples Lake (1979) 7.5' quadrangle.

Schoettgen Pass [TUOLUMNE]: *pass,* 1.5 miles west-northwest of Crandall Peak (lat. 38°10'10" N, long. 120°10'10" W; near W line sec. 25, T 4 N, R 16 E). Named on Crandall Peak (1979) 7.5' quadrangle. Big Trees (1891) 30' quadrangle has the name "Shotgun" near the site.

Schofield Peak [TUOLUMNE]: *peak,* 8 miles west-southwest of Tower Peak (lat. 38°05'35" N, long. 119°40'40" W). Altitude 9935 feet. Named on Tower Peak (1956) 15' quadrangle. Major W.W. Forsyth, acting superintendent of Yosemite National Park, named the peak for Lieutenant General John McAllister Schofield (United States Board on Geographic Names, 1934, p. 22).

Schoolhouse Gulch [CALAVERAS]: *canyon,* drained by a stream that flows less than 1 mile to Chili Gulch 4 miles northwest of San Andreas (lat. 38°14'30" N, long. 120°43'30" W; sec. 35, T 5 N, R 11 E). Named on San Andreas (1962) 7.5' quadrangle.

School Land Gulch [AMADOR]: *canyon,* drained by a stream that flows 1 mile to Mokelumne River 4 miles south of Jackson (lat. 38°17'20" N, long. 120°46'25" W; sec. 16, T 5 N, R 11 E). Named on Jackson (1962) 7.5' quadrangle.

Sciata Creek: see **Curry Creek** [PLACER].

Sciots Camp [EL DORADO]: *locality,* 4 miles south of Pyramid Peak along South Fork American River (lat. 38°47'15" N, long. 120°09'10" W; near W line sec. 19, T 11 N, R 17 E). Named on Pyramid Peak (1955) 7.5' quadrangle.

Scorpion Gulch [CALAVERAS]: *canyon,* 1 mile long, opens into the canyon of Stanislaus River 6.5 miles south-southeast of Copperopolis (lat. 37°53'25" N, long. 120°35'45" W). Named on Melones Dam (1962) 7.5' quadrangle. Water of Tulloch Lake floods much of the canyon.

Scotch Gulch [MARIPOSA]: *canyon,* drained by a stream that flows nearly 3 miles to Lake McClure 5.5 miles south-southeast of Coulterville (lat. 37°28'10" N, long. 120°09'50" W; sec. 36, T 3 S, R 16 E). Named on Coulterville (1947, photorevised 1973) 7.5' quadrangle.

Scotchman Creek [NEVADA]: *stream,* flows 3.5 miles to South Yuba River 1 mile east of Washington (lat. 39°21'25" N, long. 120°46'55" W; sec. 7, T 17 N, R 11 E). Named on Washington (1950) 7.5' quadrangle. Called Scotchman's Creek on Whitney's (1873) map, which has the name "Krumbacker's Rav." for a canyon that opens into the canyon of Scotchman's Creek from the southwest less than 0.5 mile above the mouth of Scotchman's Creek. Gudde (1975, p. 88) used the form "Crumbecker" for the name of the side canyon. Whitney's (1873) map also has the name "Baltimore Rav." for a canyon that enters the canyon of Scotchman's Creek from the southeast less than 1 mile above the mouth of Scotchman's Creek. Gudde (1975, p. 44, 295) listed two mining places, Boulder Bar and Rocky Bar, that were situated at the mouth of Scotchman Creek, but Bancroft (1888, p. 358) indicated that these two places were one and

the same. Gudde (1975, p. 177, 197) also listed places called Long Bar and Jimmy Brown Bar that were situated along South Yuba River above the mouth of Scotchman Creek.

Scott Creek [EL DORADO]: *stream,* flows 16 miles to South Fork Cosumnes River 0.5 mile south-southeast of Aukum (lat. 38°32'50" N, long. 120°43'15" W; near W line sec. 13, T 8 N, R 11 E). Named on Aukum (1952), Caldor (1951), and Omo Ranch (1952) 7.5' quadrangles. Called South Fork Cosumnes River on Placerville (1893) 30' quadrangle, which has the name "South Fork of South Fork Cosumnes River" for present South Fork Cosumnes River.

Scott Creek [MARIPOSA]: *stream,* flows 2.25 miles to North Fork Merced River 6 miles east-southeast of Smith Peak (lat. 37°45'20" N, long. 120°00'20" W; sec. 17, T 2 S, R 18 E); the stream is east of Scott Ridge. Named on Jawbone Ridge (1947) 7.5' quadrangle.

Scott Hill [PLACER]: *ridge,* south-southwest-trending, 0.5 mile long, 3.25 miles south of Emigrant Gap (1) (lat. 39°15'15" N, long. 120° 39'50" W; sec. 18, T 16 N, R 12 E). Named on Blue Canyon (1955) 7.5' quadrangle.

Scott Peak [PLACER]: *peak,* 4.5 miles west-southwest of Tahoe City (lat. 39°09'30" N, long. 120°13'20" W; sec. 9, T 15 N, R 16 E). Altitude 8289 feet. Named on Tahoe City (1955) 7.5' quadrangle.

Scott Ridge [MARIPOSA]: *ridge,* south- to southwest-trending, 2.25 miles long, 5.25 miles east-southeast of Smith Peak (lat. 37°46'30" N, long. 120°00'35" W); the ridge is west of Scott Creek. Named on Jawbone Ridge (1947) 7.5' quadrangle.

Scotts Flat [NEVADA]:

(1) *valley,* 6 miles south of North Bloomfield along Deer Creek (lat. 39°16'30" N, long. 120°55' W). Named on Colfax (1938) 30' quadrangle.

(2) *locality,* 6 miles south of North Bloomfield (lat. 39°16'45" N, long. 120°54'45" W); the place is at Scotts Flat (1). Named on Colfax (1898) 30' quadrangle. Whitney's (1873) map shows a place called Six Mile Ho. [House] located 1 mile west-northwest of Scotts Flat (2).

Scotts Flat Reservoir [NEVADA]: *lake,* behind a dam on Deer Creek 7 miles south-southwest of North Bloomfield (lat. 39°16'20" N, long. 120°55'50" W; on S line sec. 2, T 16 N, R 9 E); water of the reservoir covers Scotts Flat (1). Named on North Bloomfield (1949, photorevised 1973) 7.5' quadrangle.

Scotts Springs: see **Deer Park** [PLACER].

Scottsville [AMADOR]: *locality,* 1.5 miles southeast of Jackson (lat. 38°20'05" N, long. 120°45'20" W; sec. 34, T 6 N, R 11 E). Named on Jackson (1962) 7.5' quadrangle.

Scraperville: see **Sonora** [TUOLUMNE].

Screech Owl Canyon [EL DORADO]: *canyon,*

drained by a stream that flows 1.5 miles to Alder Creek 4.5 miles west-southwest of Kyburz (lat. 38°45'20" N, long. 120°22'20" W; sec. 35, T 11 N, R 14 E). Named on Kyburz (1952), Leek Spring Hill (1951), Riverton (1950), and Stump Spring (1951) 7.5' quadrangles.

Screech Owl Creek [EL DORADO]: *stream,* flows 1.5 miles to Carson Creek near Clarksville (lat. 38°39'10" N, long. 121°03'20" W; sec. 12, T 9 N, R 8 E). Named on Clarksville (1953) 7.5' quadrangle.

Screwauger Canyon [PLACER]: *canyon,* drained by a stream that flows 6 miles to Middle Fork American River 5 miles west-southwest of Duncan Peak (lat. 39°07'20" N, long. 120°35'35" W; sec. 25, T 15 N, R 12 E). Named on Duncan Peak (1952) and Greek Store (1952) 7.5' quadrangles. Whitney's (1880) map has the form "Screw Auger Gulch" for the name.

Screw Auger Gulch: see **Screwauger Canyon** [PLACER].

Sears' Diggings: see **Saint Louis** [SIERRA].

Sears Ravine [SIERRA]: *canyon,* drained by a stream that flows 0.5 mile to Slate Creek 4.5 miles west-southwest of Mount Fillmore (lat. 39°42'15" N, long. 120°55'50" W; near SW cor. sec. 1, T 21 N, R 9 E). Named on La Porte (1951) 7.5' quadrangle.

Sears Ridge: see **Port Wine Ridge** [SIERRA].

Seavey Pass [TUOLUMNE]: *pass,* 7 miles south-southeast of Tower Peak (lat. 38°02'45" N, long. 119°31'15" W). Named on Tower Peak (1956) 15' quadrangle. R.B. Marshall of United States Geological Survey named the pass for Clyde L. Seavey, a member of California State Board of Control from 1911 until 1915 and from 1917 until 1921, state civil service commissioner from 1921 until 1923, and president of the California State Railroad Commission after 1923 (Hanna, p. 298).

Sebastopol [NEVADA]: *locality,* 1 mile west-southwest of North San Juan (lat. 39°21'45" N, long. 121°07'10" W; sec. 6, T 17 N, R 8 E). Named on Nevada City (1948) 7.5' quadrangle. The place was named at the time of the Crimean War, when the siege of Sebastopol was of world-wide interest (Gudde, 1975, p. 313).

Second Brushy Canyon [PLACER]: *canyon,* 2.25 miles long, opens into the head of Brushy Canyon (1) 2.25 miles west-northwest of Foresthill (lat. 39°02'15" N, long. 120°51'15" W; near N line sec. 28, T 14 N, R 10 E). Named on Foresthill (1949) 7.5' quadrangle.

Second Creek [TUOLUMNE]: *stream,* flows nearly 2 miles to Hatch Creek 4 miles south-southwest of Moccasin (lat. 37°45'25" N, long. 120°19'30" W; sec. 16, T 2 S, R 15 E); the stream is north of First Creek. Named on Moccasin (1948) and Penon Blanco Peak (1962) 7.5' quadrangles.

Second Crossing: see **North Branch** [CALA-

VERAS].

Second Divide [SIERRA]: *pass,* nearly 3 miles north-northeast of Downieville on the ridge between Lavezzola Creek and Pauley Creek (lat. 39°35'40" N, long. 120°47'55" W; near SE cor. sec. 12, T 20 N, R 10 E); the pass is 1 mile northeast of First Divide. Named on Downieville (1951) 7.5' quadrangle.

Second Garrotte [TUOLUMNE]: *locality,* 2 miles east-southeast of Groveland (lat. 37°49'30" N, long. 120°11'40" W; near W line sec. 26, T 1 S, R 16 E); the place is along Garrotte Creek. Named on Groveland (1947) 7.5' quadrangle. After present Groveland became known as Garrotte from the hanging there of Mexican thieves, Second Garrotte received its name from a similar incident— *garrote* is the Spanish term for capital punishment by strangulation (Gudde, 1949, p. 324). Wheeler (1879, p. 161) referred to "2^d Garrotta, a mining village."

Second Garrotte Basin [TUOLUMNE]: *valley,* 2 miles southeast of Groveland (lat. 37°49'20" N, long. 120°12' W; mainly in sec. 27, T 1 S, R 16 E); the valley is west-southwest of Second Garrotte. Named on Groveland (1947) 7.5' quadrangle.

Second Garrotte Ridge [TUOLUMNE]: *ridge,* south- to west-trending, 2 miles long, center 3 miles southeast of Groveland (lat. 37°48'40" N, long. 120°11'20" W); the ridge is 1 mile south-southeast of Second Garrotte. Named on Groveland (1947) 7.5' quadrangle.

Second Sugarloaf [PLACER]: *peak,* 6.25 miles north-northwest of Foresthill (lat. 38°06' N, long. 120°52'20" W; near S line sec. 32, T 15 N, R 10 E); the peak is less than 0.5 mile southwest of First Sugarloaf. Altitude 3066 feet. Named on Foresthill (1949) 7.5' quadrangle. This peak and First Sugarloaf together are called Sugar Loaves on Colfax (1898) 30' quadrangle.

Secreta: see **Clinton** [AMADOR].

Secret Canyon [PLACER]: *canyon,* drained by a stream that flows 9 miles to North Fork of Middle Fork American River 7.5 miles northeast of Michigan Bluff (lat. 39°07' N, long. 120°38' W; near E line sec. 28, T 15 N, R 12 E). Named on Duncan Peak (1952), Michigan Bluff (1952), and Westville (1952) 7.5' quadrangles.

Secret Canyon [SIERRA]: *canyon,* drained by a stream that flows 2.5 miles to North Yuba River 2.25 miles east-southeast of Downieville (lat. 39°33'10" N, long. 120°47'05" W; near S line sec. 31, T 20 N, R 11 E). Named on Downieville (1951) 7.5' quadrangle. Gudde (1975, p. 235) listed a mining place called Negro Bar that was located opposite Secret Canyon, and (p. 251) a mining place called Omits Flat that also was located opposite Secret Canyon.

Secret Canyon: see **Little Secret Canyon** [PLACER]; **Secret House** [PLACER].

Secret House [PLACER]: *locality,* 4.5 miles west-northwest of Duncan Peak (lat. 39°11'15" N, long. 120°35'05" W; sec. 1, T 15 N, R 12 E); the place is northwest of Little Secret Canyon. Named on Duncan Peak (1952) 7.5' quadrangle. Colfax (1898) 30' quadrangle has the name "Secret Canyon" for an inhabited place at or near present Secret House.

Secret Lake [EL DORADO]: *lake,* 400 feet long, 2.25 miles west-northwest of Pyramid Peak (lat. 38°51'10" N, long. 120°11'50" W). Named on Pyramid Peak (1955) 7.5' quadrangle.

Secret Lake [NEVADA]: *lake,* 550 feet long, 1 mile northeast of English Mountain (lat. 39°27'25" N, long. 120°32'15" W; sec. 5, T 18 N, R 13 E). Named on English Mountain (1983) 7.5' quadrangle.

Secret Meadow [SIERRA]: *area,* 10 miles south-southeast of Sierraville (lat. 39°27'40" N, long. 120°16'20" W; at SE cor. sec. 26, T 19 N, R 15 E). Named on Independence Lake (1981) 7.5' quadrangle.

Secret Ravine [PLACER]:
(1) *canyon,* drained by a stream that flows 3.5 miles to North Fork American River 3 miles east-northeast of Colfax (lat. 39°07' N, long. 120°53'55" W; near S line sec. 30, T 15 N, R 10 E); the canyon heads near the site of Secret Town. Named on Chicago Park (1949), Colfax (1949), and Dutch Flat (1950) 7.5' quadrangles. Called Robbers Ravine on Colfax (1938) 30' quadrangle.
(2) *canyon,* drained by a stream that flows 11 miles to Miners Ravine 1.5 miles east-northeast of downtown Roseville (lat. 38° 45'35" N, long. 121°15'20" W; sec. 36, T 11 N, R 6 E). Named on Rocklin (1967) and Roseville (1967) 7.5' quadrangles.

Secret Ravine: see **Newcastle** [PLACER].

Secret Ridge [SIERRA]: *ridge,* north-northeast-trending, 1.25 miles long, 1.5 miles southeast of Downieville (lat. 39°32'40" N, long. 120°48'15" W; sec. 1, T 19 N, R 10 E); the ridge is northwest of Secret Canyon. Named on Downieville (1951) 7.5' quadrangle.

Secret Town [PLACER]: *locality,* 5 miles northeast of Colfax (lat. 39°09'30" N, long. 120°52'45" W; near SW cor. sec. 8, T 15 N, R 10 E). Site named on Chicago Park (1949) 7.5' quadrangle.

Selby Flat [NEVADA]: *area,* 2 miles north-northwest of Nevada City (lat. 39°17'30" N, long. 121°01'45" W; sec. 36, T 17 N, R 8 E). Named on Nevada City (1948) 7.5' quadrangle. Smartsville (1895) 30' quadrangle shows a place called Shelby Flat situated 2 miles north-northwest of Nevada City.

Sellier Creek [PLACER]: *stream,* flows 2.25 miles to Brimstone Creek 5.5 miles north-northeast of Foresthill (lat. 39°05'10" N, long. 120°45'50" W; sec. 5, T 14 N, R 11 E). Named on Foresthill (1949) and Michigan Bluff

(1952) 7.5' quadrangles.

Sentinel Creek [MARIPOSA]: *stream,* flows 3 miles to Merced River 1.5 miles southwest of Yosemite Village (lat. 37°44'10" N, long. 119°36'15" W); the stream goes past Sentinel Dome and Sentinel Rock. Named on Yosemite (1956) 15' quadrangle.

Sentinel Dome [MARIPOSA]: *peak,* nearly 2 miles south of Yosemite Village (lat. 37°43'25" N, long. 119°35' W). Altitude 8122 feet. Named on Yosemite (1956) 15' quadrangle. The men who discovered Yosemite Valley in 1851 called the peak South Dome (Hanna, p. 131).

Sentinel Fall [MARIPOSA]: *waterfall,* 1.5 miles south-southwest of Yosemite Village (lat. 37°43'30" N, long. 119°35'40" W); the feature is along Sentinel Creek.. Named on Yosemite (1956) 15' quadrangle.

Sentinel Rock [MARIPOSA]: *promontory,* 1.5 miles south-southwest of Yosemite Village on the south side of Yosemite Valley (lat. 37° 43'45" N, long. 119°35'35" W). Named on Yosemite (1956) 15' quadrangle. The name is from the resemblance of the feature to a gigantic watch tower (Whitney, 1870, p. 62).

Sequoia: see **Rush Creek** [TUOLUMNE] (3).

Serena Creek [PLACER]: *stream,* flows 3 miles to North Fork American River 5.25 miles south-southwest of Donner Pass (lat. 39°15'20" N, long. 120°22'45" W; near W line sec. 14, T 16 N, R 14 E); the stream heads at Ice Lakes, one of which formerly was called Serena Lake. Named on Soda Springs (1955) 7.5' quadrangle. Called Sereno Creek on Truckee (1895) 30' quadrangle.

Serena Lake: see **Ice Lakes** [PLACER].

Sereno Creek: see **Serena Creek** [PLACER].

Sereno Lake: see **Ice Lakes** [PLACER].

Sesame: see **Bellview** [MADERA].

Seven Mile House: see **Camino** [EL DORADO].

"77" Corral: see **Corral Meadow** [MADERA].

Shad Gulch [CALAVERAS]: *canyon,* 0.5 mile long, 3 miles west-northwest of Paloma (lat. 38°16'30" N, long. 120°48'45" W; on W line sec. 19, T 5 N, R 11 E). Named on Jackson (1962) 7.5' quadrangle. Water of Pardee Reservoir floods the lower part of the canyon.

Shadow Creek [MADERA]: *stream,* flows 4.5 miles to Middle Fork San Joaquin River 5.25 miles north-northwest of Devils Postpile (lat. 37°41'45" N, long. 119°07'05" W); the stream goes through Shadow Lake. Named on Devils Postpile (1953) 15' quadrangle.

Shadow Lake [EL DORADO]:
(1) *lake,* 850 feet long, 7.5 miles east-northeast of Robbs Peak (lat. 38°58'10" N, long. 120°16'20" W; on W line sec. 14, T 13 N, R 15 E). Named on Loon Lake (1952) 7.5' quadrangle.
(2) *lake,* 900 feet long, 2.25 miles north of Phipps Peak (lat. 38°59'20" N, long. 120°08'45" W; sec. 7, T 13 N, R 17 E). Named

on Rockbound Valley (1955) 7.5' quadrangle.

Shadow Lake [MADERA]: *lake,* 2400 feet long, 5.5 miles north-northwest of Devils Postpile (lat. 37°41'40" N, long. 119°07'50" W). Named on Devils Postpile (1953) 15' quadrangle. Called Garnet Lake on some early maps (Browning, 1988, p. 128).

Shadow Lake: see **Little Shadow Lake**, under **Ediza Lake** [MADERA]; **Merced Lake** [MARIPOSA].

Shady Creek [NEVADA]: *stream,* flows 10.5 miles to South Yuba River 6 miles west-north-west of Nevada City (lat. 39°17'40" N, long. 121°07'20" W; sec. 31, T 17 N, R 8 E). Named on Nevada City (1948) and North Bloomfield (1949) 7.5' quadrangles. A miner used the name "Big Shady Creek" for the stream in 1852 (Canfield, p. 230).

Shady Creek: see **Little Shady Creek** [NEVADA]; **Little Shady Creek**, under **Blind Shady Creek** [NEVADA].

Shady Flat: see **Mobile Ravine** [SIERRA].

Shady Glen [PLACER]: *settlement,* 1.25 miles north of Colfax (lat. 39°07'05" N, long. 120°56'55" W; near SE cor. sec. 27, T 15 N, R 9 E). Named on Colfax (1949) 7.5' quadrangle.

Shady Grove Run [PLACER]: *stream,* flows 1 mile to North Fork of Middle Fork American River 6.5 miles west-southwest of Duncan Peak (lat. 39°07'10" N, long. 120°37'30" W; sec. 27, T 15 N, R 12 E). Named on Greek Store (1952) 7.5' quadrangle.

Shady Run [PLACER]: *stream,* flows 1.25 miles to Blue Canyon (1) 5 miles east of Dutch Flat (lat. 38°12' N, long. 120°44'50" W). Named on Colfax (1898) 30' quadrangle.

Shady Run: see **Midas** [PLACER].

Shakeflat Creek [MADERA]: *stream,* flows 3.25 miles to San Joaquin River 5.5 miles east-southeast of Shuteye Peak (lat. 37°18'50" N, long. 119°20' W). Named on Shuteye Peak (1953) 15' quadrangle.

Shake Hill: see **Washington** [NEVADA].

Shake Ridge: see **Lockwood** [AMADOR].

Shallow Lake [TUOLUMNE]: *lake,* 2000 feet long, 8 miles west of Tower Peak (lat. 38°09'40" N, long. 119°41'55" W). Named on Tower Peak (1956) 15' quadrangle.

Shamrock Lake [TUOLUMNE]: *lake,* 700 feet long, 6.25 miles southwest of Matterhorn Peak (lat. 38°01'25" N, long. 119°27'15" W). Named on Matterhorn Peak (1956) 15' quadrangle.

Shanahan Flat [TUOLUMNE]: *area,* 5 miles east-southeast of Groveland (lat. 37°43'30" N, long. 120°08'50" W; sec. 31, T 1 S, R 17 E). Named on Groveland (1947) 7.5' quadrangle.

Shands [NEVADA]: *locality,* 2.5 miles west-southwest of Graniteville (lat. 39°24'55" N, long. 120°46'50" W). Named on Colfax (1898) 30' quadrangle.

Shanghai Ridge [MARIPOSA]: *ridge,* south-east-trending, 1 mile long, 4.25 miles north-

northwest of the settlement of Catheys Valley (lat. 37°29'30" N, long. 120°07'30" W). Named on Catheys Valley (1962) and Indian Gulch (1962) 7.5' quadrangles.

Shanks Cove [PLACER]: *relief feature,* 4 miles south-southwest of Granite Creek (lat. 39°08'20" N, long. 120°18'05" W; near N line sec. 21, T 15 N, R 15 E). Named on Granite Chief (1953) 7.5' quadrangle.

Shannon Ravine [SIERRA]: *canyon,* drained by a stream that flows 1 mile to Jim Crow Creek nearly 4 miles east-southeast of Downieville (lat. 39°32' N, long. 120°45'55" W; near N line sec. 8, T 19 N, R 11 E). Named on Downieville (1951) 7.5' quadrangle.

Sharon [MADERA]: *locality,* 4 miles east-northeast of Fairmead along Atchison, Topeka and Santa Fe Railroad (lat. 37°06' N, long. 120°07'50" W; near SE cor. sec. 32, T 9 S, R 17 E). Named on Berenda (1961) 7.5' quadrangle. Postal authorities established Sharon post office in 1898 and discontinued it in 1927 (Frickstad, p. 86). The place began as part of a real estate promotion on land that had been owned by San Francisco financier William Sharon (Clough, p. 91). California Mining Bureau's (1917d) map shows a place called Watt located 2.5 miles north-northwest of Sharon along the railroad.

Sharon Lake [TUOLUMNE]: *lake,* 725 feet long, 5 miles southwest of Sonora Pass (lat. 38°16'35" N, long. 119°42' W; near SE cor. sec. 18, T 5 N, R 21 E). Named on Sonora Pass (1979) 7.5' quadrangle.

Sharps Ravine [PLACER]: *canyon,* drained by a stream that flows less than 1 mile to Middle Fork American River 8 miles east-northeast of Auburn (lat. 38°56'35" N, long. 120°56'15" W; at S line sec. 26, T 13 N, R 9 E). Named on Greenwood (1949) 7.5' quadrangle.

Shaughnessy Place: see **Mobile Flat**, under **Mobile Ravine** [SIERRA].

Shaughnessy Ravine [SIERRA]: *canyon,* drained by a stream that flows nearly 2 miles to North Yuba River 4 miles east of Downie-ville (lat. 39°33'35" N, long. 120°45'10" W; at W line sec. 33, T 20 N, R 11 E). Named on Downieville (1951) 7.5' quadrangle.

Shaw Flat [EL DORADO]: *area,* 7 miles west-southwest of Kirkwood (lat. 38°39'15" N, long. 120°11'20" W; near SE cor. sec. 3, T 9 N, R 16 E). Named on Tragedy Spring (1979) 7.5' quadrangle.

Shawmut: see **Chinese Camp** [TUOLUMNE].

Shaws Flat [TUOLUMNE]: *locality,* 2 miles south-southwest of Columbia (lat. 38°00'25" N, long. 120°24'30" W; near S line sec. 23, T 2 N, R 14 E). Named on Columbia (1948) 7.5' quadrangle. Mandeville Shaw planted an orchard at the place in 1849 (Hoover, Rensch, and Rensch, p. 572). Perkins (p. 199) referred to Shaw's Flats in 1851. Stoddart (p. 64) mentioned a place called Dragoon Flat that was located "at the lower end of Shaws Flat"—a group of discharged dragoons settled there to mine gold in 1848.

Shealor Lakes [EL DORADO]: *lakes,* largest 700 feet long, 5.25 miles southwest of Kirkwood (lat. 38°39'30" N, long. 120°09' W; mainly in sec. 1, T 9 N, R 16 E). Named on Tragedy Spring (1979) 7.5' quadrangle.

Sheepcamp Spring [MARIPOSA]: *spring,* less than 0.5 mile northeast of Santa Cruz Mountain (lat. 37°27'40" N, long. 120°11'50" W; at N line sec. 34, T 5 S, R 16 E). Named on Indian Gulch (1962) 7.5' quadrangle.

Sheep Crossing [MADERA]: *locality,* 8 miles west-southwest of Devils Postpile along North Fork San Joaquin River (lat. 37°33'40" N, long. 119°12'30" W). Named on Devils Postpile (1953) 15' quadrangle. A trail used by cattlemen crossed the river at the place on a bridge known as Sheep Crossing (McLaughlin and Bradley, p. 556).

Sheep Gap [MARIPOSA]: *pass,* 4 miles east-southeast of the settlement of Catheys Valley (lat. 37°24'10" N, long. 120°01'40" W; near NW cor. sec. 20, T 6 S, R 18 E). Named on Catheys Valley (1962) 7.5' quadrangle.

Sheep Hollow: see **Steephollow Creek** [NEVADA].

Sheep Peak [TUOLUMNE]: *peak,* 6.5 miles northwest of Tioga Pass (lat. 37°59' N, long. 119°20'25" W; sec. 33, T 2 N, R 24 E). Named on Tuolumne Meadows (1956) 15' quadrangle.

Sheep Ranch [CALAVERAS]: *village,* 5 miles north of Murphys (lat. 38°12'35" N, long. 120°27'50" W; near SW cor. sec. 7, T 4 N, R 14 E). Named on Murphys (1948) 7.5' quadrangle. Postal authorities established Sheep Ranch post office in 1877 and changed the name to Sheepranch in 1895; the name was from Sheep Ranch mine (Salley, p. 202).

Sheep Ranch Ravine [SIERRA]: *canyon,* drained by a stream that flows 0.5 mile to Cedar Grove Ravine 3.25 miles southwest of Mount Fillmore (lat. 39°41'55" N, long. 120°53'55" W; sec. 7, T 21 N, R 10 E). Named on La Porte (1951) 7.5' quadrangle.

Sheering Creek [TUOLUMNE]: *stream,* flows nearly 2 miles to North Fork Tuolumne River 0.5 mile south-southeast of Pinecrest (lat. 38°11' N, long. 119°59'35" W; at W line sec. 22, T 4 N, R 18 E). Named on Pinecrest (1979) 7.5' quadrangle.

Shelby Flat: see **Selby Flat** [NEVADA].

Sheldon Ravine [PLACER]: *canyon,* drained by a stream that flows less than 1 mile to North Fork American River 4.25 miles south of Dutch Flat (lat. 39°08'40" N, long. 120°50'35" W; near W line sec. 15, T 15 N, R 10 E). Named on Dutch Flat (1950) 7.5' quadrangle.

Shellback: see **Omega** [NEVADA].

Shellenbarger Lake [MADERA]: *lake,* 450 feet long, 6.25 miles west of Devils Postpile (lat. 37°38'35" N, long. 119°11'40" W). Named on Devils Postpile (1953) 15' quadrangle.

Shenandoah Valley [AMADOR]: *valley,* 3.5

miles west-northwest of Fiddletown (lat. 38°31'15" N, long. 120°48'45" W). Named on Fiddletown (1949) 7.5' quadrangle. John Jameson settled in the valley in the early 1850's and named it for his birthplace in Virginia (Gudde, 1949, p. 328).

Shenanigan Flat [SIERRA]: *area,* 8 miles west-southwest of Goodyears Bar along North Yuba River (lat. 39°30'20" N, long. 121°01'25" W; near NE cor. sec. 24, T 19 N, R 8 E). Named on Strawberry Valley (1948) 7.5' quadrangle.

Shepherd Crest [TUOLUMNE]: *ridge,* northwest-trending, 2 miles long, 6.5 miles southsoutheast of Matterhorn Peak (lat. 38°00'35" N, long. 119°19'30" W). Named on Matterhorn Peak (1956) 15' quadrangle.

Shepherd Lake [TUOLUMNE]: *lake,* 700 feet long, 6 miles southeast of Matterhorn Peak (lat. 38°01'10" N, long. 119°19'05" W; sec. 15, T 2 N, R 24 E); the lake is northeast of Shepherd Crest. Named on Matterhorn Peak (1956) 15' quadrangle.

Sheridan [PLACER]: *village,* 7.5 miles northwest of Lincoln (lat. 38° 58'50" N, long. 121°22'20" W; sec. 13, T 13 N, R 5 E). Named on Lincoln (1953) and Sheridan (1953) 7.5' quadrangles. Postal authorities established Sheridan post office in 1868 and discontinued it for a brief time in 1870 (Frickstad, p. 121). A crossroads station called Union Shed was located 0.5 mile south of present Sheridan before the railroad came (Hoover, Rensch, and Rensch, p. 268).

Sheridans [PLACER]: *locality,* 7.5 miles east-northeast of Auburn (lat. 38°57'35" N, long. 120°57'15" W). Named on Placerville (1893) 30' quadrangle.

Sherlock: see **Sherlock Creek** [MARIPOSA].

Sherlock Creek [MARIPOSA]: *stream,* flows 7 miles to Merced River 3.25 miles northeast of the village of Bear Valley (lat. 37°35'50" N, long. 120°04'10" W; sec. 11, T 4 S, R 17 E). Named on Bear Valley (1947) and Feliciana Mountain (1947) 7.5' quadrangles. The name commemorates Jimmy Sherlock, who discovered gold in the stream in 1849; a mining camp by the creek was called Sherlock, Sherlock Town (Sargent, Shirley, 1976, p. 34-35), and Sherlock's Diggings (Morgan *in* Gardiner, p. 351).

Sherlock's Diggings: see **Sherlock Creek** [MARIPOSA].

Sherlock Town: see **Sherlock Creek** [MARIPOSA].

Sherman Acres [CALAVERAS]: *settlement,* 0.5 mile north-northeast of Tamarack (lat. 38°26'45" N, long. 120°04'20" W; sec. 23, T 7 N, R 17 E). Named on Tamarack (1979) 7.5' quadrangle. Called Lombardi on Big Meadow (1956) 15' quadrangle.

Sherman Canyon [EL DORADO]: *canyon,* drained by a stream that flows 5.5 miles to Silver Fork American River 7 miles west of Kirkwood (lat. 38°41'40" N, long. 120°12' W).

Named on Tragedy Spring (1979) 7.5' quadrangle.

Sherwood Forest [TUOLUMNE]: *settlement,* less than 1 mile southeast of Twain Harte (lat. 38°01'45" N, long. 120°13'20" W; sec. 16, T 2 N, R 16 E). Named on Twain Harte (1979) 7.5' quadrangle.

Shields Camp [NEVADA]: *locality,* 3 miles west-northwest of North Bloomfield (lat. 39°22'40" N, long. 120°57'20" W; sec. 34, T 18 N, R 9 E). Named on Pike (1949) 7.5' quadrangle.

Shingle: see **Shingle Springs** [EL DORADO].

Shingle Creek [EL DORADO]:
(1) *stream,* flows nearly 3 miles to South Fork American River 1.25 miles west of Coloma (lat. 38°48' N, long. 120°54'45" W; near W line sec. 18, T 11 N, R 10 E). Named on Coloma (1949) 7.5' quadrangle.
(2) *stream,* flows 3 miles to French Creek 5 miles north-northeast of Latrobe (lat. 38°37'15" N, long. 120°55'45" W; near E line sec. 24, T 9 N, R 9 E); the stream heads near Shingle Springs. Named on Latrobe (1949) and Shingle Springs (1949) 7.5' quadrangles.

Shingle Hill [MARIPOSA]: *ridge,* southeast- to east-trending, 2.5 miles long, 4 miles south-southeast of Smith Peak (lat. 37°45' N, long. 120°04' W). Named on Buckhorn Peak (1947) and Jawbone Ridge (1947) 7.5' quadrangles.

Shingle Mill Creek [EL DORADO]: *stream,* flows 3 miles to Middle Fork Cosumnes River 4.5 miles southeast of Caldor (lat. 38°34'05" N, long. 120°22'05" W; near SW cor. sec. 6, T 8 N, R 15 E). Named on Peddler Hill (1951) 7.5' quadrangle.

Shingle Mill Gulch [EL DORADO]: *canyon,* drained by a stream that flows 1.5 miles to Steely Fork Cosumnes River 11.5 miles southeast of Camino (lat. 38°37'50" N, long. 120°31'05" W; near SE cor. sec. 15, T 9 N, R 13 E). Named on Omo Ranch (1952) and Sly Park (1952) 7.5' quadrangles.

Shingle Spring [TUOLUMNE]: *spring,* 14 miles south-southeast of Pinecrest on Kibbie Ridge (lat. 38°00'45" N, long. 119°53' W; near W line sec. 22, T 2 N, R 19 E). Named on Cherry Lake North (1979) 7.5' quadrangle.

Shingle Spring: see **Shingle Springs** [EL DORADO].

Shingle Spring House: see **Shingle Springs** [EL DORADO].

Shingle Springs [EL DORADO]: *village,* 8 miles southwest of Placerville (lat. 38°39'55" N, long. 120°55'35" W; near W line sec. 6, T 9 N, R 10 E). Named on Shingle Springs (1949) 7.5' quadrangle. Called Shingle on California Mining Bureau's (1909a) map. Postal authorities established Shingle Spring post office in 1853 and discontinued it in 1855; they established Shingle Springs post office in 1865, changed the name to Shingle in 1895, and changed it back to Shingle Springs in 1955 (Salley, p. 203). The name is

from springs at the place, and from a shingle mill built there in 1849; mining began at the site in 1850 and a hostelry called Shingle Spring House was erected the same year (Hoover, Rensch, and Rensch, p. 83). Postal authorities established Canyon post office 5 miles southeast of Shingle post office in 1897 and discontinued it in 1906; the name was from the location of the post office along Big Canyon Creek (Salley, p. 36). California Division of Highways' (1934) map shows a place called Bennett situated 2.25 miles southwest of Shingle Springs along Southern Pacific Railroad (near N line sec. 14, T 9 N, R 9 E). A mining camp of 1849 called Euchre Diggings was located near Shingle Springs; the name was for the game miners played in the winter (Gudde, 1975, p. 111).

Shirley Creek [CALAVERAS]: *stream,* heads in Calaveras County and flows 10 miles to Hoods Creek 10.5 miles north of Oakdale in Stanislaus County (lat. 37°55'20" N, long. 120°49'30" W; sec. 24, T 1 N, R 10 E); the stream goes through Shirley Gulch. Named on Bachelor Valley (1968) 7.5' quadrangle.

Shirley Creek [MADERA]: *stream,* flows 1 mile to Madera Creek nearly 6 miles south-south-east of Merced Peak (lat. 37°33'30" N, long. 119°20'50" W). Named on Merced Peak (1953) 15' quadrangle.

Shirley Gulch [CALAVERAS]: *canyon,* on Calaveras-Stanislaus county line, along Shirley Creek above a point 10.5 miles north-northeast of Oakdale (lat. 37°54' N, long. 120°45'50" W; near N line sec. 33, T 1 N, R 11 E). Named on Bachelor Valley (1968) and Copperopolis (1962) 7.5' quadrangles.

Shirley Lake [MADERA]: *lake,* 600 feet long, 5.25 miles south of Merced Peak (lat. 37°33'35" N, long. 119°22'30" W). Named on Merced Peak (1953) 15' quadrangle.

Shirley Mountain [CALAVERAS]: *ridge,* west-trending, 1 mile long, about 5 miles southwest of Copperopolis (lat. 37°55'45" N, long. 120°42'35" W); the ridge is south of Shirley Gulch. Named on Copperopolis (1962) 7.5' quadrangle.

Shirley Lake [PLACER]: *lake,* 350 feet long, 1 mile east-northeast of Granite Chief (lat. 39°12'10" N, long. 120°16'10" W; near SW cor. sec. 25, T 16 N, R 15 E). Named on Granite Chief (1953) 7.5' quadrangle.

Shirttail Canyon [PLACER]: *canyon,* drained by a stream that flows 12 miles to North Fork American River 5 miles southeast of Colfax (lat. 39°02'30" N, long. 120°54'05" W; near S line sec. 19, T 14 N, R 10 E). Named on Colfax (1949) and Foresthill (1949) 7.5' quadrangles. The name was given in the summer of 1849 after two men chanced upon a miner who wore nothing but a shirt to cover his nakedness (Hoover, Rensch, and Rensch, p. 275). Whitney's (1873) map shows a place called Old Bar located along North Fork

American River nearly 1 mile below the mouth of Shirttail Canyon.

Shirttail Canyon: see **North Shirttail Canyon** [PLACER].

Shirttail Peak [EL DORADO]: *peak,* 5 miles southwest of the village of Pilot Hill (lat. 38°47'35" N, long. 121°05'20" W; sec. 21, T 11 N, R 8 E). Altitude 1217 feet. Named on Pilot Hill (1954) 7.5' quadrangle.

Shoemake: see **Chinese Station** [TUOLUMNE].

Shoemaker Hill [EL DORADO]: *peak,* 2.25 miles southeast of Georgetown (lat. 38°53'05" N, long. 120°48'20" W; sec. 13, T 12 N, R 10 E). Named on Georgetown (1949) 7.5' quadrangle.

Shoofly Creek [TUOLUMNE]: *stream,* flows 6 miles to Middle Fork Stanislaus River nearly 7 miles southeast of Liberty Hill (lat. 38°18'05" N, long. 120°00'30" W; at E line sec. 8, T 5 N, R 18 E). Named on Liberty Hill (1979) 7.5' quadrangle.

Shoofly Meadow [TUOLUMNE]: *area,* 4 miles east of Liberty Hill (lat. 38°21'30" N, long. 120°01'40" W; near E line sec. 19, T 6 N, R 18 E); the place is by the head of Shoofly Creek. Named on Liberty Hill (1979) 7.5' quadrangle.

Shotgun: see **Schoettgen Pass** [TUOLUMNE].

Shotgun Creek [TUOLUMNE]: *stream,* flows 1.5 miles to Stanislaus River nearly 6 miles north-northwest of Keystone (lat. 37°54'15" N, long. 120°33'45" W; sec. 29, T 1 N, R 13 E). Named on Melones Dam (1962) 7.5' quadrangle.

Shotgun Lake [NEVADA]: *lake,* 1000 feet long, 3.25 miles southwest of English Mountain along South Fork Canyon Creek (lat. 39°25'20" N, long. 120°36'15" W; on W line sec. 14, T 18 N, R 12 E). Named on English Mountain (1983) 7.5' quadrangle.

Shower Branch [SIERRA]: *stream,* flows 2.25 miles to Canyon Creek 6 miles west-northwest of Goodyears Bar (lat. 39°34'55" N, long. 120°59' W; near E line sec. 20, T 20 N, R 9 E). Named on Goodyears Bar (1951) 7.5' quadrangle.

Showers Lake [EL DORADO]: *lake,* 750 feet long, 3.25 miles northeast of Kirkwood (lat. 38°44'30" N, long. 120°02'05" W; on E line sec. 6, T 10 N, R 18 E). Named on Caples Lake (1979) 7.5' quadrangle.

Shriner Lake [AMADOR]: *lake,* 750 feet long, 3.5 miles west of Mokelumne Peak (lat. 38°32'10" N, long. 120°09'30" W; on N line sec. 24, T 8 N, R 16 E). Named on Bear River Reservoir (1979) 7.5' quadrangle.

Shrub [EL DORADO]: *locality,* 2.5 miles north-northeast of Latrobe along Southern Pacific Railroad (lat. 38°35'30" N, long. 120°57'10" W; sec. 35, T 9 N, R 9 E). Named on Latrobe (1949) 7.5' quadrangle.

Shultz Mountain [MARIPOSA]: *ridge,* south- to southeast-trending, 2.5 miles long, 3.25

miles east-southeast of Santa Cruz Mountain (lat. 37°26'45" N, long. 120°08'35" W). Named on Indian Gulch (1962) 7.5' quadrangle.

Shumake Knoll [TUOLUMNE]: *ridge,* east- to east-northeast-trending, nearly 1 mile long, 8 miles south-southwest of Liberty Hill (lat. 38°15'30" N, long. 120°09'50" W). Named on Boards Crossing (1979) 7.5' quadrangle.

Shuteye Creek [MADERA]: *stream,* flows 2.5 miles to West Fork Chiquito Creek 3 miles northeast of Shuteye Peak (lat. 37°22'50" N, long. 119°23'20" W; sec. 30, T 6 S, R 24 E); the stream heads at Shuteye Peak. Named on Shuteye Peak (1953) 15' quadrangle.

Shuteye Pass [MADERA]: *pass,* 1 mile southeast of Shuteye Peak (lat. 37°20'20" N, long. 119°24'45" W; near NW cor. sec. 12, T 7 S, R 23 E). Named on Shuteye Peak (1953) 15' quadrangle.

Shuteye Pass: see **Little Shuteye Pass** [MADERA].

Shuteye Peak [MADERA]: *peak,* 11 miles east of Yosemite Forks (lat. 37°21' N, long. 119°25'40" W; sec. 2, T 7 S, R 23 E). Altitude 8351 feet. Named on Shuteye Peak (1953) 15' quadrangle. The name commemorates a mountaineer who was called Old Shuteye because he was blind in one eye (Hanna, p. 304).

Shuteye Peak: see **Little Shuteye Peak** [MADERA].

Sierra: see **Sierra City** [SIERRA].

Sierra Buttes [SIERRA]: *relief feature,* multiple peaks 2 miles north-northwest of Sierra City along a northwest-trending ridge (lat. 39°35'30" N, long. 120°38'20" W). Named on Sierra City (1981) 7.5' quadrangle. Called Yuba Butte on Goddard's (1857) map.

Sierra Campground [SIERRA]: *locality,* 6 miles northeast of Sierra City along North Yuba River (lat. 39°37'50" N, long. 120°33'30" W; at N line sec. 6, T 20 N, R 13 E). Named on Clio (1981) 7.5' quadrangle.

Sierra Campground [TUOLUMNE]: *locality,* 3.5 miles south-southwest of Strawberry along North Fork Tuolumne River (lat. 38°09'15" N, long. 120°02'35" W). Named on Strawberry (1979) 7.5' quadrangle.

Sierra City [SIERRA]: *village,* 10.5 miles east of Downieville along North Yuba River (lat. 39°34' N, long. 120°38' W; at S line sec. 28, T 20 N, R 12 E). Named on Sierra City (1981) 7.5' quadrangle. Postal authorities established Sierra post office in 1855, discontinued it in 1856, reestablished it with the name "Sierra City" in 1864, discontinued it in 1865, and reestablished it in 1867 (Salley, p. 204). Kane Flat, also known as Buttes Flat, is at the west end of Sierra City; it was the site of a stamp mill for Sierra Buttes mine (Gudde, 1975, p. 182).

Sierra del Monte Diablo: see "Regional setting."

Sierra de San Marcos: see "Regional setting."

Sierra House [EL DORADO]: *locality,* 5 miles

northwest of Freel Peak (lat. 38°54'25" N, long. 119°57'50" W; near NW cor. cor. sec. 11, T 12 N, R 18 E). Site named on South Lake Tahoe (1955) 7.5' quadrangle.

Sierra Point [MARIPOSA]: *promontory,* 2.25 miles southeast of Yosemite Village on the north side of Merced River (lat. 37°43'40" N, long. 119°33'15" W). Named on Yosemite (1956) 15' quadrangle. Charles A. Bailey named the place in 1897 to honor the Sierra Club after he found that Illilouette Fall, Vernal Fall, Nevada Fall , Upper Yosemite Fall, and Lower Yosemite Fall all can be seen from the spot (Browning, 1986, p. 198).

Sierra Valley [SIERRA]: *valley,* extends north and northeast from Sierraville into Plumas County. Named on Antelope Valley (1981), Calpine (1981), Loyalton (1981), Sattley (1981), and Sierraville (1981) 7.5' quadrangles.

Sierra Valley: see **Sierraville** [SIERRA].

Sierra Valley Channels [SIERRA]: *water feature,* braided streams that extend from the south part of Sierra Valley north into Plumas County, where they enter marsh. Named on Antelope Valley (1981) and Calpine (1981) 7.5' quadrangles. United States Board on Geographic Names (1974b, p. 3) noted that the feature is a network of ditches and drains that converge in Plumas County at the head of Middle Fork Feather River—the Board gave the variant name "Middle Fork Feather River" for Sierra Valley Channels.

Sierra Village [TUOLUMNE]: *settlement,* 4 miles northeast of Twain Harte (lat. 38°04'20" N, long. 120°10'20" W; near W line sec. 36, T 3 N, R 16 E). Named on Twain Harte (1979) 7.5' quadrangle.

Sierraville [SIERRA]: *village,* 25 miles east of Downieville (lat. 39° 35'20" N, long. 120°22' W; sec. 13, T 20 N, R 14 E); the place is at the south end of Sierra Valley. Named on Sierraville (1981) 7.5' quadrangle. Postal authorities established Sierra Valley post office in 1862 and changed the name to Sierraville in 1899 (Frickstad, p. 185).

Sierraville Creek [SIERRA]: *stream,* formed by the confluence of Bonita Creek and Cold Stream (1), flows less than 1 mile to Sierra Valley 1.25 miles south of Sierraville (lat. 39°34'20" N, long. 120° 21'55" W; sec. 24, T 20 N, R 14 E); the stream goes past Sierraville. Named on Sierraville (1981) 7.5' quadrangle.

Sierra Vista [MADERA]: *locality,* 2.5 miles north-northwest of Chowchilla along Southern Pacific Railroad (lat. 37°09' N, long. 120°17'10" W; sec. 13, T 9 S, R 15 E). Named on Plainsburg (1919) 7.5' quadrangle.

Sierra Vista Mountain: see **Quiggs Mountain** [CALAVERAS].

Siesta Lake [TUOLUMNE]: *lake,* 500 feet long, 1.5 miles south-southwest of White Wolf (lat. 37°51' N, long. 119°39'35" W; near SE cor. sec. 16, T 1 S, R 21 E). Named on Hetch Hetchy Reservoir (1956) 15' quadrangle.

Signal Peak [NEVADA]: *peak,* 4.5 miles east-northeast of Yuba Gap (lat. 39°20'20" N, long. 120°32'05" W; sec. 17, T 17 N, R 13 E). Altitude 7841 feet. Named on Cico Grove (1955) 7.5' quadrangle.

Signal Peak: see **Devil Peak** [MARIPOSA].

Silverado: see **Camp Silverado** [AMADOR].

Silver Creek [EL DORADO]: *stream,* heads at Union Valley Reservoir and flows 16 miles to South Fork American River 2 miles north of Pollock Pines (lat. 38°47'20" N, long. 120°35'20" W; sec. 24, T 11 N, R 12 E). Named on Pollock Pines (1950) and Riverton (1950) 7.5' quadrangles. Jones Fork flows 16 miles to Union Valley Reservoir 6.5 miles north-northwest of Riverton (near S line sec. 26, T 12 N, R 14 E); it is named on Kyburz (1952), Pyramid Peak (1955), and Rockbound Valley (1955) 7.5' quadrangles. Kyburz (1952) 7.5' quadrangle shows Jones place situated along Jones Fork (NE cor. sec. 35, T 12 N, R 14 E). Jones Fork has the name "Middle Fork Silver Creek" on Pyramid Peak (1896) 30' quadrangle. South Fork enters Silver Creek 5.5 miles north of Riverton (sec. 30, T 12 N, R 14 E); it is 25 miles long and is named on Kyburz (1952), Pyramid Peak (1955), and Riverton (1950) 7.5' quadrangles.

Silver Creek [PLACER]: *stream,* flows 2.5 miles to Truckee River 5 miles northwest of Tahoe City (lat. 39°13'30" N, long. 120°12' W; sec. 21, T 16 N, R 16 E); the stream heads near Silver Peak. Named on Tahoe City (1955) 7.5' quadrangle.

Silver Creek: see **Big Silver Creek** [EL DORADO]; **Deer Creek** [PLACER]; **Litttle Silver Creek** [EL DORADO].

Silver Creek Campground [EL DORADO]: *locality,* nearly 5 miles northeast of Riverton along South Fork Silver Creek (lat. 38°48'55" N, long. 120°22'45" W; sec. 11, T 11 N, R 14 E). Named on Riverton (1950) 7.5' quadrangle.

Silver Creek Campground [PLACER]: *locality,* 5 miles northwest of Tahoe City along Truckee River (lat. 39°13'25" N, long. 120°12'05" W; sec. 21, T 16 N, R 16 E); the place is near the mouth of Silver Creek. Named on Tahoe City (1955) 7.5' quadrangle.

Silver Fork: see **American River** [EL DORADO-PLACER].

Silver Fork Meadow [EL DORADO]: *area,* 4.5 miles west-southwest of Kirkwood (lat. 38°41'30" N, long. 120°09' W); the place is north of Silver Fork American River. Named on Tragedy Spring (1979) 7.5' quadrangle.

Silver Gulch [TUOLUMNE]: *canyon,* 1.25 miles long, opens into the canyon of South Fork Stanislaus River 4.5 miles northeast of Columbia (lat. 38°04'30" N, long. 120°20'10" W; sec. 33, T 3 N, R 15 E). Named on Columbia SE (1948) 7.5' quadrangle.

Silver Hill [EL DORADO]: *peak,* 4 miles west-southwest of Robbs Peak (lat. 38°53'55" N, long. 120°28'05" W; sec. 12, T 12 N, R 13 E). Altitude 6081 feet. Named on Robbs Peak (1950) 7.5' quadrangle.

Silver Knob [MARIPOSA]: *peak*, 4 miles southwest of Fish Camp (lat. 37°26' N, long. 119°41' W; near S line sec. 4, T 6 S, R 21 E). Named on Bass Lake (1953) 15' quadrangle.

Silver Knoll: see **Douglas Flat** [CALAVERAS].

Silver Lake [AMADOR]: *lake*, 2 miles long, behind a dam 9 miles north of Mokelumne Peak (lat. 38°40'05" N, long. 120°07'15" W; sec. 32, T 10 N, R 17 E). Named on Caples Lake (1979) and Tragedy Spring (1979) 7.5' quadrangles. Postal authorities established Caminettis post office—probably at a resort near Silver Lake—in 1916 and discontinued it in 1920; the name was for for Elizabeth B. Caminetti, first postmaster (Salley, p. 33).

Silver Lake: see **Plasse** [AMADOR].

Silver Lake West Campground [AMADOR-EL DORADO]: *locality*, 3.5 miles southwest of Kirkwood (lat. 38°40'20" N, long. 120°07'15" W; sec. 32, T 10 N, R 17 E); the place is north of Silver Lake. Named on Caples Lake (1979) 7.5' quadrangle.

Silver Mine Creek [TUOLUMNE]: *stream*, flows 2.5 miles to Relief Reservoir 6.5 miles west-southwest of Sonora Pass (lat. 38°16'35" N, long. 119°44'10" W; sec. 14, T 5 N, R 20 E). Named on Dardanelle (1979) and Sonora Pass (1979) 7.5' quadrangles.

Silver Peak [EL DORADO]: *peak*, 4.5 miles west-southwest of Phipps Peak (lat. 38°56'05" N, long. 120°13'45" W; sec. 32, T 13 N, R 16 E). Altitude 8930 feet. Named on Rockbound Valley (1955) 7.5' quadrangle.

Silver Peak [PLACER]: *peak*, 6.5 miles west-northwest of Tahoe City (lat. 39°13'15" N, long. 120°14'45" W; sec. 19, T 16 N, R 16 E). Altitude 8424 feet. Named on Tahoe City (1955) 7.5' quadrangle.

Silver Strand Falls [MARIPOSA]: *waterfall*, 5.5 miles southwest of Yosemite Village along Meadow Brook (lat. 37°42'15" N, long. 119°40'05" W). Named on Yosemite (1956) 15' quadrangle. United States Board on Geographic Names (1933, p. 694) rejected the name "Widows Tears Falls" for the feature. Early stage drivers told tourists that the name "Widows Tears Falls" was given to the feature because the waterfall lasted only two weeks; François E. Matthes suggested the present name (Browning, 1986, p. 201).

Simmons Peak [MADERA-TUOLUMNE]: *peak*, 10.5 miles south of Tioga Pass on Madera-Tuolumne county line (lat. 37°45'40" N, long. 119°17'35" W). Altitude 12,503 feet. Named on Tuolumne Meadows (1956) 15' quadrangle. R.B. Marshall of United States Geological Survey named the peak in 1909 for Dr. Samuel E. Simmons of Sacramento (United States Board on Geographic Names, 1934, p. 22).

Simmons Point [CALAVERAS]: *peak*, 5.5

miles southeast of San Andreas (lat. 38°08'05" N, long. 120°36'50" W; near SE cor. sec. 2, T 3 N, R 12 E). Named on Calaveritas (1962) 7.5' quadrangle.

Simpson Gulch [EL DORADO]: *canyon*, drained by a stream that flows 2.5 miles to Middle Dry Creek 1.5 miles south-southwest of Caldor (lat. 38°35'05" N, long. 120°26'20" W; sec. 33, T 9 N, R 14 E). Named on Caldor (1951) 7.5' quadrangle.

Simpsonville: see **Bear Valley** [MARIPOSA] (2).

Sims Cove [MARIPOSA]: *locality*, nearly 5 miles south-southwest of El Portal along South Fork Merced River (lat. 37°37'10" N, long. 119°49'40" W; sec. 2, T 4 S, R 19 E). Named on Buckingham Mountain (1947) 7.5' quadrangle. The name should have the form "Simm's Cove" (Mendershausen, p. 18).

Singleton Springs [EL DORADO]: *springs*, 10 miles west-southwest of Kirkwood at the head of North Fork Cosumnes River (lat. 38° 38'15" N, long. 120°14'20" W; near SW cor. sec. 8, T 9 N, R 16 E). Named on Tragedy Spring (1979) 7.5' quadrangle.

Sing Peak [MADERA]: *peak*, 5.5 miles south of Merced Peak (lat. 37°33'15" N, long. 119°23'15" W). Altitude 10,552 feet. Named on Merced Peak (1953) 15' quadrangle. R.B. Marshall of United States Geological Survey named the peak in 1899 for Tie Sing, cook for the Survey from 1888 until he died in an accident in 1918 (United States Board on Geographic Names, 1934, p. 22).

Sister Lake [TUOLUMNE]: *lake*, 1500 feet long, 7.25 miles southwest of Matterhorn Peak (lat. 38°01'05" N, long. 119°28'30" W). Named on Matterhorn Peak (1956) 15' quadrangle.

Sivels Mountain [MARIPOSA]: *peak*, 3.5 miles northeast of Yosemite Forks (lat. 37°23'50" N, long. 119°34'45" W; at W line sec. 21, T 6 S, R 22 E). Altitude 5813 feet. Named on Bass Lake (1953) 15' quadrangle, which shows Sivels ranch situated 0.5 mile southwest of the peak. The misspelled name recalls Thomas Sivils, who patented land in section 20 in 1891 (Browning, 1986, p. 201).

Six-Bit Gulch [TUOLUMNE]: *canyon*, drained by a stream that flows 5.5 miles to Don Pedro Reservoir 4 miles south-southeast of Chinese Camp (lat. 37°49'05" N, long. 120°24'45" W; sec. 27, T 1 S, R 14 E). Named on Chinese Camp (1947, photorevised 1973) 7.5' quadrangle. Sonora (1897) 30' quadrangle has the form "Sixbit Gulch" for the name, which was given in derision because of the scarcity of gold at the place (Paden and Schlichtmann, p. 63).

Sixmile Creek [CALAVERAS]: *stream*, flows nearly 7 miles to Angels Creek less than 1 mile south of Angels Camp (lat. 38°03'25" N, long. 120°32'30" W; near W line sec. 3, T 2 N, R 13 E). Named on Angels Camp (1962) and Columbia (1948) 7.5' quadrangles. Jackson (1902) 30' quadrangle has the form "Six Mile Creek" for the name.

Six Mile House [EL DORADO]: *locality,* 5.5 miles east of Placerville (lat. 38°44'15" N, long. 120°41'55" W). Named on Placerville (1893) 30' quadrangle.

Sixmile House [MADERA]: *locality,* 14 miles south-southwest of Raymond (lat. 37°00'45" N, long. 119°57'50" W; near SW cor. sec. 36, T 10 S, R 18 E). Named on Daulton (1921) 7.5' quadrangle.

Six Mile House: see **Scotts Flat** [NEVADA] (2).

Sixmile Valley [PLACER]: *valley,* 3.5 miles west of Cisco Grove (lat. 39°18'45" N, long. 120°36'15" W; on E line sec. 27, T 17 N, R 12 E). Named on Cisco Grove (1955) 7.5' quadrangle.

Skelton Creek [MARIPOSA]: *stream,* flows 4.5 miles to Devil Gulch 7 miles south-southwest of El Portal (lat. 37°34'45" N, long. 119° 48'45" W; near N line sec. 24, T 4 S, R 19 E). Named on Buckingham Mountain (1947) 7.5' quadrangle.

Skelton Lakes [TUOLUMNE]: *lakes,* two, largest 1000 feet long, 3 miles northwest of Tioga Pass (lat. 37°56'05" N, long. 119°18' W). Named on Tuolumne Meadows (1956) 15' quadrangle. Browning (1986, p. 202) associated the name with Henry A. Skelton, who was a ranger at Yosemite National Park from 1916 until 1932.

Skillman Flat [NEVADA]: *area,* nearly 3 miles south of Washington (lat. 39°19'10" N, long. 120°47'25" W; near SW cor. sec. 19, T 17 N, R 11 E). Named on Washington (1950) 7.5' quadrangle.

Skinners [EL DORADO]: *locality,* 4.25 miles west-northwest of Shingle Springs (lat. 38°42' N, long. 120°59'40" W; near N line sec. 28, T 10 N, R 9 E). Named on Shingle Springs (1949) 7.5' quadrangle.

Skull Creek [TUOLUMNE]: *stream,* formed by the confluence of North Fork and South Fork, flows nearly 6 miles to Griswold Creek 6.5 miles northwest of Crandall Peak (lat. 38°14'20" N, long. 120°12'35" W; sec. 33, T 5 N, R 15 E). Named on Boards Crossing (1979), Crandall Peak (1979), and Liberty Hill (1979) 7.5' quadrangles. North Fork is 3 miles long and South Fork is 2.5 miles long. Both forks are named on Liberty Hill (1979) 7.5' quadrangle.

Skull Flat [CALAVERAS]: *area,* 1.5 miles north-northeast of West Point (lat. 38°25'15" N, long. 120°30'50" W; mainly in sec. 35, T 7 N, R 13 E). Named on West Point (1948) 7.5' quadrangle.

Skunk Canyon [EL DORADO]: *canyon,* 1.5 miles long, opens into the canyon of South Fork American River 4.25 miles south-south-west of the village of Pilot Hill (lat. 38°46'25" N, long. 121°02' W; sec. 25, T 11 N, R 8 E). Named on Pilot Hill (1954) 7.5' quadrangle.

Skunk Canyon [PLACER]: *canyon,* drained by a stream that flows 1.5 miles to North Fork of Middle Fork American River 1.5 miles south of Michigan Bluff (lat. 39°01'05" N, long. 120°44' W; sec. 34, T 14 N, R 11 E). Named on Michigan Bluff (1952) 7.5' quadrangle. Called Skunk Gulch on Whitney's (1873) map.

Skunk Creek [TUOLUMNE]: *stream,* flows 5 miles to Jawbone Creek 8 miles west-north-west of Mather (lat. 37°55'40" N, long. 119°59'30" W; sec. 22, T 1 N, R 18 E). Named on Lake Eleanor (1956) and Tuolumne (1948) 15' quadrangles.

Skunk Gulch [CALAVERAS]: *canyon,* drained by a stream that flows nearly 2 miles to Stanislaus River 2.5 miles southeast of Vallecito (lat. 38°03'40" N, long. 120°26'35" W; sec. 4, T 2 N, R 14 E). Named on Columbia (1948) 7.5' quadrangle.

Skunk Gulch [MARIPOSA]: *canyon,* drained by a stream that flows 2.25 miles to Bull Creek 11.5 miles west of El Portal (lat. 37°42'25" N, long. 119°58'55" W; near E line sec. 4, T 3 S, R 18 E). Named on Buckhorn Peak (1947) and Kinsley (1947) 7.5' quadrangles.

Skunk Gulch: see **Skunk Canyon** [PLACER].

Skunk Spring [PLACER]: *spring,* 3.5 miles northwest of Duncan Peak (lat. 39°11'15" N, long. 120°33'50" W; sec. 6, T 15 N, R 13 E). Named on Duncan Peak (1952) 7.5' quadrangle.

Skyhigh [CALAVERAS]: *settlement,* 1.5 miles southwest of Tamarack (lat. 38°25'30" N, long. 120°05'45" W; sec. 27, T 7 N, R 17 E). Named on Tamarack (1979) 7.5' quadrangle.

Skyhigh [SIERRA]: *peak,* 2.25 miles south-southwest of Mount Fillmore (lat. 39°42' N, long. 120°51'45" W; sec. 9, T 21 N, R 10 E). Altitude 6443 feet. Named on Mount Fillmore (1951) 7.5' quadrangle.

Skylake Camp [EL DORADO]: *locality,* 6 miles west-northwest of Freel Peak along Upper Truckee River (lat. 38°54'15" N, long. 119°59'35" W; sec. 9, T 12 N, R 18 E). Named on Freel Peak (1956) 15' quadrangle.

Slab Creek [EL DORADO]: *stream,* flows 12 miles to South Fork American River 5.5 miles west-northwest of Pollock Pines (lat. 38° 47'15" N, long. 120°41' W; sec. 19, T 11 N, R 12 E). Named on Pollock Pines (1950) and Slate Mountain (1950) 7.5' quadrangles.

Slab Creek Reservoir [EL DORADO]: *lake,* behind a dam on South Fork American River 6.25 miles west of Pollock Pines (lat. 38°46'40" N, long. 120°41'50" W; sec. 25, T 11 N, R 11 E); Slab Creek joins South Fork American River in the lake. Named on Slate Mountain (1950, photorevised 1973) 7.5' quadrangle.

Slab Lakes [MADERA]: *lakes,* largest 800 feet long, 2.5 miles east-southeast of Merced Peak (lat. 37°37'05" N, long. 119°21'25" W). Named on Merced Peak (1953) 15' quadrangle.

Slabtown: see **Jackson Butte** [AMADOR].

Slacks Ravine [NEVADA]: *canyon,* drained by a stream that flows 4 miles to Deer Creek 6 miles northwest of Pilot Peak (lat. 39°13'25" N, long. 121°16'20" W; at S line sec. 23, T 16 N, R 6 E). Named on Rough and Ready (1949) and Smartville (1951) 7.5' quadrangles.

Slat Creek [EL DORADO]: *stream,* flows 2 miles to Traverse Creek 7.25 miles north of Chili Bar (lat. 38°52'20" N, long. 120°49' W; sec. 24, T 12 N, R 10 E). Named on Garden Valley (1949) and Georgetown (1949) 7.5' quadrangles.

Slate Canyon [EL DORADO]: *canyon,* drained by a stream that flows 2.5 miles to Whaler Creek 9 miles northwest of Pollock Pines (lat. 38°50'40" N, long. 120°42'50" W; sec. 35, T 12 N, R 11 E); the canyon is on the northeast side of the ridge called Slate Mountains. Named on Slate Mountain (1950) 7.5' quadrangle. Logan's (1938) map has the name "Slate Mtn. Cr." for the stream in the canyon.

Slate Castle [SIERRA]: *relief feature,* 2 miles south-southeast of Downieville (lat. 39°32'10" N, long. 120°48'35" W; near N line sec. 12, T 19 N, R 10 E). Altitude 5236 feet. Named on Downieville (1951) 7.5' quadrangle.

Slate Castle Creek [SIERRA]: *stream,* flows 1.5 miles to North Yuba River less than 1 mile east-southeast of Downieville (lat. 39° 33'30" N, long. 120°48'50" W; near W line sec. 36, T 20 N, R 10 E); the stream heads near Slate Castle. Named on Downieville (1951) 7.5' quadrangle.

Slate Creek [AMADOR]: *stream,* flows 2.25 miles to South Fork Cosumnes River 3 miles north of Fiddletown (lat. 38°32'55" N, long. 120°44'45" W; sec. 15, T 8 N, R 11 E). Named on Aukum (1952) 7.5' quadrangle.

Slate Creek [CALAVERAS]: *stream,* flows 5.5 miles to New Hogan Reservoir nearly 6 miles south-southeast of Valley Springs (lat. 38°07'35" N, long. 120°48'35" W; sec. 7, T 3 N, R 11 E). Named on Jenny Lind (1962) and Valley Springs (1962) 7.5' quadrangles.

Slate Creek [EL DORADO]:

(1) *stream,* flows 2 miles to Dutch Creek 3.5 miles northwest of Chili Bar (lat. 38°48'30" N, long. 120°51'25" W; near NW cor. sec. 15, T 11 N, R 10 E). Named on Garden Valley (1949) 7.5' quadrangle.

(2) *stream,* flows 6.25 miles to Big Canyon Creek 4 miles east-northeast of Latrobe (lat. 38°34'40" N, long. 120°54'35" W; near E line sec. 6, T 8 N, R 10 E). Named on Fiddletown (1949), Latrobe (1949), and Placerville (1949) 7.5' quadrangles.

(3) *stream,* flows 6.5 miles to Dry Creek 3.5 miles north-northeast of Shingle Springs (lat. 38°42'40" N, long. 120°54'05" W; sec. 20, T 10 N, R 10 E). Named on Placerville (1949) and Shingle Springs (1949) 7.5' quadrangles. Called North Slate Cr. on Logan's (1938) map.

Slate Creek [NEVADA]: *stream,* flows 2.5 miles to Deer Creek 2.25 miles northwest of Grass Valley (lat. 39°14'35" N, long. 121°05'20" W; near SW cor. sec. 16, T 16 N, R 8 E). Named on Grass Valley (1949) 7.5' quadrangle.

Slate Creek [SIERRA]: *stream,* heads in Sierra County and flows 26 miles, partly in Plumas County, to North Yuba River nearly 3 miles south-southeast of Strawberry Valley in Yuba County (lat. 39°31'35" N, long. 121°05'25" W; sec. 9, T 19 N, R 8 E). Named on American House (1948), Blue Nose Mountain (1951), La Porte (1951), Onion Valley (1950), and Strawberry Valley (1948) 7.5' quadrangles. The stream forms part of Sierra-Plumas county line. Downieville (1897) 30' quadrangle has the name "Little Slate Creek" for present Slate Creek above the mouth of East Branch, which enters the main stream 3.5 miles west of Mount Fillmore. East Branch is 5.5 miles long and is named on La Porte (1951) and Mount Fillmore (1951) 7.5' quadrangles.

Slate Creek [TUOLUMNE]: *stream,* flows 1.5 miles to Woods Creek 6.5 miles south-southwest of Sonora (lat. 37°53'50" N, long. 120° 26' W; sec. 33, T 1 N, R 14 E). Named on Sonora (1948) 7.5' quadrangle.

Slate Creek: see **Dry Creek** [AMADOR].

Slate Gulch [MARIPOSA]: *canyon,* drained by a stream that flows 5 miles to Bear Creek (2) 2 miles east-southeast of Santa Cruz Mountain (lat. 37°26'35" N, long. 120°10'20" W; sec. 1, T 6 S, R 16 E). Named on Indian Gulch (1962) 7.5' quadrangle.

Slate Gulch [TUOLUMNE]: *canyon,* drained by a stream that flows 1 mile to Algerine Creek 6 miles south of Sonora (lat. 37°53'55" N, long. 120°21'40" W; near E line sec. 31, T 1 N, R 15 E). Named on Standard (1948) 7.5' quadrangle.

Slate Gulch: see **Feliciana Creek** [MARIPOSA].

Slate Mountain [EL DORADO]: *peak,* 7 miles northwest of Pollock Pines (lat. 38°49'25" N, long. 120°41' W; at S line sec. 6, T 11 N, R 12 E). Altitude 3892 feet. Named on Slate Mountain (1950) 7.5' quadrangle.

Slate Mountain Creek: see **Slate Canyon** [EL DORADO].

Slate Mountains [EL DORADO]: *ridge,* generally southeast-trending, 5.5 miles long, 8.5 miles northwest of Pollock Pines (lat. 38°50' N, long. 120°42' W); Slate Mountain is near the southeast end of the ridge. Named on Slate Mountain (1950) 7.5' quadrangle.

Slatington: see **Kelsey** [EL DORADO].

Slaughter Ravine [PLACER]: *canyon,* drained by a stream that flows 1.5 miles to North Fork American River 1.5 miles east of Colfax (lat. 39°05'55" N, long. 120°55'25" W; near N line sec. 1, T 14 N, R 9 E). Named on Colfax (1949) 7.5' quadrangle.

Slaughter's Bar: see **Goodyears Bar** [SI-

ERRA].

Sleepy Hollow [PLACER]: *canyon,* drained by a stream that flows 0.5 mile to Live Oak Ravine 3.5 miles south of Colfax (lat. 39°03'05" N, long. 120°57'45" W; sec. 22, T 14 N, R 9 E). Named on Colfax (1949) 7.5' quadrangle.

Sleighville Creek [SIERRA]: *stream,* heads in Sierra County and flows 1 mile to Williamson Creek nearly 2 miles north-northeast of Camptonville in Yuba County (lat. 39°28'35" N, long. 121° 02'20" W; near NW cor. sec. 36, T 19 N, R 8 E); the stream heads north of Sleighville House. Named on Camptonville (1948) 7.5' quadrangle.

Sleighville House [SIERRA]: *locality,* 2.25 miles north-northwest of Pike (lat. 39°28'15" N, long. 121°00'35" W; sec. 31, T 19 N, R 9 E). Named on Camptonville (1948) 7.5' quadrangle. Peter Yore built the original structure at the site in 1849; goods were transferred from wagons to sleighs at the place in winter months (Hoover, Rensch, and Rensch, p. 495).

Sleighville Ridge [SIERRA]: *ridge,* generally west-trending, 2 miles long, 1.5 miles northeast of Camptonville on Sierra-Yuba county line (lat. 39°27'50" N, long. 121°01'20" W); Sleighville House is at the east end of the ridge. Named on Camptonville (1948) 7.5' quadrangle.

Slick Rock [EL DORADO]: *peak,* 7 miles east-southeast of Robs Peak (lat. 38°53' N, long. 120°17'15" W; near SW cor. sec. 15, T 12 N, R 15 E). Altitude 7242 feet. Named on Loon Lake (1952) 7.5' quadrangle.

Slide: see **The Slide** [TUOLUMNE].

Slide Canyon [TUOLUMNE]: *canyon,* 5 miles long, on upper reaches of Piute Creek (2) above a point 5 miles southwest of Matterhorn Peak (lat. 38°03'10" N, long. 119°27'25" W); the canyon is east of the feature called The Slide. Named on Matterhorn Peak (1956) 15' quadrangle.

Slide Creek [MADERA]:
(1) *stream,* flows 3.5 miles to Bass Lake (1) nearly 4 miles southeast of Yosemite Forks (lat. 37°19'50" N, long. 119°34'40" W; sec. 9, T 7 S, R 22 E). Named on Bass Lake (1953) 15' quadrangle.
(2) *stream,* flows 2.5 miles to Rock Creek 5.5 miles southeast of Shuteye Peak (lat. 37°17'15" N, long. 119°21'25" W; sec. 28, T 7 S, R 24 E). Named on Shuteye Peak (1953) 15' quadrangle.
(3) *stream,* flows 2.5 miles to North Fork San Joaquin River 8 miles west of Devils Postpile (lat. 37°38'20" N, long. 119°13'25" W). Named on Devils Postpile (1953) 15' quadrangle.

Slide Lakes [FRESNO]: *lakes,* largest 600 feet long, 10 miles west-southwest of Marion Peak (lat. 36°53'30" N, long. 118°41' W); the lakes are at the head of Slide Creek. Named on Marion Peak (1953) 15' quadrangle.

Slide Fall: see **Pywiack Cascade** [MARIPOSA].

Slide Mountain [TUOLUMNE]:
(1) *peak,* 3.5 miles west of Tower Peak on Tuolumne-Mono county line (lat. 38°05'35" N, long. 119°26'45" W); the peak is at the head of the feature called The Slide. Named on Matterhorn Peak (1956) 15' quadrangle.
(2) *ridge,* west-southwest-trending, 1.25 miles long, 5.5 miles southwest of Matterhorn Peak (lat. 38°02'05" N, long. 119°27'15" W). Named on Matterhorn Peak (1956) 15' quadrangle.

Slide Ravine [NEVADA]: *canyon,* 0.5 mile long, in the north part of Grass Valley (lat. 39°13'35" N, long. 121°03'50" W; on S line sec. 22, T 16 N, R 8 E). Named on Grass Valley (1949) 7.5' quadrangle.

Slippery Ford: see **Kyburz** [EL DORADO].

Slocum Gulch [CALAVERAS]: *canyon,* drained by a stream that flows 0.5 mile to Mokelumne River 1 mile northwest of Mokelumne Hill at Big Bar (lat. 38°18'50" N, long. 120°43' W; sec. 1, T 5 N, R 11 E). Named on Mokelumne Hill (1948) 7.5' quadrangle.

Sloss: see **Clearing House** [MARIPOSA].

Slug Canyon [SIERRA]: *canyon,* drained by a stream that flows 2 miles to North Yuba River 0.25 mile southwest of Downieville (lat. 39°33'25" N, long. 120°49'55" W; at E line sec. 34, T 20 N, R 10 E); the canyon is east of City of Six Ridge. Named on Downieville (1951) 7.5' quadrangle. Gudde (1975, p. 73) listed a mining place called City of Six Diggings that was located "on Slug Canyon," and noted (p. 172) that Jackassville was a popular name for City of Six—the popular name was an abbreviation of the name "Camp of Half a Dozen Jackasses." The name "Slug" is from the coarse lump gold, or slug gold, found at the place (Hoover, Rensch, and Rensch, p. 492).

Slug Gulch [EL DORADO]:
(1) *canyon,* 2 miles long, opens into the canyon of Middle Fork Cosumnes River 3.25 miles northwest of Omo Ranch (lat. 38°36'45" N, long. 120°37'15" W; near S line sec. 23, T 9 N, R 12 E). Named on Omo Ranch (1952) 7.5' quadrangle.
(2) *canyon,* 1.25 miles long, opens into an unnamed canyon 2.25 miles east of Latrobe (lat. 38°33'55" N, long. 120°56'25" W; sec. 12, T 8 N, R 9 E). Named on Latrobe (1949) 7.5' quadrangle.
(3) *locality,* 2 miles west-northwest of Omo Ranch (lat. 38°35'40" N, long. 120°37' W). Named on Placerville (1893) 30' quadrangle.

Slug Gulch [PLACER]: *canyon,* drained by a stream that flows 2 miles to Middle Fork American River 11 miles east-northeast of Auburn (lat. 38°57'35" N, long. 120°53'05" W; sec. 20, T 13 N, R 10 E). Named on Greenwood (1949) 7.5' quadrangle.

Sluice Box: see **Big Sluice Box** [EL DORADO]; **Little Sluice Box** [EL DORADO].

Slumgullion: see **Carson Hill** [CALAVERAS]

(2).

Sly Park [EL DORADO]: *valley,* 13 miles east of Placerville (lat. 38° 43'15" N, long. 120°33'30" W). Named on Placerville (1893) 30' quadrangle. Water of Jenkinson Lake now covers the valley. The name is for James Sly, one of a group of Mormons who discovered the place in 1848 (Gudde, 1969, p. 313). Park post office was located at Sly Park (Beverly Cola, personal communication, 1985). Postal authorities established Park post office in 1891, moved it 1 mile east in 1900, moved it 2.5 miles northwest in 1907, and discontinued it in 1919 (Salley, p. 167).

Sly Park Creek [EL DORADO]: *stream,* flows 14 miles to Camp Creek 5.5 miles southeast of Camino (lat. 38°41'15" N, long. 120° 35'45" W; near E line sec. 25, T 10 N, R 12 E); the stream goes through Sly Park. Named on Sly Park (1952) 7.5' quadrangle. Called Park Creek on Stump Spring (1951) 7.5' quadrangle, but United States Board on Geographic Names (1978a, p. 8) rejected this name for the stream. On Placerville (1893) 30' quadrangle, the part of present Sly Park Creek above present Jenkinson Lake is called Empire Creek, and present Hazel Creek is shown as the upper part of Sly Park Creek.

Sly Park Creek: see **North Sly Park Creek** [EL DORADO].

Sly Park House [EL DORADO]: *locality,* 13 miles east of Placerville (lat. 38°43'30" N, long. 120°33'10" W); the place is located near the east end of Sly Park. Named on Placerville (1893) 30' quadrangle.

Sly Park Reservoir: see **Jenkinson Lake** [EL DORADO].

Smarts Gulch [TUOLUMNE]: *canyon,* drained by a stream that flows nearly 2 miles to Don Pedro Reservoir 3.25 miles east-southeast of Chinese Camp (lat. 37°51'05" N, long. 120°22'35" W; near E line sec. 13, T 1 S, R 14 E). Named on Chinese Camp (1947) 7.5' quadrangle.

Smedberg Lake [TUOLUMNE]: *lake,* 0.5 mile long, 8 miles southwest of Matterhorn Peak (lat. 38°00'50" N, long. 119°29' W). Named on Matterhorn Peak (1956) 15' quadrangle. Lieutenant H.C. Benson named the lake in 1895 for Lieutenant William Renwick Smedberg, Jr. (United States Board on Geographic Names, 1934, p. 23).

Smiley Mountain [MADERA]: *peak,* 3.25 miles west-northwest of the town of North Fork (lat. 37°14'35" N, long. 119°33'55" W; near SE cor. sec. 9, T 8 S, R 22 E). Altitude 3648 feet. Named on North Fork (1965) 7.5' quadrangle.

Smith Creek [CALAVERAS]: *stream,* flows 2 miles to Peachy Creek 7.5 miles south-south-west of Copperopolis (lat. 37°52'25" N, long. 120°40'20" W); the stream goes through Smith Flat. Named on Copperopolis (1962) and Knights Ferry (1962) 7.5' quadrangles.

Smith Creek [MARIPOSA]: *stream,* flows 6.5 miles to Bean Creek 6.5 miles north-north-east of Buckhorn Peak (lat. 37°44'45" N, long. 120°04'10" W; sec. 23, T 2 S, R 17 E). Named on Buckhorn Peak (1947), Groveland (1947), and Jawbone Ridge (1947) 7.5' quadrangles.

Smith Creek [SIERRA]: *stream,* flows 1.25 miles to Levezzola Creek 8.5 miles northwest of Sierra City (lat. 39°39'20" N, long. 120°44'40" W; sec. 28, T 21 N, R 11 E); the stream heads at Smith Lake. Named on Gold Lake (1981) 7.5' quadrangle.

Smith Flat [CALAVERAS]: *area,* nearly 7 miles south of Copperopolis (lat. 37°53' N, long. 120°39'30" W); the place is along Smith Creek. Named on Copperopolis (1962) 7.5' quadrangle.

Smithflat [EL DORADO]: *village,* 2.5 miles east of downtown Placerville (lat. 38°44'10" N, long. 120°45'15" W; sec. 10, T 10 N, R 11 E). Named on Placerville (1949) 7.5' quadrangle. Called Smiths Flat on Placerville (1893) 30' quadrangle, but United States Board on Geographic Names (1965c, p. 11) rejected the forms "Smiths Flat" and "Smith Flat" for the name. Postal authorities established Smith's Flat post office in 1876 and changed the name to Smithflat in 1895 (Frickstad, p. 29). The name commemorates Jeb Smith, a pioneer rancher (Gudde, 1949, p. 335).

Smith Lake [EL DORADO]: *lake,* 850 feet long, 2 miles west-northwest of Pyramid Peak (lat. 38°51'30" N, long. 120°11'15" W). Named on Pyramid Peak (1955) 7.5' quadrangle.

Smith Lake [SIERRA]: *lake,* 450 feet long, 8 miles northwest of Sierra City (lat. 39°39'30" N, long. 120°43'15" W; at E line sec. 27, T 21 N, R 11 E); the lake is at the head of Smith Creek. Named on Gold Lake (1981) 7.5' quadrangle.

Smith Meadow [TUOLUMNE]: *area,* 6.25 miles east-northeast of Mather along Cottonwood Creek (3) (lat. 37°55'15" N, long. 119° 45'05" W; near NE cor. sec. 27, T 1 N, R 20 E); the place is southwest of Smith Peak (2). Named on Hetch Hetchy Reservoir (1956) and Lake Eleanor (1956) 15' quadrangles. Cyril C. Smith built a cabin in the area in 1885 (Uhte, p. 64).

Smith Mill: see **Old Smith Mill** [SIERRA]; **Winnie Smith Mill** [SIERRA].

Smithneck Creek [SIERRA]: *stream,* flows 9.5 miles to Sierra Valley 1.25 miles south-south-east of Loyalton (lat. 39°39'40" N, long. 120°13'50" W; sec. 19, T 21 N, R 16 E). Named on Antelope Valley (1981), Loyalton (1981), and Sardine Peak (1981) 7.5' quadrangles.

Smith Peak [MARIPOSA-TUOLUMNE]: *peak,* 7.5 miles east-southeast of Groveland on Mariposa-Tuolumne county line (lat. 37°48'05" N, long. 120°06' W; sec. 34, T 1 S, R 17 E); the peak is 1.5 miles southeast of Smith Station. Altitude 3877 feet. Named on Jawbone Ridge (1947) 7.5' quadrangle.

Smith Peak [TUOLUMNE]: *peak,* 6 miles northwest of White Wolf (lat. 37°55'35" N, long. 119°44' W; on W line sec. 24, T 1 N, R 20 E); the peak is 1 mile east-northeast of Smith Meadow at the head of Cottonwood Creek (3). Altitude 7751 feet. Named on Hetch Hetchy Reservoir (1956) 15' quadrangle. United States Board on Geographic Names (1933, p. 701) rejected the names "Smith's Peak" and "Cottonwood Peak" for the feature.

Smith Ridge [MARIPOSA]: *ridge,* south- to southeast-trending, 2.5 miles long, 2 miles southeast of Smith Peak (lat. 37°46'45" N, long. 120°04'35" W). Named on Jawbone Ridge (1947) 7.5' quadrangle.

Smith's Flat: see Smith Station [TUOLUMNE].

Smith's Peak: see Smith Peak [TUOLUMNE].

Smiths: see Colfax [PLACER].

Smith's Flat: see Smithflat [EL DORADO].

Smith's Neck: see Loyalton [SIERRA].

Smiths Point [PLACER]: *ridge,* west-trending, less than 1 mile long, 1.5 miles northwest of Foresthill (lat. 39°02' N, long. 120°50'20" W; sec. 27, T 14 N, R 10 E). Named on Foresthill (1949) 7.5' quadrangle. Called Smith Point on Colfax (1950) 15' quadrangle.

Smith Station [TUOLUMNE]: *locality,* 6.25 miles east-southeast of Groveland in Burch Meadow (lat. 37°48'45" N, long. 120°07'15" W; near W line sec. 33, T 1 S, R 17 E). Named on Jawbone Ridge (1947) 7.5' quadrangle. The name commemorates John B. Smith, who homesteaded at the place and ran a stage station there at what became known as Smith's Flat (Paden and Schlichtmann, p. 186, 188).

Smoky Jack Campground [TUOLUMNE]: *locality,* 5 miles southwest of White Wolf (lat. 37°49'05" N, long. 119°42'45" W; near NW cor. sec. 31, T 1 S, R 21 E). Named on Hetch Hetchy Reservoir (1956) 15' quadrangle. Browning (1986, p. 203) associated the name with John Connell, a sheepman who had the nickname "Smoky Jack."

Smoky Mountain [MARIPOSA]: *peak,* 3 miles east of the settlement of Catheys Valley in the Guadalupe Mountains (lat. 37°26'25" N, long. 120°02'05" W; sec. 6, T 6 S, R 18 E). Named on Catheys Valley (1962) 7.5' quadrangle.

Smoothwire Camp [TUOLUMNE]: *locality,* 8 miles south-southeast of Liberty Hill (lat. 38°15'45" N, long. 120°02'40" W; near NE cor. sec. 25, T 5 N, R 17 E); the place is along Smoothwire Creek. Named on Big Meadow (1956) 15' quadrangle.

Smoothwire Creek [TUOLUMNE]: *stream,* flows 2.5 miles to Middle Fork Stanislaus River 9 miles south-southeast of Liberty Hill (lat. 38°15'15" N, long. 120°01'40" W; near E line sec. 30, T 5 N, R 18 E). Named on Liberty Hill (1979) 7.5' quadrangle.

Smuthers Ravine [PLACER]: *canyon,* drained by a stream that flows 2 miles to Bunch Can-

yon 3 miles south-southeast of Colfax (lat. 39°03'35" N, long. 120°56'20" W; sec. 14, T 14 N, R 9 E). Named on Colfax (1949) 7.5' quadrangle.

Snag Lake [SIERRA]: *lake,* 2050 feet long, 7.25 miles north of Sierra City (lat. 39°40'10" N, long. 120°37'40" W; near E line sec. 21, T 21 N, R 12 E). Named on Gold Lake (1981) 7.5' quadrangle.

Snag Lake Campground [SIERRA]: *locality,* 7.25 miles north of Sierra City (lat. 39°40'10" N, long. 120°37'30" W; at W line sec. 22, T 21 N, R 12 E); the place is at the northeast end of Snag Lake. Named on Sierra City (1955) 15' quadrangle.

Snail Canyon [PLACER]: *canyon,* drained by a stream that flows 1.5 miles to North Shirttail Canyon 6 miles north of Foresthill (lat. 39° 06'35" N, long. 120°48'15" W; at N line sec. 36, T 15 N, R 10 E). Named on Foresthill (1949) 7.5' quadrangle.

Snake Flat: see Drytown [AMADOR].

Snake Gulch [AMADOR]: *canyon,* drained by a stream that flows 1.25 miles to Dry Creek 2.5 miles south of Plymouth at Drytown (lat. 38°26'35" N, long. 120°51'05" W; sec. 23, T 7 N, R 10 E). Named on Amador City (1962) 7.5' quadrangle.

Snake Gulch [CALAVERAS]: *canyon,* drained by a stream that flows 2 miles to Stanislaus River 3.5 miles south-southeast of Vallecito (lat. 38°02'15" N, long. 120°27'15" W; sec. 8, T 2 N, R 14 E). Named on Columbia (1948) 7.5' quadrangle.

Snakehead Point [PLACER]: *peak,* 3.5 miles east-southeast of Dutch Flat (lat. 39°10'35" N, long. 120°46'50" W; sec. 6, T 15 N, R 11 E). Altitude 2437 feet. Named on Dutch Flat (1950) 7.5' quadrangle.

Snake Lake [SIERRA]: *lake,* 800 feet long, 8 miles north-northwest of Sierra City (lat. 39°40'40" N, long. 120°41'25" W; sec. 13, T 21 N, R 11 E). Named on Gold Lake (1981) 7.5' quadrangle.

Snake Meadow [MADERA]: *area,* 7.5 miles southwest of Devils Postpile (lat. 37°33'35" N, long. 119°11'20" W). Named on Devils Postpile (1953) 15' quadrangle.

Snow Canyon [MADERA]: *canyon,* 2.5 miles long, 1.5 miles southwest of Devils Postpile along King Creek (lat. 37°36'35" N, long. 119°06'45" W). Named on Devils Postpile (1953) 15' quadrangle.

Snow Creek [CALAVERAS]: *stream,* heads in Calaveras County and flows 5 miles to Hoods Creek 12 miles north-northeast of Oakdale in Stanislaus County (lat. 37°56'50" N, long. 120°47'30" W; sec. 8, T 1 N, R 11 E). Named on Bachelor Valley (1968) 7.5' quadrangle.

Snow Creek [EL DORADO]: *stream,* flows 4 miles to Camp Creek 4.5 miles west of Old Iron Mountain (lat. 38°42' N, long. 120°28'25" W; near SW cor. sec. 19, T 10 N, R 14 E). Named on Stump Spring (1951) 7.5' quadrangle.

Snow Creek [MARIPOSA]:
(1) *stream,* flows 7.25 miles to Tenaya Creek 3 miles east-northeast of Yosemite Village (lat. 37°45'35" N, long. 119°32' W). Named on Hetch Hetchy Reservoir (1956) and Tuolumne Meadows (1956) 15' quadrangles. United States Board on Geographic Names (1933, p. 703) rejected the names "Glacier Brook," "Hoffman Creek," and "Hoffmann Creek" for the stream.
(2) *stream,* flows 8 miles to join Jones Creek and form West Fork Chowchilla River 5 miles east of Mariposa (lat. 37°28'55" N, long. 119°52'25" W; sec. 22, T 5 S, R 19 E). Named on Buckingham Mountain (1947) and Stumpfield Mountain (1947) 7.5' quadrangles.

Snow Creek [SIERRA]: *stream,* flows 1.5 miles to Eureka Creek 3 miles north of Goodyears Bar (lat. 39°35' N, long. 120°53'20" W; near E line sec. 19, T 20 N, R 10 E). Named on Goodyears Bar (1951) 7.5' quadrangle.

Snow Creek: see **Darrah** [MARIPOSA].

Snow Creek Falls [MARIPOSA]: *waterfall,* 3 miles east-northeast of Yosemite Village on Snow Creek (1) (lat. 37°46' N, long. 119° 32' W). Named on Hetch Hetchy Reservoir (1956) 15' quadrangle.

Snowden Hill [SIERRA]: *ridge,* west-southwest-trending, 1 mile long, 3.5 miles west-south-west of Goodyears Bar (lat. 39°30'55" N, long. 120°56'35" W; on W line sec. 14, T 19 N, R 9 E). Named on Goodyears Bar (1951) 7.5' quadrangle.

Snow Flat [MARIPOSA]: *area,* 5 miles west-southwest of Cathedral Peak (lat. 37°50' N, long. 119°29'30" W; near W line sec. 19, T 1 S, R 23 E); the area is along Snow Creek (1). Named on Tuolumne Meadows (1956) 15' quadrangle. The place was called Snow's Flat in 1893 (Browning, 1988, p. 133).

Snow Lake [EL DORADO]: *lake,* 1400 feet long, 1 mile northwest of Mount Tallac (lat. 38°55'05" N, long. 120°06'50" W; on E line sec. 5, T 12 N, R 17 E). Named on Emerald Bay (1955) 7.5' quadrangle. The feature first was called Katrine Lake for Katherine Brigham Ebright (Lekisch, p. 108).

Snow Lake [TUOLUMNE]: *lake,* 2300 feet long, 4.5 miles west-northwest of Tower Peak (lat. 38°10'20" N, long. 119°37'30" W). Named on Tower Peak (1956) 15' quadrangle.

Snowline Camp [EL DORADO]: *locality,* 3 miles east-northeast of Camino (lat. 38°44'45" N, long. 120°37'25" W; sec. 2, T 10 N, R 12 E). Named on Sly Park (1952) 7.5' quadrangle.

Snow Mountain [PLACER]: *peak,* 10 miles west-northwest of Granite Chief (lat. 39°14'30" N, long. 120°27'40" W; sec. 24, T 16 N, R 13 E). Altitude 8014 feet. Named on Royal Gorge (1953) 7.5' quadrangle.

Snow Peak [TUOLUMNE]: *peak,* 2.25 miles south-southwest of Tower Peak (lat. 38°06'55"

N, long. 119°34'15" W). Altitude 10,950 feet. Named on Tower Peak (1956) 15' quadrangle.

Snow Point [NEVADA]: *locality,* 6.25 miles northeast of North Bloomfield (lat. 39°25'15" N, long. 120°48'45" W). Named on Colfax (1898) 30' quadrangle. Whitney's (1873) map shows a place called Eureka located 4 miles east of Snow Point.

Snow Ridge [EL DORADO]: *ridge,* generally west-trending, 3.25 miles long, 1.5 miles south of Camino (lat. 38°42'45" N, long. 120° 40'45" W). Named on Camino (1952) 7.5' quadrangle.

Snowshoe Lake [CALAVERAS]: *lake,* 600 feet long, 6 miles east-southeast of Blue Mountain (lat. 38°17'35" N, long. 120°16'25" W; near W line sec. 13, T 5 N, R 15 E). Named on Dorrington (1979) 7.5' quadrangle.

Snow Tent [NEVADA]: *locality,* 3 miles northeast of North Bloomfield (lat. 39°23'45" N, long. 120°51'55" W). Named on Colfax (1898) 30' quadrangle. Whitney's (1873) map shows a place called Mt. Zion located 1.5 miles east-southeast of Snow Tent.

Snowtent Spring [NEVADA]: *spring,* 3.25 miles north-northwest of Washington (lat. 39°24' N, long. 121°49'45" W; near W line sec. 26, T 18 N, R 10 E). Named on Alleghany (1949) 7.5' quadrangle. Colfax (1938) 30' quadrangle has the form "Snow Tent Spring" for the name.

Snowy Mountains: see "Regional setting."

Snowy Range: see "Regional setting."

Snyder Camp [TUOLUMNE]: *locality,* 2 miles east of Liberty Hill in Randalls Meadow (lat. 38°22'20" N, long. 120°03'40" W; sec. 13, T 6 N, R 17 E). Named on Liberty Hill (1979) 7.5' quadrangle.

Snyder Canyon [PLACER]: *canyon,* drained by a stream that flows 1.25 miles to Middle Fork American River 1.5 miles south-southeast of Foresthill (lat. 39°00'05" N, long. 120°48'30" W; sec. 1, T 13 N, R 10 E). Named on Foresthill (1949) 7.5' quadrangle. Called Yankee Jim Gulch on Whitney's (1880) map.

Snyder Gulch [MARIPOSA]: *canyon,* drained by a stream that flows nearly 3 miles to Devil Gulch 5.5 miles south-southwest of El Portal (lat. 37°36'20" N, long. 119°49'20" W); the canyon is north of Snyder Ridge. Named on Buckingham Mountain (1947) 7.5' quadrangle. Browning (1988, p. 134) associated the name with John W. Snyder, a homesteader in the neighborhood in 1885.

Snyder Gulch: see **Big Snyder Gulch** [PLACER].

Snyder Ridge [MARIPOSA]: *ridge,* south-trending, 2 miles long, 7 miles south-south-west of El Portal (lat. 37°34'50" N, long. 119°50'15" W); the ridge is south of Snyder Gulch. Named on Buckingham Mountain (1947) 7.5' quadrangle.

Snyders Bar: see **Coloma** [EL DORADO].

Soap Creek [TUOLUMNE]: *stream,* flows 7.25

miles to Griswold Creek 7.5 miles northeast of Stanislaus (lat. 38°12'25" N, long. 120°15'50" W; near NE cor. sec. 13, T 4 N, R 15 E). Named on Crandall Peak (1979) and Stanislaus (1948) 7.5' quadrangles.

Soap Creek Pass [TUOLUMNE]: *pass,* 4 miles north of Crandall Peak (lat. 38°13' N, long. 120°08'45" W; sec. 7, T 4 N, R 17 E); the pass is near the head of Soap Creek. Named on Crandall Peak (1979) 7.5' quadrangle.

Soap Creek Pass Camp: see **Camp Pendola** [TUOLUMNE].

Soapstone Hill [CALAVERAS]: *peak,* 10.5 miles east-southeast of San Andreas (lat. 38°08'15" N, long. 120°30'05" W; near W line sec. 1, T 3 N, R 13 E). Altitude 1625 feet. Named on Calaveritas (1962) 7.5' quadrangle.

Soapstone Ridge [MARIPOSA]: *ridge,* south-trending, 2 miles long, 8.5 miles west-northwest of El Portal (lat. 37°42' N, long. 119°56'15" W). Named on Kinsley (1947) 7.5' quadrangle.

Soapweed [EL DORADO]: *locality,* 7.5 miles northwest of Pollock Pines (lat. 38°50'30" N, long. 120°40'30" W; sec. 31, T 12 N, R 12 E). Named on Slate Mountain (1950) 7.5' quadrangle. Placerville (1893) 30' quadrangle has the form "Soap Weed" for the name. Logan's (1938) map shows a place called Golden located at or near present Soapweed. Postal authorities established Golden post office in 1923 and discontinued it in 1926; the name was for Miss Callie L. Golden, first postmaster (Salley, p. 86).

Soapweed Creek [EL DORADO]: *stream,* flows 2.25 miles to Slab Creek 6 miles northwest of Pollock Pines (lat. 38°49'35" N, long. 120°39'30" W; sec. 5, T 11 N, R 12 E). Named on Slate Mountain (1950) 7.5' quadrangle.

Soda Canyon [TUOLUMNE]: *canyon,* drained by a stream that flows 2.5 miles to Kennedy Creek 4.5 miles south-southwest of Sonora Pass (lat. 38°16'15" N, long. 119°40'45" W; near E line sec. 20, T 5 N, R 21 E); Soda Spring is in the canyon. Named on Sonora Pass (1956) and Tower Peak (1956) 15' quadrangles.

Soda Spring [MADERA]: *spring,* 8 miles southwest of Devils Postpile near Sheep Crossing (lat. 37°33'15" N, long. 119°12'30" W). Named on Mount Lyell (1901) 30' quadrangle.

Soda Spring [TUOLUMNE]: *spring,* 5.5 miles south-southwest of Sonora Pass (lat. 38°15'15" N, long. 119°40'25" W; sec. 28, T 5 N, R 21 E); the spring is in Soda Canyon. Named on Sonora Pass (1979) 7.5' quadrangle.

Soda Spring Dome: see **Fairview Dome** [TUOLUMNE].

Soda Spring Flat: see **Pumice Flat** [MADERA].

Soda Springs [NEVADA]: *village,* nearly 3 miles west of Donner Pass (lat. 39°19'25" N, long. 120°22'45" W; on W line sec. 23, T 17

N, R 14 E). Named on Soda Springs (1955) 7.5' quadrangle. Truckee (1895) 30' quadrangle shows Soda Springs Station at the place. Postal authorities established Summit Valley post office in 1870, changed the name to Soda Springs in 1875, discontinued it in 1881, and reestablished it in 1929 (Frickstad, p. 115). They established Hopkins post office, named for Mark Hopkins, at the place in 1885 and discontinued it in 1886 (Salley, p. 100). The resort that Mark Hopkins and Leland Stanford developed at present Soda Springs in the 1870's was known as Hopkins Springs; from 1867 until 1873 the railroad station at the place was called Tinkers Station for J.A. Tinker, a teamster who hauled freight between Soda Springs and the mines (Gudde, 1969, p. 315, 339).

Soda Springs [PLACER]: *springs,* 4 miles north-northwest of Granite Chief along North Fork American River (lat. 39°14'50" N, long. 120°19'35" W; near W line sec. 9, T 16 N, R 15 E). Named on Granite Chief (1953) 7.5' quadrangle. Anderson (p. 95) used the name "Berkeley Soda Springs" for present Soda Springs. G. A. Waring (p. 231) used the name "Summit Soda Springs" for the resort that operated there before the hotel burned in 1898. G.A. Waring (p. 232) also listed Florence Spring, located 0.25 mile northeast of Summit Soda Springs.

Soda Springs [TUOLUMNE]: *spring,* 6.25 miles west-southwest of Tioga Pass in Tuolumne Meadows (lat. 37°52'45" N, long. 119°21'55" W; sec. 5, T 1 S, R 24 E). Named on Tuolumne Meadows (1956) 15' quadrangle. G. A. Waring (p. 237-238) called the feature Lambert Soda Springs, and noted that the water could be used to make biscuits without baking soda, the carbon dioxide in the water serving to lighten the dough.

Soda Springs Butte: see **Fairview Dome** [TUOLUMNE].

Soda Springs Campground [MADERA]: *locality,* 3 miles northeast of Shuteye Peak (lat. 37°22'50" N, long. 119°23'20" W; sec. 30, T 6 S, R 24 E). Named on Shuteye Peak (1953) 15' quadrangle.

Soda Springs Station: see **Soda Springs** [NEVADA].

Soldier Creek [EL DORADO]: *stream,* formed by the confluence of North Fork and South Fork, flows 3.5 miles to South Fork American River 1.5 miles northeast of Pollock Pines (lat. 38°46'40" N, long. 120°33'35" W; near E line sec. 19, T 11 N, R 13 E). Named on Pollock Pines (1950) 7.5' quadrangle. North Fork is 1.5 miles long and South Fork is 2.25 miles long; both forks are named on Pollock Pines (1950) and Riverton (1950) 7.5' quadrangles.

Soldier Creek [TUOLUMNE]: *stream,* flows 1.5 miles to South Fork Tuolumne River 6.25 miles southwest of Mather (lat. 37°48'40" N, long. 119°55'40" W; sec. 31, T 1 S, R 19 E). Named on Lake Eleanor (1956) 15' quadrangle.

Soldier Creek: see **Little Soldier Creek** [EL DORADO].

Soldier Gulch [TUOLUMNE]: *canyon,* drained by a stream that flows 1 mile to New Melones Lake 6.5 miles west-northwest of Sonora (lat. 38°00' N, long. 120°29'50" W; sec. 25, T 2 N, R 13 E). Named on Sonora (1948) 7.5' quadrangle. A group of soldiers discovered gold in the canyon in 1848 (Stoddart, p. 64).

Soldier Lake [TUOLUMNE]: *lake,* 1300 feet long, 3.5 miles south-southeast of Matterhorn Peak (lat. 38°02'50" N, long. 119°21'20" W). Named on Matterhorn Peak (1956) 15' quadrangle.

Soldier Meadow [MADERA]: *area,* 10 miles southeast of Merced Peak (lat. 37°32'35" N, long. 119°15' W). Named on Devils Postpile (1953) and Merced Peak (1953) 15' quadrangles. The place first was called Little Jackass Meadow; the present name is from use of the area as a patrol camp when the army administered Yosemite National Park (Browning, 1986, p. 204).

Soldiers Gulch: see **Jackson Butte** [AMADOR]; **Volcano** [AMADOR].

Solinsky Camp [CALAVERAS]: *locality,* 4 miles northeast of Blue Mountain (lat. 38°23' N, long. 120°18'50" W; sec. 10, T 6 N, R 15 E); the place is 0.5 mile west-southwest of Solinsky Crossing. Named on Blue Mountain (1956) 15' quadrangle.

Solinsky Crossing [CALAVERAS]: *locality,* 7 miles south-southwest of Garnet Hill along Middle Fork Mokelumne River (lat. 38°23'20" N, long. 120°18'35" W; sec. 10, T 6 N, R 15 E). Named on Garnet Hill (1979) 7.5' quadrangle.

Solomon Gulch [MARIPOSA]: *canyon,* drained by a stream that flows 6 miles to Lake McClure 2.5 miles north-northeast of the village of Bear Valley (lat. 37°36'20" N, long. 120°06'20" W; sec. 9, T 4 S, R 17 E). Named on Bear Valley (1947, photorevised 1973) and Buckhorn Peak (1947) 7.5' quadrangles.

Solomons Hole: see **Moaning Caves** [CALAVERAS].

Solsbury: see **Soulsbyville** [TUOLUMNE].

Solsby: see **Soulsbyville** [TUOLUMNE].

Somerset [EL DORADO]: *village,* 6.25 miles south of Camino (lat. 38°38'50" N, long. 120°41'05" W; at W line sec. 8, T 9 N, R 12 E). Named on Camino (1952) 7.5' quadrangle. Placerville (1893) 30' quadrangle shows Sommerset House at the place. Called Youngs on California Division of Highways' (1934) map. Postal authorities established Youngs post office, named for Morgan W. Young, first postmaster, in 1924 and discontinued in 1950, when they moved it 1 mile south and changed the name to Somerset (Salley, p. 245). The first settlers, who came from Somerset, Ohio,

named the village (Gudde, 1975, p. 327). California Division of Highway's (1934) map also shows a place called Rodwell located nearly 2 miles east of Youngs along Diamond Caldor Railroad (near E line sec. 9, T 9 N, R 12 E), and a place called River Hill located along the railroad nearly 2 miles northwest of Youngs (sec. 1, T 9 N, R 11 W).

Somerville: see **Summersville**, under **Soulsbyville** [TUOLUMNE].

Sommerset House: see **Somerset** [EL DORADO].

Sonntag Hill: see **Sontag Hill** [NEVADA].

Sonny Meadow [MARIPOSA]: *area,* 4 miles west-southwest of Fish Camp (lat. 37°27' N, long. 119°42' W). Named on Bass Lake (1953) 15' quadrangle. Called Sonny Meadows on Mariposa (1912) 30' quadrangle; United States Board on Geographic Names (1947, p. 2) once approved this plural form of the name, while rejecting the names "Bruener Meadow," "Groves Meadow," "Hogan Meadow," and "Hogan's Meadow" for the feature.

Sonora [TUOLUMNE]: *town,* at the confluence of Woods Creek and Sonora Creek (lat. 37°59' N, long. 120°22'50" W; in and near sec. 36, T 2 N, R 14 E). Named on Sonora (1948) 7.5' quadrangle. Called Sonoran Camp on Derby's (1849) map. Postal authorities established Sonora post office in 1851 (Frickstad, p. 217), and the town incorporated the same year. The place started with a preponderance of miners from Sonora in Mexico, and was called Sonora Camp in the middle of 1848 (Bancroft, 1888, p. 469). When the town was made the seat of government of newly formed Tuolumne County, the state legislature gave the name "Stewart" to the community, probably to honor Malcolm M. Stewart, assemblyman from San Joaquin district, but soon restored the name "Sonora" to the place (DeFerrari *in* Stoddart, p. 86). Gudde (1975, p. 312) listed a place called Scraperville that was located about 2 miles west of Sonora on the east side of Table Mountain.

Sonora Bar: see **Lancha Plana** [AMADOR].

Sonora Camp: see **Sonora** [TUOLUMNE].

Sonora Creek [TUOLUMNE]: *stream,* flows 4 miles to Woods Creek in Sonora (lat. 37°58'45" N, long. 120°23'15" W; sec. 36, T 2 N, R 14 E). Named on Columbia SE (1948), Sonora (1948), and Standard (1948) 7.5' quadrangles. The canyon of the stream was called Bassett's Gulch for Charles Bassett, who prospected there early in 1849 (Stoddart, p. 82-83).

Sonoran Camp: see **Sonora** [TUOLUMNE].

Sonora Pass [TUOLUMNE]: *pass,* 47 miles east-northeast of Sonora, where Tuolumne County, Mono County, and Alpine County meet (lat. 38°19'40" N, long. 119°38'10" W). Named on Sonora Pass (1979) 7.5' quadrangle. The name is from the town of Sonora—the wagon road from Sonora to mining camps east of the crest of the Sierra Nevada went through the pass (Hanna, p. 311).

Sontag Hill [NEVADA]: *peak,* nearly 3 miles north of Chicago Park (lat. 39°11'10" N, long. 120°57'45" W; near W line sec. 3, T 15 N, R 9 E). Named on Chicago Park (1949) 7.5' quadrangle. United States Board on Geographic Names (1984a, p. 5) approved the form "Sonntag Hill" for the name, and noted that it commemorates Herman E. Sonntag, who settled in the neighborhood in 1890 and owned part of the feature.

Sopiago Creek [EL DORADO]: *stream,* flows 11.5 miles to Middle Fork Cosumnes River 0.5 mile north-northeast of Omo Ranch (lat. 38°35'20" N, long. 120°33'45" W; sec. 32, T 9 N, R 13 E). Named on Caldor (1951) and Omo Ranch (1952) 7.5' quadrangles.

Soquel Campground [MADERA]: *locality,* 4.5 miles northeast of Yosemite Forks along North Fork Willow Creek (2) (lat. 37°24'15" N, long. 119°33'40" W; near SE cor. sec. 16, T 6 S, R 22 E). Named on Bass Lake (1953) 15' quadrangle.

Soquel Meadow [MADERA]: *area,* 6 miles northeast of Yosemite Forks (lat. 37°25'40" N, long. 119°33'15" W; in and near sec. 10, T 6 S, R 22 E). Named on Bass Lake (1953) 15' quadrangle. Smith Comstock moved his sawmill to the place from Soquel in Santa Cruz County in 1881, and applied the name of the old site to the new one (Browning, 1986, p. 205).

Sore Finger Point [PLACER]: *ridge,* southeast-trending, 0.5 mile long, 6 miles south-southeast of Colfax (lat. 39°01' N, long. 120° 55'20" W; sec. 36, T 14 N, R 9 E). Named on Colfax (1949) 7.5' quadrangle.

Sotcher Lake [MADERA]: *lake,* 1600 feet long, 0.5 mile east of Devils Postpile (lat. 37°37'35" N, long. 119°04'25" W). Named on Devils Postpile (1953) 15' quadrangle. Called Satcher Lake on Mount Lyell (1901) 30' quadrangle. The name commemorates "Red" Sotcher (or Satcher), for whom Reds Meadows was named; the feature also is known as Pond Lily Lake for the mass of yellow lilies that cover its surface near the outlet (Smith, p. 14).

Source Point [MADERA]: *peak,* 9 miles south-southeast of Shuteye Peak (lat. 37°13'30" N, long. 119°23'20" W; near N line sec. 19, T 8 S, R 24 E). Altitude 6182 feet. Named on Shaver Lake (1953) 15' quadrangle.

Soulsbys Flat: see **Soulsbyville** [TUOLUMNE].

Soulsbyville [TUOLUMNE]: *village,* 6.5 miles east of Sonora (lat. 37°59'05" N, long. 120°15'45" W; near W line sec. 31, T 2 N, R 16 E). Named on Standard (1948) 7.5' quadrangle. Postal authorities established Soulsbyville post office in 1877 (Frickstad, p. 217). The name commemorates Benjamin Soulsby and his sons, who found a rich gold mine at the place in 1858 (Gudde, 1969, p.

317). The village also was known as Solsby, Solsbury, and Soulsbys Flat (Gudde, 1975, p. 328). A place called Summersville was situated about 2.5 miles southeast of Soulsbyville; the name, which also had the form "Somerville," was from Franklin Summers and Elizabeth Summers, who settled near the site in 1854 (Gudde, 1975, p. 341). Postal authorities established Carters post office at Summersville in 1888 and discontinued it in 1908; the name was for Charles H. Carter, first postmaster (Salley, p. 39). California Mining Bureau's (1917d) map shows a place called Nashton located about 7 miles east of Soulsbyville between North Fork and Middle Fork Tuolumne River. Postal authorities established Nashton post office in 1900 and discontinued it in 1904; the name was for John F. Nash, first postmaster (Salley, p. 150). Gudde (1975, p. 249) listed a place called Ohio Diggings that was located 3 miles north of Soulsbyville. California Division of Highways' (1934) map shows Pooley's Ranch located 1.5 miles north-northwest of Soulsbyville (at E line sec. 25, T 2 N, R 15 E).

Sourdough Hill [EL DORADO]: *peak,* 5.25 miles west of the town of Meeks Bay (lat. 39°01'35" N, long. 120°13'05" W; near SW cor. sec. 28, T 14 N, R 16 E). Altitude 7976 feet. Named on Homewood (1955) 7.5' quadrangle.

Sourgrass Lake [TUOLUMNE]: *intermittent lake,* 250 feet long, 5 miles west of Strawberry (lat. 38°12'30" N, long. 120°06'10" W); the feature is 0.5 mile east-northeast of Sourgrass Meadow. Named on Strawberry (1979) 7.5' quadrangle.

Sourgrass Meadow [TUOLUMNE]: *area,* 5.5 miles west of Strawberry (lat. 38°12'15" N, long. 120°06'45" W; sec. 16, T 4 N, R 17 E); the place is 0.5 mile west-southwest of Sourgrass Lake. Named on Strawberry (1979) 7.5' quadrangle.

South Canyon [EL DORADO]: *canyon,* drained by a stream that flows 3 miles to South Fork American River 8.5 miles west of Pollock Pines (lat. 38°46'20" N, long. 120°44'15" W); the canyon is west of North Canyon (2). Named on Camino (1952) and Slate Mountain (1950) 7.5' quadrangles.

South Canyon: see **Illinois Canyon** [EL DORADO].

South Canyon Creek: see **Illilouette Creek** [MADERA-MARIPOSA].

South Creek [EL DORADO]: *stream,* flows 2 miles to South Fork Rubicon River 4 miles northwest of Robbs Peak (lat. 38°57'55" N, long. 120°27'30" W; near NW cor. sec. 19, T 13 N, R 14 E). Named on Robbs Peak (1950) 7.5' quadrangle.

South Dome: see **Sentinel Dome** [MARIPOSA].

South Fork [MADERA]: *village,* 9 miles south-southeast of Shuteye Peak along South Fork Willow Creek (2) (lat. 37°14' N, long. 119° 29'30" W; sec. 18, T 8 S, R 23 E). Named on Shaver Lake (1953) 15' quadrangle.

South Fork [MARIPOSA]: *locality,* 6 miles west-southwest of El Portal (lat. 37°39'15" N, long. 119°53'10" W); the place is at the mouth of South Fork Merced River. Named on Kinsley (1947) 7.5' quadrangle.

South Fork: see **Poorman Creek** [NEVADA] (1).

South Fork Bluffs [MADERA]: *relief feature,* 6 miles south-southwest of Shuteye Peak on the east side of South Fork Willow Creek (2) (lat. 37°16'30" N, long. 119°29' W). Named on Shuteye Peak (1953) 15' quadrangle.

South Fork Camp Ground [EL DORADO]: *locality,* 1.5 miles north of Robbs Peak (lat. 38°56'55" N, long. 120°24' W; sec. 27, T 13 N, R 14 E); the place is along South Fork Rubicon River. Named on Robbs Peak (1950) 7.5' quadrangle.

South Gulch [CALAVERAS]: *canyon,* mainly in Calaveras County, but a small part is in Stanislaus County; drained by a stream that flows 9 miles to Calaveras River 9.5 miles south-southwest of Valley Springs (lat. 38°04'10" N, long. 120°54'15" W; sec. 32, T 3 N, R 10 E). Named on Jenny Lind (1962) and Valley Springs SW (1962) 7.5' quadrangles.

South Hill [CALAVERAS]: *peak,* 1.25 miles southeast of Jenny Lind (lat. 38°04'55" N, long. 120°51'05" W; near W line sec. 26, T 3 N, R 10 E); the peak is between South Gulch and Calaveras River. Named on Jenny Lind (1962) 7.5' quadrangle.

South Indian Creek: see **Little Indian Creek** [AMADOR].

South Lake Tahoe [EL DORADO]: *town,* 7 miles northwest of Freel Peak at the south end of Lake Tahoe (lat. 38°56'30" N, long. 119° 59' W). Named on Emerald Bay (1955, photorevised 1969) and South Lake Tahoe (1955, photorevised 1969 and 1974) 7.5' quadrangles. Postal authorities established South Lake Tahoe post office in 1967 (Salley, p. 209). The communities of Al Tahoe, Bijou, Bijou Park, Stateline, Tahoe Valley, and Tallac Village combined to form the new town, which incorporated in 1965. United States Board on Geographic Names (1985b, p. 2) approved the name "Jakes Peak" for a peak located 7 miles northwest of South Lake Tahoe (lat. 38°58'12" N, long. 120°07'18" W; sec. 17, T 13 N, R 17 E; altitude 9187 feet); the name commemorates Jeffery J. Smith, who died with others in an avalanche in 1982.

South Long Point [PLACER]: *ridge,* west-trending, 1.5 miles long, 3.25 miles north-north-west of Foresthill (lat. 39°03'40" N, long. 120°51' W); the ridge is situated south across Shirttail Canyon from Long Point (1). Named on Foresthill (1949) 7.5' quadrangle.

South Shore Campground [AMADOR]: *local-*

ity, 8 miles west of Mokelumne Peak (lat. 38°32' N, long. 120°14'30" W; on E line sec. 19, T 8 N, R 16 E); the place is on the south shore of Lower Bear River Reservoir. Named on Bear River Reservoir (1979) 7.5' quadrangle.

South Steely Creek [EL DORADO]: *stream,* flows 3.5 miles to join North Steely Creek and form Steely Fork Cosumnes River 2 miles west-northwest of Caldor (lat. 38°37' N, long. 120°28' W; sec. 19, T 9 N, R 14 E). Named on Caldor (1951) and Stump Spring (1951) 7.5' quadrangles.

South Wallace Canyon [PLACER]: *canyon,* drained by a stream that flows 4.5 miles to Wallace Canyon 2 miles north-northeast of Davis Peak (lat. 38°59' N, long. 120°31'35" W; near N line sec. 16, T 13 N, R 13 E). Named on Bunker Hill (1953), Devil Peak (1950), and Robbs Peak (1950) 7.5' quadrangles. Called Middle Wallace Canyon on Placerville (1893) 30' quadrangle.

South Wawona [MARIPOSA]: *settlement,* 1 mile east-northeast of Wawona (lat. 37°32'25" N, long. 119°38'20" W; sec. 35, T 4 S, R 21 E); the place is 0.5 mile south of North Wawona. Named on Yosemite (1956) 15' quadrangle.

South Wolf Creek [NEVADA]: *stream,* flows 10.5 miles to Wolf Creek 1.5 miles north of Higgins Corner (lat. 39°03'45" N, long. 121°05'20" W; sec. 16, T 14 N, R 8 E). Named on Chicago Park (1949), Grass Valley (1949), and Lake Combie (1949) 7.5' quadrangles.

South Yuba River [NEVADA-PLACER]: *stream,* heads near Donner Pass in Placer County and flows 62 miles to Yuba River 2.5 miles west-southwest of French Corral in Nevada County (lat. 39°17'45" N, long. 121°12'25" W; near NE cor. sec. 32, T 17 N, R 7 E). Named on Blue Canyon (1955), Cisco Grove (1955), French Corral (1948), Nevada City (1948), Norden (1955), North Bloomfield (1949), Soda Springs (1955), and Washington (1950) 7.5' quadrangles. Called Yuba River on Truckee (1895) 30' quadrangle, and called South Fork Yuba River on Colfax (1898), Smartsville (1895), and Truckee (1940) 30' quadrangles. United States Board on Geographic Names (1950, p. 6) rejected the names "South Fork" and "South Fork Yuba River" for the feature. Giffen (*in* Decker, p. 291) noted that a mining place called Ohio Bar was located on the south side of Yuba River 1 mile below the mouth of South Fork (present South Yuba River).

Spangle Gold Creek [MADERA]: *stream,* flows 3.5 miles to Fresno River 5.5 miles east-northeast of Knowles (lat. 37°14'15" N, long. 119°46'25" W; sec. 15, T 8 S, R 20 E). Named on Horsecamp Mountain (1947) and Knowles (1962) 7.5' quadrangles. Crawford (1896, p. 207) referred to Spangle Gold Gulch.

Spangle Gold Gulch: see **Spangle Gold Creek** [MADERA].

Spanish Camp: see **Martinez** [TUOLUMNE].

Spanish Corral: see **Ophir** [PLACER].

Spanish Creek [EL DORADO]: *stream*, formed by the confluence of North Fork and South Fork, flows 4.5 miles to Middle Fork Cosumnes River 11 miles south of Placerville (lat. 38°34'30" N, long. 120°46'45" W; near E line sec. 5, T 8 N, R 11 E). Named on Aukum (1952) and Fiddletown (1949) 7.5' quadrangles. North Fork is 2 miles long and South Fork is 3 miles long; both forks are named on Aukum (1952) 7.5' quadrangle.

Spanish Diggings: see **Spanish Dry Diggings** [EL DORADO].

Spanish Dry Diggings [EL DORADO]: *locality*, 3.25 miles north of Greenwood (lat. 38°56'45" N, long. 120°54'45" W; near W line sec. 30, T 13 N, R 10 E). Named on Greenwood (1949) 7.5' quadrangle. Called Spanish Diggings on Placerville (1893) 30' quadrangle. Postal authorities established Spanish Dry Dggings post office in 1875 and discontinued it the same year (Frickstad, p. 29). Andreas Pico and a party of Spaniards were the first prospectors at the place in 1848; the next year a group of Germans set up a trading center nearby that was known as Dutchtown (Hoover, Rensch, and Rensch, p. 87).

Spanish Flat [EL DORADO]: *locality*, 4 miles north of Chili Bar (lat. 38°49'25" N, long. 120°48'25" W; on N line sec. 12, T 11 N, R 10 E). Named on Garden Valley (1949) 7.5' quadrangle. Postal authorities established Spanish Flat post office in 1853, discontinued it in 1872, reestablished it in 1888, and discontinued it that same year (Frickstad, p. 29). The name was for Spanish-speaking miners at the place (Gernes, p. 39). A mining camp called Union Flat started in 1852 about 0.5 mile north of Spanish Flat; many of the early miners there were from Union County, Ohio (Gernes, p. 41, 42). A mining camp called Stag Flat was located about 0.5 mile south of Spanish Flat (Gernes, p. 49), and a mining place called Chicken Flat was located north of South Fork American River 1 mile west of Spanish Flat (Gudde, 1975, p. 69).

Spanish Gulch [AMADOR]: *canyon*, drained by a stream that flows 1.25 miles to Dry Creek 6.5 miles southwest of Plymouth (lat. 38°24'35" N, long. 120°55'40" W). Named on Irish Hill (1962) 7.5' quadrangle.

Spanish Gulch [CALAVERAS]: *canyon*, drained by a stream that flows 1.25 miles to Mokelumne River 2 miles north of Paloma (lat. 38°17'25" N, long. 120°46' W; sec. 16, T 5 N, R 11 E). Named on Jackson (1962) 7.5' quadrangle.

Spanish Hill [EL DORADO]: *ridge*, north-northwest-trending, less than 1 mile long, 4.5 miles north of Chili Bar (lat. 38°49'40" N, long. 120°48'45" W; sec. 1, T 11 N, R 10 E); the ridge is northwest of Spanish Flat. Named on Garden Valley (1949) 7.5' quadrangle.

Spanish Hill: see **Big Spanish Hill**, under **Span-ish Ravine** [EL DORADO].

Spanish Ravine [EL DORADO]: *canyon*, drained by a stream that flows 0.5 mile to Hangtown Creek 0.5 mile east of downtown Placerville (lat. 38°43'50" N, long. 120°47'15" W; sec. 8, T 10 N, R 11 E). Named on Placerville (1949) 7.5' quadrangle. Whitney's (1880) map shows a feature called Big Spanish Hill located just east of Spanish Ravine, and has the name "Taylor's Rav." for the canyon east of Big Spanish Hill.

Spanish Ravine [PLACER]: *canyon*, drained by a stream that flows 0.5 mile to Duncan Canyon 5.5 miles south of Duncan Peak (lat. 39°04'30" N, long. 120°32' W; sec. 9, T 14 N, R 13 E). Named on Greek Store (1952) 7.5' quadrangle.

Spanish Spring [AMADOR]: *spring*, 6.5 miles southwest of Plymouth (lat. 38°24'50" N, long. 120°55'50" W; sec. 36, T 7 N, R 9 E); the spring is in Spanish Gulch. Named on Irish Hill (1962) 7.5' quadrangle.

Spaulding: see **Camp Spaulding** [NEVADA]; **Lake Spaulding** [NEVADA].

Spaulding Point [PLACER]: *peak*, 2.5 miles northeast of Dutch Flat (lat. 39°13'30" N, long. 120°48' W; sec. 25, T 16 N, R 10 E). Named on Dutch Flat (1950) 7.5' quadrangle.

Specimen Gulch [MARIPOSA]: *canyon*, drained by a stream that flows 0.5 mile to Agua Fria Creek 5.5 miles northeast of Catheys Valley (2) (lat. 37°29'15" N, long. 120°21'05" W). Named on Catheys Valley (1962) 7.5' quadrangle.

Specimen Gulch [PLACER]: *canyon*, drained by a stream that flows 1.25 miles to Bunch Canyon 4.25 miles south-southeast of Colfax (lat. 39°02'35" N, long. 120°55'30" W; at S line sec. 24, T 14 N, R 9 E). Named on Colfax (1949) 7.5' quadrangle.

Specimen Springs [MADERA]: *spring*, 6.25 miles north-northeast of Raymond (lat. 37°18'25" N, long. 119°52'05" W; sec. 23, T 7 S, R 19 E). Named on Horsecamp Mountain (1947) 7.5' quadrangle.

Speckerman Mountain [MADERA]: *peak*, 6.5 miles north-northeast of Yosemite Forks (lat. 37°27'15" N, long. 119°34'45" W; near E line sec. 32, T 5 S, R 22 E). Altitude 7137 feet. Named on Bass Lake (1953) 15' quadrangle. The name, given in the 1850's, commemorates a settler who lived near the feature (Gudde, 1949, p. 340).

Spencer Creek [SIERRA]: *stream*, flows 1.5 miles to Lavezzola Creek 11 miles north-northwest of Sierra City (lat. 39°41'55" N, long. 120°44'50" W; sec. 9, T 21 N, R 11 E); the stream heads at Spencer Lakes. Named on Gold Lake (1981) 7.5' quadrangle.

Spencer Lakes [SIERRA]: *lakes*, two, each 850 feet long, 10.5 miles north-northwest of Sierra City (lat. 39°41'55" N, long. 120°43'25" W; on and near E line sec. 10, T 21 N, R 11 E); the lakes are at the head of Spencer Creek.

Named on Gold Lake (1981) 7.5' quadrangle.

Spenceville [NEVADA]: *locality,* 6 miles southwest of Pilot Peak along Dry Creek (2) at the mouth of Little Dry Creek (lat. 39°06'50" N, long. 121°16' W; near NE cor. sec. 35, T 15 N, R 6 E). Site named on Camp Far West (1949) 7.5' quadrangle. Postal authorities established Spenceville post office in 1872, discontinued it in 1878, reestablished it in 1879, and discontinued it in 1932 (Frickstad, p. 115). The name commemorates Edward F. Spence of Nevada City, who donated lumber for the first school at the place in 1868 (Hanna, p. 313).

Spicer Canyon [EL DORADO]: *canyon,* drained by a stream that flows 1 mile to Sherman Canyon 9 miles west-southwest of Kirkwood (lat. 38°38'45" N, long. 120°13'15" W; at E line sec. 8, T 9 N, R 16 E). Named on Tragedy Spring (1979) 7.5' quadrangle.

Spicer Meadow [EL DORADO]: *area,* 9.5 miles west-southwest of Kirkwood (lat. 38°38'55" N, long. 120°13'55" W; near N line sec. 8, T 9 N, R 16 E); the place is in Spicer Canyon. Named on Tragedy Spring (1979) 7.5' quadrangle.

Spicer Meadow Reservoir [TUOLUMNE]: *lake,* behind a dam on Highland Creek 10 miles west-northwest of Dardanelle (lat. 38°23'35" N, long. 119°59'45" W). Named on Spicer Meadow Reservoir (1979) 7.5' quadrangle.

Spider Lake [EL DORADO]: *lake,* 3150 feet long, 3.5 miles east of Wentworth Springs (lat. 39°00'50" N, long. 120°16'20" W; on E line sec. 34, T 14 N, R 15 E). Named on Wentworth Springs (1953, photorevised 1973) 7.5' quadrangle.

Spiller Creek [TUOLUMNE]: *stream,* flows 6.5 miles to Return Creek 6.5 miles south of Matterhorn Peak (lat. 38°00' N, long. 119° 23'05" W). Named on Matterhorn Peak (1956) 15' quadrangle. Members of the Wheeler survey named the stream for J. Calvert Spiller, a topographer (United States Board on Geographic Names, 1934, p. 23). A Wheeler survey map has the name "Spiller's Cañon," and a map of the 1890's has the designation "Spiller or Randall Canon" (Browning, 1988, p. 135).

Spiller Lake [TUOLUMNE]: *lake,* 1700 feet long, 3 miles south of Matterhorn Peak (lat. 38°02'50" N, long. 119°22'10" W); the lake is at the head of a tributary to Spiller Creek. Named on Matterhorn Peak (1956) 15' quadrangle.

Spiller's Cañon: see **Spiller Creek** [TUOLUMNE].

Spillway Lake [TUOLUMNE]: *lake,* 1700 feet long, 5 miles south-southeast of Tioga Pass along Parker Pass Creek (lat. 37°50'30" N, long. 119°13'55" W). Named on Mono Craters (1953) 15' quadrangle.

Spinecup Ridge [MADERA]: *ridge,* southwest-trending, 1.5 miles long, 1.5 miles east-north-

east of Raymond (lat. 37°13'30" N, long. 119°53' W). Named on Raymond (1962) 7.5' quadrangle.

Spirito: see **Camp Spirito**, under **Bummerville** [CALAVERAS].

Spiritsville: see **Omega** [NEVADA].

S.P. Lakes [PLACER]: *lakes,* largest 1000 feet long, about 1 mile west-southwest of Cisco Grove (lat. 39°18'15" N, long. 120°33'35" W; sec. 30, T 17 N, R 13 E). Named on Cisco Grove (1955) 7.5' quadrangle.

Split Pinnacle [MARIPOSA]: *relief feature,* 2.25 miles west-southwest of Yosemite Village on the north side of Yosemite Valley (lat. 37°44'10" N, long. 119°37'15" W). Named on Yosemite (1956) 15' quadrangle. Members of the Sierra Club began using the name in the 1930's (Browning, 1986, p. 206).

Split Rock [MARIPOSA]: *peak,* 9.5 miles south of Mariposa (lat. 37° 21' N, long. 119°55'55" W; sec. 6, T 7 S, R 19 E). Named on Ben Hur (1947) 7.5' quadrangle.

Split Rock: see **Split Rock Ferry** [MARIPOSA].

Split Rock Creek [MARIPOSA]: *stream,* flows 5.5 miles to Chowchilla River 14 miles south of Mariposa at Mariposa-Madera county line (lat. 37°17' N, long. 119°55'35" W; near E line sec. 31, T 7 S, R 19 E). Named on Ben Hur (1947) 7.5' quadrangle.

Split Rock Ferry [MARIPOSA]: *locality,* 4.5 miles south-southeast of Coulterville along Merced River (lat. 37°38'40" N, long. 120°10'30" W). The site of the abandoned ferry is named on Coulterville (1947) 15' quadrangle. Split Rock post office, named for the ferry, was established in 1855 and discontinued in 1858 (Salley, p. 210).

Sport Hill: see **Mokelumne Hill** [CALAVERAS].

Spotted Fawn Lake [TUOLUMNE]: *lake,* 3000 feet long, 14 miles southeast of Pinecrest (lat. 38°04'20" N, long. 119°46'35" W). Named on Pinecrest (1956) 15' quadrangle.

Spotted Lakes [MADERA]: *lakes,* largest 1400 feet long, nearly 6 miles south of Merced Peak (lat. 37°33'05" N, long. 119°24' W). Named on Merced Peak (1953) 15' quadrangle.

Sportsmans Hall: see **Placerville** [EL DORADO].

Sprague [CALAVERAS]: *locality,* nearly 3 miles east-northeast of Blue Mountain (lat. 38°21'35" N, long. 120°19'20" W). Named on Big Trees (1891) 30' quadrangle.

Spring Canyon [EL DORADO]: *canyon,* 1 mile long, opens into String Canyon 10 miles southeast of Camino (lat. 38°38'40" N, long. 120°32'20" W; near SE cor. sec. 9, T 9 N, R 13 E); the canyon heads at Spring Flat. Named on Sly Park (1952) 7.5' quadrangle.

Spring Canyon [PLACER]: *canyon,* drained by a stream that flows 1.5 miles to Grouse Creek 6.25 miles northeast of Michigan Bluff (lat. 39°05'30" N, long. 120°38'25" W; sec. 4, T

14 N, R 12 E). Named on Michigan Bluff (1952) 7.5' quadrangle.

Spring Cove Campground [MADERA]: *locality,* 6.5 miles southeast of Yosemite Forks on the southwest side of Bass Lake (1) (lat. 37° 18' N, long. 119°32'30" W; near S line sec. 23, T 7 S, R 22 E). Named on Bass Lake (1953) 15' quadrangle.

Spring Creek [MARIPOSA]: *stream,* flows 2 miles to Mariposa Creek 2.5 miles south-southeast of Mariposa (lat. 37°27'05" N, long. 119°56'45" W). Named on Mariposa (1947) 7.5' quadrangle. The canyon of the stream is called Spring Gulch on Mariposa (1912) 30' quadrangle, and it is called Australia Gulch on Laizure's (1928) map.

Spring Creek [NEVADA]: *stream,* flows 6 miles to South Yuba River 5.5 miles west-southwest of North Bloomfield (lat. 39°19'55" N, long. 120°59'15" W; sec. 17, T 17 N, R 9 E). Named on North Bloomfield (1949) and Pike (1949) 7.5' quadrangles. Called Knapp Cr. on Hobson's (1890a) map.

Spring Creek [TUOLUMNE]: *stream,* flows 4 miles to West Fork Cherry Creek 11 miles east of Pinecrest (lat. 38°11' N, long. 119° 47'25" W). Named on Pinecrest (1956) and Tower Peak (1956) 15' quadrangles.

Springfield [TUOLUMNE]: *locality,* 1 mile south-southwest of Columbia (lat. 38°01'20" N, long. 120°24'45" W; near SW cor. sec. 14, T 2 N, R 14 E). Named on Columbia (1948) 7.5' quadrangle. Postal authorities established Springfield post office in 1857 and discontinued it in 1868 (Frickstad, p. 217). The name is from large springs at the place (Hanna, p. 314). Stoddart (p. 127) noted the early names "Pietra Blanca" and "Tim's Springs" for the locality; Timothy Eastman filed a preemption claim on the site in 1850 (DeFerrari *in* Stoddart, p. 130).

Spring Flat [EL DORADO]: *area,* 11 miles southeast of Camino (lat. 38°38'55" N, long. 120°30'40" W; sec. 11, T 9 N, R 13 E). Named on Sly Park (1952) 7.5' quadrangle.

Spring Gap [TUOLUMNE]: *locality,* 5.5 miles west-southwest of Strawberry (lat. 38°10'05" N, long. 120°06'05" W; near SW cor. sec. 27, T 4 N, R 17 E). Named on Strawberry (1979) 7.5' quadrangle.

Spring Garden [PLACER]: *locality,* 11 miles northeast of Auburn (lat. 38°59'55" N, long. 120°54'45" W). Named on Placerville (1893) 30' quadrangle.

Spring Garden Ravine [PLACER]: *canyon,* drained by a stream that flows 2.5 miles to Gas Canyon 11 miles northeast of Auburn (lat. 38°59'50" N, long. 120°54'30" W; near SE cor. sec. 1, T 13 N, R 9 E); Spring Garden was in the canyon. Named on Foresthill (1949) and Greenwood (1949) 7.5' quadrangles.

Spring Gulch [CALAVERAS]:
(1) *canyon,* 1.25 miles long, 1 mile south-southeast of Mokelumne Hill (lat. 38°17'20" N,

long. 120°41'45" W; in and near sec. 18, T 5 N, R 12 E). Named on Mokelumne Hill (1948) 7.5' quadrangle.
(2) *canyon,* drained by a stream that flows 2.25 miles to Jesus Maria Creek 7 miles southwest of Rail Road Flat (lat. 38°15'35" N, long. 120°35'10" W; sec. 30, T 5 N, R 13 E). Named on Rail Road Flat (1948) 7.5' quadrangle.
(3) *canyon,* drained by a stream that flows nearly 2 miles to Chili Gulch 2.5 miles northwest of San Andreas (lat. 38°13'35" N, long. 120°42'30" W). Named on San Andreas (1962) 7.5' quadrangle. Called Old Woman Gulch on San Andreas (1947) 15' quadrangle.

Spring Gulch [MARIPOSA]: *canyon,* drained by a stream that flows 1 mile to Willow Creek 2.5 miles south of Penon Blanco Peak (lat. 37°42' N, long. 120°15'45" W; sec. 1, T 3 S, R 15 E). Named on Penon Blanco Peak (1962) 7.5' quadrangle.

Spring Gulch: see **Alabama Gulch**, under **Alabama Hill** [CALAVERAS]; **Spring Creek** [MARIPOSA].

Spring Hill [NEVADA]: *locality,* 1.25 miles northeast of Grass Valley (lat. 39°13'55" N, long. 121°02'35" W; sec. 23, T 16 N, R 8 E). Named on Grass Valley (1949) 7.5' quadrangle.

Spring Meadow [TUOLUMNE]: *area,* 12 miles east of Pinecrest (lat. 38°11'15" N, long. 119°46'35" W); the place is along Spring Creek. Named on Pinecrest (1956) 15' quadrangle.

Spring Valley [CALAVERAS]: *valley,* 2.25 miles east-northeast of Valley Springs (lat. 38°12'25" N, long. 120°47'25" W; on S line sec. 8, T 4 N, R 11 E). Named on Valley Springs (1962) 7.5' quadrangle.

Spring Valley [EL DORADO]: *locality,* 3 miles east-northeast of Pollock Pines (lat. 38°46'45" N, long. 120°31'35" W; sec. 21, T 11 N, E 13 E). Named on Pollock Pines (1950) 7.5' quadrangle.

Spring Valley: see **Valley Springs** [CALAVERAS].

Spring Valley Branch [AMADOR]: *stream,* flows 1 mile to Little Indian Creek 2 miles west-northwest of Plymouth (lat. 38°29'05" N, long. 120°52'55" W; sec. 4, T 7 N, R 10 E). Named on Amador City (1962) and Irish Hill (1962) 7.5' quadrangles.

Spring Valley Creek [CALAVERAS]: *stream,* flows 4.5 miles to Cosgrove Creek less than 1 mile south-southeast of Valley Springs (lat. 38°11' N, long. 120°49'25" W; sec. 24, T 4 N, R 10 E); the stream goes through Spring Valley. Named on Valley Springs (1962) 7.5' quadrangle.

Spring Valley House: see **Wheats** [CALAVERAS].

Spruce [PLACER]: *locality,* 5.5 miles west of Donner Pass along Southern Pacific Railroad (lat. 39°18'55" N, long. 120°25'40" W; near N line sec. 29, T 17 N, R 14 E). Named on Truckee (1940) 30' quadrangle.

Spruce Bar: see **Spruce Creek** [PLACER].
Spruce Cañon: see **Spruce Creek** [PLACER].
Spruce Creek [PLACER]: *stream,* flows 2.5 miles to Duncan Canyon 7.25 miles south-southwest of Duncan Peak (lat. 39°03'05" N, long. 120°32'35" W; sec. 20, T 14 N, R 13 E). Named on Greek Store (1952) 7.5' quadrangle. Logan's (1925) map shows a place called Spruce Bar located at the mouth of the stream, and has the name "Spruce Cañon" for the canyon of the stream. Logan's (1925) map also shows a place called Greek Store situated at the head of the canyon (near the center of W line sec. 8, T 14 N, R 13 E), where Greek Store (1952) 7.5' quadrangle shows Greek Store guard station.
Spruce Gulch [CALAVERAS]: *canyon,* drained by a stream that flows nearly 4 miles to South Fork Mokelumne River 1.25 miles north-northeast of Rail Road Flat (lat. 38°21'35" N, long. 120°30'10" W; near W line sec. 24, T 6 N, R 13 E). Named on Fort Mountain (1979) and Rail Road Flat (1948) 7.5' quadrangles.
Squabbletown [TUOLUMNE]: *locality,* 1.5 miles south-southeast of Columbia along Woods Creek (lat. 38°00'55" N, long. 120°23'05" W; sec. 24, T 2 N, R 14 E). Named on Columbia (1948) 7.5' quadrangle. According to Jackson (p. 326), the place was noted for fights.
Squaw Creek [PLACER]: *stream,* flows 5.5 miles to Truckee River 4.25 miles northwest of Tahoe City (lat. 39°12'40" N, long. 120°11'55" W; near NE cor. sec. 28, T 16 N, R 16 E); the stream goes through Squaw Valley. Named on Granite Chief (1953) and Tahoe City (1955) 7.5' quadrangles. California Division of Highways' (1934) map has the name "Squaw Creek" for a locality along Southern Pacific Railroad near the mouth of Squaw Creek (near SE cor. sec. 21, T 15 N, R 16 E), and has the name "Old Road" for a place along the railroad about 1 mile farther south (near SE cor. sec. 28, T 16 N, R 16 E). Postal authorities established Squaw Creek post office at a vacation resort along Squaw Creek in 1917 and discontinued it in 1918 (Salley, p. 211). Hobson's (1890b) map shows a place called Claraville situated south of the mouth of Squaw Creek on the east side of Truckee River (near W line sec. 27, T 16 N, R 16 E); Wheeler (1877, p. 1237) described the place as a deserted mining camp. Hobson's (1890b) map also shows a place called Knoxville located north of the mouth of Squaw Creek on the east side of Truckee River (sec. 21, T 16 N, R 16 E); Wheeler (1877, p. 1237) identified this place as a tollhouse on Truckee and Tahoe turnpike road.
Squaw Dome [MADERA]: *peak,* about 13 miles northeast of Shuteye Peak (lat. 37°28'55" N, long. 119°15'50" W; sec. 20, T 5 S, R 25 E). Altitude 7818 feet. Named on Shuteye Peak (1953) 15' quadrangle. Called Squaw Nipple

Peak on California Mining Bureau's (1917d) map.
Squaw Flat [PLACER]:
(1) *area,* 5.5 miles east-northeast of Auburn (lat. 38°56'25" N, long. 120°59'10" W; near NW cor. sec. 33, T 13 N, R 9 E). Named on Greenwood (1949) 7.5' quadrangle.
(2) *area,* 8 miles west-northwest of Devil Peak (lat. 38°59'25" N, long. 120°41'30" W; sec. 12, T 13 N, R 11 E). Named on Tunnel Hill (1950) 7.5' quadrangle.
Squaw Gulch [PLACER]: *canyon,* flows 1.5 miles to Middle Fork American River 11 miles east-northeast of Auburn (lat. 38°57'35" N, long. 120°53' W; sec. 20, T 13 N, R 10 E). Named on Georgetown (1949) and Greenwood (1949) 7.5' quadrangles.
Squaw Hill [MARIPOSA]: *peak,* 11.5 miles east of Mariposa (lat. 37° 27'45" N, long. 119°45'25" W; near SW cor. sec. 26, T 5 S, R 20 E). Named on Stumpfield Mountain (1947) 7.5' quadrangle.
Squaw Hollow [CALAVERAS]: *area,* 6.25 miles southeast of Blue Mountain (lat. 38°16'10" N, long. 120°17'15" W; sec. 23, T 5 N, R 15 E). Named on Blue Mountain (1956) 15' quadrangle. Big Trees (1891) 30' quadrangle has the name "Squaw Hollow" for a cluster of buildings at or near the place.
Squaw Hollow [EL DORADO]: *valley,* 5 miles south-southeast of Placerville (lat. 38°40'05" N, long. 120°44'55" W; at N line sec. 3, T 9 N, R 11 E). Named on Camino (1952) and Placerville (1949) 7.5' quadrangles.
Squaw Hollow Campground [CALAVERAS]: *locality,* 6.25 miles southeast of Blue Mountain (lat. 38°16'25" N, long. 120°17'20" W; sec. 23, T 5 N, R 15 E); the place is at or near Squaw Hollow. Named on Dorrington (1979) 7.5' quadrangle.
Squaw Hollow Creek [EL DORADO]: *stream,* flows 9 miles to Martinez Creek 6.5 miles south of Placerville (lat. 38°38'05" N, long. 120°19' W; near E line sec. 13, T 9 N, R 10 E); the stream goes through Squaw Hollow. Named on Camino (1952) and Placerville (1949) 7.5' quadrangles.
Squaw Lake [SIERRA]: *lake,* 700 feet long, 7.25 miles north of Sierra City (lat. 39°40'10" N, long. 120°39'05" W; sec. 20, T 21 N, R 12 E). Named on Gold Lake (1981) 7.5' quadrangle.
Squaw Nipple Peak: see **Squaw Dome** [MADERA].
Squaw Peak [PLACER]: *peak,* 1.5 miles southeast of Granite Chief (lat. 39°10'50" N, long. 120°16'05" W; sec. 2, T 15 N, R 15 E); the peak is west of Squaw Valley. Altitude 8885 feet. Named on Granite Chief (1953) 7.5' quadrangle.
Squaw Ridge [AMADOR]: *ridge,* southwest-trending, 8 miles long, 4.5 miles north of Mokelumne Peak on Amador-Alpine county line (lat. 38°36' N, long. 120°06'30" W). Named on Bear River Reservoir (1979),

Caples Lake (1979), and Mokelumne Peak (1979) 7.5' quadrangles.

Squaw Valley [PLACER]: *valley,* 4.5 miles west-northwest of Tahoe City (lat. 39°12'15" N, long. 120°13' W); the feature is along Squaw Creek. Named on Tahoe City (1955) 7.5' quadrangle. The valley was called Ladies Paradise in the early days (Stewart, p. 85). Postal authorities established Squaw Village post office in the valley in 1959 and changed the name to Olympic Valley when Winter Olympic Games were held there in 1960 (Salley, p. 161, 211).

Squaw Village: see **Squaw Valley** [PLACER].

Squires Canyon [PLACER]: *canyon,* drained by a stream that flows nearly 2 miles to Bear River 2 miles southwest of Dutch Flat (lat. 39°11'20" N, long. 120°51'50" W" W; near E line sec. 5, T 15 N, R 10 E). Named on Dutch Flat (1950) 7.5' quadrangle.

Squirrel Creek [MARIPOSA]: *stream,* flows 1.5 miles to South Fork Merced River 2 miles west-northwest of Wawona (lat. 37°33' N, long. 119°41'05" W; near NE cor. sec. 32, T 4 S, R 21 E). Named on Yosemite (1956) 15' quadrangle.

Squirrel Creek [NEVADA]: *stream,* flows 11 miles to Deer Creek 5.25 miles northwest of Pilot Peak (lat. 39°13'45" N, long. 121°14'40" W; sec. 24, T 16 N, R 6 E). Named on Grass Valley (1949) and Rough and Ready (1949) 7.5' quadrangles.

Squirrel Creek [SIERRA]: *stream,* flows 2 miles to Grouse Creek 3 miles east of Pike (lat. 39°26'05" N, long. 120°56'30" W; near SW cor. sec. 11, T 18 N, R 9 E). Named on Pike (1949) 7.5' quadrangle.

Squirrel Gulch [CALAVERAS]: *canyon,* drained by a stream that flows less than 0.5 mile to Coyote Creek 5 miles south-southwest of Vallecito (lat. 38°00'55" N, long. 120°29'35" W; sec. 24, T 2 N, R 13 E). Named on Columbia (1948) 7.5' quadrangle.

Stafford Creek [EL DORADO]: *stream,* flows 1.5 miles to Big Canyon Creek nearly 3 miles southeast of Shingle Springs (lat. 38°37'50" N, long. 120°53'50" W; sec. 17, T 9 N, R 10 E). Named on Shingle Springs (1949) 7.5' quadrangle.

Stafford Mountain [SIERRA]: *peak,* 1.5 miles east-northeast of Mount Fillmore on Sierra-Plumas county line (lat. 39°44'30" N, long. 120°49'30" W; sec. 26, T 22 N, R 10 E). Altitude 7019 feet. Named on Mount Fillmore (1951) 7.5' quadrangle.

Stafford Ravine [SIERRA]: *canyon,* drained by a stream that flows 0.5 mile to West Branch Canyon Creek 1 mile east-northeast of Mount Fillmore (lat. 39°44'15" N, long. 120°49'55" W; sec. 26, T 22 N, R 10 E); the canyon is west of Stafford Mountain. Named on Mount Fillmore (1951) 7.5' quadrangle.

Stage [TUOLUMNE]: *locality,* 10 miles northeast of Columbia near Knight Creek (lat.

38°08' N, long. 120°16'20" W). Named on Big Trees (1891) 30' quadrangle.

Stag Flat: see **Spanish Flat** [EL DORADO].

Stahls Ravine [SIERRA]: *canyon,* drained by a stream that flows 1 mile to Cedar Grove Ravine 4 miles southwest of Mount Fillmore (lat. 39°41'35" N, long. 120°54'35" W; sec. 7, T 21 N, R 10 E). Named on La Porte (1951) 7.5' quadrangle.

Staircase Falls [MARIPOSA]: *waterfall,* 1.25 miles southeast of Yosemite Village on the south side of Yosemite Valley (lat. 37°44'10" N, long. 119°34'30" W). Named on Yosemite (1956) 15' quadrangle.

Stairway Creek [MADERA]: *stream,* flows 4.5 miles to Middle Fork San Joaquin River 6.5 miles south-southwest of Devils Postpile (lat. 37°32'25" N, long. 119°08'15" W); the stream heads near Granite Stairway. Named on Devils Postpile (1953) 15' quadrangle.

Stairway Meadow [MADERA]: *area,* 3.25 miles southwest of Devils Postpile (lat. 37°35'50" N, long. 119°07'45" W); the place is northwest of Granite Stairway. Named on Devils Postpile (1953) 15' quadrangle.

Stallman Corners [PLACER]: *locality,* 4.25 miles east-southeast of Rocklin (lat. 38°46' N, long. 121°09'45" W; on S line sec. 26, T 11 N, R 7 E). Named on Rocklin (1967) 7.5' quadrangle.

Stampede Canyon [PLACER]: *canyon,* drained by a stream that flows 1 mile to Bear River 5.25 miles north-northeast of Colfax (lat. 39°09'55" N, long. 120°54'20" W; near W line sec. 7, T 15 N, R 10 E). Named on Chicago Park (1949) 7.5' quadrangle.

Stampede Reservoir [SIERRA]: *lake,* behind a dam on Little Truckee River 5.5 miles south of Crystal Peak (lat. 39°28'30" N, long. 120°06'10" W; at NW cor. sec. 28, T 19 N, R 17 E). Named on Boca (1955, photorevised 1969), Dog Valley (1981), Hobart Mills (1981), and Sardine Peak (1981) 7.5' quadrangles.

Stampede Valley [SIERRA]: *valley,* 4.5 miles south-southwest of Crystal Peak (lat. 39°29'30" N, long. 120°07'30" W). Named on Loyalton (1955) and Truckee (1955) 15' quadrangles. Water of Stampede Reservoir now covers most of the valley.

Standard [TUOLUMNE]: *village,* 4 miles east-southeast of Sonora (lat. 38°58' N, long. 120°18'40" W; sec. 3, T 1 N, R 15 E). Named on Standard (1948) 7.5' quadrangle. Postal authorities established Standard post office in 1910; Standard Lumber Company had a lumber mill, box factory, and homes for employees at the place (Salley, p. 211).

Standard Mill [MADERA]: *locality,* 4 miles northeast of O'Neals (lat. 37°09'55" N, long. 119°38'20" W; near W line sec. 12, T 9 S, R 21 E). Named on Mariposa (1912) 30' quadrangle.

Stanford [PLACER]: *locality,* 3.5 miles east-southeast of Donner Pass along Southern Pacific Railroad (lat. 39°17'45" N, long. 120° 15'45" W; sec. 25, T 17 N, R 15 E). Named on Truckee (1940) 30' quadrangle.

Stanford Lakes [MADERA]: *lakes,* largest 1100 feet long, nearly 6 miles south-southeast of Merced Peak (lat. 37°33'15" N, long. 119° 21'40" W). Named on Merced Peak (1953) 15' quadrangle. Billy Brown, a local packer, applied the misspelled name about 1920; he intended to honor the Kenneth J. Staniford family of Fresno (Browning, 1986, p. 207).

Stanford Point [MARIPOSA]: *promontory,* 5.25 miles southwest of Yosemite Village on the south side of Yosemite Valley (lat. 37°42'25" N, long. 119°40' W). Named on Yosemite (1956) 15' quadrangle. The name commemorates Leland Stanford (Browning, 1988, p. 137).

Stanford Rock [PLACER]: *peak,* 3.5 miles northwest of Homewood (lat. 39°07'25" N, long. 120°12'15" W; sec. 27, T 15 N, R 16 E). Altitude 8473 feet. Named on Homewood (1955) 7.5' quadrangle. The name commemorates Leland Stanford (Lekisch, p. 110).

Stanford Wood Camp: see **Old Stanford Wood Camp** [PLACER].

Stanislaus [TUOLUMNE]: *locality,* 7.25 miles north-northeast of Columbia (lat. 38°08'15" N, long. 120°22'10" W; sec. 6, T 3 N, R 15 E); the place is along Stanislaus River. Named on Stanislaus (1948) 7.5' quadrangle. Postal authorities established Stanislaus post office in 1911 and discontinued it in 1962 (Salley, p. 211). California Division of Highways' (1934) map shows Petty Reservoir 1 mile northeast of Stanislaus (near NW cor. sec. 5, T 3 N, R 15 E).

Stanislaus: see **Stanislaus River** [CALAVERAS-TUOLUMNE].

Stanislaus City: see **Stanislaus River** [CALAVERAS-TUOLUMNE].

Stanislaus Mesa: see **Table Mountain** [CALAVERAS-TUOLUMNE].

Stanislaus River [CALAVERAS-TUOLUMNE]: *stream,* formed by the confluence of North Fork and Middle Fork in Tuolumne County, flows 93 miles to San Joaquin River 13 miles west of Modesto in Stanislaus County (lat. 37°39'50" N, long. 121°14'25" W). Named on Sacramento (1957, limited revision 1964) and San Jose (1962) 1°x 2° quadrangles. Ensign Gabriel Moraga and Padre Pedro Muñoz gave the name "Rio de Nuestra Señora de Guadalupe" to the stream in 1806, but in mission records it usually has the designation "Rio del Laquisimes," a name derived from an Indian tribe that lived along its lower reaches (Brotherton, p. 47). In 1829 some Mexicans had a bloody battle near the river with a band of Indians led by a mission-trained Indian called Estanislao, who probably was named for a Polish saint; by 1839 the stream was known as Rio Estanislao, and

later it was called Stanislaus River (Gudde, 1949, p. 342). Middle Fork, formed by the confluence of Summit Creek and Kennedy Creek, is 45 miles long; it is named on Crandall Peak (1979), Dardanelle (1979), Donnell Lake (1979), Liberty Hill (1979), Sonora Pass (1979), Stanislaus (1948), and Strawberry (1979) 7.5' quadrangles. United States Board on Geographic Names (1980a, p. 3) rejected the name "Middle Fork Stanislaus River" for Kennedy Creek. North Fork heads in Alpine County and flows for 31 miles along Calaveras-Tuolumne county line; it is named on Boards Crossing (1979), Calaveras Dome (1979), Dorrington (1979), Stanislaus (1948), and Tamarack (1979) 7.5' quadrangles. South Fork is 45 miles long and joins Stanislaus River 3 miles north-northeast of Columbia; it is named on Pinecrest (1956) 15' quadrangle, and on Columbia (1948), Columbia SE (1948), Crandall Peak (1979), Strawberry (1979), and Twain Harte (1979) 7.5' quadrangles. In 1846 a party of Mormons under Samuel Brannan started a community called New Hope on the north side of Stanislaus River about 1.5 miles above the mouth of the stream, but the place was abandoned by the autumn of 1847; another attempt at settlement, called Stanislaus City, was made at the same place during the gold rush (Hoover, Rensch, and Rensch, p. 376). Bancroft's (1864) map shows Stanislaus City situated on the south side of Stanislaus River near the mouth of the stream. Postal authorities established Stanislaus post office at the junction of Stanislaus River and San Joaquin River in 1874 and discontinued it in 1875 (Salley, p. 211). Sirey and Clarke's Ferry operated in 1850 on Stanislaus River about 5 miles above the mouth of the stream (Morgan and Scobie *in* Perkins, p. 315). Hillyer and Burnham Ferry was started on Stanislaus River in 1864 about 4.5 miles in a strait line from the mouth of the stream; C. and Frederick Meineckes took over the ferry in 1866, and a small settlement grew nearby, chiefly on the north side of the river (Brotherton, p. 51-52). Postal authorities established Meinecke post office at the place (NW quarter sec. 2, T 3 S, R 7 E) in 1866 and discontinued it in 1872 (Salley, p. 137). The ferry was called Taylor's Ferry after C.E. Taylor acquired it in 1869 (Brotherton, p. 52). Thompson and West's (1879) map shows Taylor's Ferry along Stanislaus River nearly 4 miles southwest of Ripon.

Stanislaus River Campground [CALAVERAS]: *locality,* 2 miles southeast of Tamarack (lat. 38°25'20" N, long. 120°02'45" W); the place is along North Fork Stanislaus River. Named on Tamarack (1979) 7.5' quadrangle.

Stanton Peak [TUOLUMNE]: *peak,* 2.5 miles south-southeast of Matterhorn Peak (lat. 38°03'30" N, long. 119°21'45" W). Altitude

11,695 feet. Named on Matterhorn Peak (1956) 15' quadrangle.

Star [TUOLUMNE]: *locality,* 7.5 miles northeast of Columbia along Rose Creek (lat. 38°06' N, long. 120°17'30" W). Named on Big Trees (1891) 30' quadrangle. Columbia SE (1948) 7.5' quadrangle shows Star mine near the place. Postal authorities established Star post office in 1896 and discontinued it in 1901; the name was from Star mine (Salley, p. 212).

Starkweather Lake [MADERA]: *lake,* 600 feet long, 2.5 miles north of Devils Postpile (lat. 37°39'50" N, long. 119°04'25" W). Named on Devils Postpile (1953) 15' quadrangle. The name commemorates a prospector who had claims above the lake in the 1920's (Smith, p. 13).

Star Lakes [MADERA]: *lakes,* largest 900 feet long, 5.5 miles south-southwest of Buena Vista Peak (lat. 37°30'55" N, long. 119°32'45" W; sec. 10, T 5 S, R 22 E). Named on Yosemite (1956) 15' quadrangle, which shows Star mine southwest of the lakes.

Star Lake [EL DORADO]: *lake,* 1800 feet long, 1.25 miles north-northeast of Freel Peak (lat. 38°52'30" N, long. 119°53'15" W; sec. 30, T 12 N, R 19 E). Named on Freel Peak (1955) and South Lake Tahoe (1955) 7.5' quadrangles.

Starr [MARIPOSA]: *locality,* 5.25 miles north-northwest of Hornitos along Yosemite Valley Railroad (lat. 37°34'05" N, long. 120°16'55" W; sec. 23, T 4 S, R 15 E). Named on Merced Falls (1944) 15' quadrangle.

Star Ridge [TUOLUMNE]: *ridge,* southwest-to west-trending, 9 miles long, 6 miles west-northwest of Long Barn between Rose Creek and Eagle Creek (1). Named on Columbia SE (1948), Crandall Peak (1979), and Twain Harte (1979) 7.5' quadrangles. Columbia SE (1948) 7.5' quadrangle shows Star mine near the west end of the ridge.

Starr King: see **Mount Starr King** [MARIPOSA].

Starr King Lake [MARIPOSA]: *lake,* 600 feet long, 4.5 miles east-southeast of Yosemite Village (lat. 37°43'05" N, long. 119°30'30" W); the lake is 1 mile north-northeast of Mount Starr King. Named on Yosemite (1956) 15' quadrangle. United States Board on Geographic Names (1934, p. 24) rejected the name "Helen Lake" for the feature.

Starr King Meadow [MARIPOSA]: *area,* 5.5 miles southeast of Yosemite Village (lat. 37°42' N, long. 119°30'10" W); the place is east of Mount Starr King. Named on Merced Peak (1953) and Yosemite (1956) 15' quadrangles. The name is from Mount Starr King (United States Board on Geographic Names, 1934, p. 24).

Starr Ravine [PLACER]: *canyon,* 1.25 miles long, opens into Deep Canyon 3.5 miles south-southwest of Duncan Peak (lat. 39°06'45" N, long. 120°32'45" W; at N line sec. 32, T 15 N, R 13 E). Named on Greek Store (1952) 7.5' quadrangle, which shows a mine called Millers Defeat at the head of the canyon. On Logan's (1925) map, present Starr Ravine is called Millers Defeat Cañon.

Star Town [PLACER]: *locality,* 6 miles west-southwest of Duncan Peak (lat. 39°07'10" N, long. 120°36'20" W; sec. 26, T 15 N, R 12 E). Named on Greek Store (1952) 7.5' quadrangle.

Starvation Bar [NEVADA]: *locality,* nearly 2 miles south-southeast of French Corral along South Yuba River (lat. 39°17'05" N, long. 121°08'40" W; near S line sec. 36, T 17 N, R 7 E). Named on French Corral (1948) 7.5' quadrangle.

Starvation Lake [TUOLUMNE]: *lake,* 350 feet long, 12.5 miles east of Pinecrest (lat. 38°11'10" N, long. 119°45'40" W). Named on Pinecrest (1956) 15' quadrangle.

Starville: see **Oakhurst** [MADERA].

Stateline [EL DORADO]: *district,* 7.5 miles north-northwest of Freel Peak in the town of South Lake Tahoe (lat. 38°57'30" N, long. 119°56'45" W; sec. 27, T 13 N, R 18 E); the place is at California-Nevada State line. Named on South Lake Tahoe (1955, photorevised 1969 and 1974) 7.5' quadrangle. Postal authorities established Stateline post office in 1901 (Salley, p. 212). Markleeville (1889) 30' quadrangle shows a place called Lakeside situated in present Stateline near the intersection of the old Von Schmidt California-Nevada State line with Lake Tahoe. The name "Laphams" shown on an old map at present Stateline refers to the hotel and landing that William W. Lapham had there in the mid-1850's (Lekisch, p. 108).

Stateline Point [PLACER]: *promontory,* 1.5 miles southeast of Kings Beach along Lake Tahoe (lat. 39°13'20" N, long. 120°00'15" W; sec. 30, T 16 N, R 18 E); the feature is at California-Nevada State line. Named on Kings Beach (1955) 7.5' quadrangle. Truckee (1895) 30' quadrangle has the form "State Line Point" for the name.

Station Creek [EL DORADO]: *stream,* flows 3.5 miles to South Fork American River 4.25 miles south-southwest of Pyramid Peak (lat. 38°47'15" N, long. 120°11' W; sec. 23, T 11 N, R 16 E). Named on Pyramid Peak (1955) 7.5' quadrangle.

Station Creek [NEVADA]: *stream,* flows 1 mile to Prosser Creek 4 miles northeast of Truckee (lat. 39°22'25" N, long. 120°07'55" W; near N line sec. 31, T 18 N, R 17 E). Named on Truckee (1955) 7.5' quadrangle.

Steamboat Canyon [PLACER]: *canyon,* drained by a stream that flows 2 miles to Five Lakes Creek 3.5 miles northeast of Bunker Hill (lat. 39°05'05" N, long. 120°19'50" W; near SE cor. sec. 6, T 14 N, R 15 E); the canyon heads near Steamboat Mountain. Named on Wentworth Springs (1953) 7.5' quadrangle.

Steamboat Mountain [PLACER]: *peak*, 4.5 miles north-northeast of Bunker Hill (lat. 39°06'40" N, long. 120°21'10" W; sec. 36, T 15 N, R 14 E). Altitude 7347 feet. Named on Wentworth Springs (1953) 7.5' quadrangle. Called Steamboat Rock on Truckee (1940) 30' quadrangle.

Steamboat Mountain: see **Little Steamboat Mountain** [PLACER].

Steamboat Rock: see **Steamboat Mountain** [PLACER].

Steele Creek [CALAVERAS]: *stream*, flows nearly 4 miles to South Fork Calaveras River 7 miles west-northwest of Angels Camp (lat. 38°07'25" N, long. 120°39'25" W; sec. 9, T 3 N, R 12 E). Named on Salt Spring Valley (1962) and San Andreas (1962) 7.5' quadrangles.

Steeley Fork: see **Steely Fork**, under **Cosumnes River** [AMADOR-EL DORADO].

Steely Creek: see **North Steely Creek** [EL DORADO]; **South Steely Creek** [EL DORADO].

Steely Fork: see **Cosumnes River** [AMADOR-EL DORADO].

Steep Gulch: see **Volunteer Gulch** [CALAVERAS].

Steephollow Creek [NEVADA]: *stream*, flows 18 miles to Bear River 4.5 miles northeast of Chicago Park (lat. 39°10'35" N, long. 120°53'40" W; near S line sec. 6, T 15 N, R 10 E). Named on Blue Canyon (1955), Chicago Park (1949), Dutch Flat (1950), and Washington (1950) 7.5' quadrangles. Colfax (1898) 30' quadrangle has the name "Sheep Hollow" along the stream. North Fork enters from the northeast 6 miles south of Washington; it is 4.5 miles long and is named on Blue Canyon (1955) and Washington (1950) 7.5' quadrangles.

Steephollow Crossing [NEVADA]: *locality*, 5.5 miles northeast of Chicago Park along Steephollow Creek (lat. 39°11'45" N, long. 120°53'05" W; near NE cor. sec. 6, T 15 N, R 10 E). Named on Chicago Park (1949) 7.5' quadrangle.

Stent [TUOLUMNE]: *village*, 5 miles south-southwest of Sonora (lat. 37°55' N, long. 120°24'45" W; near NW cor. sec. 26, T 1 N, R 14 E). Named on Sonora (1948) 7.5' quadrangle. Stent post office, which originally was 2 miles south of present Stent, was established in 1895 and discontinued in 1925; the place also was known as Utterville (Salley, p. 213). William Utter settled at the site in 1850, which then was called Utters Bar (Gudde, 1975, p. 275). The village is on a prominence known as Poverty Hill, and was itself sometimes called by that name (Gudde, 1975, p. 335). DeFerrari (*in* Stoddart, p. 93) noted that a place called Yorktown was situated about 0.5 mile from Poverty Hill.

Stephens: see **Mount Stephens**, under **Donner Lake** [NEVADA].

Sterling: see **Lake Sterling** [NEVADA].

Stevenson Meadow [MADERA]: *area*, 8.5 miles west-northwest of Devils Postpile (lat. 37°39'35" N, long. 119°13'50" W). Named on Devils Postpile (1953) 15' quadrangle.

Stevens Ravine [PLACER]: *canyon*, drained by a stream that flows 1 mile to the head of Third Brushy Canyon 2.5 miles north of Foresthill (lat. 39°03'20" N, long. 120°49'25" W; sec. 14, T 14 N, R 10 E). Named on Foresthill (1949) 7.5' quadrangle.

Stewart: see **George R. Stewart Peak**, under **Donner Pass** [NEVADA-PLACER]; **Sonora** [TUOLUMNE].

Stewarts Flat: see **Penryn** [PLACER].

Stockings Flat: see **Newtown** [NEVADA].

Stockton Creek [MARIPOSA]: *stream*, flows 5.5 miles to Mariposa Creek 1.5 miles southeast of Mariposa (lat. 37°28'10" N, long. 119°56'55" W). Named on Feliciana Mountain (1947) and Mariposa (1947) 7.5' quadrangles. The stream first was called Ave Maria River, and a mining camp at the mouth of the stream was called Ave Maria (Gudde, 1975, p. 23-24). Laizure's (1928) map has the name "Stockton Ridge" for the ridge located between Stockton Creek and Mariposa Creek.

Stockton Hill [CALAVERAS]: *peak*, at the southwest edge of the town of Mokelumne Hill (lat. 38°17'50" N, long. 120°42'30" W; sec. 12, T 5 N, R 11 E). Named on Mokelumne Hill (1948) 7.5' quadrangle.

Stockton Ridge: see **Stockton Creek** [MARIPOSA].

Stoddard Spring [TUOLUMNE]: *spring*, nearly 7 miles southwest of Strawberry (lat. 38°07'50" N, long. 120°06' W; sec. 10, T 3 N, R 17 E). Named on Strawberry (1979) 7.5' quadrangle.

Stonebreaker Creek [EL DORADO]: *stream*, flows 4.5 miles to Camp Creek 8.5 miles east of Camino (lat. 38°43'30" N, long. 120° 31' W; near NE cor. sec. 15, T 10 N, R 13 E). Named on Sly Park (1952) and Stump Spring (1951) 7.5' quadrangles. Logan's (1938) map has the name "Bryant Cr." for the feature.

Stone Cellar [EL DORADO]: *locality*, 4 miles northeast of Robbs Peak (lat. 38°57'40" N, long. 120°20'45" W; at W line sec. 19, T 13 N, R 15 E). Named on Loon Lake (1952) 7.5' quadrangle.

Stone City: see **Lost City** [CALAVERAS].

Stone Corral [CALAVERAS]: *locality*, 3 miles west of Jenny Lind (lat. 38°06' N, long. 120°55'40" W). Named on Jackson (1902) 30' quadrangle. The place consisted of a hotel, barns, and the corral for which it was named (California Department of Parks and Recreation, p. 13).

Stone Creek Settlement: see **Lost City** [CALAVERAS].

Stonehill: see **Westville** [PLACER].

Stonehouse [MARIPOSA]: *locality*, nearly 2

miles south of the settlement of Catheys Valley (lat. 37°24'35" N, long. 120°05'05" W; near E line sec. 15, T 6 S, R 17 E). Named on Catheys Valley (1962) 7.5' quadrangle.

Stoney Creek [EL DORADO]: *stream,* flows 2 miles to Perry Creek 4.5 miles northeast of Aukum (lat. 38°36'05" N, long. 120°39'35" W; sec. 28, T 9 N, R 12 E). Named on Aukum (1952) 7.5' quadrangle.

Stony Bar: see **Big Bar** [CALAVERAS].

Stony Bar [PLACER]: *locality,* 2 miles south of Michigan Bluff (lat. 39°00'45" N, long. 120°44'10" W; sec. 34, T 14 N, R 11 E). Named on Michigan Bluff (1952) 7.5' quadrangle.

Stony Bar: see **Coloma** [EL DORADO]; **Otter Creek** [EL DORADO].

Stony Creek [AMADOR]: *stream,* flows 2.5 miles to Sutter Creek (1) 7 miles south of Plymouth (lat. 38°22'35" N, long. 120°50'50" W; sec. 14, T 6 N, R 10 E). Named on Amador City (1962) and Jackson (1962) 7.5' quadrangles.

Stony Creek [EL DORADO]: *stream,* flows nearly 2 miles to Rubicon River 5 miles northnorthwest of Robbs Peak (lat. 38°59'15" N, long. 120°27' W). Named on Robbs Peak (1950) 7.5' quadrangle.

Stony Gulch [TUOLUMNE]:
(1) *canyon,* drained by a stream that flows 4.25 miles to Stanislaus River 5.5 miles north of Columbia (lat. 38°06'50" N, long. 120°23'20" W; sec. 13, T 3 N, R 14 E). Named on Columbia (1948), Columbia SE (1948), and Stanislaus (1948) 7.5' quadrangles.
(2) *canyon,* drained by a stream that flows 1.5 miles to South Fork Stanislaus River 2.5 miles north of Columbia (lat. 38°04'25" N, long. 120°24'20" W; sec. 35, T 3 N, R 14 E). Named on Columbia (1948) 7.5' quadrangle.

Stony Hill [PLACER]: *peak,* 6 miles northeast of Auburn (lat. 38°56'50" N, long. 120°59' W; sec. 28, T 13 N, R 9 E). Altitude 1898 feet. Named on Greenwood (1949) 7.5' quadrangle.

Stony Ridge Lake [EL DORADO]: *lake,* 2900 feet long, nearly 2 miles north-northeast of Phipps Peak (lat. 38°58'45" N, long. 120° 08'15" W; on N line sec. 18, T 13 N, R 17 E). Named on Rockbound Valley (1955) 7.5' quadrangle. The feature also was known as Upper Tallant Lake (Lekisch, p. 114).

Storey [MADERA]: *locality,* 2.5 miles eastnortheast of Madera along Atchison, Topeka and Santa Fe Railroad (lat. 37°58'30" N, long. 120°01'05" W; near W line sec. 16, T 11 S, R 18 E). Named on Madera (1963) 7.5' quadrangle. Madera (1946) 15' quadrangle has the designation "Storey (Madera Sta.)" at the place.

Storms' Station: see **Chicago Park** [NEVADA].

Stoutenburg: see **Murphys** [CALAVERAS].

Stovepipe Campground [MARIPOSA]: *locality,* 4.5 miles west of Wawona (lat. 37°32'30" N, long. 119°44' W; sec. 35, T 4 S, R 20 E).

Named on Yosemite (1956) 15' quadrangle.

Straight Spring Gulch [CALAVERAS]: *canyon,* drained by a stream that flows less than 1 mile to Walla Gulch 3.5 miles east-northeast of San Andreas (lat. 38°12'45" N, long. 120°37' W; sec. 11, T 4 N, R 12 E). Named on Calaveritas (1962) 7.5' quadrangle.

Strand Falls [MARIPOSA]: *waterfall,* 5.5 miles southwest of Yosemite Village along Meadow Brook (lat. 37°42'15" N, long. 119°40'05" W). Named on Yosemite (1956) 15' quadrangle.

Strap Miner Creek [EL DORADO]: *stream,* flows 1.25 miles to Deer Creek (2) nearly 4 miles south-southeast of Clarksville (lat. 38°36'25" N, long. 121°01' W; sec. 29, T 9 N, R 9 E). Named on Folsom SE (1954) 7.5' quadrangle.

Strap Ravine [PLACER]: *canyon,* drained by a stream that flows 3.5 miles to Linda Creek 2.5 miles southeast of Roseville (lat. 38°43'50" N, long. 121°15' W; near S line sec. 7, T 10 N, R 7 E). Named on Folsom (1967) 7.5' quadrangle.

Strawberry [EL DORADO]: *locality,* 3.25 miles south-southeast of Pyramid Peak along South Fork American River (lat. 38°47'55" N, long. 120°08'35" W; sec. 18, T 11 N, R 17 E); the place is in Strawberry Valley. Named on Pyramid Peak (1955) 7.5' quadrangle.

Strawberry [TUOLUMNE]: *settlement,* 10 miles northeast of Long Barn (lat. 38°11'50" N, long. 120°00'35" W). Named on Pinecrest (1979) and Strawberry (1979) 7.5' quadrangles. Postal authorities established Strawberry post office in 1949 (Frickstad, p. 217). Big Trees (1891) 30' quadrangle has the name "Parsons" at the place. Postal authorities established Parsons post office in 1891 and discontinued it in 1895; the name was for Edmond Parsons, who settled in Tuolumne County in 1856 and was a county supervisor (Salley, p. 167).

Strawberry Bar [NEVADA]: *locality,* nearly 3 miles northeast of North San Juan along Middle Yuba River on Nevada-Yuba county line (lat. 39°23'25" N, long. 121°03'40" W; near SE cor. sec. 27, T 18 N, R 8 E). Named on Camptonville (1948) 7.5' quadrangle.

Strawberry Creek [EL DORADO]: *stream,* flows 7.25 miles to South Fork American River 4 miles south of Pyramid Peak in Strawberry Valley (lat. 38°47'20" N, long. 120°09'10" W; near W line sec. 19, T 11 N, R 17 E). Named on Caples Lake (1979), Echo Lake (1955), and Pyramid Peak (1955) 7.5' quadrangles.

Strawberry Creek [MARIPOSA]: *stream,* flows 1.5 miles to Elevenmile Creek 9.5 miles southwest of Yosemite Village (lat. 37°38'10" N, long. 119°41'10" W; near NE cor. sec. 32, T 3 S, R 21 E). Named on Yosemite (1956) 15' quadrangle.

Strawberry Flat [EL DORADO]: *locality,* 5 miles northwest of Kyburz (lat. 38°49'45" N, long. 120°21' W; at E line sec. 1, T 11 N, R 14 E). Named on Robbs Peak (1952) 15' quadrangle. Water of Ice House Reservoir now covers the place.

Strawberry Flat [PLACER]: *area,* 7 miles north of Foresthill (lat. 39°07'15" N, long. 120°49'30" W; at W line sec. 26, T 15 N, R 10 E). Named on Foresthill (1949) 7.5' quadrangle. Whitney's (1873) map has the name for an inhabited place at the site.

Strawberry Lake: see **Pinecrest Lake** [TUOLUMNE].

Strawberry Peak [TUOLUMNE]: *peak,* 1.25 miles west of Strawberry (lat. 38°11'45" N, long. 120°01'55" W; near SE cor. sec. 18, T 4 N, R 18 E). Named on Strawberry (1979) 7.5' quadrangle.

Strawberry Valley [EL DORADO]: *valley,* 3.5 miles south of Pyramid Peak along South Fork American River (lat. 38°47'30" N, long. 120°09' W). Named on Pyramid Peak (1896) 30' quadrangle. According to Gudde (1949, p. 345), the name is from a Mr. Berry, who ran a travelers stop at the place, and from the straw that Berry used to stuff the mattresses that he provided for his customers.

Streeter Mountain [MARIPOSA]: *peak,* 5.5 miles east-southeast of Mariposa (lat. 37°26'50" N, long. 119°52'45" W; near S line sec. 34, T 5 S, R 19 E). Altitude 2553 feet. Named on Mariposa (1947) and Stumpfield Mountain (1947) 7.5' quadrangles. Called Cedar Mtn. on Mariposa (1912) 30' quadrangle.

String Canyon [EL DORADO]: *canyon,* drained by a stream that flows nearly 3 miles to Steely Fork Cosumnes River 9 miles southeast of Camino (lat. 38°37'45" N, long. 120°34'25" W; near SE cor. sec. 18, T 9 N, R 13 E). Named on Sly Park (1952) 7.5' quadrangle.

String Town: see **Gertrude**, under **Ahwanee** [MADERA].

Striped Rock [MARIPOSA]: *peak,* 6.5 miles south-southeast of Mariposa (lat. 37°23'50" N, long. 119°55'05" W; sec. 20, T 6 S, R 19 E). Altitude 2152 feet. Named on Mariposa (1947) 7.5' quadrangle.

Striped Rock Creek [MADERA-MARIPOSA]: *stream,* heads in Mariposa County and flows 11 miles to Chowchilla River 6.25 miles north-northeast of Raymond in Madera County (lat. 37°18'05" N, long. 119°51'45" W); the stream goes past Striped Rock. Named on Ben Hur (1947), Horsecamp Mountain (1947), and Mariposa (1947) 7.5' quadrangles.

Strong Diggings: see **Damascus** [PLACER].

Strychnine City: see **Brandy City** [SIERRA].

Stubblefield Canyon [TUOLUMNE]: *canyon,* drained by a stream that flows 9.5 miles to Rancheria Creek 8 miles south-southwest of Tower Peak (lat. 38°02'20" N, long. 119°37'10" W). Named on Tower Peak (1956) 15' quadrangle.

Studhorse Meadow [TUOLUMNE]: *locality,* 9

miles east-southeast of Pinecrest along Piute Creek (1) (lat. 38°08'45" N, long. 119° 50'40" W). Named on Pinecrest (1956) 15' quadrangle.

Studhorse Ravine [SIERRA]: *canyon,* drained by a stream that flows 1.25 miles to Canyon Creek 2.25 miles south-southeast of Mount Fillmore (lat. 39°41'50" N, long. 120°50'15" W). Named on Mount Fillmore (1951) 7.5' quadrangle.

Stump Canyon [NEVADA]: *canyon,* 0.5 mile long, opens into the canyon of Bear River 9.5 miles northeast of Chicago Park (lat. 39° 13'35" N, long. 120°49'15" W; sec. 26, T 16 N, R 10 E). Named on Dutch Flat (1950) 7.5' quadrangle.

Stumpfield Mountain [MARIPOSA]: *ridge,* north-trending, 2 miles long, 9.5 miles east-southeast of Mariposa (lat. 37°26'30" N, long. 119°48'10" W). Named on Stumpfield Mountain (1947) 7.5' quadrangle.

Stumps Bar [PLACER]: *locality,* 2.25 miles south of Michigan Bluff along North Fork of Middle Fork American River (lat. 39°00'35" N, long. 120°44'30" W; near SW cor. sec. 34, T 14 N, R 11 E). Named on Michigan Bluff (1952) 7.5' quadrangle.

Stump Spring [EL DORADO]: *spring,* less than 1 mile west of Old Iron Mountain (lat. 38°42'20" N, long. 120°24'15" W; sec. 22, T 10 N, R 14 E). Named on Stump Spring (1951) 7.5' quadrangle. The name is from the location of the spring in the stump of a tree (Beverly Cola, personal communication, 1985).

Stumpy Meadows [EL DORADO]: *area,* 9.5 miles north of Pollock Pines along Pilot Creek (1) (lat. 38°54' N, long. 120°35'30" W). Named on Saddle Mountain (1950) 15' quadrangle. Water of Stumpy Meadows Lake now covers the place.

Stumpy Meadows Lake [EL DORADO]: *lake,* behind a dam on Pilot Creek (1) 10 miles north of Pollock Pines (lat. 38°54'15" N, long. 120°36'10" W; sec. 11, T 12 N, R 12 E). Named on Devil Peak (1950, photorevised 1973) 7.5' quadrangle. United States Board on Geographic Names (1973, p. 3) gave the names "Lake Edson" and "Mark Edson Reservoir" as variants.

Sturdevant Ridge [EL DORADO]: *ridge,* west-southwest-trending, 3 miles long, 6 miles southeast of Camino (lat. 38°40'30" N, long. 120°35'45" W). Named on Sly Park (1952) 7.5' quadrangle.

Succor Flat [PLACER]: *area,* 7 miles north of Foresthill (lat. 39°07'15" N, long. 120°48'15" W; near W line sec. 25, T 15 N, R 10 E). Named on Foresthill (1949) 7.5' quadrangle. Colfax (1898) 30' quadrangle has the name for an inhabited place at the site—the inhabited place is called Sucker Flat on Whitney's (1873) map, but United States Board on Geographic Names (1933, p. 725) rejected this name.

Sucker Flat: see **Succor Flat** [PLACER].

Suckertown: see **Bridgeport** [MARIPOSA];

Dry Creek [AMADOR].

Sugar Bowl [PLACER]: *canyon,* drained by a stream that flows 1 mile to South Yuba River 1 mile southwest of Donner Pass (lat. 39°18'30" N, long. 120°20'25" W; sec. 20, T 17 N, R 15 E). Named on Norden (1955) 7.5' quadrangle.

Sugarbowl Dome: see Bunnell Point [MARIPOSA].

Sugar Loaf [PLACER]: *peak,* less than 0.25 mile northeast of Michigan Bluff (lat. 39°02'40" N, long. 120°44' W; near W line sec. 22, T 14 N, R 11 E). Named on Michigan Bluff (1952) 7.5' quadrangle.

Sugar Loaf: see Big Sugar Loaf, under China Mountain [EL DORADO]; Kolana Rock [TUOLUMNE]; Sugarloaf Mountain [NEVADA] (1); Sugarloaf Peak [AMADOR]; Sugarloaf Peak [NEVADA].

Sugarloaf [CALAVERAS]: *peak,* nearly 6 miles west-northwest of Valley Springs (lat. 38°13'20" N, long. 120°55'40" W; near NE cor. sec. 12, T 4 N, R 9 E). Altitude 390 feet. Named on Wallace (1962) 7.5' quadrangle.

Sugarloaf [EL DORADO]:
(1) *peak,* 12 miles northwest of Pollock Pines (lat. 38°52'55" N, long. 120°44'05" W; near S line sec. 15, T 12 N, R 11 E). Altitude 3419 feet. Named on Tunnel Hill (1950) 7.5' quadrangle.
(2) *peak,* less than 1 mile west of Kyburz (lat. 38°46'35" N, long. 120°18'25" W; on N line sec. 28, T 11 N, R 15 E). Named on Kyburz (1952) 7.5' quadrangle. Pyramid Peak (1896) 30' quadrangle has the form "Sugar Loaf" for the name.
(3) *peak,* 2.25 miles northeast of Latrobe (lat. 38°34'50" N, long. 120°56'55" W; near E line sec. 2, T 8 N, R 9 E). Named on Latrobe (1949) 7.5' quadrangle. Logan's (1938) map has the form "Sugar Loaf" for the name.

Sugarloaf [PLACER]:
(1) *peak,* 5 miles east-northeast of Rocklin (lat. 38°49'40" N, long. 121°09'10" W; at W line sec. 1, T 11 N, R 7 E). Named on Rocklin (1967) 7.5' quadrangle.
(2) *peak,* 5 miles east-southeast of Dutch Flat (lat. 39°10'20" N, long. 120°45'20" W; sec. 5, T 15 N, R 11 E). Altitude 4184 feet. Named on Dutch Flat (1950) 7.5' quadrangle.

Sugarloaf [SIERRA]:
(1) *peak,* 2.5 miles west-southwest of Mount Fillmore (lat. 39°42'55" N, long. 120°53'50" W; near N line sec. 6, T 21 N, R 10 E). Altitude 5818 feet. Named on La Porte (1951) 7.5' quadrangle.
(2) *peak,* 4.5 miles north-northwest of Goodyears Bar (lat. 39°36'15" N, long. 120°55'05" W; sec. 13, T 20 N, R 9 E). Altitude 5663 feet. Named on Goodyears Bar (1951) 7.5' quadrangle.

Sugarloaf [TUOLUMNE]: *peak,* 6.5 miles southeast of Tuolumne (lat. 37°53'50" N, long. 120°08'40" W; sec. 31, T 1 N, R 17 E). Alti-

tude 3880 feet. Named on Tuolumne (1948) 15' quadrangle.

Sugarloaf: see First Sugarloaf [PLACER]; Second Sugarloaf [PLACER].

Sugarloaf Hill [CALAVERAS]: *peak,* 2.25 miles south-southeast of Vallecito (lat. 38°03'20" N, long. 120°27'50" W; sec. 5, T 2 N, R 14 E). Altitude 2179 feet. Named on Columbia (1948) 7.5' quadrangle.

Sugarloaf Hill [NEVADA]: *peak,* 6.5 miles northwest of Pilot Peak (lat. 39°14'40" N, long. 121°15'35" W; sec, 14, T 16 N, R 6 E). Named on Smartville (1951) 7.5' quadrangle.

Sugarloaf Mountain [CALAVERAS]: *peak,* 6 miles southeast of Copperopolis (lat. 37°55'10" N, long. 120°33'45" W; near SE cor. sec. 20, T 1 N, R 13 E). Altitude 1072 feet. Named on Melones Dam (1962) 7.5' quadrangle.

Sugarloaf Mountain [NEVADA]:
(1) *peak,* less than 1 mile north of downtown Nevada City (lat. 39°16'25" N, long. 121°01' W; near SW cor. sec. 6, T 16 N, R 9 E). Named on Nevada City (1948) 7.5' quadrangle. Called Sugar Loaf on Smartsville (1895) 30' quadrangle. California Division of Highways' (1934) map has the name "Sugar Loaf Res." for a lake about 1 mile north of downtown Nevada City.
(2) *peak,* 3.25 miles north-northwest of Wolf (lat. 39°06'15" N, long. 121°09'30" W; near SE cor. sec. 35, T 15 N, R 7 E). Altitude 1514 feet. Named on Wolf (1949) 7.5' quadrangle.

Sugarloaf Peak [AMADOR]: *peak,* 3 miles southwest of Plymouth (lat. 38°26'45" N, long. 120°52'55" W; sec. 21, T 7 N, R 10 E). Altitude 1070 feet. Named on Irish Hill (1962) 7.5' quadrangle. Called Sugar Loaf on Jackson (1902) 30' quadrangle.

Sugarloaf Peak [NEVADA]: *peak,* 7.25 miles north of Nevada City (lat. 39°22'15" N, long. 121°00'30" W; sec. 6, T 17 N, R 9 E). Named on Nevada City (1948) 7.5' quadrangle. Called Chimney Hill on Whitney's (1873) map, and called Sugar Loaf on Smartsville(1895) 30' quadrangle.

Sugar Loaf Reservoir: see Sugarloaf Mountain [NEVADA] (1).

Sugar Loaves: see First Sugarloaf [PLACER].

Sugar Pine [MADERA]: *village,* 5 miles north of Yosemite Forks (lat. 37°26'30" N, long. 119°37'45" W; near W line sec. 1, T 6 S, R 21 E). Named on Bass Lake (1953) 15' quadrangle. Postal authorities established Sugar Pine post office in 1907 and discontinued it in 1934 (Frickstad, p. 86). Madera Sugar Pine Company built a town at the site in 1899 and 1900 (Clough, p. 47).

Sugarpine [TUOLUMNE]: *settlement,* 2.25 miles northeast of Twain Harte (lat. 38°03'35" N, long. 120°11'50" W; sec. 3, T 2 N, R 16 E). Named on Twain Harte (1979) 7.5' quadrangle. Postal authorities established Sugar Pine post office in 1866 and discontinued it in 1900; the place was the site of Sugar Pine Lumber Company's sawmill (Salley, p. 215). They established Raspberry post office 15 miles east of Sugar Pine in 1880 and discontinued it in 1881 (Salley, p. 181).

Sugar Pine Canyon [EL DORADO]: *canyon*, drained by a stream that flows 1.5 miles to Cat Creek 5.5 miles east of Caldor (lat. 38°35'35" N, long. 120°19'45" W; near NW cor. sec. 33, T 9 N, R 15 E). Named on Peddler Hill (1951) 7.5' quadrangle.

Sugar Pine Canyon [PLACER]: *canyon*, drained by a stream that flows 3 miles to Brimstone Creek 5.5 miles north-east of Foresthill (lat. 39°05'30" N, long. 120°45'50" W; near N line sec. 5, T 14 N, R 11 E). Named on Foresthill (1949) and Michigan Bluff (1952) 7.5' quadrangles.

Sugar Pine Creek [AMADOR]: *stream*, flows nearly 2 miles to Lower Bear River Reservoir 8 miles west of Mokelumne Peak (lat. 38°32'45" N, long. 120°14'20" W; sec. 17, T 8 N, R 16 E). Named on Bear River Reservoir (1979) 7.5' quadrangle.

Sugar Pine Creek [EL DORADO]: *stream*, flows 2.5 miles to Silver Creek 6 miles north-northeast of Pollock Pines (lat. 38°50'25" N, long. 120°32'10" W; at E line sec. 32, T 12 N, R 13 E). Named on Pollock Pines (1950) 7.5' quadrangle.

Sugarpine Creek [TUOLUMNE]: *stream*, flows 6.5 miles to North Fork Tuolumne River 4.5 miles east-northeast of Twain Harte (lat. 38°03'40" N, long. 120°09'05" W; sec. 6, T 2 N, R 17 E). Named on Hull Creek (1979), Strawberry (1979), and Twain Harte (1979) 7.5' quadrangles.

Sugarpine Flat: see **Sugar Pine Point** [PLACER] (2).

Sugar Pine Gap [TUOLUMNE]: *pass*, 8 miles northwest of Crandall Peak (lat. 38°14'50" N, long. 120°14'55" W; sec. 31, T 5 N, R 16 E). Named on Crandall Peak (1979) 7.5' quadrangle.

Sugar Pine Mill [PLACER]: *locality*, 7 miles north-northeast of Foresthill along Brimstone Creek (lat. 39°06'30" N, long. 120°45'40" W). Named on Colfax (1898) 30' quadrangle.

Sugar Pine Mountain [PLACER]: *ridge*, east-southeast-trending, 3 miles long, 6.5 miles north of Auburn (lat. 38°59'35" N, long. 121°03'15" W). Named on Auburn (1953) and Lake Combie (1949) 7.5' quadrangles.

Sugar Pine Mountain: see **Little Sugar Pine Mountain** [EL DORADO].

Sugar Pine Point [EL DORADO]: *promontory*, 1.5 miles north-northeast of the town of Meeks Bay along Lake Tahoe (lat. 39°03'40" N, long. 120°06'45" W; sec. 16, T 14 N, R 17 E). Named on Meeks Bay (1955) 7.5' quadrangle. United States Board on Geographic Names (1963a, p. 7) rejected the form "Sugarpine Point" for the name.

Sugar Pine Point [PLACER]:

(1) *relief feature*, 3.5 miles northeast of Dutch Flat (lat. 39°14'05" N, long. 120°46'50" W; sec. 19, T 16 N, R 11 E). Named on Dutch Flat (1950) 7.5' quadrangle.

(2) *peak*, 6.5 miles north-north-west of Duncan Peak (lat. 39°14'45" N, long. 120°32'40" W; near SW cor. sec. 17, T 16 N, R 13 E). Altitude 6322 feet. Named on Duncan Peak (1952) 7.5' quadrangle. Colfax (1898) 30' quadrangle shows Sugarpine Flat at or near present Sugar Pine Point (2).

Sugar Spring [CALAVERAS]: *spring*, less than 1 mile east-southeast of Devils Nose (lat. 38°27'25" N, long. 120°24'25" W; sec. 14, T 7 N, R 14 E). Named on Devils Nose (1979) 7.5' quadrangle.

Suicide Ridge [TUOLUMNE]: *ridge*, south-southwest-trending, 3 miles long, 4.5 miles west-southwest of Matterhorn Peak (lat. 38°04'35" N, long. 119°27'45" W). Named on Matterhorn Peak (1956) 15' quadrangle.

Sullivan: see **Dan Sullivan Gulch** [MARIPOSA].

Sullivan Creek [TUOLUMNE]: *stream*, flows 20 miles to Woods Creek nearly 7 miles south-southwest of Sonora (lat. 37°53'25" N, long. 120°25'15" W; at S line sec. 34, T 1 N, R 14 E). Named on Columbia SE (1948), Sonora (1948), Standard (1948), and Twain Harte (1979) 7.5' quadrangles. The name commemorates John Sullivan, an Irishman who discovered gold in the canyon in 1848; the mining camp there was called Sullivan's Diggings (Buffum, p. 126).

Sullivan's Diggings: see **Sullivan Creek** [TUOLUMNE].

Sulphur Creek [SIERRA]: *stream*, flows 5 miles to Plumas County 11 miles north-northeast of Sierra City (lat. 39°42'25" N, long. 120°31'50" W; at W line sec. 4, T 21 N, R 13 E). Named on Calpine (1981) and Clio (1981) 7.5' quadrangles. United States Board on Geographic Names (1960a, p. 17) rejected the name "Mohawk Creek" for the stream.

Sulphur Spring: see **Campbell Hot Springs** [SIERRA].

Summerdale [MARIPOSA]: *locality*, 0.25 mile north of Happy Camp (present Fish Camp) (lat. 37°28'50" N, long. 119°38'15" W; sec. 23, T 5 S, R 21 E). Named on Mariposa (1912) 30' quadrangle. Postal authorities established Summerdale post office in 1893 and discontinued it in 1908; the place was a summer-vacation camp (Salley, p. 215).

Summerdale Campground [MARIPOSA]: *locality*, less than 1 mile north of Fish Camp (lat. 37°29'20" N, long. 119°38'10" W; sec. 23, T 5 S, R 21 E). Named on Bass Lake (1953) 15' quadrangle.

Summersville: see **Soulsbyville** [TUOLUMNE].

Summit Campground [MARIPOSA]: *locality*, 3.25 miles southwest of Wawona (lat. 37°30'20" N, long. 119°42' W; sec. 8, T 5 S,

R 21 E). Named on Yosemite (1956) 15' quadrangle.

Summit City [NEVADA]: *locality,* 3.5 miles southeast of English Mountain (lat. 39°24'35" N, long. 120°30'10" W; sec. 22, T 18 N, R 13 E). Site named on English Mountain (1983) 7.5' quadrangle. Postal authorities established Meadow Lake post office at the place in 1866 and discontinued it in 1869; the community also was called Excelsior (Salley, p. 137). A place called Hudsonville was situated across Meadow Lake from Summit City (Fatout, p. 48).

Summit Creek [TUOLUMNE]: *stream,* flows 10 miles to join Kennedy Creek and form Middle Fork Stanislaus River 5.5 miles west-southwest of Sonora Pass (lat. 38°17'40" N, long. 119°43'45" W; sec. 12, T 5 N, R 20 E). Named on Sonora Pass (1956) and Tower Peak (1956) 15' quadrangles. Called Relief Creek on Dardanelles (1898) 30' quadrangle, which also applies the name "Relief Creek" to present Middle Fork Stanislaus River on its course through present Kennedy Meadow (1), and has the name "East Fork" for present Kennedy Creek.

Summit Creek: see **Cold Creek** [NEVADA-PLACER].

Summit Hill [EL DORADO]: *peak,* 4 miles north of Greenwood (lat. 38°57'10" N, long. 120°55'25" W; sec. 25, T 13 N, R 9 E). Altitude 2168 feet. Named on Greenwood (1949) 7.5' quadrangle.

Summit House [MADERA]: *locality,* 6 miles northeast of Raymond (lat. 37°16'50" N, long. 119°49'30" W; sec. 31, T 7 S, R 20 E). Named on Horsecamp Mountain (1947) 7.5' quadrangle.

Summit House [SIERRA]: *locality,* 8 miles east-northeast of Sierra City along North Fork Yuba River (present North Yuba River) (lat. 39°37' N, long. 120°30'30" W). Named on Downieville (1897) 30' quadrangle.

Summit Inn [MARIPOSA]: *locality,* nearly 2 miles south-southwest of Midpines (lat. 37°31'15" N, long. 119°56'10" W; near SW cor. sec. 6, T 5 S, R 19 E). Named on Feliciana Mountain (1947) 7.5' quadrangle.

Summit Lake [MADERA]: *lake,* 600 feet long, 8 miles north-northwest of Devils Postpile (lat. 37°44' N, long. 119°08'35" W; sec. 31, T 2 S, R 26 E). Named on Devils Postpile (1953) 15' quadrangle.

Summit Lake [NEVADA]: *lake,* 850 feet long, 2.25 miles north of Donner Pass (lat. 39°21' N, long. 120°19'25" W; sec. 4, T 17 N, R 15 E). Named on Norden (1955) 7.5' quadrangle.

Summit Lake [SIERRA]: *lake,* 350 feet long, 7 miles north-northwest of Sierra City (lat. 39°39'40" N, long. 120°40'30" W; at S line sec. 19, T 21 N, R 12 E). Named on Gold Lake (1981) 7.5' quadrangle.

Summit Lake [TUOLUMNE]: *lake,* 600 feet long, 4.5 miles south-southeast of Tioga Pass

(lat. 37°51'15" N, long. 119°12'50" W). Named on Mono Craters (1953) 15' quadrangle.

Summit Level Ridge [CALAVERAS]: *ridge,* generally southwest- to west-trending, 11 miles long, extends from Cottage Springs to a point 3.5 miles south-southwest of Blue Mountain. Named on Boards Crossing (1979), Dorrington (1979), and Fort Mountain (1979) 7.5' quadrangles.

Summit Meadow [MADERA]:
(1) *area,* 5.5 miles east-northeast of Shuteye Peak (lat. 37°22'30" N, long. 119°19'45" W; sec. 27, T 6 S, R 24 E). Named on Shuteye Peak (1953) 15' quadrangle.
(2) *area,* nearly 3 miles southwest of Devils Postpile (lat. 37°36' N, long. 119°07'15" W). Named on Devils Postpile (1953) 15' quadrangle.

Summit Meadow [TUOLUMNE]: *area,* 4.5 miles west-northwest of Tower Peak (lat. 38°10'35" N, long. 119°37' W). Named on Tower Peak (1956) 15' quadrangle.

Summit Ridge [TUOLUMNE]: *ridge,* south-southwest-trending, 0.5 mile long, 4.25 miles east-northeast of Twain Harte (lat. 38°01'30" N, long. 120°09'15" W). Named on Twain Harte (1979) 7.5' quadrangle.

Summit Soda Springs: see **Soda Springs** [PLACER].

Summit Station: see **Donner Pass** [NEVADA-PLACER].

Summit Valley [NEVADA-PLACER]: *valley,* 2 miles west of Donner Pass along South Yuba River on Nevada-Placer county line (lat. 39°18'55" N, long. 120°21'45" W). Named on Norden (1955) 7.5' quadrangle. Water of Lake Van Norden now covers most of the valley. Morgan (p. 425) identified present Summit Valley as the place called Meadow-Vale on Jefferson's (1849) map, and noted that it was known as Yuba Valley in 1846.

Summit Valley: see **Lake Van Norden** [NEVADA-PLACER]; **Soda Springs** [NEVADA].

Sunbeam: see **Tallac** [EL DORADO].

Sunday Ridge [EL DORADO]: *ridge,* west-trending, 0.5 mile long, 9.5 miles southeast of Camino (lat. 38°39'10" N, long. 120°32'20" W). Named on Sly Park (1952) 7.5' quadrangle.

Sunflower Hill [PLACER]: *peak,* 9.5 miles west-southwest of Granite Chief (lat. 39°10'10" N, long. 120°27'15" W; sec. 7, T 15 N, R 14 E). Altitude 7045 feet. Named on Royal Gorge (1953) 7.5' quadrangle.

Sunnybrook [AMADOR]: *locality,* 3 miles east of Ione along Mountain Spring Creek (lat. 38°20'35" N, long. 120°52'30" W; sec. 28, T 6 N, R 10 E). Named on Ione (1962) and Jackson (1962) 7.5' quadrangles. Postal authorities established Vogans post office at the place in 1888 and discontinued it in 1889; the name was from the operator of Mountain Spring

House, a travelers stop at present Sunnybrook (Salley, p. 233). They established Ranlett post office 0.5 mile west of present Sunnybrook at Newton mine in 1895 and discontinued it in 1905; the name was for Arthur G. Ranlett, first postmaster (Andrews, p. 47; Salley, p. 181).

Sunnyside [PLACER]: *settlement,* 2 miles south-southwest of Tahoe City along Lake Tahoe (lat. 39°08'30" N, long. 120°09'15" W). Named on Tahoe City (1955) 7.5' quadrangle. The name is from a resort that Mrs. Hayes developed in the early 1880's (Lekisch, p. 115).

Sunnyside Creek [SIERRA]: *stream,* flows 2.25 miles to Lavezzola Creek nearly 6 miles east-southeast of Mount Fillmore (lat. 39°41'45" N, long. 120°45'05" W; sec. 9, T 21 N, R 11 E); the stream heads near Sunnyside Meadow. Named on Mount Fillmore (1951) 7.5' quadrangle.

Sunnyside Meadow [SIERRA]: *area,* 4.5 miles east-southeast of Mount Fillmore (lat. 39°41'55" N, long. 120°46'45" W; on E line sec. 7, T 21 N, R 11 E); the stream is near the head of Sunnyside Creek. Named on Mount Fillmore (1951) 7.5' quadrangle.

Sunny South [PLACER]: *locality,* 4 miles north-northeast of Michigan Bluff (lat. 39°05'45" N, long. 120°42'40" W; near SW cor. sec. 35, T 15 N, R 11 E). Site named on Michigan Bluff (1952) 7.5' quadrangle. The place was in a sheltered nook that escaped the heavy winter snows of the surrounding neighborhood (Hoover, Rensch, and Rensch, p. 276).

Sunrise Creek [SIERRA]: *stream,* flows 2.5 miles to the State of Nevada 5 miles east-southeast of Crystal Peak (lat. 39°31'25" N, long. 120°00'05" W; at E line sec. 7, T 19 N, R 18 E). Named on Dog Valley (1981) 7.5' quadrangle.

Sunrise Creek [MARIPOSA]: *stream,* flows 5.5 miles to Merced River 4 miles east-southeast of Yosemite Village in Little Yosemite Valley (lat. 37°44' N, long. 119°30'45" W); the stream heads at the south end of Sunrise Mountain. Named on Merced Peak (1953), Tuolumne Meadows (1956), and Yosemite (1956) 15' quadrangles.

Sunrise Lakes [MARIPOSA]: *lakes,* largest 1100 feet long, 4 miles southwest of Cathedral Peak (lat. 37°48'20" N, long. 119°26'45" W; sec. 33, 34, T 1 S, R 23 E); the lakes are north of Sunrise Mountain. Named on Tuolumne Meadows (1956) 15' quadrangle.

Sunrise Mountain [MARIPOSA]: *ridge,* south-trending, 2.5 miles long, 4.5 miles south-southwest of Cathedral Peak (lat. 37°47'15" N, long. 119°26'30" W). Named on Tuolumne Meadows (1956) 15' quadrangle.

Sun Rock [EL DORADO]: *peak,* nearly 4 miles east of Robbs Peak (lat. 38°55'35" N, long. 120°20' W; sec. 31, T 13 N, R 15 E). Named on Loon Lake (1952) 7.5' quadrangle.

Sunset Camp [TUOLUMNE]: *locality,* 5.5

miles south-southwest of Mather (lat. 37°48'25" N, long. 119°53'45" W; sec. 33, T 1 S, R 19 E). Named on Lake Eleanor (1956) 15' quadrangle.

Sunset View [NEVADA]: *settlement,* 2.25 miles west-northwest of Grass Valley (lat. 39°13'45" N, long. 121°05'50" W; near S line sec. 20, T 16 N, R 8 E). Named on Grass Valley (1949) 7.5' quadrangle.

Sunset View Reservoir [NEVADA]: *lake,* 150 feet long, 2 miles west-northwest of Grass Valley (lat. 39°13'50" N, long. 121°05'35" W; near E line sec. 20, T 16 N, R 8 E); the lake is near the northeast end of Sunset View. Named on Grass Valley (1949) 7.5' quadrangle.

Sunshine Camp [TUOLUMNE]: *settlement,* 5.5 miles east of Sonora (lat. 37°59'15" N, long. 120°16'55" W; sec. 36, T 2 N, R 15 E). Named on Sonora (1948) 15' quadrangle.

Sunshine Valley [NEVADA]: *area,* nearly 2 miles west-northwest of Chicago Park (lat. 39°09'20" N, long. 120°59'40" W; sec. 17, T 15 N, R 9 E). Named on Chicago Park (1949) 7.5' quadrangle.

Superior Lake [MADERA]: *lake,* 850 feet long, 3.25 miles west of Devils Postpile (lat. 37°38'05" N, long. 119°08'25" W). Named on Devils Postpile (1953) 15' quadrangle.

Surprise Lake [TUOLUMNE]: *lake,* 800 feet long, 7.5 miles southwest of Matterhorn Peak (lat. 38°01'20" N, long. 119°29'15" W). Named on Matterhorn Peak (1956) 15' quadrangle.

Susie Lake [EL DORADO]: *lake,* 0.5 mile long, 5 miles south-southeast of Phipps Peak (lat. 38°52'55" N, long. 120°07'35" W). Named on Emerald Bay (1955) and Rockbound Valley (1955) 7.5' quadrangles.

Sutter: see **Sutter Creek** [AMADOR] (2).

Sutter Creek [AMADOR]:

(1) *stream,* flows 32 miles to Dry Creek 3.25 miles west of Ione (lat. 38°21'35" N, long. 120°59'30" W). Named on Amador City (1962), Ione (1962), Jackson (1962), Pine Grove (1948), and West Point (1948) 7.5' quadrangles. John A. Sutter came to mine at the stream in 1848 (Bancroft, 1888, p. 77). South Branch, which enters from the southeast near Volcano, is 7.25 miles long and is named on Pine Grove (1948) and West Point (1948) 7.5' quadrangles.

(2) *town,* 6.5 miles south-southeast of Plymouth (lat. 38°23'35" N, long. 120°48'05" W; around NE cor. sec. 7, T 6 N, R 11 E); the town is along Sutter Creek (1). Named on Amador City (1962) 7.5' quadrangle. Postal authorities established Sutter Creek post office in 1852 (Frickstad, p. 6), and the town incorporated in 1913. The town was named for the stream; it also was called Sutter and Suttersville in the early 1850's (Gudde, 1975, p. 342).

Sutter Hill [AMADOR]: *village,* 7.25 miles south-southeast of Plymouth (lat. 38°22'45"

N, long. 120°48'05" W; near NE cor. sec. 18, T 6 N, R 11 E). Named on Amador City (1962) 7.5' quadrangle.

Sutters Mill [EL DORADO]: *locality,* along South Fork American River at Coloma (lat. 38°48'10" N, long. 120°53'30" W; sec. 17, T 11 N, R 10 E). Site named on Coloma (1949) 7.5' quadrangle. James Marshall's discovery of gold in the mill race set off the California gold rush.

Suttersville: see **Sutter Creek** [AMADOR] (2).

Swamp Creek [CALAVERAS]: *stream,* flows 5 miles to South Fork Mokelumne River 2 miles southeast of Blue Mountain (lat. 38°19'20" N, long. 120°20'20" W; near N line sec. 5, T 5 N, R 15 E). Named on Dorrington (1979) 7.5' quadrangle.

Swamp Lake [MADERA]: *lake,* 500 feet long, 7 miles south-southwest of Merced Peak (lat. 37°32'50" N, long. 119°27'15" W). Named on Merced Peak (1953) 15' quadrangle.

Swamp Lake [TUOLUMNE]:
(1) *lake,* 650 feet long, 2.5 miles west-north-west of Liberty Hill (lat. 38°22'35" N, long. 120°08'35" W). Named on Calaveras Dome (1979) 7.5' quadrangle.
(2) *lake,* 1200 feet long, 5 miles north-north-east of Mather (lat. 37° 57' N, long. 119°49'40" W; at NW cor. sec. 18, T 1 N, R 20 E). Named on Lake Eleanor (1956) 15' quadrangle.

Swan Lake Jr. [PLACER]: *lake,* 400 feet long, 3.5 miles south of Colfax (lat. 39°03' N, long. 120°57'45" W; sec. 22, T 14 N, R 9 E). Named on Colfax (1949) 7.5' quadrangle.

Sweeneys: see **Sweeneys Crossing** [EL DORADO].

Sweeneys Crossing [EL DORADO]: *locality,* 6.5 miles south-southeast of Camino along North Fork Cosumnes River (lat. 38°39'10" N, long. 120°37'25" W; near N line sec. 11, T 9 N, R 12 E). Named on Sly Park (1952) 7.5' quadrangle. Called Sweeneys on Placerville (1893) 30' quadrangle.

Sweetland [NEVADA]: *locality,* 2 miles south-southwest of North San Juan (lat. 39°20'35" N, long. 121°07'10" W; at S line sec. 7, T 17 N, R 8 E). Named on Nevada City (1948) 7.5' quadrangle. Postal authorities established Sweetland post office in 1857 and discontinued it in 1905 (Frickstad, p. 115). The name commemorates the Sweetland brothers, who started mining at the place in 1850 (Gudde, 1975, p. 343).

Sweetland Creek [NEVADA]: *stream,* flows 3.5 miles to Yuba River 3 miles north-northeast of French Corral (lat. 39°21' N, long. 121°08'35" W; sec. 12, T 17 N, R 7 E); the stream goes past Sweetland. Named on French Corral (1948) and Nevada City (1948) 7.5' quadrangles.

Sweetwater [MARIPOSA]: *locality,* 9 miles southwest of El Portal (lat. 37°34'20" N, long. 119°52'40" W; sec. 21, T 4 S, R 19 E); the

place is near the head of Sweetwater Creek. Named on Yosemite (1909) 30' quadrangle.

Sweet Water Campground [MADERA]: *locality,* 4.5 miles east of Shuteye Peak along Chiquito Creek (lat. 37°21'30" N, long. 119° 20'40" W; near E line sec. 33, T 6 S, R 24 E). Named on Shuteye Peak (1953) 15' quadrangle.

Sweetwater Creek [AMADOR]: *stream,* flows 2.25 miles to Tiger Creek 5.5 miles southwest of Hams Station (lat. 38°29'15" N, long. 120°26'40" W; near W line sec. 4, T 7 N, R 14 E). Named on Caldor (1951) and Devils Nose (1979) 7.5' quadrangles.

Sweetwater Creek [EL DORADO]: *stream,* flows 7.5 miles to South Fork American River nearly 6 miles south-southwest of the village of Pilot Hill near the site of Salmon Falls (2) (lat. 38°45'25" N, long. 121°03'30" W; sec. 35, T 11 N, R 8 E). Named on Auburn (1954) 15' quadrangle, and on Clarksville (1953) and Shingle Springs (1949) 7.5' quadrangles. The creek now joins South Fork in Folsom Lake.

Sweetwater Creek [MARIPOSA]: *stream,* flows 6.25 miles to Merced River 8 miles west-southwest of El Portal (lat. 37°38'15" N, long. 119°55'30" W); the stream heads near Sweetwater Point. Named on Feliciana Mountain (1947) and Kinsley (1947) 7.5' quadrangles.

Sweetwater Point [MARIPOSA]: *peak,* 2.5 miles northeast of Midpines (lat. 37°34'10" N, long. 119°53'05" W; sec. 20, T 4 S, R 10 E); the peak is near the head of Sweetwater Creek. Altitude 4615 feet. Named on Feliciana Mountain (1947) 7.6' quadrangle.

Sweetwater Ridge [MARIPOSA]: *ridge,* northwest-trending, 3.5 miles long, 8 miles west-southwest of El Portal (lat. 37°37'15" N, long. 119°54'45" W); the ridge is west of Sweetwater Creek. Named on El Portal (1947) 15' quadrangle.

Swiss Ranch [CALAVERAS]: *locality,* 6.5 miles southwest of Blue Mountain along Jesus Maria Creek (lat. 38°16'30" N, long. 120°27'30" W). Named on Big Trees (1891) 30' quadrangle.

Swetts Bar: see **Indian Bar** [TUOLUMNE].

Swift: see **Flonellis** [EL DORADO].

Switch [PLACER]: *locality,* 0.5 mile east of Emigrant Gap (1) along Southern Pacific Railroad (lat. 39°18'10" N, long. 120°39'10" W). Named on Colfax (1898) 30' quadrangle.

Swortzels Camp [MADERA]: *locality,* 5.5 miles north of Shuteye Peak (lat. 37°26' N, long. 119°24'45" W; near E line sec. 2, T 6 S, R 23 E). Named on Shuteye Peak (1953) 15' quadrangle.

Sylvan Lodge [TUOLUMNE]: *locality,* 1.5 miles west-southwest of Long Barn (lat. 38°05' N, long. 120°09'20" W; near E line sec. 25, T 3 N, R 16 E). Named on Long Barn (1956) 15' quadrangle.

Sylvia: see **Lake Sylvia** [EL DORADO].

— T —

Tabeaud Reservoir: see **Lake Tabeaud** [AMADOR].

Table Lake [TUOLUMNE]: *lake,* 1700 feet long, 9 miles north-northeast of White Wolf (lat. 37°59' N, long. 119°33'45" W). Named on Hetch Hetchy Reservoir (1956) 15' quadrangle.

Table Mountain [CALAVERAS-TUOL-UMNE]: *ridge,* on Calaveras-Tuolumne county line, mainly in Tuolumne County; extends along Stanislaus River for 28 miles from a point northeast of Murphys to the entrance of the river into Stanislaus County 10 miles south of Copperopolis. Named on Columbia (1948), Keystone (1962), Knights Ferry (1962), Melones Dam (1962), Murphys (1948), and Sonora (1948) 7.5' quadrangles. The feature also is called Stanislaus Mesa (Gudde, 1975, p. 344).

Table Mountain: see **Little Table Mountain** [MADERA].

Table Mountain [MARIPOSA]: *peak,* 16 miles south of the settlement of Catheys Valley (lat. 37°11'35" N, long. 120°03'10" W; near E line sec. 36, T 8 S, R 17 E). Named on Raynor Creek (1961) 7.5' quadrangle.

Table Mountain [SIERRA]: *ridge,* west-trending, 0.5 mile long, 3.5 miles south-southwest of Downieville (lat. 39°30'40" N, long. 120° 50'50" W; near SW cor. sec. 15, T 19 N, R 10 E). Named on Downieville (1951) 7.5' quadrangle.

Table Rock [EL DORADO]: *ridge,* southwest-trending, 0.5 mile long, 5 miles north of Kyburz (lat. 38°50'45" N, long. 120°17'15" W; sec. 34, T 12 N, R 15 E). Named on Kyburz (1952) 7.5' quadrangle.

Table Rock [SIERRA]: *peak,* 2.5 miles southwest of Mount Fillmore (lat. 39°42'15" N, long. 120°52'50" W; near S line sec. 5, T 21 N, R 10 E). Altitude 6908 feet. Named on La Porte (1951) 7.5' quadrangle.

Table Rock: see **Howland Flat** [SIERRA]; **Little Table Rock** [SIERRA].

Tadpole Campground [PLACER]: *locality,* 2.5 miles northwest of Duncan Peak (lat. 39°11'05" N, long. 120°32'10" W; sec. 4, T 15 N, R 13 E); the place is near the head of Tadpole Creek. Named on Duncan Peak (1952) 7.5' quadrangle. Colfax (1938) 30' quadrangle shows Tadpole Spring at present Tadpole Campground.

Tadpole Canyon: see **Tadpole Creek** [PLACER].

Tadpole Creek [PLACER]: *stream,* flows nearly 3 miles to North Fork American River 5 miles northwest of Duncan Peak (lat. 39° 12'50" N, long. 120°34'05" W; near NE cor. sec. 36, T 16 N, R 12 E). Named on Duncan Peak (1952) 7.5' quadrangle. Colfax (1898) 30' quadrangle has the name "Tadpole Canyon" for the canyon of the stream.

Tadpole Spring: see **Tadpole Campground** [PLACER].

Taft Point [MARIPOSA]: *promontory,* 2.5 miles south-southwest of Yosemite Village on the south side of Yosemite Valley (lat. 37° 42'45" N, long. 119°36'15" W). Named on Yosemite (1956) 15' quadrangle. R.B. Marshall of United States Geological Survey named the feature for President William Howard Taft (United States Board on Geographic Names, 1934, p. 24).

Taho: see **Tallac** [EL DORADO].

Tahoe: see **Lake Tahoe** [EL DORADO-PLACER]; **Tahoe City** [PLACER].

Tahoe City [PLACER]: town, 14 miles southeast of Donner Pass along Lake Tahoe (lat. 39°10'15" N, long. 120°08'25" W; sec. 6, 7, T 15 N, R 17 E). Named on Tahoe City (1955) 7.5' quadrangle. Called Tahoe on Truckee (1940) 30' quadrangle, but United States Board on Geographic Names (1954, p. 4) rejected this name for the place. Postal authorities established Tahoe post office in 1871, discontinued it for a time in 1896, and changed the name to Tahoe City in 1949 (Frickstad, p. 122). The town site was surveyed in 1863, and William Pomin built Tahoe House there in 1864 (Hanna, p. 324).

Tahoe House: see **Tahoe City** [PLACER].

Tahoe Keys: see **Tahoe Valley** [EL DORADO].

Tahoe Mountain [EL DORADO]: *ridge,* south-to east-trending, 2 miles long, 3.5 miles east of Mount Tallac (lat. 38°54'30" N, long. 120°01'55" W). Named on Emerald Bay (1955) 7.5' quadrangle.

Tahoe Paradise: see **Meyers** [EL DORADO].

Tahoe Pines [PLACER]: *settlement,* 1 mile north of Homewood along Lake Tahoe (lat. 39°06'15" N, long. 120°09'45" W; sec. 36, T 15 N, R 16 E). Named on Homewood (1955) 7.5' quadrangle. Postal authorities established Tahoe Pines post office in 1912 and discontinued it in 1959 (Salley, p. 218). Messers. Ferguson and Breuner started the settlement in 1909 and named it for the large number of ponderosa pine trees there (Hanna, p. 324).

Tahoe Tavern [PLACER]: *locality,* less than 1 mile south of Tahoe City along Lake Tahoe (lat. 39°09'40" N, long. 120°08'30" W; sec. 7, T 15 N, R 17 E). Named on Tahoe (1955) 15' quadrangle.

Tahoe Valley [EL DORADO]: *district,* 5 miles east of Mount Tallac in South Lake Tahoe (lat. 38°54'50" N, long. 120°00'10" W). Named on Emerald Bay (1955) and South Lake Tahoe (1955, photorevised 1969 and 1974) 7.5' quadrangles. Postal authorities established Tahoe Valley post office in 1940 (Salley, p. 218). They established Tahoe Keys post office at a marina located 2 miles north of Tahoe Valley post office in 1959 and discontinued it in 1962 (Salley, p. 218). California Division of Highways' (1934) map shows a place called Mays located in present Tahoe Valley district (near SE cor. sec. 5, T 12 N, R 18 E).

Tahoe Vista [PLACER]: *settlement,* 1.5 miles west of Kings Beach along Lake Tahoe (lat. 39°14'25" N, long. 120°03' W; sec. 13, 14, T 16 N, R 17 E). Named on Kings Beach (1955) 7.5' quadrangle. Postal authorities established Tahoe Vista post office in 1911 (Frickstad, p. 122).

Tahoma [PLACER]: *town,* 2 miles southeast of Homewood along Lake Tahoe at El Dorado-Placer county line (lat. 39°04'10" N, long. 120°07'45" W; near SW cor. sec. 8, T 14 N, R 17 E). Named on Homewood (1955) and Meeks Bay (1955) 7.5' quadrangles. Truckee (1940) 30' quadrangle shows Chambers Lodge at the site. Postal authorities established Tahoma post office in 1946 (Frickstad, p. 122).

Tailings Gulch [MARIPOSA]: *canyon,* less than 1 mile long, 5 miles north-northeast of the settlement of Catheys Valley on upper reaches of Sand Creek (lat. 37°29'40" N, long. 120°02'25" W). Named on Catheys Valley (1962) 7.5' quadrangle.

Talbot [MADERA]: *locality,* 9 miles east of Fairmead along Southern Pacific Railroad (lat. 37°04'30" N, long. 120°11'45" W; sec. 8, T 10 S, R 18 E). Named on Kismet (1920) 7.5' quadrangle.

Talbot Campground [PLACER]: *locality,* 4.5 miles west of Granite Chief along Middle Fork American River (lat. 39°11'15" N, long. 120°22'20" W; near E line sec. 2, T 15 N, R 14 E); the place is at the mouth of Talbot Creek. Named on Granite Chief (1953) 7.5' quadrangle.

Talbot Creek [PLACER]: *stream,* flows 2.5 miles to Middle Fork American River 4.5 miles west of Granite Chief (lat. 39°11'15" N, long. 120°22'20" W; near E line sec. 2, T 15 N, R 14 E). Named on Granite Chief (1953) 7.5' quadrangle.

Talking Mountain [EL DORADO]: *peak,* 2.5 miles west-northwest of Echo Summit (lat. 38°50' N, long. 120°04'05" W; sec. 2, T 11 N, R 17 E). Altitude 8824 feet. Named on Echo Lake (1955) 7.5' quadrangle.

Tallac [EL DORADO]: *locality,* 3.25 miles northeast of Mount Tallac along Lake Tahoe (lat. 38°56'20" N, long. 120°03'30" W). Named on Pyramid Peak (1896) 30' quadrangle. Postal authorities established Lake Valley post office in 1861, changed the name to Taho in 1863, to Tallac in 1870, back to Lake Valley in 1871, and discontinued the post office in 1895; they established Tallac post office again in 1875, moved it 0.5 mile east in 1883, moved it 0.5 mile west in 1888, and discontinued it in 1927 (Salley, p. 116, 217, 218). Bancroft's (1864) map shows a locality called Lake Valley situated just south of Lake Tahoe about half way between Yanks and California-Nevada State line. Postal authorities established Sunbeam post office 9 miles north

of Tallac in 1888 and discontinued it in 1893 (Salley, p. 215).

Tallac: see **Mount Tallac** [EL DORADO].

Tallac Creek [EL DORADO]: *stream,* flows 3.5 miles to Lake Tahoe 3.25 miles northeast of Mount Tallac (lat. 38°56'25" N, long, 120° 03'30" W; near W line sec. 25, T 13 N, R 17 E); the stream heads near Mount Tallac. Named on Emerald Bay (1955) 7.5' quadrangle.

Tallac Lake [EL DORADO]: *lake,* 400 feet long, nearly 1 mile north-northwest of Mount Tallac (lat. 38°54'45" N, long. 120°06'40" W). Named on Emerald Bay (1955) 7.5' quadrangle.

Tallac Village [EL DORADO]: *district,* 4.25 miles east-northeast of Mount Tallac in South Lake Tahoe (lat. 38°55'15" N, long. 120°01'15" W; near W line sec. 5, T 12 N, R 18 E). Named on Emerald Bay (1955) 7.5' quadrangle.

Tallant Lake: see **Upper Tallant Lake,** under **Stony Ridge Lake** [EL DORADO].

Tallulah Lake [TUOLUMNE]: *lake,* 1000 feet long, nearly 6 miles southwest of Matterhorn Peak (lat. 38°01'50" N, long. 119°27' W). Named on Matterhorn Peak (1956) 15' quadrangle.

Tamarack [CALAVERAS]: *settlement,* 36 miles east-northeast of San Andreas (lat. 38°26'20" N, long. 120°04'35" W; near S line sec. 23, T 7 N, R 17 E). Named on Tamarack (1979) 7.5' quadrangle. W.H. Hutchins built the first store at the site in the early 1920's and called the place Camp Tamarack—the word "Camp" in the name was from a cow camp located at the place (Browning, 1986, p. 212).

Tamarack [PLACER]: *locality,* 9 miles west of Donner Pass along Southern Pacific Railroad (lat. 39°18'20" N, long. 120°29'20" W; near W line sec. 26, T 17 N, R 13 E). Named on Truckee (1940) 30' quadrangle.

Tamarack Creek [EL DORADO]: *stream,* flows 1.25 miles to South Fork American River 4 miles west of Echo Summit (lat. 38°48'15" N, long. 120°06'20" W; sec. 16, T 11 N, R 17 E). Named on Echo Lake (1955) 7.5' quadrangle.

Tamarack Creek [MARIPOSA]: *stream,* flows 5 miles to Cascade Creek 7 miles west-southwest of Yosemite Village (lat. 37°43'40" N, long. 119°42'45" W; sec . 25, T 2 S, R 20 E); the stream goes past Tamarack Flat. Named on Hetch Hetchy Reservoir (1956) and Yosemite (1956) 15' quadrangles.

Tamarack Flat [MARIPOSA]: *area,* 8.5 miles west of Yosemite Village (lat. 37°45'05" N, long. 119°44'20" W; near NW cor. sec. 23, T 2 S, R 20 E); the place is near Tamarack Creek. Named on Hetch Hetchy Reservoir (1956) 15' quadrangle. George W. Coulter and Lafayette H. Bunnell named the area in 1856; Alva Hamilton operated a small stopping place there that he called Tamarack House (Paden and Schlichtmann, p. 235).

Tamarack Flat [SIERRA]: *area,* 4 miles south of Mount Fillmore (lat. 39°40'25" N, long. 120°51'05" W). Named on Mount Fillmore (1951) 7.5' quadrangle.

Tamarack House: see **Tamarack Flat** [MARIPOSA].

Tamarack Lake [EL DORADO]: *lake,* 1750 feet long, 4.5 miles west-northwest of Echo Summit (lat. 38°50'50" N, long. 120°05'50" W; on W line sec. 34, T 12 N, R 17 E). Named on Echo Lake (1955) 7.5' quadrangle.

Tamarack Lakes [SIERRA]: *lakes,* largest 650 feet long, 3.25 miles north-northwest of Sierra City (lat. 39°36'35" N, long. 120°39'15" W; sec. 8, T 20 N, R 12 E). Named on Sierra City (1981) 7.5' quadrangle.

Tamaroo Bar [PLACER]: *locality,* 1.5 miles east-southeast of downtown Auburn along North Fork American River (lat. 38°53'15" N, long. 121°03' W; near S line sec. 14, T 12 N, R 8 E). Named on Auburn (1953) 7.5' quadrangle.

Tanglefoot Canyon [AMADOR]: *canyon,* drained by a stream that flows 4 miles to Salt Springs Reservoir 4 miles southwest of Mokelumne Peak (lat. 38°29'50" N, long. 120°09'05" W). Named on Bear River Reservoir (1979) and Calaveras Dome (1979) 7.5' quadrangles.

Tanner Reservoir [AMADOR]: *lake,* 600 feet long, 7.5 miles south-southeast of Plymouth (lat. 38°22'55" N, long. 120°47'15" W; sec. 8, T 6 N, R 11 E). Named on Amador City (1962) 7.5' quadrangle.

Tanners Point [PLACER]: *ridge,* northwest-trending, 0.5 mile long, 5.5 miles east of Michigan Bluff (lat. 39°01'55" N, long. 120°38'15" W; near E line sec. 28, T 14 N, R 12 E). Named on Michigan Bluff (1952) 7.5' quadrangle.

Tars Mill [AMADOR]: *locality,* 13 miles east of present Fiddletown (lat. 38°30'15" N, long. 120°30'40" W). Named on Placerville (1893) 30' quadrangle.

Taylor Creek [EL DORADO]: *stream,* heads at Fallen Leaf Lake and flows 2 miles to Lake Tahoe 3.25 miles northeast of Mount Tallac (lat. 38°56'25" N, long. 120°03'25" W; sec 25, T 13 N, R 17 E). Named on Emerald Bay (1955) 7.5' quadrangle.

Taylor Crossing [NEVADA-PLACER]: *locality,* 2 miles west-northwest of Colfax along Bear River on Nevada-Placer county line (lat. 39°06'40" N, long. 120°59' W; near W line sec. 33, T 15 N, R 9 E). Named on Colfax (1949) 7.5' quadrangle.

Taylor Hill [TUOLUMNE]: *peak,* 1.25 miles south-southwest of Chinese Camp (lat. 37°51'20" N, long. 120°26'35" W; on S line sec. 9, T 1 S, R 14 E). Altitude 1680 feet. Named on Chinese Camp (1947) 7.5' quadrangle. The feature also was called Red Mountain, Mount Pleasant, and Taylor Mountain (Paden and Schlichtmann, p. 62).

Taylor Mountain [MADERA]: *ridge,* west-northwest-trending, 1.5 miles long, 2 miles southeast of Yosemite Forks (lat. 37°20'50" N, long. 119°36' W; on E line sec. 6, T 7 S, R 22 E). Named on Bass Lake (1953) 15' quadrangle.

Taylor Mountain: see **Taylor Hill** [TUOLUMNE].

Taylor Reservoir [NEVADA]: *lake,* 350 feet long, 2.5 miles east-northeast of Grass Valley (lat. 39°14'15" N, long. 121°01'05" W; at W line sec. 19, T 16 N, R 9 E). Named on Grass Valley (1949) 7.5' quadrangle.

Taylors Bar: see **San Andreas** [CALAVERAS].

Taylor's Ferry: see **Stanislaus River** [CALAVERAS-TUOLUMNE].

Taylor's Landing: see **Bijou** [EL DORADO].

Taylor's Ravine: see **Spanish Ravine** [EL DORADO].

Teaford Saddle [MADERA]: *pass,* 6 miles south-southeast of Yosemite Forks (lat. 37°17'15" N, long. 119°34'55" W; near SW cor. sec. 28, T 7 S, R 22 E). Named on Bass Lake (1953) 15' quadrangle, which shows Teaford ranch located 1 mile south of the pass.

Teapot Dome: see **Pywiack Dome** [MARIPOSA].

Tehama Ravine [NEVADA]: *canyon,* drained by a stream that flows nearly 2 miles to Middle Yuba River 10 miles northeast of North Bloomfield (lat. 39°27'15" N, long. 120°45'15" W; at E line sec. 5, T 18 N, R 11 E). Named on Alleghany (1949) and Graniteville (1982) 7.5' quadrangles.

Tehuantepec Valley: see **Haypress Valley** [SIERRA].

Telegraph City [CALAVERAS]: *locality,* 6.25 miles west-southwest of Copperopolis (lat. 37°56'10" N, long. 120°44'25" W; near W line sec. 14, T 1 N, R 11 E); the place is along Telegraph Creek. Named on Copperopolis (1962) 7.5' quadrangle. Postal authorities established Telegraph City post office in 1862 and discontinued it in 1894; the post office name was from a telegraph station on the Stockton to Sonora line (Salley, p. 219).

Telegraph Creek [CALAVERAS]: *stream,* heads in Calaveras County and flows 8 miles to Shirley Creek 10.5 miles north of Oakdale in Stanislaus County (lat. 37°54'55" N, long. 120° 48'50" W; near SW cor. sec. 19, T 1 N, R 11 E); the stream goes past Telegraph City. Named on Bachelor Valley (1968) and Copperopolis (1962) 7.5' quadrangles.

Telegraph Hill [MARIPOSA]: *peak,* 5 miles east-northeast of the village of Bear Valley (lat. 37°35'55" N, long. 120°02'05" W; near E line sec. 12, T 4 S, R 17 E). Altitude 3402 feet. Named on Bear Valley (1947) 7.5' quadrangle.

Telegraph Hill [PLACER]: *peak,* 6 miles north of Roseville (lat. 38° 50'05" N, long. 121°15'50" W; at W line sec. 1, T 11 N, R 6 E). Named on Roseville (1967) 7.5' quadrangle.

Telegraph Hill [TUOLUMNE]: *peak,* nearly 3 miles east of Columbia (lat. 38°01'55" N, long. 120°21' W; sec. 17, T 2 N, R 15 E). Altitude 3738 feet. Named on Columbia SE (1948) 7.5' quadrangle.

Telephone Ridge [EL DORADO]:
(1) *ridge,* generally west-trending, 4.5 miles long, center 4.5 miles east-northeast of Pollock Pines (lat. 38°47'20" N, long. 120°30'30" W). Named on Pollock Pines (1950) and Riverton (1950) 7.5' quadrangles.
(2) *ridge,* generally south-trending, 2.5 miles long, 3.5 miles east of Caldor (lat. 38°36'15" N, long. 120°21'45" W). Named on Peddler Hill (1951) 7.5' quadrangle.

Tells Creek [EL DORADO]: *stream,* flows 6.5 mile to Union Valley Reservoir nearly 2.5 miles southeast of Robbs Peak (lat. 38°53'55" N, long. 120°22'35" W; sec. 11, T 12 N, R 14 E). Named on Loon Lake (1952) 7.5' quadrangle.

Tells Peak [EL DORADO]: *peak,* 8.5 miles east-northeast of Robbs Peak (lat. 38°57'35" N, long. 120°15'15" W; sec. 19, T 13 N, R 16 E). Altitude 8872 feet. Named on Loon Lake (1952) 7.5' quadrangle. The name commemorates William Pedrini, a Swiss known as Bill Tell, who owned land in the neighborhood in the 1860's (Gernes, p. 58).

Temperance Arm: see Lake McClure [MARIPOSA].

Temperance Creek [MARIPOSA]: *stream,* flows 3.5 miles to Lake McClure 7.25 miles north of Hornitos (lat. 37°36'25" N, long. 120°14'25" W; near NW cor. sec. 8, T 4 S, R 16 E). Named on Hornitos (1947, photorevised 1973) 7.5' quadrangle.

Temperance Creek [PLACER]: *stream,* flows about 1.5 miles to Shirttail Canyon 3.5 miles north-northeast of Foresthill (lat. 39°04'10" N, long. 120°47'20" W; at W line sec. 7, T 14 N, R 11 E). Named on Foresthill (1949) 7.5' quadrangle.

Tenaya Canyon: see Tenaya Creek [MARIPOSA].

Tenaya Creek [MARIPOSA]: *stream,* flows 12.5 miles to Merced River 1 mile east-south-east of Yosemite Village (lat. 37°44'40" N, long. 119°34'10" W). Named on Hetch Hetchy Reservoir (1956), Tuolumne Meadows (1956), and Yosemite (1956) 15' quadrangles. Called Tenaya Fork on King and Gardner's (1865) map. Whitney (1870, p. 65) used the name "Tenaya Fork of the Merced" for the stream. On Yosemite (1909) 30' quadrangle, the name "Tenaya Canyon" applies to the canyon of Tenaya Creek above Yosemite Valley.

Tenaya Fork: see Tenaya Creek [MARIPOSA].

Tenaya Lake [MARIPOSA]: *lake,* 1 mile long, 3 miles west-southwest of Cathedral Peak (lat. 37°49'50" N, long. 119°27'30" W; sec. 20, 21, T 1 S, R 23 E). Named on Tuolumne Meadows (1956) 15' quadrangle. Lafayette H.

Bunnell named the lake for the chief of the Indians who occupied Yosemite Valley when the valley was discovered by white men (Bunnell, p. 163).

Tenaya Peak [MARIPOSA]: *peak,* 2.5 miles southwest of Cathedral Peak (lat. 37°49'45" N, long. 119°26'30" W; near W line sec. 22, T 1 S, R 23 E). Altitude 10,301 feet. Named on Tuolumne Meadows (1956) 15' quadrangle.

Tenaya Peak: see Tresidder Peak [MARIPOSA].

Ten-ieya Dome: see Pywiack Dome [MARIPOSA].

Ten Lakes [TUOLUMNE]: *lakes,* largest 1400 feet long, 7.5 miles east-northeast of White Wolf (lat. 37°54' N, long. 119°31'15" W). Named on Hetch Hetchy Reservoir (1956) 15' quadrangle.

Tennessee Creek [EL DORADO]:
(1) *stream,* flows 4 miles to Dry Creek 4 miles north of Shingle Springs (lat. 38°43'20" N, long. 120°56' W; sec. 13, T 10 N, R 9 E). Named on Shingle Springs (1949) 7.5' quadrangle.
(2) *stream,* flows nearly 3 miles to North Fork Cosumnes River 7 miles south-southeast of Camino (lat. 38°39' N, long. 120°36'40" W; at W line sec. 12, T 9 N, R 12 E). Named on Sly Park (1952) 7.5' quadrangle.

Tennessee Gulch [TUOLUMNE]: *canyon,* drained by a stream that flows 1 mile to Woods Creek 2.5 miles south-southeast of Columbia at Browns Flat (lat. 38°00'10" N, long. 120°23' W; sec. 25, T 2 N, R 14 E). Named on Columbia (1948) and Columbia SE (1948) 7.5' quadrangles.

Tennessee Mountain [SIERRA]: *peak,* 3 miles south-southeast of Mount Fillmore (lat. 39°41'20" N, long. 120°49'50" W); the peak is southwest of Tennessee Ravine. Altitude 6401 feet. Named on Mount Fillmore (1951) 7.5' quadrangle.

Tennessee Ravine [SIERRA]: *canyon,* drained by a stream that flows 1 mile to Canyon Creek 2.25 miles southeast of Mount Fillmore (lat. 39°42'15" N, long. 120°49'35" W); the canyon is northeast of Tennessee Mountain. Named on Mount Fillmore (1951) 7.5' quadrangle, which shows Tennessee mine in the canyon.

Tesaiyak: see Half Dome [MARIPOSA].

Texas Bar [EL DORADO]: *locality,* nearly 5 miles west-northwest of Greenwood along Middle Fork American River (lat. 38°55'10" N, long. 120°59'45" W; sec. 5, T 12 N, R 9 E). Named on Greenwood (1949) 7.5' quadrangle.

Texas Bar: see Beals Point [PLACER]; Chili Bar [EL DORADO]; Goodyears Bar [SIERRA]; Red Mountain Bar [TUOLUMNE].

Texas Canyon [EL DORADO]: *canyon,* drained by a stream that flows 1.5 miles to Kelsey Canyon nearly 1 mile north-northwest of Chili

Bar (lat. 38°46'40" N, long. 120°49'40" W; sec. 26, T 11 N, R 10 E). Named on Garden Valley (1949) 7.5' quadrangle.

Texas Charlie Gulch [CALAVERAS]: *canyon,* drained by a stream that flows 3.5 miles to Melones Reservoir 5 miles east of Copperopolis (lat. 37°59'35" N, long. 120°33'05" W; sec. 28, T 2 N, R 13 E). Named on Angels Camp (1962) and Melones Dam (1962) 7.5' quadrangles.

Texas Creek [EL DORADO]: *stream,* flows 1.25 miles to Slab Creek nearly 7 miles north-northwest of Pollock Pines (lat. 38°50'35" N, long. 120°39' W; at E line sec. 32, T 12 N, R 12 E). Named on Slate Mountain (1950) 7.5' quadrangle.

Texas Creek [NEVADA]: *stream,* flows 5 miles to Canyon Creek 4 miles southeast of Graniteville (lat. 39°24'15" N, long. 120°41'05" W; at S line sec. 24, T 18 N, R 11 E). Named on English Mountain (1983) and Graniteville (1982) 7.5' quadrangles.

Texas Creek: see **Cavallada Creek** [MARIPOSA].

Texas Diggins: see **Texas Hill** [PLACER].

Texas Flat [MADERA]: *area,* 7.25 miles north-northwest of Shuteye Peak (lat. 27°26'25" N, long. 119°29'45" W; sec. 6, T 6 S, R 23 E). Named on Shuteye Peak (1953) 15' quadrangle.

Texas Flat: see **Anthony House** [NEVADA]; **Coarsegold** [MADERA]; **Gold Spring** [TUOLUMNE].

Texas Gulch [CALAVERAS]: *canyon,* drained by a stream that flows less than 1 mile to Buckham Gulch 5 miles west-southwest of Copperopolis (lat. 37°57'20" N, long. 120°43'35" W; sec. 11, T 1 N, R 11 E). Named on Copperopolis (1962) 7.5' quadrangle.

Texas Gulch [MARIPOSA]: *canyon,* drained by a stream that flows 1 mile to Agua Fria Creek 4.5 miles northeast of the settlement of Catheys Valley (lat. 37°28'45" N, long. 120°01'45" W). Named on Catheys Valley (1962) 7.5' quadrangle. United States Board on Geographic Names (1964a, p. 15) rejected the name "Cavallada Gulch" for the feature.

Texas Gulch [TUOLUMNE]: *canyon,* drained by a stream that flows less than 1 mile to Big Creek (1) 3 miles east of Groveland (lat. 37°50'05" N, long. 120°10'20" W; sec. 24, T 1 S, R 16 E). Named on Groveland (1947) 7.5' quadrangle.

Texas Hill [EL DORADO]: *ridge,* generally west-trending, 2 miles long, 2 miles east-southeast of downtown Placerville (lat. 38°43'20" N, long. 120°45'45" W). Named on Placerville (1949) 7.5' quadrangle.

Texas Hill [MARIPOSA]: *peak,* 6.25 miles east-northeast of Buckhorn Peak (lat. 37°41'35" N, long. 120°00'55" W; near NW cor. sec. 8, T 3 S, R 18 E). Altitude 3251 feet. Named on Buckhorn Peak (1947) 7.5' quadrangle.

Texas Hill [PLACER]: *ridge,* generally north-

west-trending, 1.5 miles long. 4.25 miles north of Westville (lat. 39°14'10" N, long. 120°38'30" W; on E line sec. 20, T 16 N, R 12 E). Named on Westville (1952) 7.5' quadrangle. Hobson's (1890b) map shows a place called Texas Diggins situated on the ridge.

Texas Hill: see **Black Mountain** [MARIPOSA].

Texas Hill Spring [PLACER]: *spring,* 4.5 miles north of Westville (lat. 39°14'15" N, long. 120°38'15" W; sec. 21, T 16 N, R 12 E); the feature is on the northeast side of Texas Hill. Named on Westville (1952) 7.5' quadrangle.

Tharsa: see **Irrigosa** [MADERA].

Thatchers Gulch [CALAVERAS]: *canyon,* drained by a stream that flows less than 1 mile to Pardee Reservoir 4 miles west of Paloma (lat. 38°15'40" N, long. 120°50' W; near W line sec. 25, T 5 N, R 10 E). Named on Jackson (1962) 7.5' quadrangle.

The Basin [TUOLUMNE]: *area,* 5 miles east-southeast of Twain Harte (lat. 38°00' N, long. 120°08'45" W); Basin Creek goes through the place. Named on Tuolumne (1948) and Twain Harte (1979) 7.5' quadrangles.

The Beartrap [NEVADA]: *relief feature,* 3.5 miles south-southeast of Graniteville (lat. 39°23'40" N, long. 120°42'25" W; sec. 26, T 18 N, R 11 E). Named on Graniteville (1982) 7.5' quadrangle.

The Buttresses [MADERA]: *escarpment,* 1 mile south-southwest of Devils Postpile on the west side of Middle Fork San Joaquin River (lat. 37°36'45" N, long. 119°05'15" W). Named on Devils Postpile (1953) 15' quadrangle.

The Cascades [MARIPOSA]: *waterfall,* 7 miles west-southwest of Yosemite Village (lat. 37°43'40" N, long. 119°42'45" W; sec. 25, T 2 S, R 20 E); the feature is along Cascade Creek. Named on Yosemite (1956) 15' quadrangle. Lafayette H. Bunnell named the waterfall in 1851; the feature also was called Cascade Falls (Browning, 1988, p. 21).

The Cedars [PLACER]: *settlement,* 4.5 miles south-southwest of Donner Pass (lat. 39°15'15" N, long. 120°21' W; sec. 13, T 16 N, R 14 E); the place is along Cedar Creek. Named on Norden (1955) 7.5' quadrangle.

The Chemisal [AMADOR]: *peak,* 6.25 miles south-southeast of Ione (lat. 38°15'50" N, long. 120°54'20" W; sec. 29, T 5 N, R 10 E). Named on Ione (1962) 7.5' quadrangle.

The Cups [SIERRA]: *relief feature,* 1.25 miles west of Sierra City (lat. 39°34'10" N, long. 120°39'25" W; near SW cor. sec. 29, T 20 N, R 12 E). Named on Sierra City (1981) 7.5' quadrangle.

The Falls [MADERA]: *locality,* 4 miles southeast of Yosemite Forks near the northwest end of Bass Lake (1) (lat. 37°19'55" N, long. 119°34'15" W; sec. 9, T 7 S, R 22 E). Named on Bass Lake (1953) 15' quadrangle.

The Fissures [MARIPOSA]: *relief feature,* 2.5 miles south-southwest of Yosemite Village on the south side of Yosemite Valley (lat. 37°

42'45" N, long. 119°36' W). Named on Yosemite (1956) 15' quadrangle.

The Forks [MADERA]: *locality,* 5 miles southeast of Yosemite Forks on the west side of Bass Lake (1) (lat. 37°18'50" N, long. 119°34'20" W; on N line sec. 21, T 7 S, R 22 E). Named on Bass Lake (1953) 15' quadrangle.

The Forks: see **Downieville** [SIERRA].

The Gate: see **Jackson Gate** [AMADOR].

The Laguna: see **Laguna** [AMADOR].

The Mounds [SIERRA]: *hills,* 3 miles north-northwest of Sierraville in Sierra Valley (lat. 39°37'30" N, long. 120°23'50" W; sec. 34, T 21 N, R 14 E). Altitude of highest hill is 5027 feet. Named on Calpine (1981) and Sattley (1981) 7.5' quadrangles.

The Oaks [NEVADA]: *settlement,* 1 mile west of downtown Grass Valley (lat. 39°13'15" N, long. 121°04'45" W; sec. 28, T 16 N, R 8 E). Named on Grass Valley (1949) 7.5' quadrangle.

The Pines [MADERA]: *settlement,* 5.25 miles southeast of Yosemite Forks on the northeast side of Bass Lake (1) (lat. 37°19'10" N, long. 119°33'15" W; sec. 15, T 7 S, R 22 E). Named on Bass Lake (1953) 15' quadrangle.

Theodore: see **Lake Theodore** [PLACER].**The Pinnacles** [PLACER]: *relief feature,* 1.25 miles northeast of Bunker Hill (lat. 39°03'30" N, long. 120°21'40" W; sec. 13, T 14 N, R 14 E). Named on Wentworth Springs (1953) 7.5' quadrangle.

The Old Piute: see **Ahwiyah Point** [MARIPOSA].

The Punchbowl [NEVADA]: *relief feature,* 1.5 miles southwest of Grass Valley (lat. 39°11'55" N, long. 121°04'55" W; at S line sec. 33, T 16 N, R 8 E). Named on Grass Valley (1949) 7.5' quadrangle. Called Devils Punch Bowl on United States Geological Survey's (1901) map.

The Slide [TUOLUMNE]: *relief feature,* 3.25 miles west of Matterhorn Peak (lat. 38°05'20" N, long. 119°26'20" W); the feature is on the southeast side of Slide Mountain (1). Named on Matterhorn Peak (1956) 15' quadrangle.

The Three Chimneys [TUOLUMNE]: *relief features,* 6.25 miles south-southeast of Dardanelle (lat. 38°15'10" N, long. 119°48'05" W; sec. 29, T 5 N, R 20 E). Named on Dardanelle (1979) 7.5' quadrangle.

The Three Graces: see **Cathedral Rocks** [MARIPOSA].

Thimbleberry Creek [NEVADA]: *stream,* flows less that 1 mile to Logan Canyon 2.5 miles west of Washington (lat. 39°21'40" N, long. 120°50'55" W; near SW cor. sec. 3, T 17 N, R 10 E). Named on Washington (1950) 7.5' quadrangle.

Third Brushy Canyon [PLACER]: *canyon,* formed by the junction of Blackhawk Canyon and Stevens Ravine, 1.5 miles long, opens into Brushy Canyon (1) 3 miles northwest of Foresthill (lat. 39°03'20" N, long. 120°51' W;

sec. 16, T 14 N, R 10 E). Named on Foresthill (1949) 7.5' quadrangle.

Third Crossing: see **Kentucky House** [CALAVERAS].

Third Divide [SIERRA]: *pass,* 5.5 miles northeast of Downieville on the ridge between Lavezzola Creek and Pauley Creek (lat. 39°36'45" N, long. 120°45'05" W; near W line sec. 9, T 20 N, R 11 E); the pass is nearly 3 miles east-northeast of Second Divide. Named on Downieville (1951) 7.5' quadrangle.

Thirteenmile Creek [TUOLUMNE]: *stream,* flows 2.5 miles to Cottonwood Creek (1) nearly 3 miles east-northeast of Duckwall Mountain (lat. 37°59'10" N, long. 120°04'20" W; sec. 35, T 2 N, R 17 E). Named on Duckwall Mountain (1948) 7.5' quadrangle.

Thompson Canyon [TUOLUMNE]: *canyon,* drained by a stream that flows 9.5 miles to Stubblefield Canyon 6.25 miles south-southwest of Tower Peak (lat. 38°03'30" N, long. 119°35'20" W). Named on Matterhorn Peak (1956) and Tower Peak (1956) 15' quadrangles.

Thompson Creek [CALAVERAS]: *stream,* flows nearly 3 miles to Greenhorn Gulch 2.25 miles south-southwest of Angels Camp (lat. 38°02'40" N, long. 120°33'35" W; sec. 9, T 2 N, R 13 E). Named on Angels Camp (1962) 7.5' quadrangle.

Thompson Flat [CALAVERAS]: *valley,* 4.5 miles southwest of Copperopolis near the head of Martells Creek (lat. 37°55'45" N, long. 120°41'45" W; on N line sec. 19, T 1 N, R 12 E). Named on Copperopolis (1962) 7.5' quadrangle.

Thompson Hill [EL DORADO]: *peak,* 2.5 miles south-southwest of Coloma (lat. 38°45'55" N, long. 120°54'15" W; sec. 31, T 11 N, R 10 E). Altitude 2035 feet. Named on Coloma (1949) 7.5' quadrangle.

Thompson Meadow [CALAVERAS]: *area,* 2.25 miles west of Tamarack along Big Meadow Creek (lat. 38°26' N, long. 120°07' W; near W line sec. 28, T 7 N, R 17 E). Named on Tamarack (1979) 7.5' quadrangle.

Thompson Meadow [TUOLUMNE]: *area,* 2.25 miles northeast of Duckwall Mountain (lat. 37°59'40" N, long. 120°05'35" W; on S line sec. 27, T 2 N, R 17 E); the place is 1.5 miles west-southwest of Thompson Peak. Named on Duckwall Mountain (1948) 7.5' quadrangle.

Thompson Meadows [SIERRA]: *area,* 4 miles east-southeast of Sierra City (lat. 39°33'10" N, long. 120°33'40" W; near SW cor. sec. 31, T 20 N, R 13 E). Named on Haypress Valley (1981) 7.5' quadrangle. Sierra City (1955) 15' quadrangle shows marsh in the area.

Thompson Peak [EL DORADO]: *peak,* nearly 5 miles south-southwest of Freel Peak on El Dorado-Alpine county line (lat. 38°47'50" N, long. 119°56'35" W; near W line sec. 13, T 11 N, R 18 E). Altitude 9340 feet. Named on Freel Peak (1955) 7.5' quadrangle.

Thompson Peak [TUOLUMNE]: *peak,* 3.5 miles northeast of Duckwall Mountain (lat. 37°59'55" N, long. 120°04'05" W; near E line sec. 26, T 2 N, R 17 E). Altitude 5294 feet. Named on Duckwall Mountain (1948) 7.5' quadrangle.

Thornberry Mountain [MADERA]: *ridge,* east- to east-northeast-trending, 4.5 miles long, 6.5 miles south of Yosemite Forks (lat. 37°16'15" N, long. 119°37' W). Named on Bass Lake (1953) 15' quadrangle.

Thorps Creek [TUOLUMNE]: *stream,* flows 1.25 miles to North Fork Dry Creek 2.5 miles west of Keystone (lat. 37°50'25" N, long. 120°33' W; sec. 21, T 1 S, R 13 E). Named on Keystone (1962) 7.5' quadrangle.

Thousand Dollar Canyon: see **Illinois Canyon** [EL DORADO].

Thousand Island Lake [MADERA]: *lake,* 1.5 miles long, 8.5 miles northwest of Devils Postpile (lat. 37°43'15" N, long. 119°11' W). Named on Devils Postpile (1953) 15' quadrangle.

Three Brothers [MARIPOSA]: *relief feature,* 1.5 miles west-southwest of Yosemite Village on the north side of Yosemite Valley (lat. 37°44'30" N, long. 119°36'45" W); the feature comprises Lower Brother, Middle Brother, and Eagle Peak (1). Named on Yosemite (1956) 15' quadrangle. The name is from three Indian brothers who were captured near the feature in 1851 by members of the Mariposa Battalion (Bunnell, p. 107-108).

Three Buttes [MARIPOSA]: *peaks,* 3 miles south-southwest of Santa Cruz Mountain (lat. 37°25'10" N, long. 120°13'35" W; near S line sec. 8, 9, T 6 S, R 16 E). Named on Indian Gulch (1962) 7.5' quadrangle.

Three Chimneys: see **The Three Chimneys** [TUOLUMNE].

Three Graces: see **The Three Graces**, under **Cathedral Rocks** [MARIPOSA].

Three Meadows [TUOLUMNE]: *areas,* 7 miles east-northeast of Pinecrest (lat. 38°14'35" N, long. 119°53' W). Named on Pinecrest (1979) 7.5' quadrangle. The group comprises Gully Meadow, Middle Three Meadow, and Upper Three Meadow (United States Board on Geographic Names, 1980b, p. 5).

Three Cornered Meadow [SIERRA]: *area,* 3 miles north-northwest of Calpine (lat. 39°42'20" N, long. 120°27'45" W; at NW cor. sec. 6, T 21 N, R 14 E). Named on Calpine (1981) 7.5' quadrangle.

Three Mile House [EL DORADO]: *locality,* 2 miles northeast of Georgetown (lat. 38°55'20" N, long. 120°48'10" W). Named on Placerville (1893) 30' quadrangle.

Three Pine Gulch: see **Yankee Hill** [TUOLUMNE] (2).

Thunder Cliff [PLACER]: *relief feature,* 2.5 miles west of Tahoe City on the east side of Truckee River (lat. 39°10'30" N, long. 120°11'05" W; sec. 2, T 15 N, R 16 E). Named on Tahoe City (1955) 7.5' quadrangle.

Thunder Hill [TUOLUMNE]: *ridge,* north-northeast-trending, less than 1 mile long, 7 miles southwest of Liberty Hill (lat. 38°17'10" N, long. 120°10'20" W; near E line sec. 14, T 5 N, R 16 E). Named on Boards Crossing (1979) 7.5' quadrangle.

Thunder Mountain [AMADOR]: *peak,* 9.5 miles north of Mokelumne Peak (lat. 38°40'30" N, long. 120°05'25" W; sec. 33, T 10 N, R 17 E). Altitude 9408 feet. Named on Caples Lake (1979) 7.5' quadrangle. Forest Service personnel gave the name because "thunderheads appear to build up in that area" (United States Board on Geographic Names, 1980b, p. 5).

Tice [CALAVERAS]: *locality,* 6 miles west of present Tamarack along Blue Creek (lat. 38°26'10" N, long. 120°11'35" W). Named on Big Trees (1891) 30' quadrangle.

Ticky Creek [EL DORADO]: *stream,* flows 1 mile to Slab Creek 7.5 miles north-northwest of Pollock Pines (lat. 38°52'05" N, long. 120°37'40" W; sec. 22, T 12 N, R 12 E). Named on Slate Mountain (1950) and Tunnel Hill (1950) 7.5' quadrangles.

Tick-Tack-Toe Hill [MADERA]: *ridge,* west-southwest-trending, 1 mile long, nearly 7 miles south of O'Neals (lat. 37°01'45" N, long. 119°42'15" W). Named on Millerton Lake West (1965) 7.5' quadrangle. Millerton Lake (1945) 15' quadrangle has the form "Tick-tack-toe Hill" for the name.

Tiger Creek [AMADOR]: *stream,* flows 9 miles to Tiger Creek Reservoir 9 miles southwest of Hams Station (lat. 38°27' N, long. 120°29'30" W; sec. 24, T 7 N, R 13 E). Named on Caldor (1951) and Devils Nose (1979) 7.5' quadrangles.

Tiger Creek: see **Little Tiger Creek** [AMADOR].

Tiger Creek Reservoir [AMADOR]: *lake,* behind a dam on North Fork Mokelumne River 9 miles east-northeast of Pine Grove on Amador-Calaveras county line (lat. 38°26'30" N, long. 120°30'15" W; sec. 23, T 7 N, R 13 E); Tiger Creek joins North Fork Mokelumne River in the lake. Named on Devils Nose (1979) and West Point (1948) 7.5' quadrangles.

Tiger Creek Reservoir [CALAVERAS]: *lake,* behind a dam on North Fork Mokelumne River 3 miles north-northeast of West Point on Calaveras-Amador county line (lat. 38°26'30" N, long. 120°30'15" W; sec. 23, T 7 N, R 13 E); Tiger Creek enters the lake in Amador County. Named on Devils Nose (1979) and West Point (1948) 7.5' quadrangles.

Tiger Lily [EL DORADO]: *locality,* 3.5 miles south-southeast of Placerville (lat. 38°40'55" N, long. 120°46'25" W; near NE cor. sec. 33, T 10 N, R 11 E). Named on Placerville (1949) 7.5' quadrangle.

Tilden Canyon [TUOLUMNE]: *canyon,* 0.5 mile long, 8.5 miles southwest of Tower Peak (lat. 38°02'25" N, long. 119°38'15" W). Named on Tower Peak (1956) 15' quadrangle.

Tilden Canyon Creek [TUOLUMNE]: *stream,* flows 5.5 miles to Rancheria Creek 9 miles south-southwest of Tower Peak (lat. 38° 01'35" N, long. 119°37'40" W); the stream goes through Tilden Canyon. Named on Tower Peak (1956) 15' quadrangle.

Tilden Creek [TUOLUMNE]: *stream,* flows 6 miles to Falls Creek 5.5 miles southwest of Tower Peak (lat. 38°05'35" N, long. 119° 37'45" W). Named on Tower Peak (1956) 15' quadrangle.

Tilden Lake [TUOLUMNE]: *lake,* 2 miles long, 4 miles southwest of Tower Peak (lat. 38°06'15" N, long. 119°36'10" W); the lake is along Tilden Creek. Named on Tower Peak (1956) 15' quadrangle. United States Board on Geographic Names (1986, p. 1) rejected the name "Lake Nina" for the feature.

Tillman [MADERA]: *locality,* 6.25 miles south-southwest of Chowchilla along Chowchilla Pacific Railroad (lat. 37°02'30" N, long. 120°19'35" W; near SW cor. sec. 22, T 10 S, R 15 E). Named on Chowchilla (1918) 7.5' quadrangle. California Division of Highways' (1934) map shows a place called Plains located along Southern Pacific Railroad nearly 2 miles southwest of Tillman (near E line sec. 32, T 10 S, R 15 E), a place called Ovejo located along the railroad 1.25 miles northeast of Tillman (near N line sec. 22, T 10 S, R 15 E), and a place called Ash located along the railroad 1.5 miles northeast of Ovejo (near S line sec. 11, T 10 S, R 15 E).

Tiltill Creek [TUOLUMNE]: *stream,* flows 6.25 miles to Hetch Hetchy Reservoir 7.5 miles northwest of White Wolf (lat. 37° 57'25" N, long. 119°43'40" W; sec. 12, T 1 N, R 20 E); the stream heads near Tiltill Mountain and goes through Tiltill Valley. Named on Hetch Hetchy Reservoir (1956) and Tower Peak (1956) 15' quadrangles.

Tiltill Mountain [TUOLUMNE]: *peak,* 10 miles southwest of Tower Peak (lat. 38°01'40" N, long. 119°39'55" W). Altitude 9005 feet. Named on Tower Peak (1956) 15' quadrangle.

Tiltill Valley [TUOLUMNE]: *valley,* 7.5 miles north-northwest of White Wolf (lat. 37°58'25" N, long. 119°41'35" W); the valley is along Tiltill Creek and a tributary to Tiltill Creek. Named on Hetch Hetchy Reservoir (1956) 15' quadrangle. Eugene Y. Ellwell homesteaded in the valley and named it in 1887 (Browning, 1986, p. 217). United States Board on Geographic Names (1933, p. 756) rejected the forms "Til Till," "Tiltil," and "Tilltill" for the name.

Timber Creek [MADERA]:
(1) *stream,* flows 2 miles to West Fork Granite Creek 6 miles southeast of Merced Peak (lat. 37°34'20" N, long. 119°19' W); the stream

heads near Timber Knob. Named on Merced Peak (1953) 15' quadrangle.
(2) *stream,* flows 2.5 miles to Sand Creek 3.5 miles west-southwest of Shuteye Peak (lat. 37°19'45" N, long. 119°29'25" W; near SE cor. sec. 7, T 7 S, R 23 E). Named on Shuteye Peak (1953) 15' quadrangle.

Timber Knob [MADERA]: *peak,* 6 miles east-southeast of Merced Peak (lat. 37°35'20" N, long. 119°18' W); the peak is east of Timber Creek (1). Altitude 9945 feet. Named on Merced Peak (1953) 15' quadrangle.

Timber Lodge [MARIPOSA]: *locality,* 0.5 mile north-northwest of Midpines (lat. 37°33'05" N, long. 119°55'25" W; near SW cor. sec. 30, T 4 S, R 19 E). Named on Feliciana Mountain (1947) 7.5' quadrangle.

Timberloft Camp [MARIPOSA]: *locality,* 3 miles southwest of Fish Camp (lat. 37°26'30" N, long. 119°40'20" W; sec. 4, T 6 S, R 21 E). Named on Bass Lake (1953) 15' quadrangle. Mariposa (1912) 30' quadrangle shows Old Miami Mill at the place.

Tim's Springs: see **Springfield** [TUOLUMNE].

Tin Cup Diggings: see **Downieville** [SIERRA].

Tinker Knob [PLACER]: *peak,* 3.25 miles north of Granite Chief (lat. 39°14'40" N, long. 120°17'05" W; near SW cor. sec. 11, T 16 N, R 15 E). Altitude 8949 feet. Named on Granite Chief (1953) 7.5' quadrangle. Called Tinkerknob on Wheeler's (1876-1877b) map. The name is for J.A. Tinker, a teamster who hauled freight from Soda Springs to mines on Forest Hill Divide (Gudde, 1969, p. 339).

Tinkers Station: see **Soda Springs** [NEVADA].

Tioga Hill: see **Gaylor Peak** [TUOLUMNE].

Tioga Meadows: see **Dana Meadows** [TUOLUMNE].

Tioga Pass [TUOLUMNE]: *pass,* 60 miles east of Sonora on Tuolumne-Mono county line (lat. 37°54'40" N, long. 119°15'25" W; near N line sec. 31, T 1 N, R 25 E). Named on Tuolumne Meadows (1956) 15' quadrangle. The name is from Tioga County, New York (United States Board on Geographic Names, 1934, p. 25), and was applied to a mine near the pass and then to the pass itself (Smith, p. 29). The feature also was known as McLean's Pass (Hubbard). Bancroft's (1864) map had the name "Browns Pass" at or near present Tioga Pass.

Tippecanoe [SIERRA]: *locality,* 2.5 miles northeast of Pike (lat. 39° 27'50" N, long. 120°57'30" W). Named on Colfax (1898) 30' quadrangle.

Tipton Hill [EL DORADO]: *ridge,* south-trending, 1 mile long, 14 miles northwest of Pollock Pines (lat. 38°55'45" N, long. 120°44'25" W). Named on Tunnel Hill (1950) 7.5' quadrangle. Gudde (1975, p. 311) listed Schleins Diggings, a mining place located on Tipton Hill.

Tip Top Peak [TUOLUMNE]: *peak,* 2.5 miles east-northeast of Moccasin (lat. 37°49'45" N,

long. 120°15'40" W; sec. 30, T 1 S, R 16 E).
Altitude 3361 feet. Named on Moccasin
(1948) 7.5' quadrangle.
Tisaiyak: see **Half Dome** [MARIPOSA].
Tisayac: see **Half Dome** [MARIPOSA].
Tis-sa-ack: see **Half Dome** [MARIPOSA].
Titcomb Flat [MADERA]: *area,* 5.25 miles
southwest of North Fork (lat. 37°10'35" N,
long. 119°34'40" W; sec. 4, T 9 S, R 22 E).
Named on North Fork (1965) 7.5' quadrangle.
Titus and Manly Ferry: see **San Joaquin City**
[MADERA].
Todd: see **Todd Valley** [PLACER].
Todd Creek [PLACER]: *stream,* flows 5.5 miles
to Middle Fork American River 9.5 miles east-
northeast of Auburn (lat. 38°57'40" N, long.
120°55'25" W; sec. 24, T 13 N, R 9 E). Named
on Foresthill (1949), Georgetown (1949), and
Greenwood (1949) 7.5' quadrangles. Called
Todd's Valley Creek on Whitney's (1880) map.
Todd's Valley: see **Todd Valley** [PLACER].
Todd's Valley Creek: see **Todd Creek**
[PLACER].
Todd Valley [PLACER]: *locality,* 13 miles east-
northeast of Auburn (lat. 38°59'55" N, long.
120°51' W; at W line sec. 3, T 13 N, R 10 E);
the place is along Todd Creek. Named on
Georgetown (1949) 7.5' quadrangle. Postal
authorities established Todd's Valley post office in 1856, discontinued it in 1884, reestablished it with the name "Todd" in 1885,
and discontinued it in 1901 (Salley, p. 222).
Dr. F. Walton Todd opened a store at the place
in 1849 (Gudde, 1949, p. 363).
Toem Lake [EL DORADO]: *lake,* 1150 feet long,
1.25 miles east-southeast of Pyramid Peak (lat.
38°50'25" N, long. 120°08'10" W). Named on
Pyramid Peak (1955) 7.5' quadrangle. The
word "Toem" was coined from letters in the
name "Tom Emery" (Lekisch, p. 65).
Tojam Lake [TUOLUMNE]: *lake,* 950 feet
long, 10.5 miles east of Pinecrest (lat.
38°11'25" N, long. 119°48' W). Named on
Pinecrest (1956) 15' quadrangle.
Toledo [MARIPOSA]: *locality,* nearly 2 miles
west of Santa Cruz Mountain (lat. 37°27'30"
N, long. 120°14'10" W; sec. 32, T 5 S, R 16
E). Site named on Indian Gulch (1962) 7.5'
quadrangle.
Toledo Gulch [MARIPOSA]: *canyon,* drained
by a stream that flows 3.25 miles to Burns
Creek 1.5 miles north-northeast of Courthouse Rock (lat. 37°26'35" N, long.
120°16'15" W; sec. 1, T 6 S, R 15 E); the site
of Toledo is in the canyon. Named on Haystack Mountain (1962) and Indian Gulch
(1962) 7.5' quadrangles.
Toledo Pond [MARIPOSA]: *lake,* 550 feet long,
1.5 miles west-northwest of Santa Cruz
Mountain (lat. 37°27'45" N, long. 120°13'50"
W; near SE cor. sec. 29, T 5 S, R 16 E); the
lake is 0.5 mile northeast of the site of Toledo. Named on Indian Gulch (1962) 7.5'
quadrangle.

Tollhouse Lake [NEVADA]: *lake,* 800 feet long,
2 miles east-southeast of English Mountain
(lat. 39°26' N, long. 120°31' W; on N line sec.
16, T 18 N, R 13 E). Named on English Mountain (1983) 7.5' quadrangle. Called Little Catfish Lake on Colfax (1938) 30' quadrangle,
but United States Board on Geographic
Names (1965a, p. 16) rejected this name.
Tolpekocking Flat: see **Chips Flat** [SIERRA].
Tombstone Mountain [EL DORADO]: *peak,*
5 miles south-southwest of Placerville (lat.
38°39'40" N, long. 120°49'35" W; sec. 1, T 9
N, R 10 E). Altitude 1785 feet. Named on
Placerville (1949) 7.5' quadrangle.
Tommy Cain Ravine [PLACER]: *canyon,*
drained by a stream that flows 1.5 miles to
North Fork American River 4.5 miles south
of Dutch Flat (lat. 39°08'25" N, long.
120°50'45" W; near NE cor. sec. 21, T 15 N,
R 10 E). Named on Dutch Flat (1950) 7.5'
quadrangle.
Toms Canyon [TUOLUMNE]: *canyon,* 1 mile
long, 9.5 miles east of Pinecrest along upper
reaches of Piute Creek (1) (lat. 38°10'40" N,
long. 119°49'15" W). Named on Pinecrest
(1956) 15' quadrangle.
Toms Creek [NEVADA]: *stream,* flows 1.5
miles to East Fork Creek 5 miles northeast of
Graniteville (lat. 39°28'40" N, long.
120°39'20" W; at N line sec. 32, T 19 N, R 12
E). Named on Graniteville (1982) 7.5' quadrangle.
Toms Valley [NEVADA]: *valley,* 9.5 miles north-
northwest of Donner Pass (lat. 39°26'10" N,
long. 120°24'35" W; near S line sec. 9, T 18
N, R 14 E). Named on Webber Peak (1981)
7.5' quadrangle.
Tonys Gulch [EL DORADO]: *canyon,* drained
by a stream that flows 1.5 miles to Salt Rock
Creek 7 miles southwest of Old Iron Mountain (lat. 38°37'40" N, long. 120°28'40" W;
near SW cor. sec. 18, T 9 N, R 14 E). Named
on Stump Spring (1951) 7.5' quadrangle.
Top Lake [EL DORADO]: *lake,* 850 feet long,
5 miles southwest of Phipps Peak (lat.
38°54'20" N, long. 120°12'55" W; sec. 9, T
12 N, R 16 E). Named on Rockbound Valley
(1955) 7.5' quadrangle.
Toutch Mill [CALAVERAS]: *locality,* 3.5 miles
southwest of Blue Mountain (lat. 38°18'20"
N, long. 120°24'20" W; near W line sec. 11,
T 5 N, R 14 E). Site named on Blue Moun-
tain (1956) 15' quadrangle.
Tower Peak [TUOLUMNE]: *peak,* 13 miles
south-southeast of Sonora Pass (lat. 38°08'35"
N, long. 119°32'50" W). Altitude 11,755 feet.
Named on Tower Peak (1956) 15' quadrangle.
First called Castle Peak, but members of the
Whitney survey renamed the feature Tower
Peak after the name "Castle Peak" was trans-
ferred by mistake to another feature (United
States Board on Geographic Names, 1934, p.
25).
Towers [CALAVERAS]: *locality,* 10 miles west-

southwest of Angels Camp in Salt Spring Valley (lat. 38°01'35" N, long. 120°43' W). Named on Jackson (1902) 30' quadrangle.

Towle [PLACER]: *locality,* 2 miles east of Dutch Flat along Southern Pacific Railroad (lat. 39°12'15" N, long. 120°48' W; sec. 36, T 16 N, R 10 E). Named on Dutch Flat (1950) 7.5' quadrangle. Called Towles on Hobson's (1890b) map. Postal authorities established Towle post office in 1891 and discontinued it in 1935 (Frickstad, p. 122). The name is for Allen Towle and George Towle, lumbermen in the region (Hanna, p. 332). California Mining Bureau's (1917b) map shows a place called Gorge located along the railroad about 1 mile east-southeast of Towle.

Towle Mill [NEVADA]: *locality,* 4 miles south of Washington (lat. 39°18'05" N, long. 120°48'40" W; near NW cor. sec. 36, T 17 N, R 10 E). Site named on Washington (1950) 7.5' quadrangle.

Townerville: see **Copper Mine Gulch** [AMADOR].

Townsley Lake [MARIPOSA]: *lake,* 1900 feet long, 5.5 miles southeast of Cathedral Peak along Fletcher Creek (lat. 37°47'40" N, long. 119°19'55" W). Named on Tuolumne Meadows (1956) 15' quadrangle. The name commemorates Forest Sanford Townsley, chief ranger of Yosemite National Park from 1916 until 1943, who planted golden trout in the lake; the feature first was called Upper Fletcher Lake (Browning, 1986, p. 219), but United States Board on Geographic Names (1991, p. 7) rejected this name.

Town Talk [NEVADA]: *locality,* 2.5 miles northeast of Grass Valley (lat. 39°14'35" N, long. 121°01'50" W; near S line sec. 13, T 16 N, R 8 E). Named on Grass Valley (1949) 7.5' quadrangle.

Toyon [CALAVERAS]: *locality,* 3.5 miles east-northeast of Valley Springs along Southern Pacific Railroad (lat. 38°12'15" N, long. 120°46' W; sec. 16, T 4 N, R 11 E). Named on Valley Springs (1962) 7.5' quadrangle.

Trabucco Creek [MARIPOSA]: *stream,* flows about 1 mile to Bear River (1) 2.5 miles north-northwest of Midpines (lat. 37°34'30" N, long. 119°56'40" W; near E line sec. 23, T 4 S, R 18 E). Named on Feliciana Mountain (1947) 7.5' quadrangle.

Trabucco Flat [MARIPOSA]: *area,* 3 miles east-southeast of the settlement of Catheys Valley (lat. 37°25'40" N, long. 120°02'25" W; sec. 7, T 6 S, R 18 E). Named on Catheys Valley (1962) 7.5' quadrangle.

Trabucco Gardens [MARIPOSA]: *locality,* less than 1 mile south-southeast of the village of Bear Valley (lat. 37°33'35" N, long. 120°06'40" W). Named on Bear Valley (1947) 7.5' quadrangle. Louis Trabucco had his home and a store at the place in 1851 (Sargent, Shirley, 1976, p. 16-17).

Trabuco Mountain [MADERA]: *peak,* 8.5

miles north-northwest of O'Neals (lat. 37°14'50" N, long. 119°44'10" W; sec. 12, T 8 S, R 20 E). Altitude 2647 feet. Named on Bass Lake (1953) and Millerton Lake (1965) 15' quadrangles.

Tragedy Creek [AMADOR]: *stream,* flows 6 miles to Bear River 7 miles west-northwest of Mokelumne Peak (lat. 38°35'15" N, long. 120°12'05" W; sec. 34, T 9 N, R 16 E); the stream heads at Tragedy Spring [EL DORADO]. Named on Bear River Reservoir (1979) and Tragedy Spring (1979) 7.5' quadrangles.

Tragedy Creek: see **Bear River** [AMADOR]; **North Tragedy Creek** [EL DORADO].

Tragedy Spring [AMADOR]: *locality,* 7.5 miles north-northwest of Mokelumne Peak (lat. 38°38'20" N, long. 120°08'40" W; sec. 7, T 9 N, R 17 E). Named on Silver Lake (1956) 15' quadrangle.

Tragedy Spring [EL DORADO]: *spring,* 6 miles southwest of Kirkwood (lat. 38°38'25" N, long. 120°08'45" W; sec. 7, T 9 N, R 17 E). Named on Tragedy Spring (1979) 7.5' quadrangle. The name was given after Indians killed three Mormons at the spring in 1848; the victims were in advance of a group traveling to Salt Lake City (Ricketts, 1983, p. 20).

Trailer Hill [NEVADA]: *ridge,* south-trending, 1.5 miles long, 3.25 miles north-northeast of Higgins Corner (lat. 39°05'15" N, long. 121°04'30" W; on N line sec. 10, T 14 N, R 8 E). Named on Lake Combie (1949) 7.5' quadrangle.

Trail Gulch [EL DORADO]: *canyon,* less than 1 mile long, opens into the canyon of Rock Creek 4 miles north-northeast of Chili Bar (lat. 38°49' N, long. 120°46'45" W; sec. 8, T 11 N, R 11 E). Named on Garden Valley (1949) 7.5' quadrangle.

Trap Canyon [EL DORADO]: *canyon,* drained by a stream that flows 1.5 miles to Park Creek (present Sly Park Creek) 2.5 miles west-north-west of Old Iron Mountain (lat. 38°42'50" N, long. 120°26'10" W; near SW cor. sec. 16, T 10 N, R 14 E). Named on Stump Spring (1951) 7.5' quadrangle.

Trap Creek [NEVADA]: *stream,* flows 2.5 miles to Fall Creek 5 miles northwest of Yuba Gap (lat. 39°21'20" N, long. 120°41'40" W; sec. 12, T 17 N, R 11 E). Named on Blue Canyon (1955) 7.5' quadrangle.

Traverse Creek [EL DORADO]: *stream,* flows 7.25 miles to Bear Creek (2) nearly 5 miles north-northeast of Chili Bar (lat. 38°49'50" N, long. 120°46'55" W; near W line sec. 5, T 11 N, R 11 E). Named on Garden Valley (1949) and Georgetown (1949) 7.5' quadrangles.

Treasure Island [AMADOR]: *island,* 2000 feet long, 8 miles north of Mokelumne Peak in Silver Lake (lat. 39°39'10" N, long. 120°07'-15" W; near S line sec. 5, T 9 N, R 17 E). Named on Caples Lake (1979) 7.5' quadrangle

Treasure Mountain [SIERRA]: *peak,* 3.5 miles south of Sierraville (lat. 39°32'25" N, long. 120°21'20" W; sec. 1, T 19 N, R 14 E). Altitude 7085 feet. Named on Sierraville (1981) 7.5' quadrangle.

Tremont House: see **Valley Springs** [CALAVERAS].

Tresidder Peak [MARIPOSA]: *peak,* 1.5 miles southwest of Cathedral Peak (lat. 37°49'50" N, long. 119°25'15" W; sec. 23, T 1 S, R 23 E). Named on Tuolumne Meadows (1956) 15' quadrangle. United States Board on Geographic Names (1959a, p. 3) rejected the name "Tenaya Peak" for the feature, and noted that the name "Tresidder" commemorates Donald E. Tresidder, president of Stanford University from 1943 until 1948. Tresidder also was president of Yosemite Park & Curry Company from 1925 until 1948 (Browning, 1986, p. 220).

Trestle Ravine [SIERRA]: *canyon,* drained by a stream that flows less than 0.5 mile to Middle Yuba River 4.5 miles southwest of Alleghany (lat. 39°25'30" N, long. 120°54'15" W; near W line sec. 18, T 18 N, R 10 E). Named on Pike (1949) 7.5' quadrangle.

Triangle Lake [EL DORADO]: *lake,* 450 feet long, 4.5 miles northwest of Echo Summit (lat. 38°51'35" N, long. 120°05'30" W). Named on Echo Lake (1955) 7.5' quadrangle. The name is from the shape of the lake (Lekisch, p. 141).

Trigo [MADERA]: *village,* 7 miles east-southeast of Madera (lat. 36° 54'35" N, long. 119°57'30" W; sec. 1, T 12 S, R 18 E). Named on Gregg (1965) 7.5' quadrangle. Called Patterson on Mendenhall's (1908) map. Postal authorities established Trigo post office in 1912 and discontinued it in 1942 (Frickstad, p. 86). Logan's (1950) map shows a place called Lankershim located about 3.5 miles northwest of Trigo along Atchison, Topeka and Santa Fe Railroad.

Trimmer Peak: see **Freel Peak** [EL DORADO].

Trinity Lakes [MADERA]: *lakes,* 3.25 miles north-northwest of Devils Postpile (lat. 37°40' N, long. 119°06' W). Named on Devils Postpile (1953) 15' quadrangle.

Triple Divide Peak [MADERA]: *peak,* 1.5 miles east of Merced Peak (lat. 37°37'55" N, long. 119°22'10" W). Altitude 11,607 feet. Named on Merced Peak (1953) 15' quadrangle. Lieutenant N.F. McClure named the peak in 1895 (Browning, 1988, p. 147).

Triple Peak Fork [MADERA]: *stream,* flows 5.5 miles to Merced Peak Fork 5 miles north-northeast of Merced Peak (lat. 37°41'45" N, long. 119°20'50" W); the stream heads near Triple Divide Peak. Named on Merced Peak (1953) 15' quadrangle. United States Board on Geographic Names (1978c, p. 4) rejected the form "Tripple Peak Fork" for the name.

Trojan: see **Fort Trojan**, under **Virginiatown** [PLACER].

Trosi Canyon [SIERRA]: *canyon,* drained by a stream that flows 3 miles to Smithneck Creek 9.5 miles southeast of Loyalton in Pats Meadow (lat. 39°33'35" N, long. 120°08'50" W; sec. 25, T 20 N, R 16 E). Named on Sardine Peak (1981) 7.5' quadrangle.

Trout Creek [EL DORADO]: *stream,* flows 10 miles to Truckee Marsh 7 miles northwest of Freel Peak (lat. 38°56' N, long. 120°59'10" W; near E line sec. 4, T 12 N, R 18 E). Named on Freel Peak (1955) and South Lake Tahoe (1955) 7.5' quadrangles.

Trout Creek [NEVADA]: *stream,* flows 5.5 miles to Truckee River 1 mile east-northeast of downtown Truckee (lat. 39°19'55" N, long. 120°09'50" W; near SE cor. sec. 11, T 17 N, R 16 E). Named on Truckee (1955, photorevised 1969) 7.5' quadrangle.

Trout Creek [TUOLUMNE]: *stream,* flows 6 miles to Clavey River nearly 7 miles east of Long Barn (lat. 38°04'55" N, long. 120°00'35" W; sec. 28, T 3 N, R 18 E). Named on Hull Creek (1979) and Pinecrest (1979) 7.5' quadrangles.

Troy [PLACER]: *locality,* 7.5 miles west of Donner Pass along Southern Pacific Railroad (lat. 39°18'40" N, long. 120°27'40" W; sec. 25, T 17 N, R 13 E). Named on Soda Springs (1955) 7.5' quadrangle.

Truckee [NEVADA]: *town,* 47 miles east of Grass Valley (lat. 39° 19'45" N, long. 120°11' W; near NE cor. sec. 15, T 17 N, R 16 E). Named on Truckee (1955) 7.5' quadrangle. Postal authorities established Truckee post office in 1868 (Frickstad, p. 115). The place was called Coburn Station, for a saloon keeper, when the railroad reached the site in 1863-1864, but it was renamed for Truckee River in 1868 (Bancroft, 1888, p. 486). Postal authorities established Donner Lake post office 7 miles west of Truckee in 1866 and discontinued it in 1868 (Salley, p. 60).

Truckee Canyon [NEVADA-SIERRA]: *canyon,* along Truckee River in Nevada County and Sierra County below a point about 6.5 miles northeast of Truckee near Boca—the canyon extends into the State of Nevada. Named on Boca (1955) and Martis Peak (1955) 7.5' quadrangles.

Truckee Lake: see **Donner Lake** [NEVADA]; **Little Truckee Lake**, under **Webber Lake** [SIERRA].

Truckee Marsh [EL DORADO]: *marsh,* 5 miles east-northeast of Mount Tallac in Lake Valley near Lake Tahoe (lat. 38°56' N, long. 120°00'45" W). Named on Fallen Leaf Lake (1955) and Freel Peak (1956) 15' quadrangles. Called Upper Truckee Marsh on Taylor's (1902) map. Development of South Lake Tahoe now partly covers the marsh.

Truckee River [NEVADA-PLACER-SIERRA]: *stream,* heads at Lake Tahoe in Placer County and flows 35 miles through Nevada County and Sierra County to the State of Nevada 7.5

miles southeast of Crystal Peak (lat. 39°28' N, long. 120°00'05" W; at E line sec. 31, T 19 N, R 18 E). Named on Boca (1955), Martis Peak (1955), Tahoe City (1955), and Truckee (1955) 7.5' quadrangles. Called Salmon Trout R. on Fremont's (1848) map, and called Truckey R. on Jefferson's (1849) map. Elisha Stevens and his party of emigrants gave the name "Truckee" to the stream in 1844 to honor a helpful Indian whom they called Truckee (Stewart, p. 8).

Truckee River: see **Little Truckee River** [NEVADA-SIERRA]; **Upper Truckee River** [EL DORADO].

Truckee Summit: see **Little Truckee Summit** [SIERRA].

Truckey Pass: see **Donner Pass** [PLACER].

Truckey River: see **Truckee River** [NEVADA-PLACER-SIERRA].

Trumbull Peak [MARIPOSA]: *peak,* 4.5 miles west-northwest of El Portal (lat. 37°41'15" N, long. 119°51'35" W). Altitude 5004 feet. Named on El Portal (1947) 7.5' quadrangle. United States Board on Geographic Names (1901, p. 125) rejected the names "Cranberry Peak" and "Mount Trumbull" for the feature. The name "Trumbull" is for a Senator Trumbull, who visited Yosemite National Park (Browning, 1988, p. 147).

Tucker Flat [EL DORADO]: *area,* 4.25 miles southwest of Freel Peak along Saxon Creek (lat. 38°49' N, long. 119°57'30" W; sec. 11, T 11 N, R 18 E). Named on Freel Peak (1955) 7.5' quadrangle. The name commemorates a stockman who took up land in the neighborhood of Upper Truckee River (Gudde, 1969, p. 346).

Tueculala Falls: see **Tueeulala Falls** [TUOLUMNE].

Tueeulala Falls [TUOLUMNE]: *waterfall,* 7 miles northeast of Mather on the north side of Hetch Hetchy Reservoir (lat. 37°57'45" N, long. 119°46'35" W; sec. 9, T 1 N, R 20 E). Named on Lake Eleanor (1956) 15' quadrangle. The name is of Indian origin (Browning, 1986, p. 221). United States Board on Geographic Names (1991, p. 7) rejected the name "Tueculala Falls" for the feature.

Tule Gulch [AMADOR]: *canyon,* less than 1 mile long, opens into the canyon of Mokelumne River 6.5 miles south-southwest of Jackson (lat. 38°16'05" N, long. 120°50'05" W; near SE cor. sec. 23, T 5 N, R 10 E). Named on Jackson (1962) 7.5' quadrangle. Water of Pardee Reservoir now covers the lower part of the canyon.

Tulloch Gulch [TUOLUMNE]: *canyon,* drained by a stream that flows 1.25 miles to Tulloch Lake nearly 5 miles northwest of Keystone (lat. 37°53'10" N, long. 120°33'50" W; sec. 5, T 1 S, R 18 E). Named on Keystone (1962) and Melones Dam (1962) 7.5' quadrangles. Copperopolis (1916) 15' quadrangle has the form "Tullock Gulch" for the name.

Tulloch Lake [CALAVERAS-TUOLUMNE]: *lake,* behind a dam on Stanislaus River 7 miles south of Copperopolis on Calaveras-Tuolumne county line (lat. 37°52'35" N, long. 120°36'15" W). Named on Melones Dam (1962) 7.5' quadrangle. United States Board on Geographic Names (1977b, p. 6) approved the name "Tulloch Reservoir" for the feature, and gave the name "Tulloch Lake" as a variant.

Tulloch Mountain [TUOLUMNE]: *peak,* 4.5 miles northwest of Keystone (lat. 37°53' N, long. 120°33'40" W; sec. 5, T 1 S, R 13 E). Altitude 943 feet. Named on Melones Dam (1962) 7.5' quadrangle. Called Tullock Mtn. on Copperopolis (1916) 15' quadrangle, but United States Board on Geographic Names (1965c, p. 12) rejected this form of the name.

Tulloch Reservoir: see **Tulloch Lake** [CALAVERAS-TUOLUMNE].

Tullock Gulch: see **Tulloch Gulch** [TUOLUMNE].

Tullock Mountain: see **Tulloch Mountain** [TUOLUMNE].

Tu-lu-la-wi-ak: see **Illilouette Creek** [MADERA-MARIPOSA].

Tuman Mill [EL DORADO]: *locality,* 2.5 miles west-northwest of Old Iron Mountain (lat. 38°42'50" N, long. 120°25'55" W; near SW cor. sec. 16, T 10 N, R 14 E). Site named on Stump Spring (1951) 7.5' quadrangle.

Tunnel Creek [EL DORADO]: *stream,* flows 1.25 miles to Whaler Creek 10 miles northwest of Pollock Pines (lat. 38°52'55" N, long. 120°41'05" W; near SW cor. sec. 18, T 12 N, R 12 E). Named on Tunnel Hill (1950) 7.5' quadrangle.

Tunnel Creek [TUOLUMNE]: *stream,* flows 1.5 miles to Middle Fork Stanislaus River 6.25 miles west of Strawberry (lat. 38°11'10" N, long. 120°07'25" W). Named on Strawberry (1979) 7.5' quadrangle.

Tunnel Hill [AMADOR]: *hill,* 1 mile southeast of Jackson (lat. 38°20'20" N, long. 120°45'30" W; near SW cor. sec. 27, T 6 N, R 11 E). Altitude 1441 feet. Named on Jackson (1962) 7.5' quadrangle.

Tunnel Hill [EL DORADO]: *ridge,* north-trending, 2.5 miles long, 15 miles north-northwest of Pollock Pines (lat. 38°57' N, long. 120°42'10" W); a tunnel along Georgetown Divide ditch is near the south end of the ridge. Named on Tunnel Hill (1950) 7.5' quadrangle. On Placerville (1893) 30' quadrangle, the name applies to a peak on the ridge.

Tunnel Mill Campground [PLACER]: *locality,* 3.5 miles south-southeast of Emigrant Gap (1) (lat. 39°15'05" N, long. 120°30'10" W; sec. 17, T 16 N, R 12 E). Named on Blue Canyon (1955) 7.5' quadrangle.

Tunnel Spring: see **Big Tunnel Spring** [NEVADA].

Tuolumne [TUOLUMNE]: *town,* 8 miles east-southeast of Sonora (lat. 37°57'45" N, long.

120°14'15" W; on N line sec. 8, T 1 N, R 16 E). Named on Tuolumne (1948) 7.5' quadrangle. Postal authorities established Tuolumne post office in 1891, discontinued it in 1893, and reestablished it in 1901 (Frickstad, p. 217).

Tuolumne Camp [TUOLUMNE]: *locality,* 6.5 miles southwest of Mather (lat. 37°48'40" N, long. 119°55'50" W; sec. 31, T 1 S, R 19 E); the place is along South Fork Tuolumne River. Named on Lake Eleanor (1956) 15' quadrangle.

Tuolumne Castle: see **Grand Mountain** [TUOLUMNE].

Tuolumne Falls [TUOLUMNE]: *waterfall,* 8.5 miles west of Tioga Pass (lat. 37°54'10" N, long. 119°24'45" W); the feature is along Tuolumne River. Named on Tuolumne Meadows (1956) 15' quadrangle. United States Board on Geographic Names (1992, p. 5) rejected the name "White Cascade" for the feature.

Tuolumne Glacier Monument: see **Fairview Dome** [TUOLUMNE].

Tuolumne Meadows [TUOLUMNE]: *valley,* 5.5 miles west-southwest of Tioga Pass (lat. 37°52'30" N, long. 119°21' W); the valley is along upper reaches of Tuolumne River and lower reaches of Lyell Fork. Named on Tuolumne Meadows (1956) 15' quadrangle. Members of the Whitney survey named the feature in 1863 (O'Neill, p. 17).

Tuolumne Meadows High Sierra Camp [TUOLUMNE]: *locality,* 4.5 miles west-southwest of Tioga Pass (lat. 37°52'40" N, long. 119°19'55" W; near E line sec. 4, T 1 S, R 24 E); the place is in Tuolumne Meadows. Named on Tuolumne Meadows (1956) 15' quadrangle.

Tuolumne Pass [MARIPOSA-TUOLUMNE]: *pass,* 8.5 miles south-southwest of Tioga Pass on Mariposa-Tuolumne county line (lat. 37°48'15" N, long. 119°20'20" W). Named on Tuolumne Meadows (1956) 15' quadrangle.

Tuolumne Peak [TUOLUMNE]: *peak,* 12.5 miles west of Tioga Pass (lat. 37°52'30" N, long. 119°29' W; sec. 6, T 1 S, R 23 E). Altitude 10,845 feet. Named on Tuolumne Meadows (1956) 15' quadrangle.

Tuolumne River [TUOLUMNE]: *stream,* formed in Tuolumne County by the confluence of Lyell Fork and Dana Fork, flows 135 miles to San Joaquin River 4 miles north-northeast of Westley in Stanislaus County (lat. 37°36'20" N, long. 121°10'20" W; sec. 11, T 4 S, R 7 E). Named on Mariposa (1957, revised 1970) and San Jose (1962) 1°x 2° quadrangles. Called Touleme River on Ellis' (1850) map, Rio d. l. Towalumnes on Fremont's (1848) map, and Tualumne River on Gibbes' (1850) map. The name also had a variety of other forms in the early days, including: Tuwalumnes (Lyman, 1849b, p. 418), Tawallamie (Turner, p. 127), Towallamie

(Evans, p. 215), Tuwaleme (Keller, p. 38), Towallome, and Towallernes (M'Collum, p. 129, 150). In the journal of the first session of California state senate the name "Tualumne" is described as a corruption of an Indian word that signifies a "cluster of stone wigwams" (DeFerrari *in* Stoddart, p. 173). North Fork enters from the north 9 miles south of Sonora; it is 33 miles long and is named on Long Barn (1956), Pinecrest (1956), Sonora (1948), and Tuolumne (1948) 15' quadrangles. United States Board on Geographic Names (1933, p. 560) rejected the name "Return Creek" for North Fork, and also rejected the name "North Fork" without the further designation "Tuolumne River." South Fork enters from the southeast 10 miles east of Groveland; it is 27 miles long and is named on Hetch Hetchy Reservoir (1956), Lake Eleanor (1956), and Tuolumne (1948) 15' quadrangles. United States Board on Geographic Names (1934, p. 17) rejected the name "Middle Fork Tuolumne River" for present Middle Tuolumne River.

Tuolumne River: see **Middle Tuolumne River** [TUOLUMNE].

Tuolumne Valley: see **Hetch Hetchy Valley** [TUOLUMNE].

Turnback Creek [TUOLUMNE]: *stream,* flows 13 miles to Tuolumne River 9 miles southeast of Sonora (lat. 37°53'20" N, long. 120°16'20" W; sec. 1, T 1 S, R 15 E). Named on Standard (1948), Tuolumne (1948), and Twain Harte (1979) 7.5' quadrangles. The name supposedly records an incident involving a group of miners who turned back after an indecisive fight with Indians at the stream (Gudde, 1969, p. 348).

Turner Canyon [SIERRA]:
(1) *canyon,* 2.5 miles long, along Turner Creek above a point 5 miles west-northwest of Sierraville (lat. 39°37'30" N, long. 120°26'40" W; near W line sec. 32, T 21 N, R 14 E). Named on Calpine (1981) and Sattley (1981) 7.5' quadrangles.
(2) *canyon,* drained by a stream that flows 2.25 miles to Bear Valley Creek 4.25 miles southeast of Loyalton (lat. 39°37' N, long. 120°13'10" W; sec. 5, T 20 N, R 16 E). Named on Sardine Peak (1981) and Sierraville (1981) 7.5' quadrangles.

Turner Creek [SIERRA]: *stream,* flows 4.25 miles to Sierra Valley 3.5 miles west-northwest of Sierraville (lat. 39°36'45" N, long. 120°25'30" W; sec. 4, T 20 N, R 14 E); the stream drains Turner Canyon (1). Named on Calpine (1981) and Sattley (1981) 7.5' quadrangles.

Turner Lake [MADERA]: *lake,* 1200 feet long, 2.5 miles east of Merced Peak (lat. 37°38'30" N, long. 119°20'50" W). Named on Merced Peak (1953) 15' quadrangle. The name is for Henry Ward Turner of United States Geological Survey, who pioneered geologic mapping in and near Yosemite National Park (United States Board on Geographic Names, 1963b, p. 15).

Turner Meadows [MARIPOSA]: *area,* 5 miles northeast of Wawona (lat. 37°35'45" N, long. 119°35'50" W; sec. 7, T 4 S, R 22 E). Named on Yosemite (1956) 15' quadrangle. United States Board on Geographic Names (1991, p. 7) approved the singular form "Turner Meadow" for the name. Browning (1986, p. 224) associated the name with Will Turner, who ran cattle in the vicinity in the 1880's, and was a ranger at Yosemite National Park for 37 years.

Turner Ridge [MARIPOSA]: *ridge,* southwest-trending, 2 miles long, 2.5 miles north of Wawona (lat. 37°34'15" N, long. 119°39'30" W). Named on Yosemite (1956) 15' quadrangle.

Turners Spring [CALAVERAS]: *spring,* 0.25 mile east-southeast of Copperopolis (lat. 37°58'45" N, long. 120°38'10" W; sec. 34, T 2 N, R 12 E). Named on Copperopolis (1962) 7.5' quadrangle.

Turtleback Dome [MARIPOSA]: *promontory,* 7 miles west-southwest of Yosemite Village on the south side of Merced River (lat. 37°42'45" N, long. 119°42'15" W). Named on Yosemite (1956) 15' quadrangle. United States Board on Geographic Names (1962a, p. 21) rejected the names "Turtle Dome" and "Turtle Back Dome" for the name.

Turtle Dome: see **Turtleback Dome** [MARIPOSA].

Turtle Rock: see **Pywiack Dome** [MARIPOSA].

Tuttle Lake [NEVADA]: *lake,* 1100 feet long, 5 miles east of Yuba Gap (lat. 39°19'10" N, long. 120°31'35" W; near SW cor. sec. 21, T 17 N, R 13 E). Named on Cisco Grove (1955) 7.5' quadrangle.

Tuttle's Creek: see **Mormon Creek** [TUOLUMNE].

Tuttletown [TUOLUMNE]: *settlement,* 4.25 miles west of Sonora near Mormon Creek (lat. 37°59'30" N, long. 120°27'30" W; on S line sec. 29, T 2 N, R 14 E). Named on Sonora (1948) 7.5' quadrangle. The name is for Judge A.A.H. Tuttle, the earliest settler at the place (Stoddart, p. 61). Postal authorities established Tuttletown post office in 1857, discontinued it in 1858, reestablished in 1890, and discontinued it in 1922 (Frickstad, p. 217). Wheeler (1878, p. 64) used the form "Tuttle Town" for the name. The community was known as Mormon Gulch in 1850 because some Mormons mined there (Jackson, p. 331). A place called Jeffersonville was situated about 1 mile southeast of Tuttletown (Gudde, 1975, p. 176); it thrived in the 1850's (Hoover, Rensch, and Rensch, p. 570).

TV Hill [SIERRA]: *peak,* 6.5 miles east-northeast of Sierraville (lat. 39°38'20" N, long. 120°15'50" W; near SE cor. sec. 26, T 21 N,

R 15 E). Altitude 6706 feet. Named on Antelope Valley (1981) 7.5' quadrangle.

Twain Harte [TUOLUMNE]: *town,* 9.5 miles east of Columbia (lat. 38°02'15" N, long. 120°13'45" W). Named on Twain Harte (1979) 7.5' quadrangle. Postal authorities established Twain Harte post office in 1931 (Frickstad, p. 217). Katurah F. Wood named the place in 1924 for writers Mark Twain and Bret Harte (Gudde, 1949, p. 373).

Twain Harte Lake [TUOLUMNE]: *lake,* 1150 feet long, less than 1 mile southwest of Twain Harte (lat. 38°01'45" N, long. 120°14'30" W; sec. 17, T 2 N, R 16 E). Named on Twain Harte (1979) 7.5' quadrangle.

Twain Harte Valley [TUOLUMNE]: *valley,* 1 mile north of Twain Harte (lat. 38°03'15" N, long. 120°13'55" W; near E line sec. 5, T 2 N, R 16 E). Named on Twain Harte (1979) 7.5' quadrangle.

Twelve Mile House [EL DORADO]: *locality,* 8 miles east of Georgetown (lat. 38°54'40" N, long. 120°41' W). Named on Placerville (1893) 30' quadrangle.

Twelvemile House [MADERA]: *locality,* 10 miles south of Raymond (lat. 37°04'20" N, long. 119°54'10" W; sec. 9, T 10 S, R 19 E). Named on Daulton (1921) 7.5' quadrangle.

Twentyfive Mile Canyon [EL DORADO]: *canyon,* drained by a stream that flows 1.5 miles to South Fork American River less than 1 mile west-northwest of Riverton (lat. 38°46'40" N, long. 120°27'35" W; near NW cor. sec. 30, T 11 N, R 14 E). Named on Riverton (1950) 7.5' quadrangle.

Twentytwo Mile House [MADERA]: *locality,* 14 miles south-southeast of Raymond (lat. 37°02'20" N, long. 119°46'50" W; near S line sec. 22, T 10 S, R 20 E). Named on Little Table Mountain (1962) 7.5' quadrangle. Called Millers Corner on Raymond (1944) 15' quadrangle.

Twin Bridges [EL DORADO]: *locality,* 5 miles west of Echo Summit along Pyramid Creek (lat. 38°48'40" N, long. 120°07'15" W; sec. 8, T 11 N, R 17 E). Named on Echo Lake (1955) 7.5' quadrangle. Postal authorities established Twin Bridges post office in 1947 (Frickstad, p. 30).

Twin Crags [PLACER]: *relief feature,* 1.25 miles west-southwest of Tahoe City on the north side of Truckee River (lat. 39°09'55" N, long. 120°09'55" W; sec. 12, T 15 N, R 16 E). Named on Tahoe City (1955) 7.5' quadrangle.

Twin Gulch [EL DORADO]: *canyon,* drained by a stream that flows 2.5 miles to Middle Fork Cosumnes River nearly 4 miles southeast of Caldor (lat. 38°33'55" N, long. 120°23'05" W; near NW cor. sec. 12, T 8 N, R 14 E). Named on Caldor (1951) and Peddler Hill (1951) 7.5' quadrangles.

Twin Gulch [TUOLUMNE]:
(1) *canyon,* drained by a stream that flows

nearly 1 mile to La Grange Reservoir 2.5 miles south-southwest of Don Pedro Camp opposite the mouth of Twin Gulch (2) (lat. 37°40'55" N, long. 120° 25'45" W; near S line sec. 9, T 3 S, R 14 E). Named on La Grange (1962) 7.5' quadrangle.

(2) *canyon,* drained by a stream that flows 1 mile to La Grange Reservoir 2.5 miles south-southwest of Don Pedro Camp opposite the mouth of Twin Gulch (1) (lat. 37°40'50" N, long. 120°25'40" W; near N line sec. 16, T 3 S, R 14 E). Named on La Grange (1962) 7.5' quadrangle.

Twin Gulch: see **Little Twin Gulch** [TUOLUMNE].

Twin Island Lakes [MADERA]: *lakes,* two, largest 1800 feet long, 9.5 miles west-north-west of Devils Postpile (lat. 37°41'30" N, long. 119°13'55" W); each lake contains a small island. Named on Devils Postpile (1953) 15' quadrangle.

Twin Lakes [EL DORADO]: *lakes,* two, each about 1200 feet long, 2.5 miles northwest of Pyramid Peak (lat. 38°52'10" N, long. 120° 11'30" W). Named on Pyramid Peak (1955) 7.5' quadrangle.

Twin Lakes [MADERA]: *lakes,* two, largest 400 feet long, 5 miles southeast of Merced Peak (lat. 37°34'30" N, long. 119°20'25" W). Named on Merced Peak (1953) 15' quadrangle.

Twin Lakes [PLACER]: *lakes,* two, largest 800 feet long, 4.5 miles west-southwest of Cisco Grove (lat. 39°17'20" N, long. 120°37' W; near N line sec. 3, T 16 N, R 12 E). Named on Cisco Grove (1955) 7.5' quadrangle.

Twin Lakes [TUOLUMNE]: *lakes,* two, largest 1.25 miles long, 6.5 miles west of Tower Peak along Kendrick Creek (lat. 38°08' N, long. 119°40' W). Named on Tower Peak (1956) 15' quadrangle.

Twin Meadows [TUOLUMNE]: *areas,* two, 8 miles west-northwest of Dardanelle (lat. 38°23' N, long. 119°58' W). Named on Spicer Meadow Reservoir (1979) 7.5' quadrangle, which shows marsh in the areas.

Twin Meadows Lake [TUOLUMNE]: *lake,* 400 feet long, 8 miles west-northwest of Dardanelle (lat. 38°23'25" N, long. 119°57'45" W); the lake is 0.5 mile north-northeast of Twin Meadows. Named on Spicer Meadow Reservoir (1979) 7.5' quadrangle.

Twin Peaks [EL DORADO]: *peaks,* 5 miles east-southeast of Mount Tallac (lat. 38°52'55" N, long. 120°00'35" W; at S line sec. 17, T 12 N, R 18 E). Altitude of highest is 6971 feet. Named on Emerald Bay (1955) 7.5' quadrangle.

Twin Peaks [PLACER]: *peaks,* 4.25 miles west-northwest of Homewood (lat. 39°06'45" N, long. 120°13'55" W; at SE cor. sec. 29, T 15 N, R 16 E). Altitude of the easternmost peak is 8878 feet. Named on Homewood (1955) 7.5' quadrangle. Called Twin Peak on Truckee (1895) 30' quadrangle.

Twin Peaks [TUOLUMNE]: *peaks,* two, 1.5 miles east-southeast of Matterhorn Peak on Tuolumne-Mono county line (lat. 38°04'55" N, long. 119°21'15" W). Named on Matterhorn Peak (1956) 15' quadrangle.

Twin Peaks: see **Mount Savage** [MARIPOSA].

Twin Pines [PLACER]: *settlement,* 5.5 miles south-southwest of Colfax (lat. 39°01'30" N, long. 120°58'40" W; sec. 33, T 14 N, R 9 E). Named on Colfax (1949) 7.5' quadrangle.

Twin Sisters [MADERA]: *peaks,* two, 11 miles northeast of Raymond (lat. 37°20'25" N, long. 119°46'15" W; sec. 10, T 7 S, R 20 E). Altitudes 2697 and 2789 feet. Named on Horsecamp Mountain (1947) 7.5' quadrangle.

Twin Valley: see **Carpenter Valley** [NEVADA].

Two Dog Pass [TUOLUMNE]: *pass,* 4.5 miles east-northeast of Tuolumne (lat. 37°58'55" N, long. 120°09'25" W; near W line sec. 31, T 2 N, R 17 E). Named on Tuolumne (1948) 7.5' quadrangle.

Two Dollar Gulch [CALAVERAS]: *canyon,* drained by a stream that flows less than 1 mile to Spruce Gulch 0.25 mile east of Rail Road Flat (lat. 38°20'35" N, long. 120°30'15" W; near E line sec. 26, T 6 N, R 13 E). Named on Rail Road Flat (1948) 7.5' quadrangle.

Twomile Creek [TUOLUMNE]: *stream,* flows 5.25 miles to Clavey River 7 miles southeast of Long Barn (lat. 38°00'50" N, long. 120° 03' W; near E line sec. 24, T 2 N, R 17 E). Named on Hull Creek (1979) 7.5' quadrangle.

Two Peaks [EL DORADO]: *peaks,* 6.5 miles east-southeast of Robbs Peak (lat. 38°54'10" N, long. 120°17' W; sec. 10, T 12 N, R 15 E). Altitude of highest is 7594 feet. Named on Loon Lake (1952) 7.5' quadrangle.

Two Sentinels [AMADOR]: *peaks,* 11 miles north of Mokelumne Peak (lat. 38°41'55" N, long. 120°05'15" W; sec. 21, T 10 N, R 17 E). Named on Caples Lake (1979) 7.5' quadrangle.

Two Sentinels: see **Camp Two Sentinels** [EL DORADO].

Two Springs: see **Wheats** [CALAVERAS].

Two Springs Campground [MADERA]: *locality,* 5 miles southeast of Yosemite Forks on the south side of Bass Lake (1) (lat. 37°18'50" N, long. 119°33'50" W; near SW cor. sec. 15, T 7 S, R 22 E). Named on Bass Lake (1953) 15' quadrangle.

Two Teats [MADERA]: *peak,* 6 miles north of Devils Postpile on Madera-Mono county line (lat. 37°42'45" N, long. 119°05'55" W). Altitude 11,387 feet. Named on Devils Postpile (1953) 15' quadrangle. This peak and nearby San Joaquin Mountain together also were called Two Teats (Gudde, 1949, p. 373-374).

Tyler [MADERA]: *locality,* 5 miles south-south-west of Chowchilla along Chowchilla Pacific Railroad (lat. 37°03'20" N, long. 120°18'50" W; sec. 15, T 10 S, R 15 E). Named on Chowchilla (1918) 7.5' quadrangle.

Tyler: see **Cherokee** [NEVADA].

Tyler Lake [EL DORADO]: *lake,* 500 feet long,

5.5 miles south-southwest of Phipps Peak (lat. 38°52'50" N, long. 120°11'50" W). Named on Rockbound Valley (1955) 7.5' quadrangle.

Tylers Corner [EL DORADO]: *locality,* 3 miles southeast of Aukum along South Fork Cosumnes River (lat. 38°31'40" N, long. 120°41'05" W; near W line sec. 20, T 8 N, R 12 E). Named on Aukum (1952) 7.5' quadrangle.

– U –

Uhlen Valley [NEVADA]: *valley,* 2 miles northwest of Donner Pass along Upper Castle Creek (lat. 39°20' N, long. 120°21'20" W). Named on Norden (1955) 7.5' quadrangle.

Umbrella Hill [EL DORADO]: *peak,* 1 mile north-northeast of the village of Pilot Hill (lat. 38°50'50" N, long. 121°00'15" W; at W line sec. 32, T 12 N, R 9 E). Named on Pilot Hill (1954) 7.5' quadrangle.

Umpa Lake [EL DORADO]: *lake,* 400 feet long, 3 miles northwest of Pyramid Peak (lat. 38°52'20" N, long. 120°12'05" W). Named on Pyramid Peak (1955) 7.5' quadrangle.

Uncle Toms Cabin [EL DORADO]: *locality,* 4.5 miles west of Robbs Peak (lat. 38°55'45" N, long. 120°29'10" W; sec. 35, T 13 N, R 13 E). Named on Robbs Peak (1950) 7.5' quadrangle. The name "Uncle Tom" is said to be from a black man who lived at the place in the early days; later a roadhouse at the site was called Uncle Toms Cabin (Yohalem, p. 199).

Underwood Creek [CALAVERAS]: *stream,* flows 2.5 miles to Littlejohns Creek 2.5 miles west-northwest of Copperopolis (lat. 37°59'45" N, long. 120°41' W; sec. 29, T 2 N, R 12 E). Named on Copperopolis (1962) and Salt Spring Valley (1962) 7.5' quadrangles.

Unicorn Creek [TUOLUMNE]: *stream,* flows 2.5 miles to Tuolumne River 6.5 miles west-southwest of Tioga Pass in Tuolumne Meadows (lat. 37°52'30" N, long. 119°22'05" W; near W line sec. 5, T 1 S, R 24 E); the stream heads near Unicorn Peak. Named on Tuolumne Meadows (1956) 15' quadrangle.

Unicorn Peak [TUOLUMNE]: *peak,* 8 miles southwest of Tioga Pass (lat. 37°50'45" N, long. 119°22'50" W). Named on Tuolumne Meadows (1956) 15' quadrangle. Members of the Whitney survey named the peak (United States Board on Geographic Names, 1934, p. 26). Brewer (p. 412) described the feature in 1863 as a "sharp needle."

Union: see **Camp Union**, under **Lancha Plana** [AMADOR].

Union Canyon [NEVADA]: *canyon,* drained by a stream that flows 1.25 miles to South Yuba River nearly 4 miles west-southwest of Washington (lat. 39°20'40" N, long. 120°52'05" W; near NW cor. sec. 16, T 17 N, R 10 E). Named on Washington (1950) 7.5' quadrangle.

Union Flat: see **Spanish Flat** [EL DORADO]; **Volcano** [AMADOR].

Union Flat Campground [SIERRA]: *locality,* 6 miles west of Sierra City along North Yuba River (lat. 39°34' N, long. 120°44'40" W; near S line sec. 28, T 20 N, R 11 E). Named on Sierra City (1981) 7.5' quadrangle.

Union Hill [EL DORADO]: *peak,* 1.5 miles east of Pollock Pines (lat. 38°45'50" N, long. 120°33'10" W; near N line sec. 32, T 11 N, R 13 E). Named on Pollock Pines (1950) 7.5' quadrangle.

Union Hill [NEVADA]: *village,* 1.5 miles east-southeast of Grass Valley (lat. 39°12'25" N, long. 121°02'15" W; on E line sec. 35, T 16 N, R 8 E). Named on Grass Valley (1949) 7.5' quadrangle. California Division of Highways' (1934) map shows a place called Union Hill located about 1.5 miles farther east (sec. 31, T 16 N, R 9 E) along Nevada County Narrow Gauge Railroad, and a place called Cedar Kress located along the railroad 0.5 mile south of this second Union Hill (near S line sec. 31, T 16 N, R 9 E).

Union Hill [SIERRA]: *locality,* 7.25 miles west-northwest of Goodyears Bar (lat. 39°35'50" N, long. 121°00'10" W; near E line sec. 18, T 20 N, R 9 E). Named on Strawberry Valley (1948) 7.5' quadrangle.

Union Hill [TUOLUMNE]: *hill,* 1 mile south of Columbia (lat. 38°01'10" N, long. 120°24'05" W; sec. 23, T 2 N, R 14 E). Named on Columbia (1948) 7.5' quadrangle. Gudde (1975, p. 99) listed a place called Douglasville that was situated opposite Union Hill.

Union House: see **Hidden Valley** [PLACER] (2).

Union Mills [NEVADA]: *locality,* 4.5 miles east-northeast of Truckee (lat. 39°21'15" N, long. 120°06'15" W; at E line sec. 5, T 17 N, R 17 E); the place is in Union Valley. Site named on Martis Peak (1955) 7.5' quadrangle.

Union Point [MARIPOSA]: *promontory,* 1 mile south of Yosemite Village on the south side of Yosemite Valley (lat. 37°44'10" N, long. 119°35'10" W). Named on Yosemite (1956) 15' quadrangle.

Union Shed: see **Sheridan** [PLACER].

Uniontown: see **El Dorado** [EL DORADO]; **Lotus** [EL DORADO].

Union Valley [EL DORADO]: *valley,* 3.5 miles south of Robbs Peak (lat. 38°52'30" N, long. 120°24'30" W). Named on Robbs Peak (1952) 15' quadrangle. Water of Union Valley Reservoir now covers most of the valley.

Union Valley [NEVADA]: *valley,* 4.5 miles east-northeast of Truckee (lat. 39°21'05" N, long. 120°05'55" W; sec. 4, 5, T 17 N, R 17 E); the site of Union Mills is in the valley. Named on Martis Peak (1955) 7.5' quadrangle.

Union Valley Reservoir [EL DORADO]: *lake,* behind a dam on Silver Creek 6.5 miles north of Riverton (lat. 38°52' N, long. 120° 26'20" W; near SW cor. sec. 20, T 12 N, R 14 E); the lake is in Union Valley. Named on Loon Lake (1952, photorevised 1973), Riverton (1950, photorevised 1973), and Robbs Peak (1950, photorevised 1973) 7.5' quadrangles.

United States Canyon [PLACER]: *canyon,* drained by a stream that flows nearly 1 mile to Middle Fork American River 8.5 miles east-northeast of Auburn (lat. 38°57'45" N, long. 120°56'20" W; sec. 23, T 13 N, R 9 E). Named on Greenwood (1949) 7.5' quadrangle.

Uno: see **Aukum** [EL DORADO].

Upper Agua Fria: see **Agua Fria** [MARI-POSA].

Upper Arkansas Bar: see **Green Valley** [PLACER].

Upper Baker Campground: see **Baker Campground** [TUOLUMNE].

Upper Bar: see **Big Bar** [CALAVERAS].

Upper Branigan Lake [TUOLUMNE]: *lake,* 900 feet long, 10 miles southwest of Tower Peak (lat. 38°02'20" N, long. 119°40'15" W); the lake is 0.25 mile upstream from Middle Branigan Lake. Named on Tower Peak (1956) 15' quadrangle.

Upper Calaveritas: see **Calaveritas** [CALA-VERAS].

Upper Castle Creek [NEVADA]: *stream,* flows 4 miles to Lake Van Norden 2.5 miles west of Donner Pass (lat. 39°19'20" N, long. 120°22'15" W; sec. 23, T 17 N, R 14 E); the stream heads at Castle Valley. Named on Norden (1955) 7.5' quadrangle.

Upper Chiquito Campground [MADERA]: *locality,* 10 miles north of Shuteye Peak (lat. 37°29'55" N, long. 119°24'30" W; sec. 13, T 5 S, R 23 E); the place is along Chiquito Creek 7 miles upstream from Lower Chiquito Campground. Named on Shuteye Peak (1953) 15' quadrangle.

Upper Corral: see **Illinoistown** [PLACER].

Upper Crossing: see **Amador Crossing**, under **Amador City** [AMADOR].

Upper Derbec Spring [NEVADA]: *spring,* 2.25 miles north-northeast of North Bloomfield (lat. 39°23'40" N, long. 120°52'35" W; sec. 29, T 18 N, R 10 E); the spring is 1000 feet north-northeast of Derbec Spring. Named on Pike (1949) 7.5' quadrangle.

Upper Echo Lake [EL DORADO]: *lake,* 3600 feet long, 3.25 miles northwest of Echo Summit (lat. 38°50'40" N, long. 120°04'30" W; sec. 35, T 12 N, R 17 E); the lake is west of Lower Echo Lake. Named on Echo Lake (1955) 7.5' quadrangle.

Upper Ferry: see **Big Bar** [CALAVERAS].

Upper Fletcher Lake [MARIPOSA]: *lake,* 1100 feet long, 5 miles southeast of Cathedral Peak (lat. 37°47'50" N, long. 119°20'25" W); the lake is along Fletcher Creek. Named on Tuolumne Meadows (1956) 7.5' quadrangle. Called Fletcher Lake on Mount Lyell (1901) 30' quadrangle, and United States Board on Geographic Names (1991, p. 4) approved this name for it. Lieutenant N.F. McClure gave the name "Fletcher Lake" to the feature in 1895 to honor Arthur C. Fletcher of California State Board of Fish Commissioners (United States

Board on Geographic Names, 1934, p. 9).

Upper Fletcher Lake: see **Townsley Lake** [MARIPOSA].

Upper Forni [EL DORADO]: *locality,* nearly 2 miles south-southwest of Pyramid Peak (lat. 38°49'20" N, long. 120°10'20" W; near NW cor. sec. 12, T 11 N, R 16 E); the place is 3.25 miles east-northeast of Lower Forni. Named on Pyramid Peak (1955) 7.5' quadrangle. Called Forni on Pyramid Peak (1896) 30' quadrangle.

Upper Hell Hole [PLACER]: *valley,* 2.5 miles north-northeast of Bunker Hill along Rubicon River (lat. 39°05' N, long. 120°21'30" W; on S line sec. 1, T 14 N, R 14 E). Named on Granite Chief (1953) 15' quadrangle. Called Hell Hole on Truckee (1895) 30' quadrangle. Truckee (1940) 30' quadrangle has the form "Upper Hellhole" for the name. Water of Hell Hole Reservoir now floods part of the valley.

Upper Iceberg Lake: see **Cecile Lake** [MADERA].

Upper Independence Creek [NEVADA]: *stream,* flows nearly 3 miles to Independence Lake 8 miles north of Donner Pass (lat. 39° 25'55" N, long. 120°19'40" W; near SE cor. sec. 5, T 18 N, R 15 E). Named on Independence Lake (1981) 7.5' quadrangle.

Upper Jones Valley [NEVADA]: *valley,* 6.5 miles west-northwest of Donner Pass at the head of Rattlesnake Creek (2) (lat. 39°20'55" N, long. 120°26'30" W; near S line sec. 7, T 17 N, R 14 E); the feature is above Jones Valley. Named on Soda Springs (1955) 7.5' quadrangle.

Upper Lola Montez Lake [NEVADA]: *lake,* 550 feet long, 6.25 miles west-northwest of Donner Pass (lat. 39°21'05" N, long. 120° 25'50" W; sec. 8, T 17 N, R 14 E); the lake is 0.25 mile west-northwest of Lower Lola Montez Lake. Named on Soda Springs (1955) 7.5' quadrangle.

Upper Long Valley [SIERRA]: *valley,* 11 miles east of Loyalton on Sierra-Lassen county line (lat. 39°42'30" N, long. 120°02'30" W). Named on Evans Canyon (1978) 7.5' quadrangle.

Upper McCabe Lake [TUOLUMNE]: *lake,* 0.5 mile long, 7 miles north-northwest of Tioga Pass (lat. 37°59'45" N, long. 119°19'20" W; on W line sec. 27, T 2 N, R 24 E); the lake is about 1 mile east of McCabe Lakes. Named on Tuolumne Meadows (1956) 15' quadrangle. On Mount Lyell (1901) 30' quadrangle, the lake apparently is included with the group called McCabe Lakes. United States Board on Geographic Names (1962a, p. 21) rejected the name "McCabe Lake" for present Upper McCabe Lake.

Upper Merced Pass Lake [MADERA]: *lake,* 450 feet long, 2.5 miles west-southwest of Merced Peak (lat. 37°37'25" N, long. 119°26'30" W); the lake is 0.5 mile north of Merced Pass. Named on Merced Peak (1953) 15' quadrangle.

Upper Mud Spring [EL DORADO]: *spring,* 6.5 miles southeast of Caldor (lat. 38°32'50" N, long. 120°20' W; near E line sec. 17, T 8 N, R 15 E); the spring is less than 0.5 mile east-northeast of Mud Spring [AMADOR]. Named on Peddler Hill (1951) 7.5' quadrangle.

Upper Narrows Reservoir: see **Englebright Lake** [NEVADA].

Upper Onion Valley [AMADOR]: *area,* 5.25 miles west-northwest of Mokelumne Peak (lat. 38°33'40" N, long. 120°11' W; sec. 11, T 8 N, R 16 E); the place is 0.5 mile south-southeast of Onion Valley. Named on Bear River Reservoir (1979) 7.5' quadrangle.

Upper Ottoway Lake [MADERA]: *lake,* 1650 feet long, 0.5 mile west-northwest of Merced Peak (lat. 37°38'25" N, long. 119°24'15" W); the lake is less than 1 mile east of Lower Ottoway Lake. Named on Merced Peak (1953) 15' quadrangle.

Upper Pardoes Camp [AMADOR]: *locality,* 4.25 miles west-northwest of Mokelumne Peak (lat. 38°33'45" N, long. 120°10' W; sec. 12, T 8 N, R 16 E). Site named on Bear River Reservoir (1979) 7.5' quadrangle.

Upper Peninsula Lake [TUOLUMNE]: *lake,* 1100 feet long, 8 miles west-southwest of Tower Peak (lat. 38°06' N, long. 119°40'45" W); the lake is 0.5 mile east of Peninsula Lake. Named on Tower Peak (1956) 15' quadrangle.

Upper Rancheria: see **Rancheria** [AMADOR].

Upper Relief Valley [TUOLUMNE]: *valley,* 12 miles east-northeast of Pinecrest at the head of Relief Creek (lat. 38°13'30" N, long. 119°46'30" W); the valley is about 1.5 miles south-southwest of Lower Relief Valley. Named on Pinecrest (1956) 15' quadrangle.

Upper Salmon Lake [SIERRA]: *lake,* 2100 feet long, 6.5 miles north of Sierra City (lat. 39°39'25" N, long. 120°39'05" W; sec. 29, T 21 N, R 12 E); the lake is along Salmon Creek 0.5 mile upstream from Lower Salmon Lake. Named on Gold Lake (1981) 7.5' quadrangle.

Upper Sardine Lake [SIERRA]: *lake,* 2950 feet long, 3 miles north of Sierra City (lat. 39°36'30" N, long. 120°38' W; sec. 9, 16, T 20 N, R 12 E); the lake is on upper reaches of Sardine Creek less than 0.25 mile upstream from Lower Sardine Lake. Named on Sierra City (1981) 7.5' quadrangle.

Upper Tallant Lake: see **Stony Ridge Lake** [EL DORADO].

Upper Three Meadow [TUOLUMNE]: *area,* 7.25 miles east-northeast of Pinecrest (lat. 38°14'25" N, long. 119°52'40" W; sec. 34, T 5 N, R 19 E); the feature is one of the group called Three Meadows. Named on Pinecrest (1979) 7.5' quadrangle.

Upper Truckee Marsh: see **Truckee Marsh** [EL DORADO].

Upper Truckee River [EL DORADO]: *stream,* heads in Alpine County and flows 18 miles to Lake Tahoe 8 miles northwest of Freel Peak in El Dorado County (lat. 38°56'30" N, long. 119° 59'45" W; sec. 31, T 13 N, R 18 E). Named on Caples Lake (1979), Echo Lake (1955), Emerald Bay (1955), and South Lake Tahoe (1955, photorevised 1969 and 1974) 7.5' quadrangles.

Upper Velma Lake [EL DORADO]: *lake,* 1300 feet long, 2 miles south of Phipps Peak (lat. 38°55'40" N, long. 120°08'50" W; on W line sec. 31, T 13 N, R 17 E); the lake is less than 1 mile south-southwest of Lower Velma Lake. Named on Rockbound Valley (1955) 7.5' quadrangle.

Upper Woolsey Spring [NEVADA]: *spring,* 3.25 miles north-northeast of North Bloomfield (lat. 39°24'40" N, long. 120°52' W; near W line sec. 21, T 18 N, R 10 E); the spring is 0.5 mile southwest of the site of Woolsey Flat (2). Named on Alleghany (1949) 7.5' quadrangle.

Upper Yosemite Fall [MARIPOSA]: *waterfall,* less than 1 mile northwest of Yosemite Village (lat. 37°45'20" N, long. 119°35'45" W); the feature is along Yosemite Creek above Lower Yosemite Fall. Named on Hetch Hetchy Reservoir (1956) 15' quadrangle. Yosemite (1909) 30' quadrangle has the name "Yosemite Falls" for Upper Yosemite Fall and Lower Yosemite Fall together. Hoffmann and Gardner's (1863-1867) map has the name "Yosemite Fall" for the two waterfalls together.

Urban: see **Pleasant Valley** [EL DORADO] (2).

Usona [MARIPOSA]: *locality,* 8 miles east-southeast of Mariposa (lat. 37°27'15" N, long. 119°49'35" W; sec. 31, T 5 S, R 20 E). Named on Mariposa (1947) 15' quadrangle. Postal authorities established Usona post office in 1913, moved it 5.5 miles north in 1940, and discontinued it in 1942; the name is from the initial letters of the term "United States of North America" (Salley, p. 228).

Utica Reservoir [TUOLUMNE]: *lake,* nearly 2 miles long, 7 miles northeast of Liberty Hill on Tuolumne-Alpine county line, mainly in Alpine County (lat. 38°26' N, long. 120°00' W). Named on Tamarack (1979) 7.5' quadrangle.

Utica Reservoir: see **Ross Reservoir** [CALAVERAS].

Utters Bar: see **Stent** [TUOLUMNE].

Utterville: see **Stent** [TUOLUMNE].

– V –

Vade: see **Phillips** [EL DORADO].

Valentine Gulch [CALAVERAS]: *canyon,* drained by a stream that flows 1 mile to Middle Fork Mokelumne River nearly 5 miles west-northwest of Rail Road Flat (lat. 38°22'25" N, long. 120°35'25" W; sec. 18, T 6 N, R 13 E). Named on Rail Road Flat (1948) 7.5' quadrangle. The name commemorates Valentine Granados, a well-known Mexican prospector of Calaveras County (Camp *in* Doble, p. 300).

Valentine Hill: see **Bummerville** [CALA-VERAS].

Vallecita: see **Catheys Valley** [MARIPOSA] (1).

Vallecito [CALAVERAS]: *village,* 4 miles east-northeast of Angels Camp (lat. 38°05'15" N, long. 120°28'20" W; sec. 30, T 3 N, R 14 E). Named on Columbia (1948) 7.5' quadrangle. Postal authorities established Vallicita post office in 1854 and changed the name to Vallecito in 1940 (Salley, p. 229). United States Board on Geographic Names (1950, p. 7) ruled against the name "Vallicita" for the place. Balaklava Hill, named for a battle site of the Crimean War, was located 2.5 miles south of Vallecito (Gudde, 1975, p. 25).

Valley Springs [CALAVERAS]: *town,* 8 miles west of San Andreas (lat. 38°11'35" N, long. 120°49'45" W; sec. 13, 24, T 4 N, R 10 E). Named on Valley Springs (1962) 7.5' quadrangle. Postal authorities established Valley Springs post office in 1872, discontinued it in 1879, and reestablished it in 1882 (Frickstad, p. 17). The place first was called Spring Valley for mineral springs there, but the words of this name were reversed when the site became the terminus of San Joaquin and Sierra Nevada Railroad (Gudde, 1949, p. 376). Camp's (1962) map has the name "Tremont House" for a stopping place located 3 miles south of Valley Springs, and the name "N. American House" for a stopping place situated 2 miles south of Valley Springs.

Valley Springs Peak [CALAVERAS]: *peak,* 1 mile north-northwest of Valley Springs (lat. 38°12'25" N, long. 120°50'15" W; near N line sec. 14, T 4 N, R 10 E). Altitude 1211 feet. Named on Valley Springs (1962) 7.5' quadrangle.

Valley Springs Reservoir: see **New Hogan Reservoir** [CALAVERAS].

Valley View [MARIPOSA]: *locality,* 5 miles west-southwest of Yosemite Village in Yosemite Valley (lat. 37°43'05" N, long. 119° 40' W). Named on Yosemite (1956) 15' quadrangle. This is the first spot from which most of Yosemite Valley can be viewed on the approach from the west; the place is called River View on a map of 1883 (Browning, 1988, p. 150).

Valley View [PLACER]: *locality,* 5.25 miles north of Lincoln (lat. 38°57'45" N, long. 121°16'30" W). Named on Sacramento (1892) 30' quadrangle. Gudde (1975, p. 369) noted that the place also was called Whiskey Diggings.

Valley View Reservoir [PLACER]: *lake,* 400 feet long, 10.5 miles west-northwest of Auburn (lat. 38°58' N, long. 121°14'45" W; on E line sec. 24, T 13 N, R 6 E). Named on Gold Hill (1954) 7.5' quadrangle.

Vallicita: see **Vallecito** [CALAVERAS].

Van Cliffe Canyon: see **Cliff Canyon** [PLACER].

Vandeburg Lake [MADERA]: *lake,* 900 feet long, 6 miles south-southeast of Merced Peak (lat. 37°32'55" N, long. 119°21'05" W); the lake is one of the group called Madera Lakes. Named on Merced Peak (1953) 15' quadrangle. United States Board on Geographic Names (1991, p. 7) approved the form "Vanderburgh Lake" for the name.

Vanderburgh Lake: see **Vandeburg Lake** [MADERA].

Vandervere Mountain [NEVADA]: *peak,* 3 miles south of Pilot Peak (lat. 39°07'40" N, long. 121°10'35" W; near NE cor. sec. 27, T 15 N, R 7 E). Altitude 1846 feet. Named on Rough and Ready (1949) 7.5' quadrangle. Called Pike Mt. on Smartsville (1895) 30' quadrangle.

Vangeisen Combie Diversion Reservoir: see **Lake Combie** [NEVADA-PLACER].

Van Horn Creek [EL DORADO]: *stream,* flows 3.25 miles to North Fork Cosumnes River 4 miles southwest of Old Iron Mountain (lat. 38°39'45" N, long. 120°26'20" W; at W line sec. 4, T 9 N, R 14 E). Named on Stump Spring (1951) 7.5' quadrangle.

Van Norden: see **Lake Van Norden** [NEVADA-PLACER].

Vantrent: see **Lincoln** [PLACER].

Van Vleck [EL DORADO]: *locality,* 4 miles east-northeast of Pollock Pines (lat. 38°46'40" N, long. 120°30'50" W; sec. 22, T 11 N, R 13 E). Named on Pollock Pines (1950) 7.5' quadrangle.

Van Winkle [EL DORADO]: *locality,* 4.5 miles west-southwest of Kirkwood (lat. 38°41'15" N, long. 120°09'10" W). Named on Pyramid Peak (1896) 30' quadrangle.

Varain: see **Exchequer** [MARIPOSA] (1).

Vaughn Cabin [EL DORADO]: *locality,* 11.5 miles north-northeast of Pollock Pines (lat. 38°55'05" N, long. 120°31'05" W; sec. 4, T 12 N, R 13 E). Named on Devil Peak (1950) 7.5' quadrangle.

Velma Lake: see **Lower Velma Lake** [EL DORADO]; **Middle Velma Lake** [EL DORADO]; **Upper Velma Lake** [EL DORADO].

Vera: see **Lake Vera** [NEVADA].

Verdi Peak [SIERRA]: *peak,* 6.25 miles southsoutheast of Crystal Peak (lat. 39°28'20" N, long. 120°02'20" W; sec. 25, T 19 N, R 17 E); the peak is at the south end of Verdi Range. Altitude 8444 feet. Named on Boca (1955) 7.5' quadrangle. Called Crystal Peak on Truckee (1895) 30' quadrangle, but United States Board on Geographic Names (1939, p. 36) rejected this name and the name "Bald Mountain" for the feature. The name "Verdi" is from nearby Verdi, Nevada, which was named for the Italian composer, Giuseppe Verdi (Hanna, p. 344).

Verdi Range [SIERRA]: *ridge,* south-trending, 5 miles long, center 4.25 miles southeast of Crystal Peak (lat. 39°30' N, long. 120°02'45" W); Verdi Peak is near the south end of the ridge. Named on Boca (1955) and Dog Valley (1981) 7.5' quadrangles.

Vermont Bar [TUOLUMNE]: *locality,* 9 miles

north of Keystone along Stanislaus River (lat. 37°58'05" N, long. 120°31'30" W; on E line sec. 3, T 1 N, R 13 E). Named on Copperopolis (1916) 15' quadrangle. Water of New Melones Lake now covers the site.

Vernal Fall [MARIPOSA]: *waterfall,* 3 miles east-southeast of Yosemite Village along Merced River (lat. 37°43'40" N, long. 119°32'35" W). Named on Yosemite (1956) 15' quadrangle. Lafayette H. Bunnell named the waterfall in 1851 (United States Board on Geographic Names, 1934, p. 26).

Vernon Lake: see **Lake Vernon** [TUOLUMNE].

Vichy Spring [MADERA]: *spring,* 7.25 miles east-southeast of Raymond (lat. 37°09'35" N, long. 119°47'35" W; sec. 9, T 9 S, R 20 E). Named on Raymond (1944) 15' quadrangle.

Victoria Gulch [MARIPOSA]: *canyon,* drained by a stream that flows 3 miles to Bear Creek (2) 4.25 miles north of the settlement of Catheys Valley (lat. 37°29'45" N, long. 120°06'05" W). Named on Catheys Valley (1962) 7.5' quadrangle.

Vine Spring [TUOLUMNE]: *spring,* nearly 2 miles north-northwest of Columbia (lat. 38°03'30" N, long. 120°25'10" W; sec. 3, T 2 N, R 14 E). Named on Columbia (1948) 7.5' quadrangle.

Virginia: see **Virginiatown** [PLACER].

Virginia Canyon [TUOLUMNE]: *canyon,* 10 miles long, along Return Creek above a point 11 miles west-northwest of Tioga Pass (lat. 37°58' N, long. 119°26'25" W). Named on Matterhorn Peak (1956) and Tuolumne Meadows (1956) 15' quadrangles.

Virginia Creek [MARIPOSA]: *stream,* flows 1 mile to Devil Gulch 9 miles south of El Portal (lat. 37°32'25" N, long. 119°47'25" W). Named on Buckingham Mountain (1947) 7.5' quadrangle.

Virginia Falls: see **Lower Virginia Falls**, under **White Cascade** [TUOLUMNE].

Virginia House: see **Boca** [NEVADA].

Virginia Lake [TUOLUMNE]: *lake,* 1700 feet long, 10 miles west-northwest of Tioga Pass (lat. 37°57'45" N, long. 119°25'35" W); the lake is less than 1 mile east-southeast of the mouth of Virginia Canyon. Named on Tuolumne Meadows (1956) 15' quadrangle.

Virginia Pass [TUOLUMNE]: *pass,* 3 miles southeast of Matterhorn Peak on Tuolumne-Mono county line (lat. 38°04' N, long. 119°20'05" W); the pass is near the head of Virginia Canyon. Named on Matterhorn Peak (1956) 15' quadrangle.

Virginia Peak [TUOLUMNE]: *peak,* 2.25 miles southeast of Matterhorn Peak (lat. 38°03'55" N, long. 119°21'25" W). Altitude 12,001 feet. Named on Matterhorn Peak (1956) 15' quadrangle. Officials of the National Park Service recommended the name "Virginia Peak" to replace the earlier name "Red Peak" (United States Board on Geographic Names, 1934, p. 27).

Virginia Point [MARIPOSA]: *relief feature,* nearly 4 miles southeast of Coulterville (lat. 37°40'15" N, long. 120°09'05" W; near SE cor. sec. 13, T 3 S, R 16 E). Named on Coulterville (1947) 7.5' quadrangle.

Virginiatown [PLACER]: *locality,* 7.5 miles west of Auburn along Auburn Ravine (lat. 38°54'05" N, long. 121°12'45" W; sec. 8, T 12 N, R 7 E). Named on Gold Hill (1954) 7.5' quadrangle. Called Virginia on Sacramento (1892) 30' quadrangle. A place called Fort Trojan, settled in 1858, was situated about 1 mile down Auburn Ravine from Virginiatown; when the town of Lincoln was founded, the inhabitants of Fort Trojan moved 3 miles on down Auburn Ravine to the new community (Hoover, Rensch, and Rensch, p. 271).

Virgin Tears Creek: see **Ribbon Creek** [MARIPOSA].

Virgin Tear's Fall: see **Ribbon Fall** [MARIPOSA].

Virner: see **Balderson Station** [EL DORADO].

Vizard Creek [TUOLUMNE]: *stream,* heads in Tuolumne County and flows 7 miles to Beltz Lake 1.5 miles east-southeast of La Grange in Stanislaus County (lat. 37°39'20" N, long. 120°26'15" W). Named on La Grange (1962) 7.5' quadrangle.

Vogans: see **Sunnybrook** [AMADOR].

Vogelsang High Sierra Camp [MARIPOSA]: *locality,* 5 miles southeast of Cathedral Peak (lat. 37°47'45" N, long. 119°20'40" W); the place is 1.25 miles north of Vogelsang Peak. Named on Tuolumne Meadows (1956) 15' quadrangle.

Vogelsang Lake [MARIPOSA]: *lake,* 1700 feet long, 5.25 miles southeast of Cathedral Peak (lat. 37°47'10" N, long. 119°20'35" W); the lake is 0.5 mile north-northeast of Vogelsang Peak. Named on Tuolumne Meadows (1956) 15' quadrangle. A pass located 0.5 mile south of the lake is called Vogelsang Pass; the same feature is called Real Pass on a map of 1896 made by Lieutenant McClure (Browning, 1988, p. 153).

Vogelsang Pass: see **Vogelsang Lake** [MARIPOSA].

Vogelsang Peak [MARIPOSA]: *peak,* nearly 6 miles south-southeast of Cathedral Peak (lat. 37°46'40" N, long. 119°20'55" W). Altitude 11,516 feet. Named on Tuolumne Meadows (1956) 15' quadrangle. Lieutenant H.C. Benson named the peak for Alexander T. Vogelsang, who was president of California State Board of Fish Commissioners from 1896 until 1901 (United States Board on Geographic Names, 1934, p. 27).

Volcanic Ridge [MADERA]: *ridge,* west- to southwest-trending, 2.25 miles long, 5.5 miles northwest of Devils Postpile (lat. 37°40'40" N, long. 119°09'15" W). Named on Devils Postpile (1953) 15' quadrangle.

Volcano [AMADOR]: *village,* 2.5 miles northeast of Pine Grove along Sutter Creek (lat.

38'26'35" N, long. 120°37'45" W; sec. 23, T 7 N, R 12 E). Named on Pine Grove (1948) 7.5' quadrangle. Postal authorities established Volcano post office in 1851 (Frickstad, p. 6). Doble (p. 101) noted in 1852 that the place was named "from the supposed Volcanic appearance that exist in & about it." Camp (map facing p. 99 *in* Doble) showed a canyon called Soldiers Gulch that opens into the canyon of Sutter Creek from the northwest at Volcano; Doble (p. 103) stated that soldiers made the first discovery of gold in Soldiers Gulch in 1848. Camp (*in* Doble, p. 301) noted that the name "Soldiers Gulch" was an early designation for Volcano. Camp (map facing p. 99 *in* Doble) also showed a canyon called Clapboard Gulch that opens into the canyon of Sutter Creek from the north at the edge of Volcano, a canyon called Jackass Gulch that opens into Clapboard Gulch from the northwest less than 0.5 mile north-northeast of Volcano, a canyon called Ballards Humbug that opens into the canyon of South Branch Sutter Creek from the south 0.5 mile south-southeast of Volcano, and a place called Mahala Flat located south-southeast of Volcano along South Branch Sutter Creek. Camp's (1962) map shows Fort Ann located 3.5 miles north of Volcano along Dry Creek (present South Fork Dry Creek), and Fort John located 4 miles northwest of Volcano along the same stream. According to local tradition, Fort Ann began as a military post (Andrews, p. 98), but Whiting and Whiting (p. 5) called the place an early mining camp and not a military post. Fort John was named for John Stuart (Gudde, 1975, p. 120). Gudde (1975, p. 356) mentioned a place called Union Flat that was situated about 1 mile north of Volcano.

Volcano: see **Bath** [PLACER].

Volcano Canyon [PLACER]: *canyon,* drained by a stream that flows 10 miles to Middle Fork American River 2 miles southeast of Foresthill (lat. 39°00' N, long. 120°47'15" W; sec. 6, T 13 N, R 11 E). Named on Foresthill (1949) and Michigan Bluff (1952) 7.5' quadrangles.

Volcano Hill [PLACER]: *peak,* 5 miles south-southeast of Rocklin (lat. 38°43'20" N, long. 121°11'50" W; sec. 15, T 10 N, R 7 E). Named on Folsom (1967) 7.5' quadrangle.

Volcano Lake [SIERRA]: *lake,* 750 feet long, 3 miles north of Sierra City (lat. 39°36'25" N, long. 120°37'25" W; at SE cor. sec. 9, T 20 N, R 12 E). Named on Haypress Valley (1981) 7.5' quadrangle.

Volcanoville [EL DORADO]: *village,* 6 miles north-northeast of Georgetown (lat. 38°58'55" N, long. 120°47'15" W; on N line sec. 18, T 13 N, R 11 E). Named on Georgetown (1949) 7.5' quadrangle. Postal authorities established Volcanoville post office in 1930 and discontinued it in 1953 (Frickstad, p. 30). The name is from the mistaken idea of early miners that a nearby peak was an extinct volcano (Gudde,

1969, p. 356). Postal authorities established Lava post office near present Volcanoville in 1880 and discontinued it in 1881 (Salley, p. 119). Whitney's (1880) map shows a place called Flora's located about 2 miles west of Volcanoville.

Volunteer Gulch [CALAVERAS]: *canyon,* drained by a stream that flows 1 mile to Mokelumne River 1 mile north-northwest of Mokelumne Hill (lat. 38°18'50" N, long. 120°42'45" W; sec. 1, T 5 N, R 11 E). Named on Mokelumne Hill (1948) 7.5' quadrangle. McKinstry (p. 362) mentioned a canyon called Steep Gulch that, from his description, probably is a branch of Volunteer Gulch.

Volunteer Peak [TUOLUMNE]: *peak,* 8.5 miles southwest of Matterhorn Peak (lat. 38°00'20" N, long. 119°29'15" W). Altitude 10,479 feet. Named on Matterhorn Peak (1956) 15' quadrangle. The feature originally had the name "Regulation Peak" (Browning, 1986, p. 181).

Vonich Gulch [CALAVERAS]: *canyon,* nearly 2 miles long, opens into the canyon of Angels Creek 5 miles south of Angels Camp (lat. 38°00'15" N, long. 120°33'10" W; near S line sec. 21, T 2 N, R 13 E). Named on Angels Camp (1962) 7.5' quadrangle.

Voss [EL DORADO]: *locality,* 3.25 miles south of Old Iron Mountain (lat. 38°39'25" N, long. 120°23'10" W; sec. 2, T 9 N, R 14 E). Named on Stump Spring (1951) 7.5' quadrangle.

Votaw Camp [AMADOR]: *locality,* 5.5 miles west of Mokelumne Peak (lat. 38°31'45" N, long. 120°11'15" W; near E line sec. 22, T 8 N, R 16 E). Named on Bear River Reservoir (1979) 7.5' quadrangle.

– W –

Wabena Creek [PLACER]: *stream,* flows 4.25 miles to North Fork American River 8.5 miles west of Granite Chief (lat. 39°13'20" N, long. 120°26'35" W; sec. 30, T 16 N, R 14 E). Named on Royal Gorge (1953) 7.5' quadrangle.

Waca Lake [EL DORADO]: *lake,* 650 feet long, 1 mile northeast of Pyramid Peak (lat. 38°51'20" N, long. 120°08'25" W). Named on Pyramid Peak (1955) 7.5' quadrangle. The word "Waca" was coined from letters in the name "Walter Campbell" (Lekisch, p. 65).

Wades Flat Gulch [CALAVERAS]: *canyon,* drained by a stream that flows 1.5 miles to Coyote Creek 1.5 miles south of Vallecito (lat. 38°03'45" N, long. 120°28'05" W; near NW cor. sec. 5, T 2 N, R 14 E). Named on Columbia (1948) 7.5' quadrangle.

Wade's Meadows: see **Ackerson Meadow** [TUOLUMNE].

Wade's Mountain: see **Bald Mountain** [TUOLUMNE] (3).

Wagner [EL DORADO]: *locality,* 3.5 miles south-southwest of Robbs Peak (lat. 38°52'40"

N, long. 120°26'10" W). Named on Pyramid Peak (1896) 30' quadrangle.

Wagner [TUOLUMNE]: *settlement,* 2.5 miles west-northwest of Dardanelle (lat. 38°21'35" N, long. 119°52'40" W). Named on Donnell Lake (1979) 7.5' quadrangle.

Wagner Ridge [MARIPOSA-TUOLUMNE]: *ridge,* east-southeast-trending, 4.5 miles long, 2.5 miles west-southwest of Smith Peak on Mariposa-Tuolumne county line (lat. 37°47' N, long. 120°08'15" W). Named on Groveland (1947) and Jawbone Ridge (1947) 7.5' quadrangles.

Wagner Valley [MARIPOSA]: *valley,* 2.5 miles southwest of Smith Peak along Smith Creek (lat. 37°46'10" N, long. 120°07'45" W); the valley is south of Wagner Ridge. Named on Groveland (1947) and Jawbone Ridge (1947) 7.5' quadrangles.

Wagon Wheel Lake [NEVADA]: *lake,* 650 feet long, 4.25 miles south-southeast of English Mountain (lat. 39°23'05" N, long. 120°31'45" W; on E line sec. 32, T 18 N, R 13 E). Named on English Mountain (1983) 7.5' quadrangle.

Wahoo [SIERRA]: *locality,* 5.5 miles southwest of Mount Fillmore (lat. 39°40'05" N, long. 120°54'55" W; near E line sec. 24, T 21 N, R 9 E). Named on La Porte (1951) 7.5' quadrangle.

Waits Station [AMADOR]: *locality,* 3.25 miles southwest of Plymouth (lat. 38°27' N, long. 120°53'50" W; sec. 20, T 7 N, R 10 E). Named on Irish Hill (1962) 7.5' quadrangle.

Wa-kal-la: see **Merced River** [MADERA-MARIPOSA].

Waldron Reservoir: see **Backbone House** [NEVADA].

Walemo Rock: see **Fresno Dome** [MADERA].

Walker [CALAVERAS]: *locality,* 2.25 miles southwest of Garnet Hill (lat. 38°27'10" N, long. 120°16'35" W; near S line sec. 13, T 7 N, R 15 E). Named on Garnet Hill (1979) 7.5' quadrangle.

Walker: see **Mike Walker Canyon** [MADERA].

Walkers Ravine: see **Cirby Creek** [PLACER].

Wallace [CALAVERAS]: *village,* 8 miles west of Valley Springs (lat. 38°11'40" N, long. 120°58'35" W; sec. 15, T 4 N, R 9 E). Named on Wallace (1962) 7.5' quadrangle. Postal authorities established Wallace post office in 1883, discontinued it in 1945, and reestablished it in 1951; the name is for J.H. Wallace, chief engineer for San Joaquin and Sierra Nevada Railroad (Salley, p. 234).

Wallace: see **Mount Wallace** [CALAVERAS].

Wallace Canyon [PLACER]: *canyon,* formed by the junction of North Wallace Canyon and South Wallace Canyon, drained by a stream that flows 4.25 miles to Long Canyon 3.25 miles west-northwest of Devil Peak (lat. 38°58'50" N, long. 120°35'55" W; sec. 14, T 13 N, R 12 E). Named on Devil Peak (1950) 7.5' quadrangle. On Placerville (1893) 30' quadrangle, present North Wallace Canyon is shown as part of Wallace Canyon.

Wallace Canyon: see **Little Wallace Canyon** [PLACER]; **North Wallace Canyon** [PLACER]; **South Wallace Canyon** [PLACER].

Wallace Creek [SIERRA]: *stream,* flows 2.5 miles, partly in Plumas County, to Slate Creek 4.25 miles west-southwest of Mount Fillmore (lat. 39°42'35" N, long. 120°55'40" W; sec. 1, T 21 N, R 9 E). Named on La Porte (1951) 7.5' quadrangle.

Wallace Spring [PLACER]: *spring,* 3 miles west-northwest of Devil Peak (lat. 38°58'05" N, long. 120°35'55" W; near NE cor. sec. 23, T 13 N, R 12 E); the spring is 1 mile south of the mouth of Wallace Canyon. Named on Devil Peak (1950) 7.5' quadrangle.

Walla Gulch [CALAVERAS]: *canyon,* drained by a stream that flows 2.25 miles to Murray Creek 3.5 miles east of San Andreas (lat. 38°12'05" N, long. 120°36'55" W; sec. 14, T 4 N, R 12 E). Named on Calaveritas (1962) 7.5' quadrangle.

Walloupa: see **You Bet** [NEVADA].

Wall's Bridge: see **Purdon Crossing** [NEVADA].

Walls Flat [NEVADA]: *area,* 2.5 miles north of North Bloomfield (lat. 39°24'15" N, long. 120°54' W; sec. 19, T 18 N, R 10 E). Named on Pike (1949) 7.5' quadrangle.

Waloupa: see **You Bet** [NEVADA].

Wally Hill [CALAVERAS]: *ridge,* west-north-west-trending, 1 mile long, 7.5 miles east-southeast of San Andreas (lat. 38°09'50" N, long. 120°33' W; on S line sec. 28, T 4 N, R 13 E). Named on Calaveritas (1962) 7.5' quadrangle.

Walton Cabin Spring [TUOLUMNE]: *spring,* 6.25 miles south-southeast of Duckwall Mountain (lat. 37°52'40" N, long. 120°05'45" W; sec. 3, T 1 S, R 17 E). Named on Duckwall Mountain (1948) 7.5' quadrangle.

Walton Lake [MADERA]: *lake,* 500 feet long, 2 miles east-southeast of Merced Peak (lat. 37°37'20" N, long. 119°21'50" W). Named on Merced Peak (1953) 15' quadrangle. John Handley of California Department of Fish and Game named the lake in 1940 (Browning, 1986, p. 231).

Wamelo Rock: see **Fresno Dome** [MADERA].

Wapama Falls [TUOLUMNE]: *waterfall,* 7.5 miles northeast of Mather on Falls Creek (lat. 37°58' N, long. 119°45'50" W; at S line sec. 3, T 1 N, R 20 E). Named on Lake Eleanor (1956) 15' quadrangle. Called Hetch Hetchy Fall on Hoffmann and Gardner's (1863-1867) map, and the feature has the name "Macomb Falls" on a map of 1896 (Browning, 1986, p. 231).

Ward Creek [PLACER]: *stream,* flows 5.5 miles to Lake Tahoe 3 miles south-southwest of Tahoe City (lat. 39°07'45" N, long. 120°09'15" W; sec. 24, T 15 N, R 16 E). Named on Homewood (1955) and Tahoe City (1955) 7.5' quadrangles. Ward Rust and William Ferguson built a cabin at the mouth of Ward Creek in 1862 (Hoover, Rensch, and Rensch, p. 266).

Ward Lakes [MADERA]: *lakes,* two, largest 1200 feet long, 4 miles east of Merced Peak (lat. 37°38'15" N, long. 119°19'10" W). Named on Merced Peak (1953) 15' quadrangle.

Ward Mountain [MADERA]: *peak,* nearly 5 miles north-northeast of O'Neals (lat. 37°11'10" N, long. 119°38'50" W; near S line sec. 35, T 8 S, R 21 E). Altitude 2788 feet. Named on O'Neals (1965) 7.5' quadrangle.

Ward Mountain [MARIPOSA]: *ridge,* northwest- to west-trending, 1.25 miles long, 6 miles southeast of the settlement of Catheys Valley (lat. 37°22'40" N, long. 120°00'30" W). Named on Catheys Valley (1962) and Illinois Hill (1962) 7'5' quadrangles.

Ward Peak [PLACER]: *peak,* nearly 6 miles west-southwest of Tahoe City (lat. 39°08'50" N, long. 120°14'40" W; at W line sec. 17, T 15 N, R 16 E). Altitude 8637 feet. Named on Tahoe City (1955) 7.5' quadrangle.

Ward's Branch: see **Henness Branch** [MARIPOSA].

Wards Ferry [TUOLUMNE]: *locality,* 9 miles southeast of Sonora along Tuolumne River (lat. 37°52'40" N, long. 120°17'35" W). Named on Sonora (1897) 30' quadrangle. Standard (1948) 7.5' quadrangle shows Wards Ferry bridge at the place. Joseph Ward ran a ferry at the site in 1850; a canyon on the south side of Tuolumne River at Ward's Ferry was called Murderers' Gulch for the danger of bandits there (Paden and Schlichtmann, p. 148-149).

Warm Lake [PLACER]: *lake,* 650 feet long, 9.5 miles west-southwest of Donner Pass (lat. 39°15'55" N, long. 120°29'15" W; sec. 11, T 16 N, R 13 E). Named on Soda Springs (1955) 7.5' quadrangle.

Warner Ravine [EL DORADO]: *canyon,* drained by a stream that flows 1 mile to Middle Fork American River 2 miles north-northwest of Cool (lat. 38°54'50" N, long. 121°01'45" W; near N line sec. 12, T 12 N, R 8 E). Named on Auburn (1953) 7.5' quadrangle.

Warren Lake [NEVADA]: *lake,* 2450 feet long, 5.5 miles north-northwest of Donner Pass (lat. 39°23'45" N, long. 120°21' W; sec. 25, T 18 N, R 14 E). Named on Independence Lake (1981) 7.5' quadrangle.

Washburn Cascade: see **Bunnell Cascade** [MARIPOSA].

Washburn Lake [MADERA]: *lake,* 0.5 mile long, 5.5 miles north-northeast of Merced Peak along Merced River (lat. 37°42'55" N, long. 119°22'15" W). Named on Merced Peak (1953) 15' quadrangle. Lieutenant N.F. McClure named the lake in 1895 for Albert Henry Washburn of Wawona (United States Board on Geographic Names, 1934, p. 27).

Washburn Point [MARIPOSA]: *relief feature,*

2 miles south-southeast of Yosemite Village on the south side of Yosemite Valley (lat. 37°43'15" N, long. 119°34'20" W). Named on Yosemite (1956) 15' quadrangle. Browning (1986, p. 232) associated the name with Albert Henry Washburn, for whom Washburn Lake was named.

Washburn Slide [MARIPOSA]: *relief feature,* 5.25 miles west-southwest of Yosemite Village on the south side of Yosemite Valley (lat. 37°42'40" N, long. 119°40'05" W). Named on Yosemite (1956) 15' quadrangle.

Washington [NEVADA]: *village,* 17 miles northeast of Grass Valley along South Yuba River (lat. 39°21'30" N, long. 120°28' W; at N line sec. 12, T 17 N, R 10 E). Named on Washington (1950) 7.5' quadrangle. Postal authorities established Washington South Yuba post office in 1852 and discontinued it in 1854; they reestablished it in 1862 with the name "Washington" (Salley, p. 235). Miners from Indiana settled at the site in 1849, and for a time the place was known as Indiana Camp; the name "Washington" was adopted in 1850 at a Fourth-of-July celebration—the village is at what is known as Washington Flat (Slyter and Slyter, p. 2). Logan's (1940) map shows a peak called Shake Hill located 3 miles south-southeast of Washington (sec. 23, T 17 N, R 10 E). Whitney's (1873) map shows a place called White Cloud located 3 miles south-southwest of Washington, a relief feature called Phelps Point situated 1 mile south-southwest of Washington, a relief feature called Phelps Hill located 2 miles south-southwest of Washington, and a relief feature called Gold Hill located 1 mile southwest of Washington—fire destroyed a mining town at Gold Hill in 1856 and the community never recovered (Slyter and Slyter, p. 10). Gudde (1975, p. 45) listed a place called Brass Wire Bar that was located along South Yuba River opposite Washington, and (p. 125) a place called Frenchmans Bar that was located along South Yuba River about 3 miles west of Washington.

Washington: see **George Washington Hill** [NEVADA]; **Camp Washington**, under **Chinese Camp** [TUOLUMNE].

Washington Column [MARIPOSA]: *relief feature,* 1.5 miles east of Yosemite Village on the north side of Yosemite Valley (lat. 37°44'55" N, long. 119°33'35" W). Named on Yosemite (1956) 15' quadrangle. The feature also was called Washington Tower (Browning, 1986, p. 232).

Washington Creek [NEVADA]: *stream,* flows nearly 3 miles to South Yuba River 0.25 mile southwest of Washington (lat. 39°21'20" N, long. 120°48'15" W; sec. 12, T 17 N, R 10 E). Named on Washington (1950) 7.5' quadrangle. The canyon of the stream is called Washington Rav. [Ravine] on Whitney's (1873) map.

Washington Flat [MARIPOSA]: *area,* 2.5 miles

north of the village of Bear Valley on the north side of Merced River (lat. 37°36'30" N, long. 120°07'15" W; on S line sec. 5, T 4 S, R 17 E). Named on Bear Valley (1947) 7.5' quadrangle.

Washington Flat: see **Old Gulch** [CALAVERAS] (2); **Washington** [NEVADA].

Washington Ravine: see **Washington Creek** [NEVADA].

Washington Ridge [NEVADA]: *ridge,* west- to west-southwest-trending, 5 miles long, center 4.5 miles southwest of Washington (lat. 39°19'20" N, long. 120°52'15" W). Named on North Bloomfield (1949) and Washington (1950) 7.5' quadrangles.

Washington South Yuba: see **Washington** [NEVADA].

Washingtonville: see **Durgans Flat**, under **Downieville** [SIERRA].

Washington Tower: see **Washington Column** [MARIPOSA].

Wasiu: see **Camp Wasiu** [EL DORADO].

Wassamma [MADERA]: *locality,* 6 miles west-southwest of present Yosemite Forks (lat. 37°21' N, long. 119°44' W; sec. 1, T 7 S, R 20 E); the place is 1.25 miles west-southwest of present Ahwahnee. Named on Mariposa (1912) 30' quadrangle. The name is from an Indian village located nearby (Kroeber, p. 66). United States Board on Geographic Names (1933, p. 803) rejected the name "Ahwahnee" for the place, which was a stage station. McLaughlin and Bradley (p. 532) gave the name "Poison Switch" as an alternate. Clough (p. 80) described Poison Switch as a crossroads just outside of Gertrude, where teamsters after unloading their cargo of lumber at the head of the flume to Madera would "switch off" to a saloon.

Water Canyon [EL DORADO]: *canyon,* drained by a stream that flows 2 miles to Slab Creek 5.5 miles northwest of Pollock Pines (lat. 38°48'50" N, long. 120°39'30" W; sec. 8, T 11 N, R 12 E). Named on Slate Mountain (1950) 7.5' quadrangle.

Water Gulch [CALAVERAS]: *canyon,* drained by a stream that flows 1.25 miles to Blue Creek nearly 4 miles west-southwest of Tamarack (lat. 38°25'20" N, long. 120°08'35" W; near N line sec. 31, T 7 N, R 17 E). Named on Calaveras Dome (1979) 7.5' quadrangle.

Water Gulch [MADERA]: *canyon,* drained by a stream that flows 3.5 miles to Fresno River 5.5 miles east of Knowles (lat. 37°13'20" N, long. 119°46'25" W). Named on Knowles (1962) and O'Neals (1965) 7.5' quadrangles.

Waterhouse Lake [TUOLUMNE]: *lake,* 1150 feet long, 5.5 miles east-northeast of Pinecrest (lat. 38°13'20" N, long. 119°54'05" W; on W line sec. 9, T 4 N, R 19 E). Named on Pinecrest (1979) 7.5' quadrangle. Called Bear Lake Reservoir on California Division on Highways' (1934) map.

Waterhouse Peak [EL DORADO]: *peak,* 6.5

miles south-southwest of Freel Peak on El Dorado-Alpine county line (lat. 38°46'35" N, long. 119°57'50" W; sec. 26, T 11 N, R 18 E). Altitude 9497 feet. Named on Freel Peak (1955) 7.5' quadrangle. Forest Service officials named the peak to honor Clark Waterhouse, a Forest Service employee who died in World War I (Gudde, 1969, p. 359).

Waterman [AMADOR]: *settlement,* 0.5 mile north-northwest of Ione (lat. 38°21'40" N, long. 120°56'15" W). Named on Sutter Creek (1944) 15' quadrangle. Postal authorities established Waterman post office in 1895 and discontinued it in 1955; the name was for Robert W. Waterman, who promoted the place (Salley, p. 235).

Waterman Creek [CALAVERAS]: *stream,* flows nearly 4 miles to Cherokee Creek 4 miles west of Angels Camp (lat. 38°05'05" N, long. 120°37'15" W; sec. 26, T 3 N, R 12 E). Named on Angels Camp (1962) 7.5' quadrangle.

Watkins: see **Mount Watkins** [MARIPOSA].

Waters Campground: see **Middle Waters Campground** [SIERRA].

Watershed Falls: see **Waterwheel Falls** [TUOLUMNE].

Waters Peak [AMADOR]: *peak,* 7.5 miles southwest of Jackson (lat. 38°16'10" N, long. 120°52'10" W; near W line sec. 22, T 5 N, R 10 E). Altitude 950 feet. Named on Jackson (1962) 7.5' quadrangle.

Waterwheel Falls [TUOLUMNE]: *waterfall,* 11 miles west of Tioga Pass on Tuolumne River (lat. 37°55'35" N, long. 119°27'30" W). Named on Tuolumne Meadows (1956) 15' quadrangle. R.M. Price gave the name "Le Conte Cascade" to the feature in 1894 to honor Professor J.N. Le Conte of University of California (Browning, 1988, p. 72-73). United States Board on Geographic Names (1991, p. 7) rejected the name "Watershed Falls" for the feature.

Watkins Bar: see **Electra** [AMADOR].

Watson: see **Mount Watson** [PLACER].

Watson Creek [PLACER]: *stream,* flows 3 miles to Lake Tahoe 3.5 miles west-southwest of Kings Beach (lat. 39°13'25" N, long. 120°05'05" W; at E line sec. 21, T 16 N, R 17 E); the stream heads near Watson Lake. Named on Kings Beach (1955) and Tahoe City (1955) 7.5' quadrangles. The name commemorates Robert Montgomery Watson, who came to Lake Tahoe in 1875 and purchased Tahoe House in 1888 (Lekisch, p. 151).

Watson Lake [PLACER]: *lake,* 750 feet long, nearly 4 miles north of Tahoe City (lat. 39°13'30" N, long. 120°08'10" W; sec. 19, T 16 N, R 17 E); the lake is 0.5 mile northeast of Mount Watson. Named on Tahoe City (1955) 7.5' quadrangle. The name is for Robert Montgomery Waston of Watson Creek (Lekisch, p. 151).

Watt: see **Sharon** [MADERA].

Wawona [MARIPOSA]: *settlement,* 18 miles

east of Mariposa (lat. 37°32'10" N, long.
119°39'15" W; near NW cor. sec. 2, T 5 S, R
21 E). Named on Yosemite (1956) 15' quadrangle. Called Clark's Ranch on Hoffmann
and Gardner's (1863-1867) map. Galen Clark
camped at the site in 1855 and returned in
1856 to build a rough overnight lodging place
for tourists that was known at different times
as Clark's Station, Clark and Moore's, and Big
Tree Station; Clark sold out to Edward
Washburn, John Washburn, and Henry
Washburn in 1874—Henry Washburn's wife
renamed the place Wawona (Sargent, Shirley,
1961, p. 6-9). Postal authorities established
Clark's Station post office in 1878, changed
the name to Wawona in 1883, and discontinued it in 1935 (Frickstad, p. 90, 92). The name
"Wawona" supposedly is from an Indian term
meaning "a Big Tree" (Bunnell, p. 37), but
Kroeber (p. 66) stated that the word "wawona"
does not appear to be Indian. Laizure's (1935)
map shows a place called Chinquapin located
8.5 miles north-northwest of Wawona, where
Yosemite (1956) 15' quadrangle shows Chinquapin Ranger Sta. (near SW cor. sec. 20, T 3
S, R 21 E). The name "Chinquapin" is from a
kind of shrub common at the place (Hanna,
p. 63). United States Board on Geographic
Names (1933, p. 217) approved the name
"Chinquapin" for a settlement, and rejected
the forms "Chincapin" and "Chinkapin."
Laizure's (1935) map also shows a place
called Elevenmile located about 1 mile south-
southeast of Chinquapin and west of present
Elevenmile Creek (near S line sec. 29, T 3 S,
R 21 E). A stage stop called Eleven Mile Station and 11-Mile House was at the place,
which was 11 miles from Wawona (Browning, 1988, p. 40). In addition, Laizure's (1935)
map shows a place called Eightmile situated
about 3 miles south-southeast of Chinquapin
(near SW cor. sec. 4, T 4 S, R 21 E).

Wawona: see **North Wawona** [MARIPOSA];
South Wawona [MARIPOSA].

Wawona Campground [MARIPOSA]: *locality,*
nearly 2 miles west-northwest of Wawona (lat.
37°33' N, long. 119°41' W; near NW cor. sec.
33, T 4 S, R 21 E). Named on Yosemite (1956)
15' quadrangle.

Wawona Dome [MARIPOSA]: *peak,* 2.5 miles
east-northeast of Wawona (lat. 37°33'20" N,
long. 119°36'45" W; near E line sec. 25, T 4
S, R 21 E). Altitude 6903 feet. Named on
Yosemite (1956) 15' quadrangle. The feature
also had the names "Granite Dome" and
"Capitol Dome" (Browning, 1986, p. 233).

Wawona Point [MARIPOSA]: *peak,* 3.25 miles
east-southeast of Wawona (lat. 37°31'05" N,
long. 119°36' W). Altitude 6810 feet. Named
on Yosemite (1956) 15' quadrangle.

We-ack: see **Rocky Point** [MARIPOSA].

Weaver Creek: see **Weber Creek** [EL DO-
RADO].

Weaver Lake [NEVADA]: *lake,* 0.5 mile long,

4.5 miles east-northeast of Graniteville (lat.
39°27'55" N, long. 120°39'25" W; at SW cor.
sec. 32, T 19 N, R 12 E). Named on
Graniteville (1982) 7.5' quadrangle.

Weavertown: see **Weber Creek** [EL DO-
RADO].

Weaverville: see **Weber Creek** [EL DORADO].

Webb: see **Webb Station** [MARIPOSA].

Webber [EL DORADO]: *locality,* 15 miles east
of Georgetown (lat. 38°53'30" N, long.
120°33' W). Named on Placerville (1893) 30'
quadrangle.

Webber Creek: see **Weber Creek** [EL DO-
RADO].

Webber Creek Reservoir: see **Weber Reservoir**
[EL DORADO].

Webber Lake [SIERRA]: *lake,* 4100 feet long,
7.5 miles south-southwest of Sierraville (lat.
39°29'10" N, long. 120°24'45" W; sec. 28, T
19 N, R 14 E); the lake is at the head of Little
Truckee River. Named on Webber Peak (1981)
7.5' quadrangle. The name commemorates
David Gould Webber, who bought land
around the lake in 1852 for stock range—the
feature previously was called Little Truckee
Lake (Gudde, 1949, p. 385).

Webber Peak [SIERRA]: *peak,* 8.5 miles south-
southwest of Sierraville (lat. 39°28'50" N,
long. 120°26'40" W; sec. 30, T 19 N, R 14 E).
Altitude 8093 feet. Named on Webber Peak
(1981) 7.5' quadrangle.

Webber's Bridge: see **Purdon Crossing** [NE-
VADA].

Webb Station [MARIPOSA]: *locality,* 8 miles
north-northwest of Hornitos along Dry Creek
(lat. 37°36'20" N, long. 120°18'25" W; sec.
10, T 4 S, R 15 E). Named on Merced Falls
(1962) 7.5' quadrangle. Called Webb on Sonora (1891) 30' quadrangle.

Weber Creek [EL DORADO]: *stream,* formed
by the confluence of North Fork and South
Fork, flows 20 miles to South Fork American
River 5 miles south of the village of Pilot Hill
(lat. 38° 45'50" N, long. 121°00'25" W; near
E line sec. 31, T 11 N, R 9 E). Named on
Camino (1952), Coloma (1949), Pilot Hill
(1954), Placerville (1949), and Shingle
Springs (1949) 7.5' quadrangles. Called Webber Creek on Placerville (1893) 30' quadrangle. North Fork is 9 miles long and is
named on Camino (1952) and Sly Park (1952)
7.5' quadrangles. South Fork is 7.5 miles long
and is named on Camino (1952) and Sly Park
(1952) 7.5' quadrangles. The name "Weber"
is for Charles M. Weber, who mined in the
neighborhood in 1848; it also had the forms
"Webber" and "Weaver" (Gudde, 1975, p.
366). Weber started a store along Weber Creek
about 2 miles from Placerville and it became
the nucleus of a mining camp called
Weberville (Hoover, Rensch, and Rensch, p.
82). The camp, which also was called Weaverville, was located at the confluence of Weber
Creek and Ringgold Creek (Morgan *in*

Pritchard, p. 170). The place also was called Weavertown; a mining camp called Ringgold was situated along Weber Creek between Weavertown and Diamond Springs (Becker *in* Christy, entry for August 7, 1850). Postal authorities established Ringgold post office in 1852 and discontinued it in 1853 (Frickstad, p. 29).

Weber Reservoir [EL DORADO]: *lake,* behind a dam on North Fork Weber Creek nearly 2 miles south-southwest of Camino (lat. 38° 42'55" N, long. 120°41'30" W; sec. 18, T 10 N, R 12 E). Named on Camino (1952) 7.5' quadrangle. Called Webber Creek Reservoir on California Division of Highways' (1934) map, which has the form "Webber Creek" for the name of present Weber Creek.

Weberville: see **Weber Creek** [EL DORADO].

Webster: see **Michigan Bluff** [PLACER].

Webster Flat [NEVADA]: *area,* 9 miles west of Donner Pass (lat. 39°19'50" N, long. 120°29'25" W; near NW cor. sec. 23, T 17 N, R 13 E). Named on Soda Springs (1955) 7.5' quadrangle.

Weed Meadow [TUOLUMNE]: *area,* 6.5 miles southeast of Pinecrest (lat. 38°07'15" N, long. 119°55' W; sec. 17, T 3 N, R 19 E). Named on Cherry Lake North (1979) 7.5' quadrangle.

Wegner Lake [MARIPOSA]: *lake,* 1000 feet long, 7 miles north-northeast of Yosemite Village (lat. 37°50'30" N, long. 119°32'10" W; sec. 22, T 1 S, R 22 E). Named on Hetch Hetchy Reservoir (1956) 15' quadrangle. The name commemorates John H. Wegner, a ranger in Yosemite National Park from 1916 until 1949 (Browning, 1986, p. 234).

Weil Lake [NEVADA]: *lake,* 850 feet long, 1.5 miles south of English Mountain along Canyon Creek (lat. 39°25'30" N, long. 120°32'45" W; on W line sec. 17, T 18 N, R 13 E). Named on English Mountain (1983) 7.5' quadrangle.

Weimar [PLACER]: *settlement,* 4.5 miles south-southwest of Colfax (lat. 39°02'10" N, long. 120°58'25" W; near E line sec. 28, T 14 N, R 9 E). Named on Colfax (1949) 7.5' quadrangle. Postal authorities established Weimar post office in 1866 (Frickstad, p. 122). United States Board on Geographic Names (1933, p. 806) rejected the form "Weimer" for the name, which is from a local Indian chief (Stewart, p. 90).

Wells Peak [TUOLUMNE]: *peak,* 2 miles southeast of Tower Peak (lat. 38°07'20" N, long. 119°31'40" W). Altitude 11,118 feet. Named on Tower Peak (1956) 15' quadrangle. R.B. Marshall of United States Geological Survey named the peak for Rush Spencer Wells, an army officer (Browning, 1986, p. 234).

Welsh: see **Nick Welsh Spring** [PLACER].

Wench Flat [EL DORADO]: *area,* 3.5 miles east-southeast of Robbs Peak (lat. 38°54' N, long. 120°20'30" W; sec. 7, T 12 N, R 15 E). Named on Loon Lake (1952) 7.5' quadrangle.

Wenger: see **Coulterville** [MARIPOSA].

Wentworth Springs [EL DORADO]: *locality,* 11.5 miles west of the town of Meeks Bay (lat. 39°00'45" N, long. 120°20'20" W; sec. 31, T 14 N, R 15 E). Named on Wentworth Springs (1953) 7.5' quadrangle.

Wentworth Springs Campground [EL DORADO]: *locality,* less than 1 mile east of Wentworth Springs (lat. 39°00'45" N, long. 120°19'25" W; sec. 32, T 14 N, R 15 E). Named on Wentworth Springs (1953) 7.5' quadrangle.

West: see **Camp Harvey West** [EL DORADO].

West Applegate: see **Applegate** [PLACER].

West Canyon [EL DORADO]: *canyon,* drained by a stream that flows 2 miles to Canyon Creek (1) 2 miles northwest of Georgetown (lat. 38°55'50" N, long. 120°51'40" W; sec. 33, T 13 N, R 10 E). Named on Georgetown (1949) 7.5' quadrangle.

Westfall Campground [MARIPOSA]: *locality,* 2.5 miles south-southwest of Fish Camp (lat. 37°26'40" N, long. 119°39'05" W; near NE cor. sec. 3, T 6 S, R 21 E). Named on Bass Lake (1953) 15' quadrangle.

Westfall Meadows [MARIPOSA]: *area,* 7 miles south-southwest of Yosemite Village (lat. 37°39'10" N, long. 119°38' W; near SE cor. sec. 23, T 3 S, R 21 E). Named on Yosemite (1956) 15' quadrangle. Hoffmann and Gardner's (1863-1867) map has the name "Westfall's" at or near present Westfall Meadows. Westfall's was a sheep camp; Charles Peregoy built Mountain View House at the site in 1869 (Russell, p. 51).

Westfalls [EL DORADO]: *locality,* 6 miles southwest of Leek Spring Hill (lat. 38°33'30" N, long. 120°30'50" W). Named on Pyramid Peak (1896) 30' quadrangle.

Westfall's: see **Westfall Meadows** [MARIPOSA].

West Juniper Creek [NEVADA]: *stream,* flows nearly 2 miles to Juniper Creek 7.25 miles east of Truckee (lat. 39°20'15" N, long. 120°03'05" W; sec. 11, T 17 N, R 17 E). Named on Martis Peak (1955) 7.5' quadrangle.

West Lakes [NEVADA]: *lakes,* nearly 2 miles north-northwest of Donner Pass (lat. 39°20'25" N, long. 120°20'15" W; near NW cor. sec. 8, T 17 N, R 15 E). Named on Norden (1955) 7.5' quadrangle.

West Martis Creek [PLACER]: *stream,* flows 4.25 miles to Martis Creek nearly 5 miles west of Martis Peak (lat. 39°18'05" N, long. 120°07'15" W; near SW cor. sec. 20, T 17 N, R 17 E). Named on Martis Peak (1955) 7.5' quadrangle.

West Meadow Creek [PLACER]: *stream,* flows nearly 3 miles to Barker Creek 4.5 miles east of Bunker Hill (lat. 39°03'40" N, long. 120°17'50" W; sec. 16, T 14 N, R 15 E). Named on Wentworth Springs (1953) 7.5' quadrangle.

Westmoreland [AMADOR]: *locality,* 4.25 miles southeast of present Hams Station (lat. 38°30'05" N, long. 120°19'05" W). Named on Pyramid Peak (1896) 30' quadrangle.

Westmoreland Bridge: see **Chaparral Hill**, under **Lancha Plana** [AMADOR].

Westmoreland's Ferry: see **Chaparral Hill**, under **Lancha Plana** [AMADOR].

West Panther Creek [AMADOR]: *stream,* flows 6.5 miles to join East Panther Creek and form Panther Creek 4.25 miles south-southwest of Hams Station (lat. 38°29'10" N, long. 120°24'05" W; sec. 2, T 7 N, R 14 E); the stream is west of Panther Ridge. Named on Caldor (1951), Devils Nose (1979), and Peddler Hill (1951) 7.5' quadrangles. Called Panther Creek on Pyramid Peak (1896) 30' quadrangle, but United States Board on Geographic Names (1959a, p. 7) rejected this name for the stream.

West Peak [TUOLUMNE]: *peak,* 14 miles west-northwest of Tioga Pass (lat. 37°58'50" N, long. 119°29'50" W). Named on Tuolumne Meadows (1956) 15' quadrangle. The feature also was called Regulation Peak (Browning, 1986, p. 234).

West Point [CALAVERAS]: *town,* 16 miles north-northeast of San Andreas on the ridge between North Fork and Middle Fork Mokelumne River (lat. 38°24' N, long. 120°31'35" W; sec. 3, T 6 N, R 13 E). Named on West Point (1948) 7.5' quadrangle. The place was called Indian Gulch in 1852, and it was called West Point in 1854 (Gudde, 1949, p. 387). Postal authorities established West Point post office in 1856, changed the name to Westpoint in 1895, and changed it back to West Point in 1947 (Salley, p. 238). United States Board on Geographic Names (1950, p. 7) rejected the form "Westpoint" for the name. According to Hanna (p. 352), Kit Carson gave the name "West Point" to his camp at the site in 1844 because it was as far west as he could go on his route before he had to retreat in order to cross North Fork Mokelumne River.

Westville [PLACER]: *locality,* 14 miles northeast of Foresthill on Forest Hill Divide (lat. 39°10'30" N, long. 120°38'50" W; at W line sec. 4, T 15 N, R 12 E). Named on Westville (1952) 7.5' quadrangle. Postal authorities established Westville post office in 1889 and discontinued it in 1919; the name was for George C. West, first postmaster (Salley, p. 238). They established Ackerman post office 4.5 miles east of Westville in 1896 and discontinued it in 1899; the name was for John Q. Ackerman, first postmaster (Salley, p. 1). They established Stonehill post office 5 miles south of Westville in 1900 and discontinued it in 1901; the name was for Frances H. Stone, first postmaster (Salley, p. 213).

Wet Gulch [CALAVERAS]:

(1) *canyon,* drained by a stream that flows 5.25 miles to Jesus Maria Creek 4 miles east-southeast of Mokelumne Hill (lat. 38°16'45" N, long. 120°38' W; sec. 15, T 5 N, R 12 E). Named on Rail Road Flat (1948) 7.5' quadrangle.

(2) *canyon,* drained by a stream that flows nearly 3 miles to South Fork Mokelumne River 2.5 miles northwest of Rail Road Flat (lat. 38°22'05" N, long. 120°32'40" W; near S line sec. 16, T 6 N, R 13 E). Named on Rail Road Flat (1948) 7.5' quadrangle.

Wet Gulch [TUOLUMNE]: *canyon,* drained by a stream that flows 1 mile to South Fork Stanislaus River 2.5 miles north-northeast of Columbia (lat. 38°04'05" N, long. 120°22'50" W; sec. 36, T 3 N, R 14 E). Named on Columbia (1948) and Columbia SE (1948) 7.5' quadrangles.

Wet Meadow [TUOLUMNE]: *area,* 5 miles east-southeast of Tuolumne (lat. 37°55'20" N, long. 120°09'40" W; near SE cor. sec. 24, T 1 N, R 16 E). Named on Tuolumne (1948) 7.5' quadrangle.

Wet Meadow Hill [TUOLUMNE]: *peak,* 5 miles southeast of Tuolumne (lat. 37°55' N, long. 120°09'45" W; sec. 25, T 1 N, R 16 E); the peak is less than 0.5 mile south-southwest of Wet Meadow. Named on Tuolumne (1948) 7.5' quadrangle.

Wet Meadows Springs [TUOLUMNE]: *springs,* two, 4.5 miles southeast of Long Barn (lat. 38°02'30" N, long. 120°04'50" W; sec. 11, T 2 N, R 17 E). Named on Hull Creek (1979) 7.5' quadrangle.

Wet Prong [CALAVERAS]: *stream,* flows 1.25 miles to Salamander Creek 5.5 miles east-northeast of San Andreas (lat. 38°14'20" N, long. 120°35'25" W; sec. 31, T 5 N, R 13 E). Named on Calaveritas (1962) 7.5' quadrangle.

Wet Ravine [SIERRA]:

(1) *canyon,* drained by a stream that flows 1 mile to Fiddle Creek 6.25 miles west-southwest of Goodyears Bar (lat. 39°31'10" N, long. 120°59'45" W; sec. 17, T 19 N, R 9 E). Named on Goodyears Bar (1951) 7.5' quadrangle.

(2) *canyon,* drained by a stream that flows 2 miles to Kanaka Creek 1.25 miles southwest of Alleghany (lat. 39°27'30" N, long. 120°51'25" W; sec. 4, T 18 N, R 10 E). Named on Alleghany (1949) 7.5' quadrangle.

Whale Boat Ferry: see **Big Bar** [CALAVERAS].

Whaler Creek [EL DORADO]: *stream,* flows 8 miles to Rock Creek 10 miles west-northwest of Pollock Pines (lat. 38°49'45" N, long. 120°44'45" W; near W line sec. 3, T 11 N, R 11 E). Named on Slate Mountain (1950) and Tunnel Hill (1950) 7.5' quadrangles.

Wheats [CALAVERAS]: *locality,* 3.25 miles east-northeast of Valley Springs (lat. 38°12'45" N, long. 120°46'30" W). Named on Jackson (1902) 30' quadrangle. Called Double Springs on Camp's (1962) map. The place also was called Pleasant Valley (Hoover, Rensch, and Rensch, p. 41) and Two Springs (Gudde, 1975, p. 99). Postal authorities established Double Springs post office in 1851 and discontinued it in 1860 (Frickstad, p. 14). Valley Springs (1944) 15' quadrangle shows

Double Springs ranch located 3 miles east-northeast of Valley Springs, and Camp's (1962) map shows Spring Valley House situated 1 mile west-southwest of Double Springs.

Wheats Cow Camp [TUOLUMNE]: *locality,* 7.25 miles west-northwest of Dardanelle (lat. 38°21'55" N, long. 119°57'40" W; near N line sec. 23, T 6 N, R 18 E); the place is in Wheats Meadow. Named on Donnell Lake (1979) 7.5' quadrangle.

Wheats Meadow [TUOLUMNE]: *area,* 7.25 miles west-northwest of Dardanelle (lat. 38°21'50" N, long. 119°57'40" W; near N line sec. 23, T 6 N, R 18 E). Named on Donnell Lake (1979) 7.5' quadrangle. The name commemorates an early settler (Browning, 1986, p. 235).

Wheats Meadow Creek [TUOLUMNE]: *stream,* flows 5 miles to Donnell Lake 5.5 miles west of Dardanelle (lat. 38°21' N, long. 119°56'05" W); the stream goes through Wheats Meadow. Named on Donnell Lake (1979) and Spicer Meadow Reservoir (1979) 7.5' quadrangles.

Wheeler Gulch [MARIPOSA]: *canyon,* drained by a stream that flows 3 miles to Lake McClure 3 miles west-southwest of Coulterville (lat. 37°41'50" N, long. 120°14'45" W; near N line sec. 7, T 3 S, R 16 E). Named on Coulterville (1947, photorevised 1973) 7.5' quadrangle.

Wheeler Peak [TUOLUMNE]: *peak,* 10.5 miles west-southwest of Tower Peak (lat. 38°06' N, long. 119°43'45" W). Altitude 9001 feet. Named on Tower Peak (1956) 15' quadrangle.

Wheelers Sheep Camp [SIERRA]: *locality,* 11 miles south of Loyalton (lat. 39°30'55" N, long. 120°14'40" W; sec. 7, T 19 N, R 16 E). Named on Sardine Peak (1981) 7.5' quadrangle.

Whiskers Campground [MADERA]: *locality,* nearly 4 miles west-southwest of Shuteye Peak along North Fork Sand Creek (lat. 37° 20'05" N, long. 119°29'35" W; sec. 7, T 7 S, R 23 E). Named on Shuteye Peak (1953) 15' quadrangle.

Whiskey Bar [EL DORADO]: *locality,* 5.25 miles west-southwest of the village of Pilot Hill along North Fork American River (lat. 38° 48'55" N, long. 121°06'20" W; sec. 8, T 11 N, R 8 E). Site named on Auburn (1954) 15' quadrangle. Water of Folsom Lake now covers the spot.

Whiskey Creek [MADERA]:
(1) *stream,* flows nearly 3 miles to Willow Creek (3) at Knowles (lat. 37°12'55" N, long. 119°52'35" W; sec. 2, T 8 S, R 19 E). Named on Knowles (1962) 7.5' quadrangle.
(2) *stream,* flows 11.5 miles to Willow Creek (2) 13 miles south of Shuteye Peak (lat. 37°09'50" N, long. 119°28'20" W; sec. 9, T 9 S, R 23 E). Named on Shaver Lake (1953) and Shuteye Peak (1953) 15' quadrangles. The stream first was called Alder Creek, but after

a store that sold a lot of whiskey opened near the feature at present Cascadel, Indians gave the stream the name "Whiskey Creek" (Clough, p. 80).

Whiskey Creek [SIERRA]: *stream,* flows 1.5 miles to Slate Creek 2.25 miles northwest of Mount Fillmore (lat. 39°45'05" N, long. 120°52'55" W; sec. 20, T 22 N, R 10 E). Named on Blue Nose Mountain (1951) and Onion Valley (1950) 7.5' quadrangles.

Whiskey Diggings [SIERRA]: *locality,* 2.25 miles northwest of Mount Fillmore (lat. 39°45'10" N, long. 120°52'50" W; sec. 20, T 22 N, R 10 E); the place is near the mouth of Whiskey Creek. Named on Onion Valley (1950) 7.5' quadrangle. Downieville (1897) 30' quadrangle has the name for a community. The place also was called Newark (Bancroft, 1888, p. 362).

Whiskey Diggings: see **Valley View** [PLACER].

Whiskey Falls [MADERA]: *locality,* 4.5 miles south of Shuteye Peak along Whiskey Creek (2) (lat. 37°17'10" N, long. 119°26'25" W; sec. 27, T 7 S, R 23 E). Named on Shuteye Peak (1953) 15' quadrangle.

Whiskey Flat [MARIPOSA]: *area,* 6 miles east of the village of Bear Valley along Sherlock Creek (lat. 37°34'10" N, long. 120°00'35" W; sec. 20, T 4 S, R 18 E). Named on Bear Valley (1947) 7.5' quadrangle.

Whiskey Hill: see **Jamestown** [TUOLUMNE].

Whiskey Slide [CALAVERAS]: *locality,* 5.25 miles east of Mokelumne Hill (lat. 38°17'30" N, long. 120°36'30" W). Named on Jackson (1902) 30' quadrangle, which has the name along a road grade. The mining camp called Whiskey Slide later was called Clear View (Hoover, Rensch, and Rensch, p. 44). Clear View post office was established 8 miles east of Mokelumne Hill in 1902 and discontinued in 1903 (Salley, p. 45).

Whisky Creek [CALAVERAS]: *stream,* flows nearly 4 miles to New Hogan Reservoir 4.25 miles east-northeast of Jenny Lind (lat. 38° 06'35" N, long. 120°47'30" W; sec. 17, T 3 N, R 11 E). Named on Jenny Lind (1962) and Valley Springs (1962) 7.5' quadrangles.

Whisky Creek [PLACER]: *stream,* flows 2 miles to Five Lakes Creek 2.5 miles south-southeast of Granite Chief (lat. 39°09'40" N, long. 120°16'10" W; sec. 11, T 15 N, R 15 E). Named on Granite Chief (1953) 7.5' quadrangle.

Whisky Creek Camp [PLACER]: *locality,* 2.25 mile south-southeast of Granite Chief (lat. 39°10' N, long. 120°16'15" W; sec. 11, T 15 N, R 15 E); the place is along Whisky Creek. Named on Granite Chief (1953) 7.5' quadrangle.

Whisky Flat [MARIPOSA]: *area,* 3 miles west-southwest of Penon Blanco Peak (lat. 37°43' N, long. 120°18'55" W; on W line sec. 34, T 2 S, R 15 E). Named on Penon Blanco Peak (1962) 7.5' quadrangle.

Whisky Gulch [AMADOR]: *canyon,* less than

1 mile long, 5.25 miles south-southeast of Plymouth (lat. 38°24'35" N, long. 120° 48' W). Named on Amador City (1962) 7.5' quadrangle.

Whisky Hill [PLACER]: *ridge,* west-southwest-trending, 1.5 miles long, 4.5 miles northwest of Duncan Peak (lat. 39°11'35" N, long. 120°34'35" W; on E line sec. 1, T 15 N, R 12 E). Named on Duncan Peak (1952) 7.5' quadrangle.

Whiskey Ridge [MADERA]: *ridge,* south-trending, 6 miles long, 5.5 miles south of Shuteye Peak (lat. 37°16' N, long. 119°24'45" W); the ridge is east of Whiskey Creek (2). Named on Shaver Lake (1953) and Shuteye Peak (1953) 15' quadrangles.

Whisky Run [PLACER]: *stream,* flows 2 miles to Coon Creek 7 miles north-northeast of Lincoln (lat. 38°59'20" N, long. 121°15'15" W; sec. 12, T 13 N, R 6 E). Named on Gold Hill (1954) and Lincoln (1953) 7.5' quadrangles.

White [EL DORADO]: *locality,* 1.25 miles east of Leek Spring Hill in Leek Spring Valley (lat. 38°38' N, long. 120°15'20" W; sec. 18, T 9 N, R 16 E). Named on Leek Spring Hill (1951) 7.5' quadrangle.

White Azalea Campground [AMADOR]: *locality,* 7.5 miles southeast of Hams Station along North Fork Mokelumne River (lat. 38°29'10" N, long. 120°15'40" W; near W line sec. 6, T 7 N, R 16 E). Named on Garnet Hill (1979) 7.5' quadrangle.

White Cascade [TUOLUMNE]: *waterfall,* 9 miles west of Tioga Pass on Tuolumne River (lat. 37°54'45" N, long. 119°25' W). Named on Tuolumne Meadows (1956) 15' quadrangle. Members of the Whitney survey named the feature in 1866 (Browning, 1986, p. 235). United States Board on Geographic Names (1992, p. 5) rejected the name "Lower Virginia Falls" for the feature.

White Cascade: see **Tuolumne Falls** [TUOLUMNE].

White Chief Branch [MADERA]: *stream,* flows 2.5 miles to Big Creek 7.5 miles north-northeast of Yosemite Forks (lat. 37°28'20" N, long. 119°35'05" W; sec. 29, T 5 S, R 22 E); the stream heads near White Chief Mountain. Named on Bass Lake (1953) 15' quadrangle.

White Chief Mountain [MADERA]: *peak,* 10 miles north-northeast of Yosemite Forks (lat. 37°29'20" N, long. 119°32' W; near N line sec. 23, T 5 S, R 22 E). Altitude 8676 feet. Named on Bass Lake (1953) 15' quadrangle.

White Cloud: see **Washington** [NEVADA].

White Fir Creek [TUOLUMNE]: *stream,* flows 2.5 miles to Cherry Lake 7.5 miles north-northwest of Mather (lat. 37°59' N, long. 119°55' W; sec. 32, T 2 N, R 19 E). Named on Cherry Lake North (1979) 7.5' quadrangle. United States Board on Geographic Names (1969a, p. 5) rejected the name "Nigger Creek" for the stream.

White Gulch: see **Whites Gulch** [MARIPOSA].

White Hall [EL DORADO]: *locality,* 2.5 miles east of Riverton along South Fork American River (lat. 38°46'30" N, long. 120°24'10" W; sec. 27, T 11 N, R 14 E). Named on Riverton (1950) 7.5' quadrangle. Logan's (1938) map has the form "Whitehall" for the name. Postal authorities established Randall post office at Whitehall in 1917 and discontinued it in 1937; the name was for Albert B. Randall, first postmaster (Salley, p. 181).

White Hall Canyon [EL DORADO]: *canyon,* drained by a stream that flows 1 mile to South Fork American River 2.25 miles east of Riverton at White Hall (lat. 38°46'35" N, long. 120°24'15" W; sec. 27, T 11 N, R 14 E). Named on Riverton (1950) 7.5' quadrangle.

White Man Ravine [EL DORADO]: *canyon,* drained by a stream that flows 1.5 miles to Little Indian Creek 2.5 miles east of Latrobe (lat. 38°33'15" N, long. 120°55'55" W; sec. 13, T 8 N, R 9 E). Named on Latrobe (1949) 7.5' quadrangle. Called White Mans Ravine on Placerville (1893) 30' quadrangle.

White Meadow [EL DORADO]: *area,* 2 miles west-northwest of Riverton (lat. 38°47' N, long. 120°29'05" W; near NE cor. sec. 23, T 11 N, R 13 E). Named on Riverton (1950) 7.5' quadrangle.

White Oak Creek [EL DORADO]: *stream,* flows 2.25 miles to Kelly Creek 3.5 miles north-northwest of Shingle Springs (lat. 38°42'45" N, long. 120°57' W; sec. 23, T 10 N, R 9 E); the stream goes through White Oak Flat. Named on Shingle Springs (1949) 7.5' quadrangle.

White Oak Flat [EL DORADO]: *area,* 3.25 miles northwest of Shingle Springs (lat. 38°42'20" N, long. 120°57'45" W). Named on Shingle Springs (1949) 7.5' quadrangle. The place first was called Cart Wheel Valley (Gudde, 1975, p. 370).

White Mountain [TUOLUMNE]: *peak,* 3.5 miles northwest of Tioga Pass on Tuolumne-Mono county line (lat. 37°56'45" N, long. 119° 18'30" W). Named on Tuolumne Meadows (1956) 15' quadrangle.

White Oak Creek [MARIPOSA]: *stream,* flows 1.5 miles to Moore Creek 2 miles east of Smith Peak (lat. 37°47'50" N, long. 120°03'45" W; near N line sec. 2, T 2 S, R 17 E). Named on Jawbone Ridge (1947) 7.5' quadrangle.

White Oak Point [EL DORADO]: *peak,* 6.5 miles west of Pollock Pines (lat. 38°46'45" N, long. 120°42'10" W; at N line sec. 25, T 11 N, R 12 E). Altitude 2888 feet. Named on Slate Mountain (1950) 7.5' quadrangle.

White Rock Canyon: see **White Rock Creek** [EL DORADO].

White Pines [CALAVERAS]: *village,* 5.5 miles south-southeast of Blue Mountain (lat. 38°15'50" N, long. 120°20'25" W; on N line sec. 29, T 5 N, R 15 E). Named on Dorrington (1979) 7.5' quadrangle. Postal authorities established White Pines post office at a lumber camp in 1940 and discontinued it in 1975 (Salley, p. 239).

White Pines Lake [CALAVERAS]: *lake,* behind a dam on San Antonio Creek 5.25 miles south-southeast of Blue Mountain (lat. 38°16'05" N, long. 120°20'35" W; sec. 20, T 5 N, R 15 E). Named on Dorrington (1979) 7.5' quadrangle.

White Rock [MARIPOSA]: *peak,* 7.25 miles south of the present settlement of Catheys Valley (lat. 37°19'50" N, long. 120°05' W; near NW cor. sec. 14, T 7 S, R 17 E). Altitude 1117 feet. Named on Indian Gulch (1920) 15' quadrangle.

White Rock Creek [EL DORADO]: *stream,* flows 3.5 miles to South Fork American River 2.25 miles east of Chili Bar (lat. 38°45'50" N, long. 120°46'50" W; near NW cor. sec. 32, T 11 N, R 11 E). Named on Camino (1952), Garden Valley (1949), and Slate Mountain (1950) 7.5' quadrangles. The canyon of the stream is called White Rock Canyon on Placerville (1893) 30' quadrangle.

White Rock Creek [NEVADA]: *stream,* flows 3.5 miles to North Creek 7.5 miles northwest of Donner Pass (lat. 39°23'50" N, long. 120°25'20" W; sec. 29, T 18 N, R 14 E). Named on Webber Peak (1981) 7.5' quadrangle.

White Rock Lake [NEVADA]: *lake,* 2900 feet long, 7.5 miles north-northwest of Donner Pass (lat. 39°25'10" N, long. 120°23' W; at SE cor. sec. 15, T 18 N, R 14 E); the lake is along White Rock Creek. Named on Webber Peak (1981) 7.5' quadrangle. Truckee (1940) 30' quadrangle has the form "Whiterock Lake" for the name.

Whites Bar: see **Electra** [AMADOR].

Whites Gulch [MARIPOSA]: *canyon,* drained by a stream that flows 2.5 miles to Lake McClure 4.5 miles south-southeast of Coulterville (lat. 37°38'55" N, long. 120°10'25" W; sec. 26, T 3 S, R 16 E). Named on Coulterville (1947, photorevised 1973) 7.5' quadrangle. Called White Gulch on Hoffmann and Gardner's (1863-1867) map.

Whites Gulch [TUOLUMNE]: *canyon,* drained by a stream that flows less than 1 mile to Big Creek (1) 2.5 miles east of Groveland (lat. 37°50'30" N, long. 120°11'05" W; sec. 23, T 1 S, R 16 E). Named on Groveland (1947) 7.5' quadrangle.

Whitesides Meadow [TUOLUMNE]: *area,* 10 miles east of Pinecrest (lat. 38°12'35" N, long. 119°48'40" W). Named on Pinecrest (1956) 15' quadrangle.

White Spring [TUOLUMNE]: *spring,* 7.5 miles south-southeast of Liberty Hill (lat. 38°15'50" N, long. 120°03'15" W; sec. 24, T 5 N, R 17 E). Named on Liberty Hill (1979) 7.5' quadrangle.

White Wolf [TUOLUMNE]: *locality,* 22 miles west of Tioga Pass (lat. 37°52'10" N, long.

119°38'55" W; sec. 10, T 1 S, R 21 E). Named on Hetch Hetchy Reservoir (1956) 15' quadrangle. Brothers Diedrich Meyer and Heinrich Meyer named the place for the chief of a group of Indians that lived there; later the brothers owned the land (Paden and Schlichtmann, p. 153).

Whitlock: see **Whitlock Creek** [MARIPOSA].

Whitlock Creek [MARIPOSA]: *stream,* flows nearly 2 miles to Sherlock Creek 6 miles east of the village of Bear Valley (lat. 37°33'35" N, long. 120°00'45" W; sec. 29, T 4 S, R 18 E). Named on Bear Valley (1947) 7.5' quadrangle. Postal authorities established Whitlock post office 3.5 miles northwest of Mariposa in 1899, moved it 1 mile north in 1904, and discontinued it in 1910 (Salley, p. 239-240).

Whitmore [AMADOR]: *locality,* 8 miles east-northeast of Pine Grove (lat. 38°27'20" N, long. 120°31' W). Named on Jackson (1902) 30' quadrangle.

Whitmore Meadow [AMADOR]: *area,* 7.5 miles southwest of Hams Station (lat. 38°28'35" N, long. 120°28'40" W; sec. 7, T 7 N, R 14 E). Named on Devils Nose (1979) 7.5' quadrangle.

Whitney [PLACER]: *locality,* nearly 6 miles north-northwest of Roseville along Southern Pacific Railroad (lat. 38°49'55" N, long. 121°18'20" W; sec. 4, T 11 N, R 6 E). Named on Roseville (1967) 7.5' quadrangle. The name commemorates Joel Parker Whitney, who had a large ranch at the place (Hanna, p. 354).

Whittakers Dardanelles [TUOLUMNE]: *ridge,* northeast-trending, 3 miles long, 9 miles west-northwest of Dardanelle (lat. 38°22' N, long. 120°00' W). Named on Donnell Lake (1979), Liberty Hill (1979), and Spicer Meadow Reservoir (1979) 7.5' quadrangles.

Whittles Upper Camp [TUOLUMNE]: *locality,* 3.25 miles southwest of Liberty Hill (lat. 38°20'25" N, long. 120°09'05" W; sec. 30, T 6 N, R 17 E). Named on Boards Crossing (1979) 7.5' quadrangle.

Whore House Gulch: see **Indian Diggins** [EL DORADO].

Whorl Mountain [TUOLUMNE]: *peak,* 1.25 miles south of Matterhorn Peak (lat. 38°04'25" N, long. 119°22'55" W). Altitude 12,029 feet. Named on Matterhorn Peak (1956) 15' quadrangle.

Wickes: see **Floriston** [NEVADA].

Widow Creek: see **Burnt Shanty Creek** [EL DORADO].

Widows Tears Falls: see **Silver Strand Falls** [MARIPOSA].

Wieland: see **Pine Grove** [AMADOR].

Wightman's Camp: see **Baltimore Town** [NEVADA].

Wild Bill Canyon [SIERRA]: *canyon,* drained by a stream that flows 2 miles to Berry Creek 4.5 miles west of Sierraville (lat. 39°35'50" N, long. 120°27' W; sec. 8, T 20 N, R 14 E).

Named on Sattley (1981) 7.5' quadrangle. On Sierraville (1955) 15' quadrangle, the stream in the canyon is called Berry Creek.

Wild Cat Bar: see **Hoosier Bar** [EL DORADO-PLACER].

Wildcat Canyon [EL DORADO]:

(1) *canyon*, drained by a stream that flows 1.5 miles to Middle Fork American River 4 miles west-northwest of Greenwood (lat. 38°55'45" N, long. 120°58'30" W; near SE cor. sec. 33, T 13 N, R 9 E). Named on Greenwood (1949) 7.5' quadrangle.

(2) *canyon*, drained by a stream that flows 1 mile to Weber Creek 6.5 miles west-southwest of Coloma (lat. 38°45'35" N, long. 121° 00' W). Named on Coloma (1949) and Pilot Hill (1954) 7.5' quadrangles.

Wildcat Canyon [PLACER]: *canyon*, drained by a stream that flows 3.5 miles to North Fork American River 10 miles west of Granite Chief (lat. 39°13'05" N, long. 120°28'25" W; near SE cor. sec. 26, T 16 N, R 13 E). Named on Royal Gorge (1953) 7.5' quadrangle.

Wildcat Creek [MADERA]: *stream*, flows 7 miles to Chowchilla River 5 miles west of Raymond (lat. 37°12'15" N, long. 119°59'55" W; sec. 28, T 8 S, R 18 E). Named on Raymond (1962) 15' quadrangle.

Wildcat Creek [MARIPOSA]: *stream*, flows 2 miles to Merced River 7.25 miles west-south-west of Yosemite Village (lat. 37°43'20" N, long. 119°42'45" W; sec. 36, T 2 S, R 20 E). Named on Yosemite (1956) 15' quadrangle.

Wildcat Creek [TUOLUMNE]: *stream*, formed by the confluence of North Fork and South Fork, flows nearly 5 miles to Stanislaus River 1.25 miles southwest of Knights Ferry in Stanislaus County (lat. 37°48'30" N, long. 120°41'05" W; sec. 31, T 1 S, R 12 E). Named on Knights Ferry (1962) 7.5' quadrangle. The stream first was called Edwards' Creek (Criswell, p. 16). North Fork is 4.5 miles long and South Fork is 5 miles long; both forks head in Tuolumne County and are named on Keystone (1962) and Knights Ferry (1962) 7.5' quadrangles.

Wildcat Falls [MARIPOSA]: *waterfall*, 7.25 miles west-southwest of Yosemite Village on Wildcat Creek (lat. 37°43'25" N, long. 119° 42'55" W; near N line sec. 36, T 2 S, R 20 E). Named on Yosemite (1956) 15' quadrangle.

Wildcat Mountain [MARIPOSA]:

(1) *ridge*, north-northwest-trending, 1 mile long, 1 mile west-northwest of the settlement of Catheys Valley (lat. 37°26'30" N, long. 120°06'30" W; sec. 4, T 6 S, R 17 E). Named on Catheys Valley (1962) 7.5' quadrangle.

(2) *peak*, 8 miles east-southeast of Mariposa (lat. 37°26'25" N, long. 119°50'05" W; sec. 1, T 6 S, R 19 E). Altitude 2920 feet. Named on Stumpfield Mountain (1947) 7.5' quadrangle.

Wildcat Point [TUOLUMNE]: *peak*, 10 miles west of Tioga Pass (lat. 37°5540" N, long.

119°26'30" W). Altitude 9455 feet. Named on Tuolumne Meadows (1956) 15' quadrangle.

Wilderness Creek [TUOLUMNE]: *stream*, heads in Alpine County and flows less than 0.25 mile in Tuolumne County to Spicer Meadow Reservoir 8.5 miles west-northwest of Dardanelle (lat. 38°24'25" N, long. 119°58'05" W). Named on Spicer Meadow Reservoir (1979) 7.5' quadrangle.

Wild Goose Flat: see **Goose Flat** [EL DO-RADO].

Wild Goose Gulch [CALAVERAS]: *canyon*, drained by a stream that flows less than 1 mile to Coyote Creek 2 miles northeast of Vallecito (lat. 38°06'50" N, long. 120°27'05" W; sec. 17, T 3 N, R 14 E). Named on Columbia (1948) 7.5' quadrangle.

Wild Hog Canyon [MADERA]: *canyon*, drained by a stream that flows 2.5 miles to Fresno River 4.25 miles east of Knowles (lat. 37°12'35" N, long. 119°47'50" W; near W line sec. 28, T 8 S, R 20 E). Named on Knowles (1962) 7.5' quadrangle.

Wild Plum Campground [SIERRA]: *locality*, nearly 2 miles east of Sierra City along Haypress Creek (lat. 39°34' N, long. 120°36' W; near SW cor. sec. 26, T 20 N, R 12 E). Named on Sierra City (1955) 15' quadrangle.

Wildwood: see **Hidden Valley** [PLACER] (2).

Wiley: see **Cooks Station** [AMADOR].

William Aches Canyon: see **Bellyache Canyon** [MARIPOSA].

Williams: see **Sam Williams Spring** [TUOL-UMNE].

Williams Creek [SIERRA]: *stream*, flows 1 mile to Deer Creek 4 miles northeast of Sierra City (lat. 39°36'40" N, long. 120°35'15" W; near E line sec. 11, T 20 N, R 12 E). Named on Haypress Valley (1981) 7.5' quadrangle. On Sierra City (1955) 15' quadrangle, the name "Williams Creek" applies to present Deer Creek below its junction with Williams Creek.

Williamson Creek [SIERRA-YOLO]: *stream*, heads in Sierra County and flows 2.25 miles to Willow Creek nearly 2 miles north of Camptonville in Yuba County (lat. 39°28'40" N, long. 121°02'30" W; near NW cor. sec. 36, T 19 N, R 8 E). Named on Camptonville (1948) 7.5' quadrangle.

Williams Peak [MARIPOSA]: *peak*, 7.5 miles north-northeast of Hornitos (lat. 37°36' N, long. 120°10'10" W; near E line sec. 11, T 4 S, R 16 E). Altitude 3205 feet. Named on Hornitos (1947) 7.5' quadrangle. The name commemorates William H. Williams, a Cornishman who settled in Hunter Valley (Sargent, Shirley, 1976, p. 27).

Williams Ravine: see **You Bet** [NEVADA].

Willmont Canyon [PLACER]: *canyon*, drained by a stream that flows 1 mile to Burnett Canyon 4 miles north-northwest of Westville (lat. 39°13'50" N, long. 120°40'35" W; at N line sec. 30, T 16 N, R 12 E). Named on Westville (1952) 7.5' quadrangle.

Willmont Saddle [PLACER]: *pass,* 3.25 miles north-northwest of Westville (lat. 39°13'10" N, long. 120°39'50" W; sec. 30, T 16 N, R 12 E); the pass is near the head of Willmot Canyon. Named on Westville (1952) 7.5' quadrangle.

Willow Bar [EL DORADO]: *locality,* 3 miles northeast of Volcanoville along Middle Fork American River (lat. 39°00'25" N, long. 120°44'45" W; near N line sec. 4, T 13 N, R 11 E). Named on Michigan Bluff (1952) 7.5' quadrangle.

Willow Bar: see **Hoosier Bar** [EL DORADO-PLACER].

Willow Creek [AMADOR]: *stream,* heads in Amador County and flows 12.5 miles to Laguna in Sacramento County 27 miles east-southeast of downtown Sacramento (lat. 38°24'35" N, long. 121°02'50" W; at S line sec. 36, T 7 N, R 8 E). Named on Carbondale (1968) and Irish Hill (1962) 7.5' quadrangles. Called Laguna on Carbondale (1909) 7.5' quadrangle, but United States Board on Geographic Names (1964a, p. 15) rejected this name.

Willow Creek [CALAVERAS]: *stream,* formed by the confluence of North Fork and South Fork, flows 5.5 miles to Calaveritas Creek 3 miles southeast of San Andreas (lat. 38°09'45" N, long. 120°38'50" W; near NE cor. sec. 33, T 4 N, R 12 E). Named on Calaveritas (1962) and San Andreas (1962) 7.5' quadrangles. North Fork is 2 miles long and South Fork is nearly 3 miles long; both forks are named on Calaveritas (1962) 7.5' quadrangle.

Willow Creek [MADERA]:
(1) *stream,* flows 6 miles to Chowchilla River nearly 4 miles north-northeast of Raymond (lat. 37°16'20" N, long. 119°53'40" W; near N line sec. 4, T 8 S, R 19 E). Named on Ben Hur (1947), Horsecamp Mountain (1947), and Knowles (1962) 7.5' quadrangles. North Branch enters from the northeast 3 miles northeast of Raymond; it is 4.5 miles long and is named on Horsecamp Mountain (1947) 7.5' quadrangle.
(2) *stream,* formed by the confluence of North Fork and South Fork, flows 6.25 miles to San Joaquin River 14 miles south of Shuteye Peak (lat. 37°08'45" N, long. 119°27'40" W; sec. 16, T 9 S, R 23 E). Named on Shaver Lake (1953) 15' quadrangle. United States Board on Geographic Names (1937, p. 32) rejected the name "North Fork, San Joaquin River" for the stream and (p. 21) for its North Fork. North Fork Willow Creek is 24 miles long and is named on Bass Lake (1953), Millerton Lake (1965), Shaver Lake (1953), and Shuteye Peak (1953) 15' quadrangles. North Fork is called Willow Creek on Mariposa (1912) 30' quadrangle. United States Board on Geographic Names (1933, p. 216), under the entry "Chilkoot," called present North Fork Willow Creek by the name "Crane Valley Creek."

South Fork is formed by the confluence of Browns Creek and Sand Creek; it is 6.5 miles long and is named on Bass Lake (1953), Shaver Lake (1953), and Shuteye Peak (1953) 15' quadrangles.
(3) *stream,* flows 12 miles to Fresno River 7.5 miles south of Raymond (lat. 37°06'15" N, long. 119°53'15" W; sec. 34, T 9 S, R 19 E). Named on Daulton (1962), Knowles (1962), and Raymond (1962) 7.5' quadrangles. Called Cottonwood Cr. on Mariposa (1912) 30' quadrangle.
(4) *stream,* flows 8 miles to Fine Gold Creek 4.5 miles south-southeast of O'Neals (lat. 37°04'15" N, long. 119°38'55" W; sec. 11, T 10 S, R 21 E). Named on Millerton Lake West (1965) and O'Neals (1965) 7.5' quadrangles.

Willow Creek [MARIPOSA]: *stream,* flows 2.5 miles to Lake McClure 3 miles west-south-west of Coulterville (lat. 37°41'50" N, long. 120°14'45" W; near N line sec. 7, T 3 S, R 16 E). Named on Penon Blanco Peak (1962) 7.5' quadrangle.

Willow Creek [PLACER]: *stream,* flows 1 mile to Bear Pen Creek 7 miles northeast of Bunker Hill (lat. 39°06'50" N, long. 120°16'45" W; sec. 27, T 15 N, R 15 E). Named on Wentworth Springs (1953) 7.5' quadrangle.

Willow Creek [SIERRA]: *stream,* heads in Sierra County and flows 5.25 miles to New Bullards Bar Reservoir 1.5 miles west of Camptonville in Yuba County (lat. 39°27'15" N, long. 121°04'35" W; near W line sec. 3, T 18 N, R 8 E). Named on Camptonville (1948, photorevised 1969) 7.5' quadrangle.

Willow Creek [TUOLUMNE]:
(1) *stream,* flows 4.5 miles to Herring Creek 8 miles southwest of Dardanelle (lat. 38°15'10" N, long. 119°55'20" W; sec. 30, T 5 N, R 19 E). Named on Dardanelles Cone (1956) and Pinecrest (1956) 15' quadrangles.
(2) *stream,* flows 1.25 miles to Don Pedro Reservoir 3.5 miles northeast of Don Pedro Camp (lat. 37°44'35" N, long. 120°21'10" W; sec. 19, T 2 S, R 15 E). Named on Penon Blanco Peak (1962, photorevised 1973) 7.5' quadrangle.

Willow Creek: see **Chilkoot Creek** [MADERA]; **Laguna** [AMADOR].

Willow Flat [AMADOR]: *area,* nearly 4 miles west-northwest of Mokelumne Peak (lat. 38°34'10" N, long. 120°09'20" W; near E line sec. 1, T 8 N, R 16 E). Named on Bear River Reservoir (1979) 7.5' quadrangle.

Willow Flat [EL DORADO]:
(1) *area,* 6 miles southwest of Phipps Peak (lat. 38°53'05" N, long. 120°13'05" W; sec. 16, T 12 N, R 16 E). Named on Rockbound Valley (1955) 7.5' quadrangle.
(2) *area,* 8 miles west-southwest of Kirkwood (lat. 38°38'55" N, long. 120°12'25" W; sec. 9, T 9 N, R 16 E). Named on Tragedy Spring (1979) 7.5' quadrangle.

Willow Flat Creek [EL DORADO]: *stream,* flows 3.25 miles to Sherman Canyon 7.5 miles west-southwest of Kirkwood (lat. 38° 40' N, long. 120°12'15" W; near S line sec. 33, T 10 N, R 16 E); the stream goes through Willow Flat (2). Named on Tragedy Spring (1979) 7.5' quadrangle.

Willow Glen [MADERA]: *locality,* 6 miles north of O'Neals (lat. 37° 12'45" N, long. 119°42'30" W; near NW cor. sec. 29, T 8 S, R 21 E). Named on Mariposa (1912) 30' quadrangle.

Willow Gulch [TUOLUMNE]: *canyon,* drained by a stream that flows 1.5 miles to Rose Creek nearly 5 miles north-northeast of Columbia (lat. 38°06'10" N, long. 120°22'45" W; sec. 24, T 3 N, R 14 E). Named on Columbia (1948) 7.5' quadrangle.

Willow Meadow [TUOLUMNE]:
(1) *area,* 6.5 miles south-southwest of Dardanelle (lat. 38°15'20" N, long. 119°53'35" W; sec. 28, T 5 N, R 19 E); the place is along Willow Creek (1). Named on Donnell Lake (1979) 7.5' quadrangle.
(2) *area,* 1.5 miles north-northeast of Duckwall Mountain (lat. 37° 59'25" N, long. 120°06'20" W; near NE cor. sec. 33, T 2 N, R 17 E). Named on Duckwall Mountain (1948) 7.5' quadrangle.

Willow Spring [NEVADA]:
(1) *spring,* nearly 2 miles north-northeast of North Bloomfield (lat. 39°23'35" N, long. 120°53'25" W; sec. 30, T 18 N, R 10 E). Named on Pike (1949) 7.5' quadrangle.
(2) *spring,* 2 miles east of Graniteville (lat. 39°26'05" N, long. 120° 41'55" W; near SE cor. sec. 11, T 18 N, R 11 E). Named on Graniteville (1982) 7.5' quadrangle.

Willow Springs: see **Willow Springs Creek** [AMADOR].

Willow Springs Creek [AMADOR]: *stream,* flows 2.5 miles to Willow Creek 4.25 miles west-southwest of Plymouth (lat. 38°26'50" N, long. 120°54'45" W; sec. 19, T 7 N, R 10 E). Named on Irish Hill (1962) 7.5' quadrangle. Camp's (1962) map shows a place called Willow Springs situated near the confluence of present Willow Springs Creek and Willow Creek.

Willow Valley [NEVADA]:
(1) *valley,* 8 miles south-southwest of North Bloomfield along Deer Creek (lat. 39°16'05" N, long. 120°58'50" W; on E line sec. 8, T 16 N, R 9 E). Named on North Bloomfield (1949) 7.5' quadrangle.
(2) *locality,* 6.5 miles south-southwest of North Bloomfield in present Willow Valley (1) (lat. 39°16'40" N, long. 120°57'50" W). Named on Colfax (1898) 30' quadrangle.

Willow Valley: see **Castle Valley** [NEVADA].

Willow Valley Creek [NEVADA]: *stream,* flows 2 miles to Deer Creek 8 miles south-southwest of North Bloomfield in Willow Valley (1) (lat. 39°16'05" N, long. 120°58'40" W; sec. 9, T 16 N, R 9 E). Named on North Bloomfield (1949) 7.5' quadrangle.

Wilma Lake [TUOLUMNE]: *lake,* 1700 feet long, 7 miles southwest of Tower Peak (lat. 38°04'15" N, long. 119°38'25" W). Named on Tower Peak (1956) 15' quadrangle. Called Wilmer Lake on Dardanelles (1898, reprinted 1947) 30' quadrangle, but United States Board on Geographic Names (1964c, p. 16) rejected this designation. R.B. Marshall of United States Geological Survey named the lake for the daughter of Clyde L. Seavey (United States Board on Geographic Names, 1934, p. 28).

Wilmer Lake: see **Wilma Lake** [TUOLUMNE].

Wilseyville [CALAVERAS]: *village,* 1.5 miles south-southeast of West Point (lat. 38°22'45" N, long. 120°30'50" W; near N line sec. 14, T 6 N, R 13 E). Named on West Point (1948) 7.5' quadrangle. Postal authorities established Wilseyville post office in 1947 and named it for Lawrence A. Wilsey, an official of Forest Products Company (Salley, p. 241).

Wilson [EL DORADO]: *locality,* 3.5 miles northeast of Slippery Ford (present Kyburz) (lat. 38°49' N, long. 120°15'30" W). Named on Pyramid Peak (1896) 30' quadrangle.

Wilson Creek [TUOLUMNE]: *stream,* flows 4.5 miles to Matterhorn Canyon (lat. 38°00'15" N, long. 119°25'30" W). Named on Matterhorn Peak (1956) 15' quadrangle. Lieutenant H.C. Benson named the stream for his friend Mountford Wilson (Browning 1986, p. 239).

Wilson Lake [CALAVERAS]: *lake,* 800 feet long, 3.25 miles southwest of Devils Nose along Bear Creek (1) (lat. 38°25'55" N, long. 120°27'45" W; near W line sec. 29, T 7 N, R 14 E). Named on Devils Nose (1979) 7.5' quadrangle.

Wilson Meadow [TUOLUMNE]: *area,* 6 miles north-northwest of Mather (lat. 37°57'40" N, long. 119°53'50" W; sec. 9, T 1 N, R 19 E). Named on Lake Eleanor (1956) 15' quadrangle. Browning (1986, p. 239) associated the name with William B. Wilson, who patented land in the neighborhood in 1892.

Wilsons Branch: see **Henness Branch** [MARIPOSA].

Wilsons Ranch: see **Emigrant Gap** [PLACER] (2).

Wilson Valley: see **Carpenter Flat** [PLACER].

Windlass Ridge [MARIPOSA]: *ridge,* north-northwest-trending, 2.5 miles long, 9 miles south of El Portal (lat. 37°32'30" N, long. 119° 48'10" W). Named on Buckingham Mountain (1947) 7.5' quadrangle.

Windmill Canyon [MARIPOSA]: *canyon,* drained by a stream that flows 2.25 miles to Del Puerto Canyon 3.5 miles northeast of Copper Mountain (lat. 37°27'15" N, long. 121°16'10" W; sec. 35, T 5 S, R 6 E). Named on Copper Mountain (1956) 7.5' quadrangle.

Windmiller Ravine [EL DORADO]: *canyon,* drained by a stream that flows 2 miles to South Fork Silver Creek 3 miles northeast of Riverton (lat. 38°48'10" N, long. 120°24'35"

W; sec. 16, T 11 N, R 14 E). Named on Riverton (1950) 7.5' quadrangle.

Windmuller [EL DORADO]: *locality,* 9 miles southeast of Robbs Peak (lat. 38°49'55" N, long. 120°17'25" W). Named on Pyramid Peak (1896) 30' quadrangle. Kyburz (1952) 7.5' quadrangle shows Windmiller cabin at or near the place.

Wind River: see **Little Truckee River** [NEVADA-SIERRA].

Windy Gap [MADERA]: *pass,* 11.5 miles northeast of Raymond (lat. 37°20'55" N, long. 119°46'10" W; sec. 3, T 7 S, R 20 E). Named on Horsecamp Mountain (1947) 7.5' quadrangle.

Windy Gap [TUOLUMNE]: *pass,* 10 miles southwest of Liberty Hill (lat. 38°15' N, long. 120°13'20" W; near N line sec. 33, T 5 N, R 16 E). Named on Boards Crossing (1979) 7.5' quadrangle.

Windy Lake [MADERA]: *lake,* 700 feet long, 1.25 miles north-northeast of Buena Vista Peak (lat. 37°36'45" N, long. 119°30'40" W; sec. 1, T 4 S, R 22 E). Named on Yosemite (1956) 15' quadrangle.

Windy Point [PLACER]: *relief feature,* 2 miles east-southeast of Colfax (lat. 39°05'20" N, long. 120°54'55" W; sec. 1, T 14 N, R 9 E). Named on Colfax (1949) 7.5' quadrangle.

Windy Point Cliffs [NEVADA]: *relief feature,* 4 miles east of Graniteville (lat. 39°25'45" N, long. 120°40' W; sec. 18, T 18 N, R 12 E). Named on Graniteville (1982) 7.5' quadrangle.

Winifred: see **Lake Winifred** [EL DORADO].

Winkle Branch: see **Little Winkle Branch**, under **Lehamite Creek** [MARIPOSA].

Winnie Smith Mill [SIERRA]:
(1) *locality,* 5 miles northeast of Sierraville in Antelope Valley (lat. 39°38' N, long. 120°17' W; near NW cor. sec. 34, T 21 N, R 15 E). Ruins named on Sierraville (1955) 15' quadrangle.
(2) *locality,* 16 miles south-southeast of Loyalton along Dry Creek (lat. 39°27' N, long. 120°08'25" W; near SW cor. sec. 31, T 31 N, R 17 E). Site named on Hobart Mills (1981) 7.5' quadrangle.

Winter Bar [CALAVERAS]: *locality,* 4 miles northwest of Valley Springs along Mokelumne River (lat. 38°13'25" N, long. 120°53'20" W; near SW cor. sec. 4, T 4 N, R 10 E). Named on Wallace (1962) 7.5' quadrangle. Water of Camanche Reservoir now covers the site. Andrews (p. 118) referred to Winter's Bar, and F. S. Cook (p. 4) mentioned Winters Bar.

Winterton: see **Altaville** [CALAVERAS].

Winton: see **Camp Winton** [AMADOR].

Wire Lakes [TUOLUMNE]: *lakes,* largest 2200 feet long, 12 miles east of Pinecrest (lat. 38°10'30" N, long. 119°46'45" W). Named on Pinecrest (1956) 15' quadrangle.

Wisconsin Bar: see **Bucks Bar** [EL DORADO]; **Grapevine Ravine** [AMADOR].

Wisconsin Gulch [EL DORADO]: *canyon,* drained by a stream that flows 1 mile to Steely Fork Cosumnes River 9 miles southeast of Camino (lat. 38°38'10" N, long. 120°34'45" W; sec. 18, T 9 N, R 13 E). Named on Sly Park (1952) 7.5' quadrangle.

Wisconsin Hill: see **Refuge Canyon** [PLACER].

Wishon: see **Wishon Cove** [MADERA].

Wishon Campground [MADERA]: *locality,* 7 miles southeast of Yosemite Forks on the west side of Bass Lake (1) (lat. 37°17'15" N, long. 119°32' W; sec. 26, T 7 S, R 22 E); the place is near Wishon Cove. Named on Bass Lake (1953) 7.5' quadrangle.

Wishon Cove [MADERA]: *embayment,* nearly 7 miles southeast of Yosemite Forks on the west side of Bass Lake (1) (lat. 37°18' N, long. 119°32'15" W; on N line sec. 26, T 7 S, R 22 E). Named on Bass Lake (1953) 7.5' quadrangle. The name "Wishon" commemorates A. Emory Wishon of San Joaquin Light and Power Corporation, later vice-president and general manager of Pacific Gas and Electric Company (Gudde, 1969, p. 366). A place called Wishon is situated along Minaret and Western Railroad on the south shore of Bass Lake (1) near the dam that forms the lake (Clough, p. 95). Postal authorities established Wishon post office in 1923 to serve a vacation community (Salley, p. 242).

W Lake: see **Emigrant Lake** [TUOLUMNE].

Wolf [NEVADA]: *locality,* 11.5 miles south-southwest of Grass Valley (lat. 39°03'35" N, long. 121°08'20" W; near SE cor. sec. 13, T 14 N, R 7 E); the place is near the head of Little Wolf Creek (2). Named on Wolf (1949) 7.5' quadrangle. Postal authorities established Wolf post office in 1888, moved it 0.5 mile south in 1940, and discontinued it in 1956 (Salley, p. 242).

Wolf Creek [NEVADA]: *stream,* flows 22 miles to Bear River nearly 2 miles south-southeast of Wolf (lat. 39°02'05" N, long. 121°07'45" W; sec. 30, T 14 N, R 8 E). Named on Chicago Park (1949), Grass Valley (1949), Lake Combie (1949), and Wolf (1949) 7.5' quadrangles. South Fork enters the main stream in downtown Grass Valley; it is nearly 3 miles long and is named on Grass Valley (1949) 7.5' quadrangle.

Wolf Creek [SIERRA]: *stream,* flows 6.5 miles to Middle Yuba River 3 miles southeast of Alleghany (lat. 39°26'40" N, long. 120°48'15" W; near N line sec. 12, T 18 N, R 10 E). Named on Alleghany (1949) and Graniteville (1982) 7.5' quadrangles.

Wolf Creek: see **Little Wolf Creek** [NEVADA]; **Little Wolf Creek** [SIERRA]; **Mill Creek** [EL DORADO] (2); **South Wolf Creek** [NEVADA].

Wolf Creek Mountain: see **Wolf Mountain** [NEVADA].

Wolfeboro: see **Camp Wolfeboro** [CALAVERAS].

Wolf Gulch [TUOLUMNE]: *canyon,* drained by a stream that flows 1.25 miles to Stanislaus River 2.25 miles northwest of Columbia (lat. 38°03'35" N, long. 120°25'50" W; sec. 3, T 2 N, R 14 E). Named on Columbia (1948) 7.5' quadrangle.

Wolfin Meadow [TUOLUMNE]: *area,* 8 miles southeast of Long Barn (lat. 38°00'50" N, long. 120°01'35" W; sec. 20, T 2 N, R 18 E). Named on Hull Creek (1979) 7.5' quadrangle.

Wolf Mountain [NEVADA]: *peak,* 6 miles south-southwest of Grass Valley (lat. 39°08' N, long. 121°05'55" W; near SW cor. sec. 21, T 15 N, R 8 E). Altitude 2632 feet. Named on Grass Valley (1949) 7.5' quadrangle. Called Wolf Creek Mountain on Smartsville (1895) 30' quadrangle—the feature is west of Wolf Creek. Whitney's (1873) map has the name "Wolf Creek Mts." near present Wolf Mountain.

Wolverine: see **Monona Flat** [PLACER].

Wood [CALAVERAS]: *locality,* 7 miles east of Blue Mountain (lat. 38°19'50" N, long. 120°14'15" W). Named on Big Trees (1891) 30' quadrangle.

Wood: see **Camp A.E. Wood**, under **Camp Hoyle** [MARIPOSA].

Woodcamp Campground [NEVADA]: *locality,* 2.5 miles north of English Mountain (lat. 39°29'10" N, long. 120°32'55" W; near E line sec. 30, T 19 N, R 13 E); the place is at the mouth of Woodcamp Creek. Named on English Mountain (1983) 7.5' quadrangle.

Woodcamp Creek [NEVADA]: *stream,* flows 1.25 miles to Jackson Meadows Reservoir 2.5 miles east of English Mountain (lat. 39° 29'10" N, long. 120°33' W; near E line sec. 30, T 19 N, R 13 E). Named on English Mountain (1983) 7.5' quadrangle.

Woodchoppers Spring [NEVADA]: *spring,* 2.25 miles east of Hobart Mills (lat. 39°24'20" N, long. 120°08'30" W; near SW cor. sec. 18, T 18 N, R 17 E). Named on Hobart Mills (1981) 7.5' quadrangle.

Woodchuck Flat [NEVADA]: *area,* 5.5 miles east-northeast of Yuba Gap (lat. 39°20'05" N, long. 120°30'55" W; near SE cor. sec. 16, T 17 N, R 13 E). Named on Cisco Grove (1955) 7.5' quadrangle.

Woodcock [CALAVERAS]: *locality,* 7.5 miles west-northwest of Blue Mountain (lat. 38°22'40" N, long. 120°29'50" W). Named on Big Trees (1891) 30' quadrangle.

Wood Lake [TUOLUMNE]: *lake,* nearly 1 mile long, 13 miles east of Pinecrest along Buck Meadow Creek (lat. 38°09'05" N, long. 119° 45'20" W). Named on Pinecrest (1956) 15' quadrangle.

Wood Meadow [TUOLUMNE]: *area,* 7.5 miles northwest of Mather (lat. 37°57'20" N, long. 119°57'25" W; on W line sec. 12, T 1 N, R 18 E). Named on Lake Eleanor (1956) 15' quadrangle.

Woodpecker Gulch [EL DORADO]: *canyon,* drained by a stream that flows 0.5 mile to Cedar Canyon 9 miles southeast of Camino (lat. 38°39'05" N, long. 120°33'10" W; at W line sec. 9, T 9 N, R 13 E). Named on Sly Park (1952) 7.5' quadrangle.

Woodpecker Ravine [NEVADA]: *canyon,* drained by a stream that flows 4.5 miles to South Wolf Creek 6 miles south-southeast of Grass Valley (lat. 39°08'15" N, long. 121°00'55" W; sec. 19, T 15 N, R 9 E). Named on Grass Valley (1949) 7.5' quadrangle.

Woodpile Gulch [AMADOR]: *canyon,* 1 mile long, 7 miles southwest of Jackson (lat. 38°16'25" N, long. 120°51'35" W; sec. 22, T 5 N, R 10 E). Named on Jackson (1962) 7.5' quadrangle. Water of North Arm Pardee Reservoir now floods most of the canyon.

Woodruff Creek [SIERRA]: *stream,* flows about 2.5 miles to Rock Creek (3) 0.25 mile south-southwest of Goodyears Bar (lat. 39°32'10" N, long. 120°53'05" W; near S line sec. 5, T 19 N, R 10 E). Named on Goodyears Bar (1951) 7.5' quadrangle.

Woods Creek [TUOLUMNE]: *stream,* flows 17 miles to Don Pedro Reservoir 1.25 miles east-northeast of Chinese Camp (lat. 37°52'30" N, long. 120°24'40" W). Named on Columbia (1948), Columbia SE (1948), and Sonora (1948) 7.5' quadrangles. According to Morgan (*in* Gardiner, p. 317), the name possibly is for Benjamin Wood, who was killed by Indians in 1849. The first discovery of gold in Tuolumne County was made in August of 1848 along Woods Creek 1 mile southwest of Jamestown at Woods' Crossing (Hoover, Rensch, and Rensch, p. 568). Derby's (1849) map has the name "Woods" southeast of Sonoran Camp (present Sonora) on upper reaches of Tuolumne River drainage. Postal authorities established Wood's Diggings post office in 1851 and discontinued it in 1853 (Frickstad, p. 217). A travelers stop called Halfway House was situated along Woods Creek halfway from Sonora to Jamestown (Gudde, 1975, p. 149).

Woods' Crossing: see **Woods Creek** [TUOLUMNE].

Wood's Diggings: see **Woods Creek** [TUOLUMNE].

Wood's Dry Diggings: see **Auburn** [PLACER].

Wooley Creek [PLACER]: *stream,* flows 4 miles to Lake Combie 7.5 miles south-southwest of Colfax (lat. 39°00'20" N, long. 121° 02'30" W; at W line sec. 1, T 13 N, R 8 E). Named on Lake Combie (1949) 7.5' quadrangle. Called Coyote Creek on Smartsville (1895) 30' quadrangle.

Woolford: see **King Woolford Mill** [NEVADA].

Wool Hollow [CALAVERAS]: *canyon,* drained by a stream that flows 1 mile to Stanislaus River 3.5 miles east-northeast of Vallecito (lat. 38°06'05" N, long. 120°24'35" W; sec. 23, T 3 N, R 14 E). Named on Columbia (1948) 7.5' quadrangle.

Woolsey Flat [NEVADA]:

(1) *locality,* 8.5 miles northeast of North Bloomfield along Middle Yuba River (lat. 39°27' N, long. 120°46'35" W; near SE cor. sec. 6, T 18 N, R 11 E). Named on Alleghany (1949) 7.5' quadrangle. Colfax (1938) 30' quadrangle shows Woolsey cabin at or near the place.

(2) *locality,* 4 miles north-northeast of North Bloomfield (lat. 39° 25' N, long. 120°51'30" W; at N line sec. 21, T 18 N, R 10 E). Named on Alleghany (1949) 7.5' quadrangle.

Woolsey Spring: see **Upper Woolsey Spring** [NEVADA].

Woosterville: see **Ione** [AMADOR].

Worn Mill Canyon [SIERRA]: *canyon,* drained by a stream that flows 3.25 miles to Little Truckee River 6 miles south of Crystal Peak (lat. 39°28'05" N, long. 120°06'05" W; near W line sec. 28, T 19 N, R 17 E). Named on Boca (1955) 7.5' quadrangle.

Wrights Creek [TUOLUMNE]: *stream,* flows 8 miles to North Fork Tuolumne River 5.25 miles east-northeast of Twain Harte (lat. 38°03'55" N, long. 120°08'15" W; at W line sec. 32, T 3 N, R 17 E). Named on Hull Creek (1979) and Twain Harte (1979) 7.5' quadrangles. Called Wright Creek on Big Trees (1891) 30' quadrangle.

Wrights Lake [EL DORADO]: *lake,* 3250 feet long, 4 miles west of Pyramid Peak (lat. 38°50'55" N, long. 120°13'55" W; near NE cor. sec. 32, T 12 N, R 16 E). Named on Pyramid Peak (1955) 7.5' quadrangle. Pyramid Peak (1896) 30' quadrangle has the name "Wrights Lakes" for present Wrights Lake, Dark Lake, and Beauty Lake together.

Wrights Lakes: see **Wrights Lake** [EL DORADO].

Wulffs [EL DORADO]: *locality,* 5 miles north-northeast of Clarksville (lat. 38°43'20" N, long. 121°01'05" W). Named on Sacramento (1892) 30' quadrangle.

– X - Y –

Yagers Gulch [AMADOR]: *canyon,* drained by a stream that flows less than 0.5 mile to Pardee Reservoir 6.25 miles southwest of Jackson (lat. 38°17'05" N, long. 120°51'15" W; sec. 15, T 5 N, R 10 E). Named on Jackson (1962) 7.5' quadrangle.

Yankee Hill [TUOLUMNE]:

(1) *ridge,* west-southwest-trending, 1.25 miles long, 2 miles east of Columbia (lat. 38°02'30" N, long. 120°21'30" W; sec. 7, 8, T 2 N, R 15 E). Named on Columbia (1948) 15' quadrangle.

(2) *locality,* 1 mile east of Columbia (lat. 38°02'20" N, long. 120° 22'40" W; near E line sec. 12, T 2 N, R 14 E); the place is 1 mile west of Yankee Hill (1). Named on Columbia (1948) 7.5' quadrangle. According to Stoddart (p. 89), Thomas Hill of New York City, a vet-

eran of Stevenson's New York Volunteers, won the right to name the camp and he called it Yankee Hill. Other accounts attribute the name to other men named Hill; a camp called Knickerbocker Flat was at or south of Yankee Hill (Gudde, 1975, p. 188, 377; Jackson, J. H., p. 326). Gudde (1975, p. 349) listed a feature called Three Pine Gulch that was situated between Yankee Hill and Columbia.

Yankee Jim Gulch: see **Snyder Canyon** [PLACER].

Yankee Jims [PLACER]: *settlement,* 2.5 miles west-northwest of Foresthill (lat. 39°01'45" N, long. 120°51'40" W; sec. 28, T 14 N, R 10 E). Named on Foresthill (1949) 7.5' quadrangle. Called Yankee Jim on Colfax (1898) 30' quadrangle. Postal authorities established Yankee Jim's post office in 1852 and discontinued it in 1940 (Frickstad, p. 122). The name is for an Australian criminal who had the nickname "Yankee" and who held stolen horses at the site before the discovery of gold there (Jackson, J.H., p. 398-399). A mining camp called Yorkville was located 1.5 miles north of Yankee Jims, where gold was discovered in 1853 (Gudde, 1975, p. 379).

Yankee Jims Cañon: see **Mexican Gulch** [PLACER].

Yankee John Creek [EL DORADO]: *stream,* flows 2.25 miles to Slab Creek nearly 6 miles west-northwest of Pollock Pines (lat. 38° 47'40" N, long. 120°40'50" W; near S line sec. 18, T 11 N, R 12 E). Named on Slate Mountain (1950) 7.5' quadrangle. Placerville (1893) 30' quadrangle has the name "Yankee John Rav." for the canyon of the stream.

Yankee John Ravine: see **Yankee John Creek** [EL DORADO].

Yankee Slough [PLACER]: *water feature,* heads in Placer County and flows for 8 miles in Sutter County to Bear River nearly 5 miles north-northeast of Nicolaus (lat. 38°58'10" N, long. 121° 32'35" W; near SE cor. sec. 17, T 13 N, R 4 E). Named on Nicolaus (1952) and Sheridan (1953, photorevised 1973) 7.5' quadrangles.

Yanks [EL DORADO]: *locality,* 3.5 miles northeast of Mount Tallac along Lake Tahoe (lat. 38°56'10" N, long. 120°02'40" W). Named on Pyramid Peak (1896) 30' quadrangle.

Yanks: see **Meyers** [EL DORADO].

Yank's Station: see **Meyers** [EL DORADO].

Yaqui Camp: see **San Andreas** [CALAVERAS].

Yaqui Gulch [MARIPOSA]: *canyon,* 1.5 miles long, opens into the canyon of Carson Creek 5.5 miles northeast of the settlement of Catheys Valley at the site of Carson (lat. 37°28'45" N, long. 120°00'35" W). Named on Catheys Valley (1962) 7.5' quadrangle.

Yea Hoo Gulch [CALAVERAS]: *canyon,* drained by a stream that flows less than 1 mile to Stanislaus River 4.5 miles east-southeast of Murphys (lat. 38°07'25" N, long. 120°23'

W; sec. 12, T 3 N, R 14 E). Named on Murphys (1948) 7.5' quadrangle.

Yellowhammer Lake [TUOLUMNE]: *lake,* 2300 feet long, 12.5 miles east-southeast of Pinecrest (lat. 38°07'10" N, long. 119° 47' W). Named on Pinecrest (1956) 15' quadrangle.

Yellow Jacket Canyon [PLACER]: *canyon,* drained by a stream that flows 1 mile to Duncan Canyon 5.25 miles south-southwest of Duncan Peak (lat. 39°04'50" N, long. 120°32' W; sec. 9, T 14 N, R 13 E). Named on Greek Store (1952) 7.5' quadrangle.

Yellow Jacket Creek [PLACER]: *stream,* drained by a stream that flows less than 1 mile to Shirttail Canyon 3.5 miles north-northeast of Foresthill (lat. 39°04'10" N, long. 120°48'05" W; sec. 12, T 14 N, R 10 E). Named on Foresthill (1949) 7.5' quadrangle.

Yeomet: see **Enterprise** [AMADOR].

Yomana: see **Forest** [SIERRA].

Yore: see **Pat Yore Flat** [NEVADA].

York: see **Little York** [NEVADA].

York Creek [CALAVERAS]: *stream,* flows 2.5 miles to Empire Creek 2.25 miles east-northeast of Copperopolis (lat. 37°59' N, long. 120°35'50" W; sec. 36, T 2 N, R 12 E). Named on Angels Camp (1962) and Melones Dam (1962) 7.5' quadrangles.

York Diggings: see **Little York Diggings** [NEVADA].

Yorktown: see **Stent** [TUOLUMNE].

Yorkville: see **Yankee Jims** [PLACER].

Yornet: see **Yeomet**, under **Enterprise** [AMADOR].

Yosemite [MARIPOSA]: *area,* in and around Yosemite Valley; this is the original grant of land made by the United States Government to the State of California for the purpose of preserving Yosemite Valley as a park (Whitney, 1870, p. 9-10). Named on Hetch Hetchy Reservoir (1956), Tuolumne Meadows (1956), and Yosemite (1956) 15' quadrangles.

Yosemite: see **Fort Yosemite**, under **Yosemite Village** [MARIPOSA]; **Yosemite Village** [MARIPOSA].

Yosemite Creek [MARIPOSA]: *stream,* flows 12.5 miles to Merced River at Yosemite Village (lat. 37°44'30" N, long. 119°35'40" W). Named on Hetch Hetchy Reservoir (1956) 15' quadrangle.

Yosemite Creek Campgrounds [MARIPOSA]: *locality,* 5.5 miles north of Yosemite Village along Yosemite Creek (lat. 37°49'50" N, long. 119°35'15" W; sec. 30, T 1 S, R 22 E). Named on Hetch Hetchy Reservoir (1956) 15' quadrangle.

Yosemite Fall: see **Lower Yosemite Fall** [MARIPOSA]; **Upper Yosemite Fall** [MARIPOSA].

Yosemite Falls: see **Upper Yosemite Fall** [MARIPOSA].

Yosemite Forks [MADERA]: *locality,* 18 miles northeast of Raymond, where the road to Yosemite Valley branches from the road to Bass

Lake (1) (lat. 37°22' N, long. 119°37'45" W; sec. 36, T 6 S, R 21 E). Named on Bass Lake (1953) 15' quadrangle.

Yosemite Junction [TUOLUMNE]: *locality,* 8.5 miles southwest of Sonora, where the road to Yosemite National Park branches from the road to Sonora (lat. 37°53'30" N, long. 120°29'15" W; near E line sec. 36, T 1 N, R 13 E). Named on Sonora (1948) 7.5' quadrangle. J.W. Goodwin founded a travelers stop known as Goodwin's at the site in 1854 and ran it for 27 years (Paden and Schlichtmann, p. 56, 57). A stopping place called New York Tent was located about 0.5 mile southwest of present Yosemite Junction (Gudde, 1975, p. 243).

Yosemite Mill: see **Clearing House** [MARIPOSA].

Yosemite National Park [post office]: see **Yosemite Village** [MARIPOSA].

Yosemite Oaks: see **Acorn Lodge** [MARIPOSA].

Yosemite Point [MARIPOSA]: *promontory,* less than 1 mile north-northwest of Yosemite Village on the north side of Yosemite Valley (lat. 37°45'30" N, long. 119°35'30" W). Named on Hetch Hetchy Reservoir (1956) 15' quadrangle.

Yosemite Valley [MARIPOSA]: *valley,* along Merced River above a point about 7 miles west-southwest of Yosemite Village (lat. 37° 43'30" N, long. 119°42'30" W). Named on Yosemite (1956) 15' quadrangle. Bunnell (p. 58-59) claimed that he proposed the name "Yosemite" in 1851 in the belief that the Indians in the valley had that designation. The name is from an Indian word that has the meaning "bear," or "grizzly bear" (Kroeber, p. 68).

Yosemite Valley: see **Little Yosemite Valley** [MARIPOSA].

Yosemite Village [MARIPOSA]: *settlement,* 27 miles northeast of Mariposa in Yosemite Valley (lat. 37°44'45" N, long. 119°35' W). Named on Hetch Hetchy Reservoir (1956) and Yosemite (1956) 15' quadrangles. Called Yosemite on Yosemite (1909) 30' quadrangle. Postal authorities established Yo Semite post office in 1869, changed the name to Yosemite in 1908, and changed it to Yosemite National Park in 1922 (Salley, p. 245). Major H.C. Benson started Fort Yosemite in 1906 at the later site of Yosemite Lodge, and troops were stationed there until creation of the National Park Service in 1916 (Whiting and Whiting, p. 88).

You Bet [NEVADA]: *locality,* 5.5 miles northeast of Chicago Park (lat. 39°12'35" N, long. 120°53'50" W; sec. 31, T 16 N, R 10 E). Named on Chicago Park (1949) 7.5' quadrangle. Postal authorities established You Bet post office in 1868 and discontinued it in 1903 (Frickstad, p. 115). The name is from the favorite expression of a saloonkeeper at the place (Browne, p. 21-22). Whitney's (1873) map shows a mining camp called Waloupa located less than 1 mile south of You Bet. The name "Waloupa" or "Walloupa" was for an Indian chief; the place started in 1852, but by 1860 the remains of the community had moved to You Bet (Browne, p. 21). Whitney's (1873) map also shows a canyon called Williams Ravine that heads near You Bet and extends west-northwest for 1.25 miles to Greenhorn Creek. Gudde (1975, p. 47) listed a feature called Browns Hill that was located about 0.25 mile east of You Bet and named for Giles S. Brown, one of the brothers who owned a mine there.

Young: see **Frank Young Gulch** [TUOLUMNE].

Young America Canyon [PLACER]: *canyon,* drained by a stream that flows less than 1 mile to Stevens Ravine 2 miles north of Foresthill (lat. 39°03' N, long. 120°49'10" W; sec. 23, T 14 N, R 10 E). Named on Foresthill (1949) 7.5' quadrangle.

Young Lakes [TUOLUMNE]: *lakes,* three, largest 1900 feet long, 5 miles west-northwest of Tioga Pass (lat. 37°56'10" N, long. 119°20'10" W). Named on Tuolumne Meadows (1956) 15' quadrangle. The name commemorates General S.M.B. Young, acting superintendent of Yosemite National Park in 1896 (United States Board on Geographic Names, 1962a, p. 21).

Youngs: see **Dad Youngs Spring** [PLACER]; **Somerset** [EL DORADO].

Youngs Creek [CALAVERAS]: *stream,* flows 4 miles to Spring Valley Creek 2.5 miles east-northeast of Valley Springs in Spring Valley (lat. 38°12'30" N, long. 120°47'20" W; near S line sec. 8, T 4 N, R 11 E). Named on Jackson (1962) and Valley Springs (1962) 7.5' quadrangles.

Yuba Butte: see **Sierra Buttes** [SIERRA].

Yuba Gap [NEVADA]: *locality,* 2 miles west of Truckee near Nevada-Placer county line (lat. 39°19' N, long. 120°37' W; near N line sec. 27, T 17 N, R 12 E). Named on Emigrant Gap (1955) 15' quadrangle. Called Yuba Pass on Colfax (1938) 30' quadrangle.

Yuba Pass [NEVADA]:
(1) *pass,* 1 mile northeast of Yuba Gap (lat. 39°19' N, long. 120°35'55" W; sec. 23, T 17 N, R 12 E). Named on Emigrant Gap (1955) 15' quadrangle.
(2) *locality,* 1 mile east-northeast of Yuba Gap along Southern Pacific Railroad (lat. 39°19'25" N, long. 120°35'55" W; sec. 23, T 17 N, R 12 E); the place is at Yuba Gap (1). Named on Cisco Grove (1955, photorevised 1973) 7.5' quadrangle.

Yuba Pass: see **Yuba Gap** [NEVADA].

Yuba Reservoir [NEVADA]: *lake,* 1100 feet long, 5.5 miles north-northwest of Chicago Park (lat. 39°13'25" N, long. 120°59'15" W; sec. 29, T 16 N, R 9 E). Named on Chicago Park (1949, photorevised 1973) 7.5' quadrangle.

Yuba River [NEVADA]: *stream,* formed by the confluence of Middle Yuba River and North Yuba River, flows 37 miles, partly along Nevada-Yuba county line, to Feather River 1.25 miles south-southwest of downtown Marysville (lat. 39°07'40" N, long. 121°35'50" W). Named on Browns Valley (1947, photorevised 1973), French Corral (1948), Oregon House (1948), Smartville (1951, photorevised 1973), and Yuba City (1952, photorevised 1973) 7.5' quadrangles. Called Rio de Yuba on Larkin's (1848) map, and called Juba C. [Creek] on Ord's (1848) map. Work called the stream Middle Fork of Feather River in 1833 (Maloney *in* Work, p. 95). The name "Yuba" is derived from the designation of an Indian village that was near the mouth of the stream (Kroeber, p. 68). The name had a variety of forms in the early days, including "Yubah" (Dana, 1949, p. 125), "Uba" (Lyman, 1849a, p. 307), "Uber" and "Yu ba" (Cook, E.W., p. 36), and "Juber" (Ingersoll, p. 42). On Smartsville (1895) 30' quadrangle, the part of present Yuba River between the mouth of present Middle Yuba River and the mouth of present South Yuba River is called Middle Fork Yuba River, but United States Board on Geographic Names (1950, p. 7) rejected the names "Middle Fork" and "Middle Fork Yuba River" for this reach. Yuba City (1911) 7.5' quadrangle shows a distributary of Yuba River, also called Yuba River, located about 1 mile southeast of the lower part of present Yuba River, and nearly parallel to it; the dry course of the distributary has the label "Old River Channel" on Yuba City (1952) 7.5' quadrangle.

Yuba River: see **Middle Yuba River** [NEVADA-SIERRA]; **North Yuba River** [SIERRA]; **South Yuba River** [NEVADA-PLACER].

Yuba Valley: see **Summit Valley** [NEVADA-PLACER].

– Z –

Zebra: see **Zebra Station** [MADERA].

Zebra Station [MADERA]: *locality,* 10 miles southeast of Raymond (lat. 37°06'45" N, long. 119°46'40" W; sec. 27, T 9 S, R 20 E). Named on Little Table Mountain (1962) 7.5' quadrangle. Postal authorities established Zebra post office 6 miles northeast of Bates in 1886, discontinued it in 1888, reestablished it in 1890, discontinued it for a time in 1894, moved it 4.5 miles southwest in 1901, and discontinued it in 1904; the name was from Zebra mine, which had light and dark ore veins that suggested the stripes of a zebra (Salley, p. 246).

Zero Spring [EL DORADO]: *spring,* 16 miles north-northwest of Pollock Pines (lat. 38°58'35" N, long. 120°41'40" W; sec. 13, T 13 N, R 11 E). Named on Tunnel Hill (1950) 7.5' quadrangle.

Zinc House: see **Mooney Flat** [NEVADA].
Zion: see **Mount Zion** [AMADOR]; **Mount Zion**, under **Snow Tent** [NEVADA].
Zion Hill [NEVADA]: *peak,* nearly 3 miles north-northwest of Yuba Gap (lat. 39°21'10" N, long. 120°38'05" W; sec. 9, T 17 N, R 12 E). Altitude 6204 feet. Named on Blue Canyon (1955) 7.5' quadrangle.
Zip Creek [MARIPOSA]: *stream,* flows 2.5 miles to South Fork Merced River nearly 5 miles south-southeast of El Portal (lat. 37° 36'35" N, long. 119°45'05" W). Named on Buckingham Mountain (1947) and El Portal (1947) 7.5' quadrangles.

Zitella: see **Lake Zitella** [EL DORADO].
Zodoc: see **Placerville** [EL DORADO].
Zumwalt [EL DORADO]: *locality,* 9.5 miles northwest of Leek Spring Hill (lat. 38°43'10" N, long. 120°24'40" W). Named on Pyramid Peak (1896) 30' quadrangle.
Zumwalt Flat: see **Downieville** [SIERRA].
Zuver [PLACER]: *locality,* 3 miles west-north-west of Devil Peak (lat. 38°58'25" N, long. 120°35'55" W; sec. 14, T 13 N, R 12 E). Named on Devil Peak (1950) 7.5' quadrangle, which shows Zuver mine situated 0.5 mile east of the place.

References Cited

BOOKS AND ARTICLES

Anderson, Winslow. 1892. *Mineral springs and health resorts of California.* San Francisco: The Bancroft Company, 347 p.

Andrews, John R. 1978. *The ghost towns of Amador.* Fresno, California: Valley Publishers, 137 p.

Bancroft, Hubert Howe, 1886. *History of California, Volume II, 1801-1824.* San Francisco: The History Company, Publishers, 795 p.

Bancroft, Hubert Howe. 1888. *History of California, Volume VI, 1848-1859.* San Francisco: The History Company, Publishers, 787 p.

Becker, Robert H. 1969. *Designs on the land.* San Francisco: The Book Club of California, (no pagination).

Blake, William P. 1857. "Geological report." *Reports of explorations and surveys, to ascertain the most practicable and economical route for a railroad from the Mississippi River to the Pacific Ocean.* Volume V, Part II. (33d Cong., 2d Sess., Sen. Ex. Doc. No. 78.) Washington: Beverley Tucker, Printer, 370 p.

Borthwick, J.D. 1857. *Three years in California.* Edinburgh and London: William Blackwood and Sons, 384 p.

Boyd, William Harland. 1972. *A California middle boarder, The Kern River country, 1772-1880.* Richardson, Texas: The Havilah Press, 226 p.

Brewer, William H.. 1949. *Up and down California in 1860-1864.* Berkeley and Los Angeles: University of California Press, 583 p.

Brewster, Edwin Tenney. 1909. *Life and letters of Josiah Dwight Whitney.* Boston and New York: Houghton Mifflin Company, 411 p.

Brotherton, I. N. 1982. *Annals of Stanislaus County, Volume I, River towns and ferries.* Santa Cruz: Western Tanager Press, 180 p.

Browne, Juanita Kennedy. 1983. *Nuggets of Nevada County history.* Nevada City, California: Nevada County Historical Society, 143 p.

Browning, Peter. 1986. *Place names of the Sierra Nevada.* Berkeley: Wilderness Press, 253 p.

_____1988. *Yosemite place names.* Lafayette, California: Great West Books, 241 p.

Buffum, E. Gould. 1850. *Six months in the gold mines; From a journal of three years' residence in Upper and Lower California, 1847-8-9.* Philadelphia: Lea and Blanchard, 172 p.

Bunnell, Lafayette Houghton. 1977. *Discovery of the Yosemite.* (Reprinted from *Discovery of the Yosemite and the Indian War of 1851 which led to that event,* first published in 1880.) Olympic Valley, California: Outbooks, 184 p.

Burchfield, Chris. 1986. "Demolishing two Mariposa legends." *The Californians*, v. 4, no. 6, p. 42-43.

Burrows, Rufus, and Hall, Cyrus. 1971. *A long road to Stony Creek.* (Introduction and annotations by Richard Dillon.) Ashland: Lewis Osborne, 71 p.

California Department of Parks and Recreation. 1979. *California historical landmarks.* Sacramento: Department of Parks and Recreation, 174 p.

California Division of Highways. 1934. *California highway transportation survey, 1934.* Sacramento: Department of Public Works, Division of Highways, 130 p. + appendices.

Canfield, Chauncey L. (editor). 1920. *The diary of a forty-niner.* Boston and New York: Houghton Mifflin Company, 253 p.

Chalfant, W.A. 1933. *The story of Inyo.* (Revised edition.) (Author), 430 p.

Chamberlain, Newell D. 1936. *The call of gold, True tales on the gold road to Yosemite.* Mariposa, California: Gazette Press, 183 p.

Christy, Thomas. 1969. *Thomas Christy's road across the Plains.* (Edited by Robert H. Becker.) Denver, Colorado: Old West Publishing Company, (no pagination).

Clark, William B. 1970. *Gold districts of California.* (California Division of Mines and Geology Bulletin 193.) San Francisco: California Division of Mines and Geology, 186 p.

Clough, Charles W. 1968. *Madera.* Madera, California: Madera County History, 96 p.

Clyman, James. 1960. *James Clyman, frontiersman.* Portland, Oregon: Champoeg Press, 352 p.

Cook, Elliott Wilkinson. 1935. *Land Ho! The original diary of a forty-niner.* Baltimore: The Remington-Putnam Book Company, 43 p.

Cook, Fred S. (No date). *Legends of the Southern Mines.* (No place): California Traveler, 64 p.

Cowan, Robert G. 1956. *Ranchos of California.* Fresno, California: Academy Library Guild, 151 p.

Coy, Owen C. 1923. *California county boundaries.* Berkeley: California Historical Survey Commission, 335 p.

Crawford, J. J. 1984. "Report of the State Mineralogist." *Twelfth report of the State Mineralogist (Second Biennial), Two years ending September 15, 1894.* Sacramento: California State Mining Bureau, p. 8-412.

_____ 1896. *Thirteenth report (Third Biennial) of the State Mineralogist for the two years ending September 15, 1896.* Sacramento: California State Mining Bureau, p. 10-646.

Criswell, John F. 1972. *Knight's Ferry's golden past.* (Author), 64 p.

Dana, James D. 1849. "Gold in California." *American Journal of Science and Arts* (series 2), v. 7, no. 19, p. 125-126.

Davis, Leonard M. 1975. *Dry diggings on the North Fork; Personal observations of Auburn, California, in the days of '49.* (No place): Placer County Museum Foundation, 47 p.

Davis, Stephen Chapin. 1956. *California gold rush merchant, The journal of Stephen Chapin Davis.* (Edited by Benjamin B. Richards.) San Marino, California: The Huntington Library, 124 p.

Day, Sherman. 1856. "Hon. Sherman Day's report on the immigrant wagon road explorations." *Annual Report of the Surveyor-General of the State of California.* (Sen. Doc.No. 5, Sess. of 1856.) Sacramento: State printer, p. 77-84.

Decker, Peter. 1966. *The diaries of Peter Decker, Overland to California in 1849 and life in the mines 1850-1851.* (Edited by Helen S. Giffen.) Georgetown, California: The Talisman Press, 338 p.

Doble, John, 1962. *John Doble's journal and letters from the mines, Mokelumne Hill, Jackson, Volcano, and San Francisco, 1851-1865.* (Edited by Charles L. Camp.) Denver, Colorado: The Old West Publishing Company, 304 p.

Eccleston, Robert. 1957. *The Mariposa Indian War, 1850-1851.* (Edited by C. Gregory Crampton.) Salt Lake City: University of Utah Press, 168 p.

Evans, George W.B. 1945. *Mexican gold trail, The journal of a forty-niner.* San Marino, California: The Huntington Library, 340 p.

Farquhar, Francis P. 1924. "Place names of the High Sierra, Part II." *Sierra Club Bulletin*, v. 12, no. 1, p. 47-64.

_____1925. "Place names of the High Sierra, Part III." *Sierra Club Bulletin*, v. 12, no. 1, p. 126-157.

_____1926. "Mountaineering Notes." *Sierra Club Bulletin*, v. 12, no. 3, p. 304-307.

_____1930. "Fremont in the Sierra Nevada." *Sierra Club Bulletin,* v. 15, no. 1, p. 74-95.

_____1965. *History of the Sierra Nevada.* Berkeley, Los Angeles, London: University of California Press, 262 p.

Fatout, Paul. 1969. *Meadow Lake gold town.* Bloomington, London: Indiana University Press, 178 p.

Fremont, J.C. 1845. *Report of the exploring expedition to the Rocky Mountains in the year 1842, and to Oregon and North California in the years 1843-'44.* Washington: Blair and Rives, Printers, 583 p.

Frickstad, Walter N. 1955. *A century of California post offices, 1848 to 1954.* Oakland, California: Philatelic Research Society, 395 p.

Gardiner, Howard C. 1970. *In pursuit of the golden dream, Reminiscences of San Francisco and the Northern and Southern Mines, 1849-1857.* (Edited by Dale L. Morgan.) Stoughton, Massachusetts: Western Hemisphere, Inc., 390 p.

Gernes, Phyllis. 1979. *Hidden in the chaparral.* Garden Valley, California: (Author), 209 p.

Gray, Thorne B. 1973. *Quest for deep gold, The story of La Grange, California.* La Grange, California: Southern Mines Press, 44 p.

Gudde, Erwin G. 1949. *California place names.* Berkeley and Los Angeles: University of California Press, 431 p.

_____1969. *California place names.* Berkeley and Los Angeles: University of California Press, 416 p.

_____1975. *California gold camps.* Berkeley, Los Angeles, London: University of California Press, 467 p.

Hanna, Phil Townsend. 1951. *The dictionary of California land names.* Los Angeles: The Automobile Club of Southern California, 392 p.

Harris, Benjamin Butler. 1960. *The Gila Trail, The Texas argonauts and the California gold rush.* (Edited by Richard H. Dillon.) Norman: University of Oklahoma Press, 175 p.

Hart, James D. 1978. *A companion to California.* New York: Oxford University Press, 504 p.

Hobson, J.B. 1890a. "Nevada County." *Tenth annual report of the State Mineralogist, for the year ending December 1, 1890.* Sacramento: California State Mining Bureau, p. 364-398.

_____1890b. "Placer County." *Tenth annual report of the State Mineralogist, for the year ending December 1, 1890.* Sacramento, California State Mining Bureau, p. 410-434.

Hoffmann, C.F. 1868. "Notes on Hetch-Hetchy Valley." *American Journal of Science and Arts* (series 2), v. 46, no. 137, p. 266-267.

Hoover, Mildred Brooke, Rensch, Hero Eugene, and Rensch, Ethel Grace. 1966. *Historic spots in California.* (Third edition, revised by William N. Abeloe.) Stanford, California: Stanford University Press, 642 p.

Hubbard, Douglass. 1958. *Ghost mines of Yosemite.* Fredericksburg, Texas: The Awani Press, (no pagination).

Ingersoll, Chester. 1937. *Overland to California in 1847.* Chicago: Black Cat Press., 50 p.

Jackson, Joseph Henry. 1941. *Anybody's gold, The story of California's mining towns.* New York, London: D. Appleton-Century Company, 468 p.

Jackson, Louise A. 1988. *Beulah, A biography of the Mineral King Valley of California.* Tucson, Arizona: Westernlore Press, 179 p.

Johnston, Hank. 1963. *Railroads of the Yosemite Valley.* Corona del Mar, California: Trans-Anglo Books, 206 p.

Keller, George. 1955. *A trip across the plains and life in California.* Oakland, California: Biobooks, 44 p.

Kelly, William. 1950. *A stroll through the diggings of California.* Oakland, California: Biobooks, 206 p.

Kip, Leonard. 1946. *California sketches, with recollections of the gold mines.* Los Angeles: N. A. Kovach, 58 p.

Kroeber, A.L. 1916. "California place names of

Indian origin." *University of California Publications in American Archæology and Ethnology,* v. 12, no. 2, p. 31-69.

Laizure, C. McK. 1928. "San Francisco field division (Mariposa County)." *Mining in California,* v. 24, no. 2, p. 72-153.

_____1935. "Current mining activities in the San Francisco district with special reference to gold." *California Journal of Mines and Geology,* v. 31, no. 1, p. 24-48.

Lekisch, Barbara. 1988. *Tahoe place names.* Lafayette, California: Great West Books, 173 p.

Leonard, Edward C. 1973. *A brief history of Angels Camp.* Murphys, California: Old Timer's Museum, 40 p.

Lindgren, Waldemar. 1897. "The gold-quartz veins of Nevada City and Grass Valley districts, California." *Seventeenth Annual Report of the United States Geological Survey, Part II,—Papers of an economic character, 1895.* Washington: Government Printing Office, p. 1-262.

_____1911. *The Tertiary gravels of the Sierra Nevada of California.* (United States Geological Survey Professional Paper 73.) Washington: Government Printing Office, 226 p.

Lippincott, Joseph Barlow. 1902. *Storage of water on Kings River, California.* (United States Geological Survey Water-Supply and Irrigation Paper 58.) Washington: Government Printing Office, 101 p.

Logan, C.A. 1925. "Sacramento field division (Ancient channels of the Duncan Canyon region, Placer County)." *Mining in California,* v. 21, no. 3, p. 275-280.

_____1929. "Sacramento field division (Sierra County)." *Mining in California,* v. 25, no. 2, p. 151-212.

_____1938. "Mineral resources of El Dorado County." *California Journal of Mines and Geology,* v. 34, no. 3, p. 206-280.

_____1941. "Sacramento field district (Mineral resources of Nevada County)." *California Journal of Mines and Geology,* v. 37, no. 3, p. 374-468.

Logan, C.A. 1950. "Mines and mineral resources of Madera County, California." *California Journal of Mines and Geology,* v. 46, no. 4, p. 445-482.

Long, Ileen Price (Chairman, The Centennial Book Committee). 1964. *Alpine heritage, One hundred years of history, recreation, lore, in Alpine County, California, 1864-1964.* Campbell, California: Craftsmen Typographers, Inc., 66 p.

Lyman, C.S. 1849a. "Observations on California." *American Journal of Science and Arts* (series 2), v. 7, no. 20, p. 290-292, 305-309.

_____1849b. "Notes on the California gold regions." *American Journal of Science and Arts* (series 2), v. 8, no. 24, p. 415-419.

Marlette, S.H. 1856. *Annual report of the Surveyor-General, of the State of California.* (Sen. Doc. No. 5, Sess. of 1856.) Sacramento: State Printer, 334 p.

M'Collum, William. 1960. *California as I saw it.* (Edited by Dale L. Morgan.) Los Gatos, California: The Talisman Press, 219 p.

McKinstry, Bruce L. 1975. *The California gold rush overland diary of Byron N. McKinstry, 1850-1852.* Glendale, California: The Arthur H. Clark Company, 401 p.

McLaughlin, R. P., and Bradley, Walter W. 1916. "Madera County." *Report XIV of the State Mineralogist.* Sacramento: California State Mining Bureau, p. 531-568.

Mendenhall, Walter C. 1908. *Preliminary report on the ground waters of San Joaquin Valley, California.* (United States Geological Survey Water-Supply Paper 222.) Washington: Government Printing Office, 52 p.

Mendershausen, Ralph Rene. 1984. *Treasures of the South Fork.* (Revised.) (Author), 96 p.

Morgan, Dale (editor). 1963. *Overland in 1846, Diaries and letters of the California-Oregon trail.* Georgetown, California: The Talisman Press, 825 p.

Morley, Jim, and Foley, Doris. 1965. *Gold cities, Grass Valley and Nevada City.* Berkeley, California: Howell-North Books, 96 p.

Mosier, Dan L. 1979. *California coal towns, coaling stations, & landings.* San Leandro, California: Mines Road Books, 8 p.

Myrick, Thomas S. 1971. *The gold rush, Letters of Thomas S. Myrick from California to the Jackson, Michigan, American Citizen, 1849-1855.* Mount Pleasant, Michigan: The Cumming Press, 117 p.

O'Neill, Elizabeth Stone. 1983. *Meadow in the sky, A history of Yosemite's Tuolumne Meadows region.* Fresno, California: Panorama West Books, 162 p.

Paden, Irene D. 1943. *The wake of the prairie schooner.* New York: The Macmillan Company, 514 p.

Paden, Irene D., and Schlichtmann, Margaret E. 1959. *The Big Oak Flat road, An account of freighting from Stockton to Yosemite Valley.* Yosemite National Park: Yosemite Natural History Association, 356 p.

Perkins, William. 1964. *Three years in California, Williams Perkins' journal of life at Sonora, 1849-1852.* (Introduction and annotations by Dale L. Morgan and James R. Scobie.) Berkeley and Los Angeles: University of California Press, 424 p.

Preston, E.B. 1893. "Sierra County." *Eleventh report of the State Mineralogist, (First Biennial,) Two years ending September 15, 1892.* Sacramento: California State Mining Bureau, p. 400-412.

Pritchard, James A. 1959. *The overland diary of James A. Pritchard from Kentucky to California in 1849.* Denver, Colorado: The Old West Publishing Company, 221 p.

Quimby, Myron J. 1969. *Scratch Ankle, U.S.A., American place names and their derivation.* New York: A.S. Barnes and Company, 390 p.

Ricketts, Norma Baldwin. 1983. *Tragedy Spring*

and the pouch of gold. Sacramento, California: Ricketts Publishing Company, 47 p.

Russell, Carl Parcher. 1968. *One hundred years in Yosemite.* Yosemite National Park: Yosemite Natural History Association, 206 p.

Salazar, Francisco. 1964. *The gold of old Hornitos.* Fresno, California: Saga-West Publishing Co., 32 p.

Salley, H.E. 1977. *History of California post offices, 1849-1976.* La Mesa, California: Postal History Associates, Inc., 300 p.

Sargent, Mrs. J.L. (editor). 1927. *Amador County history.* (No place): Amador County Federation of Women's Clubs, 127 p.

Sargent, Shirley. 1961. *Wawona's yesterdays.* Yosemite National Park: Yosemite Natural History Association, 44 p.

_____1976. *Mariposa County guidebook.* Yosemite, California: Flying Spur Press, 37 p.

Scamehorn, Howard L. (editor). 1965. *The Buckeye Rovers in the gold rush.* Athens, Ohio: Ohio University Press, 195 p.

Sinclair, C.H. 1901. *Oblique boundary line between California and Nevada.* (United.States Coast and Geodetic Survey, Report for 1900, Appendix 3.) Washington: Government Printing Office, p. 255-484.

Slyter, Robert I., and Slyter, Grace I. (No date.) *Historical notes of the early Washington, Nevada, County, California, mining district.* (Authors), 160 p.

Smith, Genny (editor). 1976. *Mammoth Lakes Sierra.* (Fourth edition.) Palo Alto, California: Genny Smith Books, 147 p.

Spence, Mary Lee, and Jackson, Donald (editors). 1973. *The expeditions of John Charles Frémont, Volume 2, The Bear Flag revolt and the court-martial.* Urbana, Chicago, and London: University of Illinois Press, 519 p.

Stewart, George R. 1960. *Donner Pass and those who crossed it.* San Francisco, California: The California Historical Society, 96 p.

Stoddart, Thomas Robertson. 1963. *Annals of Tuolumne County.* (With introduction, critical notes, and index by Carlo M. DeFerrari.) Sonora, California: The Mother Lode Press. 188 p.

Taylor, L.H. 1902. *Water storage in the Truckee basin, California-Nevada.* (United States Geological Survey Water-Supply and Irrigation Papers No. 68.) Washington: Government Printing Office, 90 p.

Thompson and West. 1879. *History of San Joaquin County, California.* Oakland, California: Thompson & West, 142 p.

Turner, Henry Smith. 1966. *The original journals of Henry Smith Turner, with Stephen Watts Kearney to New Mexico and California, 1846-1847.* Norman: University of Oklahoma Press, 173 p.

Tyson, Philip T. 1850. "Report of P.T. Tyson, esq., upon the geology of California." *Report of the Secretary of War, communicating information in relation to the geology and topography of California.* (31st Cong., 1st Sess., Sen. Ex. Doc. No. 47.) Washington: Government Printing Office, p. 3-74.

Uhte, Robert F. 1951. "Yosemite's pioneer cabins." *Sierra Club Bulletin,* v. 36, no. 5, p. 49-71.

United States Board on Geographic Names. 1901. *Second report of the United States Board on Geographic Names, 1890-1899.* Washington: Government Printing Office, 150 p.

_____(under name "United States Geographic Board"). 1933. *Sixth report of the United States Geographic Board, 1890 to 1932.* Washington: Government Printing Office, 834 p.

_____(under name "United States Geographic Board"). 1934. *Decisions of the United States Geographic Board, No. 30—June 30, 1932.* (Yosemite National Park, California.) Washington: Government Printing Office, 29 p.

_____(under name "United States Board on Geographical Names"). 1936. *Decisions of the United States Board on Geographical Names, Decisions rendered between July 1, 1935, and June 30, 1936.* Washington: Government Printing Office, 44 p.

_____(under name "United States Board on Geographical Names"). 1937. *Decisions of the United States Board on Geographical Names, Decisions rendered between July 1, 1936, and June 30, 1937.* Washington: Government Printing Office, 33 p.

_____(under name "United States Board on Geographical Names"). 1939. *Decisions of the United States Board on Geographical Names, Decisions rendered between July 1, 1938, and June 30, 1939.* Washington: Government Printing Office, 41 p.

_____(under name "United States Board on Geographical Names"). 1942. *Decisions of the United States Board on Geographical Names, Decisions rendered between July 1, 1940, and June 30, 1941.* Washington: Government Printing Office, 89 p.

_____(under name "United States Board on Geographical Names"). 1947. *Decision lists nos. 4701, 4702, 4703.* Washington: Department of the Interior, 14 p.

_____1949a. *Decision lists nos. 4810, 4811, 4812, October, November, December, 1948.* Washington: Department of the Interior, 25 p.

_____1949b. *Decision list no. 4903, March 1949.* Washington: Department of the Interior. 26 p.

_____1949c. *Decision lists nos. 4907, 4908, 4909, July, August, September, 1949.* Washington: Department of the Interior, 24 p.

_____1950. *Decisions on names in the United States and Alaska rendered during April, May, and June 1950.* (Decision list no. 5006.) Washington: Department of the Interior, 47 p.

_____1954. *Decisions on names in the United States, Alaska and Puerto Rico, Decisions rendered from July 1950 to May 1954.* (Decision list no. 5401.) Washington: Department of the Interior, 115 p.

_____1957. *Decisions on names in the United States, Alaska and Hawaii, Decisions rendered from May 1954 through March 1957.* (Decision list no. 5701.) Washington: Department of the Interior, 23 p.

_____1959a. *Decisions on names in the United States, Puerto Rico and the Virgin Islands, Decisions rendered from April 1957 through December 1958.* (Decision list no. 5901.) Washington: Department of the Interior, 100 p.

_____1959b. *Decisions on names in the United States, Decisions rendered from January, 1959 through April, 1959.* (Decision list no. 5902.) Washington: Department of the Interior, 49 p.

_____1960a. *Decisions on names in the United States and Puerto Rico, Decisions rendered in May, June, July, and August, 1959.* (Decision list no. 5903.) Washington: Department of the Interior, 79 p.

_____1960b. *Decisions on names in the United States, Decisions rendered from September 1959 through December 1959.* (Decision list no. 5904.) Washington: Department of the Interior, 68 p.

_____1960c. *Decisions on names in the United States, Puerto Rico and the Virgin Islands, Decisions rendered from January through April 1960.* (Decision list no. 6001.) Washington: Department of the Interior, 79 p.

_____1961. *Decisions on names in the United States, Decisions rendered from May through August 1961.* (Decision list no. 6102.) Washington: Department of the Interior, 81 p.

_____1962a. *Decisions on names in the United States, Decisions rendered from January through April 1962.* (Decision list no. 6201.) Washington: Department of the Interior, 72 p.

_____1962b. *Decisions on names in the United States, Decisions rendered from May through August 1962.* (Decision list no. 6202.) Washington: Department of the Interior, 81 p.

_____1963a. *Decisions on names in the United States, Decisions rendered from September through December 1962.* (Decision list no. 6203.) Washington: Department of the Interior, 59 p.

_____1963b. *Decisions on geographic names in the United States, May through August 1963.* (Decision list no. 6302.) Washington: Department of the Interior, 81 p.

_____1964a. *Decisions on geographic names in the United States, September through December 1963.* (Decision list no. 6303.) Washington: Department of the Interior, 66 p.

_____1964b. *Decisions on geographic names in the United States, January through April 1964.* (Decision list no. 6401.) Washington: Department of the Interior, 74 p.

_____1964c. *Decisions on geographic names in the United States, May through August 1964.* (Decision list no. 6402.) Washington: Department of the Interior, 85 p.

_____1965a. *Decisions on geographic names in the United States, January through March 1965.* (Decision list no. 6501.) Washington: Department of the Interior, 85 p.

_____1965b. *Decisions on geographic names in the United States, April through June 1965.* (Decision list no. 6502.) Washington: Department of the Interior, 39 p.

_____1965c. *Decisions on geographic names in the United States, July through September 1965.* (Decision list no. 6503.) Washington: Department of the Interior, 74 p.

_____1966. *Decisions on geographic names in the United States, October through December 1965.* (Decision list no. 6504.) Washington: Department of the Interior, 38 p.

_____1967a. *Decisions on geographic names in the United States, January through March 1967.* (Decision list no. 6701.) Washington: Department of the Interior, 20 p.

_____1967b. *Decisions on geographic names in the United States, April through June 1967.* (Decision list no. 6702.) Washington: Department of the Interior, 26 p.

_____1968a. *Decisions on geographic names in the United States, January through March 1968.* (Decision list no. 6801.) Washington: Department of the Interior, 51 p.

_____1968b. *Decisions on geographic names in the United States, April through June 1968.* (Decision list no. 6802.) Washington: Department of the Interior, 42 p.

_____1969a. *Decisions on geographic names in the United States, October through December 1968.* (Decision list no. 6804.) Washington: Department of the Interior, 33 p.

_____1969b. *Decisions on geographic names in the United States, April through June 1969.* (Decision list no. 6902.) Washington: Department of the Interior, 28 p.

_____1970a. *Decisions on geographic names in the United States, January through March 1970.* (Decision list no. 7001.) Washington: Department of the Interior, 31 p.

_____1970b. *Decisions on geographic names in the United States, April through June 1970.* (Decision list no. 7002.) Washington: Department of the Interior, 20 p.

_____1971. *Decisions on geographic names in the United States, January through March 1971.* (Decision list no. 7101.) Washington: Department of the Interior, 19 p.

_____1972. *Decisions on geographic names in the United States, January through March 1972.* (Decision list no. 7201.) Washington: Department of the Interior, 32 p.

_____1973. *Decisions on geographic names in the United States, January through March 1973.* (Decision list no. 7301.) Washington: Department of the Interior, 20 p.

_____1974a. *Decisions on geographic names in the United States, October through December 1973.* (Decision list no. 7304.) Washington: Department of the Interior, 15 p.

_____1974b. *Decisions on geographic names in the United States, January through March*

1974. (Decision list no. 7401.) Washington: Department of the Interior, 27 p.

_____1975. *Decisions on geographic names in the United States, April through June 1975.* (Decision list no. 7502.) Washington: Department of the Interior, 32 p.

_____1976a. *Decisions on geographic names in the United States, October through December 1975.* (Decision list no. 7504.) Washington: Department of the Interior, 45 p.

_____1976b. *Decisions on geographic names in the United States, April through June 1976.* (Decision list no. 7602.) Washington: Department of the Interior, 26 p.

_____1976c. *Decisions on geographic names in the United States, April through June 1976.* (Decision list no. 7603.) Washington: Department of the Interior, 25 p.

_____1977a. *Decisions on geographic names in the United States, January through March 1977.* (Decision list no. 7701.) Washington: Department of the Interior, 32 p.

_____1977b. *Decisions on geographic names in the United States, April through June 1977.* (Decision list no. 7702.) Washington: Department of the Interior, 40 p.

_____1978a. *Decisions on geographic names in the United States, October through December 1977.* (Decision list no. 7704.) Washington: Department of the Interior, 29 p.

_____1978b. *Decisions on geographic names in the United States, April through June 1978.* (Decision list no. 7802.) Washington: Department of the Interior, 30 p.

_____1978c. *Decisions on geographic names in the United States, October through December 1978.* (Decision list no. 7804.) Washington: Department of the Interior, 48 p.

_____1980a. *Decisions on geographic names in the United States, October through December 1979.* (Decision list no. 7904.) Washington: Department of the Interior, 26 p.

_____1980b. *Decisions on geographic names in the United States, April through June 1980.* (Decision list no. 8002.) Washington: Department of the Interior, 33 p.

_____1981a. *Decisions on geographic names in the United States, October through December 1981.* (Decision list no. 8004.) Washington: Department of the Interior, 21 p.

_____1981b. *Decisions on geographic names in the United States, January through March 1981.* (Decision list no. 8101.) Washington: Department of the Interior, 23 p.

_____1981c. *Decisions on geographic names in the United States, April through June 1981.* (Decision list no. 8102.) Washington: Department of the Interior, 28 p.

_____1982. *Decisions on geographic names in the United States, April through June 1982.* (Decision list no. 8202.) Washington: Department of the Interior, 21 p.

_____1984a. *Decisions on geographic names in the United States, April through June 1984.*

(Decision list no. 8402.) Washington: Department of the Interior, 22 p.

_____1984b. *Decisions on geographic names in the United States, October through December 1984.* (Decision list no. 8404.) Washington: Department of the Interior, 18 p.

_____1985a. *Decisions on geographic names in the United States, April through June 1985.* (Decision list no. 8502.) Washington: Department of the Interior, 12 p.

_____1985b. *Decisions on geographic names in the United States, July through September 1985.* (Decision list no. 8503.) Washington: Department of the Interior, 19 p.

_____1986. *Decisions on geographic names in the United States, April through June 1986.* (Decision list no. 8602.) Washington: Department of the Interior, 10 p.

_____1988. *Decisions on geographic names in the United States, October through December 1988.* (Decision list no. 8804.) Washington: Department of the Interior, 20 p.

_____1990. *Decisions on geographic names in the United States.* (Decision list 1990.) Washington: Department of the Interior, 35 p.

_____1991. *Decisions on geographic names in the United States.* (Decision list 1991.) Washington: Department of the Interior, 40 p.

_____1992. *Decisions on geographic names in the United States.* (Decision list 1992.) Washington: Department of the Interior, 21 p.

_____1994. *Decisions on geographic names in the United States.* (Decision list 1994.) Washington: Department of the Interior, 17 p.

_____1995. *Decisions on geographic names in the United States.* (Decision list 1995.) Washington: Department of the Interior, 19 p.

Waring, Clarence A. 1919. "Placer County." *Report XV of the State Mineralogist.* San Francisco: California State Mining Bureau, p. 309-399.

Waring, Gerald A. 1915. *Springs of California.* (United States Geological Survey Water-Supply Paper 338.) Washington: Government Printing Office, 410 p.

Watts, W. L. 1890. "Stanislaus County." *Tenth annual report of the State Mineralogist, for the year ending December 1, 1890.* Sacramento: California State Mining Bureau, p. 680-690.

Watson, Jeanne Hamilton (editor). 1988. *To the land of gold and wickedness, The 1848-59 diary of Lorena L. Hayes.* St. Louis, Missouri: The Patrice Press, 486 p.

Wayman, John Hudson. 1971. *A doctor on the California Trail, The diary of Dr. John Hudson Wayman from Cambridge City, Indiana, to the gold fields in 1852.* (Edited by Edgeley Woodman Todd.) Denver, Colorado: Old West Publishing Company, 136 p.

Wedertz, Frank S. 1978. *Mono Diggings.* Bishop, California: Chalfant Press, Inc., 245 p.

Wheat, Carl I. 1963. *Mapping the Transmississippi West.* Volume Five. San Francisco: The Institute of Historical Cartography, 487 p.

Wheeler, George M. 1877. *Annual report upon the geographical surveys west of the one-hundredth meridian in the states and territories of California, Oregon, Nevada, Texas, Arizona, Colorado, Idaho, Montana, New Mexico, Utah, and Wyoming.* (Appendix NN of *The Annual Report of the Chief of Engineers for 1877.*) Washington: Government Printing Office, p. 1211-1334.

_____1878. *Annual report upon the geographical surveys of the territory of the United States west of the 100th meridian, in the states and territories of California, Colorado, Kansas, Nebraska, Nevada, Oregon, Texas, Arizona, Idaho, Montana, New Mexico, Utah, Washington, and Wyoming.* (Appendix NN of *The Annual Report of the Chief of Engineers for 1878.*) Washington: Government Printing Office, 234 p.

_____1879. *Annual report upon the geographical surveys of the territory of the United States west of the 100th meridian, in the states and territories of California, Colorado, Kansas, Nebraska, Nevada, Oregon, Texas, Arizona, Idaho, Montana, New Mexico, Utah, Washington, and Wyoming.* (Appendix OO of *The Annual Report of the Chief of Engineers for 1879.*) Washington: Government Printing Office, 340 p.

Whiting, J.S., and Whiting, Richard J. 1960. *Forts of the State of California.* (Authors), 90 p.

Whitney, J.D. 1865. *Report of progress and synopsis of the field-work from 1860 to 1864.* (Geological Survey of California, Geology, Volume I.) Published by authority of the Legislature of California, 498 p.

_____1870. *The Yosemite guide-book.* Published by authority of the Legislature [of California], 155 p.

_____1880. *The auriferous gravels of the Sierra Nevada of California.* Cambridge: University Press, John Wilson & Son, 569 p.

Wierzbicki, F.P. 1970. *California as it is & as it may be, or a guide to the gold region.* New York: Burt Franklin, 101 p.

Wilkes, Charles. 1958. *Columbia River to the Sacramento.* Oakland, California: Biobooks, 140 p.*udson's Bay Company.* (Edited by Alice Bay Malony.) San Francisco: California Historical Society, 112 p.

Wood, Harvey. 1954. *Personal recollections of Harvey Wood.* (Introduction and notes by John B. Goodman, III.) Pasadena, California: (Privately published), 27 p.

Work, John. 1945. *Fur brigade to the Bonaventura. John Work's California expedition, 1832-1833, for the Hudson's Bay Company.* (Edited by Alice Bay Malony.) San Francisco: California Historical Society, 112 p.

Wright, James W. A. 1984. *The Lost Cement Mine.* (Edited by Genny Smith.) Mammoth Lakes, California: Genny Smith Books, 95 p.

Yohalem, Betty. 1977. *"I remember . . ." , Stories and pictures of El Dorado County pioneer families.* Placerville, California: El Dorado County Chamber of Commerce, 237 p.

Zauner, Phyllis. 1982. *Lake Tahoe.* Tahoe Paradise, California: Zanel Publications, 63 p.

MISCELLANEOUS MAPS

Arrowsmith. 1860. "Map of the American River and Natoma Water and Mining Compys. Canals." A.T. Arrowsmith, C.E.

Bancroft. 1864. "Bancroft's map of the Pacific States." Compiled by Wm. H. Knight. Published by H.H. Bancroft & Co., Booksellers and Stationers, San Francisco, Cal.

California Division of Highways. 1934. (Appendix "A" *of* California Division of Highways.)

California Mining Bureau. 1909a. "Sutter, Yuba, Sierra, Nevada, Placer, and El Dorado Counties." (*In* California Mining Bureau Bulletin 56.)

_____1909b. "Sacramento, San Joaquin, Amador, and Calaveras Counties." (*In* California Mining Bureau Bulletin 56.)

_____1909c. "Stanislaus, Merced, Tuolumne, and Mariposa Counties." (*In* California Mining Bureau Bulletin 56.)

_____1910. "Map of California showing the approximate location of the principal mineral deposits." Compiled by the State Mining Bureau.

_____1917a. (Untitled map *in* California Mining Bureau Bulletin 74, p. 161.)

_____1917b. (Untitled map *in* California Mining Bureau Bulletin 74, p. 163.)

_____1917c. (Untitled map *in* California Mining Bureau Bulletin 74, p. 165.)

_____1917d. (Untitled map *in* California Mining Bureau Bulletin 74, p. 165.)

Camp. 1962. (Untitled map *in* Doble.)

DeGroot. 1863. "Bancroft's map of Nevada Territory exhibiting a portion of southern Oregon & eastern California." Published by Warren Holt, San Francisco, Cal.

Derby. 1849. "A Sketch of General Riley's route through the mining districts, July and Aug. 1849."

_____1850. "Reconnaissance of the Tulares Valley." Lieut. G.H. Derby, Topl. Engrs., April and May, 1850.

Eddy. 1851. "A complete map of the Feather & Yuba Rivers, with towns, ranches, diggings, roads, distances." Compiled from the recent surveys of M. Milleson & R. Adams, C. Engineers. Published by R.A. Eddy, Book & Stationer, Marysville Calia.

_____1854. "Approved and declared to be the official map of the State of California by an act of the Legislature passed March 25th 1853." Compiled by W.M. Eddy, State Surveyor General. Published for R.A. Eddy, Marysville, California, by J.H. Colton, New York.

Ellis. 1850. "Map of the gold region of California." Taken from a recent survey by Robert H. Ellis.

Fremont. 1845. "Map of an exploring expedition to the Rocky Mountains in the year 1842 and to Oregon & North California in the years 1843-44." By Brevet Capt. J.C. Frémont.

_____1848. "Map of Oregon and Upper California from the surveys of John Charles Frémont, and other authorities." Drawn by Charles Preuss. Washington City.

Gibbes. 1850. "Map of San Joaquin River." By Charles D. Gibbes.

_____1852. "A new map of California." By Charles Drayton Gibbes, from his own and other recent surveys and explorations. Published by C.D. Gibbes, Stockton, Cal.

Goddard. 1857. "Britton & Rey's map of the State of California." By George H. Goddard.

Hobson. 1890a. "Geological map of Nevada County." By J.B. Hobson. (*In* Hobson, 1890a.)

_____1890b. "Geological map of Placer County." By J.B. Hobson. (*In* Hobson, 1890b.)

Hoffmann and Gardner. 1863-1867. "Map of a portion of the Sierra Nevada adjacent to Yosemite Valley." From surveys made by Chs. F. Hoffmann and J.T. Gardner, 1863-1867. Geological Survey of California.

Jackson. 1850. "Map of the mining district of California." By Wm. A. Jackson.

Jefferson. 1849. "Map of the emigrant road from Independence, Mo. to St. Francisco, California." By T.H. Jefferson.

King and Gardner. 1865. "Map of the Yosemite Valley." From surveys made by order of the Commissioners to Manage the Yosemite Valley and Mariposa Big Tree Grove, by C. King and J.T. Gardner.

Laizure. 1928. "'Las Mariposa' of the Mariposa Commercial & Mining Company, Mariposa County, California." (*In* Laizure, 1928.)

_____1935. "Map of Mariposa County showing principal gold mines." (*In* Laizure, 1935.)

Larkin. 1848. "Map of the valley of the Sacramento, including the gold region." This map is a correct tracing of the map of Bidwell (land surveyor) by Thos. O. Larkin Esq. late Consul of the U.S. for California. Boston. Published by T. Wiley Jr.

Lindgren. 1911a. "Map of the northern part of the Sierra Nevada, California and Nevada." (Plate I *in* Lindgren, 1911.)

_____1911b. "Map of the deep placer mines near North Bloomfield and Relief, Nevada County, California." (Plate XX *in* Lindgren, 1911.)

Lippincott. 1902. "Map of drainage basin of Kings River, California, showing route traversed by exploring parties." (Plate I *in* Lippincott.)

Logan. 1925. "Region of Duncan Cañon, Placer County, Cal." (*In* Logan, 1925.)

_____1929. "Mineral map of western part of Sierra County, California." (*In* Logan, 1929.)

_____1938. "Map of western portion of El Dorado County, showing mining claims." Prepared by C.A. Logan, District Mining Engineer, July 1938. (Plate 2 *in* Logan, 1938.)

_____1940. "Map of western portion Nevada County, California, showing mining claims." By C.A. Logan, District Mining Engineer, 1940. (*In* Logan, 1941.)

_____1950. "Map of Madera County showing location of mines and mineral deposits." (Plate 73 *in* Logan.)

Mendenhall. 1908. "Artesian areas and groundwater levels in the San Joaquin Valley, California." (Plate I *in* Mendenhall.)

Ord. 1848. "Topographical sketch of the gold & quicksilver district of California, July 25th 1848." By E.O.C.O. [E.O.C. Ord] Lt. U.S.A.

Postal Route. 1884. (Map reproduced in *Early California, Northern Edition.* Corvallis, Oregon: Western Guide Publishers, p, 34-43.)

Reynolds. 1899. "Mining map of Tuolumne County, California." By A.M. Reynolds, mining engineer. (Follows p. 358 in *California mines and minerals,* published by California Miners' Association in 1899 at San Francisco.)

Sage. 1846. "Map of Oregon, California, New Mexico, N.W. Texas, & the proposed Territory of Ne-Bras-ka." By Rufus B. Sage.

Scholfield. 1851. "Map of southern Oregon and northern California." Compiled from the best authorities, and from personal surveys and explorations, by N. Scholfield, Civil Engineer. Published by Marvin & Hitchcock, San Francisco.

Sinclair. 1901. "Oblique boundary between California and Nevada, Lake Tahoe to Colorado River." (In 7 sections.) By C.H. Sinclair, Assistant, Chief of Party. (*In* Sinclair.)

Taylor. 1902. "Map of Lake Tahoe." (Figure 5 *in* Taylor.)

Thompson and West. 1879. (Maps *in* Thompson and West, 1879.)

Trask. 1853. "Topographical map of the mineral districts of California." Being the first map ever published from actual survey. By John B. Trask. Lithog. & Published by Britton & Rey. San Francisco.

United States Geological Survey. 1901. "Grass Valley quadrangle." (Scale 1:14,400.)

Wescoatt. 1861. "Official surveys." By N. Wescoatt. [Nevada] County Surveyor.

Wheeler. 1876-1877a. "Parts of eastern California and western Nevada." (Atlas Sheet No. 56B.) Expeditions of 1876 & 1877 under the command of 1st Lieut. Geo. M. Wheeler.

_____1876-1877b. "Parts of eastern California and western Nevada." (Atlas Sheets 47(B) & 47 (D).) Expeditions of 1876 and 1877 under the command of 1st Lieut. Geo. M. Wheeler.

Whitney. 1870. "Map showing the extent of the hydraulic mining operations near Gold Run, Dutch Flat, Little York, You Bet, Chalk Bluffs, Red Dog, Hunt's Hill and Quaker Hill, on Bear River and Cañon, Steep Hollow and Greenhorn Creeks." From surveys made for the Geological Survey of California in 1870. By W.H. Pettee and A. Bowman. Revised and corrected in 1879 by W.H. Pettee. (*In* Whitney, 1880.)

_____1873. "Map of the Tertiary Auriferous Gravel deposits lying between the Middle Fork of the American and the Middle Yuba Rivers." (*In* Whitney, 1880.)

_____1880. "Sketch map showing the distribution of the volcanic and gravel formations over a portion of Placer and El Dorado Counties, California." (Plate B *in* Whitney, 1880.)

Wilkes. 1841. "Map of Upper California." By the U.S. Ex. Ex. and best authorities.

_____1849. "Map of Upper California." By the best authorities.

Williamson. 1849. "Sketch of the route of Capt. Warner's exploring party in the Sacramento Valley and Sierra Nevada. During the months of August, September, and October, 1849." By R.S. Williamson, Lieut. Top. Engrs.

Wyld. 1849. "Map of the gold regions of California." Compiled from original surveys by James Wyld, Geographer to the Queen & Prince Albert, Charing Cross East & 2 Royal Exchange, London.

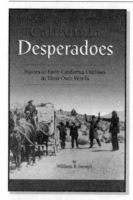

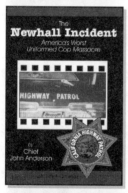

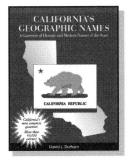

About the Author

Many years ago in connection with his more than three-decade-long career as a geologist with the United States Geological Survey, David L. Durham often needed to know the whereabouts of some obscure or vanished place in California. He searched for a suitable gazetteer to help him locate these features but found no such volume. To meet his needs he began compiling his own gazetteer for part of the state and, as his interests expanded, so did his gazetteer.

For the first twelve years of his retirement, Mr. Durham compiled information for the gazetteer nearly full-time. Eventually he extended coverage to all of California. The definitive gazetteer of California, *California's Geographic Names: A Gazetteer of Historic and Modern Names of the State* is the result. The Durham's Place-Names of California series, of which this volume is one, contains the same information as *California's Geographic Names* but in fourteen regional divisions.

Mr. Durham was born in California, served as an infantryman in France and Germany during World War II and holds a Bachelor of Science degree from the California Institute of Technology. He and his wife Nancy have two grown children.